Sca

lonely planet

Iceland
p219

Norway
p285

Sweden
p386

Finland
p127

Tallinn
p210

Denmark
p42

THIS EDITION WRITTEN AND RESEARCHED BY
Andy Symington,
Carolyn Bain, Cristian Bonetto,
Anthony Ham, Anna Kaminski

PLAN YOUR TRIP

ON THE ROAD

SÁMI WOMAN,
KAUTOKEINO (P370)

OLD TOWN (P211), TALLINN

FRANZ ABERHAM/GETTY IMAGES ©

DOUG PEARSON/GETTY IMAGES ©

CHRISTOPHER GROENHOUT/GETTY IMAGES ©

Contents

UTNE, HARDANGERFJORD
(P331)

ON THE ROAD

ICEHOTEL
(P465)

BIRDLIFE IN NORWAY

Contents

JOSTEDALSBREEN
(P339)

BRYGGEN (313), BERGEN

Welcome to Scandinavia

Outdoors

The great outdoors is rarely greater than in Europe's big north. Epic expanses of wilderness – forests, lakes, volcanoes – and intoxicatingly pure air mean that engaging with nature is utter pleasure. A network of well-cared-for protected areas stretches across the region, offering some of Europe's best hiking as well as anything from kayaking to glacier-walking to bear-watching. Spectacular coasts, whether rugged fjords, cliffs teeming with seabirds, or archipelagos so speckled with islands it looks like the artist who designed this canvas flicked a paintbrush at it, invite exploration from the sea. It's rare to find such inspiring landscapes that are so easily accessed.

City Style

Stolid Nordic stereotypes dissolve completely in the region's vibrant capitals. Crest-of-the-wave design can be seen across them all, backed up by outstanding modern architecture, excellent museums, imaginative solutions for 21st-century urban living, some of Europe's most acclaimed restaurants and a nightlife that fizzes along wildly despite the hefty beer prices. Live music is a given: you're bound to come across some inspiring local act whether your taste is Viking metal or chamber music. Style here manages to be conservative and innovative at the same time, or perhaps it's just that the new and the old blend with less effort here than

Effortlessly chic cities balance remote forests, enchanting style gurus and wilderness hikers alike. Endless day, perpetual night. Rocking festivals, majestic aurora borealis. Scandinavia's menu is anything but bland.

(left) Ice cave in Skaftafell (261)
(below) Waterfront living in Sweden

in other places. A side trip to seductive Tallinn will add an eastern Baltic kick to your Scandinavian city experiences.

Seasons

They have proper seasons up here. Long, cold winters with feet of snow carpeting the ground and the sun making only cameo appearances – if at all. Despite the scary subzero temperatures, there's a wealth of things to do: skiing, sledding behind huskies or reindeer, taking snowmobile safaris to the Arctic Sea, dangling a fishing line through a hole in the ice, spending romantic nights in snow hotels, visiting Santa Claus and gazing at the soul-piercing Northern Lights. Spring sees nature's tentative awakening before the explosive summer with its long, long days filled with festivals, beer terraces and wonderful boating, hiking and cycling. Autumn in Scandinavia's forested lands can be the most beautiful of all, as the birches and other deciduous trees display a glorious array of colours, offering marvellous woodland walking before the first snows.

Green Choices

You'll rarely come across the word *ecotourism* in Scandinavia, but those values have long been an important part of life here. Generally, green, sustainable solutions are a way of living, rather than a gimmick to attract visitors.

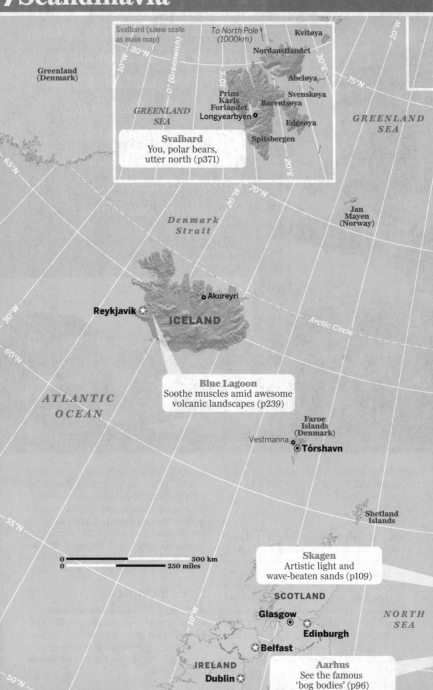

Svalbard (same scale
as main map)

**Greenland
(Denmark)**

To North Pole
(1000km)

Kvitøya

Nordaustlandet

Abeløya

Svenskøya

**Prins
Karls
Forlandet**

Barentsøya

*GREENLAND
SEA*

Longyearbyen ○

Edgeøya

*GREENLAND
SEA*

Spitsbergen

Svalbard
You, polar bears,
utter north (p371)

*Denmark
Strait*

**Jan
Mayen
(Norway)**

○ Akureyri

Arctic Circle

Reykjavík ✪

ICELAND

Blue Lagoon
Soothe muscles amid awesome
volcanic landscapes (p239)

*ATLANTIC
OCEAN*

**Faroe
Islands
(Denmark)**

Vestmanna ○

◎ **Tórshavn**

**Shetland
Islands**

0 ———————— 500 km
0 ———————— 250 miles

Skagen
Artistic light and
wave-beaten sands (p109)

SCOTLAND

Glasgow ◉

✪
Edinburgh

*NORTH
SEA*

✪ **Belfast**

IRELAND

Dublin ✪

Aarhus
See the famous
'bog bodies' (p96)

0° (Greenwich)

10°E

20°E

30°E

40°E

75°N

50°E

Novaya
Zemlya
(Russia)

Svalbard
(Norway)

See Svalbard inset

**BARENTS
SEA**

Icehotel
Subzero sleeping in
ethereal beauty (p465)

Lofoten Islands
Epic rock, timeless fishing
communities (p355)

Lapland
Discover reindeer-herding
Sámi culture (p369)

Nordkapp o

o Vardø

o Murmansk

Inarijärvi

50°E

70°N

**NORWEGIAN
SEA**

Tromsø o

Narvik o

o Kiruna

Lofoten
Islands

Bodø o

o Rovaniemi

65°N

RUSSIA

Norway's Fjords
Investigate these awesome
geological serrations (p311)

Oulu
o

Oulujärvi

Lake
Onega

SWEDEN

FINLAND

NORWAY

Umeå o

o Kuopio

Saimaa

Trondheim o

o Östersund

o Vaasa

o **Jyväskylä**

Lake
Ladoga

o **Ålesund**

Gulf of
Bothnia

Lappeenranta

Galdhøpiggen
(2469m)

Tampere o

o Vyborg

Lillehammer o

Turku o

Helsinki ☆

60°N

St Petersburg ◉

o **Bergen**

Åland

Gulf of Finland

Oslo ☆

Västerås o

o Uppsala

o ☆ **Tallinn**

Lake
Peipsi

o Stavanger

Örebro o

☆ **Stockholm**

ESTONIA

RUSSIA

Vänern

o Norrköping

Kristiansand o

Vättern

o Linköping

LATVIA

Skagen

o Jönköping

Gotland

Skagerrak

Kattegat

Göteborg o

**BALTIC
SEA**

Rīga ☆

Aalborg o

Öland

Tallinn
Evocative medieval
city centre (p211)

DENMARK

Aarhus
o

Helsingør o

LITHUANIA

o Helsingborg

Vilnius ☆

Copenhagen ●

o Malmö

☆ **Minsk**

Esbjerg o

o **Odense**

Kaliningrad ◉ **RUSSIA**

55°N

Funen

Bornholm

BELARUS

19 TOP EXPERIENCES

National Park Hiking

1 Scandinavia's unspoilt wilderness areas are the finest in Europe. If you like dark pine woods populated by foxes and bears, head for northeastern Finland's Karhunkier-ros trail (p188). Norway's Jotunheimen National Park (p310) encompasses hundreds of lofty mountain peaks and crystal-blue lakes. Lying inside the Arctic Circle, Abisko National Park in Sweden begins the epic 440km Kungsleden hiking trail (p467). Walkers will never forget the bleak volcanic slopes, steaming pools and mossy valleys of Iceland's Landmannalaugar to Þórsmörk trek (p268). Laugavegurinn Trek, Iceland

Fjords, Norway

2 The drama of Norway's fjords (p311) is difficult to overstate. Seen from above, they cut deep gashes into the Norwegian interior, adding texture and depth to the map of northwestern Scandinavia. Up close, sheer rock walls plunge from high, green meadows into water-filled canyons shadowed by pretty fjord-side villages. Sognefjorden (p335), more than 200km long, and Hardangerfjord (p331) are Norway's most extensive fjord networks, but the quiet, precipitous beauty of Nærøyfjorden (part of Sognefjorden), Lysefjord (p334) and – the king of Norwegian fjords – Geirangerfjorden (p342) are prime candidates for Scandinavia's most beautiful corner. Geirangerfjorden (p342)

Lofoten Islands, Norway

3 Few visitors forget their first sighting of the Lofoten Islands (p355), laid out in summer greens and yellows or drowned in the snows of winter, their razor-sharp peaks poking dark against a cobalt-clear sky. In the pure, exhilarating air, there's a constant tang of salt and, in the villages, more than a whiff of cod, that giant of the seas whose annual migration brings wealth. A hiker's dream and nowadays linked by bridges, the islands are simple to hop along, whether by bus, car or bicycle. Svolvær (p355)

Aurora Borealis, Lapland & Iceland

4 Whether caused by the collision of charged particles in the upper atmosphere, or sparked, as Sámi tradition tells, by a giant snow fox swishing its tail as it runs across the Arctic tundra, the haunting, humbling splendour of the aurora borealis, or Northern Lights, is an experience never to be forgotten. Though it is theoretically visible year-round, it's much easier to see and more spectacular in the darker winter months. The further north you go, such as the Lapland region (p188) in Finland, the better your chances of gazing on nature's light show.

3

Old Town, Tallinn

5 The jewel in Tallinn's crown is its Unesco-protected Old Town (p211), a 14th- and 15th-century two-tiered jumble of turrets, spires and winding streets. Most travellers' experiences of Tallinn begin and end with the cobblestoned, chocolate-box landscape of intertwining alleys and picturesque courtyards. Enjoy it from up high (climb one of the observation towers) or down below (refuel in one of the vaulted cellars turned into cosy bars and cafes), or simply stroll and soak up the medieval magic.

Svalbard, Norway

6 The subpolar archipelago of Svalbard (p371) is a true place of the heart. Deliciously remote and yet surprisingly accessible, Svalbard is Europe's most evocative slice of the polar north and one of the continent's last great wilderness areas. It is blessed with shapely peaks, massive ice fields (60% of Svalbard is covered by glaciers) and heartbreakingly beautiful fjords. All this provides the backdrop for a rich array of Arctic wildlife (including around one-fifth of the world's polar bears, which outnumber people up here) and for summer and winter activities that get you out amid the ringing silence of the snows.

Icehotel, Sweden

7 Somewhere between a chandelier and an igloo, the famed Icehotel (p465) at Jukkasjärvi is a justifiably popular destination – it may be a gimmick, but it's also really cool (and not just literally). Sleep among bearskin rugs in a hotel sculpted anew from ice each winter and hang out in the attached Icebar, sipping chilled vodka out of ice glasses. Beyond its own appeal, the hotel makes a good base for admiring the aurora borealis and learning about Sámi culture in this part of Lapland. Pillar hall

New Nordic Food

8 With Noma (p57) widely considered the world's finest restaurant, Copenhagen's culinary prowess is a byword. Once known for *frikadeller* (meatballs) and *smørrebrød* (open sandwiches), Denmark's capital has re-invented itself as a hotbed of gastronomic innovation, with the revamped Nordic cuisine and its forage ethos turning heads around the globe. Other countries have followed Denmark's lead, and exciting new restaurants now stock all the region's capitals. Not bad for a region once derided for its bland food by the sophisticates of southern Europe. Chefs at work at Noma

Island Cycling

9 A lazy bike ride around the perimeters of Gotland (p451), the holiday-friendly Baltic Sea island, is one of the most rewarding ways to spend your time in Sweden. The mostly flat, paved Gotlandsleden cycle path (p454) circles the island, passing fields of poppies, shady woodlands, historic churches and ancient rune stones at regular intervals. Also a short ferry ride from Stockholm, the autonomous Åland islands (p153) have a network of bridges and ferries that makes them a pleasure to pedal around. Or try the 105km-long ride around Bornholm (p74), one of Denmark's National Routes, from the hilly north to the flat, scenic south. Bornholm (p74)

9

Skagen, Denmark

10 Sweeping skies, moving sands and duelling seas: the appeal of Skagen (p109) is both ephemeral and constant. The lure of the light has drawn many – packing paintbrushes – from far beyond its coastline, and its blending colour of sky, sea and sand can inspire awe in the most hardened of souls. This is both Jutland's northern tip and Denmark's 'end of the line': where gentle fields give way to ghostly dunes, a buried church and the shapeshifting headland of Grenen; where the Baltic meets its murky North Sea rival. Sand dunes, Skagen

10

LOUISE MURRAY/GETTY IMAGES ©

M.CANTARERO/GETTY IMAGES ©

RICHARD ASHWORTH/GETTY IMAGES ©

Sledding

11 Once there's healthy snow cover in the north, a classic experience is to hitch up a team of reindeer or husky dogs to a sled and swish away under the pale winter sun. Short jaunts are good for getting the hang of steering, stopping and letting the animals know who's boss. Once your confidence is high, take off on an overnight trip, sleeping in a hut in the wilderness and thawing those deserving bones with a steaming sauna. Pure magic. Dog sledding in Karelia, Finland

Viking History

12 Mead-swilling pillaging hooligans or civilising craftspeople, poets and merchants? Your preconceptions of the Vikings will likely be challenged here. A series of memorable burial sites, rune stones, settlements and museums across the region brings this fascinating age to life. The Scandinavians' gods and beliefs, their stupendous feats of navigation, their customs, their longships, their intricate jewellery, carvings and sagas – it's all here. Just forget about the horned helmets – they didn't wear them. Viking ship, Oslo, Norway

Bog Bodies, Denmark

13 If you've ever read Seamus Heaney's 'bog people' poems, you'll know all about the eerily preserved, millennia-old bodies exhumed from Denmark's peat bogs. Skin still intact and frown lines clear, these ancient locals seem caught in perpetual slumber. The Grauballe Man (p96) near Aarhus is a compelling Bronze Age whodunit: was he a noble sacrifice or the victim of foul play? More serene is the Tollund Man (p101), his face so breathtakingly preserved that people mistook him for a modern-day crime victim upon discovery in 1950. Tollund Man

Sámi Culture

14 The indigenous Sámi have a near-mystical closeness to nature: in their case the awesome wildernesses of Lapland (p188). Reindeer-herding is still a primary occupation, but these days it's done with all-terrain vehicles and snowmobiles, leaving much more time to pursue other endeavours. The Sámi are a modern people, but still in touch with their roots. Check out the great museums, the parliament building, and craft workshops in Karasjok (p369) and Inari (p195), and try to coincide with a festival or cultural event while up here, whether reindeer-racing or *yoiking* (singing). Sámi man and reindeer, Finland

Thermal Springs & Saunas

15 Geothermal pools are Iceland's pride. The most famous one is the Blue Lagoon (p239), packed with skin-softening minerals. Visitors can also relax in warm milky-blue waters at Mývatn Nature Baths (p255), or even inside a volcanic crater at Stóra-Víti (p255). The sauna (p199) is as deeply entrenched in Finnish tradition: participants steam in the nude, whisk themselves with birch twigs and cool off with a cold shower or icy plunge. Experience the soothing springs and saunas yourself, and emerge from your visit a calmer, wiser person. Blue Lagoon (p239), Iceland

Design Shopping

16 If design is defined as making the practical beautiful, then Scandinavia rules the roost. Elegant, innovative yet functional takes on everyday items mean that you won't have to look far before you get an 'I need that!' moment. There's great design and handicrafts to be found right across the region, but Copenhagen (p60) and Helsinki (p143), closely followed by Stockholm (p407), are where modern flagships can be found alongside the best of the edgier new ideas. Marimekko store, Helsinki, Finland

Bar Life

17 In Scandinavia's capital cities summer is short and winter is long and bitter. Driving away the darkness is a necessity – so it's no wonder that a near-legendary nightlife has evolved in these cities. After all, what could be better than gathering your friends into a snug, sleek bar to talk, drink, joke, sing, laugh, flirt and dance the night away? Natural Nordic reserve melts away with the application of such local firewaters as *brennivín*, *salmiakkikossu*, *snaps* or aquavit, or plain old beer – join the party and make new friends fast. Laundromat Café, Reykjavík, Iceland (p235)

ROBIN SMITH/GETTY IMAGES ©

ARCTIC IMAGES/ALAMY ©

HAUKE DRESSLER/GETTY IMAGES ©

Historic Wooden Towns

18 Wooden buildings are a feature of Scandinavia, once comprising whole towns. But 'great fires' – whether through somebody smoking in bed or burning the toast – were understandably common and comparatively few of these historic districts remain. They are worth seeking out for their quaint, unusual beauty. Among others, Rauma (p164), Bergen (p313), Stavanger (p332) and Göteborg (p430) preserve excellent 'timbertowns', perfect neighbourhoods for strolling around. Eighteenth-century wooden houses, Bergen (p313), Norway

A Cottage Somewhere

19 Vast numbers of Scandinavians head to summer cottages at the first hint of midyear sunshine. The typical one is simple, by a lake or on an island, with few modern comforts, but probably has a rowing boat or canoe, a barbecue, a bit of old fishing line and maybe a sauna. The holidays are spent enjoying nature and getting away from city life. Across the region there are numerous rental cottages that can become venues for you to experience a slice of authentic Nordic peace. Summer cottage, Norway

need to know

Buses
» Comprehensive network throughout the region. The only choice in further-flung corners, such as Lapland.

Trains
» Efficient services in the continental nations, none in Iceland.

When to go?

Warm to hot summers, mild winters
Warm to hot summers, cold winters
Mild year round
Mild summers, cold to very cold winters
Polar climate

Svalbard
GO Mar–Aug

Iceland
GO Jun–Aug

Lapland
GO Feb–Mar, Aug–Sep

Fjords
GO Mar–Sep

Helsinki/Tallinn
GO Jun–Jul

Copenhagen
GO May–Oct, Dec

High Season (Jun–Aug)
» Expect warm, long days throughout most of the region.

» Hotel prices are down in many countries.

» Christmas and February to March are very busy in winter-sports destinations.

Shoulder Season (Apr & May, Sep & Oct)
» Expect chilly nights and even snow.

» It's not the cheapest time to travel as summer hostels and camping grounds have closed.

» Many attractions close or shorten their opening hours.

Low Season (Nov–Mar)
» Outside the cities, it's very quiet except in winter-sports centres.

» Prepare for serious cold.

» Most outdoor attractions are shut and other tourist services closed or severely restricted.

Your Daily Budget

Budget up to
€130

» Dorm beds: €15–40

» Supermarkets and market halls for self-caterers: €20 per day

» Cheap lunch specials: €8–15

» National parks: free

Midrange
€130–250

» Double room: €80–150

» Car hire: €40–80 per day

» Lunch and light dinner in restaurants: €70 for two

» Major museum admission: €7–15

Top end over
€250

» Double room: €140–230

» Three-course meal for two with wine: €150–200

» Cocktail in the glitziest designer bar: €15-25

Driving

» Drive on the right. Car hire is easy but not cheap. There are few motorways so travel times can be long. Compulsory winter tyres mean hassle-free snow driving.

Ferries

» Top way to travel the region: great-value network around the Baltic; spectacular Norwegian coastal ferry; and a service to Iceland via the Faroe Islands.

Bicycles

» Very bike-friendly cities and lots of options for longer cycling routes. Most ferries, buses and trains carry bikes for little or no charge and hire is widely available.

Planes

» Decent network of budget flights connecting major centres. Full-fare flights with the major carriers are comparatively expensive.

Websites

» Lonely Planet (www.lonelyplanet.com/europe) Destination information, accommodation bookings, traveller forum and more.

» Go Scandinavia (www.goscandinavia.com) Combined tourist board website for the five major Nordic countries.

» IceNews (www.icenews.is) Presents the latest English news snippets from the Nordic nations.

» Direct Ferries (www.directferries.co.uk) Useful booking site for Baltic and Atlantic ferries.

Money

» Debit and credit cards used throughout; ATMs widespread, accept all cards.

» Finland and Tallinn use the euro; St Petersburg uses the rouble.

» Iceland (króna), Norway (krone), Sweden (krona) and Denmark/Faroe Islands (krone) each have their own currency.

» The euro is commonly accepted in major centres; all major currencies are easily exchanged throughout the region.

Visas

Norway, Iceland, Denmark, Sweden, Estonia and Finland are all part of the Schengen area.

A valid passport or EU identity card is required to enter the Schengen area. Citizens of the EU, USA, Canada, Australia and New Zealand don't need a tourist visa for stays of less than three months; others may need a Schengen visa.

Arriving in Scandinavia

» **Copenhagen Kastrup Airport**
Trains: every 10 minutes into the centre.
Taxis: around Dkr250 for the 20-minute ride

» **Stockholm Arlanda Airport**
Trains: express trains all day from Stockholm; airport buses cheaper but slower
Taxis: think Skr520 for the 45-minute drive

» **Oslo Gardermoen Airport**
Buses: regular shuttle buses make the 40 minute journey to the centre
Trains: from the airport into the centre of Oslo in 20 minutes

What to Take

» For winter visits: decent thermal underwear, waterproof boots and top layer, woolly hat, gloves and a neck warmer.

» A credit or debit card: plastic's an easy option throughout, and saves working out which country that 50-krone banknote is from.

» An HI membership card, towel and sleep sheet if you plan to use hostels.

» A tent and sleeping bag if you're going hiking – huts fill up fast.

» Powerful insect repellent in summer, especially in Finland and Iceland.

» An eye mask for sleeping under the never-setting summer sun.

» Swimsuit – there are lots of hot springs, spa hotels and lakes to jump in.

» Mobile phone – buying a local SIM card is the easiest way to get connected.

if you like...

Coastal Scenery

Scoured by glaciers, speckled with islands and buffeted by wind and rain, the Nordic coastlines are spectacular and capable of inspiring profound awe. The Atlantic coasts are the most jagged, while the more sedate Baltic archipelagos offer a gentler beauty.

Dueodde On Bornholm, Nordic forest and snow white dunes back one of Europe's most spectacular beaches (p77)

Møns Klint Gleaming white cliffs against the Baltic blue (p72)

Kvarken A constantly changing pattern of land and water as the Earth's crust bounces back from the weight of the glaciers in the last Ice Age (p166)

The High Coast See northern Sweden's dramatic Höga Kusten (p455)

Lofoten Marvel at nature's sheer improbability in these northern Norwegian islands (p355)

Svalbard Be spellbound where vast glaciers meet the Arctic Ocean at this remote outpost (p371)

Jökulsárlón Watch glaciers float to sea from this glittering lagoon (p260)

Ingólfshöfði An isolated Iceland headland and nature reserve, accessible only by tractor-towed hay cart (p262)

Hiking

Wide open spaces, majestic landscapes and bracing air offer brilliant hiking. Multiday treks are easily accomplished with the great network of national parks, camping grounds and huts. Norway and Iceland offer magnificent scenery, while Finland and Sweden have spectacular autumn forestscapes.

Northern Sweden Trek along the Kungsleden (King's Trail) in Swedish Lappland (p467)

Norwegian peaks Traverse the roof of Norway in the Jotunheimen National Park (p310)

Rjukan Hike in search of wild reindeer atop Norway's Hardangervidda plateau (p331)

Hornstrandir Accessible only by boat in high summer, this isolated Icelandic peninsula is the ultimate escape (p245)

Laugavegurinn Trek Iceland's most famous hike, from Landmannalaugar to Þórsmörk, over rainbow-coloured mountains and through deserts of pumice (p268)

Finnish Lapland Hit Lapland's Urho K Kekkonen (UKK) National Park for some top trekking in one of Europe's last great wildernesses (p195)

Cycling

Bikes are part of life in here: the cities are full of cycle lanes, grab-a-bike stands and marked routes. There are great options for multiday cycling holidays, particularly in the Baltic islands. Bikes are easily transported throughout the region.

Bornholm Pedal your way across this perfect Danish island (p74)

Tallinn Get out of the Old Town and take a bike tour to the far-flung corners of the capital (p215)

City cruising Hire a bike and join the locals in cycle-friendly Örebro (p417), Oulu (p184) or Reykjavík (p227)

Gotland Make the easy loop around this Swedish island (p451)

Rjukan Ride across Norway's Hardangervidda, Europe's highest mountain plateau (p306)

Mývatn The best way to explore the charms of Iceland's Lake Mývatn is on a day-long bicycle circuit (p253)

Åland This archipelago between Finland and Sweden is ideal for two-wheeled touring, with numerous flat islands to explore (p153)

YOSHIO TOMII/GETTY IMAGES ©

» Santa Claus Village (p189), Lapland, Finland

Vikings

Whether you're interested in the structured society, extensive trade networks, dexterous handicrafts and well-honed navigational skills of this advanced civilisation or you glorify in tales of plunder, pillage, dragon ships and the twilight of the gods, there's something for you here.

Roskilde Set sail on a faithful Viking replica in Denmark (p68)

Ribe Vikingecenter Schmooze with modern-day Danish Vikings (p115)

Gotland Visit this Swedish island's numerous rune stones and ship settings (p453)

Oslo Admire a Viking longboat at Oslo's marvellous Viking-skipshuset (p292)

Lofotr Vikingmuseum Norway's largest Viking-era building (p358)

Reykjavík 871 +/-2 Fascinating hi-tech exhibition, based around an original Viking longhouse (p223)

Saga Museum A kind of Viking Madame Tussauds, this Reykjavík museum is heaps of fun (p223)

Northern seas Follow the mighty wake of the Viking colonists by taking the boat from Denmark to Iceland via the Faroes (p36)

The Active Winter

Once the snow has carpeted the land, northern Scandinavia is a wonderful place to get active. March and April are the best months to enjoy winter sports, with more daylight and less-extreme temperatures than you get earlier in the winter.

Sled safaris Head out pulled by huskies or reindeer, or aboard a snowmobile to explore the frozen wildernesses; there are excellent places to do this right across northern Norway, Sweden and Finland, whether it's a short hour-long swoosh or a multiday adventure (p380)

Skiing and snowboarding There are excellent resorts in Norway and flatter, family-friendly slopes in northern Sweden and Finland; these places usually offer a host of other wintry activities like snowshoe treks and ice fishing (p204)

Breaking the ice Crunch a passage through the frozen Gulf of Bothnia aboard an icebreaker and go for a dip – with a hi-tech drysuit – at Kemi in Finland (p193)

Winter Wonders

Winter's magic isn't confined to the active. There are other enticing attractions aplenty up north, and the southern cities are feel-good places in December, with spectacular street lighting and festive drinks.

Snow hotels It's tough to beat the romance of snow hotels, ethereally beautiful creations sculpted from snow and ice; the most famous is at Jukkasjärvi (p465, near Kiruna) in Sweden but others we like are at Alta (p365) and Kirkenes (p368) in Norway, and Kemi in Finland (p193)

Santa Claus Visit the world's most famous beardie in his eerie Finnish grotto (p189)

Stockholm Christmas Shop at Gamla Stan's delightful Christmas Market (p389)

Tivoli Put the magic back into Christmas with wonderful lights and warming mulled wine (p45)

Aurora borealis (Northern Lights) Get as far north as you can and find a place without much light, then you'll need patience and a slice of luck; one of the best viewing spots is Abisko in Sweden (p466)

» Puffins on Runde (p346), Norway

Food & Drink

Once pooh-poohed by the gourmets, Scandinavia is now at the forefront of modern and molecular cuisine. Michelin stars twinkle across the region's capitals: Copenhagen has the most sophisticated scene, but heartier traditional cookery still warms the cockles in local restaurants throughout the region.

Noma Push the culinary envelope in Copenhagen, at the world's hottest restaurant (p57)

Arctic ingredients Norwegian elk, salmon, Arctic char and even whale come together in the Arctic Menu scheme (p286)

Smörgåsbord Try the Veranda at the Grand Hôtel, Stockholm, open all year (p403)

Brennivín Known as 'Black Death', this Icelandic schnapps is swiggable in all good bars (p220)

Rudolf and friends Reindeer is a staple in Lapland; elk and bear make regular appearances on menus in other parts of Finland (p128)

Pony No, not the meat; the Copenhagen restaurant – New Nordic brilliance at mere-mortal prices (p56)

Canoeing & Kayaking

It's hard to beat this region for kayaking and canoeing. Numerous suppliers, handily placed camping grounds and plenty of wildlife to silently approach make it a pleasure, whether you're planning a multiday sea-kayaking or afternoon lake-canoeing adventure.

Danish Lake District Glide silent lakes in bucolic Jutland (p93)

Stockholm Rent a canoe for the day from Djurgårdsbrons Sjöcafe (p399)

Sweden Set out on a multiday canoe adventure (p475)

Norway Kayak some of Norway's prettiest corners, such as Svalbard (p373) or the World Heritage–listed Geirangerfjorden (p342) and Sognefjorden (p335)

Ísafjörður This Icelandic destination is perfect for beginners (p244)

Seyðisfjörður Guided kayaking tours with the affable Hlynur in Iceland (p259)

Åland Paddle around the low, rocky islands of this quietly picturesque Finnish archipelago (p155)

Seal Lakes Explore these watery Finnish national parks by boat and try to spot a rare inland seal (p172)

Modern Art & Architecture

Nordic lands tend to be at the forefront of these things, with designers and artists given a freer rein than elsewhere. The region has a huge amount to offer for anyone interested in contemporary art and architecture.

Louisiana Art meets vistas at this Copenhagen modern-art must (p62)

ARoS Walk among giants at this Danish cultural showpiece (p93)

Stockholm Visit one of Scandinavia's best modern-art museums, Moderna Museet (p395)

Malmö Marvel at the Turning Torso (p423)

Oslo Enjoy a modern architectural icon: the Oslo Opera House (p287) or the young-at-20 Astrup Fearnley (p287) modern-art museum

Helsinki Iconic Kiasma (p131) still turns heads with its exuberant exterior and excellent exhibitions and the adjacent new Musiikkitalo (p142) is a stunning concert venue

Alvar Aalto Make an architectural pilgrimage to Jyväskylä, the city where one of the giants made his name (p173)

If you like... Sámi culture, visit Jokkmokk (p463), see the museum at Inari (p196), experience traditional activities in Lemmenjoki (p197), and admire the parliament at Karasjok (p369) and the silver gallery at Kautokeino (p370).

Historic Buildings & Churches

It's not all 'out with the old' and 'bring in the new' in Scandinavia. Creaky, ancient wooden churches dot the countryside, and the older towns and cities in the region are replete with treasures. A series of muscular castles fortified the kingdoms around the ever-turbulent Baltic.

Kronborg Slot Channel Shakespeare at Hamlet's old haunt in Helsingør (p64)

Tallinn Stroll back to the 14th century around the Old Town's narrow, cobbled streets (p211)

Gotland Historic churches dot this Swedish island (p451)

Norwegian stave churches Admire World Heritage–listed Urnes Stave Church on the banks of a fjord (p339)

Gamle Stavanger One of Europe's most spectacular districts of wooden buildings sits at the heart of this Norwegian city (p332)

Olavinlinna From its island perch, Finland's most spectacular castle presides over the centre of its prettiest town (p169)

Roskilde Domkirke Eight centuries of Danish architecture under one roof (p67)

Wildlife Watching

Seabirds clamour in the Atlantic air while whales roll beneath. Elk are widespread, Finnish forests harbour serious carnivores and mighty polar bears still lord it – for now – over Svalbard. Low population densities make it excellent for observing wildlife in summer.

Fanø Witness mass migration of the feathered kind in Denmark (p116)

Puffins A hundred thousand pairs of these comical seabirds nest on the island of Runde, Norway (p346)

Reindeer These roam at will across the north of Sweden, Norway and Finland; learn about reindeer in Jukkasjärvi, in Sweden (p465)

Central Norway Track down the prehistoric musk ox (p308)

Svalbard Watch out for Europe's last polar bears in Svalbard (p371)

Whale watching Head to Norway's **Lofoten Islands** (p357) or Húsavík in **Iceland** (p252)

Látrabjarg These dramatic cliffs are the world's biggest bird breeding grounds (p246)

Bear watching Head out to the Finnish forests to observe bears, elk or wolverines (p183)

Design

Why is Scandinavian design so admired? Because substance comes first and style second. The cities showcase innovative, beautiful creations, but underlying efficiency and practicality keeps contact with the rural past. In Lapland, Sámi artists weave modern interpretations and ancient traditions.

Copenhagen Hit Designmuseum Danmark (p51) then revamp your home at Hay House, a Danish design mecca (p60)

Helsinki A design epicentre with everything from flagship stores to cutting-edge studios (p143)

Stockholm DesignTorget puts chic gadgetry within reach (p407)

Bergen Browse designer jewellery around the ancient warehouses of Bryggen (p313)

Hafnarhús This central modern-art gallery sells cutting-edge Icelandic design (p226)

Lapland Visit workshops at Inari (195) for the best Sámi handicrafts and browse jewellery that evokes the Arctic north in Kautokeino (p370)

month by month

Top Events

1 **Midsummer** June

2 **Sled safaris & skiing** March

3 **Roskilde Festival** June

4 **Aurora watching** November

5 **Christmas** December

January

It's cold. Very cold and very dark. But this is the beginning of the active winter; there's enough snow for ice hotels, and sledding, snowmobiling and skiing are reliable.

☆ Skábmagovat, Finland

In the third week of January, this film festival (p196) with an indigenous theme is held in the Finnish Sámi village of Inari. Associated cultural events also happen here throughout the winter.

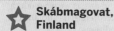 Kiruna Snöfestivalen, Sweden

This Lapland snow festival in Kiruna, based around a snow-sculpting competition that draws artists from all over, is held on the last weekend in January. There's also a husky dog competition and a handicrafts fair.

February

There's enough light now for it to be prime skiing season in northern Scandinavia. Local holidays mean it gets very busy (and pricey) on the slopes around the middle of the month.

☆ Jokkmokk Winter Market, Sweden

The biggest Sámi market (p463) of the year with all manner of crafts for sale, preceded by celebrations of all things Sámi and featuring reindeer races on the frozen lake.

☆ Þorrablót, Iceland

Held all across the country, nominally in honour of the god Thor, this midwinter festival's centrepiece is a feast for the fearless that includes delicacies such as putrid shark.

☆ Rørosmartnan, Norway

A old-fashioned and traditional winter fair (p309; www.rorosmartnan.no) livens the streets of this historic Norwegian town, whose old wooden buildings make it a World Heritage area.

March

As the hours of light dramatically increase and temperatures begin to rise again, this is an excellent time to take advantage of the hefty snow cover and indulge in some winter activities.

Sled Safaris & Skiing, Northern Norway, Sweden & Finland

Whizzing across the snow pulled by a team of huskies or reindeer is a pretty spectacular way to see the northern wildernesses. Add snowmobiling or skiing to the mix and it's a top time to be at high latitude.

☆ Reindeer Racing, Finland

Held over the last weekend of March or first of April, the King's Cup (p196) is the grand finale of Finnish Lapland's reindeer-racing season and a great spectacle.

☆ Vasaloppet, Sweden

Held on the first Sunday in March, this ski race (p422; www.vasaloppet.se) salutes Gustav Vasa's history-making flight on skis in 1521; it has grown into a week-long ski fest and celebration with different races – short, gruelling or just for fun.

April

Easter is celebrated in a traditional fashion across the region. Spring is underway in Denmark and the southern parts, but there's still solid snow cover in the northern reaches.

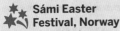

Sámi Easter Festival, Norway

Thousands of Sámi participate in reindeer racing, theatre and cultural events (www.samieasterfestival.com) in the Finnmark towns of Karasjok and Kautokeino. The highlight is the Sámi Grand Prix, a singing and *yoiking* (traditional Sámi form of song) contest attended by artists from across Lapland.

Valborgsmässoafton, Sweden

This public holiday (Walpurgis Night) on 30 April is a pagan hold-over that's partly to welcome the arrival of spring. Celebrated across the country, it involves lighting huge bonfires, singing songs and forming parades.

Jazzkaar, Tallinn

Late April sees jazz greats from all around the world converge on Estonia's picturesque capital for a series of performances (www.jazzkaar.ee).

May

A transitional month in the north, with snow beginning to disappear and signs of life emerging after the long winter. In the south, spring's in full flow. This is a quiet but rewarding time to visit.

Copenhagen Marathon, Denmark

Scandinavia's largest marathon (www.copenhagenmarathon.dk) is on a Sunday in mid-May and draws around 5000 participants and tens of thousands of spectators. A series of shorter, lead-up races in the preceding months are a fun way to see the city.

Reykjavík Arts Festival, Iceland

Running for two weeks from late May to June, this wide-ranging festival (www.artfest.is) sees Iceland's capital taken over by local and international theatre performances, films, lectures and music.

Bergen International Festival, Norway

One of the biggest events on Norway's cultural calendar, this two-week festival (p315), beginning in late May, showcases dance, music and folklore presentations, some international, some focusing on traditional local culture.

June

Midsummer weekend in late June is celebrated with great gusto, but it's typically a family event; unless you've got local friends it's not the best moment to visit. Lapland's muddy, but the rest of the region is warm and welcoming.

Old Town Days, Tallinn

This week-long Estonian festival (www.vanalinnapaevad.ee) in early June features dancing, concerts, costumed performers and plenty of medieval merrymaking in the heart of Tallinn's stunning historic centre.

Stockholm Jazz Festival, Sweden

Held on the island of Skeppsholmen, this internationally known jazz fest (p400) brings artists from all over, including big names like Van Morrison and Mary J Blige.

Skagen Festival, Denmark

Held over four days in late June, this festival (p109) at Denmark's picturesque northern tip features folk and world music performed by Danish and international artists.

Independence Day, Iceland

Held on 17 June, this is the largest nationwide festival in the country. It commemorates the founding of the Republic of Iceland in 1944 with big parades and general celebration.

Roskilde Festival, Denmark

Northern Europe's largest music festival (p68) rocks Roskilde for four consecutive days each summer. It takes place from late June to early July, but advance ticket sales are on offer in December and the festival usually sells out.

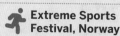 **Midsummer, Denmark, Norway, Sweden & Finland**

The year's biggest event in continental Nordic Europe sees fun family feasts, joyous celebrations of the summer, heady bonfires and copious drinking, often at peaceful lakeside summer cottages. It takes place on the weekend that falls between 19 and 26 June.

Extreme Sports Festival, Norway

Adventure junkies from across the world converge on Voss in late June for a week of skydiving, paragliding, parasailing and base jumping (p330); local and international music acts keep the energy flowing.

July

Peak season sees long, long days and sunshine. This is when the region really comes to life, with many festivals, boat trips, activities, cheaper hotels and a celebratory feel. Insects in Lapland and Iceland are a nuisance.

Frederikssund Vikingespil, Denmark

Held in Frederikssund over a two-week period from late June to early July, this Viking festival (www. vikingespil.dk) includes a costumed open-air drama followed by a banquet with Viking food and entertainment.

Copenhagen Jazz Festival, Denmark

This is the biggest entertainment event of the year in the capital, with 10 days of music at the beginning of July. The festival (p53) features a range of Danish and international jazz, blues and fusion music, with more than 500 indoor and outdoor concerts.

Ruisrock, Finland

Finland's oldest and possibly best rock festival (p148) takes place in early July on an island just outside the southwestern city of Turku. Top Finnish and international acts take part.

Wife-Carrying World Championships, Finland

Finland's, nay, the world's premier wife-carrying event (p175) is held in the village of Sonkajärvi in early July. Winning couples (marriage not required) win the woman's weight in beer as well as significant kudos.

Moldejazz, Norway

Norway has a fine portfolio of jazz festivals, but Molde's version (p346) in mid-July is the most prestigious. With 100,000 spectators, world-class performers and a reputation for consistently high-quality music, it's easily one of Norway's most popular festivals.

Ólavsøka, Faroe Islands

The largest and most exciting traditional festival in the Faroes celebrates the 10th-century Norwegian king Olav the Holy, who spread Christian faith on the isles. The big days are 28 and 29 July.

Savonlinna Opera Festival, Finland

A month of excellent performances (p169) in the romantic location of one of Europe's most picturesquely situated castles makes this Finland's biggest summer drawcard for casual and devoted lovers of opera.

August

Most Scandinavians are back at work, so it's quieter than in July but there's still decent weather across most of the region. It's a great time for hiking in Lapland, biking the islands or cruising the archipelagos.

Medieval Week, Sweden

Find yourself an actual knight in shining armour at this immensely popular annual Swedish fest (p454) in Visby, Gotland's medieval jewel. It takes place over a week in early August.

Aarhus Festival, Denmark

The 10-day Aarhus Festival (p96) starts in late August and features scores of musical performances, theatre, ballet, modern dance, opera, films and sports events at indoor and outdoor venues across Denmark's second-largest city.

Air Guitar World Championships, Finland

Tune your imaginary instrument and get involved in this crazy rockstravaganza (p184) held in Oulu in late August. This surfeit of cheesy guitar classics and seemingly endless beer is all in the name of world peace.

Reykjavík Jazz Festival, Iceland

A fun, yearly cultural event is the Reykjavík Jazz Festival (www.reykjavikjazz.is) with jazz concerts around the city. It tends to move around the calendar, so be sure to check the month.

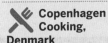

Copenhagen Cooking, Denmark

Scandinavia's largest food festival (p54) focuses on the gourmet. It's a busy event that will let you catch up on the latest trends in fashionable New Nordic cuisine.

September

The winter is fast approaching: pack something warm for those chilly nights. Autumn colours are spectacular in northern forests, making it another great month for hiking. Many attractions and activities close down or go onto winter time.

Reykjavík International Film Festival, Iceland

This annual event (p231) right at the end of September sees blockbusters make way for international art films in cinemas across the city, as well as talks from film directors from home and abroad.

Ruska Hiking, Finland & Sweden

Ruska is the Finnish word for the autumn colours, and there's a mini high season in Finnish and Swedish Lapland as hikers take to the trails to enjoy nature's brief artistic flourish.

October

Snow is already beginning to carpet the region's north. It's generally a quiet time to be in Scandinavia, as locals face the realities of yet another long winter approaching.

Iceland Airwaves, Iceland

This five-day event in Reykjavík is one of the world's most cutting-edge music festivals (www.icelandairwaves.com): don't expect to sleep. It focuses on new musical trends rather than mainstream acts.

November

Once the clocks change in late October, there's no denying the winter. November's bad for winter sports as there's little light and not enough snow. It can be a good month to see the aurora borealis (Northern Lights), though.

Aurora-Watching, Iceland, Norway, Sweden & Finland

Whether you are blessed with seeing the aurora borealis is largely a matter of luck, but the further north you are, the better the chances. Dark, cloudless nights, patience and a viewing spot away from city lights are other key factors.

Stockholm International Film Festival, Sweden

Screenings of new international and independent films, director talks and discussion panels draw cinephiles to this important annual festival (p400); tickets go quickly, so book early.

December

The Christmas period is celebrated enthusiastically across the region, with cinnamon smells, warming mulled drinks, romantic lights and festive traditions putting the meaning back into the event.

Christmas, Regionwide

Whether visiting Santa and his reindeer in Finnish Lapland, admiring the magic of Copenhagen's Tivoli at night or sampling home-baked delicacies, Christmas – especially if you know a friendly local family to spend it with – is a heartwarming time to be here.

Itineraries
Scandinavia in a Nutshell

One or Two Weeks

This quick hop jaunts around southern Scandinavia's classic sights. With just a week, it's essentially one city in each of Denmark, Sweden and Norway; extra time allows more detailed exploration and side trips.

» Start in **Copenhagen** (p45), admiring the waterfront, museums and lights of Tivoli at night. Day-trip to the cathedral and Viking Ship Museum at **Roskilde** (p67) or Hamlet's castle at **Helsingør** (p64).

» Next, train it to **Stockholm** (p389) and get into the design scene and the stately, watery town centre. An overnight train takes you to **Oslo** (p287), to check out Munch's work. From Oslo, a long but very scenic day includes the rail trip to **Flåm** (p336) and a combination boat/bus journey along the Sognefjord to **Bergen** (p313), Norway's prettiest city. Out of time? Fly out from Bergen.

» Otherwise, head to **Kristiansand** (p303), where there's a ferry to **Hirtshals** (p111). Nose on down to **Aarhus** (p93) – don't miss the ARoS art museum. From here, it's an easy train to Copenhagen.

» Extra days? A side trip from Stockholm on a Baltic ferry could take you to **Helsinki** (p130) or picturesque **Tallinn** (p210). Other stops could include **Göteborg** (p430) or **Kalmar** (p447); more fjord-y Norwegian experiences at **Fjærland** (p340) and **Geiranger** (p342); or extra Danish time at **Odense** (p81).

Clockwise from top left
1 Ice skating in Oslo (p287) 2 Bryggen (p313), Bergen
3 Gamla Stan (p389), Stockholm

Finland & the Baltic

Two to Three Weeks

Starting in Stockholm, this itinerary follows the old trading routes around the Baltic and covers plenty of Finland, including the capital, Helsinki, and beautiful Lakeland, it also takes in the sumptuous Baltic city of Tallinn.

» Kick things off in **Stockholm** (p389), for centuries a Baltic trading powerhouse. Take a day trip to ancient **Uppsala** (p415) before taking advantage of Stockholm's cheap, luxurious overnight ferries to Finland. Enjoy the spectacular arrival in **Helsinki** (p130), where you should investigate the cathedrals, market halls, modern architecture and design scene. Catch a classical concert at the new Musiikkitalo or a rock gig at legendary Tavastia.

» From Helsinki, a good excursion heads east to **Porvoo** (p145), with its picturesque wooden warehouses and cathedral. Back in Helsinki, it's an easy boat ride across the Baltic to medieval **Tallinn** (p210), a historic treasure trove that's worth a couple of days' exploration. If time's short, take a day trip.

» In summer, take the train to the shimmering lakes of **Savonlinna** (p169), with its awesome medieval castle and opera festival, and/or **Kuopio** (p174), to steam up in its large smoke sauna. Historic lake boats travel between these and other inland Finnish towns, a fabulously leisurely way to travel on a sunny day. A side trip from either of these towns can take you to **Joensuu** (p178), from where you can visit the Orthodox monastery of **Valamo** (p178) or what is claimed to be Finland's best view at **Koli** (p181).

» Head to the dynamic cultural city of **Tampere** (p157), visiting its quirky museums, re-imagined fabric mills and interesting cafes and restaurants. Then it's on to intriguing **Turku** (p147), with excellent museums, a towering castle and cathedral, and some very quirky drinking dens. From here you can get a ferry back to Sweden via the **Åland islands** (p153). Stop off here for as long as you wish and tour the archipelago by bike.

Clockwise from top left
1 Old Town (p211), Tallinn 2 Musiikkitalo (p142), Helsinki
3 Olavinlinna (p169), Savonlinna 4 Mariehamn (p155)

Beyond the Arctic Circle

Three to Four Weeks

This visit to the north takes in Santa, Sámi culture, spectacular coastal scenery viewed from the sea and opportunities for excellent activities. It'll be a completely different experience in summer or in winter.

» Take the overnight train from **Helsinki** (p130) to **Rovaniemi** (p188). Stock up here on anything you might need for your wilderness adventure. Head north, crossing the Arctic Circle to **Saariselkä** (p195), a base for great activities.

» From here it's a short hop to **Inari** (p195), where Siida is a wonderful Lapland exhibition. Check out the craft shops too, and the impressive parliament building. Head onwards to **Karasjok** (p369), Inari's Norwegian counterpart and an important meeting place for representatives of different Sámi groups.

» From Karasjok (and Inari) summer buses run to **Nordkapp** (p366), where you can gaze out towards the utter north. From nearby **Honningsvåg** (p366), catch the *Hurtigruten* coastal steamer to the stunning **Lofoten Islands** (p355), possibly stopping in lively **Tromsø** (p360. From Tromsø

there are flights north to **Svalbard** (p371), demesne of polar bears and an epic Arctic experience.

» Enjoy the Lofoten Islands before taking the *Hurtigruten* down to **Narvik** (p353) and take the train to **Kiruna** (p464), a remote mining town, and, in winter, home to the famous Icehotel. On the way, stop off for some hiking or aurora-watching at **Abisko National Park** (p466). Check out the Sámi village and reindeer-herding region of **Jokkmokk** (p462).

» From here, you could go to Stockholm, Norway, or to the Finnish border at **Haparanda/Tornio** (p194) to head back to Helsinki.

Clockwise from top left
1 A Sámi *kota* (dwelling) 2 Arktikum (p189), Rovaniemi
3 Abisko National Park (p466) 4 *Hurtigruten* ferry (p383)

Northern Islands

Three to Four Weeks

Of course you can fly to Iceland, but it's much more fun to do it like the Vikings did and go by boat. Start in Denmark and head into the North Atlantic to this fabulous volcanic island, with a stop in the Faroes en route.

» Fly into **Copenhagen** (p45), taking some time to absorb its addictive atmosphere. Then hit north Jutland and the beautiful dunes at **Skagen** (p109), where two seas meet at Denmark's northernmost tip.

» Jump aboard the Smyril Line ferry at nearby **Hirtshals** (p111). In summer there are two ferries running per week, so you can make a three-day stop in the remote **Faroe Islands** (p112); in the off season it's either nine hours there or a whole week. If you manage some time on the islands, giggle at the comical puffins on the cliffs of **Mykines** (p112) and take a boat trip to visit the immense seabird colonies at **Vestmanna** (p112).

» The ferry (April to late October) continues to Iceland, arriving at **Seyðisfjörður**

(p258). From here journey to Reykjavík along the south coast past **Skaftafell** (p261), a national-park area that is one of Iceland's most spectacularly scenic regions, with great hiking and glacier walks. In **Reykjavík** (p221), enjoy the nightlife, visit the Saga Museum and take trips to the Viking village of Hafnarfjörður and the Blue Lagoon.

» Head to the desolate interior for the amazing geoscapes of **Landmannalaugar** (p268). Take the spectacular three-day hike to Þórsmörk. The tough day's extension to **Skógar** (p264) takes you across some of the country's newest lava fields. Next, you could head out to the **Vestmannaeyjar** (p264) islands, then travel to the north of the island, where an R&R stop at **Akureyri** (p247) can include a side trip to the **Mývatn** (p253) natural thermal baths and the volcanic landscape of **Krafla** (p254).

» Head back to Denmark on the ferry, or fly back from Reykjavík.

Clockwise from top left
1 Icelandic fish and chips 2 Landmannalaugar (p268)
3 Vatnajökull glacier (p260) 4 Mývatn baths (p253)

countries at a glance

The seductive call of the north is one of wild landscapes, crisp air and cutting-edge city style coloured by the epic changes of the Scandinavian seasons. Scenically, it's hard to beat. Norway's noble, breathtaking coastline, serrated with fjords, competes with Iceland's harsh, volcanic majesty. Soothing Swedish and Finnish lake- and forest-scapes offer a gentler beauty.

Though the towns and cities all have a definite allure – Copenhagen is the one worth the most time – the big attraction is the outdoors. There are so many ways to get active on land, water and snow. Hiking, kayaking and wildlife-watching are among Europe's best, while the bike-friendly culture makes it great for cyclists too, particularly in Denmark, southern Sweden and various Baltic islands.

Denmark

Cycling ✓✓✓
History ✓✓
Gastronomy ✓✓

Two-Wheeled Pleasure
With a highest point as lofty as your average big-city office building, it's no surprise to find that Denmark is a paradise for cycling. With thousands of kilometres of dedicated cycle routes and islands designed for two-wheeled exploration, it's the best way to get around.

Past Echoes
Denmark's historical sites are excellent. Hauntingly preserved bog bodies take us back to prehistoric times, while Roskilde's Viking boats and majestic cathedral are important remnants of other periods. Hamlet may have been a fictional character, but his home, Elsinore Castle (Kronborg Slot), is a major attraction.

New Nordic Cuisine
Nordic food has taken a big upward swing, and Denmark is at the forefront of modern trends in Scandinavian cuisine. Copenhagen has a great eating scene, with Noma one of the world's most highly regarded restaurants.

p42

Finland

Hiking ✓✓
Winter Activities ✓✓✓
Design ✓✓✓

Wild Nature

Finland's vast forested wildernesses are some of Europe's least populated areas. Large national parks with excellent networks of trails, huts and camping grounds make this prime hiking country. Kayaking and canoeing are also great options.

Active Winters

Northern Finland's numerous ski resorts aren't very elevated but are great for beginners and families. Skiing's just the start, though: snowy wildernesses crossed in sleds pulled by reindeer or huskies, snowmobile safaris, ice-breaker cruises, nights in snow hotels and a personal audience with Santa Claus are other wintry delights.

Design & Architecture

Finnish design is world-famous; browsing Helsinki's shops, from flagship emporia to edgy bohemian studios, is one of the city's great pleasures. Some of the world's finest modern architecture can also be found scattered around Finland's towns.

p127

Tallinn

Medieval Streets ✓✓✓
Culture ✓
Bars & Cafes ✓✓

Historic Jewel

A short trip across the water from Helsinki, Estonia's capital, Tallinn, is the jewel of the nation. The medieval Old Town is its highlight, and weaving your way along its narrow, cobbled streets is like strolling back to the 14th century.

Traditional Culture

Despite (or perhaps because of) centuries of occupation, Estonians have tenaciously held onto their national identity and are deeply, emotionally connected to their history, folklore and national song traditions.

Bar Life

Tallinn has numerous cosy cafes decorated in plush style, ideal spots to while away a few hours if the weather's not being kind. Nightlife, with alcohol not such a wallet drain as in other Nordic countries, is pretty vibrant.

p210

Iceland

Scenery ✓✓✓
Activities ✓✓
Wildlife ✓✓

Volcanic Landscapes

Iceland, forged in fire, has a scenic splendour matched by few other nations. It's a bleak, epic grandeur that seems designed to remind visitors of their utter insignificance in the greater scheme of things. Get among the steaming pools, spouting geysers and majestic glaciers to really appreciate the unique nature of this country.

Outdoors

There are so many ways to get active. Truly spectacular hikes give awesome perspectives of Iceland's natural wonder; kayaks let you see it all from the seaward side. And what better way to soothe those aching muscles than luxuriating in a thermal spring?

Whales & Birds

The land may seem inhospitable, but the seas and skies teem with life. Iceland is one of the world's premier spots for whale-watching, and the quantity of seabirds has to be seen to be believed.

p219

Norway

Fjords ✓✓✓
Activities ✓✓
Wildlife ✓✓✓

Coastal Majesty

The famous serrations of the coast are justly renowned; from base to tip, Norway's jagged geography is deeply momentous, inspiring profound awe.

Outdoor Appeal

The rough and rugged contours make this a prime outdoors destination. Mountains and plateaux attract hikers and cyclists, while the coastline invites getting out on the water in anything from a kayak to a cruise ship. Winter switches over to husky-sledding and snowmobile safaris, as well as the region's best skiing.

Unusual Creatures

For a modern European country, Norway has an impressive range of beasts, from whales frolicking off-shore to roaming elk and reindeer. There's even a reintroduced population of the weird-looking musk ox, as well as plentiful seabird life. Right up north, Svalbard is bossed by polar bears and walruses.

p285

Sweden

Winter Activities ✓✓✓
Museums ✓✓
Boating ✓✓

Snowy Seduction

Northern Sweden has several top-drawer winter attractions, one of which is the aurora borealis (Northern Lights). Dark places like Abisko, in the country's top-left corner, make great observatories; other attractions up here include dog-sledding, skiing and Kiruna's famous Ice Hotel.

Proud Heritage

Sweden, which once controlled much of northern Europe, has a rich history and proud artistic heritage, which is displayed at great galleries and museums in the country. But it's not all about the rich and famous. Excellent open-air displays dotted across the country document the humbler traditions of everyday life.

Water World

The abundance of water once the snow melts means Sweden is perfect for boating, whether you're canoeing inland waterways, boating in an archipelago, or exploring the coastline in a yacht or kayak.

p386

On the
Road

Norway
p285

Iceland
p219

Finland
p127

Sweden
p386

Tallinn
p210

Denmark
p42

Denmark

Includes »

Best Places to Eat

» Noma (p57)

» Kødbyens Fiskebar (p56)

» Schønnemann (p57)

» Kadeau (p78)

» St Pauls Apothek (p97)

Best Places to Stay

» Hotel Nimb (p54)

» Helenekilde Badehotel (p66)

» Dragsholm Slot (p69)

» Pension Vestergade 44 (p92)

» Stammershalle Badehotel (p80)

Why Go?

Denmark is the bridge between Scandinavia and northern Europe. To the rest of Scandinavia, the Danes are fun-loving, frivolous party animals, with relatively liberal, progressive attitudes. Their culture, food, architecture and appetite for conspicuous consumption owe as much, if not more, to their German neighbours to the south as to their former colonies – Sweden, Norway and Iceland – to the north.

Packed with intriguing museums, shops, bars, nightlife and award-winning restaurants, Denmark's capital, Copenhagen, is one of the hippest, most accessible cities in Europe. And while Danish cities such as Odense and Aarhus harbour their own cultural gems, Denmark's other chief appeal lies in its photogenic countryside, sweeping coastline and historic sights such as neolithic burial chambers, the bodies of well-preserved Iron Age people exhumed from their slumber in peat bogs, and atmospheric Viking ruins and treasures.

When to Go
Copenhagen

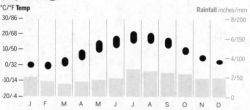

Jun & Jul Long days, buzzing beachside towns, Copenhagen Jazz and A-list rock fest Roskilde.

Sep & Oct Fewer crowds, golden landscapes and snug nights by crackling open fires.

Dec Twinkling Christmas lights, ice-skating rinks and gallons of warming *gløgg* (mulled wine).

DENMARK

Connections

Denmark's modern, efficient transport network is well connected to the region and the rest of the world. Located in Copenhagen, its main airport, Kastrup, offers excellent and numerous long- and short-haul connections, while Billund and Aarhus in Jutland (regional airports) offer numerous European short-haul options. Good road and rail connections link Sweden and Germany to Denmark. Plentiful ferries link Denmark with all major Baltic destinations and with Atlantic Coast destinations in Norway, the Faroe Islands, Iceland and the UK.

ITINERARIES

One Week

You could comfortably spend four days in Copenhagen exploring the museums, hunting down Danish design and taste-testing its lauded restaurants and bars. A trip north along the coast to the magnificent modern-art museum, Louisiana, and then further north still to Kronborg Slot, before returning south via Frederiksborg Slot and Roskilde, would be a great way to spend the other three days. If the weather is on your side, head for the north coast of Zealand for historic fishing villages and gorgeous sandy beaches.

Two Weeks

After time in Copenhagen, a quick catamaran ride will take you to the Baltic island of Bornholm, reputedly the sunniest slice of Denmark, and famed for cycling, beaches and its cheap, tasty smoke-houses. Alternatively, head west, stopping off on the island of Funen to see Hans Christian Andersen's birthplace in Odense. Continue further west to the Jutland peninsula for the understated hipster cool of Aarhus and further north to magnificent Skagen, where the Baltic and North Seas clash.

Essential Food & Drink

» **Smørrebrød** Rye bread topped with anything from beef tartar to egg and shrimp, the open sandwich is Denmark's most famous culinary export.

» **Sild** Smoked, cured, pickled or fried, herring is a local staple and best washed down with generous serves of akvavit (schnapps).

» **Kanelsnegle** A calorific delight, 'cinnamon snails' are sweet, buttery scrolls, sometimes laced with chocolate.

» **Akvavit** Denmark's best-loved spirit is caraway-spiced akvavit from Aalborg, drunk straight down as a shot, followed by a chaser of øl (beer).

» **Lashings of beer** Carlsberg may dominate, but Denmark's expanding battalion of microbreweries includes Rise Bryggeri, Brøckhouse and Grauballe.

AT A GLANCE

- » **Capital** Copenhagen
- » **Area** 43,098 sq km
- » **Population** 5.58 million
- » **Country code** ☑45
- » **Language** Danish
- » **Currency** Danish krone (Dkr)

Exchange Rates

Australia	A$1	Dkr5.98
Canada	C$1	Dkr5.59
Europe	€1	Dkr7.45
Japan	¥100	Dkr6.03
New Zealand	NZ$1	Dkr4.77
UK	UK£1	Dkr8.72
USA	US$1	Dkr5.72

For current exchange rates see www.xe.com.

Set Your Budget

» **Double room in hostel** Dkr300–700

» **Two-course evening meal** Dkr300

» **Museum entrance** free–Dkr95

» **Beer** Dkr45

» **Copenhagen transport pass (72 hours)** Dkr190

Resources

» **Visit Denmark** (www.visitdenmark.com) Comprehensive tourist information.

» **AOK** (www.aok.dk) Up-to-date reviews and listings for Copenhagen events, restaurants, bars and nightlife.

» **Rejseplanen** (www.rejseplanen.dk) Great journey planner.

» **Lonely Planet** (www.lonelyplanet.com/denmark) Info, hotel bookings, forums and more.

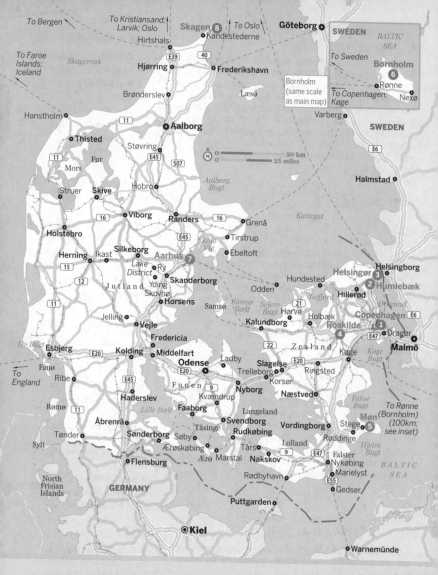

Denmark Highlights

1 Shop, nosh and chill in Scandinavia's capital of cool, **Copenhagen** (p45)

2 Be inspired by the art and the views at the **Louisiana Museum of Modern Art** (p62) in Humlebæk

3 Snoop around **Kronborg Slot** (p64), Hamlet's epic home in Helsingør

4 Get your groove on at Denmark's top annual music event, **Roskilde Festival** (p68)

5 Tackle the Colgate-white cliffs of **Møns Klint** (p72) on picture-perfect Møn

6 Lose yourself in nature and smoked fish on the Baltic island of **Bornholm** (p74)

7 See Aarhus through Technicolor glass at impressive art museum **ARoS** (p93)

8 Watch angry seas duel above luminous, northern **Skagen** (p109)

COPENHAGEN

POP 1.9 MILLION

Copenhagen is the coolest kid on the Nordic block. Edgier than Stockholm and worldlier than Oslo, the Danish capital gives Scandinavia the X-factor.

While this thousand-year-old harbour town has managed to retain much of its historic good looks – think copper spires and cobbled squares – the focus here is on the innovative and cutting edge. Denmark's overachieving capital is home to a thriving design scene, its streets awash with effortlessly hip shops, cafes and bars; world-class museums and art collections; intelligent new architecture; and no fewer than 13 Michelin-starred restaurants. This is also a royal city, home to the multitalented Queen Margrethe II and her photogenic family.

And as if this wasn't impressive enough, a bounty of beautiful beaches, wooded parks and elegant lakes await just minutes away.

History

For more millennia than anyone can be sure of, Copenhagen was a fishing settlement on the shores of what we now call the Øresund Strait, the narrow belt of water between Denmark and Sweden.

Wendish pirates, who marauded the coast in the 12th century, prompted the locals, led by Bishop Absalon, to build a fort on a small island in the harbour – where the modern-day Danish parliament stands on Slotsholmen; you can still see the foundations of the original fort in the cellar museum.

The city of København ('købe' means 'to buy,' 'havn' is 'harbour') gradually grew to the north of Slotsholmen, where the restaurants of Gammel Strand now stand, founded on the wealth that came from the herring caught by the local fishermen. But it wasn't until the 15th century that Copenhagen stole Roskilde's thunder as the new capital of Denmark.

Denmark's great Renaissance king, Christian IV (1588–1648), transformed Copenhagen into an impressive capital. From there he controlled much of Scandinavia – with numerous ambitious buildings including Rosenborg Slot and the Rundetårn. Eventually Christian IV brought the country to its knees with overspending and reckless foreign forays.

By the early 19th century the once-mighty Danish empire was greatly diminished. Twice in the early 19th century the British navy bombarded the city but its people bounced back with a cultural Golden Age, led by the likes of Hans Christian Andersen and Søren Kierkegaard.

COPENHAGEN CARD

The **Copenhagen Card** (www.cphcard.com; 24hr adult/child 249/135Dkr, 72hr 479/245Dkr) secures unlimited travel on buses and trains around Copenhagen and North Zealand. This covers the city's metro system, as well as suburban trains. It also gives free or discounted admission to around 70 of the region's museums and attractions. Cards can be purchased directly online and are also sold at the Copenhagen tourist office, Central Station, major Danske Statsbaner (DSB) stations and at many hotels, camping grounds and hostels. Be aware, though, that several of the city's attractions are either free or at least free one day of the week.

◎ Sights

Two of the great things about Copenhagen are its accessibility and size. You can walk across the city centre in an hour, and travel further with great ease thanks to the cycle paths, metro, trains and buses, all of which mean you can pack many of the sights into two days.

AROUND TIVOLI

TOP CHOICE Tivoli AMUSEMENT PARK
(www.tivoli.dk; adult/child under 8 Dkr95/free; ⊙11am-10pm Sun-Thu, to 12.30am Fri, to midnight Sat early Apr-late Sep, reduced hr rest of yr) It ain't Disneyland, but Copenhagen's iconic amusement park has been winning hearts since 1843. There's a timeless quality about the place, especially as the sun sets and the park's Moorish domes, arches and manicured gardens sparkle in a sea of twinkling lights. You'll find pantomime and live-music acts, food pavilions (including some very decent restaurants), carnival games, not to mention amusement rides, from the soothing to the hair-raising.

Tivoli's numerous open-air performances are free of charge, but there's usually an admission fee for the indoor performances – check the website for venue details, line-ups and prices. Amusement ride tickets cost 25Dkr (some rides require up to three tickets),

Central Copenhagen (København)

Assistens
Kierkegård

To Coffee Collective
Nørrebro (350m);
Relæ (500m)

NØRREBRO

Møllegade

Guldbergsgade

Sankt
Hans Torv

Læssøesgade

Ryesgade

Fredensbro

69

46

Elmegade

Nørrebrogade

Fælledvej

Sankt Hans Gade

Ramsborggade

Sortedam Dossering

Sortedams
Sø

Øster Søgade

Sølvgade

Sølvtorvet

Stengade

Baggesensgade

Dronning
Louises
Bro

Øster Farimagsgade

Botanisk Have

12
2

Blågårds
Plads

Korsgade

Frederiksborggade

25

Gothersgade

Nørre Voldgade

Åblvd

Peblinge Dossering

Peblinge
Sø

Nørre Søgade

Vendersgade

Romersgade

Linnésgade

Nørreport

Rosenborggade

To Coffee Collective
Frederiksberg (1.2km)

Rosenørns Allé

Gyldenløvesgade

Turesensgade

Nansensgade

Nørre Farimagsgade

Israels
Plads

Nørre Voldgade

Nørregade

Rosengården

Hausergade

Hauser
Plads

Forum

Sankt Marcus Allé

VESTERBRO

Vester Søgade

Nyropsgade

Ørsteds
Parken

Larslejsstræde

Holstræde

38

73

Krystalgade

16

51

Kannikestræde

Skindergade

Danasvej

Kampmannsgade

Vester Farimagsgade

H C Andersens Blvd

Nørre Voldgade

61

59

20

Vor Frue
Plads

36
21

Studiestræde

45

Vimmelskaftet

Sankt
Jørgens Sø

Vestergade

Gammeltorv

Nytorv

Vesterport

Hammerichsgade

35

Vestergade

Frederiksberggade

58

STRØGET

68

64

Bertrams Hotel
Guldsmeden
(400m); Pony
(800m)

Ved Vesterport

Jernbanegade

39

Rådhuspladsen

62

Rådhusstræde

33

Stormbro

Gammel Kongevej

Axeltorv

Lavendelstræde

Tivoli

TIVOLI

Bag Rådhuset

Nationalmuseet

Vesterbrogade

57

Banegårdspladsen

Dantes
Plads

Vester Voldgade

Stormgade

30

28

Viktoriagade

Istedgade

København
Hovedbanegården
(Central Station)

Tietgensgade

Ny Carlsberg
Glyptotek

Dannebrogsgade

Gasværksvej

Eskildsgade

Absalonsgade

Skydebanegade

Halmtorvet

29

Hambrosgade

32

To Ideal
Bar
(500m)

Sønder Blvd

54

52

Kødbyen
(Meatpacking
District)

VESTERBRO

23

Ingerslevsgade

40

Kalvebod Brygge

60

44

Sydhavnen

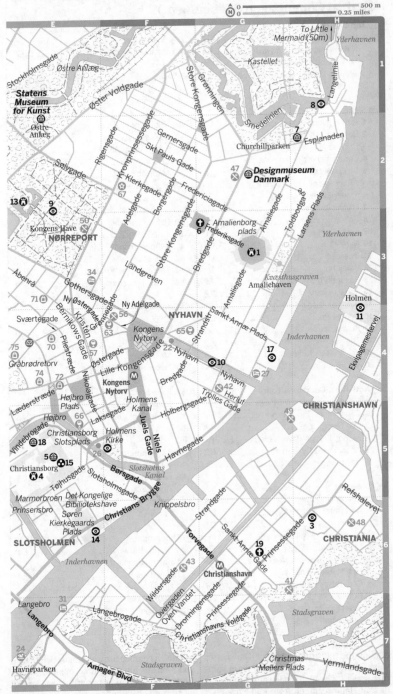

N 0 ——————— 500 m
0 ——————— 0.25 miles

To Little
Mermaid (50m)
Yderhavnen

Kastellet

Langelinie

Stockholmsgade
Østre Anlæg

**Statens
Museum
for Kunst**

Østre
Anlæg

Øster Voldgade

Store Kongensgade

Grønningen

Smedelinien

8⊚

7🏛

Churchillparken

Esplanaden

Gernersgade

Skt Pauls Gade

Sølgade

47⊗

**Designmuseum
Danmark**

Regensgade

Kronprinsessegade

Fredericiagade

Amaliegade

13🏛

9⊕

50

Kongens Have

NØRREPORT

Adelgade

Borgergade

Store Kongensgade

Bredgade

6✝

**Amalienborg
plads**

Frederiksgade

🏛1

Amaliehaven

Kvæsthusgraven

Toldbodgade

Larsens Plads

Yderhavnen

Landgreven

Amaliegade

Åbenrå

Gothersgade

34🏛

71🔒

Ny Østergade

Ny Adelgade

NYHAVN

Sankt Annæ Plads

Strandstr

Holmen

⊚
11

Sværtegade

Bernikows Gade

Kristen

56⊗

63⊗

57⊗

Kongens
Nytorv

65⊗

22 Nyhavn

⊚10

Nyhavn

17
⊚

Inderhavnen

75⊗

70⊕

Pilestræde

Østergade

Lille Kongensgade

Bredgade

42⊗

27🏛

Ekvipagemestervej

Gråbrødretorv

74🔒

72🔒

Nikolajgade

**Kongens
Nytorv**
Ⓜ

Herluf

Nyhavn

Læderstræde

Højbro
Plads

66⊗

Holmens
Kanal

Holbergsgade

Trolles Gade

CHRISTIANSHAWN

49⊗

Højbro

Laksegade

Juels Gade

Niels

Vindebrogade

18🏛

Christiansborg
Slotsplads

26

Holmens
Kirke

Havnegade

5🏛

15⊕

Børsgade

Slotsholms
Kanal

Refshalevej

Christiansborg

4⊕

Tøjhusgade

Slotsholmsgade

Marmorbroen

Prinsensbro

Det Kongelige
Bibiliotekshave

Søren

Christians Brygge

Knippelsbro

Strandgade

3⊚

48⊗

SLOTSHOLMEN

Kierkegaards
Plads

14⊚

Sankt Annæ Gade

Prinsessegade

CHRISTIANIA

Inderhavnen

Torvegade

19
ℹ

41⊗

Langebro

31🏛

Wildersgade

43⊗

Overgaden

Oven Vandet

Christianshavn
Ⓜ

Dronningensgade

Prinsessegade

Christianshavns Voldgade

Stadsgraven

24⊗

Havneparken

Langebrogade

Amager Blvd

Stadsgraven

Christmas
Møllers Plads

Vermlandsgade

Central Copenhagen (København)

making the multiride ticket (199Dkr) better value in most cases. Outside the main summer season, Tivoli also opens for around 10 days at Halloween and from mid-November to late December for Christmas. See the Tivoli website for up-to-date opening times, as well as upcoming performances, special events and evening fireworks.

COPENHAGEN IN...

Two Days

Oriente yourself with a **canal tour** before strolling **Nyhavn** and design shopping at **Hay House** and **Illums Bolighus**. Gourmet graze at **TorvehallerneKBH** and dive into Danish history at the **Nationalmuseet**. If dining at **Kadeau**, cap the night at **Ruby**. If eating at **Kødbyens Fiskebar**, kick on at **Mesteren & Lærlingen**. The following day, visit **Statens Museum for Kunst**, sample smørrebrød at **Schønnemann** and take in the panorama atop **Rundetårn**. Amble through free-spirited **Christiania** before New Nordic noshing at **Noma** (assuming you booked months ahead!) or wallet-friendly **Pony**. If it's summer, indulge your inner child at **Tivoli**. If it's not, opt for crafty cocktails at **1105**.

Four Days

Spend day three gazing at art and Sweden at the **Louisiana Museum of Modern Art** or head further north to Hamlet's 'home' in Helsingør, **Kronborg Slot**. Head back into town for dinner at **Le Sommelier**, followed by jazz at **La Fontaine** or clubbing at **Simons**. Spend day four exploring **Ny Carlsberg Glyptotek**, lunching at romantic **Orangeriet**, and eyeing the crown jewels at **Rosenborg Slot**. After dark, catch an aria at Copenhagen's head-turning opera house, **Operaen**.

TOP CHOICE **Nationalmuseet**   MUSEUM
(National Museum; www.natmus.dk; Ny Vestergade 10; admission free; ⏱10am-5pm Tue-Sun) Take 'Danish History 101' at Denmark's National Museum. With first claims on virtually every antiquity found on Danish soil, its treasures includes Stone Age tools, Viking weaponry and impressive Bronze Age, Iron Age and rune-stone collections. Don't miss the exhibition of bronze lurs, some of which date back 3000 years and are still capable of blowing a tune, and the finely crafted 3500-year-old Sun Chariot, unearthed in a Zealand field a century ago. There are sections related to the Norsemen and Inuit of Greenland, collections of 18th-century Danish furniture, even a re-created 18th-century Copenhagen apartment. The museum also has an excellent Children's Museum, a fine collection of Greek, Roman and medieval coins, and a Classical Antiquities section complete with Egyptian mummies. A cafe and gift shop provide cerebral relief.

TOP CHOICE **Ny Carlsberg Glyptotek**   MUSEUM
(www.glyptoteket.dk; Dantes Plads 7, HC Andersens Blvd; adult/child Dkr75/free, Sun free; ⏱11am-5pm Tue-Sun) Fin de siècle architecture dallies with top-notch art at eclectic Ny Carlsberg Glyptotek. Across the road from Tivoli, the museum is celebrated for its antiquities, French impressionist works and Danish Golden Age paintings. Particularly impressive is the collection of Rodin sculptures – the largest outside of France –

as well as the numerous works by Gauguin. At its heart is a beautiful tropical winter garden and cafe.

SLOTSHOLMEN

An island separated from the city centre by a moatlike canal on three sides and the harbour on the other side, Slotsholmen is the site of Christiansborg Palace, home to Denmark's parliament.

Christiansborg Palace   PALACE
Of Christiansborg Palace's numerous museums (which include a theatre museum and an armoury museum), the cake-taker is De Kongelige Repræsentationslokaler (Royal Reception Chambers; www.ses.dk; adult/child Dkr80/40; ⏱guided tours in Danish 11am, in English 3pm), an ornate Renaissance hall where the queen entertains heads of state.

Beneath the building lurk the Ruins of Absalon's Fortress (adult/child Dkr40/20; ⏱10am-5pm, closed Mon Oct-Apr), the excavated foundations of Bishop Absalon's original castle of 1167 and of its successor, Copenhagen Slot.

Thorvaldsens Museum   MUSEUM
(www.thorvaldsensmuseum.dk; Bertel Thorvaldsens Plads; adult/child Dkr40/free, Wed free; ⏱10am-5pm Tue-Sun) The striking Thorvaldsens Museum stars the imposing statues by the famed Danish sculptor Bertel Thorvaldsen. Like his works, the building's Pompeian-style interiors reflect the artist's obsession with Greek and Roman mythology.

Royal Library
ARCHITECTURE

(www.kb.dk; Søren Kierkegaards Plads; ⊙8am-7pm Mon-Sat Jul & Aug) While the Royal Library dates from the 17th century, the focal point these days is its ultramodern walkway-connected extension, dubbed the 'Black Diamond' for its shiny black-granite facade. The sleek, seven-storey building houses 21 million books and other precious literary items, such as Hans Christian Andersen's original manuscripts. The building itself is open for visits, with rotating exhibitions, as well as a cafe, restaurant and bookshop.

AROUND NYHAVN & HARBOURFRONT

Just east of Kongens Nytorv, the bustling waterfront and the surrounding area are home to a number of iconic landmarks and cultural riches.

Nyhavn
CANAL

Built to connect Kongens Nytorv to the harbour, the mast-flanked Nyhavn canal was long a haunt for sailors and writers, including Hans Christian Andersen, who lived there for most of his life at, variously, numbers 20, 18 and 67. These days it's the city's default postcard image, defined by pastel-hued gabled town houses and smitten tourists. While the strip's mediocre 'tourist menus' are best avoided, you can do a lot worse than kicking back with a beer here when the sun pours over Copenhagen.

Skuespilhuset
ARCHITECTURE

(Royal Danish Playhouse; ☑33 69 69 69; www.kglteater.dk; Sankt Anne Plads 36) Around the corner from Nyhavn, nostalgia gives way to edge at Skuespilhuset, Copenhagen's striking, three-stage playhouse. A very contemporary take on Italian Renaissance architecture, it's home to the Royal Danish Theatre. Guided tours in English (Dkr2500) are only for groups. Most productions are in Danish and tickets must be bought in advance from www.kglteater.dk, www.billetnet.dk or at the box office.

Operaen
NOTABLE BUILDING

(www.kglteater.dk; Ekvipagemestervej 10) Across the harbour stands Copenhagen's altogether more controversial opera house, Operaen (see also p60). Upon its completion in 2005, the building's architect, Henning Larsen, declared the project 'a compromise which failed', referring to project investor Maersk McKinney Moller's insistence on adding metal strings to the bubble-shaped glass facade. The tweak led Danish newspaper *Politiken* to compare it to the grille of a 1955 Pontiac.

Amalienborg Palace
PALACE

(www.dkks.dk; adult/child Dkr65/free; ⊙10am-4pm May-Oct, reduced the rest of yr) Amalienborg Palace, 300m north of Skusepilhuset, has been home to the royal family since 1794. Its four austere mansions surround a central square. The buildings are guarded by sentries, relieved at noon by a ceremonial changing of the guard. You can view the interior of the northwestern mansion, with its royal memorabilia and the study rooms of three kings. A combined ticket including Rosenborg Slot costs 110Dkr.

Frederikskirken
CHURCH

(www.marmorkirken.dk; Frederiksgade 4; admission free, dome adult/child Dkr25/10; ⊙10am-5pm Mon-Thu & Sat, noon-5pm Fri & Sun, dome 1pm & 3pm

---

WORTH A TRIP

KLAMPENBORG

Klampenborg is a favourite spot for family outings from Copenhagen. It is only 20 minutes from Central Station on the S-train's line C (Dkr48). **Bellevue Beach**, 400m east of Klampenborg station, is a sandy strand that gets packed with sunbathers in summer. A large grassy area behind the beach absorbs some of the overflow.

About 700m west from the station is **Bakken** (www.bakken.dk; Dyrehavevej 62; multiride wristband adult/child Dkr249/159; ⊙varies), the world's oldest amusement park. A blue-collar version of Copenhagen's Tivoli, it's a pleasantly old-fashioned carnival of bumper cars, slot machines and beer halls.

Bakken is on the southern edge of **Dyrehaven**, an extensive expanse of beech woods and meadows crossed with peaceful walking and cycling trails. Dyrehaven was established in 1669 as a royal hunting ground and is the capital's most popular picnic area – it's excellent for cycling and running too. At its centre, 2km north of Bakken, is the old manor house **Eremitagen**, a good vantage point for spotting herds of deer.

Sat & Sun) Inland along Frederiksgade is the glorious, neo-baroque Frederikskirken, universally known as Marmorkirken (Marble Church). The view from its great dome – inspired by St Peter's in Rome – is spectacular.

TOP CHOICE Designmuseum Danmark   MUSEUM
(www.designmuseum.dk; Bredgade 68; adult/child Dkr75/free; ⊙11am-5pm Tue & Thu-Sun, to 9pm Wed) The outstanding Designmuseum Danmark lies 250m north of Frederikskirken along Bredgade. Its collection includes ancient Chinese and Japanese ceramics, 18th- and 19th-century European porcelain, and a fabulous collection of Danish design pieces from pioneers like Poul Henningsen, Finn Juhl and Arne Jacobsen.

FREE Frihedsmuseet   MUSEUM
(www.natmus.dk; Churchillparken 7; ⊙10am-4pm Tue-Sun May-Sep, to 3pm Oct-Apr) Bredgade ends at Churchillparken, where you'll find Frihedsmuseet, with moving relics from the history of the Danish Resistance against Nazi occupation.

About 150m north of the Frihedsmuseet stands the spectacular Gefion Fountain (Gefionspringvandet), which captures the goddess Gefion ploughing the island of Zealand with her four sons yoked as oxen. Less impressive yet much more iconic is the somewhat forlorn Little Mermaid (Den Lille Havfrue) statue, another 400m north along the waterfront. Artist Bjørn Nørgaard's Genetically Modified Little Mermaid, which sits just a few hundred metres from Edvard Eriksen's original statue, is a much more interesting interpretation.

AROUND STRØGET

The streets running off the main shopping strip of Strøget are a treat for flâneurs. Especially beautiful is the so-called Latin Quarter, to the north of Strøget. Also known as Pisserenden (which needs no translation), it's the city's historic university quarter, its grid of narrow streets and, often, half-timbered town houses crammed with independent shops and cafes. On the northern side of the Latin Quarter is Kultorvet, a lively square known for its impromptu street entertainment, beer gardens, flower stalls and produce stands.

Rundetårn   HISTORIC BUILDING, LOOKOUT
(www.rundetaarn.dk; Købmagergade 52; adult/child Dkr25/5; ⊙10am-8pm late May-late Sep, astronomy programs 7-10pm Tue & Wed mid-Oct–mid-Mar)

Haul yourself to the top of the 34.8m-high, red-brick 'Round Tower' and you'll be following in the footsteps of such luminaries as King Christian IV, who built it in 1642 as an observatory for the famous astronomer Tycho Brahe. You'll also be following in the hoofsteps of Tsar Peter the Great's horse and, according to legend, the track marks of a car that made its way up the tower's spiral ramp in 1902. The tower houses the oldest functioning observatory in Europe and offers evening astronomy programs.

Vor Frue Kirke   CHURCH
(⊙8am-5pm, closed during services & concerts) Opposite the university stands Vor Frue Kirke, Copenhagen's neoclassical cathedral. The building dates from 1829, but stands on the site of earlier churches. Inside are imposing neoclassical statues of Christ and the 12 Apostles, the most acclaimed works of the Golden Age sculptor Bertel Thorvaldsen.

AROUND KONGENS HAVE

TOP CHOICE Statens Museum for Kunst   MUSEUM
(www.smk.dk; Sølvgade 48-50; special exhibitions adult/child Dkr95/free; ⊙10am-5pm Tue & Thu-Sun, to 8pm Wed) Perfect on a rainy day, Denmark's art museum heavyweight straddles seven centuries of European art. There's an interesting collection of old masters by Dutch and Flemish artists, including Rubens and Frans Hals, as well as more contemporary European paintings by luminaries such as Matisse, Picasso and Munch. Not surprisingly, the museum also has an inspiring collection of Danish art from icons including CW Eckersberg, Jens Juel, Christen Købke, Asger Jorn and Per Kirkeby. It's also home to Bjørn Nørgaard's infamous works *The Horse Sacrifice* and *Objects from The Horse Sacrifice*, which document the Danish artist's ritualistic sacrifice of a horse in 1970 in protest at the Vietnam War. Critique the controversy at the museum's light-filled cafe, or stock up on books, art cards and gifts at the museum shop. From Nørreport S-train station, the museum is 800m northeast along Nørre Voldgade (which becomes Øster Voldgade).

Rosenborg Slot   CASTLE
(www.dkks.dk; Øster Voldgade 4a; adult/child 75Dkr/free; ⊙10am-5pm Jun-Aug, 11am-4pm Sep & Oct, reduced hrs rest of yr) Christian IV's fabulous Dutch Renaissance–style castle stands at the edge of Kongens Have (p52). Built in the early 17th century, it's one of Copenhagen's great landmarks, home to glorious marbled

MARTIN KALHØJ, ARTIST & GALLERY OWNER

Copenhagen artist and gallery owner Martin Kalhøj (www.kalhoej.dk) lets us in on his favourite city hang-outs.

Must-See

Copenhagen has a lot of inspiring museums and galleries. One of my favourites is Designmuseum Danmark (p51). It's a great place to get a feeling for what Danish and Scandinavian design is all about. You'll find works by my favourite designer, Arne Jacobsen. Look out for his Swan Chair, designed especially for Copenhagen's Royal Hotel in 1958. Another personal favourite is his Series 7 Chair, created in 1955.

Must-Do

Walk or cycle through Christianshavn. It's my favourite city neighbourhood. It has everything; nice cafes, old-fashioned pubs, trendy restaurant and lots of water. I also think it has the best *hygge* (cosiness) factor in town. Another beautiful spot to cycle is along the lakes separating the city centre from Nørrebro. The city side has some especially elegant architecture.

Must-Eat

The best place to try Denmark's famous *smørrebrød* (open sandwich) is Schønnemann (p57). The quality of the food and service is high and the place is wonderfully *hyggelig* (cosy). Order the caramelised herring open sandwich, a glass of schnapps and a good brewed beer from Bornholm or Copenhagen's Nørrebro Bryghus. Follow it up with the potatoes with smoked mayonnaise...and another schnapps, of course.

and painted ceilings, gilded mirrors, priceless Dutch tapestries, solid-silver lions, and gold- and enamel-ware. The Royal Treasury, in the castle basement, houses the Danish crown jewels. A combined ticket including Amalienborg Palace (p50) costs Dkr110.

Kongens Have — GARDENS

(King's Gardens; admission free) The stretch of green along Øster Voldgade offers a refuge from the city traffic. Behind Rosenborg Slot lie the manicured box hedges, lush lawns and heavenly rose beds of Kongens Have, Copenhagen's oldest public park. A hit with sunbathers and the picnic set, it's also the site of a free marionette theatre that performs on summer afternoons.

Botanisk Have — GARDENS

(Botanical Gardens; botanik.snm.ku.dk; main entrance Gothersgade 140; ⊙8.30am-6pm May-Sep, reduced hr rest of yr) To the west of Rosenborg Slot is the recently revamped Botanisk Have, its tranquil trails are dotted with quotes from Danish poets and writers (in Danish). If Denmark's fickle weather leaves you longing for Phuket, don't miss a walk through the gardens' elegant Palmehus (⊙10am-3pm May-Sep, closed Mon Oct-Apr), a walk-through glasshouse lavished with tropical plants.

CHRISTIANSHAVN

Christiania — NEIGHBOURHOOD

(www.christiania.org; Prinsessegade) Escape the capitalist crunch at Freetown Christiania, a hash-scented, collectively run commune straddling the eastern side of Christianshavn. Since its establishment by squatters in 1971, the area has drawn nonconformists and free-spirited souls from across the globe, attracted by the concept of collective business, workshops, recycling programs and communal living. While Pusher St – lined with shady hash and marijuana dealers – may be its most infamous attraction, beyond it lies a semibucolic wonderland of whimsical DIY homes, cosy gardens, rambling paths, as well as a handful of craft shops, cheap eateries, beer gardens and music venues. The main entrance into Christiania is on Prinsessegade, 200m northeast of its intersection with Bådsmandsstræde. Guided tours (⊉32 57 96 70; www.rundvisergruppen.dk; tours Dkr40; ⊙3pm daily late Jun-Aug, 3pm Sat & Sun Sep-Jun) of Christiania depart from just inside the main entrance.

FREE **Vor Frelsers Kirke** CHURCH, LOOKOUT

(www.vorfrelserskirke.dk; Sankt Annæ Gade 29; admission free, tower adult/child Dkr35/10; ⊘11am-3.30pm, closed during services, tower 10am-6.45pm late Jun–mid-Sep) Close to Christiania stands the 17th-century Vor Frelsers Kirke, featuring an impressive baroque altar and a breathtaking pipe organ, carved in 1698 and propped up by two unhappy-looking decorative elephants. For a panoramic view of the city and across to Sweden, climb the 400 steps of the church's 95m-high spiral tower. The last 160 steps run spectacularly along the outside rim, narrowing to the point where they disappear at the top.

OUTSIDE THE CENTRE

Carlsberg Brewery BREWERY

(www.visitcarlsberg.dk; Gamle Carlsberg Vej 11; adult incl 2 beers or soft drinks Dkr70, child incl 2 soft drinks Dkr50; ⊘10am-5pm May-Aug, closed Mon rest of yr) The Carlsberg Brewery's visitor center serves up an evocative exhibition on the history of Danish beer from 1370 BC (yes, they carbon-dated a bog girl who was found in a peat bog caressing a jug of well-aged brew). The self-guided tour ends at the in-house bar where you can knock back two free beers. To get here, take bus 18 or 26 westbound or the S-Tog (S-Train) to Enghave station.

🏃 **Activities**

Weather permitting, there are reasonably good opportunities to swim, sunbathe and appreciate the Danish scenery at bathing spots in and around the city.

Amager Strandpark BEACH

(🏖) Less than 5km southeast of the city centre, this sand-sational artificial lagoon has acres of sandy beach and, during summer, a festive vibe with cafes and bars. Playground facilities and shallow water make it ideal for kids. Take the metro to Amager Strand.

FREE **Islands Brygge**

Havnebadet SWIMMING

(Islands Brygge; ⊘7am-7pm Mon-Fri, 11am-7pm Sat & Sun Jun-Aug) Copenhagen's knack for good design extends to this architect-designed outdoor pool complex, right *in* the city's main canal. Water quality is rigorously monitored, so don't worry about pollution. On warm summer days, this is the place to see and be seen.

DGI-byen SWIMMING, GYM

(www.dgi-byen.dk; Tietgensgade 65, Vesterbro; day pass adult/child Dkr60/40; ⊘6.30am-10pm Mon-Thu, 6.30am-8pm Fri, 9am-7pm Sat, 9am-6pm Sun; 🏊) Splash year-round at this heated indoor fitness centre, complete with an ellipse-shaped pool with 100m lanes, a deep 'mountain pool' with climbing wall, a hot-water pool and a children's pool. You can hire togs or towels (Dkr25 each), assuming you have photo ID as a deposit. There's also a small gym (Dkr75).

👉 **Tours**

Canal Tours

The best way to see Copenhagen is from the water. There are several ways to take a boat tour around the city's canals and harbour, with multilingual guides giving a commentary in English.

Canal Tours Copenhagen BOAT TOUR

(www.stromma.dk; adult/child Dkr75/37.50; ⊘tours every 30min 9.30am-8pm, to 7.15pm from Gammel Strand, mid-Jun–late Aug, reduced hr rest of yr) Tours leave from Nyhavn and Gammel Strand, taking one hour and passing by the *Little Mermaid*, Christianshavn and Christiansborg Palace.

Netto-Bådene BOAT TOUR

(www.netto-baadene.dk; adult/child Dkr40/15; ⊘2-5 hours per hr, 10am-7pm Jul & Aug, to 5pm Apr-Jun & Sep–mid-Oct) Covers the same route as Canal Tours Copenhagen, with embarkation points at Holmens Kirke and Nyhavn.

Cycling & Jogging

Bike Copenhagen With Mike CYCLING

(📞26 39 56 88; www.bikecopenhagenwithmike.dk; tour incl bike rental Dkr290) Go local and hit the saddle on Mike's daily three-hour cycling tours of the city. Tours depart from Skt Peders Stræde 47, slap bang in the central Latin Quarter. Come summer, themed tours include a contemporary architecture tour.

Jogging Tours RUNNING

(📞20 29 64 19; www.joggingtours.dk; 1-2 persons 200Dkr, 3-5 persons Dkr300) Huff and puff your way across the city on a jogging tour. Choose from four neighbourhood-based routes: Royal Tour, Nørrebro Tour, Christianhavn Tour or Frederiksberg Tour.

⭐ **Festivals & Events**

Copenhagen Jazz Festival MUSIC

(www.jazz.dk) Copenhagen's largest music event and the largest jazz festival in northern

Europe means 10 swinging days of world-class music in early July. A scaled-back winter edition, **Vinterjazz**, takes places over 17 days in late January or February.

Copenhagen Distortion
MUSIC

(www.cphdistortion.dk) Thumping across five days in late May or early June, Copenhagen Distortion delivers raucous block parties and top-name DJs in bars and clubs across town.

Copenhagen Cooking
FOOD

(www.copenhagencooking.dk) Scandinavia's largest food festival usually takes place from mid-August to early September. Events include cooking demonstrations, tastings and foodie tours of Copenhagen. A winter edition takes place in February.

🛏 Sleeping

Copenhagen's slumber spots cover all bases: boutique luxury (Nimb and Hotel Guldsmeden), artistic kookiness (Hotel Fox), floating (CPH Living) and budget chic (Generator Hostel and Wakeup Copenhagen).

Most of the city's main budget hotels are centred in Vesterbro, the neighbourhood directly west of Central Station (Hovedbanegården). Ironically, what was once a relatively downtrodden part of town is now one of its hippest, home to a healthy quota of hot-spot eateries and bars.

It's a good idea to book in advance – rooms in many of the most popular midrange hotels fill quickly, particularly during the convention season, typically from August to October, when prices increase significantly too. That said, prices for rooms do fluctuate greatly, depending on the time of year or even the time of week, with most hotels tempting guests with special offers throughout the year.

The tourist office (p61) can book rooms in private homes (Dkr350/500 for singles/doubles); there is a Dkr100 booking fee if you do it via the tourist office when you arrive, otherwise it's free online.

🏆 TOP CHOICE Hotel Nimb
BOUTIQUE HOTEL €€€

(✆88 70 00 00; www.nimb.dk; Bernstorffsgade 5; r from Dkr2200; @) Posh slumber at its finest, svelte, discerning Nimb sits right in Tivoli. Live glam in its 14 individually styled rooms and suites, all of which fuse crisp Scandi style with beautiful art and antiques, and hi-tech touches. On-site perks include four top restaurants and some fabulous drinking spots (think cocktails by the fire).

🏆 TOP CHOICE Generator Hostel
HOSTEL €

(www.generatorhostel.com; Adelgade 5-7; dm/s/d from Dkr127.50/200/400; @) It might be pricier than a standard hostel, but Generator is also a lot funkier, with contemporary hues, designer touches and slick communal areas (including a bar and outdoor terrace). Some rooms are a little small but all are bright, modern and have private bathrooms (including dorms). Social butterflies will appreciate the regular events.

Hotel Fox
BOUTIQUE HOTEL €€

(✆33 95 77 55; www.hotelfox.dk; Jarmers Plads 3; s Dkr700-1495, d Dkr850-2095; @) Outrageous Fox delivers the city's most original rooms, each one individually designed by a group of 21 international artists and designers. Standouts include room 302 (Moroccan bathhouse meets Stanley Kubrick), room 409 (Swiss chalet kitsch) and room 510 (regal fairy tale). Breakfast is an extra 155Dkr.

Hotel Guldsmeden
BOUTIQUE HOTEL €€

(www.hotelguldsmeden.dk; @) Sandra and Marc Weinert's excellent Guldsmeden group now has three attractive and welcoming hotels in Copenhagen. The **Axel** (✆33 31 32 66; Helgolandsgade 7-11; s Dkr765-1250, d Dkr895-1630) boasts a spa and hints of Balinese style, while both **Bertrams** (✆70 20 81 07; Vesterbrogade 107; s Dkr895-1295, d Dkr995-1595) and **Carlton** (✆33 22 15 00; Vesterbrogade 66; s Dkr695-1195, d Dkr795-1495; 🚃6A) ooze French-colonial flair. The Axel is four-star, Bertrams and the Carlton are three-star. The Axel is the most central, while Bertrams and Carlton are close to the hipster nightlife and retail of Vesterbro.

CPH Living
FLOATING HOTEL €€

(✆61 60 85 46; www.cphliving.com; Langebrogade 1c; r Dkr1180-1460) Sleep on water at this smart floating hotel, right on Copenhagen's main canal. Set on a converted freight boat, its 12 contemporary, light-filled rooms feature floor-to-ceiling windows, modern bathrooms with rainforest shower and a communal sun deck. To get here, follow HC Andersens Blvd southeast from Tivoli and cross Langebro bridge; the hotel is on the north side of the bridge.

Wakeup Copenhagen
HOTEL €€

(✆44 80 00 10; www.wakeupcopenhagen.com; Carsten Niebuhrs Gade 11; s Dkr400-1300, d Dkr500-1400; @) Cheap chic is what you get at contemporary, 510-room Wakeup Copenhagen, assuming you've booked ahead and online (walk-in reservations can be anything but 'budget'). Located 1km south of Central Station, rooms are generic and compact, yet fresh and stylish (we love the podlike showers). Clean linen is under the bed (cost-cutting in action) and three floors feature wooden flooring for the allergy-inclined.

Square
HOTEL €€€

(℡33 38 12 00; www.thesquarecopenhagen.com; Rådhuspladsen 14; s/d from Dkr1000/1100; @) Pimped with Jacobsen chairs and red leather, the Square is a solid slumber option with design touches and amenities generally associated with greater expense and stiffness. Standard rooms are a little small but comfortable, and some have sterling views of Copenhagen's main square.

Hotel Alexandra
HOTEL €€€

(℡33 74 44 44; www.hotelalexandra.dk; HC Andersens Blvd 8; s Dkr853-1741, d Dkr1053-1941; @) Design geeks will adore refined, homely Alexandra, graced with the furniture of Danish greats such as Arne Jacobsen, Ole Wanscher and Kaare Klint. Rooms are effortlessly cosy, each adorned with modern art. Staff are attentive, and the hotel's vintage air makes a refreshing change from all that Nordic minimalism.

71 Nyhavn Hotel
HOTEL €€€

(℡33 43 62 00; www.71nyhavnhotel.com; Nyhavn 71; s Dkr1025-2995, d Dkr1090-3495; @) Superbly located at the harbour end of Nyhavn, this beautiful converted grain house delivers four-star luxury. Rooms facing Nyhavn are quite small, while those without the magical view compensate with more space. Popular with business travellers, the hotel can be a bargain on weekends.

First Hotel Twentyseven
HOTEL €€

(℡70 27 56 27; www.hotel27.dk; Løngangstræde 27; s/d Dkr1086/1395; P) Rooms at the Twentyseven might be a little small, but their minimalist styling and cool furniture fit the hipster bill. We love the black-slate bathrooms, friendly staff, and in-house bars – yes, there's even an ice bar. (If you're a light sleeper, request a room away from the action.)

Hotel Skt Petri
HOTEL €€€

(℡33 45 91 00; www.hotelsktpetri.com; Krystalgade 22; s Dkr995-2895, d Dkr1195-3095) Despite looking a little tired in parts, Skt Petri remains one of Copenhagen's coolest luxury

---

ⓘ LAST-MINUTE CHEAP SLEEPS

If you arrive in Copenhagen without a hotel booking, luck may yet be on your side. The Copenhagen Visitor Centre (p61) offers over-the-counter, last-minute deals on hotel rooms at very low prices. A double room at a four-star hotel can cost as little as 600Dkr, with three-star options at around 500Dkr per night. Breakfast is often included, as well as the perk of a central location.

---

hotels. The rooms are cosseting, and some have balconies or gorgeous city views or both: request a room on level 4 or higher for the best outlook. Guests have access to the gym next door.

Danhostel Copenhagen City
HOSTEL €

(℡33 11 85 85; www.danhostel.dk/copenhagencity; HC Andersens Blvd 50; dm/d Dkr225/600; @) In a tower block overlooking the harbour (yes, the views are fabulous), this friendly, buzzing favourite features bright, modern rooms, each with its own bathroom. Book ahead.

Cabinn City
HOTEL €€

(℡33 46 16 16; www.cabinn.com; Mitchellsgade 14; s/d/tr Dkr545/675/805; @) Although cookie-cutter Cabinns are a little clinical (with narrow beds and no character), they're clean, reliable and cheap. This is the best located of all the chain's Copenhagen branches, just a short walk south of Tivoli. You do usually have to book well in advance here as it is pretty much unrivalled for price and location.

✖ Eating

Copenhagen's dining scene is hot, with more Michelin-starred restaurants than any other city in Scandinavia. Among these is New Nordic pioneer Noma, topping the World's Best 50 Restaurants list three years running. Beyond the fine-dining meccas a growing number of smart-yet-casual hot spots – among them Pony, Kødbyens Fiskebar and Relæ – putting new-school Nordic gastronomy in the reach of kroner-conscious gourmands.

New Nordic scene aside, you can expect a multifaceted culinary landscape, spanning everything from superlative sushi restaurants to hipster pizza bars, cheap-eat cafes and old-school institutions like Schøn-nemann, where *smørrebrød*, herring and akvavit come with a side of nostalgia.

You'll find many of Copenhagen's coolest nosh spots in the Vesterbrø neighbourhood, while bohemian Nørrebro has its fair share of cheaper, student-friendly eateries.

Before you tuck in, consider the following: Copenhagen is not Barcelona, meaning that if you like to eat late, you'll have trouble finding an open kitchen after 10pm. Secondly, hot-spot 'New Nordic' Scandinavian restaurants should always be booked ahead; tables are highly coveted and often booked out days ahead (three months ahead in Noma's case!). Conveniently, a growing number of restaurants allow you to book tables on their website.

AROUND TIVOLI & VESTERBRO

TOP
CHOICE Kødbyens

Fiskebar MODERN SCANDINAVIAN €€€
(☑32 15 56 56; www.fiskebaren.dk; Flæsketorvet 100; mains Dkr195-245; ⊗5.30pm-midnight Mon-Thu, to 2am Fri, noon-4pm & 5.30pm-2am Sat, noon-4pm & 5.30-11pm Sun) Concrete floors, industrial tiling and a 1000-litre aquarium meets impeccable seafood at this Michelin-listed must, slap-bang in Vesterbro's trendy Kødbyen (meat-packing district). Consider ditching the mains for three of four starters; the silky razor clam, served with fennel and tarragon on crispy maltbread, is simply sublime. While you can book a table, dining at the Manhattan-style bar is much more fun.

Pony MODERN SCANDINAVIAN €€
(☑33 22 10 00; www.ponykbh.dk; Vesterbrogade 135; mains Dkr110-175; ⊗5.30-10pm Tue-Sun; 🖐) If your accountant forbids dinner at Kadeau, opt for its cheaper bistro spin-off, Pony. While the New Nordic grub here is simpler, it's no less stunning, with seasonal gems like tartar with black-trumpet mushrooms, blackberries and mushroom broth, or slated cod paired with mussel foam, dried seaweed, and raw-and-roasted Jerusalem artichoke. Despite the dizzying standards, the vibe is convivial, relaxed and intimate. Book ahead, especially on Friday and Saturday.

Paté Paté INTERNATIONAL €€
(☑39 69 55 57; www.patepate.dk; Slagterboderne 1; mains 145-195Dkr; ⊗lunch & dinner) Another Kødbyen must, this pâté factory-turned-restaurant-and-wine bar gives Euro classics a modern twist. Hip, yet warm and convivial, its bonus extras include clued-up staff,

a well-versed wine list and welcoming alfresco summertime tables. The kitchen closes at 11pm; late for Copenhagen.

Madklubben EUROPEAN €€
(☑38 41 41 43; www.madklubben.info; Vesterbrogade 62; 2/3/4 courses Dkr150/200/250; ⊗5.30pm-midnight Mon-Sun) It's a winning concept: hip industrial fit-out, electric buzz and fancy food at absurdly reasonable prices. Portions are generous and the flavours fresh and contemporary; think sweet crab spiked with creamy avocado, chilli, soy sauce and coriander, or reconfigured tarte flambé served flat, long and flaky on a chopping block. Service can be a little patchy.

Siciliansk Is ICE CREAM €
(www.sicilianskis.dk; Skydebanegade 3, Vesterbro; ice creams from Dkr25; ⊗noon-9pm Jun-Aug, 1-6pm Apr, May & Sep) Honing their skills in Sicily, gelato meisters Michael and David churn out Copenhagen's best gelato. Lick yourself out on smooth, seasonal flavours like *havtorn* (sea buckthorn) and *koldskål* (a frozen take on the classic Danish buttermilk and lemon dessert).

AROUND NYHAVN & HARBOURFRONT

TOP
CHOICE Damindra JAPANESE €€€
(www.damindra.dk; Holbergsgade 26; lunch dishes Dkr168-398, dinner dishes Dkr285-398, 8-course tasting menu Dkr700; ⊗11am-3pm & 5-10pm Tue-Sat) Ditch Nyhavn's tacky tourist traps for this unforgettable Japanese gem. While we commend the owner for designing almost everything in sight (yes, even the chairs and cutlery), we reserve a standing ovation for the food itself. From the buttery sashimi to an unforgettable prawn tempura, it's all obscenely fresh, flavoursome and beautifully presented.

Le Sommelier FRENCH €€
(☑33 11 45 15; www.lesommelier.dk; Bredgade 63; 3 courses 395kr; ⊗dinner daily, also lunch Mon-Fri mid-Aug–Jun) White linen, wooden floorboards and vintage French and Italian posters set a cosy, elegant scene at Le Sommelier, where French traditions and in-season produce meet refreshing twists. Dishes are delicate and memorable, with creations like buttersoft Duroc pork, with apple puree, ginger and pickled cabbage. The wine list has a particularly impressive French selection and service is smooth and attentive.

AROUND STRØGET

TOP CHOICE **Schønnemann** DANISH €€

(☑33 12 07 85; Hauser Plads 16; smørrebrød Dkr65-158; ⊘lunch Mon-Sat) Schønnemann has been nourishing Danes with *smørrebrød* and schnapps since 1877. Originally a hit with peasant farmers, its current fan base includes René Redzepi, head chef at world-famous Noma. There are two daily sittings, from 11.30am to 2pm and from 2.14pm to 5pm. A local institution, it's best booked one day in advance.

TorvehallerneKBH MARKET €

(www.torvehallernekbh.dk; Israels Plads; ⊘10am-7pm Mon-Thu, to 8pm Fri, to 6pm Sat, 11am-5pm Sun) Copenhagen's indoor food market is a gourmet paradise, its two slick halls packed with enough artisan produce and ready-to-eat delights to leave you a drooling mess. Hunt for Nordic herbs, seafood, meats and charcuterie; and treat yourself to handmade cheeses, bread and chocolates. If you're pressed for time, chow down a succulent panino from Il Fornaio Bottega (stall C9-10). If not, kick back with thin, crisp, real-deal pizza at hot-spot Gorm's (stall G1-H1; pizzas Dkr55-85).

Paludan Bogcafe INTERNATIONAL €

(www.paludan-cafe.dk; Fiolstræde 10-12; dishes Dkr49-119; ⊘9am-10pm Mon-Fri, 10am-10pm Sat, 10am-8pm Sun) Packed with scribbling students, gossiping professors and Mac-tapping writers, this sprawling, multiroom cafe-bookstore is a supersnug scene of soaring bookshelves, crooked paintings, chintzy chandeliers and the odd Danish design piece. While the menu isn't amazing, it is good value, satisfying and covers all bases, from morning muesli to stir-fries, burgers, cheese platters and pancakes. Order at the counter.

La Glace BAKERY €

(www.laglace.dk; Skoubougade 3; cake slices Dkr52, pastries from Dkr39; ⊘8.30am-6pm Mon-Fri, 9am-6pm Sat, 10am-6pm Sun, closed Sun Apr-Sep) Copenhagen's oldest *konditori* (pastry shop) has been compromising waistlines since 1870. Succumb to a slice of the classic *valnøddekage* (walnut cake), a sinful concoction of crushed and caramelised walnuts, whipped cream and Mocca glacé. Alternatively, betray your personal trainer with the *sportskage* (think crushed nougat, cream and caramelised profiteroles). Your secret is safe.

Wokshop Cantina THAI, VIETNAMESE €€

(www.wokshop.dk; Ny Adelgade 6; noodle dishes Dkr65-145, dinner mains Dkr119-145; ⊘noon-10pm Mon-Sat) This basement canteen in a street just off Kongens Nytorv (beside the grand Hotel d'Angleterre) serves excellent and cheap Thai and Vietnamese staples.

AROUND KONGENS HAVE

Orangeriet FRANCO-DANISH €€€

(☑33 11 13 07; www.restaurant-orangeriet.dk; Kronprinsessegade 13; 3-course lunch Dkr255, 3-/5-course dinner Dkr355/465; ⊘11.30am-3pm & 6-10pm Mon-Sat, noon-4pm Sun) *Ja*, we adore the setting (a romantic conservatory in Kongens Have), but it's the affordable, fine-dining brilliance we keep coming back for. At the helm is award-winning chef Jasper Kure, whose contemporary Franco-Danish creations pair premium seasonal produce with masterful texture and flavour combinations. Sharp service and an inspired wine list seal the deal. The Sunday menu is a simpler affair, offering gourmet *smørrebrød* and cakes. Book ahead.

CHRISTIANSHAVN

TOP CHOICE **Kadeau** MODERN SCANDINAVIAN €€€

(☑33 25 22 23; www.kadeau.dk; Wildersgade 10a; fixed 4-/8-course menu Dkr550/850; ⊘noon-3.30pm Wed-Fri & from 6pm Tue-Sun) Watch out Noma, there's a new kid in town. Bornholm's critically acclaimed Kadeau now has a big-city sibling, serving the same outstanding New Nordic cuisine and flaunting the same superlative Bornholm produce. Dishes are artful and intensely flavoursome: whether it's salted and burnt scallops drizzled with clam bouillon, or the 'porridge' of creamy cereal grains, egg yolk, mushrooms and pickled rhubarb, expect course after course of culinary enlightenment. An equally exciting wine list and warm, seamless service make this place obligatory. Book ahead.

TOP CHOICE **Noma** MODERN SCANDINAVIAN €€€

(☑32 96 32 97; www.noma.dk; Strandgade 93; fixed menu Dkr1500; ⊘noon-4pm & 7pm-12:30am Tue-Sat) Can this place do no wrong? Topping the San Pellegrino 'World's 50 Best Restaurants' list in 2010, 2011 and 2012, Michelin-starred Noma continues to seduce international gastronomes with its breathtaking, boundary-pushing modern Scandinavian creations. Check the website for the next reservation window period, usually two to three months ahead. Or try your luck by joining the waiting list; like miracles, cancellations do happen.

Bastionen og Løven
DANISH €€

(www.bastionen-loven.dk; Christianshavn Voldgade 50; mains Dkr125; ☺11am-midnight Mon-Fri, 10am-midnight Sat, 10am-4pm Sun) The elegant bare wood interior and storybook garden of this old miller's cottage induce bucolic Nordic fantasies. Dream of your own Danish getaway over gems like sweet, freshwater crayfish cooked in beer and dill. The whole place feels like a snug little secret, although the much-loved weekend brunch sessions (Dkr169) that run from 10am to 2pm can get mighty packed. Cash only.

🍴 Morgenstedet
VEGETARIAN €

(www.morgenstedet.dk; Langgaden; mains Dkr75-90; ☺noon-9pm Tue-Sun; 🖉) This is a long-established vegetarian/vegan bolthole with a pretty little garden in the heart of Christiania, Copenhagen's famous alternative neighbourhood. You'll usually find a simple, salubrious choice of three hot dishes, six salads, plus vegan soup, cakes and chai.

NØRREBRO

Relæ
MODERN SCANDINAVIAN €€

(📠36 96 66 09; www.restaurant-relae.dk; Jægersborggade 41, Norrebrø; 4-course menu Dkr375; ☺7.30pm-midnight Wed-Sat, noon-3pm Sat) One of the more affordable New Nordic hotspots, pared-back Relæ is where you'll find ex-Noma chef Christian Puglisi. Simple seasonal ingredients are the starting point for his cutting-edge cooking techniques, which might see veal tongue paired with anchovy, or mandarin granita topped with raw egg yolk. To ensure a table on Friday or Saturday nights, book three weeks ahead.

Laundromat Cafe
INTERNATIONAL €€

(www.thelaundromatcafe.com; Elmegade 15; meals Dkr85-155; ☺8am-midnight Mon-Fri, 10am-midnight Sat & Sun) A cafe, bookstore and launderette in one, this retrolicious Nørrebro institution is never short of a crowd. It's an especially popular brunch spot, with both 'clean' (vegetarian) and 'dirty' (carnivorous) brunch platters, strong coffee and fresh juices. All-day comforters include hamburgers (there's a flesh-free option), cannelloni, chilli con carne and finger-stickin' buffalo wings.

🍷 Drinking

Drinking is one of the Danes' chief pastimes and Copenhagen is packed with a huge range of places, from cosy, old-school cellar bars or bodegas to slinky cocktail dens and many more quirky, grungy, boozy, artsy,

stylish places elsewhere. The line between cafe, bar and restaurant is often blurred, with many places changing role as the day progresses. Nørrebro and Vesterbro (especially along Istedgade, west of the red-light district, and Kødbyen, closer to the station) are well worth exploring.

TOP CHOICE Ved Stranden 10
WINE BAR

(www.vedstranden10.dk; Ved Stranden 10; ☺noon-10pm Mon-Sat) Politicians and well-versed oenophiles make a beeline for this canalside wine bar, famed for its classic European vintages, biodynamic wines and more obscure drops. Adorned with modernist Danish design and oil paintings, its succession of rooms lend the place an intimate air. Roving staff offer excellent recommendations, while vino-friendly nibbles include a selection of tapas dishes (25Dkr to 150Dkr), from olives and cheeses to smoked meats and fried sardines.

🍴 Coffee Collective
CAFE

(www.coffeecollective.dk; TorvehallerneKBH, Israels Plads,; ☺7am-8pm Mon-Fri, 8am-7pm Sat & Sun) Aptly located inside gourmet food market TorvehallerneKBH, Coffee Collective brews Copenhagen's best cups of Joe. Beans are house-roasted and sourced ethically and directly from farmers. There are two other outlets, in Frederiksberg (Godthåbsvej 34b; ☺7.30am-9pm Mon-Fri, 9am-9pm Sat, 10am-9pm Sun) and Nørrebro (Jægersborggade 10; ☺7am-8pm Mon-Fri, 8am-6pm Sat & Sun).

Ruby
COCKTAIL BAR

(www.rby.dk; Nybrogade 10) If you are looking for one of the coolest cocktail bars in Copenhagen, this discreet (from the outside at least) place beside the canal is it. You'll find self-proclaimed cocktail nerds behind the bar, and enough nooks, crannies and vintage chic for long, lingering tête-à-têtes.

Mesteren & Lærlingen
BAR

(Flæsketorvet 86, Vesterbro; ☺8pm-3am Wed-Sat) A stripped-back combo of concrete floors and wax-splashed tables, this former slaughterhouse bodega in Vesterbro's gritty-cool Kødbyen district packs in a friendly, hipster crowd. Join them for rum and ginger (the house speciality) and DJ-spun retro, soul, reggae and country.

Union Bar
BAR

(www.theunionbar.dk; Store Strandstræde 16; ☺Wed-Sat) Inspired by the speakeasy bars of old New York (even the cocktails are named after 1920s slang), the Union hides behind an unmarked black door. Ring the buzzer and head down the stairs to a suitably dim, decadent scene of handsome bartenders, in-the-know revellers and smooth tunes.

1105 — COCKTAIL BAR

(www.1105.dk; Kristen Bernikows Gade 4; ⊘Wed-Sat) Perfect cocktails in dark, svelte surrounds await at 1105. The star libation remains the No 4 (Tanqueray gin, cardamom seeds, pepper, lime and honey). Whisky connoisseurs will be equally enthralled.

Palæ Bar — PUB

(www.palaebar.dk; Ny Adelgade 5; ⊘11am-1am Mon-Wed, to 3am Thu-Sat, 4pm-1am Sun) Nostalgia and cigarette smoke fill the air at Palæ, one of Copenhagen's best old-school drinking dens. Grab an øl and reminisce with a loyal crowd spanning journalists and writers to beer-swilling politicians.

Gay & Lesbian Venues

Denmark was the first country to permit same-sex marriage and has had a swinging gay scene for more than 30 years. Beyond the city's string of LGBT cafes, bars and clubs, queer drawcards include Copenhagen Pride (www.copenhagenpride.dk) in August and queer film fest Mix Copenhagen (www.mixcopenhagen.dk) in October. For listings and events, see www.out-and-about.dk.

Oscar Bar & Cafe — GAY

(www.oscarbarcafe.dk; Rådhuspladsen 77; ⊘11am-11pm Sun-Thu, to 2am Fri & Sat) Oscar remains the gay community's see-and-be-seen cafe-cum-bar, with cute bar staff and a healthy quota of eye-candy guests. In the warmer months, its alfresco tables are packed with preparty crowds, one eye on friends, the other on Grindr.

Jailhouse CPH — GAY

(www.jailhousecph.dk; Studiestræde 12; ⊘3pm-2am Sun-Thu, to 5am Fri & Sat) With less 'attitude' than Oscar, this popular, smoker-friendly bar promises plenty of penal action, with uniformed 'guards' and willing guests.

Centralhjørnet — GAY

(www.centralhjornet.dk; Kattetsundet 18; ⊘noon-2am Sun-Thu, to 3am Fri & Sat) The oldest gay bar in the village offers attitude-free camaraderie, a more mature crowd, and pop and *schlager* (kitsch Euro pop) classics. The cabaret shows are especially fun, held from 9pm Thursdays and 4pm Sundays, October to April.

WANT MORE?

For in-depth information, reviews and recommendations at your fingertips, head to the Apple App Store to purchase Lonely Planet's *Copenhagen City Guide* iPhone app.

Alternatively, head to Lonely Planet (www.lonelyplanet.com/denmark/copenhagen) for planning advice, author recommendations, traveller reviews and insider tips.

Never Mind — GAY

(www.nevermindbar.dk; Nørre Voldgade 2; ⊘10pm-6am) Tiny, smoky and often packed to the rafters, Never Mind is a seriously fun spot for shameless pop and late-night flirtation.

☆ Entertainment

Copenhagen's 'X factor' fuels its entertainment options. Its live-music and club scene are healthy and kicking, with choices spanning intimate jazz and blues boltholes to mega rock venues and secret clubs dropping experimental beats. While you can hit the dance floor most nights of the week, the scene really revs into gear from Thursday to Saturday. Club admission is usually around 70Dkr, though you can often get in for free before a certain time in the evening. Keep in mind that Danes tend to be late-nighters and, unlike the restaurants, many nightspots don't start heaving until 11pm or midnight.

Further up the entertainment ladder, a string of arresting, 21st-century cultural venues, including Operaen (Copenhagen Opera House) and Skuespilhuset (p50), have injected the city's cultural scene with new verve.

Most events can be booked through Billetnet (☏70 15 65 65; www.billetnet.dk). You can also try Billetlugen (☏70 26 32 67; www.billetlugen.dk). For listings, scan www.aok.dk and www.visitcopenhagen.com.

TOP CHOICE Simons — CLUB

(www.simonscopenhagen.com; Store Strandstræde 14; ⊘Fri & Sat) Occupying a former art gallery, hip Simons' biggest (and smallest) claims to fame are top-shelf DJ talent and dwarfs behind the bar. Expect selective electronica and an even more selective door policy (Fridays are more accessible than Saturdays).

If you have a Danish SIM card, register for updates online.

TOP CHOICE **La Fontaine** JAZZ
(www.lafontaine.dk; Kompagnistræde 11; ⊙7pm-5am, live music from 10.30pm Fri & Sat, from 9pm Sun) Cosy La Fontaine is a stalwart of the city's thriving jazz scene, with emerging homegrown talent and the occasional big name. Expect live gigs Friday to Sunday and legendary late-night jam sessions.

Vega Live LIVE MUSIC, CLUB
(www.vega.dk; Enghavevej 40) The daddy of all Copenhagen's live-music and club venues, Vega hosts everyone from big-name pop, rock, blues and jazz acts to underground indie, hip hop and electro up-and-comers. Gigs take place on either the main stage (Store Vega), small stage (Lille Vega), or the ground-floor **Ideal Bar** (Enghavevej 40; ⊙8pm-1am Wed, 9pm-2am Thu, 10pm-5am Fri & Sat). The venue itself is a fabulous 1950s former trade union HQ by Vilhelm Lauritizen.

Operaen OPERA
(Copenhagen Opera House; ☑box office 33 69 69 69; www.kglteater.dk; Ekvipagemestervej 10) Dubbed 'The Toaster' by its critics, Copenhagen's state-of-the-art opera house hosts world-class opera, both classic and contemporary. It also features regular free music events in its foyer. Productions usually sell out well in advance but any unsold tickets are offered at half-price at the Opera House box office one hour before performances.

Rust LIVE MUSIC, CLUB
(www.rust.dk; Guldbergsgade 8) A thriving, smashing place that pulls one of the largest, coolest club crowds in Copenhagen. Spaces range from club to live-music hall and lounge, with an equally diverse musical policy. From 11pm, entrance is available only to over 18s (Wednesday and Thursday) and over 20s (Friday and Saturday).

Culture Box CLUB
(www.culture-box.com; Kronprinsessegade 54a; ⊙bar 9pm-late Fri & Sat, club 11pm-5am Fri & Sat) Spread over two levels, Culture Box ditches commercial hits for innovative, edgy electronic beats spun by top local and visiting DJ talent. Deliciously dark and Berlin-esque, it's all about the music, not the attitude.

🔒 Shopping

Copenhagen is a superb, if expensive, shopping destination. The city heaves with small, independent boutiques selling must-have Danish homewares, fashion and jewellery. Be aware that aside from major retail chains, department stores and supermarkets, most shops are closed on Sunday.

Illums Bolighus DESIGN
(www.illumsbolighus.dk; Amagertorv 8-10, Strøget) Drool your way through the city's dedicated design department store, packed with eye-candy homewares, clothing, jewellery and furniture from established and up-and-coming local and international designers.

Hay House DESIGN
(www.hay.dk; Østergade 61, Strøget) Generally more affordable than Illums Bolighus, Rolf Hay's fabulous interior-design store sells well-chosen design gifts such as ceramic cups, funky textiles and art books, as well as delectable Danish furniture.

Bruuns Bazaar FASHION
(www.bruunsbazaar.com; Kronprinsensgade 8 & 9) Bruuns Bazaar is now an internationally recognised fashion label selling archetypal, contemporary Scandinavian style around the world. And it's here that it all began. Man or woman, the look is clean, svelte and sharp.

THE SHOPPING-STREET LOW DOWN

Strøget (City Centre) Local and global fashion chains, Danish design stores, department stores; downmarket at its western end, upmarket at its eastern end.

Kronprinsensgade, Store Regnegade, Pilestræde, Købmagergade (City Centre) High-end independent fashion labels, local jewellery and homewares.

Istedgade (Vesterbro) Street fashion, vintage threads, shoes and food.

Elmegade, Blågårdsgade and Ravnsborggade (Nørrebro) Antiques, hipster fashion labels, homewares.

Bredgade (Nyhavn) Upmarket art and antiques.

Han Kjøbenhavn   FASHION

(www.hankjobenhavn.com; Vognmagergade 7) While the modernist Nordic fit-out is reason enough to go, it's what's on the racks that will hook you: original, beautifully crafted men's threads that fuse classic design principles with retro irreverence and trademark Danish cool. Accessories include sublime leathergoods from America's Kenton Sorensen.

Henrik Vibskov   FASHION

(www.henrikvibskov.com; Krystalgade 6) Not just a drummer and prolific artist (past exhibition venues include New York's PS1 MOMA), Danish *enfant terrible* Henrik Vibskov pushes the fashion envelope too. Dive in for multiprinted creations for progressive guys and girls, as well as other fashion-forward labels such as Surface to Air, Comme des Garçons and Walter Van Beirendonck.

Pop Cph   FASHION

(www.popcph.dk; Gråbrødretorv 4) Mikkel Kristensen and Kasper Henriksen began hosting parties for Copenhagen's creative community in 2005. The parties continue to inspire the duo's fashion creations, which span graphic-print T-shirts to dinner-party glamour fused with subversive detailing.

ℹ Information

Emergency

Dial ☑112 to contact police, ambulance or fire services.

Politigården (☑33 14 14 48; Polititorvet; ⊙24hr) Police headquarters; south of Tivoli.

Internet Access

Hovedbiblioteket (15 Krystalgade; ⊙10am-7pm Mon-Fri, to 2pm Sat) The main public library – computers on all floors provide free internet access. Free wi-fi too.

Medical Services

Frederiksberg Hospital (☑38 16 38 16; www.frederiksberghospital.dk; Nordre Fasanvej 57) West of the city centre; has a 24-hour emergency ward.

Steno Apotek (Vesterbrogade 6c; ⊙24hr) Pharmacy opposite Central Station.

Money

Banks are plentiful throughout Copenhagen. Banks in the airport arrival and transit halls are open 6am to 10pm daily.

Post

Central Station post office (⊙8am-9pm Mon-Fri, 10am-4pm Sat & Sun) In the main train station, with long opening hours.

Post office (Købmagergade 33; ⊙10am-6pm Mon-Fri, to 2pm Sat) Handy central-city location.

Tourist Information

Copenhagen Visitor Centre (☑70 22 24 42; www.visitcopenhagen.com; Vesterbrogade 4a; ⊙9am-6pm Mon-Sat, 10am-2pm Sun May & Jun, 9am-8pm Mon-Sat, 10am-6pm Sun Jul & Aug, 9am-4pm Mon-Fri, 9am-2pm Sat rest of yr) Copenhagen's impressive tourist office distributes a free city map, and brochures covering Copenhagen and all of Denmark's regions. It also offers free wi-fi.

ℹ Getting There & Away

Air

Copenhagen International Airport (p124) is Scandinavia's busiest hub, with direct connections to other destinations in Denmark, as well as in Europe, North America and Asia. The airport is located in Kastrup, 9km southeast of the city centre.

Boat

DFDS Seaways (☑33 42 30 10; www.dfds-seaways.com; Dampfærgevej 30) operates daily ferries to Oslo. See p491 for details.

Bus

Long-distance buses leave from opposite the DGI-byen sports complex on Ingerslevsgade, a quick walk southwest of Central Station. Advance reservations on most international routes can be made at Eurolines (p124).

Car & Motorcycle

The main highways into Copenhagen are the E20, which goes west to Funen and east to Malmö, Sweden; and the E47, which connects to Helsingør. If you're coming into Copenhagen from the north on the E47, exit onto Lyngbyvej (Rte 19) and continue south to get into the heart of the city.

As well as airport booths, the following rental agencies have city branches:

Avis (☑70 24 77 07; www.avis.com; Kampmannsgade 1)

Europcar (☑33 55 99 00; www.europcar.com; Gammel Kongevej 13)

Hertz (☑33 17 90 20; www.hertzdk.dk; Ved Vesterport 3)

Train

Long-distance trains arrive and depart from **Central Station** (⊙5.30am-1am Mon-Sat, 6am-1am Sun). *Billetautomats* (coin-operated ticket machines) are the quickest way to purchase a ticket, but only if you've mastered the zone-system prices. They are best for S-Tog (S-Train) tickets. **DSB Billetsalg** (www.dsb.dk; ☉7am-8pm Mon-Fri, 8am-4pm Sat, 8am-5pm Sun, international ticket sales 9.30am-6pm Mon-Fri) is best for reservations and for purchasing international train tickets. Alternatively, you can make reservations on its website, and while online booking options are in Danish, there's an English-language file that explains how to buy them.

Central Station also offers **left luggage services** (☑24 68 31 77; per 24hr, max 10 days luggage per piece Dkr45-55, pram, bike per piece Dkr55, luggage lockers per 24hr, max 72hr small/large Dkr40/50) lockers are in the lower level near the Reventlowsgade exit.

❶ Getting Around

To/From the Airport

TRAIN **DSB trains** (www.dsb.dk) link the airport with Central Station (Dkr36, 14 minutes, every 10 minutes).

METRO **Copenhagen Metro** (www.m.dk) runs every four to 20 minutes around the clock between the airport (Lufthavnen station) and central Copenhagen. It does not stop at Central Station but is handy for Christianshavn, Nyhavn (alight at Kongens Nytorv station) and Nørreport. Journey time to Kongens Nytorv is 13 minutes and costs Dkr48.

TAXI Taxa 4x35 charges about Dkr250 from the city centre, with a journey time of around 20 minutes, subject to traffic.

Bicycle

Bycykler (City Bikes; www.bycyklen.dk) Offers free-use bikes from mid-April to November at 110 City Bike racks throughout central Copenhagen. Deposit a Dkr20 coin in the stand to release the bike. You can return the bicycle to any rack to get your money back.

Københavns Cyklerbørs (www.cykelboersen. dk; Gothersgade 157; bicycle hire per day/week Dkr75/350; ☉9am-5.30pm Mon-Fri, 10am-1.30pm Sat) Bike hire close to the Botanisk Have (Botanical Gardens) on the northwest edge of the city centre.

Bikes can be carried free on S-Train, but are forbidden at Nørreport station during weekday peak hours.

» Bikes can be carried on the metro (except from 7am to 9am and 3.30pm to 5.30pm on weekdays from September to May). Bike tickets cost Dkr12.

Bus & Train

Copenhagen has a large, modern and efficient public transport system.

» Buses, Metro and trains use a common fare system based on zones. The basic fare of Dkr24 for up to two zones covers most city runs and allows transfers between buses and trains on a single ticket within one hour.

» If you're day-tripping it to Louisiana Museum of Modern Art, Helsingør and other North Zealand coastal towns, purchase a 24-hour pass (adult/child Dkr130/65), which allows unlimited travel in all zones. Two children under 12 travel free when accompanied by an adult.

DON'T MISS

LOUISIANA: A MODERN ART MUST

Even if you don't have a burning passion for art, Denmark's outstanding Louisiana Museum of Modern Art (www.louisiana.dk; Gl Strandvej 13; adult/child Dkr95/free; ☉11am-10pm Tue-Fri, to 6pm Sat & Sun; ▣) should be high on your 'To-Do' list. It's a striking modernist-art mecca, sprawling across a sculpture-laced park, burrowing down into the hillside and nosing out again to wink at the sea (and Sweden).

The museum's permanent collection, mainly postwar paintings and graphic art, covers everything from constructivism, COBRA movement artists and minimalist art, to abstract expressionism and pop art. Pablo Picasso, Francis Bacon, Andy Warhol and Robert Rauschenberg are some of the international luminaries you'll encounter, while Henry Moore's monumental bronzes and Max Ernst's owl-eyed creatures lurk behind the hillocks of the garden. Then there's the homegrown stars, among them Asger Jorn, Carl-Henning Pedersen, Robert Jacobsen and Richard Mortensen.

Adding extra X-factor is the museum's program of fantastic temporary exhibitions, its dedicated (and diverting) children's wing, fantastic gift shop, not to mention its airy cafe (complete with sunny terrace and international vista).

Louisiana is in the leafy commuter town of Humlebæk, 30km north of central Copenhagen and roughly 35 minutes from there on the S-train's C line. From Humlebæk station, the museum is a 900m signposted walk north along Strandvej. If day-tripping it from Copenhagen, the 24-hour ticket (adult/child 130/65Dkr) is better value.

» The website www.rejseplanen.dk offers a handy journey planner, with transport routes, times and prices.

Bus (www.moviatrafik.dk) Copenhagen's vast bus system has its main terminus at Rådhuspladsen. Night buses (1am to 5am) run on a few major routes. Purchase tickets on board from the driver (bring coins, not notes!).

Metro (www.m.dk) Consists of two lines (M1 and M2) and runs a minimum of every two minutes. Connects Nørreport and Kongens Nytorv (near Nyhavn) to Christianshavn and the airport. Purchase tickets from *billetautomats* (automated ticket machine) at the station. Trains run around the clock, with reduced frequency at night.

S-Tog (S-train; www.dsb.dk) Operates seven metropolitan lines, each passing through Central Station (København H). Popular tourist towns covered by the network include Helsingør and Køge. Purchase tickets at the station and punch them in the yellow time clock on the platform. Services run from approximately 5am to 12.30am Sunday to Thursday, with all-night services on Friday and Saturday.

Car & Motorcycle

» Weekday morning and evening rush hour aside, traffic is usually manageable, though parking can be hard to find. It's far better to explore sights within the city centre on foot or by using public transport.

» For street parking, buy a ticket from a streetside *billetautomat* and place it inside the windscreen. Ticket machines accept credit cards.

» Parking in Copenhagen costs from Dkr3 to Dkr29 depending on the time of day or night and how close you are to the city centre.

Taxi

» Taxis can be flagged on the street and there are ranks at various points around the city centre. If the yellow *taxa* (taxi) sign is lit, the taxi is available for hire.

» The basic fare is Dkr24 (Dkr37 if you book over the phone), plus Dkr14 per kilometre between 7am and 4pm, Dkr15 between 4pm and 7am Monday to Friday and all day Saturday and Sunday, and Dkr17.90 from 11pm to 7am Friday to Saturday and on public holidays. Credit cards are accepted. Fares include a service charge, so tipping is not expected.

» Two of the main companies are **DanTaxi** (☑70 25 25 25; www.dantaxi.dk) and **Taxa 4x35** (☑35 35 35 35; www.taxa.dk).

ZEALAND

Though Copenhagen is the centre of gravity for most visitors to Denmark's eastern island, there is no shortage of drawcards beyond the city limits. Zealand is an island with a rich history, beautiful coastline and plenty of rolling countryside. Then there are the region's pedigree castles, most notably Kronborg Slot (famously known as Hamlet's castle, Elsinore) and Renaissance showstopper Frederiksborg Slot. Older still are the remarkable Viking ships of Roskilde, excavated from Roskilde fjord in the 1950s and housed in a purpose-built museum.

North Zealand

One of the most popular day trips from Copenhagen is a loop tour taking in Frederiksborg Slot in Hillerød and Kronborg Slot in Helsingør. With an early start you might even have time to reach one of the north-shore beaches before making your way back to the city, although it is more rewarding to allow an extra day for wandering between shoreline towns along this gorgeous coastline.

If you're driving between Helsingør and Copenhagen, ditch the motorway for the coastal road, Strandvej (Rte 152), which is far more scenic (though admittedly quite crowded on summer weekends).

FREDERIKSBORG SLOT

Hillerød, 30km northwest of Copenhagen, is the site of Frederiksborg Slot (www.frederiksborgmuseet.dk; adult/child Dkr75/20; ⊙10am-5pm Apr-Oct, reduced hr rest of year), an impressive Dutch Renaissance castle spread across three islands. The oldest part of the castle dates from Frederik II's time, though most of the present structure was built by his son Christian IV in the early 17th century. After parts of the castle were ravaged by fire in 1859, Carlsberg beer baron JC Jacobsen spearheaded a drive to restore the castle and make it a national museum.

The sprawling castle has a magnificent interior, with gilded ceilings, full wall-sized tapestries, royal paintings and antiques. The richly embellished Riddershalen (Knights' Hall) and the coronation chapel, where Danish monarchs were crowned between 1671 and 1840, are well worth the admission fee.

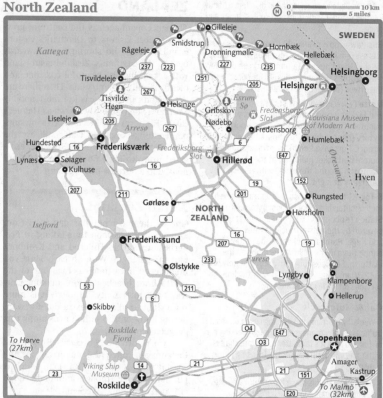

The S-train (E line) runs every 10 minutes between Copenhagen and Hillerød (24-hour travel card adult/child Dkr130/65k, a 40-minute ride. From Hillerød station follow the signs to Torvet, then continue along Slotsgade to the castle, a 1.5km walk in all. Alternatively, take bus 301 or 302, which can drop you at the gate.

HELSINGØR (ELSINORE)
POP 46,400

Generally, visitors come to the charming harbour town of Helsingør, at the northeastern tip of Zealand, for one of two reasons. If they are Swedish, they come to stock up on cheap(er) booze (this is the closest point to Sweden, and ferries shuttle back and forth across the Øresund frequently). Or, more often, they come to soak up the atmosphere of Denmark's most famous and awe-inspiring castle, Elsinore, home of Shakespeare's indecisive antihero, Hamlet.

The **tourist office** (☑49 21 13 33; www.visit-nordsjaelland.com; Havnepladsen 3; ◷10am-5pm Mon-Fri, to 2pm Sat & Sun late Jun-early Aug) is opposite the train station.

◉ Sights

TOP CHOICE Kronborg Slot   CASTLE

(www.kronborg.dk; adult/child Dkr75/30; ◷10am-5.30pm Jun-Aug, 11am-4pm Apr, May, Sep & Oct, reduced hr rest of yr) Helsingør's top sight is Kronborg Slot, made famous as the Elsinore Castle of Shakespeare's Hamlet (it's the venue for August performances of the play during the annual Shakespeare festival – often with major English or US stars in the lead role). Kronborg's primary function was not as a royal residence, but rather as a grandiose tollhouse, wresting taxes (the infamous and lucrative 'Sound Dues') for more than 400 years from ships passing through the narrow Øresund. Stand by the cannons facing Sweden and you immediately see what a key strategic military and naval choke point this was. The castle is on the northern side of the harbour within easy walking distance of the station.

Medieval Quarter NEIGHBOURHOOD
From the tourist office head up Brostræde and along Sankt Anna Gade. This will take you through the medieval quarter and past the old cathedral, **Sankt Olai Kirke** (⊙10am-4pm May-Aug), the small **City History Museum** (admission free; ⊙noon-4pm Tue-Fri, 10am-2pm Sat, noon-4pm Sun) and Sct Mariæ Kirke and **Karmeliter-klostret** (adult/child Dkr20/5; ⊙10am-3pm Tue-Sun mid-May–mid-Sep), one of Scandinavia's best-preserved medieval monasteries. From here Sudergade leads to the tree-lined, cobbled central square of **Axeltorv**, where you will find several cafes and takeaways.

Danmarks Tekniske Museum MUSEUM
(www.tekniskmuseum.dk; Fabriksvej 25; adult/child Dkr65/free; ⊙10am-5pm Tue-Sun) A little out of town, this museum has historic aeroplanes and motor cars among other exhibits.

Øresundsakvariet AQUARIUM
(www.oresundsakvariet.ku.dk; Strandpromenaden 5; adult/child Dkr60/35; ⊙10am-5pm Jun-Aug) An aquarium with local sea life.

Fredensborg Slot CASTLE, GARDENS
(www.ses.dk; combined palace, herb garden & orangerie tour adult/child Dkr85/30, gardens free; ⊙palace & chapel tours every 15min 1-4.30pm Jul-early Aug, herb garden & orangerie tour every 20min 1-4.20pm Jul-early Aug) A 20-minute train ride southwest of Helsingør takes you to a very different kind of royal castle from Kronborg Slot. Fredensborg Slot evolved during the early 18th century as a royal hunting lodge. Its present-day role is as the royal family's summer residence and number-one party palace: this is where the wedding reception of Crown Prince Frederik and Australian Mary Donaldson took place. It is a peaceful spot for a stroll or a picnic, with lush rolling lawns, forest and formal gardens beside Esrum Sø (Lake Esrum).

🛏 Sleeping

The tourist office website (www.visitnordsjaelland.com) offers a list of private accommodation options, with links to each property. Prices start at Dkr450 for both singles and doubles.

Hotel & Casino Marienlyst HOTEL €€
(☑49 21 40 00; www.marienlyst.dk; Nordre Strandvej 2; s Dkr985-1275, d Dkr1185-1475; P@☀) This is the closest that things get to glamour and luxury in these parts, as this modern conference hotel has a casino, swimming pool and views across the sea to Sweden.

Danhostel Helsingør HOSTEL €
(☑49 28 49 49; www.helsingorhostel.dk; Nordre Strandvej 24; dm/d/q Dkr185/495/550; P@) Housed in the imposing red-brick Villa Moltke, 2km northwest of the centre, this hostel is right by the water with its own beach. The run-of-the-mill dorms are in one of the smaller detached buildings. From Helsingør, bus 842 will get you there.

Hotel Sleep2Night MOTEL €€
(☑49 27 01 00; www.sleep2night.com; Industrivej 19; s/d Dkr595/675; P@) Denmark's beautifully designed take on the US motel, with simple but well-equipped rooms and free internet connections throughout. It's good value (check the website for discounted-rate offers) but it's a 20-minute journey from the centre of town, to the south of Helsingør. From the train station, buses 353 and 802 stop close to the hotel.

Helsingør Camping CAMPGROUND €
(☑49 28 49 50; www.helsingorcamping.dk; Strandalleen 2; campsites per adult/child 70/35kr, cabins from 350kr) A well-spaced beachside camping ground that is east of the Danhostel Helsingørand, close to one of the area's best beaches.

🍴 Eating

Rådmand Davids Hus DANISH €
(☑49 26 10 43; Strandgade 70; dishes Dkr32-98; ⊙10am-5pm Mon-Sat) What better place to tuck into Danish classics than a snug, lopsided 17th-century house. Gobble down honest, solid staples like *smørrebrød*, herring, fried pork and homemade *fiskefrikadeller* (Danish fish cakes) with remoulade. Leave room for the Grand Marnier pancakes.

Café Vivaldi INTERNATIONAL €€
(Stengade 9; sandwiches Dkr95-119, dinner mains Dkr169-199; ⊙10am-10pm Sun-Thu, to 2am Fri & Sat) Expect tasty cafe standards at this relaxed, mock-bistro chain. The menu spans nachos, omelettes, salads and quiches to more substantial evening mains like pasta and steaks. There's a good-value daily brunch buffet (Dkr119) and live music on weekends.

Kulturværftets Spisehus INTERNATIONAL € (www.kulturvaerftet.dk; Allegade 2; meals Dkr66-99; ☺10am-6.30pm Mon-Thu, to 7pm Fri, to 5pm Sat & Sun) Part of the Culture Yard, a striking waterfront cultural centre housing theatres, exhibition spaces and the town library, this casual, contemporary cafe peddles fresh, straightforward grub. Gaze out over Hamlet's pad while nibbling on open sandwiches, soup, salads or the more substantial daily special.

❶ Getting There & Away

BOAT For information on ferries to Helsingborg (Sweden), see p491.

TRAIN Trains between Copenhagen and Helsingør run several times hourly (Dkr108, 45 minutes). If you're day-tripping it from Copenhagen, buy a 24-hour pass (Dkr130). Trains between Helsingør and Hillerød (Dkr72, 30 minutes) run at least once hourly.

Zealand's North Coast

The entire stretch of coast from Helsingør west to Liseleje is in effect Zealand's holiday zone, with literally thousands of traditional Danish summer houses packing the woodlands and beachfronts. Long, sandy beaches and the festive summer vibe that grips its half-timbered fishing villages make the region worth a visit.

Hornbæk, the next main town west of Helsingør, has the best and most easily accessible beach on the north coast. The beach is a vast expanse of white sand and grassy dunes that run the entire length of the town, and it has a **Blue Flag** (www.blueflag.org) eco-friendly label. From the train station, it's just a five-minute walk directly down Havnevej to the harbour, where you'll find a great seafood kiosk and the yacht marina. Simply climb the dunes to the left and you're on the beach. The library doubles as the **tourist office** (www.hornbaek.dk; Vestre Stejlebakke 2a; ☺1-5pm Mon & Thu, 10am-3pm Tue, Wed & Fri, to 2pm Sat).

Zealand's northernmost town, **Gilleleje**, has the island's largest fishing port. Visitors usually head straight for the harbour and adjacent sandy beach. The harbour has several wonderful seafood kiosks, selling platters of freshly caught crayfish, fish and chips and even sushi. The **tourist office** (www.visitnordsjaelland.com; Hovedgade 6f; ☺10am-6pm Mon-Sat mid-Jun–Aug) is in the centre. There are excellent beaches either side of the town and others along the coast to the west, especially

at **Rågeleje**, **Dronningmølle** and at **Smidstrup Strand**, where conditions are often good for windsurfing. All have Blue Flags.

Tisvildeleje is a pleasant seaside village known for its bohemian and artistic communities, with a long, straggling main street that leads to an even longer beach. It really transforms in July when the holidaymakers arrive. Behind the beach is **Tisvilde Hegn**, a windswept forest of twisted trees and heather-covered hills laced with good walking paths. You can pick up brochures and tourist information at the train station. Out of season the town feels desolate.

🛏 Sleeping

TOP CHOICE Helenekilde

Badehotel BOUTIQUE HOTEL €€€ (☎48 70 70 01; www.helenekilde.com; Strandvejen 25, Tisvildeleje; s Dkr1295-1595, d Dkr1395-1695; ℗) An enchanting, renovated bathing hotel with interiors designed by the ballet dancer Alexander Kolpin. Built on the cliffs overlooking the beaches at Tisvildeleje, it's about a 10-minute walk from the main street.

TopCamp

Dronningmølle Strand CAMPGROUND € (☎49 71 92 90; www.dronningmolle.dk; Strandkrogen 2b, Dronningmølle; campsites per adult/child Dkr85/55, tent Dkr155; ☺late Mar-late Aug) An excellent four-star camping ground on the coast road between Hornbæk and Gilleleje. You have to cross the main road to get to the beach, but it is a beauty and has a Blue Flag. Tent sites come with all amenities – electricity, water and, in some cases, even cable TV.

Gilleleje Badehotel HOTEL €€
(☎48 30 13 47; www.gillelejebadehotel.dk; Hulsøvej 15, Gilleleje; s/d Dkr990/1490; ℗) On Gilleleje beach, the grandest of the north coast's bathing hotels has been renovated in Gustavian style. Request a room with a sea view.

Hotel Villa Strand HOTEL €€
(☎49 70 00 88; www.villastrand.dk; Kystvej 12; s/d from Dkr895/995; ☺Jun-Aug; ℗) Villa Strand is a pleasant, quiet place to the west of Hornbæk centre and very close to the beach. There are cheaper doubles in garden bungalows, and plusher rooms with balconies in the main building.

Ewaldsgården Guest House GUESTHOUSE €€
(☎49 70 00 82; www.ewaldsgaarden.dk; Johannes Ewalds Vej 5, Hornbæk; s/d Dkr565/875; ☺mid-Jun–mid-Aug; ℗@) Though not close to the

beach, this cosy and elegant guesthouse is a delight, with a picture-perfect garden and a homely mix of antiques and cottage-style furnishings.

✗ Eating

For eating out along Zealand's northern coast you can't beat the seafood restaurants – usually little more than a few kiosks, really – that you find in the harbours.

Fiskehuset Hornbæk SEAFOOD **€**
(Havenevej 32, Hornbæk; fish & chips Dkr50; ⊙11am-8pm summer, reduced hr rest of yr) Hornbæk's seafood kiosk is the Fiskehuset. Here you can dine like a lord, albeit outdoors with paper serviettes, on smoked cod's roe, cured herring, smoked mackerel, fresh prawns, *fiskfrikadeller*, mussel soup and all manner of fresh, local seafood – for under Dkr60.

Adamsen's Fish SEAFOOD, SUSHI **€**
(Gilleleje Harbour; fish & chips Dkr65; ⊙11am-9pm, sushi bar to 8pm, reduced hr rest of yr) Gilleleje's popular harbourside takeaway peddles fish, seafood, sides of chips and more salubrious salads. The fish and seafood are heavily battered, so delicate stomachs may prefer the grilled options. For those who prefer their fish raw, Adamsen's has a sushi bar next door.

Hansens Café DANISH **€€**
(☑49 70 04 79; www.hansenscafe.dk; Havnevej 19, Hornbæk; mains Dkr248; ⊙from 6pm Mon & Thu-Sat, noon-8pm Sun) Hansens occupies Hornbæk's oldest house, an earthen-roofed half-timbered building with a pleasant, pub-like atmosphere. The menu changes regularly but you can find solid Danish grub like *fiskfrikadeller* with homemade remoulade.

Restaurant Søstrene Olsen FRANCO-DANISH **€€€**
(☑49 70 05 50; www.sostreneolsen.dk; Øresundsvej 10, Hornbæk; mains Dkr168-298; ⊙noon-4pm & from 6pm Thu-Mon) Hornbæk is hardly a gourmet mecca, but you will find refined, ambitious Franco-Danish food at husband-and-wife team Thorleif and Minne Aagaard's charming thatched cottage right on the beach.

❶ Getting There & Away

Train connections to/from Helsingør include the following:

Gilleleje Dkr72, 43 minutes, every 30 minutes on weekdays, every 30 to 60 minutes on weekends.

Hornbæk Dkr36, 25 minutes, every 30 minutes on weekdays, every 30 to 60 minutes on weekends.

Tisvildeleje via Hillerød Dkr84, one hour, every 30 minutes on weekdays, hourly on weekends.

Although buses service the area, trains are usually the quicker, more convenient option. Hillerød trains run to Gilleleje and to Tisvildeleje (Dkr60, 30 minutes, every 30 minutes Monday to Saturday, hourly on Sunday), though with no rail link between the two.

Roskilde

POP 47,800

Most foreigners who have heard of Roskilde know it either as the home of one of northern Europe's best outdoor music festivals, or the site of several remarkable Viking ship finds, now housed in an excellent, purpose-built museum. To the Danes, however, it is a city of great royal and religious significance, as it was the capital city long before Copenhagen and is still the burial place of 39 monarchs stretching back several hundred years. Located on the southern tip of Roskilde Fjord, the city was a thriving trading port throughout the Middle Ages. It was also the site of Zealand's first Christian church, built by Viking king Harald Bluetooth in AD 980.

◉ Sights

Roskilde Domkirke CHURCH
(www.roskildedomkirke.dk; Domkirkepladsen; adult/child Dkr60/free; ⊙9am-5pm Mon-Sat, 12.30-5pm Sun Apr-Sep, reduced hr rest of yr) Not merely the crème de la crème of Danish cathedrals, this twin-towered, red-brick giant is a designated Unesco World Heritage Site. Started by Bishop Absalon in 1170, the building has been rebuilt and tweaked so many times that it's now a superb catalogue of 800 years' worth of Danish architecture.

As the royal mausoleum, it contains the crypts of 37 Danish kings and queens. The **Chapel of King Christian IV**, off the northern side of the cathedral, contains the builder king himself. His ocean-green coffin, surrounded by a procession of angels, is ironically low-key given his reputation as an extravagant spender.

The **Chapel of the Magi** is adorned with fantastic 15th-century frescos (the largest in Denmark), as well as the incomparably ornate Renaissance sepulchres of Christian III and Frederik II. The chapel is also home to the curious Royal Column, marked with the heights of visiting princes – from Christian I at a lofty 219.5cm down to Christian VII at 164.1cm.

For more light relief, look up at the 15th-century clock above the cathedral entrance, where a tiny St George on horseback marks the hour by slaying a yelping dragon (a pair of bellows and three out-of-tune organ pipes create its cry for help).

TOP CHOICE Viking Ship Museum MUSEUM

(www.vikingeskibsmuseet.dk; Vindeboder 12; adult/child May-Sep Dkr115/free, Oct-Apr Dkr80/free, boat trip excl museum admission Dkr80; ☉10am-5pm late Jun-Aug, to 4pm rest of yr, boat trips daily May-Sep) From the northern side of the cathedral, walk across a field where wildflowers blanket the unexcavated remains of Roskilde's original medieval town, and continue through a green belt all the way to the well-presented Viking Ship Museum. Here you'll find five reconstructed Viking ships (c 1000), excavated from Roskilde Fjord in 1962 and brought to shore in thousands of fragments. The five ships – all different – had been filled with stones and scuttled to block the entrance to the fjord to protect the town (at that time, the capital of Denmark) from attack by Norwegian Vikings.

The museum also incorporates fascinating **waterfront workshops** where replicas of Viking ships are built using Viking-era techniques. The smells and sounds here are just as they would have been 1000 years ago.

From May to the end of September, you can take a **boat trip** on the waters of Roskilde Fjord in a replica Viking ship; call the museum to confirm daily sailing times. As well as this, MS *Sagafjord* is a veteran cruiser that offers sailing **tours** (☑46 75 64 60; adult/child Dkr100/59; ☉tours daily Jun-Aug, reduced hr May & Sep-Oct) of the fjord.

West of the Viking Ship Museum is the **Sankt Jørgensbjerg quarter**, where the cobbled Kirkegade walkway leads through a neighbourhood of old straw-roofed houses into the courtyard of the 11th-century **Sankt Jørgensbjerg Kirke**.

Museum for Samtidskunst MUSEUM

(www.samtidskunst.dk; Stændertorvet 3d; adult/child Dkr40/free, Wed free; ☉11am-5pm Tue-Fri, noon-4pm Sat & Sun) In the town centre, a terrific surprise awaits art fans at the Museum for Samtidskunst. Housed in the elegant 18th-century Roskilde Palace, this is a sur-prisingly cutting-edge contemporary art space, fond of perplexing installations by Danish and international artists.

Sagnlandet Lejre MUSEUM

(www.sagnlandet.dk; Slangealleen 2, Lejre; adult/child 3-11 Dkr130/85; ☉10am-5pm Jun-early Aug, to 6pm Aug, reduced hr rest of yr) If the Viking Ship Museum has given you a taste for the history of the region, 7km southwest of Roskilde is the fascinating Sagnlandet Lejre, a historic, 43-hectare open-air park – they call it a centre for 'experimental archaeology' – with re-created buildings from the Iron Age, Stone Age, Viking era and the 19th century, and a variety of activi-ties and special events. You get there by train from Roskilde (Dkr14.50, eight minutes).

Roskilde Museum MUSEUM

(www.roskildemuseum.dk; Sankt Olsgade 18; adult/child Dkr25/free; ☉11am-4pm) The well-presented Roskilde Museum has displays on Roskilde's rich history.

★ Festivals & Events

Roskilde Festival MUSIC

(www.roskilde-festival.dk) The Roskilde Festival takes place over a long weekend in early July, in fields just outside the city centre. It attracts the biggest international rock and pop names (Queens of the Stone Age and Slip-knot headlined in 2013), along with 75,000 music fans. It is renowned for its relaxed, friendly atmosphere. Most visitors camp on-site, as the accommodation in Roskilde itself tends to get booked up well in advance.

🛏 Sleeping & Eating

Roskilde has limited accommodation for its size; being so close to Copenhagen, it's a popular day-trip destination. The tourist office can book singles and doubles in private homes for between Dkr450 and Dkr600, plus a Dkr45 booking fee.

Danhostel Roskilde HOSTEL €

(☑46 35 21 84; www.danhostel.dk/roskilde; Vindeboder 7; dm/s/d/tr Dkr250/500/650/750; ℗) While this harbourside hostel is smart and modern, we found the private bathrooms less than pristine on our last visit. Equally unim-pressive is the wi-fi charge (Dkr20 per hour). Though made up of small three-, four-, five-, six- or eight-bed dorms, most are offered as private rooms. It's adjacent to the Viking Ship Museum.

DRAGSHOLM SLOT

Fancy a night in a culinary castle? Then pack your bag and your appetite and check in at **Dragsholm Slot** (⌨59 65 33 00; www.dragsholm-slot.dk; Dragsholm Allé, Hørve; s/d from Dkr1895/1995; P). Located at the edge of Zealand's fertile Lammefjorden (Denmark's most famous 'vegetable garden'), its medieval walls are home to **Slotskøkkenet** (Castle Kitchen; 5/7 courses Dkr650/800; ⊙dinner Tue-Sat summer, Fri & Sat winter), a New Nordic hot spot headed by ex-Noma chef Claus Henriksen. From the area's prized carrots to herbs from the castle's own garden, 'locally sourced' is the catch-cry here. The end results are deceptively simple, sublime creations such as candied herbs with *skyr* (Icelandic yoghurt) and celeriac. Upstairs, the more casual **Spisehus** (2-course lunch Dkr195, 3-course dinner Dkr325; ⊙lunch & dinner Mon-Sun) offers cheaper, pared-back Nordic dishes using the same top-notch ingredients (think herb-marinated herring or hay-smoked salmon). Bookings are a must for Slotskøkkenet and recommended for Spisehuset.

Nosh aside, whitewashed Dragsholm is famed for its 800-year history, which includes the imprisonment of Roskilde's last Catholic bishop and the secret burial of a love-struck girl in the castle walls (eerily visible behind a plexiglass panel). While some rooms – spread across the castle and the nearby porter's lodge – feature contemporary styling, most ooze a distinguished baronial air, with anything from canopy beds to fleur-de-lis wallpaper and (in some cases) jacuzzis. Add to this a string of Late Romantic salons and ballrooms and rambling fairy-tale gardens, and you'll soon be feeling like a well-fed noble.

Check the website for dinner and accommodation packages (often cheaper than the official room rates), and request a room with field or garden views. Dragsholm Slot is located 91km west of Copenhagen via motorway 21.

Hotel Prindsen   HOTEL €€€
(⌨46 30 91 00; www.prindsen.dk; Algade 13; s/d from Dkr1395/1495; P@) The town's grandest accommodation, with plenty of chintz and all the trimmings. Rates drop dramatically on weekends and public holidays; check the website.

Restaurant Mumm   INTERNATIONAL €€€
(⌨46 37 22 01; www.restaurantmumm.dk; Karen Olsdatters Stræde 9; 3/5/7 courses Dkr445/585/700; ⊙5.30pm-midnight Mon-Sat) Intimate, fine-dining Mumm takes Danish, French and Spanish influences and gives them a palate-pleasing revamp. The result is nothing short of inspired, with dishes like pickled halibut with pomegranate and hazelnuts, or silky cheesecake with blue cornflour and plums. Book ahead.

Café Vivaldi   INTERNATIONAL €€
(Stændertorvet 8; mains Dkr149-199; ⊙10am-10pm Sun-Thu, to midnight Fri & Sat) Right on the main square with views to the cathedral, bistro chain Vivaldi serves wraps, sandwiches, burgers, salads and pasta dishes (Dkr99 to Dkr119), as well as evening mains.

Rådhuskælderen   DANISH, EUROPEAN €€€
(www.raadhuskaelderen.dk; Fondens Bro 1; mains Dkr168-332; ⊙11am-9pm Mon-Sat) Right next to the cathedral, this atmospheric, red-brick cellar serves simple modern European and Danish dishes.

Gimle   INTERNATIONAL €
(www.gimle.dk; Helligkorsvej 2; meals Dkr30-88; ⊙noon-midnight Tue & Wed, to 2am Thu, to 5am Fri & Sat, to 5pm Sun; ☎) Gimle does it all; laid-back cafe, cultural hub, live-music venue and weekend club. Munch on simple, tasty standards like bagels, salads, nachos and burgers (including a vegetarian version). Free wi-fi.

❶ Information

Nordea Bank (Algade 4)
Post office (Jernbanegade 3)
Tourist office (www.visitroskilde.com; Stændertorvet 1; ⊙10am-5pm Mon-Fri, 10am-2pm Sat Jul & Aug, reduced hr rest of yr)

❶ Getting There & Around

Trains from Copenhagen to Roskilde are frequent (Dkr96, 25 minutes). From Copenhagen by car, Rte 21 leads to Roskilde; upon approaching the city, exit onto Rte 156, which leads into the centre.

Parking discs are required in Roskilde and can be purchased at the tourist office. There are free car parks at Gustav Weds Plads and near the Viking Ship Museum.

Jupiter Cykler (www.jupitercykler.dk; Gullandsstræde 3; per day Dkr75-90), just off Skomagergade, rents out bikes.

Køge

POP 35,300

Køge is a pretty town that, if not worth a special visit, offers a pleasant diversion if you're passing through on your way to Bornholm (by ferry) or the south islands. The one-time medieval trading centre, 42km south of Copenhagen, retains a photogenic core of narrow cobbled streets flanked by Denmark's best-preserved 17th- and 18th-century buildings. At its heart is broad and bustling **Torvet**, the nation's largest square.

◎ Sights

A short stroll through the central part of Køge takes you to Denmark's oldest **half-timbered building** (c 1527) at Kirkestræde 20, a marvellous survivor with a fine raked roof. Køge's **historical museum** (Nørregade 4; adult/child Dkr30/free; ⊙11am-5pm Tue-Sun Jun-Aug) is in a splendid building that dates from 1619. Another gem is **Brogade 23**, decorated with cherubs carved by the famed 17th-century artist Abel Schrøder. Elsewhere best efforts have been made to improve a not-very-attractive industrial harbour with open-air cafes and restaurants. Køge also has Denmark's only museum dedicated to the artistic process, **KØS** (www.koes.dk; Vestergade 1; adult/18-24yr/child Dkr50/20/free; ⊙10am-5pm Tue-Sun), which includes the sketches for the statue of the *Little Mermaid* and for Queen Margrethe II's birthday tapestries.

🛏 Sleeping & Eating

The tourist office can book double rooms in private homes for around Dkr500 per double, plus a Dkr25 booking fee.

Hotel Hvide Hus HOTEL €€
(☎56 65 36 90; www.helnan.info; Strandvejen 111; s/d Dkr1195/1495; P) Well located if a little characterless, this 127-room modern hotel is on the beach, and has a cafe and restaurant. Price drop dramatically on weekends (to Dkr750/950 for a single/double).

Danhostel Køge HOSTEL €
(☎56 67 66 50; www.danhostel.dk/koege; Vamdrupvej 1; dm Dkr200, r from Dkr380; P) Located 2km northwest of the centre, this friendly hostel offers small but cosy rooms. Catch bus 101A from Køge train station and get off at Norsevej, from there the hostel is a 1km walk.

Café Vanilla INTERNATIONAL €€
(☎56 65 01 75; Torvet 17; sandwiches Dkr89-99, wok dishes Dkr119, dinner mains Dkr169-199; ⊙10am-10pm Sun-Thu, to 2am Fri & Sat) Square-side Vanilla covers a lot of ground, from toast, yoghurt and croissants to generous salads, burgers, stir-fries, pasta and steaks. Servings are generous and the value better than at its main rival on the square.

StigAnn EUROPEAN €€
(www.stigann.dk; Sankt Gertruds Stræd 2; lunch meals Dkr70-110, 3-course dinner menu Dkr350; ⊙4-11pm Mon & Tue, noon-4pm & 5-11pm Wed-Sat) One of Køge's best restaurants by some margin, StigAnn offers refined and ambitious retro-classic dishes such as tournedos rossini and chateaubriand.

Café T CAFE
(www.cafe-t.dk; Nyportstræde 17; ⊙10am-6pm Tue-Fri, to 4pm Sat) Just off the main square, this oversized doll's house peddles coffee, cakes and 38 types of loose-leaf tea. If you just can't live without the old sofas, retro lamps, or dainty tea sets, buy them; the place doubles as a bric-a-brac shop.

❶ Information

Tourist office (☎56 67 60 01; www.visitkoege.com; Vestergade 1; ⊙9am-6pm Mon-Fri, to 3pm Sat, 11am-1pm Sun Jul & Aug, reduced hr rest of yr) Just off the main square.

❶ Getting There & Away

You can park in Torvet, but for one hour only during the day; there are longer-term car parks near the train station. Time discs are required.

Boat

Bornholmer Færgen (☎56 95 18 66; www.bornholmerfaergen.dk; adult/child 12-15/under 11 Dkr284/142/free, car incl 5 passengers Dkr1645) operates an overnight service from Køge to Bornholm, departing daily at 12.30am and arriving at 6am. It is quicker and almost as cheap to take a train via Copenhagen to Ystad in Sweden, and then a catamaran to Rønne from there (total journey time would be around 3½ hours), although it can make sense to sleep while you sail if your itinerary is tight.

Train

Køge's train and bus stations are at Jernbanegade 12 on the east side of town. The train station is the last stop on the E line on Copenhagen's S-Tog network. Trains to Copenhagen run at least three times an hour (Dkr108, 40 minutes).

Trelleborg

In the countryside of western Zealand, **Trelleborg** (www.vikingeborg.dk; Trelleborg Allé 4, Hejninge; adult/child Dkr60/free; ☺10am-4pm Tue-Sun Apr, May, Sep & Oct, to 5pm Tue-Sun Jun-Aug) is the best preserved of Denmark's four Viking ring fortresses.

There isn't an awful lot to see here, it must be said – there is a reconstructed Viking hall, a small visitor centre and the earthen-walled fortress itself, dating from AD 980. This is made up of various grassy earthworks, hillocks and trenches divided into four symmetrical quadrants. In Viking times, each quadrant contained four long elliptical buildings of wood that surrounded a courtyard. Each of the 16 buildings, which served as barracks, was exactly 100 Roman feet (29.5m) long. Concrete blocks mark the outlines of the house foundations. Plaques point out burial mounds and other features.

Trelleborg is 7km west of Slagelse. To get there, take the train to Slagelse (Dkr73, 33 minutes from Roskilde) and then either catch the hourly bus 439 to Trelleborg (12 minutes) or take a taxi from Slagelse (around Dkr190 on weekdays, Dkr220 on weekends). There is no bus service to Trelleborg on Saturdays.

Vordingborg

POP 11,700

Vordingborg's modern-day quaintness is deceptive. Now best known as Zealand's gateway to the south islands, the town played a starring role in early Danish history. It was the royal residence and Baltic power base of Valdemar I (Valdemar the Great), famed for reuniting the Danish kingdom in 1157 after a period of civil war. And it was here that Valdemar II (Valdemar the Victorious) signed the Law of Jutland in 1241, a civil code which declared that legitimate laws must be based on objective and sovereign justice. The code would become a forerunner to Danish national law.

Starting as a small wooden fortification in the 1160s, the town's historic fortress expanded over the following two centuries, becoming one of Denmark's most important castles. The remnants of that 14th-century giant, the 26m **Gåsetårnet** (Goose Tower; ☎55 37 25 51; Slotsruinen 1; adult/child incl Sydsjællands Museum Dkr45/free, tower only Dkr30/free; ☺10am-5pm Jun-Aug, reduced hr rest of yr),

is Vordingborg's most prominent landmark (and lookout) today. Beside it stands the striking, multimillion-dollar **Danmarks Borgcenter** (www.danmarksborgcenter.dk; Slotsruinen 1). Due to open in autumn 2013, the redeveloped museum will use cutting-edge technology to bring to life both the history of the fortress and the medieval world in which it thrived. The project will also see the original castle moat restored. Check the museum website for updates and opening hours.

The centre will house the **Vordingborg tourist office** (☎55 34 11 11; www.visitvordingborg.dk; Danmarks Borgcenter, Slotsruinen 1; ☺10am-5pm Mon-Sun Jun-Aug, reduced hr rest of yr).

SOUTH ISLANDS

The three islands of Møn, Falster and Lolland mark the southernmost part of Denmark. Of these, Møn and Falster are the most beautiful. Though just a 1½-hour drive from Copenhagen, these rural oases, with their gently rolling, unspoiled landscape, can seem centuries removed. Though bridges connect all three islands to each other and Zealand, they often appear disconnected from the modern world, which of course is part of their appeal. Cycling holidays are popular here, as are fishing, sailing, birdwatching and hiking, and there are several good golf courses. There is also a thriving arts scene on Møn, although the island is most celebrated for its striking chalk sea cliffs.

Møn

POP 9900

Prepare to fall head over heels for Møn. By far the most bewitching of the south islands, its most famous drawcards are its spectacular white cliffs, Møns Klint. Soft, sweeping and crowned by deep green forest, they're the stuff paintings are made of...which possibly explains the island's healthy quota of artists.

Yet the inspiration doesn't end there, with beautiful beaches spanning sandy expanses to small secret coves, haunting Neolithic graves and medieval churches lined with some of Denmark's most vivid medieval frescos.

Stege, the main settlement on Møn, is an everyday place, but it is enlivened by its role as the island's gateway town and main commercial centre.

So hit the peddle or get behind the wheel (Møn has no trains and the bus service is sketchy), and let the island work its magic.

◉ Sights

Møns Klint
OUTDOORS

The chalk cliffs of Møns Klint, at the eastern tip of the island, were created during the last Ice Age when the calcareous deposits from aeons of compressed seashells were lifted from the ocean floor. The gleaming white cliffs rise sharply for 128m above an azure sea, presenting one of the most striking landscapes in Denmark. The chalk subsoil of the land above the cliffs supports a terrific variety of wildflowers including vivid orchids. There is a strict embargo on picking wildflowers.

The woods of **Klinteskoven**, behind the cliffs, have a network of paths and tracks. From near the cafeteria you can descend the cliffs by a series of wooden stairways. It's quite a long descent and a strenuous return up the 500-odd stairs. From the base of the steps, turn south along the narrow beach, which leads in about 1km to another stairway at **Gråryg Fald**. These take you steeply to the top of the cliff, from where a path leads back to the car park. Warning notices and barriers should be heeded.

Geocenter Møns Klint
MUSEUM

(www.moensklint.dk; Stengårdsvej 8, Borre; adult/child Dkr115/75; ◷10am-6pm end Jun–mid-Aug, reduced hr rest of yr) The history of the cliffs, and why you should be careful climbing them, are explained at the swish museum Geocenter Møns Klint, which also houses a collection of fossils found on the beaches here. The museum is located on the clifftop at Borre and has a lovely cafe-restaurant with views over the sea.

FREE Passage Graves
HISTORIC SITE

Møn has a wealth of prehistoric remains, although many are vestigial burial mounds. The best-preserved sites are the late–Stone Age passage graves of Kong Asgers Høj and Klekkende Høj. Both are on the west side of the island within a 2km radius of the village of **Røddinge**, from where they are signposted.

Kong Asgers Høj is close to the narrow road and parking space is limited. The site is extremely well preserved and comprises a grassy mound pierced by a low passageway that leads to a splendid stone-lined chamber. Take a torch and mind your head.

Klekkende Høj is on a hilltop amid fields. From a car park, follow a signposted track to reach the site. The grave has a double chamber and again you need a torch and some agility to creep inside.

FREE Stege Kirke
CHURCH

(Provstesstræde, Stege; ◷9am-5pm) It looks as though a demented nine-year-old has been let loose inside Stege Kirke, built in the 13th century by one of the powerful Hvide family. Walls and ceiling are covered in endearingly naive 14th- and 15th-century frescos in red and black paint: monkeylike faces sprout from branches, a hunter chases unidentifiable animals, and a sorrowful man is covered in big red blobs...measles?

🏃 Activities

Although testing at times, cycling on Møn is rewarding given the island's uncharacteristic hilliness. The tourist office has maps of cycling routes on the island. Bike rental is available at **Møns Dækservice** (☏55 81 42 49; Storegade 91, Stege; 8.30am-5pm Mon-Fri, 9am-1pm Sat; bike rental per day/week Dkr65/300).

A FEAST OF FRESCOS

Given Møn's artistic sensibility, it seems apt that the island should claim some of the best-preserved primitive frescos in Denmark. You'll find them in many of Møn's churches, most of which are of medieval origin. The frescos depict biblical scenes, often interpreted through light-hearted rustic imagery. Fearful of what they saw as too much Roman exuberance, post-Reformation Lutherans whitewashed them, ironically preserving the artworks. The style of Møn fresco painting owes much to the Emelundemesttteren (the Elmelunde Master), an accomplished stylist whose name is unknown. Some of his finest work can be seen at **Elmelunde Kirke** (Kirkebakken 41; admission free; ◷8am-4pm Mon-Sun) on the road to Møns Klint.

Sejlkutteren

Discovery Boat Tours   BOAT TOUR

(☑21 40 41 81; www.sejlkutteren-discovery.dk; adult/child 165/80kr) During summer, boat tours of the coast around the cliffs run with MS *Discovery* from Klintholm harbour every two hours from 10am to 4pm.

🛏 Sleeping & Eating

The tourist office has a brochure with a list of B&Bs on the island. You're welcome to use the tourist office phone free of charge to book accommodation or you can pay Dkr25 to have the staff call for you.

In Stege, there are bakeries and super-markets and a handful of cafes.

TOP CHOICE Tohøjgaard

Gæstgivern   GUESTHOUSE €€

(☑55 81 60 67; www.tohoejgaard.com; Rytsebækvej 17, Hjelm; r Dkr420-700; ⊙Mar-Dec; P) Book ahead to slumber at one of Denmark's most coveted guesthouses: an 1875 farmhouse surrounded by fields, a 4000-year-old burial mound and soothing sea views. Choose from five eclectic, individually themed guest rooms, adorned with flea-market finds, books and fluffy bathrobes. If booked two days in advance, host Christine can whip up a fabulous Scandinavian dinner (Dkr210, Friday to Sunday only) for guests, using local produce and vegies and herbs straight from the garden. A daily 'Biker's Supper' light meal is also available (Dkr130). The guest-house lies 9.5km southwest of Stege.

Motel Stege   MOTEL €€

(☑55 81 35 35; www.motel-stege.dk; Provstestræde 4; s Dkr550-650, d Dkr575-750; P) This is your best bet in central Stege, with 12 simple, smart rooms. Those in the main building have a mezzanine level (accessible by ladder), and sleep up to four. Rooms in the annexe have their own kitchenette, while all guests have access to a homely communal kitchen and dining area. Added comforts include a washer, dryer, umbrellas and lock-able bike garage.

Camping Møns Klint   CAMPING GROUND €

(☑55 81 20 25; www.campingmoensklint.dk; Klintevej 544, Børre Møn; campsites per adult/child/tent Dkr89/65/30; ⊙late Apr-Oct; @🏊) The best located of Møn's camping grounds is about 3km from the cliffs. The camping ground is in a pleasant woodland setting with swim-

ming pool (June to August), tennis court, minigolf, guest kitchen, as well as bike and boat hire.

Danhostel Møns Klint   HOSTEL €

(☑55 81 20 30; www.danhostel.dk; Klintholm Havnevej 17a, Borre; dm/d/tr/q from Dkr165/330/420/460; P) This two-star hostel 5km from the beach and cliffs occupies an enchanting lakeside spot opposite the camping ground.

TOP CHOICE Gourmet Gaarden

    DANISH €€

(☑55 81 17 00; www.gourmetgaarden.com; Store-garden 68, Stege; 3-course menu Dkr385-400; ⊙5.30-11pm Tue-Sat) If you like your food seasonal and beautifully prepared by a chef who hails from one of Copenhagen's top restaurants, secure a table here. Henrik Bajer and his wife, Lina, are seriously passionate about Danish produce and flavours, and Henrik's simple yet sophisticated dishes allow the prime ingredients to shine. Always check the website for updated opening times. Note that the kitchen closes much earlier here (8pm Tuesday to Thursday; 8.30pm Friday and Saturday) than most.

David's   INTERNATIONAL €€

(www.davids.nu; Storegade 11a, Stege; lunches Dkr80-145, 2-course menus Dkr255; ⊙10am-5pm Mon-Thu, to 10pm Fri & Sat, to 4pm Sun) David's open kitchen prepares flavoursome, contemporary cafe fare. Tuck into the speciality Danish 'tapas' platter or refreshing options like a roll of smoked salmon and apples with trout mousse and green salad. Housemade cakes and real-deal espresso make for a perfect between-meals pit stop.

Klintholm Røgeri   SEAFOOD €€

(Thyravej 25, Klintholm Havn; lunch/dinner buffet Dkr108/155; ⊙noon-3pm & from 6pm) You'll find this excellent-value smoke-house in the one-road village of Klintholm Havn. You can buy fish by the piece and enjoy it at a picnic table. Alternatively, head into the restaurant and tackle the drool-inducing buffet of grilled, smoked and marinated sea-born treats.

Bryghuset Møn   INTERNATIONAL €€

(Storegade 18, Stege; lunch Dkr69-125, dinner Dkr69-279; ⊙lunch & dinner Mon-Sun end May-Sep) This casual microbrewery is a sound bet for simple, honest grub. It has outdoor seating in summer.

❶ Information

Møn tourist office (☎55 86 04 00; www.
visitvordingborg.dk; Storegade 2, Stege;
☉9.30am-5pm Mon-Fri, 9.30am-12.30pm &
2.30-5pm Sat Jul–mid-Aug, reduced hr rest of
yr) is at the entrance to Stege. As well as offering
information on the island, the website allows you
to book accommodation online out of hours.

❶ Getting There & Around

From Copenhagen take the train to Vordingborg
(Dkr128, 1¼ hours, at least once hourly); from
there it's a 45-minute ride to Stege on bus 660R
(Dkr48, half-hourly on weekdays, hourly on
weekends).

From July to September, bus 678 runs from
Stege to Møns Klint (Dkr24, 22 minutes, every
two hours from 9.45am to 5.45pm), stopping
at Elmelunde Kirke, the hostel and camping
ground en route. To reach Møns Klint outside
this period, take bus 667 (hourly to every two
hours weekdays, every two hours weekends) to
Magleby, from where the cliffs are an incovenient
6km walk further east.

Falster

POP 43,400

Falster is the middle of the three islands to
the south of Zealand and, as with Møn and
Lolland, the people who live here – most
of whom live in the only town of any significance, **Nykøbing** – are largely concerned
with farming and tourism. The east coast
of Falster is lined with white sandy beaches
that attract huge numbers of German and
Danish holidaymakers, many of whom own
tree-shrouded cabins along the wooded
coastline.

The most glorious stretch of beach is at
Marielyst, which is 12km from Nykøbing.
The beach draws crowds in summer, but it's
so long that you can always achieve some
sense of escape. The southern tip of the island, **Gedser Odde**, is the southernmost
point of Denmark.

⏣ Sleeping

Hotel Nørrevang   HOTEL €€€
(☎54 13 62 62; www.norrevang.dk; Marielyst
Strandvej 32; s/d from Dkr945/1195, cottages
Dkr1300 plus cleaning fee Dkr400; Ⓟ⛳) Marielyst's most upmarket hotel offers smart
rooms under a thatched roof, as well as an
indoor pool with spa and waterslide. Also
on offer are 54 kitchen-equipped cottages
accommodating four to six people. The 'upmarket' restaurant charges high-end prices
for often bland, mediocre food.

Danhostel Nykøbing Falster   HOSTEL €
(☑54 85 66 99; www.danhostel.dk/nykoebingfal-
ster; Østre Allé 110; dm Dkr300, s Dkr350-450, d
Dkr480-560; ☉mid-Jan–mid-Dec; Ⓟ) This is the
nearest hostel to Marielyst, being just 1km
east of Nykøbing F, Falster's train station.
It is a large, institutional-style place about
10km from the beach. Take bus 742 (741 on
Sundays) from the train station.

**Marielyst Feriepark &
Camping**   CAMPGROUND €
(☑54 13 53 07; www.marielyst-camping.dk; Marielyst Strandvej 36; campsites per adult/child
Dkr75/35; ☉Apr-Sep; @⛺) This central camping ground is popular with families. It's
400m from the beach.

❶ Information

The **tourist office** (www.visitlolland-falster.com;
Marielyst Strandpark 3; ☉9am-4pm Mon-Fri, to
5pm Sat, 10am-2pm Sun Jul & Aug, reduced hr
rest of yrr) is in a modern complex on the western entrance to the resort as you come in from
the E55. Go left at the big roundabout. There
is also a tourist office in **Nykøbing F** (☑5485
1303; Færgestræde 1a; ☉10am-4pm Mon-Sat
summer, reduced hr rest of yr).

❶ Getting There & Around

BOAT Ferries connect Gedser to Rostock,
Germany. See p491 for details.

TRAIN Trains leave Copenhagen one to two
times hourly for Nykøbing F (Dkr159, 80 to 110
minutes), on the island's western side. From
here, buses reach Marielyst (Dkr24, 25 minutes) in the east or Gedser (Dkr36, 50 minutes)
further south.

BORNHOLM

POP 41,300

Bornholm is a little Baltic pearl: a Danish
island, yet lying some 200km east of the
mainland, north of Poland. It boasts more
hours of sunshine than any other part of the
country, as well as gorgeous sandy beaches,
idyllic fishing villages, numerous historic
sights, endless cycling paths and a burgeon-
ing reputation for culinary curiosities and
ceramic artists and glassmakers.

Unique among Bornholm's attractions
are its four 12th-century round churches,
splendid buildings with whitewashed walls,
2m thick, that are framed by solid buttresses
and crowned with black, conical roofs. Each
was designed as both a place of worship
and a fortress against enemy attacks, with

Bornholm

a gunslot-pierced upper storey. All four churches are still used for Sunday services, but are otherwise open to visitors. The island's tourist website, with information on accommodation, activities, events and transport, is at www.bornholm.info.

History

Bornholm's history reflects its position at the heart of the Baltic and, in its time, Sweden, Germany and Soviet Russia have occupied it. A Danish possession since the Middle Ages, the island fell into Swedish hands in the 17th century, but was won back for Denmark by a fierce local rebellion.

The island suffered cruelly in the chaos at the end of WWII. It was occupied by the Nazis, but when Germany surrendered in May 1945 the commander on Bornholm resisted and Rønne and Nexø suffered heavy damage from Soviet air raids. On 9 May the island was handed over to the Soviets, who remained in situ until the following year, when Bornholm was returned to Denmark.

❶ Getting There & Away

AIR Danish Airport Transport (DAT; www.bornholmerflyet.dk) runs numerous daily flights between Copenhagen and Rønne (one way around Dkr1095, 35 minutes). Tickets booked online and in advance can be significantly cheaper.

BOAT & TRAIN Bornholmer Færgen (☏70 23 15 15; www.faergen.com; adult/child 12-15/ under 11 Dkr284/142/free, car incl 5 passengers Dkr1645) operates an overnight ferry service from Køge, 39km south of Copenhagen, to Bornholm. The ferry departs daily at 12.30am and arrives at 6am. On the upside, the overnight journey makes good use of your travel time. On the downside, the trip to Køge (around 30 minutes by train) adds additional cost and time if travelling from Copenhagen.

From Copenhagen, **DSB** (www.dsb.dk) offers a combined train/catamaran ticket (one way Dkr310, three hours) that includes train travel to Ystad (Sweden) and high-speed catamaran from Ystad to Rønne on Bornholm. This is the most cost- and time-effective option from Copenhagen. It's also possible to drive to Ystad and cross with your car from there.

❶ Getting Around

TO/FROM THE AIRPORT Bornholms Lufthavn is 5km southeast of Rønne, on the road to Dueodde. Bus 3 connects the airport to Rønne.

BICYCLE Bornholm is criss-crossed by more than 200km of bike trails. Download cycle routes free at www.bornholm.info, or purchase a more detailed cycling booklet with maps (Dkr129) from the island's tourist offices.

In Rønne, **Bornholms Cykeludlejning** (www.bornholms-cykeludlejning.dk; Nordre Kystvej 5; per day/week Dkr70/360), next to the tourist office, has bikes for hire. Rental bikes are commonly available at hostels and camping grounds for about Dkr70 a day.

BUS Bornholms Amts Trafikselskab
(BAT; www.bat.dk; pass per day adult/child Dkr150/75, per week Dkr500/250) operates bus services on the island. Fares cost Dkr13 per zone; the maximum fare is for five zones. Ask the bus driver about the 'RaBATkort' (10 rides; Dkr80), which can be used by more than one person and saves about 20%. Day/week passes cost Dkr150/500. Children travel for half-price. Buses operate all year, but services are less frequent from October to April. From early May to late September, buses 7 and 8 circumnavigate the island, stopping at all major towns and settlements.

CAR & SCOOTER Europcar (56 95 43 00; www.europcar.com; Nordre Kystvej 1, Rønne) rents cars from Dkr580 per day as well as scooters. The office is at the Q8 petrol station, 100m north of the ferry terminal. You'll find another branch at the airport.

Rønne
POP 13,900

Though Rønne is not the most charming of the island's harbour towns, virtually everyone who visits Bornholm will end up spending time here. The town boasts engaging museums and an old quarter of cobbled streets flanked by pretty single-storey dwellings, as well as having a reasonable-sized shopping area. It is the island's largest settlement and is a popular shopping destination for Swedes on day trips.

⊙ Sights

Two very pleasant streets with period buildings are the cobblestoned **Laksegade** and **Storegade**.

Bornholms Museum   MUSEUM
(www.bornholmsmuseum.dk; Sankt Mortensgade 29; adult/child Dkr50/free, combined ticket incl Hjorths Fabrik Dkr70/free; ⊗10am-5pm Jul & Aug, closed Sun mid-May–Jun & Sep–mid-Oct, reduced hr rest of yr) The wonderfully atmospheric Bornholms Museum has a surprisingly large collection of local-history exhibits, some interesting displays about Christiansø, along with many prehistoric finds and a good maritime section decked out like the interior of a ship.

Hjorths Fabrik   MUSEUM
(www.bornholmsmuseer.dk; Krystalgade 5; adult/child Dkr50/free, combined ticket incl Bornholms

Museum Dkr70/free; ⊗10am-5pm Mon-Sat mid-May–late Oct, reduced hr rest of yr) This intimate ceramics museum features a working studio.

TOP CHOICE Nylars Rundkirke   CHURCH
(Kirkevej 10K, Nylars; ⊗8am-6pm Apr-Sep, to 3.30pm Oct-Mar) Built in 1150, handsome Nylars Rundkirke is the most well-preserved and easily accessible round church in the Rønne area. Its central pillar is painted with wonderful 13th-century, Creation-themed frescos, the oldest in Bornholm. Inside the church, the front door is flanked by two of Bronholm's 40 rune stones (carved memorial stones dating back to the Viking era). It's a 25-minute ride from Rønne on bus 5 or 6. The cycle path between Rønne and Åkirkeby also passes the church.

🛏 Sleeping

The tourist office books rooms (singles/doubles Dkr225/400) in private homes.

BB-Hotel   HOTEL €
(70 22 55 30; www.bbhotels.dk; Store Torv 17, Rønne; d/tr/q Dkr530/690/850; P) Accommodation doesn't get much more spartan than this self-service place above some shops on the main square, but the rooms are clean and all have en suite bathrooms, plus breakfast is included in the price. Above all, it's cheap.

Danhostel Rønne   HOSTEL €
(56 95 13 40; www.danhostel-roenne.dk; Arsenalvej 12; dm/s/d/tr Dkr200/350/450/530; ⊗Apr-late Oct; P) Immaculately kept and close to town, rooms here sleep up to eight. There is a shared kitchen, laundry, minigolf and bike rental on site.

🍴 Eating & Drinking

You'll find numerous fast-food places on Store Torv.

Poul P   INTERNATIONAL €€
(www.restaurantpoulp.dk; Store Torvegade 29; lunch Dkr78-148, dinner mains Dkr152-328; ⊗10am-late Mon-Sun) Pimped with the Technicolor artwork of its artist-owner, this relaxed, beach-chic cafe-restaurant is one of the better options in Rønne. Lunch options include gourmet salads, sandwiches and burgers, as well as a graze-alicious 'tapas plate' (Dkr108) of Bornholm specialities. Dinner options are a little more ambitious, though some work better than others.

Kvickly Supermarket SUPERMARKET €
(Nordre Kystvej 28; ⊙8am-8pm Mon-Fri, to 6pm Sat, 10am-5pm Sun) Opposite the tourist office; the decent bakery opens at 7am daily.

① Information

Public library (Pingels Allé; ⊙9.30am-6pm Mon-Fri, to 2pm Sat) Free internet access.

Tourist office (Bornholms Velkomstcenter; ☑56 95 95 00; www.bornholm.info; Nordre Kystvej 3; ⊙9am-6pm late Jun–mid-Aug, reduced hr rest of yr) A few minutes' walk from the harbour; has masses of information on all of Bornholm.

Dueodde

Backed by deep green woodlands and dramatic dunes, Dueodde has a vast stretch of white-sand beach that most of Europe can only dream about. The only 'sight' is the slender **lighthouse** (adult/child Dkr10/5; ⊙11.30am-3pm daily Jul–mid-Aug, 11am-2pm Tue-Thu & Sun, May, Jun & mid-Aug–Sep), which you can climb for views of sea and strand that stretch to the horizon. There's no village, just a bus stop with a single hotel, a restaurant, a cluster of kiosks selling ice cream and hot dogs, and the necessary public toilets to cope with the rush from tour coaches in summer.

It can be a crowded trek for a couple of hundred metres along boardwalks to reach the superb beach. Once there, head left or right for wide-open spaces.

🛏 Sleeping & Eating

Bornholms Familie Camping CAMPGROUND €
(☑56 48 81 50; www.bornholms-familiecamping.dk; Krogegårdsvejen 2; campsites per adult/child/tent Dkr75/45/60, 4-person family tent from Dkr425, apt per week from Dkr3900; ⊙mid-May–mid-Sep; ℗) One of the loveliest camping grounds in Denmark, this place is set amid beech and pine trees right beside the wonderful soft, white-sand beach at Dueodde. Facilities include laundry, shared kitchen, minigolf and table tennis.

Dueodde Vandrerhjem & Camping Ground CAMPGROUND €
(☑56 48 81 19; www.dueodde.dk; Skorkkegårdsvejen 17; s/d/tr/q Dkr225/375/450/530, tent Dkr30-40, campsites per adult/child Dkr72/37; ⊙May-Sep; ℗☒) Another lovely, low-cost spot to stay on Dueodde beach is this cabin-style, single-storey hostel and camping ground. It has an indoor pool (Dkr22), as well as pleasant, pine-clad cabins/apartments for rent from Dkr3000 per week for two people.

LOCAL KNOWLEDGE

RASMUS KOFOED: SOMMELIER

Bornholm native Rasmus Kofoed is the founder of Dueodde restaurant Kadeau.

Must-Eats

Don't miss smoked herring and a beer at a *rogeri* (smoke-house). Smoke-houses are part of Bornholm's history, and one of the island's simple pleasures. One of the best and most consistent is Rogeriet i Svaneke (p78). Ditch the chips (they're for the tourists) and ask the staff for a platter of whatever is best that day.

Must-Dos

Walk around Svaneke (p78). The locals have been very active in protecting its built heritage and I think it's the most beautiful town on Bornholm. Then there's Paradisbakkerne (p78), with its changing landscapes and sublime views. It's called 'Paradise Hills' with good reason.

Did You Know?

We can grow figs on Bornholm. The island is one of the mildest areas of Denmark. It takes a while to warm up in June but then it stays warm for longer, which allows some exotic things to grow. Bornholm is also home to Denmark's biggest chef competition, Sol Over Gudhjem (Sun Over Gudhjem; www.solovergudhjemkonkurrence.dk). It takes place in June and sees some of the country's best chefs battle it out using local produce.

TOP
CHOICE Kadeau   MODERN SCANDINAVIAN €€€
(🖉56 97 82 50; www.kadeau.dk; Baunevej 18; 3-/5-course dinner Dkr450/700; ◷lunch & dinner Jul–mid-Aug, dinner Thu-Sun Easter-Jun & mid-Aug–mid-Sep) Not simply Bornholm's top restaurant, but a rising star on the national stage, Kadeau wows with unforgettable New Nordic creations, spectacular wines and near-faultless service. The emphasis is on foraged and regional ingredients, transformed into revelations like sugar-cured scallops in chamomile-infused milk, served with pickled celeriac. If the budget allows, opt for the seven-course tasting menu. The restaurant is 8km southeast of Âkirkeby, in a cosy, converted shack right on the beach. Book two days in advance.

Bornholm's East Coast

Bornholm's east coast tends to be fairly built-up and is punctuated by several settlements, all with some interest as stopping-off places.

Snogebæk is a small shoreside fishing village that hangs on to its authenticity because of its small fleet of working boats and its scattering of fishing huts and cabins. Just north of Snogebæk is the fine beach of Balka Strand.

Nexø is Bornholm's second-largest town. It took a hammering from Soviet bombers in WWII and today much of what you see from the harbour outwards is a fairly functional reconstruction. Nexø Museum (Havnen 2; adult/child Dkr30/10; ◷10am-4pm Mon-Fri, to 2pm Sat Jul-late Aug) is at the harbour and is packed with maritime flotsam and jetsam including an old-fashioned diving suit, cannons, WWII mines and the inner workings of a lighthouse. Nexø-Dueodde Turist-information (Sdr Hammer 2g; ◷10am-5pm Mon-Fri, also 9am-2pm Sat May–mid-Sep) is down by the harbour.

Three kilometres northwest of Nexø lies Paradisbakkerne, a natural wonderland of forest, high-heath bogs and rift valleys. To get here from Nexø, take Paradisvej (which becomes Klintebyvejen) inland and turn right at Lisegårdsvejen, which leads to a car park, toilets and a map of the area's colour-coded walking tracks.

The harbour town of Svaneke has award-winning historic buildings, especially those near the village church, a few minutes' walk south of the centre. The tourist office (Peter F Heerings Gade 7; ◷10am-4pm Mon-Fri mid-Jun–mid-Sep) is open only in summer.

🛏 Sleeping

Hotel Balka Strand   HOTEL €€
(🖉56 49 49 49; www.hotelbalkastrand.dk; Boulevarden 9; s Dkr700-850, d Dkr800-1050; 🅿🕸) A good base in the Snogebæk–Nexø area, this friendly, smart hotel is located about 150m from Balka Strand beach. On-site perks include a heated outdoor pool, sauna, bar and restaurant.

Nexø Hostel   HOSTEL €€
(🖉70 22 08 98; www.nexohostel.dk; Gammel Rønnevej 17a, Nexø; s Dkr375-485, d Dkr495-595, q Dkr625-750) One of the more unusual places to stay on Bornholm is this major glass and ceramic workshop and hostel on the outskirts of Nexø. It hosts various events, courses and exhibitions throughout the year, and you can even rent the workshop. Rooms are extremely basic, but clean and tidy.

Danhostel Svaneke   HOSTEL €
(🖉56 49 62 42; www.danhostel-svaneke.dk; Reberbanevej 9; dm/s/d Dkr160/450/510; ◷Apr-late Oct; 🅿) This quiet complex of bungalow-style chalet dorms and rooms is 1km south of the centre of Svaneke and close to the water.

🍴 Eating & Drinking

TOP
CHOICE Rogeriet i Svaneke   SEAFOOD €
(Fiskergade 12; counter items Dkr35-99; ◷9am-8.30pm summer, reduced hr rest of yr) Down by the harbour, this superlative smoke-house serves smoked trout, cod's roe, herring, salmon and fish *frikadeller,* traditionally washed down with a cool beer while sitting at the outdoor picnic tables.

Svaneke Chokoladeri   CHOCOLATE €
(www.svanekechokoladeri.dk; Torv 5; 3 chocolate truffles Dkr30; ◷10am-5pm Mon-Fri, to 3pm Sat & Sun; 🚼) Chocolate fans, prepare to worship at Bornholm's top chocolatier. Freshly made on-site, the sublime cocoa creations include a zesty white chocolate, coconut and lime truffle, as well as a very Bornholm *stout øl* (stout beer) truffle.

Bryghuset   BREWERY
(Torv 5; lunch Dkr69-125, dinner mains Dkr145-280) This is one of the most popular nosh-and-slosh options on the island, known throughout Denmark for its excellent beers, brewed on-site. Soak up the liquid amber with decent, meat-centric pub grub.

WORTH A TRIP

CHRISTIANSØ

If you think Bornholm is as remote as Denmark gets, you're wrong. Even further east, way out in the merciless Baltic, is tiny Christiansø, an intensely atmospheric 17th-century fortress-island about 500m long and an hour's sail northeast of Bornholm. It's well worth making time for a day trip: its rugged, moss-covered rocks, historic stone buildings and even hardier people are reminiscent of the Faroe Islands. A seasonal fishing hamlet since the Middle Ages, the island fell briefly into Swedish hands in 1658, after which Christian V decided to turn the island into an invincible naval fortress. Bastions and barracks were built; a church, school and prison followed.

By the 1850s the island was no longer needed as a forward base against Sweden and the navy withdrew. Soldiers who wanted to stay on as fishermen were allowed to live as free tenants in the old cottages. Their offspring, and a few latter-day fisherfolk and artists, currently comprise Christiansø's 100 residents. The entire island is an unspoiled reserve – there are no cats or dogs, no cars and no modern buildings – allowing the rich birdlife, including puffins, to prosper.

There's a small **local history museum** (☎56 46 20 71; adult/child Dkr20/5; ☉11am-4pm Mon-Fri, 11.30am-4pm Sat & Sun late Jun-Aug, reduced hr rest of yr) in Frederickson's tower and a great 360-degree view from **Christiansø lighthouse**. Otherwise the main activity is walking the footpaths along the fortified walls and batteries that skirt the island. There are skerries with nesting seabirds and a secluded **swimming cove** on Christiansø's eastern side.

In summer, camping is allowed at **Christiansø Teltplads** (☎24 42 12 22; campsite Dkr75-100), a small field called the Duchess Battery. **Christiansø Gæstgiveriet** (☎56 46 20 15; www.christiansoekro.dk; s/d without bathroom Dkr950/1050; ☉closed late Dec-Jan), the island's only inn, has six rooms with shared bathroom and a restaurant. Booking ahead for a room is advised. There's a small food store and a kiosk.

Christiansøfarten (☎56 48 51 76; www.bornholmexpress.dk; return ticket adult/child 6-14 Dkr240/120) sails daily to Christiansø from Gudhjem between late April and mid-October, with reduced services the rest of the year. It also sails daily from Allinge from mid-June to late August, with reduced services from early May to mid-June and from late August to late September. Check the website for up-to-date timetables.

Gudhjem

POP 740

Gudhjem is the best-looking of Bornholm's harbour towns. Its rambling high street is crowned by a squat windmill standing over half-timbered houses and sloping streets that roll down to the picture-perfect harbour. The town is a good base for exploring the rest of Bornholm, with cycle and walking trails, convenient bus connections, plenty of places to eat and stay and a boat service to Christiansø. Interestingly, the harbour was one of the settings for the Oscar-winning film *Pelle the Conqueror*, based on the novel by Bornholm writer Martin Andersen Nexø.

There's a public car park northwest of the harbour.

☉ Sights

A bike path leads inland 4km south from Gudhjem to the thick-walled, buttressed

Østerlars Rundkirke, the most impressive of the island's round churches – buses 1 and 9 go by the church.

Oluf Høst Museet   MUSEUM
(www.ohmus.dk; Løkkegade 35; adult/child Dkr75/35; ☉11am-5pm Tue-Sun early May-early Jun, 11am-5pm early Jun-end Sep; ⏹) The former home and studio of 20th-century Danish painter Oluf Høst is now a beautiful museum dedicated to his life and work. Though inspired by Cézanne, Høst's work is distinctly Scandinavian in his depiction of Bornholm's light and moods. The beautiful backyard hosts a children's art space and Høst's former summer atelier, and you can even purchase coffee, tea and chocolate for a cultured pit stop.

Bornholms Kunstmuseum   MUSEUM
(www.bornholms-kunstmuseum.dk; Helligdommen, Rø; adult/child Dkr70/free; ☉10am-5pm Jun-Aug, reduced hr rest of yr) Six kilometres north of

Gudhjem along the coast road is Bornholm's leading art museum. Housed in a striking modern building overlooking the famously vertiginous Heligdoms cliffs and coastal path, it boasts some of the finest 19th- and early-20th-century art to have been made on the island by Danish artists such as Richard Mortensen and Michael Ancher. There is also an excellent cafe. Buses 1, 2, 4, 7 and 8 stop in front of the museum.

📇 Sleeping & Eating

TOP CHOICE ▷ Stammershalle Badehotel
BOUTIQUE HOTEL €€

(📞56 48 42 10; www.stammershalle-badehotel.dk; Sdr Strandvej 128, Rø; s Dkr4700-1050, d Dkr900-1250; P) This has to be one of the island's most charismatic places to stay. Set in an imposing 19th-century bathing hotel overlooking a rocky part of the coast 8.5km northwest of Gudhjem, it's a soothing blend of whitewashed timber and understated Cape Cod–esque chic. It's also home to one of Bornholm's top New Nordic restaurants, Lassens. Book ahead.

Jantzens Hotel
HOTEL €€€

(📞56 48 50 17; www.jantzenshotel.dk; Brøddegade 33; s/d Dkr750/1100) The central Jantzens Hotel is a fine old building, its cosy rooms laced with original Danish art and crafts. Rooms in the main building all feature renovated bathrooms, and the hotel garden is nothing short of gorgeous. Suites with private kitchenette are available for Dkr1275.

Danhostel Gudhjem
HOSTEL €

(📞56 48 50 35; www.danhostel-gudhjem.dk; dm/s/d Dkr200/360/460) About 50m from the bus stop, this hostel is in an attractive spot right by the harbour with small, cosy, bright-white, six-bed dorms.

Therns Hotel
HOTEL €€

(📞56 48 50 99; www.therns-hotel.dk; Brøddegade 31; s Dkr650, d Dkr750-1050) The management from Danhostel Gudhjem also handles this pleasant place to stay.

TOP CHOICE ▷ Lassens Restaurant
MODERN SCANDINAVIAN €€€

(📞56 48 42 10; www.stammershalle-badehotel.dk; Sdr Strandvej 128, Rø; 3-course dinner Dkr395; ◷6-11pm Tue-Sun) Located 8.5km northwest of Gudhjem, elegant, seafronting Lassens is the domain of up-and-coming Daniel Kruse, voted Denmark's best chef in 2012. Taste the talent in delicate dishes like smoked scal-

lops with Icelandic *skyr*, dehydrated olives, truffle mayonnaise, persille sauce and malt chips. Kruse's desserts are arguably the country's best. Book ahead.

Gudhjem Rogeri
SEAFOOD €

(Gudhjem Harbour; buffet Dkr115; ◷10am-10pm Jul–mid-Aug, to 9pm early May-Jun & mid-Aug–mid-Sep, reduced hr rest of yr) Dating from 1910, Gudhjem's waterfront smoke-house is the oldest on the island. It has an all-you-can-eat buffet and some challenging seating, including on the upper floor, which is reached by rope ladder. There's live folk, country and rock music most nights in summer.

ℹ Information

Tourist office (📞56 48 64 48; Ejnar Mikkelsensvej 17, Gudhjem Harbour; ◷10am-4pm Mon-Sun Jun-Aug) On the harbour.

Sandvig & Allinge

Sandvig and Allinge have grown together over the years and are generally referred to as Sandvig-Allinge. They are tucked away to the east of Bornholm's rocky northwestern tip and boast an excellent sandy beach to add to their beguiling appeal. Sandvig is a small fishing village, while Allinge has as good a range of restaurants, grand hotels and nightlife as you will find outside Rønne.

◉ Sights

Bornholm's best-known sight, **Hammershus Slot**, is 3km south on the road to Rønne. The impressive, substantial ruins of this 13th-century castle are the largest of their kind in Scandinavia. They are perched dramatically over the sea, flanked by cliffs and a deep valley. One of the best ways of reaching the castle is by following footpaths from Sandvig through the heather-covered hills of Hammeren – a wonderful hour-long hike. The trail begins by the camping ground. If there is a must-see sight on Bornholm, this castle is it.

📇 Sleeping

Byskriviergarden
GUESTHOUSE €€

(📞56 48 08 86; www.byskrivergaarden.dk; Løsebækegade 3, Allinge; s/d Dkr690/940; ◷mid-May–mid-Sep; P) An enchanting, white-walled, black-beamed converted farmhouse right on the water in Allinge. The rooms are smartly, if sparsely, decorated in traditional Danish style; try to get the sea-facing ones. There's a pleasant garden and swimmable, kelp-filled rock pools around the corner if you fancy braving the water.

Hotel Romantik
HOTEL €€

(☑20 23 15 24; www.hotelromantik.dk; Stranvejen 68, Sandvig; s/d from Dkr650/800, 2- to 4-person apt per week from Dkr3402; ℗@) The coast-hugging Romantik offers simple, smart and comfortable hotel rooms, some with sea views. Even better are the 40 stylish apartments, complete with modern kitchenettes. The hotel also offers comfy, simpler budget rooms (singles/doubles from Dkr600/700) in a nondescript building across the road.

Eating

Nordbornholms Rogeri
SEAFOOD €

(Kæmpestranden 2, Allinge; meals Dkr58-99; ⊙11am-9pm) If you ask us, you can't have too many good smoke-houses, and this is another great one, right on the harbour in Allinge. The Dkr179 all-you-can-eat fish buffet is nothing short of sumptuous.

FUNEN

POP 485,200

Funen is Denmark's proverbial middle child. Lacking Zealand's capital-city pull or Jutland's geographic dominance, it's often overlooked by visitors, who perhaps make a whistle-stop visit to Hans Christian Andersen's birthplace and museum in the island's capital, Odense. But there is more to Funen (Fyn in Danish): the beautiful harbour towns of Svendborg and Faaborg, Denmark's only Viking ship grave at Ladby, not to mention the island's manor houses and castles, some dating back to the 14th century.

If you are visiting Funen by bike – as many Danish holidaymakers do – a useful guide is the *Cykelguide Fyn* (Dkr119), available from most tourist offices, which shows cycle routes throughout Funen and its neighbouring islands. Virtually all towns on Funen have places that rent bicycles by the day or week from around Dkr75 per day.

Odense

POP 168,800

Funen's millennium-old capital is a cheerful, compact city, ideal for feet and bicycles, with enough diversions to keep you hooked for a day or two. It was here that Hans Christian Andersen was born, a fact hard to miss given the city's string of Andersen-related attractions, not to mention its Andersen-themed

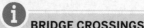

BRIDGE CROSSINGS

Funen is connected to Zealand by the Storebælts Forbindlesen (Great Belt's Bridge) and to Jutland by the Lillebælts Bro (Little Belt's Bridge). Storebælts Forbindlesen is an impressive span, running between the industrial towns of Korsør and Nyborg. It covers 18km – even longer than the Øresunds Fixed Link to Sweden. If you're taking a train, the cost of crossing is included in your fare; however, if you're driving, there's a costly bridge toll each way (under-/over-6m vehicle Dkr230/350; Dkr120 for a motorbike). For more information, click onto www.storebaelt.dk.

pedestrian lights. Yet there's more to the place than hatted storytellers, including contemporary-art-hub Brandts Klædefabrik, Denmark's best zoo, and a buzzing cafe and bar scene.

◉ Sights

TOP CHOICE HC Andersens Hus
MUSEUM

(www.museum.odense.dk; Bangs Boder 29; adult/child Dkr70/free; ⊙10am-5pm Jul & Aug, reduced hr rest of yr) Lying amid the miniaturised streets of the old poor quarter, the 'City of Beggars', now often referred to as the 'HCA Quarter', HC Andersens Hus delivers a thorough and lively telling of the amazing life Andersen lived, put into an interesting historical context and leavened by some good audiovisual material. Andersen was supposedly born in the corner room of the building, although the author himself denied this in later life and there is no concrete evidence to support this view.

TOP CHOICE Brandts Klædefabrik
CULTURAL BUILDING

(☑65 20 70 00; www.brandts.dk; Brandts Passage; combined ticket adult/child Dkr80/free; ⊙10am-5pm Tue, Wed & Fri-Sun, noon-9pm Thu) What was once a textile mill is now a savvy, multilevel cultural centre housing a number of fascinating museums. The **Museet for Fotokunst** (Museum of Photographic Art; adult Dkr40) offers permanent and temporary collections from both national and international practitioners; **Kunsthallen Brandts** (Art Gallery; adult Dkr50) focuses on new trends in the visual arts; while the **Danmarks Mediemuseum** (Danish Media Museum; adult Dkr40) traces the development of printing in Denmark. Topping it off is an excellent art-book and gift shop on the ground floor.

Fyrtøjet – Et Kulturhus for Børn
CULTURAL BUILDING

(Tinderbox – A Cultural Centre for Children; www.fyrtoejet.com; Hans Jensens Stræde 21; admission Dkr95; ◎10am-5pm Jul–mid-Aug, 10am-4pm Fri-Sun mid-Aug–Jun; ⊕) Charming Fyrtøjet – Et Kulturhus for Børn encourages youngsters to explore the magical world of Hans Christian Andersen through storytelling and music (in English as well as Danish during summer). They can dress up as Andersen characters, have their face painted, act out stories and draw fairy-tale pictures in the art room. All materials are included in the price.

Odense Zoo
ZOO

(☑66 11 13 60; www.odensezoo.dk; Sønder Blvd 306; adult/child Dkr175/95; ◎10am-7pm Jul–mid-Aug reduced hr rest of yr; ⊕) Denmark's show-piece zoo borders both banks of the river, 2km south of the city centre. An active supporter of conservation and educational programs, its residents include tigers, lions, giraffes, zebras, chimpanzees and manatees. The true highlight is the Kiwara area, a massive space that mimics the African savannah (yes, you can even feed the giraffes). Child-friendly drawcards also include petting donkeys, a playground and animal-related games. Last admission is one hour before closing.

From late June to early August, **Odense Åfart** (☑66 10 70 80; www.aafart.dk; adult/child return Dkr80/60) boats sail from **Munke Mose** to the zoo. City buses 41, 51, 141, 151 and 152 (22kr, 15 minutes) run there frequently.

Den Fynske Landsby
OPEN-AIR MUSEUM

(www.museum.odense.dk; Sejerskovvej 20; adult/child Dkr80/free; ◎10am-6pm daily Jul–mid-Aug, 10am-5pm Tue-Sun Apr-Jun & mid-Aug–late Oct)

Odense

Wind back the clock at this seriously delightful open-air museum. Furnished with period Funen buildings authentically laid out like a small country village, it includes all the once-upon-a-time essentials, from costumed 'peasants' tending to the geese, to children in knickerbockers getting crafty with hoops and sticks.

The museum is located in a green zone 4km south of the city centre; city bus 42 (Dkr19, 25 minutes) runs nearby. From May to early September, you can take a boat from Munke Mose down the river to Erik Bøghs Sti, from where it's a 15-minute woodland walk along the river to Den Fynske Landsby.

Fyns Kunstmuseum　　　MUSEUM
(www.museum.odense.dk; Jernbanegade 13; adult/child Dkr50/free; ☺10am-4pm Tue-Sun) In a stately, neoclassical building, serene Fyns Kunstmuseum houses a quality collection of Danish art from the 18th century to the present. Highlights include Gustava Emilie Grüner's cheerful *Portraegruppe Familien Leunbach* and HA Brendekilde's powerful, harrowing *Udslidt* (Worn Out), depicting a dead farm worker and distressed woman in a vast, flat field. Changing exhibitions are also staged.

Sankt Knuds Kirke　　　CHURCH
(Flakhaven; ☺10am-4pm Mon-Sat, noon-4pm Sun, to 5pm Sat Apr-Oct) Odense's 13th-century Gothic cathedral reflects Odense's medieval wealth and stature. The stark white interior has a handsome rococo pulpit, a dazzling 16th-century altarpiece and a gilded wooden triptych crowded with more than 300 carved figures and said to be one of the finest pieces of religious art in northern Europe.

HC Andersens Barndomshjem　　　MUSEUM
(www.museum.odense.dk; Munkemøllestræde 3-5; adult/child Dkr30/free; ☺10am-4pm daily Jul & Aug, reduced hr rest of yr) Expect a couple of rooms of mildly diverting exhibits in the small house where Hans Christian lived from the age of two to 14. Interestingly, it's this very place that Andersen describes in his autobiographies and which features in a couple of his fairy stories.

FREE **Carl Nielsen Museet**　　　MUSEUM
(www.museum.odense.dk; Claus Bergs Gade 11; ☺11am-3pm Wed-Sun May-Aug, 3-7pm Wed-Fri, 11am-3pm Sat & Sun Sep-Apr) This museum, which is located in Odense's concert hall, details the career of the city's native son Carl Nielsen, Denmark's best-known

Odense

STORYBOOK SIDESTREETS

The east side of Odense's city centre has some of the city's oldest buildings. You can follow a rewarding walking route from the centre by crossing the busy Torvegade and strolling down Nedergade, a cobblestoned street lined with leaning, half-timbered houses and antique shops, and then returning via Overgade. En route you'll pass the 13th-century **Vor Frue Kirke** (☉10am-2pm Tue-Fri, to noon Sat).

From Overgade turn right into Overstræde, which spills into Sortebrødre Torv. This square (and adjoining Claus Bergs Gade) is the setting for Odense's belly-rumble-inducing outdoor **produce market** (Sortebrødre Torv, Claus Bergs Gade; ☉7am-1pm Wed & Sat), where vendors peddle a sprawling feast of fruits, vegetables, meats and seafood, bread, pastries, cheeses and flowers.

From the square, turn left into Bangs Boder, and then immediately right into what is a continuation of Bangs Boder. Awaiting is a charming cobblestoned street lined with pastel-coloured cottages. At the end of Bangs Boder, turn left into Hans Jensens Stræde, which leads back to busy Thomas B Thriges Gade and the centre of town beyond (note the Hans Christian Andersen–themed pedestrian lights).

composer. It also sheds light on the life of sculptor Anne Marie Brodersen, with whom Nielsen had a tempestuous affair. At various points there are earphones to sample Nielsen's music.

Jernbanemuseet MUSEUM
(www.jernbanemuseet.dk; Dannebrogsgade 24; adult/child Dkr90/45; ☉10am-4pm) Clamber aboard a diverting collection of 19th-century locomotives at Odense's rail museum, located just behind the train station. Expect around two dozen engines and wagons, including the Royal Saloon Car belonging to Christian IX. Cranking up the nostalgia is a huge collection of Märklin model trains.

Bymuseet Møntergården MUSEUM
(www.museum-odense.dk; Overgade 48-50; adult/child Dkr50/free; ☉10am-4pm Tue-Sun) Odense's modest city museum has various displays on the city's history from the Viking Age and a couple of 16th- and 17th-century half-timbered houses.

🛏 Sleeping

TOP CHOICE First Hotel Grand HOTEL €€€
(☎66 11 71 71; www.firsthotels.dk; Jernbanegade 18; s/d from Dkr1200/1400; ℗@) Close to the station, this refurbished member of the First Hotels chain is the height of modernity compared with most of Odense's accommodation. Rooms feature comfortable beds and understated style, while the excellent breakfast features lots of seasonal and healthy options.

Hotel Plaza HOTEL €€
(☎66 11 77 45; www.millinghotels.dk; Østre Stationsvej 24; s Dkr815-1275, d Dkr895-1475; @) Overlooking the green spaces of Kongens Have in the city centre, the comfortable Plaza is one of Odense's best slumber spots. Its spacious rooms are decorated in a rather chintzy, provincial, Old English style but are fairly luxurious. There's a gym and free snacks between 3pm and 6pm. You'll get the best rates online.

Cabinn HOTEL €€
(☎63 14 57 00; www.cabinn.com; Østre Stationsvej 7; s/d/tr from Dkr495/675/805; ℗@) Right by the station, the low-cost Cabinn chain offers modern, clean, no-frills rooms. The beds are narrow and the rooms lacks charm, but the price, free wi-fi and central location make it an excellent choice for the kronor-conscious.

Hotel Domir HOTEL €€
(☎66 12 14 27; www.domir.dk; Hans Tausensgade 19; s/tw/d/tr Dkr575/650/700/800; ℗@) One of the better midrange options, a short walk from the train station. Decked out in white, the modern, good-value rooms have phone, desk, TV and bathroom; some singles are cramped. There's free wi-fi and a computer in the lobby. The car park only holds six cars.

Danhostel Odense City HOSTEL €
(☎63 11 04 25; www.cityhostel.dk; Østre Stationsvej 31; dm/s/d/tr from Dkr250/450/620/655; @) An excellent, modern 139-bed place, with four- and six-bed dorms, a kitchen and laundry facilities, located alongside the train and bus stations. All rooms have a bathroom and wi-fi is free.

DCU-Odense City Camp CAMPGROUND €

(☑66 11 47 02; www.camping-odense.dk; Odensevej 102; campsites per adult/child/tent Dkr78/48/48, cabins from Dkr550; @☒⊞) Set in a wooded area 3.5km south of the city centre, this neat, three-star camping ground features a TV lounge, outdoor pool, shop and kids' amusements. You'll also find simple cabins for rent, with kitchenettes and either with or without private bathroom. Take bus 21, 22 or 28.

✖ Eating

Numerous, mainly fast-food, places line Kongensgade. Odense Banegård Center, which incorporates the train and bus stations, has low-priced options including bakery **Bager From** (sandwiches from Dkr40; ⊘5.45am-6.30pm Mon-Fri, 7am-5.30pm Sat & Sun), a supermarket, cafe and fast-food outlets.

Kvægtorvet MODERN SCANDINAVIAN €€€

TOP CHOICE (☑65 91 50 01; www.kvaegtorvet.com; Rugårdsvej 25; 6-/12-course tasting menu Dkr425/575; ⊘noon-3pm Fri, 5.30pm-midnight Tue-Sat) Klavs Styrbæk is one of Funen's leading chefs and his superb restaurant is renowned for its accomplished, ambitious modern Danish food made using locally sourced meat and seafood, such as pheasant with chestnuts and grilled scallops with coconut and lime. The restaurant is 1km west of the train station.

Simoncini ITALIAN €€€

(www.simoncini.dk; Vestergade 70; 3 courses Dkr375; ⊘5.30-11pm Mon-Wed, to midnight Thu-Sat) Rustic, authentic Italian grub created with flair is what you can expect at this snug, welcoming place in an old Odense house. The menu is short, seasonal and delicious, whether you're nibbling on crustacean-stuffed homemade ravioli or tucking into a butter-soft beef fillet splashed with red vino. *Buon appetito!*

Olivia Brasserie INTERNATIONAL €€

(www.oliviabrasserie.dk; Vintapperstræde 37; lunch Dkr68-135, 2-/3-course dinner from Dkr200/250; ⊘10am-11pm Mon-Fri, 9am-11pm Sat, 9am-3pm Sun) A *hyggelig* (cosy) combo of chintzy chandeliers, old portraits and vested waiters, this relaxed local favourite draws everyone from ladies-who-lunch to shopped-out teens. Fuelling the conversation is a solid selection of fresh, homely grub, from soup, quiche and burgers to giant salads made with beautiful ingredients. Dinner is a more elaborate pan-European affair.

Den Gamle Kro DANISH, FRENCH €€€

(www.dengamlekro.eu; Overgade 23; open sandwiches Dkr71-145, 2/3 courses Dkr298/365; ⊘11am-10pm Mon-Sat, to 9pm Sun) Atmospheric Gamle Kro runs through several 17th-century houses, with a glass-roofed courtyard and medieval cellar. Simpler lunch options include classic open sandwiches, while dinner offers decadent Franco-Danish affairs like French onion soup with cognac and cheese croutons, or steamed local plaice with *gambas* soufflé, butter-tossed leek and shellfish créme. The wine list is suitably seductive.

Odense Chokoladehus CHOCOLATE €

(Norregade 32; ⊘10am-5pm Tue-Sat) We dare you to practice self-restraint at this den of sweet, melt-in-your-mouth bliss. Beyond the sublime cocoa creations are obscenely fresh pastries (the lemon and white chocolate tart is absurdly good) and pretty macaroons with flavours like liquorice and sea salt. Come summer, join the queue for ice-cream combos like Icelandic *skyr* with ginger and passionfruit.

Il Gusto ICE CREAM €

(☑66 19 26 04; Vindegade 84-86; gelato 2 flavours Dkr30; ⊘noon-10pm daily summer, reduced hr rest of yr, closed Nov-Feb) Run by Sicilian expat Stefano Di Gaetano, this tiny gelateria is a mecca for gelato connoisseurs. Flavours are seasonal and everything is made from scratch, the proper Italian way. For a double dose of dolce vita, knock back a mighty espresso.

🍷 Drinking

Carlsens Kvarter BAR

(www.carlsens.dk; Hunderupvej 19; ⊘noon-1am Mon-Sat, 1-7pm Sun) If soulful sipping appeals more than thumping party crowds, this affable neighbourhood bar has you covered. Ale and whisky connoisseurs will be especially impressed with the fine selection. You'll find it 400m south of HC Andersens Barndomshjem.

Viggos PUB

(www.cafeviggos.dk; Vindegade 76; ⊘noon-2am Mon-Thu, to 3am Fri, 2pm-3am Sat, to 11pm Sun) A big hit with students, this three-level pub sees punters table-dancing to *schlager*, bonding at big tables or kicking back 10 beers to earn their own personalised beer mug (triumphantly suspended from the ceiling). We wish you luck.

Joe & the Juice
JUICE BAR

(Vestergade 20; juices from Dkr38, sandwiches Dkr48; ☺10am-6pm Mon-Thu, to 7pm Fri, to 5pm Sat) Attached to the Magasin department store, this youthful chain squeezes fresh juices with names like 'Stress Down' and 'Sex Me Up'. You'll also find decent coffee and freshly made sandwiches.

☆ Entertainment

Nightlife is centred on Brandts Passage, a pedestrian corridor lined with boutiques, restaurants, bars and cafes, many with outdoor seating in summer, leading to Brandts Klædefabrik.

On Thursdays, from July to mid-August, **Kongens Have** is the setting for free and highly popular weekly music concerts. Tunes span anything from '60s pop to contemporary rock, mostly performed by Danish acts. Concerts normally start at 7pm, though it's best to check www.odense.dk for updates.

Room
CLUB

(Brandts Passage 6-8; ☺to 3am Fri & Sat) This light, slick cafe-bistro-club turns into a house-music nightspot on weekends.

The Gym
CLUB

(www.facebook.com/TheGymOdense; Overgade 45-47; ☺10pm-5am Thu-Sat) The Gym keeps hedonists active with sweat-soaked DJ sessions and oh-so-retro table-tennis tables.

Jazzhus Dexter
LIVE MUSIC

(www.dexter.dk; Vindegade 65) Jazzhus Dexter has good live-music (mostly of the jazz variety) groups virtually every night of the week starting around 8pm or 9pm.

Brandts
LIVE MUSIC

(☑65 20 70 01; Brandts Passage) Has an outdoor amphitheatre that's a venue for free summer weekend concerts.

❶ Information

Main post office (Dannebrogsgade 2; ☺9am-6pm Mon-Fri, to 1pm Sat) North of the train station.

Nordea (Vestergade 64) Bank

Odense Central Library (Odense Banegård Center; ☺10am-7pm Mon-Thu, to 4pm Fri, to 2pm Sat, also to 2pm Sun Oct-Mar) Free internet access.

Tourist office (☑66 12 75 20; www.visitodense.com; Vestergade 2; ☺9.30am-6pm Mon-Fri, 10am-3pm Sat, 11am-2pm Sun Jul & Aug, reduced hr rest of yr) Located at Rådhus, a 900m walk from the train station.

❶ Getting There & Away

BUS Buses leave from the bus station at the rear of the train station. Fynbus (www.fynbus.dk) runs bus services between Odense and all major towns on Funen.

CAR & MOTORCYCLE Odense is just north of the E20; access from the highway is clearly marked. Rte 43 connects Odense with Faaborg; Rte 9 connects Odense with Svendborg.

TRAIN Odense is on the main railway line between Copenhagen (Dkr258, 1½ hours, at least twice hourly), Aarhus (Dkr224, 1¾ hours, twice hourly), Aalborg (Dkr346, three hours, once or twice hourly) and Esbjerg (Dkr204, 80 minutes, one to two times hourly). At the train station, left-luggage lockers cost Dkr20 to Dkr40 for 24 hours.

❶ Getting Around

BICYCLE Odense is best seen on foot or on a bicycle. From May to September, bikes can be rented at **CVS Cykeludlejning** (☑63 75 39 64; www.odensecykler.dk; Nedergade 36) for Dkr100 a day. Year-round bike rental is available at **City Hotel Odense** (www.city-hotel-odense.dk; Hans Mules Gade 5) for the same price.

CAR & MOTORCYCLE You'll find substantial car parks around Brandts Klædefabrik and the Carl Nielsen Museet. Parking costs around Dkr12 per hour. Car-rental companies in town include the following:

Avis (☑70 24 77 87; www.avis.com; Rugaardsvej 3)

Europcar (☑66 14 15 44; www.europcar.com; Vestre Stationsvej 13)

Ladbyskibet & Vikingemuseet Ladby

Denmark's only Viking Age **ship grave** is a captivating site. Around the year 925, a Viking chieftan was laid to rest in a splendid 21.5m-long warship, surrounded by weapons, jewellery, clothing, riding equipment, pots and pans, coins and a gaming board. All the wooden planks from the Ladby ship decayed long ago, leaving the imprint of the hull moulded into the earth, along with iron nails, an anchor and the grinning skulls of sacrificed dogs and horses.

The site's **museum** (www.vikingemuseet-ladby.dk; Vikingevej 123, Ladby; adult/child Dkr60/free; ☺10am-5pm Jun-Aug, to 9pm Wed in Jul, reduced hr rest of year) does a great job of recounting what is known of the story, displaying finds from the grave and a reconstructed mock-up of the boat before it was interred. The result is a vivid sense of the scale and trouble taken over the chieftan's burial.

To get here by car, in Ladby, 4km southwest of Kerteminde via Odensevej, turn north onto Vikingevej, a one-lane road through fields that ends after 1.2km at the Ladbyskibet car park. You enter through the little museum, from where it's a few minutes' walk along a field path to the mound.

From Banegården Plads C in Odense, catch bus 151 or 152 to Kerteminde (Dkr41, 35 minutes, hourly), then change to bus 482 for the village of Ladby (seven minutes, hourly). Once in Ladby, you'll have to walk the Vikingevej section to the museum about 750m away. See www.rejseplanen.dk for bus times.

Egeskov Slot

This magnificent **castle** (www.egeskov.dk; Egeskovgade 18, Kværndrup; park & exhibitions adult/child Dkr180/110, all inclusive incl castle adult child Dkr210/130; ⊙10am-7pm late Jun–mid-Aug, reduced hr rest of yr, closed late Oct-late Apr), complete with moat and drawbridge, is an outstanding example of the lavish efforts that sprang up during Denmark's Golden Age, the Renaissance. There are enough sights and activities here to keep anyone happily occupied for a day. The castle exteriors are the best features. The interior is heavily Victorian in its furnishings and hunting trophies of now rare beasts. The grounds include century-old privet hedges, free-roaming peacocks, topiary, aerial woodland walkways, English gardens and a bamboo grass labyrinth.

Admission to the grounds includes entry to a large **antique-car museum**, which also features some vintage aircraft swooping from the rafters. The castle opens until 11pm on Wednesday nights in July and early August, with a program of evening concerts, falconry displays, ghost hunts and fireworks.

Egeskov Slot is 2km west of Kvændrup on Rte 8. From Odense and Svendborg, take a train to Kvændrup station (Dkr60, hourly) and either catch a Faaborg-bound 920 bus or take a taxi.

Faaborg

POP 7200

In its 17th-century heyday, Faaborg claimed one of the country's largest commercial fishing fleets. It might be a lot sleepier these days, but vestiges of those golden years live on in cobblestone streets like Holkegade, Adelgade and Tårngade. Add to this a fine art museum and you have a deeply pleasant pit stop on your way to or from the unmissable, time-warped island of Ærø.

⊙ Sights & Activities

Faaborg Museum for
Fynsk Malerkunst   MUSEUM
(www.faaborgmuseum.dk; Grønnegade 75; adult/child Dkr60/free; ⊙10am-4pm Apr-Oct, reduced hr rest of yr) Occupying a handsome Nordic classicist building designed by Carl Petersen, the Faaborg Museum for Fynsk Malerkunst houses a notable collection of Funen art, including works by artists such as Peter Hansen, Jens Birkholm and Anna Syberg. Kai Nielsen's original granite sculpture of the *Ymerbrønd* is also here. The town landmark is the nearby **belltower of St Nikolai**.

Den Gamle Gaard   MUSEUM
(Øhavsmuseet Faaborg; Holkegade 1; adult/child Dkr40/free; ⊙11am-3pm Jun-Aug) A well-presented museum, Den Gamle Gaard sits in a timber-framed house dating back to about 1725. The 22 rooms, arranged to show how a wealthy merchant lived in the early 19th century, brim with antique furniture, porcelain, toys, maritime objects and even a hearse carriage. One room contains personal items belonging to Riborg Voigt, a merchant's daughter with whom Hans Christian Andersen had a lifelong infatuation. Mementos include one of Andersen's business cards with a lock of his hair sewn onto it.

Torvet   SQUARE
The star of Faaborg's main square, Torvet, is sculptor Kai Nielsen's striking bronze fountain group *Ymerbrønd*. Causing a minor uproar upon its unveiling, the work depicts a Norse fertility myth: the naked frost giant Ymir (from whose body the sky and earth were made) suckling at the udder of a cow.

🛏 Sleeping & Eating

There are a couple of unremarkable cafes and fast-food places in the town square and more upmarket restaurants along the harbour front.

Hotel Færgegaarden
HOTEL €€

(☎62 61 11 15; www.hotelfg.dk; Christian IX Vej 31; s/d Dkr795/950) Located close to the harbour and town centre, the Færgegaarden offers 15 simply decorated, comfortable rooms. The hotel's cosy restaurant (mains Dkr185 to Dkr245) is a little more ambitious than it used to be, with attention-grabbing dishes like smoked salad with horseradish and aquavit granita.

Hotel Faaborg
HOTEL €€

(☎62 61 02 45; www.hotelfaaborg.dk; Torvet; s/d Dkr750/950; P@) This very central hotel in Faaborg has good, welcoming rooms and a sweet courtyard. There's a bar and restaurant downstairs.

Danhostel Faaborg
HOSTEL €

(☎62 61 12 03; www.danhostel.dk/faaborg; Grønnegade 71-72; dm/s/d Dkr175/325/375; ☺Apr-Sep; P) This 69-bed, three-star hostel occupies two handsome historic buildings, close to the Faaborg Museum and the town's indoor swimming baths.

Det Hvide Pakhus
DANISH, INTERNATIONAL €€

(www.dethvidepakhus.dk; Christian IXs Vej 2, Faaborg Harbour; lunch dishes Dkr88-155, 2-/3-course dinner Dkr285/355; ☺lunch & dinner daily mid-Jun–late Aug, reduced hr Apr-Jun & Sep-Dec, closed Jan-Mar) Set in a light, airy harbourside warehouse, Det Hvide Pakhus is as much a hit with locals as it is with out-of-towners. Lunch is an old-school Danish affair, while the dinner menu is a little more adventurous. This said, the evening standouts are often the simpler dishes. All fish served is bought from local fishermen and the kitchen proudly uses Funen produce as much as possible.

Faaborg Røgeri
SEAFOOD €

(Vestkaj; fish dishes Dkr29-74; ☺10am-9pm daily mid-Jun–Aug, reduced hr rest of yr) Situated to the west of the harbour, this takeaway serves cheap, tasty, home-smoked fish, plus ice cream (from Dkr30).

❶ Information

Tourist office (☎63 75 94 44; www.visit-faaborg-midtfyn.dk; Torvet 19; ☺9am-5pm Mon-Sat Jun-Aug, reduced hr rest of yr) Head here for bike rental (Dkr60 a day), cycling maps and fishing licences.

❶ Getting There & Away

BOAT Ærøfærgerne (www.aeroe-ferry.com) runs car ferries between Faaborg and Søby on the island of Ærø. See the table on p93 for details.

BUS Faaborg's bus station is on Banegårdspladsen, at the defunct train station on the southern side of town. From Odense, buses 111 and 141 (Dkr71, 1¼ hours) run at least hourly to 11.20pm. From Svendborg, bus 931 (Dkr51, one hour) runs at least hourly to 10.40pm.

CAR & MOTORCYCLE From the north, simply follow Rte 43. From Svendborg, Rte 44 leads directly west into Faaborg.

Lyø, Avernakø & Bjørnø

This trio of islands off the coast of Faaborg make pleasant day trips – fans of feathered creatures will especially love the rich bird life. Of the three, Lyø has the most to see: an old village with an unusual **circular church-yard**; the **Klokkesten**, a 1000-year-old dolmen that rings like a bell when struck; and several bathing **beaches**.

From Faaborg, **Ø-Færgen** (☎62 61 23 07; www.oefaergen.com; adult/child return Dkr115/80, bicycle Dkr30) sails around five times daily to Avernakø and Lyø, taking between 30 and 70 minutes. For Bjørnø, the passenger-only **M/S Lillebjørn** (☎20 29 80 50; www.bjoernoe-faergen.dk; adult/child return Dkr56/28, bicycle Dkr17) runs seven times Monday to Friday, and three times on weekends. Journey time is approximately 20 minutes.

Svendborg
POP 26,900

Darling of the Danish yachting fraternity, who pack the town's cafe-dotted streets each summer, hilly Svendborg is a major sailing and kayaking centre. There are more Danish boats registered here than anywhere else beyond Copenhagen, and the place is the main gateway to Funen's beautiful southern islands. Although predominantly a modern industrial settlement, the town has no shortage of elegant old buildings, not to mention a harbour packed with beautiful old wooden boats from across the Baltic.

◉ Sights & Activites

Sejlskibsbroen
WATERFRONT

At the southern end of Havnepladsen's cobbled quayside, opposite where the Ærø ferry docks, is Sejlskibsbroen, a jetty lined with splendidly preserved sailing ships and smaller vessels and with an adjoining marina catering for the great number of yachts that sail local waters. Ask at the tourist centre about the various trips that can be arranged on the old sailing ships.

Naturama   MUSEUM
(☑62 21 06 50; www.naturama.dk; Dronninge-maen 30; adult/child Dkr140/free; ⊙10am-4pm Tue-Sun, to 5pm daily school holidays; ⊞) Make a date with nature at Svendborg's impressive natural history museum, a three-level, spiral-shaped ode to critters great and small. Get close and personal with giant whale bones, taxidermied Scandinavian mammals, and birds frozen-in-flight, from the tiny Pallas' leaf warbler to the golden eagle. State-of-the-art sound and lighting, regular film shows and hands-on exhibits make it an especially great choice for kids.

Svendborg Cykeludlejning   CYCLING
(www.svendborgcykeludlejning.dk; Jessens Mole 9b; ⊙9am-1pm late Jun–mid-Aug) Bicycle rental.

Nicus Nature
(www.nicusnature.com; Vindebyoerevej 31b) Kayak rental and tours.

🛏 Sleeping & Eating

The nearest camping grounds are located on Tåsinge. You'll find a number of cafes, pubs and restaurants on pretty Gerritsgade.

Hotel Ærø   HOTEL €€
(☑62 21 07 60; www.hotel-aeroe.dk; Brogade 1; s/d Dkr850/1025; ℗@) Right by the water, the Ærø has cosy, classic, yet spacious rooms. You'll find a bathtub in most bathrooms, though some crank up the decadence with jacuzzis. Looking like an old sea captain's den, the hotel's atmospheric restaurant serves solid Danish lunch classics (Dkr90 to Dkr185), though less impressive 'gourmet' dinner options (three-course set menu Dkr345).

Danhostel Svendborg   HOSTEL €
(☑62 21 66 99; www.danhostel-svendborg.dk; Vestergade 45; dm/s/d Dkr250/535/680; ℗) This five-star-rated hostel offers smart, modern rooms in a renovated 19th-century iron foundry in the town centre. Dorm beds are available only from July to mid-September.

Citronen   INTERNATIONAL €€
(☑62 20 21 95; www.citronen.dk; Brogade 33; mains Dkr126-178; ⊙lunch & dinner Mon-Sat) Food made from fresh ingredients on the premises rather than taken from the catering truck is the appeal of Citronen. Options include tasty salads, pasta dishes and lip-smacking burgers. Head in around 11.30pm on Friday and Saturday for live music.

Pizzeria La Pupa   ITALIAN €€
(☑62 20 21 70; Møllergard 78; pizzas Dkr60-90, mains Dkr185-249; ⊙5.30-10pm) Run by a real-deal Italian family, this pizzeria-trattoria a short walk back from the harbour is a local favourite. Hit the spot with authentic pasta dishes (try the heavenly tortellini with gorgonzola cheese), juicy grilled seafood and meats, and a tiramisu any nonna would approve of.

ℹ Information

Tourist office (☑62 23 57 00; www.visitsyd fyn.dk; Centrumpladsen 4; ⊙9.30am-5pm Mon-Fri, to 12.30pm Sat) Has lots of information on the greater south Funen area.

ℹ Getting There & Around

The train and bus stations are two blocks northwest of the ferry terminal.

Trains run from Odense to Svendborg (Dkr73, 40 minutes, once or twice hourly).

Ærøfærgerne (☑62 52 40 00; www.aeroe-ferry.dk) runs car ferries to Ærøskøbing on Ærø. See p93 for details. The ticket is valid for any one of Ærø's four ferry routes.

SOUTH FUNEN ARCHIPELAGO

Tåsinge

Just over the bridge from Svendborg is the island of Tåsinge, with its pretty harbour-side village of **Troense** and the nearby 17th-century castle **Valdemars Slot** (www.valdemarsslot.dk; Slotsalléen 100; adult/child castle & hunting museum Dkr85/45, castle & all museums Dkr100/50; ⊙10am-5pm daily Jun-Aug, closed Mon May & Sep). The castle was built in the early 17th century by Denmark's great Renaissance king, Christian IV, for his son, but later awarded to the naval hero Admiral Niels Juel; it remains in his family to this day. Its lavish interior is crammed with paintings and eccentric objects. In the grounds are the **Danish Yachting Museum** and the **Big Game Trophy Museum**, the latter packed with ethnographic objects and animal trophies collected by hunter Boerge Hinsch and others. The grounds of the castle and the nearby **white-sand beach** have free access.

You can get to Valdemars Slot by bus but a better way is by **MS Helge** (www.svendborghavn.dk; Svendborg–Valdemars Slot 55 minutes, Svendborg–Troense 80 minutes; return fare adult/child Dkr120/60), an old-style ferry that carries passengers from Svendborg to Troense and Valdemars Slot every few hours from mid-May to early September. The castle also has a good Danish **restaurant** (meals Dkr105-175, buffet Dkr149; ☺lunch Tue-Sun Jun-Aug), which offers a good-value Sunday lunch buffet.

Langeland

POP 13,100

The long, narrow grain-producing island of Langeland, connected by bridge to Funen via Tåsinge, is a natural haven and popular holiday destination for Danes. It has some excellent sandy beaches, enjoyable cycling and rewarding birdwatching. A large part of the island around Dovns Klint has been protected as a wildlife reserve. It is also well known in Denmark for its annual **Langeland Festival** (www.langelandsfestival.dk; ☺late Jul–early Aug), a popular family-oriented music festival often referred to as 'Denmark's largest garden party'.

◉ Sights

Langeland's main town of **Rudkøbing** has a fairly desolate harbour area, but the town centre is attractive and there's a booty of fine old buildings around Rudekøbing Kirke, to the north of Brogade, the street leading inland from the harbour to the main square of Torvet.

For beaches, head for **Ristinge** about 15km south of Rudkøbing.

Tranekær Slot   GARDENS, MUSEUM

Langeland's top sight is the red stucco Tranekær Slot, a handsome medieval castle that has been in the hands of the one family since 1672. The castle is not open to the public, but its grounds are home to the **Tickon** (Tranekær International Centre for Art & Nature; adult/child Dkr25/free), a collection of intriguing

art installations created by international artists and sited around the wooded grounds and lake.

Castle Mill   HISTORIC BUILDING

(Lejbøllevej 3; adult/child Dkr30/free; ☺10am-5pm Mon-Fri, 1-5pm Sun Jun–mid-Sep) Situated about 1km north of Tranekær Slot is the Castle Mill, a 19th-century windmill, with its remarkable wooden mechanics still intact.

🏃 Activities

Cycling is a good way to explore Langeland. The tourist office in Rudkøbing sells a bicycle map of Langeland (Dkr30) and you can hire bikes at **Lapletten** (☏62 51 10 98; www.lapletten.dk; Engdraget 1, Rudkøbing; per day Dkr60).

For birdwatching you'll find a sighting tower at **Tryggelev Nor**, 5km south of Ristinge, and a sanctuary at **Gulstav Bog**, the island's southern tip.

🛌 Sleeping & Eating

The tourist office maintains a list of rooms for rent in private homes, with doubles ranging from Dkr400 to Dkr600.

Tranekær Gæstgivergaard   GUESTHOUSE €€

(☏62 59 12 04; www.tranekaerkro.dk; Slotsgade 74; s/d Dkr750/950; ℗) This village inn 200m south of Tranekær Slot dates from 1802 and retains its period ambience. Most rooms have peaceful garden views and there's one lovely, bright family apartment. The highly rated restaurant (mains Dkr230 to Dkr290) is strong on local seafood and game, with at least one vegetarian option. There are also good-value bed, breakfast and dinner packages.

Skrøbelev Gods   HOTEL €€€

(☏62 51 45 31; www.ritz-resorts.com; Skrøbelev Hedevej 4; r from Dkr1695) This secluded converted manor farm 3km from Rudkøbing in the centre of the island is based in buildings dating from the 17th century. The decor is wonderfully camp and over the top, and there is a very impressive wine cellar.

Danhostel Rudkøbing & Camping   HOSTEL €

(☏62 51 18 30; www.danhostel.dk/rudkobing; Engdraget 11, Rudkøbing; campsites/dm Dkr65/200, d from Dkr350; ☺Apr-end Oct) Langeland's only hostel is a 10-minute walk from Torvet, but it's a rather cheerless place, with very basic cabin accommodation. Tents can be plonked in the adjoining field.

TOP CHOICE **Skovsgaard Café** INTERNATIONAL €

(Kågårdsvej 12; light lunches Dkr60-99; ⊘11am-5pm daily mid-Jun–mid-Aug, reduced hr rest of yr, closed Oct–mid-May) Snugly set at the entrance of Skovsgaard estate, this bright, squeaky-clean organic cafe is our favourite lunch spot on the island. Expect a small menu of freshly brewed coffee, homemade bread and cakes, salads, burgers and sandwiches. If the weather's on your side, nibble blissfully in the cafe garden.

❶ Information

Pick up information about the island from Langeland's **tourist office** (www.langeland.dk; Torvet 5, Rudkøbing; ⊘9am-5pm Mon-Fri, to 3pm Sat Jul & Aug, reduced hr rest of yr).

❶ Getting There & Away

Boat

Ærøfærgerne (www.aeroe-ferry.com) runs car ferries from Rudkøbing to Marstal on Ærø. See p93 for details.

Bus

Buses 911, 912S and 913S make the 20km run from Svendborg to Rudkøbing (Dkr41, 25 minutes) at least hourly.

Ærø

POP 6600

Just 30km long and 8km wide, Ærø (pronounced 'with difficulty') holds a special place in the hearts of Danes. Mention it and they will sigh wistfully and perhaps recall a long-ago childhood visit to the quaint old town of Ærøskøbing, or cycling holidays amid the beautiful, gentle countryside peppered with crooked, half-timbered houses with traditional hand-blown glass windows and decorative doorways beautified by hollyhocks. Most young residents leave as soon as they can, however, as, though Ærø is one of the most enchanting of all the islands of the south Funen archipelago, there isn't a great deal going on here out of season. There are some good, small beaches, one of the best being Risemark Strand on the southern tip of the island; it's a great place to tour by bicycle, not least as this is in keeping with the spirit of an island that is run almost entirely on sustainable energy sources such as wind and solar power.

Ærø has three main towns: Ærøskøbing, Marstal and Søby. The island's tourist website is www.arre.dk.

ÆRØSKØBING

POP 980

The words 'higgledy' and 'piggledy' could have been invented to describe the idyllic town of Ærøskøbing. A prosperous merchants' town in the late 17th century, the town's winding cobblestone streets meander between crooked houses, cheerfully painted and gently skewed, with hand-blown glass windows, doorways bursting with bright hollyhocks, and half-timbered courtyards offering glimpses into snug, private worlds. The tourist office sells an illustrated leaflet (Dkr10) describing the finest buildings in the town, many of them impressively preserved.

Apart from Ærøskøbing's overall charm, the main tourist attraction is **Flaske Peters Samling** (Smedegade 22; admission incl Æro Museum adult/child Dkr40/free; ⊘10am-5pm late Jun–mid-Aug, reduced hr rest of yr), a museum in the former poorhouse with displays on the life's work of ship's cook Peter Jacobsen, 'Bottle Peter', who crafted 1700 ships-in-a-bottle. **Æro Museum** (www.arremus.dk; Brogade 3-5; admission incl Flaske Peters Samling adult/child Dkr30/free; ⊘10am-4pm Mon-Fri, 11am-3pm Sat & Sun late Jun-Aug) charts the local cultural history.

Ærøskøbing tourist office (Ærøskøbing Havn 4; ⊘9am-6pm Mon-Fri, 10am-6pm Sat & Sun mid-Jul–early Aug) is by the waterfront.

SØBY

This quiet little port has a shipyard, which happens to be the island's biggest employer, a sizeable fishing fleet and a busy yacht marina. Five kilometres beyond Søby, at Ærø's northern tip, there's a pebble beach with clear water and a stone lighthouse with a view.

MARSTAL

On the southeastern end of the island, Marstal is Ærø's most modern-looking town and has a web of busy shopping streets at its centre. Marstal has an emphatically maritime history; even its street names echo the names of ships and famous sailors. Its **Søfartsmuseum** (Prinsensgade 1; adult/child Dkr55/free; ⊘9am-6pm Jul & Aug, to 5pm Jun, to 4pm May, Sep & Oct) has an absorbing collection of nautical artefacts including 250 ships' models and full-size boats. There is a reasonably good beach on the southern side of town.

ANCIENT ÆRØ

Ærø once had more than 100 prehistoric sites and, although many have been lost, the island still has some atmospheric Neolithic remains, especially in its southeast district, to the west of Marstal. At the small village of Store Rise is the site of **Tingstedet**, the remains of a passage grave in a field behind an attractive **12th-century church**.

At **Lindsbjerg** is the superb hilltop site of a long barrow and two passage graves, one of which has a nicely poised capstone. Just over 1km south of here, follow signs to a spot right on the coast where you'll find the fascinating medieval relic of **Sankt Albert's Kirke**. It's within a Viking defensive wall from about the 8th century.

Another striking site is at **Kragnæs**, about 4km west of Marstal. Head through the village of Græsvænge and follow the signs for 'Jættestue' along narrow lanes to reach a small car park, from where it's about 600m along field tracks to the restored grave site.

🛏 Sleeping

The island's tourist offices have a list of countryside B&Bs around the island for around Dkr375/600 per single/double. There are camping grounds at Søby (☑62 58 14 70; www.soeby-camping.dk), Ærøskøbing (☑62 52 18 54; www.aeroecamp.dk) and Marstal (☑63 52 63 69; www.marstalcamping.dk).

TOP **CHOICE** **Pension**
Vestergade 44 GUESTHOUSE €€
(☑62 52 22 98; www.vestergade44.com; Vestergade 44, Ærøskøbing; r Dkr990; @) Next door to Hotel Ærohus is this delightful 18th-century house with beautifully appointed, cosy interiors. Host Susanna Greve is impeccably gracious and we won't be surprised if you decide to stay an extra night or two. Predictably popular and with just six rooms, it's best to book ahead.

Tolbodhus GUESTHOUSE €€
(www.toldbodhus.com; Brogade 8, Ærøskøbing; s/d Dkr750/890; P) A close second to Pension Vesterbroagde 44 for charm and warmth, this doll's house of a B&B – with just four nostalgic rooms – also serves good breakfasts.

Hotel Ærøhus HOTEL €€
(☑62 52 10 03; www.aeroehus.dk; Vestergade 38, Ærøskøbing; s/d Dkr990/1250; P@) This hotel occupies a large period building near the harbour. Rooms are comfortable and modernised, and there's a smart garden annexe. The in-house restaurant (mains Dkr210 to

310) specialises in local seafood. Rent a bike for Dkr75 per day.

Danhostel Marstal HOSTEL €
(☑62 53 39 50; www.marstalvandrerhjem.dk; Færgestræde 29, Marstal; dm Dkr200, s/d from Dkr325/400; ☺May–mid-Sep; P) South of Marstal harbour, this modest, 82-bed hostel is right by the sea. A couple of rooms have sea views. Dorms are available in the summer.

🍴 Eating

All three towns have bakeries, restaurants and food stores.

Edith MODERN SCANDINAVIAN €€€
(☑62 25 25 69; www.restaurantedith.dk; Kirkestræde 8, Marstal; 3-/6-course menu Dkr425/625; ☺6-11pm Mon-Sun) Smart yet refreshingly relaxed, Edith is a showcase for foraged ingredients and mostly organic island produce. While the presentation can be whimsical – think slow-cooked egg yolk served in a sealed sardine tin – chef Rasmus Kristiensen keeps the focus firmly on rustic, natural flavours. Outside the summer season, the restaurant is only open for dinner Thursday to Saturday, and only if booked one day ahead.

Ærøskøbing Røgeri SEAFOOD €
(Havnen 15, Ærøskøbing; meals Dkr32-78; ☺11am-9pm mid-Jun–mid-Aug, to 7pm Apr–mid-Jun & mid-Aug–late Sep) This traditional fish smokehouse in Ærøskøbing harbour serves excellent-value plates – you eat outside on picnic benches. Wash it down with some of the excellent ale from the island's Rise Bryggeri microbrewery.

Kongensgade 34 INTERNATIONAL €€
(www.kongensgade34.dk; Kongensgade 34, Marstal; meals Dkr76-199; ☺10am-midnight Sun-Thu, to 2am Fri & Sat; ☑) This homely, art-slung cafe peddles Danish classics, global standbys like burgers and *moules-frites*, and plenty of vegetarian dishes. The owners also run adjoining ice-cream shop **Smageriet** (Kirkestræde 6; ice creams Dkr19-36; ☺9am-10pm May-Aug), known for its seasonal, gelatin-free delights (try the blueberry with chocolate chunks).

Café Aroma INTERNATIONAL €€
(www.cafe-aroma.dk; Havnepladsen, Ærøskøbing; lunch Dkr75-118, dinner mains Dkr145-198; ☺11am-11pm Jul–mid-Aug, to 9pm mid-late Jun & rest of Aug) Pimped with film posters, old cinema seats, even a barber's chair, this eclectic

Return tickets for the following routes: adult/child/bike/car Dkr199/115/41/437

ROUTE	FREQUENCY (DAILY)	DURATION (MIN)
Faaborg-Søby	5-6 (Mon-Fri), 2-3 (Sat & Sun)	60
Fynshav-Søby	4 (Mon-Fri), 2-5 (Sat), 3-4 (Sun)	70
Svendborg-Ærøskøbing	6 (Mon-Fri), 5 (Sat), 5-6 (Sun)	75
Rudkøbing-Marstal	5-6 Mon-Fri, 4 (Sat), 5 (Sun)	60

cafe serves simple, quality grub, including salads, *smørrebrød* and burgers made with homemade bread and dressing. Even the ice cream is proudly homemade.

ℹ Getting There & Away

Ærøfærgerne (www.aeroe-ferry.com) runs car ferries year-round. If you have a car it's a good idea to make reservations, particularly at weekends and in midsummer. Tickets are valid on all four routes.

ℹ Getting Around

BICYCLE Both the tourist offices in Ærøskøbing and Marstal sell a Dkr20 cycling map of the island.

Pilebækkens Cykler (☑62 52 11 10; Pilebækken 11; per day from Dkr60) Opposite the car park on the outskirts of Ærøskøbing; rents out bikes.

Søby Cykeludlejning (☑62 58 14 60; Havnevejen 2; per day Dkr75) Rents out bikes in Søby.

BUS Bus 790 is a free service, running from Søby to Marstal via Ærøskøbing (up to 17 times daily on weekdays, up to eight times daily on weekends).

JUTLAND

Denmark doesn't have a north–south divide; culturally, spiritually and to a great extent politically, it is divided into Jutland...and all the rest. Jutlanders are different. Sturdy, down to earth, unpretentious, hard-working. You will find an old-fashioned hospitality here and an engaging frankness. Then there are those Jutland landscapes, an arresting melange of windswept islands, duelling seas, and brooding lakes that have inspired centuries of great Danish art. Add to this fine-art museums, Denmark's oldest town, and the understated cool of 'second-city' Aarhus, and you too might concede that there's something about Jutland.

Aarhus

POP 252,200

Always the bridesmaid, never the bride, Aarhus (*oar*-hus) stands in the shadow of its bigger, brasher sibling, Copenhagen. But just like Montreal or Melbourne (albeit on a much smaller scale), Denmark's affable runner-up city has a few unexpected surprises up its sleeve, from hipster boutiques, bars and cafes to world-class dining and some fantastic museums. The city is home to ARoS (one of Denmark's best art museums), a thriving student population, as well as the country's best music scene. Quietly confident and on its way up, it's time to join the party.

◉ Sights & Activities

There are sandy beaches on the outskirts of Aarhus. The most popular one to the north is **Bellevue**, about 4km from the city centre (bus 17 or 20), while the favourite to the south is **Moesgård Strand** (take bus 18 or 31).

| TOP CHOICE | ARoS | MUSEUM |

(www.aros.dk; adult/child Dkr100/free; ☉10am-6pm Tue & Fri-Sun, to 10pm Wed & Thu) One of the top three art galleries in Denmark, ARoS lures with its Golden Age masterpieces, Danish modernist works and arresting contemporary creations from A-listers like Andy Warhol, Robert Rauschenberg and Denmark's Per Kirkeby.

Curiously, Dante's *The Divine Comedy* provides the museum's main theme: from the building's entrance on level 4, you can either descend into 'Hell' or ascend towards 'Heaven'. On the bottom floor, 'Hell' manifests itself in the form of **De 9 Rum** (The 9 Spaces), a dark, brooding collection of installation pieces from the likes of James Turrell, Mariko Mori and Danish-Icelandic 'it kid' Olafur Eliasson.

Aarhus

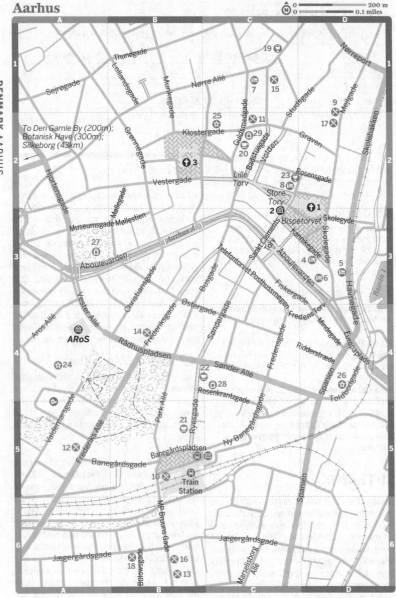

N

0 ———————— 200 m
0 ———————— 0.1 miles

To Den Gamle By (200m);
Botanisk Have (300m);
Silkeborg (43km)

Topping the building, 'Heaven' is Eliasson's spectacular **Your Rainbow Panorama**, a 360-degree rooftop walkway offering Technicolour views of the city. Hard to miss is Australian artist Ron Mueck's startlingly life-like giant *Boy* on level 1, a jaw-dropping, 5m-high sculpture of an eerily lifelike crouching child. The museum's temporary exhibitions are varied and often impressive, while both the gift shop and cafe are top notch.

Aarhus

Den Gamle By   MUSEUM
(Old Town; www.dengamleby.dk; Viborgvej 2; adult/child Dkr135/free; ⊙9am-6pm late Jun–mid-Aug, 10am-5pm Apr-late Jun & mid-Aug–mid-Nov, reduced hr rest of yr) The Danes' seemingly limitless enthusiasm for dressing up and re-creating history reaches its zenith at Den Gamle By. It's an engaging open-air museum of 75 half-timbered houses brought here from around Denmark and reconstructed as a provincial town, complete with a functioning bakery, silversmith and bookbinder. Re-created neighbourhoods include one from 1927 and another from 1974.

The museum is on Viborgvej, 1.1km from the central train station. Buses 3A, 4A, 11, 15 and 19 will take you there. You'll find a detailed schedule of opening hours and admission prices (set according to the time of year and number of activities) on the museum's website.

The recently revamped **Botanisk Have** (Botanic Gardens; Vesterbrogade), with its thousands of plants and re-created Jutland environments, occupies the high ground above Den Gamle By and can be reached through an exit from the Old Town or directly from Vesterbrogade.

FREE **Aarhus Domkirke**   CHURCH
(Bispetorv; ⊙9.30am-4pm Mon & Wed-Sat, 10.30am-4pm Tue) This impressive cathedral is Denmark's longest, with a lofty nave that spans nearly 100m. The original Romanesque chapel at the eastern end dates from the 12th century, while most of the rest of the church is 15th-century Gothic.

Like other Danish churches, the cathedral was once richly decorated with **frescos** that served to convey biblical parables to unschooled peasants. After the Reformation, church authorities who felt the frescos smacked too much of Roman Catholicism had them all whitewashed, but many have now been uncovered and restored. They range from fairy-tale paintings of St George slaying a dragon to scenes of hellfire. The cathedral's splendid, five-panel, gilt **altarpiece** is a highlight. It was made in Lübeck by the renowned woodcarver Bernt Notke in the 15th century.

Vor Frue Kirke   CHURCH
(Frue Kirkeplads; ⊙10am-2pm Tue-Fri & Sun, to noon Sat) This church, off Vestergade, has a carved wooden **altarpiece** dating from the 1530s. But far more interesting is what's in its basement: the **crypt** of the city's original cathedral, dating from about 1060.

Enter via the stairway beneath the altar. To enter a third chapel, this one with 16th-century frescos, go through the courtyard and take the left door.

FREE **Vikingemuseet** MUSEUM
(Sankt Clements Torv 6; ⊙10.15am-5pm Mon-Fri) There's more than the expected vaults in the basement of Nordea bank, where there's a small exhibition of artefacts from the Viking Age town that was excavated at this site in 1964 during the bank's construction. The display includes a skeleton, a reconstructed house, 1000-year-old carpentry tools and pottery, and photos of the excavation.

Festivals & Events

Sculpture by the Sea ARTS
(www.sculpturebythesea.dk) This is a biennial, month-long festival in June, which transforms the city's beachfront into an outdoor gallery, around 60 sculptures from both Danish and foreign artists are displayed beside (and in) the water.

Aarhus Festival ARTS
(www.aarhusfestival.com) This 10-day festival in late August and/or early September turns the city into a stage for nonstop revelry, with world-class jazz, rock, classical music, theatre, dance and film events (many of which are free). Performances take place all over the city.

Sleeping

Hotel Guldsmeden BOUTIQUE HOTEL €€
(☑86 13 45 50; www.hotelguldsmeden.com; Guldsmedgade 40; s/d from Dkr1225/1375, without bathroom from Dkr795/895; @) On the northern side of the city centre, this is our midrange choice in town for friendly staff, delightfully bright French-colonial-style rooms with polished wood floors, large four-poster beds with soft white linen, a small garden terrace and a generally relaxed, stylish ambience. Further perks include organic toiletries and good (mainly organic) breakfasts.

Hotel Ferdinand BOUTIQUE HOTEL €€€
(☑87 32 14 44; www.hotelferdinand.dk; Åboulevarden 28; s/d studio from Dkr950/1150, ste from Dkr1100/1300) Right on the buzzing canalside, this boutique hotel is divided into fully equipped studio apartments (washing machine and dryer included!) and svelte, large suites (with Nespresso machines). Topping it all off is a cracking ground-floor French brasserie. Check the website for special packages, which may include champagne, wine and food.

Havnhotellet HOTEL €
(www.havnehotellet.dk; Marselisborg Havnevej 20; s/d/tr Dkr565/565/775; P) These good-looking, good-value rooms down at the marina are fresh off the Ikea production line. All booking is done online (hence no phone number), and check-in is via a computer too. The hotel is about 1.5km south of the

WORTH A TRIP

MOESGÅRD

Visit Moesgård, 5km south of the Aarhus city centre, for its glorious beech woods and the trails threading through them towards sandy beaches. Closed until autumn 2014 due to redevelopment, the **Moesgård Museum of Prehistory** (www.moesmus.dk; Moesgård Allé 20, Højbjerg) features well-presented history exhibits from the Stone Age to the Viking Age. Its most dramatic exhibit is the 2000-year-old 'bog body' **Grauballe Man**, or Grauballe-manden, whose astonishingly well-preserved body was found in 1952 at the village of Grauballe, 35km west of Aarhus.

Behind the museum is an enjoyable trail dubbed the 'prehistoric trackway' or Old-tidsstien, which leads across fields of wildflowers, past grazing sheep and through beech woods down to **Moesgård Strand**, Aarhus' best sandy beach. The trail, marked by red-dotted stones, passes reconstructed historic sights including a dolmen, burial cists and an Iron Age house. The museum has a brochure with details. You can walk one way and catch a bus back to the city centre, or follow the trail both ways as a 5km round trip. It's all well worth a half-day or full-day visit, with a picnic perhaps if the weather behaves itself.

Bus 18 from Aarhus train station terminates at the museum year-round and runs two to three times per hour.

centre (off Strandvejen; catch bus 16 or 18). Tip: choose a room on the 1st floor (1.sal), as ground-floor rooms lack privacy. Room rates decrease for stays of two nights or more.

Cabinn Aarhus
HOTEL €€

(☑86 75 70 00; www.cabinn.com; Kannikegade 14; s/d/tr from Dkr495/625/805; ☻) In an ideal central location opposite the Domkirke, the style here is standard Cabinn, with small, rather bare but usually clean rooms. If you're a light sleeper, request a room not facing Åboulevarden, especially on Thursday to Saturday nights. Parking costs Dkr80. Free internet and wi-fi access.

Hotel Royal
HOTEL €€€

(☑86 12 00 11; www.hotelroyal.dk; Store Torv 4; s/d Dkr1495/1850; ℗) Aarhus' premiere place to bed down comes with chandeliers, murals and a fish-tank reception desk. The rooms are lavish and ornate (check out the blingy white-and-gold bathrooms) and the staff are reassuringly warm and friendly.

Danhostel Aarhus
HOSTEL €

(☑86 21 21 20; www.aarhus-danhostel.dk; Marienlundsvej 10; dm Dkr200, r from Dkr456; ☺early Jan-mid-Dec; ℗☻) It may be 4km north of the city centre but it's well worth considering for the lovely parkland setting in a renovated 1850s dance hall. It's at the edge of the Risskov Woods and a few minutes from the beach. Buses 17, 18 and 20 pass nearby.

City Sleep-In
HOTEL €

(☑86 19 20 55; www.citysleep-in.dk; Havnegade 20; dm Dkr180, d Dkr500, without bathroom Dkr450; ☻) Run by a youth organisation, the City Sleep-In is in a central former mariners' hotel. It's casual, the rooms are a bit run-down, but it's a cheerful place and by far the best budget option in the centre. Sheet hire costs Dkr50kr and towels are Dkr20 if you don't have your own.

DCU-Camping Blommehaven
CAMPGROUND €

(☑86 27 02 07; www.blommehaven.dk; Ørneredevej 35; campsite Dkr48-70, plus adult/child Dkr78/48; ☺late Mar-late Oct; ☷) Huge, beachside camping ground 6km south of the city centre with loads of family-oriented facilities and activities, plus simple cabins (Dkr625kr to 700). Take bus 18 from Aarhus train station.

✕ Eating

Away from the generic, touristy eatries lining Åboulevarden, Aarhus' dining scene is burgeoining and exciting. While the Latin Quarter is good for bistro-style cafes, Skolegade (and its extension, Mejlgade) deliver a handful of excellent budget options. For fashionable New Nordic hot psots, head to the cool Frederiksbjerg neighbourhood (centred on MP Bruuns Gade and Jægergårdsgade), just south of the train station.

The train station has a convenience store and fast-food outlets. Adjoining the station is **Bruuns Galleri**, a major shopping centre with supermarket chain **Kvickly** and a **bakery**.

Two blocks west of the station is **Føtex supermarket** (Frederiks Allé 22), with a cheap bakery and deli.

TOP CHOICE St Pauls
Apothek
MODERN SCANDINAVIAN €€

(☑86 12 08 33; www.stpaulsapothek.dk; Jægergårdsgade 76; sharing plates Dkr85-135; ☺5.30pm-midnight Tue-Thu, to 2am Fri & Sat) What was once a pharmacy is now one of Aarhus' hottest, best-value dining destinations; a Brooklyn-esque combo of hipster mixologists and vintage architectural detailing. At the helm is young-gun chef Christian Bøjlund, whose stint at restaurant heavyweight Noma translates into confident New Nordic dishes like pillow-soft pork neck with rosehip chutney, or cauliflower with yoghurt and liquorice. The focus is on sharing plates (three dishes per head should suffice), impressively paired with killer cocktails. Book ahead.

TOP CHOICE Nordisk
Spisehus
MODERN SCANDINAVIAN €€€

(☑86 17 70 99; www.nordiskspisehus.dk; MP Bruuns Gade 31; lunch Dkr65-85, 3-/5-/8-course dinner Dkr350/500/700; ☺noon-10pm Mon-Sat) It may have changed hands in 2012, but this simple, elegant restaurant remains one of Aarhus' best-value foodie experiences. While lunch focuses on simpler dishes, dinner pushes regional produce to soaring heights in dishes like marinated walleye with celery crème and ravioli, and home-pasteurised mini egg yolks. Book ahead.

TOP CHOICE Kähler
Spisesalon
MODERN SCANDINAVIAN €€

(www.spisesalon.dk; MP Bruuns Gade 33; open sandwiches from Dkr75, 3-/4-course menu Dkr275/325; ☺9am-10pm Mon-Sat, 10am-10pm Sun) Wooden panels, classic Danish furniture and coveted ceramics (made by Kähler, a historic ceramic company with a handy store down the road at No 41) set a smart yet warm vibe at this ode to outstanding seasonal food. Brunch, lunch or dinner, expect clean, fresh, creative dishes like baked corn salad with chorizo, fried chantarelle mushrooms and honey-pickled shallot rings. Wash it down with house made schnapps.

Aperto & Vino
EUROPEAN, MEDITERRANEAN €€

(☑86 12 30 24; www.apertoogvino.dk; Baggården, Mejlgade 35; 4/6/8 sharing plates Dkr185/230/275; ⊙5-11.30pm Tue-Sun) Up one flight of anonymous stairs, in a building used as a creative lab, you'll find a door with a 'Daily Specials' blackboard on it. Open it and stumble into this swinging nosh spot. Divided into casual bistro space and fine-dining room, its focus is on contemporary antipasti 'sharing plates', from creamy buffalo mozzarella to wicked pan-fried ox fillet with foie gras terrine, truffle and butter-fried bread. While some dishes work better than others, the overall quality, price and vibe hit the spot.

Oli Nico
INTERNATIONAL €

(www.olinico.dk; Mejlgade 35; classic dishes Dkr50-125; ⊙11.30am-2pm & 5.30-9pm Mon-Fri, noon-2pm & 5.30-9pm Sat, 5.30-9pm Sun) You may need to fight for one of the prized tables at Oli Nico, a small deli-restaurant with a menu of classic dishes at astoundingly good prices (*moules-frites* for Dkr60, rib-eye steak for Dkr125 – both with homemade chips!). The daily changing three-course menu may be Aarhus' best-kept secret.

Mo & Fro
INTERNATIONAL €

(www.moogfro.dk; Borggade 16; breakfast items Dkr17-60, sandwiches Dkr49; ⊙8am-4.30pm Mon-Fri, 9am-3.30pm Sat) Decked out in sheepskin stools, old cookie tins and books, this cute-as-a-button cafe/health-food store keeps locals glowing with epic, made-on-the-spot sandwiches, salads, warming winter soups and homemade sweet treats. Breakfast grub is served all day, and most of the menu items are organic and homemade. Students enjoy a small discount on sandwiches.

Manu Italienskis
ICE CREAM €

(Frederiksgade 88; gelato 2 scoops Dkr30; ⊙noon-10pm May–mid-Sep, reduced hr rest of yr) Head here for sublime gelato, made by Florentine expat Emanuele ('Manu') Iezzi. Flavours include *lakrids* (liquorice), watermelon and Manu's favourite, mango (made with Indian mangos).

Emmery's
BAKERY €

(Guldsmedgade 24-26; sandwiches Dkr50-65, brunch Dkr100-130; ⊙7am-6pm Mon-Thu, to 7pm Fri, to 4pm Sat & Sun; 🖋) A stylish and friendly cafe/delicatessen/wine-shop hybrid that serves its own delicious bread and sandwiches, some with vegetarian fillings.

Drinking & Entertainment

Aarhus is the nation's music capital, with no shortage of quality music gigs in venues from dignified concert halls to beer-fuelled boltholes. For the lowdown on what's happening around town, click onto www.visitaarhus.com or www.aoa.dk.

Sigfred's Kaffebar
CAFE

(Ryesgade 28; sandwiches Dkr46-56; ⊙8.30am-6.30pm Mon-Thu, to 8pm Fri, 9.30am-6pm Sat) Head here for Jutland's best cup of Joe, perfectly paired with flaky pastries (the *pain au raisin* is addictive) and foodie-licious sandwiches. There are two other outlets: on **Ryesgade** (Ryesgade 3; ⊙10am-5.30pm Mon-Thu, to 7pm Fri, to 4pm Sat) inside the Vangsgaards bookstore and **Guldsmedgade** (Guldsmedgade 20; ⊙8am-6.30pm Mon-Thu, to 7pm Fri, 9.30am-4pm Sat).

Løve's Bog- & VinCafé
BAR, CAFE

(Nørregade 32; ⊙9am-midnight Mon-Fri, from 10am Sat, 10am-5pm Sun) This snug, bookish wine cafe is full of book-lined shelves, old furniture and laptop-tapping regulars. Occasional poetry readings and jazz bands add to the cultured air, while the short, simple menu nicely fills in any writer's-block moments.

Under Masken
BAR

(Bispegade 3; ⊙noon-2am Mon-Sat, to 10pm Sun) Artist-run Under Masken keeps things kooky with its jumble of gilded mirrors, African tribal masks, sailor pictures and glowing fish tanks. Slide in for a loud, smokey, boozalicious night on the tiles. Note no food is served.

Train
LIVE MUSIC, CLUB

(www.train.dk; Toldbodgade 6; ⊙club from midnight Fri & Sat) One of Denmark's biggest venues, staging concerts by international rock, pop and country stars. Expect late-night clubbing events most Fridays and Saturdays, with top-notch DJ talent. Club entry is restricted to over 18s on Friday, and over 21s on Saturday.

Radar
LIVE MUSIC

(www.radarlive.dk; Godsbanen, Skovgaardsgade 3; ☺live music Thu-Sat) You'll find this rocking live music hot spot inside the Godsbanen freight yard, a new cultural hub for Aarhus (see www.godsbanen.dk). On offer is both home grown and international alternative-music acts, with sounds spanning metal, rock and jazz to electropop, techno and folk.

Social Club
CLUB

(www.socialclub.dk; Klostergade 34; ☺11pm-6am Thu-Sat) Completely focused on the student crowd, and attracting them in droves, Social Club is a packed and sweaty dance affair; cheap shots, two-for-one drink offers and other social lubricants help the night along. Free entry all night on Thursday, and before 1am on Friday and Saturday nights.

Musikhuset Aarhus
LIVE MUSIC

(www.musikhusetaarhus.dk; Thomas Jensens Allé 2) The city concert hall cuts a broad swath through the arts, from Damien Rice and *Rigoletto* to performances from Det Kongelige Ballet (the Royal Danish Ballet). Its large, airy foyer also delivers a range of events spanning everything from art-house films and piano concerts to jazz jams, many of them free.

🛍 Shopping

Wood Wood
FASHION

(www.woodwood.dk; Guldsmedgade 22b) Male and female trendsetters head here for one-of-a-kind, high-end threads and streetwear, suitably matched with in-the-know shoes, sneakers and accessories. Wood Wood aside, labels include Band of Outsiders, Junya Watanabe and Opening Ceremony.

Hay
DESIGN

(www.hay.dk; Rosenkrantzgade 24) Well-chosen examples of the latest Danish furniture as well as fabulous designer homewares, textiles and rugs.

Foreningen Flagstang
MARKET

(Mølleparken; ☺10am-4pm Sun monthly Apr-Sep) Aarhus' fantastic monthly flea market washes up anything from Cheap Monday jeans and Karen Millen frocks to Royal Copenhagen porcelain, Stelton candle holders and plastic-fantastic '70s Danish kitchenware. Email the organisers (foreningenflagstang@gmail.com) directly for updated market dates.

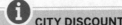

ℹ CITY DISCOUNTS

If you're planning to tick off the city sights, the AarhusCard is a worthy investment. Available from the bus station, most hotels, as well as from ARoS (p93) and Den Gamle By (p95), it comes as a 24-hour pass (adult/child Dkr129/69) or a 48-hour pass (adult/child Dkr179/79), both of which include free transport on local buses as well as free or discounted admission to most city sights.

ℹ Information

VisitAarhus closed down its central tourist office in 2011 and now provides information online (www.visitaarhus.com), by phone (☎87 31 50 10), at mobile info booths in peak periods, and via touchscreen computers at many of the city's attractions, transport hubs and accommodation providers. Smartphone users can also download the free VisitAarhus app.

Aarhus Universitetshospital (☎78 45 00 00; Nørrebrogade 44) Has a 24-hour emergency room.

Post office (Banegårdspladsen 1A) Beside the train station.

ℹ Getting There & Away

AIR SAS (www.flysas.com) have frequent daily connections to Copenhagen (one-way ticket from around Dkr570). Budget airline **Ryanair** (www.ryanair.com) operates four weekly flights between Aarhus and London Stansted. **Aarhus airport** (www.aar.dk) is in Tirstrup, 44km northeast of central Aarhus.

BOAT Mols-Linien (☎70 10 14 18; www.mols-linien.dk; adult/child/car Dkr399/174/850) operates high-speed ferries from Aarhus to Odden in northwest Zealand (70 minutes). It's worth checking the website for special, low-price fares.

BUS The **bus station** (Fredensgade) has a DSB cafe and a small supermarket. **Abildskou** (☎70 21 08 88; www.abildskou.dk) runs express bus line 888 up to nine times daily between Aarhus and Copenhagen's Valby station (adult/child Dkr300/150, three hours), with connections to Copenhagen airport (Kastrup). Students and seniors travel for Dkr150 Monday to Thursday. For information on travel to other destinations in Jutland visit www.dsb.dk. Bus-station lockers cost Dkr10 for 24 hours.

CAR & MOTORCYCLE The main highways to Aarhus are the E45 from the north and south and Rte 15 from the west. The E45 curves around the western edge of the city as a ring road. There are a number of turn-offs from the ring road into the city, including Åohavevej from the south and Randersvej from the north.

Cars can be rented from **Europcar** (📞89 33 11 11; www.europcar.com; Sønder Allé 35).

TRAIN Aarhus is well connected by train.There's a ticket-queuing system at the station: red for internal; green for international. For local journeys, unless you have mastered the use of the quicker ticket machines, be prepared for quite long waits at busy times. Friday trains are always very busy and it's advisable to reserve a seat for long journeys. Train-station lockers cost Dkr20 to Dkr40 for 24 hours.

Destinations include the following:

Aalborg Dkr181, 1½ hours, twice hourly.

Copenhagen via Odense Dkr358, three hours, twice hourly.

Esbjerg Dkr248, 2½ hours, once or twice hourly.

ⓘ Getting Around

TO/FROM THE AIRPORT The airport bus (route 925X) to Aarhus train station costs Dkr100/75 per adult/child and takes approximately 50 minutes. The changeable schedule is geared to meet all incoming and outgoing flights. For times, see www.midttrafik.dk or check the timetable at the bus stop. The taxi fare to the airport is about Dkr650.

BICYCLE **Bikes4Rent** (📞20 26 10 20; www. bikes4rent.dk; per day Dkr95) Rents out good-quality bikes. At the time of writing, the owners were looking for a new shop location in Aarhus. Check the website for updates.

Aarhus Bycykel (www.bycykler.foundry. aarhuskommune.dk) Aarhus Bycykel offers free-use bikes, available from special bike racks around the city from April to October. Check the website for a list of all 56 locations. If you're lucky enough to find a bike rack with an actual bike in it, simply deposit a Dkr20 coin in the stand to release the bike. You can return the bicycle to any rack to get your money back

BUS Most in-town buses stop in front of the train station or around the corner on Park Allé. City bus tickets (Dkr20) are bought from a machine at the back of the bus and allow unlimited rides within the time period stamped on the ticket, which is two hours. You can also buy the good-value *klipperkort* ticket, valid for 10 rides, for Dkr130.

CAR & MOTORCYCLE A car is convenient for getting to sights such as Moesgård on the city outskirts, though the city centre is best explored on foot. There's paid parking along many streets and in municipal car parks, including one on the southern side of Musikhuset Aarhus. Parking costs Dkr12/15 for the first/second hour and

Dkr20 per hour after that. Overnight (7pm to 9am) is free, as is Saturday from 4pm and all day Sunday.

TAXI Taxis congregate outside the Aarhus mainline station and at Store Torv. All taxis have a meter – expect to pay up to Dkr100 for destinations within the inner city.

Randers Regnskov

One of Jutland's most popular (and smelliest) attractions in Jutland is Randers' dome-enclosed tropical **zoo** (www.regnskoven.dk; Tørvebryggen 11, Randers; adult/child Dkr175/105; ⊙10am-6pm end Jun–mid-Aug, to 5pm mid-end Aug). Trails within the sultry trio of domes, which re-create the tropical environments of South America, Africa and Asia, pass through enclosures housing crocodiles, monkeys, iguanas, a manatee, orchids, hibiscus and various other tropical fauna and flora.

The zoo is in the town of Randers, 40km north of Aarhus on the E45 motorway to Aalborg. By train Aalborg is 49 to 57 minutes away (Dkr103); Aarhus is 30 minutes (Dkr60).

Jelling

The tiny, apparently nondescript village of Jelling is a kind of spiritual touchstone for the Danes, and virtually all of them will visit it at some point during their lives. This is the location of one of Denmark's most important historic sites, the **Jelling Kirke** (📞75 87 16 28; www.jellingkirke.dk; Vejlevej; admission free; ⊙8am-8pm May-Aug, reduced hr rest of yr). Inside the small whitewashed church are frescos dating from the 12th century, and outside the door are two impressive and historically significant rune stones. The smaller stone was erected in the early 900s by King Gorm the Old, Denmark's first king, in honour of his wife, Queen Thyra. The larger one, raised by Harald Bluetooth and dubbed 'Denmark's baptismal certificate', is adorned with the oldest representation of Christ found in Scandinavia and reads: 'Harald king bade this be ordained for Gorm his father and Thyra his mother, the Harald who won for himself all Denmark and Norway and made the Danes Christians.'

Two huge **burial mounds** flank the church; the one on the northern side is said to be that of King Gorm and the other of Queen Thyra, although excavators in the 19th century found no human remains and few artefacts. This could suggest much earlier grave robbing.

During the 1970s archaeologists excavated below Jelling Kirke and found the remains of three **wooden churches**. The oldest of these was thought to have been erected by Harald Bluetooth. A **burial chamber** within this site was also uncovered and revealed human bones and gold jewellery that shared characteristics with artefacts previously discovered within the large northern burial mound. Archaeologists now believe that the skeletal remains found beneath the church ruins are those of King Gorm, moved there from the old pagan burial mound by Harald Bluetooth out of respect for his recently acquired Christian faith. The bones of Queen Thyra have yet to be found. The Jelling mounds, church and rune stones are a designated Unesco World Heritage Site.

Kongernes Jelling (www.kongernesjelling. dk; Gormsgade 23; admission free; ⏰10am-5pm Tue-Sun Jun-Aug, noon-4pm Tue-Sun Sep-May), opposite the church, is an enthralling modern museum, providing further insight into the town's magnificent monuments and its importance in Danish royal history.

Jelling makes a good two-hour side trip off the Odense–Aarhus run. Change trains at Vejle for the ride to Jelling (20 minutes). The church is 100m straight up Stationsvej from the Jelling train station.

The Lake District

This is a perhaps misleading name for what is more like a gently hilly region with a few medium-sized lakes and Denmark's highest point, Yding Skovhø. It is unlikely to induce nosebleeds, but this is a delightful area for rambling. There is also ample opportunity for canoeing, biking and longer-distance hiking here. This is also where you'll find Denmark's longest river, the Gudenå, and Mossø, Jutland's largest lake. This area is south and southwest of Silkeborg, slap bang in the centre of Jutland, half an hour's drive west of Aarhus.

SILKEBORG
POP 42,800

Silkeborg overcomes its rather bland modern character with a friendly openness. It is the Lake District's biggest town and is an ideal base for exploring the surrounding forests and waterways. The town has some good restaurants and lively bars and cafes. A compelling reason to visit is to see the Tollund Man, the body of a preserved Iron Age 'bog man' who looks as if he's merely asleep.

⊙ Sights

Silkeborg Museum   MUSEUM
(www.silkeborgmuseum.dk; Hovedgårdsvej 7; adult/child Dkr50/free; ⏰10am-5pm May–mid-Oct, reduced hr rest of yr) The main (actually virtually the only) attraction at the Silkeborg Museum is the Tollund Man. He is believed to have been executed in 300 BC and his leathery body, complete with the rope still around his neck, was discovered in a bog in 1950. The well-preserved face of the Tollund Man is hypnotic in its detail, right down to the stubble on his chin. The museum is about 150m east of the main town square.

Museum Jorn   MUSEUM
(www.museumjorn.dk; Gudenåvej 7-9; adult/child Dkr70/free; ⏰10am-5pm Tue-Sun Apr-Oct, reduced hr rest of yr) This wonderful art space contains some striking work, such as the large ceramic walls by Jean Dubuffet and Pierre Alechinsky that greet visitors at the entrance. It displays many of the works of native son Asger Jorn and other modern artists, including Max Ernst, Le Corbusier and Danish artists from the influential CoBrA group. It's 1km south of the town centre.

KunstCentret Silkeborg Bad   MUSEUM
(www.silkeborgbad.dk; Gjessøvej 40; adult/child Dkr60/free; ⏰10am-5pm Tue-Sun May-Sep, reduced hr rest of yr) Kunst Centret Silkeborg Bad, a former spa dating from 1883, is now a beautiful, modern art space – Art Centre Silkeborg Baths – with permanent works and changing exhibitions of art, sculpture, ceramics, glassware, design and architecture, surrounded by parkland featuring contemporary sculpture. It's about 2km southwest of the town; catch local bus 10.

Aqua   AQUARIUM
(www.visitaqua.dk; Vejsøvej 55; adult/child Dkr140/75; ⏰10am-6pm end Jun–mid-Aug, reduced hr rest of yr) Situated 2km south of central Silkeborg, Aqua is an entertaining aquarium and exhibition centre exploring the ecosystems of the lakes and surrounding area with lots of fishy creatures, otters and fishing birds among the imaginative displays.

✦ Activities

Outdoor activities are at the heart of the Lake District's appeal. The track of the old railway from Silkeborg to Horsens is now an excellent **walking** and **cycling** trail of about 50km or so. It passes through the beech forest of **Nordskoven**, itself criss-crossed with hiking and bike trails. To reach Nordskoven head south down Åhavevej from the tourist office, then go left over the old railway bridge down by the hostel.

Canoeing is a marvellous way to explore the Lake District and you can plan trips for several days staying at lakeside camping grounds along the way. The canoe-hire places can help plan an itinerary. Rent canoes for Dkr100/380 per hour/day at **Slusekiosken** (☎86 80 30 03; www.silkeborgkanocenter.dk; Østergade 36) at the harbour.

The world's oldest operating **paddle steamer** (☎86 82 07 66; www.hjejlen.com; return to Himmelbjerget per adult/child Dkr120/65; ☉times vary) offers tours on the lake during summer, departing opposite Slusekiosken.

🛏 Sleeping

Budget and midrange options in town are limited, making B&B accommodation an especially good option. The tourist office publishes a B&B booklet, with singles/doubles costing around Dkr300/525.

Radisson BLU Hotel   HOTEL €€
(☎88 82 22 22; www.radissonblu.com; Papirfabrikken 12; s Dkr1145-1365, d Dkr1145-1565; P @) A comfortable, business-class hotel in a converted mill by the riverbank, the Radisson is simply the best place to stay in town. The huge rooms, in a simple, appealing modern Scandinavian style, have large beds and all modern conveniences. Added perks include a cosy bar and renowned restaurant. Rates include wi-fi.

Danhostel Silkeborg   HOSTEL €
(☎86 82 36 42; www.danhostel-silkeborg.dk; Åhavevej 55; dm Dkr275, s Dkr545-695, d Dkr570-720; ☉Mar–Nov; P @) The riverbank location (650m southeast of the town's main square), modern facilities and lack of decent alternative options make this hostel very popular, so book ahead. It's east of the train station. Dorms are available only from July to mid-September, while private rooms are available all year.

WORTH A TRIP

THE HEART OF ART

If you're a fan of modern art, chances are you've heard of Italian conceptual artist Piero Manzoni (1933–63). What you may not know is that the biggest public collection of his work is not in Milan, but on the eastern fringe of Herning, a regional textile centre 40km west of Silkeborg.

You'll find Manzoni's work, and that of visionaries like Mario Merz and Man Ray, at **HEART** (www.heartmus.dk; Birk Centerpark 8, Herning; admission Dkr75; ☉10am-5pm Tue-Sun), Herning's striking contemporary-art museum. Designed by US architect Steven Holl, its shirtlike crumpled walls and sleeve-inspired roof honour the collection's founder, Danish shirt manufacturer and passionate art collector Aage Damgaard (1917–91). In the summers of 1960 and 1961, Damgaard invited Manzoni to indulge his creative spirit in Herning. The result was a string of masterpieces and the forging of Herning's Manzoni legacy. But HEART doesn't stop at 20th-century conceptual art, with several world-class exhibitions of contemporary art staged annually.

Across the street, the **Carl-Henning Pedersen & Else Alfelts Museum** (www.chpea-museum.dk; Birk Centerpark 1; adult/child Dkr40/free; ☉10am-5pm Tue-Sun May-Oct) showcases the riotously colourful paintings, watercolours, mosaics, ceramics and sculptures of artists Carl-Henning Pedersen (1913–2007) and Else Alfelt (1910–74). Next door to HEART stands Danish architect Jørn Utzon's 1970-designed **Prototype House** (closed to the public), while further south on Birk Centerpark street you'll stumble across artist Ingvar Cronhammar's ominous **Elia**. Attracting lightning, shooting random flames of gas, and looking like it comes straight off a *Dr Who* set, it's northern Europe's largest sculpture.

HEART and its neighbours aside, there's little else to keep you in Herning, so consider it a day trip from Silkeborg, easily reached by train (one way Dkr60k, 36 minutes). Alight at Birk Centerpark station (not at Herning station), from where the sights are a quick walk up the street. If you're driving, follow the signs to Herning Ø and Birk.

Gammel Skovridergaard
HOTEL €€

(📞87 22 55 00; www.glskov.dk; Marienlundsvej 36; s/d Dkr1265/1595, Sat, Sun & summer s/d Dkr825/1195; P@) This magnificent former manor farm is now a hotel and conference centre with oodles of charm and an idyllic location close to the lakes and forests of Silkeborg, yet only 2km south of the town centre.

✖ Eating

Nygade, lined with grill bars and pizza places, is the street to head to for quick, inexpensive fast food. You'll find a number of cheap food outlets on Søndergade, and plenty of cafes to the west on pleasant Tværgade. The **Føtex supermarket** (Torvet) has a bakery.

Michael D
EUROPEAN €€

(📞88 82 22 00; www.michaeld.dk; Radisson BLU, Papirfabrikken 12; 3-course brasserie menu Dkr295, 3-/5-course gourmet menu Dkr375/525; ⏱5.30-9.30pm Mon-Sun) White linen and French techniques make Michael D a special-occasion favourite with locals. Nosh on classic, well-executed brasserie fare like *coq au vin* with toasted brioche, pearl onions and potatoes, or opt for the more ambitious gourmet menus. It's a good idea to book ahead, especially on Friday and Saturday.

Restaurant Gastronomisk Institut
EUROPEAN €€€

(📞86 82 40 97; www.gastronomiske.dk; Søndergade 20; lunch Dkr85-135, dinner mains Dkr199-270; ⏱11.30am-3pm & 5.30-9.30pm Tue-Sat) This cosy brasserie-restaurant, located 200m south of the main square, serves good salads, steaks, sandwiches and soups for lunch and more ambitious Euro-centric dishes in the evenings. Dinner bookings are recommended.

Bagel Shop
BAGELS €

(Tværgade 24; bagels from Dkr38; ⏱10am-6pm Mon-Fri, 11am-3pm Sat) Fresh, customised bagels is what you get at this tiny takeaway. From bagel type to fillings and sauces, the choice is yours. Toast your health with a freshly squeezed OJ.

ℹ Information

Jsyke Bank (Vestergade 16) Branch with an ATM.

Library (Hostrupsgade 41) Has free internet terminals.

Tourist office (www.silkeborg.com; Åhavevej 2a; ⏱9.30am-4pm Mon-Fri, 10am-2pm Sat Jul-late Aug) Near the harbour; has lots of leaflets including detailed route descriptions of walks and cycle routes.

ℹ Getting There & Away

Hourly or half-hourly trains connect Silkeborg with Skanderborg (Dkr48, 30 minutes) and Aarhus (Dkr66, 50 minutes) via Ry.

SKANDERBORG & RY

Two smaller, quieter Lake District towns east of Silkeborg are Ry and Skanderborg. Ry, the closer of the two to Silkeborg, is a particularly peaceful place from which to base your exploration of the Lake District. Skanderborg is a rather humdrum town, but it has a lovely setting on Skanderborg Lake. It is best known in Denmark for the Smukfest.

◉ Sights & Activities

Himmelbjerget
OUTDOORS

The Lake District's most visited spot is the ambitiously named Himmelbjerget (Sky Mountain), which, at just 147m, is one of Denmark's highest hills. It was formed by water erosion during the final Ice Age as a *kol* (false hill), the sides of which are quite steep. There are a number of interesting memorials surrounding the hilltop's crowning glory, the 25m tower (admission Dkr10), reached via a marked 6km footpath northeast of Ry, or by bus or boat.

Ry Kanofart
CANOEING

(www.kanoferie.dk; Kyhnsvej 20, Ry) If you want to explore the lakes in the district, Ry Kanofart rents out canoes for Dkr400 per day.

Cykeludlejning
CYCLING

(www.rycykler.dk; Parallelvej 9b, Ry; per day Dkr75) Rents out bikes. For walking and cycling routes, ask at Ry's tourist centre.

✦ Festivals & Events

Smukfest
MUSIC

(www.smukfest.dk) Smukfest bills itself as Denmark's most beautiful music festival, and is second only to Roskilde in terms of scale. It takes place during the second weekend in August in Dyrehaven, a parkland a couple of kilometres east of the town, and attracts up to 45,000 people with a mix of – mostly Danish – rock, pop and dance artists. 2012 acts included David Guetta, Joan Armatrading and Bryan Adams.

⌱ Sleeping & Eating

Knudhule
CABIN, BUNGALOW €€

(📞86 89 14 07; www.knudhule.dk; Randersvej 88, Ry; 4-person cabins from Dkr700) An appealing budget holiday camp on a picturesque lake. There are cabins without bathrooms, and bungalows (sleeping up to four) with bathrooms. There's also a small restaurant, minigolf, boat hire and swimming/diving platforms on the lake. To get there from the train station, cross the tracks, turn left and go 2.5km.

Ry Park Hotel
HOTEL €€

(☑86 89 19 11; www.ryparkhotel.dk; Kyhnsvej 2, Ry; renovated s/d Dkr1050/1250, unrenovated Dkr790/990; ℗@) There are two room categories at Ry's only hotel – the fresh, newly renovated rooms are a better bet. A pleasant-enough place, the hotel can help arrange canoeing and cycling in the surrounding countryside. The hotel is also home to **La Saison** (lunch dishes 55-128kr, 2-/3-/5-course dinner 278/326/428kr; ☺lunch & dinner), a smart, competent restaurant-bar with Danish classics for lunch and seasonal dishes like lamb carpaccio with pickled and fresh apple, aged pecorino, beer-marinated mushrooms and mustard sauce for dinner.

Ristorante Italia
ITALIAN €€

(Skanderborgvej 3, Ry; mains Dkr132-161) There are several restaurants and fast-food places on Skanderborgvej, including Ristorante Italia, which offers tasty pasta dishes (Dkr74 to Dkr82) and more substantial mains.

Le Gâteau
BAKERY €

(Klostervej 12, Ry; sandwiches Dkr42; ☺7am-5.30pm Mon-Fri, to 2pm Sat, to noon Sun) Fragrant loaves of bread, flaky pastries (succumb to the chocolate croissant), and handy sandwiches await at this smart little bakery, opposite the Ry train station and tourist office.

ⓘ Information

Tourist office (☑86 69 66 00; www.visitskanderborg.com; Klostervej 3, Ry; ☺7am-5pm Mon-Fri, 10am-2pm Sat early Jul–mid-Aug, reduced hr rest of yr)In the train station.

ⓘ Getting There & Away

Twice-hourly trains connect Ry and Skanderborg with Silkeborg and Aarhus. See www.dsb.dk for details.

VIBORG
POP 37,600

It might be quieter and sleepier than Silkeborg, but Viborg claims a rich religious and historic heritage. In 1060 Viborg became one of Denmark's eight bishoprics and grew into a major religious centre. Prior to the Reformation, the town had no less than 25 churches and abbeys lining its streets. Though ecclesiastical remnants from that period are few, its handsome cathedral, cobbled lanes and storybook buildings lend the place a cosy, romantic air. It makes another good base for exploring the nearby lakes and surrounding woodland.

⊙ Sights & Activities

The tourist office has excellent printouts, including English-language versions, which describe **walks** around the town with historical and cultural themes. Sankt Mogens Gade, between the cathedral and the tourist office, has some handsome old houses, including **Den Hauchske Gård** at No 7 and the **Villadsens Gård** at No 9, both dating back to the first half of the 1500s.

From mid-May to the end of August, you can take a **boat trip** on the Viborg lakes on the *Margrethe I* (adult/child Dkr50/30). The boat departs from the jetty at Golf Salonen.

Viborg Domkirke
CHURCH

(Sankt Mogens Gade 4; admission Dkr10; ☺11am-4pm Mon-Sat, noon-4pm Sun) Dominating the town, this multitowered marvel is Scandinavia's largest granite church. The first church on the site dated from the Viking period, of which only the crypt survives. Almost entirely rebuilt in 1876, the cathedral's interior is awash with evocative, biblically themed frescos created over five years (1908–13) by artist Joakim Skovgaard. Of the paintings, two are especially notable: God creating women (on the left as you enter), and the 12 Apostles and four evangelists with St Paul replacing Judas (the centrepiece on the roof).

Skovgaard Museet
MUSEUM

(www.skovgaardmuseet.dk; Domkirkestræde 2-4; adult/child Dkr50/free; ☺10am-5pm Tue-Sun Jun-Aug, reduced hr rest of yr) Just outside the cathedral, this art museum also features work by Joakim Skovgaard, but here the scenes include portraits, landscapes and nudes. The museum also features work by Skovgaard's relatives and contemporaries, as well as changing exhibitions.

Kunsthallen Brænderigården
GALLERY

(www.braenderigaarden.dk; Riddergade 8; adult/child Dkr40/free; ☺1-5pm Tue-Sun mid-Jun–Aug, reduced hr rest of yr) Brænderigården is an engaging modern art space showcasing changing exhibitions of architecture, photography, art and sculpure.

Viborg Stiftsmuseum
MUSEUM

(www.viborgstiftsmuseum.dk; Hjultorvet 4; adult/child Dkr40/free; ⊙11am-5pm Tue-Sun mid-Jun–mid-Aug, reduced hr rest of yr) Viborg's local- history museum tells the story of the town's rich religious past.

📂 Sleeping & Eating

The tourist office website (www.visitviborg.dk) has a list of private accommodation options with singles/doubles starting at Dkr200/350.

The Sankt Mathias Gade Centre has cafes, a supermarket, bakery, fruit shop and a butcher.

TOP CHOICE **Niels**
Bugges Hotel
BOUTIQUE HOTEL €€

(☑86 63 80 11; www.nielsbuggeskro.dk; Egeskovvej 26, Hald Ege; d Dkr1250-1450, without bathroom Dkr790; Ⓟ) A true destination hotel, where design and gastronomy are taken seriously. Rooms epitomise farmhouse chic, adorned with florals, patchwork and antiques. Add a library, romantic grounds and the wonderful, New Nordic–inspired restaurant Skov (meaning 'forest') and you too will be dreading check out. From Viborg, catch bus 53.

Palads Hotel
HOTEL €€€

(☑86 62 37 00; www.hotelpalads.dk; Sankt Mathiasgade; s Dkr895, d Dkr995-1195; Ⓟ@) Straddling four sites, this chintzy yet charming hotel is part of the Best Western chain and has bright, pleasant rooms (some with kitchenettes). Hotel guests have complimentary access to the nearby Viborg swimming pool. The hotel is a short walk north of the train station.

Danhostel Viborg
HOSTEL €

(☑86 67 17 81; www.danhostel.dk/viborg; Vinkelvej 36; dm Dkr160, s/d from Dkr325/400; ⊙mid-Jan–Nov; Ⓟ@) Located 3km from town, this soothing, modern hostel feels like a rural escape. Adjacent to DCU-Viborg Camping, it's also backed by botanic gardens down to the lakeside. From Viborg, bus 770 stops 400m from the hostel. On weekends, catch bus 4 or 62.

DCU-Viborg Camping
CAMPGROUND €

(☑86 67 13 11; www.camping-viborg.dk; Vinkelvej 36b; campsites per adult/child/tent Dkr78/48/48; ⊙late Mar–late Oct; @) Viborg is a well-ordered, three-star camping ground at a pleasant, leafy location on the east side of Lake Søndersø. Wi-fi access costs Dkr20 for four hours.

Arthur
INTERNATIONAL €€

(Vestergade 4; tapas platters Dkr110-150, dinner mains Dkr169-248; ⊙11am-4pm & 6-11pm Mon-Thu, 11am-4pm & 6pm-midnight Fri & Sat) Bare-brick walls, stripped floors and candlelight make for a cosy setting at Arthur. While lunch dishes include sandwiches, pasta and pies, tapas is the lunch speciality, with tasty morsels straddling both Danish and global flavours. Come evening, things get a little fancier (and rather carnivorous), with mains such as New Zealand lamb with grain mustard, thyme and roasted garlic.

Café Morville
INTERNATIONAL €€

(Hjultorvet; lunch Dkr78-118, dinner dishes Dkr89-185; ⊙10am-10pm Mon & Tue, to 11pm Wed & Thu, to 1am Fri & Sat, 11am-5pm Sun) A bustling place on the main square with a modern bistro look, decent bistro-style dishes and great coffee (they have soy milk!).

❶ Information

The post office and several banks with ATMs line Sankt Mathias Gade, just south of the main square.

Tourist office (☑87 87 88 88; www.visitviborg.dk; Nytorv 9; ⊙9am-5pm Mon-Fri, to 2pm Sat Jun-Aug) Located in the centre of town; rents out bikes (per day Dkr100).

❶ Getting There & Around

Viborg is 66km northwest of Aarhus on Rte 26 and 41km west of Randers on Rte 16. Trains from Aarhus (Dkr128, 70 minutes) run once or twice hourly on weekdays, and hourly at weekends. There is ample and convenient free parking behind the Sankt Mathias Gade Centre on the south side of town, but you must use a time disc.

Aalborg

POP 104,900

While Odense gave the world superscribe Hans Christian Andersen, Denmark's fourth-biggest city gave it late, great architect Jørn Utzon, creator of the Sydney Opera House. His namesake Utzon Center – a museum of architecture and design – is a key component of Aalborg's slowly evolving waterfront redevelopment. Refocusing attention towards the water is a smart idea given the city's setting on the mighty Limfjord, the long body of water that slices Jutland in two. Yet, despite this focus on the future, many of Aalborg's finer features belong to the past: a sprinkling of imposing Renaissance facades, half-timbered houses down quiet side streets, not to mention Denmark's largest Viking burial ground, Lindholm Høje. Add a healthy dose of students and a lively bar scene, and chances are you'll be glad you checkedin for a night or two.

◉ Sights

Old Town
NEIGHBOURHOOD

The whitewashed **Budolfi Domkirke** (Budolfi Cathedral; Algade 40; admission free; ⊙9am-4pm Mon-Fri, to 2pm Sat) marks the centre of the old town, and has colourful early-16th-century frescos in the foyer. Northeast of the cathedral on Østerågade are three noteworthy historic buildings: the **old town hall** (c 1762), the five-storey **Jens Bangs Stenhus** (built c 1624 by wealthy merchant Jens Bangs) and **Jørgen Olufsens House** (c 1616).

In addition, the half-timbered neighbourhoods around **Vor Frue Kirke** (Peder Barkes Gade) are worth a stroll, particularly the cobbled Hjelmerstald. **Aalborghus Slot** (castle; Slotspladsen, City Centre), near the waterfront, is more administrative office than castle, but there's a small **dungeon** (⊙8am-3pm Mon-Fri May-Oct) you can enter for free.

Aalborg Historiske Museum
MUSEUM

(www.nordmus.dk; Algade 48; adult/child Dkr30/free; ⊙10am-5pm Tue-Sun) About 75m west of the cathedral is the Aalborg Historiske Museum, with artefacts from prehistory to the present and furnishings and interiors that hint at the wealth Aalborg's merchants enjoyed during the Renaissance.

Helligåndsklostret
MONASTERY

(Monastery of the Holy Ghost; CW Obels Plads; adult/child Dkr50/free; ⊙guided tours in English 2pm Tue Jul–mid-Aug) The alley between the Aalborg Historiske Museum and Budolfi Domkirke leads to the rambling monastery Helligåndsklostret, which dates from 1431 and features frescos from the early 16th century.

Utzon Center
ARCHITECTURE

(www.utzoncenter.dk; Slotspladsen 4; adult/child incl Kunsten Dkr60/free; ⊙10am-5pm Tue-Sun) An impressive 700-sq-metre design and architecture space, the Utzon Centre, with its distinctive silver roofscape, sits pretty on the harbour. It bills itself as 'a dynamic and experimental centre of culture and knowledge' and is close to where Jørn Utzon (1918–2008), the celebrated Danish architect, went to school. Sadly, the starchitect died shortly after the eponymous centre was finished. It hosts a changing program of exhibitions

on architecture, design and art; there's also a high-quality restaurant here. Admission includes same-day entry to the art museum Kunsten.

Kunsten
MUSEUM

(www.kunsten.dk; Kong Christian Allé 50; adult/child incl Utzon Center Dkr60/free; ⊙10am-5pm Tue-Sun, to 9pm Tue Feb-Apr & Sep-Nov; 🚗) Housed in a striking modular marble building by the great Finnish architect Alvar Aalto, Aalborg's regional art museum has a fine collection of predominately Danish modern and contemporary art, including work by JF Willumsen, Asger Jorn and Richard Mortensen. In the warmer months, kids will appreciate artist Jeppe Hein's Water Pavilion, an interactive outdoor fountain that encourages a good soaking.

To get to the museum, take the tunnel beneath the train station; it leads to **Kildeparken**, a green space with statues and water fountains. Go directly through the park, cross Vesterbro and then continue through a wooded area to the museum, a 10-minute walk in all. Alternatively, take bus 15. Note that admission includes entry to the Utzon Center.

FREE Lindholm Høje
HISTORIC SITE

(⊙dawn-dusk) The Limfjorden (Chalk Fjord) was a kind of Viking motorway providing easy and speedy access to the Atlantic for longboat raiding parties. It's perhaps not surprising then that by far the most important piece of Aalborg's historical heritage is a predominantly Viking one. The hugely atmospheric Lindholm Høje is a Viking burial ground where nearly 700 graves from the Iron Age and Viking Age are strewn around a hilltop pasture ringed by a wall of tall beech trees. Many of the Viking graves are marked by stones placed in the outline of a Viking ship, with two larger end stones as stem and stern.

The **museum** (☎99 31 74 40; Vendilavej 11; adult/child Dkr60/free; ⊙10am-5pm Apr-Oct, reduced hr rest of yr), adjacent to the field, depicts the site's history, while huge murals behind the exhibits speculate on what the people of Lindholm looked like and how they lived.

Lindholm Høje is 15 minutes from Aalborg centre on bus 2C. With your own wheels, head north from the centre over Limfjordsbroen to Nørresundby, and follow the signs, taking Lindholmsvej north.

FREE Nordkraft   CULTURAL CENTRE
(www.nordkraft.dk; Kjellerups Torv) What was once a foreboding power station is now an impressive cultural centre, complete with theatre, concert hall, art-house cinema, art gallery, fitness centre, plus a couple of eateries. It's big and well done but still finding its feet. The tourist office is also here, so it's worth popping in to see what's on.

Sleeping

While Aalborg's slumber options are somewhat uninspiring, they are relatively inexpensive compared with other Danish destinations and not generally in massive demand.

Villa Rosa   GUESTHOUSE €€
(98 12 13 38; www.villarosa.dk; Grønnegangen 4; r & apt Dkr500-800; P) Book early to snare one of only six theatrically decorated rooms over three floors (no lift) at this centrally located, late-19th-century villa. The three small self-contained apartments are the standout bargain here – the English Room is especially lovely. Three rooms share a large bathroom and guest kitchen.

Cabinn Aalborg   HOTEL €€
(96 20 30 00; www.cabinn.com; Fjordgade 20; s/d/tr from Dkr495/625/805; @) The cheap and reliable Cabinn chain delivers this modern, centrally located option. Beds are narrow, but all 239 rooms have TV and private bathroom. Conveniently, the hotel is steps away from the Utzon Center and next door to the Friis shopping centre; if you're driving, the hotel offers discounted undercover parking in the shopping centre car park (Dkr80, valid from 3pm to 11am).

Hotel Hvide Hus   HOTEL €€
(98 13 84 00; www.helnan.info; Vesterbro 2; s Dkr795-975, d Dkr995-1195) A quick walk from the city centre, this large, high-rise hotel may not scream 'character', but its rooms are comfortable, the views are superb, and the rates are good for a hotel of this class in Denmark (weekend rates are the cheapest). Fitness freaks can sweat it out at the modest in-house gym.

First Hotel Aalborg   HOTEL €€
(98 10 14 00; www.firsthotels.com; Rendsburggade 5; d from Dkr660; P @) Some of the newly renovated rooms at this smart fjordside hotel near the Utzon Center feature water views. The free parking and central location are an added bonus. Book online for the best rates.

Danhostel Aalborg   HOSTEL €
(98 11 60 44; www.danhostelaalborg.dk; Skydebanevej 50; dm/s/d from Dkr250/390/455; P @) Handy for boating activities on the fjord but hardly central, the hostel is at the marina 4km west of the centre. Dorm beds are available in the summer, and the hostel also runs an adjacent camping ground with cabins (two-person cabins from Dkr415 to Dkr480). Otherwise the facilities are rather basic. Catch bus 13.

Aalborg Camping   CAMPGROUND €
(98 11 60 44; www.aalborgcamping.dk; Skydebanevej 50; campsites per adult/child under 12/tent Dkr52/26/52) This pleasant two-star camping ground is popular with naturists.

Eating

TOP CHOICE Mortens Kro   MODERN SCANDINAVIAN €€€
(98 12 48 60; www.mortenskro.dk; Møllea 4-6; 3-/5-/7-course menu Dkr498/698/898; 5.30-10pm Mon-Sat) Hands down both the best and priciest nosh spot in town, sleek Mortens Kro serves confident, contemporary fare using local, seasonal ingredients – think home-smoked organic trout from Thy marinated with juniper berries, or lobster pearl barley risotto with anise liqueur, roasted langoustine tails, local cheese, truffle, crispy basil and basil puree. Book ahead and dress to impress.

Ristorante Fellini   ITALIAN €€
(98 11 34 55; www.fellini.dk; Vesterå 13; pizzas Dkr75-95, mains Dkr149-239; 11.30am-11pm Mon-Sat, 5-10pm Sun) Fellini film stills, Eros Ramazzotti ballads, cocky Italian chefs in the kitchen – you can almost hear the rush of the Trevi Fountain at this linen-and-candles heart-stealer. Pine for Il bel paese (the beautiful country) over authentic thin-crust pizzas, pasta classics and a heavenly lasagne with ricotta, mushroom and spinach. Book ahead on Friday and Saturday nights.

Penny Lane   CAFE, DELI €
(Boulevarden 1; pastries from Dkr30, sandwiches Dkr85; 8am-6pm Mon-Thu, to 7pm Fri, to 4pm Sat) From fragrant bread and local cheeses to wine and pantry treats, this charming cafe-cum-deli even has a little shop out back peddling well-picked vintage threads, shoes and gifts. Fill up the picnic hamper or grab a table and devour just-made pastries and

cakes, salubrious sandwiches, or the satisfying tapas plate (Dkr115).

Pingvin Tapas & Vincafé INTERNATIONAL **€€** (www.cafepingvin.dk; Adelgade 12; plate of 4/6/8 tapas Dkr188/228/258; ◎noon-11pm Mon-Sat) This chic, contemporary wine and tapas bar offers a selection of 30 'tapas', best approached as individual tasting plates rather than dishes to share. Graze on flavoursome dishes like duck confit and lamb tagine, then tackle dessert tapas options like almond rice with cherries and crunchy almond biscuits. The wine list is equally global and competent.

🍷 Drinking

If it's a flirt, a drink or loud repetitive beats in the form of banging techno, Euro-rock or house music you're after, trawl Jomfru Ane Gade, Aalborg's take-no-prisoners party street. Only really crowded later in the week, the venues themselves are pretty homogenous, so simply explore until you hear your kind of tunes.

TOP CHOICE **Den Fede Ælling** CAFE, BAR (www.denfedeaelling.dk; Strandvejen 12c; ◎from noon Tue-Sun) The Fat Duckling is a fabulous 'fjordbar' and cafe under Limfjordsbroen, set on a funky converted houseboat. Sip and sup (the changing, creative three-course menu dinner menu is Dkr295) inside or on the top deck; the latter is perfect on a mild summer night. Service is a little hit-and-miss, but with views like this all is forgiven.

Irish House PUB (www.theirishhouse.dk; Østerågade 25) Tucked inside a 17th-century building packed with stained glass and wooden carvings, this cheerful Irish pub serves up cheap pub grub, a mouthwatering range of beers, and live music Thursday to Saturday.

Søgaards Bryghus BREWERY (www.soegaardsbryghus.dk; CW Obels Plads 4) Every Danish town worth its salt now has a microbrewery, and Aalborg's is a cracker. With a swank interior, loads of outdoor seating and a long menu of beer accompaniments, you could easily lose an afternoon or evening here comparing the seven locals brews.

❶ Information

Danish Emigration Archives (www.emiarch. dk; Arkivstræde 1; ◎10am-4pm Mon-Wed, to 5pm Thu, to 3pm Fri) Behind Vor Frue Kirke,

helps foreigners of Danish descent trace their roots.

Hovedbiblioteket (City library; Rendsburggade 2; ◎10am-7pm Mon-Thu, to 6pm Fri, to 3pm Sat) Free internet access.

Jyske Bank (Nytorv 1)

Post office (Algade 42)

Tourist office (🖀99 31 75 00; www.visitaalborg.com; Nordkraft, Kjellerups Torv 5; ◎10am-8pm Mon-Fr, to 1pm Sat late Jun-Aug, reduced hr rest of yr) A small, noncentral office inside Nordkraft, with roving info booths in the summer.

❶ Getting There & Away

BUS & TRAIN Trains run to Aarhus (Dkr181, 1½ hours, at least hourly) and Frederikshavn (Dkr110, one hour, hourly). **Abildskou** (www. abildskou.dk)runs express bus 888 to Copenhagen (Dkr340, 5¾ hours), twice daily Sunday to Friday, once daily Saturday.

CAR & MOTORCYCLE The E45 bypasses the city centre, tunnelling under the Limfjord, whereas the connecting Rte 180 leads into the centre. To get to Lindholm Høje or points north from Aalborg centre, take Rte 180 (Vesterbro), which crosses Limfjordsbroen.

Avis (🖀70 24 77 40; www.avis.com; John F Kennedys Plads 3a) At the train station.

Europcar (🖀98 13 23 55; www.europcar.com; cnr Jyllandsgade & Dag Hammarskjølds Gade) Located 450m to the east of the train station.

❶ Getting Around

BUS Almost all city buses leave from the south of JF Kennedys Plads and pass the city-centre stops of Østerågade and Nytorv, near Burger King. The standard local bus bus fare is Dkr18.

From late June to late August, a free City Circle bus runs half-hourly from 10am to 5.30pm (until 1.30pm on weekends). The circuit takes in major sites, including Kunsten and the waterfront.

CAR Despite a few one-way streets, central Aalborg is a fairly easy place to get around by car. There's free (but time-restricted) parking on many side streets, and metered parking in the city centre (Dkr13 to Dkr16 per hour). Cheaper, undercover parking can be found at the **Friis Shopping Centre** (Nytorv), which charges Dkr10 per hour from 10am to 7pm Monday to Friday (to 4pm on weekends) and Dkr6 per hour at all other times.

Frederikshavn

TRANSPORT HUB / POP 23,300

If you plan on catching a ferry to Sweden or Norway, you may find yourself boarding

in Frederikshavn. Those with time to kill can head to **Bangsbo Museum** (☑98 42 31 11; www.bangsbo.com; Dronning Margrethes Vej 6; adult/child Dkr50/free; ⊙10am-4pm Mon-Fri, 11am-4pm Sat & Sun Jun-Aug, reduced hr rest of yr), an old country estate with eclectic exhibits. Among these are the reconstructed remains of a 12th-century, Viking-style merchant ship dug up from a nearby stream bed. Located 3km south of the centre, the museum can be reached by bus 3, which stops near the estate's entrance.

🛏 Sleeping

In case you have a late or early ferry, here are a couple of decent options within walking distance of the port.

Hotel Herman Bang　　　　　HOTEL **€€**
(☑98 42 21 66; www.hermanbang.dk; Tordenskjoldsgade 3; s/d from Dkr795/945) These midpriced rooms are bright and comfortable, and the most expensive are huge and luxurious. Avoid the cheapest ('standard') rooms, which offer poor value – you're better off at the hotel's newly decorated budget annex, **Herman Bang Bed & Breakfast** (Skolegade 2; s/d Dkr500/600, without bathroom Dkr400/500). The hotel has an upmarket spa and American-style diner.

Danhostel Frederikshavn City　HOSTEL **€**
(☑98 42 14 75; danhostelfrederikshavn.dk; Læsøgade 18; dm/s/d Dkr200/500/550; 🅿@) All rooms at this fresh, new hostel have private bathroom and the communal areas are topnotch. It's perfectly positioned behind the tourist office, which faces the ferry terminal.

🍴 Eating

Numerous, mainly fast-food, places line central Danmarkgade. You'll also find a cluster of eateries at the eastern end of Lodsgade, the best of which is **Karma Sushi** (☑98 43 22 01; Lodsgade 10; 8-piece signature sushi Dkr125-165; ⊙dinner Tue-Sat).

❶ Getting There & Away

BOAT Ferries connects Frederikshavn with Gothenburg in Sweden and Oslo in Norway. See p493 for details.

TRAIN Frederikshavn is the northern terminus of the DSB train line. Trains run about hourly south to Aalborg (Dkr110) and then onto Copenhagen (Dkr416). **Nordjyske Jernbaner** (www.njba.dk) runs trains to Skagen (Dkr60) once or twice hourly on weekdays, and every two hours on weekends. The train station and adjacent bus

terminal are 600m north of the ferry terminal and tourist office.

Skagen

POP 8400

Skagen is a magical place, both bracing and beautiful. If you are driving from the south, to get there you pass through kilometre after kilometre of, well, pretty much nothing really, until first pine forests and then an extraordinary landscape of grassy sand dunes herald this popular vacation region. The town of Skagen (pronounced 'skain') is a busy working harbour and is Denmark's northernmost settlement, just a couple of kilometres from the dramatic sandy spit where the country finally peters out at Grenen, a slender point of wave-washed sand, where seals bask and seagulls soar.

Artists discovered Skagen's luminous light and its colourful, wind-blasted, heath-and-dune landscape in the mid-19th century and fixed eagerly on the romantic imagery of the area's fishing life that had earned the people of Skagen a hard living for centuries. Painters such as Michael and Anna Ancher and Oscar Björck followed the contemporary fashion of painting *en plein air* (out of doors), often regardless of the weather. Their work established a vivid figurative style of painting that became known internationally as the 'Skagen School'.

Today, Skagen is a highly popular tourist resort, completely packed during high summer. But the sense of a more picturesque Skagen survives and the town's older neighbourhood, Gammel Skagen, 5km west, is filled with distinctive, single-storey, yellow-walled, red-roofed houses (they're traditionally painted every Whitsuntide with lime and ochre).

The peninsula is lined with fine beaches, including a sandy stretch on the eastern end of Østre Strandvej, a 15-minute walk from the town centre.

The **Skagen Festival** (www.skagenfestival.dk) packs the town out with official performers, buskers and appreciative visitors during the first weekend of July; book accommodation well in advance.

◉ Sights

Grenen　　　　　　　　　　　OUTDOORS
Appropriately for such a neatly kept country, Denmark doesn't end untidily at its northernmost point, but on a neat finger of sand

just a few metres wide. You can actually paddle at its tip where the waters of the Kattegat and Skagerrak clash and you can put one foot in each sea; but not too far. Bathing is strictly forbidden here because of the ferocious tidal currents and often turbulent seas that collide to create mane-tossing white horses.

The tip is the culmination of a long, curving sweep of sand at Grenen, about 3km northeast of Skagen along Rte 40. Where the road ends there's a car park (Dkr12 per hour between 9am and 6pm), cafe-restaurant and souvenir shop plus, in high summer, what seems like the entire population of Denmark. Crowds head along the last stretch of beach for the 30-minute walk to the tip. From Easter to October, a special tractor-drawn bus, the *Sandormen*, leaves from the car park every half hour, waits for 15 minutes at the beach end, then returns (adult/child Dkr25/15). From late June to mid-August, bus 99 runs from Skagen station to Grenen hourly (Dkr15) five times daily until 5pm. **Taxis** (②98 43 34 34) are available at the train station.

Skagens Museum MUSEUM
(www.skagensmuseum.dk; Brøndumsvej 4; adult/child Dkr90/free; ⊙10am-5pm Thu-Tue, to 9pm Wed Jun-Aug, closed Jan) This fine museum showcases the paintings of Michael and Anna Ancher, PS Krøyer and other artists who flocked to Skagen between 1830 and 1930, many of them kitchen-sink portraits of the lives and deaths of the fishing community.

Tilsandede Kirke RUIN
(adult/child Dkr10/5; ⊙11am-5pm Jun-Aug) This whitewashed medieval church tower still rises above the sand dunes that buried the church and surrounding farms in the late 18th century. The tower, in a nature reserve, is 5km south of Skagen and well signposted from Rte 40. By bike, take Gammel Landevej from Skagen.

Råbjerg Mile OUTDOORS
These undulating 40m-high hills comprise Denmark's largest expanse of shifting dunes and are great fun to explore. Råbjerg Mile is 16km south of Skagen, off Rte 40 on the road to Kandestederne. It's about 4km from Hulsig station on the Frederikshavn–Skagen train line.

Michael & Anna Ancher's Hus MUSEUM
(www.anchershus.dk; Markvej 2-4; adult/child Dkr70/20; ⊙10am-5pm May-Sep) This poignant domestic museum occupies the house that

the Anchers bought in 1884 and in which their daughter Helga lived until 1960.

🛏 Sleeping

Hotel accommodation can be scarce at summer weekends, especially during the Skagen Festival at the end of June and in weeks 28 and 29 (mid-July), when Denmark's VIP party crowd hits town to party. The tourist office books singles/doubles in private homes for around Dkr325/450, plus a Dkr75 booking fee for the first night and Dkr25 for subsequent nights.

TOP CHOICE **Finns Hotel Pension** GUESTHOUSE €€
(②98 45 01 55; www.finnshotelpension.dk; Østre Strandvej 63; s Dkr525-775, d Dkr750-975; ⊙May-late Sep) Take a 1923-vintage 'log cabin' built for a Norwegian count, fill it with art, antiques and memorabilia, and you have this fabulously atmospheric slumber spot. Gay friendly, TV-free and adults-only (no kids under 15), Finns offers six individually decorated rooms, and accommodating hosts who'll even cook you dinner (from Dkr275 for two courses). Best of all, it's a stone's throw from the beach.

Badepension Marienlund GUESTHOUSE €€
(②98 44 13 20; www.marienlund.dk; Fabriciusvej 8; s/d Dkr630/1060; ⊙mid-Mar–late Oct; ℗) A cosy atmosphere and picture-perfect garden make this immaculately kept place a solid choice for quiet R&R. There are only 14 rooms, so book ahead, especially in the high season. You'll find it on the quieter western side of town; bikes are available for rent.

Grenen Camping CAMPGROUND €
(②98 44 25 46; www.grenencamping.dk; Fyrvej 16; campsites per adult/child Dkr89/53; ⊙Apr–mid-Sep; @) A fine seaside location, semiprivate campsites and pleasant four-bunk huts, 1.5km northeast of Skagen centre. The only downside is the rather tightly bunched sites.

Danhostel Skagen HOSTEL €
(②98 44 22 00; www.danhostel.dk/skagen; Rolighedsvej 2; dm/s/d Dkr180/475/625; ⊙Mar-Nov; ℗) Well kept, very popular and 1km from the centre; book ahead in summer. Rates drop sharply in low season.

🍴 Eating & Drinking

Around half a dozen seafood shacks line the harbour selling good seafood to eat inside, outside or take away. Freshly caught prawns are the favourite fare, costing around Dkr95 for a generous helping. You'll also find a bakery here.

There are a couple of pizzerias, Mexican restaurants, a burger joint and an ice-cream shop clustered near each other on Havnevej. The supermarket **Super Brugsen** (Sankt Laurentii Vej 28) has a bakery.

TOP CHOICE **Ruths Hotel** FRENCH €€€
(☑98 44 11 24; www.ruths-hotel.dk; Hans Ruths Vej 1; brasserie 3-course dinner Dkr395, restaurant 3/4/5 courses Dkr650/750/950; ☺brasserie lunch & dinner year-round, gourmet restaurant dinner Tue-Sat early Jun-Aug, reduced hr rest of yr) One of Denmark's grand bathing hotels, Ruths also has two top-notch dining options. Ruths Brasserie serves an all-day menu of classic French dishes showcasing fabulous local produce; the in-house bakery starts peddling sublime pastries from 7.30am.

If the budget permits, lift your fork at the more formal, fine-dining Ruths Gourmet. Heading the kitchen is Michelin-starred chef Michael Michaud, whose Gallic talents sparkle in dishes like pigeon cassoulet.

Brøndum's Hotel FRENCH, DANISH €€
(☑98 44 15 55; www.broendums-hotel.dk; Anchersvej 3; mains Dkr140-210; ☺11.30am-9pm) French cuisine is the main influence on the otherwise classic, well-executed Danish dishes, with abundant seafood such as lobster and turbot, as well as tenderloin and chateaubriand. Meals are served in an elegant, old-world dining room and, in the warmer months, a picture-perfect garden. The hotel's simple, cosy rooms (single/double Dkr935/1485) charm with old-school Nordic style: stripped-back floorboards, striped wallpaper and antique furniture.

Pakhuset SEAFOOD €€
(Rødspættevej 6; lunch Dkr85-145, mains Dkr160-235; ☺lunch & dinner) Seafood is the star at harbourside Pakhuset, from simple fish cakes with remoulade, cranberry compote and salad to the swoon-inducing flambéed Norwegian lobster tails with risotto and cherry tomatoes. It has long hours and a superb ambience both outdoors (slap bang on the harbour) and indoors (think wooden-beams, jovial ship mastheads and Impressionist paintings). Fine dine upstairs or keep it cheaper in the downstairs cafe.

Jakobs Café & Bar INTERNATIONAL €€
(Havnevej 4; dinner mains Dkr180-265; ☺11am-11.30pm Sun-Thu, 11am-12.30am Fri, 10am-1am Sat)

Jakobs is a popular restaurant on Skagen's busy main street. It does good homemade brunches (Dkr65 to Dkr120), salads and open sandwiches (80kr to 95kr). By night it's a popular bar staging live music at weekends (usually cover bands).

ℹ Information

Sankt Laurentii Vej, Skagen's main street, runs almost the entire length of this long thin town, and is never more than five minutes from the waterfront.
Tourist office (☑98 44 13 77; www.skagen.dk; Vestre Strandvej 10; ☺9am-4pm Mon-Sat, 10am-2pm Sun late Jun–mid-Aug) By the harbour.

ℹ Getting There & Away

TRAIN Nordjyske Jernbaner (www.njba.dk) runs trains to Frederikshavn (Dkr60, 36 minutes, once or twice hourly on weekdays, every two hours on weekends).
BUS Bus 99 runs between Hirtshals and Skagen (Dkr50, one hour and 20 minutes, two to four daily) from late June to mid-August only. The same bus continues on to Hjørring.

ℹ Getting Around

CYCLING Cycling is an excellent way of exploring Skagen and the surrounding area. Close to the tourist office, **Cykelhandler** (Vestre Strandvej 4; per day Dkr70) rents out bicycles through the liquor shop next door.
CAR & MOTORCYCLE Skagen is very busy with traffic in high season. There is little free parking but you will find convenient car parks (Dr12 per hour, free between 6pm and 9am) by the harbour; one between the tourist office and the waterfront, the other just to the left of the tourist office.

Hirtshals

TRANSPORT HUB / POP 6200
Situated 50km southwest of Skagen, the port town of Hirtshals services year-round ferries to Norway and seasonal ferries to the Faroe Islands and Iceland. Its one notable sight is **Nordsøen Oceanarium** (www.nordsoenoceanarium.dk; Willemoesvej 2; adult/child Dkr165/90; ☺9am-8pm mid-late Jul, reduced hr rest of yr, closed mid-Dec–early Jan), an impressive aquarium that re-creates a slice of the North Sea in a massive four-storey tank.

☕ Sleeping

Hotel Hirtshals HOTEL €€
(☑98 94 20 77; www.hotelhirtshals.dk; Havnegade 2; s/d Dkr795/895) In case you have a late

WORTH A TRIP

FAROE ISLANDS

The far-flung Faroes (Føroyar) may be under Danish sovereignty, but this self-governing slice of Scandinavia is a universe unto itself. Midway between Iceland and Scotland, it's an 18-piece jigsaw of majestic rocks jutting out of the frothing North Atlantic swells, a place where multicoloured cottages and grass-roofed wooden churches add focus to grandly stark, treeless moorlands. It's a curiously bewitching place, infused with ancient Norse legends and tight-knit rural communities alive with art and music.

Running the show is capital-city **Tórshavn** (Thor's Harbour), its transport links, solid restaurants and hotels making the place an excellent base from which to explore the rest of the country. Take a day or two to explore the turf-roofed cottages of its historic Tinganes district, as well as the islands' idiosyncratic culture at museums such as **Føroya Fornminnissavn** (www.fornminni.fo; Brekkutún 6, Hoyvík; adult/child Dkr30/free; ☉ 10am-5pm Mon-Fri, 2-5pm Sat & Sun mid-May–mid-Sep) and **Listasavn Føroya** (www.art.fo; Gundadalsvegur 9; adult/child Dkr50/free; ☉11am-5pm Mon-Fri, 2-5pm Sat & Sun May-Aug, reduced hr rest of yr).

The Faroes' ethereal pull, however, lurks beyond the city limits. Sharing the island of **Streymoy** with Tórshavn is tiny Vestmanna, from where tour boats reach the inspirational **Vestmanna Bird Cliffs**, bobbing beneath towering cliff faces, passing spiky rock pinnacles and squeezing through tight stone arches. You'll spy the breeding areas of guillemots and razorbills as screeching fulmars and kittiwakes soar above like thousands of white dots.

Another birdwatchers' paradise is the far western island of **Mykines**. Its hiking trail to the 1909 Mykinesholmur Lighthouse leads through densely packed puffin burrows and across a 35m footbridge over a sea gorge brimming with birdlife, including the Faroes' only significant gannet colonies.

Long and thin enough to make a supermodel cry, the northeast island of **Kalsoy** delivers a surreal succession of abrupt peaks and swales. Nicknamed the 'flute' for its many tunnel holes, the scenery glimpsed all too briefly between them is nothing short of majestic.

Arresting scenery is something the island of **Eysturoy** does especially well. Wedged between the Kalsoy and Streymoy, it's here that you'll find the country's grandest fjords and highest peaks. Northern Eysturoy serves up especially spectacular scenery at every turn, and travelling between its criminally cute villages makes for one of the most magical experiences in the country.

Facing Kalsoy's jagged northern tip, the petite village of **Elduvík** is a dreamily cute snaggle of tar-blackened traditional cottages divided into two photogenic clumps by the meandering mouth of the Stórá stream. Then there's **Gøta**. Caught in a fjord end between two jagged mountain arms, this sprawling three-villages-in-one wakes the neighbours in late July with the Faroes' foremost rock festival, **G!** (www.gfestival.com), improbably held on a sandy little beach.

While July and August cover the main tourist season, consider visiting in June, when the days are dreamily long, most hotels and museums are open, yet tourist numbers are low. From September to May, rain abounds and much infrastructure is shut, though the brooding skies, pounding ocean and haunting landscapes will speak to more meditative travellers.

All flights fly into the Faroe Islands' only airport, **Vágar** (www.floghavn.fo). National carrier **Atlantic Airways** (www.atlantic.fo) runs direct flights to/from Copenhagen (daily), Billund (two to seven times weekly) Bergen (twice weekly) and Reykjavík (once or twice weekly). In summer it also flies directly to Aalborg (one to three times daily), London Gatwick (twice weekly) and Barcelona (once weekly). **Air Iceland** (www.airiceland.is) also has flights to Reykjavík.

For details on ferry connections to/from Hirtshals (Denmark) and Seyðisfjörður (Iceland), see p493. For more information on the Faroe Islands themselves, click onto www.faroeislands.com.

or early ferry, this is a decent option 750m southwest of the ferry terminal. It's on the main square above the fishing harbour and has bright, comfortable rooms with high, steepled ceilings and good sea views at the front.

Eating

There are cafes at the northern end of Hjør-ringgade, and there are also a couple of pizza and kebab places on Nørregade. Your best bet for a decent feed is seafood-centric **Hirtshals Kro** (Havnegade; lunch Dkr55-189, dinner mains Dkr118-238), beside Hotel Hirtshals.

Getting There & Away

BOAT Ferries connect Frederikshavn to five Norwegian ports: Bergen, Kristiansand, Stavanger, Langesund and Larvik. Seasonal ferries run to Tórshavn (Faroe Islands) and Seyðisfjörður (Iceland). For details, see p493.

TRAIN Hirtshals' main train station is 500m south of the ferry harbour. There is a second stop near the Color Line terminal. The privately run line connects Hirtshals with Hjørring (Dkr30, 22 minutes). Trains run at least hourly. From Hjørring you can take a DSB train to Aalborg (Dkr90, 45 minutes, once or twice hourly) or Frederikshavn (Dkr60, 30 minutes, once or twice hourly).

Esbjerg

POP 71,600

Esbjerg fails to pull heartstrings on first impressions. Made big and rich from North Sea oil, its silos and smokestacks hardly compete with the crooked, storybook streets of nearby Ribe. Away from the industrial grit, however, Esbjerg redeems itself with a handsome town square, fantastic art museum and easy access to the beautiful, time-warped island of Fanø – a quick 12-minute ferry ride away.

Sights & Activities

Esbjerg Kunstmuseum MUSEUM
(www.eskum.dk; Havnegade 20; adult/child Dkr60/free; ☉10am-4pm) The single most worthwhile place to visit in town is the Esbjerg Kunstmuseum, an impressive gallery with an important collection of Danish modern art, including work by Asger Jorn.

Esbjerg Museum MUSEUM
(www.esbjergmuseum.dk; Torvegade 45; adult/child Dkr40/free; ☉10am-4pm Jun–mid-Sep) Also in

the town centre, the small Esbjerg Museum contains a few historical artefacts from the area and an amber display, offering a short diversion if it's raining.

Sleeping

The tourist office books rooms in private homes from around Dkr250 per person per night.

Cabinn Esbjerg HOTEL €€€
(☎75 18 16 00; www.cabinn.com; Skolegade 14; s/d from Dkr545/675; @) Clean, functional but good-value, cabin-style rooms (with small dimensions and rather narrow bunk beds) right in the centre. The superior rooms are larger and a little less clinical. Free wi-fi.

Hotel Britannia HOTEL €€€
(☎75 13 01 11; www.britannia.dk; Torvet 24; s/d Dkr1399/1599; @) The town's largest and most business-oriented hotel has good service, revamped rooms and good on-site eateries in a central location. While the rack rates are clearly aimed at expense-account travellers, the hotel offers regular online specials, with rates dropping as low as Dkr800/900 per single/double.

Ådalens Camping CAMPGROUND €
(☎75 15 88 22; www.adal.dk; Gudenåvej 20; campsites adult/child Dkr67/39; @⚡) The nearest camping to Esbjerg (5km north of the city via bus 1 or 7), this place has great facilities including a pool, solarium and jacuzzi.

Danhostel Esbjerg HOSTEL €
(☎75 12 42 58; www.danhostel.dk/esbjerg; Gammel Vardevej 80; dm Dkr180, s/d Dkr550/650, without bathroom Dkr350/500; ☉Jan–mid-Dec; P@) Occupying a handsome former high school 3km northwest of the city centre, this hostel is close to sports facilities including a pool. Take bus 4.

Eating & Drinking

Most restaurants and grocery stores are east of Torvet on Kongensgade.

Sand's Restaurant DANISH €€
(www.sands.dk; Skolegade 60; lunch Dkr42-135, mains Dkr109-249; ☉11.30am-9.30pm Mon-Sat) You'll find superb, real-deal Danish staples such as *smørrebrød*, Danish hash, meatballs, smoked eel and *pariserbof* (a fried beef patty on bread with a raw egg yolk, pickles and fresh horseradish) in this snug, old-fashioned dining room.

Dronning Louise
INTERNATIONAL €€

(www.dr-louise.dk; Torvet 19; lunch Dkr49-100, dinner mains Dkr140-255; ⊗10am-1am Mon-Wed, to 3am Thu, to 4am Fri, to 5am Sat, to midnight Sun) This cosy, jack-of-all-trades restaurant-pub turns out decent salads, bagels and burgers for under Dkr120, as well as slightly more ambitious brasserie fare and pastries. There's a disco upstairs on Friday and Saturday nights, with tunes spanning Top 40 pop to commercial dance. The kitchen closes 10.30pm Monday to Saturday, 9.30pm Sunday.

Industrien
CAFE, BAR

(☑75 13 61 66; Skolegade 27; ⊗Tue-Sat) This Bar-studded Skolegade is where to head when you're thirsty, and cool Industrien is a local favourite. Dive in for changing art exhibitions, live music and late, late hours (until 5am Friday and Saturday). If you're peckish, tackle its thumpin' burgers (flesh-free option available); the kitchen closes at 9pm.

Paddy Go Easy
PUB

(Skolegade 42) A friendly Irish pub actually run by Irish proprietors, just off the main square.

ⓘ Information

Central Library (Nørregade 19; ⊗10am-7pm Mon-Thu, to 5pm Fri, to 2pm Sat) Free internet access.

Danske Bank (Torvet 18)

Post office (Torvet 20)

Tourist office (☑75 12 55 99; www.visitesbjerg.dk; Skolegade 52; ⊗10am-4.30pm Mon-Fri, to 1pm Sat)

ⓘ Getting There & Away

BOAT Ferries sail between Esbjerg and Harwich, England. See p491 for details.

CAR If you're driving into Esbjerg from the east, the E20 leads into the city centre. If you're coming from the south, Rte 24 merges with the E20 on the city outskirts. From the north, Rte 12 makes a beeline into the city, ending at the harbour.

TRAIN Trains to Copenhagen (Dkr358, 2¼ hours, hourly) run until 9.42pm.

ⓘ Getting Around

Most city-bound buses (Dkr19) call at the train station. Parking is free in Esbjerg. There's also a convenient car park on Danmarksgade, but it has a two-hour limit; some unlimited parking is available in the car park on Nørregade, east of the library.

Ribe
POP 8200

The charming, crooked cobblestone streets of Ribe date from AD 869, making it one of Scandinavia's oldest and Denmark's most attractive towns. It is a delightful chocolate-box confection of half-timbered, 16th-century houses, clear-flowing streams and water meadows. Almost everything, including the hostel and train station, is within a 10-minute walk of Torvet, the town square, which is dominated by the huge Romanesque cathedral.

◉ Sights

For a charmed stroll that takes in some of Ribe's handsome half-timbered buildings and winding cobbled lanes, head along any of the streets radiating out from Torvet, in particular Puggårdsgade or Grønnegade, from where narrow alleys lead down and across Fiskegarde to Skibbroen and the picturesque old harbour.

Ribe Domkirke
CHURCH

(Torvet; steeple adult/child Dkr10/5; ⊗10am-5pm Mon-Sat, noon-5pm Sun) Dominating the heart of the town, Ribe Domkirke claims a variety of hugger-mugger styles from Romanesque to Gothic. The cathedral's monumental presence is literally sunk into the heart of Ribe. The highlight is the climb up the steeple for breathtaking views.

Ribe Kunstmuseum
MUSEUM

(www.ribekunstmuseum.dk; Sankt Nicolajgade 10; adult/child Dkr70/free; ⊗10am-5pm Thu-Tue, to 8pm Wed Jul & Aug, 11am-4pm Tue-Sun Sep-Jun) Ribe's restored art museum claims some of Denmark's best works, including those by 19th-century 'Golden Age' painters. Among the luminaries are Jens Juel, Nicolaj Abildgaard, Christoffer Wilhelm Eckersberg and Michael Ancher.

Museet Ribes Vikinger
MUSEUM

(www.ribesvikinger.dk; Odins Plads 1; adult/child Dkr70/free; ⊗10am-6pm Thu-Tue, to 9pm Wed Jul & Aug, reduced hr rest of yr) Get up to speed on Ribe's intriguing history at the town's dedicated Viking museum. Rare archaeological finds and reconstructions explore Ribe's Viking past, with two rooms providing snapshots of the town in 800 and during medieval times in 1500.

LEGOLAND

Revisit your tender years at Denmark's most visited tourist attraction (beyond Copenhagen), **Legoland** (www.legoland.dk; Nordmarksvej, Billund; adult/child Dkr299/279; ☺late Mar-late Oct, see website for specific times; 🖼). While clearly family focused, even those sans ankle-biters should set a day aside for a little playtime magic. The sprawling theme park is a gob-smacking ode to those little plastic building blocks, with everything from giant Lego models of famous cities, landmarks and wild beasts to re-created scenes from the Star Wars film series. And while the park's booty of rides and activities is mostly geared to preteens, adrenalin junkies can scream to their heart's content on the X-treme Racers roller coaster, not to mention the gravity-defying Power Builder.

Consider buying your tickets online to avoid the queues, and be mindful that rides close one or two hours before the park does.

Legoland is in the town of Billund, 63km northeast of Esbjerg. Bus 44 runs between them (80 minutes). If travelling from Aarhus, catch the train to Velje, from where bus 43 continues to Billund airport, located opposite Legoland (95 minutes).

Ribe VikingeCenter　　　　　　MUSEUM
(www.ribevikingecenter.dk; Lustrupvej 4; adult/child Dkr90/45; ☺11am-5pm daily late Jun-late Aug, 10am-3.30pm Mon-Fri early May-late Jun & late Aug–mid-Oct) More hands-on than the museum, this re-created Viking village lets you get in touch with your inner Viking. Dressed in period costumes, the staff demonstrate daily 'Viking life', from baking bread over open fires, to demonstating Viking crafts like archery, pottery and leathermaking. The centre is 3km south of town; catch bus 417 (bus 135 on weekends).

Old Town Hall　　　　　　　　MUSEUM
(adult/child Dkr15/free; ☺1-3pm Jun-Aug, reduced hr rest of yr) The town also has a couple of interesting local-history museums, including one at the Old Town Hall, the former debtors' prison, displaying a small arsenal of viciously spiked medieval weaponry and the formidable axe of the town executioner.

☞ Tours

Night-Watchman Tour　　　　　　TOUR
There isn't any new-fangled CCTV fad in Ribe; instead, a costumed night watchman takes care of security, making the rounds from Torvet at 10pm from May to mid-September (also at 8pm June to August). Now an entertaining, song-laced stroll through Ribe's medieval streets, the night-watchman's evening walk dates back to the 14th century. Aside from ensuring the safety of the streets, these guardians were also charged with looking out for floods or fires threatening the town. Abolished in 1902, the role was reinstated as a tourist attraction in 1935.

☕ Sleeping

The tourist office maintains a brochure of rooms in private homes from around Dkr300/400 per single/double.

Weis Stue　　　　　　　　　　HOTEL €
(☎75 42 07 00; www.weisstue.dk; Torvet; s/d Dkr395/495) This is the poorer, quirkier but no less charming alternative to the Dagmar opposite. A small, ancient wooden-beamed house, it has rather small, crooked rooms right above its restaurant, but they have bags of character. The restaurant is an old-school feast (herbivores beware), offering hearty plates of herring, salmon or meatballs (lunch Dkr129 to Dkr245, two/three courses Dkr249/298), best washed down with locally brewed beer.

Danhostel Ribe　　　　　　　HOSTEL €
(☎75 42 06 20; www.danhostel-ribe.dk; Sankt Pedersgade 16; dm Dkr180, s/d from Dkr380/400; 🅿@) Knowledgeable staff, sparkling rooms (all with bathroom) and impressive facilities make this hostel a top choice for both backpackers and families. A stone's throw from Ribe's historic heart, it also rents out bikes.

Ribe Byferie　　　　　　　　RESORT €€
(☎79 88 79 88; www.ribe-byferie.dk; Damvej 34; apt for 2-4 people Dkr745-2055; 🅿@🖼) This well-run 'village' of roomy, modern, self-catering apartments lies southwest of the town centre. It is, in effect, a holiday centre and perfect for families of up to seven. Facilities include a wellness centre, games room, bike and canoe hire, playground, kids' club and a barbeque area.

Hotel Dagmar

HOTEL €€€

(☑75 42 00 33; www.hoteldagmar.dk; Torvet; s/d from Dkr1045/1245; @) The central Hotel Dagmar claims to be the oldest hotel in Denmark; it has plush (if mostly rather small) rooms and a great period atmosphere.

✗ Eating & Drinking

Sælhunden

DANISH €€

(Skibbroen 13; lunch Dkr75-125, mains Dkr125-210; ⏰lunch & dinner) This cosy, old restaurant is right on the quayside. Look out for a West Jutland speciality called *bakskuld* (Dkr95), consisting of dried, salted and smoked dab (flatfish) served with rye bread. It's also a good spot for a coffee and (if you're lucky) crêpes.

Postgaarden

CAFE €

(Nederdammen 36; meals Dkr59-119; ⏰10am-8pm Mon-Sat, to 5pm Sun) Postgaarden has a wide range of Danish and international microbrews for sale in its delicatessen. It also offers a changing selection of boutique (and sometimes obscure) brews on tap to accompany its cafe-style grub, best chowed down in the photogenic courtyard. You'll also find a good stock of hamper-friendly picnic goodies (ask about picnic baskets to go).

Café Valdemar

CAFE, BAR

(Sct Nicolajgade 6; ⏰10am-10pm Tue-Thu, to 5am Fri & Sat, to 6pm Sun) This buzzing cafe and bar offers frequent live music, youthful flirting and, most attractive of all, a waterside summer terrace in the heart of the old town.

ⓘ Information

Danske Bank (Saltgade 10-14)

Post office (Sct Nicolaj Gade 12)

Tourist office (☑75 42 15 00; www.visitribe. dk; Torvet 3; ⏰9am-6pm Mon-Fri, 10am-5pm Sat, 10am-2pm Sun Jul & Aug, reduced hr rest of yr)

ⓘ Getting There & Away

There are trains from Esbjerg to Ribe (Dkr60, 35 minutes, once or twice hourly) and from Aarhus to Ribe (Dkr258, three hours, hourly).

Fanø

POP 3300

If Esbjerg has one silver lining, it is that one of the treasures of the Danish Wadden Sea – famed for its seals, birdlife and national park status – is just a short ferry ride away.

The island of Fanø, a popular holiday island for Danes and Germans, pulls in the punters with its picture-perfect villages; broad, endless sandy beaches; and lively summertime vibe. Its two fishing villages, northerly Nordby (where the majority of the islanders live) and southerly Sønderho, are time-warped jumbles of historic, thatched cottages and cobblestone streets. Sønderho in particular is one of Denmark's most charming villages, dating back to the 16th century and radiating more than a hint of Middle Earth.

⊙ Sights & Activities

Families and water-sports fans come to Fanø above all else for the magnificent **beaches** – the best of which are around **Rindby Strand**, **Sønderho** and **Fanø Bad** (Denmark's first international seaside resort). All three villages have shops and restaurants. Further north is the vast and breathtaking sand spit, **Søren Jessens Sand**. Amber hunters also flock to the island to hunt along Fanø's beaches.

Nordby and Sønderho are home to a few low-key museums detailing Fanø's history.

Fanø Skibsfarts og Dragtsamling

MUSEUM

(www.fanoskibs-dragt.dk; Hovedgaden 28, Nordby; adult/child Dkr25/5; ⏰11am-4pm Mon-Sat May-Sep, reduced hr rest of yr) The island's Golden Age peaked in the 19th century, when it claimed the largest maritime fleet beyond Copenhagen. Indeed, over a period of 150 years, it was the site for the construction of over 1000 vessels. The modest Skibsfarts og Dragtsamling covers the nautical history and traditional costumes of this ancient fishing island.

Fanø Kunstmuseum

MUSEUM

(www.fanoekunstmuseum.dk; Nordland 5, Sønderho; adult/child Dkr30/15; ⏰1-5pm Tue-Sat, 11am-5pm Sun Jul & Aug, reduced hr rest of yr) Art is the focus of the Fanø Kunstmuseum, which features paintings from the 19th and early 20th centuries by homegrown artists and other Danish creatives who have been inspired by Fanø's ethereal light and atmosphere.

Fanø Museum

MUSEUM

(www.fanomuseerne.dk; Skolevej 2, Nordby; adult/child Dkr25/5; ⏰11am-4pm Mon-Fri Jul & Aug, reduced hr rest of yr) Housed in a 300-year-old building, Skibsfarts og Dragtsamling's sibling, Fanø Museum, covers the nonmaritime history of Fanø; fans of period furniture will appreciate its particularly fine collection.

Fanø Klitplantage NATURE RESERVE
Wildlife watchers and nature lovers will be in their element in the centre of the island, where 1162 hectares make up the Fanø Klitplantage nature reserve. Hit the walking tracks and you'll find birds, deer and rabbits in abundance. There's a popular picnic site and forest playground near Pælebjerg.

🛏 Sleeping & Eating
There are seven campsites on Fanø, virtually all within a short walk of the coast. For more information see www.visitfanoe.dk.

For information on booking summer holidays houses and flats (which typically sleep four to six people and are rented by the week), contact the tourist office.

As well as the inns serving good food (listed below), take a stroll along Nordby's Hovedgaden and Sønderho's Sønderland for appealing eateries and sunny courtyard gardens.

You'll find supermarkets and bakeries in all the main villages. The Nordby butcher **Slagter Christiansen** (Hovedgaden 17) is known throughout Denmark for his *Fanø skinke* (Fanø ham), which is in the style of Italian prosciutto. The **Fanø Bryghus** (www.fanoebryghus.dk; Strandvejen 5, Nordby) is a microbrewery concocting well-respected beers: stop in and swill a few at its on-site bar.

TOP CHOICE Sønderho Kro INN €€€
(☑75 16 40 09; www.sonderhokro.dk; Kropladsen 11, Sønderho; s Dkr1100-1200, d Dkr1300-1800; ℗) The loveliest place to stay on the island (and renowned around the country) is this thatched-roof slice of *hyggelig* heaven, dating back to 1722. Its 14 individually decorated rooms are filled with charming local antiques and the inn also has a notable gourmet restaurant (lunch Dkr118k to Dkr178, dinner three/six courses Dkr460/700), which showcases local and seasonal produce.

Fanø Krogaard INN €€
(☑76 66 01 66; www.fanoekrogaard.dk; Langelinie 11, Nordby; d from Dkr895) Going strong since 1664, this charming old inn on the waterfront in Nordby has an intimate vibe and cosy, antique-filled rooms (plus more modern ones in a newer annexe). We also love the fabulous large terrace and long menu of local specialities, especially fishy favourites (lunch Dkr79 to Dkr119, dinner mains Dkr169 to Dkr219).

ℹ Information
Tourist office (☑70 26 42 00; www.visitfanoe.dk; Færgevej 1, Nordby; ◷9am-5pm Mon-Fri, 10am-4pm Sat & Sun Jul & Aug, reduced hr rest of yr) Close to the harbour in Nordby.

ℹ Getting There & Around
If you're doing a day trip or overnight stay from Esbjerg, it's much cheaper to leave your car on the mainland and hire a bike or take the bus once on the island.

Fanø Færgen (☑70 23 15 15; www.fanoefaergen.dk; return adult/child/bike Dkr40/20/40, return car incl passengers May-Oct Dkr400, Nov-Apr Dkr 290) ferries depart from Esbjerg for Nordby one to three times hourly from 4.50am to around midnight. Sailing time is 12 minutes.

You can rent bicycles in Nordby from **Fanø Cykler** (www.fanoecykler.dk; Hovedgaden 96, Nordby; per day Dkr50).

Fanø has a limited bus service connecting Nordby with Fanø Bad, Rindby Strand and Sønderho.

UNDERSTAND DENMARK

History
Humble Hunters to Mighty Vikings
First settled around 4000 BC, most probably by prehistoric hunter-gatherers from the south, Denmark has been at the centre of Scandinavian civilisation ever since, and there are plenty of reminders of that past in the shape of the ancient burial chambers that pepper the countryside and the traces of fortifications at, for example, Trelleborg.

The Danes themselves are thought to have migrated south from Sweden in around AD 500 but it was their descendants, who were initially a peaceful, farming people, who are better known today. What we think of as modern Denmark was an important trading centre within the Viking empire and the physical evidence of this part of Denmark's history is to be found throughout the country today. In the late 9th century, warriors led by the Viking chieftain, Hardegon, conquered the Jutland peninsula. The Danish monarchy, Europe's oldest, dates back to Hardegon's son, Gorm the Old, who reigned in the early 10th century. Gorm's son, Harald Bluetooth, completed the conquest of Denmark and spearheaded the conversion of the Danes to Christianity; his story and his legacy is well showcased in the tiny hamlet of Jelling. Successive Danish kings sent their subjects to row their longboats to England and conquer most of the Baltic region. They were accomplished fighters, swordsmiths, shipbuilders and sailors, qualities well illustrated at the excellent Viking Ship Museum in Roskilde.

Reformation & Renaissance

In 1397 Margrethe I of Denmark established a union between Denmark, Norway and Sweden to counter the influence of the powerful Hanseatic League that had come to dominate the region's trade. Sweden withdrew from the union in 1523 and over the next few hundred years Denmark and Sweden fought numerous border skirmishes and a few fully fledged wars, largely over control of the Baltic Sea. Norway remained under Danish rule until 1814.

In the 16th century the Reformation swept through the country, accompanied by church burnings and civil warfare. The fighting ended in 1536, the Catholic Church was ousted and the Danish Lutheran Church headed by the monarchy was established.

Denmark's Golden Age was under Christian IV (1588–1648), with Renaissance cities, castles and fortresses flourishing throughout his kingdom. A superb example is Egeskov Slot on Funen. In 1625 Christian IV, hoping to neutralise Swedish expansion, entered an extremely ill-advised and protracted struggle known as the Thirty Years War. The Swedes triumphed and won large chunks of Danish territory. Centuries worth of Danish kings and queens are laid to rest in sarcophagi on dramatic display at Roskilde's cathedral.

The Modern Nation

Literature, the arts, philosophy and populist ideas flourished in the 1830s, and Europe's Year of Revolution in 1848 helped inspire a democratic movement in Denmark. Overnight, and in typically orderly Danish fashion, the country adopted male suffrage and a constitution on 5 June 1849, forcing King Frederik VII to relinquish most of his power and become Denmark's first constitutional monarch. Denmark lost the Schleswig and Holstein regions to Germany in 1864.

Denmark remained neutral throughout WWI and also declared its neutrality at the outbreak of WWII. Nevertheless, on 9 April 1940 the Germans invaded, albeit allowing the Danes a degree of autonomy. For three years the Danes managed to walk a thin line, running their own internal affairs under Nazi supervision, until in August 1943 the Germans took outright control. The Danish Resistance movement mushroomed and 7000 Jewish Danes were smuggled into neutral Sweden.

Although Soviet forces heavily bombarded the island of Bornholm, the rest of Denmark emerged from WWII relatively unscathed. Postwar Social Democrat governments introduced a comprehensive social welfare state in the postwar period, and still today Denmark provides its citizens with extensive cradle-to-grave social security.

Denmark joined NATO in 1949, and the European Community, now the EU, in 1973. The Danes offer tepid support for an expanding EU. In 1993 they narrowly voted to accept the Maastricht Treaty, which established the terms of a European economic and political union, only after being granted exemptions from common-defence and single-currency provisions. They also voted not to adopt the euro in 2000.

Political Controversies

In 2004 the country's most eligible bachelor, Crown Prince Frederik, married Australian Mary Donaldson in a hugely popular and exhaustively covered storybook wedding. They now have four children.

It has not all been fairy tales, though. The growing political sway of the nationalist, right-wing Danish People's Party (DPP) in the late 1990s and early 2000s led Denmark to impose some of the toughest immigration laws in Europe in 2002. Its influence also contributed to Denmark's joining the USA, UK and other allies in the 2003 Iraq War, as well as to its commitment to maintain its role in Afghanistan.

In 2006 the country became the focus of violent demonstrations around the Middle East following the publication of a cartoon depicting the prophet Mohammed – a deep taboo for many Muslims but an issue of freedom of speech for liberal news editors – in the *Jyllands-Posten* newspaper.

Discontent over the country's stuttering economic performance influenced the election of a new, centre-left coalition in 2011, led by Social Democrat Helle Thorning-Schmidt.

It has not been smooth sailing for Denmark's first female prime minister. While the rolling back of anti-immigration legislation enacted by the previous government was welcomed by many, Thorning-Schmidt alienated a significant number of her supporters by agreeing on a tax package with the centre-right opposition. Driven by mounting concerns over Denmark's rapidly ageing population and the increasing pressure on the country's welfare system, the reforms aimed at stimulating labour output by cutting corporate tax, increasing the tax threshold for higher income earners, and reducing unemployment benefits and pensions.

The package was strongly condemned by the socialist Red-Green Alliance, on whose votes Thorning-Schmidt's minority government relies to stay in power. Needless to say, the government worked a little closer with its far-left ally when drawing up its 2013 budget.

People

Denmark's 5.58 million people are a generally relaxed bunch. It takes a lot to shock a Dane, and even if you do, they probably won't show it. This was the first country in the world to legalise same-sex marriages, and it became (in)famous during the 1960s for its relaxed attitudes to pornography.

They are an outwardly serious people, yet with an ironic sense of humour. They have a strong sense of family and an admirable environmental sensitivity. Above all, they are the most egalitarian of people – they officially have the smallest gap between rich and poor in the world – proud of their social equality in which none have too much or too little.

The vast majority of Danes are members of the National Church of Denmark, an Evangelical Lutheran denomination (a proportion of each Dane's income tax goes directly to the church), though less than 5% of the population are regular churchgoers.

Arts

Literature

By far the most famous Danish author is Hans Christian Andersen. Other prominent Danish writers include religious philosopher Søren Kierkegaard, whose writings were a forerunner of existentialism, and Karen Blixen, who wrote under the name

Isak Dinesen and penned *Out of Africa* and *Babette's Feast*, both made into acclaimed movies in the 1980s.

Another successful novel-turned-screenplay is Peter Høeg's 1992 world hit *Miss Smilla's Feeling for Snow*, a suspense mystery about a Danish Greenlandic woman living in Copenhagen. And while the hugely popular genre of Scandinavian crime fiction is dominated by authors from Sweden (Henning Mankell and Stieg Larsson) and Norway (Jo Nesbø), Denmark is not without its noteworthy contributors. Among them is Jussi Adler-Olsen, whose novel *The Message That Arrived in a Bottle* won the 2010 Glass Key award, an annual prize given to a Nordic crime novel. The prize was once again swagged by a Dane in 2012, this time by Erik Valeur for his debut work, *The Seventh Child*.

Architecture & Design

For a small country Denmark has had a massive global impact in the fields of architecture and design. Arne Jacobsen, Verner Panton, the late Jørn Utzon and Hans J Wegner are now considered among the foremost designers of the 20th century, and the tradition of great furniture and interior design remains strong in the country's design schools, museums and independent artisanal workshops.

In recent years, a new league of eco-conscious architectural firms has emerged on the world stage. Among them is Effekt, designers of Tallinn's striking new Estonian Academy of Arts building, and BIG (Bjarke Ingels Group), the head-turning projects of which include the cascading VM Bjerget housing complex in Copenhagen's Ørestad district. Indeed, Copenhagen is Denmark's architectural and design powerhouse, with museums such as Desigmuseum Danmark and architectural show-stealers like the Opera House and Royal Library extension maintaining the country's enviable international reputation.

Film

As with its design prowess, Denmark punches well above its weight in the realm of cinema. The country has scored regular Oscar success with films such as *Babette's Feast* (1987), Gabriel Axel's adaptation of a Karen Blixen novel; Bille August's *Pelle the Conqueror* (1988); and Anders Thomas Jensen's short film *Valgaften* (1998). In 2011 Susanne

Bier's family drama *In a Better World* (2010) won Best Foreign Film at both the Academy Awards and the Golden Globe Awards. In 2010 Mads Brügger's subversively comic documentary about North Korea, *The Red Chapel* (2009), swooped the World Cinema Documentary Jury Prize at the Sundance Film Festival.

The most prolific and controversial of Denmark's 21st-century directors remains Lars von Trier, whose most recent film, *Melancholia* (2010), delivers a surreal, visually arresting take on the apocalypse. His best-known films to date include the melodrama *Breaking the Waves* (1996), which took the Cannes Film Festival's Grand Prix; *Dancer in the Dark* (2000), a musical starring Icelandic singer-songwriter Björk and Catherine Deneuve, which won Cannes' Palme d'Or; and experimental *Dogville* (2003), starring Nicole Kidman. Dubbed the enfant terrible of contemporary cinema, von Trier first scored international attention as a cofounder of the Dogme95, an artistic manifesto pledging a minimalist approach to filmmaking using only hand-held cameras, shooting in natural light and rejecting special effects and prerecorded music. The movement scored notable international hits with Thomas Vinterberg's *The Celebration* (1998) and Lone Scherfig's *Italian for Beginners* (2000).

Visual Arts

Before the 19th century, Danish art consisted mainly of formal portraiture, exemplified by the works of Jens Juel (1745–1802). A Golden Age ushered in the 19th century with such fine painters as Wilhelm Eckersberg (1783–1853) and major sculptors like Bertel Thorvaldsen (1770–1844), although he chose to spend most of his life in Rome.

Later in the century the Skagen School evolved from the movement towards alfresco painting of scenes from working life, especially of fishing communities on the northern coasts of Jutland and Zealand. Much of it is exhibited at the Skagens Museum. Leading exponents of the Skagen School were PS Krøyer and Michael and Anna Ancher. In the mid-20th century, a vigorous modernist school of Danish painting emerged, of which Asger Jorn (1914–73) was a leading exponent. Many of his works are on display at the art museum in Silkeborg.

A number of contemporary Danish artists enjoy international acclaim, including conceptual artists Jeppe Hein, duo Elmgreen & Dragset, and Danish–Icelandic Olafur Eliasson. The latter's famously large-scale projects have included four temporary 'waterfalls' along New York's East River, as well as a whimsical multicoloured walkway atop the acclaimed ARoS gallery in Aarhus.

Like Aarhus, many Danish towns and cities contain a vibrant selection of home-grown and international contemporary art; even the smallest towns can surprise. Two of the best small art museums and galleries outside the capital are Faaborg's art museum and Herning's contemporary-art museum, HEART. Topping it all off is the magnificent Louisiana Museum of Modern Art, on the coast north of Copenhagen.

Wildlife

On the nature front, common critters include wild hare, deer and many species of bird, including eagles, magpies, coots, swans, and ducks. Stretching along Jutland's west coast from Ho Bugt to the German border (and including the popular island of Fanø), the Nationalpark Vadehadet (Wadden Sea National Park) provides food and rest for between 10 and 12 million migratory birds each spring and autumn. Among the feathered regulars are eiders, oystercatchers, mallards and wigeons, as well as brent geese and barnacle geese. The park, Denmark's largest and newest, is part of an ambitious plan to restore many of Denmark's wetlands and marshes, and to help endangered species such as the freshwater otter make a comeback.

Environmental Issues

When it comes to sustainability, Denmark puts much of the world to shame. Over 20% of Denmark's energy already comes from renewable energy, a figure expected to reach 100% by 2050. Much of this renewable energy comes from wind turbines, a technology that Denmark excels at.

Denmark also leads the world in peddle power. According to the **Cycling Embassy of Denmark** (www.cycling-embassy.dk), nine out of 10 Danes own a bicycle, 16% of all trips are by bike, and 45% of all Danish children cycle to school. In Copenhagen alone, a staggering 40% of the workforce commute on two wheels. The country has over 12,000km of signposted cycle routes, covering urban and rural areas. On the roads themselves, cyclists enjoy a level of respect and consideration from motorists that borders on the utopian. An efficient, well-integrated public-transport network is also helping to shrink the nation's carbon footprint.

Food & Drink

Denmark has rebranded itself from 'dining dowager' to 'cutting-edge gastronome' in less than two decades. At the heart of the revolution is Copenhagen, home to 13 Michelin-starred restaurants and 2010, 2011 and 2012 San Pellegrino World's Best Restaurant winner, Noma. Along with restaurants like Kadeau, Kødbyens Fiskebar and Pony, Noma has helped redefine New Nordic cuisine by showcasing native produce and herbs, prepared using traditional techniques and contemporary experimentation, and focused on clean, natural flavours.

Staples & Specialities

Proud of it though they are, even the Danes would concede that their traditional cuisine is rather heavy and unhealthy. They eat a great deal of meat, mostly pork and usually accompanied by something starchy and a gravylike sauce. However, one Danish speciality has conquered the world: *smørrebrød*, or the Danish open sandwich.

Meaty staples include *frikadeller* (fried minced-pork balls) and *fiskefrikadeller* (the fish version), *flæskesteg* (roast pork with crackling), *hvid labskovs* (beef-and-potato stew), *hakkebøf* (beefburger with fried onions) and the surprisingly tasty *pariserbøf* (rare beef patty topped with capers, raw egg yolk, beets, onions and horseradish).

It's not all turf, with coast-sourced classics including *sild* (herring), fresh *rejer* (shrimp) and *hummer* (lobster). The Danes are great fish smokers too; you'll find smoke-houses (called *røgeri* in Danish) preserving herring, eel, cod livers, shrimp and other seafood all around the coast. The most renowned are on Bornholm.

Where to Eat

Beyond Copenhagen, Denmark's food scene can be less inspiring. Culinary cliches – from nachos and burgers, to inauthentic pasta, pizza and Thai – continue to plague too many menus. Yet things are slowly changing. Seasonality and local produce are informing an ever-growing number of kitchens. In Aarhus, New Nordic hot spots such as St Pauls Apothek, Nordisk Spisehus and Kähler Spisesalon have pushed the city onto the foodie radar. Beyond the big cities, destinations like Zealand's Dragsholm Slot, Bornholm's Kadeau and Lassens, and Ærø's Edith fly the flag for quality and innovation. And then there are the country's traditional *kroer* (inns), many of which serve authentic Danish home cooking.

Drinks

The Danes are enthusiastic drinkers, and not just of their world-famous domestic beers. The most popular spirit in Denmark is caraway-spiced Aalborg aquavit; it's drunk straight down as a shot, followed by a chaser of beer. *Øl* (beer), *vin* (wine) and spirits are reasonably cheap and easily bought here compared with other Scandinavian countries.

SURVIVAL GUIDE

Directory A–Z

Accommodation

PRICE RANGES

The following price indicators are for a double room with private bathroom and breakfast unless stated otherwise. Rates include all taxes.

€€€   more than Dkr1500

€€   Dkr600 to Dkr1500

€   less than Dkr600

CAMPING & CABINS

With over 500 registered camping grounds, Denmark is well set up for campers, although many grounds are open only in the summer, while others open from spring to autumn. The 200 camping grounds that open all year often offer cheaper off-peak rates.

Grounds typically charge between Dkr50 and Dkr85 per adult and half that per child. Electricity will typically cost between Dkr20 and Dkr40 per day. Some camping grounds also charge an environmental fee (around Dkr25).

Many camping grounds offer cabins for rent; expect to pay around Dkr3500 per week during the peak summer season.

A camping pass (available at any camping ground) is required (Dkr110) and covers a family group with children aged under 18 years for the season. If you do not have a seasonal pass you pay an extra Dkr35 a night for a transit pass.

See www.danishcampsites.dk and www.dk-camp.dk for further details.

HOSTELS

The national Hostelling International office is **Danhostel** (☑33 31 36 12; www.danhostel.dk; Vesterbrogade 39, 1620 Copenhagen V). Most of Denmark's 95 *vandrerhjem* (hostels) in its Danhostel association have private rooms in addition to dorms, making hostels an affordable and popular alternative to hotels (so book ahead from June to August).

Dorm beds cost from about Dkr150 to Dkr300, while private rooms range from about Dkr300 to Dkr650 for singles, and Dkr350 to Dkr700 for doubles. Blankets and pillows are provided, but not sheets; bring your own or hire them for Dkr50 to Dkr75. Sleeping bags are not allowed.

A Hostelling International Card costs Dkr160. Without one you pay Dkr35 extra per person per night. You can buy the card at all Danhostels. In a few places, reception closes as early as 6pm – check ahead. In most hostels, reception is closed between noon and 4pm.

HOTELS

Budget hotels start at around Dkr500 for single rooms and Dkr650 for double rooms. A *kro*, a name that implies a country inn but is more often the Danish version of a motel, is generally simpler and cheaper, and often occupies homely period buildings. Both hotels and *kros* usually include an all-you-can-eat breakfast. You can find out more about some of Denmark's inns and make online bookings at www.krohotel.dk.

Many large chain or business-oriented hotels operate on a flexi-rate system or offer discounts at weekends year-round and from May to September; booking online in advance is often cheaper.

OTHER ACCOMMODATION

Many tourist offices book rooms in private homes for a small fee, or provide a free list of the rooms on their website so travellers can book online or phone on their own. Rates vary, averaging about Dkr400/600 for singles/doubles. Standards of accommodation vary widely. **Dansk Bed & Breakfast** (☑39 61 04 05; www.bedandbreakfast.dk) handles a large number of homes throughout Denmark, offering private rooms at similar rates.

Activities

Denmark is well set up for a diversity of outdoor activities, from walking and cycling to fishing and water sports. The official **Visit Denmark** (www.visitdenmark.com) tourist website offers useful information and links.

Dansk Cyklist Forbund (DCF; ☑33 32 31 21; www.dcf.dk; Rømersgade 5-7, 1362 Copenhagen K) publishes a 1:500,000-scale *Cycling Map of Denmark* (Dkr25), showing all national biking routes. It also publishes more detailed 1:100,000 regional cycle touring maps (Dkr129). Purchase them online from DCF or at most tourist offices.

Business Hours

The liberalisation of trading hours in 2012 has seen an increase in opening times. More shops are trading on Sundays, especially in Copenhagen, and supermarkets hours have been noticeably extended across Denmark.

Opening hours can vary significantly between high and low seasons. Hours provided here are for the high season. There is no strict rule defining 'high season' and it can vary from sight to sight. Most commonly, high season refers to the period from late June to mid-August (sometimes early June to late August, though in some places the season covers May to September, inclusive). Standard opening hours are as follows:

Banks 10am to 4pm Monday to Friday, to 5pm or 6pm Thursday

Bars 4pm to 1am or 2am Sunday to Wednesday, to 3am or 5am Thursday to Saturday

Post offices 9am or 10am to 5pm or 6pm Monday to Friday, to noon or 2pm Saturday

Restaurants 11am to 10pm

Shops 9.30am to 5.30pm Monday to Thursday, to 7pm or 8pm Friday, to 5pm Saturday

Supermarkets 8am to 8pm or 10pm Monday to Friday, 8am to 6pm, 8pm or 10pm Saturday and Sunday

Food

Generally speaking, eating out in Denmark is not cheap. You can expect to pay Dkr400 for a decent three-course meal in the capital, rising easily to Dkr1000 and above in the finest restaurants.

The following price indicators refer to the cost of a main course:

€€€   more than Dkr200

€€   Dkr100 to Dkr200

€   less than Dkr100

Gay & Lesbian Travellers

Denmark is a popular destination for gay and lesbian travellers. Copenhagen in particular has an active, open gay community with a healthy number of gay venues.

Landsforeningen for Bøsser, Lesbiske, Biseksuelle og Transpersoner (LBL; ☑33 13 19 48; www.lbl.dk; Nygade 7, Copenhagen) is the national organisation for the GLBT community. **Out & About** (www.out-and-about.dk) is a useful website for visitors, with listings, upcoming events and links to GLBT organisations. Also useful is the free GAY CPH app.

Internet Access

Wi-fi hot spots, many of them free, are mushrooming across Denmark. Many cafes offer free wi-fi and most public libraries offer free access to internet-enabled computers. Most hotels, guesthouses and hostels also offer wi-fi access, often free.

Money

ATMs Major bank ATMs accept Visa, MasterCard and the Cirrus and Plus bank cards.

Cash If you're exchanging cash, there's a Dkr30 fee for a transaction. Post offices exchange foreign currency at comparable rates to those at banks.

Credit cards Visa and MasterCard are widely accepted in Denmark. American Express and Diners Club are occasionally accepted. A surcharge of up to 3.75% is imposed on foreign credit-card transactions in some restaurants, shops and hotels. Bring photo ID when using a credit card in Denmark as it may be requested.

Euros Denmark remains outside the euro zone, though acceptance of euros is commonplace. Most hotels and restaurants will take euros, as do many bars, cafes and shops, although you may find reluctance to do so in more remote areas or from very small businesses. Government institutions do not accept euros.

Tipping Restaurant bills and taxi fares include service charges in the quoted prices. Further tipping is not expected, although rounding up the bill is not uncommon when service has been particularly good.

Public Holidays

Many Danes take their main work holiday during the first three weeks of July. Banks and most businesses close on public holidays and transport schedules are commonly reduced.

New Year's Day 1 January

Maundy Thursday Thursday before Easter

Good Friday to Easter Monday March/April

Great Prayer Day Fourth Friday after Easter

Ascension Day Sixth Thursday after Easter

Whit Sunday Seventh Sunday after Easter

Whit Monday Seventh Monday after Easter Monday

Constitution Day 5 June

Christmas Eve 24 December from noon

Christmas Day 25 December

Boxing Day 26 December

Telephone

To call Denmark from abroad dial your country's international access code, then ☑45 (Denmark's country code), then the local number. There are no regional area codes within Denmark.

To call internationally from Denmark dial ☑00, then the country code for the country you're calling, followed by the area code (without the initial zero if there is one) and the local number.

Public payphones accept coins, phone cards and credit cards. Phonecards come in denominations of Dkr30, Dkr50 and Dkr100 and are available from newspaper kiosks and post offices.

Time

Denmark is normally one hour ahead of GMT/UTC. Clocks are moved forward one hour for daylight-saving time from the last Sunday in March to the last Sunday in October. Denmark uses the 24-hour clock.

Tourist Information

Visit Denmark (www.visitdenmark.com), Denmark's official tourism website, lists tourist offices throughout the country.

Travellers with Disabilities

Overall, Denmark is a user-friendly destination for travellers with disabilities. Most Danish tourist literature indicates which establishments have disability-friendly rooms and facilities. Disabled travellers with specific questions can contact **Dansk Handicap Forbund** (☑39 29 35 55; http://dhf-net.dk; Hans Knudsens Plads 1a).

Visas

Citizens of the USA, Canada, Australia and New Zealand need a valid passport to visit Denmark, but do not need a visa for stays of less than three months. In addition, no entry visa is required by citizens of EU and Scandinavian countries. Citizens of many African, South American, Asian and former Soviet bloc countries do require a visa. See www.nyidanmark.dk/en-us/coming_to_dk/visa/visa.htm for details.

Women Travellers

Women travellers are less likely to encounter problems in Denmark than in most other countries. Naturally, use common sense when it comes to potentially dangerous situations such as hitching or walking alone at night. Dial ☑112 for emergencies.

Getting There & Away

Flights, cars and tours can be booked online at lonelyplanet.com.

Air

If you're coming from European destinations, consider flying into an airport other than Copenhagen, such as Aarhus or Billund; airfares are competitive, and the airports are well connected by bus with neighbouring towns and afford fast access to Northern and Central Jutland. Another option involves flying into Sweden's Malmö Airport, located across the Oresund Bridge. Shuttle buses connect the airport to central Malmö, from where frequent train services run to Copenhagen.

The main Danish airports include the following:

Aarhus (www.aar.dk) Nonstop flights include London (Stansted), Manchester, Stockholm, Gothenburg, Oslo, Girona (Barcelona) and Málaga.

Billund (www.bll.dk) Nonstop flights include London (City and Stansted), Manchester, Edinburgh, Stockholm, Oslo, Frankfurt, Düsseldorf, Amsterdam, Brussels, Paris, Krakow, Venice (Treviso), Rome (Ciampino), Girona (Barcelona), Málaga and Istanbul.

Copenhagen International Airport (www.cph.dk) Nonstop flights include most major European destinations, New York, Washington DC, Chicago, San Francisco, Toronto, Bangkok, Beijing, Shanghai, Singapore, Tokyo, Casablanca, Tel Aviv, Cairo, Damascus, Doha and Bahrain.

Land

GERMANY

The E45 is the main motorway running between Germany and Denmark's Jutland peninsula.

Bus

Eurolines (www.eurolines-travel.com; Halmtorvet 5) operates buses from Copenhagen to 18 destinations in Germany.

Berlin Dkr349, seven hours, one to three daily

Frankfurt Dkr869, 13 hours, one daily

Hamburg Dkr389, six hours, one to two daily

Services to Germany also depart from Aarhus and Aalborg. Note that promotional fares booked online in advance can be substantially cheaper than the prices listed here.

Train

There are both direct and indirect train services from Copenhagen to Germany, see www.bahn.com for more information. Direct services serve the following cities:

Berlin From Dkr1005, 6¾ to 10 hours, one daily

Frankfurt From Dkr1215, 12½ hours, one daily

NORWAY

Bus

Eurolines runs three weekly services between Oslo and Copenhagen (Dkr385, nine hours) via Gothenburg.

Train

There are numerous daily services between Copenhagen and Oslo, although most require several interchanges. One to two daily services require only one interchange in Göteborg, Sweden (from Dkr1021, 8¼ hours). See www.sj.se for more information.

SWEDEN

Bus

Eurolines runs three weekly buses to Göteborg (Dkr275, 4½ hours) and Stockholm (Dkr385, 9¾ hours).

Train

Trains run many times a day between Denmark and Sweden via the Øresund bridge linking Copenhagen with Malmö (Dkr90, 35 minutes). If you're travelling by train, the bridge crossing is included in the fare, but for those travelling by car, there's a Dkr325 toll per vehicle. For train timetables, ticket offers and bookings, see www.sj.se. From Copenhagen, other direct Swedish connections include the following:

Göteborg From Dkr418, 3¾ hours, 15 daily

Stockholm From Dkr485, 5½ hours, six daily

Sea

International ferries run between Denmark and the UK, Sweden, Norway, Iceland, Germany and Poland. See p491 for details.

Getting Around

Air

Denmark's small size and efficient train network mean that domestic air travel is mostly the domain of business folk and people connecting from international flights through Copenhagen.

Danish Airport Transport (DAT; ☎76 92 30 40; www.dat.dk) Operates numerous daily flights between Copenhagen and Rønne (Bornholm). It also connects Copenhagen to Sønderborg.

SAS (☎70 10 20 00; www.flysas.com) Numerous daily connections from Copenhagen to Billund, Aarhus and Aalborg.

Bicycle

» Cycling is a practical way to get around Denmark. There are extensive bike paths linking towns throughout the country and bike lanes through most city centres.
» You can rent bikes in most towns for around Dkr75 per day, plus a deposit of about Dkr500.
» Bikes can be taken on ferries and most trains for a modest cost. From May to

August, you must make a reservation to carry a bicycle on InterCity and InterCityLyn trains, either at the station or by calling ☎70 13 14 15. Outside this period, it is still wise to make a booking to guarantee that your bike gets on board.
» Bikes can be carried for free on Copenhagen's S-trains.

Boat

Ferries link virtually all of Denmark's populated islands. See listings in the destination chapters for details.

Bus

All large cities and towns have a local and regional bus system; many connect with trains. Long-distance buses run a distant second to trains. Yet, some cross-country bus routes work out 25% cheaper than trains. Popular routes include Copenhagen to Aarhus or Aalborg.

The following main bus companies operate in Denmark.

Abildskou (☎70 21 08 88; www.abildskou.dk) Runs from Copenhagen to Aarhus, Silkeborg and Aalborg.

Gråhund Bus (☎44 68 44 00; www.graahundbus.dk) Operates between Copenhagen and Bornholm, Copenhagen and Malmö and Copenhagen and Berlin.

Thinggaard Express (☎98 11 66 00; www.expressbus.dk) Operates between Frederikshavn and Esbjerg via Viborg and Aalborg.

Car & Motorcycle

Denmark is perfect for touring by car. Roads are in good condition and well signposted. Traffic is manageable, even in major cities such as Copenhagen (rush hours excepted). Denmark's extensive network of ferries carries motor vehicles for reasonable rates. It's always a good idea for drivers to call ahead and make reservations, especially in the summer.

CAR HIRE

The following applies when renting a car:
» You must be 21.
» You must have a valid home driving licence.
» You must have a major credit card.
» You may need to supply a passport.
» Independent local companies are often much cheaper than the international

chains, but the big companies offer one-way rentals.

» You may get the best deal by booking through an international rental agency before you arrive. Be sure to ask for promotional rates.

» Ensure you get a deal covering unlimited kilometres.

» Check car-rental websites for special online deals.

» Drivers aged 21 to 25 may need to pay an additional 'young driver fee'.

Car-hire companies in Denmark:

Avis (www.avis.com)

Europcar (www.europcar.com)

Hertz (www.hertzdk.dk)

ROAD RULES

» Drive on the right-hand side of the road.

» The use of seatbelts is mandatory.

» Cars and motorcyles must have dipped headlights on at all times.

» Motorcyclists (but not cyclists) must wear helmets.

» Speed limits: 50km/h in towns and built-up areas, 80km/h on major roads, 110km/h or 130km/h on motorways.

» The legal blood-alcohol limit is 0.05%.

» Using a hand-held mobile phone while driving is illegal; hands-free use is permitted.

» Use of a parking disc (P-skive) is usually required. Resembling a clock, the device is placed on the dashboard to indicate the time of arrival at a car-parking space. Discs are commonly available at petrol stations and tourist offices.

Train

With the exception of a few short private lines, **Danish State Railways** (DSB; www.dsb. dk) runs all Danish train services. Overall, train travel in Denmark is not expensive, in large part because distances are short.

Reservations During morning and evening peak times, it's advisable to make reservations (Dkr30) if travelling on the speedy InterCityLyn (ICL) and Intercity (IC) trains.

Discounts and Passes People aged 65 and older are entitled to a 25% discount on Friday and Sunday and a 50% discount on other days. Children under the age of 12 years usually travel for free if accompanied by an adult, and one adult can bring two children for free.

Finland

Best Places to Eat

» Musta Lammas (p177)

» Olo (p138)

» Figaro (p174)

» Tuulensuu (p161)

» Huvila (p171)

Best Places to Stay

» Lossiranta Lodge (p169)

» Dream Hostel (p161)

» Lumihotelli (p193)

» Hotel Fabian (p135)

» Hotel Kantarellis (p165)

Why Go?

There's something pure in the Finnish air and a spirit that's incredibly vital and exciting. It's an invitation to get out and active year-round. A postsauna dip in an ice hole under the majestic aurora borealis (Northern Lights), after whooshing across the snow behind a team of huskies, isn't a typical winter's day just anywhere. And canoeing or hiking under the midnight sun through pine forests populated by wolves and bears isn't your typical tanning-oil summer either.

Although socially and economically in the vanguard of nations, large parts of Finland remain gloriously remote; trendsetting modern Helsinki is counterbalanced by vast forested wildernesses elsewhere.

Nordic peace in lakeside cottages, summer sunshine on convivial beer terraces, avant-garde design, dark melodic music and cafes warm with baking aromas are other facets of Suomi (Finnish) seduction. As are the independent, loyal, warm and welcoming Finns, who tend to do their own thing and are much the better for it.

When to Go
Helsinki

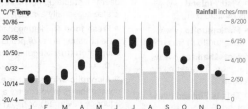

| **Mar** There's still plenty of snow, but enough daylight to enjoy winter sports. | **Jul** Everlasting daylight, countless festivals and discounted accommodation. | **Sep** The stunning colours of the *ruska* (autumn) season make this prime hiking time up north. |

AT A GLANCE

» **Capital** Helsinki

» **Area** 338,145 sq km

» **Population** 5.4 million

» **Country code** ☑358

» **Languages** Finnish, Swedish and Sámi languages

» **Currency** euro (€)

Exchange Rates

Australia	A$1	€0.73
Canada	C$1	€0.71
Japan	¥100	€0.83
New Zealand	NZ$1	€0.54
UK	UK£1	€1.12
USA	US$1	€0.67

Set Your Budget

» **Budget hotel room** €70

» **Two-course evening meal** €40

» **Museum entrance** €7

» **Beer** €6

» **City transport ticket** €3

Resources

» **Visit Finland** (www.visitfinland.com)

» **Matkahuolto** (www.matkahuolto.fi) Bus travel.

» **Metsähallitus** (www.outdoors.fi) Great hiking resource.

» **This is Finland** (www.finland.fi) Informative and entertaining.

» **VR** (www.vr.fi) Train travel.

Connections

Road connections with Norway and Sweden are way up north, but ferries are big on the Baltic; an overnight boat can take you to Stockholm or even as far as Germany. Helsinki's harbour also offers quick and easy connections to Tallinn in Estonia, launch pad for the Baltic states and Eastern Europe. Finland's also a springboard for Russia, with boat, bus and train services available, some visa-free.

ITINERARIES

One Week

Helsinki demands at least a couple of days and is a good base for a day trip to Tallinn (Estonia) or Porvoo. In summer, head to the eastern Lakeland and explore Lappeenranta, Savonlinna and Kuopio; catch a lake ferry between the latter towns). In winter, take an overnight train or budget flight to Lapland (Rovaniemi) for a few days, visiting Santa, exploring Sámi culture and mushing with the huskies. A Helsinki–Savonlinna–Kuopio–Rovaniemi–Helsinki route is a good option.

Two Weeks

Spend a few days in Helsinki and Porvoo, visit the harbour town of Turku and lively Tampere. Next stops are Savonlinna and Kuopio in the beautiful eastern Lakeland. Head up to Rovaniemi, and perhaps as far north as Inari. You could also fit in a summer festival, some hiking in Lapland or North Karelia, or a quick cycling trip to Åland.

Essential Food & Drink

» **Coffee** To fit in, eight or nine cups a day is about right, best accompanied with a cardamom-flavoured pastry.

» **Offbeat meats** Unusual meats appear on menus: reindeer is a staple up north, elk is commonly eaten, and bear is also seasonally available.

» **Fresh food** The kauppahalli (market hall) is where to go for a stunning array of produce. In summer, stalls at the kauppatori (market square) sell delicious fresh vegetables and fruit.

» **Alcoholic drinks** Beer is a staple. Finns also love dissolving things in vodka; try a shot of *salmiakkikossu* (salty-liquorice flavoured) or *fisu* (Fisherman's Friend–flavoured).

» **Fish** Salmon is ubiquitous; tasty lake fish include arctic char, pike-perch and scrumptious fried *muikku* (vendace).

Finland Highlights

1 Immerse yourself in harbourside **Helsinki** (p130), creative melting pot for the latest in Finnish design and nightlife

2 Marvel at the shimmering lakescapes of handsome **Savonlinna** (p169), and see top-quality opera in its medieval castle

3 Cruise Lakeland waterways, gorge on tiny fish, and sweat it out in the huge smoke sauna at **Kuopio** (p174)

4 Cross the Arctic Circle, hit the awesome Arktikum museum, and visit Santa in his official grotto at **Rovaniemi** (p188)

5 Trek the Bear's Ring Trail in the **Oulanka National Park** (p188)

6 Learn about Sámi culture and reindeer at **Inari** (p195)

7 Cycle the picturesque islands of the **Åland archipelago** (p153)

8 Check out the quirky museums of **Tampere** (p157)

9 Take an unusual pub crawl around the offbeat watering holes of **Turku** (p147)

10 Crunch out a shipping lane aboard an ice-breaker and spend a night in the ethereal Snow Castle at **Kemi** (p193)

HELSINKI

♪09 / POP 596,200

It's fitting that harbourside Helsinki, capital of a country with such a watery geography, melds so graciously into the Baltic Sea. Half the city seems to be liquid, and the tortured writhing of the complex coastline includes any number of bays, inlets and a smattering of islands.

Though Helsinki can seem like a younger sibling to other Scandinavian capitals, it's the one that went to art school, scorns pop music, is working in a cutting-edge design studio and hangs out with friends who like black and plenty of piercings. The city's design shops are legendary and its music and pub scene kicking.

On the other hand, much of what is lovable in Helsinki is older. Its understated yet glorious art nouveau buildings, the spacious elegance of its centenarian cafes, the careful preservation of Finnish heritage in its dozens of museums, and restaurants that have changed neither menu nor furnishings since the 1930s are all part of the city's quirky charm.

Like all of Finland, though, Helsinki has a dual nature. In winter, although it still hums along with skaters, cafe chat and cultural life, you can sometimes wonder where all the people are. In spring and summer they are back again, though, packing green spaces and outdoor tables to get a piece of blessed sun, whirring around on thousands of bicycles, and revving the city's nightlife into overdrive.

History

Helsinki (Swedish: Helsingfors) was founded in 1550 by the Swedish king Gustav Vasa, who hoped to compete with the Hanseatic trading port of Tallinn across the water. In the 18th century the Swedes built a mammoth fortress on the nearby island of Suomenlinna, but it wasn't enough to keep the Russians out. Once the Russians were in control of Finland, they needed a capital closer to home than the Swedish-influenced west coast. Helsinki was it, and took Turku's mantle in 1812. Helsinki grew rapidly, with German architect CL Engel responsible for many noble central buildings. In the bitter postwar years, the 1952 Olympic Games symbolised the city's gradual revival.

⊙ Sights

Kauppatori
SQUARE

Finnish cities are traditionally centred on their market squares; Helsinki's sits right by the passenger harbour in the old part of town. It's a forum for selling fish fresh off the boats, as well as other fresh garden produce and seasonal berries. Check out the fountain and mermaid **Havis Amanda statue**, a symbol of Helsinki. Nearby, the Vanha Kauppahalli (p140) is a classic Finnish market hall.

Tuomiokirkko
CHURCH

(Lutheran Cathedral; www.helsinginseurakunnat.fi; Unioninkatu 29; ⊙9am-6pm) Presiding over Senate Sq just north of the kauppatori, chalk white neoclassical Tuomiokirkko was designed by CL Engel but not completed until 1852, 12 years after his death. Its interior is fairly unadorned, unlike the red-brick Uspenskin Katedraali on nearby Katajanokka island.

HELSINKI IN...

One Day

Finns are the world's biggest coffee drinkers, so first up it's a caffeine shot with a cardamom *pulla* (bun) at one of the centre's classic cafes. Then down to the **kauppatori** (market square), and the fresh produce in the adjacent **kauppahalli** market building. Put a picnic together and boat out to the island fortress of **Suomenlinna**. Back in town, check out the **Tuomiokirkko** and nearby **Uspenski Katedraali**. Then take the metro to legendary **Kotiharjun Sauna** for a predinner sweat. Eat traditional Finnish at **Kuu** or **Sea Horse**.

Two Days

Investigate the art and design scene. Head to the **Ateneum** for a perspective on the Golden Age of Finnish painting, and then see contemporary works at still-iconic **Kiasma**. Feet tired? Catch the **No 3 tram** for a circular sightseeing trip around town, before browsing some of the design shops around **Punavuori**. In the evening head up to the **Ateljee Bar** for great views and on to **Tavastia & Semifinal** for a rock gig.

Uspenskin Katedraali
CHURCH

(Uspenski Cathedral; www.ort.fi; Kanavakatu 1; ⊙9.30am-4pm Tue-Fri, to 2pm Sat, noon-3pm Sun) Tuomiokirkko and Uspenskin Katedraali face each other high above the city like two queens on a theological chessboard. Built as a Russian Orthodox church in 1868, Uspenskin features onion-topped domes and now serves the Finnish Orthodox congregation. The high, square interior has a lavish iconostasis.

Kiasma
GALLERY

(www.kiasma.fi; Mannerheiminaukio 2; adult/child €10/free; ⊙10am-5pm Sun & Tue, to 8.30pm Wed & Thu, to 10pm Fri, to 6pm Sat) Now just one of a series of elegant contemporary buildings in this part of town, curvaceous and quirky metallic Kiasma, designed by Steven Holl and finished in 1998, is still a symbol of the city's modernisation. It exhibits an eclectic collection of Finnish and international modern art and keeps people on their toes with its striking contemporary exhibitions. The interior, with its unexpected curves and perspectives, is as invigorating as the outside.

Kiasma's outstanding success is due to the fact that it's been embraced by the people of Helsinki. Its sleek, glass-sided cafe and terrace are hugely popular, locals sunbathe on the grassy fringes, and skateboarders perform aerobatics under the stern gaze of Mannerheim's statue outside.

Ateneum
GALLERY

(www.ateneum.fi; Kaivokatu 2; adult/child €12/free; ⊙10am-6pm Tue & Fri, to 8pm Wed & Thu, 11am-5pm Sat & Sun) The top floor of Finland's premier art gallery is an ideal crash course in the nation's art. It houses Finnish paintings and sculptures from the Golden Age of the late 19th century through to the 1950s' including works by Albert Edelfelt, Hugo Simberg, Helene Schjerfbeck, the Von Wright brothers and Pekka Halonen. Pride of place goes to the prolific Akseli Gallen-Kallela's triptych from the *Kalevala* (Finland's national epic) depicting Väinämöinen's pursuit of the maiden Aino. There's also a small but interesting collection of 19th- and early-20th-century foreign art. Downstairs is a cafe, good bookshop and reading room.

Kansallismuseo
MUSEUM

(www.kansallismuseo.fi; Mannerheimintie 34; adult/child €8/free; ⊙11am-6pm Tue-Sun) The impressive National Museum, built in National Romantic style in 1916, looks a bit like a Gothic church with its heavy stonework and tall square tower. This is Finland's premier historical museum and is divided into rooms covering different periods of Finnish history, including prehistory and archaeological finds, church relics, ethnography and changing cultural exhibitions. It's a very thorough, old-style museum – you might have trouble selling this one to the kids – but it provides a comprehensive overview. Admission is free from 4pm on Fridays.

Temppeliaukion Kirkko
CHURCH

(www.helsinginseurakunnat.fi; Lutherinkatu 3; ⊙10am-5.45pm Mon-Sat, 11.45am-5.45pm Sun Jun-Sep, 10am-5pm Mon-Sat, 11.45am-5pm Sun Oct-May) The Temppeliaukio church, designed by Timo and Tuomo Suomalainen in 1969, remains one of Helsinki's foremost attractions. Hewn into solid stone, it feels close to a Finnish ideal of spirituality in nature – you could be in a rocky glade were it not for the stunning 24m-diameter roof covered in 22km of copper stripping. There are regular concerts, with great acoustics.

Seurasaaren Ulkomuseo
MUSEUM

(www.seurasaari.fi; adult/child €8/2.50; ⊙11am-5pm Jun-Aug, 9am-3pm Mon-Fri, 11am-5pm Sat-Sun late May & early Sep) The peaceful, forested island of Seurasaari, northwest of the centre, is home to this sprawling open-air folk museum with more than 80 wooden buildings from the 18th and 19th centuries. In summer, guides dressed in traditional costume demonstrate folk dancing and crafts. Seurasaari is the best place in Helsinki to see the **Midsummer bonfires**, a popular local tradition on Midsummer's Eve.

For Seurasaari, take bus 24 from central Helsinki, or tram 4 and walk.

Design Museum
MUSEUM

(www.designmuseum.fi; Korkeavuorenkatu 23; adult/child €8/free; ⊙11am-8pm Tue, to 6pm Wed-Sun Sep-May, to 6pm daily Jun-Aug) This museum has a permanent collection that looks at the roots of Finnish design in the nation's traditions and nature. It's a good introduction to the foundations of the discipline and the towering 20th-century figures that put Finland at the forefront of it. Changing exhibitions focus on contemporary designers' work.

Helsingin Kaupunginmuseo
MUSEUM

(Helsinki City Museum; www.hel.fi/kaumuseo; Sofiankatu 4; ⊙9am-5pm Mon-Fri, to 7pm Thu, 11am-5pm Sat & Sun) Just off Senate Sq, this

Helsinki

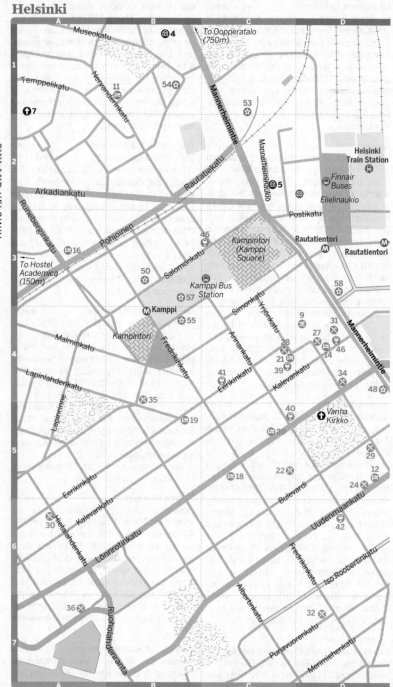

Museokatu

To Oopperatalo
(750m)

Temppelikatu

Neryandenrinkatu

11

54

7

53

Mannerheimintie

Helsinki
Train Station

Rautatiekatu

Mannerheiminaukio

5

Finnair
Buses

Elielinaukio

Arkadiankatu

Postikatu

Runeberginkatu

Pohjoinen

16

45

Kampintori
(Kamppi
Square)

Rautatientori

To Hostel
Academica
(150m)

Salomonkatu

50

Kamppi Bus
Station

57

Rautatientori

58

Kamppi

55

Simonkatu

9

31

Malminkatu

Kampintori

Fredrikinkatu

Annankatu

Yrjönkatu

28

27

46

14

Lapinlahdenkatu

41

Eerikinkatu

21

39

Kalevankatu

34

Lapinrinne

35

19

40

Vanha
Kirkko

48

20

29

18

22

12

Eerikinkatu

Kalevankatu

24

Hietalahdenkatu

Bulevardi

Uudenmaankatu

30

Lönnrotinkatu

42

Fredrikinkatu

Iso-Roobertinkatu

36

Albertinkatu

32

Ruoholahdenranta

Punavuorenkatu

Mermiehenkatu

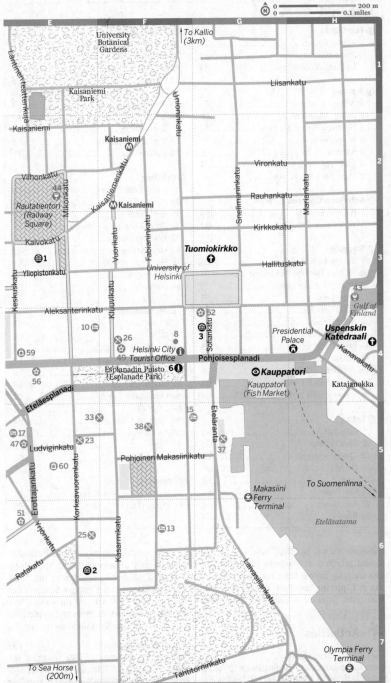

0   200 m
0   0.1 miles

University Botanical Gardens

To Kallio (3km)

Liisankatu

Kaisaniemi Park

Kaisaniemi

Lähtinen teatterikuja

Kaisaniemi

Unioninkatu

Kaisaniemi M

Vironkatu

Vilhonkatu

44

Mikonkatu

Rautatientori (Railway Square)

Kaisaniemenkatu

M **Kaisaniemi**

Snellmaninkatu

Rauhankatu

Mariankatu

Kalvokatu

Fabianinkatu

Kirkkokatu

1

Keskuskatu

Yliopistonkatu

Vuorikatu

Tuomiokirkko ✝

Hallituskatu

43

Gulf of Finland

Aleksanterinkatu

Kluuvikatu

University of Helsinki

52

Uspenskin Katedraali ✝

10

26

8

Sofiankatu

3

Presidential Palace

Kanavakatu

59

49

Helsinki City Tourist Office

Pohjoisesplanadi

◎ **Kauppatori**

56

Esplanadin Puisto (Esplanade Park) 6

Kauppatori (Fish Market)

Katajanokka

Eteläesplanadi

33

38

15

Etelaranta

17

23

37

47

Ludviginkatu

Pohjoinen Makasiinikatu

To Suomenlinna

60

Makasiini Ferry Terminal

Erottajankatu

Korkeavuorenkatu

Eteläsatama

51

Vyönkatu

25

Kasarmikatu

13

2

Ratakatu

Laivasillankatu

To Sea Horse (200m)

Tähtitorninkatu

Olympia Ferry Terminal

Helsinki

museum has an excellent collection of historical artefacts and photos backed up by entertaining information on the history of the city, piecing together Helsinki's transition from Swedish to Russian hands and into independence.

 Activities

TOP CHOICE **Kotiharjun Sauna** SAUNA
(www.kotiharjunsauna.fi; Harjutorinkatu 1; adult/child €12/6; ⏰2-9.30pm Tue-Sat,) A traditional

public wood-fired sauna dating back to 1928. These largely disappeared with the advent of shared saunas in apartment buildings, but it's a classic experience, where you can also get a scrub-down and massage. There are separate saunas for men and women. It's a short stroll from Sörnäinen metro station.

Yrjönkadun Uimahalli POOL
(Yrjönkatu 21; swimming €5-5.40, swimming plus saunas €12; ⏰men 6.30am-8pm Tue & Thu, 8am-8pm Sat, women noon-8pm Sun & Mon, 6.30am-8pm

Wed & Fri) For a sauna and swim, these art deco baths are a Helsinki institution – a fusion of soaring Nordic elegance and Roman tradition. There are separate hours for men and women. Nudity is compulsory in the saunas; bathing suits are optional in the pool.

☞ Tours

There are several cruise companies departing hourly on harbour jaunts from the kauppatori in summer. These cost between €15 and €20, with lunch buffets available for an extra €15 or so.

Leaving from near the tourist office, **Helsinki Expert** (☑2288 1500; www.helsinkiexpert. com; Pohjoisesplanadi 19; adult/child €28/15) runs multilingual 90-minute sightseeing tours in its bright-orange bus. The same company offers walking tours.

An excellent budget alternative is to catch the 3T/3B tram and pick up the free *Sightseeing on 3T/3B* brochure as your guide around the city centre and out to Kallio.

✸✸ Festivals & Events

There's something going on in Helsinki year-round. Some of the biggies:

Vappu STUDENT
On May Day the student graduation festival is celebrated around the Havis Amanda (p130) statue, which receives a graduation cap.

Helsinki Day CITY FESTIVAL
(www.hel.fi) Celebrating the city's anniversary brings many free events to Esplanadin Puisto on 12 June.

Helsinki Festival ARTS
(Helsingin Juhlaviikot; www.helsinginjuhlaviikot.fi) From late August to early September, this arts festival features chamber music, jazz, theatre, opera and more.

Helsinki Design Week DESIGN
(www.helsinkidesignweek.com) Held over two weeks in mid-September, this has talks, exhibitions, forums, and a big design market in various Helsinki venues.

Baltic Herring Fair FOOD
(www.portofhelsinki.fi) In early October fisherfolk and chefs gather at the kauppatori to cook the time-honoured fish.

🛌 Sleeping

Bookings are advisable year-round, as there's nearly always some event or conference on. Helsinki has plenty of big, central business hotels, including the Sokos, Radisson, Scandic and Cumulus chains.

TOP CHOICE ⫸ Hotel Fabian HOTEL €€€
(☑6128 2000; www.hotelfabian.fi; Fabianinkatu 7; r around €190; ❋@) Central, but in a quiet part without the bustle of the other designer hotels, this place gets everything right. Elegant standard rooms with whimsical lighting and restrained modern design are extremely comfortable; they vary substantially in size. Higher-grade rooms add extra features and a kitchenette. There's no restaurant, but breakfast is cooked in front of you. Staff are superhelpful and seem happy to be there.

TOP CHOICE ⫸ Hotelli Helka HOTEL €€€
(☑613 580; www.helka.fi; Pohjoinen Rautatiekatu 23; s/d €153/189; P@) One of the centre's best midrange hotels, the Helka has competent, friendly staff and excellent facilities, including free parking if you can bag one of the limited spots. Best are the rooms, which smell of pine with their Artek furniture, ice-block bedside lights and print of an autumn forest that hangs over the bed and is backlit to give rooms a moody glow. You can nearly always bag it cheaper than the listed price, with big discounts at weekends and in summer.

TOP CHOICE ⫸ Hostel Academica HOSTEL €
(☑1311 4334; www.hostelacademica.fi; Hietaniemenkatu 14; dm/s/d €24/62/72; ☉Jun-Aug; P@⊠) Finnish students live well, so in

ⓘ HELSINKI CARD

The **Helsinki Card** (www.helsinkiexpert. com; adult per 24/48/72 hr €36/46/56, child €15/18/21) gives you free travel, entry to more than 50 attractions in and around Helsinki, and discounts on day tours to Porvoo and Tallinn. It's cheaper to buy it online; otherwise get it at the tourist office, hotels, R-kioskis and transport terminals. To get value for money, you'd need to pack a lot of sights in to a short time.

DON'T MISS

SUOMENLINNA

Just a 15-minute ferry ride from the kauppatori (market square), a visit to the 'fortress of Finland' is a Helsinki must-do. Set on a tight cluster of four islands connected by bridges, the Unesco World Heritage Site was originally built by the Swedes as Sveaborg in the mid-18th century. The impressive island fortress used to be a larger settlement than Helsinki but was taken by the Russians in 1808 and gradually fell into disuse.

From the main quay, a blue-signposted walking path connects the main attractions. By the bridge that connects Iso Mustasaari and the main island, Susisaari, is **Suomenlinnakeskus** (☑029-533 8410; www.suomenlinna.fi; ◷10.30am-4.30pm Oct-Apr, 10am-6pm May-Sep), which has tourist information, internet access, maps and guided walking tours. Here too is **Suomenlinna-museo** (adult/child €6.50/free; ◷10.30am-4.30pm Oct-Apr, 10am-6pm May-Sep), a two-level museum of the fortress's history.

The most atmospheric part of Suomenlinna is at the end of the blue trail, the southern end of Susisaari. Exploring the old bunkers, crumbling fortress walls and cannons will give you an insight into this fortress, and there are plenty of grassy picnic spots. In summer you can get a boat back to Helsinki from here, saving you the walk back to the main quay.

Several other museums dot the islands, including **Ehrensvärd-museo** (adult/child €3/1; ◷11am-4pm May & Sep, 11am-6pm Jun-Aug), once the home of the man responsible for designing and running the fortress; and **Vesikko** (admission €5; ◷11am-6pm Jun-Aug), a WWII-era submarine.

Ferries depart from the kauppatori in Helsinki to the main quay at Suomenlinna, also stopping at other points on the islands in summer. Tickets (return €5, 15 minutes, three times hourly, 6.20am to 2.20am) are available at the pier. In addition, **JT-Line** (www.jt-line.fi; single/return €4.50/7; ◷May–mid-Sep) runs a waterbus at least hourly from the kauppatori, making two stops on Suomenlinna.

Taking a picnic is a great way to make the most of the grass, views and (hopefully) sunshine. There are also several cafes and restaurants. At around 5.15pm it's worth finding a spot to watch the enormous Baltic ferries pass through the narrow gap.

summer take advantage of this residence, a superclean spot packed with features (pool and sauna) and cheery staff. The modern rooms are great, and all come with bar fridges and their own bathrooms. Dorms have only two to four berths so even the cheapest rooms feel uncrowded. They're also environmentally sound, offsetting all their carbon emissions among other positive steps. HI discount.

Hotel Finn HOTEL €€
(☑684 4360; www.hotellifinn.fi; Kalevankatu 3B; s/d/q €79/89/129; ☐) High in a perfectly located, central city building, this small, friendly hotel is great value for Helsinki if you don't expect luxury. The corridors are darkly done out in sexy chocolate and red, with art from young Finnish photographers on the walls, but rooms are bright white and blond parquet. They vary – some haven't been renovated yet. No breakfast.

GLO Hotel Kluuvi HOTEL €€€
(☑010-344 4400; www.glohotels.fi; Kluuvikatu 4; r around €205; ☀@) There are no starched suits at reception at this laid-back designer spot, and the relaxed atmosphere continues through the comfortably modish public areas to the rooms. Beds: exceptionally inviting. Facilities: top-notch and mostly free. Location: on a pedestrian street in the heart of town. Cute extra: a stuffed tiger toy atop the covers. Online prices are the best; if there's not much difference between the standard and the deluxe, go for the latter as you get quite a bit more space.

Klaus K HOTEL €€€
(☑020-770 4700; www.klauskhotel.com; Bulevardi 2; d €145-220; ☀@) Boasting excellent service and extremely comfortable beds, this central, independent design hotel has a theme of *Kalevala* quotes throughout, and easy-on-the-eye space-conscious architecture.

Free fast wi-fi and other amenities ease the stay, but the best bit is the fabulous breakfast, with all sorts of original and tasty morsels sourced from small Finnish producers. Room prices vary substantially according to demand – book well ahead and you can get good bargains.

Hotel Haven
HOTEL €€€

(✆681 930; www.hotelhaven.fi; Unioninkatu 17; s/d from €179/209; P✳@🖥) The closest hotel to the kauppatori is an elegant and welcoming central choice. All room grades feature excellent beds and linen, soft colour combinations, classy toiletries, and thoughtful extras like sockets in the personal safes. 'Comfort' rooms face the street and are very spacious; higher grades give you a couple of add-ons – like a Nespresso machine in 'Lux' category –and the chance of a harbour view. There's a great bar for rum and whisky fans, a gym, bikes to use and limited (expensive) parking.

Hellsten Helsinki Parliament
APARTMENTS €€

(✆5110 5700; www.hellstenhotels.fi; Museokatu 18; studio apt €130-180; ⊙reception 8am-8pm Mon-Fri; @🖥) A good-value base, especially for families, the apartments here are in a quiet but central location and have sleek modern furnishings, kitchenette, internet connections and cable TV. Prices vary seasonally and there are discounts for longer stays. They'll give you a key code if you arrive after hours.

Rastila Camping
CAMPGROUND, COTTAGES €

(✆3107 8517; www.rastilacamping.fi; Karavaanikatu 4; campsites €14, plus per adult/child €5/1, hostel dm/s/d €21/36/62, 2- to 4-person cabins €79, cottages €107-213; P@🖥🖥) Only 20 minutes on the metro from the heart of town, in a pretty waterside location, this camping ground makes sense. As well as tent and van sites, there are wooden cabins and more upmarket log cottages, as well as a summer hostel (open mid-June to early August). There are all sorts of facilities including rowing-boat and canoe hire. Great for families.

Hostel Erottajanpuisto
HOSTEL €

(✆642 169; www.erottajanpuisto.com; Uudenmaankatu 9; dm/s/d €27/54/68; @🖥) Helsinki's smallest and most laid-back hostel occupies the top floor of a building in a lively street of bars and restaurants close to the heart of the city. Forget curfews, lockouts, school kids and bringing your own sleeping sheet – this is more like a guesthouse with (crowded) dormitories. Private rooms offer more

peace but aren't great value. Great lounge and friendly folk. HI discount.

Eurohostel
HOSTEL €

(✆622 0470; www.eurohostel.eu; Linnankatu 9; s without bathroom €45-51, d without bathroom €54-62; @) On Katajanokka Island less than 500m from the Viking Line terminal, this sizable place is busy but a bit soulless and offers both backpacker and 'hotel' rooms. The small cafe-bar serves a breakfast buffet (€7.90) and other meals, and there's a morning sauna included. There's a discount for HI members and for booking online. Tram 4 stops right alongside.

Omenahotelli
HOTEL €€

(✆0600 18018; www.omenahotels.com; r €60-120; 🖥) This staffless, keyless hotel chain is good value and has three handy Helsinki locations on **Eerikinkatu** (Eerikinkatu 24), **Lönnrotinkatu** (Lönnrotinkatu 13) and **Yrjönkatu** (Yrjönkatu 30). As well as a double bed, rooms have fold-outs that can sleep two more, plus there's a microwave and minifridge. Book online or via a terminal in the lobby.

Hostel Stadion
HOSTEL €

(✆477 8480; www.stadionhostel.fi; Pohjoinen Stadiontie 3; dm/s/d €22/42/50; P@) An easy tram ride from town, this well-equipped hostel is actually part of the Olympic Stadium. There are no views, though, and it feels old-style with big dorms and not much light-heartedness. It's the cheapest bed in town though. HI discount.

Matkamajoitus
APARTMENTS €€

(Traveller's Home; ✆044-2119 526; www.matkamajoitus.fi; Lönnrotinkatu 16D; d/q €99/125) These guys kit you out with a fully furnished apartment somewhere in the city centre so you'll feel like you're living in Helsinki. Some are better than others; you may have to walk

---

FINLAND HELSINKI

SCANDINAVIA? NOT US!

Despite its proximity, Finland isn't actually geographically part of Scandinavia, and Finns will be quick to remind you of the fact. Technically, Scandinavia refers to the Scandinavian peninsula (Norway plus Sweden) along with Denmark. Linguistically, Scandinavia includes Iceland, the Faroe Islands and Swedish-speaking Finns, while the term Nordic countries is a more general term for all these lands.

ALEXIS KOUROS, FILM MAKER & FOUNDING EDITOR OF THE HELSINKI TIMES

What Finnish film would you recommend? People could watch a couple of the Kaurismäki brothers' movies. Aki has *Man Without a Past*, for example, which won a prize at the Cannes festival. His films are always a bit exaggerated, like a sort of carica-ture of Finnish society. But that sort of exaggerated view that gives you an idea about the Finnish people's shyness.

Favourite building in Helsinki? My favourite building is the Temppeliaukion Kirkko, which is a round church built into the environment which is basically a big hill with stones. It's a fantastic building and I really am amazed that the church authorities let it happen, because the roundness is pointing back to the pagan religions before Christianity.

For Finnish food? In the summertime there are some tents in the kauppatori (market square) which will give you an assortment of fish, potatoes, these kind of things. Those are really very typically Finnish. Then there is a newish restaurant called Juuri, with Finnish tapas: *sapas*.

For design shopping? Well, there is a design district, which goes from the centre of the city towards Punavuori. It evolves all the time, and there are always new shops. Lots of Finnish design.

Helsinki in one word? One word! I would say fresh. From the top of my head.

a while from the office, which is open only from 2pm to 6pm.

🍴 Eating

Helsinki has by far the nation's best range of restaurants, whether for Finnish classics, new Suomi cuisine or international food. Good budget options are in shorter sup-ply but lunch specials are available in most places and there are plenty of self-catering opportunities.

TOP CHOICE Olo   MODERN FINNISH €€€
(☑665 565; Kasarmikatu 44; lunch/dinner menus from €33/59; ☺11.30am-1.30pm Mon, 11.30am-1.30pm & 5-9.30pm Tue-Fri, 5-9pm Sat) Casual street surveys always seem to flag this up as Helsinki's favourite restaurant. It's one of ours too. Despite the quality, Olo is refresh-ingly unpretentious with a dining room of muted greys and whites. All meals come with house-baked breads (try the fruity malt) and the wine list is broad enough to appeal to all palates.

TOP CHOICE Kuu   FINNISH €€
(☑2709 0973; www.ravintolakuu.info; Töölönkatu 27; mains €15-25; ☺11am-midnight Mon-Fri, from 1pm Sat, 1-10pm Sun) Tucked away on a cor-ner behind the Crowne Plaza hotel on Man-nerheimintie, this is an excellent choice for traditional Finnish fare given a confident

modern touch and served in an upbeat bistro atmosphere. Salmon is smoked to order, the staff are eager to explain every dish, and there's a general ambience of good cheer. Prices are very reasonable for the quality on offer. Don't confuse this spot with another (good) place, Kuu Kuu, not far away.

Zucchini   VEGETARIAN €
(Fabianinkatu 4; lunch €7-11; ☺11am-4pm Mon-Fri; ☑) One of the city's few vegetarian cafes, this is a top-notch lunchtime spot; queues out the door are not unusual. Piping-hot soups banish winter chills, and fresh-baked quiche on the sunny terrace out the back is a summer treat.

Demo   MODERN FINNISH €€€
(☑2289 0840; www.restaurantdemo.fi; Uuden-maankatu 9; mains €32-41; ☺4-11pm Tue-Sat) Book to get a table at this chic spot, where young chefs wow a designer-y crowd with modern Finnish cuisine. The quality is excellent, the combinations innovative, the presentation top-notch and the slick contemporary decor appropriate. A place to be seen, but not a place for quiet contemplation.

Kitchen & Co   FINNISH €€
(☑010-322 2940; www.kitchenco.fi; Yrjönkatu 18; mains €21-28; ☺11am-3pm Mon, to 11pm Tue-Fri, 4-11pm Sat, closed first half Jul) The high ceilings in this stylish conversion of a noble, old,

central building mean minimal noise, so it's a sound bet for a romantic dinner. Quality Finnish ingredients, including recommended organic beef, are presented with French-style sauces. Excellent, friendly service backs up an impressive package.

KarlJohan FINNISH €€

(☑612 1121; www.ravintolakarljohan.fi; Yrjönkatu 21; mains €21-24; ⊙11am-3pm Mon, 11am-3pm & 5-11pm Tue-Fri, 2-11pm Sat) Welcoming service and an elegant but relaxed atmosphere provide a fitting backdrop for carefully prepared Finnish cuisine that's strong on both local fish dishes and rich, delicious meat options. The central location is another plus point. Wines are rather pricey.

Chez Dominique FRENCH €€€

(☑612 7393; www.chezdominique.fi; Rikhardinkatu 4; mains €60, set menus €99-145; ⊙6pm-midnight Tue, 11.30am-2pm & 6pm-midnight Wed-Fri, noon-3pm & 6pm-midnight Sat) Helsinki's most renowned restaurant is still one of its best. The focus these days is increasingly on its degustation menus, which present quality Finnish fare alongside French gourmet morsels and avant-garde combinations. The à la carte options have a more traditionally Gallic feel. There's an excellent wine list, with various matched suites available to accompany the set menus.

Juuri MODERN FINNISH €€€

(☑635 732; www.juuri.fi; Korkeavuorenkatu 27; mains €25-27; ⊙11am-2.30pm & 4-10pm Mon-Fri, noon-10pm Sat, 3-10pm Sun) Creative takes on classic Finnish ingredients draw the crowds to this stylish modern restaurant, but the best way to eat is to sample the *sapas*, which are tapas with a Suomi twist (€4.50 a plate). You might graze marinated fish, smoked beef or homemade sausages. It also operates a wholefoods shop with takeaway salad and sandwiches next door.

Sea Horse FINNISH €€

(☑010-837 5700; www.seahorse.fi; Kapteeninkatu 11; mains €16-22; ⊙10.30am-midnight) Sea Horse dates back to the '30s and is as traditional a Finnish restaurant as you'll find anywhere. Locals gather in the gloriously unchanged interior to meet and drink over hefty dishes of Baltic herring, Finnish meatballs and cabbage rolls.

Café Bar 9 CAFE €

(www.bar9.net; Uudenmaankatu 9; mains €8-14; ⊙kitchen 11am-11pm Mon-Fri, from noon Sat & Sun)

It's tough to find low-priced food at dinnertime in Helsinki that's not shaved off a spinning stick, so this place stands out. It would anyway, with its retro red formica tables and unpretentious artsy air. Plates vary, with some solid Finnish fare backed up by big sandwiches, Thai-inspired stir-fries and pasta. Portions are generous so don't overdo it: you can always come back.

Kosmos FINNISH €€

(☑647 255; www.kosmos.fi; Kalevankatu 3; mains €19-32; ⊙11.30-1am Mon-Fri, from 4pm Sat, closed Jul) Designed by Alvar Aalto, and with a bohemian, artsy history, this place is a Helsinki classic. It combines a staid, very traditionally Finnish atmosphere with tasty not-very-modern dishes including tasty reindeer options. If you think you'll like an authentic pre-war ambience, you'll love it here.

Lupolo GASTROPUB €

(☑050-554 4050; www.lupolo.fi; Punavuorenkatu 3; dishes €8-12; ⊙11.30am-2pm, 5-11pm Tue-Fri, 5-11pm Sat; ☑) Fashionably retro with a modern twist, this compact Punavuori eatery is a favourite of the barrio's bohemian young design crowd. The chef turns out a nice line in well-prepared fusion cookery, accompanied by a range of tasty bottled beers and ciders from around the world. Portions are on the small side, so you might want to order three dishes between two or go for the tasting menu (€45).

Salve FINNISH €€

(☑010-766 4280; www.ravintolasalve.fi; Hietalahdenranta 11; mains €16-28; ⊙10am-midnight Mon-Sat, 10am-11pm Sun) Down by the water in the west of town, this centenarian establishment has long been a favourite of nautical types, and has appropriately high-seas decor, with paintings of noble ships on the walls. They serve great Finnish comfort food like meatballs, fried Baltic herring and steaks in substantial quantities. The atmosphere is warm and the service kindly.

Konstan Möljä FINNISH €

(☑694 7504; www.konstanmolja.fi; Hietalahdenkatu 14; lunch/dinner buffet €8.70/18; ⊙11am-2.30pm & 5-10pm Tue-Fri, 4-10pm Sat) The maritime interior of this old sailors' eatery hosts an impressive husband-and-wife team who turn out a great-value Finnish buffet for lunch and dinner. Though these days it sees plenty of tourists, it provides solid traditional fare with salmon, soup, reindeer and friendly explanations of what goes with what. There's also à la carte available. It tends to close for a month or so in summer, so ring ahead to check it's open.

Ravintola Martta
FINNISH €€

(www.ravintolamartta.fi; Lapinlahdenkatu 3; lunches €8-10, mains €19-25; ⊙11am-3pm Mon, to 10pm Tue-Fri, 4-10pm Sat) One of the best-value lunch stops around, Martta is run by a historic women's organisation. The light, bright dining room is matched by the tasty, wholesome food.

Orchid Thai Restaurant
THAI €

(www.thaimaalainenravintola.fi; Yrjönkatu 15; mains €13-19; ⊙11am-3pm Mon, to 11pm Tue-Thu, to midnight Fri, noon-midnight Sat, 2-8pm Sun; 🖉) In a new, larger location, this reliably good Helsinki Thai eatery does good-value lunch deals and tasty curries, stir-fries and soups. Rice is included in the cost of a main dish. There's even a weekend karaoke bar here too.

Kitch
CAFE €€

(www.kitch.fi; Yrjönkatu 30; mains €14-22; ⊙11am-10pm Mon & Tue, to 11pm Wed-Fri, noon-11pm Sat; 🖉) Handily located in a central area, this place offers good-value lunches as well as tapas portions (€4 to €8), original salads and decent burgers. Most of the produce is sustainably sourced.

Karl Fazer
CAFE €

(www.fazer.fi; Kluuvikatu 3; light meals €4-11; ⊙7.30am-10pm Mon-Fri, 9am-10pm Sat, 10am-6pm Sun) This classic cafe can feel a little cavernous, but it's the flagship for the mighty confectionery empire of the same name. The cupola famously reflects sound, so locals say it's a bad place to gossip. It is ideal, however, for buying delicious Fazer chocolates, fresh bread, sandwiches and light meals or enjoying the towering sundaes or slabs of cake.

Tin Tin Tango
CAFE €

(www.tintintango.info; Töölöntorinkatu 7; light meals €7-10; ⊙7am-midnight Mon-Thu, to 2am Fri, 9am-2am Sat, 10am-midnight Sun) This buzzy neighbourhood cafe decorated with prints from the quiffed Belgian's adventures has a bit of everything. There's a laundry and a sauna (handy if you need to wash your only pair of jeans), as well as cosy tables to sip a drink or get to grips with delicious rolls absolutely stuffed full. The welcoming, low-key

bohemian vibe is the real draw, though. It's on a square a block west of Mannerheimintie some 750m north of Kiasma.

Café Ekberg
CAFE €

(www.cafeekberg.fi; Bulevardi 9; lunches €9-10; ⊙7.30am-7pm Mon-Fri, 8.30am-5pm Sat, 9am-5pm Sun) There's been a bakery of this name in Helsinki since 1852, and today it continues to be a family-run place renowned for its pastries such as the Napoleon cake. Its buffet breakfasts and lunches are also popular, and there is fresh bread to take away.

Quick Eats & Self-Catering

In summer there are food stalls, fresh produce and berries at the kauppatori (p130).

TOP CHOICE Vanha Kauppahalli
MARKET €

(www.wanhakauppahalli.fi; Eteläranta 1; ⊙8am-6pm Mon-Fri, to 5pm Sat, plus 10am-4pm Sun Jun-Aug; 🖉) Near the kauppatori, this traditional market hall was built in 1889. Some of it is touristy these days (reindeer kebabs?) but it's still a glorious place full of picnic treats like filled rolls, cheeses, breads, smoked fish and an array of other Finnish snacks and delicacies. There are several places serving good, cheap light meals here too.

Hakaniemen Kauppahalli
MARKET €

(www.hakaniemenkauppahalli.fi; ⊙8am-6pm Mon-Fri, 8am-4pm Sat; 🖉) The fabulous traditional market hall by Hakaniemi metro station is less visited by tourists. Here you'll find some great salmon-on-rye sandwiches.

Soppakeittiö
SOUP BAR €

(www.sopakeittio.fi; Vanha Kauppahalli; soups €8-9; ⊙lunch Mon-Sat) A great place to warm the cockles in winter. There's another branch at Hakaniemen Kauppahalli.

🍷 Drinking

Helsinki has some of Scandinavia's most diverse nightlife. In winter locals gather in cosy bars, while in summer early-opening beer terraces sprout all over town.

The centre is full of bars and clubs, with the Punavuori area around Iso-Roobertinkatu one of the most worthwhile for trendy alternative choices. For the cheapest beer in Helsinki (under €3 a pint during the seemingly perpetual happy hours), hit working-class Kallio (near Sörnäinen metro station), north of the centre.

Teerenpeli TOP CHOICE
PUB

(www.teerenpeli.com; Olavinkatu 2; ⊘noon-2am Mon-Thu, to 3am Fri & Sat, 3pm-midnight Sun) Get away from the Finnish lager mainstream with this excellent pub right by the bus station. It serves very tasty ales, stouts and berry ciders from a microbrewery in Lahti in a long, split-level place with romantically low lighting, intimate tables, and an indoor smokers' patio. A top spot.

Bar Loose
BAR

(www.barloose.com; Annankatu 21; ⊘4pm-2am Mon & Tue, to 4am Wed-Sat, 6pm-4am Sun) The opulent blood red interior and comfortably cosy seating seem too stylish for a rock bar, but this is what this is, with portraits of guitar heroes lining one wall and an eclectic mix of people filling the upstairs, served by two bars. Downstairs is a club area, with live music more nights than not and DJs spinning everything from metal to retro-mod classics.

A21 Cocktail Lounge
COCKTAIL BAR

(☏040-021 1921; www.a21.fi; Annankatu 21; ⊘6pm-2am Wed & Thu, to 3am Fri & Sat) You'll need to ring the doorbell to get into this chic place but it's worth the intrigue to swing with Helsinki's arty set. The interior is sumptuous in gold, but the real lushness is in the cocktails, particularly the Finnish blends that toss Lakka (cloudberry liqueur) and rhubarb to create the city's most innovative tipples.

Corona Bar & Kafe Moskova
BAR

(www.andorra.fi; Eerikinkatu 11-15; ⊘Corona 11am-2am Mon-Sat, noon-2am Sun, Moskova 6pm-2am Mon-Sat, Roska 10pm-4am daily) Those offbeat film-making Kaurismäki brothers are up to their old tricks with this pair of conjoined drinking dens. Corona plays the relative straight man with pool tables and cheap beer, while Moskova is back in the USSR with a bubbling samovar and Soviet vinyl. At closing they clear the place out by playing Brezhnev speeches. But wait, there's more: Dubrovnik, in the same complex, does regular live jazz, and separate Roska ('rubbish'), downstairs, is completely decorated in recycled materials.

Majakkalaiva Relandersgrund
BOAT BAR

(Pohjoisranta; ⊘noon-10pm or later May–mid-Oct) The deck of this elegant old lightship provides a fabulous and unusual venue for a coffee, beer or cider on a sunny afternoon.

Kokomo Tikibar
COCKTAIL BAR

(www.kokomo.fi; Uudenmaankatu 16; ⊘11am-9pm Mon-Tue, to 11pm Wed, to midnight Thu, to 4am Fri, 1pm-4am Sat, 1-9pm Sun) Appended to a Pacific-themed restaurant, this small bamboo-lined lounge is a relaxing hang-out for some upbeat and expertly mixed fruity cocktails (€8 to €10). You'll feel positively tropical until you step out into the biting winter wind again. Once the food's done, they crank up the music and open the less-inspiring dancefloor area out the back. It's more romantic before that happens.

Ateljee Bar
BAR

(www.ateljeebar.fi; Yrjönkatu 26, Sokos Hotel Torni; ⊘2pm-1am Mon-Thu, to 2am Fri, noon-2am Sat, 2pm-midnight Sun) It's worth heading up to this tiny perch on the roof of the Sokos Hotel Torni for the city panorama. Take the lift to the 12th floor, then there's a narrow spiral staircase to the top. Downstairs, the summer courtyard Tornin Piha is a cute little terrace with good wines by the glass.

U Kaleva
PUB

(www.ukaleva.fi; Kalevankatu 3A; ⊘2pm-2am) Part of a knot of bars on this street just off Mannerheimintie in the heart of town, this unpretentious place stands out for its old-time Finnish atmosphere, cordial owners, eclectic local crowd and heated terrace.

Pub Tram Spårakoff
PUB TRAM

(www.koff.net; adult/child €8/4; ⊘departs hourly 2-3pm & 5-8pm Tue-Sat mid-May–Aug) Not sure whether to go sightseeing or booze the day away? Do both in this bright-red pub tram, the tipsy alternative to traditional tours around town. Departs from Mikonkatu, east of the train station.

Roskapankki
PUB

(Helsinginkatu 20; ⊘9am-2am) There's a string of earthy local pubs along Helsinginkatu, such as this grungy local favourite – the name of which means 'trash bank'.

☆ Entertainment

Clubs

Helsinki has a dynamic club scene; some nights have age limits, most commonly 20 or 22.

Tiger
CLUB

(www.thetiger.fi; Urho Kekkosen katu 1A; admission €10; ⊘10pm-4am Fri-Sun) Ascend into clubbing heaven at this superslick club with

FINLAND HELSINKI

stellar lighting and high-altitude cocktails. Music runs from chart hits to R&B; drinks are expensive but the view from the terrace is stunning. Entrance via Kamppi Sq.

Kuudes Linja
CLUB
(www.kuudeslinja.com; Hämeentie 13; entry from €8; ☺10pm-4am Wed-Sat) Between Hakaniemi and Sörnäinen metro stops, this is the place to find Helsinki's more experimental beats from top visiting DJs playing techno, industrial, postrock and electro. There are also live gigs.

Cuba! Cafe
CLUB
(☑050-505 0425; www.cubacafe.fi; Erottajankatu 4; ☺5pm-midnight Tue, to 2am Wed & Thu, to 4am Fri & Sat) Certainly one of Helsinki's brighter bars, this place doesn't take itself too seriously. Beers, cocktails and dancing – on the tables once the mojitos start flowing – are the order of the night in this party place; it packs out, but you'll hear more Suomi pop than salsa. There's no cover charge except the cloakroom fee (€2.50).

Teatteri
CLUB
(www.royalravintolat.com; Pohjoisesplanadi 2; ☺to 1am Mon-Thu, to 4am Fri & Sat) Occupying part of the stylish Swedish Theatre building, this club has three floors of fun, from the sophisticated Long Bar, with its modernist paintings and web-spun light fixtures, to the summer-swelling terraces. It gets an older, more relaxed crowd and can be packed on weekends.

Cinemas
Cinemas in Helsinki show original versions with Finnish and Swedish subtitles.

Kino Engel
CINEMA
(☑020-155 5801; www.cinemamondo.fi; Sofiankatu 4; adults €9) This independent theatre shows art-house and Finnish indie film.

FinnKino
CINEMA
(☑0600 007 007; www.finnkino.fi; adult €8-17) Operates several Helsinki cinemas with big-name films; there are branches at Tennispalatsi (Salomonkatu 15) and Maxim (Kluuvikatu 1). It's substantially cheaper midweek.

Gay & Lesbian
Helsinki has a low-key but solid gay scene. Check out www.gayfinland.fi for more listings.

DTM
GAY
(www.dtm.fi; Mannerheimintie 6; ☺9pm-4am) Finland's most famous gay venue (Don't Tell Mama) now occupies smart new premises in an very out-of-the-closet location on the city's main street. There are various club nights with variable entry fees.

Hugo's Room
GAY
(www.roombar.fi; Iso Roobertinkatu 3; ☺noon-2am Mon-Sat, 2pm-2am Sun) This popular gay lounge bar is elegant but doesn't take itself too seriously. It's got a great streetside terrace on this always-intriguing pedestrian thoroughfare.

Theatre & Concerts
For upcoming performances, see *Helsinki This Week*, inquire at the tourist office, or check the website of ticket outlet Lippupiste (☑0600 900 900; www.lippu.fi).

TOP CHOICE Musiikkitalo
CLASSICAL MUSIC
(www.musiikkitalo.fi; Mannerheimintie 13) As cool and crisp as a gin and tonic on a glacier, this striking modern building is a great addition to central Helsinki. The interior doesn't disappoint either – the main auditorium, visible from the foyer, has stunning acoustics, particularly for symphony orchestras; some musicians have wept after playing here for the first time. There are regular classical concerts, and prices are kept low, normally around €15. The bar is a nice place to hang out for a drink.

Oopperatalo
OPERA, BALLET
(☑4030 2211; www.opera.fi; Helsinginkatu 58, Opera House; tickets from €14) Opera and ballet performances.

Live Music
Various bars and clubs around Helsinki host live bands. Big-name rock concerts and international acts often perform at Hartwall Areena.

Tavastia & Semifinal
LIVE MUSIC
(www.tavastiaklubi.fi; Urho Kekkosenkatu 4; tickets from €12; ☺8pm-late) One of Helsinki's legendary rock venues, Tavastia attracts both up-and-coming local acts and bigger international groups. There's a band every night of the week. Also check out what's on at Semifinal, the smaller venue next door (tickets €6 to €8).

Storyville
JAZZ

(www.storyville.fi; Museokatu 8; ⊙6pm-late Tue-Sat) Helsinki's number-one jazz club attracts a refined older crowd swinging to boogie-woogie, trad jazz, Dixieland and New Orleans most nights. As well as the club section (closed Tuesdays), there's a stylish bar which has a cool outside summer terrace in the park opposite. It's on a corner just south of the Kansallismuseo.

Juttutupa
JAZZ, FUSION

(www.juttutupa.com; Säästöpankinranta 6) This imposing stone building near Hakaniemi metro is one of Helsinki's top live-music bars, focusing on contemporary jazz and rock fusion. The best day is Wednesday, when there's nearly always a high-quality jazz act.

Virgin Oil Co
LIVE MUSIC, CLUB

(⊉010-766 4000; www.virginoil.fi; Mannerheimintie 5) While it does pizzas and has a cosy front bar area and weekend club, the big attraction of this central spot is the top-drawer Finnish bands it attracts on a regular basis.

Sport

Hartwall Areena
SPECTATOR SPORTS, CONCERTS

(⊉0600 900 900; www.hartwall-areena.com; Areenakuja 1) If you're around between September and April, take the opportunity to see an ice-hockey game. Big matches are played at this huge arena in Pasila, north of the centre (tram 7A or 7B). The stadium is home to Helsinki superleague side Jokerit. Tickets cost €15 to €35.

Shopping

Known for design and art, Helsinki is an epicentre of Nordic cool from fashion to the latest furniture and homewares. The central but touristy Esplanadi has the chic boutiques of Finnish classics like Marimekko, Stockmann, Aarikka and Artek. The hippest area is definitely Punavuori, with cutting-edge studios and galleries to explore.

Design Forum Finland
DESIGN

(⊉6220 810; www.designforum.fi; Erottajankatu 7; ⊙10am-7pm Mon-Fri, to 6pm Sat, noon-5pm Sun) For design, you can get some good pointers at this place, which operates a shop that hosts many designers' work. You're often better off pricewise hunting down your own bargains, though. It has regular free exhibitions downstairs. It's closed Sundays from mid-September to May.

Design District Helsinki
DESIGN

(www.designdistrict.fi) A loose confederation of innovative design shops and galleries spread through the central area, particularly between Esplanadi and Punavuori. Grab their brochure map from the tourist office.

Akateeminen Kirjakauppa
BOOKS

(www.akateeminenkirjakauppa.fi; Pohjoisesplanadi 39; ⊙9am-9pm Mon-Fri, to 6pm Sat, noon-6pm Sun) Finland's biggest bookshop has a huge travel section, maps, Finnish literature and an impressive English section.

ⓘ Information

Emergency
General Emergency (⊉112)

Internet Access

Internet access at public libraries is free. Large parts of the city centre have free wi-fi, as do many bars and cafes – some also have terminals for customers' use.

Kirjasto 10 (Elielinaukio 2G; ⊙8am-10pm Mon-Thu, to 8pm Fri, noon-6pm Sat & Sun) On the 1st floor of the main post office. Several half-hour terminals and others are bookable.

Mbar (www.mbar.fi; Mannerheimintie 22; per hr €5; ⊙9am-midnight, later Fri & Sat) In the Lasipalatsi building. Heaps of terminals and proper drinks.

Sidewalk Express (www.sidewalkexpress.com; per hr €2) There are several of these no-staff stand-up access points around town. Buy your ticket from the machine; it's valid for all of them. Handy locations include the central train station (far left as you look at the trains) and Kamppi bus station (outside the ticket office).

Medical Services

Haartman Hospital (⊉3106 3231; Haartmaninkatu 4; ⊙24hr) For emergency medical assistance.

Money

There are currency-exchange counters at the airport and ferry terminals. ATMs are plentiful in the city.

Forex (www.forex.fi; ⊙8am-8pm Mon-Fri, 9am-7pm Sat & Sun) At the train station; the best place to change cash or travellers cheques.

Post

Main post office (www.posti.fi; Mannerheiminaukio 1; ⊙8am-8pm Mon-Fri, 10am-2pm Sat & Sun) Between the bus and train stations.

Tourist Information

Helsinki City Tourist Office (⊉3101 3300; www.visithelsinki.fi; Pohjoisesplanadi 19;

ST PETERSBURG

A short side trip from Finland, beguiling St Petersburg makes a tempting destination. Russia's most outward-looking metropolis is a fascinating hybrid where one moment you can be inhaling the incense in the mosaic-heavy interior of an Orthodox church or strolling the gilded halls of a tsar's palace, the next knocking back vodka shots in a trendy bar or taking in cutting-edge contemporary art.

One of the world's premier museums and art galleries, the **Hermitage** (☑571 3420; www. hermitagemuseum.org; Dvortsovaya nab 34; adult/student/child R350/free/free; ◷10.30am-6pm Tue-Sat, to 5pm Sun) is sumptuously located in the Winter Palace. It's a scarcely believable collection of archaeological treasures and Western art which would take days to fully appreciate. Buy tickets online to avoid the frightening queues. Nearby, Nevsky Prospekt is the city's main boulevard and well worth a stroll to observe a slice of St Petersburg life. It bridges canals that criss-cross the city and takes you close to several other principal sights. The **Russian Museum** (www.rusmuseum.ru; Inzhenernaya ul 4; adult/student R300/150; ◷10am-6pm Wed & Fri-Sun, to 5pm Mon, 1-9pm Thu; MGostiny Dvor) offers a comprehensive overview of Russian art, while adjacent **Church of the Saviour on Spilled Blood** (Konyushennaya pl; adult/student R250/150, audioguide R100; ◷10am-6pm Thu-Tue; MNevsky Pr) is a multidomed dazzler with impressive interior mosaics.

The tsars' lavish lifestyle is best appreciated at one of their summer palaces outside town. The best, **Petrodvorets** (www.peterhof.ru; ul Razvodnaya 2; ◷grounds daily, individual sights vary), has a series of splendid chambers and ballrooms overlooking the sumptuously over-the-top Grand Cascade water feature.

Getting out on the water lets you appreciate St Petersburg's noble buildings along the Neva and the intricate network of canals. One of many operators, **Anglo Tourismo** (☑921-989 4722; www.anglotourismo.com; nab reki Fontanki; adult/student R600/500; MNevsky Pr) has the advantage of offering good English commentary.

◷9am-8pm Mon-Fri, to 6pm Sat & Sun mid-May–mid-Sep, 9am-6pm Mon-Fri, 10am-4pm Sat & Sun mid-Sep–mid-May) Busy multilingual office with booking desk. In summer it sends out uniformed 'Helsinki Helpers' – grab one on the street and ask away. Its website links to various useful phone apps.

❶ Getting There & Away

Small/large lockers cost €3/4 per 24 hours at the bus and train station. There are similar lockers and left-luggage counters at the ferry terminals. See the Getting There & Away sections for destinations in this chapter for more details on fares and services.

AIR There are direct flights to Helsinki from many major European cities and several intercontinental ones. There are domestic flights to some 20 Finnish cities. The airport is at Vantaa, 19km north of Helsinki.

BOAT Ferries (p491) travel to Sweden (via the Åland archipelago), Estonia, Russia, Germany and Poland from Helsinki.

There are five main terminals, three close to the centre: Katajanokka terminal is served by bus 13 and trams 2, 2V and 4, and Olympia and Makasiini terminals by trams 3B and 3T. Länsiterminaali (West Terminal) is served by bus 15, while further-afield Hansaterminaali (Vuosaari) can be reached on bus 90A.

Ferry tickets may be purchased at the terminal, from a ferry company's office (and often its website) or (in some cases) from the city tourist office. Book in advance during the high season (late June to mid-August) and for weekend travel.

BUS Regional and long-distance buses dock at underground **Kamppi Bus Station** (www.matkahuolto.fi), below the Kamppi Centre. There are services to all major towns in Finland.

TRAIN Helsinki's **train station** (rautatieasema; www.vr.fi; ◷tickets 6.30am-9.30pm) is central. It's linked to the metro (Rautatientori stop), and is a short walk from the bus station.

The train is the fastest and cheapest way to get from Helsinki to major centres: express trains run daily to Turku, Tampere, Kuopio and Lappeenranta among others, and there's a choice of day and overnight trains to Oulu, Rovaniemi and Joensuu. There are also daily trains to Russia.

❶ Getting Around

TO/FROM THE AIRPORT Bus 615 (€4.50, 30 to 45 minutes) shuttles between Vantaa airport and platform 5 at Rautatientori by the train station. Bus stops are marked with a blue sign featuring a plane. Faster Finnair buses (€6.20, 30 minutes, every 20 minutes) depart from Elielinaukio platform 30 on the other side of the train station, stopping once en route. Bus 415

The historic centre offers plenty of choice for sleeping, from the stunning designer interiors of **W Hotel** (📞610 6161; www.wstpetersburg.com; Voznesensky pr 6; r from R13,000; ❄🛜🏊; Ⓜ Admiralteyskaya) to the Italianate boutique charm of **Casa Leto** (📞812 314 6622; www.casaleto.com; Bolshaya Morskaya ul 34; s/d incl breakfast €160/225; ❄🛜; Ⓜ Nevsky Pr). One of several central 'mini-hotels', **Guest House Nevsky 3** (📞812 710 6776; www.nevsky3.ru; Nevsky pr 3; s/d incl breakfast R4700/5300; 🛜; Ⓜ Admiralteyskaya) offers excellent value. Budget travellers have **Friends Hostel** (📞812 571 0151; www.friendsplace.ru; nab kanala Griboyedova 20; dm/d R500/2500; 🛜; Ⓜ Nevsky Pr) at four distinct, appealing locations.

For restaurants, look around the side streets rather than along Nevsky Prospekt itself, which is tourist-trap territory. If you are up for a night of bar-hopping, **Dumskaya ulitsa** (Ⓜ Gostiny Dvor) has dozens of St Petersburg's hottest spots for drinking and dancing crammed into a crumbling, classical facade. St Petersburg's Kirov ballet company are world-famous, and seeing a performance in the **Mariinsky Theatre** (📞326 4141; www.mariinsky.ru; Teatralnaya pl 1; ⊙performances 7pm; Ⓜ Sadovaya/Sennaya Ploshchad) is an unforgettable experience. Book tickets online in advance.

You can travel to St Petersburg from Helsinki by air, overnight ferry (13 hours, from €55), bus (10 hours, €40) or train. The fast Allegro train does the trip in just 3½ hours (€86.10). St Petersburg is an hour ahead of Finland in summer and two in winter.

Visas are required by all. Applying in your home country is easiest; in Finland, it's best via a travel agent. Think €60 to €100 for the normal seven working days processing time, plus a hefty fee for express processing (three to four working days). You'll require a 'visa support' document – essentially an invitation that can be obtained via a hotel booking or by paying a fee to a travel agent. You can travel visa-free to St Petersburg by ferry from Helsinki, or by taking a canal cruise from Lappeenranta (maximum stay three days).

---

departs from the adjacent stand but it's slower than the other two.

Door-to-door **airport taxis** (📞0600 555 555; www.airporttaxi.fi) need to be booked the previous day before 6pm if you're leaving Helsinki (one to two people costs €29).

BICYCLE Helsinki is ideal for cycling, as it's flat and has well-marked bicycle paths. Pick up a copy of the city cycling map from the tourist office.

Greenbike (📞050 404 0400; www.greenbike.fi; Kampintori; single-speed bike per day/24hr/week €25/30/75; ⊙10am-6pm Jun-early Sep) rents out quality bikes including 24-speed hybrids.

LOCAL TRANSPORT The city's public transport system, **HSL** (www.hsl.fi) operates buses, metro and local trains, trams and the Suomenlinna ferry. The number 3 trams run a circular route around town (3B runs the eastern half, 3T the western), excellent as a cheap sightseeing tour. A one-hour ticket for any transport costs €2.70 when purchased on-board, or €2.20 when purchased in advance. The ticket allows unlimited transfers but must be validated in the stamping machine on-board when you first use it. Tram-only tickets are slightly cheaper. Day or multiday tickets (€7/10.50/14 for 24/48/72 hours) are the best option if you're in town for a short period of time. The Helsinki Card (p135) gives you free travel anywhere within Helsinki.

A ticket office at the Rautatientori metro station sell tickets and passes, as do the city's R-kiosks, K-market supermarkets and the tourist office. The *Helsinki Route Map,* available at HSL offices and the city tourist office, is an easily understood public-transport map.

SOUTH COAST

The south coast of Finland meanders east and west of Helsinki. It's a summer playground for Finnish families, with a handful of fading resort towns and the pretty bays, beaches, and convoluted islands and waterways of the southern archipelago. Medieval churches, old manors and castles show the strong influence of early Swedish settlers, and Swedish is still a majority language in some of the coastal towns.

Porvoo

📞19 / POP 49,000

A great day trip from Helsinki, charming medieval Porvoo is Finland's second-oldest town (founded in 1346). There are three distinct sections to the city: Vanha Porvoo (the Old Town), the New Town and the 19th-century Empire quarter, built Russian-style under the rule of Tsar Nicholas I of Russia.

◉ Sights

Vanha Porvoo
HISTORIC AREA

(Old Town) The old town, with its tightly clustered wooden houses, cobbled streets and riverfront setting, is one of the most picturesque in Finland. During the day, its craft shops are bustling with visitors; if you can stay the night, you'll have it more or less to yourself. The old painted buildings are spectacular in the setting sun. Crossing the old bridge to the west bank of the Porvoo River (Porvoonjoki) provides a fantastic view of the photogenic, rust-red **shore houses** lining the river bank.

Tuomiokirkko
CATHEDRAL

(www.porvoonseurakunnat.fi; ⊙10am-6pm Mon-Fri, 10am-2pm Sat, 2-5pm Sun May-Sep, 10am-2pm Tue-Sat, 2-4pm Sun Oct-Apr) The historic stone-and-timber cathedral sits atop a hill looking over the quaint Old Town. Vandalised by fire in 2006, it has been completely restored, so you can admire the ornate pulpit and tiered galleries. The magnificent exterior, with free-standing belltower, remains the highlight.

Porvoon Museo
MUSEUM

(www.porvoonmuseo.fi; Vanha Raatihuoneentori; adult/child €6/3; ⊙10am-4pm Mon-Sat, 11am-4pm Sun May-Aug, noon-4pm Wed-Sun Sep-Apr) Porvoo's town museum is located in two adjacent buildings on the beautiful cobbled Old Town Hall Sq.

🛏 Sleeping

Hotelli Onni
BOUTIQUE HOTEL €€€

(☑044 534 8110; www.onniporvoo.fi; Kirkkotori 3; s/d €152/182; 🅿) Right opposite the cathedral, this gold-coloured wooden building couldn't be better placed. There's a real range here, from the four-poster bed and slick design of the Funk room to the rustic single Peasant room. Breakfast is downstairs in the terraced cafe that serves as a popular coffee shop.

Gasthaus Werneri
GUESTHOUSE €

(☑0400 494 876; www.werneri.net; Adlercreutzinkatu 29; s/d/tr without bathroom €45/60/90; 🅿) This cosy family-run guesthouse, in an apartment block a 10-minute walk from the Old Town (the street is about seven blocks east of the bridge along the main road Mannerheiminkatu), is decent value for Finland with just five rooms and a self-contained apartment.

Porvoon Retkeilymaja
HOSTEL €

(☑523 0012; www.porvoohostel.fi; Linnankoskenkatu 1-3; dm/s/d €20/35/48; ⊙check-in 4-7pm; 🅿) A 10-minute walk southeast of the Old Town, this historic wooden house holds a well-kept hostel in a grassy garden. It's a bit old school, but it's the cheapest bed in town. There's a great indoor pool and sauna complex over the road. HI discount.

✗ Eating & Drinking

Porvoo's most atmospheric cafes, restaurants and bars are in the Old Town and along the riverfront. Porvoo is famous for its sweets; the Runeberg pastry is ubiquitous.

Timbaali
FINNISH €€

(☑523 1020; www.timbaali.com; Jokikatu 43; mains €20-26; ⊙11am-11pm Mon-Sat, noon-6pm Sun) In the heart of the Old Town, this rustic restaurant specialises in slow food: locally farmed snails prepared in a variety of innovative ways. There's also a broad menu of gourmet Finnish cuisine, served in quaint dining rooms or the inner courtyard. It does an upmarket fish buffet weekday lunchtimes (€30).

TOP CHOICE Porvoon Paahtimo
CAFE, PUB

(www.porvoonpaahtimo.fi; Mannerheiminkatu 2; ⊙10am-midnight, to 3am Fri & Sat) Right at the main bridge, this atmospheric red-brick former storehouse is a cosy, romantic spot for drinks of any kind: it roasts its own coffee and have tap beer and several wines by the glass. There's a terrace and boat deck, which come with blankets on cooler evenings.

ⓘ Information

Tourist Office (☑040-489 9801; www.visitporvoo.fi; Läntinen Aleksanterinkatu 1; ⊙9am-7pm Mon-Sat, 10am-6pm Sun) Across the river from the centre. **Kompassi** (Rihkamatori; ⊙9am-4pm Mon-Fri, 10am-2pm Sat), on the edge of the old town, also offers tourist information.

ⓘ Getting There & Away

Buses run every half hour between Porvoo's kauppatori and Helsinki's bus station (€11.40, one hour), but the best way to reach Porvoo in summer is by boat. The historic steamship **JL Runeberg** (☑524 3331; www.msjlruneberg.fi; 1 way/return €25/36) sails daily, except Thursday, from Helsinki in summer (exact dates vary). The trip takes 3½ hours each way, so you may prefer to return by bus.

Turku

♪02 / POP 179,500

Turku is Finland's oldest town, but today it's a modern maritime city, brimming with museums and boasting a robust harbourside castle and magnificent cathedral. Its heart and soul is the lovely Aurajoki, a broad ribbon spilling into the Baltic Sea harbour and lined with riverboat bars and restaurants.

Once the capital under the Swedes, Turku (Swedish: Åbo) was founded in 1229, and grew into an important trading centre despite being ravaged by fire many times. In 2011 it shone again as one of the EU's Capitals of Culture.

⊙ Sights & Activities

Soak up Turku's summertime vibe by walking or cycling along the riverbank between the cathedral and the castle, crossing via bridges or the pedestrian *föri* (ferry).

Turun Linna　　　　　　　　CASTLE
(Turku Castle; www.museumcentreturku.fi; adult/child €8/4.50; ⊙10am-6pm Tue-Sun) A visit to lofty Turku Castle, near the harbour, should be your first stop. Founded in 1280 at the mouth of the Aurajoki, the castle has been rebuilt a number of times since. Notable occupants have included Count Per Brahe, founder of many towns in Finland, and Sweden's King Eric XIV, who was imprisoned in the castle's Round Tower in the late 16th century, having been declared insane. Guided tours of the stronghold area are available daily in English from June to August, but do not include the Renaissance rooms on the upper floor, or the extensive museums in the bailey section of the castle, so allow time to explore those yourself. You can also download a free audioguide from www.turku.fi.

TOP CHOICE Aboa Vetus & Ars Nova　　MUSEUM, GALLERY
(♪020-718 1640; www.aboavetusarsnova.fi; Itäinen Rantakatu 4-6; adult/child €8/5.50; ⊙11am-7pm, closed Mon late Sep–mid-Mar; ⏷) Aboa Vetus and Ars Nova are two museums under one roof. Aboa Vetus is an absolutely fascinating museum of live archaeology. You descend into the comprehensively excavated remains of medieval Turku; these are brought to life by lively commentary, plenty of info and activities for kids, and replica items that make sense of the fragments. Ars Nova is a museum of contemporary art with temporary exhibitions, the highlight of which is the **Turku Biennaali**, held in summer in odd years.

TOP CHOICE Luostarimäen Käsityöläismuseo　　MUSEUM
(www.museumcentreturku.fi; Vartiovuorenkatu 2; adult/child €6/4; ⊙10am-6pm Tue-Sun May–mid-Sep) The open-air Luostarinmäki Handicrafts Museum, in the only surviving 18th-century area of this medieval town, is one of the best of its kind in Finland and much more intriguing than the name suggests – it's a Turku must-see. In summer artisans work inside its 40 old wooden houses, and musicians stroll its paths. It also opens in December as a Christmas market.

Forum Marinum　　　　　　MUSEUM
(www.forum-marinum.fi; Linnankatu 72; adult/child €8/5, plus museum ships €6/4; ⊙11am-7pm May-Sep, 11am-6pm Tue-Sun Oct-Apr) Forum Marinum is an impressive maritime museum near Turku Castle. As well as a nautically crammed exhibition space devoted to Turku's shipping background, it incorporates a fleet of **museum ships** including the mine layer *Keihässalmi*, the three-masted barque *Sigyn* and the impressive 1902 sailing ship *Suomen Joutsen* (Swan of Finland). The ships can be visited independently of the museum.

Turun Tuomiokirkko　　　CATHEDRAL
(www.turuntuomiokirkko.fi; museum adult/child €2/1; ⊙9am-8pm May–mid-Sep, 9am-7pm mid-Sep–Apr) Commanding Turku Cathedral, dating from the 13th century, is the national shrine and 'mother church' of the Lutheran Church of Finland. In the south gallery of the cathedral is a small **museum** containing church relics and artworks. Opposite the cathedral, the **Vanha Suurtori** was once the main town square. It's surrounded by elegant buildings, the old town hall and trading mansions.

TURKU CARD

The **Turku Card** (www.turkutouring.com; 24/48hr €21/28, 24hr family card €45) gives free admission to most museums and attractions in the region, free public transport and various other discounts. Available from the tourist office or any participating attraction.

Turku

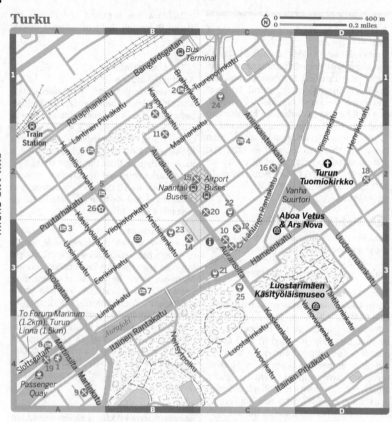

SS Ukkopekka
CRUISE

(www.ukkopekka.fi; 1 way/return €22/29; ⊘Naantali Tue-Sat mid-Jun–mid-Aug, other cruises mid-May–mid-Sep) Archipelago cruises are popular in summer, with daily departures from Martinsilta bridge at the passenger quay. The best option is this two-hour cruise out to Naantali aboard the steamship SS *Ukkopekka*.

🎉 Festivals & Events

Ruisrock
MUSIC

(www.ruisrock.fi) A major music festival held on Ruissalo Island in early July.

🛏 Sleeping

Park Hotel
HOTEL €€

(☎273 2555; www.parkhotelturku.fi; Rauhankatu 1; s/d €127/159; Ⓟ) This art nouveau house is a genuine character right down to Jaakko, the parrot that squawks a welcome when you check in. Rooms themselves, though showing signs of age, are lavishly decorated in individual styles, and the other facilities, such as a pool table, fireplace-warmed drawing room and breakfast, make for a great stay. There are discounts on weekends and in summer.

Centro Hotel
HOTEL €€

(☎211 8100; www.centrohotel.com; Yliopistonkatu 12; s/d €111/129; Ⓟ@) Central but far enough from the raucous kauppatori to still be quiet, this place has a good balance. Attentive service always feels friendly, and blonde-wood rooms are a good compromise between size and price, with superiors that have a more designer feel. The breakfast buffet has fresh pastries and a varied spread that's worth getting out of bed for. There are discounts on weekends and in summer.

Turku

Radisson Blu Marina Palace Hotel HOTEL €€
(☏020-123 4710; www.radissonblu.com; Linnankatu 32; d €120-160; P❄@) This modern, competitively priced business hotel has pleasant, efficient staff, great amenities and stylish, Scandinavian-style dark-wood rooms. It's worth paying extra for a superior room with one of the stunning river views; and couples who have grown weary of sleeping in pushed-together twin beds will be delighted to learn of real doubles on the 7th floor! Higher-grade rooms have extra luxuries like private saunas and in-room espresso machines.

Bed & Breakfast Tuure B&B €
(☏233 0230; www.tuure.fi; Tuureporinkatu 17C; s/d/tr €39/58/78; @🛜) Very handy for the bus station, and close to the market square, this tidy and friendly guesthouse makes an excellent place to stay. The rooms are bright and thoughtfully decorated, you get your own keys, and there's a microwave, a fridge and free internet use for guests. Reception is open 8am to 9pm.

Turku Hostel HOSTEL €
(☏262 7680; www.turku.fi/hostelturku; Linnankatu 39; dm/s/tw €23/43/54; P@🛜) Well located near the river a pleasant stroll from the town centre, this is a friendly, neat place with good lockers, spacious dorms, keycard

security and a minifridge in each private room. There's also cheap bike hire, breakfast available and free internet. There's a 2am curfew if you're dorming it. HI discount.

Bridgettine Sisters' Guesthouse GUESTHOUSE €
(☏250 1910; www.kolumbus.fi/birgitta.turku; Ursininkatu 15A; s/d €45/65; P) Behind a church and run by the friendly nuns of a Catholic convent, this tucked-away guesthouse offers excellent value. It's a peaceful place with spotless, spacious rooms with narrow beds and compact en suite bathrooms. There's a common lounge with fridge and stove and a few free parking places. They don't accept cards.

Omenahotelli HOTEL €
(☏0600 18018; www.omenahotels.com; Humalistonkatu 7; r €50-80; 🛜) This larger hotel, part of a chain that takes internet bookings, is in a refurbished Alvar Aalto–designed building. It represents the usual excellent value of the 'apple hotels' with spaces that can sleep up to four. You can also book via the lobby terminal.

Ruissalo Camping CAMPGROUND €
(☏262 5100; www.turkutouring.fi; campsites €16, plus per person €5, 2-/4-person cottage €38/78; ⊙Jun-Aug; P🛖) On Ruissalo Island, 10km west of the city centre, this camping ground

has lots of room for tents and a few cabins, along with saunas, a cafeteria and nice beaches. It's the bunkhouse for Ruisrock so expect it to be booked out around festival time (early July). Bus 8 runs from the kauppatori.

✗ Eating

There are plenty of cheap eateries on and around Turku's bustling central **kauppatori** (☺8am-4pm Mon-Sat May-Sep).

TOP CHOICE Tintå
GASTROPUB €€

(☏230 7023; www.tinta.fi; Läntinen Rantakatu 9; mains €13-20; ☺11am-midnight Mon, to 1am Tue-Thu, to 2am Fri, noon-2am Sat, noon-9pm Sun) On the riverfront, this cosy wine bar offers more than 50 choices by the glass, including some very interesting selections. The food is fabulous: large, innovative pizzas and a short, eclectic array of other dishes bursting with flavour. Top quality, top value.

Mami
BISTRO €€

(☏231 1111; www.mami.fi; Linnankatu 3; lunch €6-9, mains €18-23; ☺11am-10pm Tue-Fri, 1-10pm Sat) Mami's summer terrace is perfect for people watching, though you'll have to fight for a table with half of Turku – the restaurant is so popular that cynics have already placed bets as to when it will jump the shark. Seasonal ingredients from local, small-scale suppliers – goat's cheese, chanterelles, perch, salmon, duck – are prepared with care, and served with a twinkle.

Bistrot Le Porc
FRENCH €€

(☏230 0030; www.porc.fi; Martinkatu 3; mains €16-21; ☺dinner Wed-Sat, 1-5pm Sun) This unpretentious favourite of the Turku scene has won a loyal fan base (read: book ahead at weekends) with its classic French bistro fare served at more-than-fair prices. The delicious changing menu, no-nonsense contemporary decor and caring service soon won us over too.

Bossa
BRAZILIAN €€

(☏251 5880; www.restaurantebossa.fi; Kauppiaskatu 12; mains €17-25; ☺4-10pm Mon-Wed, to 11pm Thu-Fri, 2-11pm Sat) Buzzy and inviting, this L-shaped Brazilian restaurant is decorated with arty photos of the carnival capital. There's good authentic eating to be done here: *feijoada* (hearty bean and meat stew) and *moqueca* (Bahian prawn casserole with a distinctive palm-oil flavour) are the highlights of a short menu. Portions are generous and service is excellent.

Enkeliravintola
FINNISH €€

(☏231 8088; www.enkeliravintola.fi; Kauppiaskatu 16; mains €18-24; ☺11am-3pm Mon, to 10pm Tue-Fri, 1-10pm Sat, 1-6pm Sun; 🖪) You can't help feeling the celestial presence in the 'angel restaurant', an atmospheric old restaurant serving thoughtfully prepared Finnish cuisine with the winged wonders omnipresent. Hearty dishes involving things like reindeer, pork, goose and snails are the mainstays of the changing menu.

Trattoria Romana
ITALIAN €

(Hämeenkatu 9; pizzas & pasta €9-15; ☺11am-10pm Mon-Fri, 1-10pm Sat, 1-8pm Sun) With that reliably comfortable trattoria decoration, this intimate spot adds to the tried-and-tested favourites with some more interesting combinations, including a changing list of daily specials. Get the waiter to translate them for you, as they're very worthwhile, and better value than the à la carte meat dishes. Delicious salads are available here too.

CaféArt
CAFE €

(www.cafeart.fi; Läntinen Rantakatu 5; ☺10am-7pm Mon-Fri, to 4pm Sat) In a noble old waterfront building on one of Turku's most pleasant stretches, this hospitable cafe has tables out along the river. There's good espresso and super-elaborate lattes and hot chocolates. The cakes are pricey but great. Opens on Sunday in summer.

Vaakahuoneen Paviljonki
FINNISH €

(www.vaakahuone.fi; Linnankatu 38; mains €13-29, fish buffet €12; ☺kitchen 11am-10pm May-Aug) A pleasant stroll away from the centre, this summer pavilion, right on the riverbank, has a big à la carte menu of snacks, pasta, pizzas and steak, and folk descend on the daily fish buffets like starving herring gulls. Best of all, evening live jazz accompanies the food and sunshine, giving it the happiest, most toe-tapping atmosphere of all Turku's restaurants.

Blanko
BISTRO €€

(www.blanko.net; Aurakatu 1; mains €14-21; ☺11am-11pm Mon-Tue, to midnight Wed-Thu, noon-3am Sat, noon-9pm Sun) This chic place by the main bridge is a top spot for its creative fusion menu that includes Asian dishes, salads and seldom-seen pasta combinations. Meat and fish mains come in good-sized portions, the downstairs vaulted dining area is atmospheric, and service is helpful and kindly. There's an outdoor terrace great for watching Turku life. Blanko opens till late at weekends, when there are DJs once the washing up is done. Sunday brunch is famous throughout the city, but get there early or queue.

Viikinkiravintola Harald SCANDINAVIAN €€

(☏044-766 8204; www.ravintolaharald.fi; Aurakatu 3; menus €31-57, mains €15-30; ⊙11am-midnight Mon-Thu, to 1am Fri, noon-1am Sat, 3-10pm Sun; 🔊) Dust off your horned helmet for this Viking theme restaurant where subtlety is run through with a berserker's broadsword. Set menus (or Voyages as they're called here) are filling three-course samplers, but picking and mixing means you can indulge in barbarian ribs on a plank or tar ice cream with cognac. It's not exactly gourmet, but it is great fun.

Kauppahalli MARKET €

(Eerikinkatu 16; ⊙7am-5.30pm Mon-Fri, 7am-3pm Sat; 🍴) Packed with great produce, and good for cheap eats. Options include a sushi bar and a recommended cafe set up like a train carriage.

🍷 Drinking & Entertainment

Turku also has some of Finland's most eccentric bars that make for an offbeat pub crawl.

Boat Bars BARS

Summer drinking begins on the decks of any of the boats lining the south bank of the river. Although most serve food, they are primarily floating beer terraces with music and shipboard socialising. If the beer prices make you wince, join locals gathering on the grassy riverbank drinking takeaway alcohol.

Cosmic Comic Café BAR

(www.cosmic.fi; Kauppiaskatu 4; ⊙3pm-2am Mon-Thu, to 3am Fri & Sat, 4pm-2am Sun) Despite the unromantic shopping-centre location, this is a destination worth seeking out for a fine selection of Finnish and foreign microbrewed beers, shelves full of comics to browse, or to try your hand at Cluedo in Finnish. Was it Professori Purppuravalo with a *tikari* in the *kirjasto*?

Uusi Apteekki PUB

(www.uusiapteekki.fi; Kaskenkatu 1; ⊙10am-2am) This characterful bar was once a pharmacy; the antique shelving and desks have been retained, but they are filled with hundreds of old beer bottles. It's a locals' spot, great for a quiet drink, and there's an array of good international beers on tap.

Panimoravintola Koulu PUB

(www.panimoravintolakoulu.fi; Eerikinkatu 18; ⊙11am-2am, to 3am Fri & Sat) They've done their homework at this brewery pub, set in a former school, with nine of their own beers and ciders. As well as inkwells, black-boards and a playground-turned-beer-garden there's a decent restaurant upstairs with cheap lunches. The only downside is that the bar staff seem grumpy enough to wield the cane any moment. Seek out the history classroom for comfy seating fit for a headmistress.

Puutorin Vessa PUB

(www.puutorinvessa.fi; Puutori; ⊙noon-midnight Tue-Sat, 4pm-midnight Sun, 3pm-midnight Mon) In the middle of a small square near the bus terminal, this novel bar was a public toilet in a former life. Toilet humour and memorabilia adorn the walls and you can even have your drink in a tin potty.

Edison PUB

(www.tokravintolat.fi; Kauppiaskatu 4; ⊙3pm-late) While there's nothing particularly quirky about this corner pub, it's a comfortable, spacious spot, and can be livelier than the other options. On boisterous weekend evenings it's a great place to meet the locals.

Klubi CLUB

(www.klubi.net; Humalistonkatu 8A; ⊙to 4am Wed-Sun) This massive complex has several speeds, from the darkened drinking of Kolo ('cave') to the DJ-fuelled club of Ilta, plus regular big Finnish bands at Live. It's part-owned by a local record label, which means it snares its fair share of prominent bands.

ℹ Information

Forex (www.forex.fi; Eerikinkatu 13; ⊙9am-7pm Mon-Fri, 10am-3pm Sat) The best place to change cash and travellers cheques.

Library (Linnankatu 2; ⊙11am-8pm Mon-Thu, to 6pm Fri, to 4pm Sat) Free internet terminals (15-minute maximum).

Tourist office (☏262 7444; www.turkutouring.fi; Aurakatu 4; ⊙8.30am-6pm Mon-Fri, 9am-4pm Sat & Sun) Busy, very helpful and with information on the entire region. From October to March, weekend opening is 10am to 3pm.

There's coin-op internet access here, and bike hire (€20 per day).

❶ Getting There & Away

AIR **Finnair** (www.finnair.com) flies regularly between Helsinki and Turku airport, 8km north of the city. SAS (p207) has cheap flights to Copenhagen and Stockholm. Ryanair (p163) flies to London, Belgium and Spain while **Wizzair** (www.wizzair.com) and AirBaltic (p163) service various eastern European cities.

BOAT The harbour, southwest of the centre, has terminals for **Tallink/Silja Line** (www.tallinksilja.fi) and **Viking Line** (www.vikingline.fi). Both companies sail to Stockholm (11 hours) and Mariehamn (six hours). Prices vary widely according to season and class.

BUS From the main **bus terminal** (www.matkahuolto.fi; Aninkaistenkatu 20) there are hourly express buses to Helsinki (€30.50, 2¾ hours) and frequent services to Tampere (€24.80, two to three hours) and other points in southern Finland.

TRAIN The **train station** (www.vr.fi) is a short walk northwest of the centre; trains also stop at the ferry harbour and at Kupittaa train station east of the centre. Bus 32 shuttles between the centre and the main train station. Express trains run frequently to and from Helsinki (from €30.76, two hours), Tampere (from €25.49, 1¾ hours) and beyond.

❶ Getting Around

BICYCLE Various places hire bikes, including the hostel and the tourist office. Ask there about the scenic 250km route around the Turku archipelago, covered in more detail in Lonely Planet's *Finland* guide.

BUS Bus 1 runs between the kauppatori and the airport (€2.50, 25 minutes). This same bus also goes from the kauppatori to the harbour. City and regional buses are frequent and you pay €2.50 for a two-hour ticket or €5.50 for a 24-hour ticket.

Naantali

🎵02 / POP 18,800

The lovely seaside town of Naantali is just 18km from Turku and is set around a picturesque horseshoe-shaped harbour. It's a delightfully peaceful, historic sort of spot... or it would be, were it not for the presence of its extraordinarily popular main attraction.

⊙ Sights

The harbour, lined with cafes and restaurants, the delightful cobbled **Old Town** and the huge **Convent Church** (⊙10am-6pm daily May, 10am-8pm daily Jun-Aug, 11am-3pm Sun, noon-2pm Wed Sep-Apr) are enough incentive for a day trip here from Turku. Out of season Muumimaailma closes its gates, and the Old Town acquires the melancholic air of an abandoned film set.

Muumimaailma   AMUSEMENT PARK
(Moomin World; www.muumimaailma.fi; 1-/2-day pass €23/32; ⊙10am-6pm early Jun–mid-Aug, noon-6pm late Aug; 🚸) Crossing the bridge from town takes you into the downright delightful world of the Moomins, Finland's most famous family. Even if you've never read the books or seen the TV series, there's still something wonderful about these white hippolike trolls. Costumed characters wander through the Moominhouse, Snork's Workshop (where kids help with inventions) and a host of places that leap to life from the books and cartoons. Merchandising is limited, and the focus is on hands-on activities and exploration, not rides.

🛌 Sleeping & Eating

Although an easy day trip from Turku, Naantali has some lovely guesthouses and a famous spa hotel.

Naantali Spa Hotel   HOTEL €€€
(☑44550; www.naantalispa.fi; Matkailijantie 2; s/d €149/186; P@🏊🚸) The last word in pampering, this spa hotel is one of the best in Finland. Luxurious rooms, exotic restaurants, awesome spa and health facilities – there's even a stationary cruise ship docked outside where you can stay in luxury shipboard cabins. It's like something out of Vegas. If this is too much for the budget, nonguests can use the spa and pool facilities (€19 to €23 for three hours).

Merisali   FINNISH €
(www.merisali.fi; Nunnakatu 1; buffet lunch/dinner €13.50/18; ⊙9am-1am May-Sep) Just below the Convent Church, this iconic restaurant in an old waterfront spa pavilion has a shaded terrace and a mind-blowing smorgasbord for lunch and dinner, including lavish seafood and salads – pack an appetite! It's slightly more expensive on Sundays.

❶ Information

Naantalin Matkailu (☑435 9800; www.naantalinmatkailu.fi; Kaivotori 2; ⊙9am-6pm Mon-Fri, 10am-4pm Sat & Sun late May-late Aug, 9am-4.30pm Mon-Fri late Aug-late May) Tourist information near the harbour; also has bikes for hire.

ⓘ Getting There & Away

Buses to Naantali (routes 11 and 110) run every 15 to 30 minutes from the kauppatori in Turku (€5.30, 30 minutes). In summer the steamship Ukkopekka (p148) cruises between Turku and Naantali.

ⓘ Getting There & Away

There's at least one daily express bus to/from Helsinki (€24.40, two to three hours) and a couple of Turku services. The train from Helsinki (€23.89, 1¾ hours) requires a change to a local train or bus at Karjaa.

Hanko

♪019 / POP 9400

With its sweep of beach and bustling marina, Hanko (Swedish: Hangö) is easily the pick of Finland's south-coast resorts. In the late 19th and early 20th centuries it was a popular and glamorous summer retreat for Russian nobles and artists. These cashed-up holidaymakers built lofty wooden villas on the sandy shore east of the harbour, and with several of them now converted to charming guesthouses, they continue to attract tourists with a taste for the romantic.

🛏 Sleeping & Eating

Accommodation can be tight in the summer months, so book ahead. A unique feature of Hanko is its Empire-era Russian-style villas, four of which operate as B&Bs. Don't go expecting luxury, but with an open mind and a lively appreciation of history!

East Harbour has a row of red wooden buildings housing four restaurants – pasta, pizza, gourmet and family. It's a lovely spot to eat, but be warned – in summer you pay for the location with high prices, crowded terraces and slow service.

TOP CHOICE Villa Maija RUSSIAN VILLA €€

(♪248 2900; www.villamaija.fi; Appelgrenintie 7; s €95-125, d €99-200; 🅿) Built in 1888, this is the best villa accommodation. Faultlessly restored rooms are so gosh-darned cosy and packed with character that it's difficult to prise yourself away. Prices vary according to the size of the room, and whether it has a private bathroom and balcony. It's a lot cheaper in the low season. Out the back are Villa Janne and Villa Anke, as light-filled and pleasant as the main building. An excellent breakfast is included.

ⓘ Information

Tourist office (♪220 3411; www.hanko.fi/tourism; Raatihuoneentori 5; ⊙9am-4pm Mon-Fri Sep-May, 9am-6pm Mon-Fri, 10am-4pm Sat & Sun Jun-Aug) Can help with accommodation and the myriad summer activities in town.

ÅLAND ARCHIPELAGO

♪018 / POP 28,400

Little known beyond the Baltic, this sweeping archipelago spattered between Finland and Sweden is a curious geopolitical entity: the islands belong to Finland, the inhabitants speak Swedish, but have their own parliament, fly their own blue, gold and red flag, issue their own stamps and have their own web suffix: 'dot ax'. Their 'special relationship' with the EU means they can sell duty-free and make their own gambling laws.

There are well over 6000 islands, although many of these are merely little mounds of granite rising centimetres above the sea. Indeed, the islands are all remarkably flat: Ålanders are even less thrilled by global warming than most.

This flatness, however, makes the islands ideal for exploration by bike. The main central island (Åland) is connected with those around it by bridge and cable ferry while, northeast and southeast of here, the archipelago islands are even more rural and remote: on places like Kökar you could be forgiven for believing you have stepped right back in time. Throughout Åland, traditions such as the Midsummer celebration bear a marked local character.

ⓘ NEED TO KNOW

» The website www.visitaland.com is very helpful, and www.alandsresor.fi lets you book much of the island's accommodation online.

» Åland uses the Finnish mobile-phone network.

» Åland uses the euro, but most businesses will also accept the Swedish krona.

» Mail sent in Åland must have Åland postage stamps.

» Åland operates on the same time as Finland – that is, one hour ahead of Sweden.

FINLAND HANKO

Åland

20 km
10 miles

Kustavi
Osnäs
To Galtby;
Turku

Jurmo
Brändö
Ava
Långö
Torsholma
Lappo

Northern
Archipelago

Kökar
Hellsö

Enklinge
Krokarno
Karlby
Kumlinge
Hamnö
Källskär

Seglinge
Husö

Skaget
Sottunga
Southern
Archipelago

Överö
Finholma

Hummelvik
Fögelö

Östra
Simskäla
Vårdö

Västra
Simskäla
Sweden/
Tengsödavik

Lumpo
Långnäs

Ödkarby
Kvarnbo
Finby
Vargata
Svinö

Getabergen
Saltvik
Sund
Lumparland
Norrby
Herrön

Dånö
Geta
Godby
Ahvenanmaan
Lemland

Hällö
Hammarland
Jomala
Lumparn

Skarpnåtö
Lillbolstad
ÅLAND

Salis
Jomala
Järsö

Skag
Kyrkoby
Gottby
Mariehamn

Eckerö
Storby
Degersand

Torp

Djurvik

GULF OF
BOTHNIA

Örödals
Klint

Bomarsund

Kastelholms
Slott

To Helsinki;
Tallinn

Åland
Sea

To Stockholm;
Kapellskär

SWEDEN

To Grisslehamn

- - - International Ferry
——— Interisland Ferry
········· Bicycle Ferry

❶ Getting There & Away

AIR NextJet (☑+46 771 90 00 90; www.nextjet.
se) has weekday flights from Mariehamn to
Turku and Stockholm, while Flybe (p207) flies
daily from Helsinki. The airport is 4km north
of Mariehamn and there's a connecting bus
service.

BOAT These are the main companies operating between the Finnish mainland and Åland
(and on to Sweden). Some services dock at
Långnäs (with connecting bus service) instead
of Mariehamn:

Eckerö Linjen (☑28300; www.eckerolinjen.ax;
Torggatan 2, Mariehamn) Sails to Grisslehamn,
Sweden (€11, three hours) from Eckerö.

Tallink/Silja Lines (☑16711; www.tallinksilja.
com; Torggatan 14, Mariehamn) Runs direct
services to Mariehamn from Turku (€17, five
hours), Helsinki (€42, 11½ hours), Stockholm
(€32, 5½ hours) and Tallinn (dorm from €38,
11 hours).

Viking Line (☑26211; www.vikingline.fi;
Storagatan 3, Mariehamn) Runs to Turku (€16,
5½ hours), Helsinki (€45, 11 hours) and Stockholm (€16, six hours). Also runs to Kapellskär,
Sweden, a quicker crossing with bus connection to Stockholm.

It's also possible to travel using the archipelago
ferries (free for foot passengers) to and from
mainland Finland via Korpo (southern route,
from Galtby passenger harbour) or Kustavi
(northern route, from Osnäs passenger
harbour); see p157.

❶ Getting Around

BICYCLE Cycling is a great way to tour these
flat, rural islands. **Ro-No Rent** (☑12820; www.
rono.ax; bicycles per day/week from €8/40,
mopeds €80/200; ☺Jun–mid-Aug), which also
rents out boats, has offices at both Mariehamn
harbours as well as Eckerö. In the low season you
can arrange a hire by calling ☑0400 529 315,
preferably a few days in advance. Green-and-
white signs trace the excellent routes through
the islands.

BOAT Timetables for all interisland ferries are
available at the main tourist office in Mariehamn
and online at www.alandstrafiken.ax. Nonstop
free ferries connect adjacent islands, while there
are programmed departures for longer routes.

BUS Five main bus lines depart from Mariehamn's regional bus terminal on Torggatan
opposite the library. Bus 1 goes to Hammarland
and Eckerö, bus 2 to Godby and Geta, bus 3 to
Godby and Saltvik, bus 4 to Godby, Sund and
Vårdö (Hummelvik) and bus 5 to Lemland and
Långnäs (Lumparland).

Mariehamn

☑018 / POP 11,300

Village-y Mariehamn is Åland's main port
and capital, a pretty place lined with linden
trees and timber houses set between two
large harbours. Compared to the rest of the
archipelago, it's a metropolis, getting quite
busy in summer with tourists off the ferries,
and yachts stocking the marinas. Outside
peak season, you could safely fire a cannon
through the town.

◉ Sights & Activities

Sjöfartsmuseum   MUSEUM
(Maritime Museum; www.sjofartsmuseum.ax; Hamngatan 2; adult/child €10/6; ☺10am-5pm May-Aug,
11am-4pm Sep-May) The stalwarts of Åland are
mariners and the best place to get a feel for
their exploits is down at the West Harbour.
The Sjöfartsmuseum is an intriguing display with everything from artefacts from the
seven seas to interactive cruise-ship karaoke.
Best of all, anchored outside, is the graceful
museum ship **Pommern** (☺May-Sep only), a
beautifully preserved four-masted barque
built in Glasgow in 1903.

Ålands Museum &
Ålands Konstmuseum   MUSEUM, GALLERY
(www.museum.ax; Stadhusparken; adult/child
€4/3; ☺10am-5pm Jun-Aug, 10am-8pm Tue & Thu,
to 4pm Wed & Fri, noon-4pm Sat & Sun Sep-May)
Housed in the same building in the centre
of town, this gallery and museum give an
account of Åland's history and culture with
displays on local music, seafaring, wildlife
and festivals. There's little info in English.
The art museum features a permanent collection of works by Åland artists – check out
the works on cardboard by Joel Pettersson,
the 'Åland Van Gogh' – as well as changing
exhibitions. It's free from October to April.

Sjökvarteret   BOATYARD
(Maritime Quarter; www.sjokvarteret.com; museum
adult/child €4/free; ☺museum 9am-6pm daily
mid-Jun–mid-Aug, 9-11am Mon-Fri mid-Aug–mid-
Jun) Over at the East Harbour is a marina,
boat-building yard and museum (no English info) with exhibitions on shipbuilding,
craft workshops and a cafe.

Ro-No Rent   CANOEING, KAYAKING
(☑12820; www.goaland.net/rono; kayak hire from
€40; ☺9am-noon & 1-6pm Jun–mid Aug) There
are various options for getting out on the

SELF-CATERING ACCOMMODATION

There's a wealth of cottages for rent on Åland. Both Eckerö (p155) and Viking Lines (p155) have a comprehensive list of places that can be booked, as does **Destination Åland** (☎0400 108 800; www.destinationaland.com; Östra Esplanadgatan 7, Mariehamn).

water yourself. Ro-No Rent hires kayaks – kayaking around the archipelago is a great way to see Åland – and small boats, which don't require a license.

🛏 Sleeping

Rates for Mariehamn's hotels and guesthouses peak in July and August. The hotels are all much of a muchness, with no standout option.

Pensionat Solhem   GUESTHOUSE €€
(☎16322; www.visitaland.com/solhem; Lökskärsvägen; s/d without bathroom €46/71; ⊗May-Oct; P🐾) Although it might be 3km south of the centre, it's only 2km from the ferries to this delightful seaside spot that can feel like your very own villa. Rooms are basic, but cheerful staff keep the place running like clockwork. Guests also have use of the rowing boats and sauna. Local buses (routes B and D) stop nearby.

Park Alandia Hotel   HOTEL €€
(☎14130; www.vikingline.fi/parkalandiahotel; Norra Esplanadgatan 3; s/d €96/114; P🐾) The Park is a modern, comfortable hotel on Mariehamn's main boulevard. A range of smart rooms with TV – some with kitchenette and bathtub – are complemented by a small swimming pool and sauna. Rooms are a bargain on a Sunday, and Viking Lines (p155) offers ferry-plus-hotel deals. There's a good restaurant, a cafe and a lively terrace bar at the front.

Gästhem Kronan   GUESTHOUSE €€
(☎12617; www.visitaland.com/kronan; Neptunigatan 52; s/d without bathroom €52/75; P) Mariehamn has no hostels, but Kronan is a good-value (for Mariehamn) guesthouse with basic but spotless, renovated rooms. It's in a quiet street a short walk from the ferry terminal. It's a lot cheaper outside high season,

though breakfast isn't included. Call ahead as they're not always there.

Gröna Udden Camping   CAMPGROUND €
(☎21121; www.gronaudden.com; campsite €8, plus per adult €8, r €80, 2-/4-person cabins €90/110; ⊗6 May-4 Sep; P🐾) A kilometre south of the centre, this camping ground is a family favourite, with a safe swimming beach, minigolf course, bike hire and sauna. If the tent plots are a little small, then opt for the spruce red cabins, which are fully equipped.

🍴 Eating & Drinking

Mariehamn's many cafes serve the local speciality, *Ålandspannkaka* (Åland pancakes), a fluffy square pudding made with semolina and served with stewed prunes.

TOP CHOICE **Indigo**   SCANDINAVIAN €€
(☎16550; www.indigo.ax; Nygatan 1; mains €27-29; ⊗11am-11pm Mon-Fri, 5pm-midnight Sat, bar until 4am weekends) Attractive and upmarket, this restaurant is in a historic brick-and-timber building but the menu is contemporary Scandinavian. Upstairs, in a beautiful loft space, it serves a good-value bistro menu in the evenings (dishes €12 to €19). It's also a stylish spot for a weekend drink.

Café Bönan   VEGETARIAN €
(www.cafebonan.ax; Sjökvarteret; snacks €6; ⊗10.30am-4pm; 🐾) An oasis in a desert of meat and fish, this organic vegetarian place does healthy soups and salads such as fresh beans with couscous, washed down with elderflower cordial. All the food is sourced from ethical producers.

Dino's Bar & Grill   BAR, BISTRO €€
(www.dinosbar.com; Strandgatan 12; mains €13-24; ⊗10.30am-10pm Mon-Thu, to 11pm Fri, noon-11pm Sat, 2-10pm Sun; 🐾) Popular as a meeting spot, this bar does thick burgers and creative pasta and steaks, best eaten on its great outdoor deck. It's a good place to hang around for a few beers, especially when the house band is playing. The bar opens till 4am at weekends.

ℹ Information

Visit Åland (☎24000; www.visitaland.com; Storagatan 8; ⊗9am-6pm daily late Jun & Jul, 9am-5pm Mon-Fri, to 4pm Sat & Sun early Jun & Aug, 9am-4pm Mon-Fri Oct-Mar, plus 10am-3pm Sat Apr-May & Sep) Plenty of island info. Books tours. There's also a booth at the ferry terminal.

Around the Islands

SUND

Crossing the bridge into the municipality of Sund brings you to Åland's most striking attraction: the medieval 14th-century **Kastelholms Slott** (www.museum.ax; adult/child €5/3.50; ⊙10am-5pm May–mid-Sep, to 6pm Jul), a striking and beautifully situated castle. Next to the castle, **Jan Karlsgårdens Friluftsmuseum** (admission free; ⊙10am-5pm May–mid-Sep) is a typical open-air museum consisting of about 20 wooden buildings, including three windmills, transported here from around the archipelago.

Further east, the ruins of the Russian fortress at **Bomarsund** are accessible all year. The impressive fortifications date from the 1830s and were destroyed during the Crimean War (1853–56). Near Bomarsund, **Puttes Camping** (☑44040; www.visitaland.com/puttescamping; Bryggvägen 2, Bomarsund; campsites per person €3, plus per tent or vehicle €2, cabins €29-43; ⊙mid-May–mid-Sep; ℙ) is a large, well-equipped site with a beach sauna, a cafe and cabins.

ECKERÖ

Finland's westernmost municipality, Eckerö is all blonde hair and tanned bodies in summer, packed with holidaying Swedish families making the short ferry-hop across. **Storby** (Big Village), at the ferry terminal, is the main centre, with a petrol station and bank. The best beach is at **Degersand** in the south, but away from the coast, Eckerö is typical rural Åland, with winding country lanes and tiny villages.

Storby was once the western extremity of the Russian Empire, and the Bear wanted a show of power for Europe, so CL Engel was commissioned to design a massive, er, post office. The **Post och Tullhuset** (☑38689; Post & Customs House) is enormous and now houses a cafe, exhibition gallery and the small **mailboat museum** (www.aland.com; admission €3; ⊙10am-3pm Tue-Sun Jun–mid-Aug), which tells the story of the gruelling archipelago mail route that cost many lives over two and half centuries. Bus 1 runs to Mariehamn.

EASTERN ARCHIPELAGO ROUTES

If you have a bit of time on your hands it's possible to island-hop eastwards through the northeast and southeast archipelago routes. Accommodation options are limited so carry a tent or make advance bookings.

To the north you can travel through Vårdö then take the ferry to **Kumlinge**. Another 1½ hours by ferry via **Lappo** brings you to **Torsholma** on the scattered island group of **Brändö**. It's then possible to hop via **Jurmo** all the way to Turku. By public transport, take bus 4 from Mariehamn to Hummelvik harbour on Vårdö island. From Turku, take a bus to Kustavi, and on to Vartsala island to reach the harbour of Osnäs (Vuosnainen).

To the south, it's an easier trip to the port of **Långnäs**, from where you can hop via **Föglö** and **Sottunga** to the far-flung but picturesque island of **Kökar**, with hiking trails, a 14th-century abbey and an 18th-century church. By local transport from Mariehamn, take bus 5 to Långnäs harbour. From Kökar there are ferries to Galtby harbour on Korppoo island (two hours), then it's 75km by bus to Turku.

If you're taking a car on these ferries, it's substantially cheaper if you spend a night en route between Finland and mainland Åland.

SOUTHWESTERN FINLAND

Tampere

☑03 / POP 215,300

Scenic Tampere, set between two vast lakes, has a down-to-earth vitality that makes it a Finland favourite for many visitors. Through its centre churn the Tammerkoski rapids, whose grassy banks contrast with the red brick of the imposing fabric mills that once gave the city the moniker 'Manchester of Finland'.

A popular short-break destination thanks to its budget flight connection, Tampere doesn't disappoint: its students ensure plenty of evening action, and its regenerated industrial buildings house quirky museums, enticing shops, pubs, cinemas and cafes.

◉ Sights

⧉ TOP CHOICE **Tuomiokirkko**　　　　CHURCH
(www.tampereenseurakunnat.fi; Tuomiokirkonkatu 3; ⊙10am-5pm May-Aug, 11am-3pm Sep-Apr) Tampere's intriguing cathedral is one of the most notable examples of National Romantic architecture in Finland. The famous artist Hugo Simberg was responsible for the frescos and stained glass; once you've

Tampere

500 m
0.25 miles

Salhojankatu

Tammelan puistokatu

Pinninkatu

Tammelankatu

Yliopistonkatu

Pinninkatu

Itsenäisyydenkatu

Kalevantie

Tullikamarinaukio

24
6
10
25

Visit
Tampere
Train
Station

Rautatienkatu

Rantatienkatu

Tuomiokirkko

Rongankatu

Tuomiokirkonkatu

9

15

21

Kyttälänkatu

Hämeenkatu

7
20
13

Verkatehtaankatu

Aleksanterinkatu

Lapintie

Espianadi

16
19

Otava

Verstank

Aleksanteri valtkatu

Tammerkoski

Itäinenkatu

1

Frenckellinaukio

Vanha
Kirkko

Koskikatu

Hatanpään valtatie

11

Laukontori
Market
Square

22

26

Laukontori
Quay

Ratinan
suvanto

Näsinpuisto Park

Aleksis Kivenkatu
18

Keskustori

Hämeenkatu

12

Kuninkaankatu

14

Finlaysoninkatu

Puutarhakatu

Kauppakatu

Hallituskatu

23

Näsilinnankatu

Mustalahti
Quay

Näsijärvi

4

Satakunnankatu

Puuvillatehtaankatu

17

8

SÄRKÄNNIEMI

3

Lahtinkatu

Näsijärvenkatu

Mustanlahdenkatu

27

Aleksanterin
Kirkko

Hämeenpuisto

Lenin-
Museo

Satamakatu

Paasikiventie

Kortelahdenkatu

Amurinkatu

Mariankatu

Amurin
Työläismuseokortteli

2

Pyynikintie

Niemikatu

Pirkankatu

To Rajaportin
Sauna (2km)

Sepänkatu

To Pyynikki
(200m)

To Camping
Härmälä
(4km)

Tampere

seen them you'll appreciate that they were controversial at the time. A procession of ghostly childlike apostles holds the 'garland of life', the garden of death shows graves and plants tended by skeletal figures, while another image shows a wounded angel being carried off on a stretcher by two children. There's a solemn, almost mournful feel about it; the altarpiece, by Magnus Enckell, is a dreamlike Resurrection in similar style. The symbolist stonework and disturbing colours of the stained glass add to the haunting ambience.

Amurin Työläismuseokortteli
MUSEUM

(Amuri Museum of Workers' Housing; www.tampere. fi/amuri; Satakunnankatu 49; adult/child €6/1; ⊙10am-6pm Tue-Sun mid-May–mid-Sep) An entire block of 19th-century wooden houses, including 32 apartments, a bakery, a shoemaker, shops and a cafe, is preserved in this fascinating museum. It's one of the most realistic house-museums in Finland – many homes look as if the tenant had left just moments ago to go shopping. Entertaining backstories (English translation available) give plenty of historical information.

Finlayson Centre
CULTURAL BUILDING

(Satakunnankatu 18) Tampere's era as an industrial city began with the arrival of Scot James Finlayson, who established a small workshop by the Tammerkoski here in 1820. He later erected a huge cotton mill, now sensitively converted into a mall of cafes and shops; you'll also find a cinema here, as well as a brewery-pub and a couple of intriguing museums.

Vakoilumuseo
MUSEUM

(Spy Museum; www.vakoilumuseo.fi; Satakunnankatu 18, Finlayson Centre; adult/child €8/6; ⊙10am-6pm Mon-Sat, 11am-5pm Sun Jun-Aug, 11am-5pm Sep-May; 🚼) This plays to the budding secret agent in all of us, with a large and well-assembled display of devices of international espionage, mainly from the Cold War era. Interactive elements liven things up; for a little extra, the kids can take a suitability test for KGB cadet school.

Lenin-Museo
MUSEUM

(www.lenin.fi; Hämeenpuisto 28; adult/child €5/3; ⊙9am-6pm Mon-Fri, 11am-4pm Sat & Sun) Admirers of bearded revolutionaries won't want to miss the small Lenin Museum, housed in the Workers' Hall where Lenin and Stalin first met at a conference in 1905. His life is evoked by way of photos and documents; it's a little dry, but it's fascinating to see, for example, Vladimir's old school report (a straight-A student). There's a gift shop where you can buy Lenin pens, badges, T-shirts and other souvenirs of the Soviet era.

Muumilaakso MUSEUM
(Moomin Valley; www.tampere.fi/muumi; Puutarhakatu 34; adult/child €7/2; ⊙9am-5pm Tue-Fri, 10am-6pm Sat & Sun; ♠) Explore the creation of Tove Jansson's enduringly popular Moomins in this museum on the ground floor of Tampere's art gallery (pending the construction of a purpose-built museum). It contains original drawings and elaborate models depicting stories from Moomin Valley (English explanations available), computer displays, toys and other memorabilia. The **gift shop** (Hämeenpuisto 20) is still located at the old address, in the public library.

🏃 Activities

Särkänniemi AMUSEMENT PARK
(www.sarkanniemi.fi; adult/child day pass up to €35/29; ⊙rides 10am-8pm mid-May–Aug; ♠) On the northern edge of town, this promontory amusement park is a large complex with a load of high-adrenalin rides, an Angry Birds–themed area and several other attractions, including a good art gallery and an aquarium. There's a bewildering system of entry tickets and opening times; it's cheaper to book online. A day pass is valid for all sights and unlimited rides, while €10 will get you up the **Näsinneula Observation Tower** (⊙11am-11.30pm), and into the gallery. Once the rides are closed for the season, you can still access the other sights, but (gallery apart) it's not great value. Take bus 4 or 16 from the train station.

Pyynikki WALKING
Rising between Tampere's two lakes, Pyynikki is a forested ridge of walking and cycling trails with fine views on both sides. There's a stone **observation tower** (Näkötorni; adult/child €2/0.50; ⊙9am-8pm) on the ridge with a cafe serving Tampere's best doughnuts. The tower is a 20-minute walk from the centre of town, west along Satamakatu, bearing left at a small park, then right up the hill.

Rajaportin Sauna SAUNA
(www.rajaportinsauna.fi; Pispalan Valtatie 9; adult/child €8/2; ⊙6-10pm Mon & Wed, 3-9pm Fri, 2-10pm Sat) This is Finland's oldest operating traditional public sauna. It's a great chance to experience the softer steam from a traditionally heated sauna rather than the harsher electric ones. It's a couple of kilometres west of the centre; buses 1, 13 and 22 among others head out there. There's a cafe on-site, and massages can be arranged. Take a towel or rent one there.

👉 Tours

Trips on Tampere's two magnificent lakes are extremely popular in summer and there are plenty of options. Trips on Näsijärvi leave from Mustalahti quay, while Laukontori quay serves Pyhäjärvi. All cruises can be booked at the tourist office.

SS Tarjanne BOAT TOUR
(☑010-422 5600; www.runoilijantie.fi) From Mustalahti quay, the glorious steamship SS *Tarjanne* does evening cruises with optional dinner, but is best boarded for the Poet's Way, one of the finest lake cruises in Finland. A one-way ticket costs €44 to Ruovesi (4¾ hours) and €54 to Virrat (8¼ hours). For €42 per person, you can sleep in this venerable boat before or after your trip. Day use of a cabin is also €42. Bicycles can be taken on board for a small fee. You can book a day trip to Virrat or Ruovesi, with one of the legs made by bus (return to Virrat/Ruovesi costs €70/62).

Suomen Hopealinja BOAT TOUR
(Finnish Silverline; ☑010-422 5600; www.hopealinja.fi) Runs cruises to Visavuori (one way/return €46/69, five hours, 9.30am, Wednesday to Saturday early June to mid-August), continuing to Hämeenlinna (one way/return €48/72, 8½ hours).

🎉 Festivals & Events

There are events in Tampere almost year-round.

Tampere Film Festival FILM
(www.tamperefilmfestival.fi) Usually held in early March, this is a respected international festival of short films.

Tammerfest ROCK
(www.tammerfest.fi) The city's premier rock-music festival, held over four days in mid-July with concerts at various stages around town.

Tampere Jazz Happening JAZZ
(www.tamperemusicfestivals.fi) October or early November brings this award-winning event

featuring Finnish and international jazz musicians.

🛏 Sleeping

TOP CHOICE Dream Hostel
HOSTEL €

(☑045-236 0517; www.dreamhostel.fi; Åkerlundinkatu 2; dm €22-27, tw/q €63/89; P ❖ 🖥) Sparky and spacious, this is Finland's best urban hostel. Helpful staff, supercomfortable, wide-berth dorms in various sizes (both unisex and female available), a heap of facilities, original decor and the right attitude about everything make it a real winner. It's a short walk from the train station in a quiet area.

🏨 Scandic Tampere Station
HOTEL €€

(☑339 8000; www.scandichotels.com; Ratapihankatu 37; s/d €150/170; P ❖ @ 🖥) The city's newest hotel is, as the name suggests, right by the train station. It's a sleek, beautifully designed place with a minimalist feel to the decor, which is based on soothing pink and mauve lighting breaking up the chic whites and blacks. The superior plus rooms are particularly enticing, with dark-wood sauna and balcony, and don't cost a whole lot more. There are also lots of accessible rooms, with motorised beds. Facilities are modern, service excellent and prices very competitive.

🏨 Scandic Tampere City
HOTEL €€€

(☑244 6111; www.scandichotels.com; Rautatienkatu 16; s/d €176/196; @ 🖥) Right opposite the train station, this hotel has modern Nordic lines and a fistful of facilities including a sauna, a gym, various restaurants and a cocktail bar. The rooms are spacious and spotless with a clean wooden feel. Superiors are almost identical, but have a coffee tray and a comfier chair. The hotel has a family-friendly feel and you can borrow bikes or walking poles from reception.

Sokos Hotel Ilves
HOTEL €€

(☑020-123 4631; www.sokoshotels.fi; Hatanpään valtatie 1; s/d €158/178; P ❖ @ 🖥) This huge tower hotel was big news in Finland when it opened in the '80s, and is still keeping standards high. Very high: the view from rooms on the upper floors is memorable, so ask for as lofty a chamber as they can give you. Rooms are attractively furnished with Finnish design classics; superiors are the same size but with even better views. The impressive facilities include an excellent restaurant as well as chain eateries, and an attractive club with a dedicated karaoke chamber.

Hotelli Victoria
HOTEL €€

(☑242 5111; www.hotellivictoria.fi; Itsenäisyydenkatu 1; s/d €119/156; P @ 🖥) Just on the other side of the railway station from the centre, this friendly hotel offers appealing summer discounts on its spruce rooms, free internet and commendable breakfast spread including waffles, sausage omelette and berry pudding options. Rooms are compact but light and quiet despite the busy road and there's a good sauna. It's closed most of December. Bike hire available.

Omenahotelli
HOTEL €

(☑0600 18018; www.omenahotels.com; Hämeenkatu 7; r €70-90; @ 🖥 👪) Very handy for the station, this receptionless hotel offers the usual comfortable rooms with double bed, a microwave, fridge, kettle and two fold-outs. There's free wi-fi, and the rooms are great value for a family of four, for example. Book online or via the terminal at the entrance. There's another location on **Hämeenkatu** (Hämeenkatu 28; r €60-90), at the western end of the main drag.

Camping Härmälä
CAMPGROUND €

(☑020-719 9777; www.suomicamping.fi; Leirintäkatu 8; campsites €15, plus per person €5, cabins €52-80; ☺early May-late Sep; P) Four kilometres south of the centre (take bus 1), this is a spacious camping ground on the Pyhäjärvi lake shore. There's a cafe, saunas and rowing boats, as well as a rather down-at-heel summer hotel with self-contained rooms (singles/doubles €45/61, open June to mid-September).

🍴 Eating

Tampere's speciality, *mustamakkara*, is a mild sausage made with cow's blood, black-pudding style. It's normally eaten with lingonberry jam and is tastier than it sounds. You can get it at the kauppahalli, or a summer kiosk at **Laukontori market** (☺8am-2pm Mon-Sat).

TOP CHOICE Tuulensuu
PUB €€

(www.gastropub.net/tuulensuu; Hämeenpuisto 23; mains €17-23; ☺food noon-midnight Mon-Sat, 3pm-midnight Sun) The best of a range of Tampere gastropubs, this corner spot has a superb selection of Belgian beers, good wines, as well as a lengthy port menu. The food is lovingly prepared and features staples such as liver and schnitzel, as well as more elaborate plates like duck *confit* and other bistro fare inspired by Belgium and northeastern France. Even the bar snacks are gourmet: fresh-roasted almonds. It's closed Sundays in summer.

Neljä Vuodenaikaa BISTRO €
(4 Saisons; www.4vuodenaikaa.fi; Kauppahalli; dishes €9-22; ⊙11am-3.45pm Mon-Fri, to 3.15pm Sat) Tucked into a corner of the kauppahalli, this recommended spot brings a Gallic flair to the Finnish lunch hour with delicious plates such as bouillabaisse and French country salad augmented by excellent daily specials and wines by the glass. The morsel of cheese of the day is a great way to finish up. Get there early for the best selection.

Ravintola C MODERN FINNISH €€€
(☑010-617 9760; www.ravintola-c.fi; Rautatienkatu 20; mains €24-28; ⊙noon-3pm Tue-Fri, 5pm-midnight Tue-Sat) In a pristine, off-white dining room near the railway station, this top Tampere restaurant creates innovative, beautifully presented modern dishes from a short menu with a focus on local ingredients and traditions. Meat tends to be slow-cooked and treated with respect, and there's always a nondull vegetarian option. Various set menus with optional matched wines are also available.

Panimoravintola Plevna BEER HALL €€
(www.plevna.fi; Itäinenkatu 8; mains €10-20; ⊙food 11am-10pm) Inside the old Finlayson textile mill, this big barn of a place offers a wide range of delicious beer, cider and perry brewed on the premises, including an excellent strong stout. Meals are large and designed for soaking it all up: massive sausage platters and enormous slabs of pork in classic beer-hall style as well as more Finnish fish and steak dishes. 'Vegetables' here mean potatoes and onions, preferably fried, but it's all tasty, and service is fast.

Valo CAFE €€
(www.kahvilavalo.fi; Puutarhakatu 11; cakes €3-6; ⊙11am-10pm Mon-Thu, to midnight Fri, to 2am Sat, 10am-7.30pm Sun) This upmarket late-opening cafe is a cosy, central place doing pricey but excellent coffees, cakes and smoothies. It's a favourite haunt for trendy coffee-hounds and Sunday brunchers (€17 for this excellent spread) but also for 50-something mothers who know they deserve a treat.

✔ Kauppahalli MARKET €
(Hämeenkatu 19; ⊙8am-6pm Mon-Fri, to 4pm Sat; ✔) This intriguing indoor market is one of Finland's best, with picturesque wooden stalls serving a dazzling array of wonderful meat, fruit, baked goodies and fish.

Runo CAFE €
(www.kahviларuno.fi; Ojakatu 3; sandwiches €4-6; ⊙9am-8pm Mon-Sat, 10am-8pm Sun) With an arty crowd and bohemian feel, Runo (meaning 'poem') is an elegant, almost baroque cafe with books, paintings, decent coffee and huge windows that allow you to keep tabs on the weather.

Vohvelikahvila CAFE €
(www.vohvelikahvila.com; Ojakatu 2; waffles €4-7; ⊙10am-8pm Mon-Fri, to 7pm Sat, 11am-7pm Sun; 📶) This cosy and quaint little place does a range of sweet delights, but specialises above all in fresh waffles, with a big variety of sweet or savoury toppings. There's another branch on **Tuomiokirkonkatu** (www.kuparitalonvohvelikahvila.fi; Tuomiokirkonkatu 34; ⊙10am-8pm Mon-Fri, 11am-7pm Sat, noon-6pm Sun).

▾ Drinking & Entertainment
Panimoravintola Plevna and Tuulensuu are also fine places for a beer or two.

🅣🅞🅟 Café Europa BAR, CAFE
(www.ravintola.fi/europa; Aleksanterinkatu 29; ⊙noon-midnight Mon-Tue, to 2am Wed & Thu, to 3am Fri & Sat, 1pm-midnight Sun) Lavishly furnished with horsehair couches, armchairs, mirrors, chandeliers and paintings, this place successfully fuses a re-creation of a 1930s-style, old-Europe cafe with a popular meeting spot for students and anyone else who appreciates comfort, board games, Belgian and German beers and generously proportioned sandwiches and salads. There's good summer seating out the front.

Teerenpeli PUB
(www.teerenpeli.com; Hämeenkatu 25; ⊙noon-2am, to 3am Fri & Sat) On the main street, this is an enticing place with excellent microbrewery beer and cider. There's a relaxing, candlelit interior, heated terrace and heaps of choice at the taps. There's a huge downstairs space too, with comfy seating.

O'Connell's PUB
(www.oconnells.fi; Rautatienkatu 24; ⊙4pm-1am Sun-Mon, to 2am Tue-Fri, 2pm-2am Sat) Popular with both Finns and expats, this rambling

Irish pub is handy for the train station and has plenty of time-worn, comfortable seating and an air of bonhomie. Its best feature is the range of interesting beers on tap and carefully selected bottled imports. Regular free live music and other events.

Suvi BOAT BAR
(www.rengasravintolat.fi; Laukontori; ⊙10am-2am Jun-Sep) Moored alongside the Laukontori quay, this is a typical Finnish boat bar offering deck-top drinking. Prepare a boarding party and lap up the afternoon sun.

Tullikamari Klubi BAR, CONCERT VENUE
(www.klubi.net; Tullikamarinaukio 2; ⊙11am-10pm Mon & Tue to 4am Wed-Sat) This cavernous place, near the train station, is Tampere's main indoor live-music venue; there are usually several bands playing every week, and big Finnish names regularly swing by for concerts.

Ruma CLUB, BAR
(www.ruma.fi; Murtokatu 1; ⊙8pm-4am Wed-Sat) A cool spot with offbeat decor, quirky lighting, friendly staff, and a mixture of Finnish and European pop and alternative rock every day of the week. There's a cover of €3 to €5, avoidable if you get there early.

❶ Information

Forex (www.forex.fi; Hämeenkatu 4; ⊙9am-9pm Mon-Fri, to 6pm Sat) Money changers in the Stockmann Building.

Internet Café Madi (Tuomiokirkonkatu 36; per hr €3; ⊙10am-10pm Mon-Fri, 11am-10pm Sat & Sun) Free tea and coffee.

Visit Tampere (☑5656 6800; www.visittampere. fi; Rautatienkatu 25; ⊙9am-6pm Mon-Fri, 11am-3pm Sat & Sun Jun-Aug, 8.30am-4.30pm Mon-Fri Sep-May) In the train station. Has a booking desk and free internet terminal.

❶ Getting There & Away

AIR A number of airlines offer services to Tempere.

AirBaltic (www.airbaltic.com) Connects Tampere with Riga, Latvia.

Finnair/Flybe (www.finnair.com) Flies to Helsinki – though it's more convenient on the train – and serves other major Finnish cities.

Ryanair (☑0200 39000; www.ryanair.com) Has budget services to several European destinations including London Stansted, Edinburgh, 'Frankfurt' Hahn and Rome. Note that there's no ATM at the Ryanair terminal, but you can buy bus tickets with a card if you're euro-less.

SAS (☑06000 25831; www.sas.fi) Flies direct to Stockholm and Copenhagen.

BUS The **bus station** (Hatanpään valtatie 7) is in the south of town. Regular express buses run to Helsinki (€26.30, 2½ hours) and Turku (€24.80, two to three hours), and most other major towns in Finland are served from here.

TRAIN The **train station** (www.vr.fi; Rautatienkatu 25) is in the centre at the eastern end of Hämeenkatu. Express trains run hourly to/from Helsinki (€24 to €31, two hours). There are direct trains to Turku (€28.41, 1¾ hours), Oulu (€60 to €70, 4¼ to seven hours) and other cities.

❶ Getting Around

Tampere's bus service is extensive and includes the airport; a ticket costs €2.50. A 24-hour Tourist Ticket costs €6. A separate company serves the Ryanair terminal (€6). To use the bikes from stands around town, get a key from the tourist office for a €3 fee and returnable €40 deposit.

Hämeenlinna

☑03 / POP 67,300

Dominated by its namesake, majestic 13th-century Häme Castle, Hämeenlinna (Swedish: Tavastehus) is the oldest inland town in Finland. The town is quiet but picturesque, and its wealth of museums will keep you busy for a day or two. It makes a good stop between Helsinki and Tampere, and you could head on to the latter by lake boat.

⊙ Sights

Hämeenlinna CASTLE
(Häme Castle; www.nba.fi; adult/child €8/4; ⊙ 11am-6pm daily Jun–mid-Aug, 10am-4pm Tue-Fri, 11am-4pm Sat & Sun mid-Aug–May) Hämeenlinna means Häme Castle so it's no surprise that this bulky twin-towered red-brick fortress is the town's pride and most significant attraction. It never saw serious military action and, after the Russian takeover, was converted into a jail. The interior is a little disappointing, with a modern exhibition annex tacked on to the original building, the bare rooms of which don't really evoke its past. The guided tour is recommended.

By the castle are three worthwhile **museums**, which can be visited individually or with the castle on a combined ticket (adult/child €14/6). The most interesting is the Prison Museum, set in a prison block that only closed in 1997.

Sibeliuksen syntymäkoti MUSEUM
(www.hameenlinna.fi; Hallituskatu 11; adult/child €5/2; ⊙10am-4pm Tue-Sun May-Jun, daily Jul-Aug, noon-4pm Tue-Sun Sep-Apr) Finland's most

famous composer, Jean Sibelius, was born in Hämeenlinna in 1865 and his childhood home is now an unassuming museum with four rooms containing photographs, letters, his upright piano and some family furniture.

Palanderin Talo
HISTORIC BUILDING

(www.hameenlinna.fi; Linnankatu 16; adult/child €5/2; ⊙noon-3pm Tue-Sun Jun-Aug, Sat & Sun Sep-May) Finland loves its house museums and Palanderin Talo is among the best as it offers a wonderful insight into well-off, 19th-century Finnish life, thanks to excellent English-speaking guided tours.

🛏 Sleeping

Aulangon Lomakylä
CAMPGROUND, COTTAGES €

(☑675 9772; www.aulangonlomakyla.fi; Aulangon heikkiläntie 168; campsite €20, d/cabin/cottage €45/50/80; ℙ🐾) There are hostel-style rooms as well as camping and cabins at this camping ground on the edge of a nature park, 6km north of the centre. It's a lovely spot.

Hotelli Emilia
HOTEL €€

(☑6122106; www.hotelliemilia.fi; Raatihuoneenkatu 23; s/d €99/119; ℙ) On the pedestrian street, this is a privately owned hotel and a good deal with its summer discounts which are in place from June through August.

ℹ Information

The tourist office (☑621 3373; www. hameenlinna.fi; Raatihuoneenkatu 11; ⊙9am-5pm Mon, 9am-4.15pm Tue-Fri, also 11am-2pm Sat Jun-Aug) has plenty of information and free internet.

ℹ Getting There & Away

Hämeenlinna is located on the Helsinki–Tampere motorway and rail line, so trains and express buses to both cities are frequent and fast. In summer you can cruise on a lake ferry to or from Tampere.

Rauma

☑02 / POP 39,800

The main attraction of this historic seaside settlement is its Old Town.

◉ Sights

TOP CHOICE Vanha Rauma
HISTORIC AREA

(www.oldrauma.fi; house museums combined ticket €7) Some 600 wooden houses from the 18th and 19th centuries make up Vanha Rauma

(Old Rauma), a Unesco Site with a Wild West feel. With narrow cobbled streets, cafes, craft shops selling the town's famous lace, **house museums** and 15th-century stone **Church of the Holy Cross**, the Old Town makes modern-day Rauma worthy of a stop along the west coast.

🛏 Sleeping & Eating

Hotelli Vanha Rauma
HOTEL €€

(☑8376 2200; www.hotelvanharauma.fi; Vanhan-kirkonkatu 26; s/d €125/150; ℙ) This sleek hotel is set in a one-time fish market on the edge of the Old Town. Despite Rauma's creaky wooden feel, rooms here are modern and chic. There's a barely believable variety available for the same price. Ground-floor rooms are darkish and unremarkable, but some upstairs rooms are enormous suites, huge, stylish chambers with views of the park. There are only 20 rooms, so book ahead. Good weekend and summer deals can be found on its website. Bike hire available.

Rauman Kesähotelli
HOSTEL €

(☑050-511 8855; www.kesahotellirauma.fi; Satamakatu 20; s/d/f €47/62/75; ⊙Jun-Aug; ℙ) About 1km west of the Old Town, this summer hostel is student accommodation most of the year. It's clean and the facilities are excellent, with a private kitchen and bathrooms shared between two rooms.

Poroholma
CAMPGROUND €

(☑533 5522; www.poroholma.fi; Poroholmantie; campsites €10, plus per person €5, cottages €75-100; ⊙May-Aug; ℙ🐾) On pretty Otanlahti Bay about 2km northwest of the town centre, this pleasant camping ground has fabulous facilities and a range of cottages. A tourist 'train' chugs out there from the centre in peak season.

TOP CHOICE Wanhan Rauman Kellari
FINNISH €€

(☑866 6700; www.wrk.fi; Anundilankatu 8; mains €14-26; ⊙11am-10pm Mon, to 11pm Tue-Thu, to midnight Fri & Sat, noon-10pm Sun) On the edge of Vanha Rauma, this stone-and-timber cellar restaurant is a great place to splurge on Finnish specialities, seafood and steak. The rooftop beer terrace is terrific in summer. Excellent value.

Café Sali
CAFE, BISTRO €

(www.cafesali.fi; Kuninkaankatu 22; lunch €7.50-10; ⊙8am-10pm Jun-Aug, 9am-9pm Sep-May) On the kauppatori, this enormous restored historic building is part cafe, part restaurant and part lounge bar. It does great coffee and is the town favourite for lunchtime salads and daily hot specials.

❶ Information

Tourist office (📞834 3512; www.visitrauma. fi; Valtakatu 2; ⊙9am-6pm Mon-Fri, 10am-6pm Sat & Sun Jun-Aug, 9am-4pm Mon, Wed & Thu, to 5pm Tue, to 3pm Fri Sep-May) Publishes the helpful free pamphlet *A Walking Tour in the Old Town*.

❶ Getting There & Away

Rauma is connected by regular buses to Pori (45 minutes) and Turku (€22, 1½ hours).

Vaasa

🎵06 / POP 60,600

The Gulf of Bothnia gets wasp-waisted around here and Sweden's a bare 45 nautical miles away, so it's no surprise that a cultural duality exists in Vaasa (Swedish: Vasa). A quarter of the population speaks Swedish and the city has a feel all of its own. You'll hear conversations between friends and colleagues in restaurants and bars flitting between Finnish and Swedish, often in the same sentence. Vaasa has a thriving art scene, with several galleries and plenty of public sculpture.

◉ Sights

TOP **Pohjanmaan Museo** MUSEUM
(www.museo.vaasa.fi; Museokatu 3; adult/child €7/ free, Fri free; ⊙noon-5pm Tue-Sun, to 8pm Wed) This two-in-one museum is Vaasa's must-see. The art collection upstairs is extraordinary. There's an excellent range of works from the Golden Age of Finnish painting; more surprisingly, there's also a high-quality selection of European masters, purchased for virtually nothing in the chaos of Russia after the Revolution. Downstairs, Terra Nova is devoted to the ecosystem of the local environment.

Vaskiluoto Island AMUSEMENT PARK
On Vaskiluoto island, linked by bridge to the town centre, the amusement park, **Wasalandia** (www.wasalandia.fi; day pass €12; ⊙from 11am mid-Jun–early Aug, closing varies 4-7pm; ⊕), and water park and spa complex, **Tropiclandia** (www.tropiclandia.fi; admission €16-21; ⊙10am-8pm Sun-Thu, to 9pm Fri & Sat, closed Sep, outdoor water park mid-Jun–early Aug;

⊕), are both popular with Finnish families and great for young kids. A summer tourist train chugs out there from the kauppatori.

Kuntsi GALLERY
(www.kuntsi.fi; Rantakatu; adult/child €6/free; ⊙11am-5pm Tue-Sun, to 8pm Thu) One of this arty town's several interesting galleries, retro-contemporary Kuntsi is by the water. Its permanent collection and temporary exhibitions cover mainly Finnish art from the '50s to the '80s.

🛏 Sleeping

TOP **Hotel Kantarellis** HOTEL €€
(📞357 8100; www.hotelkantarellis.fi; Rosteninkatu 6; s/d €128/148; ❄@) Handy for the train or bus, this excellent modern independent hotel combines great facilities with lavish individual style. Rooms are gleamingly new and contrast elegant, old-time, polished-wood fittings and artistic toilets with trendy, spotlit nature photos behind the beds and a huge rotating flat-screen TV. All come with a sauna and most have a jacuzzi too. The reception and bar area is like something out of a Finnish fable, with two autumnal trees presiding over the fireplace and fountain.

TOP **Kenraali Wasa Hostel** GUESTHOUSE €
(📞0400 668 521; www.kenraaliwasahostel.com; Korsholmanpuistikko 6-8; s/d/tr €50/60/65; 🅿@) Decorated true to its origins as a former military hospital, this place is more guesthouse than hostel, with cosy private rooms, a slick iMac to get online, grassy surrounds, bike hire and a good kitchen. There's an intimate, peaceful feel to the place that's most appealing.

Hotel Astor HOTEL €€
(📞326 9111; www.astorvaasa.fi; Asemakatu 4; s/d €111/128; 🅿@) This stylish, intimate hotel opposite the train station is in a lovely old building with a classy, noble interior. The nicest rooms are in the old wing of the building, with polished floors and dark-wood furnishings. Weekend and summer discounts.

Omenahotelli HOTEL €
(📞0600 18018; www.omenahotels.com; Hovioikeudenpuistikko 23; r €60-90) This is one of the smaller hotels in this chain that takes internet bookings (you can also book using the terminal in the foyer). Rooms sleep up to four and come with fridge and microwave.

KVARKEN ARCHIPELAGO

This part of the Gulf of Bothnia is a World Heritage area known as the Kvarken (www.kvarken.fi); the land is still rising as the crust 'rebounds' after the last Ice Age weighed it down. New islets appear, expand and join other islands, forming a fascinating changing landscape across the shallow sea. You can drive or bike out to Replot to examine the phenomenon, but the area cries out for exploration by canoe; the Vaasa tourist office has details of where you can rent one. Terranova, in the Pohjanmaan Museo (p165), is the best place to go for more info about the area.

✖ Eating

Gustav Wasa   MODERN FINNISH €€€
(☎050-466 3208; www.gustavwasa.com; Raastuvankatu 24; set menus €49-72; ⊙6pm-midnight Tue-Fri, from 4pm Sat) This underground restaurant is one of Finland's best with a concise gourmet menu that blends classic Finnish with modern cuisine. Once a coal cellar, the transformation to suave restaurant is achieved through low lighting and attentive service. The pride of the house is the seven-course tasting menu that changes daily, but à la carte dishes are also available.

Strampen   FINNISH €€
(☎041-451 4512; www.strampen.com; Rantakatu 6; lunch buffet €9-12, mains €16-26; ⊙11am-10pm mid-Apr–Sep) This favourite in a lovely 19th-century waterside pavilion manages to do top-end meals inside, with various themed set menus, and affordable burgers and pastas for drinkers on its harbourside terrace. Both clienteles are happy, and staff keep the outdoor bar pumping until late in summer, when it's also open Sundays.

Fondis   FINNISH €€
(☎280 0400; www.fondis.fi; Hovioikeudenpuistikko 15; mains €14-21; ⊙11am-11pm Mon-Sat) There's a bit of everything here on the main pedestrian thoroughfare; Fondis has hearty Finnish meals with good service, there's a stylish lounge bar with sunny terrace and an upstairs club, and around the corner in El Gringo you'll find just about the cheapest beer in town.

❶ Information

Tourist office (☎325 1145; www.visitvaasa.fi; Raastuvankatu 30; ⊙9am-5pm Mon-Fri Jun-Aug, plus 10am-6pm Sat & Sun Jul, 9am-4pm Mon-Fri Sep-May) Books accommodation and rents out bikes. There's also an information kiosk open on the square in summer.

❶ Getting There & Away

From the combined bus and train station, there are frequent buses up and down the coast, and trains connecting via Seinäjoki to Tampere (€35.78, 2½ to three hours) and Helsinki (€56.93, four to five hours) among other destinations.

Finnair/Flybe and SAS fly daily to Helsinki. The airport is 12km southeast and is serviced by local buses on weekdays. SAS serves Stockholm.

There's a ferry service from Vaasa to Umeå in Sweden, see p491.

Jakobstad

☑06 / POP 19,700

The quaint town of Jakobstad (Finnish: Pietarsaari), about 100km north of Vaasa, has a Swedish-speaking majority and is one of the most distinctive and enchanting spots on this part of the Finnish west coast known as *parallelsverige* (parallel Sweden).

◉ Sights

Skata   HISTORIC AREA
Skata is filled with around 300 wonderfully preserved 18th-century wooden houses. It is just north of the centre and is Jakobstad's highlight. Most of the old town remains residential so it feels refreshingly untouristy.

🛏 Sleeping & Eating

There are cheap places to eat and drink along the partly pedestrian Kanalesplanaden, one block north of the market square.

Jugend Home   HOTEL, HOSTEL €
(☎781 4300; www.visitjugend.fi; Skolgatan 11; hostel s/d/f €39/52/72, hotel s/d €72/95; P❋@🖶) The lovely new rooms here, just on the edge of Skata, are light, peaceful and filled with understated pieces of Finnish design; the smaller 'hostel' rooms (without breakfast) for budget travellers are also pleasant.

Hotel Epoque   HOTEL €€
(☎788 7100; www.hotelepoque.fi; Jakobsgatan 10; s €102-125, d €122-187) This restored Customs House is the most upmarket place in town –

service is great (although reception hours are limited), and with just 16 rooms, it feels quiet, private and exclusive. From the extreme close-up mirrors to the blonde-wood floors, every aspect has been well thought out. The restaurant downstairs does a blend of Finnish and modern European that will have you dining in.

Westerlunds Inn　　　　　　GUESTHOUSE €

(☑723 0440; www.multi.fi/westerlund; Norrmalmsgatan 8; s/d/tr €29/45/55; ℗) Old-fashioned charm in the heart of the historic Skata part of town makes this lovely family-run guesthouse a romantic choice. There are kitchen facilities, a sauna and spotless shared bathrooms. Breakfast is €5 extra. Look for the signs saying Resandehem/Matkustajakoti.

🍴 **After Eight**　　　　　　CAFE €

(www.aftereight.fi; Storgatan; lunch €8.80; ⊗10am-7pm Mon-Fri; ☑) This smashing cafe-cum-cultural-centre is the best hang-out in town, with a relaxed atmosphere, friendly service and a grassy courtyard garden. Lunches feature simple but tasty choices, such as pea-and-bacon soup or chicken stir-fry, and big slabs of homemade cake are on offer at all times. They also run a hostel here, hire out bikes and offer internet access.

ℹ **Information**

Tourist office (☑723 1796; www.jakobstad.fi; Salutorget 1; ⊗8am-6pm Mon-Fri, 9am-3pm Sat Jun-Aug, 8am-5pm Mon-Fri Sep-May) Next to the town square.

ℹ **Getting There & Away**

There are regular buses to Jakobstad from Vaasa (€21.30, 1½ to 2½ hours) and other towns along the west coast.

Bennäs (Finnish: Pännäinen), 11km away, is the closest train station to Jakobstad. A shuttle bus (€3.80, 10 minutes) meets arriving trains.

LAKELAND, KARELIA & THE EAST

Most of southern Finland could be dubbed 'lakeland', but this spectacular area takes it to extremes. It often seems there's more water than land here, and what water it is: sublime, sparkling and clean, reflecting sky and forests as cleanly as a mirror. It's a land that leaves an indelible impression on every visitor.

The greater Lakeland area encompasses Karelia, once the symbol of Finnish distinctiveness and the totem of the independence movement. Most of Karelia today lies over the other side of the Russian border; much of the gruelling attrition of the Winter and Continuation Wars against the Soviet Union took place in this area, and large swaths of territory were lost in ceasefire and reparation agreements.

Lappeenranta

☑05 / POP 72,200

The South Karelian capital of Lappeenranta was a frontier garrison town until the construction of the Saimaa Canal in 1856 made it an important trading centre. These days the canal is a major attraction for tourists, with boats cruising through Russia to the Baltic at Vyborg, Finland's second-largest city until it was lost to its large neighbour. Finland's largest lake, Saimaa, spreads out from Lappeenranta's harbour, and the town itself is vibrant, with plenty of historical links in its old fortress; it's a good place to sample Karelian food and culture.

⊙ **Sights**

Linnoitus　　　　　FORTRESS, MUSEUM

(www.lappeenranta.fi/linnoitus; fortress free, adult/child combined museum ticket €8.50/free; ⊗10am-6pm Mon-Fri, 11am-5pm Sat & Sun Jun-late Aug, 11am-5pm Tue-Sun late Aug-May) On a small hill overlooking the harbour, Linnoitus is a fortress started by the Swedes and finished by the Russians in the 18th century. Some of the fortress buildings house galleries and craft workshops; others have been turned into museums. These include the **South Karelia Museum**, with a variety of folk costumes, local history and a scale model of Vyborg as it looked before it fell to the Russians in 1939, and the **South Karelia Art Museum**, with a permanent collection of paintings by Finnish and Karelian artists.

FREE **Hiekkalinna**　　　　　SANDCASTLE

(http://hiekkalinna.lappeenranta.fi; ⊗10am-9pm Jun-Aug; 🚸) An unlikely sight in inland Finland, Hiekkalinna is a giant sandcastle that uses around 3 million kg of sand for its ramparts and themed sculptures. It's great for kids, and has a small village of nearby rides (many free).

☞ Tours

Cruises on Lake Saimaa and the Saimaa Canal are popular, and there are daily departures from mid-May to mid-September from the passenger quay at the harbour. The cruise along the Saimaa Canal to Vyborg (Russia) is one of Lappeenranta's biggest drawcards. At the time of writing you didn't need a visa, even if you stayed overnight in Vyborg or took an onward minibus to St Petersburg, but check this ahead of time.

Saimaan Matkaverkko　　　CRUISE
(☏541 0100; www.saimaatravel.fi; Valtakatu 49; ⊙mid-May–early Sep) Runs various trips, including cruises to Savonlinna and visa-free trips to Vyborg and St Petersburg in Russia. They need a copy of your passport at least three days before departure to arrange the latter. Booking these cruises well in advance is advisable in any case, as they are very popular. It's on the roundabout at the eastern end of the main street through town.

⌂ Sleeping

Contact the Lappeenranta tourist office for details of some of the many appealing farmhouse stays available in the area.

⌗ Scandic Hotel Patria　　　HOTEL €€
(☏677 511; www.scandichotels.com; Kauppakatu 21; s/d €120/140; P❋@) Definitely one of the best places to stay in Lappeenranta, especially since its recent revamp, the Scandic is also close to the harbour and fortress. The better doubles feature balconies with park views, but all rooms are fitted out with minimalist Scandic chic, and air-con.

Huhtiniemi　　　CAMPGROUND €
(☏451 5555; www.huhtiniemi.com; Kuusimäenkatu 18; campsites €14 plus per person €5, 2-/4-person cottages €35/45, apt €75-90; ⊙mid-May–Sep; P⌕) This large complex 2km west of the centre has a bed for just about everyone. There's the expansive camping ground by the lake (mosquito repellent is a must in summer) as well as tidy cottages with bunks and fridges, and self-contained apartments. But wait, there's more. **Finnhostel Lappeenranta** (☏451 5555; www.huhtiniemi.com; s/d €65/78) offers hotel-style accommodation with HI discount and pool and sauna access in a nearby sports centre, while **Huhtiniemi Hostel** (☏451 5555; www.huhtiniemi.com; dm €15; ⊙Jun-Aug) offers two simple six-bed dorms in summer. Buses 1, 3 and 5 run past; most incoming intercity buses will also stop here.

✕ Eating & Drinking

Stalls at the harbour, kauppatori and kauppahalli sell local Karelian specialities such as *vety* (bread roll or pie with ham, sliced boiled egg, mince and spices), the similar *atomi* (either smoked ham or egg), rice pies, or waffles with jam and whipped cream.

In town, Kauppakatu has a lively strip of bars.

Kahvila Majurska　　　CAFE €
(www.majurskantalo.fi; Kristiinankatu 1; pastries €3-5; ⊙10am-7pm Jul-early Aug, to 6pm Jun & late Aug, 10am-5pm Mon-Sat, 11am-5pm Sun rest of yr) In a beautifully furnished 18th-century wooden building at the fortress complex, Majurska oozes Tsarist-era charm, serves tea from the samovar and does a good range of homemade cakes and quiches.

Wanha Makasiini　　　BISTRO €€
(☏010-666 8611; www.ravintolawanhamakasiini.fi; Satamatie 4; mains €9-25; ⊙4-10pm Mon-Thu, to 11pm Fri, noon-11pm Sat, noon-6pm Sun; ⌕) With something for everyone, this handsome double dining room sits in a thick-walled old harbour storehouse by the water under the fortress. Cheap pizzas are balanced on the menu by succulent pork dishes, toothsome pastas and tasty vegetarian options. The kitchen shuts like a guillotine an hour before close though, so get there with plenty of time if you don't want impatient foot-tapping while you try to enjoy a meal. Opens extended hours in summer.

**SS Suvi-Saimaa &
Prinsessa Armaada**　　　BOAT BAR
In summer a top place for a drink is down at the harbour where these two boats welcome you to their busy beer terraces.

ℹ Information

Tourist kiosk (⊙10am-8pm Jul, to 6pm late Jun & Aug) Summer info at the Hiekkalinna (giant sandcastle by the water).

Go Saimaa (☏667 788; www.gosaimaa.com; Valtakatu 37; ⊙10am-6pm Jun-Aug, 10am-5pm Mon-Fri, to 2pm Sat rest of yr) Tourist information in the centre of town.

ℹ Getting There & Away

From Lappeenranta's airport, Ryanair serves Milan Bergamo and Düsseldorf Weeze, while AirBaltic flies to Riga. Take bus 4 to the airport, a 20-minute walk from the centre.

The bus and train stations are together about 500m south of the centre along Ratakatu, though most buses stop in the centre too. Trains are significantly speedier than buses to Helsinki (€42.77, 2½ hours) and Joensuu (€37.05, 2¼ hours). For Savonlinna, change trains at Parikkala. For Kuopio change at Mikkeli.

Savonlinna

015 / POP 27,600

Finland's prettiest town, Savonlinna shimmers on a sunny day as the water ripples around its centre. Set on two islands between Haapavesi and Pihlajavesi lakes, it's a classic Lakeland settlement with a major attraction: perched on a rocky islet, one of Europe's most visually dramatic castles lords it over the picturesque centre and hosts July's world-famous opera festival in a spectacular setting.

Sights & Activities

Olavinlinna   CASTLE
(www.olavinlinna.fi; adult/child €8/4; 10am-6pm Jun–mid-Aug, to 4pm Mon-Fri, 11am-4pm Sat & Sun mid-Aug–May) Standing immense and haughty on a rock in the lake, 15th-century Olavinlinna is one of the most spectacularly situated castles in northern Europe and, as well as being an imposing fortification, is also the venue for the month-long Savonlinna Opera Festival. The castle's been heavily restored, but is still seriously impressive, not least in the way it's built directly on the rock in the middle of the lake. To visit the upper part of the interior, including the towers and chapel, you must join a guided tour (around 45 minutes). Tours are multilingual depending on demand and depart on the hour, the last tour leaves one hour before closing.

Savonlinnan Maakuntamuseo   MUSEUM
(www.savonlinna.fi/museo; Riihisaari; adult/child €5/2; 10am-5pm daily, closed Mon Sep-May) Across from the castle, the provincial museum tells of local history and the importance of water transport. Here also is **Nestori** (0205 645 929; www.outdoors.fi; Akselinkatu 8), a national parks visitor and information centre for the Saimaa region. Moored alongside are four **historic ships**, all with exhibitions open from May to September during museum hours (same ticket). It's a bargain to visit if you're going to the castle too; just a euro extra for a combined ticket.

Boat Trips   CRUISE
From June to August, Savonlinna passenger harbour is buzzing with dozens of daily scenic cruises that last about an hour and cost around €10 to €16. The boats anchor alongside the kauppatori and you can soon see which is the next departure. The **SS Heinävesi** (www.savonlinnanlaivat.fi) runs daily at 11am to Retretti art gallery in Punkaharju (adult one way/return €25/33, two hours, July to early August), giving you 2½ hours there.

There are also longer cruises to Kuopio and Lappeenranta.

Festivals

Savonlinna Opera Festival   OPERA
(476 750; www.operafestival.fi; Olavinkatu 27) Finland's most famous festival, with an enviably dramatic setting: the covered courtyard of Olavinlinna Castle. It offers four weeks of high-class opera performances from early July to early August. The atmosphere in town during the festival is reason enough to come; it's buzzing, with restaurants serving postshow midnight feasts, and animated discussions and impromptu arias on all sides.

The festival's excellent website details the program. There are tickets in various price bands. The top grades (€117 to €180) are fine, but the penultimate grade (€82 to €99) puts you in untiered seats, so it helps to be tall. The few cheap seats (€40) have a severely restricted view. Buy tickets up to a year in advance from **Lippupalvelu** (0600 10800; www.lippupalvelu.fi).

Ballet Festival   BALLET
(www.savonlinnaballet.net) When the opera's done, this worthwhile festival runs for four days in early August.

Sleeping

Prices rise sharply during the opera festival, when hotel beds are scarce. Fortunately, students are out of town and their residences are converted to summer hotels and hostels. Book accommodation well in advance if you plan to visit during July.

Lossiranta Lodge   GUESTHOUSE €€€
(044-511 2323; www.lossiranta.net; Aino Acktén Puistotie; d €160-200; P) To get up close and personal with the castle, this lakeside spot is the place to be: its impressive form looms just opposite. Offering five snug little nests

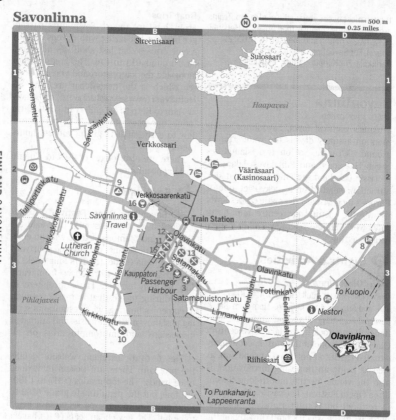

in an outbuilding, this is one of Finland's most charming hotels. All are very different but decorated with love and style; they come with a small kitchen (yes, that's it in the cupboard) and numerous personal touches. The best has a wood sauna and jacuzzi – a honeymoon special. Breakfast is served on the lawn if weather allows; when the snows fall, an outdoor spa bath will keep the chills out. This is like a rural retreat but in the middle of town; warm personal service seals the experience. The same people run **Tavis Inn** (Kalkkiuuninkatu), further along the lakeside. There are no castle views but rooms and suites are larger than at Lossiranta, and summer art exhibitions give it its own discrete ambience.

Perhehotelli Hospitz
HOTEL **€€**

(☑515 661; www.hospitz.com; Linnankatu 20; s/d €88/98; ☉Apr-Dec; ℗) This cosy place near the castle is a Savonlinna classic, built in the 1930s and redolent of that period's elegance, with striped wallpaper, ornate public areas and an orchard garden down to the water. The rooms are also stylish, although most bathrooms are small. Superior doubles offer a more upmarket experience, with modern styling, balconies and extra space.

Spa Hotel Casino
HOTEL **€€**

(☑73950; www.spahotelcasino.fi; Vääräsaari; s/d €99/115, large d €147-165; ℗❄@☒) Charmingly situated on an island across a footbridge from the kauppatori, this is old-fashioned in parts but a good option. Nearly all rooms have a balcony; those that don't have their own sauna. Some have dreamy outlooks west over water. Many rooms have been recently renovated, and the new installation of air-con is a bonus. Guests have access to the spa facilities, and the location is fantastic. Nonguests can use the spa for €10 in the afternoons.

Savonlinna

Kesähotelli Vuorilinna   HOTEL €€

(✆73950; www.spahotelcasino.fi; Kylpylaitoksentie; s/d from €65/85; ☺Jun-Aug; ℙ🛜) Set in several buildings mostly used by students, this friendly complex shares the spa hotel's appealing location across a footbridge from the centre. Rooms are clean and comfortable; the cheaper ones share a bathroom and kitchen between two. Prices include breakfast and afternoon sauna.

Vuohimäki   CAMPGROUND €

(✆537 353; www.suncamping.fi; campsite €15, q €58-76, cabins €65-90; ☺early Jun-late Aug; ℙ) Located 7km southwest of town, this campground has good facilities but fills quickly in July. Prices for rooms and cabins are cheaper in June and August. It hires out canoes, bikes and rowing boats.

SS Heinävesi   BOAT CABINS €

(✆533 120; www.savonlinnanlaivat.fi; d upper/lower deck €70/60) During summer this steamer offers cramped-but-cute two-bunk cabins after the last cruise every afternoon or evening. It's moored right in the centre of things. Breakfast is extra.

Lake Star   BOAT CABINS €

(✆0400 200 117; www.lakestar.info; d €50) Offers tight, basic cabins on board a boat after the last cruise every evening.

✖ Eating & Drinking

The lively lakeside **kauppatori** is the place for casual snacking. A *lörtsy* (turnover) is typical and comes savoury with *lihalörtsy* (meat) or sweet with *omenalörtsy* (apple) or *lakkalörtsy* (cloudberry). Savonlinna is also famous for fried *muikku* (vendace, tiny lake fish); try these at **Kalastajan Koju** (www.kalastajankoju.com; Kauppatori; ☺10am-10pm Mon-Tue, to midnight Wed-Sat, 11am-10pm Sun Jun-Aug), or the **Muikkubaari** (www.sokoshotels.fi; Kauppatori 4-6, top fl, Hotel Seurahuone; ☺11am-10pm Mon-Tue, to midnight Wed-Sat, noon-10pm Sun May-Aug) at the Seurahuone hotel.

The opera festival peps up Savonlinna's nightlife, with restaurants open late and pubs thronged with postperformance merriment. Near the castle, on lovely Linnankatu, several handsome cafe-bars compete for the pre- and postopera crowd with mini bottles of fizz and traditional, if priced-up, Finnish plates. In the low season, options are few.

🏆 CHOICE Huvila   FINNISH, BREWERY €€

(✆555 0555; www.panimoravintolahuvila.fi; Puistokatu 4; mains €16-28; ☺noon-midnight Jun-Aug) This noble wooden building was formerly a fever hospital then a mental asylum, but these days writes happier stories as an excellent microbrewery and restaurant just across the harbour from the town centre. The food focuses on fresh local ingredients and might feature unusual fare like goose or wild boar, all expertly prepared and served in generous quantities. The staff will recommend a beer match, whether it be fresh, hoppy Joutsen, traditional sweet *sahti*, or the deliciously rich dessert stout. The terrace is a wonderful place on a sunny afternoon, with live music some weekends.

Majakka
FINNISH €€

(⌨206 2825; www.ravintolamajakka.fi; Satamakatu 11; mains €14-20; ⊙11am-10pm Mon-Thu, to midnight Fri & Sat, noon-9pm Sun; ⊕) This restaurant has a decklike terrace fitting the nautical theme (the name means 'lighthouse'). Local meat and fish specialities are tasty, generously sized and fairly priced and the select-your-own appetiser plate is a nice touch. It's child friendly too.

Liekkilohi
SEAFOOD €€

(www.liekkilohi.fi; fish buffet per kg €42; ⊙11am-9pm Mon-Sat, 1-9pm Sun late Jun-mid Aug) This bright-red pontoon, anchored just off the kauppatori, specialises in 'flamed' salmon, a delicious plate that forms part of an excellent pay-by-weight fish buffet. It opens until 1am on opera nights.

Torikahvio
CAFE €

(www.torikahvio.fi; Kauppatori; snacks €2-5; ⊙9am-3pm) Run by a stout grandmotherly figure, this is a worthwhile option on the square to try the local speciality, *lörtsy*, available here with all sorts of fillings. Delicious!

Olutravintola Sillansuu
PUB

(Verkkosaarenkatu 1; ⊙2pm-2am Tue-Sat, to midnight Sun & Mon) Savonlinna's best pub by some distance is compact and cosy, offering an excellent variety of international bottled beers, a decent whisky selection and friendly service. There's a downstairs area with a pool table; during the festival, amateur arias are sometimes sung as the beer kegs empty.

❶ Information

Savonlinna Travel (⌨0600 30007; www.savonlinna.travel; Puistokatu 1; ⊙9am-5pm Mon-Fri Aug-Jun, 10am to 6pm Mon-Sat Jul) Tourist information including accommodation reservation, farmstays, festival tickets and tours. Free internet. Usually also opens 10am to 2pm Sundays in July.

❶ Getting There & Away

AIR Flybe flies daily between Helsinki and Savonlinna in summer and more seldom in winter. The airport is 13km from the centre and is connected by **taxi shuttle** (⌨044-025 2471) in July and August (€14, 20 minutes).

BOAT Boat services include the following.

MS Brahe (⌨05-541 0100; www.saimaatravel.fi) MS Brahe heads to/from Lappeenranta (€87, eight hours) once a week during summer; the fare includes lunch and return bus transfer to Savonlinna.

MS Puijo (www.mspuijo.fi) From mid-June to mid-August, MS Puijo travels to Kuopio on Monday, Wednesday and Friday at 9am (€88 one way, 10½ hours), returning on Tuesday, Thursday and Saturday. You can book a return from Savonlinna with overnight cabin accommodation for €175.

BUS Buses run to the following destinations.

Helsinki €51.90, 4½ to six hours, several per day

Joensuu €25.50, three hours, Mondays to Fridays

Kuopio €31.80, three hours

Mikkeli €23.30, 1½ hours

TRAIN Trains departing from Helsinki (€56.93, 4¼ hours) and Joensuu (€29.47, 2¼ hours),

---

THE SEAL LAKES

Linnansaari (www.outdoors.fi) and **Kolovesi**, two primarily water-based national parks in the Savonlinna area, offer fabulous lakescapes dotted with islands; all best explored by hiring a canoe or rowing boat. Several outfitters offer these services, and free camping spots dot the lakes' shores. This is perhaps the best part of the Lakeland to really get up close and personal with the region's extraordinary natural beauty. It makes a good winter destination too, with laketop skating tracks, snowshoe walks and ice fishing.

This is the habitat of the Saimaa ringed seal, an endangered freshwater species whose population levels have stabilised and are on the increase, although there remain only a precarious 300-odd of the noble greyish beasts. Late May is the best time to glimpse them.

A convenient place for information on these parks is the Nestori centre (p169) in the Savonlinna museum. **Saimaaholiday** (⌨Oravi 015-647290, Porosalmi 020-729 1760; www.saimaaholiday.net) can set you up with anything you need for Linnansaari, from maps and canoe/equipment hire to hostel and hotel accommodation at the two main embarkation points for park exploration, Oravi and Rantasalmi. For the Kolovesi park, **Kolovesi Retkeily** (⌨040-558 9163; www.sealtrail.com) is the best and most experienced operator.

both require a change in Parikkala. For Kuopio, Jyväskylä and Tampere, rail buses will shuttle you the two-hour trip to Pieksämäki to connect with trains.

Around Savonlinna

PUNKAHARJU

Situated between Savonlinna and Parikkala, Punkaharju is a renowned sand ridge covered with pines; the surrounding forest and lakes are beautiful and it is a great area for cycling or walking. Worth the trip in itself is wonderful **Retretti** (www.retretti.fi; adult/child €16/5, with Lusto €23/9; ◷10am-6pm early Jun-late Aug), one of the world's most unusual galleries. An innovative annual exhibition of contemporary art is displayed inside an enormous subterranean cavern complex, artificial but authentic in atmosphere.

Not far away, **Lusto** (www.lusto.fi; adult/child €10/5, with Retretti €23/9; ◷10am-7pm Jun-Aug, 10am-5pm May & Sep, 10am-5pm Tue-Sun Oct-Apr) is dedicated to forests and forestry and is a good visit, with plenty of English information. There's also tourist information here.

Trains between Savonlinna and Parikkala stop at Retretti, Lusto and Punkaharju train stations (35 minutes, five to six daily). You can also get here on less-regular buses from Savonlinna or by boat.

KERIMÄKI

Unexpectedly, the world's largest wooden church, the **Kerimäen Kirkko** (Kerimäki Church; www.kerimaki.fi; ◷10am-7pm Jul, to 6pm Jun & early Aug, to 4pm late Aug) can be found here, about 23km east of Savonlinna. It was built in 1847 to seat a (very optimistic) congregation of 5000 people. Regular buses run here from Savonlinna.

Jyväskylä

☏ 014 / POP 132,000

Vivacious and young at heart, central Lakeland's main town has a wonderful waterside location and an optimistic feel that makes it a real drawcard. Thanks to Alvar Aalto, the city also has a global reputation for its architecture, and petrolheads know it as the legendary venue for the Finnish leg of the World Rally Championships. Along with Alvar Aalto-Museo, Jyväskylä has several other worthwhile museums, all free on Friday, and closed on Monday.

◉ Sights & Activities

Alvar Aalto-Museo   MUSEUM
(www.alvaraalto.fi; Alvar Aallon katu 7; adult/child €6/free, Fri Sep-May free; ◷11am-6pm Tue-Sun, from 10am Tue-Fri Jun-Aug) Alvar Aalto, a giant of 20th-century architecture, was schooled here, opened his first offices here and spent his summers in nearby Muuratsalo. The city has dozens of Aalto buildings, but stop first at one of his last creations: this museum, near the university to the west of the centre. It's very engaging, and you get a real feel for the man and his philosophy. It stocks the free pamphlet *Alvar Aalto's Jyväskylä*, which plots some of his significant buildings in and around the city. Outside town, at **Säynätsalo Town Hall** (Säynätsalon Kunnantalo; ☏015-623 801; Mon-Fri by donation, Sat & Sun €4; ◷8.30am-3.30pm Mon-Fri year-round, also 1-4pm Sat & Sun mid-Jul–Aug), you can sleep in a room that the man himself slept in, and at Muuratsalo you can visit his experimental summer cottage.

Cruises   BOAT TOUR
(www.jyvaskyla.fi) In summer there are numerous cruise options, from short lake trips to longer journeys on the Keitele canal or as far as the city of Lahti.

Laajavuori Winter Sports Centre   SKIING
(www.laajis.fi; Laajavuorentie; ♿) Four kilometres from town, this centre has 12 slopes including a kids' run, as well as 62km of cross-country trails. It's easily reached on bus 25 from the town centre.

⌁ Sleeping

TOP CHOICE **Hotel Yöpuu**   BOUTIQUE HOTEL €€
(☏333 900; www.hotelliyopuu.fi; Yliopistonkatu 23; s/d/ste €105/132/185; P @) Among Finland's most enchanting boutique hotels, this exquisite spot has lavishly decorated rooms, all individually designed in markedly different styles and offering excellent value for this part of Europe. The Africa room is really something to behold, while the Aalto room is the one to go for if you like a cleaner, more Nordic look. Service is warm and hospitable with an assured personal touch – including a welcome drink – that makes for a delightful stay. There's an excellent restaurant too, and discounts on weekends.

Kesähotelli Harju   HOTEL €
(☏010-279 2004; www.hotelharju.fi; Sepänkatu 3; s/d/tr €49/60/72; ◷early Jun-early Aug; P @)

Five minutes uphill from the centre, this excellent summer hotel has modern, light and spacious student rooms with kitchenette (no utensils, but there's an equipped kitchen downstairs) and good bathrooms. It's a real bargain, especially given that breakfast and an evening sauna are included.

Hotelli Milton   HOTEL €€
(☑337 7900; www.hotellimilton.com; Hannikaisenkatu 29; s/d €85/120) Right in the thick of things, this family-run hotel has an old-fashioned dark foyer, but the modern rooms offer plenty of natural light, space and attractive wooden floors; most have a balcony. An evening sauna on weekdays is included and it's very handy for the bus and train stations. Weekend prices are great (singles/doubles €60/80).

✗ Eating & Drinking

TOP CHOICE Figaro   FINNISH €€€
(☑212 255; www.figaro-restaurant.com; Asemakatu 4; mains €23-28; ⊙11am-11pm Mon-Fri, noon-11pm Sat, 2-10pm Sun; ▣) With a warm drawing-room feel and cordial service, this place backs up the atmosphere with excellent food served in generous portions. The fish is especially good, served with creamy sauces and inventive garnishes. Sizeable steaks are a given, and reindeer and bear make occasional appearances. There are good vegetarian mains too, and it's youngster friendly. Next door, in the 'Winebistro', a number of interesting drops are available by the glass, and good-value bistro plates are served (€16 to €22).

Soppabaari   SOUP BAR €
(☑449 8001; www.soppabaari.fi; Väinönkeskus; soups, pasta €7.90; ⊙11am-8pm Mon-Thu, to 10pm Fri, noon-10pm Sat) This cute little licensed soup bar is situated in a small arcade in the heart of town. It does three daily soups and three pastas, all of which are pretty much guaranteed to be delicious. There are also tapas-sized portions of Finnish treats like meatballs for €2 to €4.

Ye Old Brick's Inn   PUB €€
(www.oldbricksinn.fi; Kauppakatu 41; mains €14-23; ⊙11am-midnight Mon, to 2am Tue-Thu, to 3am Fri, noon-3am Sat, noon-midnight Sun) In the liveliest part of the pedestrian zone, this warm and welcoming pub has several excellent beers on tap, a cosy interior and an outdoor terrace screened by plastic plants – the place to be on a summer evening. It also has a good upmarket bar menu featuring steaks, pasta and more adventurous choices like duck. Opens longer hours midweek in summer.

Katriinan Kasvisravintola   VEGETARIAN €
(www.maijasilvennoinen.fi; Kauppakatu 11; lunch €6-9; ⊙11am-2.30pm Mon-Fri; ▣) A couple of blocks west of the pedestrian zone, this vegetarian lunch restaurant is an excellent bet – €6 gets you soup and salad bar, €7 buys a hot dish instead of the soup, and €9 gets you the lot. It changes daily – you might get pasta, ratatouille or curry – but it's always tasty.

Sohwi   PUB
(www.sohwi.fi; Vaasankatu 21; ⊙2pm-late Mon-Fri, noon-2am Sat, 2-10pm Sun) A short walk from the centre is an excellent bar with a spacious wooden terrace, a good menu of snacks and soak-it-all-up bar meals (mains €14 to €19), and plenty of lively student and academic discussion lubricated by a range of good bottled and draught beers. It's open longer hours in summer. A great place.

❶ Information

Tourist Office (☑266 0113; www.jyvaskyla region.fi; Asemakatu 6; ⊙9am-5pm Mon-Fri, also 9am-2pm Sat Jun-Aug) Good info and ticket sales, including day passes for the local buses (€8 or €12 depending on distance), handy if you're following Aalto's footsteps.

❶ Getting There & Away

AIR Finnair/Flybe operates daily flights from Helsinki to Jyväskylä. Jyväskylä airport is 21km north of the centre; buses meet flights.

BUS The bus terminal shares the Matkakeskus building with the train station and has many daily express buses connecting Jyväskylä to southern and central Finnish towns, including hourly departures to Helsinki (€48.70, 4½ hours), some requiring a change.

TRAIN The train station is between the town and the harbour, in the Matkakeskus building. There are regular trains from Helsinki (€50.30, three to 3½ hours), some requiring a change at Tampere.

Kuopio
☑017 / POP 97,600

Most things a reasonable person could desire from a summery lakeside town are in Kuopio, with pleasure cruises on the azure water, spruce forests to stroll in, wooden

SHE AIN'T HEAVY, SHE'S MY WIFE

If the thought of grabbing your wife by the legs, hurling her over your shoulder and running for your life sounds appealing, make sure you're in Sonkajärvi, 100km north of Kuopio near the town of Iisalmi, in early July, for the **Wife-Carrying World Championships** (www.eukonkanto.fi). What began as a heathenish medieval habit of pillaging neighbouring villages in search of nubile women has become one of Finland's oddest – and most publicised – events.

The championship is a race over a 253.5m obstacle course, where competitors must carry their 'wives' through water traps and over hurdles to achieve the fastest time. Dropping your cargo means a 15-second penalty. The winners get the wife's weight in beer and, of course, the prestigious title of Wife-Carrying World Champions. To enter, you need only €50 and a consenting female.

There's also a sprint and a team competition; the championship is accompanied by a weekend of drinking, dancing and typical Finnish frivolity.

Buses and trains connect Kuopio with Iisalmi, from where buses run to Sonkajärvi, 18km northeast.

waterside pubs, and local fish specialities to taste. And what could be better than a traditional smoke sauna to give you the necessary impetus to jump into the admittedly chilly waters?

⊙ Sights & Activities

Puijo   HILL

Even small hills have cachet in flat Finland, and Kuopio was so proud of Puijo that it was crowned with a tower. Take the lift to the top of the 75m-high **Puijo Torni** (Puijo Tower; www.puijo.com; adult/child €6/3; ☺10am-9pm Mon-Sat, to 7pm Sun Jun-Aug, 10am-7pm Mon-Thu, to 9pm Fri, 11am-9pm Sat, 11am-4pm Sun Sep-May) for vast perspectives of (yes, you guessed correctly) lakes and forests. The spruce-wooded hill is a popular spot for mountain biking, walking and, in winter, cross-country skiing, and there's a giant all-season ski jump here where you can often see jumpers in training. Bus 22 runs from the north side of the kauppatori twice daily Monday to Friday, early June to mid-August or you can walk to the top from the town centre in 30 to 40 minutes.

Kuopion Museo   MUSEUM

(www.kuopionmuseo.fi; Kauppakatu 23; adult/child €6/free; ☺10am-5pm Tue, Thu & Fri, to 7pm Wed, 11am-5pm Sat & Sun) In a castlelike, art nouveau mansion, this museum has a wide scope. The top two floors are devoted to cultural history, but the real highlight is the natural-history display, with a wide variety of beautifully presented Finnish wildlife, including a mammoth and an ostrich wearing snow boots. The ground floor has temporary exhibitions. Pick up English explanations at the ticket desk.

Kuopion Korttelimuseo   MUSEUM

(www.korttelimuseo.kuopio.fi; Kirkkokatu 22; adult/child €4/free; ☺10am-5pm Tue-Sun mid-May–Aug, to 3pm Tue-Fri, to 4pm Sat & Sun Sep–mid-May) This museum is a block of old town houses, and a it's a real delight. Several homes – all with period furniture and decor – are very detailed and thorough, and the level of information (in English) is excellent.

Pikku-Pietarin Torikuja   MARKET

(www.pikkupietarintorikuja.net; ☺10am-5pm Mon-Fri, to 3pm Sat Jun-Aug) Pikku-Pietarin Torikuja is an atmospheric narrow lane of renovated red wooden houses converted into quirky shops stocking jewellery, clothing, handicrafts and other items. Halfway along is an excellent cafe (open from 8am). Also opens in December as a Christmas market.

[TOP CHOICE] Jätkänkämppä   SAUNA

(☎030-60830; www.rauhalahti.fi; adult/child €12/6; ☺4-10pm Tue, also Thu Jun-Aug) Time your Kuopio visit for a Tuesday (also Thursday in summer) so you can sweat in Jätkänkämppä smoke sauna, a memorable and sociable experience that draws locals and visitors. This giant *savusauna* (smoke sauna) seats 60; it's mixed, and guests are given towels to wear. Bring a swimsuit for a dip in the lake – devoted locals and brave tourists do so even when it's covered with ice. The restaurant in the adjacent loggers' cabin serves traditional dinners (adult/child buffet €21/10.50) when the sauna's on, with accordion entertainment and a lumberjack show. Bus 7 goes every half hour from the kauppatori to the Rauhalahti hotel complex, from where it's a 600m walk to the sauna, or you could take a lake boat from the passenger harbour in summer.

Lake Cruises
BOAT TOUR

From late May to late August there are regular lake and canal cruises from the harbour. Ninety-minute jaunts cost €13 to €16 (half-price for children) and depart hourly from 11am to 6pm. There are cruises to Rauhalahti tourist centre (€14 return) Monday to Saturday from late June to mid-August; a good way to get to the smoke sauna. Special theme cruises include dinner and dancing, wine tasting or a trip to a local berry farm. There are also canal cruises and a monastery cruise to Valamo and Lintula, with return bus transport (€79). One of the companies offering most options is **Roll** (📞266 2466; www.roll. fi; Minna Canthinkatu 4). Cruises can be paid for at the harbour or booked at the tourist office.

★ Festivals & Events

Kuopion Tanssii ja Soi
DANCE

(www.kuopiodancefestival.fi) In mid-June, this festival brings open-air classical and modern dance performances, comedy and theatre gigs, and the town is generally buzzing.

🛏 Sleeping

Hotel Atlas
HOTEL €€

(📞020-789 6101; www.hotelatlas.fi; Haapaniemenkatu 22; s/d €120/140; P✳@) A historic Kuopio hotel that reopened in 2012 after complete remodelling, the Atlas is now the city's most appealing option, not least for its prime location on the kauppatori. The commodious modern rooms, with a sofa, are well soundproofed and offer perspectives over the square or, more unusually, the interior of a department store. Prices are variable and there are three grades of room (superiors are €25 to €35 more than standards) plus suites.

Hotelli Jahtihovi
HOTEL €€

(📞264 4400; www.jahtihovi.fi; Snellmaninkatu 23; s/d €89/109; P✳@) Well-located near the harbour on a quiet street, this cordial independent hotel makes a good address. Regular rooms are good-sized and pleasant; the superiors, in a modern wing, add big windows, extra mod cons and a stylish look for only €10 extra. A session in the smart new sauna is included, and parking's free. Prices drop €20 at weekends.

Spa Hotel Rauhalahti
HOTEL €€

(📞030-60830; www.rauhalahti.com; Katiskaniementie 8; s/d €109/144; P@🏊✉) Though it feels a bit faded in parts, this still makes a great place to stay, largely because of the huge scope for activities here. The spa complex is good (available to nonguests for €12), and the rooms are spacious, with low beds and decent in-room facilities. In the same complex is the cheaper **Hostelli Rauhalahti** (s/d €77/92), with simple Nordic rooms and full use of the hotel's facilities, as well as **Apartment Hotel Rauhalahti** (2-/4-person apt from €144/220) which has excellent modern pads with all the trimmings, including (for not much extra dough) a sauna. There are some excellent family packages offered on their website. It's 5km south of town; take bus 7, or it's €20 in a cab.

Matkustajakoti Rautatie
GUESTHOUSE €

(📞580 0569; www.kuopionasemagrilli.com; Asemakatu 1; s/d €60/79, without bathroom €50/65; P↩) This friendly place, run out of the *grilli* (takeaway) at the train station, actually offers en suite rooms in the station itself, which are very comfortable, spacious and surprisingly peaceful. Across the road, at Vuorikatu 35, it has some cheaper but also acceptable rooms, this time with shared bathroom. No wi-fi.

Camping Rauhalahti
CAMPGROUND €

(📞473 000; www.visitrauhalahti.fi; Kiviniementie; campsites €13, plus per person €4, cabins €32-60, cottages €120; ☺late May-late Aug; P🏠) Next to the Rauhalahti spa complex, this camping ground has a great location, plenty of facilities and is well set up for families. As well as simple cabins and well-equipped cottages, there are swish year-round holiday homes with all the mod cons. Bus 7 or 16 will get you here.

Hostelli Hermanni
HOSTEL €

(📞040-910 9083; www.hostellihermanni.fi; Hermanninaukio 3D; dm/s/d €30/50/55; P@) Tucked away in a quiet area 1.5km south of the kauppatori (follow Haapaniemenkatu and bear left when you can: the hostel's in the Metsähallitus building), this is a well-run little hostel with comfy wooden bunks and beds, high ceilings and decent shared bathrooms and kitchen. Check-in is between 2pm and 9pm; if you are going to arrive later, call ahead. Bus 1 from the centre makes occasional appearances nearby.

✖ Eating

TOP CHOICE Musta Lammas
FINNISH €€€

(☎581 0458; www.mustalammas.net; Satamakatu 4; mains €27-32, degustation menu €55; ⊙5-9pm Mon-Thu, to 11pm Fri & Sat; ⊘) One of Finland's best restaurants, the Black Sheep has a golden fleece. Set in an enchantingly romantic brick-vaulted space, it offers a short menu of delicious gourmet mains using top-quality Finnish meat and fish, with complex sauces that complement but never overpower the natural flavours. Starter portions are stronger on presentation than quantity but also undeniably toothsome. The wine list includes a fabulous selection of bin ends that will need a healthy credit card to do it justice.

Kummisetä
FINNISH €€

(www.kummiseta.com; Minna Canthinkatu 44; mains €16-24; ⊙kitchen 4-8pm Mon & Tue, to 9.30pm Wed & Thu, 3-10.30pm Fri & Sat) The sober brown colours of the 'Godfather' restaurant give it a traditional and romantic feel that's replicated on the menu, with a variety of excellent sauces featuring fennel, berries, and morel mushrooms garnishing prime cuts of beef, tender-as-young-love lamb, and succulent pike-perch. Food and service are both excellent. There's also a popular back terrace and an attractive bar that is open longer hours.

Lounas-Salonki
FINNISH €

(☎017-281 1210; www.lounassalonki.fi; Kasarmikatu 12; lunches €7-9, mains €13-20; ⊙9am-9pm Mon-Sat, noon-9pm Sun; ⊘⚹) This charming wooden building west of the city centre is warm and friendly, with little rooms sporting elegant imperial furniture. It does a salad buffet and daily hot lunch featuring traditional Finnish fare. It's reliably delicious, and offers excellent value, including dessert, soft drinks and coffee. There are also à-la-carte options including vegetarian choices like crêpes filled with blue cheese and vegetables. Lunch is from 11am to 3pm (noon to 4pm Sundays, when the expanded buffet costs €15.70).

🖉 Kauppahalli
MARKET €

(⊙8am-5pm Mon-Fri, to 3pm Sat; ⊘) At the southern end of the kauppatori is a classic Finnish indoor market hall. Here stalls sell local speciality *kalakukko*, a large rye loaf stuffed with whitefish and then baked. It's delicious hot or cold. A whole one – a substantial thing – costs around €25, but the bakery by the western door sells mini-ones for €2 if you just want a taste.

Muikkuravintola Sampo
FINNISH €

(www.wanhamestari.fi; Kauppakatu 13; dishes €12-16; ⊙11am-10pm Mon-Thu, to midnight Fri & Sat, noon-10pm Sun) Have it stewed, fried, smoked or in a soup, but it's all about *muikku* here. This is one of Finland's most famous spots to try the small, locally caught lake fish that drives Savo stomachs. The 70-year-old restaurant is cosy and most typical.

Kaneli
CAFE €

(www.kahvilakaneli.net; Kauppakatu 22; cakes €4-5; ⊙8am-6pm Mon, Tue, Thu & Fri, to 9pm Wed, 11am-4pm Sat, 11am-3pm Sun) This cracking cafe just off the kauppatori evokes a bygone age with much of its original decor, but offers modern comfort in its shiny espresso machine, as well as many other flavoured coffees to accompany your toothsome and sticky *pulla* (bun). Opens shorter hours in winter.

🍷 Drinking & Entertainment

Kuopio's nightlife area is around Kauppakatu, east of the kauppatori. There are many options in this block, some with summer terraces.

Wanha Satama
PUB

(www.wanhasatama.net; mains €13-20; ⊙11am-11pm Sun-Tue, to 4am Wed-Sat late Apr-Aug) In a noble blue building by the harbour, this place has one of Lakeland's best terraces, definitely the place to be on a sunny day to watch the boats come and go. There's Finnish fish and meat dishes and regular live music.

Helmi
PUB

(www.satamanhelmi.fi; Kauppakatu 2; ⊙11am-midnight or later) This historic 19th-century sailors' hang-out by the harbour has recently been remodelled and is a cosy, comfortable spot with a range of local characters. There's a decent pool table, tasty pizzas (€7 to €9) and a sociable enclosed terrace.

Ilona
CLUB

(www.ilonacity.fi; Vuorikatu 19; ⊙10pm-4am) The city's best club has an attractive London-themed bar with a smoking cabin done out like a red bus, and a separate karaoke bar where enthusiastic punters belt out Suomi hits. There's a fat list of English-language songs if you don't fancy trying out your Finnish vowels.

WORTH A TRIP

VALAMO MONASTERY

Finland's only Orthodox monastery, **Valamo** (☎017-570 111; www.valamo.fi; Valamontie 42, Uusi-Valamo) is one of Lakeland's most popular attractions. One of the great, ancient Russian monasteries, old Valamo was eventually re-established here, after the Revolution and the Winter War. Monks and novices, almost a thousand strong at old Valamo a century ago, now number in single figures, but the complex in general is thriving.

The first church was made by connecting two sheds; the rustic architecture contrasts curiously with the fine gilded icons. The new church, completed in 1977, has an onion dome and is redolent of incense. Visitors are free to roam and enter the churches. A one-hour **guided tour** (tours €5) is highly recommended for insights into the monastery and Orthodox beliefs.

Valamo makes an excellent place to stay, more peaceful once evening descends. Two **guesthouses** (s/d without bathroom €40/60; P) in picturesque wooden buildings provide comfortable, no-frills sleeping; the **hotel** (s/d €70/110; P) offers a higher standard of accommodation. The complex's eatery, **Trapesa** (⊙7am-9pm), has high-quality buffet spreads and evening meals with not a hint of monastic frugality; try the monastery's range of berry wines.

Valamo is clearly signposted 4km north of the main Varkaus–Joensuu road. A couple of daily buses run to Valamo from Joensuu and from Helsinki via Mikkeli and Varkaus. From Heinävesi change at Karvio.

The most pleasant way to get to Valamo (and nearby Lintula Convent, which also has simple accommodation) in summer is on a **Monastery Cruise** (☎015-250 250; www.mspuijo.fi; adult €69-79; ⊙Mon-Sat mid-Jun–mid-Aug) from Kuopio.

Henry's Pub   PUB, CONCERT VENUE
(www.henryspub.net; Käsityökatu 17; ⊙9pm-4am) An atmospheric underworld with bands playing several times a week, usually free, and usually at the heavier end of the rock/metal spectrum. Opens at 11pm Sunday and Monday.

❶ Information
Kuopio Tourist Service (☎182 584; www.visitlakeland.fi; Haapaniemenkatu 22; ⊙9.30am-5pm Jun-Aug, plus 9.30am-3pm Sat Jul, 9.30am-4pm Mon-Fri,) In the basement of the Carlson department store on the kauppatori. Information on regional attractions and accommodation.

❶ Getting There & Away
AIR Kuopio airport is 14km north of town. **Buses** (☎020-141 5710) leave from the kauppatori by the Anttila department store 55 minutes before most departures (€5 one-way, 30 minutes).
SAS (☎06000 25831; www.sas.fi) Daily flights to Helsinki.
Finnair/Flybe (☎580 7400; www.finnair.com) Daily flights to Helsinki.
BOAT From mid-June to mid-August, **MS Puijo** (www.mspuijo.fi) travels to Savonlinna (€88 one way, 10½ hours) on Tuesday, Thursday and Saturday at 9am, returning on Monday, Wednesday and Friday. It passes through scenic waterways, canals and locks. A return with overnight cabin accommodation costs €175.
BUS The bus terminal is just north of the train station. Regular express services to/from Kuopio include:
Helsinki €64.30, 6½ hours
Jyväskylä €24.80, 2¼ hours
TRAIN The train station is 400m north of the centre on Asemakatu.
Helsinki €61 to €76, 4½ hours
Kajaani €28,40, 1¾ hours
Oulu €51.63, four hours

Joensuu
☎013 / POP 73,900
The capital of North Karelia is a bubbly young university town, with students making up almost a third of the population. Today Joensuu looks pretty modern – bombing raids during the Winter and Continuation Wars flattened many of its older buildings. It's also the gateway to the deep, quiet depths of the Karelian wilderness. The gentle Pielisjoki rapids divide the town into two parts: most of the town centre is west of the river, but the bus and train stations are to the east.

⊙ Sights

In summer there are scenic cruises on the Pielisjoki, a centuries-old trading route.

Carelicum   MUSEUM
(www.pohjoiskarjalanmuseo.fi; Koskikatu 5; admission €5; ⊙9am-5pm Mon-Fri, to 7pm Wed, 10am-3pm Sat & Sun) This excellent museum on the square has detailed modern exhbitions on all aspects of northern Karelian life and history, including plenty on the parts that are now in Russia. The war is covered in detail, as are Karelian musical traditions from rune-singing to Nightwish. Try your hand singing regional classics in the Karelia Karaoke Room. Changing temporary exhibitions occupy the floor above.

✯✯ Festivals

Ilosaarirock   ROCK MUSIC
(www.ilosaarirock.fi) Held over a weekend in mid-July, this is a highly charged rock festival with big Finnish and international headliners.

⌷ Sleeping

Finnhostel Joensuu   HOSTEL €
(☑267 5076; www.islo.fi; Kalevankatu 8; s/tw €56/70, s without bathroom €46; ℗) This super spot offers great value in sizeable new rooms with minikitchen and small balconies, across the road from reception, located in a sports institute. Some rooms share a bathroom and kitchen with one other room. Prices include breakfast and access to facilities that include a bookable private sauna session and a gym. HI discount.

Hotel GreenStar   HOTEL €
(☑010-423 9390; www.greenstar.fi; Torikatu 16; r €59-65; ℗) This bright modern hotel has all the usual facilities without environmental guilt: it's designed for low energy consumption. Rooms sleep up to three for the same price with a pull-out armchair for a third bed. It's very central and a great deal for two. There's automatic check-in in the foyer as well as part-time reception and internet booking. Breakfast is €7 extra.

Linnunlahti   CAMPGROUND €
(☑010-666 5520; www.linnunlahti.fi; Linnunlahdentie 1; campsites €7, plus per adult €2, 4- to 6-person cottages €89-160; ℗) Just south of the centre and right next to the Ilosaari festival stage, this site has a pleasant lakeside location and good-value year-round cottages.

✗ Eating & Drinking

The kauppatori is packed with *grillis* and stalls selling cheap snacks: try the *karjalanpiirakka,* a savoury rice pastry of local origin but eagerly munched all over Finland.

Kielo   MODERN FINNISH €€€
(☑227 874; www.ravintolakielo.fi; Suvantokatu 12; mains €26-27; ⊙4-10pm Mon-Fri, noon-10pm Sat) At the high end of Karelian cuisine, this upmarket but welcoming locale gives a New Nordic touch to quality dishes with slow-cooked meats, artfully presented miniature starters and the best of local ingredients. The €44 tasting menu is the best way to appreciate what it's about.

Astoria   HUNGARIAN €€
(☑229 766; www.astoria.fi; mains €18-30; ⊙4-10pm Mon-Thu, to midnight Fri, noon-midnight Sat, noon-8pm Sun) This rustic but stylish riverfront restaurant specialises in Hungarian cuisine with a paprika kick, as well as a wide range of roast meats, with several specials for two or more diners. There's a great summer terrace with bar serving pizzas and pasta.

Gaude   PIZZERIA €
(www.gaude.fi; Länsikatu 18; pizzas €9; ⊙3pm-11.30pm Mon-Thu, 2pm-midnight Fri & Sat, 2-10pm Sun) Curiously set in a student residence that turns into a guesthouse in summer, this compact place does Joensuu's best pizzas, which have a reassuringly homemade taste. There are no set combinations: tick boxes to choose what you want. Last orders are at 9.30pm.

Wanha Jokela   PUB
(www.ravintolawanhajokela.fi; Torikatu 26; ⊙10am-late) The oldest and best pub in town, this bohemian hang-out is always interesting. It's full of characters and cheap beer and also has inexpensive rooms (single/double €35/60) with shared bathroom upstairs in case you have one too many.

ⓘ Information

Karelia Expert Joensuu (☑0400 239 549; www.visitkarelia.fi; Koskikatu 5; ⊙9am-5pm Mon-Fri, also 10am-3pm Sat mid-May–mid-Sep, 10am-3pm Sun Jul) In the Carelicum; tourist information and activity bookings.

ⓘ Getting There & Away

Finnair/Flybe flies daily to/from Helsinki. Joensuu's airport is 11km from town; the bus service costs €5 one way and departs weekdays only from the bus station.

The bus station is across the river on Itäranta. Services go to Savonlinna (€25.50, three hours), Kuopio (€29, 2½ hours) as well as Helsinki and closer Karelian destinations.

The train station is next to the bus station. Direct trains run frequently to/from Helsinki (€65 to €73, 4½ to 6½ hours) and Lieksa (€14, 1¼ hours). For northern and western destinations change at Pieksämäki; for Savonlinna change at Parikkala.

Ilomantsi

📋 013 / POP 5720

Pushing up against the border that separates Finland from Russia, Ilomantsi is Finland's most Karelian, Orthodox and eastern municipality, and the centre of a charming region where a wealth of wilderness hiking opens up before you.

Parppeinvaara (www.parppeinvaara.fi; adult/child €5/free; ☺10am-6pm Jul, to 4pm Jun & Aug) is the oldest and most interesting of Finland's Karelian theme villages, where you can hear the *kantele* (Karelian stringed instrument) played and try traditional food at the excellent **Parppeinpirtti** (www.parppeinpirtti.fi; lunch €20; ☺10am-7pm Jul, to 5pm Jun & early Aug, to 3pm Mon-Fri late Aug-Jun).

Ilomantsi celebrates the traditional Orthodox festivals **Petru Praasniekka** on 28 and 29 June and **Ilja Praasniekka** on 19 and 20 July.

Originally built in 1751, **Anssilan Maatila** (📞040-543 1526; www.ilomantsi.com/anssila; Anssilantie; r per person €30-40; 🅿♿), a former dairy farm, is on a hill 4km south of the village and about 500m off the main road. It's family friendly with rides on horses and sleds for kids; rooms are available in a range of converted farmhouse buildings.

The excellent tourist centre, **Karelia Expert** (📞0400 240 072; www.visitkarelia.fi; Kalevalantie 13; ☺8am-4pm Mon-Fri Sep-May, 9am-5pm

KARELIAN COTTAGES

Karelia's gorgeous scenery, sparkling lakes and deep forests make it an appealing part of the country to rent a cabin or cottage and relax for a few days. As well as national operators, Karelia Expert (p179) has a great portfolio.

Mon-Fri Jun-Aug), can help with just about everything, from cottage reservations to information on trekking routes and hire of camping equipment, snowshoes and cross-country ski gear.

Treks around Karelia

Karelia's best trekking routes form the **Karjalan Kierros** (Karelian Circuit), a loop of really lovely marked trails with a total length of over 1000km between Ilomantsi and Lake Pielinen. For more information on these and other routes contact Karelia Expert in Ilomantsi or Lieksa (p182), or **Metsähallitus** (www.outdoors.fi).

KARHUNPOLKU

The **Bear's Trail** (not to be confused with the Bear's Ring near Kuusamo) is a 133km marked hiking trail of medium difficulty leading north from Patvinsuo National Park near Lieksa, through a string of stunning national parks and peaceful nature reserves along the Russian border. The trail ends at Teljo, about 50km south of Kuhmo. You will need to arrange transport from either end.

SUSITAIVAL

The 97km **Wolf Trail** is a marked trail running south from the marshlands of Patvinsuo National Park to the forests of Petkeljärvi National Park, 21km east of Ilomantsi. This links with the Bear's Trail. It's a three-day trek of medium difficulty (the marshland can be wet underfoot). It passes through some important Winter War battlegrounds near the Russian border.

Lake Pielinen Region

In a land full of lakes, Pielinen, Finland's sixth largest, is pretty special. In summer it's the shimmering jewel of North Karelia and is surrounded by some of the most beautiful wilderness areas and action-packed countryside in the country.

KOLI NATIONAL PARK

Finns, with reason, consider the stunning views from the heights of Koli, overlooking Lake Pielinen, as the best in the country – the same views inspired several Finnish artists from the National Romantic era. In summer the national park offers scenic hiking routes; in winter it offers skiing, with two slalom centres and more than 60km of cross-country trails, including 24km of illuminated track.

The hill has road access with a short **funicular** (free) from the lower car park to the hilltop Sokos hotel. From here it's a brief walk to **Ukko-Koli**, the highest point with the best vistas. It really is an incredible panorama as you stand on weatherbeaten rocks with the vast island-studded lake stretched out far below you and pine forest as far as the eye can see.

By the hotel, **Luontokeskus Ukko** (📞020-564 5654; www.outdoors.fi; exhibition adult/child €5/2; ☺10am-7pm Jul, to 5pm rest of yr) is a modern visitor centre with exhibitions on history, nature and the park's geology, and information on hiking. There's a craft shop, free internet terminal and a cafe.

In Koli village, 3km below the Luontokeskus, the helpful **tourist office** (📞045-138 7429; www.koli.fi; Ylä-Kolintie 2; ☺10am-6pm daily Jun-Aug, 9am-5pm Mon-Fri, 10am-5pm Sat & Sun Sep-May) books activities and has a comprehensive range of information and maps. The village also has a supermarket, but the last stop for fuel is on the main road.

Vanhan Koulun Majatalo (📞050-343 7881; www.vanhankoulunmajatalo.fi; Niinilahdentie 47; s/d/q €36/52/88, 2-person apt €80; P@🐾), on a gravel road 6km from Koli village (follow signs to Kolin Retkeilymaja), is a great place to base yourself for walking, skiing and exploring the area. A tranquil setting with a grassy garden, smoke sauna and outdoor games is complemented by large kitchen and common areas inside and simple, comfortable private rooms with beds and bunks as well as studio apartments.

There's a summer car **ferry** (📞0400 228 435; www.pielis-laivat.fi; adult/child/car/bicycle 1 way €16/8/11/3) twice daily mid-June to mid-August, between Koli and Lieksa (1½ hours). Apart from the boat, year-round *kimppakyyti* (car pool) **shuttle taxis** (📞040-104 4687; adult/child €25/13) run from Joensuu to Koli (one hour), picking up door-to-door, including the *majatalo*. It's best to book the service the day before; if your phone Finnish isn't great, get the tourist office or your hotel to call for you. There are also bus connections from Joensuu to Koli-kylä (Koli village) via Ahmovaara.

LIEKSA & RUUNAA
📞013 / POP 12,600

The small lakeside town of Lieksa is primarily a base and service town for outdoor activities in the region. In winter, husky tours and snowmobile safaris along the Russian border are popular; in summer hiking, fishing and white-water rafting are all the rage.

◎ Sights & Activities

Pielisen Museo MUSEUM
(📞689 4151; Pappilantie 2; adult/child €5/€1.50; ☺10am-4pm mid-May–mid-Sep) One of Finland's largest open-air museums is a slightly jumbled complex of almost 100 Karelian buildings (many relocated from Russia) and historical exhibits, along with an indoor museum of local war and folk history. The indoor hall is also open (€3, 10am to 3pm Tuesday to Friday) in winter.

Ruunaa Recreation Area ACTIVITY PARK
(www.outdoors.fi) Karelia Expert in Lieksa handles information and bookings for all manner of activities around Lieksa and at this park, 30km east. This is a superb, carefully managed wilderness area perfect for fishing, white-water rafting, wildlife spotting and easy hiking. There's a nature centre (open daily May to September) with trail information and various cabin and camping accommodation available. On Mondays and Fridays only, a shared taxi service operates from Lieksa: phone 📞040 1044 683. Otherwise, you should be able to hitch (or go with an organised tour) in summer.

🛌 Sleeping

There are numerous options in the countryside around Lieksa. In town, there's campsite, hostel and hotel accommodation.

TOP
CHOICE **Ruunaan**
Retkeilykeskus CAMPGROUND, COTTAGES **€€**
(📞533 170; www.ruunaa.fi; Ruunaa; campsites €12, plus per person €3, cabins/cottages €35/100; P🐾) At Ruunaa, in addition to accommodation and services near the bridge over the Naarajoki, this hiking centre has a large cafe (May to October), campsites, a kitchen, a sauna and cabins ranging from simple to luxurious. A boardwalk goes a short distance from here to the Neitikoski rapids, a popular fishing and kayaking spot.

Hotelli Puustelli HOTEL **€€**
(📞511 5500; www.puustelliravintolat.fi; Hovileirinkatu 3; s/d €95/120; P@) By the riverside in Lieksa, with good-sized rooms with affordable rates that include breakfast and sauna. Popular restaurant; discounts on weekends and in summer.

KESTIKIEVARI HERRANNIEMI

For a relaxing break, it's worth going out of the way and catching a train to Vuonislahti, 28km south of Lieksa, for **Kestikievari Herranniemi** (☑013-542 110; www.herranniemi. com; Vuonislahdentie 185; s/d from €56/78, cabins €30-78, apt €115-135; P) a brilliant lakeside retreat. Attractive wooden buildings house a variety of excellent rooms and cottages, with some particularly appealing ones for families. The welcoming owners offer meals by arrangement and a variety of treatments, and there are all sorts of extras, with several saunas, rowing boats and a fantastic lakeside with its own pavilion and auditorium. It's a magically peaceful place that seems close to the soul of Finnishness. Various discounts are available in winter.

ℹ Information

Karelia Expert Lieksa (☑0400 175 323; www. visitkarelia.fi; Pielisentie 22; ⊗9am-5pm Mon-Fri Jun-Aug, also 9am-2pm Sat Jul, 8am-4pm Mon-Fri Sep-May) On the main street, this is the place to stop for information on accommodation and activities.

ℹ Getting There & Away

Buses head from Joensuu and Nurmes to Lieksa, as do trains. A car ferry (p181) runs across the lake to Koli in summer.

NURMES

☑013 / POP 8400

On the northern shores of Lake Pielinen, Nurmes is another base for activities such as snowmobiling, ice fishing, dog-sledding and cross-country skiing tours in winter, and wildlife-watching, canoeing, hiking and farmhouse tours in summer. It's a pleasant town in its own right though, with an 'old town' area (Puu-Nurmes) of historical wooden buildings along Kirkkokatu. A highlight is Bomban Talo, the largest building of a re-created Karelian village 3km east of the centre featuring a summer market, craft shops and cafes.

The best places to stay in Nurmes are side by side on the lake shore about 3.5km east of the town centre. **Sokos Hotel Bomba** (☑020-1234 908; www.sokoshotels.fi; Tuulentie 10; s/d €132/157, apt €191-224; P❄@☀) has a great indoor pool and spa area overlooking the lake, and slick modern rooms in a stylish new wing. There are also fully equipped apartment cottages available, and cheaper rooms in wooden buildings within the replica Karelian village. Prices can be up to 40% lower at quiet times. Just beyond, **Hyvärilä** (☑020-746 6780; www.hyvarila.com; Lomatie 12; campsites €10, plus per person €4, cabins €42-59, hostel dm/s €12.50/21, hotel s/d €74/89; ⊗camping Jun–mid-Sep; P) is a sprawling lakefront holiday resort with a manicured camping ground, hostel accommodation, cabins, upmarket cottages, a hotel, restaurant and even a golf course.

Karelia Expert (☑050-336 0707; www.visit karelia.fi; Kauppatori 3; ⊗9am-5pm Mon-Fri) has local information and bookings. It's opposite the bus and train stations.

Buses run regularly to Joensuu, Kajaani and Lieksa. For Kuhmo there are direct buses Monday to Friday during the school year; otherwise change at Sotkamo. Trains go to Joensuu via Lieksa.

NORTH-CENTRAL FINLAND

Kuhmo

☑08 / POP 9270

Kuhmo, once a major tar producer, is a good launch pad for the wilderness; it makes a natural base for hiking the Urho K Kekkonen (UKK) route, Finland's longest marked trek. The vast taiga forest runs from here right across Siberia and harbours 'respect' animals like wolves, bears and lynx. Kuhmo is also the unofficial capital of Vienan Karjala, the Karelian heartland that is now in Russia. This was the region that artists explored in the Karelian movement, a crucial part of the development of Finnish national identity.

◎ Sights & Activities

Hiking is the big drawcard in Kuhmo, but there are plenty of other ways to get active; Petola visitor centre (p183) has more walking info and can arrange fishing permits.

Juminkeko   CULTURAL CENTRE
(www.juminkeko.fi; Kontionkatu 25; adult/child €4/free; ⊗noon-6pm Mon-Fri, daily in Jul) If you

are interested in the *Kalevala* or Karelian culture, pay a visit to the excellent centre, which offers everything from audiovisual presentations, to Finland's largest collection of *Kalevala* books and multimedia translations.

Kalevalakylä   THEME PARK

(📞0440 755 500; www.kalevalaspirit.fi) Four kilometres from the centre of town is this theme park about traditional Karelian life, with a number of Karelian wooden buildings including a sauna, craft shops and Pohjolantalo, a large hall that functions as cafe, restaurant and gallery. The rest of the area, with tar-making, fishing, etc, is basically designed for group visits; ask if there are any tours scheduled that you can join.

Petola Luontokeskus   NATURE CENTRE

(www.outdoors.fi; Lentiirantie 342; ⊙9am-5pm daily mid-Jun–mid-Aug, 9am-4pm Mon-Fri Dec–mid-Jun & mid-Aug–mid-Oct) An excellent nature centre focusing on carnivore species and with useful information on walking routes in the area. On the main road near the Kalevala turn-off.

Wild Brown Bear   WILDLIFE-WATCHING TRIPS

(📞040-546 9008; www.wbb.fi) Organises trips to view bears, wolves and wolverines from hides for around €150.

Taiga Spirit   WILDLIFE-WATCHING TRIPS

(📞040-746 8243; www.taigaspirit.com) Wildlife safaris, elk-spotting and bear-viewing.

⭐ Festivals & Events

Kuhmon Kamarimusiikki   MUSIC

(Kuhmo Chamber Music Festival; 📞652 0936; www.kuhmofestival.fi; tickets €15-25) Runs for two weeks in late July and has a full program of about 80 top-quality concerts performed by a variety of Finnish and international musicians. Tickets are a steal at around €15 for most events.

🛏 Sleeping

TOP CHOICE Hotelli Kalevala   HOTEL €€

(📞655 4100; www.hotellikalevala.fi; Väinämöinen 9; s/d €91/126; P@) Four kilometres from central Kuhmo, by the Kalevala village, this striking building of wood and concrete is a great place to stay. The pretty rooms in pastel colours mostly have tantalising lake views, with the sound of the lapping water. It's the facilities that win you over here,

though, with boat, bike and snowmobile rental, a gym and spa complex, peat sauna and various tailored trips on foot or skis.

Matkakoti Parkki   GUESTHOUSE €

(📞655 0271; matkakoti.parkki@elisanet.fi; Vienantie 3; s/d/tr without bathroom €30/50/70; P) Run in a most kindly manner, this quiet and handsome little family guesthouse offers excellent value near the centre of town. Rooms are spotless and need to be booked ahead during the festival. There's a kitchen you can use, and breakfast is included. No wi-fi.

Kalevala Camping   CAMPGROUND €

(📞044-0755 500; www.kalevalaspirit.fi; Väinämöinen 13; campsites €10, 2-/4-person cabins €40/50, cottages €90-110; ⊙Jun-Aug) This has basic facilities but a most attractive lakeside location, 4km from town and among tall pines. Reception is at adjacent Kalevalakylä.

ℹ Information

The main tourist information point is at **Petola Luontokeskus** (📞205-646 380; petola@metsa.fi; Lentiirantie 342; ⊙10am-5pm Jun-Aug, to 4pm Mon-Fri Sep-Dec). The nature centre, bookshop and Hotelli Kainuu in the centre of town also give out info.

ℹ Getting There & Away

Numerous daily buses head to/from Kajaani (€19.80, 1¾ hours), which is on the main Kuopio–Oulu train line, and to Nurmes, usually requiring a change at Sotkamo. For other destinations, you'll have to go via Kajaani.

Oulu

📞08 / POP 143.988

Thriving Oulu is spread across several islands, elegantly connected by pedestrian bridges, and water never seems far away. In summer the angled sun bathes the kauppatori in light and all seems well with the world. Locals, who appreciate daylight when they get it, crowd the terraces, and stalls groan under the weight of Arctic berries.

Founded in 1605, Oulu grew prosperous in the 18th century from tar, which was floated down the river from the Kainuu region and shipped to Sweden for shipbuilding. Although pulp factories are a major industry, it's the IT boom that's leading the way in Oulu now and plenty of expat professionals live and work here.

Oulu

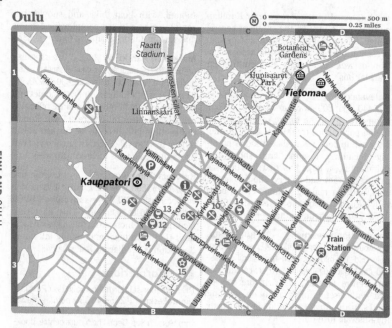

◉ Sights & Activities

Kauppatori
SQUARE

By the waterside, this is one of the liveliest and most colourful market squares in Finland, with its red wooden storehouses (now housing restaurants, bars and craft shops), market stalls, bursting summer terraces, boat cruises and the rotund **Toripolliisi statue**, a humorous representation of the local police.

Tietomaa
MUSEUM

(www.tietomaa.fi; Nahkatehtaankatu 6; adult/child €15/11; ⊙10am-5pm or 6pm; ☑) This huge, excellent science museum can occupy kids for the best part of a day with a giant Imax screen, hands-on interactive exhibits on the universe, the human body and gender differences, as well as a planetarium and an observation tower. There's a yearly mega-exhibition that's the focal point.

Oulun Taidemuseo
GALLERY

(www.ouka.fi/taidemuseo; Kasarmintie 7; adult/child €3/free, Fri free; ⊙10am-5pm Tue-Thu, Sat & Sun, noon-7pm Fri) Oulu's art museum is a bright, spacious gallery with excellent temporary exhibitions of both international and Finnish contemporary art, and a cafe.

Cycling
CYCLING

Oulu's extensive network of wonderful bicycle paths is among the best in Finland, and nowhere is the Finns' love of two-wheeled transport more obvious than here in summer. Bikes can be hired from **Pyörä-Suvala** (☑338 175; www.pyorasuvala.fi; Lakatie 2), and from Nallikari Camping. The tourist office has a free cycle-route map.

✪ Festivals & Events

Tervahiihto
SKIING

(Oulu Tar Ski Race; www.tervahiihto.fi) Held in early March. This 70km skiing race (40km for women) has been going strong since 1889.

Oulu Music Video Festival
MUSIC

(www.omvf.net) In late August. Includes the **Air Guitar World Championships** (www.airguitarworldchampionships.com). Contestants from all over the world take the stage to show what they can do with their imaginary instruments.

⌂ Sleeping

TOP CHOICE Hotel Lasaretti
HOTEL €€

(☑020-757 4700; www.lasaretti.com; Kasarmintie 13; s/d €128/150, Sat & Sun €75/87; ℗@⊠)

Oulu

Bright, modern and optimistic, this inviting hotel sits in a group of renovated brick buildings that were once a hospital. It's close to town but the parkside location by the babbling stream makes it feel rural. The artistically modern rooms have floorboards and flat-screen TVs; some have fold-out sofa beds for families. Ask for a room with water view. Facilities and staff are excellent; there's also a busy restaurant with a sun-kissed terrace.

Sokos Hotel Eden HOTEL €€
(☎123 4603; www.sokoshotels.fi; Holstinsalmentie 29, Nallikari; s/d €123/138, superior €143/158; P@⌘⛱) This excellent spa hotel by the beach on Hietasaari offers great watery facilities – slides, intricate indoor pools, saunas – and massage treatments. Superior rooms on the new side of the building are bigger and have air-conditioning (handier than you may think) as well as a sea-view balcony. Nonguests can use the whole spa facilities for the day for a pretty reasonable €15 (€9 for kids). Prices are usually lower than listed above; check online.

Hotel Scandic Oulu HOTEL €€€
(☎543 1000; www.scandic-hotels.com; Saaristonkatu 4; s/d €166/185; P@) This sleek hotel occupies half a city block right in the middle of town. From the space-opera lights in its spacious foyer to the high-ceilinged rooms with clean Nordic decor and flatscreen TV, it's a temple to efficiency, hygiene and modern design (art, individuality: look elsewhere). Above rates are a guide, but demand-pricing operates.

Omenahotelli HOTEL €€
(☎0600-18018; www.omenahotels.com; Uusikatu 26; r €60-90) The latest branch of this no-staff hotel is in a good central location and features comfortable plasticky rooms with giant TV, spacious double bed and fold-out chairs sleeping two more. Book online or via the terminal in the lobby.

Forenom House HOTEL €
(☎020-198 3420; www.forenom.fi; Rautatienkatu 9; s/d €60/70; P@) You can't beat this spot for convenience: it's bang opposite the train station. Rooms are a little uncared-for but have plenty of space as well as fridge and microwave; there's a range of them, sleeping up to five. Book online or via the terminal in the lobby. Rates are variable and can be excellent value. It also offers good-value apartments elsewhere in Oulu on the same webpage. Reception is staffed Monday to Friday during working hours.

Nallikari Camping CAMPGROUND €
(☎044-703 1353; www.nallikari.fi; Hietasaari; campsite €13, plus per adult/child €4/2, cabins €36-42, cottages €98-139; P@⛱) Resembling a small town, this excellent camping ground offers all sorts of options in a location close to the beach on Hietasaari, a 40-minute walk to town via pedestrian bridges. Bus 17 gets you there from the kauppatori, as does the tourist train.

🍴 Eating

Local specialities can be found in and around the lively kauppatori.

Hella TOP CHOICE BISTRO
(☎371 180; www.hellaravintola.fi; Isokatu 13; mains €18-27; ☉10.30am-2pm & 5-11pm Mon-Fri, 3-11pm Sat, noon-6pm Sun) This sweet little corner spot is a welcoming two-person show that offers excellent Italian-inspired fare. Attentive

service is backed up by the food, which changes seasonally but features great salads, canneloni stuffed with goat cheese, and tender, well-treated meat dishes.

Puistola
BISTRO, FINNISH €€

(☑020-792 8210; www.ravintolapuistola.fi; Pakkahuoneenkatu 15; bistro mains €16-25, restaurant mains €23-29; ☺bistro 10.45am-10pm Mon-Thu, to 11pm Fri, noon-11pm Sat, noon-6pm Sun) This ambitious, handsome place offers a deli-cafe and two restaurant areas. The entry-level bistro is a comfortable space, and turns out tasty, sizeable dishes – think pastas, ribs, burgers, fish, salads and steaks – from its open kitchen with plenty of flair, and also does good-value lunches. Downstairs is a more formal restaurant (open dinner only, Tuesday to Saturday), with somewhat higher prices. Service throughout is excellent. Be sure to check out the toilets – highly original.

Café Bisketti
CAFE €

(www.cafebisketti.fi; Kirkkokatu 8; lunches €6-9; ☺10am-10pm Mon & Tue, to midnight Wed & Thu, to 2am Fri & Sat, noon-8pm Sun) This top double-sided spot transforms itself throughout the day. Think twice before getting that pastry with your morning coffee; they're enormous and might not leave room for lunch, with its cheap deals on soup, salad, coffee and a pastry, and hot dishes for not much extra. In the evenings the terrace is a decent spot for people watching with a beer.

Kauppahalli
MARKET €

(☺8am-5pm Mon-Thu, to 6pm Fri, to 3pm Sat; ☑) On the square, the kauppahalli has freshly filleted salmon glistening in the market stalls and plenty of spots to snack on anything from cloudberries to sushi.

Sokeri-Jussin Kievari
FINNISH €€

(☑376 628; www.sokerijussi.fi; Pikisaarentie 2; mains €17-33; ☺11am-10pm) An Oulu classic, this timbered local on Pikisaari was once a shipbuilding workshop and has outdoor tables that have good views of the centre. Although the renovated interior has lost a bit of the original character, it's still an attractive spot to eat, with no-frills traditional dishes, including reindeer, and a selection of much more upmarket plates. It's also a nice place to go for a few beers away from the bustle of the city but just a few steps from it.

Fit Wok
ASIAN €

(www.fitwok.fi; Hallituskatu 10; dishes €6-10; ☺10.30am-8pm Mon-Fri, noon-6pm Sat & Sun; ☑) It's a simple procedure to create your own stir-fry at this attractive showroom-style eatery. Choose your noodles or rice, choose your toppings, and choose your sauce. Good value and plenty of veg and healthy options.

🍷 Drinking & Entertainment

There's plenty going on in Oulu at night. The kauppatori is the spot to start in summer: the terraces lick up every last drop of the evening sun. Keltainen Aitta and Makasiini are the main ones, set in traditional wooden warehouses.

Never Grow Old
BAR

(www.ngo.fi; Hallituskatu 17; ☺8pm-2am Sun & Tue, 6pm-2am Wed & Thu, 4pm-3am Fri & Sat) This enduringly popular bar hits its stride after 10pm, with plenty of dancing, DJs and revelry in the tightly packed interior. The goofy decor includes some seriously comfortable and extremely uncomfortable places to sit, and a log-palisade bar that seems designed to get you to wear your drink. It opens earlier in summer.

Kaarlenholvi & Jumpru Pub
PUB

(www.jumpru.fi; Kauppurienkatu 6; ☺11am-2am Mon & Tue, to 4am Wed-Sat, noon-2am Sun) This Oulu institution is a great place for meeting locals and its enclosed outdoor area always seems to be humming with cheerfully sauced-up folk. There's a warren of cosy rooms inside, as well as a club opening from 10pm Wednesday to Saturday.

Graali
PUB

(www.graali.fi; Saaristonkatu 5; ☺2pm-2am) When it's cold and snowy outside, there's nowhere cosier than this pub, decorated with suits of armour and sporting trophies. Sink into a leather armchair by the open fire and feel the warmth return to your bones. A good whisky selection will help you along.

45 Special
CLUB

(www.45special.com; Saaristonkatu 12; ☺8pm-4am Mon, 6pm-4am Tue-Thu, 3pm-4am Fri & Sun) This grungy three-level club pulls a youngish crowd for its downstairs rock and chartier top floor. There's a cover charge at weekends and regular live gigs.

ℹ Information

Free wireless internet is available throughout the city centre on the PanOulu network.

Tourist office (☑5584 1330; www.visitoulu.fi; Torikatu 10; ☺9am-5pm Mon-Thu, to 4pm Fri) Publishes the useful guide *Look at Oulu*.

ℹ Getting There & Away

AIR Bus 19 runs between the centre and the airport (€3.60, 25 minutes, every 20 minutes).

Finnair/Flybe has several daily direct flights from Helsinki, as does SAS. Norwegian also flies the Helsinki route. SAS also serve Stockholm and Copenhagen.

BUS The bus station, near the train station, has services connecting Oulu with all the main centres.

Helsinki €95.40, 10 hours
Kajaani €30.50, 2½ hours
Rovaniemi €42.60, 3½ hours
Tornio €27.90, 2½ hours

TRAIN The station is just east of the centre. Six to 10 trains a day (€72 to €82, six to 10 hours) run from Helsinki to Oulu. There are also trains via Kajaani, and trains north to Rovaniemi.

Kuusamo & Ruka

☑08 / POP 16,400

Kuusamo is a remote frontier town 200km northeast of Oulu and close to the Russian border, while Ruka is its buzzy ski resort 30km north. Both make great activity bases: wonderful canoeing, hiking and wildlife watching is available in the surrounding area.

⊙ Sights & Activities

There are many tour operators based in Kuusamo, Ruka and the surrounding area, offering a full range of winter and summer activities from husky sledding to fishing to bear watching. The Ruka webpage, www.ruka.fi, is a good place to look for active ideas. Apart from skiing (downhill and cross-country), there's also great hiking as well as fast, rugged rapids on the Kitkajoki and Oulankajoki.

TOP CHOICE **Kuusamon Suurpetokeskus**   ZOO
(☑861 713; Keronrannantie 31; adult/child €10/5; ☺10am-5pm Apr-Sep) There's a great backstory to this bear sanctuary situated 33km south of Kuusamo on the Kajaani road. The bears were rescued as helpless orphans and nursed by their 'father' Sulo Karjalainen,

who then refused to have them put down – they can't return to the wild – when the government research project wound up. He casually takes them fishing and walking in the forest, but you'll meet them in their cages here; the guide introduces you to all of them. It's a real thrill to see these impressive, intelligent animals up so close and appreciate their different personalities. There are also lynx, foxes and reindeer.

🛏 Sleeping & Eating

Numerous holiday cottages dot the area. Contact Lomarengas (p203) or the Kuusamo tourist office for a wide choice. For rooms, apartments and chalets in Ruka, go for **Ruka Booking** (☑860 0300; www.ski-inn.fi; apt weekend/weeknight May-Aug €75/55, Sep-Oct €85/75, apt Nov-Apr €100-450), which rents out most of the central ones. The www.ruka.fi webpage has links to other providers of apartments and cottages.

Kuusamon Kansanopisto   GUESTHOUSE €
(☑050-444 1157; www.kuusamo-opisto.fi; Kitkantie 35, Kuusamo; s/d €30/50, without bathroom €25/42; P) Around the corner from the bus station, this folk high school offers great budget accommodation in comfortable spacious rooms with en suites (some have shared facilities) in a variety of buildings. There are kitchen and laundry facilities available; the bad news is that you have to arrive during office hours (8am to 3.45pm Monday to Friday).

Kalakeidas   SEAFOOD €€€
(☑868 1800, 0400 836 023; www.kalakeidas.fi; Rukatunturintie 2; mains €25-30; ☺5-11pm Sep & Nov-Apr) Built in the style of a Sámi *kota* (wigwam) just outside the central area of Ruka, this intimate restaurant is a top destination to try lake fish. The owners catch them themselves – ask about fishing trips – and prepare them simply but deliciously. Portions are most generous in quantity, and there are various more-elaborate dishes that you can preorder a day or two before. Outside normal operating hours they are more than happy to open up if they're around, even if it's only for one or two people, so it's always worth calling.

Riipisen Riistaravintola   GAME €€
(☑868 1219; www.ruka.fi; mains €16-40; ☺1-9pm Mon-Sat) At the Kelo ski-lift area, a five-minute walk from Ruka square, this friendly

log cabin has an attractively rustic interior. It specialises in game dishes, and you'll find Rudolf, Bullwinkle and, yes, poor Yogi (€61) on the menu here in various guises, depending on availability and season. Arctic hare also features, while capercaillie in a creamy sauce will get bird lovers twitching too.

❶ Information

Karhuntassu (☑040-860 8365; www.ruka.fi; Torangintaival 2; ⊙9am-5pm Mon-Fri, plus Sat & Sun high season) This large visitor centre is at the highway junction, 2km from the centre of Kuusamo. There's comprehensive tourist information, free internet, a desk for booking rental cottages, and a cafe-shop. The nationalparks service has an information desk here too, as well as an excellent exhibition of wildlife photography.

Ruka Info (☑860 0250; www.ruka.fi; ⊙9am-5pm early Jun & late Aug, 9.30am-7pm Sep & late Jun–mid-Aug, 10am-8pm daily Oct-May) Located in the Kumpare building in Ruka's village square, offers tourist information and accommodation booking.

❶ Getting There & Away

There are flights from Helsinki to Kuusamo airport, with bus links to both Ruka and Kuusamo. Regular buses run to Kuusamo from Kajaani, Oulu and Rovaniemi, and there are regular services making the half-hour journey between Kuusamo and Ruka.

Oulanka National Park

This is one of the most visited national parks in Finland, thanks mainly to the 80km **Karhunkierros** (Bear's Ring Trail), a spectacular three- or four-day trek through rugged hills, deep gorges and swinging suspension bridges, starting from either the Hautajärvi Visitor Centre or the Ristikallio parking area and ending at the resort village of Ruka, which is located 30km north of Kuusamo.

There are shelters and free overnight huts on the trail. The *Rukatunturi-Oulanka Map* (1:40,000) has trail and hut information. The best online resource is the excellent Metsähallitus website, www.outdoors.fi.

Juuma is another gateway to the region, with accommodation and accessibility to some of the main sights, such as the charming, idyllic **Myllykoski** and **Jyrävä** waterfalls. If you don't have the time or resources for the longer walk, you can do the 12km **Pieni Karhunkierros** (Little Bear's Ring)

from Juuma in around four hours. There's camping, cabin and lodge accommodation in Juuma.

LAPLAND

Lapland, extending hundreds of kilometres above the Arctic Circle, is Finland's true wilderness and casts a powerful spell. While you won't see polar bears or fjords, there is something intangible here that makes it magical. The midnight sun, the Sámi peoples, the aurora borealis (Northern Lights) and the wandering reindeer are all components of this magic, as is good old ho-ho-ho himself, who 'officially' resides in this part of the world.

Lapland, which occupies 30% of Finland's land area but houses just 3% of its people, has vast and awesome emptinesses, ripe for exploring on foot, skis or sledge. The sense of space, pure air and big skies is what is memorable here, rather than the settlements.

Lapland's far north is known as Sápmi, the homeland of the Sámi people. Their main communities are around Inari, Hetta and Utsjoki. Rovaniemi is the main gateway to the north.

Rovaniemi

☑016 / POP 60,700

The 'official' terrestrial residence of Santa Claus is the capital of Finnish Lapland and a more-or-less obligatory northern stop. Its wonderful Arktikum museum is the perfect introduction to the mysteries of these latitudes, and Rovaniemi is a good place to organise activities.

Thoroughly destroyed by the retreating Wehrmacht in 1944, the town was rebuilt to a plan by Alvar Aalto, with the major streets in the shape of a reindeer's head and antlers (don't worry, it took us years to work it out). Its unattractive buildings are compensated for by its marvellous location on the fast-flowing (when it's not frozen over...) Kemijoki.

Though the museum is by far the most impressive sight, the tour buses roll north of town, where everyone's favourite beardie-weirdie has an impressive grotto among an array of tourist shops that straddle the Arctic Circle marker. It's free to visit, if not to photograph, the personable chap.

⊙ Sights & Activities

TOP CHOICE **Arktikum** MUSEUM

(www.arktikum.fi; Pohjoisranta 4; adult/child/family €12/5/27; ☉10am-6pm Dec–mid-Jan, 10am-6pm Tue-Sun mid-Jan–May, 9am-6pm Jun–mid-Aug) With its beautifully designed glass tunnel stretching out to the Ounasjoki, Arktikum is one of Finland's best museums and well worth the admission if you are interested in the north. There are two main exhibitions; one side deals with Lapland, with some information on Sámi culture. The highlight, though, is the other side, with a wide-ranging display on the Arctic itself, with superb static and interactive displays focusing on Arctic flora and fauna, as well as on the peoples of Arctic Europe, Asia and North America.

Napapiiri TOURIST COMPLEX

The southernmost line at which the sun doesn't set at least one day a year, the Arctic Circle, is called Napapiiri in Finland. It crosses the road here, 8km north of Rovaniemi – and built right on top of it is the 'official' **Santa Claus Village** (www.santa-clausvillage.info; ☉9am-7pm Dec–mid-Jan, 10am-5pm mid-Jan–May & Sep-Nov, 9am-6pm Jun-Aug), a touristy complex of shops, reindeer, winter activities and cottage accommodation. Here too is the **Santa Claus Post Office** (www.santaclaus.posti.fi; ☉9am-7pm Jun-Aug & Dec, 10am-5pm Sep-Nov & Jan-May), which receives nearly three-quarters of a million letters each year from children and adults all over the world. Your postcard sent from here will bear an official Santa stamp, and you can arrange to have it delivered at Christmas time. You can also order a letter from Santa (€7). At the tourist information desk you can get your Arctic Circle certificate (€4.20) or stamp for your passport (€0.50).

But the big attraction is **Santa** himself, who receives visitors year-round in a rather impressive **grotto** (www.santaclauslive.com), where a huge clock mechanism (it slows the earth's rotation so that Santa can visit the whole world's children on Christmas night) eerily surrounds those queuing for an audience. The portly saint is quite a linguist, and an old hand at chatting with kids and adults alike. A private chinwag – around two minutes – with the man is absolutely free, but you can't photograph the moment... and official photos of your visit start at an outrageous €25.

LAPLAND SEASONS

It's important to pick your time in Lapland carefully. In the far north there's no sun for 50 days of the year, and no night for 70-odd days. In June it's very muddy, and in July insects can be hard to deal with. If you're here to walk, August is great, and in September the stunning *ruska* (autumn) colours can be seen. There's thick snow cover from mid-October to May; the best time for skiing and husky/reindeer/snowmobile safaris is March and April, when you get a decent amount of daylight and less-extreme temperatures.

Bus 8 heads to Napapiiri from the train station, passing through the centre (adult/child €7/3.80 return).

Pilke MUSEUM

(www.sciencecentre-pilke.fi; Ounasjoentie 6; adult/child €7/5; ☉9am-6pm Tue-Fri, 10am-6pm Sat & Sun) Run by the forest and park service, this museum has permanent interactive displays and changing summer exhibitions on sustainable forestry in Finland, as well as a national-parks information point. It closes Mondays in autumn and spring. There's a decent discount for combined admission with the Arktikum museum, which is alongside.

Ounasvaara SKIING

(www.ounasvaara.fi) This long fell across the river to the east of town is a place to get active. In winter it's a downhill ski centre, which also has three ski jumps, plus more than 100km of cross-country tracks around the hill and further afield. These tracks are great for walking in the summer months, when there's also a toboggan run and a mountain-bike park, with rental available.

Europcar BIKE HIRE

(☏040-306 2870; www.europcar.fi; Pohjanpuistikko 2) Rent bicycles for €20 a day, with discounts given for multiday hire.

☞ Tours

Rovaniemi is Lapland's most popular base for winter and summer activities, offering the convenience of frequent departures and professional trips with multilingual guides.

In summer tours offered include guided walks, mountain biking (€55 to €60), river cruises (€25), visits to a reindeer farm (€50

Rovaniemi

to €60) or huskies (€80), rafting, canoeing and wilderness camping.

Winter activities are snowmobiling (€100 to €165 for a two- to six-hour trip), snowshoe-walking (€50), reindeer-sledding (€100 to €120), husky-sledding (€70 to €250), cross-country skiing (€50 to €60), or a combination. These can include ice fishing, a sauna, a shot at seeing the aurora borealis or an overnight trip to a wilderness cottage (€350 to €450). Longer safaris might take you to the Arctic Ocean or across Lapland (€300 to €500 per day).

Lapland Safaris　　　OUTDOOR ACTIVITIES
(🗺331 1200; www.laplandsafaris.fi; Koskikatu 1) Reliable and well-established outfit for most activities.

Husky Point　　　DOG SLEDDING
(🗺0400-790 096; www.huskypoint.fi; Kittiläntie 1638, Sinettä) From short rides to multiday treks. You can visit the huskies in summer (adult/child €30/15), with pick-ups from Rovaniemi possible for an extra €26/13. In winter it operates a central office at Koskikatu 9.

Safartica　　　OUTDOOR ACTIVITIES
(🗺311 485; www.safartica.com; Koskikatu 9) One of the best companies for snowmobiling and river activities.

✦ Festivals & Events

Napapiirinhiihto　　　SKIING
(www.napapiirinhiihto.fi) In March Rovaniemi hosts skiing and ski-jumping competitions as well as a reindeer race in the centre of town.

Christmas　　　RELIGIOUS
A huge event here, and there are plenty of festive activities throughout December.

Rovaniemi

🛏 Sleeping

Most places offer good discounts in summer.

TOP CHOICE City Hotel HOTEL €€

(☏330 0111; www.cityhotel.fi; Pekankatu 9; s/d €124/144; P@) There's something very pleasing about this warm and welcoming place a block off the main drag. It retains an intimate feel, with excellent service and plenty of extras included free of charge. All the rooms are comfortable and compact; they've been recently refurbished and look very stylish with their large windows, silver objects, new beds and plush maroon and brown fabrics. Lux rooms offer a proper double bed, while the smart suites come with their own sauna. Prices are significantly cheaper from June to August.

Hotel Santa Claus HOTEL €€€

(☏321 321; www.hotelsantaclaus.fi; Korkalonkatu 29; s/d €158/188; @) Thankfully this excellent hotel is devoid of sleigh bells and 'ho-ho-ho' kitsch. It's right in the heart of town and very upbeat and busy, with helpful staff and a great bar and restaurant. The rooms have all the trimmings and are spacious, with a sofa and good-sized beds; a €20 supplement gets you a superior room, which is slightly bigger. Prices drop a little in summer.

Hostel Rudolf HOSTEL €

(☏321 321; www.rudolf.fi; Koskikatu 41; dm/s/d Dec-Mar €48/62/89, Apr-Nov €38/46/59; P♠) Run by Hotel Santa Claus, where you inconveniently have to go to check in, this staffless hostel is Rovaniemi's only one and can fill up fast. Private rooms are good for the price, with spotless bathrooms, solid desks and bedside lamps; dorm rates get you the same deal. There's also a kitchen available and free wi-fi. HI discount.

Guesthouse Borealis GUESTHOUSE €

(☏342 0130; www.guesthouseborealis.com; Asemieskatu 1; s/d/tr €51/64/88; P@♠) The cordial hospitality and proximity to the train station make this family-run spot a winner. The rooms have no frills but are bright and clean; some have a balcony. The airy dining room is the venue for breakfast, which features Finnish porridge; a sauna's also available for a small extra charge. Guests have use of a kitchen, and there are also two self-contained apartments. Prices are a little higher in winter, and substantially so over Christmas.

Santa Claus Holiday Village COTTAGES €€

(☏356 1513; www.schv.fi; Tähtikuja 2, Napapiiri; d €99-149; P♻) This complex of holiday cottages is right in the Napapiiri complex, official terrestrial residence of Santa Claus, but it's off to one side so the tour buses aren't revving outside your front door. Reception rents out bikes and organises excursions. The cottages are comfortable, with sauna and kitchenette; they are semidetached with connecting doors so families can rent out a whole one. Prices are reasonable except over December and New Year, when they double. Book many months in advance for this period.

Santasport HOTEL €€

(☏020-798 4202; www.santasport.fi; Hiihtomajantie 2; s €70-95, d €90-140; P♻♻) A 20-minute stroll from the centre at the base of Ounasvaara hill, this sports complex offers modern rooms – including excellent family suites – with heaps of space and facilities.

RANUA ZOO

The small town of Ranua is 82km south of Rovaniemi on Road 78 and famous for its excellent zoo (Ranuan Eläinpuisto; www.ranuazoo.com; Ranua; adult/child €15/12; 9am-7pm Jun-Aug, 10am-4pm Sep-May;), which focuses almost entirely on Finnish animals, although there are also polar bears and musk oxen from further north. A boardwalk takes you on a 2.5km circuit past all the creatures, which include minks and stoats, impressive owls and eagles, wild reindeer, elk, a big bear paddock (they hibernate from mid-autumn to mid-spring), lynx and wolverines. Apart from the animals, there's plenty to do for kids. It's slightly cheaper in winter.

Ranua has hotel and camping accommodation. There are four to six daily buses from Rovaniemi (€16.80, 1¼ hours) as well as connections from Kajaani and Oulu.

On-site is a full-size pool, spa facilities, bowling, gym, indoor playpark, and bike and ski rental. There are also older, cheaper, student-style rooms and upmarket cottages sleeping six.

Ounaskoski Camping CAMPGROUND €
(345 304; www.ounaskoski-camping-rovaniemi.com; Jäämerentie 1; campsites €14, plus per adult/child €7.50/3; late May-late Sep) Just across the elegant bridge from the town centre, this camping ground is perfectly situated on the riverbank.

🍴 Eating

Gaissa & ZoomUp FINNISH €€
(321 321; www.hotelsantaclaus.fi; Korkalonkatu 29; mains €15-30; Gaissa 5.30-11pm Mon-Sat, ZoomUp 11am-2pm & 4-11pm Mon-Fri, noon-11pm Sat, 1-10pm Sun) The upstairs restaurant of the Hotel Santa Claus is split into two attractive areas. Elegant Gaissa offers petite, reindeer-heavy cuisine. ZoomUp is a bar and serves excellent salads, pastas, grilled meats, and succulent fish in a more casual atmosphere aimed at pulling a local crowd. In ZoomUp, you can mix and match dishes from either menu.

Monte Rosa FINNISH €€
(330 0111; www.monterosa.fi; Pekankatu 9; mains €16-25; 11am-10.30pm Mon-Thu, to 11pm Fri, 3-11pm Sat, 3-10.30pm Sun) Attached to the City Hotel, this place goes for the romance vote with a low candlelit interior and chummy booth seating. Good-sized portions of Finnish and Lapland fare are very tasty; the house salad comes with slabs of reindeer and arctic char on top, and the reindeer carpaccio is also worth trying. Downstairs, the Bull Bar serves ribs and huge burgers out of the same kitchen.

Nili FINNISH €€€
(0400 369 669; www.nili.fi; Valtakatu 20; mains €17-30; 6-11pm Mon-Sat) There's much more English than Finnish heard at this popular central restaurant, with an attractive interior and a Lapland theme. There are a few glitches – the staff, who wear 'Lapp' smocks, are obviously instructed to sell as much as they can – but the meals are very tasty, with wild-mushroom sauces garnishing fish, reindeer and even bear dishes. Portions are longer on presentation than size.

Mariza FINNISH €
(www.ruokahuonemariza.fi; Ruokasenkatu 2; lunch €8.20; 10am-2pm Mon-Fri) A couple of blocks from the centre in untouristed territory, this simple lunch place is a real find, and offers a buffet of home-cooked Finnish food, including daily changing hot dishes, soup and salad. Authentic and excellent. Opens slightly longer hours in summer.

🍷 Drinking & Entertainment

Excluding ski resorts, Rovaniemi is the only place north of Oulu with a half-decent nightlife.

TOP CHOICE Kauppayhtiö CAFE, BAR
(Valtakatu 24; light meals €4-7; 10.30am-8pm Mon, Tue & Thu, to midnight Wed, to 4am Fri & Sat) Rovaniemi's best cafe, this is an oddball collection of retro curios with a coffee-bean and gasoline theme and colourful plastic tables. An espresso machine, bottomless coffee, outdoor seating, salads, sundaes and a bohemian Lapland crowd keep the place ticking. It also does food, including sushi some days, and has regular live music.

Oliver's Corner PUB
(www.oliverscorner.fi; Koskikatu 9; 2pm-2am Sun-Tue, to 3am Wed-Sat) On a central crossroads, Oliver's goes for the standard sports-bar

look upstairs, with big screens wherever your gaze may wander. Downstairs is cosier, with a pool table and weekly live music.

Roy Club BAR, CLUB
(www.royclub.fi; Maakuntakatu 24; ⏰9pm-4am) This friendly bar has a sedate, comfortable top half with cosy seating, a very cheap happy hour until midnight or 1am nightly, and well-attended karaoke. There's also a downstairs club that gets cheerily boisterous with students and goes late.

❶ Information

There are lockers (€2 per 24 hours) at both train and bus stations, and a storage counter at the train station. Check out the website www.rovaniemi24.com for current news and happenings.

Metsähallitus (☑020-564 7820; www.outdoors.fi; Ounasjoentie 6, Pilke Bldg; ⏰8am-4pm Mon, to 6pm Tue-Fri, 10am-6pm Sat & Sun) Information centre for the national parks, with information on hiking and fishing in Lapland and an exhibition on sustainable forestry. The office sells maps and fishing permits, and books cottages.

Tourist Information (☑346 270; www.visit rovaniemi.fi; Maakuntakatu 29; ⏰9am-5pm Mon-Fri) On the square in the middle of town. Free internet. It opens until 6pm from mid-June to mid-August, when it also opens weekends from 9am to 1pm. It uses the same opening hours over the Christmas high season.

❶ Getting There & Away

AIR There are numerous winter charter flights from all around Europe. Minibuses to the centre meet each arriving flight (€7, 15 minutes), doing hotel drop-offs. They pick up along the same route an hour before flight departures.

Finnair/Flybe and Norwegian fly between Helsinki and Rovaniemi.

BUS Rovaniemi is Lapland's main transport hub. Daily connections from the bus station serve just about everywhere in Lapland. Some buses head on north into Norway.

Helsinki €126.30, 12½ hours, night buses.

Kemi €20 to €24.80, 1½ to two hours, frequent buses.

Oulu €42.60, 3½ hours, frequent express buses.

TRAIN Helsinki (€84 to €97, 9¾ to 13 hours) trains are quicker, cheaper and more commodious than buses. There are three daily direct services (via Oulu), including overnight services (high-season total prices go from €108 in a berth up to €169 in a smart modern cabin with en suite) with car transport possibilities.

❶ Getting Around

Major car-rental agencies have offices in the centre and at the airport. **Europcar** (☑0403 062 870; www.europcar.fi; Pohjanpuistikko 2) is at the Rantasipi Pohjanhovi hotel. Sixt (p208), based at the airport, often has the best prices and will bring your car into town.

Kemi

☑016 / POP 22,300

Kemi is an industrial town and important deep-water harbour. Although not hugely appealing (in summer only its gem museum and wide waterfront have any sort of siren song), Kemi is home to two of Finland's blockbuster winter attractions: the Arctic ice-breaker *Sampo*, and the Lumilinna (Snow Castle), complete with ice hotel.

⊙ Sights

Sampo ICE-BREAKER
(☑258 878; www.sampotours.com) Plough through the Gulf of Bothnia pack ice aboard the *Sampo*, a genuine Arctic ice-breaker. The four-hour cruise includes lunch and ice-swimming in special drysuits – a remarkable experience. The *Sampo* sails twice or more weekly from December to mid-April, and costs €260 per adult. If you choose to approach and leave the good ship on snowmobiles (with a reindeer visit included), the price is €425. The best time to go is when the ice is thickest, usually in March. See the website for departure dates and booking.

Snow Castle CASTLE
(☑258 878; www.snowcastle.net; adult/child €10/5; ⏰10am-7pm late Jan–mid-Apr) Few things conjure the fairy-tale romance of a snow castle, and few can compete with Kemi's, a favoured destination for weddings, honeymoons, or just general marvelling at the weird light and sumptuously realised decoration of the multistoreyed interior. The design changes every year but always includes an ethereally beautiful **chapel**, a **snow hotel** and a **restaurant** (3-course menu €38-47).

🛏 Sleeping

TOP CHOICE **Lumihotelli** SNOW HOTEL €€€
(☑258 878; www.snowcastle.net; s/d/ste €175/290/340; ℗) Between late January and early April you can spend the night in the snow hotel. The interior temperature is -5°C, but a woolly sheepskin and sturdy sleeping bag

keep you warm(ish) atop the ice bed. In the morning you can thaw out in the sauna of a nearby hotel.

Hotelli Palomestari HOTEL €€
(☑257117; www.hotellipalomestari.com; Valtakatu 12; s/d €75/87; P @) This likeable family place is one block south and one west of the train and bus stations and offers friendly service and decent if faded rooms with trademark Finnish furniture including a desk and sofa. There's also a convivial bar. Summer prices are great value.

❶ Information

Tourist office (☑040-680 3120; www.visit kemi.fi; Valtakatu 26; ◷8am-3.30pm Mon-Fri) In the town hall.

❶ Getting There & Away

Kemi/Tornio airport is 6km north, and Flybe/ Finnair has regular Helsinki flights. A trip in a shared airport taxi costs €20.

Buses run to Tornio (€6.60, 40 minutes) more than hourly (fewer at weekends), Rovaniemi (€20 to €24.80, 1½ to two hours) and Oulu (€21 to €25, 1¾ hours), among other places.

Trains on the Helsinki–Oulu–Rovaniemi line stop at Kemi.

Tornio

☑016 / POP 22,500

Right on the impressive Tornionjoki, the longest free-flowing river in northern Europe, Tornio is joined to its Swedish counterpart Haparanda (Finnish: Haaparanta) by short bridges. Cross-border shopping has boomed here in recent years, with new malls popping up like mushrooms. Don't forget that Finland is an hour ahead of Sweden.

◉ Sights

Tornion Kirkko CHURCH
(www.tornio.seurakunta.net; Seminaarinkatu; ◷10am-6pm Mon-Fri, 1.30-6pm Sat & Sun Jun-Jul, 10am-5pm Mon-Fri Aug) Tornio's Lutheran church was completed in 1686 and is one of the most beautiful wooden churches in Finland.

Aineen Taidemuseo GALLERY
(www.tornio.fi/aine; Torikatu 2; adult/child €4/free; ◷11am-6pm Tue-Thu, to 3pm Fri-Sun) Interesting collection of Finnish art from the 19th and 20th centuries backed up by temporary exhibitions.

🏃 Activities

River-rafting is popular in summer on the Kukkolankoski, using inflatable rubber rafts or traditional wooden boats. There are also **kayaking** trips and winter excursions such as snowmobile, reindeer and husky **safaris**. The tourist office can make bookings for all trips and handles **fishing** permits; there are several excellent spots along the Tornionjoki.

Green Zone Golf Course GOLF
(☑431711; www.torniogolf.fi; Näräntie; green fee €35-40) The famous course straddles Finland and Sweden, allowing you to fire shots into a different country and time zone, or play under the midnight sun. You'll need a Green Card or handicap certificate. There's also a driving range and pitch-and-putt course here.

🛏 Sleeping & Eating

There's a good hostel and upmarket hotel across the bridge in Haparanda.

E-City GUESTHOUSE €
(☑044-509 0358; www.ecity.fi; Saarenpäänkatu 39; d €80, s/d without bathroom €50/65; P) Tornio's best budget option, this is a friendly guesthouse in the north of town run by a welcoming young family. Cosy rooms feature comfortable beds and colourful fabrics; the shared bathrooms are clean and have good showers, and breakfast includes traditional Finnish porridge.

Umpitunneli TEX-MEX, PUB €
(www.umpitunneli.fi; Hallituskatu 15; mains €12-19; ◷food 3-9.30pm Mon-Fri, 1-9.30pm Sat, 1-8pm Sun) The 'Dead-End Tunnel' may be a road to nowhere, but it's a most enjoyable one, with a huge terrace, plenty of pissed-up patrons adding entertainment value at weekends, and large plates of food, from creamy pasta to steaks and Tex-Mex. There are often live bands.

❶ Information

Green Line Centre (☑050-590 0562; www. haparandatornio.com; ◷9am-7pm Mon-Fri, 10am-6pm Sat & Sun Jun–mid-Aug, 9am-5pm Mon-Fri mid-Aug–May) Acts as the tourist office for both towns.

❶ Getting There & Away

There are a few daily buses from Rovaniemi (€18 to €24.40, two hours), although there are more connections (bus and train) via Kemi (€6.60, 45 minutes, more than hourly, less at weekends, free with rail pass). Many Tornio-bound buses continue to Haparanda, although the distance is so short you can walk.

From Haparanda, there are buses to Luleå, from where buses and trains run to other Swedish destinations.

Rovaniemi to Inari

North from Rovaniemi, Hwy 4 (E75) heads up to the vast, flat expanse of northern Lapland and Sápmi, home of the Sámi people and their domesticated reindeer herds wandering the forests and fells. Subtle landscape changes become more severe as you head north, and the feeling of entering one of Europe's last great wildernesses is palpable. The resort town of Saariselkä is the base for hiking or ski-trekking do-it-yourself itineraries in the wonderful **UKK National Park**, while the Sámi capital of Inari is the place to learn about their traditions and a base for visiting the Lemmenjoki National Park.

SODANKYLÄ
016 / POP 5540

Likeable Sodankylä is the main service centre for one of Europe's least populated areas, with a density of just 0.75 people per sq km. It makes a decent staging post on the way between Rovaniemi and the north.

At the intersection of the Kemijärvi and Rovaniemi roads, the **Vanha Kirkko** (0400-190 406; 9am-6pm early Jun–mid-Aug, by request rest of yr) is the region's oldest church and dates back to 1689.

Sodankylä books out in mid-June for the **Midnight Sun Film Festival** (www.msff.fi), which has a comprehensive range of intriguing screenings in three venues.

Across the river from the town, **Camping Sodankylä Nilimella** (612 181; www.naturexventures.fi; campsites €6, plus per adult/child €4/2, 2-/4-person cabins €38/54, apt €80-150; Jun-Aug) has simple but spacious cabins, as well as cottage apartments with private kitchen and sauna. Some accommodation is available outside the summer season.

Majatalo Kolme Veljestä (0400 539 075; www.majatalokolmeveljesta.fi; Ivalontie 1; s/d/tr €46/64/75 without bathroom; P@) 500m north of the centre, has small spotless rooms. Price includes kitchen use, breakfast, sauna and free tea and coffee. Central **Hotelli Karhu** (020-1620 610; www.hotel-bearinn.com; Lapintie 7; r €105-115; P@) is a great deal,

offering buzzy staff, offbeat lobby decor and really inviting chambers, with big fluffy beds, greywood floors and great modern bathrooms.

The **tourist office** (040-746 9776; www.sodankyla.fi; Jäämerentie 3; 9am-5pm Mon-Fri plus 10am-3pm Sat mid-Jun–mid-Aug) is next to the Vanha Kirkko.

There are regular buses from Rovaniemi, Ivalo and Kemijärvi. The bus terminal is on the main road.

SAARISELKÄ
016

Between Sodankylä and Inari, this collection of enormous hotels and holiday cottages makes a great stop for the active. It's on the edge of one of Europe's great wilderness areas, much of which is covered by the UKK National Park. You could hike for weeks here; there's a good network of huts and a few marked trails. In winter this is a ski resort and a very popular base for snowmobiling and husky trips. In the Siula centre there's tourist information and a **national parks office** (020-564 7200; www.outdoors.fi; Siula Centre; 9am-5pm Mon-Fri, plus 10am-4pm Sat & Sun high season) that sells maps and reserves wilderness cabins. Hit the website www.saariselka.com for cottage accommodation; the cheapest place to stay is **Saariselän Panimo** (675 6500; www.saariselanpanimo.fi; Saariseläntie 10; s/d €45/58; P), a cosy brewpub with spacious, clean rooms that are a real bargain. Buses run regularly to Ivalo (€7.20, 30 minutes) and further north, and south to Rovaniemi.

Inari
016 / POP 550

The tiny village of Inari (Sámi: Anár) is the place to begin to learn something of Sámi culture, and has the excellent Siida museum, as well as worthwhile handicrafts shops. It's also a great base for heading off to further-flung locations like Lemmenjoki National Park.

Inari is the seat of the Finnish Sámi parliament, and the impressive wooden Sajos centre is where it meets; the building also contains a Sámi-language library and music archive. The village sits on Lapland's largest lake, Inarijärvi, a spectacular body of water with more than 3000 islands in its 1153-sq-km area.

◉ Sights & Activities

TOP CHOICE Siida MUSEUM

(www.siida.fi; adult/child €9/5; ⊙9am-8pm Jun–mid-Sep, 10am-5pm Tue-Sun mid-Sep–May) One of Finland's finest museums, Siida should not be missed. It's a comprehensive overview of the Sámi and their Arctic environment that's actually two museums skilfully interwoven. Outside is the original museum, a complex of **open-air buildings** that reflect facets of nomadic and postnomadic Sámi life. There's also a fine craft shop and a cafe with a lunch deal.

Siida's website is worth a mention itself: hidden away via the 'web exhibitions' page is a series of excellent pages on the Inari and Skolt Sámi cultures.

✂ Handicrafts CRAFT WORKSHOPS

Inari is the main centre for Sámi handicrafts and there are several studios and boutique shops in the village. **Sámi Duodji Ry** (Inarintie 51; ⊙ 10am-6pm daily Jul & Aug, to 5pm Mon-Fri & to 3pm Sat Sep-Jun), in the Sajos building, is the main shop of the Finnish association of Sámi craftspeople.

Inari Event CULTURAL TOUR

(Sami Experience; ☑040-179 6069; www.visitinari.fi; Inarintie 38) This outfit operates an excellent year-round activities program.

RideNorth HORSES, HUSKIES

(☑040-737 8181; www.ridenorth.fi; Kotiniemi, Inari) RideNorth offers sled trips with well-cared-for huskies, and trips with beautiful, hardy Norwegian fjording horses.

Inarin Porofarmi REINDEER TOUR

(☑050-066 6444; www.reindeerfarm.fi; Kittiläntie 1445) Inarin Porofarmi is a reindeer farm that runs sled-trips in winter and visits in summer with plenty of information on reindeer herding and Sámi culture. The two-hour visit costs €20, or €50 including transport from Inari.

Lake & Snow BOAT TOUR

(☑671 108; www.saariselka.fi/lakesnow; Inarintie 26) Daily cruises sail on Inarijärvi from early June to late September (€20, two hours).

✲✲ Festivals & Events

Skábmagovat FILM

(www.skabmagovat.fi) A recommended film festival in the third week of January, with an indigenous theme.

King's Cup REINDEER RACING

(www.paliskunnat.fi) Held over the last weekend of March or first of April, the King's Cup is the grand finale of Lapland's reindeer-racing season and a great spectacle as the beasts race around the frozen lake, jockeys sliding like waterskiers behind them.

🛏 Sleeping & Eating

TOP CHOICE Hotel Kultahovi HOTEL €€

(☑511 7100; www.hotelkultahovi.fi; Saarikoskentie 2; s/d €69/90, new wing €109/125; ⓟ@) Just off the main road towards Lemmenjoki, this cosy family-run place overlooks the rapids and has spruce rooms, some with a great river view. Chambers in the new wing have appealing, light wood Nordic decoration, riverside balcony/terrace, and most have a sauna. There's a restaurant (mains €14 to €25, open 11am to 11pm) that serves well-presented, tasty Lappish specialities.

Villa Lanca GUESTHOUSE €€

(☑040-748 0984; www.villalanca.com; s/d €55/79, with kitchen €68/95; ⓟ) On the main road in the heart of town, this is Inari's most characterful lodging, with boutique rooms decorated with Asian fabrics, feather charms and real artistic flair. The cute attic rooms are spacious and cheaper but lack a bit of headroom. An excellent breakfast with delicious homemade bread is included.

Lomakylä Inari CAMPGROUND €

(☑671 108; www.saariselka.fi/lomakylainari; 2-/4-person cabins €65/75, without bathroom €43/48, cottages €80-170, campsites for 1/2/4 people €10/15/18; ⊙Jun-Sep; ⓟ@🛜) The closest cabin accommodation to town, this place is 500m south of the centre and a good option. Some cottages are available in winter.

Inari Hostel HOSTEL €

(☑040-748 0984; www.inarihostel.com; Inarintie 51; dm/s/d €28/50/60; ⓟ) This simple but attractive hostel is in the heart of town and has eye-catching views over the lake. There's a kitchen and an open fire to keep the winter chills away. Dorms have just three single beds. Linen is extra. Check in at Villa Lanca just down the road.

ⓘ Information

Tourist office (☑040-168 9668; www.inari.fi; ⊙9am-8pm Jun–mid-Sep, 10am-5pm Tue-Sun mid-Sep–May) In the Siida museum. There's also a nature information point here.

❶ Getting There & Away

Buses run to Inari from Ivalo (€8, 30 minutes), which has a popular winter airport. There are two daily services from Rovaniemi (€58.30, 5¼ hours), which continue to Norway, one to Karasjok (and Nordkapp in summer), another to Tana Bru.

Lemmenjoki National Park

Lemmenjoki is Finland's largest national park, covering a remote wilderness area between Inari and Norway. It's prime hiking territory, with desolate wilderness rivers, rough landscapes and the mystique of gold, with solitary prospectors sloshing away with their pans in the middle of nowhere. Boat trips on the river allow more leisurely exploration of the park.

Lemmenjoki Nature Centre (www.outdoors.fi) is near the park entrance just before the village of Njurgulahti, about 50km southwest of Inari.

As well as hiking and gold panning, there's a boat cruise along the Lemmenjoki valley in summer, from Njurgulahti village to the Kultahamina wilderness hut at Gold Harbour. A 20km marked trail also follows the course of the river, so you can take the boat one way, then hike back. There are departures at 10am and 5pm from mid-June to mid-August; in early June and from mid-August to mid-September, only the evening one goes (€21 one way, 1½ hours). There are several places offering camping and/or cabin accommodation, food and boat trips. Inside the park, a dozen wilderness huts provide free accommodation.

There is one taxi-bus running Monday to Saturday between Inari and Njurgulahti from early June to early August. Otherwise, check school-bus times with the tourist office.

Northwestern Lapland

There's plenty going on above the Arctic Circle in northwestern Lapland, with several ski resorts (Levi, Ylläs, Olos), and a wonderful range of activities in Muonio, including memorable husky-sled treks. The long, lonely journey up Finland's left 'arm' culminates in Kilpisjärvi, tucked in between Sweden and Norway. These are Finland's 'highlands' and, though not especially high altitude, they offer excellent walking and some outstanding views.

MUONIO

☑016

The village of Muonio is the last significant stop on Road 21 before Kilpisjärvi and Norway. It sits on the scenic Muonionjoki that forms the border between Finland and Sweden, and is a fine base for summer and winter activities. There are plenty of places to stay around here and there's low-key skiing in winter.

Three kilometres south, the excellent **Harriniva** (☎530 0300; www.harriniva.fi) centre has a vast program of summer and winter activities, ranging from short jaunts to multiday adventures. In summer these include guided hikes, canoe and boat trips, horse trekking, quad safaris and fishing on the salmon-packed Muonionjoki. You can also rent bikes, boats and rods, and there are various accommodation options here. In winter wonderful **dog-sledding safaris** range from 1½ hours (€70) to two days (€560), or trips of a week or longer, perhaps adding reindeer-sledding and snowmobiling to the mix. In summer you can visit the **Arktinen Rekikoirakeskus** (Arctic sled-dog centre; Harriniva; guided tour adult/child €7/€4) with over 400 lovable dogs, all with names and personalities; their guided tour is great.

LEVI

☑016

Levi is one of Finland's two most popular ski resorts, but it's also a very popular destination for *ruska* (autumn) hiking and a cheap base in summer. The **tourist office** (☎639 3300; www.levi.fi; Myllyjoentie 2; ◷9am-4.30pm Mon-Fri, 11am-4pm Sat & Sun) organises accommodation bookings as well as activities like snowmobile safaris and dog-sledding.

The **ski resort** (www.levi.fi) has 45 downhill slopes, many lit. Cross-country skiing is also good, with hundreds of kilometres of trails. There's enough going on in summer to make it a worthwhile base for exploring this part of Finland.

There are several good sprawling hotel complexes. Accommodation prices go through the roof in December, and between February and May. Virtually the whole town consists of holiday apartments and cottages, typically sleeping four to six, with sauna, fully equipped kitchen and many other mod cons. In summer they are a real bargain, costing €45 to €60 per night; in winter €1100 a week is average.

Four to five daily buses run between Rovaniemi and Levi (€33.70, 2½ hours).

HETTA/ENONTEKIÖ & PALLAS-YLLÄSTUNTURI NATIONAL PARK

🍴016 / POP 1880

One of Lapland's signature long-distance walks is the excellent 55km trekking route between the northern village of Hetta (also known as Enontekiö) and **Hotelli Pallas** (🍴323 355; www.laplandhotels.com; Pallastunturi; s/d €138/166, summer €78/92; ⊙Dec-Sep; **P⊛**). The marked trail crosses Pallas-Yllästunturi National Park, and can easily be completed in four days. There are free wilderness huts, but these pack out in summer so it's wise to carry a tent. See www.outdoors.fi for details of the route and huts.

Hetta has a large Sámi population and, though a bit spread out, makes a good stop for a night or two. Here, **Skierri** (🍴020-564 7950; www.outdoors.fi; Peuratie 15; ⊙9am-5pm Jun-late Sep, to 4pm Mon-Fri late Sep-Jun) is the combined local tourist office and national park visitor centre. At the trek's southern end, **Pallastunturi Luontokeskus** (🍴020-564 7930; www.outdoors.fi; ⊙9am-5pm Jun-Sep & late Feb-Apr, to 4pm Mon-Fri rest of yr) by the Hotelli Pallas provides information and makes hut reservations.

Hetan Majatalo (🍴554 0400; www.hetan-majatalo.fi; Riekontie 8; s/d hotel €65/90, guesthouse €40/64; **P@**) is in the centre of Hetta, but set back in its own garden away from the road. This welcoming pad offers two types of accommodation in facing buildings: clean and simple guesthouse rooms sharing bathrooms, and very handsome, spacious wood-clad hotel rooms. It's an excellent deal that includes breakfast and sauna.

Buses from Hetta head to Rovaniemi (€55.20, five hours) and Kilpisjärvi (€30.20, 3¼ hours) via a swap over at Palojoensuu. There's a summer service from Rovaniemi to Tromsø in Norway via Hetta, Kautokeino and Alta.

KILPISJÄRVI

🍴016

The remote village of Kilpisjärvi, the northernmost settlement in the 'arm' of Finland, is in a memorable setting among lakes and snowy mountains on the doorstep of both Norway and Sweden. At 480m above sea level, this small border post, wedged between the lake of Kilpisjärvi and the magnificent surrounding fells, is also the highest village in Finland.

The Kilpisjärvi area offers fantastic long and short hikes. The ascent to slate-capped **Saana Fell** (1029m) takes two to three hours

return. Also popular is the route through **Malla Nature Park** to the Kolmen Valtakunnan Raja, a concrete block in a lake that marks the **treble border** of Finland, Sweden and Norway. Alternatively, a summer **boat service** (🍴0400 669 392) drops you a light 3km away (one way/return €15/20, 30 minutes).

Lining the main road are several camping grounds with cabins. Many places are open only during the trekking season, which is from June to September.

Two daily buses connect Rovaniemi and Kilpisjärvi (€70.70, six to eight hours) via Kittilä, Levi and Muonio, with a connection to Hetta. In summer one heads on to Tromsø in Norway.

UNDERSTAND FINLAND

History

Finnish history is the story of a people who for centuries were a tug-of-war rope between two sides, Sweden and Russia, and the nation's eventful emergence from their grip to become one of the world's most progressive and prosperous nations.

Prehistory

Though evidence of pre–Ice Age habitation exists, it wasn't until around 9000 years ago that settlement was re-established after the big chill. Things are hazy, but the likeliest scenario seems to be that the Finns' ancestors moved in to the south and drove the nomadic ancestors of the Sámi north towards Lapland.

Sweden & Russia

The 12th and 13th centuries saw the Swedes begin to move in, Christianising the Finns in the south, and establishing settlements and fortifications. The Russians were never far away, though. There were constant skirmishes with the power of Novgorod, and in the early 18th century Peter the Great attacked and occupied much of Finland. By 1809 Sweden was in no state to resist, and Finland became a duchy of the Russian Empire. The capital was moved to Helsinki, but the communist revolution of October 1917 brought the downfall of the Russian tsar and enabled Finland to declare independence.

Winter & Continuation Wars

Stalin's aggressive territorial demands in 1939 led to the Winter War between Finland and the Soviet Union, conducted in horribly low temperatures. Little Finland resisted heroically, but was defeated and forced to cede a tenth of its territory. When pressured for more, Finland accepted assistance from Germany. This 'Continuation War' against the Russians cost Finland almost 100,000 lives. Eventually Mannerheim negotiated an armistice with the Russians, ceding more land, and then waged a bitter war in Lapland to oust the Germans. Against the odds, Finland remained independent, but at a heavy price.

Recent Times

Finland managed to take a neutral stance during the Cold War, and once the USSR collapsed, it joined the EU in 1995, and adopted the euro in 2002.

In the new millennium, Finland has boomed on the back of a strong technology sector, the traditionally important forestry industry, design and manufacturing and, increasingly, tourism. Despite the global economic climate, Finland remains a major success story of the new Europe with a strong economy, robust social values and superlow crime and corruption.

The 2011 parliamentary elections in Finland sent a shock wave through Europe as the nationalistic, populist True Finns party came from nowhere to seize 19% of the vote.

Their absolute rejection of bailouts of other EU economies meant that rather than compromise their principles by entering a coalition government, they opted to become the major opposition party instead, establishing them as a serious political force. The True Finns' success reflected both concerns about rising immigration and a widespread feeling of frustration that Finnish taxpayers were being forced to pay for other countries' problems. It evoked a common stereotype of the lonely Finn sitting at home and not caring much about the rest of the world.

People

Finland is one of Europe's most sparsely populated countries, with 16 people per sq km, falling to fewer than one in parts of Lapland. Both Finnish and Swedish are official languages, with some 5% of Finns having Swedish as their mother tongue, especially on the west coast and the Åland archipelago. Around 5% of all Finnish residents are immigrants, a low percentage but one that has increased substantially in recent years.

Finland's minorities include some 6000 Roma in the south and, in the north, the Sámi, from several distinct groups. About 80% of Finns describe themselves as Lutherans, 1.1% are Orthodox and most of the remainder are unaffiliated. Only 4% of Finns are weekly churchgoers, one of the world's lowest worship rates.

THE SAUNA

Nothing is more traditionally or culturally Finnish than the sauna. For centuries it has been a place to bathe, meditate, warm up during cold winters and even give birth, and most Finns still use the sauna at least once a week. An invitation to bathe in a family's sauna is an honour.

There are three principal types of sauna around these days. The most common is the electric sauna stove, which produces a fairly dry harsh heat compared with the much-loved chimney sauna, which is driven by a log fire and is the staple of life at Finnish summer cottages. Even rarer is the true *savusauna* (smoke sauna), which is without a chimney.

Bathing is done in the nude (there are some exceptions in public saunas, which are almost always sex-segregated anyway) and Finns are quite strict about the nonsexual – even sacred – nature of the sauna.

According to sauna etiquette you should wash or shower first. Once inside the sauna (with a temperature of 80°C to 100°C), water is thrown onto the stove using a *kauhu* (ladle), producing *löyly* (steam). A *vihta* (whisk of birch twigs and leaves) is sometimes used to lightly strike the skin, improving circulation. Once you're hot enough, go outside and cool off with a cold shower or preferably by jumping into a lake or pool – enthusiastic Finns do so even in winter by cutting a hole in the ice. Repeat the process. The sauna beer afterwards is also traditional.

A capacity for silence and reflection are the traits that best sum up the Finnish character, though this seems odd when weighed against their global gold medal in coffee consumption, their production line of successful heavy bands, and their propensity for a tipple. The image of a log cabin with a sauna by a lake tells much about Finnish culture: independence, endurance (*sisu* or 'guts') and a deep love of nature.

Arts

Architecture

Finland's modern architecture – sleek, functionalist and industrial – has been admired throughout the world ever since Alvar Aalto started making a name for himself during the 1930s. His works can be seen all over Finland today, from the angular Finlandia Talo in Helsinki to the public buildings and street plan of Rovaniemi. Jyväskylä is another obligatory stop for Aalto fans.

Earlier architecture in Finland can be seen in churches made from stone or wood – Kerimäki's oversized church is a highlight, as are the cathedrals at Turku and Tampere. Low-rise Helsinki boasts a patchwork of architectural styles, including the neoclassical buildings of Senate Square, the rich ornamentation of art nouveau (Jugendstil), the modern functionalism of Aalto's buildings and the postmodern Kiasma museum.

Design

Finland, like Scandinavia as a whole, is also famous for its design. Aalto again laid a foundation with innovative interior design, furniture and the famous Savoy vase. Finns have created and refined their own design style through craft traditions and using natural materials such as wood, glass and ceramics. Glassware and porcelain such as Iittala and Arabia are world famous, while Marimekko's upbeat, colourful fabric is a Finnish icon. A new wave of young designers is keeping things from stagnating. Stereotypes are cheerfully broken without losing sight of the roots: an innate practicality and the Finns' almost mystical closeness to nature.

Cinema

Although around 20 films are produced in Finland annually, few make it onto screens beyond the Nordic countries. The best-known Finnish film maker is Aki Kaurismäki,

famous for films such as *Le Havre* (2011), *Drifting Clouds* (1996), and the wonderful *Man Without a Past* (2002), an ultimately life-affirming story about a man who loses his memory. Aki Kaurismäki's brother, Mika, has made a reputation for insightful documentaries like *Sonic Mirror* (2008), partially looking at Finland's jazz scene.

Recent home-grown hits include *Musta jää* (Black Ice; 2007), a characteristically complex Finnish film of infidelity, and *The Home of Dark Butterflies* (2008), a stark look at a Finnish boys' home. For something completely different, check out *Dudesons Movie* (2006), featuring the painful madness of a group of Finnish TV nuts in the style of *Jackass,* or *Miesten Vuoro* (Steam of Life; 2010), a fabulous doco-film featuring Finnish men sweating and talking about life in the confessional of the sauna.

Hollywood's most famous Finn is Renny Harlin, director of action movies such as *Die Hard II, Cliffhanger* and *Deep Blue Sea.*

Finland hosts some quality film festivals, notably the Midnight Sun Film Festival (p195) in Sodankylä and the Tampere International Short Film Festival (p160).

Literature

The *Kalevala,* a collection of folk stories, songs and poems compiled in the 1830s by Elias Lönnrot, is Finland's national epic and a very entertaining read. As part of the same nationalistic renaissance, poet JL Runeberg wrote *Tales of the Ensign Stål,* capturing Finland at war with Russia, while Aleksis Kivi wrote *Seven Brothers* (1870), the nation's first novel, about brothers escaping conventional life in the forest, allegorising the birth of Finnish national consciousness.

This theme continued in the 1970s with *The Year of the Hare,* looking at a journalist's escape into the wilds by the prolific, popular and bizarre Arto Paasilinna. Other 20th-century novelists include Mika Waltari, who gained international fame with *The Egyptian,* and FE Sillanpää, who received the Nobel Prize for Literature in 1939. The national bestseller during the postwar period was *The Unknown Soldier* by Väinö Linna. The seemingly endless series of autobiographical novels by Kalle Päätalo and the witty short stories by Veikko Huovinen are also very popular in Finland. Finland's most internationally famous author is the late Tove Jansson, whose books about the fantastic Moomin family have long captured the imagination.

Music

Music is huge in Finland, and in summer numerous festivals all over the country revel in everything from mournful Finnish tango to soul-lifting symphony orchestras to crunchingly potent metal.

Revered composer Jean Sibelius (1865–1957) was at the forefront of the nationalist movement. His stirring tone-poem *Finlandia* has been raised to the status of a national hymn. Classical music is thriving in Finland, which is an assembly line of orchestral and operatic talent: see a performance if you can.

The Karelian region has its own folk-music traditions, typified by the stringed *kantele*, while the Sámi passed down their traditions and beliefs not through the written word but through the songlike chant called the *yoik*.

Finnish bands have made a big impact on the heavier, darker side of the music scale in recent years. The Rasmus, Nightwish, Apocalyptica, Lordi, HIM and the 69 Eyes are huge worldwide. But there is lighter music, such as the Von Hertzen Brothers, indie band Disco Ensemble, emo-punks Poets of the Fall and melodic Husky Rescue. Then there are rock legends like Hanoi Rocks and the Flaming Sideburns.

Dance

Finns' passion for dance is typified by the tango, which, although borrowed from Latin America, has been refined into a uniquely Finnish style. Older Finns are tango-mad and every town has a dance hall or dance restaurant. A similar form of Finnish dancing is the waltzlike *humppa*.

Visual Art

Finland's Golden Age in painting and sculpture was the 19th-century National Romantic era, when artists such as Akseli Gallen-Kallela, Albert Edelfelt, Pekka Halonen and the Von Wright brothers were inspired by the country's forests and pastoral landscape. Gallen-Kallela and Helene Schjerfbeck are probably Finland's most famous artists. Schjerfbeck is especially famous for her self-portraits, which seem to define the situation of Finnish women a century ago; Gallen-Kallela is known for *Kalevala*-inspired works – don't miss his frescos on display in the Kansallismuseo (National Museum) in Helsinki.

The best of Finnish art can be seen at Ateneum (National Gallery) in Helsinki, but there's a *taidemuseo* (art gallery) in just about every Finnish city.

Environment

People often describe Finland offhand as a country of 'forests and lakes', and the truth is that they are spot on. Some 10% of Suomi is taken up by bodies of water, and nearly 70% is forested with birch, spruce and pine. It's a fairly flat expanse of territory: though the fells of Lapland add a little height to the picture, they are small change compared to the muscular mountainscapes of Norway.

Measuring 338,000 sq km and weighing in as Europe's seventh-largest nation, Finland hits remarkable latitudes: its southernmost point is comparable with Anchorage in Alaska, or the lower reaches of Greenland. Its watery vital statistics are also impressive, with 187,888 large lakes and numerous further wetlands and smaller bodies of water. Geographers estimate that its total coastline, including riverbanks and lake shores, measures 315,000km, not far off the distance to the moon.

Finland has one of the world's highest tree coverages; much of this forest is managed, and timber-harvesting and the associated pulp-milling is an important industry.

Wildlife

Brown bears, lynx, wolverines and wolves are native to Finland, although sightings are rare. You're more likely to see an elk, though hopefully not crashing through your windscreen; drive cautiously. In Lapland, the Sámi keep commercial herds of some 230,000 reindeer. Finland is a birdwatcher's paradise, with species like the capercaillie and golden eagle augmented by hundreds of migratory arrivals in spring and summer.

National Parks

Finland's excellent network of national parks and other protected areas is maintained by **Metsähallitus** (Finnish Forest & Park Service; www.outdoors.fi). In total, over 30,000 sq km, some 9% of the total area, is in some way protected land. The largest and most pristine national parks are in northern Finland, particularly Lapland, where vast

WILDLIFE WATCHING

The deep forests in eastern and north-eastern Finland offer excellent wildlife-spotting opportunities. While you're unlikely to spot bears, wolves, lynx or wolverines on a casual hike, there are plenty of reliable operators, especially in eastern Finland, that specialise in trips to watch these creatures in their domain. The excellent birdlife, both migratory and local, offers further opportunities. Ask at tourist offices for local services.

swaths of wilderness invite trekking, cross-country skiing, fishing and canoeing.

Sustainable Finland

As a general model for environmentally sustainable nationhood, Finland does very well. Though it has a high per-capita carbon-emission rate, this is largely due to its abnormal heating requirements and is offset in many ways. As in much of northern Europe, cycling and recycling were big here decades ago, littering and waste-dumping don't exist, and sensible solutions for keeping the houses warm and minimising heat loss have long been a question of survival, not virtue. Finns in general have a deep respect for and understanding of nature and have always trodden lightly on it, seeing the forest as friend, not foe.

But the forest is also an important part of Finland's economy. Most of the forests are periodically logged, and privately owned plots are long-term investments for many Finns. Hunting is big here, and animals are kept at an 'optimum' population level by the keen hunting contingent.

And, despite the rushing rivers and clean air, Finland manages to produce only some 16% of its energy needs from hydro- and wind-generated sources. Nevertheless, it plans to meet EU targets for 38% of energy to be produced from renewables by 2020, with woodpulp byproducts a large part of the proposal.

Finland is a strong supporter of nuclear energy, with several operational reactors.

Climate Change

Southern Finland has already noticed dramatically changed weather patterns, and the almost unthinkable prospect of a nonwhite Christmas in Helsinki looks ever-likelier. Scientists in the Arctic are producing increasingly worrying data and it seems that northern nations like Finland may be some of the earliest to be seriously affected.

Food & Drink

Typically Finnish food is similar to the fare you get elsewhere in Scandinavia – lots of fish, such as Baltic herring, salmon and whitefish, along with heavy food such as potatoes, meatballs, sausages, soups, stews and dark rye bread. Finns tend to make lunch the main meal of the day. Breakfast can be anything from coffee and a *pulla* (bun) to a buffet of cold cuts, porridge, eggs, berries and pickled fish.

Staples & Specialities

Simple hamburgers, hot dogs and kebabs are a cheap, common snack, served from *grillis* (takeaways). Fish is a mainstay of the Finnish diet. Fresh salmon, herring and Arctic char are common, and the tiny lake fish *muikku* is another treat. Elk and bear make occasional appearances, while in Lapland, reindeer is a staple on every menu.

Regional specialities from Karelia include *vety*, a sandwich made with ham, eggs and pickles, and the *karjalanpiirakka,* a savoury rice pasty folded in a thin, open crust. In Tampere, try *mustamakkara,* a thick sausage made from cow's blood. In Savo, especially Kuopio, a highlight is *kalakukko,* fish baked in a rye loaf. Åland is known for its fluffy semolina pancakes. Seasonal berries are a delight in Finland – look out for cloudberries and lingonberries from Lapland, and market stalls selling blueberries, strawberries and raspberries.

Finns drink plenty of beer, and among the big local brews are Lapin Kulta and Karhu. Cider is also popular, as is *lonkero,* a ready-made mix of gin and fruity soft drink, usually grapefruit. Other uniquely Finnish drinks include *salmiakkikossu,* which combines dissolved liquorice sweets with the iconic Koskenkorva vodka (an acquired taste); *fisu,* which does the same but with Fisherman's Friend pastilles; *sahti,* a sweet, high-alcohol beer; and cloudberry or cranberry liqueurs.

Where to Eat & Drink

Big towns all have a kauppahalli (market hall), the place to head for all sorts of Finnish specialities, breads, cheeses, fresh and smoked fish and cheap sandwiches and snacks. The summer kauppatori (market square) also has food stalls and market produce.

Meals in a *ravintola* (restaurant) can be expensive, particularly dinner, but Finns tend to eat their main meal in the middle of the day, so most restaurants and some cafes put on a generous *lounas* (lunch) buffet for between €7 and €10. These include all-you-can-eat salad, bread, coffee and dessert, plus big helpings of hearty fare – sausage and potatoes or fish and pasta are common.

Finns are big lovers of chain restaurants (Golden Rax Pizza Buffet, Rosso, Amarillo, Koti Pizza, Hesburger, Fransmanni and many more), which can be found in most towns. Quality isn't wonderful, but they can be cheap refuelling options and tend to open long hours.

Finns are the world's biggest coffee drinkers, so cafes are everywhere, ranging from 100-year-old imperial classics to trendy networking joints and simple country caffeine stops.

Beer, wine and spirits are sold by the state network, Alko. There are stores in every town. The legal age for drinking is 18 for beer and wine, and 20 for spirits. Beer and cider with less than 5% alcohol can be bought easily at supermarkets, service stations and convenience stores.

Vegetarians & Vegans

Most medium-sized towns in Finland will have a *kasvisravintola* (vegetarian restaurant), usually open weekday lunchtimes only. It's easy to self-cater at markets, or eat only the salad and vegetables at lunch buffets (which is usually cheaper). Many restaurants also have a salad buffet. The website www.vegaaniliitto.fi has a useful listing of vegetarian and vegan restaurants; follow 'ruoka' and 'kasvisravintoloita' (the Finnish list is more up to date than the English one).

SURVIVAL GUIDE

Directory A–Z
Accommodation
PRICE RANGES
The following three price categories are based on the cost of a standard double room at its most expensive. In the budget category

expect shared bathrooms; midrange will have private bathroom, good facilities and breakfast buffet included, while top end has business-class or five-star facilities. Double beds are rare; family or group rooms are common.

€€€ more than €160
€€ €70 to €160
€ less than €70

CAMPING
Most camping grounds are open only from June to August (ie summer) and popular spots are crowded during July and the Midsummer weekend. Campsites usually cost around €13 plus €4/2 per adult/child. Almost all camping grounds have cabins or cottages for rent, which are usually excellent value from €35 for a basic double cabin to €120 for a cottage with kitchen, bathroom and sauna.

The **Camping Key Europe** (www.campingkeyeurope.com) offers useful discounts. You can buy it at most camping grounds for €16. The **Finnish Camping Association** (www.camping.fi) carries an extensive listing of campsites across the country.

Finland's *jokamiehenoikeus* (everyman's right) allows access to most land and means you can pitch a tent almost anywhere on public land or at designated free campsites in national parks.

FARMSTAYS
A growing, and often ecologically sound, accommodation sector in Finland is that of farmstays. Many rural farms, particularly in the south, offer B&B accommodation, a unique opportunity to meet local people and experience their way of life. Plenty of activities are also usually on offer. **ECEAT** (www.eceat.fi) lists a number of organic, sustainable farms in Finland that offer accommodation. Local tourist offices keep lists of farmstay options in the surrounding area; the website www.visitfinland.com links to a few (click on accommodation), and **Lomarengas** (☑0306 502502; www.lomarengas.fi) also has many listed on its website. In general, prices are good – from around €30 per person per night, country breakfast included. Evening meals are also usually available. Your hosts may not speak much English; if you have difficulties the local tourist office will be happy to help arrange the booking.

HOSTELS & SUMMER HOTELS

For solo travellers, hostels generally offer the cheapest bed, and can be good value for twin rooms. Finnish hostels are invariably clean, comfortable and very well equipped, though most are in somewhat institutional buildings.

Some Finnish hostels are run by the Finnish Youth Hostel Association (SRM), and many more are affiliated. It's worth being a member of HI (www.hihostels.com), as members save 10% per night at affiliated places. You'll save money with a sleeping sheet or your own linen, as hostels tend to charge €4 to €8 for this.

From June to August, many student residences are made over as summer hostels and hotels. These are often great value, as you usually get your own room, with kitchen (bring your own utensils, though) and bathroom either to yourself or shared between two.

HOTELS

Most hotels in Finland cater to business travellers and the majority belong to one of a few major chains, including Sokos (www.sokoshotels.fi), Scandic (www.scandichotels.com) and Cumulus (www.cumulus.fi). Finlandia Hotels (www.finlandiahotels.fi) is an association of independent hotels, while Omenahotelli (www.omenahotels.com) offers great-value staffless hotels booked online.

Hotels in Finland are designed with business travellers in mind and tend to charge them robustly. But at weekends and during the summer holidays, they bring their prices crashing down to try and lure people who aren't on company expense accounts. Prices in three- and four-star hotels tend to drop by 40% or so at these times; so take advantage.

All Finnish hotels have a large, plentiful and delicious buffet breakfast included in the rate and most include a sauna session.

SELF-CATERING ACCOMMODATION

One of Finland's joys is its plethora of cottages for rent, ranging from simple camping cabins to fully equipped bungalows with electric sauna and gleaming modern kitchen. These can be remarkably good value and are perfect for families. There are tens of thousands of cabins and cottages for rent in Finland, many in typical, romantic forest lakeside locations. By far the biggest national agent for cottage rentals is Lomarengas. Another good choice is Villi Pohjola

(☏020-344122; www.villipohjola.fi). This arm of the Finnish Forest & Park Service has cottages and cabins for rent all over Finland, but especially in Lapland and the north. Local tourist offices and town websites also have lists.

Activities

Boating, Canoeing, Kayaking Every waterside town has a place (most frequently the camping ground) where you can rent a canoe, kayak or rowing boat by the hour or day. Rental cottages often have rowing boats that you can use free of charge to investigate the local lake and its islands. Canoe and kayak rentals range in price from €20 to €40 per day, and €80 to €200 per week. The website www.canoeinfinland.com has details of several Lakeland routes.

Fishing Several permits are required of foreigners (between the ages of 18 and 64) but they are very easy to arrange. Buy them online via the website www.mmm.fi or talk to the local camping ground, tourist office or fishing shop. Ice fishing is popular and requires no licence.

Hiking Hiking is best from June to September, although in July mosquitoes and other biting insects can be a big problem in Lapland. Wilderness huts line the northern trails (both free shared ones and private bookable ones). According to the law, a principle of common access to nature applies, so you are generally allowed to hike in any forested or wilderness area. The website www.outdoors.fi provides comprehensive information on trekking routes and huts in national parks.

Saunas Many hotels, hostels and camping grounds have saunas that are free with a night's stay. Large towns have public saunas.

Skiing The ski season in Finland runs from late November to early May and slightly longer in the north, where it's possible to ski from October to May. You can rent all skiing or snowboarding equipment at major ski resorts for about €30/110 per day/week. A one-day lift pass costs around €35/170 per day/week. Cross-country skiing is popular: it's best during January and February in southern Finland, and from December to April in the north.

Snowmobiles (Skidoos) You'll need a valid drivers licence to use one.

Business Hours

Following are the usual business hours in Finland.

Alko (state alcohol store) 9am to 8pm Monday to Friday, to 6pm Saturday

Banks 9am to 4.15pm Monday to Friday

Clubs As late as 4am

Post offices 9am to 6pm Monday to Friday

Pubs 11am to 1am (often later on Friday and Saturday)

Restaurants 11am to 10pm, lunch 11am to 3pm

Shops 9am to 6pm Monday to Friday, to 3pm Saturday

Children

Finland is an excellent country to travel in with children, with many kid-friendly attractions and outdoor activities, whether you visit in winter or in summer.

All hotels will put extra beds in rooms, restaurants have family-friendly features and there are substantial transport discounts.

Food

Restaurants are classified as follows (the price of an average main course):

€€€   more than €25

€€   €15 to €25

€   less than €15

Gay & Lesbian Travellers

Finland's cities are open, tolerant places and Helsinki, though no Copenhagen or Stockholm, has a small but welcoming gay scene.

Internet Access

Public libraries Always have at least one free internet terminal.

Tourist offices Most have an internet terminal that you can use for free (usually 15 minutes).

Wireless internet access Very widespread; several cities have extensive networks, and nearly all hotels, as well as many restaurants, cafes and bars, offer free access to customers and guests.

Money

ATMs Using ATMs with a credit or debit card is by far the easiest way of getting cash in Finland. ATMs have a name, Otto, and can be found even in small villages.

Credit cards Widely accepted; Finns are dedicated users of plastic even to buy a beer or cup of coffee.

Currency Finland adopted the euro (€) in 2002. Euro notes come in five, 10, 20, 50, 100 and 500 denominations and coins in five, 10, 20, 50 cents and €1 and €2. Note that one- and two-cent coins are not used in Finland.

Money changers Travellers cheques and cash can be exchanged at banks; in the big cities, independent exchange facilities such as **Forex** (www.forex.fi) usually offer better rates.

Tipping Service is considered to be included in bills, so there's no need to tip at all unless you want to reward exceptional service.

Public Holidays

Finland grinds to a halt twice a year: around Christmas and New Year, and during the Midsummer weekend. National public holidays:

New Year's Day 1 January

Epiphany 6 January

Good Friday March/April

Easter Sunday & Monday March/April

May Day 1 May

Ascension Day May

Whitsunday Late May or early June

Midsummer's Eve & Day Weekend in June closest to 24 June

All Saints' Day First Saturday in November

Independence Day 6 December

Christmas 24 and 25 December

Boxing Day 26 December

Telephone

Public telephones Basically no longer exist on the street in Finland, so if you don't have a mobile you're reduced to making expensive calls from your hotel room or talking over the internet.

Mobile phones The cheapest and most practical solution is to purchase a Finnish SIM card and pop it in your own phone. Make sure your phone isn't blocked from doing this by your home network. If coming from outside Europe, check that it will work in Europe's GSM 900/1800 network. You can buy a prepaid SIM-card at any R-kioski shop. There are always several deals on offer, and you might be able to pick up a card for as little as €10, including some call credit. Top the credit up at the same outlets, online or at ATMs.

Phonecards At the R-kioski you can also buy cut-rate phonecards that substantially lower the cost of making international calls.

Phone codes The country code for Finland is ☑358. To dial abroad it's ☑00. The number for the international operator is ☑020208.

Time

Finland is on Eastern European Time (EET), an hour ahead of Sweden and Norway and two hours ahead of UTC/GMT (three hours from late March to late October).

Toilets

Public toilets are widespread in Finland but expensive – often €1 a time. On doors, 'M' is for men and 'N' is for women.

Tourist Information

The main website of the Finnish Tourist Board is www.visitfinland.com.

Visas

See the main Directory section (p489) for entry requirements. For more information contact the nearest Finnish embassy or consulate, or check the website www.formin.finland.fi.

Getting There & Away

Air

Finland is easily reached by air, with a growing number of direct flights to Helsinki from European, American and Asian destinations. It's also served by various budget carriers from several European countries, especially Ryanair and Air Baltic. Most other flights are with Finnair or Scandinavian Airlines (SAS). Most flights to Finland land at Helsinki-Vantaa airport, situated 19km north of the capital. Winter charters hit **Rovaniemi** (RVN; www.finavia.fi), Lapland's main airport, and other smaller airports in the region.

Other international airports include Tampere (TMP), Lappeenranta (LPP), Turku (TKU), Oulu (OUL) and Vaasa (VAA). The website www.finavia.fi includes contact details and other information for all Finnish airports.

Land

Border crossings There are several border crossings from northern Sweden and Norway to northern Finland, with no passport or customs formalities. There are eight main border crossings between Finland and Russia, including several in the southeast and two in Lapland. They are more serious frontiers; you must already have a Russian visa.

Vehicles Can easily be brought into Finland on the Baltic ferries provided you have registration papers and valid insurance (Green Card).

SWEDEN

The only bus route between Finland and Sweden is between the linked towns of Tornio, Finland, and Haparanda, Sweden, from where you can get onward transport into their respective countries. The other possible crossing points are the towns of Kaaresuvanto (Finland) and Karesuando (Sweden), separated by a bridge and both served sporadically by buses.

NORWAY

There are four daily bus routes linking Finnish Lapland with northern Norway, some running only in summer. These are operated by **Eskelisen Lapin Linjat** (www.eskelisen-lapinlinjat.com), the website of which has detailed maps and timetables, as does the Finnish bus website for **Matkahuolto** (☑0200 4000; www.matkahuolto.fi).

All routes originate or pass through Rovaniemi; the two northeastern routes continue via Inari to either Tanabru/Vadsø or Karasjok. The Karasjok bus continues in summer to Nordkapp (North Cape). On the western route, one Rovaniemi-Kilpisjärvi bus runs on daily to Tromsø in summer, and a Rovaniemi–Hetta bus continues to Kautokeino and Alta.

RUSSIA

Bus

There are daily express buses to Vyborg and St Petersburg from Helsinki and Lappeenranta (one originates in Turku). These services appear on the website of Matkahuolto (www.matkahuolto.fi). Helsinki–Vyborg one way is €32 (five hours) and to St Petersburg it's €40 (8½ to nine hours). Book at the bus station in Helsinki. There are also semiofficial buses and minibuses that can be cheaper options. Costs and travel times vary substantially. Think €20 to €25 in a bus, or around €30 in a minibus, which is faster, and also quicker at the border.

Goldline (www.goldline.fi) runs three weekly buses from Rovaniemi via Ivalo to Murmansk, and there are also cross-border services from Kuhmo.

Train

The only international train links with Finland are to and from Moscow and St Petersburg. There are two high-speed *Allegro* train services daily from Helsinki to the Finland Station in St Petersburg (2nd/1st class €86/137, 3½ hours). The *Tolstoi* sleeper train runs from Helsinki via St Petersburg (Ladozhki station) to Moscow (2nd/1st class €107/152, 13 hours). See www.vr.fi for details. All trains go via the Finnish towns of Lahti and Kouvola, and the Russian city of Vyborg. Tickets are sold at the international ticket counter at Helsinki station. You must have a valid Russian visa; passport checks are carried out onboard.

Sea

For ferry company and route information, see p491.

Getting Around

Finland is well served by public transport. A resource to find the best way between two points is the online route planner at www.journey.fi.

Air

Finnair/Flybe runs a fairly comprehensive domestic service, mainly out of Helsinki. Standard prices are expensive, but check the website for offers. Budget carriers fly some routes.

Major airlines flying domestically:

Finnair (www.finnair.com) Extensive domestic network in partnership with Flybe.

Flybe (☑06-009 4477; www.flybe.com) Extensive domestic network in association with Finnair.

SAS (☑06000-25831; www.flysas.com) Links some Finnish cities.

Bicycle

Bikes can be carried on most trains, buses and ferries.

Bike paths Finland is flat and as bicycle friendly as any country you'll find, with many kilometres of bike paths. The Åland islands are particularly good cycling country.

Bike hire Daily/weekly hire around €20/75 is possible in most cities. Camping grounds, hotels and hostels often have cheap bikes available for local exploration.

Boat

Lake and river passenger services were once important means of summer transport in Finland. These services are now largely kept on as cruises, and make a great, leisurely way to journey between towns.

Popular routes Tampere–Hämeenlinna, Savonlinna–Kuopio, Lahti–Jyväskylä.

Main coastal routes Turku–Naantali, Helsinki–Porvoo and the archipelago ferries to the Åland islands.

Bus

Discounts For student discounts (50% over long distances) you need to be studying full time in Finland. If booking three or more adult tickets together, a 25% discount applies: great for groups.

Fares Buses may be *pikavuoro* (express) or *vakiovuoro* (regular). Fares are based on distance travelled. The one-way fare for a 100km trip is €18.10/21.30 for normal/express.

Ticket offices Long-distance bus ticketing is handled by Matkahuolto (www.matkahuolto.fi); its excellent website has all timetables. Each town has a *linja-autoasema* (bus terminal), with local timetables displayed (*lähtevät* is departures, *saapuvat* arrivals). Ticket offices work normal business hours, but you can always buy the ticket from the driver.

Car & Motorcycle

Petrol is expensive in Finland. Many petrol stations are unstaffed, with machines that take cards or cash. Change is not given.

HIRE

Car rental is expensive, but between a group of three or four it can work out at a reasonable cost. From the major rental companies a small car costs from €60/280 per day/week with 300km free per day. As ever, the cheapest deals are online. While the daily rate is high, the weekly rate offers some respite. Best of all, though, are the weekend rates. These can cost little more than the rate for a single day, and you can pick up the car early afternoon on Friday and return it late Sunday or early Monday.

Rental companies:

Avis (www.avis.com)

Budget (www.budget.com)

Europcar (☑0200 12154; www.europcar.com)

Hertz (☑0200 11 22 33; www.hertz.com)

Sixt (www.sixt.com) One of the cheapest. HI discount.

ROAD CONDITIONS & HAZARDS

Road network Finland's road network is excellent, although there are only a few motorways. When approaching a town or city, look for signs saying *keskusta* (town centre). There are no road tolls but lots of speed cameras.

Snow and ice Possible from September to April, and as late as June in Lapland, making driving a serious undertaking. Snow chains are illegal: instead, people use either snow tyres, which have metal studs, or special all-weather tyres. The website www.liikennevirasto.fi/alk/kelikamerat has road webcams around Finland, good for checking conditions on your prospective route.

Wildlife Beware of elk and reindeer, which don't respect vehicles and can dash onto the road unexpectedly. This sounds comical, but elk especially constitute a deadly danger. Notify the police if there is an accident involving these animals.

Reindeer are very common in Lapland: slow right down if you see one, as there will be more nearby.

ROAD RULES

Alcohol The blood alcohol limit is 0.05%.

Driving Finns drive on the right.

Headlights Use at all times.

Right of way An important feature of Finland is that there are fewer give-way signs than in many countries. Traffic entering an intersection from the right has right of way. While this doesn't apply to highways or main roads, you'll find that in towns cars will nip out from the right without looking: you must give way, so be careful at every intersection in towns.

Seatbelts Compulsory for all.

Speed limit Set at 50km/h in built-up areas, from 80km/h to 100km/h on highways, and 120km/h on motorways.

Train

Finnish trains are run by the state-owned **Valtion Rautatiet** (VR; ☑0600 41900; www.vr.fi) and are an excellent service: they are fast, efficient and cheaper than the bus.

VR's website has comprehensive timetable information. Buy tickets online (to print out at the station), or at VR offices and automated machines in stations. There are sometimes advance purchase discounts on the VR website.

CLASSES

The main classes of trains are the high-speed Pendolino (the fastest and most expensive class), fast Intercity (IC), Express and Regional trains. The first three have both 1st- and 2nd-class sections, while regional trains ('H' on the timetable) are the cheapest and slowest services, and have only 2nd-class carriages.

On longer routes there are two types of sleeping carriage currently in operation. The traditional blue ones offer berths in one-, two-, or three-bed cabins; the newer sleeping cars offer single and double compartments in a double-decker carriage. There are cabins equipped for wheelchair use, and ones with bathroom. Berths cost from €19 to €86 in high season. Sleeper trains transport cars, handy if you've brought your own vehicle.

COSTS

Second class A one-way ticket for a 100km express-train journey costs approximately €20.

First class Cost 50% more than a 2nd-class ticket.

Return fare About 10% less than two one-way tickets.

Discounts Children under 17 pay half-price, and children aged under six travel free (but without a seat). A child travels free with every adult on long-distance trips, and there are also discounts for seniors, local students and any group of three or more adults travelling together.

TRAIN PASSES

International rail passes accepted in Finland include the Eurail Scandinavia Pass, Eurail Global Pass and InterRail Global Pass. For more information on these passes, see p496.

Finland Eurail Pass (www.eurail.com) Three/five/10 days' 2nd-class travel in a one-month period within Finland for €132/174/236.

InterRail Finland Pass (www.interrail. eu) Offers travel only in Finland for three/four/six/eight days in a one-month period, costing €119/150/201/243 in 2nd class. It's about 35% cheaper if you're under 26.

Finnrail Pass Available to travellers residing outside Finland and offers a similar deal to the Finland Eurail pass at a similar price. See the VR website for details.

FINLAND SURVIVAL GUIDE

Tallinn

Best Places to Eat

» nAnO (p216)

» Ö (p217)

» Must Puudel (p216)

» Olde Hansa (p216)

» Sfäär (p217)

Best Places to Stay

» Villa Hortensia (p216)

» Tallinn Backpackers (p216)

» Old House Apartments (p216)

» Old House Hostel & Guesthouse (p216)

» Nordic Hotel Forum (p216)

Why Go?

Estonia doesn't have to struggle to find a point of difference; it's completely unique. It shares a similar geography and history with Baltic neighbours Latvia and Lithuania, but it's culturally very different. Estonia's closest ethnic and linguistic buddy is Finland, and although they may love to get naked together in the sauna, fifty years of Soviet rule separated the two countries.

In recent decades, and with a newfound confidence, Estonia has crept from under the Soviet blanket and leapt into the arms of Europe. The love affair is mutual: Europe has fallen for the allure of Estonia's capital, Tallinn and its two-tiered, Unesco-protected Old Town, a 14th- and 15th-century jumble of turrets, spires and winding streets.

A Tallinn visit from Helsinki is just too easy to overlook – ferries ply the 85km separating the two capitals so frequently that Finns almost think of Tallinn as a distant suburb.

When to Go
Tallinn

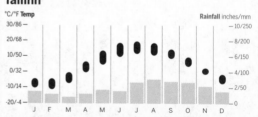

Apr–May See the country shake off winter's gloom, with forests thickening and gardens blooming.

Jun–Aug White nights, beach parties and loads of summer festivals.

Dec Christmas markets, mulled wine and long cosy nights.

⊙ Sights

The medieval Old Town, just south of Tallinn Bay, comprises the lower town, still surrounded by much of its 2.5km defensive wall, and Toompea (the upper town). Immediately east of Old Town is the modern city centre.

OLD TOWN

LOWER TOWN

Raekoja Plats SQUARE
(Town Hall Sq) Photogenic Raekoja plats has been the heart of Tallinn life since markets began here in the 11th century. It's ringed by historic, pastel-coloured buildings and al fresco restaurant tables.

Town Hall HISTORIC BUILDING
(www.tallinn.ee/raekoda; Raekoja plats; adult/student €4/2; ☺10am-4pm Mon-Sat Jul-Aug, by appointment Sep-Jun) Raekoja plats is dominated by the only surviving Gothic town hall in northern Europe, built between 1371 and 1404. You can climb the **town hall tower** (Raekoja plats; adult/student €3/1; ☺11am-6pm May–mid-Sep) for red-rooftop views.

Town Council Pharmacy HISTORIC BUILDING
(Raeapteek; Raekoja plats 11; ☺10am-6pm Tue-Sat) This is another ancient Tallinn institution; there's been a pharmacy or apothecary's shop here since at least 1422, though the present facade is from the 17th century.

Holy Spirit Church CHURCH
(Pühavaimu 2; adult/concession €1/0.50; ☺Mon-Sat) Duck through the arch beside the Town Council Pharmacy into the narrow **Saiakang** (White Bread Passage), which leads to this striking 14th-century church.

Estonian History Museum MUSEUM
(www.ajaloomuuseum.ee; Pikk 17; adult/student €5/3; ☺10am-6pm, closed Wed Sep-Apr) This newly renovated museum has filled the striking 1410 Great Guild Hall with a series of ruminations on the Estonian psyche, presented through interactive and unusual displays.

Pikk STREET
Pikk (Long Street) runs north to the **Great Coast Gate** – the medieval exit to Tallinn's port. Pikk is lined with the 15th-century houses of merchants and gentry, as well as the buildings of several old Tallinn guilds.

St Olaf's Church CHURCH
(entry at Lai 50) At the northern end of Pikk stands this gargantuan church. Anyone

NEED TO KNOW

» **Population** 416,500
» **Country code** ☑372, no area codes
» **Language** Estonian
» **Currency** euro (€)

unafraid of a few stairs (258, to be precise) should head up to the **observation tower** (adult/student €2/1; ☺10am-6pm Apr-Oct, to 8pm Jul & Aug), halfway up the church's 124m structure.

Lower Town Wall HISTORIC SITE
Suur-Kloostri leads to a long and photoworthy stretch of the Lower Town Wall, which has nine towers along Laboratooriumi. Here, as well as at various points around the town wall, you can enter the towers.

Vene STREET
Several 15th-century warehouses and merchant residences surround Raekoja plats at its southeast corner, as you head towards Vana turg and Vene (Vene means 'Russian' in Estonian, named for the Russian merchants who traded here). Vene is home to some gorgeous passageways and courtyards – **Katariina käik** (Vene 12) is lined with artisans' studios, and **Masters' Courtyard** (Vene 6) is a cobblestoned delight partially dating from the 13th century.

Tallinn City Museum MUSEUM
(www.linnamuuseum.ee; Vene 17; adult/student €3.20/1.90; ☺10am-5pm Wed-Mon) A medieval merchant's home houses the City Museum, tracing Tallinn's development from its early beginnings.

TOOMPEA

A regal approach to Toompea hill is through the red-roofed 1380 **Pikk jalg Gate Tower** at the western end of Pikk in Lower Town, and then heading uphill along Pikk jalg (Long Leg). Alternatively, a winding stairway connects Lühike jalg (Short Leg), off Rataskaevu, to Toompea.

Alexander Nevsky Cathedral CHURCH
(Lossi plats) The 19th-century icon-filled Russian Orthodox cathedral greets you at the top of Toompea in all its onion-domed splendour. It was built as a part of Alexander III's policy of Russification, and is sited strategically across from Toompea Castle, Estonia's traditional seat of power.

Tallinn

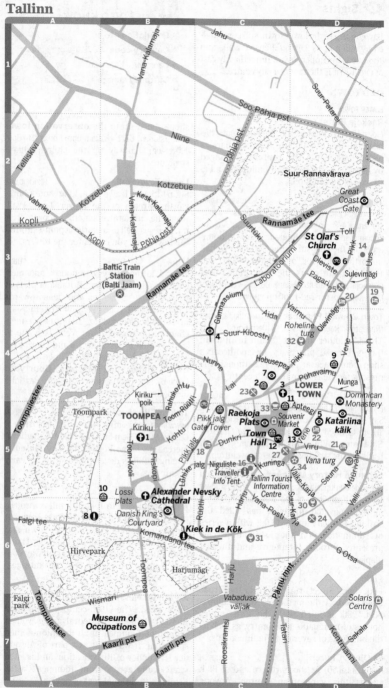

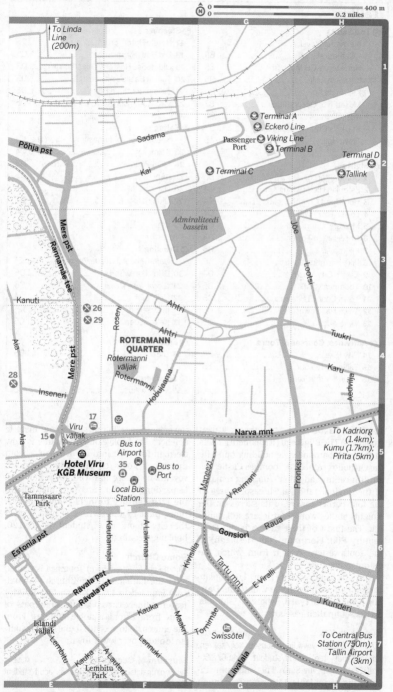

TALLINN

0   400 m
0   0.2 miles

To Linda Line (200m)

Põhja pst

Sadama

Kai

Terminal A
Eckerö Line
Passenger Port — Viking Line
Terminal B
Terminal D
Terminal C
Tallink

Admiraliteedi bassein

Mere pst

Rannamäe tee

Kanuti

Roseni
Ahtri
Ahtri

ROTERMANN QUARTER

Rotermanni väljak
Rotermanni

Jõe
Lootsi
Tuukri
Karu
Aedvilja

26
29

28

Inseneri

Aia

Mere pst

Hobujaama

17
Viru väljak
15

Narva mnt

To Kadriorg (1.4km); Kumu (1.7km); Pirita (5km)

Hotel Viru
KGB Museum

Bus to Airport
35
Bus to Port
Local Bus Station

Tammsaare Park

Aia

Maleezi
V Reimani
Pronksi
Raua

Estonia pst

Kaubamaja

Gonsiori

Kivisilla
Tartu mnt
E Viralli

Rävala pst
Rävala pst

Islandi väljak

Lembitu

Kauka

Kauka

A Laikmaa

Maakri

Tõnismäe

Lenmuki

Swissôtel

J Kunderi

To Central Bus Station (750m); Tallin Airport (3km)

Lembitu Park

A Lauteri

Liivalaia

Tallinn

Toompea Castle　　　　　HISTORIC BUILDING
(Lossi plats) The Riigikogu (Parliament) meets in the pink baroque-style building opposite the Orthodox cathedral. Toompea Castle was an 18th-century addition – nothing remains of the original 1219 Danish castle; three of the four corner towers of its successor, the Knights of the Sword's Castle, are still standing. The finest of these towers is the 14th-century **Pikk Hermann** (Tall Hermann) at the southwestern corner, from which the Estonian flag flies.

A path leads down from Lossi plats through an opening in the wall to the **Danish King's Courtyard**, where in summer artists set up their easels.

Kiek in de Kök　　　　　TOWER, MUSEUM
(☎644 6686; www.linnamuuseum.ee/kok/en; Komandandi tee; adult/student €4.50/2.60; ⊙10.30am-6pm Tue-Sun) The museum inside this formidable 15th-century cannon tower examines Tallinn's elaborate historic defences. Its kooky-sounding name is Low German for 'Peep into the Kitchen' – from the upper floors of the tower, medieval voyeurs could see into Old Town kitchens. Departing from here are tours that take in the **17th-century tunnels** connecting bastions, built by the Swedes to help protect the city (tours adult/student €5.80/3.20, bookings required).

Dome Church　　　　　CHURCH
(Toom-Kooli 6; ⊙9am-5pm) Toompea is named after the Lutheran Dome Church (Toomkirik), founded in 1233. The austere interior features finely carved tombs and coats of arms from Estonia's noble families. From the church, follow Kohtu to the city's favourite **lookout** over lower town.

Museum of Occupations　　　　　MUSEUM
(www.okupatsioon.ee; Toompea 8; adult/student €4/2; ⊙10am-6pm Tue-Sun) This absorbing

museum, just downhill from Toompea, has displays covering Estonia's 20th-century occupations. Photos and artefacts illustrate five decades of oppressive rule, under the Nazis, briefly, and the Soviets.

CITY CENTRE

Hotel Viru KGB Museum MUSEUM

(✆680 9300; www.sokoshotels.fi; Viru väljak 4; tour €8; ⊗closed Mon Nov-Mar) When Hotel Viru was built in 1972 it was not only Estonia's first skyscraper, it was the only place for tourists to stay in Tallinn – and we mean that literally. Having all the foreigners in one place made it easier to keep tabs on them and the locals they had contact with, which is exactly what the KGB did from its 23rd-floor spy base. The hotel offers insightful and entertaining guided tours; call ahead for times and to book a place.

KADRIORG

To reach the lovely, wooded **Kadriorg Park**, 2km east of Old Town along Narva mnt, take tram 1 or 3 to the Kadriorg stop. There are a number of museums in the park, plus a playground and a fine cafe.

Kadriorg Palace PALACE, MUSEUM

(A Weizenbergi 37) Kadriorg Park and its centrepiece, Kadriorg Palace (1718–36), were designed for Peter the Great's wife Catherine I (Kadriorg means 'Catherine's Valley' in Estonian). Kadriorg Palace is now home to the **Kadriorg Art Museum** (www.ekm.ee; A Weizenbergi 37; adult/student €4.50/2.50; ⊗10am-5pm Tue-Sun May-Sep, 10am-5pm Wed-Sun Oct-Apr). The 17th- and 18th-century foreign art is mainly unabashedly romantic, and the palace and its gardens are unashamedly splendid.

Kumu MUSEUM

(www.ekm.ee; Weizenbergi 34; adult/student €5.50/3.20; ⊗11am-6pm Tue-Sun May-Sep, 11am-6pm Wed-Sun Oct-Apr) This seven-storey building is a spectacular structure of limestone, glass and copper, nicely integrated into the landscape. Kumu (the name is short for *kunstimuuseum* or art museum) contains the largest repository of Estonian art.

☞ Tours

Traveller Info Tent WALKING, CYCLING

(✆5837 4800; www.traveller.ee; Niguliste) This tour company runs entertaining, good-value walking and cycling tours – including a free, two-hour walking tour of Tallinn,

departing at noon daily. Three-hour bike tours (€13) take in the town's well-known eastern attractions (Kadriorg, Pirita beach etc), or they can take you to more offbeat areas to the west. From mid-May to mid-September, the tours run from the tent itself; the rest of the year they need to be booked in advance.

City Bike CYCLING, WALKING

(✆511 1819; www.citybike.ee; Uus 33) Has a great range of Tallinn tours, by bike or on foot. Two-hour cycling tours (€16) run year-round.

Tallinn City Tour BUS

(✆627 9080; www.citytour.ee; 24hr pass €16) Runs red double-decker buses that give you hop-on, hop-off access to the city's top sights. Buses leave from Mere pst, just outside Old Town.

✨ Festivals & Events

For a complete list of Tallinn's festivals throughout the year, visit www.culture.ee and the 'Events' pages of Tallinn Tourism (www.tourism.tallinn.ee).

The following are some of the big-ticket events.

Jazzkaar MUSIC

(www.jazzkaar.ee) Jazz greats from around the world converge on Tallinn in late April.

Old Town Days ARTS, CULTURE

(www.vanalinnapaevad.ee) Week-long festival in late May/early June featuring dancing, concerts and plenty of medieval merry-making.

☐ Sleeping

The website **Tallinn** (www.tourism.tallinn.ee) has a full list of options. Whatever your preference, book in advance in summer.

TALLINN IN ONE DAY

Get your bearings by climbing the **town hall tower** on Raekoja plats, then explore the cobbled **Old Town** streets below – museums, churches, courtyards, whatever takes your fancy. In the afternoon, catch a tram to **Kadriorg** for a first-rate greenery and art fix, and/or consider a **cycling tour**. Finish with a locally flavoured feast at **Olde Hansa** or **Õ**.

The following price ranges are for a double room in high season.

€€€   more than €140

€€   €50 to €140

€   less than €50

Villa Hortensia   APARTMENTS €€

(☑504 6113; www.hoov.ee/villa-hortensial; Vene 6, Masters' Courtyard; studio s/d €40/55, apt s/d from €60/80) Villa Hortensia is a small collection of apartments in the Masters' Courtyard. There are six apartments (the website has pics) – four compact, split-level studios, with private bathroom, kitchenette and access to a shared communal lounge. The two larger apartments are the real treats. Great value in a winning location – book ahead.

Tallinn Backpackers   HOSTEL €

(☑644 0298; www.tallinnbackpackers.com; Olevimägi 11; dm without bathroom €12-15; @) In an ideal Old Town location, this 26-bed place has a global feel and a roll-call of traveller-happy features: cheap dinners, free wi-fi, lockers, free sauna, and day trips to nearby attractions. Staff organise pub crawls and city tours. Private rooms are available at the offshoot **Tallinn Boutique Hostel** (☑644 6050; www.tallinnboutiquehostel.com; Viru 5, 3rd fl; s/d without bathroom €25/40; @), also known as Viru Backpackers.

Old House Apartments   APARTMENTS €€

(☑641 1464; www.oldhouse.ee; Rataskaevu 16; per night €89-229; P) 'Old House' is an understatement for this 14th-century merchant's house. It's been split into eight beautifully furnished apartments, and there are a further 13 properties scattered around the Old Town.

Old House Hostel & Guesthouse   GUESTHOUSE €

(☑641 1281; www.oldhouse.ee; Uus 22 & Uus 26; dm/s/d without bathroom €15/30/44; P@) Although one is called a hostel, these twin establishments feel much more like cosy guesthouses, decorated with antiques, plants, lamps and bedspreads, with minimal bunks. Dorms and private rooms are available at both (all bathrooms are shared); guest kitchen, free wi-fi and parking are quality extras.

Nordic Hotel Forum   HOTEL €€

(☑622 2900; www.nordichotels.eu; Viru väljak 3; r from €95; P@☀) The Forum shows surprising style and personality for a large, business-style hotel – witness the artwork on the hotel's facade and the trees on the roof. It stands out among its competitors for its facilities and prime location.

Eating

Tallinn is a wonderful city for food lovers. Global cuisines are well represented and prices are low compared with most other European capitals. Places listed under Drinking also offer food.

There's a small, 24-hour grocery store, **Kolmjalg** (Pikk 11), in Old Town. Supermarkets include **Rimi** (Aia 7; ⊗8am-10pm), on the outskirts of Old Town; and **Kaubamaja Toidumaailm** (Viru väljak 4, Viru Keskus; ⊗9am-9pm), in the basement of Viru Keskus shopping centre.

These price ranges indicate the average cost of a main course.

€€€   more than €20

€€   10 to €20

€   below €10

OLD TOWN

nAnO   CAFE €

(☑5552 2522; www.nanohouse.ee; Sulevimägi 5; meals around €6; ⊗12.30-4pm Tue-Fri) There's no real sign to indicate you've found this place, nor firm hours, nor a written menu. Instead, this is a whimsical world concocted by Beatrice, an Estonian model, and her DJ partner Priit, who welcome guests into part of their colourful home and courtyard garden. Diners are offered fresh, affordable, home-style meals along the lines of herb-filled borscht, Russian-style pastries and pasta with in-season chanterelles or salmon. Wander past, or call ahead to check hours.

Must Puudel   CAFE €

(Müürivahe 20; mains under €5) The Black Poodle is a near-perfect loungey cafe-bar: mismatched 1970s furniture, eclectic soundtrack, courtyard seating, excellent coffee, cooked breakfasts, tasty light meals and long opening hours.

Olde Hansa   SCANDINAVIAN €€

(www.oldehansa.ee; Vana turg 1; mains €13-26) Candlelit Olde Hansa is the place to indulge in a gluttonous medieval feast. And if the music, staff clad in ye-olde garb, and aromas of red wine and roast meats sound a bit much, take heart – the chefs have done their research in producing historically authentic fare. It may be pitched heavily at tourists, but even locals rate this place.

OUTSIDE OLD TOWN

Ö
ESTONIAN €€€

(☑661 6150; www.restoran-o.ee; Mere pst 6e; mains €14-28) With angelic chandelier sculptures and charcoal-and-white overtones, the dining room at award-winning Ö is an understated work of art – as are the meals coming out of the kitchen, showcasing winning ways with seasonal local produce. Bookings advised.

Sfäär
INTERNATIONAL €€

(www.sfaar.ee; Mere pst 6e; mains €8-18) Chic Sfäär delivers an inventive menu highlighting the best Estonian produce in a warehouse-style setting that's like something out of a Nordic design catalogue.

Drinking & Entertainment

Hell Hunt
PUB

(www.hellhunt.ee; Pikk 39) See if you can score a few of the comfy armchairs out the back of this trouper of the pub circuit. It boasts an amiable air and reasonable prices for local-brewed beer and cider, plus decent pub grub. Don't let the menacing-sounding name put you off – it means 'Gentle Wolf'.

Drink Bar & Grill
PUB

(Väike-Karja 8) You know a bar means business when it calls itself Drink. This place takes its beer (and cider) seriously and offers plenty of beer-friendly accompaniments: traditional pub grub, happy hours, big-screen sports, and comedy and quiz nights.

Gloria Wine Cellar
WINE BAR

(www.gloria.ee; Müürivahe 2; ☺noon-11pm Mon-Sat) This romantic, mazelike cellar has a number of nooks and crannies where you can secrete yourself with a date and/or a good bottle of shiraz.

Clazz
LIVE MUSIC

(www.clazz.ee; Vana turg 2) Behind the cheesy name (a contraction of 'classy jazz') is a popular restaurant–bar, featuring live music every night (cover charge varies), and food served into the wee hours.

Kehrwieder
CAFE

(www.kohvik.ee; Saiakang 1; ☺8am-midnight) Sure, Kehrwieder has seating-with-a-view on Raekoja plats (and in a delightful garden oasis off Saiakang), but inside the city's cosiest cafe is where ambience is found in spades.

III Draakon
CAFE

(Raekoja plats; ☺8am-midnight) There's bucket-loads of atmosphere at this Lilliputian cafe below the town hall, and super-cheap elk soup or oven-hot pies (€1!).

Cafe-Chocolaterie de Pierre
CAFE

(www.pierre.ee; Vene 6, Masters' Courtyard; ☺10am-11pm) Nestled inside the picturesque Masters' Courtyard, this snug, antique-filled cafe makes you feel like you're hiding away at your granny's place. It's renowned for its handmade chocolates.

🛍 Shopping

Dozens of shops sell Estonian-made handicrafts (käsitöö) including: knitwear, linen, jewellery and objects carved from limestone or made from juniper wood. The quintessential Estonian souvenir is a bottle of Vana Tallinn (a syrupy, sweet liqueur of indeterminate origin). In summer a **souvenir market** is set up weekly (Wednesday) on Raekoja plats.

Viru Keskus
SHOPPING MALL

(www.virukeskus.com; Viru väljak) Tallinn's showpiece shopping mall, aka Viru Centre, lies just outside Old Town. It's home to mainstream fashion boutiques and a great bookstore. In summer there's a rooftop cinema. The bus terminal for local buses is in the basement.

ℹ Information

Discount Cards

Tallinn Card (www.tallinncard.ee; 1-/2-/3-day card €24/32/40) Offers free rides on public transport, admission to museums, free excursions and discounts at restaurants (cheaper children's cards are available). Buy online from the tourist information centre or from many hotels.

Internet Access

Tallinn is flooded with free wi-fi, but if you're not packing a laptop or smartphone you'll find internet cafes are scarce in the city. Most hostels and hotels offer a computer for guest use.

Tourist Information

Like a Local (www.likealocalguide.com/tallinn) Produces an invaluable map of Tallinn, highlighting recommended spots. The website has great info too (download the app).

Tallinn In Your Pocket (www.inyourpocket.com) Full of useful listings. The booklets are on sale at bookshops, or can be downloaded free from Tallinn In Your Pocket's website.

Tallinn Tourist Information Centre (www.tourism.tallinn.ee; cnr Kullassepa & Niguliste;

⊘9am-8pm Mon-Fri, to 6pm Sat & Sun mid-Jun–Aug, shorter hrs daily Sep–mid-Jun) Maps and brochures for the capital and further afield. Note that it doesn't offer an accommodation-booking service.

Traveller Info Tent (www.traveller.ee; Niguliste; ⊘9am-9pm mid-May–mid-Sep) Great source of information, set up by local students in a tent opposite the official tourist info centre. Dispenses local tips and maps, keeps a 'what's on' board, and operates excellent walking and cycling tours.

 Getting There & Away

Air

Tallinn airport (www.tallinn-airport.ee) is just 4km southeast of the city centre on Tartu mnt. Frequent buses connect it with the city centre.

Boat

See p491 for full details of Scandinavian ferry information.

FINLAND

A fleet of ferries services the 85km separating Helsinki and Tallinn. There are dozens of crossings daily (ships two to 3½ hours; hydrofoils 1½ hours). Note that in high winds or bad weather, hydrofoils are often cancelled; they operate only when the sea is free from ice, while larger ferries sail year-round.

All companies provide concessions, allow bikes (for a fee) and charge higher prices for peak services and weekend travel. Expect to pay around the price of an adult ticket extra to take a car. There's lots of competition, so check the following companies for special offers and packages.

Eckerö Line (www.eckeroline.ee; Terminal A; adult one way from €19; ⊘year-round) Large new vessel sails once or twice daily in both directions (2½ hours).

Linda Line (www.lindaliini.ee; Linnahall Terminal; from €31) Small, passenger-only hydrofoils run up to seven times daily from late March to late December (1½ hours).

Tallink (www.tallinksilja.com/en; Terminal D; adult from €19-54; ⊘year-round) Up to seven services daily in each direction. The huge *Baltic Princess* takes 3½ hours; newer high-speed ferries take two hours.

Viking Line (www.vikingline.com; Terminal A; adult €19-47; ⊘year-round) Operates a giant car ferry, with two departures daily (2½ hours).

SWEDEN

Tallink (www.tallinksilja.com/en) sails every night between Tallinn's Terminal D and Stockholm, via the Aaland islands (passage from €39, 16 hours). Book ahead.

Bus

Central Bus Station (Autobussijaam; ☑12550; Lastekodu 46) Located about 2km southeast of Old Town. Tram 2 or 4 will take you there, as will bus 17, 23 or 23A.

TPilet (www.tpilet.ee) Useful website with times, prices and durations for all national bus services.

ⓘ Getting Around

To/From the Ferry Terminals

» Tallinn's sea-passenger terminal is at the end of Sadama, a short, 1km walk northeast of Old Town.

» Bus 2 runs every 20 to 30 minutes between the bus stop by Terminal A and the street A Laikmaa in the city centre; if you're heading to the terminal, the bus stop is out the front of the Tallink Hotel.

» Also from the heart of town (around the Viru Keskus transport hub), trams 1 and 2, and bus 3 go to the Linnahall stop, by the Statoil Petrol Station, five minutes' walk from terminals A, B and C, and the Linda Line terminal.

» Terminal D is at the end of Lootsi, better accessed from Ahtri; bus 2 services the terminal (the same bus route that services terminal A and the airport).

» A taxi between the city centre and any of the terminals will cost about €5.

Public Transport

» Excellent network of buses, trams and trolleybuses running from 6am to 11pm.

» Major local bus station is under Viru Keskus shopping centre; local buses may also terminate their route on the surrounding streets, just east of Old Town.

» Local public transport timetables are online at Tallinn (www.tallinn.ee).

» Public transport is free for all registered Tallinn residents. Visitors still need to pay, using the new e-ticketing system, which covers all three modes of local transport. Buy a plastic smartcard to top up with credit, then validate the card at the start of each journey using the orange card-readers. Fares using the e-ticketing system cost €1.10/3/5 for an hour/day/three days. Alternatively, you will still be able to buy a paper ticket *(piletid)* from the driver when you board (€1.60 for a single journey).

» Note that the Tallinn Card gives free public transport.

Taxi

Taxis are plentiful in Tallinn, but if you hail a taxi on the street you may be overcharged. Order a taxi by phone: try **Krooni Takso** (☑638 1212, 1212) and **Reval Takso** (☑601 4600).

Iceland

Best Places to Eat

» Dill (p234)

» Bergsson Mathús (p234)

» Narfeyrarstofa (p253)

» Pallurinn (p253)

» Vogafjós (p256)

Best Places to Stay

» Icelandair Hotel Reykjavík Marina (p231)

» Hótel Egilsen (p242)

» Hótel Aldan (p259)

» Skjaldarvík (p248)

» Kaldbaks-Kot (p252)

Why Go?

Iceland is literally a country in the making, a vast volcanic laboratory where mighty forces shape the earth: geysers gush, mudpots gloop, sulphurous clouds puff from fissures and glaciers grind great pathways through the mountains. Experience the full weirdness of Icelandic nature by bathing in turquoise pools, kayaking under the midnight sun or crunching across a dazzling-white ice cap.

Iceland's creatures are larger than life too: minke, humpback and even blue whales are common visitors to the deeper fjords. Record-breaking numbers of birds nest in the sea cliffs: cutest are the puffins who flutter here in their millions.

Despite the devastating recession, signs of recovery have arrived surprisingly fast. Clean, green Reykjavík must contain the world's highest concentration of dreamers, authors, poets and musicians. Little wonder, as the magnificent scenery of this Atlantic island forged in fire and ice make it one of the world's most awe-inspiring sights.

When to Go
Reykjavík

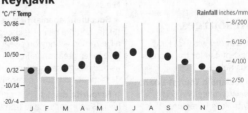

May–Jun Prime birdwatching season happily coincides with the two driest months of the year.

Aug Reykjavik runs at full throttle, culminating in the Culture Night arts festival and firework display.

Nov–Apr The best months for viewing the aurora borealis (Northern Lights).

ICELAND

Exchange Rates

Australia	A$1	Ikr128.98
Canada	C$1	Ikr120.74
Europe	€1	Ikr158.68
Japan	¥100	Ikr130.66
New Zealand	NZ$1	Ikr102.88
UK	UK£1	Ikr187.13
USA	US$1	Ikr123.28

For current exchange rates, see www.xe.com.

Set Your Budget

» **Budget hotel room**
Ikr12,000-16,000

» **Two-course evening meal** Ikr5000

» **Museum entrance**
free-Ikr1500

» **Beer (500mL)** Ikr900

» **Reykjavík bus ticket**
Ikr350

Resources

» **BSI** (www.bsi.is) First port-of-call for the island's bus network

» **Icelandic Tourist Board** (www.visiticeland.com) With links to regional websites

» **Reykjavík Tourist Office** (www.visitreykjavik.is)

Connections

Little Iceland, way out on the edge of nothing, is nevertheless connected by regular flights from Keflavík airport to Scandinavian and other European capitals – see p238 for details.

For those who like more romance, the ferry from Denmark (p494) via the Faroes along the jaw-dropping fjord to Seyðisfjörður is the most stylish way to arrive.

ITINERARIES

Three Days

Arrive in Reykjavík on Friday to catch the decadent *djammið* (pub crawl). Sober up in Laugardalslaug geothermal pool, admire the views from Hallgrímskirkja, then absorb some Viking history at the National Museum. On Sunday, visit Gullfoss, Geysir and Þingvellir on a Golden Circle tour. Stop to soak in the Blue Lagoon on the way home.

One Week

Head for the countryside: chill out on serene Snæfellsnes in the west; view the volcanic Vestmannaeyjar in the south with their immense puffin colonies; or drive east to Skaftafell for wonderful hiking and glacier walking.

Essential Food & Drink

» **Traditional Icelandic dishes** These reflect a nightmarish historical need to eat every last scrap: brave souls might try *svið* (singed sheep's head), *súrsaðir hrútspungar* (pickled ram's testicles) and *hákarl* (putrefied shark meat), bought from the butcher, fishmonger or old-school workers' canteens. More palatable offerings include *harðfiskur* (dried strips of haddock with butter), *plokkfiskur* (a hearty dish of leftover fish stew, served au gratin) and delicious yoghurt-like *skyr*.

» **Succulent specialities** Icelandic lamb is some of the tastiest on the planet – sheep roam free in the mountains all summer, grazing on sweet grass and wild thyme. Iceland also takes great pride in its fishing industry, and superfresh fish dishes grace most menus. Pink-footed goose and reindeer meat from the eastern highlands are high-end treats.

» **Favourite drinks** The traditional alcoholic brew *brennivín* is schnapps made from potatoes and caraway seeds. It's fondly known as *svarti dauði* (black death). Coffee is a national institution.

REYKJAVÍK

POP 202,300

The world's most northerly capital combines colourful buildings, quirky people, eye-popping design, a wild nightlife and a capricious soul to devastating effect. Most visitors fall helplessly in love, returning home already saving to come back.

In many ways Reykjavík is strikingly cosmopolitan for its size. It is, after all, merely a town by international standards. But on the flip side of the coin, the island's capital is also very much a global city in disguise –

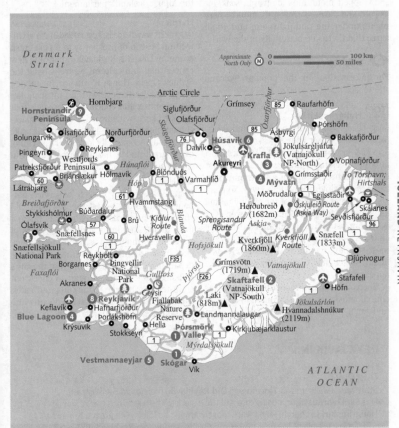

Iceland Highlights

① Hike from **Þórsmörk to Skógar** (p263) and see the lava formed in the 2010 Eyjafjallajökull eruptions

② Don crampons for an easy but exhilarating glacier walk at glorious **Skaftafell** (p261)

③ Tour the smouldering volcanic wastelands of **Krafla** (p254)

④ Swim through steam clouds at Iceland's world-famous **Blue Lagoon** (p278) spa or **Mývatn Nature Baths** (p255)

⑤ Set sail for **Vestmannaeyjar's** (p264) dazzling stone towers, millions of comical puffins, and a small town nestled between the lava flows

⑥ Admire the giants of the ocean on a **whale-watching** (p252) trip in Húsavík

⑦ **Kayak** (p278) the coastline, with just the paddle's splash and majestic fjord-scapes for company

⑧ Cavort with happy drunks on the **Reykjavík djammið** (p235)

⑨ Rove around saw-toothed cliffs and lonely coves during a life-changing hike across **Hornstrandir** (p245)

peek under the shiny holiday veneer to find a place that is utterly quaint and embraces its know-your-neighbours smallness.

It's that striking contrast that gives the city its charm, much like tectonic plates clashing against one another, creating an earthquake of energy. Add a backdrop of snowtopped mountains, churning seas, air as cold and clean as frozen diamonds, fiery nights under the midnight sun, and you'll agree that there's no better city in the world.

◉ Sights

For information on the popular 'volcano shows', see p237.

TOP CHOICE Hallgrímskirkja   CHURCH

(Map p228; ☎510 1000; www.hallgrimskirkja.is; Skólavörðuholt; tower admission Ikr600; ⊘9am-9pm Jul & Aug, to 5pm Sep-Jun) Reykjavík's most attention-seeking building, this immense concrete church is star of a thousand post-cards and visible from 20km away. You can get an unmissable view of the city by taking an elevator trip up the 75m-high tower.

In contrast to the high drama outside, the church's interior is puritanically plain. The most startling feature is the vast 5275-pipe organ, which has a strangely weapon-like appearance.

There are many opportunities to hear church music as well – from mid-June to mid-August there are concerts held at noon on Wednesdays, Thursdays and Saturdays, and on Sundays at 5pm.

Gazing proudly into the distance out front is a **statue of the Viking Leifur Eiríksson** (Map p228), the first European to stumble across America. It was a present from the USA on the 1000th anniversary of the Alþing, Iceland's parliament.

Harpa   CULTURAL BUILDING

(Map p228; www.harpa.is; Austurbakki 2) An architectural beacon of prosperity in a post-crash economy, Harpa is Reykjavík's sparkling new concert hall and cultural centre. Giving the Sydney Opera House a run for its money, Harpa dazzles the eye with an intricate lattice of convex and concave glass panels that sparkle like a switchboard of an alien spaceship at night. To some it's an acquired taste, but to most – especially locals – it's a symbol of progress and a harbinger of wonderful events and artist endeavours still to come.

Old Harbour   NEIGHBOURHOOD

(Map p228; Geirsgata) Largely a service harbour until recent years, the so-called Old Harbour has blossomed into a hotspot for tourists. Photo ops abound, as views of snowcapped mountains scallop the horizon, and whale-watching and puffin-viewing trips depart from the pier, as do many of the city's walking tours. Swing through to check out a cluster of excellent restaurants and cafes, shop for souvenirs, and watch a documentary about Iceland's temperamental tectonics.

REYKJAVÍK IN...

One Day

Start with a walk around **Tjörnin** and **Old Reykjavík**, then follow Bankastræti and **Skólavörðustígur**, nosing into its little galleries. The hilltop has the immense **Hallgrímskirkja** church, Reykjavík's most dramatic building, with great city views.

Take in a couple of the best museums, like the impressive **Reykjavík 871 +/-2**, or the **National Museum**, then wander the **Old Harbour** or join a whale-watching tour.

Keep evening plans loose, as many of the more laid-back restaurants turn into wild party beasts later on. You're going to need some energy if you're going to join Reykjavík's notorious Bacchanalian pub crawl.

Two Days

After a sleep-in and relaxing brunch at **Bergsson Mathús**, catch the bus to **Perlan**, with its tremendous vistas and superb Saga Museum, which brings Iceland's early history to life.

Head back to the city centre for design-shopping, then splash out on an authentically Icelandic feast at one of the capital's finer restaurants. After dinner treat yourself to a show at **Harpa**.

What about the **Blue Lagoon**? Well, here's the clever part – you can visit Iceland's number-one attraction on your way back to the airport. Wallowing in its warm, sapphire-blue waters is certainly a fantastic last memory to take home.

Reykjavík 871 +/-2 MUSEUM
(Settlement Exhibition; Map p228; www.reykjavik
871.is; Aðalstræti 16; adult/child Ikr1100/free;
☉10am-5pm) The city's best-curated museum
is based around a single 10th-century Viking house but shows what miracles can be
achieved when technology, archaeology and
imagination meet. Through 21st-century
wizardry, a fire leaps from the hearth, while
around the walls ghostly settlers materialise
to tend crops, hunt, launch a boat and bury
their dead. The information on the display
panels is refreshingly objective, providing a
balanced and uninflated account of Iceland's
settlement. It's interesting to note that scientists have found no evidence of religion
among the earliest settlers.

Across the street you'll find an active excavation site where archaeologists are in the
process of uncovering new artefacts from
the Viking era. Ask at the ticket booth about
daily tours of the new dig – they usually run
in English at 11am on weekdays.

Old Reykjavík NEIGHBOURHOOD
(Map p228) Old Reykjavík grew up around
Tjörnin (The Pond), a large lake that echoes
with the honks and hoots of thousands of
geese, swans, ducks and gulls. The pleasant
park at the southern end is laced with walking and cycling paths.

Rising on stilts from the northern shore
of Tjörnin is Reykjavík's postmodern City
Hall, **Ráðhús** (Vonarstræti; admission free;
☉8am-7pm Mon-Fri, noon-6pm Sat & Sun). It contains a tourist information desk, a cafe and a
huge, impressive 3-D map of Iceland: a mass
of mountains, fjords and volcanoes.

The neat grey basalt building on the
southern side of Austurvöllur, the main
square, houses **Alþingi** (Map p228; www.althin-
gi.is; Túngata), the Icelandic parliament. **Dóm-
kirkja** (Map p228; www.domkirkjan.is; Lækjargata
14a; admission free; ☉10am-5pm Mon-Fri) is a
small but perfectly proportioned cathedral.

National Museum MUSEUM
(Þjóðminjasafn; Map p228; www.nationalmuseum.
is; Suðurgata 41; adult/child Ikr1200/free; ☉10am-
5pm May–mid-Sep, 11am-5pm Tue-Sun mid-Sep–
Apr) Displays at the National Museum are
well thought out and give an excellent overview of Iceland's history and culture. The
strongest section delves into the Settlement
Era, with swords, silver hoards and a great
little bronze model of Thor on display. But
the most treasured artefact in the museum
is a beautiful 13th-century church door,

carved with the touching story of a knight
and his faithful lion! Upstairs, you really get
a sense of the country's poverty over the following 600 years. Simple, homey artefacts
make use of every scrap: check out the gaming pieces made from cod ear bones, and
the wooden doll that doubled as a kitchen
utensil.

Perlan NOTABLE BUILDING
(Map p224; www.perlan.is; ☉10am-10pm, cafe to
9pm) Looking like half of Barbarella's bra,
Perlan is a complex based around the huge
hot-water tanks on Öskjuhlíð hill. The hex-
agonal viewing deck offers a tremendous
360-degree panorama of Reykjavík and the
mountains: multilingual recordings explain
the scenery. There's a busy cafe on the same
level. It's about 2km from the city centre
(take bus 18 from Hlemmur).

Saga Museum MUSEUM
(Map p224; www.sagamuseum.is; adult/child
Ikr1800/800; ☉10am-6pm Apr-Sep, noon-5pm
Oct-Mar) Part of the Perlan complex, the
endearingly bloodthirsty Saga Museum is
where Icelandic history is brought to life
by eerie silicon models and a soundtrack
of thudding axes and hair-raising screams.
Don't be surprised if you see some of the
characters wandering around town, as
moulds were taken from Reykjavík residents
(the museum's owner is Ingólfur Arnarson,
and his daughters are the Irish princess and
the little slave gnawing a fish). Take bus 18
from Hlemmur.

Iceland Phallological Museum MUSEUM
(Hið Íslanska Reðasafn; Map p224; www.phallus.is;
Laugavegur 116; adult/child Ikr1000/free; ☉11am-
6pm) Oh, the jokes are endless here. This
unique museum houses a bizarre collection
of penises. From pickled pickles to petrified
wood, there are over 300 different types of
family jewels on display. Featured items
include contributions from a walrus, the
silver castings of each member of the Icelandic handball team and a singular human

ICELAND REYKJAVÍK

Reykjavík

Fiskislóð

Grandagarður

Old Harbour

6

Ananaust

Mýrargata

Framnesvegur

Geirsgata

Bræðraborgarstígur

Öldugata

Tryggvagata

Sólvallagata

Austurvöllur

Ásvallagata

Hofsvallagata

Hringbraut

See Central Reykjavík Map (p228)

Kalkofnsvegur

Lindargata

Skúlagata

Hverfisgata

Laugavegur

Tjörnin

Óðinsgata

Freyjugata

Njálsgata

Borgartún

Hlemmur Bus Terminal

Baronsstígur

1

10

Birkimelur

Dunhagi

12

Hallargarðurinn

Viðeyjarsund

Smáragata

Laufásvegur

Barónsstígur

Snorrabraut

Rauðarárstígur

Einholt

Háteigsvegur

Flókagata

BSÍ/Bus Terminal

Eiríksgata

Gamla

Sæmundargata

Njarðargata

Sturlagata

Suðurgata

Aragata

Oddagata

11

Hringbraut

Miðbú

Eskihlíð

Reykjahlíð

Miklabraut

Langahlíð

3

Barmahlíð

Mávahlíð

Dráuphlíð

Blönduhlíð

VATNSMÝRI

Þorragata

Reykjavík Domestic Airport

Flugvallarvegur

Bústaðavegur

Hörgshlíð

Einarsnes

Bauganes

Skeljanes

5

Öskjuhlíð

NORTH ATLANTIC OCEAN

Fossvogur

Nauthólsvík Geothermal Beach

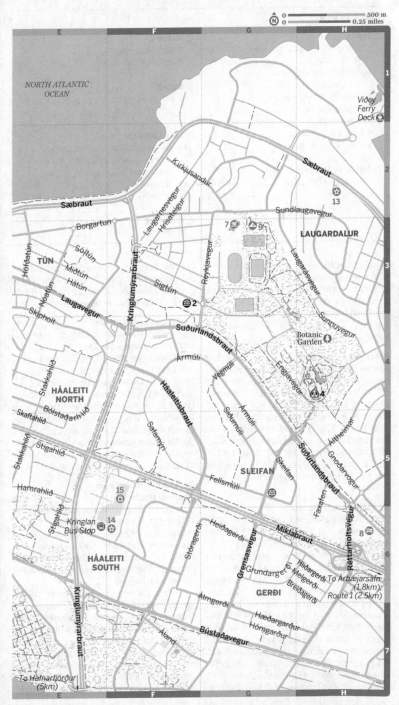

NORTH ATLANTIC
OCEAN

Viðey
Ferry
Dock

Sæbraut

13

Sundlaugavegur

LAUGARDALUR

Kirkjusandur

Sæbraut

Borgartún

7   9

Laugarnesvegur

Hrísateigur

TÚN

Sóltún

Reykjavegur

Laugarásvegur

Höfðatún

Miðtún

Hátún

Sigtún

Nóatún

Laugavegur

Kringlumýrarbraut

Suðurlandsbraut

2

Sunnuvegur

Skipholt

Ármúli

Botanic
Garden

Stakkahlíð

HÁALEITI
NORTH

Vegmúli

Háaleitisbraut

Engjavegur

Bólstaðarhlíð

4

Skaftahlíð

Ármúli

Síðumúli

Altheimar

Stakkahlíð

Stígahlíð

Safamýri

Gnoðarvogur

Hamrahlíð

Fellsmúli

SLEIFAN

Skeifan

Suðurlandsbraut

Faxafen

Réttarholtsvegur

15

8

Stígahlíð

Kringlan
Bus Stop

14

Miklabraut

Heiðargerði

Grensásvegur

Stóragerði

HÁALEITI
SOUTH

Álmgerði

Grundargerði

Hæðargarður

Hlíðargerði
Melgerði
Breiðagerði

To Árbæjarsafn
(1.8km);
Route 1 (2.5km)

GERÐI

Kringlumýrarbraut

Álfand

Bústaðavegur

Hólmgarður

To Hafnarfjörður
(5km)

Reykjavík

sample from the museum's previous owner who recently passed away. But don't rush to volunteer – three other donors-in-waiting have already promised to bequeath their manhood (signed contracts are mounted on the wall). Quirky sidenote: all displays are translated into Esperanto.

Þjóðmenningarhúsið   MUSEUM

(Culture House; Map p228; www.thjodmenning.is; Hverfisgata 15; adult/child Ikr1000/free, free Wed; ⊙11am-5pm) Creeping into the darkened rooms of the Culture House is a true thrill for saga lovers. A permanent exhibition covers saga history: from a who's who of Norse gods to a tragic account of Árni Magnússon, who devoted his life to saving Icelandic manuscripts, and died of a broken heart when his Copenhagen library went up in flames.

Víkin Maritime Museum   MUSEUM

(Víkin Sjóminjasafnið; Map p224; ☎517 9400; www.sjominjasafn.is; Grandagarður 8; adult/child Ikr1200/free; ⊙10am-5pm Jun–mid-Sep, 11am-5pm Tue-Sun mid-Sep–May) Based appropriately in a former freezing plant for fish, the small Víkin Maritime Museum celebrates the country's seafaring heritage, focusing on the trawlers that transformed Iceland's economy. Much of the information is in Icelandic only, but silent film footage of trawler crews in action is worth a look. Your ticket also allows you aboard the coastguard ship Óðin, a veteran of the Cod Wars (of the 1970s when British and Icelandic fishermen quite literally came to blows over fishing rights in the North Atlantic), as part of guided tours at 1pm, 2pm and 3pm (2pm and 3pm only at weekends in winter, closed January and February). There's also an adorable on-site cafe.

Einar Jónsson Museum   MUSEUM

(Map p228; www.lej.is; Njarðargata; adult/child Ikr600/free, garden admission free; ⊙2-5pm Tue-Sun Jun–mid-Sep, 2-5pm Sat & Sun mid-Sep–Nov & Feb-May) Einar Jónsson (1874–1954) is Iceland's foremost sculptor, famous for his intense symbolist works. Chiselled allegories of Hope, Earth, Spring and Death burst from basalt cliffs, weep over naked women, sprout wings and slay dragons. For a taster, the **sculpture garden** behind the museum is dedicated to the artist and contains 26 bronze casts; they're particularly effective at dusk.

Reykjavik Art Museum –
Ásmundarsafn   GALLERY

(Ásmundur Sveinsson Museum; Map p224; Sigtún; ⊙10am-5pm May-Sep, 1-5pm Oct-Apr) The excellent Reykjavík Art Museum is split over three sites: this one, known as Ásmundarsafn, as well as two others, **Hafnarhús** (Map p228; Tryggvagata 17) and **Kjarvalsstaðir** (Map p224; Flókagata).

There's something immensely tactile about Ásmundur Sveinsson's monumental concrete creations – see for yourself in the **garden** outside the rounded, white Ásmundarsafn. Duck inside the museum for smaller, spikier works in wood, clay and metals, exploring themes as diverse as folklore and physics. Ásmundur (1893–1982) designed the building himself; getting into the spirit of things, the council later added an igloo-shaped bus stop in front. Buses 14, 15, 17, 19 and S2 pass close by.

National Gallery of Iceland   MUSEUM
(Listasafn Íslands; Map p228; www.listasafn.is; Fríkirkjuvegur 7; admission Ikr1000; ⊙11am-5pm Tue-Sun) Surreal mud-purple landscapes are intermingled with visions of trolls, giants and dead men walking at the National Gallery of Iceland's main art gallery. Overlooking Tjörnin, it certainly gives an interesting glimpse into the nation's psyche. As well as a huge collection of 19th- and 20th-century paintings by Iceland's favourite sons and daughters (including Ásgrímur Jónsson, Jóhannes Sveinsson Kjarval and Nína Sæmundsson), there are works by Picasso and Munch.

Árbæjarsafn   MUSEUM
(www.reykjavikmuseum.is; Kistuhylur 4; adult/child Ikr1100/free; ⊙10am-5pm Jun-Aug, by tour only 1pm Mon-Fri Sep-May) Quaint old buildings have been uprooted from their original sites and rebuilt at the open-air Árbæjarsafn, a kind of zoo for houses, 4km east of the city centre beyond Laugardalur. Alongside the 19th-century homes are a turf-roofed church, and various stables, smithies, barns and boathouses – all very picturesque. There are summer arts-and-crafts demonstrations, and it's a great place for kids to let off steam. Take bus 12.

Activities

Reykjavík Bike Tours   BICYCLE TOUR
(Map p228; ☑694 8956; www.reykjavikbiketours.is) A fantastic Icelandic-German outfit offering active tours of the capital and the surrounding attractions. Prices start at Ikr4800. You can also rent a bike and go at it on your own (Ikr3000/5000 for a half/whole day).

FREE ATTRACTIONS

Reykjavík can be costly, but there are some free sights to enjoy:

» Reykjavik Art Museum (p226) There's at least a day's worth of viewing at Reykjavík Art Museum, with its three galleries scattered across the city.

» Perlan (p223) Gorge on gorgeous views from the top of the city's hot-water tanks.

» Einar Jónsson Museum garden (p226) Free sculpture garden behind the museum.

Elding Whale Watching   WHALE WATCHING
(Map p228; ☑555 3565; www.whalewatching.is) Elding is the original whale-watching operator off the coast of the capital. It is also considered the most professional and the most ecofriendly, limiting its power expenditure on its wooden boats. Refreshments are sold onboard, and every trip is staffed by a scientist. Guests walk through a small museum as they board the boat, which gives a bit of background to the life of the local whales.

Laugardalslaug   SWIMMING POOL
(Map p224; Sundlaugavegur 30a; ⊙6.30am-10.30pm Mon-Fri year-round, 8am-10pm Sat & Sun Apr-Oct, 8am-8pm Sat & Sun Nov-Mar) The biggest and best of Reykjavík's many geothermal swimming pools is found next door to the camping ground. There's an Olympic-size indoor pool, an outdoor pool, seven jacuzzi-like 'hot-pots', a steam bath and a curling 86m water slide for kids big and small. Right next door to Laugardalslaug is a five-star health resort, Laugar (Map p224; ☑553 0000; www.laugarspa.is), with themed saunas, steam rooms and beauty treatments. Catch bus 14 from Lækjartorg or Hlemmur.

Inside the Volcano   ADVENTURE TOUR
(☑863 6640; www.insidethevolcano.com; admission Ikr37,000) Iceland's media darling when it opened in 2012, this one-of-a-kind experience takes a limited number of adventure-seekers down into one of the only perfectly intact magma chambers in the entire world. From a geological perspective this is truly a mind-blowing experience; a mining cart lowers visitors in groups of four deep down into the bottom of a vase-shaped chasm that once gurgled with hot lava. The lights are dim and time is very limited; but those who can use their imagination will be dazzled. The trip also includes a hearty bowl of home-made lamb stew after returning from the bowels of the earth. Whispers about altering the experience to make it more tourist-friendly (allowing greater amounts of visitors) were circulating during the research of this guide – check the website for regularly updated details. The site is 30km southeast of Reykjavík, but the price includes transfers from town, with hotel pick-up.

Festivals & Events

For forthcoming live music festivals, see www.musik.is.

In May, the capital comes awake with the two-week **Reykjavík Arts Festival**

Central Reykjavík

ICELAND REYKJAVÍK

Jetty for Whale Watching

Old Harbour

Bakkast.

Nýlendugata

Mýrargata

25

34 55

43

10

11

6

Vesturgata

Ránargata

Bárugata

Öldugata

Marar

Hrannarst.

Stýrimannast.

Ægisgata

Vesturgata

Norðurst.

31 19 28

Geirsgata

57

Bárugata

Öldugata

Túngata

Garðastræti

9

36

Tryggvagata

Naustin

Sæbraut

Geirsgata

Hólavallagata

Grjótag.

Mjöstræti

Main Tourist Office

Ingólfstorg

65

Hafnarstræti

42

Pósthst.

32

39

Lækjartorg Bus Terminal

53

54

Austurstr.

Stjórnarráðið

62

Reykjavík 871 +/-2

7

Kirkjustræti

Austurvöllur

1

2

Lækjargata

Bankastr.

60

41

Skólastræti

Amtmannsst.

Hávallagata

Sólvallagata

Björnvallagata

Ásvallagata

Garðastræti

Suðurgata

Vonarstræti

Raðhús

8

47

33

Lækjargata

Bókhlöðust.

Þingholtsstræti

Hólavellir Cemetery

Tjörnin

Miðstr.

Spítalast.

Skálholtsst.

5

14

Bjargarst.

Ljósvallagata

Suðurgata

Tjarnargata

Hringbraut

Skothúsvegur

Frikirkjuvegur

Hallargarðurinn

Laufásvegur

Hellus.

58

22

Þingholtsstræti

Grundarst.

Baldursgata

13

Bjarkargata

Birkargata

Tjörnin

Fjölugata

Sóleyjargata

Bragagata

National Museum

Hringbraut

Suðurgata

Hljómskálagarðurinn

Viðarmarstaðir

17

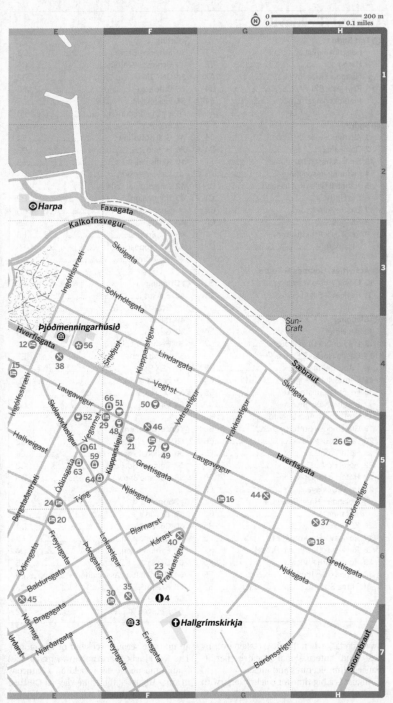

0 — 200 m
0 — 0.1 miles

Harpa

Faxagata

Kalkofnsvegur

Skúlgata

Ingólfsstræti

Sölvhólsgata

Sun-Craft

Hverfisgata

Þjóðmenningarhúsið

12

56

Smiðjust

Lindargata

Klapparstígur

Sæbraut

Skúlagata

38

15

Veghst

Vatnsstígur

Laugavegur

Ingólfsstræti

Skólavörðustígur

66 51

50

Frakkastígur

26

Hallveigast

52

29

48

46

Hverfisgata

Vegamót

61

21

27

49

59

Laugavegur

Óðinsgata

63

64

Grettisgata

Klapparstígur

Bergstaðastræti

Njálsgata

16

44

Baronsstígur

24

Týsg

20

37

Freyjugata

Pórsgata

Bjarnarst

18

Lokastígur

Kárast

40

Grettisgata

Óðinsgata

Baldursgata

23

Njálsgata

45

35

Frakkastígur

Nönnug

Bragagata

30

4

Njarðargata

Freyjugata

Eiríksgata

3

Hallgrímskirkja

Urðarst

Barónsstígur

Snorrabraut

(www.artfest.is), when the city is taken over by local and international theatre performances, films, lectures and music.

August is a big time for celebrations, with the **Gay Pride** (Gay; www.gaypride.is) parade around the second weekend of the month. The **Reykjavík Marathon** (www.marathon.is) is an atmospheric event held on a Saturday in mid-August – the same day as **Culture Night**, a lively time of art, music and dance with a grand fireworks finale. The annual **Reykjavík Jazz Festival** (www.reykjavikjazz.is) has two weeks of performances.

In September the annual **Reykjavík International Film Festival** (www.riff.is) sees blockbusters make way for international art films in cinemas across the city.

Iceland Airwaves (www.icelandairwaves.com) is a last blast of music and noise before winter sets in. This five-day event, held in the third week of October, is one of the world's most cutting-edge music festivals: don't expect to sleep.

🛏 Sleeping

Reykjavík has loads of accommodation choices, with midrange guesthouses and business-class hotels predominating. From June through the end of August accommodation fills up very quickly; reservations are a must. Most places open year-round (though we've noted where accommodation is summer only) and offer significant discounts from October to April; summer prices are listed here. Reykjavík is packed with *gistiheimili* (guesthouses), and there are new places opening every year. Most are in converted houses, so rooms often have shared bathrooms, kitchens and TV lounges. Some offer sleeping-bag accommodation.

TOP CHOICE **Icelandair Hotel Reykjavík Marina**   BOUTIQUE HOTEL €€€
(Map p228; ☑560 8000; www.icelandairhotels.is/hotels/reykjavikmarina; Mýrargata 2; d Ikr30,000; @) A gorgeous addition to the capital's accommodation scene sits next to the Old Harbour, with excellent sea views from the even-numbered rooms on the 4th floor. Captivating murals, blonde-wood trimming, up-to-the-second mod cons, and clever ways to conserve space make the small rooms a winner overall. The lobby also benefits from the eye-catching design scheme, with a menagerie of strange furniture and a live satellite feed to Blue Lagoon.

Grettisborg Apartments   APARTMENTS €€
(Map p228; ☑694 7020; www.grettisborg.is; Grettisgata 53b; apt from €145) Staying here is like sleeping in a magazine for Scandinavian home design. These thoroughly modern apartments come in 50 shades of grey (no, not like that), sporting fine furnishing and sleek built-ins.

101 Hotel   BOUTIQUE HOTEL €€€
(Map p228; ☑580 0101; www.101hotel.is; Hverfisgata 10; d from Ikr53,000; @) The 101 aims to tickle the senses – with yielding downy beds, iPod sound docks and Bose speakers, rich wooden floors and glass-walled showers – it may mean you skip the bars and opt for a night in instead. A spa with masseurs, a small gym and a glitterati restaurant–bar add to the opulence. Some people have been underwhelmed by the service but, all in all, this is one of the city's boutique-iest places to stay.

Baldursbrá Guesthouse   GUESTHOUSE €€
(Map p228; ☑552 6646; baldursbra@centrum.is; Laufásvegur 41; d incl breakfast from Ikr16,000; @) This exceptional little guesthouse, on a quiet street close to Tjörnin and the BSÍ bus terminal, stands out thanks to the care and kindness of its owners. The decent-sized, comfy rooms all have washbasins, and the additional facilities are admirable – a sociable sitting room–TV lounge, and a private garden with a fab hot-pot (hot tub), sauna and barbecue.

KEX Hostel   HOSTEL €
(Map p228; ☑561 6060; www.kexhostel.is; Skúlagata 28; 4-/16-person dm Ikr5100/3200, d without bathroom Ikr14,400) Like some kind of unofficial headquarters of backpackerdom, KEX is a mega-hostel with heaps of style (think retro vaudeville meets rodeo) and sociability. Overall it's not as prim as the other options in this category – and the bathrooms are shared by many – but if you're searching for a friendly vibe with a fun lobby bar, look no further.

Hótel Holt   LUXURY HOTEL €€€
(Map p228; ☑552 5700; www.holt.is; Bergstaðastræti 37; d from Ikr30,400; @) Cross the threshold and enter a world of luxury. Original

SCRUB UP

Reykjavík's many outdoor swimming pools, heated by volcanic water, are the social hubs of the city: children play, teenagers flirt, business deals are made and everyone catches up with the latest gossip.

Geothermal pools are the nation's pride and joy. And as chemical cleaners like chlorine aren't used, it's vital that visitors wash thoroughly without a swimsuit before getting in. To do otherwise is to cause great offence. For further information, see www.spacity.is.

paintings, drawings and sculptures adorn the rooms here (Holt houses the largest private art collection in Iceland), set off by warm-toned decor and rose-coloured carpets. Downstairs is a handsome amber-hued library, a bar with flickering fire and a huge selection of single-malt whiskys, and one of the country's best restaurants.

Reykjavík Downtown Hostel HOSTEL €

(Map p228; ☎553 8120; www.hostel.is; Vesturgata 17; dm from Ikr9400; @) Squeaky clean and well run, this effortlessly charming hostel gets such excellent reviews by the backpacker crowd that it regularly lures large groups and an older legion of savvy travellers.

Castle House & Embassy Apartments APARTMENTS €€

(Map p228; ☎511 2166; www.hotelsiceland.net; Skálholtsstígur 2a & Garðastræti 40; apt from Ikr20,500) Turn to these pleasant self-contained apartments for satisfyingly central and commendably quiet accommodation. The two sets of apartments (located on opposite sides of Tjörnin) are much more personal than a hotel, but come with room service: fresh towels appear daily and washing-up seems to magically clean itself.

Reykjavík Backpackers HOSTEL €

(Map p228; ☎578 3700; www.reykjavikbackpackers.com; Laugavegur 28; dm/d from Ikr4990/17,490; @) A major player in the capital's hostel scene, this place has had a recent facelift and boasts spick-and-span rooms (try to score one on the upper floors), quirky bus seats in the lobby, a fantastic roof deck, and a climbing wall tucked in the back.

Guesthouse Butterfly GUESTHOUSE €€

(Map p228; ☎894 1864; www.kvasir.is/butterfly; Ránargata 8a; d with/without bathroom Ikr21,900/16,900; ☻mid-May–Aug) On a quiet residential street within fluttering distance of the centre, Butterfly has neat, simply furnished rooms. There's a guest kitchen, and the friendly Icelandic–Norwegian owners make you feel right at home. The top floor has two self-contained apartments with kitchen and balcony.

CenterHótel Þingholt HOTEL €€€

(Map p228; ☎595 8530; www.centerhotels.com; Þingholtsstræti 3-5; d from €220; @) Compact, quirky and full of character, Þingholt opened in 2006 and still retains a fresh, new feel. It was designed by architect Gulla Jónsdóttir, who used natural materials and some very Icelandic ideas to create one of Reykjavík's most distinctive boutique hotels. Rooms are compact, but feel cosy rather than cramped. This snuggly effect is heightened by moody lighting, stylish dark-grey flooring and black-leather headboards and furniture.

Hótel Óðinsvé HOTEL €€€

(Map p228; ☎511 6200; www.hotelodinsve.is; Þórsgata 1; d from Ikr28,900; @) A boutique hotel with bags of personality, Oðinsvé contains 43 sun-drenched rooms with wooden floors, original artwork and classic furnishings. They're all very different – some are split-level, some have balconies and many have bathtubs – but only room 117 has a resident ghost! The hotel also owns some stunning apartments, which overlook the prison a short walk away on Skólavörðustígur.

Sunna Guesthouse GUESTHOUSE €€

(Map p228; ☎511 5570; www.sunna.is; Þórsgata 26; d/apt from Ikr18,500/31,500; P@) Rooms at this guesthouse are simple and sunny with honey-coloured parquet floors. Nine rooms have private bathrooms, and several at the front have good views of Hallgrímskirkja. Families are made to feel welcome; choose between neat studio apartments holding up

---

REYKJAVÍK FOR CHILDREN

Those travelling with children will find ample facilities (baby-changing tables in toilets, high chairs in restaurants etc) and a gently welcoming attitude. But the only attraction in Reykjavík aimed specifically at (youngish) children is **Reykjavík Zoo & Family Park** (Map p224; ☎575 7800; www.mu.is; Laugardalur; adult/5-12yr Ikr750/550, 1-/10-/20-ride tickets Ikr270/2300/4300; ☻10am-6pm mid-May–mid-Aug, to 5pm mid-Aug–mid-May). Don't expect lions and tigers: think seals, foxes, farm animals and a small aquarium. The Family Park contains child-size bulldozers, a giant trampoline and mini fairground rides. Buses 14, 15, 17, 19 and S2 pass within 400m.

Tots love to feed the birds on Tjörnin, the city's central lake, and the open-air Árbæjarsafn has plenty of appeal for kids of all ages. The dramatic Saga Museum will delight some but may be too frightening for younger children.

to four people, or more spacious apartments with accommodation for up to eight.

Galtafell Guesthouse GUESTHOUSE €€

(Map p228; ☑551 4344; www.galtafell.com; Laufásvegur 46; d/apt Ikr16,600/20,200; Ⓟ) In the quiet, well-to-do 'Embassy District', and within easy walking distance of town. The four spruce apartments here each contain a fully equipped kitchen, a cosy seating area and a separate bedroom, and there are three doubles with access to a guest kitchen. The only drawback is that they're basement rooms, so there are no views of anything but the pavement!

Guesthouse Óðinn GUESTHOUSE €€

(Map p228; ☑561 3400; www.odinnreykjavik.com; Óðinsgata 9; s/d incl breakfast Ikr13,500/16,900) This family-run guesthouse has simple white rooms with splashes of colourful artwork. An excellent buffet breakfast is served in a handsome room with sea views. Some en-suite rooms are available.

Forsæla Guesthouse GUESTHOUSE €€

(Map p228; ☑863 4643, 551 6046; www.apartmenthouse.is; Grettisgata 33b; d/apt from Ikr17,200/26,800) This is a really lovely option in Reykjavík's conservation area. Star of the show is the 100-year-old wood-and-tin house for four to eight people, which comes with all the old beams and tasteful mod-cons you could want. Three apartments have small but cosy bedrooms and sitting rooms, fully equipped kitchens and washing machines. There's a minimum three-night stay.

Three Sisters GUESTHOUSE €€

(Þrjár Systur; Map p228; ☑565 2181; www.threesisters.is; Ránargata 16; apt from €133; ⊘mid-May–Aug; @) A twinkly-eyed former fisherman runs the Three Sisters, a lovely town house in old Reykjavík, now divided into eight studio apartments. Comfy beds are flanked by old-fashioned easy chairs and state-of-the-art flatscreen TVs. Each room comes with a cute fully equipped kitchen (including fridge, microwave and two-ringed hob).

Room With A View APARTMENTS €€€

(Map p228; ☑552 7262; www.roomwithaview.is; Laugavegur 18; apt from Ikr28,000) This ridiculously central apartment hotel offers one- to four-bedroom apartments, decorated in Scandinavian style and with private bathrooms, kitchenettes, CD players, TVs and washing machines. Half have those eponymous sea and city views, and most have

access to a Jacuzzi. Rooms vary – check the website for a wealth of details. It has a bang-on-centre location; the downside is Friday- and Saturday-night street noise.

Hótel Frón HOTEL €€€

(Map p228; ☑511 4666; www.hotelfron.is; Laugavegur 22a; d incl breakfast from Ikr22,900; @) This bright blue hotel has lots in its favour – particularly its excellent location overlooking Laugavegur (although rooms at the front can be noisy at weekends), and the stylish apartments in a newer wing. Older rooms are less inspiring.

Hótel Leifur Eiríksson HOTEL €€€

(Map p228; ☑562 0800; www.hotelleifur.is; Skólavörðustígur 45; d incl breakfast from Ikr25,500) This hotel glories in one of the best locations in Reykjavík: it's slap on the end of arty Skólavörðustígur, and more than half its 47 rooms have inspiring views of Hallgrímskirkja. They're fairly small and basic, but you're paying for the hotel's coordinates rather than its interior design.

Reykjavík Campsite CAMPGROUND €

(Map p224; ☑568 6944; www.reykjavikcampsite.is; Sundlaugavegur 32; campsites per person Ikr1400; ⊘mid-May–mid-Sep; Ⓟ@) The only camping option in the city (right next door to Reykjavík City Hostel, 2km east of the centre in the Laugardalur valley) gets very busy in summer, but with space for 650 people in its three fields, you're likely to find a place. Facilities include free showers, bike hire, a kitchen and barbecue area.

✖ Eating

From take-away hot dogs to gourmet platters on white-cloth tables, little Reykjavík has an astonishing assortment of eateries. Although you can go round the world in 80 plates, we much prefer the slew of Icelandic and 'new Nordic' restaurants serving tried-and-true variations of seafood and lamb.

Of all the dining options, it's Reykjavík's cool and cosy cafes that are the city's best features. Lingering is encouraged – many offer magazines and free wi-fi access. They're the best places to go for morning coffee and light lunches. As the evening wears on, most undergo a Jekyll-and-Hyde transformation – coffee becomes beer, DJs materialise in dark corners, and suddenly you're not in a cafe but a kick-ass bar! Magic. Because the dividing line is so blurred, also refer to the Drinking listings.

TOP CHOICE Dill

SCANDINAVIAN €€€

(Map p224; www.dillrestaurant.is; Sturlugata 5; 3-course meal from Ikr5900; ☉11.30am-2.30pm & 5-10pm) 'New Nordic' par excellence is the major draw card at this elegant yet simple venue at the local culture house. The focus is very much on the food – locally sourced nibbles served as a parade of courses.

TOP CHOICE Bergsson Mathús

CAFE €€

(Map p228; www.bergsson.is; Templarasund 3; mains Ikr1190-1890; ☉7am-7pm Mon-Fri, to 5pm Sat & Sun) If this prim, Scandi-simple cafe were located in your hometown, we're pretty sure that you'd eat here every day. Meals are assembled with the utmost care – the owners pride themselves on providing the freshest produce and ingredients available.

Snaps

SCANDINAVIAN €€

(Map p228; www.snapsbistro.is; Þórsgata 1; mains Ikr1980-3100; ☉11.30am-11pm) Snaps' secret to success is simple: serve scrumptious seafood mains at surprisingly affordable prices. Lunch specials are a reasonable Ikr1690, and you'll score a three-course dinner for a wallet-friendly Ikr4800. Seats are squished into a social greenhouse-like space that receives plenty of light; or cosy up to the cute bar with its bold brass rim.

Kaffismiðjan

CAFE €

(Map p228; www.kaffismidja.is; Kárastígur 1; snacks Ikr180-600; ☉8.30am-5pm Mon-Fri, 10am-5pm Sat) Coffee cupping is now virtually akin to wine tasting in Reykjavík, and leading the trend is the effortlessly hip Kaffismiðjan, easily spotted with its smattering of wooden tables and potato sacks dropped throughout the paved square outside during the warmer months. Swig a perfect latte prepared by award-winning baristas, and snuggle up on velvety sofas when the weather isn't at its finest.

Við Tjörnina

SEAFOOD €€€

(Map p228; ☎551 8666; www.vidtjornina.is; Templarasund 3; Ikr2200-5900; ☉from 6pm) People keep coming back to this famed establishment, tucked away near Tjörnin. It serves up beautifully presented Icelandic feasts such as guillemot with port, garlic langoustine, or the house speciality marinated cod chins (far more delicious than they sound!).

Sægreifinn

SEAFOOD €

(Sea Baron; Map p228; www.saegreifinn.is; Geirsgata 8; mains Ikr1190; ☉11am-10pm) This spot dishes out the most famous lobster curry soup in the capital. If the eponymous sea baron isn't dishing out bowlfuls to customers then he's probably upstairs taking a nap on one of the bunk beds. Feel free to copy him; siestas come free with your meal.

Friðrik V

ICELANDIC €€€

(Map p228; www.fridrikv.is; Laugavegur 60; lunch mains/3-course dinner Ikr1590/5900; ☉11.30am-1.30pm Tue-Fri, 5.30-10pm Tue-Sat) One of the top spots to splash out on a gourmet Icelandic meal, Friðrik's eponymous master chef is known throughout the country for championing the 'slow food' movement, and his darling family helps him prepare every meal. Each dish is a carefully prepared medley of locally sourced items presented in a forward-thinking manner.

Fiskfélagið

INTERNATIONAL €€€

(Fish Company; Map p228; www.fishcompany.is; Vesturgata 2a; mains Ikr2900-5400; ☉11.30am-2pm & 6-11.30pm) The 'Fish Company' takes Icelandic seafood recipes and spins them through a variety of far-flung continents. Try the local catch marinated in Asian spices, amid copper lamps and quirky furnishings.

Fiskmarkaðurinn

SEAFOOD €€€

(Fish Market; Map p228; ☎578 8877; www.fiskmarkadurinn.is; Aðalstræti 12; mains Ikr1690-3390; ☉11.30am-2pm & 6-11.30pm Mon-Fri, 6-11.30pm Sat & Sun) Don't let the weird dead-bony-fish logo put you off – this restaurant excels in infusing Icelandic seafood with Far Eastern flavours. Ingredients have a strong focus on local produce. For example, there's the 'Farmers' Market' menu, which takes specialities from around Iceland (lobsters from Höfn, salmon from the Þjórsá, halibut from Breiðafjörður) and introduces them to spicy chillis, papaya, mango, coconut, satay glazes and *ponzu* sauce.

Þrír Frakkar

ICELANDIC €€€

(Map p228; ☎552 3939; www.3frakkar.com; Baldursgata 14; mains Ikr3000-5300; ☉noon-2.30pm & 6-10pm Mon-Fri, 6-11pm Sat & Sun) Owner-chef Úlfar Eysteinsson has built an excellent reputation at this snug little restaurant – apparently a favourite of Jamie Oliver's. Specialities include salt cod, anglerfish and *plokkfiskur* (fish stew served au gratin) with black bread. You can also sample nonfish items, such as seal, puffin, reindeer and whale steaks.

Tíu Droppar

CAFE €

(Map p228; Laugavegur 27; soup Ikr1290; ☉9am-10pm) Tucked away in a cosy basement off the main drag, Tiú Droppar feels like granny's den, with floral wallpaper and pictures of seascapes in small gilded frames. Check out the locals' latest footwear fashions through the street-level windows while slurping tasty homemade soup. In the evenings, the quaint space reimagines itself as the **Château des Dix Gouttes**, offering tipples of the wine variety, instead of coffee brews.

Grái Kötturinn
CAFE €

(Map p228; Hverfisgata 16a; mains Ikr800-1800; ⊙7.15am-3pm Mon-Fri, 8am-3pm Sat-Sun) This tiny six-table cafe (a favourite of Björk's) looks like a cross between an eccentric bookshop and a lopsided art gallery – quite charming! You'll be treated to a delicious breakfast of toast, bagels, American pancakes, or bacon and eggs served on thick, buttery slabs of freshly baked bread.

Lækjarbrekka
ICELANDIC €€€

(Map p228; ☑551 4430; www.laekjarbrekka.is; Bankastræti 2; mains Ikr3220-5580; ⊙11.30am-11pm) This top-notch restaurant has built up its reputation over more than 20 years, cooking traditional Icelandic dishes (game, lobster, juicy pepper steak and mountain lamb) with half an eye on the tourist dollar.

Laundromat Café
INTERNATIONAL €€

(Map p228; www.thelaundromatcafe.com/en; Austurstæti 9; mains Ikr990-3990; ⊙8am-1am Mon-Thu, to 3am Fri, 10am-3am Sat, 10am-1am Sun) This Danish import has seen a lot of success after crashlanding on one of Reykjavík's main drags. Locals devour heaps of hearty mains in a cheery environment surrounded by tattered paperbacks. Go for the 'Dirty Brunch' on weekends, to sop up an evening's worth of booze.

Bæjarins Beztu
FAST FOOD €

(Map p228; Tryggvagata; hot dogs Ikr320; ⊙10am-1am Sun-Thu, 11am-4am Fri & Sat) Icelanders are addicted to hot dogs, and swear the best are those from this converted van near the harbour. Use the vital sentence *Eina með öllu* ('One with everything') to get the quintessential favourite with mustard, tomato sauce (ketchup), remoulade and crunchy onions.

Ban Thai
ASIAN €€

(Map p224; www.banthai.name; Laugavegur 130; mains Ikr1690-1890; ⊙6-10pm) When it comes to Thai food, Iceland has a surprisingly decent selection of places to get your *pad thai* on. Though it's not the most centrally located, Ban Thai is by far the local favourite –

it's located just beyond the Hlemmur bus terminal.

Café Loki
ICELANDIC €€

(Map p228; Lokastígur 28; mains Ikr450-2590; ⊙10am-6pm Mon-Fri, noon-6pm Sun) Ignore the garish signage slapped across the exterior of this cafe located close to Hallgrímskirkja, and you'll discover it has a tasteful interior. Café Loki serves up very traditional dishes, from light snacks such as eggs and herring on home-made rye bread to Icelandic platters of sheep's-head jelly and sharkmeat.

Café Haiti
CAFE €

(Map p228; Geirsgata 7b; ⊙8.30am-6pm Mon-Thu, to 7.30pm Fri, 10am-6pm Sat) If you're a coffee fan, this tiny cafe in the Old Harbour is the place for you. Owner Elda buys her beans from her home country of Haiti, and roasts and grinds them on-site, producing what regulars swear are the best cups of coffee in the country.

Svarta Kaffið
CAFE €€

(Map p228; Laugavegur 54; mains Ikr900-1750; ⊙11am-1am Sun-Thu, to 3am Fri & Sat) Order the thick home-made soup (one meat and one veg option daily) at this quirky cave-like cafe – it's served piping hot in fantastic bread bowls.

Hornið
ITALIAN €€

(Map p228; www.hornid.is; Hafnarstræti 15; mains Ikr1500-4000; ⊙11.30am-11pm) There's an easy-going air at this bright art deco cafe-restaurant, with its warm terracotta tiles, weeping-fig plants and decently spaced tables. Pizzas are freshly made before your eyes, the prettily presented pasta meals will set you up for the day, and you can sample traditional Icelandic fish dishes.

🍷 Drinking

Reykjavík is renowned for its Friday- and Saturday-night *djammið,* when industrious Icelanders abandon work and party with passion (midweek drinking is not part of Icelandic culture). Beer is expensive. Most people visit a government-owned Vínbúð (the only shops licensed to sell alcohol), tipple at home, then hit the town from midnight to 5am. There's a central **Vínbúð** (Map p228; www.vinbudin.is; Austurstræti 10; ⊙11am-6pm Mon-Thu & Sat, to 7pm Fri).

Sometimes it's hard to distinguish between cafes, bars and entertainment venues in Reykjavík, because when night time rolls around (be it light or dark out) many of the city's coffee shops turn the lights down, the volume up, and swap cappuccinos for cocktails. Some even turn into full-blown nightclubs in the wee hours of the evening. Peruse the Eating section for some of these cafe-to-bar transformers.

Most of the action is concentrated on Laugavegur and Austurstræti. You'll pay around Ikr700 to Ikr800 per pint of beer, and some venues have cover charges (about Ikr1000) after midnight. Things change fast – check *The Reykjavik Grapevine* for the latest listings. You should dress up in Reykjavík, although there are pub-style places with a more relaxed dress code. The minimum drinking age is 20.

TOP CHOICE Kaffibarinn
BAR

(Map p228; www.kaffibarinn.is; Bergstaðastræti 1) This old house, with the London Underground symbol over the door, contains one of Reykjavík's coolest bars; it even had a starring role in the cult movie *101 Reykjavík* (2000). At weekends you'll feel like you need a famous face or a battering ram to get in.

TOP CHOICE KEX Bar
BAR

(Map p228; www.kexhostel.is; Skúlagata 28) This might be the only hostel bar in the world where locals actually hang out. And we completely understand why – the vibe is 1920 Vegas, with saloon doors, an old-school barber station, scuffed floors, and the ambient sound of snarky chatter and slot clinks. The food, however, is worth a miss.

Micro Bar
BAR

(Map p228; Austurstræti 6) Boutique brews are the name of the game at this low-key spot near Austurvöllur. Bottles of beer represent a slew of brands and countries, but more importantly you'll discover a handful of local draughts from the island's best microbreweries. Swing by during happy hour (5pm) for Ikr500 tipples.

Bakkus
BAR

(Map p228; Laugavegur 22) The double-decker dive bar fulfils all of your *djammið* needs with plenty of room to dance and a bar for swigging swill. Expect all-night romp fests on weekends.

Boston
BAR

(Map p228; Laugavegur 28b) Boston is cool, arty – and easily missable. It's accessed through a doorway on Laugavegur that leads you upstairs to its laid-back lounge, decorated in cool black wallpaper grown over with silver leaves. Expect the occasional bout of live music; you'll also find a DJ spinning beats.

Hemmi & Valdi
CAFE

(Nýlenduvöruverslun Hemma og Valda; Map p228; Laugavegur 21) At night, this relaxed cafe transmutes into a great little bar selling some of the cheapest booze in Reykjavík.

Dillon
PUB

(Map p228; 578 2424; Laugavegur 30) Beer, beards and the odd flying bottle...atmospheric Dillon is a RRRRROCK pub, drawing lively crowds. There are frequent concerts on its tiny corner stage, a great beer garden and an unusual DJ, the white-haired white-wine-and-rum-swilling 'rokkmamman' Andrea Jons.

Gay 46
GAY

(Map p228; Hverfisgata 46) Reykjavík's gay scene can feel twice as changeable as the rest of the city's nightlife culture; at the time of research this was the venue of choice for boys who want to meet boys.

Lebowski Bar
BAR

(Map p228; Laugavegur 20a) Named after the eponymous 'Dude' of moviedom, the Lebowski Bar is smack dab in the middle of the action with tons of Americana smothering the walls, and a long list of white Russians – a favourite from the film.

☆ Entertainment

Cinemas

Films are shown in their original language with Icelandic subtitles. The newspaper *Morgunblaðið* lists cinema programs, or click on the 'Bíó' tab at www.kvikmyndir.is.

Reykjavík has several multiplexes: the closest to the city centre are **Sambíóin** (Map p224; 575 8900; www.sambio.is; Kringlunni 4-6) in Kringlan shopping centre and **Laugarásbíó** (Laugarás; Map p224; www.laugarasbio.is) near Reykjavík Campsite.

Theatre

National Theatre
THEATRE

(Map p228; 551 1200; www.leikhusid.is; Hverfisgata 19; ☉theatre closed Jul & Aug) The National Theatre has three separate stages and puts on around 12 plays, musicals and operas per year, from modern Icelandic works to Shakespeare.

Reykjavík City Theatre THEATRE

(Map p224; 568 8000; www.borgarleikhus.is; Kringlan, Listabraut 3; closed Jul & Aug) Stages at least six plays and musicals per year. The **Icelandic Dance Company** (Map p224; www.id.is) is in residence there.

Live Music

The Reykjavík live-music scene is chaotic, ever-changing and strangely organic, with new venues mushrooming up over the stumps of the old. There are frequent live performances at the various bars and cafes listed in this chapter. For gig listings, see the excellent English-language newspaper *The Reykjavik Grapevine,* available free from cafes, hostels and tourist offices. Also look for flyers or ask the staff in the record shop **12 Tónar**. Tickets for larger live-music gigs are available at www.midi.is/concerts.

One stalwart is the **Iceland Symphony Orchestra** (Map p224; 545 2500; www.sinfonia.is; Háskólabíó, Hagatorg), now based in the flashy new Harpa (p222) concert hall and conference centre. There are around 60 classical performances per season, normally on Thursday at 7.30pm.

Volcano Shows

There are several spots around town where you can watch brilliantly captured footage of the island's biggest eruptions. Try **Volcano Show** (Red Rock Cinema; Map p228; 845 9548; Hellusund 6a; admission Ikr1500), **Cinema No2** (Map p228; 899 7953; www.lifsmynd.is/cinemano2; Tryggvagötu 10; admission Ikr1000-1500) and **Volcano House** (Map p228; 555 1900; www.volcanohouse.is; Tryggvagata 11; admission Ikr2000). Shows at all theatres run throughout the day every day in both English and German.

🔒 Shopping

Shopping in Iceland's capital is a great way to access the city's culture of design that acts as a wonderful counterpoint to the surrounding nature.

TOP CHOICE Kraum SOUVENIRS

(Map p228; www.kraum.is; Aðalstræti 10) The brainchild of a band of local artists; expect a carefully curated assortment of unique designer wares, all on display in Reykjavík's oldest house.

TOP CHOICE 66° North CLOTHING

(Map p228; 535 6680; www.66north.is; Bankastræti 5) This outdoor-clothing company began by making all-weather wear for Arctic fishers.

Eymundsson BOOKS

(Map p228; www.eymundsson.is; Austurstræti 18; 9am-10pm Mon-Fri, 10am-10pm Sat & Sun) Superb choice of English-language books, newspapers, magazines and maps. There's also a second **branch** (Map p228; Skólavörðustígur 11) in town.

Leynibuðin CLOTHING

(Map p228; www.leynibudin.is; Laugavegur 21) A consortium of young designers, Leynibuðin is a veritable mini-market of locally crafted apparel.

Netagerðin SOUVENIRS

(Map p228; www.netagerdin.is; Nýlendugata 12) Once a warehouse that stored and produced fishing nets, this unique space near the harbour is now home to three inspired design studios and a local music label.

Geysir SOUVENIRS

(Map p228; www.geysir.net; Skólavörðustígur 16) An elegant selection of Icelandic essentials: sweaters, postcards, figurines etc.

Handknitting Association of Iceland CLOTHING

(Map p228; www.handknit.is; Skólavörðustígur 19) Traditional handmade hats, socks and sweaters are sold at this knitting collective.

12 Tónar MUSIC

(Map p228; www.12tonar.is; Skolavörðustígur 15) In the three-floor shop you can listen to CDs, drink coffee and maybe catch a live performance on Friday afternoons.

Kringlan SHOPPING CENTRE

(Map p224; www.kringlan.is; Kringlan) Reykjavík's biggest shopping centre, 1km from town, has 150 shops. Take buses S1-4, S6, 13 or 14.

ℹ️ Information

Emergency

Dial 112.

Landspítali University Hospital (543 2000; Fossvogur) 24-hour casualty department.

Internet Access

Libraries have the cheapest internet access (Ikr250 per hour).

Aðalbókasafn (www.borgarbokasafn.is; Tryggvagata 15; 10am-7pm Mon-Thu, 11am-7pm Fri, 1-5pm Sat & Sun) Excellent main library in the heart of Reykjavík.

Kringlusafn (580 6200; www.borgarbokasafn.is; cnr Borgarleikhús & Listabraut; 10am-6.30pm Mon-Thu, 11am-6.30pm Fri, 1-5pm Sat, also 1-5pm Sun Sep-Apr) Branch by the Kringlan shopping centre.

Money

Truthfully, you don't need to take money out, as almost every place accepts credit cards (except the municipal buses). Changing currencies at hotels or private bureaus can be obscenely high.

Íslandsbanki (☏440 4000; www.islandsbanki. is; Lækjargata 12)

Kaupþing (☏444 7000; www.kaupthing.com; Austurstræti 5)

Landsbanki Íslands (☏410 4000; www.landsbanki.is; Austurstræti 11)

Post

Main post office (Pósthússtræti 5; ☺9am-6pm Mon-Fri)

Telephone

Public phones are elusive in mobile-crazy Reykjavík: try the main tourist office and the Kringlan shopping centre.

Tourist Information

Reykjavík has a very good main tourist information centre, and an increasing number of private centres run by travel agencies that specialise in booking visitors on trips.

The excellent English-language newspaper *The Reykjavik Grapevine*, widely distributed, has the lowdown on what's new in town.

BSÍ Bus Terminal Tourist Desk (Vatnsmýrarvegur 10)

Main tourist office (Upplýsingamiðstöð Ferðamanna; ☏590 1550; www.visitreykjavik. is; Aðalstræti 2; ☺8.30am-7pm Jun–mid-Sep, 9am-6pm Mon-Fri, to 4pm Sat, to 2pm Sun mid-Sep–May)

ℹ Getting There & Away

Air

The city airport, Innanlandsflug, serves all domestic destinations, the Faroe Islands and Greenland. Internal flight operator **Air Iceland** (☏570 3030; www.airiceland.is; Flugfélag Íslands) has a desk at the airport, but it's cheaper to book tickets over the internet.

International flights operate through **Keflavík Airport** (www.kefairport.com), 48km west of Reykjavík.

Bus

There are scheduled summer services to other parts of the country from Reykjavík's **BSÍ bus terminal** (☏562 1011; www.bsi.is; Vatnsmýrarvegur 10); winter services are reduced or non-existent.

ℹ Getting Around

To/From the Airport

It's a 1km walk into town from the city airport terminal (domestic flights), or there's a taxi rank. Bus 15 runs from here to Hlemmur bus station.

From Keflavík International Airport it's easy: the **Flybus** (☏580 5400; www.re.is) meets all international flights; it is not worth taking a taxi as they are very expensive and take roughly the same amount of time as the bus. One-way bus tickets cost Ikr1950, or Ikr2500 if you want to be dropped off at your hotel. Buy tickets from the booth just inside the airport doors. The journey to Reykjavík takes around 50 minutes.

Bus

Reykjavík's superb **city bus system** (www.straeto.is/english) uses two central terminals: Hlemmur and Lækjartorg. Buses only stop at designated bus stops, marked with the letter 'S'.

BUS SERVICES FROM REYKJAVÍK

Note that bus service in winter runs on a reduced schedule.

DESTINATION	PRICE	DURATION	FREQUENCY	YEAR-ROUND
Akureyri	Ikr11,800	6hr	daily	Yes
Blue Lagoon	Ikr1400	45min	several daily	Yes
Geysir/Gullfoss	Ikr3800-4400	2½hr	daily	Jun–Aug
Höfn	Ikr13,700	8½hr	daily	Yes
Keflavík	Ikr1400	40min	several daily	Yes
Kirkjubæjarklaustur	Ikr8100	5hr	daily	Yes
Landmannalaugar	Ikr7700	5½hr	daily	mid-Jun–Aug
Skaftafell	Ikr10,100	6½hr	daily	Yes
Þórsmörk	Ikr6200	3½hr	two daily	Jun–mid-Sep

ℹ REYKJAVÍK WELCOME CARD

The **Reykjavík Welcome Card** (24/48/72hr Ikr2400/3300/4000) is available at various outlets including the tourist office. The card gives you free travel on the city's buses and on the ferry to Viðey, as well as free admission to Reykjavík's municipal swimming pools and to most of the main galleries and museums. It's worth it if you make use of the buses and swimming pools but might not be good value if you're just visiting a few museums and galleries.

Fare Adult Ikr350 (exact fare only)

Day buses Run 7am to 11pm or midnight (from 10am Sunday)

Night buses Run until 2am Friday and Saturday

Reykjavík Welcome Card Includes a bus pass

Transfer tickets (*Skiptimiði*) Available from driver if you need two buses to reach your destination

Taxi

Taxi prices are high; flag fall starts at around Ikr500. There are usually taxis outside the bus stations, domestic airport, and pubs and bars (expect queues) on weekend nights. Alternatively, call **BSR** (☑561 0000) or **Hreyfill-Bæjarleiðir** (☑588 5522). Tipping is not expected.

AROUND REYKJAVÍK

Blue Lagoon

As the Eiffel Tower is to Paris, as Disney World is to Florida, so the **Blue Lagoon** (Bláa Lónið, ☑420 8800; www.bluelagoon.com; admission from €33; ⊙9am-9pm Jun-Aug, 10am-8pm Sep-May) is to Iceland...with all the positive and negative connotations that implies. Those who say it's too expensive, too clinical, too crowded are kind of right, but ignore them anyway. The Blue Lagoon is a must see, and you'll be missing something special if you don't go.

Set in a vast black lava field, the milky-blue spa is fed by water (a perfect 38°C, and at Blue Flag standards) from the futuristic Svartsengi geothermal plant, which provides an off-the-planet scene-setter for your swim. Add in steaming silver vents and people coated in silica mud, and you're in another world.

Be careful on the slippery bridges and bring plenty of conditioner for your hair. There's a snack bar, top gourmet restaurant and souvenir shop on site, plus roaming masseurs.

The lagoon is 50km southwest of Reykjavík, but there are plenty of bus services that run there year-round. You'll need to book in advance. Go to www.bluelagoon.com and click on the How to Get There link for detailed information. The best and cheapest option is **Reykjavík Excursions** (☑580 5400; www.re.is), which runs on the hour from 9pm to 6pm for Ikr8000 including lagoon admission.

The Golden Circle

Gulp down three of Iceland's most famous natural wonders – Gullfoss, Geysir and Þingvellir – in one day-long circular tour.

⊙ Sights

Gullfoss (Golden Falls) is a spectacular rainbow-tinged double cascade, falling 32m before thundering down a narrow ravine.

All spouting hot springs are named after **Geysir**, 10km away. Tourists clogged the **Great Geysir** in the 1950s with rocks and rubbish, thrown in an attempt to set it off. Since earthquakes in 2000, it has begun erupting again, though infrequently. Luckily for visitors, the world's most reliable geyser, **Strokkur**, is right next door. You rarely have to wait more than five to ten minutes for the water to swirl up an impressive 15m to 30m plume before vanishing down what looks like an enormous plughole.

Þingvellir National Park is Iceland's most important historical site: the Vikings established the world's first democratic parliament, the Alþing, here in AD 930. It also has a superb natural setting, on the edge of an immense rift caused by the separating North American and Eurasian tectonic plates. Þingvellir was (finally!) made a Unesco World Heritage Site in 2004. Above the park, on top of the rift, is an interesting **multimedia centre** (admission free; ⊙9am-5pm) exploring the area's nature and history.

Interesting features, concentrated in a small area of the park, include **Lögberg** (marked by a flagpole), the podium for the Alþing; the remains of **búðir** (booths) where Vikings attending Alþing camped; a **church** and **farm**, now the prime minister's summer house; **Drekkingarhylur**, where adulterous

WORTH A TRIP

GLJÚFRASTEINN LAXNESS MUSEUM

On the way to Þingvellir via Rte 36, literature fans should drop in on the **Gljúfrasteinn Laxness Museum** (☑586 8066; www.gljufrasteinn.is; Mosfellsbær; adult/under 16yrs Ikr800/free; ◷9am-5pm Jun-Aug, 10am-5pm Tue-Sun Sep-May), former home of Nobel Prize-winning author Halldór Laxness (1902–98). Highlights include the study where Laxness wrote his defining works and the author's beloved Jaguar parked outside in the car park (making three-point turns in the car park a nerve-wracking experience!).

From June to August, Sunday music recitals (Ikr1000; 4pm) provide an additional reason to drop by. You'll need your own transport to get here.

women were drowned; **Þingvallavatn**, Iceland's largest lake; and several fissures, including **Peningagjá** (wishing spring), **Flosagjá** (named after a slave who jumped his way to freedom) and **Nikulásargjá** (after a drunken sheriff discovered dead in the water).

🛏 Sleeping & Eating

There is a **cafe** (◷approx 9am-5pm winter, to 8pm summer) at each of the three sites.

Hótel Geysir   HOTEL, CAMP **€€**
(☑480 6800; www.geysircenter.is; Geysir; s/d from Ikr17,500/21,900, campsite per person Ikr1200; ◷Feb-Dec, campsite May-Sep; @) A campus of alpine-style cabins across the street from Strokkur; this busy spot also has a popular restaurant, a geothermal pool and two hot-pots. It also maintains a **camping ground**, and campers can use the pool for Ikr500.

Hótel Gullfoss   HOTEL **€€€**
(☑486 8979; www.hotelgullfoss.is; s/d incl breakfast Ikr22,000/27,500) A few kilometres before the waterfall, tucked into a crevice in the hills, this simple bungalow hotel has modest en suite rooms, two hot-pots and a good restaurant.

Þingvellir Camping Grounds   CAMPGROUND **€**
(☑482 2660; campsites per adult Ikr1000; ◷May–mid-Sep) The Park Service Centre oversees

five camping grounds at Þingvellir. The best are those around Leirar (near the centre).

ℹ Information

Just by the turnoff to Þingvellir, the **Service Centre** (Þjónustumiðstöð; ☑482 2660; www.thingvellir.is; ◷9am-8pm May-Sep) has a cafe (open from 8.30am to 10pm from February and mid-November) and a tourist information desk with helpful details about the national park.

ℹ Getting There & Away

From mid-June to August the daily **Reykjavík Excursions** (☑580 5400; www.re.is) bus service 6/6A runs from Reykjavík to Þingvellir, stopping for 45 minutes at the Park Service Centre before continuing to Geysir, Gullfoss and back to Reykjavík.

From June to August, scheduled **Trex** (☑551 1166; www.bogf.is) bus 2/2a runs from the BSÍ bus station in Reykjavík to Geysir and Gullfoss (at 8.30am, plus also at 11am in July and August) and back, a circuit of around 8½ hours.

Hafnarfjörður

POP 26,640

The 'Town in the Lava' rests on a 7000-year-old flow and hides a parallel elfin universe, according to locals. Its old tin-clad houses and lava caves are worth a visit on a sunny summer's day.

◉ Sights & Activities

FREE **Hafnarfjörður Museum**   MUSEUM
(☑585 5780) Hafnarfjörður Museum is spread across several historic buildings in different locations across the town. **Pakkhúsið** (Vesturgata 8; ◷11am-5pm daily Jun-Aug, Sat & Sun Sep-May) is the main section, with interesting displays on the town's history. **Sívertsen Hús** (Vesturgata 6; ◷11am-5pm Jun-Aug) is an upper-class 19th-century house. At the other end of the social scale is **Siggubær** (Sigga's House; Kirkjuvegur 10; ◷11am-5pm Sat & Sun Jun-Aug), a restored fisherman's hut.

FREE **Hafnarborg**   ART GALLERY
(☑585 5790; www.hafnarborg.is; Strandgata 34; ◷11am-5pm Wed-Mon, to 9pm Thu) Well worth a look, this upbeat modern-art gallery has two floors of regularly changing exhibitions and occasional musical concerts.

✪ Festivals & Events

In mid-June, the peace is shattered as Vikings invade the town for the four-day **Viking Festival**, with staged fights and traditional craft demonstrations.

❶ Getting There & Away

Hafnarfjörður is a short, easy bus trip from Reykjavík: take bus S1 (Ikr280, 30 minutes, every 10 minutes) from Hlemmur or Lækjartorg bus stations.

Krýsuvík (Reykjanesfólkvangur)

For a taste of Iceland's empty countryside, you could visit this 300-sq-km wilderness reserve, a mere 40km from Reykjavík. Its three showpieces are **Kleifarvatn**, a deep grey lake with submerged hot springs and black-sand beaches; the spitting, bubbling geothermal zone at **Seltún**; and the southwest's largest bird cliffs, the epic **Krýsuvíkurberg**.

The whole area is crossed by dozens of **walking trails**, which mostly follow old paths between abandoned farms. They're detailed in the good pamphlet map *Walking & Hiking in Krýsuvík* (in English), available from the tourist office at Hafnarfjörður. There are parking places at the trailheads of the popular walks, including the loop around Kleifarvatn, and the tracks along the craggy Sveifluháls and Núpshlíðarháls ridges.

WORTH A TRIP

STOKKSEYRI

If you like screaming, it might be worth detouring to tiny Stokkseyri, a fishing village 60km southeast of Reykjavík. Creep round 24 dark, dry ice-filled rooms at the **Draugasetrið** (Ghost Centre; www.draugasetrid.is; Hafnargata 9; adult/child Ikr1500/1000; ⊙12.30-6pm Jun-Aug) while a 50-minute iPod-guide (in a multitude of languages) tells blood-curdling Icelandic ghost stories. Be warned, it's not for the faint-hearted. Suitable for over-12s.

There's fine dining to be had next door at **Við Fjöruborðið** (www.fjorubordid.is; Eyrarbraut 3a; mains Ikr2050-4850; ⊙noon-9pm Jun-mid-Sep, 5-9pm Mon-Fri, noon-9pm Sat-Sun mid-Sep–May), a seashore restaurant renowned for its lobster dishes.

THE WEST

Upper Borgarfjörður

A must for saga fans, the lakes and lava flows of this region feature in *Egil's Saga,* and its author, Snorri Sturluson, lived here. Upper Borgarfjörður is 90km north of Reykjavík.

REYKHOLT
POP 40

You'd never guess it, but tiny **Reykholt** (www.reykholt.is), 22km east of the Ring Rd, was once a political and religious power centre. During the bloodthirsty Sturlung Age (1230–62), it was the home of Snorri Sturluson, Iceland's greatest saga writer, historian and social climber. Close to the cellar where he was eventually murdered you can see his circular medieval hot tub, Snorri's Pool (Snorralaug). The medieval study centre **Snorrastofa** (☑433 8000; www.snorrastofa.is; admission Ikr1000; ⊙10am-6pm May-Aug, to 5pm Mon-Fri Sep-Apr) explores Snorri's fascinating life.

Sleeping and eating options are limited, but **Fosshótel Reykholt** (☑562 4000, 435 1260; www.fosshotel.is; s/d incl breakfast Ikr24,900/26,500; P@) has large rooms, hot tubs and a restaurant.

Reykholt is 40km northeast of Borgarnes along Rte 518. Buses from Reykjavík leave at 5pm on Friday and Sunday. In the opposite direction, the bus leaves Reykholt at 7.10pm.

AROUND REYKHOLT
Deildartunguhver, 4km west of Reykholt, is Europe's most powerful, prolific and pongy hot spring, spouting out at 180L per second. About 18km northeast of Reykholt is **Hraunfossar**, a 1km-long stretch of 'magic waterfalls' mysteriously emerging from beneath a lava flow. Just upstream is **Barnafoss**, where the Hvítá river thunders through a narrow gorge. According to legend, two children drowned here when a natural bridge collapsed.

Snæfellsnes

Lush fjords, haunting volcanic peaks, dramatic sea cliffs, sweeping golden beaches and crooked crunchy lava flows make up the diverse and fascinating landscape of the 100km-long Snæfellsnes Peninsula. The area is crowned by the glistening ice cap Snæfellsjökull, immortalised in Jules Verne's

WORTH A TRIP

SETTLEMENT CENTRE, BORGARNES

You could easily zip straight through the elongated settlement of Borgarnes without realising you were missing something special. The **Settlement Centre** (Landnáms-setur Íslands; ☑437 1600; www.landnam.is; Brákarbraut 13-15; 1 exhibition adult/child Ikr1900/1500, 2 exhibitions Ikr2500/1900; ☺10am-9pm Jun-Sep, 11am-5pm Oct-May) comprises two excellent multimedia exhibitions: one covers the settlement of Iceland, and the other recounts the most dramatic parts of *Egil's Saga*, bringing the violent Viking to life with unusual sculptures, lighting and sound effects.

The centre's restaurant, **Búðarklettur** (☑437 1600; mains Ikr2200-4500; ☺10am-9pm Jun-Sep, 11am-5pm Oct-May), housed in the town's oldest building, is a stylish choice for morning coffee or a more substantial meal, with plenty of traditional Icelandic eats and a good vegie selection.

fantasy tale *Journey to the Centre of the Earth* (1864). Good roads and regular buses mean that it's an easy trip from Reykjavík and ideal for a short break, offering a cross-section of the best Iceland has to offer in a very compact region.

STYKKISHÓLMUR
POP 1090

The charming town of Stykkishólmur, the largest on the Snæfellsnes Peninsula, is built up around a natural harbour protected by a dramatic basalt island. It's a picturesque place with a laid-back attitude and a sprinkling of brightly coloured buildings from the late 19th century. With a comparatively good choice of accommodation and restaurants, and convenient transport links, quaint Stykkishólmur makes an excellent base for exploring the region.

◎ Sights & Activities

TOP
CHOICE **Breiðafjörður**   BAY

Stykkishólmur's jagged peninsula pushes north into stunning Breiðafjörður, a gaping waterway (breiðafjörður means 'broad fjord') separating the torpedo-shaped Snæfellsnes from the looming cliffs of the distant Westfjords. According to local legend,

there are only two things in the world that cannot be counted: the stars in the night sky and the craggy islets in the bay. Despite the numerical setback, those who visit beautiful Breiðafjörður can count on epic vistas – idyllic tapestries of greens and blues – and its menagerie of wild birds (puffins, white-tailed sea eagles, guillemots etc). Try mounting the basalt island of **Súgandisey**, which features a scenic lighthouse and offers grand views across Breiðafjörður.

Eldfjallasafn   MUSEUM

(Volcano Museum; ☑433 8154; www.eldfjallasafn. is; Aðalgata 6; admission Ikr800; ☺11am-5pm May-Sep) Get the back story on the neighbouring lava flows at this brainchild of vulcanologist Haraldur Sigurdsson in the old cinema. It features art and artefacts relating to the study of eruptions and their devastating effects – including 'magma bombs' from the Eyjafjallajökull eruption in 2010.

Norska Húsið   MUSEUM

(Norwegian House; ☑433 8114; www.norskahusid. is; Hafnargata 5; admission Ikr800; ☺noon-5pm Jun-Aug) The town's oldest building, it's one of the places William Morris stayed on his 1871 tour of Iceland. Today it contains a sweet little museum and art gallery.

☞ Tours

Sæferðir   BOAT TOUR

(Seatours; ☑438 2254; www.seatours.is; Smiðjustígur 3; ☺8am-8pm mid-May–mid-Sep, 9am-5pm mid-Sep–mid-May) Seatours runs a variety of boat tours, its main trip being the 'Unique Tour' – a 2¼-hour boat ride (adult/child Ikr6690/free), which takes in postcard-worthy views of the bay and its myriad islands.

🛏 Sleeping

TOP
CHOICE **Hótel Egilsen**   BOUTIQUE HOTEL €€€

(☑554 7700; www.egilsen.is; Aðalgata 2; s/d Ikr19,000/25,000; @) Bold statement alert: this might just be our favourite little inn in all of Iceland, set inside a lovingly restored timber house that creaks in the most charming way when the fjord winds come howling off the bay. Follow the yellow stairwell up to find cosy (tiny!) rooms outfitted in adorable accoutrements; complimentary iPads and a locally sourced breakfast sweeten the already-sweet deal.

Bænir og Brauð   B&B €€

(☑820 5408; www.baenirogbraud.is; Laufásvegur 1; d Ikr14,200-16,200; @) A fine example of

Stykkishólmur's quality B&B scene, this homely spot sits along the fjord waters with lovely views of the modernist church.

Sjónarhóll Hostel
HOSTEL €

(☑438 1417; Höfðagata 1; sleeping bag in dm Ikr2500, d Ikr7000; ⊙May-Oct; ℗) The dorm rooms in this charming (if rickety) hostel have fantastic views of the harbour. You can also catch fish on its Breiðafjörður boat tours, then barbecue them on the patio.

Camping Ground
CAMPGROUND €

(☑438 1075; mostri@stykk.is; Aðalgötu 27; campsites per person Ikr1000; ⊙mid-May–Aug) A huge but rather exposed spot on the way into town. Facilities include a laundry.

✗ Eating

TOP CHOICE Narfeyrarstofa
ICELANDIC €€€

(☑438 1119; www.narfeyrarstofa.is; Aðalgata 3; mains Ikr1990-4250; ⊙11.30am-10pm Apr–mid-Oct, 6pm-10pm Sat & Sun mid-Oct–Mar) If we handed out prizes for the best fish soup and the top lamb stew, this charming restaurant would win both. Run by an award-winning chef (famous in Denmark for his superlative desserts – the caramel ice cream could induce swoons), Narfeyrarstofa is the Snæfellsnes' darling dining destination and the undoubted favourite of visiting tour groups. Book a table on the 2nd floor and dine under gentle eaves and the romantic lighting of antique lamps.

Sjávarpakkhúsið
ICELANDIC €€

(Hafnargata 2; mains Ikr1890-2950; ⊙noon-10pm Jun-Aug, reduced hr Sep-May) This old fishing packing house has been transformed into a harbourside restaurant with appealing outdoor seating in warmer weather. The speciality here is the blue shell mussels straight from the bay out back.

❶ Information

The town's **tourist information centre** (www.west.is; ⊙8am-10pm Jun-Aug) changes location every summer depending on municipal funding. At the time of research it was located at the golf course, though in years past it has also been found at the swimming pool. Wherever it may be located during your visit, expect a plethora of brochures and assistance with guesthouse accommodation bookings in the area.

❶ Getting There & Away

From June to August, at least one bus plies daily between Reykjavík and Stykkishólmur (Ikr5500, 2½ hours), with a change to a connecting bus in

Vatnaleið. No Wednesday or Saturday service in winter.

The ferry **Baldur** (☑438 1450; www.seatours.is) operates between Stykkishólmur and Brjánslækur (one way per car/passenger Ikr4950/4950, three hours). Advance booking strongly advised.

DEPART	EARLY JUN-LATE AUG	LATE AUG-EARLY JUN
Stykkishólmur	9am & 3.15pm	3pm Sun-Fri
Brjánslækur	12.15pm & 7pm	6pm Sun-Fri

SNÆFELLSJÖKULL NATIONAL PARK & AROUND

The volcano Snæfell, at the tip of the peninsula, is the heart of Snæfellsjökull National Park. Its dramatic glacial summit can be reached when conditions are right: the easiest approach is from the southern end of Rte F570, linking up with one of the **snowmobile tours** run by **Snjófell** (☑435 6783; www.snjofell.is; Arnarstapi; snowcat/snowmobile tour Ikr8500/21,900; ⊙mid-Apr–early Sep). Rte F570's northern approach from Ólafsvík is 4WD-only. Park rangers at the visitor centre in Hellnar can provide on-the-spot information, including weather forecasts.

ÓLAFSVÍK
POP 1010

As a base, Stykkishólmur has the best facilities, but Ólafsvík is much closer to the park. It has a sheltered **camping ground** (☑433 9930; campsites per adult/tent Ikr500/500; ⊙Jun-Aug) 1km east of the village. Central **Hringhótel Ólafsvík** (☑436 1650; www.hotelolafsvik.is; Ólafsbraut 40; d Ikr 21,600; ⊙mid-May–mid-Sep; @) is rather spartan. If you don't mind sharing a bathroom, prices fall by almost 50%.

Eating options in Ólafsvík are limited. The hotel has a rather overpriced restaurant; otherwise there's a fast-food joint and a bakery.

HELLNAR

The spirit of the glacier, Bárður, once lived at tiny Hellnar, 6km outside the main park boundary on the south coast. He couldn't have chosen a more idyllic spot. The park's visitor centre, **Gestastofa** (☑436 6888; admission free; ⊙10am-5pm 20 May-10 Sep) and a small cafe overlook a bay in a deep, narrow cleft between hills, echoing with the shrieks of seabirds. **Hótel Hellnar** (☑435 6820; www.hellnar.is; s/d incl breakfast from €130/140; ⊙May-Sep; ℗) is the area's choice sleeping option. Recently, the comfortable inn has shifted away from its yogic reputation, proffering comfortable sun-filled rooms at reasonable prices instead. At the time of research, a new wing was under construction – it all looked very promising. It's quite common to see whales from the window.

THE WESTFJORDS

The Westfjords is where Iceland's dramatic landscapes come to a riveting climax. Jagged cliffs and broad sweeping beaches flank the south, while dirt roads snake along the tortuous coastline dotted with tiny fishing villages clinging doggedly to a traditional way of life. Further on, stone towers rise from the deep, hoisting tundra-ridden buffs up towards the northern elements. The Hornstrandir hiking reserve crowns the quiet region; it is, undoubtedly, the island's most scenic terrain, with countless fjords and cairn-marked walking paths.

Buses to, from and around the Westfjords are patchy and usually only possible in high season. Stjörnubílar (p282) runs local buses in this region.

Ísafjörður

POP 2540

You feel as though you've reached the end of the earth when you get to Ísafjörður, the Westfjord's largest settlement. Surrounded by vertiginous mountains and deep fjord waters, the town is remote and peaceful, apart from the croaking of ravens.

Sights

Westfjords Heritage Museum   MUSEUM
(www.nedsti.is; Neðstíkaupstaður; adult/child Ikr550/free; ☺10am-5pm Mon-Fri, 1-5pm Sat & Sun Jun, 10am-5pm daily Jul & Aug) The knowledgeable staff at the Westfjords Heritage Museum, based in a cluster of atmospheric 18th-century wooden warehouses, bring the excellent nautical, whaling and accordion exhibits to life.

Tours

Ísafjörður is base for a range of unusual tours available in the surrounding fjords and valleys. The tourist office has detailed walking maps.

Borea   BOAT TOUR
(✆456 3322; www.borea.is; Aðalstræti 22b) Borea is an adventure outfitter par excellence, offering a variety of mind-blowing experiences that could have you coming back to the Westfjords for years. High-quality tours often involve multiday trips aboard the yacht *Aurora*. These days Borea is really upping the ante on adventures in Hornstrandir; besides running regular ferry services from Bolungarvík, it also offers a variety of trips like multiday kayaking trips, springtime skiing and guided day-long hiking.

West Tours   ADVENTURE TOUR
(Vesturferðir; ✆456 5111; www.vesturferdir.is) Housed in the same building as the tourist information centre, the popular and professional West Tours organises a mind-boggling array of trips in the area. There are tours of Vigur and kayaking excursions all year. You can visit the abandoned village at Hesteyri on a day trip, or organise an extended tour package to explore Hornstrandir over several days. Biking, birdwatching and cultural excursions are but a few of the other activities on offer.

Festivals & Events

Ísafjörður's usual tranquillity is crumpled up and hurled away in the week after Easter, when the town gears up for two hugely important celebrations: Aldrei Fór Ég Suður and Skíðavikan.

Aldrei Fór Ég Suður   MUSIC
(I Never Went South; www.aldrei.is) Two-day music festival in March/April, dreamed up by Ísafjörður-born singer-songwriter Mugison.

Skíðavikan   SKIING
(Skiing Week; www.skidavikan.is) Annual skiing festival in early April.

Mýrarbolti   SOCCER
(www.myrarbolti.com) On the August bank holiday comes the Mýrarbolti tournament, an indescribably filthy day of swamp soccer. Visitors can abandon their sanity too, and register to join a team.

Sleeping

TOP CHOICE Gamla Gistihúsið   GUESTHOUSE €€
(✆456 4146; www.gistihus.is; Mánagata 5; sleeping bag in dm Ikr4800, s/d Ikr13,800/18,200; @) This former hospital and aged-care home is a tonic, with sunlight dappling through the

windows and homely touches everywhere. The nine neat rooms (with plentiful shared bathrooms) all come with TV, plus there's a guest kitchen and free internet access. Breakfast is Ikr1700 for those in sleeping-bag accommodation.

Litla Guesthouse
GUESTHOUSE €€
(⌨474 1455; www.guesthouselitla.is; Sundstræti 43; s/d Ikr12,000/14,000) Wooden floors, crisp white linen, fluffy towels and TVs are available in the high-quality rooms of Litla, another cosy guesthouse with tasteful decor. Two rooms share each bathroom, and there's a guest kitchen.

Hótel Ísafjörður
HOTEL €€€
(⌨456 4111; www.hotelisafjordur.is; Silfurtorg 2; s/d from Ikr22,500/27,500; @) On the main square, the town's only hotel is right at the hub of things. Rooms are clean and business-like – it's worth paying extra for the larger deluxe versions, which come with fine views and bathtubs. Readers recommend the restaurant.

Hotel Edda
HOTEL €
(⌨444 4960; www.hoteledda.is; sleeping bag in dm from Ikr3000, s/d Ikr11,900/14,200; ☺mid-Jun–mid-Aug) This is a no-frills summer option in the secondary school. Sleeping-bag accommodation is in classrooms, or you can upgrade to a private room.

Camping Ground
CAMPGROUND €
(⌨444 4960; campsites per adult plus tent Ikr1000; ☺mid-Jun–mid-Aug) Centrally located behind the secondary school.

✗ Eating

Tjöruhisið
ICELANDIC €€
(Tar House; Hólgata 10; Ikr2000-5000; ☺Jun-Sep) The faux-rustic summer restaurant at the folk museum offers some of the best fish and seafood dishes in town, and at very reasonable prices! Go for the *plokkfiskur* – flaked fish stew, potatoes and onions served au gratin – or try the catch of the day fresh off the boat from the harbour up the street.

Bræðraborg
CAFE €
(www.borea.is; Aðalstræti; mains Ikr550-1190; ☺8am-10pm Mon-Fri, to 1am Sat & Sun Jun-Aug, reduced hr Sep–May) Fancying itself a traveller's cafe, Bræðraborg is a comfy spot to update your blog while munching on healthy snacks and chatting with other visitors who have gathered to earn their Hornstrandir stripes.

Thai Koon
THAI €€
(Neisti Centre, Hafnarstræti 9; mains Ikr1590-1790; ☺11.30am-9pm Mon-Sat, 5-9pm Sun) After a few weeks of limited choice for meals, this small Thai canteen seems decidedly exotic. Although there's no atmosphere here whatsoever, the food is reliable and served up in heaping portions.

❶ Information

Library (Eyrartúni; per hr Ikr200; ☺1-7pm Mon-Fri, to 4pm Sat) Internet access is available in the fine library, once the town's hospital.

Tourist office (www.isafjordur.is; Aðalstræti 7; ☺8am-6pm Mon-Fri, 8.30am-2pm Sat, 11am-2pm Sun Jun-Aug, reduced hr Sep–May) By the harbour in the Edinborgarhús, built in 1907. Has a single internet terminal that travellers can use for a free 10-minute session. Luggage storage is available for Ikr200 a day.

❶ Getting There & Away

Air

Air Iceland (⌨456 3000; www.airiceland.is) is based at the airport and flies to/from Reykjavík two or three times daily. Flights to Akureyri connect through Reykjavík.

Bus

There are two ways of travelling from Reykjavík to Ísafjörður by bus. One service, changing in Hólmavík, runs on Tuesday, Friday and Sunday (7 hours total). The price for this journey is Ikr13,400, but it makes better sense to buy a West Iceland & Westfjords bus passport (see p282 for details). The second service, via the Stykkishólmur–Brjánslækur ferry, runs on Monday, Wednesday and Saturday. A daily bus in summer leaves Reykjavík at 8am and arrives in Stykkishólmur at 10.35am. On the other side of the water, buses meet both ferry services to Brjánslækur on Monday, Wednesday and Saturday. See www.sterna.is for updated timetables.

Hornstrandir Peninsula

Craggy mountains, precarious sea cliffs and plunging waterfalls ring the wonderful uninhabited Hornstrandir Peninsula at the northern end of the Westfjords. This is one of Europe's last true wilderness areas, covering some of the most extreme and inhospitable parts of the country. It's a fantastic destination for hiking, with challenging terrain and excellent opportunities for spotting Arctic foxes, seals, whales and teeming bird life.

A handful of hardy farmers lived in Hornstrandir until the 1950s, but since 1975 the

580 sq km of tundra, fjord, glacier and alpine upland have been protected as a national monument and nature reserve.

There are no services available in Hornstrandir and hikers must be fully prepared to tackle all eventualities. The passes here are steep and you'll need to carry all your gear, so hiking can be slower than you might expect. In addition, most trails are unmarked, so it's essential to carry a good map and a GPS.

The best time to visit is in July. Outside the summer season (late June to mid-August) there are few people around and the weather is unpredictable. If travelling in the off season, it is essential to plan ahead and get local advice. Ask some of the local operators about current conditions before setting off. Guided trips can also be easily arranged.

Where to hike? Locals and tourists agree: the Royal Horn (or 'Hornsleið') is, hands down, your best option to take in all of what the reserve has to offer. Follow this four-to-five-day hike from Veiðileysufjörður to Hesteyri and you'll get a good picture of the region; the itinerary can also be easily modified if you run into bad weather. Download the PDF of the Westfjords chapter from Lonely Planet's *Iceland* guide for a detailed route description.

🛏 Sleeping

Wild-camping in Hornstrandir is free (make sure to take all of your rubbish with you). Staying on private grounds with facilities costs around Ikr1000. Expect to pay upwards of Ikr2000 for sleeping-bag space. There are three options for sleeping-bag accommodation in the main part of the Hornstrandir reserve: **Hesteyri** (☑456 1123), which has accommodation for 18 people in the old doctor's house, with coffee and pancakes available; **Hornbjargsviti** (☑566 6762; www.fi.is), attached to the lighthouse; and **Grunnavík** (☑852 4819; www.grunnavik.is), which has space for around 20 people – the owner heats a hot-pot by fire and stirs it like human soup.

❶ Getting There & Away

Getting to Hornstrandir requires a boat trip from Ísafjörður or Bolungarvík, from where there are regular ferry services from June to mid-August. Typically a one-way ride costs Ikr6000 to Ikr7500, depending on your destination.

Látrabjarg

The world's biggest bird breeding grounds are the towering, 14km-long Látrabjarg cliffs. Fulmars, kittiwakes and fearless puffins fight for nesting space at the westernmost point of the Westfjords. It's a truly impressive sight, but wrap up well; the wind is bitter.

For accommodation, try the beautifully located working farm **Breiðavík** (☑456 1575; www.breidavik.is; campsites per person Ikr1700, d with/without bathroom incl breakfast Ikr25,500/17,500; ⊙mid-May–mid-Sep), 12km from the cliffs and located near an incredible cream-coloured beach of the same name. The large guesthouse offers homey rooms with patchwork quilts and wobbly furniture. Sleeping-bag accommodation costs Ikr4750 per person. Camping's also an option.

On Monday, Wednesday and Saturday from June to August, buses from Ísafjörður route through Látrabjarg on their way to Brjánslækur, where you can pick up the *Baldur* ferry to Stykkishólmur. The buses stop at the cliffs for two hours, leaving you plenty of time to explore.

THE NORTH

Siglufjörður

POP 1360

Iceland's northernmost town enjoys a dramatic setting at the very tip of the Tröllaskagi Peninsula. In the past, herring fishing brought frenzied activity and untold riches; today the town's appeal is its peaceful isolation and thrumming community spirit. The recent opening of tunnels linking it with Olafsfjörður have seen a new spring in the town's step, and it won't be long until travellers start paying it more attention.

◉ Sights

Herring Era Museum — TOP CHOICE — MUSEUM
(Síldarminjasafnið; ☑467 1604; www.sild.is; Snorragata 15; adult/child Ikr1200/free; ⊙10am-6pm Jun-Aug, 1-5pm Mar-May & Sep-Nov, by appointment in winter) Lovingly created over 16 years, this award-winning museum does a stunning job of re-creating Siglufjörður's boom days between 1903 and 1968. Set in three buildings that were part of an old Norwegian herring station, the museum brings the work and lives of the town's inhabitants vividly to life.

✷ Festivals

Herring Adventure Festival   CULTURE
Siglufjörður's biggest shindig, this lively festival takes place on the August bank holiday and recreates the gold-rush atmosphere of the town's glory days.

Þjóðlagahátíðin á Siglufirði   MUSIC
(www.folkmusik.is) Folk-music fans will enjoy this festival, a delightfully relaxed five-day affair held in early July.

🛏 Sleeping & Eating

TOP CHOICE Herring Guesthouse   GUESTHOUSE €€
(☑868 4200; www.theherringhouse.com; Hávegur 5; s/d without bathroom Ikr11,000/15,000, apt Ikr40,000) Þorir is a charming, knowledgeable host (he's a former town mayor) at this comfy new four-room guesthouse, with guest kitchen. He also offers a two-bedroom apartment, plus a nearby five-bedroom house that sleeps nine (check it out on www.580.is).

Siglufjörður HI Hostel   HOSTEL €
(Gistihúsið Hvanneyri; ☑467 1506; www.hvanneyri.com; Aðalgata 10; dm/d without bathroom Ikr3800/10,000) Chipped cherubs and faded gilt make up the dated decor of this quirky 1930s hotel, whose stately proportions hint at wealthier times. There are 19 rooms with kitsch furnishings, a couple of TV lounges, a mighty dining room and a guest kitchen. HI members get a discount of Ikr600 per person; linen hire costs Ikr1250.

Campsite   CAMPGROUND €
(☑460 5600; site per person Ikr800; ☉Jun-Aug) Oddly placed right in the middle of town near the harbour and town square, this municipal campsite has showers and a laundry.

TOP CHOICE Hannes Boy   ICELANDIC €€
(☑461 7730; www.raudka.is; Rauðka ehf, Suðurgata 10; mains Ikr2350-5390; ☉6-10pm daily plus noon-2pm Sat & Sun Jun-Aug, 6pm-midnight Fri & Sat Sep-May) Dressed in sunny yellow, this stylish, light-filled space is furnished with funky seats made from old herring barrels. The upmarket menu is fish-focused (natch), with lobster soup and catch-of-the-day fresh from the boats outside. Reservations recommended.

ℹ Getting There & Away

From June to August, **Sterna** (☑551 1166; www.sterna.is) bus 580/580a runs three times a week between Varmahlíð and Siglufjörður.

Hópferðabílar Akureyrar (☑898 5156; www.hba.is) runs bus 620/620a year-round between Akureyri and Ólafsfjörður, running three times daily on weekdays only, two of which were continuing to Siglufjörður (from Akureyri Ikr2100, 80 minutes) at time of research.

Akureyri

POP 17,300

Fertile, sheltered Akureyri, situated alongside Iceland's greatest fjord, has the warmest weather in a cold country. The best restaurants, cafes and cinemas outside the capital nestle beneath a range of snowcapped peaks. It's a place of small pleasures and gentle strolling: admire the flowery gardens, maple trees, sculptures and bobbing boats.

◉ Sights & Activities

Horse tours are available from a range of outlying farms. Most can arrange town pick-up if needed.

Akureyrarkirkja   CHURCH
(Eyrarlandsvegur) Akureyrarkirkja was designed by Gudjón Samúelsson, the architect of Reykjavík's Hallgrímskirkja. Although the basalt theme connects them, Akureyrarkirkja looks more like a stylised 1920s US skyscraper than its big-town brother. The church admits visitors in summer; check the board outside for opening times, as they change frequently.

Akureyri Museum   MUSEUM
(Minjasafnið á Akureyri; www.akmus.is; Aðalstræti 58; adult/child Ikr800/free; ☉10am-5pm Jun–mid-Sep, 2-4pm Sat & Sun mid-Sep–May) Akureyri Museum houses local historical items, including an interesting Settlement Era section. The tranquil garden out front set the fashion for Iceland's 19th-century tree-planting craze.

Nonnahús   MUSEUM
(www.nonni.is; Aðalstræti 54; adult/child Ikr700/free; ☉10am-5pm Jun-Aug) Children's writer Reverend Jón Sveinsson (1857–1944) spent his childhood in Akureyri and his old-fashioned tales of derring-do have a rich Icelandic flavour. You can visit Nonnahús, the author's higgledy-piggledy childhood home, and pick up an English translation of his book *At Skipalón*.

Lystigarður Akureyrar   GARDEN
(www.lystigardur.akureyri.is; Eyrarlandsholt; ☉8am-10pm Mon-Fri, 9am-10pm Sat & Sun Jun-Sep)

Akureyri

The most northerly botanical garden in the world makes a delightful picnic spot on sunny days. Opened in 1912, it includes most native Icelandic species and a further 6600 tough plants from high altitudes and latitudes.

Sundlaug Akureyrar   SWIMMING POOL
(Þingvallastræti 21; adult/child Ikr470/150, sauna Ikr750; ⊘6.45am-9pm Mon-Fri, 8am-7.30pm Sat & Sun) Akureyri has one of the country's best pools, with hot-pots, saunas and flumes.

🛏 Sleeping

Accommodation fills fast in summer – book ahead. Bear in mind, too, that there are plenty of options outside the town centre – Akureyri is surrounded by excellent rural farmstay properties (you'll need your own car for these). Consult the handy *Ideal Holiday* booklet available at www.farmholidays.is.

TOP CHOICE **Skjaldarvík**   GUESTHOUSE €€
(☑552 5200; www.skjaldarvik.is; s/d without bathroom incl breafast Ikr12,900/16,900, restau-

Akureyri

rant 2-course dinner Ikr4500; ⊘restaurant dinner mid-May–mid-Sep; **@**) A slice of guesthouse nirvana, this superb option lies in a bucolic farm setting 6km north of town. It's owned by a young family and features quirky design details everywhere you look (plants sprouting from shoes, vintage typewriters as artwork on the walls). Want more? How about a bumper breakfast buffet, horse riding, hotpot, bookswap, and honesty bar in the comfy lounge. The pretty-as-a-picture restaurant prepares a small but well-executed menu using home-grown herbs and veggies.

TOP CHOICE⟩ Icelandair Hótel
Akureyri   HOTEL €€€
(☑518 1000; www.icelandairhotels.is; Þingvallastræti 23; r from Ikr23,870; **@**) Newly opened in 2011, this brilliant hotel showcases Icelandic designers and artists among its fresh, white-and-caramel-toned room decor. We love the outdoor terrace, the lounge serving high tea of an afternoon and happy-hour cocktails in the early evening, and the elegant restaurant. The bountiful breakfast buffet is optional (Ikr1700).

Hrafninn   HOTEL €€
(☑661 9050; www.hrafninn.is; Brekkugata 4; s/d Ikr10,400/15,300; **P**) Priced below the competition yet delivering well above, beautiful Hrafninn ('The Raven') feels like an elegant manor house without being pretentious or stuffy. The 3rd-floor rooms have recently been renovated, and there's now a spacious 2nd-floor guest kitchen.

Akureyri Backpackers   HOSTEL €
(☑578 3700; www.akureyribackpackers.com; Hafnarstræti 67; dm Ikr3990-4990, d without bathroom Ikr11,990; **@**) Supremely placed in the heart of town, this new backpackers has a chilled travellers' vibe and includes a tour-booking service and popular cafe-bar. Rooms are spread over four floors: four- to eight-bed dorms, plus private rooms with made-up beds on the 4th floor.

Gula Villan   GUESTHOUSE €€
(☑896 8464; www.gulavillan.is; Brekkugata 8; s/d without bathroom Ikr9,200/12,200) New owner Sigríður has a background in travel, and this cheerful yellow-and-white villa shines under her care. Bright, well-maintained rooms are in a good central location. A second building, **Gula Villan II** (Þingvallastræti 14; ⊘Jun-Aug) is run by the same people and offers extra space in summer. Both guesthouses have guest kitchens and breakfast served on request (Ikr1600); BYO sleeping bags to reduce the price.

Edda Hotel   HOTEL €€
(☑444 4900; www.hoteledda.is; entry on Þórunnarstræti 14; d with/without bathroom Ikr 21,900/11,800; ⊘mid-Jun–late Aug; **P@**) Around 200 summer rooms are up for grabs in the grammar school: just over half are superior rooms with TVs and private bathrooms. There's a cafe and large restaurant on site.

City Campsite   CAMPGROUND €
(☑462 3379; Þórunnarstræti; sites per person Ikr1000; ⊘mid-Jun–mid-Sep) This central site has a washing machine, dining area and toilets (showers are over the road and cost Ikr100). There's no kitchen. It's handily placed for the swimming pool and a supermarket.

✖ Eating

TOP CHOICE Café Björk · CAFE €

(www.cafebjork.is; Eyrarlandsvegur 30; lunch buffet Ikr1550; ⊙11am-6pm) What could be better than a designer cafe in a botanical garden? This brand-new cafe has gorgeous picture windows, a Scandi-chic feel, good coffee, a big sun terrace and a popular lunchtime soup-and-salad buffet.

TOP CHOICE Strikið · INTERNATIONAL €€

(www.strikid.is; Skipagata 14; light meals Ikr1800-2900, mains Ikr3500-4900; ⊙11.30am-11pm) Huge windows with panoramic fjord views lend a magical glitz to this 5th-floor restaurant. The menu covers all options: go for pizzas and burgers if you must, or order superb-tasting mains showcasing prime Icelandic produce (superfresh sushi, salmon with hollandaise, lobster soup, reindeer burger, beef tenderloin). The three-course chef's menus (Ikr6600-6900) are good value.

RUB23 · INTERNATIONAL €€€

(☑462 2223; www.rub23.is; Kaupvangsstræti 6; dinner mains Ikr3790-5990; ⊙lunch Mon-Fri, dinner nightly) This supersleek restaurant revolves around a novel idea: you choose your fish (or meat) main, then pick one of the 11 'rubs', or marinades, that the chef then uses to cook your dish. Go with the chef's suggestions for catfish with smoked barbecue rub, or lamb fillet with citrus-rosemary rub. There's also a separate sushi menu.

Blaá Kannan · CAFE €

(Hafnarstræti 96; lunchtime buffet Ikr1250; ⊙8.30am-11.30pm) Prime people watching is on offer at this much-loved cafe (the 'Blue Teapot', in the dark-blue Cafe Paris building) on the main drag. The interior is timber-lined and blinged up with chandeliers, the menu offers paninis, bagels, a cornucopia of cakes and good-value daily lunchtime specials (Ikr1590). It's a popular drinking hole of an evening.

Greifinn · INTERNATIONAL €€

(www.greifinn.is; Glerárgata 20; mains Ikr1640-4830; ⊙11.30am-11pm) Family-friendly and *always* full to bursting, Greifinn is one of the most popular spots in town. The menu favours comfort food above all: juicy burgers, sizzling Tex-Mex, pizzas, salads and devilish ice-cream desserts.

Bautinn · INTERNATIONAL €€

(www.bautinn.is; Hafnarstræti 92; mains Ikr1460-5250; ⊙lunch & dinner) A local favourite, this unpretentious, family-friendly option has an excellent all-you-can-eat soup and salad bar (Ikr1880) and a big menu featuring everything from pizza, burgers, fish and lamb to such Icelandic specialties as whale.

Brynja · ICE CREAM €

(Aðalstræti 3; ice cream from Ikr310; ⊙9am-11.30pm May-Aug, 11am-11pm Sep-Apr) Slightly out of the centre, this legendary sweetshop is known across Iceland for having the best ice cream in the country.

🍷 Drinking & Entertainment

Compared to Reykjavík, Akureyri's nightlife is quite tame.

Brugghúsbarinn · BAR

(Kaupvangsstræti 23; ⊙from 6pm) It's not just any old beer on tap at this candlelit space – it's delicious Kaldi, brewed up the road at a microbrewery in Árskógsströnd. Friendly staff will walk you through the options – five draught variants. Food isn't offered, but you can order dishes from the tapas bar upstairs.

Græni Hatturinn · BAR, VENUE

(Hafnarstræti 96) More traditional and usually less boisterous than some other options, this popular pub is down a lane behind Blaá Kannan. It's the best place in town to see live music.

Café Amour · CAFE, BAR

(Ráðhústorg 9; ⊙11am-1am Sun-Thu, to 4am Fri & Sat) Sophisticated Café Amour tries hard to lure in Akureyri's bright young things with its lengthy cocktail list and New World wines. The small club upstairs is pretty garish but draws the crowds at weekends.

ⓘ Information

Akureyri Hospital (☑463 0100; www.fsa.is; Eyrarlandsvegur)

Library (Amtsbókasafnið á Akureyri; www.amtsbok.is; Brekkugata 17; ⊙10am-7pm Mon-Fri mid-May–mid-Sep, 10am-7pm Mon-Fri, 11am-4pm Sat mid-Sep–mid-May) This impressive complex holds a vast assortment of books, DVDs and magazines in Icelandic and English. The cafe and internet kiosks often lure travellers.

Tourist office (☑450 1050; www.visitakureyri.is; Hof, Strandgata 12; ⊙8am-7pm mid-Jun–Aug, 8am to 5pm Mon-Fri, 10am-2pm Sat & Sun Sep, 8am-4pm Mon-Fri Oct-Apr, 8am-5pm

Mon-Fri, 8am-4pm Sat & Sun May–mid-Jun) Inside Hof, the town's new cultural centre, is this friendly, efficient office. There are loads of brochures, maps, internet access and a design store. Knowledgeable staff can book tours and transport for free, and accommodation in the area (Ikr500).

 Getting There & Away

Air

Air Iceland (www.airiceland.is) Runs frequent daily flights between Akureyri and Reykjavík's domestic airport, and from Akureyri to Grímsey, Vopnafjörður and Þórshöfn. Online deals have one-way tickets from around €60.

Icelandair (www.icelandair.com) Has flights from June to September from Keflavík, meaning international travellers arriving into Iceland don't need to travel to Reykjavík's domestic airport to connect to Akureyri.

Bus

Buses, mainly operated by **SBA-Norðurleið** (☑550 0700; www.sba.is; Hafnarstræti 82), run from the central bus station.

The **Sterna** (Bílar og fólk; ☑551 1166; www.sterna.is) bus company operates the main route between Reykjavík and Akureyri, with buses departing at least once daily (Ikr11,800, six hours) year-round. SBA-Norðurleið buses travelling over the Kjölur route run from mid-June to early September, leaving at 8am daily from both Reykjavík and Akureyri (Ikr12,900, 10½ hours).

A bus to Mývatn (Ikr3600, 1½ hour) runs daily from June to mid-September (four per week rest of year), continuing to Egilsstaðir (Ikr8700, four hours), where you can catch another bus (sometimes a good connection, sometimes not) to Seyðisfjörður. Buses to Húsavík (Ikr3300, 1¼ hours) depart one to four times daily, depending on the time of year.

Around Akureyri

South of town is Iceland's most visited 'forest' (other Scandinavian countries would laugh at what qualifies for this term in almost-treeless Iceland), **Kjarnaskógur**, popular for family outings. A good day walk from Akureyri follows the **Glerárdalur** valley as far as Lambi mountain hut. From Akureyri you can hike up and down **Mt Súlur** (1213m) in about eight hours; if possible, get a lift to the signposted turn-off (it's a dull walk out of town), from where the summit is a 5km climb.

About 50km east of town is the curving waterfall **Goðafoss**, where Þorgeir Ljósvetningagoði, when asked to decide whether Iceland should adopt Christianity, symbolically threw his statues of the old Norse gods. Buses from Akureyri to Mývatn pass the waterfall.

Grímsey

POP 90

The main attraction of Grímsey, a windblown island 40km from the north coast, is that it's the only part of Iceland that lies (partly) inside the Arctic Circle. A large signpost marks the theoretical line; once you've crossed into polar realms, buy a commemorative certificate from the harbourside cafe. Abundant birdlife (puffins, razorbills, guillemots, gulls and Arctic terns) outnumber the close-knit community by around a thousand to one. The boat ride adds to the mystique of reaching this isolated place.

The **Sæfari** (☑458 8970; www.saefari.is) sails from Dalvík (44km north of Akureyri) to Grímsey island at 9am on Monday, Wednesday and Friday (return Ikr8000, three hours), returning from Grímsey at 4pm. In summer, connecting buses (Ikr1300) leave Akureyri at 7.45am.

From mid-June to mid-August, **Air Iceland** (☑467 3148; www.airiceland.is) flies daily to/from Akureyri; flights operate three times weekly the rest of the year. The bumpy 25-minute journey takes in the full length of Eyjafjörður and is an experience in itself. One-way online fares cost from around €60.

Húsavík

POP 2240

Most people visit the 'whale-watching capital of Europe' to do just that; in season, you're almost guaranteed to see these aweinspiring ocean giants feeding in Skjálfandi Bay.

⊙ **Sights & Activities**

Húsavík Whale Museum   MUSEUM
(Hvalasafnið; ☑414 2800; www.whalemuseum.is; Hafnarstétt; adult/child Ikr1250/500; ⊙9am-7pm Jun-Aug, 10am-5pm May & Sep) Best visited before you head out on a whale-watching trip, this excellent museum tells you all you ever needed to know about these gracious creatures, interpreting the ecology and habits of whales, conservation and the history of whaling in Iceland through beautifully curated displays, including several huge skeletons soaring high above.

LOCAL KNOWLEDGE

THE WHALES OF HÚSAVÍK

Edda Elísabet Magnúsdóttir is a local marine biologist at the Húsavík Research Center (a branch of the University of Iceland), established with a focus on marine mammal studies.

What's so special about Húsavík's geology that brings whales to the area? Húsavík sits on a scenic bay known as Skjálfandi, which means 'the tremulous one' in Icelandic. The name is appropriate, since little earthquakes occur very frequently in the bay, usually without being noticed. Skjálfandi's bowl-shaped topography and the infusion of freshwater from two river estuaries means that there is a great deal of nutrients collecting in the bay. The nutrient deposits accumulate during the winter months, and when early summer arrives – with its long sunlit days – the cool waters of Skjálfandi bay come alive with myriad plankton blooms.

These rich deposits act like a beacon, attracting special types of mammals that are highly adapted to life in the cold subarctic waters.

What species of whale visit Húsavík? Every summer roughly nine to 11 species of whale are sighted in the bay, ranging from the tiny harbour porpoise (*Phocoena phocoena*) to the giant blue whale (*Balaenoptera musculus*), the biggest animal known to roam the earth.

Plankton blooming kick-starts each year's feeding season; that's when the whales start appearing in greater numbers in the bay. The first creatures to arrive are the humpback whales (*Megaptera novaeangliae*) and the minke whales (*Balaenoptera acutorostrata*). The humpback whale is known for its curious nature, equanimity and spectacular surface displays, whereas the minke whale is famous for its elegant features: a streamlined and slender black body, and white striped pectoral fin.

Several minke and humpback whales stay in the bay throughout the year, but most migrate south during the winter. The blue whale, undoubtedly the most exciting sight in Skjálfandi, is a recent summer visitor – they only started arriving around seven years ago. They usually start coming in mid-June and stay until the middle of July. Watching these highly developed hydrodynamic giants in their natural environment is just spectacular.

Other summer sightings in Skjálfandi include the orca, also known as the killer whale (*Orcinus orca*; some come to the bay to feed on fish, others come to hunt mammals), bottlenose whales (*Hyperoodon ampullatus*; a mysterious, deep-diving beaked whale), fin whales (*Balaenoptera physalus*), sei whales (*Balaenoptera borealis*), pilot whales (*Globicephala melas*) and sperm whales (*Physeter macrocephalus*).

Culture House MUSEUM
(Safnahúsið á Húsavík; www.husmus.is; Stórigarður 17; adult/child Ikr600/free; ⊙10am-6pm Jun-Aug, 10am-4pm Mon-Fri Sep-May) A folk, maritime and natural-history museum rolled into one complex (together with the town library and a top-floor art gallery), the Culture House is one of the best local museums you'll find in Iceland.

TOP CHOICE Whale Watching WHALE WATCHING
From April to October (although the main season is June to August), **North Sailing** (☑464 7272; www.northsailing.is; Hafnarstétt; adult/child €58/29) and **Gentle Giants** (☑464 1500; www.gentlegiants.is; Hafnarstétt; adult/child €56/24) offer three-hour whale-watching trips on sturdy oaken boats. There's a 97% chance of sightings – mostly minkes and

harbour porpoises. Prices are more-or-less set, and services between the two operators are comparable for the standard three-hour tour.

🛏 Sleeping

TOP CHOICE Kaldbaks-Kot COTTAGES €€
(☑464 1504; www.cottages.is; 2-4 person cabins excl linen €135-195; ⊙May-Sep; @) Located 3km south of Húsavík, this cluster of charming timber cottages all feel like grandpa's cabin in the woods. Choose your level of service (BYO linen or hire it), bring supplies or buy breakfast here (€10) in the magnificent converted cowshed. Then just relax and enjoy the grounds, the hot-pots, the views, the serenity and the prolific birdlife.

Sigtún GUESTHOUSE **€€**
(☑864 0250; www.guesthousesigtun.is; Tún-gata 13; s/d without bathroom incl breakfast Ikr10,500/17,500; @) Free coffee machine, free laundry and fancy kitchen are draws at this first-rate guesthouse, under friendly new ownership. Only the downstairs section is open in winter (alas, without the fancy kitchen, but still with cooking facilities).

Árbót HOSTEL **€**
(☑464 3677; www.hostel.is; dm/d without bath-room Ikr3800/10,000; ☉Jun–mid-Sep; @) One of two HI hostels on rural properties in the area, both about 20km south of Húsavík, but the area's only true budget options (you'll need your own transport). Remote Árbót is on a cattle farm off Rte 85 and offers high-quality facilities and comfy common areas. Members get a discount of Ikr600 per person; linen costs Ikr1250.

Árból GUESTHOUSE **€€**
(☑464 2220; www.arbol.is; Ásgarðsvegur 2; s/d without bathroom incl breakfast Ikr10,300/17,500) Auður is a sunny hostess at this 1903 heritage house, with a pretty stream and town park as neighbours. Spacious, spotless rooms are over three levels – those on the ground and top floor are loveliest (the pine-lined attic rooms are particularly sweet). The kitchen can be used by guests of an evening.

Camping Ground CAMPGROUND **€**
(☑464 1105; campsites per person Ikr1000; ☉mid-May–mid-Sep) Next to the sportsground at the north end of town, this popular campsite has such luxuries as heated toilets, and laundry and cooking facilities.

✖ Eating

TOP CHOICE Pallurinn ICELANDIC **€€**
(www.pallurinn.is; Hafnarstétt; mains Ikr1400-2000; ☉from 6pm Jun-late Aug) This summertime 'gourmet tent' behind the Gentle Giants ticket office is run by Iceland's answer to Jamie Oliver, award-winning Völundur Völundarson. The concept is 'Icelandic street food' cooked on a giant barbecue. Lamb and seafood are at the forefront.

TOP CHOICE Gamli Baukur ICELANDIC **€€**
(www.gamlibaukur.is; Hafnarstétt 9; mains Ikr3150-4710; ☉11.30am-1am Jun-Aug, shorter hr Sep-May) Owned by North Sailing, this timber-framed restaurant-bar serves excellent food (juicy burgers, fish stew, organic lamb)

among shiny nautical relics. Live music and a sweeping terrace make it one of the most happenin' places in northeast Iceland. Kitchen closes at 10pm.

Salka ICELANDIC **€€**
(Garðarsbraut 6; mains Ikr1750-4800; ☉11.30am-9pm) Once home to Iceland's first coopera-tive, this historic building houses a popular restaurant, serving everything from smoked puffin to pizza, by way of langoustine and arctic char.

❶ Information

Library (Stórigarður 17; ☉11am-5pm Mon & Fri, 10am-6pm Tue-Thu) At the Culture House; free wi-fi plus internet access (Ikr300, untimed).
Tourist Information Centre (☑464 4300; www.visithusavik.is; Hafnarstétt; ☉9am-7pm Jun-Aug, 10am-5pm May & Sep) The ticket desk for the Whale Museum acts as the town's info centre, with plentiful maps and brochures.

❶ Getting There & Away

Air
Air Húsavík's airport is 12km south of town.
Eagle Air (☑562 2640; www.eagleair.is) flies year-round between Reykjavík and Húsavík (one way €134).

Bus
SBA-Norðurleið (☑550 0700; www.sba.is) runs a bus service between Akureyri and Húsavík (Ikr3300, 1¼ hours), at least once daily in winter and up to four times daily in summer. From mid-June to August, there are two services daily to Reykjahlíð at Mývatn (Ikr2700, 40 min-utes), and one daily service to Ásbyrgi and the waterfall Dettifoss (Ikr5000, 2¾ hours).

Mývatn

Mývatn is the calm, shallow lake at the heart of a volatile volcanic area. Nature's violent masterpieces are everywhere – crazy-coloured mudpots, huge craters and still-smouldering eruption debris. Once you've had your fill of geology gone wild, mellow out with cycle rides, birdwatching (geese, golden plovers, swans and ducks, includ-ing Barrow's goldeneye) and a bathe in the north's version of the Blue Lagoon.

Reykjahlíð, at the northern end of the lake, is more an assortment of accommoda-tion than a true town, but it makes the best base (Skútustaðir, at the southern end, also has summer facilities).

The down side to Mývatn (Midge Lake) are the dense midge clouds that appear

Mývatn & Krafla

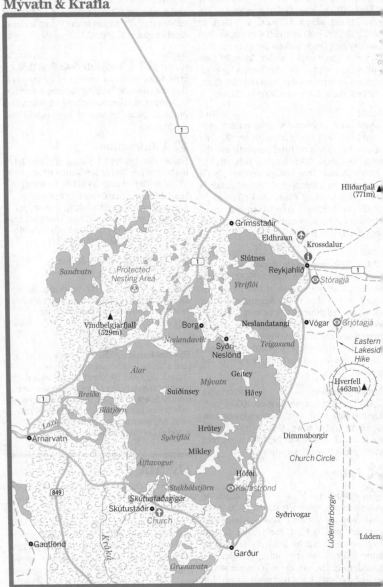

during summer, intent on flying up your nose – you may want to bring a head net. Also, if hiking, keep a look out for deep fissures, especially if you are travelling with children.

⊙ Sights & Activities

Krafla
VOLCANIC AR

The colourful, sulphurous mud hole **Leir'njúkur** is Krafla's prime attraction. Fro there you can meander round the **Kraf Caldera**, where several different lava flov

around the volcano; step into the **visitor centre** (Gestastofa; admission free; ⊙10am-4pm Jun-Aug) for an explanatory film. One of the power station's preliminary searches produced the whopping crater **Sjálfskapar Víti** (Homemade Hell; near the Krafla car park) when a team drilled into a steam chamber, which exploded. Bits of the rig were found 3km away.

From mid-June to early September, **SBA-Norðurleið** (☎550 0770; www.sba.is) operates bus 661/661a, running from Reykjahlíð to Krafla at 8am and 11.30am (Ikr1500, 15 minutes), returning at 2.15pm. The latter morning service continues on to Dettifoss.

Námafjall & Hverir
VOLCANIC AREA

Vaporous vents cover the pinky-orange Námafjall ridge. At its foot, fumaroles and solfataras in the Hverir geothermal field scream steam and belch mud. The area rests on the mid-Atlantic rift (hence all the activity), and can be seen from quite a distance. It's just off the Ring Rd, 6km east of Reykjahlíð.

TOP CHOICE Mývatn Nature Baths
SPA

(Jarðböðin; www.jardbodin.is; adult/child Ikr2800/free; ⊙9am-midnight Jun-Aug, noon-10pm Sep-May) Ease aching muscles at the Mývatn Nature Baths, the north's answer to the Blue Lagoon. Three kilometres east of Reykjahlíð, it's much smaller than the Blue Lagoon but is nicely landscaped, with a hot-pot and saunas.

Scenic Circuit
HIKING

One of the most interesting walks around the lake begins at **Stóragjá**, a hot spring near the village. After a few minutes, the path comes to a dead end at a pipeline. Go left and walk a few hundred metres until the track turns south. It crosses a lava field to **Grjótagjá**, a 50°C hot spring in a spooky fissure, then continues to the tephra crater **Hverfell** (sadly scarred by graffiti) and **Dimmuborgir**, a 2000-year-old maze of twisted lava, the highlight of which is the 'Church' (Kirkjan), a natural arched cave that looks man-made. A series of non-taxing, colour-coded walking trails runs through Dimmuborgir's easily anthropomorphised landscape. The most popular path is the easy **Church Circle** (2.3km).

Around the Lake
LAKE

One of the best ways to experience the 37-sq-km lake is by either bicycle or horse; there are several places in Reykjahlíð to rent them. We recommend a ride round the shores, taking in the forested lava headland of **Höfði**;

overlie each other; some from the 1984 eruptions are still smoking.

Nearby **Stóra-Víti** is a 320m-wide explosion crater and lake (now inactive...allegedly). The 30-megawatt **Kröflustöð power station** sources steam from 17 boreholes pinnacle formations at **Kálfaströnd**; pseudo-craters at **Skútustaðir**, where ponds, bogs and marshlands create havens for nesting birds; the climb up **Vindbelgjarfjall** (529m); and a high-density waterfowl **nesting area** on the northwestern shore (off-road entry is restricted between 15 May and 20 July), where you'll also find **Fuglasafn Sigurgeirs** (www.fuglasafn.is; adult/child Ikr950/500; ⊙10am-7pm Jun-Aug, reduced hr Sep-May), a taxidermic collection of all of Iceland's breeding birds bar one.

☞ Tours

SBA-Norðurleið
VOLCANO

(☏550 0700; www.sba.is; ⊙mid-Jun-Aug) SBA-Norðurleið operates scheduled buses to visit Krafla and Dettifoss/Ásbyrgi, which depart from Akureyri, Húsavík and Reykjahlíð. SBA also runs three-day sightseeing tours to Askja, Kverkfjöll and the glacier Vatnajökull.

Mývatn Tours
VOLCANO

(☏464 1920; www.askjatours.is; per person €130; ⊙mid-Jun–Aug) Runs a trip to the Askja caldera and Herðubreiðarlindir nature reserve from the tourist office at Reykjahlíð.

🛏 Sleeping

Mývatn's popularity means that room rates have soared, and demand is far greater than supply, so don't think twice about booking ahead! Most prices are overinflated, with €200 being the norm for a hotel double room around the lake in summer.

The following options are located either in and around Reykjahlíð. Additional options can be found at Dimmuborgir and along the southern shore at Skútustaðir. The website www.myvatn-hotels.com gives a rundown of most options.

Hótel Reynihlíð
HOTEL €€

(☏464 4170; www.myvatnhotel.is; s/d incl breakfast €155/195; @) Scores of tour groups shack up at Mývatn's most upmarket option. It's a smartly dressed 40-room hotel (plus nine rooms at its new acquisition, the pretty lakeside Hótel Reykjahlíð). The superior rooms aren't a noticeable upgrade; they only have slightly better views, plus a little more space. Also here is an upmarket restaurant, plus lounge-bar and sauna.

Helluhraun 13
GUESTHOUSE €€

(☏464 4132; www.helluhraun13.blogspot.com; Helluhraun 13; s/d without bathroom incl breakfast Ikr11,000/15,500; ⊙Jun-Sep) There are just three rooms and one bathroom at this small, homely guesthouse, but they're bright and tastefully decorated. Breakfast is included, as are the views of the lava field out the kitchen window.

Eldá
GUESTHOUSE €€

(☏464 4220; www.elda.is; Helluhraun 15; s/d without bathroom incl breakfast Ikr12,700/17,900; @) This friendly, family-run operation owns four properties along Helluhraun and offers cosy accommodation in each (plus one studio apartment sleeping five). There are guest kitchens and TV lounges, and an impressive buffet breakfast is included. All guests check in at this location.

Hlíð
CAMPGROUND, GUESTHOUSE €

(☏464 4103; www.hlidmyv.is; Hraunbrún; campsites per person Ikr1300, dm Ikr4100, d incl breakfast Ikr21,000, cottage Ikr30,000; @) Sprawling, well-run Hlíð is 300m uphill from the church and offers the full spectrum: camping, sleeping-bag dorms and rooms with kitchen access, no-frills huts, self-contained cottages sleeping six, and new en-suite guesthouse rooms. There's also a laundry, a playground and bike hire.

🍴 Eating

Look out for dark, sticky *hverabrauð* (rye bread), baked using geothermal heat.

⌜TOP⌝
⌞CHOICE⌟ Vogafjós
ICELANDIC €€

(www.vogafjos.net; mains Ikr2200-4700; ⊙7.30am-11pm Jun-Aug, shorter hr Sep-May) The 'Cowshed', 2.5km south of Reykjahlíð, is a memorable restaurant where you can enjoy views of the lush surrounds, or of the dairy shed of this working farm (cows milked at 7.30am and 6pm). Breakfast is open to all. The menu is an ode to local produce: raw smoked lamb, housemade mozzarella, dill-cured arctic char, geysir bread, homebaked cakes. It's all delicious. There are also 20 pleasant rooms (priced from Ikr27,000) in two neat wooden longhouses on the farm.

Gamli Bærinn
ICELANDIC €€

(mains Ikr1900-4900; ⊙10am-11pm) The cheerfully busy 'Old Farm' tavern beside Hótel Reynihlíð serves up pub-style meals, including fish and steak options. In the evening it becomes the local hang-out – the opening hours are often extended during weekend revelry, but the kitchen closes at 10pm.

ℹ️ Information

Tourist Information Centre (☎ 464 4390; www.visitmyvatn.is; Hraunvegur 8; ⊗8am-8pm Jun-Aug, 9am-4pm Sep & May, 9am-noon Fri-Mon Oct-Apr) This well-informed centre has good displays on the local geology, and can book accommodation, tours and transport. Pick up a copy of the hugely useful *Visit Mývatn* brochure and *Mývatn Lake* map.

ℹ️ Getting There & Around

SBA-Norðurleið (p256) bus services:

Bus 62/62a Akureyri–Mývatn–Egilsstaðir. Operates year-round: daily June to mid-September, four times weekly rest of year. Stops at Reykjahlíð and at Sel-Hótel in southern Mývatn.

Bus 650/650a Twice daily from mid-June to August, running between Reykjahlíð and Húsavík (Ikr2700, 40 minutes).

Bus 661/661a Daily from mid-June to August, running from Reykjahlíð to Krafla and Dettifoss. From Dettifoss you have the option of linking with bus 641a to return to Húsavík.

You can hire brand-new 24-gear mountain bikes from **Hike & Bike** (☎ 899 4845; www. hikeandbike.is; per day Ikr4000; ⊗8.30am-6pm Jun-Aug). The accommodation options listed above also hire bikes.

Jökulsárgljúfur (Vatnajökull National Park – North)

Birch forests, orchids and bizarre rock formations fill the rift of **Jökulsárgljúfur**, sometimes called 'Iceland's Grand Canyon'. One of its major highlights is **Ásbyrgi**, a hoof-shaped chasm formed by a flood of biblical proportions from a glacier 200km away. The swirls, spirals and strange acoustics at **Hljóðaklettar** (Echo Rocks) are similarly unearthly, and near the park's southern boundary is **Dettifoss**, Europe's most forcefully flowing waterfall, where around 200 cu metres of water per second thunder over the edge. Part of the Vatnajökull National Park network, the Jökulsárgljúfur **visitor centre** (Gljúfrastofa; ☎ 470 7100; www.vjp.is; ⊗9am-9pm mid-Jun–mid-Aug, 9am-7pm rest of Jun & Aug, 10am-4pm May & Sep) is located at the entrance to the Ásbyrgi canyon.

Camping (☎ 470 7100; www.vjp.is; campsites per person Ikr1200; ⊗mid-May–Sep) is strictly limited to the official campsites at Ásbyrgi, **Vesturdalur** and Dettifoss. Ásbyrgi has well-maintained showers (Ikr400) and laundry facilities. Vesturdalur has no power

Jökulsárgljúfur ⊗ 0 — 2 km / 0 — 1 mile

or hot water – toilets are the only luxury here. The free campsite at Dettifoss has limited freshwater supplies, and is reserved for hikers.There is a snack bar and small supermarket inside the **Ásbyrgi petrol station** (Rte 85; ⊗9am-10pm Jun-Aug, 10am-6pm Sep-May).

From 18 June to 31 August, there's a daily bus from Akureyri (Ikr7800, 4¼ hours) and Húsavík (Ikr5000 return, three hours) to major sites in the park. There's also a daily Mývatn–Dettifoss (Ikr3300, one hour) bus via Krafla (Ikr1500, 20 minutes).

ICELAND JÖKULSÁRGLJÚFUR (VATNAJÖKULL NATIONAL PARK – NORTH)

THE EAST

Wild reindeer roam the mountains of the empty east, and Iceland's version of the Loch Ness monster calls the area home. The harsh, inhospitable highlands are a complete contrast to the sparkling fjords, which are surrounded by tumbling waterfalls and dotted with tight-knit communities, such as those in picturesque Seyðisfjörður.

Egilsstaðir

TRANSPORT HUB / POP 2270

Egilsstaðir is a rather grey service town and the main regional transport hub. Its saving grace is lovely **Lagarfljót** (Lögurinn), Iceland's third-largest lake. Since saga times, tales have been told of a monster, the Lagarfljótsörmurinn, who lives in its depths. All amenities are clustered near the central crossroads.

🛏 Sleeping & Eating

Book ahead for Wednesday nights in summer, as the ferry to Europe sails from nearby Seyðisfjorður on Thursday mornings.

Egilsstaðir Guesthouse   HOTEL €€€
(✆471 1114; www.egilsstadir.com; s/d incl breakfast Ikr21,890/28,490;) The town was named after this splendid heritage guesthouse and farm, on the banks of Lagarfljót, 300m west of the crossroads. Its sensitively renovated en-suite rooms retain a sense of character, and are decorated with antique furniture.

Hotel Edda   HOTEL €€
(✆444 4880; www.hoteledda.is; Tjarnarbraut 25; s/d Ikr17,500/21,900; ☺Jun–mid-Aug;) Based in the school opposite the swimming pool, this is a typical Edda hotel. Rooms have private bathrooms, and there's a bar and restaurant with panoramic views.

Campsite   CAMPGROUND €
(✆470 0750; Kaupvangur 17; campsites per person Ikr1000; ☺Jun–Sep;) Camping pitches are in utilitarian rows, but it's central and facilities are good – there's a kitchen and laundry, and on-site cafe.

Café Nielsen   INTERNATIONAL €€
(Tjarnarbraut 1; light meals Ikr1250-2400, dinner mains Ikr2550-6900; ☺11.30am-11.30pm Mon-Fri, 1-11.30pm Sat & Sun) We've never had a duff meal at bustling Café Nielsen, based in Egilsstaðir's oldest house and straddling the divide between bar and restaurant. There's a

wide choice, from vegie burgers to reindeer – a speciality of this region.

❶ Information

Tourist Information Centre (✆471 2320; www.east.is; Miðvangur 1-3; ☺8.30am-6pm Mon-Fri, 9am-5pm Sat & Sun mid-May–mid-Sep, 9am-5pm Mon-Fri, 11am-3pm Sat rest of yr) The excellent regional information centre has enough free brochures to paper your living room.

❶ Getting There & Away

Air

Egilsstaðir's airport is 1km north of town.
Air Iceland (Flugfélag Íslands; ✆580 3000; www.airiceland.is) flies daily year-round from Egilsstaðir to Reykjavík (one way from €60).

Bus

Egilsstaðir is a major crossroads on the Ring Rd. Buses generally arrive at and depart from the N1 petrol station or the nearby tourist information centre.

SBA-Norðurleið (✆550 0770, 550 0700; www.sba.is) Runs Akureyri–Mývatn–Egilsstaðir services. Operates year-round: daily June to mid-September, four times weekly rest of year. Akureyri–Egilsstaðir takes four hours (Ikr8700).

Ferðaþjónusta Austurlands (✆852 9250, 472 1515) Runs a bus service between Egilsstaðir and Seyðisfjörður (Ikr1000, around 45 minutes). Services operate year-round, one to three times daily Monday to Saturday (Sunday services operate from mid-June to mid-August). Extra services run to coincide with the ferry arrival and departure.

Seyðisfjörður

POP 680

Things get lively when the Smyril Line's ferry *Norröna* sails majestically up the 17km-long fjord and docks at pretty little Seyðisfjörður. The picturesque houses in the town, snowcapped mountains and cascading waterfalls make the perfect welcome for visitors to Iceland.

◎ Sights & Activities

Bláa Kirkjan   CHURCH
(www.blaakirkjan.is; Ránargata; ☺8.30pm Jul–mid Aug) Like many of the town's 19th-century timber buildings, this pretty little church was brought in kit form from Norway when the herring boom was at its height. On Wednesday evenings in summer, it's the setting for a popular series of musical performances.

SKÁLANES

You might think Seyðisfjörður is the end of the line, but further retreat is possible. The remote farm **Skálanes** (☎861 7008, 690 6966; www.skalanes. com; ☺May-Sep, by arrangement Oct-Apr), 19km east of Seyðisfjörður along the fjord edge, is a beautiful nature and heritage field centre, surrounded by sea cliffs full of abundant birdlife. Accommodation is simple and cosy; there is a guest kitchen, but meals may be provided on request.

Getting there is an adventure in itself. By foot, you could walk the 19km; you can get there on a hired mountain bike or canoe; the 4WD track is accessible for jeeps; or you can have the centre pick you up from Seyðisfjörður (Ikr8000 per vehicle).

Kayaking & Mountain-Biking
KAYAKING, MOUNTAIN-BIKING

(☎865 3741; www.iceland-tour.com; 1/3hr tours Ikr3500/8000, mountain-bike tours 4hr Ikr5500; ☺Jun-Aug) We highly recommend a guided kayaking trip out on the fjord, led by the good-humoured and informative Hlynur. More experienced paddlers can go on longer trips to Austdalur or Skálanes, or arrange other tailor-made tours. Hlynur also does mountain-bike tours, or hire a bike and go off on your own (half/full day Ikr2500/3000).

Hiking
HIKING

The Seyðisfjörður to Vestdalur hike is a fine taste of the countryside around Mt Bjólfur to the Seyðisfjörður–Egilsstaðir road. You could also walk along the fjord to Skálanes.

🛌 Sleeping

TOP CHOICE **Hótel Aldan**
HOTEL €€

(☎472 1277; www.hotelaldan.com; reception at Norðurgata 2; s/d incl breakfast from Ikr15,900/21,900) The wonderful hotel is shared across three old wooden buildings. Reception and the bar–restaurant (where breakfast is served) are at the Norðurgata location. The Snæfell location (in the old post office at Austurvegur 3) is a creaky, characterful three-storey place with the cheapest rooms, fresh white paintwork, draped muslin curtains and Indian bedspreads. The Old Bank location (at Oddagata 6) houses a boutique guesthouse with all mod-cons. Its

luxurious rooms are bright, spacious and furnished with antiques, and beds snuggle under hand-embroidered bedspreads.

Hafaldan HI Hostel
HOSTEL €

(☎472 1410; www.simnet.is/hafaldan; Hafaldan; dm/d without bathroom Ikr3800/10,000; ☺Apr–mid-Oct; @) This peaceful hostel is split over two sites. The main building, a short walk out of town, has harbour views, a sunny lounge, kitchen, laundry and internet access. The annexe used to be the old hospital, but you'd never guess – Indian hangings and funky old furniture cosy it up.

Campsite
CAMPGROUND €

(☎472 1521; Ránargata; campsites per person Ikr1000; ☺May-Sep) There are two areas for camping – one sheltered, grassy site opposite the church for tents, and another nearby area for vans. The service building houses kitchen, showers (Ikr350) and laundry facilities.

🍴 Eating

TOP CHOICE Skaftfell
INTERNATIONAL €

(www.skaftfell.is; Austurvegur 42; snacks & mains Ikr890-2690; ☺noon-11pm or later May-Aug, 5pm-2am ferry days & Fri-Sun Sep-Apr) This fabulous, artsy bistro-bar/cultural centre is where you can chill, snack and/or meet locals against a cool backdrop, and with a great soundtrack. There's free internet and wi-fi, and a tempting menu (curries, salads, pizzas) that includes decent vegie options. If we lived in Seyðisfjörður, we'd probably come here every day. Be sure to check out the exhibitions in the gallery space upstairs.

Hótel Aldan
ICELANDIC €€€

(☎472 1277; www.hotelaldan.is; Norðurgata 2; lunch Ikr2250-3250, dinner mains Ikr3500-7200; ☺7am-9pm mid-May–mid-Sep) Coffee and delicious cakes are served all day in this country-chic spot, and lunches feature the likes of mussels or lamb chops. In the evening, damask tablecloths and flickering candles prettify the tables, and the menu features traditional Icelandic ingredients (lamb, langoustine, reindeer, fish) with a contemporary touch. Reservations advised.

ℹ️ Information

Tourist office (☎472 1551; ☺8am-noon & 1-5pm Mon-Fri) In the ferry terminal building.

ℹ️ Getting There & Away

For bus information, see the Egilsstaðir's Getting There & Away section. See p494 for details of the ferry service from mainland Europe.

THE SOUTH

Containing glittering glaciers, toppling waterfalls, the iceberg-filled Jökulsárlón lagoon and Iceland's favourite walking area, Skaftafell, it's no wonder that the south is the country's most-visited region. Various places along the coast offer skiing, ice climbing, snowmobiling, dog-sledding and hiking opportunities; or head offshore to the charming Vestmannaeyjar (Westman Islands) to see puffins and experience life on an active volcano.

Vatnajökull

Mighty Vatnajökull is Earth's largest ice cap outside the poles. It's 8100 sq km (three times the size of Luxembourg), reaches a thickness of 1km in places and, if you could find a scale big enough, you'd find it weighs 3000 billion tonnes! Scores of glaciers flow down from the centre as rivers of crevassed ice.

In 2008 **Vatnajökull National Park** (www.vatnajokulsthjodgardur.is) was founded, chiefly to draw attention to the alarming speed at which the ice cap is melting. Its boundaries encompass the ice cap and the former Skaftafell and Jökulsárgljúfur National Parks, forming a 12,000-sq-km megapark that covers 12% of the entire country. There are major park visitor centres at Skaftafell in the south and Ásbyrgi (Vatnajökull National Park – North) in the north.

If you have your own transport, you can park at the junction of Rte 1 and F985, and then get a **Glacier Jeep** (☑478 1000; www.glacierjeeps.is; trip incl snowmobile ride Ikr18,500; ☉9.30am & 2pm May-Oct) ride up the mountain to the ice cap, where they'll take you on an unforgettable snowmobile ride.

There are no scheduled buses that work in with the Glacier Jeeps schedule to drop you at a suitable time at the F985 car park. If you're without your own wheels, consider using the services of Höfn-based **Vatnajökull Travel** (☑894 1616; www.vatnajokull.is), which can take you up to Jöklasel, and then drive you to Jökulsárlón for a lagoon boat trip.

WARNING

Dangerous crevasses criss-cross the ice cap – hiking is not recommended without proper equipment and a knowledgeable guide.

Around Vatnajökull

JÖKULSÁRLÓN

A ghostly procession of luminous-blue icebergs drifts through the 17-sq-km **Jökulsárlón lagoon**, before floating out to sea. This surreal scene (right next to the Ring Rd between Höfn and Skaftafell) is a natural film set: in fact, you might have seen it in *Batman Begins* (2005) or *Die Another Day* (2002). The ice breaks off from Breiðamerkurjökull glacier, an offshoot of Vatnajökull.

Amphibious boat trips (☑478 2222; www.icelagoon.is; adult/child Ikr3700/1000; ☉9am-7pm Jun-Aug, 10am-5pm May & Sep) among the 'bergs are available.

Sterna's Reykjavík–Skaftafell–Höfn bus passes here – on its eastbound run, it stops long enough for you to take a boat trip. From early June to mid-September, Reykjavík Excursions run two buses a day between here and Skaftafell (Ikr4400 return, 45 minutes).

HÖFN
POP 1640

Little Höfn (pronounced 'herp', more or less) makes a handy base for trips to the glacier. At last visit, an historic wooden warehouse moved to the Höfn harbourfront to be fitted out as the town's shiny new **visitor information centre**, possibly incorporating some of the folk exhibits and the glacier expo that resided in the town's old visitor centre. Undoubtedly, it will also cover the marvels of the region's flagship national park. Check www.visitvatnajokull.is for the latest details, including opening hours and contact information.

🛏 Sleeping

TOP CHOICE **Guesthouse Dyngja** GUESTHOUSE €€
(☑690 0203; www.dyngja.com; Hafnarbraut 1; d with out bathroom incl breakfast Ikr15,500-18,000; @) A lovely young couple have opened this petite five-room guesthouse in a prime harbour front locale, and filled it with charm and good cheer: rich colours, record player and vinyl selection, delicious breakfasts, outdoor deck and good local knowledge to impart.

Höfn Camping & Cottages CAMPGROUND €
(☑478 1606; www.campsite.is; Hafnarbraut 52; campsites Ikr1100, dm Ikr3500, cabins Ikr12,000; ☉May–mid-Oct; @) Lots of travellers stay at the campsite on the main road into town where super-helpful owners and extensive local info are among the draws. There are 11 good-value cabins, sleeping up to six, plus playground, laundry and bike rental.

ICELAND VATNAJÖKULL

HI Hostel
HOSTEL €

(📞478 1736; www.hostel.is; Hvannabraut; dm/d without bathroom Ikr3800/10,000) Follow the signs from the N1 to find Höfn's best budget option, hidden away in a residential area and with some primo views. It's a sprawling space (a former aged-care home) that's usually bustling with travellers in summer.

✗ Eating
Humar (langoustine, or 'Icelandic lobster') is the speciality on Höfn menus.

TOP CHOICE Humarhöfnin
ICELANDIC €€€

(📞478 1200; www.humarhofnin.is; Hafnarbraut 4; mains Ikr3900-6700; ⊙noon-10pm Jun-Aug, 6-10pm Apr-May & Sep) Humarhöfnin offers 'gastronomy langoustine' in a cute, cheerfully Frenchified space with superb attention to detail. Mains centred on pincer-waving little critters cost upwards of Ikr6000, but there's also a 'small courses' menu boasting a fine langoustine baguette.

Pakkhús
ICELANDIC €€€

(📞478 2280; www.pakkhus.is; harbourfront; mains Ikr2790-5990; ⊙noon-10pm May–mid-Sep) Newly opened in a harbourside warehouse and proudly showcasing local produce, busy Pakkhús has kitchen creativity you don't often find in rural Iceland.

Kaffi Hornið
ICELANDIC €€

(www.kaffihorn.is; Hafnarbraut 42; mains Ikr2120-5250; lunch buffet Ikr1980; ⊙11.30am-11pm) This unpretentious bar-restaurant serves food in stomach-stretching portions. There's a lunchtime soup-and-salad buffet, and a menu stretching from burgers to local trout.

❶ Getting There & Away

Air

Höfn's airport is 4km northwest of town. **Eagle Air** (📞562 2640; www.eagleair.is) flies year-round between Reykjavík and Höfn (one way €179).

Bus

Buses arrive at and depart from the N1 petrol station, a 10-minute walk from the town centre.

Reykjavík Excursions (📞580 5400; www.re.is) Bus 19/19a Höfn–Skaftafell (two hours), once daily June to mid-September (IKr4500). From Skaftafell there are buses further west.

Sterna (📞551 1166; www.sterna.is) Bus 12/12a Reykjavík–Höfn (nine hours), once daily mid-May to mid-September (Ikr13,700); and bus 9/9a Höfn–Egilsstaðir (four hours), once daily mid-May to mid-September

Strætó (📞540 2700; www.straeto.is) Bus 51 Reykjavík–Höfn (seven hours, Ikr10,150) twice daily June to August, dropping to three times a week in winter (with a need to prebook).

Hópferðabílar Akureyri (📞898 5156; www.hba.is) Bus 1/1a Höfn–Egilsstaðir (four hours, Ikr7500), once daily June to mid-September.

Skaftafell (Vatnajökull National Park – South)

Skaftafell, the jewel in the crown of Vatnajökull National Park, encompasses a breathtaking collection of peaks and glaciers. It's the country's favourite wilderness: 170,000 visitors per year come to marvel at thundering waterfalls, twisted birch woods, the

Skaftafell

tangled web of rivers threading across the sandar, and brilliant blue-white Vatnajökull with its lurching tongues of ice.

Activities

Appearing on postcards and calendars across the land, Skaftafell's most recognisable feature is **Svartifoss**, a gloomy waterfall that thunders over black basalt columns. It's an easy 1.8km stroll from the visitor centre. Due to erosion in this area, rangers are encouraging visitors to explore elsewhere, for example, the easy one-hour return route to **Skaftafellsjökull** – at the glacier face, you can witness the bumps, groans and brilliant blue hues of the ice. The **Icelandic Mountain Guides** (☎478 2559, Reykjavík office 587 9999, Skaftafell 894 2959; www.mountainguide.is) lead invigorating glacier walks from March to October (adult/child Ikr6500/4100, minimum age eight years).

In fine weather, the circular walk around **Skaftafellsheiði** is a treat. There are some enjoyable day walks from the camping ground to **Kristínartindar** (1126m), **Kjós** or the glacial lagoon in **Morsárdalur**; plan on about seven hours for each return trip.

DON'T MISS

A CART RIDE TO CAPE INGÓLFSHÖFÐI

The dramatic headland Ingólfshöfði is an isolated nature reserve just east of Skaftafell. The only way to access this almost-island, 6km away over treacherous glacial sands, is by **tractor-towed haycart** (☎894 0894; www.oraefaferdir. is; adult/8-16yrs Ikr4000/1000; ⊙noon Mon-Sat early May–mid-May). Book through **Local Guide** (Öræfaferðir; ☎894 0894; www.localguide.is; tour adult/child Ikr5000/1000; ⊙noon Mon-Sat May-Aug), or simply turn up outside the farm at Hofsnes (signposted, just off the Ring Rd) 15 minutes before the tour is due to start. There are additional tours at 9am and 3pm from mid-June to early August. Once there, local guides take you on a fascinating one-hour bird and nature walk along the 76m-high cliffs and grassy heath, teeming with puffins, guillemots, razorbills, gulls and great skuas.

Tours

The Laki eruptions of 1783 caused utter devastation to the area. Over 30 billion tonnes of lava spewed from the Laki fissure, the largest recorded flow from a single eruption. The still-volatile **Lakagígar area**, with its spectacular 25km-long crater, is now part of Vatnajökull National Park. In July and August, daily 11-hour **Reykjavík Excursions** (☎580 5400; www.re.is) trips from Skaftafell (Ikr13,800, departs 8am) and Kirkjubæjarklaustur (Ikr10,400, departs 9am) visit the craters.

🛏 Sleeping

Fosshótel Skaftafell   HOTEL €€
(☎478 1945; www.fosshotel.is; Freysnes; s/d from €155/172; @) This is the closest hotel to the Skaftafell visitor centre, 5km east at Freysnes. Its 63 rooms are functional rather than luxurious, but staff are helpful.

Visitor Centre Campsite   CAMPGROUND €
(☎470 8300; www.vjp.is; campsites per person Ikr1200; ⊙May-Sep) Most visitors bring a tent to this large, gravelly campsite (with laundry facilities, and hot showers for Ikr400). It gets very busy (and loud) in summer. The only other place you're allowed to camp is at the Kjós campsite (free, but you must obtain a permit from the visitor centre before you set off).

ℹ Information

The **visitor centre** (Skaftafellsstofa; ☎470 8300; www.vjp.is; ⊙8am-9pm Jun-Aug, 9am-7pm May & Sep, 10am-5pm Mar-Apr & Oct, 11am-3pm Nov-Feb) contains exhibitions and film screenings about the area, and is staffed by people who really know their stuff. It contains a busy cafe.

ℹ Getting There & Away

Skaftafell is a stop on Reykjavík–Höfn bus routes (see the Höfn Getting There & Away section) and also a departure point for wilderness areas, such as Landmannalaugar. Buses stop in front of the visitor centre.

Kirkjubæjarklaustur
POP 120

Kirkjubæjarklaustur (which translates as 'church-farm-cloister') is a tiny settlement lost in the staggeringly vast and empty sandur. This tranquil village was first settled by Irish monks before the Vikings arrived.

Later, in 1186, a convent of Benedictine nuns was founded (near the modern-day church).

◎ Sights

The regular basalt columns of **Kirkjugólf**, cemented with moss, were once mistaken for an old church floor rather than a work of nature, and it's easy to see why. The 'floor' lies in a field about 400m northwest of the petrol station.

Systrastapi (Sisters' Pillar) marks the spot where two nuns were reputedly executed and buried after sleeping with the devil and other such no-nos. **Systrafoss** is the prominent waterfall located near Klausturhof. The lake **Systravatn**, a short saunter up the cliffs, was once a place where nuns went to bathe.

See p262 for information about tours to the **Lakagígar craters**.

🛏 Sleeping & Eating

Klausturhof GUESTHOUSE **€**
(📞567 7600; www.klausturhof.is; Klausturvegur 1-5; dm Ikr3800-4300, d with/without bathroom Ikr16,200/13,500) With the pretty Systrafoss waterfall as its neighbour, this bright new complex offers an assortment of compact rooms at reasonable prices, plus guest kitchen and an on-site cafe (breakfast Ikr1400). Room prices listed are for made-up beds, BYO sleeping bag to save.

Kirkjubæ II CAMPGROUND **€**
(📞894 4495; www.kirkjubaer.com; campsites per person Ikr1100; ⊙Jun-Sep) Neat green site with sheltering hedges, right in town. Good facilities include kitchen, hot showers and laundry.

Icelandair Hótel Klaustur HOTEL **€€€**
(📞487 4900; www.icelandairhotels.is; Klausturvegur 6; d from Ikr27,600; ⊙closed mid-Dec–mid-Jan) The Klaustur has sweet management and attractive business-hotel decor, plus a sunny enclosed dining terrace and bar–lounge.

Systrakaffi INTERNATIONAL **€€**
(www.systrakaffi.is; Klausturvegur 12; mains Ikr900-3600; ⊙noon-10pm Jun-Aug, 6-10pm mid-Apr–May & Sep) This beloved cafe-bar is the liveliest place in town. Its varied menu offers pizzas and burgers but plays favourites with local trout and lamb.

❶ Information

Tourist office (📞487 4620; www.klaustur.is; Klausturvegur 10; ⊙9am-7pm Mon-Fri, 10am-

THE FIRE PRIEST

In 1783 the largest flow of lava in recorded history began spewing from the Laki fissure. Fountains of molten rock shot almost 1.5km into the air, and a fiery flood of lava poured steadily southwards into the lowlands.

On July 20, as a tongue of lava crept towards Kirkjubæjarklaustur, the villagers stumbled to church through thick fog and lightning flashes to hear the Sunday sermon. The Reverend Jón Steingrímsson, who was not expecting his church to survive, prayed fervently to God for mercy as earthquakes shook the building and thunderclaps caused the bells to ring.

After the sermon, the congregation left the building to discover that the all-consuming lava flow had stopped in its tracks. Jón Steingrímsson and his Eldmessa ('Fire Sermon') were given the credit for this miracle, and the humble priest became an Icelandic hero.

6pm Sat & Sun Jun-Aug, 10am-6pm daily 1-15 Sep) Local info plus coverage of Vatnajökull National Park, and a short film on the Laki eruption.

❶ Getting There & Away

Kirkjubæjarklaustur is a stop on all Reykjavík–Höfn bus routes (see the Höfn Getting There & Away section) and also serves as a crossroads to Landmannalaugar and Laki.

Þórsmörk

A hidden valley deep in the Icelandic outback, The Woods of Thor is a verdant realm filled with curling gorges, flower-filled leas, icy streams, and views to three looming glaciers that guard the quiet hamlet from harsher weather. Be warned, though: Þórsmörk's ravishing appearance and proximity to Reykjavík (130km) make it a popular spot in summer.

Þórsmörk is the end of the Landmannalaugar to Þórsmörk trek (see p268), although walkers can extend the journey with the spectacular 23km **Þórsmörk-Skógar hike**. It crosses Fimmvörðuháls Pass, where a new lava field was formed in the 2010 Eyjafjallajökull eruptions. Go prepared – the terrain is tough, the pass is high and bad

WORTH A TRIP

SKÓGAR

As you're barrelling along the south coast, be sure to stop at the excellent **Skógar Folk Museum** (☑487 8845; www.skogasafn.is; adult/child Ikr1500/500; ◉museum 9am-6pm Jun-Aug, 10am-5pm May & Sep, 11am-4pm Oct-Apr), built by charming nonagenarian Þórður Tómasson. There are various restored buildings (church, turf-roofed farmhouse, school building, cowsheds etc) in the grounds, and a hangar-like building at the back houses an interesting transport museum, plus a cafe and souvenir shop. Nearby is the 62m waterfall **Skógafoss**, shrouded in mist and rainbows.

weather can descend very quickly even in midsummer. The hut on this stretch, **Fimmvörðuháls** (www.utivist.is; N 63° 37.320', W 19° 27.093'), is run by travel association Útivist. Ironically, in bad weather it can be difficult to find.

🛏 Sleeping

Wild camping is discouraged, but the three Þórsmörk huts have **campsites** around them. The huts themselves have showers and cooking facilities; reservations are strongly advised, particularly for weekends.

Básar   HUT €
(☑562 1000; www.utivist.is; campsites per person Ikr1100, hut per person Ikr3600)

Húsadalur   HUT €
(Volcano Huts Thorsmork; ☑552 8300; www.volcanohuts.com; campsites per person Ikr1100, dm/d Ikr6000/7000; ◉May-Sep)

Langidalur   HUT €
(Þórsmörk; ☑893 1191; www.fi.is; N 63°40.960', W 19°30.890'; campsites per person Ikr1100, per person Ikr5000; ◉mid-May–Sep)

❶ Getting There & Away

Reykjavík Excursions (☑580 5400; www.re.is) bus service from Reykjavík to Þórsmörk departs Reykjavík at 8am, arriving at Húsadalur at noon. At 12.30pm it departs for Básar, arriving at 1pm. At 3pm the bus continues to Langidalur, and at 3.15pm it leaves Langidalur returning back to Húsadalur at 3.30pm before continuing on to Reykjavík at 4pm. There's a second bus that

leaves Reykjavík at 4.30pm arriving in Húsadalur around 8pm – it makes no other stops.

Basically, forget about driving into Þórsmörk with your private vehicle. If you have your own 4WD with excellent clearance you can plough down Rtes 249 and F249 until the deep river ford, where you should leave your car. The bus that takes passengers is a special amphibious vehicle.

Vestmannaeyjar

POP 4140

Black and brooding, the Vestmannaeyjar islands form 15 eye-catching silhouettes off the southern shore. They were formed by submarine volcanoes around 11,000 years ago, except for sulky-looking Surtsey, the archipelago's newest addition, which rose from the waves in 1963. Ten years later, unforgettable pictures of Heimaey were broadcast across the globe when a huge eruption buried a third of the town under 30 million tonnes of lava. Surtsey was made a Unesco World Heritage Site in 2008, but its unique scientific status means that it is not possible to land there.

Heimaey is the only inhabited island. Its little town and sheltered harbour lie between dramatic *klettur* (escarpments) and two ominous volcanoes – blood-red Eldfell and conical Helgafell. Heimaey's cliffs are a breeding ground for 10 million puffin pairs.

◎ Sights & Activities

Skansinn   HISTORICAL AREA
The oldest structure on the island is a ruinous 15th-century fort built by English marauders; nearby is a picturesque replica **Norse stave church**, and old water tanks crushed by the 1973 lava.

Sagnheimar Byggðasafn   MUSEUM
(Folk Museum; ☑488 2040; Raðhústræti; adult/child Ikr1000/600; ◉11am-7pm mid-May–mid-Sep, 1-4pm Sat mid-Sep–mid-May) This interactive folk museum tells the story of Heimaey from the era of marauding pirates all the way up to the 1973 eruptions and beyond. Displays also shed some light on local sports heroes and native birdlife.

**House Graveyard &
Pompei of the North**   LANDMARK
(www.pompeinordursins.is) Four hundred buildings lie buried under the lava from the 1973 eruption. On the edge of the flow is a strange graveyard where beloved homes rest in peace. 'Pompei of the North' is a modern

'archaeological' excavation in which 10 houses are being dug up. So far, the crumpled concrete remains of a handful of houses have been unearthed along what was formerly Suðurvegur.

Sæheimar MUSEUM
(Náttúrugripasafn Vestmannæyja; ☎4811997; www. saeheimar.is; Heiðarvegur 12; adult/child Ikr1000/free; ⊙11am-5pm mid-May–mid-Sep, 1-4pm Sat mid-Sep–mid-May) The Aquarium & Natural History Museum has an interesting collection of stuffed birds and animals, plus fish tanks of hideous Icelandic fish. It's great fun for the family, and there's often a baby puffin wobbling about – the museum is an informal bird hospital as well.

Surtseyjarstofa MUSEUM
(Surtsey Visitors Centre; ☎591 2140; www.ust.is/surtsey; Heidarvegi 1; adult/child Ikr1000/free; ⊙11am-5pm Jun-Aug, 1-4pm Sep-May) A beautiful space dedicated to all things Surtsey, this museum offers interactive insight into the formation of one of the world's newest islands.

Hiking HIKING
Opportunities for hiking abound, including walks to Stórhöfði and up the volcanoes Helgafell and Eldfell. It's a treacherous 30-minute climb to the top of **Stóraklif**, 'assisted' by ropes and chains, but worth it for the breathtaking views.

☞ Tours

Viking Tours BOAT TOUR, BUS TOUR
(☎488 4884; www.vikingtours.is; small boat harbour, off Ægisgata; adult/child Ikr4900/3900; ⊙mid-May–mid-Sep) Stop by Cafe Kró to sign up for boat or bus trips with the friendly folks at Viking Tours. Leaving at 11am and 3.30pm every day, they zip right around the island, slowing for the big bird-nesting sites on the south coast. Boat-lunch-bus combos are available for a cool Ikr9720. Trips coincide with ferry departure times for the

ICELAND VESTMANNAEYJAR

Vestmannaeyjar

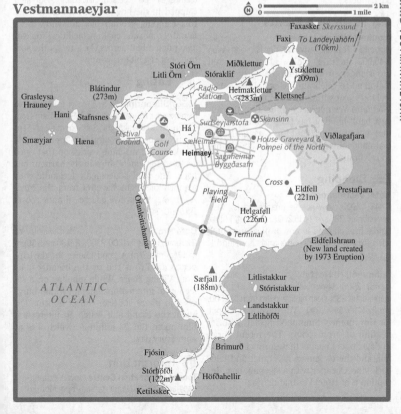

N 0 — 2 km
0 — 1 mile

Faxasker *Skerssund*
Faxi *To Landeyjahöfn (10km)*
Stóri Örn Miðklettur
Litli Örn Stóraklif Ystiklettur (209m)
Blátindur (273m) *Radio Station* Heimaklettur (283m) Klettsnef
Grasleysa Hrauney Hani Stafsnses
Smæyjar Hæna *Festival Ground* Há Surtseyjarstofa Skánsinn
  Golf Course Sæheimar *House Graveyard & Pompei of the North* Viðlagafjara
  Heimaey Sagnheimar Byggðasafn
  Cross Eldfell (221m) Prestafjara
  Playing Field Helgafell (226m)
  Terminal Eldfellshraun (New land created by 1973 Eruption)
Ofanleitishamar
ATLANTIC OCEAN Sæfjall (188m) Litlistakkur Stóristakkur
  Landstakkur Lítlihöfði
  Fjósin Brimurð
  Stórhöfði (122m) Höfðahellir
  Ketilssker

PUFFINS – CLOWNS OF THE OCEAN

Iceland is famous for its puffins (*Fratercula arctica*). It's hard not to get dewy-eyed over these sociable little 'clowns of the ocean', but really they're as tough as old boots, living out on the stormy winter seas and surviving on salt water.

It's easy to spot puffins: they're the clumsiest things in the air. Wings beat frantically 300 to 400 times per minute to keep them aloft, and the birds often crash-land. Underwater, it's a different story – their flight beneath the waves is so graceful that they were once thought to be a bird-fish hybrid.

Every spring the puffins return to land to breed. They're discerning birds: 60% of the world's population breed in Iceland. From late May to August, the best places to see them include offshore Reykjavík (p227), Látrabjarg (p246) and Heimaey, which has the world's biggest puffin colony. Pufflings start leaving their nests in August. On Heimaey, the young birds are often confused by the town's lights, so every year the town's children stay up late to collect them and point them seawards.

Sadly, a sudden decline in sand eel numbers (the birds' main food source) has led to a corresponding drop in puffin numbers. It remains to be seen whether the populations will recover or continue to fade away. Puffins and their eggs are a traditional part of the Icelandic diet: if you can bring yourself to devour them, you'll often find them on restaurant menus.

mainland, making it a convenient option for daytrippers.

Festivals & Events

Þjóðhátíð Vestmannaeyjar   CULTURE
(National Festival; www.dalurinn.is; admission Ikr18,900) In 1874, foul weather prevented the islanders from joining the party on the mainland to celebrate the establishment of Iceland's constitution. The earth-shaking Þjóðhátíð Vestmannaeyjar, held on the August bank holiday, has been making up for that day ever since; and these days, half the mainland joins *them* for the wild and drunken celebrations.

🛏 Sleeping

Hótel Vestmannæyjar   HOTEL €€
(☑481 2900; www.hotelvestmannaeyjar.is; Vestmannabraut 28; s/d Ikr15,200/21,500; @) Iceland's first cinema is now a pleasant hotel, with freshly redone rooms and the friendliest staff in town.

Sunnuhöll HI Hostel   HOSTEL €
(☑481 2900; www.hotelvestmannaeyjar.is; Vestmannabraut 28b; sleeping bag in dm from Ikr2500, s/d Ikr4400/6900; @) We have a soft spot for tiny, homely Sunnuhöll hostel, with its handful of prim rooms. The recent surge in daytrippers means that dorms are rarely full, and there's generally a quiet and laid-back vibe. Cheaper with a sleeping bag. Reception is at Hótel Vestmannæyjar.

Campsite   CAMPGROUND €
(campsites per person Ikr1200; ⊙Jun-Aug) Cupped in the bowl of an extinct volcano, this camping ground has hot showers, a laundry room and cooking facilities. You can also pitch a tent across the street – the second spot is a bit less windy.

🍴 Eating

TOP CHOICE Slippurinn   ICELANDIC €€
(Strandvegur 76; mains Ikr1790-3690; ⊙11am-11pm Tue-Fri, 11.30am-midnight Sat-Sun mid-Apr–Sep) Family owned and operated, Slippurinn sits inside an old machine workshop that once serviced the lonely ships in the harbour out back. The food is decidedly Icelandic with a pinch of bright flavours from the Med. A fresh, three-/five-course dinner costs Ikr5490/7490.

Café Kró   INTERNATIONAL €€
(Harbour; mains Ikr1200-2300; ⊙9.30am-5.30pm mid-May–mid-Sep) A good choice for daytrippers, Café Kró is run by the friendly folks from Viking Tours. While nibbling on a selection of international staples (think burgers and pizza) you can collect information about the island and watch an interesting film about the '73 eruption (which airs at 4pm every day).

❶ Information

Tourist Information Centre (www.vestmannaeyjar.is; Strandvegur; ⊙9am-6pm Mon-Fri,

10am-5pm Sat, 1-5pm Sun Jun-Aug) The summer tourist office staffed by local teens; consider it more of a place to pick up pamphlets.

Library (Ráðhústræti; ☺10am-5pm Mon-Fri Jun-Aug, 11am-2pm Sat Sep-May) Internet access is available for Ikr100 per 30 minutes.

❶ Getting There & Away

Air

There are two daily flights between Reykjavík's domestic airport and Vestmannæyjar on **Eagle Air** (☑562 4200; www.eagleair.is) for Ikr25,000 return.

Boat

Eimskip's ferry **Herjólfur** (☑481 2800; www.herjolfur.is; adult/car Ikr1150/1840) sails from Landeyjahöfn (about 12km off the Ring Rd between Hvolsvöllur and Skógar) to Heimaey four to five times a day all throughout the year. The journey takes about 30 minutes. Car reservations are essential in summer.

Bus

Sterna (☑553 3737; www.sterna.is) runs some connecting buses from Reykjavík to the harbour (Ikr3500), setting off around 2½ hours before the ferry departs. But not all the ferry journeys have a bus connection, and there is nothing whatsoever to do or see at or near Landeyjahöfn, so do check bus schedules carefully.

THE INTERIOR

The desolate interior is so vast, barren and remote that the Apollo astronauts held training exercises here before the 1969 lunar landings. The highlands are true wilderness, with practically no services, accommodation, mobile-phone signals or bridges, and no guarantees if things go wrong: careful preparations are essential. Routes are only accessible in July and August.

Routes of Central Iceland

Historically, the interior routes were used as summer short cuts between north and south, places of terror to be traversed as quickly as possible. Some *útilegumenn* (outlaws) fled into these harsh highlands: those who survived gained legendary status, like the superhuman Grettir; or Fjalla-Eyvindur, an Icelandic Robin Hood/Butch Cassidy figure.

Routes in this section are summer-only, and (apart from the Kjölur route) are strictly for high-clearance 4WD vehicles. It's recommended that vehicles travel in pairs.

Many mountain huts are run by **Ferðafélag Íslands** (Map p224; ☑568 2533; www.fi.is; Mörkin 6, Reykjavík); accommodation is on a first-come, first-served basis, so book in advance. Facilities tend to be spartan, and if there are kitchens, they generally lack utensils.

KJÖLUR ROUTE

The Kjölur route (35) was once believed to be infested with bloodthirsty outlaws. Nowadays, it's a favourite with visitors: it's greener and more hospitable than the Sprengisandur route; it forms a neat shortcut between Reykjavík and Akureyri; and it's accessible to all vehicles, as there are no rivers to ford. The route's name (Keel) refers to the perceived shape of its topography.

Kjölur's main attraction is **Hveravellir**, a geothermal area of fumaroles and multicoloured hot pools at the northern end of the pass. A camping ground and two mountain huts with kitchens are run by **Hveravallafélag** (☑summer 452 4200, year-round 894 1293; www.hveravellir.is; campsite/dm per person Ikr1200/4000; ☺mid-Jun–mid-Sep).

Daily from mid-June to early September, scheduled buses travel along the Kjölur route between Reykjavík and Akureyri (in both directions). **SBA-Norðurleið** (☑550 0770, 550 0700; www.sba.is) bus 610/610a takes 10½ hours for the complete journey, with various stops. **Sterna** (☑551 1166; www.sterna.is) bus 35/35a from Reykjavík is a 15-hour longer day, which more resembles a tour if you travel the whole way to Akureyri.

Drivers with 4WD vehicles will have no problems on the Kjölur route. You won't find a car-rental agency that provides insurance to those with plans of taking a 2WD.

SPRENGISANDUR ROUTE

The Sprengisandur route (F26) is long and desolate, but it does offer some wonderful views of Vatnajökull, Tungnafellsjökull and Hofsjökull, as well as Askja and Herðubreið. The bus passes the photogenic waterfall **Aldeyjarfoss**, which topples over clustered basalt columns.

A good place to break your journey is **Nýidalur**, which has a campsite, two Ferðafélag Íslands **huts** (☑Jul-Aug 860 3334; www.fi.is; N 64° 44.130′, W 18° 04.350′; dm Ikr5000) and lots of hiking possibilities. A recommended, challenging day hike takes you to the **Vonarskarð Pass** (1000m), a colourful saddle between Vatnajökull, Tungnafellsjökull and the green Ógöngur hills.

From July to August, **Reykjavík Excursions** (☎580 5400; www.re.is) operate two scheduled services along the Sprengisandur route between Reykjavík or Landmannalaugar and Lake Mývatn. Daily buses (Ikr7700, four hours) run between Reykjavík (departs 8am) and Landmannalaugar (departs 3.30pm) early-June to mid-September.

ÖSKJULEIÐ ROUTE (ASKJA WAY)

The Öskjuleið route runs across the highlands to Herðubreið, and to the desert's most popular marvel, the immense Askja caldera.

HERÐUBREIÐ

Iceland's most distinctive mountain, Herðubreið (1682m), has been described as a birthday cake, a cooking pot and a lampshade, but the tourist industry calls it (more respectfully) the 'Queen of the Desert'. The track around it makes a nice day hike from **Herðubreiðarlindir Nature Reserve**, a grassy oasis created by springs flowing from beneath the lava. There's a **campsite** (per person Ikr1100) and the 30-bed **Þorsteinsskáli hut** (☎mid-Jun–Aug 854 9301; www.ffa.is; N 65° 11.544', W 16° 13.360'; dm Ikr4500), a comfy lodge with showers, kitchen and summer warden.

ASKJA

Askja is an immense 50-sq-km caldera, created by a colossal explosion of tephra (volcanic rock and lava) in 1875. Part of the volcano's collapsed magma chamber contains sapphire-blue **Öskjuvatn**, Iceland's deepest lake at 217m. At its northeastern corner is **Víti**, a hot lake in a tephra crater where the water (around 25°C) is ideal for swimming.

The two **Dreki Huts** (Askja Camp; ☎mid-Jun–Aug 853 2541; www.ffa.is; N 65° 02.503', W 16° 35.690'; campsite/dm per person Ikr1100/5000) at **Drekagil** (Dragon Ravine), 8km away, accommodate 60 people.

For tours to the Askja caldera, see p256.

Landmannalaugar & Fjallabak Nature Reserve

The Fjallabak route (F208) is a spectacular alternative to the coast road between Hella and Kirkjubæjarklaustur. It passes through the scenic nature reserve to **Landmannalaugar**, an area of rainbow-coloured rhyolite peaks, rambling lava flows, blue lakes and hot springs, which can hold you captive for days. Much of the route is along

(and in!) rivers and therefore unsuitable for 2WD vehicles.

The star attractions around Landmannalaugar are **Laugahraun**, a convoluted lava field; the soothing **hot springs** 200m west of the Landmannalaugar hut; multi-coloured vents at **Brennisteinsalda**; the incredible red crater lake **Ljótipollur**; and the blue lake **Frostastaðavatn**, just over the rhyolite ridge north of Landmannalaugar. **Bláhnúkur**, immediately south of Laugahraun, offers a scree scramble and fine views from the 943m peak.

The chaotic **hut and camping complex** (☎863 1175; N 63° 59.600', W 19° 03.660'; per person Ikr5000; ☻early Jun-Sep) is operated by Ferðafélag Íslands. It accommodates 85 people in closed (and close) quarters. There's a kitchen area, showers (Ikr500 for five minutes of hot water), and several wardens on site. Campers can pitch a tent in the designated areas (Ikr1100 per person) – they have access to the toilet and shower facilities as well.

Daily buses (Ikr7700, four hours) run between Reykjavík (departs 8am) and Landmannalaugar (departs 3.30pm) early-June to mid-September. From mid-June to mid-September, there's a parallel bus from Skaftafell (Ikr6600, 5 hours, departs 8am), also heading back at 3.30pm.

Laugavegurinn Trek

This 55km trek from Landmannalaugar to Þórsmörk, commonly known as Laugavegurinn, deserves the same fame as great world walks such as the Inca Trail. The best map is Landmælingar Íslands' *Þórsmörk/ Landmannalaugar* (1:100,000), which you can purchase online through **Ferðakort** (www.ferdakort.is).

The track is usually passable from mid-July to early September. You shouldn't have any problems if you're in reasonable condition, but don't take the walk lightly: it requires substantial river crossings, all-weather gear, sturdy boots and sufficient food and water.

Most people walk from north to south (because of the net altitude loss), taking three to four days. Some continue on to Skógar, making it a four-to-six-day trip: see p263 for details of the Þórsmörk–Skógar stretch.

As the route is very well travelled, you'll find a constellation of carefully positioned

Landmannalaugar–Þórsmörk Trek

Ⓝ 0 _____ 5 km
0 _____ 2.5 miles

Vondugljáaurar

Hot Springs ●
Landmannalaugar
Hut & Camping Ground

Laugahraun
Lava Field

Landmannalaugar
to Þórsmörk Track
Brennisteinsalda
(840m)

Grænagil

To Þórsmörk   Steam Vents
& Fumaroles
Bláhnúkur
(943m)

Stóra-Brandsgil

0 _____ 1 km
0 _____ 0.5 miles

Ljótipollur

Frostastaðavatn

F208

See Enlargement

Brennisteinsalda
(840m)▲

To Eldgjá (21km);
Kirkjubæjarklaustur (81km)

Bláhnúkur
(943m)▲

Kirkjufell

F208

Fjallabak
Nature
Reserve   ● Stórihver

● Hrafntinnusker
Hut

Jökultungur

Háskerðingur
(1278m)

Torfajökull

Kaldaklofsfjöll

Álftavatn
Huts

Álftaskarð

Torfahlaup

Strutslaug
Hot Springs

Álftavatn   Hvanngil Hut &
Camping Ground

Stóra Grænafell
(850m)▲

Mælifellssandur

F210

Blessárjökull

Stórasúla
(820m)▲

Tindfjallajökull

Sléttjökull

Mosar

Markarfljótsgljúfur

Botnar
(Emstrur) Huts

Markarfljót

● Slyppagil

Entujökull

F261

Ljósá

Húsadalur
Hut

Prongá

Þórsmörk
Hut

Merkurjökull

Sottarhellir

Básar
Hut

Þórsmörk

Krossá   Krossárjökull

Goðaland

Mýrdalsjökull

Eyjafjallajökull

Goðalandsjökull

Fimmvörðuháls
Hut

Fimmvörðuháls

Skógaheiði

Skógá

Skógafoss

Skógar

ICELAND LAUGAVEGURINN TREK

huts along the way – all are owned and maintained by **Ferðafélag Íslands** (☑568 2533; www.fi.is). These huts sleep dozens of people and must be booked well in advance – the wardens recommend booking in early spring even if you plan on travelling at the end of summer.

You can also camp in the designated areas around the huts, although these spaces tend to be open to the elements, making it difficult to steady your tent.

Leg 1: Landmannalaugar to Hrafntinnusker (12km; three to five hours) A relatively easy start to your adventure, the walk to the first hut passes the boiling earth at Stórihver and sweeping fields of glittering obsidian. You'll need to fill up on fresh water before you depart as there's no source until you reach the first hut.

Leg 2: Hrafntinnusker to Álftavatn (12km; four to five hours) At Hrafntinnusker you can try a couple of short local hikes without your pack before setting off – there are views at Söðull (20 minutes return) and Reykjafjöll (one hour return), and a hidden geothermal area behind the ice caves (three hours return) – ask the warden for walking tips. Views aplenty are found on the walk to Álftavatn as well – hike across the northern spur of the Kaldaklofsfjökull ice cap for vistas from the summit. Walking into Álftavatn you'll see looming Tindfjallajökull, Mýrdalsjökull and the infamous Eyjafjallajökull before reaching the serenely beautiful lake at which you'll spend the night.

Leg 3: Álftavatn to Emstrur (16km; six to seven hours) To reach Emstrur you'll need to ford at least one large stream – you can take your shoes off and get wet or wait at the edge of the river for a 4WD service car to give you a lift over. Not to be missed is the detour to Markarfljótsgljúfur – a gaping green canyon. It's well marked from Emstrur, and takes about an hour to reach (you come back the same way).

Leg 4: Emstrur to Þórsmörk (15km; six to seven hours) Bleakness and barrenness quickly turn to the lush arctic flowers of a brilliantly verdant kingdom. If you're not planning on staying in Þórsmörk you should aim to arrive by 3.30pm, as the amphibious bus departs for the Ring Rd and Reykjavík at 4pm sharp. For more information on Þórsmörk, see p263.

UNDERSTAND ICELAND

History

Viking Beginnings

Irish monks were probably the first people to come to Iceland in around AD 700. Their solitude was rudely shattered by the Settlement Era (871–930), when a wave of Nordic people descended, driven from the Scandinavian mainland by political clashes. Many raided Ireland and the Scottish islands on the way, bringing Celtic slaves to the new country.

Ingólfur Arnarson, a Norwegian fugitive, became the first official Icelander (AD 871). He settled at Reykjavík (Smoky Bay), which he named after steam he saw rising from geothermal vents. According to 12th-century sources, Ingólfur built his farm on Aðalstræti. Recent archaeological excavations have unearthed a Viking longhouse on that very spot; the dwelling is now the focus of the Reykjavík 871+/-2 museum.

The settlers rejected monarchy and established the world's first democratic parliament at Þingvellir (Parliament Plains; p239), outside Reykjavík. The country converted to Christianity in the year 1000.

Six-Hundred Years of Misery

Two hundred years of peace ended during the Sturlung Age (1230–62), when Iceland's chieftains descended into bloody territorial fighting. The era is epitomised by the life and violent death of historian and political schemer, Snorri Sturluson (p241). Iceland ceded control of the country to Norway in 1262, then was placed under Danish rule in 1397. For the next six centuries, the forgotten country endured a Dark Age of famine, disease and disastrous volcanic eruptions.

In the early 17th century, the Danish king imposed a trade monopoly that was utterly exploited by foreign merchants. In an attempt to bypass the crippling embargo, weaving, tanning and wool-dyeing factories were built, which led to the foundation of the city of Reykjavík.

Iceland's next calamity was volcanic. In 1783 the vast crater row Lakagígar (Laki) erupted for 10 months, devastating southeastern Iceland and creating a lingering poisonous haze. Nearly 75% of Iceland's livestock and 20% of the human population perished in the resulting famine, and an evacuation of the country was discussed.

ICELAND'S ECONOMIC MELTDOWN

Everything was looking so rosy. Between 2003 and early 2008, Iceland was full of confidence and riding high. But much of the country's wealth was built over a black hole of debt – its banks' liabilities were more than 10 times the country's annual GDP. The ripples of the worldwide financial crisis became a tidal wave by the time they reached Icelandic shores, washing away the country's entire economy.

By October 2008 the Icelandic stock market had crashed; the króna plummeted, losing almost half its value overnight; all three national banks went into receivership; and the country teetered on the brink of bankruptcy.

Help came for Iceland in November 2008 with a US$2.1 billion International Monetary Fund (IMF) loan and a US$3 billion bailout from Scandinavian neighbours. Nevertheless, spiralling inflation, wage cuts and redundancies meant that Icelanders' incomes fell by a quarter in real terms. Protesters rioted in Reykjavík, furious with a government they felt had betrayed them by not downsizing the bloated banking system. Prime Minister Geir Haarde resigned in January 2009.

One of the new government's first acts was to apply for EU membership, with a view to changing their currency from the króna to the euro (although subsequent events made this look a distinctly less attractive prospect).

The crash was a terrible blow to Icelanders, but incredibly the economic situation has already begun to right itself. Unlike other countries in financial straits, Iceland allowed its banks to fail, and refused to make cuts to its welfare system. The decision to favour taxpayers over financiers appears to be paying off

Birth of a New Nation

In spite (or perhaps because) of such neglectful foreign rule and miserable living conditions, a sense of Icelandic nationalism slowly began to grow. The Republic of Iceland was established on 17 June 1944, symbolically at Þingvellir.

Perversely, while the rest of Europe endured the horrors of WWII, Iceland went from strength to strength. British and then US troops were stationed at Keflavík (right up until September 2006), bringing with them undreamt of wealth. Subsistence farming gave way to prosperity and a frenzy of new building, funded mainly by American dollars. The Ring Rd, Iceland's main highway that circles the whole country, was finally completed in 1974.

Boom...and Bust

A corresponding boom in the fishing industry saw Iceland extend its fishing limit in the 1970s to 200 miles (322km). This precipitated the worst of the 'cod wars', when the UK initially refused to recognise the new zone and continued fishing inside what were now deemed to be Icelandic waters. During the seven-month conflict, Icelandic ships cut the nets of British trawlers, shots were fired and ships on both sides were rammed.

Iceland's booming economy suffered when the world financial crisis dealt the country a sledgehammer blow in 2008, thanks to massive foreign debt and a severely overvalued currency. The government fell, following four months of furious protests in the capital. In May 2009 a new left-wing government was elected, headed by Jóhanna Sigurðardóttir, Iceland's first female prime minister. Later that year, the government voted by a narrow margin to apply for EU membership, and the application process is well underway. But polls from 2010 onwards suggest Icelanders are likely to strongly reject any referendum on joining. Economic indicators are rising steadily now, with unemployment back at low levels and a sense that the future is looking bright again.

In volcano news, the ash cloud from the April 2010 eruption under Eyjafjallajökull glacier shut down European air traffic for six days, causing travel chaos across much of the continent. The airline industry, which is estimated to have lost over US$200 million per day, breathed a sigh of relief when the eruption stopped on May 23 – as did media broadcasters and commentators, who struggled woefully to pronounce the glacier's name correctly. The Grimsvötn volcano, which erupted the following year, was a mere trifle by comparison: its ash cloud only managed three days of air-traffic disruption. However, erupting volcanoes tickled people's interest and this, combined with the devalued króna, gave the nation's tourism industry an unforeseen jolt. Recently, Iceland has been registering record-breaking tourist numbers; the island is expected to hit one million annual visitors some time soon, and there are no signs of slowing down in sight.

People

Though Icelanders are reserved, they are notably welcoming, recently being voted the world's friendliest country to visitors in a poll conducted by the World Economic Forum. They value independence and have a live-and-let-live attitude. But they are fiercely proud of their seafaring culture and many hold strong pro-whaling views. Icelanders recently discovered that much of their genetic makeup is Celtic, suggesting that far more of the Viking settlers had children by their Celtic slaves than originally thought.

Icelanders' names are constructed from a combination of their first name and their father's (or mother's) first name. Girls add the suffix *dóttir* (daughter) to the patronymic and boys add *son*. Therefore, Jón, the son of Einar, would be Jón Einarsson. Guðrun, the daughter of Halldór, would be Guðrun Halldórsdóttir. Icelanders always call each other by their first names.

The country has one of the world's highest life expectancies: 79 years for men and 83 years for women. Of a population of 313,000, almost two-thirds live in or around Reykjavík.

Iceland officially converted to Christianity around 1000, although followers of the old pagan gods were allowed to worship in private. The Danes imposed Lutheranism in the 1550 Reformation: 84% of Icelanders are Lutheran today. Nevertheless, a recent survey showed that more than 60% were prepared to believe that elves existed on the island.

Arts

Literature

Bloody, black, humorous and powerful, the late 12th- and 13th-century sagas are without doubt Iceland's greatest cultural achievement. Written in terse Old Norse, these epics continue to entertain Icelanders and provide them with a rich sense of heritage. One of the best known, *Egil's Saga,* revolves around the complex, devious Egill Skallagrímsson. A renowned poet and skilled lawyer, he's also the grandson of a werewolf and a murderous drunk. You can admire original saga manuscripts in Reykjavík's Þjóðmenningarhúsið.

The best-known modern Icelandic writer is Nobel Prize-winner Halldór Laxness, who lived just outside Reykjavík. His darkly comic work gives a superb insight into Icelandic life. His most famous book, *Independent People* (1934), concerning the fatally proud farmer Bjartur and the birth of the Icelandic nation, is an unmissable read.

Modern Icelandic writers include Einar Kárason, who wrote the outstanding *Devil's Island* (1983; about Reykjavík life in the 1950s); Hallgrímur Helgason, creator of *101 Reykjavík* (1996; about a modern-day city slacker); and Arnaldur Indriðason, whose Reykjavík-based crime fiction, including the award-winning *Silence of the Grave* (2001), regularly tops Iceland's bestseller lists.

Music

Internationally famous Icelandic musicians include (of course) Björk. Sigur Rós have followed Björk to stardom; their biggest-selling album *Takk* (2005) garnered rave reviews around the world. It was followed by the poppier *Með suð í eyrum við spilum endalaust* (2007); and after a long hiatus the band released their sixth studio album *Valtari* in 2012.

Indie-folk newcomers Of Monsters and Men stormed the US charts in 2011 with their debut album *My Head is an Animal.* You may also be familiar with Emiliana Torrini, the Icelandic–Italian singer who sang the spooky *Gollum's Song* in the Lord of the Rings film *The Two Towers* (2002).

Back home, Reykjavík has a flourishing music scene with a constantly changing line-up of new bands and sounds – see www.icelandmusic.is for an idea of the variety. Those who have stayed the course include FM Belfast; Múm (electronica mixed with real instruments); Mínus (their thrashy guitars have supported Foo Fighters and Metallica); Hafdís Huld (spiky female popstress); and ebullient garage-rockers Benny Crespo's Gang.

The fabulous Iceland Airwaves music festival (held in Reykjavík in October) showcases Iceland's talent along with international acts.

Visual Arts

Various artists have wrestled with Iceland's enigmatic soul, including the prolific Ásgrímur Jónsson (1876–1958). His work, depicting Icelandic landscapes and folk tales, can be seen at the National Gallery of Iceland in Reykjavík. Pop-art icon Erró (b 1932) is honoured with a permanent collection in Listasafn Reykjavíkur.

Sculptors are well represented: the mystical work of Einar Jónsson (1874–1954) dwells on death and resurrection, and can be viewed at the Einar Jónsson Museum in Reykjavík. Ásmundur Sveinsson's (1893–1982) sculptures, on display at Ásmundarsafn in Reykjavík, celebrate Iceland and its stories.

Cinema

Iceland's film industry is young but distinctive, often containing quirky, dark subject matter and superb cinematography, using Iceland's powerful landscape as a backdrop.

Director Friðrik Þór Friðriksson is something of a legend in Icelandic cinema circles, although some of his films are definitely better than others. *Children of Nature* (1992), *Cold Fever* (1994), *Angels of the Universe* (2000) and *The Sunshine Boy* (2009) are four that are well worth watching.

If one Icelandic film has put Reykjavík on the cinematic stage, it's *101 Reykjavík* (2000), directed by Baltasar Kormákur and based on the novel by Hallgrímur Helgason. This dark comedy explores sex, drugs and the life of a loafer in downtown Reykjavík. Kormákur's *Jar City* (2006) stars the ever-watchable Ingvar E Sigurðsson as Iceland's favourite detective, Inspector Erlendur. His latest film *The Deep* (2012) has been a hit with both critics and the public.

Iceland's immense alien beauty is a lure for foreign filmmakers too; try to spot the island's scenery in blockbusters such as *Tomb Raider* (2001), *Die Another Day* (2002), *Batman Begins* (2005), *Flags of Our Fathers* (2006), *Stardust* (2007), *Journey to the Centre of the Earth* (2008), *Prometheus* (2012), *Oblivion* (2013), *Star Trek: Into Darkness* (2013) and the HBO series *Game of Thrones* (2011–).

Environment

The Land

Iceland, a juvenile among the world's land masses, is shaped by desert plateaus (52%), lava fields (11%), sandur (sand deltas; 4%) and ice caps (12%). Over half of Iceland lies above 400m and its highest point, Hvannadalshnúkur, rises 2119m above sea level. Only 21% of Iceland is considered habitable.

Iceland's active volcanic zone runs through the middle of the country, from southwest to northeast. Active-zone geological features include lava flows, tubes, geysers, hot springs and volcanoes, and rocks such as basalt, pumice and rhyolite. Geysir, Krýsuvík and Krafla are very accessible active areas.

There are very few trees. Most of the native flora consists of grasses, mosses, lichens and wildflowers. *Plöntukort Íslands* (Botanical Map; Ikr1690), available from Reykjavík's bookshops, is a good guide.

Wildlife

The wild-eyed Arctic fox is the only indigenous land mammal; introduced species include reindeer and mice. Polar bears occasionally turn up on the north coast, but their life expectancy in Iceland is short.

The lack of land mammals is compensated for by vast numbers of birds and marine fauna. Kittiwakes, fulmars and gannets form large coastal colonies (best seen at Látrabjarg); there are Arctic terns, golden plovers, ducks, swans, divers and geese at Mývatn; and Vestmannaeyjar has the largest population of puffins. The website www.fuglar.is lists what rarities are about. *Fuglakort Íslands* (Birdwatcher's Map; Ikr1690), sold in Reykjavík's bookshops, is a good reference.

Four different seal species and 12 species of cetacean have been spotted: boat trips run from various coastal towns, including Reykjavík, although the best sightings are at Húsavík.

National Parks & Nature Reserves

Iceland's three national parks (*þjóðgarður*) are Snæfellsjökull (Snæfellsnes); Þingvellir (The Golden Circle), a Unesco World Heritage Site; and the newly created Vatnajökull National Park (Vatnajökull), which combines the former Jökulsárgljúfur and

WEIGHING UP THE WHALE DEBATE

After centuries of hunting, many whale species are now facing extinction. To give populations a chance to recover, the International Whaling Commission (IWC) called for a suspension of commercial whaling in 1986. Most countries complied; however, Iceland continued 'scientific' whaling, a loophole that allows whales to be hunted for DNA samples and then permits the meat to be sold to restaurants.

Following international pressure, there was a lull between 1989 and 2003, after which Icelandic whalers resumed 'scientific' whaling. In 2006, Iceland also began commercial whaling again, with the governmental Icelandic Marine Institute tentatively suggesting that an annual catch of 100 minke and 150 fin whales was sustainable. In response, 26 countries issued a formal protest to the Icelandic government, and conservationists called for a boycott of Iceland and Icelandic goods. Though the protests appeared to have had little effect, in 2012, after pressue from the USA, Iceland announced that the endangered fin whale will no longer be hunted. Demand for minke whale meat seemed to have dried up too, as whalers didn't come close to reaching the proposed quota of 216.

Whaling is an emotional topic, and has become deeply entwined with national pride. A strong majority of Icelanders support the hunt, though only some 1% of households consume the meat. (A significant proportion of whale meat consumed in Iceland is eaten by tourists.) Supporters believe minke whales are depleting fish stocks and need culling; whereas antiwhalers fear for the animals and for the flourishing whale-watching industry, which brings in about US$18 million annually.

Whaling in Iceland is regulated by the International Whaling Commission. For more information, see the websites of the International Whaling Commission (www.iwcoffice. org), WWF (www.wwf.org), Icelandic Ministry of Fisheries and Agriculture (www.fisheries. is) and Greenpeace (www.greenpeace.org).

Skaftafell parks. There are more than 80 nature reserves (friðland), the most significant being Mývatn. Parks and reserves are open to visitors at all times. Wild camping is restricted. For further information, contact the government's environment agency, **Umhverfisstofnun** (☑591 2000; www.ust.is).

Environmental Issues

Historically, sheep farming and timber extraction caused immense environmental damage. The Iceland Forest Service estimates that a mere 1% of Iceland's original woodland remains. Large-scale aerial seeding and intensive tree-planting programs are combating erosion.

Concerns over declining fish stocks have led the government to invest in other areas, particularly heavy industry (in early 2008, aluminium smelting products accounted for 40% of Iceland's total exports, overtaking fish for the first time). The most controversial project in Icelandic history was the dam built in the Kárahnjúkar peaks in eastern Iceland to power an American aluminium smelting plant. Completed in 2008, it altered the courses of two glacial rivers and flooded a vast area of untouched wilderness.

Iceland is endeavouring to free itself of fossil fuels by 2050, relying instead on geothermal power, hydrogen cells and solar energy. Little wonder that Iceland is keenly interested in averting climate change; there are worrying signs that Iceland's major ice caps have been melting at an unprecedented rate since 2000. Icelandic Met Office glaciologists believe that some of their attendant glaciers could disappear completely within a few decades.

Food & Drink

Cafes and restaurants in Reykjavík cater to most tastes, but fresh fish, seafood and Icelandic lamb get top billing on most upmarket menus.

The government levies high taxes on alcohol to discourage excessive drinking. Check out Friday-night Reykjavík to see the success of this policy!

Staples & Specialities

Born from centuries of near-starvation, Iceland's traditional dishes reflect a 'waste not, want not' austerity. Specialities include *svið* (singed sheep's head complete with eyeballs), *súrsaðir hrútspungar* (pickled rams' testicles) and *hákarl* (putrefied shark meat, buried and rotted for three months to make it digestible). These gruesome dishes are generally only eaten nowadays during the February celebration of Þorri. You can try cubes of shark meat at Kolaportið Flea Market in Reykjavík, but be warned that the smell alone makes many foreigners ill! Some restaurants serve whale meat *(hval)*.

Icelanders consume *lundi* (puffin), which looks and tastes like calf liver. Most of the birds are netted on the Vestmannaeyjar. *Harðfiskur* is an everyday snack: these brittle pieces of wind-dried haddock are usually eaten with butter. Delicious yoghurt-like *skyr,* made from curdled milk, is a unique treat; sugar, fruit and cream are often added to turn it into a rich dessert. Around Mývatn look out for a regional pudding: *hverabrauð* (hot-spring bread) is a sweet, dark, sticky loaf, baked in the ground using geothermal heat. *Kleinur* (twisted doughnuts, traditionally deep-fried in lard) are popular snacks to dip in coffee.

Coffee is a national institution, and most cafes offer free refills. The traditional Icelandic alcoholic brew is *brennivín* (burnt wine), a sort of schnapps made from potatoes and caraway seeds with the foreboding nickname *svarti dauði* (black death). Note that if you buy *syrmjolk* from the supermarket, it's sour milk.

Where to Eat & Drink

Reykjavík has no shortage of cosy cafes (commonly open from 11am until 1am, later at weekends) that turn into bars at night. They're great for lingering coffees, light lunches (from about Ikr1500) and late-night beers. Restaurants are more upmarket, often serving gourmet food, with mains from about Ikr2700 to Ikr5000 per person. Some are open for lunch (between 11am and 2pm), and most open nightly (between 6pm and 10pm). In other towns, choice is much reduced and opening times shorter.

Every village has at least one *kaupfélagið* (cooperative supermarket), with Bónus and Netto being the cheapest. Petrol stations and grills sell relatively inexpensive fast-food snacks (a hot dog and chips cost around Ikr900).

Beer, wine and spirits are available to people aged over 20 years from licensed hotels, bars, restaurants and Vínbúð (state monopoly) stores. A pint of beer in a pub costs about Ikr700 to Ikr800; a bottle of house wine in a restaurant will cost at least Ikr3000.

Vegetarians & Vegans

You'll have no problem in Reykjavík – there are several excellent meat-free, organic cafe-restaurants in the city, and many more eateries offer vegetarian choices. Outside the capital most restaurants have at least one vegie item on the menu – although as this is routinely cheese-and-tomato pasta or pizza, you could get very bored. Vegans will have to self-cater.

SURVIVAL GUIDE

Directory A–Z

Accommodation

Iceland has a full spectrum of accommodation options, from spartan mountain huts through hostels, working farms, guesthouses and school-based summer rooms to luxury hotels. It must be said, however, that accommodation is often of a lower standard than you might expect from a developed European destination. Although rooms are generally spotless, they are usually small, with thin walls and limited facilities.

Sleeping-bag accommodation is a peculiarly Icelandic concept, and a boon for those on a budget. Many hostels and guesthouses let you have a bed without bedding for a discount on their standard prices, if you use your own sleeping bag.

We have given high-season prices throughout. Out of season, prices at some B&Bs, guesthouses and hotels drop by as much as 50%. Many places close in winter; check first.

In this chapter accommodation prices are based on a double room, usually with private bathroom and breakfast. The following price indicators apply:

€€€   more than Ikr22,000 (€140)

€€   Ikr12,000 to 22,000 (€75–140)

€   less than Ikr12,000 (approx €75)

CAMPING

» Make sure your tent is up to Icelandic weather: storm-force winds and deluges aren't uncommon throughout the year, even in summer. Wild camping is possible in some areas (although not on fenced land without permission, or in national

WARNING – POTENTIAL PRICE HIKE

See p223 for details of a proposed VAT price hike in Iceland. Needless to say, prices may rise and look quite different to those listed in this book. Our best advice is to always check websites for up-to-date information.

parks and nature reserves), but is often discouraged. With approximately 130 *tjaldsvæði* (organised camping grounds) in towns and at rural farmhouses, there's usually a campsite close at hand.

» Camping with a tent or campervan/caravan usually costs between Ikr800 and Ikr1200 per person. Electricity is often an additional Ikr800. Some campsites charge for showers.

» A new 'lodging tax' of Ikr100 per site per night was introduced in 2012; some places absorb this cost in the per-person rate, others make you pay it in addition to the per-person rate.

» Campfires are not allowed, so bring a stove. Butane cartridges and petroleum fuels are available in petrol stations and hardware shops.

» Most campsites open from June to August or early September only. If it's a large campsite that also offers huts or cottages, these may be open year-round.

» Consider purchasing the **Camping Card** (www.campingcard.is; €99), which covers unlimited camping for the season at 44 campsites throughout the country for two adults and up to four children.

» The free directory *Tjaldsvæði Íslands* (available from tourist information centres) lists many of Iceland's campsites.

FARMHOUSE ACCOMMODATION

» Many rural farmhouses offer campsites, sleeping-bag spaces, made-up guest rooms and cabins and cottages. Over time, some 'farmhouses' have evolved into large country hotels.

» Facilities vary: some farms provide meals or have a guest kitchen, some have outdoor hot-pots (hot tubs) or a geothermal swimming pool, and many provide horse riding or can organise activities such as fishing.

» Rates are similar to guesthouses in towns, with sleeping-bag accommodation

costing around Ikr4500 and made-up beds from Ikr7000 to Ikr10,000 per person.

» Some 180 farm properties are members of **Icelandic Farm Holidays** (www.farmholidays.is), which publishes a free annual guide available from tourist information centres.

GUESTHOUSES

» The Icelandic term *gistiheimilið* (guesthouse) covers a wide variety of properties, from family homes renting out a few rooms to custom-built motels.

» Most are comfortable and homey, with guest kitchens, TV lounges and buffet-style breakfast (either included in the price or for around Ikr1500 to Ikr2000 extra).

» Some guesthouses offer sleeping-bag accommodation at a price significantly reduced from that of a made-up bed. Note that some places don't advertise a sleeping-bag option, so it pays to ask.

» As a general guide, sleeping-bag accommodation costs Ikr4500 to Ikr5000, double rooms from Ikr12,000 to Ikr18,000, and self-contained units from Ikr14,000 per night.

HOSTELS

» Iceland has 36 well-maintained youth hostels administered by **Hostelling International Iceland** (www.hostel.is). In Reykjavík and Akureyri, there are also independent backpacker hostels. Bookings are recommended at all of them, especially from June to August.

» If you don't have a sleeping bag, you can hire linen (Ikr1100 per stay at HI hostels).

» Breakfast (where available) costs Ikr1500 to Ikr2000.

» Join **Hostelling International** (HI; www.hihostels.com) in your home country to benefit from HI member discounts. Pay Ikr2700 to Ikr3200 for a dorm bed; nonmembers pay Ikr600 extra per night. Single/double rooms for members cost roughly Ikr5000/8000. Children aged five to 12 years pay half price.

HOTELS

» Every major town has at least one business-style hotel, usually featuring comfortable but innocuous rooms with private bathroom, phone, TV and sometimes minibar. Invariably the hotels also have decent restaurants.

» Summer prices for singles/doubles start at around Ikr17,000/22,000 and include a buffet breakfast. Prices drop substantially outside peak season (June to August), and cheaper rates can often be found if you book online.

Two of the largest local hotel chains are **Fosshótel** (☏562 4000; www.fosshotel.is) and **Icelandair Hotels** (☏444 4000; www.icelandairhotels.is).

SUMMER HOTELS

» Once the school holidays begin, many schools, colleges and conference centres become summer hotels offering simple accommodation. Most are open from early June to late August, and 12 of them are part of a chain called **Hotel Edda** (www.hoteledda.is).

» Rooms are plain but functional, usually with twin beds, a washbasin and shared bathrooms, although four of the 12 hotels offer 'Edda Plus' rooms, with private bathroom, TV and phone. Some Edda hotels have dormitory sleeping-bag spaces; most Edda hotels have a restaurant.

» Expect to pay around Ikr4000 for sleeping-bag accommodation, Ikr9500/11,800 for a single/double with washbasin and Ikr17,500/21,900 for an 'Edda Plus' single/double.

MOUNTAIN HUTS

» *Sæluhús* (mountain huts) sprout up on popular hiking routes, mostly in wilderness areas. The best huts have showers, kitchens, wardens and potable water; they cost Ikr4000 to Ikr5000 for nonmembers. Simpler huts cost Ikr3500 and usually just have bed space, toilet and a basic cooking area. Camping is available at some huts for around Ikr1100 per person.

» The huts are open to anyone, but members get a discount. Book in advance, as places fill quickly.

» The main mountain-hut provider is **Ferðafélag Íslands** (Icelandic Touring Association; ☏568 2533; www.fi.is; Mörkin 6, Reykjavík), with 38 huts around Iceland.

» Bright orange huts are dotted about the mountain passes and coastline and are for emergencies only

Activities
FISHING

» A one-day fishing licence may cost anything up to Ikr200,000, but you can fish for rainbow trout, sea trout and Arctic char on a more reasonably priced voucher system.

» Trout fishing runs from April to mid-September, and ice fishing is possible in some areas in winter. For further information, contact the **National Angling Association** (☏553 1510; www.angling.is).

GLACIER WALKING

» Several companies offer exhilarating guided walks, with crampons and ice axes, on the south-coast glaciers. The **Icelandic Mountain Guides Reykjavík** (☏587 9999; www.mountainguides.is); **Skaftafell** (☏894 2959; www.mountainguides.is) and the **Glacier Guides** (☏571 2100; www.glacierguides.is) both have huts in the Skaftafell visitor-centre car park in summer.

HIKING, TREKKING & MOUNTAINEERING

» Rain, fog and mist are common, and snow may fall in any season at higher altitudes.

» In the highlands, straightforward hiking only becomes possible in July, August and early September. At other times, routes are impassable without complete winter gear; in late spring, melting snow turns many tracks into quagmires where whole vehicles have sunk without trace! Unbridged rivers can be difficult to cross at any time of year.

» Use caution when walking with children, especially in fissured areas such as Mývatn and Þingvellir, where narrow cracks in the earth can be hundreds of metres deep. Tough boots are needed for negotiating lava fields.

» For details on hiking and mountaineering, contact **Ferðafélag Íslands** (Map p224; ☏568 2533; www.fi.is; Mörkin 6, Reykjavík), **Íslenski Alpaklúbburinn** (www.isalp.is) or the **Icelandic Mountain Guides** (☏587 9999; www.mountainguides.is; Vagnhöfði 7b, Reykjavík).

HORSE RIDING

» The Icelandic horse *(Equus scandinavicus)* is known for its *tölt,* a smooth, distinctive gait that makes riding easy, even for beginners.

» You can hire horses through farms and tour agencies throughout the country, with a one-hour/one-day ride costing around Ikr 4000/15,000. In September experienced riders can also volunteer for the *réttir* (sheep round-up); contact local tourist offices to arrange this.

KAYAKING & RAFTING

Arctic Rafting (☎571 2200; www.rafting.is; ☺May-Sep) run trips in south Iceland on the Hvítá river (near Gullfoss and Geysir); and in north Iceland on two glacial rivers near the small service town of Varmahlíð. Both bases offer gentler journeys suitable for ages 12-plus; but if it's wild white water that you want, head for Varmahlíð and the exhilarating three-hour trip on the **Austari Jökulsá** (East Glacial River; Ikr20,000) with Grades III to IV-plus rapids (over 18s only). There's also a three-day adventure (Ikr70,000) that speeds you downstream from the Sprengisandur desert and the river's glacial source.

SCUBA DIVING & SNORKELLING

Dive.is (☎663 2858; www.dive.is; 2 dives at Þingvellir Ikr30,000) runs daily tours year-round to the Silfra fissure in Lake Þingvellir, giving you the chance to dive between the North American and European continental plates. Scuba-diving certification is required; nondivers can drift overhead with drysuits and snorkels. The company also runs three- and seven-day diving tours to other sites around the country.

SKIING & SNOWBOARDING

» Both Reykjavík and Akureyri have winter resorts for downhill skiing or snowboarding (one-day lift passes around Ikr3000), with rentals (Ikr4500) and instructors:

Skíðasvæðin (www.skidasvaedi.is)

Hlíðarfjall (www.hlidarfjall.is)

SWIMMING

» Admission to a *sundlaug* or *sundhöll* (public swimming hall)is usually around Ikr400 to Ikr500 (half price for children) for an unlimited swim session.

» The following are the best resources for getting into hot water, so to speak:

Friends of Water (www.vatnavinir.is/home)

Swimming in Iceland (www.swimminginiceland.com)

Thermal Pools in Iceland (by Jón G Snæland) Comprehensive guide to Iceland's naturally occurring springs (with images); sold in most Icelandic bookstores.

Blue Lagoon (Bláa Lónið; ☎420 8800; www.bluelagoon.com; admission from €33; ☺9am-9pm Jun-Aug, 10am-8pm Sep-May) Iceland's favourite hot spring and undisputed top attraction.

WHALE WATCHING

» The most common sightings are of minke whales, but you can also spot humpback, fin, sei and blue whales, among others.

» Prices hover around €50 for a two- or three-hour tour. Sailings do in fact run all year, with the best chances of success from mid-June to August.

Business Hours

Opening hours in general tend to be far longer from June to August, and shorter from September to May. Standard opening hours are as follows:

Banks 9.15am to 4pm Monday to Friday

Cafe-bars 10am to 1am Sunday to Thursday, 10am to between 3am and 6am Friday and Saturday

Cafes 10am to 6pm

Offices 9am to 5pm Monday to Friday

Petrol stations 8am to 10pm or 11pm

Post offices 9am to 4pm or 4.30pm Monday to Friday (to 6pm in larger towns)

Restaurants 11.30am to 2.30pm and 6pm to 10pm

Shops 10am to 6pm Monday to Friday, 10am to 4pm Saturday; some Sunday opening in Reykjavík malls and major shopping strips

Supermarkets 9am to 8pm (later in Reykjavík)

Vinbuð (state alcohol stores) Variable; many outside Reykjavík only open for a couple of hours per day

Children

» Icelanders have a relaxed attitude to kids, but there are not many activities provided especially for them. Frequent bad weather may put you off family camping, but everyone can enjoy a ride on a mild-mannered Icelandic horse or a swim in an open-air pool.

» Children aged between two and 11 years pay half fare on Flugfélag Íslands (Air Iceland) flights and tours, and are charged half price for farmhouse and some other accommodation. Bus fares are half price for children aged four to 11. Reykjavík Excursions tours are free for children under 11, and half fare for those aged between 12 and 15. There's a 50% discount at pools, and admission to museums and cinemas varies from full price to free.

Food

In this chapter restaurant prices are based on the average cost of a main course, unless stated otherwise. The following price indicators apply:

€   less than Ikr1500 (approx €10)

€€   Ikr1500 to 3500 (€10–25)

€€€   more than Ikr3500 (€25)

Gay & Lesbian Travellers

» Icelanders have an open attitude toward gays and lesbians; indeed the prime minister Jóhanna Sigurðardóttir married her female partner in a same-sex union in 2010.

» Check out www.gayice.is for news and events.

Internet Access

» Public internet access is available in most Icelandic libraries for about Ikr200 to Ikr400 per hour.

» Wi-fi access is common: with a wireless-enabled laptop, you can surf in most cafes, bars, hotels and many guesthouses.

Maps

» Maps are widely available from tourist offices and bookshops all over Iceland. Ask tourist offices for the free *Map of Reykjavík* and *Around Iceland* booklets (with bags of information plus town plans).

» The map publisher **Ferðakort** (☏517 7210; www.ferdakort.is; Brautarholt 8, Reykjavík) has a good selection of road and walking maps, available through its website or at its dedicated map shop in Reykjavík. Most drivers use the general 1:500,000 *Ísland Touring Map*. Also useful are the 1:25,000 and 1:100,000 maps of Skaftafell, the 1:50,000 map of the Vestmannaeyjar and the 1:100,000 maps of Hornstrandir, Mývatn and the Landmannalaugar to Þórsmörk trek.

Money

Currency Iceland uses the króna (plural krónur), written as Ikr in this book, and often written elsewhere as ISK. Coins come in denominations of 1, 5, 10, 50 and 100 krónur. Notes come in 500-, 1000-, 2000- and 5000-krónur denominations.

Some accommodation providers and tour operators give their prices in euro. Where this is the case, we have listed the euro prices in this book.

VAT *(söluskattur)* Included in marked prices: spend over Ikr4000 in a shop offering 'Iceland Tax-Free Shopping' and you can claim back up to 15%. Shop staff will give you a tax-refund form; hand it in at the tourist office, the airport or the ferry terminal for a rebate.

ATMs Almost every town in Iceland has a bank with an ATM, where you can withdraw cash using MasterCard, Visa, Maestro or Cirrus cards.

Tipping Not required.

Public Holidays

New Year's Day 1 January

Easter March or April (Maundy Thursday and Good Friday to Easter Monday; changes annually)

First Day of Summer First Thursday after 18 April

Labour Day 1 May

Ascension Day May or June (changes annually)

Whit Sunday and Whit Monday May or June (changes annually)

National Day 17 June

Commerce Day First Monday in August

Christmas 24 to 26 December

New Year's Eve 31 December

Telephone

Public phones Elusive these days; there may be one outside the post office or bus station, and at the local petrol station. Many payphones accept credit cards. Local calls are charged at around Ikr20 per minute.

Mobile phones The cheapest and most practical way to make calls at local rates is to purchase an Icelandic SIM card and pop it into your own mobile (cell) phone (see also p488). You can buy a prepaid SIM card at bookstores, grocery stores, post offices and petrol stations throughout the country. Top-up credit is available from the same outlets. Starter packs including local SIM cards can be bought for as little as Ikr2000 (including Ikr2000 in call credit).

Phone codes Direct dialling is available to Europe, North America and elsewhere.

After dialling the international access code (☏00 from Iceland), dial your country code, area/city code and the telephone number. For dialling into Iceland from abroad, the country code is ☏354. There are no area codes: just follow the country code with the seven-digit number. Within Iceland, just dial the seven-digit number. Most Icelandic mobile phone numbers begin with an '8'.

Time

Iceland has no GMT/UTC offset and doesn't observe daylight-saving. So from late October to late March, Iceland is on the same time as London, five hours ahead of New York and 11 hours behind Sydney. Between April and September, Iceland is one hour behind London, four hours ahead of New York and 10 hours behind Sydney.

Tourist Information

You'll find tourist offices with friendly staff in towns all over the country. Pick up the useful *Around Iceland* (general tourist guide) and *Áning* (accommodation guide): both are free annual publications.

Visit Iceland (☏511 4000; www.visiticeland. com; Borgartún 35, Reykjavík) You can order or download free brochures from their website.

Travellers with Disabilities

» For details on accessible facilities, get in touch with **Sjálfsbjörg** (☏550 0360; www. sjalfsbjorg.is; Hátún 12, Reykjavík). Sjálfsbjörg's website (click on English, then For Travellers) has excellent information on resources and organisations.

» Most museums and other attractions offer reduced admission prices for travellers with disabilities. For travel, Air Iceland offers reduced rates, as does the Smyril Line ferry.

» Reykjavík's city buses have a 'kneeling' function so that wheelchairs can be lifted onto the bus; elsewhere, however, public buses don't have ramps or lifts.

» **Hertz** (www.hertz.is) has a wheelchair-accessible minivan for hire.

» The company **All Iceland Tours** (www. allicelandtours.is/Disabled_Travel) offers tailor-made trips around the country. Its website also has good general info.

» Sjálfsbjörg has guest apartments for rent. Otherwise, the website www.whenwetravel. com lists which hotels in Iceland are wheelchair accessible. All farms in the **Icelandic Farm Holidays** (www.farmholidays. is) network have been evaluated for accessibility.

Visas

See the main Directory section (p489) for entry requirements. For more information contact the nearest Icelandic embassy or consulate, or check the website www.utl.is.

Getting There & Away

Air

Iceland's main international airport is **Keflavík International Airport** (www.kefairport. is), 48km southwest of Reykjavík.

Internal flights and those to Greenland and the Faeroes use the small **Reykjavík Airport** (www.reykjavikairport.is) in central Reykjavík.

A couple of international flights from Copenhagen land at tiny **Akureyri Airport** (www.akureyriairport.is) in Iceland's 'second city' in the north.

AIRLINES FLYING TO/FROM ICELAND

A growing number of airlines fly to Iceland; many have scheduled services only in the peak summer months (June to August).

Air Berlin (www.airberlin.com)

Air Greenland (www.airgreenland.com)

Atlantic Airways (www.atlantic.fo)

Austrian (www.austrian.com)

Delta (www.delta.com)

easyJet (www.easyjet.com)

Germanwings (www.germanwings.com)

Iceland Express (www.icelandexpress.com)

Icelandair (www.icelandair.com)

Lufthansa (www.lufthansa.com)

Norwegian (www.norwegian.com)

SAS (www.flysas.com)

Transavia France (www.transavia.com)

WOW air (www.wowair.com)

Sea

Smyril Line (www.smyrilline.com) operates a pricey but well-patronised weekly car ferry, the *Norröna*, on a somewhat convoluted schedule from Hirsthals (Denmark) through Tórshavn (Faroe Islands) to Seyðisfjörður in east Iceland. See p494 for more details.

Getting Around

There is no train network in Iceland. The most common way for visitors to get around the island is to rent a car and drive. There is also a good bus network operating from approximately mid-May to mid-September, to get you between major destinations, but don't discount internal flights that can help you maximise your time in Iceland.

Air

Iceland has an extensive network of domestic flights, which locals use almost like buses. In winter a flight can be the only way to get between destinations, but weather at this time of year can play havoc with schedules.

Note that almost all domestic flights depart from the small Reykjavík Airport in central Reykjavík (not the major international airport at Keflavík).

AIRLINES

Air Iceland (Flugfélag Íslands; www.airiceland.is) Destinations covered in its network: Reykjavík, Akureyri, Grimsey, Ísafjörður, Vopnafjörður, Egilsstaðir and Þórshöfn. Offers some fly-in day tours from Reykjavík (including to destinations in Greenland). Online deals for domestic flights start at around €60 one way.

Eagle Air (www.eagleair.is) Operates scheduled flights to smaller airstrips: Vestmannaeyjar, Húsavík, Höfn, Bíldudalur and Gjögur. Flights cost between €130 and €170 one way. There is also a number of day tours.

AIR PASSES

Air Iceland offers a couple of air passes, available year-round, which must be purchased either outside Iceland or in Icelandic travel agencies catering for foreign visitors.

Air Iceland Pass Available with four/five/six sectors for €384/445/512 in high season (mid-June to mid-August).

Fly As You Please Gives 12 consecutive days of unlimited flights in Iceland for €508 in high season, excluding airport taxes (€8 per departure).

Bicycle

» Cycling is an interesting if hardcore way to view Iceland's incredible landscape. Gale-force winds, sandstorms, sleet and sudden flurries of snow add to the challenge.

SAFE TRAVEL

In geothermal areas avoid thin crusts of lighter-coloured soil around steaming fissures and mudpots. Snowfields may overlie fissures, sharp lava chunks or slippery slopes of scoria (volcanic slag). Don't underestimate the weather: only attempt isolated hiking and glacier ascents if you know what you're doing. The supercautious can read www.safetravel.is for further information.

» Bring the best waterproofing money can buy; remember, you can always put your bike on a bus if things become intolerable.
» A mountain bike is probably more practical than a touring rig – you can get off the Ring Rd onto minor roads and unsurfaced tracks.
» Bring plenty of spares and several puncture repair kits.
» An excellent resource: the English pages of the website of the **Icelandic Mountain Bike** (www.fjallahjolaklubburinn.is).
» Most airlines will carry your bike in the hold if you pack it correctly. You should remove the pedals, lower the saddle, turn the handlebars parallel to the frame and deflate the tyres.
» The Smyril Line ferry from Denmark transports bikes for €15 each way.
» Buses charge Ikr2500 or Ikr3000, but space may be a problem so show up early or book ahead.
» If you've brought your own bicycle, you can store your bike box at Guesthouse Alex in Keflavík for free for the duration of your visit.
» Various places around Iceland rent out mountain bikes, but in general these are intended for local use only, and often aren't up to long-haul travel. If you intend to go touring, it's wise to bring your bike from home or purchase one when you arrive.

Boat

The following Icelandic car ferries are in operation:

Herjólfur (p267) Between Landeyjahöfn and Vestmannaeyjar.

Baldur (p243) Between Flatey, Stykkishólmur and Brjánslækur.

Sæfari (p251) Between Dalvík, Hrísey and Grímsey.

Bus

» Iceland has an extensive network of long-distance bus routes with services operated by a number of bus companies. They're overseen by **BSÍ** (Bifreiðastöð Íslands; ☑562 1011; www.bsi.is), based in the BSÍ bus terminal in Reykjavík.

» The booking desk at the BSÍ bus terminal sells tickets and distributes the free *Iceland on Your Own* brochure, which contains timetables for some (but not all) services.

» From roughly mid-May to mid-September there are regular scheduled buses to most places on the Ring Rd, and to larger towns in the Westfjords and on the Reykjanes and Snæfellsnes Peninsulas. There are also services along the highland Kjölur and Sprengisandur routes (inaccessible to 2WD cars). During the rest of the year services range from daily to nonexistent.

» In small towns and villages, buses stop at the main petrol station.

COMPANIES

The following are the main bus companies:

Reykjavík Excursions (Kynnisferðir; ☑580 5400; www.re.is) Serves the Reykjanes Peninsula and operates the Flybus to Keflavík airport, plus some scheduled southern routes, and summer buses across the interior.

SBA-Norðurleið (☑550 0770, 550 0700; www.sba.is) Services to north Iceland.

Sterna (☑551 1166; www.sterna.is) Services countrywide.

Stjörnubílar (☑456 5518; www.stjornubilar.is) Services to Westfjords.

BUS PASSES

Got to www.re.is/IcelandOnYourOwn/Passports and www.sterna.is/en/bus-passport for a longer list of passports.

Beautiful South Passport (3/7/11 days Ikr20,700/37,600/51,000) Valid from June to mid-September. Unlimited travel along the south coast and to Þórsmörk, Landmannalaugar and Lakagígar. Offered by Reykjavík Excursions.

Combo Passport (7/11/15 days Ikr49,000/65,000/77,000) The Big Kahuna of passports, from Reykjavík Excursions (working with SBA-Norðurleið) and taking in the Ring Rd, the northeast circuit (Húsavík to Þórshöfn), Golden Circle and both highland routes (but not Westfjords

or Snæfellsnes), valid from early June to mid-September.

Full Circle Passport (Ikr37,000) Sterna's pass is valid from mid-May to mid-September for one circuit of the Ring Rd in one direction, stopping wherever you like. Reykjavík Excursions has a similar pass for Ikr35,000 (the Ring Rd Passport), with slightly shorter validity.

Golden Circle Passport (Ikr9000) Valid from June to mid-September, and a decent alternative to taking a day-excursion. Covers Þingvellir, Geysir and Gullfoss, and Selfoss. Offered by Reykjavík Excursions.

Highland Circle Passport (Ikr35,600) Valid from mid-June to early September (depending on when the highlands roads are open) for one circular route taking in the Sprengisandur and Kjölur routes. Offered by Reykjavík Excursions.

Hiking Passport (Ikr10,500) Reykjavík Excursions offers return bus journey to southwest hikers from their start/end point, choosing two of three destinations: Skógar, Landmannalaugar and Þórsmörk.

Snæfellsnes & National Park (Ikr17,000) Valid from mid-June to August for one circuit of Snæfellsnes Peninsula, starting and ending in Reykjavík. Offered by Sterna.

West & Westfjords Passport (Ikr27,000) Valid from June to August for one circuit of the Westfjords, to/from Reykjavík and including the ferry across Breiðfjörður. Offered by Sterna (in conjunction with Stjörnubílar). Sterna also offers a Full Circle (Ring Rd) plus Westfjords option (Ikr59,000).

Car & Motorcycle

» Driving in Iceland gives you unparalleled freedom to discover the country and, thanks to good roads and light traffic, it's all fairly straightforward.

» The Ring Rd (Rte 1) circles the country and is mostly paved. Beyond the Ring Rd, fingers of sealed road or gravel stretch out to most communities.

» In coastal areas driving can be spectacularly scenic, and really slow as you weave up and down over unpaved mountain passes and in and out of long fjords. Still, a 2WD vehicle will get you almost everywhere in summer (note: not into the highlands).

» In winter heavy snow can cause many roads to close and mountain roads generally remain closed until June. Some mountain roads start closing as early as September after the warm summer months. For up-to-date information on road conditions, visit www.vegagerdin.is.

» Car hire in Iceland is shockingly expensive, so taking your own vehicle to the country on the ferry from Denmark may not be as crazy as it sounds.

FUEL & SPARE PARTS

» In the highlands check fuel levels and the distance to the next station before setting off on a long journey.

» At the time of research, unleaded petrol cost about Ikr260 (€1.70) per litre, diesel about Ikr265 per litre.

» Most smaller petrol stations are unstaffed, and almost all pumps are automated – put your card in and follow the instructions. It's a good idea to check that your card will work by visiting a staffed station while it is open, in case you have any problems.

» Some Icelandic roads can be pretty lonely, so carry a jack, a spare tyre and jump leads just in case. Although the Icelandic motoring association **Félag Íslenskra Bifreiðaeigenda** (FÍB; ☑414 9999; www.fib.is) is only open to residents of Iceland, if you have breakdown cover with an automobile association affiliated with ARC Europe you may be covered by the FÍB – check with your home association.

» FÍB's round-the-clock breakdown number is ☑511 2112. Even if you're not a member, they can provide information and phone numbers for towing and breakdown services all around Iceland.

HIRE

» Driving is often the only way to get to parts of Iceland. Although car hire is expensive, it compares favourably against bus or internal air travel within the country, especially if you can split the costs.

» To rent a car you must be 20 years old (23 to 25 years for a 4WD) and you will need to show a valid licence.

» The cheapest cars cost from around Ikr16,000 per day in high season (June to August). Figure on paying from around Ikr25,000 for the smallest 4WD. Rates include unlimited mileage and VAT, and usually CDW (collision damage waiver). Book well ahead in summer.

» Most companies are based in the Reykjavík and Keflavík areas, with city and

DRIVE SAFELY

Road Rules

» Drive on the right

» Front and rear seat belts are compulsory

» Dipped headlights must be on at all times

» Blood alcohol limit is 0.05%

» Mobile-phone use is prohibited except with a hands-free kit

» Children under six must use a car seat

» Do not drive off-road

Speed Limits

» Built-up areas 50km/h

» Unsealed roads 80km/h

» Sealed roads 90km/h

airport offices. Larger companies have extra locations around the country (usually in Akureyri and Egilsstaðir).

» Ferry passengers entering Iceland via Seyðisfjörður will find car-hire agencies in nearby Egilsstaðir.

CAR-HIRE COMPANIES

The following list is far from exhaustive.

Budget (www.budget.is)

Europcar (www.europcar.is) The biggest hire company in Iceland.

Geysir (www.geysir.is) Lists its daily/weekly summer and winter prices for each of its vehicles on its website.

Go Iceland (www.goiceland.com) Also rents out camping equipment (tents, mattresses, stoves).

Hasso (www.hasso.is)

SADcars (www.sadcars.com) Older fleet, therefore cheaper prices.

Saga (www.sagacarrental.is)

CAMPERVAN HIRE

Combining accommodation and transport costs into campervan rental is a popular option. The large car-hire companies usually have campervans for rent, but following are some more offbeat choices.

Camper Iceland (www.campericeland.is)

Happy Campers (www.happycampers.is)

JS Camper Rental (www.campers.is) Truck campers on 4WD pickups.

Kúkú Campers (www.kukucampers.is) Artwork-adorned campers.

Snail.is (www.snail.is)

HITCHING

» Hitching anywhere in the world is never fully without risk and we don't recommend it. Nevertheless, we met scores of tourists that were hitching their way around Iceland and most of them had very positive reports.

» If the idea of hitching makes you uncomfortable, check out www.samferda.is, a handy car-sharing site.

ROAD CONDITIONS & HAZARDS

Good road surfaces and light traffic make driving in Iceland relatively easy, but there are some specific hazards that drivers will encounter. Watch the 'How to Drive in Iceland' video on www.drive.is.

Livestock Sheep graze in the countryside over the summer, and often wander onto roads.

Gravel Roads Not all roads are sealed, and most accidents involving foreign drivers in Iceland are caused by the use of excessive speed on unsurfaced roads. If your car does begin to skid, take your foot off the accelerator and gently turn the car in the direction you want the front wheels to go. Do not brake.

F roads Roads suitable for 4WD vehicles only are F-numbered. It's a good idea to travel in tandem on these roads and carry emergency supplies and a full tool and repair kit. Always let someone know where you are going and when you expect to be back.

River crossings Few interior roads have bridges over rivers. Fords are marked on maps with a 'V', but you may need to check the depth and speed of the river by wading into it.

Norway

Why Go?

Norway is a once-in-a-lifetime destination and the essence of its appeal is remarkably simple: this is one of the most beautiful countries on earth.

The drama of Norway's natural world is difficult to overstate. Impossibly steep-sided fjords cut deep gashes into the interior. But this is also a land of glaciers, grand and glorious, snaking down from Europe's largest ice fields, and a land with the primeval appeal of the Arctic.

The counterpoint to so much natural beauty is found in the country's vibrant cultural life. Norwegian cities are cosmopolitan and brimful of architecture that showcases the famous Scandinavian flair for design. At the same time, a busy calendar of festivals, many of international renown, are worth planning your trip around.

Yes, Norway is one of the most expensive countries on Earth. But Norway will pay you back with never-to-be-forgotten experiences many times over.

Best Places to Eat

» Pingvinen (p318)
» Potetkjelleren (p319)
» Emma's Under (p362)
» Sjøbua (p345)

Best Places to Stay

» Det Hanseatiske Hotel (p315)
» Stalheim Hotel (p338)
» Hotel Brosundet (p345)
» Svinøya Rorbuer (p355)
» Engholm Husky Design Lodge (p369)

When to Go

Oslo

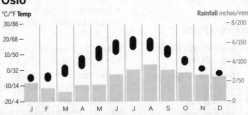

Mid-Jun–mid-Aug Summer fjords and endless days. Accommodation prices fall.

Dec-Feb The aurora borealis (Northern Lights) and wonderful winter activities.

May–mid-Jun & mid-Aug–Sep Generally fine weather and without the crowds.

AT A GLANCE

» **Capital** Oslo

» **Area** 385,186 sq km

» **Population** 5.02 million

» **Country code** ☏47

» **Language** Norwegian

» **Currency** kroner (Nkr)

Exchange Rates

Australia	A$1	Nkr5.86
Canada	C$1	Nkr5.73
Euro Zone	€1	Nkr7.42
Japan	¥100	Nkr7.13
New Zealand	NZ$1	Nkr4.64
UK	UK£1	Nkr9.12
USA	US$1	Nkr5.70

Set Your Budget

» **Budget hotel room** Up to Nkr750

» **Two-course evening meal** Nkr300–400

» **Museum entrance** Free–Nkr120

» **Beer** Nkr50–Nkr80

» **Oslo bus or tram ticket** Nkr75 (daily pass)

Resources

» **Fjord Norway** (www.fjordnorway.com)

» **Norway Guide** (www.norwayguide.no)

» **Visit Norway** (www.visitnorway.com)

Connections

Trains and buses link Norway with Russia, Sweden and Finland. Frequent ferries head to Germany and Denmark from several Norwegian ports. Airports in Oslo and Bergen connect Norway to the world, with a handful of international flights to Stavanger, Trondheim and distant Tromsø, way up in the Arctic Circle.

ITINERARIES

One Week

Spend a day in Oslo, then take the Norway in a Nutshell tour to Bergen via Myrdal, Flåm and Nærøyfjorden. Spend two nights in Bergen before taking an unhurried jaunt around Hardangerfjord. Return to Sognefjord, stay at the Stalheim Hotel and visit glaciers around Fjærland. Return to Oslo.

Two Weeks

Instead of returning to Oslo, head back to Bergen and take the *Hurtigruten* along the coast, pausing for stays of a night or two in Ålesund and Trondheim. Continue to the fishing villages of the craggy Lofoten Islands, where you should spend at least a couple of days exploring. Finally, take the *Hurtigruten* to Tromsø, the north's most vibrant city, before returning to Oslo.

One Month

Tromsø is your gateway to Norway's High Arctic. After a night in this engaging town, make for the prehistoric paintings of Alta, the area around Nordkapp, the activities of Kirkenes and, depending on the season, dog sledding or hiking around the Sámi capital of Karasjok. At journey's end, allow a week in Svalbard, taking in as many activities and excursions as you can.

Essential Food & Drink

» **Reindeer** Grilled or roasted, Scandinavia's iconic species is also its tastiest red meat; you'll find it on menus from Oslo to Svalbard.

» **Elk** Call it what you like (many prefer moose), but this tasty meat usually appears as steaks or burgers.

» **Salmon** World-renowned Norwegian salmon is so popular that you'll eat it for dinner (grilled) or breakfast (smoked).

» **Arctic char** The world's northernmost freshwater fish is a star of northern Norway's seafood-rich menus.

» **Arctic menu** A popular scheme (www.arktiskmeny.no) in northern Norway that encourages restaurants to use natural local ingredients.

» **Fish markets** Often the best (and cheapest) places to eat along the Norwegian coast, with the freshest seafood at fresh-off-the-boat prices.

OSLO

POP 613,285

Oslo is home to world-class museums and galleries to rival anywhere else on the European art trail. That may be the main reason to come here, but Mother Nature has also left her mark and Oslo is fringed with forests, hills and lakes awash with opportunities for hiking, cycling, skiing and boating. Add to this mix a thriving cafe and bar culture, top-notch restaurants and good nightlife and the result is a fine place to spend your time when you've had your fill of fjords.

History

Founded by Harald Hardråda in 1049, Oslo is the oldest Scandinavian capital. In 1299 King Håkon V constructed the Akershus Festning here, to counter the Swedish threat from the east. Levelled by fire in 1624, the city was rebuilt in brick and stone on a more easily defended site by King Christian IV, who renamed it Christiania, after his humble self.

In 1814 the framers of Norway's first constitution designated it the official capital of the new realm but their efforts were effectively nullified by Sweden, which had other ideas about Norway's future and unified the two countries under Swedish rule. In 1905, when that union dissolved, Christiania flourished as the capital of modern Norway. The city reverted to its original name, Oslo, in 1925.

⊙ Sights

Many sights are clustered together within easy walking distance of Karl Johans gate with another important concentration on the Bygdøy Peninsula; the latter is easily accessible by boat.

CENTRAL OSLO & AKER BRYGGE

TOP CHOICE Oslo Opera House   OPERA HOUSE

(Den Norske Opera & Ballett; Map p296; www.operaen.no; Kirsten Flagstads plass 1; admission to foyer free; ⊙foyer 9am-11pm Mon-Fri, 11am-11pm Sat, noon-10pm Sun) Hoping to transform the city into a world-class cultural centre, the city authorities have embarked on a massive waterfront redevelopment project (which is scheduled to last until 2020), the centrepiece of which is the magnificent new Opera House. Designed by Oslo-based architectural firm Snøhetta and costing around €500 million to build, the Opera House was designed to resemble a glacier floating in the waters off Oslo. It's a subtle building that at first doesn't look all that impressive, but give it time and it'll leave you spellbound.

Before venturing inside be sure to walk up onto the roof, which was designed to act as a 'carpet' of sloping angles and flat surfaces. The main entrance to the Opera House is purposefully small and unimpressive, which serves only to add to the sense of vastness that greets you on entering the main foyer (the windows alone are 15m high and flood the foyer with light).

Nasjonalgalleriet   GALLERY

(National Gallery; Map p296; www.nasjonalmuseet.no; Universitetsgata 13; adult/child Nkr50/free, Sun free; ⊙10am-6pm Tue, Wed & Fri, to 7pm Thu, 11am-5pm Sat & Sun) One of Oslo's major highlights, the National Gallery houses the nation's largest collection of Norwegian art, including some of Edvard Munch's best-known creations such as *The Scream*. There's also an impressive collection of European art with works by Gauguin, Picasso, El Greco and many of the impressionists: Manet, Degas, Renoir, Matisse, Cézanne and Monet.

Museet for Samtidskunst   GALLERY

(National Museum for Contemporary Art; Map p296; www.nasjonalmuseet.no; Bankplassen 4; adult/child Nkr50/free, Sun free; ⊙11am-5pm Tue, Wed & Fri, to 7pm Thu, noon-5pm Sat & Sun) Contemporary collections are housed in this museum. Some of the 3000-piece collection is definitely an acquired taste, but it's a timely reminder that Norwegian art didn't cease with Edvard Munch.

Astrup Fearnley Museet   GALLERY

(Astrup Fearnley Museum; Map p290; ☏22 93 60 60; www.afmuseet.no; Aker Brygge; adult/student/child Nkr100/60/free) This museum has all manner of zany contemporary art – don't miss the gilded ceramic sculpture *Michael Jackson and Bubbles* by Jeff Koons. Even so, the building itself – the latest stunning architectural creation to adorn Oslo's waterfront – may be the main attraction.

FREE Rådhus   ARCHITECTURE

(Map p296; Fridtjof Nansens plass; ⊙9am-6pm, guided tours 10am, noon & 2pm Mon-Sat, also 4pm Sun Jun-Aug, Wed only rest of yr) The town hall's retro red-brick towers provide a stark contrast to the flowing lines of contemporary Scandinavian architecture that elsewhere provide a backdrop to the waterfront. Inside there are echoing monumental halls covered in colourful murals that depict Norwegian

Norway Highlights

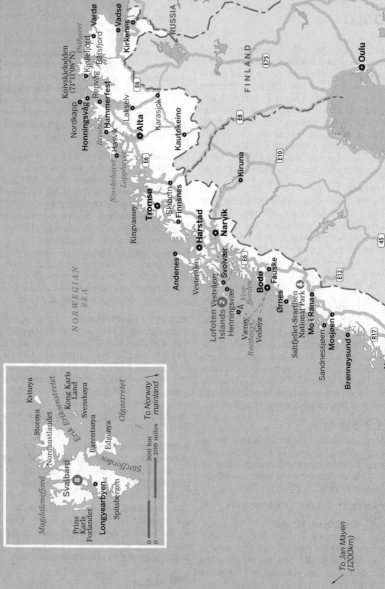

1 Take the ferry from **Flåm to Gudvangen** (p336) through some of Norway's most spectacular fjord scenery

2 Sleep in a fisherman's *robu* (shanty) on the craggy **Lofoten Islands** (p355)

3 Journey by train from Oslo to **Bergen** (p313), arguably Norway's most attractive coastal city

4 Ride Norway's jagged, beautiful coast aboard the **Hurtigruten coastal ferry** (p383)

5 Hike amid the soaring peaks and countless glaciers of **Jotunheimen National Park** (p310)

To Svalbard (550km)
(see inset)

To Norway mainland

To Jan Mayen
(1200km)

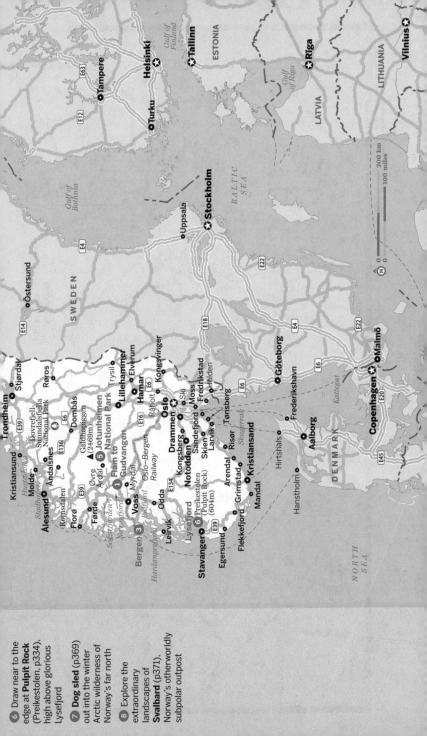

6 Draw near to the edge at **Pulpit Rock** (Preikestolen, p334), high above glorious Lysefjord

7 **Dog sled** (p369) out into the winter Arctic wilderness of Norway's far north

8 Explore the extraordinary landscapes of **Svalbard** (p371), Norway's otherworldly subpolar outpost

Oslo

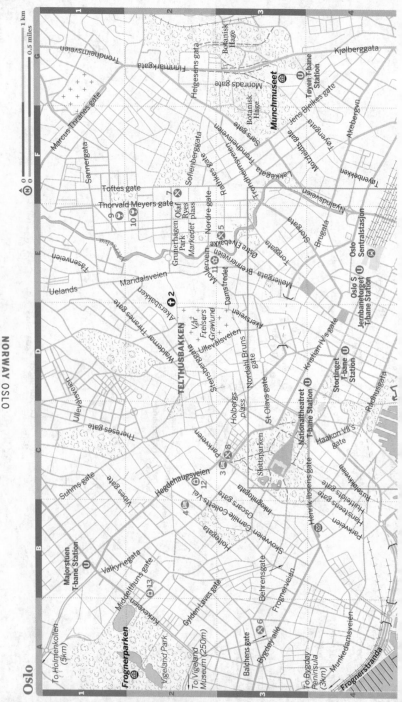

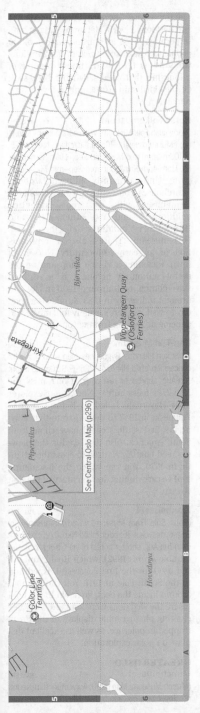

Oslo

history and mythology. The Nobel Peace Prize is awarded here every 10 December.

Akershus Slott & Festning FORTRESS
(Map p296) King Håkon V began construction of the earthen-walled **Akershus Festning** (Akershus Fortress; ⊙7am-9pm Mon-Fri, 8am-9pm Sat & Sun) in 1299. It's strategically positioned on the eastern side of the harbour; clamber up tree-lined twisting paths to stand precariously above the city and enjoy excellent views over Oslofjord. The grounds are the venue for a host of concerts, dances and theatrical productions during summer. An **information centre** recounts the building of the fortress. Changing of the guard occurs at 1.30pm.

In the 17th century Christian IV renovated **Akershus Slott** (Akershus Castle; adult/child Nkr70/30; ⊙10am-4pm Mon-Sat, 12.30-4pm Sun May-Aug, guided tours 11am, 1pm, 2pm & 4pm daily Jul–mid-Aug, shorter hr rest of yr) into a Renaissance palace, though the front remains decidedly medieval. In its dungeons you'll find dark cubby holes where outcast nobles were kept under lock and key, while the upper floors have banquet halls and staterooms. The chapel is still used for army events and the crypts of Kings Håkon VII and Olav V lie beneath it.

Ibsen Museet
MUSEUM

(Ibsen Museum; Map p296; www.ibsenmuseet.no; Arbins gate 1; adult/child Nkr85/25; ☺guided tours hourly 11am-6pm mid-May–mid-Sep) Housed in the last residence of Norwegian playwright Henrik Ibsen, this is a must-see for Ibsen fans. The study remains exactly as he left it and other rooms have been restored in the style and colours popular in Ibsen's day.

Nobels Fredssenter
MUSEUM

(Nobel Peace Center; Map p296; www.nobelpeace center.org; Rådhusplassen 1; adult/student/child Nkr80/55/free; ☺10am-6pm daily mid-May–Sep, closed Mon rest of yr) Head inside for hi-tech screens flashily exploring themes of peace and conflict. In addition to presenting the history of the prize and its patron, Alfred Nobel (a dynamite fellow), it has exhibits on winners from 1901 to present.

FREE Oslo Domkirke
CHURCH

(Oslo Cathedral; Map p296; www.oslodomkirke. no; Stortorget 1; ☺10am-4pm) Oslo's cathedral dates from 1697. It is worth seeing for its elaborate stained glass by Emanuel Vigeland and painted ceiling (completed between 1936 and 1950). The exceptional 1748 altarpiece is a model of the Last Supper and the Crucifixion by Michael Rasch. The organ front and pulpit also require your attention.

BYGDØY PENINSULA

Ferry 91 operates from early April to early October, making the 15-minute run to Bygdøy (adult/child Nkr50/25) from Rådhusbrygge 3 (opposite the Rådhus) every 20 minutes from 8am to 8.45pm in summer; earlier final departures the rest of the year. If you buy your tickets from one of the kiosks or ticket machines on the departure jetties the prices are lower (adult/child Nkr30/15). You can also take bus 30 to the Folke museum from Jernbanetorget, next to Oslo S train station.

Vikingskipshuset
MUSEUM

(Viking Ship Museum; www.khm.uio.no; Huk Aveny 35; adult/child Nkr60/30; ☺9am-6pm May-Sep, 10am-4pm Oct-Apr) The magnificent Vikingskipshuset houses three Viking ships excavated from the Oslofjord region. The ships had been brought ashore and used as tombs for nobility, who were buried with all they were expected to need in the hereafter, including jewels, furniture, food and servants.

The impressive **Oseberg**, buried in AD 834 and festooned with elaborate dragon and serpent carvings, is 22m long and took 30 people to row. A second ship, the 24m-long **Gokstad**, is the world's finest example of a longship that once sailed the high seas. Of the third ship, **Tune**, only a few boards remain.

Norsk Folkemuseum
MUSEUM

(Norwegian Folk Museum; www.norskfolkemuseum. no; Museumsveien 10; adult/child Nkr100/25; ☺10am-6pm mid-May–mid-Sep, 11am-3pm Mon-Fri, 11am-4pm Sat & Sun mid-Sep–mid-May) Dirt paths wind past sturdy old barns, *stabbur* (storehouses on stilts), rough-timbered farmhouses with sod roofs sprouting wildflowers, and 140 other 17th- and 18th-century buildings at the Norsk Folkemuseum. There's also a reproduction of an early-20th-century Norwegian town, including a village shop and an old petrol station. A highlight is a restored stave church, built around 1200 in Gol and brought to Bygdøy in 1885. Sunday is a good day to visit, as there's usually folk music and dancing at 2pm (in summer only).

Kon-Tiki Museum
MUSEUM

(www.kon-tiki.no; Bygdøynesveien 36; adult/concession/child Nkr70/40/25; ☺9.30am-5.30pm Jun-Aug, shorter hr rest of yr) Don't miss the *Kon-Tiki* balsa raft – Norwegian explorer Thor Heyerdahl sailed on it from Peru to Polynesia in 1947 to demonstrate that Polynesia's first settlers could have come from South America. Also displayed is the papyrus reed boat *Ra II*, used to cross the Atlantic in 1970. You can watch the fascinating 1951 Oscar-winning documentary of the first voyage.

Frammuseet
MUSEUM

(Polar Ship Fram Museum; www.frammuseum.no; Bygdøynesveien 36; adult/child Nkr60/25; ☺9am-6pm Jun-Aug, shorter hr rest of yr) Check out the durable *Fram* (1892), which Roald Amundsen used for the first successful expedition to the South Pole in 1911. You can clamber around inside the boat, go down to the hold where the sled dogs were kept and view fascinating photographic displays of the *Fram* trapped in polar ice, as well as excellent displays on polar exploration.

GREATER OSLO

Munchmuseet
GALLERY

(Munch Museum; Map p290; www.munch.museum. no; Tøyengata 53; adult/child Nkr75/40, free with

Oslo Pass; ⊘10am-6pm Jun-Aug) Dedicated to the life's work of Norway's most renowned artist, Munchmuseet contains more than 1100 paintings, 4500 watercolours and 18,000 prints that Munch bequeathed to the city of Oslo. As such, this landmark museum provides a comprehensive look at the artist's work, from dark (*The Sick Child*) to light (*Spring Ploughing*). To get there, take the T-bane (underground train) to Tøyen, followed by a five-minute signposted walk.

Frognerparken   GALLERY, PARK
(Map p290; ⊘year-round) Frognerparken, which has as its centrepiece Vigeland Park, is an extraordinary open-air showcase of work by Norway's best-loved sculptor, Gustav Vigeland. The park is brimming with 212 granite and bronze Vigeland works. His highly charged work ranges from entwined lovers and tranquil elderly couples to contempt-ridden beggars. His most renowned work, *Sinataggen* (the 'Little Hothead'), portrays a London child in a mood of particular ill humour. To get there, take tram 12 or 15, marked Frogner, from the city centre.

Vigeland Museum   GALLERY
(www.vigeland.museum.no; Nobels gate 32; adult/child Nkr50/25; ⊘10am-5pm Tue-Sun Jun-Aug) For a more in-depth look at the development of Gustav Vigeland's work, visit the Vigeland Museum. The museum was built by the city as a home and workshop for Vigeland in exchange for the bulk of his life's work and

contains his early statuary, plaster moulds, woodblock prints and sketches.

Gamle Aker Kirke   CHURCH
(Map p290; Akersbakken 26; ⊘noon-2pm Mon-Sat) This medieval stone church, located north of the centre, dates from 1080 and is Oslo's oldest building. Take bus 37 from Jernbanetorget to Akersbakken then walk up past the churchyard.

🏃 Activities

Hiking   HIKING
An extensive network of trails leads into Nordmarka from Frognerseteren, at the end of T-bane line 1. One good, fairly strenuous walk is from Frognerseteren to Sognsvann, where you can take T-bane line 5 back to the city. If you're interested in wilderness hiking, contact **Den Norske Turistforening** (DNT; Map p296; ☑22 82 28 22; www.turistforeningen.no; Youngstorget 1; ⊘10am-4pm Mon-Wed & Fri, to 6pm Thu, to 2pm Sat, open 1hr earlier May-Sep).

Cycling   CYCLING
Cyclists and mountain bikers will find plenty of trails on which to keep themselves occupied in the Oslo hinterland. The tourist office has free cycling maps; *Sykkelkart Oslo* traces the bicycle lanes and paths throughout the city, and *Idrett og friluftsliv i Oslo* covers the Oslo hinterland. The tourist office also has a pamphlet, *Opplevelsesturer i Marka,* which contains six possible cycling and/or hiking itineraries within reach of Oslo.

NORWAY OSLO

OSLO IN...

Two Days

Start your day at the Nasjonalgalleriet for a representative dose of artwork by Edvard Munch. Afterwards try an alfresco, pierside lunch of peel-and-eat shrimp on **Aker Brygge** from one of the local fishing boats. Take a ferry from here to **Bygdøy** and spend your afternoon learning about the exploits of Norway's greatest explorers at the **Frammuseet** or **Vikingskipshuset**.

On day two head to the breathtaking new **Oslo Opera House**, after which take a look at all that's cool and modern at the **Museet for Samtidskunst**. In the afternoon explore the medieval **Akershus Slott** and learn how to make the world a better place at the **Nobels Fredssenter**.

Four Days

With a couple of extra days you will have time to wander among the bold, earthy statues of Gustav Vigeland at **Vigeland Park** in **Frognerparken**.

The energetic might also spend a day walking, skiing or cycling in the **Nordmarka** wilderness area.

Skiing

(www.holmenkollen.com) Oslo's ski season is roughly from December to March. There are more than 2400km of prepared Nordic tracks (1000km in Nordmarka alone), many of them floodlit, as well as a ski resort within the city limits. Easy-access tracks begin right at the T-bane stations Frognerseteren and Sognsvann. The downhill slopes at **Tryvann Vinterpark** (✆40 46 27 00) are open in the ski season.

☞ Tours

For the popular **Norway in a Nutshell** (✆81 56 82 22; www.norwaynutshell.com), book at tourist offices or at train stations. From Oslo, the typical route includes a rail trip across Hardangervidda to Myrdal, descent to Flåm along the dramatic Flåmbanen, a cruise along Nærøyfjorden to Gudvangen, a bus to Voss, a connecting train to Bergen for a short visit, then an overnight return rail trip to Oslo (including a sleeper compartment); the return tour costs Nkr2240. You can also book one-way tours to Bergen (Nkr1430).

Oslo Sightseeing

BUS

(✆48 17 44 44; www.opentopsightseeing.no; adult/child/family Nkr220/110/600; ⊙mid-May–mid-Sep) Oslo's version of the hop-on hop-off phenomenon covers the overwhelming proportion of city sights, which you can explore at your own pace. The tourist offices have a list of stops where you can board and buy your ticket.

Båtservice Sightseeing

BOAT

(Map p296; ✆23 35 68 90; www.boatsightseeing.com; Pier 3, Rådhusbrygge; per person Nkr175-665)

OSLO PASS

Providing entry to most museums and attractions and free travel on public transport, the **Oslo Pass** (www.visitoslo.com/en/activities-and-attractions/oslo-pass; adult 1/2/3 days Nkr270/395/495, child Nkr120/145/190) is outstanding value, but always do your sums first. For example, if you're going to visit the museums on the Bygdøy Peninsula and travel there by boat, Oslo Pass repays itself quickly, less so if you're planning on just visiting city-centre museums and galleries, many of which are free. Oslo Pass is sold online and at tourist offices and hotels.

If you want to get out on the water, try one of these eight different boat tours including everything from 90-minute hop-on-hop-off minicruises to the 7½-hour 'Grand Tour of Oslo' city tour to the Bygdøy museums, Vigeland Park and the Holmenkollen ski jump.

Oslo Guidebureau

WALKING

(✆22 42 28 18; www.osloguide.no; adult/child Nkr150/70; ⊙2pm Sat & Sun May-Oct) Official guides lead two-hour walking tours through Oslo. Pick up their 'Oslo Weekend Walks' brochure from the tourist offices.

Viking Biking

CYCLING

(✆41 26 64 96; www.vikingbikingoslo.com; Nedre Slottsgate 4; per person Nkr250-350, bike rental per hour/half day/full day Nkr50/125/200; ⊙tours 10am, 1pm & 2pm Apr-Oct) Bicycle tours called 'Oslo Highlights' and 'Vikings and Beaches'.

✯ Festivals & Events

Oslo's most festive annual event is the **17 May Constitution Day** celebration, when city residents descend on the royal palace in the finery of their native districts.

Inferno Metal Festival

MUSIC

(www.infernofestival.net) Held in late April.

Norwegian Wood Festival

MUSIC

(www.norwegianwood.no) One of Oslo's bigger music festivals; June.

Oslo International Jazz Festival

MUSIC

(www.oslojazz.no) Jazz and long summer evenings; August.

Øya Festival

MUSIC

(www.oyafestivalen.com) Norway's largest rock-and-indie music festival; August.

Oslo Opera Festival

OPERA

(www.operafestival.no) Live opera for three weeks in September.

🛏 Sleeping

CENTRAL OSLO

TOP CHOICE Grims Grenka

HOTEL €€€

(Map p296; ✆23 10 72 00; www.firsthotels.no; Kongens gate 5; s/d from Nkr1315/1491; 🅿❄) Oslo's answer to the exclusive, cosmopolitan experience offered by boutique hotels in London and New York, Grims Grenka has minimalist, modern-designed rooms themed around summer and winter, and a hipster rooftop bar. It is, without doubt, the most exciting hotel in Oslo.

Cochs Pensjonat
PENSION €

(Map p290; ☎23 33 24 00; www.cochspens-jonat.no; Parkveien 25; s/d with kitchenette from Nkr600/820, without bathroom Nkr500/720; ❄ @) Opened as a guesthouse for bachelors in the 1920s, the well-run Cochs has sparsely furnished, clean rooms, some with kitch-enettes. It's nicely located behind the royal palace; walking distance from the centre but quieter than downtown. Some rooms have partial views of the park. The wireless connection is rather slow.

P-Hotel
HOTEL €€

(Map p296; ☎23 31 80 00; www.p-hotels.com; Grensen 19; r Nkr795-1295; ❄) In addition to offering some of the best prices in central Oslo, the P-Hotel has comfortable if slightly sterile rooms with decent bathrooms. The included breakfast is delivered to your door in a bag, and there are tea- and coffee-making facilities in the rooms. The hotel is right in the heart of the city.

Anker Hostel
HOSTEL €

(Map p296; ☎22 99 72 00; www.ankerhostel.no; Storgata 55; dm Nkr220-260, d/tr Nkr600/800; ❄ @) This huge traveller-savvy hostel boasts an international atmosphere, spick-and-span rooms, a laundry, luggage room, kitchens (some rooms also contain kitchens) and small bar. Breakfast costs an extra Nkr55, linen Nkr50 and parking Nkr175 per 24 hours. They were about to downsize when we were there, but for a good cause – a second hostel is planned further north in Gruner-løkka (check the website for location) and should have opened by the time you read this.

Anker Hotel
HOTEL €€

(Map p296; ☎22 99 75 00; www.anker-hotel.no; Storgata 55; s/d from Nkr690/890; ❄) Owned by the same people as the neighbouring Anker Hostel, this place could be described as a 'budget business hotel' and the plain and simple rooms are perfect for those who feel a bit too old for the hostel. The rooms were completely overhauled in 2010 and are outstanding value. Even so, we're at a loss to explain how it won a citation as one of Norway's trendiest hotels in 2012.

GREATER OSLO

TOP CHOICE Ellingsens Pensjonat
PENSION €

(Map p290; ☎22 60 03 59; www.ellingsenspens-jonat.no; Holtegata 25; s/d Nkr500/700, without bathroom Nkr430/640) Located in a quiet,

B&B IN THE CITY

One of the cheapest ways to stay in Oslo, and one that promises a much more personable stay than anything a hotel can offer, is to take a room in one of the city's handful of B&Bs. **B&B Norway** (www.bbnorway.com) is an online source of information listing many of Norway's better B&Bs. The tourist office can also point you towards some options (but only if you visit in person).

If you're still lucky enough to be under 26, then Use-It (p300), the Oslo Youth Information Service, will also help with bookings at hostels and private homes; there's no minimum stay and bookings are free.

pleasant neighbourhood, this homey pension offers one of the best deals in the capital. The building dates from 1890 and many of the original features (high ceilings, rose designs) remain. Rooms are bright and airy, with refrigerators and kettles, and there's a small garden to lounge about in on sunny days if you can't face the 20-minute walk into town.

Holmenkollen Park Hotel Rica
HISTORIC HOTEL €€

(☎22 92 20 00; www.holmenkollenparkhotel.no; Kongeveien 26; r Nkr795-1400; P❄@≋) Founded in 1891 as a sanatorium by Dr Ingebrigt Christian Lund, this castlelike hotel offers luxury, history, great views and, all things considered, a very reasonable price.

✕ Eating
CENTRAL OSLO

TOP CHOICE Feinschmecker
MODERN NORWEGIAN €€€

(Map p290; ☎22 12 93 80; www.feinschmecker.no; Balchens gate; set menus Nkr575-1175, mains from Nkr365; ⏰5-9pm Mon-Sat) If you're starting to think Norwegian food is all about burgers and pizzas then this absolutely sublime restaurant, with its modern take on old Norwegian dishes, will quickly change your mind. The menu changes regularly – the roasted scallops with French wild asparagus, orange and mustard caught our eye when we were there. Despite the quality of the food and the high prices, the atmosphere is surprisingly laid-back. Book ahead.

Central Oslo

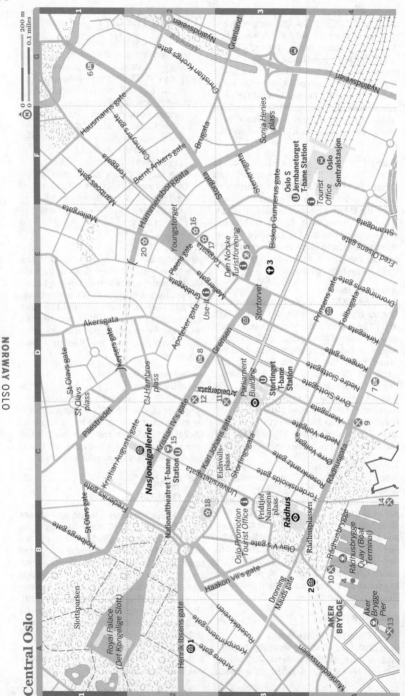

Central Oslo

◎ Top Sights

◎ Sights

◯ Activities, Courses & Tours

◰ Sleeping

◈ Eating

◉ Drinking

◈ Entertainment

Kaffistova NORWEGIAN €€

(Map p296; ☎23 21 42 10; Rosenkrantz gate 8; mains Nkr149-175; ☺11am-9pm Mon-Fri, to 7pm Sat & Sun) Don't be put off by the cafeteria-style atmosphere here because this is one of the most affordable places in town to order what locals eat at home. Its signature dish is a Norwegian staple – meatballs with mashed potatoes and gravy – but you might also find baked salmon, reindeer cakes and open sandwiches.

Rust INTERNATIONAL €

(Map p290; www.rustoslo.com; Hegehaugsveien 22; tapas Nkr42-86, mains Nkr129-195; ☺11am-1am Mon-Sat, noon-2am Sun) On a small side street lined with cafes and restaurants, Rust is bright, colourful and 100% modern Oslo. It has plenty of outdoor seating and loads of blankets for when it gets cold. Its menu ranges across the world but it's good for a quiet cocktail, burgers, hearty salads or tapas late into the night.

Café Skansen
MEDITERRANEAN €€

(Map p296; ☑24 20 13 11; www.cafeskansen.no; Rådhusgata 32; mains Nkr128-192) One of the new wave of sophisticated cafes and restaurants currently taking Oslo by storm. As in many such places this one looks south to the Mediterranean for both style and taste inspiration and on sunny summer days its outdoor terrace does indeed feel very far from the popular images of a frozen Norway. We enjoyed the creamy fish soup.

Grand Café
NORWEGIAN €€€

(Map p296; www.grand.no; Karl Johans gate 31; mains Nkr235-335) At 11am sharp, Henrik Ibsen would leave his apartment on Drammens-veien (now Henrik Ibsens gate) and walk to the Grand Café for a lunch of herring, beer and one shot of aquavit (alcoholic drink made from potatoes and caraway liquor). His table is still there. Don't worry though, there's more than herring on the menu. Take your pick from whale, turbot and other classy, traditionally Norwegian options.

AKER BRYGGE

Aker Brygge, the old shipyard turned trendy shopping complex west of the main harbour, has numerous waterside restaurants.

Onda
INTERNATIONAL €€€

(Map p296; ☑45 50 20 00; www.onda.no; Stranden 30; set menu Nkr1995, lunch mains Nkr175-189, shellfish platter Nkr695; ☺11am-11pm Mon-Sat, noon-11pm Sun) A sleek outpost of sophistication jutting out into the harbour along Aker Brygge, this place serves up fabulous shellfish and exciting fusion dishes that combine international with local Norwegian tastes. The upstairs mezzanine is the realm of the set menu, whereas downstairs is more casual, especially at lunchtime. Reservations recommended.

Fisherman's Coop
SEAFOOD €

(Map p296; Rådhusbrygge 3/4; shrimp per kg Nkr150; ☺7am-5pm Tue-Sat) If the weather is nice, the local meal of choice is peel-and-eat shrimp, eaten dockside with a fresh baguette, mayonnaise and just a touch of lemon. In the summer, you can buy the shrimp from here.

Solsiden Seafood
SEAFOOD €€€

(Map p296; ☑22 33 36 30; www.solsiden.no; Søndre Akershus Kai 34; mains Nkr175-305; ☺4.30-11pm May-Sep) Solsiden means 'sunny side' in Norwegian, which explains why this place is so popular among sun-craving Oslo dwellers. It's located inside a grey warehouse – often overlooked by massive cruise ships – on the opposite side of Pipervika from Aker Brygge. Solsiden serves up some of the city's best seafood and has an ideal view over the fjord. Try the pan-fried Arctic char, steamed mussels or Norwegian crayfish.

GRÜNERLØKKA

Oslo's Greenwich Village, while always lively and frequented by a well-dressed, youthful crowd, is especially pleasant in summer, when life spills out onto the sidewalks from the numerous cafes, bars and restaurants around Olaf Ryes plass.

Dr Kneipp's Vinbar
NORWEGIAN €€€

(Map p290; ☑22 37 22 97; www.markveien.no; Torv-bakkgt 12; mains Nkr195-249; ☺4pm-12.30am Mon-Sat) You could try just about any of Grünerløkka's restaurants and leave happy, but slide into one of the dark wooden booths at Dr Kneipp's for finger food or a sumptuous dessert, not to mention an amazing wine list.

Fru Hagen
CAFE €€

(Map p290; ☑22 38 24 26; www.fruhagen.no; Thorvald Meyers gate 40; mains Nkr109-155) The low-key and always full Fru Hagen (Mrs Garden), was one of the first places to start the Grünerløkka style revolution and serves sandwiches and burgers, all with a healthy side portion of vegetables. Its location facing Olaf Ryes plass makes it good for people watching and it fills up with 30-something revellers as the night deepens.

BYGDØY PENINSULA

Café Hemma Hos
MODERN NORWEGIAN €€

(www.cafehemmahos.no; Fredrikborgsveien 16; mains Nkr135-175) The owners of the Café Hemma Hos, close to the Viking Ship Museum, know there is more to culinary life than hot dogs and sandwiches, and have created an oasis of good food in a sea of tourist traps. Sit out in the pleasant gardens and choose from a menu that includes pickled herrings, crayfish and a variety of tapas.

NORWAY OSLO

🍷 Drinking & Entertainment

The tourist office's free monthly brochure *What's On in Oslo* lists current concerts, theatre and special events, but the best publication for night owls is the free *Streetwise*, published annually in English by Use-It.

Bars, Clubs & Live Music

Many Oslo nightspots have an unwritten dress code that expects patrons to be relatively well turned out – at the very least, don't show up in grubby gear and hiking boots. For most bars and clubs that serve beer and wine, you must be over 18 years of age, but many places, especially those that serve spirits, impose a higher age limit. On weekends, most Oslo nightspots remain open until at least 3am.

The city's best neighbourhood bar scene is along Thorvald Meyers gate and the surrounding streets in Grünerløkka. The Youngstorget area has some of the most popular places close to the city centre, while the Grønland neighbourhood has a more alternative feel.

Bar Boca   BAR
(Map p290; Thorvald Meyers gate 30; ⊙noon-1am Sun-Tue, 11am-2pm Wed & Thu, 11am-3am Fri & Sat) Squeeze into what is quite possibly the smallest bar in Oslo and you'll find that you has slid back in time to the 1960s. It's retro cool and has a cocktail selection as great as its atmosphere.

Tea Lounge   BAR
(Map p290; www.tealounge.no; Thorvald Meyers gate 33b; ⊙11am-1am Mon-Wed, 11am-3am Thu-Sat, noon-1am Sun) During the bright and cheerful daylight hours this split-personality bar is a mellow cafe with a superb range of teas and a chilled-out soundtrack, but in the dark of night it transforms itself into one of the hippest bars in Oslo with a list of cocktails to suit.

Icebar Oslo   BAR
(Map p296; www.icebaroslo.no; Kristian IV's gate 12; admission incl 1st drink Nkr160; ⊙noon-midnight Mon-Thu, noon-1am Fri & Sat, 4-10pm Sun Jun-Aug, shorter hr rest of yr) It's a cliché by now, but if you've never experienced the ice-bar-ice-hotel thing there's still considerable novelty in sipping your cocktail surrounded by ice in minus -5°C while its summer outside. It's pricey and a real scene in the afternoon when punters from cruise ships and buses

file in, but come in the evening and you may just be pleasantly surprised.

🔺TOP CHOICE Blå   JAZZ
(Map p290; www.blaaoslo.no; Brenneriveien 9c; admission Nkr100-150) It would be a pity to leave Oslo without checking out Blå, which features on a global list of 100 great jazz clubs compiled by the savvy editors at the US jazz magazine *Down Beat*. Sometimes it veers into other musical styles such as salsa and when there's no live music DJs get the crowds moving.

Fish Og Vilt Club   CLUB
(Map p296; Pløens gate 1) With DJs rocking the crowd in the covered backyard of this bar-club, and an impressive selection of beers and cocktails, this is a popular central spot for a cool crowd. On a Monday night it's really the only place worth considering.

Villa   CLUB
(Map p296; www.thevilla.no; Møllergata 23; ⊙11pm-3am Fri & Sat) With arguably the best sound system in the city, this is a diehard house-and-electro music club. It's also open on some Thursdays.

Mono   LIVE MUSIC
(Map p296; www.cafemono.no; Pløens gate 4; ⊙11am-3.30am Mon-Sat, 6pm-3.30am Sun) An upbeat place with fabulous retro wallpaper, this is the rock club of choice with the cool and beautiful of Oslo. It's known for booking the best up-and-coming new indie bands. Most live acts take the stage on Tuesday, Friday and Saturday.

Theatre

Oslo Opera House   OPERA
(Den Norske Opera & Ballett; Map p296; www.operaen.no; Kirsten Flagstads plass 1; tickets Nkr100-795; ⊙foyer 10am-11pm Mon-Fri, 11am-11pm Sat, noon-10pm Sun) Oslo Opera House is one of Norway's most impressive examples of contemporary architecture and is also known as the venue for world-class opera and ballet performances.

Nationaltheatret   THEATRE
(National Theatre; Map p296; www.nationaltheatret.no; Stortingsgata 15; tickets Nkr160-400) Norway's showcase theatre, with its lavish rococo hall, was constructed specifically as a venue for the works of Norwegian playwright Henrik Ibsen, whose works are still performed here.

Shopping

Oslo excels in upmarket shopping and there are many fine shops on Grensen and Karl Johans gate. For art, try the galleries on Frognerveien, for exclusive boutiques head to Hegdehaugsveien or Skovveien and for funky shoes or T-shirts go no further than Grünerløkka.

Vestkanttorget Flea Market MARKET
(Map p290; Amaldus Nilsens plass; ☉10am-4pm Sat) If you're happy with pot luck and sifting through heaps of junk, take a chance here. It's at the plaza that intersects Professor Dahls gate, a block east of Vigeland Park, and it's a more-than-pleasant way to pass a Saturday morning.

Moods of Norway FASHION
(Map p290; www.moodsofnorway.com; Hegdehaugsveien 34; ☉10am-7pm Mon-Fri, to 5pm Sat) Three young Norwegian designers set up shop in 2003 and transformed the country's fashion industry in the process. Combining candy-bright colours with surprising takes on Norwegian traditional crafts add up to some really fun and funky clothes.

ⓘ Information

Emergency
Ambulance (☎113)
Fire (☎110)
Police (☎112; Hammersborggata 10)

Internet Access
Arctic Internet Café (Oslo S; per hr from Nkr25; ☉8am-midnight) On the 1st floor of Oslo S train station.

Use-It (Møllergata 3; free access; ☉11am-5pm Mon-Fri, noon-5pm Sat)

Medical Services
Jernbanetorget Apotek (Fred Olsens gate; ☉24-hour) Pharmacy opposite Oslo S.

Oslo Kommunale Legevakten (Oslo Emergency Clinic; ☎22 93 22 93; Storgata 40; ☉24hr) Casualty and emergency medical clinic.

Money
There are banks with ATMs throughout the city centre, with a particular concentration along Karl Johans gate.

Forex (www.forex.no; Fridtjof Nansens plass 6 & Oslo S; ☉9am-6pm Mon-Fri) is the largest foreign-exchange service in Scandinavia.

Tourist Information
DNT (Norwegian Mountain Touring Club; www.turistforeningen.no; Storget 3; ☉10am-5pm Mon-Wed & Fri, to 6pm Thu, to 3pm Sat)

Information, maps and brochures on hiking in Norway.

Oslo Promotion Tourist Office (☎81 53 05 55; www.visitoslo.com; Fridtjof Nansens plass 5; ☉9am-7pm Jun-Aug, to 4pm Mon-Fri Sep-May)

Tourist office (☎81 53 05 55; Jernbanetorget 1, Oslo S; ☉7am-8pm Mon-Fri, 8am-6pm Sat & Sun)

Use-It (Ungdomsinformasjonen; Youth Information Office; ☎24 14 98 20; www.use-it.no; Møllergata 3; ☉11am-5pm Mon-Fri, noon-5pm Sat) Exceptionally helpful and savvy office aimed at (but not restricted to) backpackers under the age of 26. Makes (free) bookings for accommodation and provides information on anything from events to hitching. Pick up its annual *Streetwise* guide to Oslo here or at tourist offices.

ⓘ Getting There & Away

There are dozens of international routes to/from Oslo (p382).

Air
Most flights land at Oslo's main international airport in **Gardermoen** (www.osl.no), 50km north of the city. It's the country's main international gateway and domestic hub. Oslo Torp, 123km south of the city, and Rygge Airport, 60km southeast of Oslo, are secondary airports.

Bus
Long-distance buses arrive at and depart from the **Galleri Oslo Bus Terminal** (Schweigaards gate 8); the train and bus stations are linked via an overhead walkway for easy connections.

Car & Motorcycle
The main highways into the city are the E6 from the north and south, and the E18 from the southeast and west.

Train
All trains arrive and depart from Oslo S in the city centre. It has **reservation desks** (☉6.30am-11pm) and an **information desk** (☎81 50 08 88, press 9 for service in English), which provides details on routes and timetables throughout the country.

Major destinations include Stavanger via Kristiansand, Bergen via Voss, Røros via Hamar, and Trondheim via Hamar and Lillehammer.

ⓘ Getting Around

Oslo has an efficient public-transport system with an extensive network of buses, trams, underground trains (T-bane) and ferries. In addition to single-trip tickets, day and transferable eight-trip tickets are also available. Children aged four to 16 and seniors over 67 years of age pay half-price on all fares.

The Oslo Pass includes access to all public-transport options within the city, with the exception of late-night buses and trams.

Trafikanten (☏177; www.trafikanten.no; Jernbanetorget; ☺7am-11pm) is located below Oslo S tower and provides free schedules and a public transport map, *Sporveiskart Oslo*.

To/From Gardermoen International Airport

Flybussen (www.flybussen.no) is the airport shuttle to Gardermoen International Airport, 50km north of Oslo. The trip costs Nkr150/250 one way/return (valid one month) and takes 40 minutes.

FlyToget (www.flytoget.no) rail services leave Gardermoen airport for Oslo S (Nkr170, 19 minutes) every 10 minutes between 4.18am and midnight. In addition, most northbound **NSB** (www.nsb.no) intercity and local trains stop at Gardermoen (Nkr90, from 26 minutes, hourly but fewer on Saturday).

To/From Torp Airport

To get to/from Torp Airport in Sandefjord, 123km south of Oslo (and serviced by Ryanair and Wizzair among others), take the **Torp-Expressen** (www.torpekspressen.no; one-way/return adult Nkr220/380, child Nkr110/220) bus between Galleri Oslo bus terminal and the airport (1½ hours). Departures from Oslo leave 3½ hours before scheduled departures.

To/From Rygge Airport

To get to/from Rygge, in Moss, 60km southeast of Oslo, take the **Rygge-Expressen** (www.ryggeekspressen.no; one-way/return adult Nkr160/290, child Nkr80/160) bus between Galleri Oslo bus terminal and the airport (one hour). Departures from Oslo leave three hours before scheduled departures.

Bus & Tram

Bus and tram lines lace the city and extend into the suburbs. There's no central local bus station, but most converge at Jernbanetorget in front of Oslo S. Most westbound buses, including those to Bygdøy and Vigeland Park, also stop immediately south of the National Theatre.

Tickets for most trips cost Nkr30/15 adult/child if you buy them in advance (at 7-Eleven, Narvesen, Trafikanten) or Nkr50/25 if you buy them from the driver. A day pass costs Nkr75/38 adult/child.

T-Bane

The six-line Tunnelbanen underground system, better known as the T-bane, is faster and extends further from the city centre than most city bus lines. All lines pass through the Nationaltheatret, Stortinget and Jernbanetorget (for Oslo S) stations. Ticket prices are the same as for the buses and trams.

SOUTHERN NORWAY

In the summer months the curving south coast is a magnet for vacationing Norwegian families, who come to the area for its beaches, offshore islands and sailing opportunities. Unless here to pilot masted vessels, first-time foreign travellers generally visit the coast's sleepy wooden towns as a pit stop en route to more-exciting locales.

Arendal

POP 33.323

Arendal, one of the larger and livelier south-coast towns, has an undeniable buzz throughout summer. It all happens around the harbour (known as Pollen), with outdoor restaurants and bars next to the water and a full calendar of festivals.

◉ Sights

Tyholmen HISTORIC NEIGHBOURHOOD
The old harbourside area of Tyholmen, with its attractively restored 19th-century wooden buildings, was in 1992 awarded the prestigious Europa Nostra prize for its expert restoration. Check out the **Rådhus** (Rådhusgata 10), which was originally a shipowner's home dating from 1815.

FREE **Bomuldsfabriken Art Hall** GALLERY
(www.bomuldsfabriken.no; Oddenveien 5; ☺noon-4pm Tue-Fri) For an excellent gallery of contemporary art, the Bomuldsfabriken Art Hall presents exhibitions and a fine permanent collection in a pretty 19th-century textile factory. It's a 10-minute walk from the town centre on Arendal's northern edge.

✦ Festivals & Events

Sørlandet Boat Show BOATS
(www.sorlandetsbatmesse.no) Held in late May.

Hove Festival MUSIC
(www.hovefestivalen.no) This music festival draws international acts to the island of Tromø in late June. Headliners in recent years have included the likes of Massive Attack, The Strokes and Snoop Dogg.

Canal Street Jazz & Blues Festival MUSIC
(www.canalstreet.no) World-class jazz and blues; late July.

≡ Sleeping & Eating

Clarion Tyholmen Hotel HISTORIC HOTEL €€
(☏37 07 68 00; www.choice.no; Teaterplassen 2; r from Nkr1525; ❋) Arendal's best hotel, the

Clarion combines a prime waterfront position with attractive rooms in a restored old building that seeks to emulate Tyholmen's old-world ambience. The corner suites offer magnificent sea views.

Thon Hotel Arendal HOTEL €€
(☎37 05 21 50; www.thonhotels.no; Friergangen 1; r from Nkr545-1350; ☀) It might not have the waterfront views, but this outpost of Thon Hotels is just 50m from the water's edge. Typical of the Thon chain, the rooms are modern, large and comfortable. There's a public pay car park opposite (Nkr149 per 24 hours).

Café Det Lindvedske Hus CAFE €
(☎37 02 18 38; Nedre Tyholmsvei 7b; light meals Nkr69-98; ☺11am-11pm Mon-Thu, 11am-1am Fri & Sat, 2-10pm Sun) With its mellow atmosphere and 200-year-old decor, this lovely place does light meals (soups, grilled sandwiches and pasta), great coffee and has the ambience of a sophisticated but casual art cafe. The kitchen closes at 9pm, whereafter music of the Stan Getz kind takes over. A terrific place.

Blom Restaurant SEAFOOD €€€
(☎37 00 14 14; www.blomrestaurant.no; Langbrygge 5; mains Nkr289-329; ☺4-10pm Mon-Sat, 3-8pm Sun) This is perhaps the classiest bar/restaurant by the Pollen harbour, a chic place and a cut above the beer-and-yobbo culture that sometimes afflicts other waterside bars in Arendal. Try the grilled fillet of reindeer served with cinnamon-baked pear and whortleberries.

ℹ Information

Tourist office (www.arendal.com; Sam Eydes plass; ☺9am-5pm Mon-Fri, 11am-4pm Sat Jul–mid-Aug, 10am-3pm Mon-Fri mid-Aug–Jun) Provides local information and also rents out bicycles for Nkr100 per day. It's signposted from the harbour.

ℹ Getting There & Away

Nor-Way Bussekspress buses between Kristiansand (Nkr190, 1½ hours, up to nine daily) and Oslo (Nkr360, four hours) call in at the Harebakken stop on the main E18 highway, from where shuttle buses head down into town.

From the Arendal Rutebilstasjon, a block west of Pollen harbour, buses connect Arendal with Grimstad (Nkr72, 30 minutes, half-hourly) and Risør (Nkr123, 1¼ hours, hourly).

Grimstad
POP 11,291

Grimstad, once a major shipbuilding centre, is at its most beautiful in the pedestrianised streets that lie inland from the waterfront; these streets are some of the loveliest on the Skagerrak coast. Grimstad was the home of playwright Henrik Ibsen and has a good museum. It's officially the sunniest spot in Norway and has a large student population.

◉ Sights

Ibsenhuset Museum MUSEUM
(www.gbm.no; Henrik Ibsens gate 14; adult/student/child Nkr80/55/free; ☺11am-4pm Mon-Sat, noon-4pm Sun, closed mid-Sep–late May) Norway's favourite playwright, Henrik Ibsen, arrived in Grimstad in January 1844. The house where he worked as a pharmacist's apprentice, and where he lived and first cultivated his interest in writing, has been converted into the Ibsenhuset Museum. It contains a re-created pharmacy and many of the writer's belongings.

Storsanden BEACH
In the neighbouring hamlet of Fevik (more an adjunct of Grimstad, 6km away), Storsanden is a pretty little beach that was voted Norway's best a few years ago. It's all relative, but it *is* a pretty cove.

⚐ Activities

Bicycle & Boat Rental CYCLING, BOATING
(3/24hr bike rental Nkr100/150, 3/24hr boat rental from Nkr450/650) In summer the tourist office rents outs bicycles (including helmets and child seats for an extra cost) and boats for four to five people.

⨋ Sleeping & Eating

For camping, there are at least six nearby camping grounds that are listed on the tourist office website (www.visitgrimstad.com).

TOP
CHOICE **Strand Hotel Fevik** HISTORIC HOTEL
(☎37 25 00 00; www.strandhotelfevik.no; r from Nkr1295; ☀) This lovely 1930s seaside hotel was built in a functionalist style and was later a favourite of writer Roald Dahl. The rooms are supremely comfortable, classy and contemporary with many boasting ocean views, and it has a private beach. The location is one of the best on Norway's southern coast. Its restaurant (mains Nkr155 to Nkr270) is similarly good.

Rica Hotel Grimstad
HISTORIC HOTEL €€

(☑37 25 25 25; www.rica.no; Kirkegata 3; r from Nkr995; P❋) One of southern Norway's nicer in-town hotels, this stylish hotel spans a number of converted and conjoined timber houses. It's the only in-town hotel and comes with loads of charm.

Haven Brasserie
SEAFOOD €€

(www.havenbrasserie.no; Storgata 4; pizza & light meals Nkr110-150, mains Nkr190-255; ⊙noon-midnight Mon-Sat, from 1pm Sun) One of the few restaurants in town that allows you to sit at a table by the water, this appealing place dishes up superb seafood and a handful of pasta and pizza staples.

Platebaren
SANDWICHES €

(Storgata 15; sandwiches Nkr85, salads & hot meals Nkr115; ⊙9am-5pm Mon-Fri, to 4pm Sat Jun-Aug) This highly recommended coffee bar spills out onto the street in summer and is a terrific place to tuck into decent-sized snacks, such as sandwiches, bacon and eggs, and hamburgers. The sandwiches are especially good.

❶ Information

Tourist office (www.visitgrimstad.com; Storgata 1a, Sorenskrivergården; ⊙9am-6pm Mon-Fri, 10am-4pm Sat mid-Jun–mid-Aug, 8.30am-4pm Mon-Fri Sep-May)

❶ Getting There & Around

Nor-Way Bussekspress buses between Oslo (Nkr360, 4½ hours) and Kristiansand (Nkr105, one hour) call at Grimstad up to six times daily. Nettbuss buses to/from Arendal run once or twice hourly (Nkr60, 30 minutes).

Kristiansand

POP 69,380

Kristiansand, Norway's fifth-largest city, calls itself 'Norway's No.1 Holiday Resort'. Sun-starved Norwegians do flock here in summer, but for everyone else it's a gateway to the charming seaside villages of Norway's southern coast.

❂ Sights & Activities

TOP CHOICE Kristiansand Dyrepark
ZOO

(www.dyreparken.com; admission incl all activities adult/child from Nkr499/399; ⊙10am-7pm mid-Jun–early Aug) The Kristiansand zoo, off the E18 10km east of Kristiansand, has gradually expanded into what is probably *the* favourite holiday destination for children in Norway. There's a **funfair**, **fantasy village**, **water park**, **zoo** and the **Nordisk Vilmark** (Northern Wilderness), where visitors are transported over the habitat of moose, wolves, lynx and wolverines on elevated boardwalks.

Posebyen
OLD TOWN

The Kristiansand Posebyen (Old Town) takes in most of the 14 blocks at the northern end of the town's characteristic *kvadraturen* (square grid pattern of streets measuring six long blocks by nine shorter blocks). It's worth taking a slow stroll around this pretty quarter, the name of which was given by French soldiers who came to *reposer* (relax). The annual *Kristiansand* guide, published by the tourist office, includes a good section, 'A Stroll through Posebyen', to guide your wandering.

FREE Christiansholm Fortress
FORTRESS

(Kristiansand Festning; ⊙grounds 9am-9pm mid-May–mid-Sep) The most prominent feature of the waterfront Strandpromenaden is the distinctive Christiansholm Fortress. It was built by royal decree between 1662 and 1672 to keep watch over the strategic Skagerrak Straits and protect the city from pirates and rambunctious Swedes. The fortress served its purpose – it was never taken by enemy forces.

One Ocean Dive Center
DIVING

(www.oneocean.no; Dvergsnesveien 571; 1/2 dives with equipment from Nkr950/1300) A professional centre that runs dives to wrecks, which include a downed plane and even a minesweeper. It's 8km east of Kristiansand.

🛏 Sleeping

Kristiansand can be expensive for what you get, which may be nothing unless you book early for summer, especially during the July school-holiday period when prices soar.

Yess Hotel
HOTEL €€

(☑38 70 15 70; www.yesshotel.no; Tordenskjolds gate 12; s/d Nkr898/995; P❋) Yess Hotel is a classic example of the good-value, new 'back-to-basics' hotels that seem to be slowly sprouting up in bigger towns throughout the country. The rooms at this new hotel – some would say simple, others minimalist – are livened up with wall-to-wall photographs of trees. The hotel is at the western entrance of town, close to the train station.

STAVE CHURCH & THE BLUES

Notodden, in the southern Norwegian interior, is an industrial town of little note, but the nearby **Heddal stave church** (www.heddalstavkirke.no; Heddal; adult/child Nkr65/free, entry to grounds free; ⊗9am-6pm Mon-Sat mid-Jun–mid-Aug, 10am-5pm rest of yr) rises out of a graveyard like a scaly wooden dragon. Of great interest are the 'rose' paintings, a runic inscription, the bishop's chair and the altarpiece. The church possibly dates from 1242, but parts of the chancel date from as early as 1147. It was heavily restored in the 1950s. On Sundays from Easter to November, services are held at 11am (visitors are welcome, but to avoid disruption, you must remain for the entire one-hour service); after 1pm, the church is again open to the public. Notodden's other claim to fame is the renowned and hugely popular **Notodden Blues Festival** (www.bluesfest.no), in early August.

Timekspressen buses run regularly to Notodden from Kongsberg (from Nkr50, 35 minutes) and Oslo (from Nkr178, two hours).

Frobusdalen Rom
B&B €€

(☑91 12 99 06; www.gjestehus.no; Frobusdalen 2; s/d/f Nkr600/800/1200; P) Probably the most personal place to stay in Kristiansand, this small B&B in a gorgeous old timber home a 10-minute walk northwest of the centre is rustic, cosy and friendly. However, the secret's out and it's often full. To get here on foot, walk through the tunnel that leads under the motorway opposite the Yess Hotel; by car it's accessible off Tordenskjoldsgate.

Scandic Kristiansand
HOTEL €€€

(☑21 61 42 00; www.scandic-hotels.com; Markens gate 39; r from Nkr1180; P@) If you value style as well as substance, the Scandic Kristiansand has both. The rooms and public areas are stylish, rooms have all the requisite bells and whistles, and the hotel adheres to the strictest environmental standards. This is another hotel at the western corner of the city centre, a block northeast of the train station.

Eating & Drinking

One of the loveliest corners of southern Norway, the fish-market harbour is surrounded by restaurants and the small fish market itself is good for picking up fish cakes and smoked salmon for a picnic.

TOP CHOICE Bølgen & Moi
SEAFOOD €€€

(☑38 17 83 00; www.bolgenogmoi.no; Sjølystveien 1a; mains Nkr215-575, 3-/4-/5-course set menu Nkr545/595/645; ⊗3pm-midnight Mon-Sat) The best restaurant around the fish-market harbour, the supercool Bølgen & Moi does a sublime fish and shellfish soup for both starter and main and a tasty range of seafood dishes. In summer the outdoor tables are packed and it's a good place for a drink after the kitchen closes.

Hos Naboen
INTERNATIONAL €€

(www.hosnaboen.no; Markens gate 19a; lunch mains Nkr99-155, dinner mains Nkr275-310; ⊗10.30am-12.30pm Mon-Thu, to 1.30am Fri & Sat) This bustling central cafe, with a warm and sociable atmosphere, pumps out great light meals (including blue mussels with lime and coconut milk, and shrimp sandwiches), huge doorstopper wedges of cake and decent coffee.

Snadderkiosken
FAST FOOD €

(Østre Strandgate 78a; dishes Nkr89-99; ⊗8.30am-11.30pm Mon-Fri, 11.30am-11.30pm Sat & Sun) We don't normally direct you to the fast-food kiosks that are everywhere in Norway, but Snadderkiosken, at the eastern end of town, is one of the best of its kind. Near the town beach, this lovely tiled 1920s-style kiosk will sort you out with temptations such as hearty meatballs and mashed potatoes, fish burgers or grilled chicken with rice and salad.

TOP CHOICE Frk Larsen
BAR

(Markens gate 5; ⊗11am-midnight Mon-Wed, 11am-3am Thu-Sat, noon-midnight Sun) One of the coolest bars in southern Norway, this trendy place towards the southeastern end of Markens gate has retro-chic fusion decor, a mellow ambience by day and late-night music for an 'in' crowd on weekend nights. The cocktail bar opens at 8pm, but it's just as popular for a midday coffee.

Information

Tourist office (☑38 12 13 14; www.visitkrs.no; Rådhusgata 6; ⊗9am-6pm Mon-Fri, 10am-6pm Sat, noon-6pm Sun mid-Jun–Aug, 9am-4pm Mon-Fri rest of yr)

❶ Getting There & Away

BUS Departures from Kristiansand include: Arendal (Nkr190, 1½ hours, up to nine daily); Oslo (Nkr360, 5½ hours, up to nine daily) and Stavanger (Nkr340, 4½ hours, two to four daily).

TRAIN There are up to four trains daily to Oslo (Nkr299 to Nkr649, 4½ hours) and up to five to Stavanger (Nkr199 to Nkr450, 3¼ hours).

Rjukan

POP 3350

Sitting in the shadow of what is arguably Norway's most beautiful peak (Gausta; 1881m) Rjukan is a picturesque introduction to the Norwegian high country as well as southern Norway's activities centre par excellence.

◉ Sights

Industrial Workers Museum   MUSEUM
(Norsk Industriarbeidermuseet; www.visitvemork. com; adult/child Nkr75/45; ⊗10am-6pm mid-Jun–mid-Aug) Housed inside a hydroelectric plant dating from 1911, 7km west of Rjukan, this museum details the Norwegian Resistance's daring sabotage of the heavy-water plant used by the Nazis in their atomic efforts.

Rjukanfossen   WATERFALL
Believed to be the highest waterfall in the world in the 18th century (Angel Falls in Venezuela now has that claim), the 104m-high Rjukanfossen is still a spectacular sight. To get the best view, take the Rv37 heading west and park just before the tunnel 9.5km west of town; a 200m walk leads to a fine viewpoint.

⫯ Activities

Rjukan stands on the cusp of the bleak Hardangervidda Plateau. The range of summer activities here is seemingly endless and includes ice climbing; Norway's highest land-based bungee jump (84m); moose safaris and rail-biking. Winter activities include horse-drawn sleigh rides, skiing and dog sledding. The tourist office can put you in touch with local operators organising these activities.

TOP CHOICE **Gaustabanen**
Cable Railway   SCENIC RAILWAY
(www.gaustabanen.no; one-way/return adult Nkr250/350, child Nkr125/175; ⊗10am-5pm late Jun–mid-Oct) For an incredible experience, ride this mind-boggling cable railway deep into a mountain core before climbing more than 1km at an improbable 40-degree angle. Built by NATO in 1952 to ensure access to a radio tower in any weather, it's an extraordinary experience promising fantastic views. The railway's base station is 10km southeast of Rjukan.

Krossobanen   CABLE CAR
(www.krossobanen.no; one-way/return adult Nkr50/100, child Nkr20/40, bike Nkr50/100; ⊗9am-8pm mid-Jun–Aug) The top station of the Krossobanen cable car, above Rjukan, serves as the trailhead for a host of hiking and cycling trails. There are also fine views down into the valley and across towards Gausta.

⫸ Sleeping & Eating

Rjukan's town centre has a few places to stay, but there are more choices up in the Gaustablikk area. For the busy winter season, contact **Gausta Booking** (⊘45 48 51 51; www.gaustatoppenbooking.com), which can help track down a spare hut.

TOP CHOICE **Rjukan Hytteby & Kro**   CABIN €€
(⊘35 09 01 22; www.rjukan-hytteby.no; Brogata 9; cabins Nkr895-1400) Easily the town centre's best choice and sitting in a pretty spot on the river bank, these carefully decorated and very well-equipped huts seek to emulate the early-20th-century hydroelectric workers' cabins. The owner is exceptionally helpful and there are good meals (Nkr85 to Nkr195) including burgers, salads, and fish and chips in the cafe. It's a pleasant 500m walk along the river bank to the town centre.

Rjukan Gjestegård   HOTEL €€
(⊘35 08 06 50; www.rgg.no; Birkelandsgata 2; dm Nkr235, d Nkr90, s/d without bathroom Nkr385/580; ℗ @) This central guesthouse occupies the buildings of the old youth hostel and is something of a travellers' centre. The rooms here are simple but fine enough, there's a guest kitchen and the location is good if you want to be in town. Breakfast costs Nkr80.

Gaustablikk Høyfjellshotell   LODGE €€
(⊘35 09 14 22; www.gaustablikk.no; s/d from Nkr975/1390; ℗) This expansive mountain lodge is one of Norway's better mountain hotels. It has a prime location overlooking the lake and mountain off the Fv651 and 10km from town. The rooms are modern if simple and many have lovely views of Gausta, while the evening buffet dinner (Nkr395)

HIKING & CYCLING FROM RJUKAN

The tourist office can give you more information on hiking and cycling routes.

Gausta

The most obvious goal for hikers is the summit of beautiful Gausta (1881m), from where you can see a remarkable one-sixth of Norway on a clear day. The popular, and easy, two- to three-hour, 4km hiking track leads from the trailhead of Stavsro (15km southeast of Rjukan) up to Den Norske Turistforening's (DNT) **Gaustahytta** (1830m). The summit is a further half-hour walk along the rocky ridge. A 13km road link, but no public transport, runs from the far eastern end of Rjukan to Stavsro (altitude 1173m) at Lake Heddersvann Taxis (☎ 35 09 14 00) charge around Nkr450 one way.

Another alternative is to take the Gaustabanen (p305) up and walk back down, although it's a 5km walk back down from Stavsro to the Gaustabanen start point if that's where you've parked your car.

Hardangervidda

The Hardangervidda Plateau, the biggest mountain plateau in Europe and home to Europe's largest herd of wild reindeer, rises up to the north of Rjukan and offers a wealth of fantastic hikes. From Gvepseborg, the summit of the Krossobanen (p305) cable car, the most rewarding day hike is the five-hour round trip to the **Helberghytta DNT Hut**. The scenery takes in icy-cold lakes, snow-streaked hills, barren moorland and views back over towards Gausta.

For something more challenging, an eight- to nine-hour route, which can also be used by cyclists, leads from the cable-car platform past the Helberghytta DNT Hut and onwards to **Kalhovd Turisthytte**. From here you can either catch a bus or hike nine hours down to **Mogen Turisthytte**. Next catch the Møsvatn ferry (Nkr270) back to Skinnarbu, west of Rjukan on Rv37; ferry timetables are available from the Rjukan tourist office.

Alternatively, follow the marked route that begins above Rjukan Fjellstue, around 10km west of Rjukan and just north of the Rv37. This historic track follows the **Sabotørruta** (Saboteurs' Route), the path taken by the members of the Norwegian Resistance during WWII. From late June until mid-August, the tourist office organises three-hour guided hikes along this route (Nkr220, noon Tuesday, Thursday and Sunday).

The best hiking map to use for this part of the plateau is Telemark Turistforening's *Hardangervidda Sør-Øst* (1:60,000), available from the tourist office (Nkr98).

is a lavish affair. Book through Fjord Pass (p379) for a cheaper one-night rate.

Gondal Taxi Burger   FAST FOOD €
(off Sam Eydes; mains Nkr85-149) A cut above most Norwegian roadside kiosks, this well-run little place offers fish and chips, hamburgers, fish burgers, kebabs and other heart-friendly delights. Eat at the shady adjacent tables.

ℹ Information

Tourist office (☎ 35 08 05 50; www.visit rjukan.com; Torget 2; ⊙ 9am-7pm Mon-Fri, 10am-6pm Sat & Sun late Jun–late Aug, 8am-3.30pm Mon-Fri rest of yr)

ℹ Getting There & Away

Regular buses connect Rjukan to Oslo (Nkr375, 3½ hours) via Notodden (where you need to change buses) and Kongsberg (Nkr220, two hours).

CENTRAL NORWAY

The central region of Norway is strewn with stunning national parks, the most spectacular of which is Jotunheimen, a popular wilderness area and national park characterised by dramatic ravines and multiple glaciers. The immensely scenic Oslo–Bergen railway line slices east to west, crossing the stark and white snowscape of the Hardangervidda Plateau, a cross-country skiing paradise. For a resort-town feel, try Lillehammer, close to several downhill slopes and host of the 1994 Winter Olympics.

Lillehammer

POP 20,673

Long a popular Norwegian ski resort, Lillehammer became known to the world after hosting the 1994 Winter Olympics, which still provide the town with some of its most interesting sights. Lying at the northern end of Lake Mjøsa and surrounded by farms, forests and small settlements, it's a laid-back place with year-round attractions, although in winter it becomes a ski town par excellence.

Lillehammer's centre is small and cute. Storgata, the main pedestrian walkway, is two short blocks east of the adjacent bus and train stations.

Sights & Activities

Olympic Sights　　OLYMPIC PARK
(wheelbob adult/10-11yr Nkr220/150, taxibobs adult around Nkr1100; ☉taxibobs Nov-Easter) Visitors can tour the main Olympic sites over a large area called the **Olympiaparken** (www.olympiaparken.no; ☉9am-6pm mid-Jun–mid-Aug), which includes the **Lygårdsbakkene** (☑info 61 25 11 40; Olympiaparken; adult/child Nkr25/15, chairlift Nkr55/50, simulator Nkr65/55; ☉9am-8pm Jun–mid-Aug, shorter hr May & mid-Aug–end Sep) ski jump, chairlift and bobsled simulator. The excellent **Norwegian Olympic Museum** (www.ol.museum.no; Olympiaparken; adult/child Nkr110/55; ☉10am-5pm Jun-Aug, 11am-4pm Tue-Sun Sep-May) provides exhibits on every Olympic Games since 1896.

At Hunderfossen, 15km north of town, you can career down the **Olympic Bobsled Run** (Hunderfossen; adult/child Nkr230/160; ☉10.30am-4pm Jul–mid-Aug, weekends only May, Jun & late-Aug–mid-Sep, closed rest of year) aboard a **wheelbob** under the guidance of a professional bobsled pilot. Wheelbobs take five passengers and hit a top speed of 100km/h. Bookings are advisable during winter.

Maihaugen Folk Museum　　MUSEUM
(www.maihaugen.no; Maihaugveien 1; adult/child/family Jun-Aug Nkr150/75/375, Sep-May Nkr110/55/275; ☉10am-5pm Jun-Aug, 11am-4pm Tue-Sun Sep-May) Olympics aside, Lillehammer's main attraction is the exceptional Maihaugen Folk Museum, which contains around 180 historic houses, shops, farm buildings and a stave church.

Sleeping

Lillehammer Vandrerhjem　　HOSTEL €
(☑61 26 00 24; www.815mjosa.no; 1st fl, Railway Station; dm/s/d Nkr350/695/980) If you've never stayed in a youth hostel, this one above the train station (with reception downstairs) is the place to break the habits of a lifetime. The rooms are simple but come with a bathroom, bed linen and free wireless internet.

Birkebeineren　　HOTEL, APARTMENT €€
(☑61 05 00 80; www.birkebeineren.no; Birkebeinervegen 24; s/d Nkr780/1080, 2-/4-bed apt Sun-Thu Nkr1235/1720, all apt Fri & Sat Nkr2100; ℗) This terrific place, on the road up to the bottom of the ski jump, offers a range of accommodation to suit different budgets; prices fall the longer you stay. Rooms are light-filled and modern, and there's a children's playground and sauna on-site.

Mølla Hotell　　HOTEL €€€
(☑61 05 70 80; www.mollahotell.no; Elvegata 12; s/d Nkr1420/1770; ℗) Fully refurbished with modern rooms in an old mill, the hotel has antique memorabilia in the public areas and flat-screen TVs and comfy beds in the rooms. The rooftop bar (open 8pm to 2am Monday to Saturday) has fine views and the architecture is distinguished. Parking costs Nkr60 per day.

Eating

Nikkers Sport　　INTERNATIONAL €€
(www.nikkers.no; Elvegata; mains Nkr139-298) Right by Lillehammer's bubbling brook, this very cool cafe-restaurant serves tasty meals and great coffee. It's a popular spot for locals. The same people also run neighbouring Nikkers, a pub where a moose has apparently walked through the wall; they also do sandwiches and lighter meals.

Blåmann　　INTERNATIONAL
(☑61 26 22 03; www.blaamann.com; Lilletorget 1; lunch mains & light meals Nkr109-189, dinner mains Nkr169-259; ☉11am-11pm) Styling itself as a gastrobar, this recommended spot has a clean-lined interior, outdoor tables overlooking the brook and a trendy menu that encompasses Mexican dishes, burgers and all manner of surprises.

Café Stasjonen　　CAFE
(Lillehammer Skysstasjon; light meals Nkr59-79, mains Nkr119-149; ☉6.30am-10pm) The cafe of Lillehammer Vandrerhjem in the bus/train station is fine value, with light meals and

CENTRAL NORWAY ACTIVITIES

It's possible to engage in a wide range of activities in central Norway. For more information, contact the following offices, which have a list of operators and local accommodation, and can provide advice on hiking in nearby national parks:

» **Otta tourist office & Rondane National Park Centre** (☑61 23 66 50; www.rondane-dovrefjell.no; Ola Dahls gate 1; ☺8am-4pm Mon-Fri mid-Jun–mid-Aug)

» **Dombås tourist office & Dovrefjell National Park Centre** (Dovrefjell Nasjonalparksenter; ☑61 24 14 44; www.rondane-dovrefjell.no; Sentralplassen; ☺9am-8pm Mon-Sat, to 4pm Sun mid-Jun–mid-Aug, shorter hr rest of yr)

» **Oppdal Booking** (☑72 40 08 00; www.oppdal-booking.no; Olav Skasliens vei 10) A privately run one-stop shop for reserving activities and accommodation; booking fees apply.

For more possibilities, pick up the *Summer Adventures* brochure from any of the region's tourist offices.

Rafting

You can raft in Sjoa or Oppdal from the middle of May until early October. Prices start at Nkr690 for a 3½-hour family trip; there are also five-hour (from Nkr1090) and seven-hour (from Nkr1190) day trips; longer excursions are available on request. In addition to rafting, most of the following operators also organise riverboarding (from Nkr990), low-level rock climbing (from Nkr590), canyoning (from Nkr990), caving (from Nkr790) and hiking.

Operators include:

» **Heidal Rafting** (☑61 23 60 37; www.heidalrafting.no; Sjoa) Just 1km west of Sjoa and the E6 along Rv257.

» **Sjoa Rafting** (☑90 07 10 00; www.sjoarafting.com; Nedre Heidal) Some 7.5km upstream from Sjoa along Rv257.

» **Sjoa Rafting Senter NWR** (☑47 66 06 80; www.sjoaraftingsenter.no; Varphaugen Gård) About 3km upstream from Sjoa along Rv257.

» **Opplev Oppdal** (☑72 40 41 80; www.opplev-oppdal.no; Olav Skasliens vei 12, Oppdal).

Moose & Musk Ox Safaris

Your best chance of seeing one of Norway's last 80 musk oxen is to take a three- to five-hour morning musk ox safari (from Nkr300), either from Oppdal or Dombås. In both places, a three-hour evening moose safari (Nkr200) is also possible.

---

more substantial main meals that include the local speciality of sour-cream porridge with cured ham/sausage.

ℹ Information

Lillehammer tourist office (www.lillehammer.com; Lillehammer Skysstasjon; ☺8am-6pm Mon-Fri, 10am-4pm Sat & Sun mid-Jun–mid-Aug) Opening hours were uncertain at the time of writing and may change.

ℹ Getting There & Away

BUS Nor-Way Bussekspress has services to/from Oslo (Nkr330, three hours, three to four daily) via Oslo's Gardermoen airport (Nkr280, 2¼ hours) and Bergen (Nkr575, 9¼ hours, one daily). Lavprisekspressen buses run less often but are cheaper if you book online at http://lavprisekspressen.no.

TRAIN Trains run to/from Oslo (Nkr363, 2¼ hours, 11 to 17 daily) and Trondheim (from Nkr677, 4¼ to seven hours, four to six daily).

Røros
POP 3689

Røros, a charming Unesco World Heritage Site set in a small hollow of stunted forests and bleak fells, is one of Norway's most beautiful villages. The Norwegian writer Johan Falkberget described Røros as 'a place of whispering history' and this historic copper-mining town (once called Bergstad, meaning 'mountain city') has wonderfully preserved and colourful wooden houses that climb the hillside, as well as fascinating relics from the town's mining past; the first mine opened in 1644 and operations ceased 333 years later. Røros has become something of a retreat for artists, who lend even more character to this enchanted place.

Sights

TOP CHOICE **Historic District** HISTORIC SITE

Røros' historic district, characterised by the striking log architecture of its 80 protected buildings, takes in the entire central area. The two main streets, Bergmannsgata (it tapers from southwest to northeast to create an optical illusion and make the town appear larger than it is) and Kjerkgata, are lined with historical homes and buildings, all under preservation orders.

Røros Kirke CHURCH

(Kjerkgata; adult/child Nkr30/free; ⊙10am-4pm Mon-Sat, 12.30-2.30pm Sun) This Lutheran church is one of Norway's most distinctive, not to mention one of the country's largest, with a seating capacity of 1640. The first church on the site was constructed in 1650, but it had fallen into disrepair by the mid-18th century and from 1780 a new baroque-style church (the one you see today) was built just behind the original.

Smelthytta MUSEUM

(www.rorosmuseet.no; Malmplassen; adult/student/child Nkr70/60/free, incl guided tour in summer; ⊙10am-6pm mid-Jun–mid-Aug, copper-smelting displays 3pm Mon-Fri early Jul-early Aug, guided tours during summer in Norwegian 11am or 2pm, in English 3.30pm) Housed in old smelting works, this mining museum is a town highlight. The building was reconstructed in 1988 according to the original 17th-century plan. Upstairs you'll find geological and conservation displays, while downstairs are some brilliant working models of the mines and the water- and horse-powered smelting processes. The museum is on the hill next to the river at the northeastern end of the village.

Just across the stream from the museum are the protected **slegghaugan** (slag heaps), from where there are lovely views over town. Off the southwestern corner of the slag heaps, the historic smelting district with its tiny turf-roofed **miners' cottages**, particularly along Sleggveien, is one of Røros' prettiest corners.

Activities

Dog sledding, canoeing, horse riding, sleigh rides and **ice fishing** are all possible. The tourist office has a full list of operators.

Husky Excursions

Alaskan Husky Tours (☑62 49 87 66; www.huskytour.no; Os; dog sledding adult/child/12-18 Nkr590/190/290, horse-drawn sleigh for 4 people, per hr Nkr600) and **Røros Husky** (☑72 41 41 94; www.roroshusky.no) both organise winter dog-sledding tours from a few hours to a few days. Alaskan Husky Tours also operates summer tours on wheel-sleds (adult/child under 16 years Nkr690/345).

Sámi Excursions

Røros Rein TOUR

(☑72 41 10 06; www.rorosrein.no; Hagaveien 17) Organises a program that includes sleigh rides, getting up close and personal with reindeer and a traditional Sámi meal in a Sámi hut.

Tours

Guided Walking Tours WALKING

(adult/child Nkr70/free; ⊙tours 10.30am, 12.30pm, 2.30pm Mon-Sat, 11.30am & 1pm Sun mid-Jun–mid-Aug) Run by the tourist office, the tours take you through the historic town centre. The 12.30pm (Monday to Friday) and 1pm (Sunday) tours are in English and Norwegian.

Festivals & Events

The biggest winter market is **Rørosmartnan** (Røros Market), begun in 1644 as a meeting place for wandering hunters to sell goods to townspeople. Thanks to an 1853 royal decree stipulating that a grand market be held annually from the penultimate Tuesday of February to the following Saturday, it continues today with street markets and live entertainment.

Fermund Race (www.femundlopet.no), one of Europe's longest dog-sled races, starts and ends in Røros in the first week of February.

Sleeping

TOP CHOICE **Erzscheidergården** GUESTHOUSE €€

(☑72 41 11 94; www.erzscheidergaarden.no; Spell Olaveien 6; s/d from Nkr895/1290; P) This appealing 24-room guesthouse is located up the hill from the centre and behind the church. The wood-panelled rooms are loaded with personality, the atmosphere is Norwegian-family warmth and the breakfasts are outstanding.

Frøyas Hus
B&B €€

(☏92 88 35 30; www.froyashus.no; Mørkstugata 4; r without bathroom Nkr400-900) This gorgeous place in the village centre, off the easternmost of the two main streets running through town, has an intimacy that you won't find elsewhere. The two rooms are small but, save for a lick of paint, they've scarcely changed in more than 300 years – rustic in the best sense of the word. The attached cafe is similarly charming.

Vertshuset Røros
HISTORIC HOTEL €€

(☏72 41 93 50; www.vertshusetroros.no; Kjerkgata 34; s/d from Nkr900/1200, 2-/4-bed apt Nkr1500/2300; ℗) Located in a historic 17th-century building on the main pedestrian thoroughfare, Vertshuset Røros is another wonderful choice. The all-wood rooms are generously sized, with numerous period touches: beds here are arguably the most comfortable in town.

✗ Eating

TOP CHOICE Vertshuset Røros
TRADITIONAL NORWEGIAN €€

(☏72 41 24 11; Kjerkgata 34; lunch mains Nkr95-139, dinner mains Nkr295-325) Lunch dishes here include fairly standard soup, sandwiches and burgers, but from 4pm onwards, the food is exquisite. You'll find the most tender fillets of reindeer or elk, while Arctic char occasionally make an appearance and desserts are always worth saving space for.

Kaffestugu Cafeteria
CAFE, NORWEGIAN €

(www.kaffestuggu.no; Bergmannsgata 18; mains Nkr88-225; ☺10am-10pm mid-Jun–mid-Aug) This historic place at the lower (southwestern) end of town offers a good range of coffee, pastries, snacks and light meals, as well as some more substantial main dishes in an atmosphere that's part cafeteria and part old-world cafe.

Skancke Bua
NORWEGIAN

(☏72 40 60 80; Kjerkgata 28; ☺11am-3.30pm) This popular, casual place does all the usual international staples, but we like it especially for the reindeer knuckle and the lemon-baked Arctic char with a warm asparagus salad.

❶ Information

Tourist office (www.roros.no; Peder Hiortsgata 2; ☺9am-6pm Mon-Sat, 10am-4pm Sun mid-Jun–mid-Aug, 9am-3pm Mon-Fri, 10am-1pm Sat rest of yr)

❶ Getting There & Away

AIR Røros has two daily **DOT LT** (www.flydot.no) flights to/from Oslo Monday to Friday and one on Sunday.

BUS There are up to four daily buses to Oslo (Nkr480, six hours), although you may have to change at Otta, and five to Trondheim (Nkr260, 2½ hours).

TRAIN Røros lies on the eastern railway line between Oslo (Nkr299 to Nkr728, five hours, six daily) and Trondheim (Nkr199 to Nkr255, 2½ hours).

Jotunheimen National Park

The Sognefjellet road (the highest mountain road in northern Europe) between Lom and Sogndal passes the northwestern perimeter of Jotunheimen National Park, Norway's most popular wilderness destination. Hiking trails lead to some of the park's 60 glaciers, up to the top of Norway's loftiest peaks, Galdhøpiggen (2469m) and Glittertind (2452m), and along ravines and valleys featuring deep lakes and plunging waterfalls. There are more than 275 summits above 2000m inside the park. There are DNT huts (p379) and private lodges along many of the routes.

❂ Sights & Activities

For park information, maps and glacier-walk arrangements contact **Lom tourist office** (www.visitjotunheimen.com; ☺9am-7pm mid-Jun–mid-Aug). Lom contains a **stave church** dating from 1170, lit to fairy-tale effect at night. It's also home to the historic Fossheim Turisthotell.

Dramatic **Galdhøpiggen**, with its cirques, arêtes, glaciers and summer ski centre, is a fairly tough eight-hour day hike from Spiterstulen, with 1470m of ascent, accessible by a toll road (Nkr95 per car). **Krossbu** is in the middle of a network of trails, including a short one to the **Smørstabbreen glacier**. From **Turtagrø**, a rock-climbing and hiking centre midway between Sogndal and Lom, there's a three-hour hike to Fannaråkhytta, Jotunheimen's highest DNT hut (2069m), offering panoramic views.

⟃ Sleeping & Eating

⟃ Elvesæter Hotell
HOTEL €€

(☏61 21 99 00; www.elveseter.no; Bøverdalen; s/d from Nkr850/1150; ℗) Run by the sixth generation of the Elvesæter family, this gorgeous hotel and restaurant (three-course dinners

Nkr325) has pretty rooms, lovely architecture and is high on novelty value, adjacent as it is to the Sagasøyla, a 32m-high carved wooden pillar tracing Norwegian history from unification in 872 to the 1814 constitution.

Turtagrø Hotel
LODGE €€€

(☑57 68 08 00; www.turtagro.no; dm from Nkr380, s/d Nkr1490/1920, tower ste Nkr2360; P) This historic hiking and mountaineering centre is a friendly yet laid-back base for exploring Jotunheimen whatever your budget. The main building has wonderful views and supremely comfortable rooms. Meals (three courses Nkr425) and full board (from Nkr1835/2690 single/double) are available.

Røisheim Hotel
HISTORIC HOTEL €€€

(☑61 21 20 31; www.roisheim.no; Bøverdalen; s/d incl breakfast, lunch & dinner from Nkr2200/3800; P) This charming place combines architecturally stunning buildings that date back to 1858 with modern comforts, although there are no TVs. Apart from the charming accommodation, the appeal lies in the meals, which are prepared by Ingrid Hov Lunde, one of the country's best-loved chefs. Quite simply, it's a wonderful place to stay.

Fossheim Turisthotell
HOTEL €€

(☑61 21 95 00; www.fossheimhotel.no; hotel s/d Nkr1150/1590, hotel annex s/d Nkr990/1290, set menus Nkr270-1600; ⊙restaurant 1-3.30pm & 7-10pm; P) This historic family hotel at the eastern end of town is one of the best hotel-restaurant combinations in Norway. The all-wood rooms in the main hotel building are lovely, while there are also luxurious log cabins with modern interiors and simpler, cheaper rooms (some with good views) in the adjacent annex. But this place is equally famous for formerly being the home kitchen of the renowned Norwegian chef Arne Brimi. Now under the care of Brimi's protégé Kristoffer Hovland, the traditional Norwegian food on offer is exquisite.

Bøverdalen Vandrerhjem
HOSTEL €

(☑61 21 20 64; boverdalen@hihostels.no; Bøverdalen; dm Nkr180, s/d without bathroom Nkr300/480; P) This fine riverside hostel has a small cafe, tidy rooms and delightful surrounds to enjoy once the day trippers have returned home. Breakfast costs Nkr75.

❶ Getting There & Away

Three daily Nor-Way Bussekspress services between Oslo (Nkr535, 6½ hours) and Måløy (Nkr360, 4½ hours) pass through Lom, and local buses to/from Otta (Nkr130, 1½ hours, six daily). Two daily summer buses run through the Jotunheimen National Park to Sogndal (Nkr260, 3½ hours, two daily) from late June to early September.

Oslo to Bergen

The Oslo–Bergen railway line, a seven-hour journey past forests and alpine villages, and across the starkly beautiful Hardangervidda Plateau, is Norway's most scenic long-haul train trip.

Midway between Oslo and Bergen is **Geilo**, a ski centre where you can practically walk off the train and onto a chairlift. There's also good summer **hiking** in the mountains around Geilo, where you'll find **Øen Turistsenter and Geilo Vandrerhjem** (☑32 08 70 60; www.oenturist.no; Lienvegen 137; dm Nkr275, huts Nkr480-825, breakfast Nkr60), a hostel near the train station that doubles as a tourist office.

From Geilo the train climbs 600m through a tundralike landscape of high lakes and snowcapped mountains to the tiny village of **Finse**, near the **Hardangerjøkulen** icecap. Finse has year-round **skiing** and is in the middle of a network of summer **hiking trails**. One of Norway's most frequently trodden trails winds from the Finse train station down to the fjord town of **Aurland**, a four-day trek. There's breathtaking mountain scenery along the way as well as a series of DNT and private mountain huts a day's walk apart – the nearest is Finsehytta, 200m from Finse station. There's also a bicycle route from Finse to Flåm (six hours, downhill) on the century-old **Rallarvegen** railway construction road.

Myrdal, further west along the railway line, is the connecting point for the spectacularly steep Flåm railway, which twists and turns its way down 20 splendid kilometres to **Flåm** on Aurlandsfjorden, an arm of Sognefjorden.

BERGEN & THE WESTERN FJORDS

This spectacular region has truly indescribable scenery. Hardangerfjord, Sognefjord, Lysefjord and Geirangerfjord are all variants

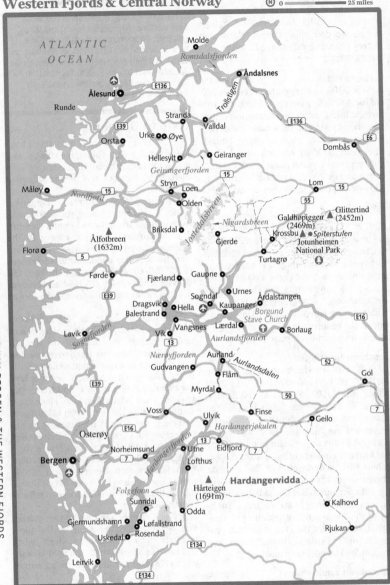

on the same theme: steep crystalline rock walls dropping with sublime force straight into the sea, often decorated with waterfalls, and small farms harmoniously blending into the natural landscape. Summer hiking opportunities exist along the fjord walls and on the enormous Jostedalsbreen glacier. Bergen is an engaging and lively city with a 15th-century waterfront.

Information on the entire region is available from **Fjord Norway** (www.fjordnorway.com).

Bergen

POP 235,046

Surrounded by seven hills and seven fjords, Bergen is a beautiful, charming city. With the Unesco World Heritage–listed Bryggen and buzzing Vågen harbour as its centrepiece, Bergen climbs the hillsides with timber-clad houses, while cable cars offer stunning views from above. Throw in great museums and a dynamic cultural life and Bergen amply rewards as much time as you can give it.

With so much else going for it, it seems almost incidental that Bergen is also a terminus of the scenic Bergen–Oslo railway line and a convenient place to stay before excursions into fjord country. The *Hurtigruten* coastal ferry begins its journey to Kirkenes from here.

History

During the 12th and 13th centuries, Bergen was Norway's capital and easily the country's most important city. By the 13th century, the city states of Germany allied themselves into trading leagues, most significantly the Hanseatic League, and the sheltered harbour of Bryggen drew the traders in droves. They established their first office here around 1360, transforming Bryggen into one of the league's four major headquarters abroad.

By the early 17th century Bergen was the trading hub of Scandinavia and Norway's most populous city, with 15,000 people. Bryggen continued as an important maritime trading centre until 1899, when the Hanseatic League's Bergen offices finally closed.

◉ Sights

TOP
CHOICE **Bryggen**   HISTORIC SITE A

The timber alleys of Bryggen, the old medieval quarter and Unesco World Heritage Site, offer an intriguing glimpse of the stacked-stone foundations and rough-plank construction of centuries past. The current 58 buildings (25% of the original) cover 13,000 sq metres and date from after the 1702 fire, although the building pattern dates back to the 12th century.

Some of Norway's creakiest floors are in the 1704 timber building housing the **Hanseatisk Museum** (www.museumvest.no; Finnegårdsgaten 1a & Øvregaten 50; adult/child Nkr60/free; ⊙9am-5pm mid-May–mid-Sep, shorter hr rest of yr). Period character flourishes, while furnishings and odd bedchambers give a glimpse of the austere living conditions of Hanseatic merchants. The entry ticket is also valid for **Schøtstuene** (Øvregaten 50), where the Hanseatic fraternity once met for its business meetings and beer guzzling.

The tiny **Theta Museum** (Enhjørningsgården; adult/child Nkr40/20; ⊙2-4pm Tue, Sat & Sun Jun-Aug) is a one-room reconstruction of a clandestine Resistance headquarters uncovered by the Nazis in 1942. Find it hidden in an upper storey at the rear of the Bryggen warehouse with the unicorn figurehead.

Rosenkrantztårnet (Rosenkrantz Tower; www.bymuseet.no; Bergenhus; adult/child Nkr60/free; ⊙10am-4pm mid-May–Aug, noon-3pm Sun Sep–mid-May) was built in the 1560s by Bergen's governor as a residence and defence post. You can climb down to bedrock and then up to the high-ceilinged bedchambers of a 16th-century tower. Detours along the way allow you to suffocate in an actual dungeon or peer into ancient toilet chambers.

Håkonshallen (www.bymuseet.no; Bergenhus; adult/child Nkr60/free; ⊙10am-4pm mid-May–Aug, shorter hr rest of yr), completed by King Håkon Håkonsson in 1261 for his son's wedding, had its roof blown off in 1944 when a Dutch munitions boat exploded in the harbour. Be pleasantly disoriented while wandering through Escherian stairways, stopping to squint through blurry antique windows.

The site of Bergen's earliest settlement is now **Bryggens Museum** (www.bymuseet.no; Dreggsallmenning 3; adult/child Nkr60/free; ⊙10am-4pm mid-May–Aug, shorter hr rest of yr). The 800-year-old foundations unearthed during the construction have been incorporated into the exhibits, along with pottery, human skulls and runes.

TOP
CHOICE **Bergen Kunst Museum**   GALLERY

(Bergen Art Museum; www.bergenartmuseum.no; Rasmus Meyers Allé 3, 7 & 9; adult/student/child Nkr100/50/free; ⊙11am-5pm mid-May–mid-Sep, closed Mon rest of yr) Three buildings opposite the lake fountain house this superb collection of Norwegian art from the 18th and 19th centuries, including many works by Munch and JC Dahl, as well as works by Picasso, Miró, Rodin, Klee and others.

Bergen Akvariet   AQUARIUM

(www.akvariet.com; Nordnesbakken 4; adult/child Jun-Aug Nkr200/150, rest of yr Nkr150/100; ⊙9am-7pm May-Aug, 10am-6pm Sep-Apr) This aquarium has a big outdoor tank with seals and penguins, as well as 70 indoor tanks, snakes, crocodiles and a shark tunnel. There are also penguin and seal feedings throughout the day. On foot, you can get there from Torget in 20 minutes; alternatively, take the Vågen ferry which runs between the Torget fish market and Tollbodhopen at Nordnes (near the Bergen aquarium).

Gamle Bergen
ARCHITECTURE

(www.bymuseet.no; Nyhavnsveien 4, Sandviken; adult/child Nkr70/free; ☺hourly tours 11am-3pm Mon-Sat, 10am-4pm Sun early May-Aug) The open-air Gamle Bergen presents around 40 buildings from the 18th and 19th centuries, including a dentist's office, bakery and houses. It's 4km north of the city centre and can be reached by city bus 20, 23 or 24.

Troldhaugen
HISTORIC BUILDING

(www.troldhaugen.com; adult/child Nkr80/free; ☺9am-6pm May-Sep, 10am-4pm Oct-Apr) If you want to tour the former lakeside home and workshop of composer Edvard Grieg, hop on any bus from platform 19, 20 or 21 of the bus station, get off at Hosbroen and follow the signs to Troldhaugen. Although Grieg fans will best appreciate this well-conceived presentation, the main house contains some excellent period furnishings and is generally quite interesting.

 Activities

Fløibanen Funicular
CABLE CAR

(www.floibanen.no; Vetrlidsalmenning 21; adult/child return Nkr80/40; ☺7.30am-11pm Mon-Fri, 8am-11pm Sat & Sun) For unbeatable city views, take the Fløibanen funicular to the top of Mt Fløyen (320m). Trails marked with dilapidated signs lead into the forest from the hilltop station. Trails 1 and 3 are the longest, each making 5km loops through hilly woodlands. For a delightful 40-minute walk back to the city, take trail 4 and connect with trail 6.

Ulriken643
CABLE CAR

(www.ulriken643.no; adult/child return Nkr145/75, with bus Nkr245/180; ☺9am-9pm May-Sep, to 5pm Oct-Apr) The Ulriksbanen cable car to the top of Mt Ulriken (642m) offers a panoramic view of Bergen, fjords and mountains. Many take the cable car one way and walk (about three hours) across a well-beaten trail to the funicular station at Mt Fløyen.

 Tours

Guided Tours of Bryggen
WALKING

(☎55 58 80 30; adult/child Nkr120/free; ☺tours 10am German, 11am & noon English, 1pm Norwegian Jun-Aug) The Bryggens Museum (p313) offers excellent 90-minute walking tours through the timeless alleys of Bryggen. The ticket

LOCAL KNOWLEDGE

BERGEN SECRETS

Sonja Krantz, a veteran campaigner to preserve Bergen's traditional wooden architecture, guides us to some of Bergen's loveliest corners.

The best undiscovered architectural gems of Bergen? The area in Sandviken, a former working-class district over the hill northwest from Bryggen. It's a large area with only wooden houses which are now mostly modernised on the inside, and you can find some charming cobbled streets. It lies within walking distance of the city centre and is located near Mt Fløyen, which is good for trekking.

Favourite corner of Bryggen? The outdoor cafes where you can watch the harbour and everyday life in Bergen.

Any restaurants that for you capture the appeal of Bergen, either for their atmosphere or food? I love to eat at Potetkjelleren (p319) in Kong Oscarsgate – excellent food, great service and a lovely atmosphere.

Where do you go in Bergen when you want to escape the crowds? When I want to escape the crowds I go to the USF at Verftet, also known as Kafé Kippers (p319). The cafe is located next to the fjord that runs into the heart of Bergen. Mt Ulriken is also a fantastic choice with a charming restaurant and beautiful views.

What's the best thing about living in Bergen? There are so many cultural events, cafes and restaurants. Also there are mountains within walking distance or you can use the funicular or the cable car if you want to be in the mountains within 10 minutes. And then there's the beautiful coastline with hundreds of unspoilt islands.

FJORD TOURS FROM BERGEN

Fjord Tours (☑81 56 82 22; www.fjordtours.com) has mastered the art of making the most of limited time with a series of tours into the fjords. Its popular year-round Norway in a Nutshell (p294) tour is a great way to see far more than you thought possible in a single day. The day ticket (adult/child Nkr1045/545) from Bergen combines a morning train to Voss, a bus to the Stalheim Hotel and then on to Gudvangen, from where a ferry takes you up the spectacular Nærøyfjord to Flåm. You join the stunning mountain railway to Myrdal and catch a train back to Bergen in time for a late dinner (or you can continue on to Oslo to arrive around 10pm, for adult/child Nkr1345/685). From May to September, it also runs the 11-hour **Hardangerfjord in a Nutshell** (adult/child Nkr820/465) and **Sognefjord in a Nutshell** (adult/child Nkr1250/630).

Details of other tours of the surrounding fjords are available from the tourist office (p329).

includes admission to Bryggens Museum, Schøtstuene and the Hanseatisk Museum.

✦ Festivals & Events

For a full list of events, see the Visit Bergen website (www.visitbergen.com).

Bergen International Festival CULTURE
(www.fib.no) Held over 14 days from late May to early June, this is the big cultural festival of the year, with dance, music and folklore presentations throughout the city.

Night Jazz Festival MUSIC
(www.nattjazz.no) Excellent jazz festival popular with Bergen's large student population; late May to early June.

Bergenfest MUSIC
(www.bergenfest.no) International music festival; mid to late June.

Bergen Food Festival FOOD
(www.matfest.no) Showcases locally grown or caught food, which includes whale meat; early to mid-September.

Bergen International Film Festival FILM
(www.biff.no) Mid- to late October.

🛏 Sleeping

Bergen has outstanding accommodation, but *always* book before arriving in town, at least in the summer months or during festivals, when Bergen fills up fast.

The tourist office (p329) has an accommodation booking service (Nkr55 for walk-ins, Nkr50 for advance booking).

TOP CHOICE **Det Hanseatiske Hotel** HISTORIC HOTEL €€€
(☑55 30 48 00; www.dethanseatiskehotell.no; Finnegårdsgaten 2; s/d from Nkr990/1090) The only hotel to be housed inside the old timber buildings that evoke Bryggen's bygone age, Det Hanseatiske Hotel is luxurious and like stepping back into a luxurious Bergen past. Flat-screen TVs cohabit with antique bathtubs and some extraordinary architectural features from Bryggen's days as a Hanseatic port.

TOP CHOICE **Kjellersmauet Gjestehus** GUESTHOUSE, APARTMENT €€
(☑55 96 26 08; www.gjestehuset.com; Kjellersmauet 22; s/d apt from Nkr800/900) This oasis of hospitality and tradition in a delightful timber-clad street southwest of the centre is outstanding. Run by the friendly Sonja, who goes the extra mile in taking care of her guests, the Kjellersmauet has a range of fabulous and recently renovated small, medium and large apartments in a building dating back to the 16th century.

Skuteviken Gjestehus GUESTHOUSE €€
(☑93 46 71 63; www.skutevikenguesthouse.com; Skutevikens Smalgang 11; d/attic Nkr1000/1100 plus per extra person Nkr200) This authentic timber guesthouse, set on a small cobbled street in Sandviken, has traditional decoration and a few modern touches. Painstakingly restored by two artists whose work adorns the rooms, the guesthouse is quite simply charming.

Hotel Park Pension HISTORIC HOTEL €€
(☑55 54 44 00; www.parkhotel.no; Harald Hårfagresgate 35; s from Nkr890, d Nkr1090-1100) Filled with character and antiques, this family-run place spreads over two beautiful 19th-century buildings. Every room is different; in the main building, expect antique writing desks, and the corner rooms are gorgeous and filled with light.

NORWAY BERGEN

Bergen

200 m
0.1 miles

To Skoltegrunnskaien
(International Ferries) (300m);
Skuteviken Gjestehus (500m)

To Bergen
Akvariet (500m)

To Kafe Kippers
(300m)

To Mt Fløyen
(100m)

STRANDSIDEN

NORDNES

Vågen

Bryggen

Dreggsallmenning

Sandbrugaten

Bryggen

Øvre Blekeveien

Stein kjeller gate Stølegate

Nikolaikirkeallmenning

Øvregaten

Øvregaten

Nedre Fjellsmug

Vetrlidsallmenning

Lille Øvregaten

Kong Oscars gate

Tvergaten

Skivebakken

Skostredet

Allehelgens gate

Nikolaikirkeallmenning

Vågsallmenning

Torgallmenningen

Torget

Strandkaien

Småstrandgaten

Strandgaten

Strandgaten

C Sundts gate

Klostergaten

Klosteret

Klosteret

Strangehagen

Haugeveien

Nøstegaten

Jon Smørs gate

Michaels gate

Markveien

V Muralim

Kjellersmauet

**Bergen
Cathedral**

**Hanseatisk
Museum**

Bryggen

Strandkaiterminal
(Express Ferries)

Vågen
Harbour
Ferry

Tourist
Office

Flybussen

Torgallmenningen

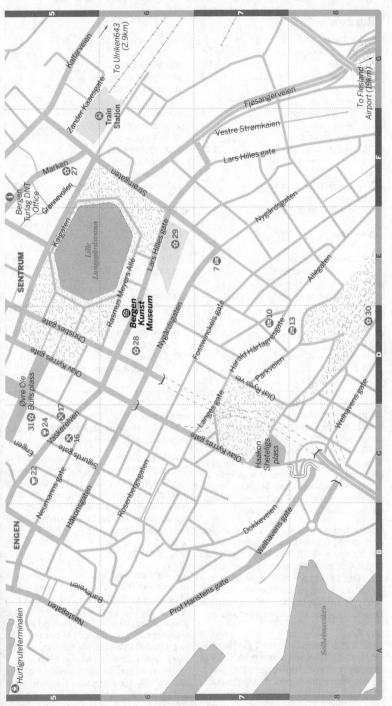

Bergen

Skansen Pensjonat   GUESTHOUSE €
(☏55 31 90 80; www.skansen-pensjonat.no; Vetrlidsalmenning 29; s/d from Nkr450/750) There are family-run guesthouses springing up all over Bergen, but this charming seven-room place is still one of our favourites. A wonderful location up behind the lower funicular station, real attention to detail and many personal touches make this a terrific choice.

Clarion Hotel Admiral   HOTEL €€€
(☏55 23 64 00; www.clarionadmiral.no; C Sundtsgate 9; s/d from Nkr780/980, Bryggen views extra Nkr300-400; ❄) With sweeping views across the water to Bryggen from the balconies of its harbour-facing rooms, this well-appointed hotel promises the best view to wake up to in Bergen, if you can get a waterside room.

City Box   HOSTEL €
(☏55 31 25 00; www.citybox.no; Nygårdsgaten 31; s/d Nkr600/900, without bathroom Nkr500/700; @) The best hostel in Bergen, City Box is a place where the owners do simple things well, such as bright modern rooms with

splashes of colour, free wireless access, a minimalist designer feel without the price tag and friendly young staff.

Steens Hotell   HISTORIC HOTEL €€
(☏55 30 88 88; www.steenshotel.no; Parkveien 22; s/d Nkr790/1100) This lovely 19th-century building oozes period charm, from the late-19th-century antiques to the gentle curve of the stairway; the bathroom facilities have recently been renovated.

✗ Eating

TOP CHOICE **Pingvinen**   NORWEGIAN €
(www.pingvinen.no; Vaskerelven 14; sandwiches Nkr98, mains Nkr149-199; ☉1pm-3am Sun-Fri, noon-3am Sat) Devoted to small-town Norwegian cooking and with a delightfully informal ambience, Pingvinen is one of our favourite restaurants in Bergen. It's the sort of place where Norwegians come for recipes their mothers and grandparents used to cook and although the menu changes regularly, there are usually fish-cake sandwiches, reindeer,

fish pie, whale, salmon, lamb shank and, our favourite, traditional Norwegian meatballs served with mushy peas and wild Norwegian berry jam.

TOP CHOICE Potetkjelleren NORWEGIAN €€€

(📞55 32 00 70; Kong Oscars gate 1a; mains Nkr295-330, 3-/4-/5-/6-course menus from Nkr535/595/655/725; ⏲4-10pm Mon-Sat) The 'Potato Cellar' is one of Bergen's finest restaurants, the sort of place that food critics rave about but which attracts more locals than tourists. The dining area has a classy wine-cellar ambience, the service is faultless, and the menu (which changes monthly) is based around the freshest ingredients, Norwegian traditions and often subtly surprising combinations of taste; the wine list is impeccable.

Torget Fish Market SEAFOOD €

(www.torgetibergen.no; Torget; ⏲7am-7pm Jun-Aug, to 4pm Mon-Sat Sep-May) For price and atmosphere, it's hard to beat the fish market. Right alongside the harbour and close to Bryggen, here you'll find everything from smoked whale meat and salmon to calamari, fish and chips, fish cakes, prawn baguettes, seafood salads, local caviar and, sometimes, nonfishy reindeer and elk. Don't miss the newer section under the tourist office.

Bryggen Tracteursted NORWEGIAN €€€

(Bryggen; lunch mains Nkr125-145, dinner mains Nkr245-375; ⏲11am-10pm May-Sep) This is one of the great Bryggen eating experiences. Housed in a 1708 building that ranges across the former stables, kitchen and Bergen's only extant *schøtstuene* (dining hall), this fine restaurant does traditional Norwegian dishes (such as fillet of reindeer with goat's cheese) that change regularly. It's classy and refined in the evenings, with a more informal atmosphere during the day.

Kafe Kippers INTERNATIONAL €€

(USF; Georgenes Verft 12; lunch mains Nkr65-89, dinner mains Nkr89-170) Away from the hub-bub of downtown Bergen, this agreeable outdoor terrace is one of the best places for a meal or just a drink when the weather's warm. Attached to a cultural centre in an old sardine-canning factory, it has an arty vibe and serves plentiful lunch dishes that include pastas and salads.

Pygmalion Økocafé ORGANIC €

(Nedre Korskirkealmenning 4; ciabatta Nkr79-99, organic pancakes Nkr99-129, salads Nkr129-179; ⏲11am-11pm; 🖊) This very cool place has contemporary art adorning its walls, a casual but classy atmosphere and tasty organic food. It's a great place at any time of the day and as good for a snack as something slightly more substantial. There are good choices for vegetarians.

Escalon TAPAS €

(Vetrlidsalmenning 21; tapas Nkr39-94, 3/5 tapas Nkr339/479; ⏲3pm-midnight Sun-Fri, 1pm-midnight Sat) Tapas has taken Bergen by storm, and Escalon has been doing it since 1998. The friendly waiters are happy to make suggestions on wine selection and the 70 varieties of tapas are tasty and the closest you'll find in Bergen to what you'll get in Spain.

Naboen SWEDISH €€

(www.grannen.no; Neumanns gate 20; lunch mains Nkr98-176, dinner mains Nkr194-266; ⏲4-11pm Mon-Sat, to 10pm Sun) Although the cook does a range of Norwegian dishes here, Naboen is best known for its Swedish specialities, such as Swedish meatballs, reindeer and wolf fish. The quality is high and it has a well-earned and devoted local following.

Pølse Kiosk SAUSAGES €

(Kong Oscars gate 1; hot dogs from Nkr50; ⏲10am-3am) If you've travelled around Norway for a while, you may be heartily sick of hot dogs bought from petrol stations, as are we. But this place has *real* sausages (including wild game, reindeer, lamb and chilli), a better-than-average range of sauces and good-sized serves.

Drinking

TOP CHOICE Altona Vinbar WINE BAR

(C Sundtsgate 22; ⏲6pm-12.30am Mon-Thu, to 1.30am Fri & Sat) Possibly our favourite wine bar in town, Altona Vinbar is in an intimate warren of underground rooms that date from the 16th century. With a huge selection of international wines, soft lighting and

---

ℹ **BERGEN CARD**

The **Bergen Card** (www.visitbergen.com/bergencard; adult/child 24hr pass Nkr200/75, 48hr Nkr260/100) allows free transport on local buses, free street parking and funicular-railway rides as well as admission to most sights. It's sold at the tourist office.

music that ranges from jazz to rock but never drowns out conversation, it's hard to find fault with this place.

Pingvinen
CAFE, BAR

(Vaskerelven 14; ☉1pm-3am Sun-Fri, noon-3am Sat) As good a bar as it is as a restaurant, 'Penguin' is laid-back and funky, and popular with a friendly 30-something crowd. The late-night snacks are good if you get the munchies, and it has all the usual beers, as well as some boutique beers from microbreweries around Norway and elsewhere.

Sakristiet
CAFE

(Jacobsfjorden 4, Bryggen; ☉11am-6pm) A charming little cafe in the heart of Bryggen's wooden lanes, 'Sacristy' is an oasis of calm, with comfy armchairs and good coffee, cakes, sandwiches and cookies. A recent change in ownership has seen mercifully little change, although more food may be on offer by the time you arrive.

Café Opera
CAFE, CLUB

(Engen 18; ☉11am-3am Mon-Sat, noon-12.15am Sun) By day, Café Opera has a literary-cafe feel, with artworks and good coffee that attracts artists and students. From Wednesday to Saturday, the crowd gets dancing around midnight.

Vågen
CAFE, BAR

(Kong Oscars gate 10; ☉10am-11.30pm Mon-Wed, 10am-2am Thu-Sat, 11am-midnight Sun) This quiet cafe is where old Norwegian meets Bob Marley, with traditional Norwegian decoration, rustic wooden tables and a laid-back feel helped by occasional reggae tunes. It's a cool combination and provides a great backdrop to a lazy afternoon.

Krog og Krinkel
CAFE

(Lille Øvregaten 14; coffee Nkr20-45; ☉11am-5pm Mon-Sat, noon-5pm Sun) This is a lovely little bookshop-cum-cafe close to the lower cable-car station but utterly removed from Bergen's clamour, this classy but casual cafe is simply lovely. When we last visited they had plans to open in the evening.

☆ Entertainment

Classical Music

Bergen has a busy program of concerts throughout summer, many of them classical performances focusing on Bergen's favourite son, composer Edvard Grieg.

Troldhaugen
CLASSICAL MUSIC

(adult/child Nkr250/75; ☉1pm daily Jun-Aug, 6pm Sun rest of yr) Concerts at the summer home of Grieg himself, close to Bergen.

Grieghallen
CLASSICAL MUSIC

(☑55 21 61 50; www.grieghallen.no; Edvard Griegs plass; ☉Aug-Jun) Performances by the respected Bergen Philharmonic Orchestra.

Nightclubs

Garage
LIVE MUSIC

(www.garage.no; Christies gate 14; ☉3pm-3am Mon-Sat, 5pm-3am Sun) Garage has taken on an almost mythical quality for music lovers across Europe. It does play live jazz and acoustic, but this is a rock venue at heart, with well-known Norwegian and international acts drawn to the cavernous basement.

Hulen
LIVE MUSIC

(www.hulen.no; Olaf Ryes vei 48; ☉9pm-3am Thu-Sat mid-Aug–mid-Jun) Going strong since 1968, Hulen is the oldest rock club in northern Europe and it's one of the classic stages for indie rock. Hulen means 'cave' and the venue is actually a converted bomb shelter. Sadly, it closes during summer when many of Bergen's students head off on holidays.

Logen
LIVE MUSIC

(Øvre Ole Bulls plass 6; ☉6pm-2am Mon-Thu, 6pm-3am Fri & Sat, 8pm-3am Sun) Upstairs above the Wesselstuen Restaurant, Logen is Bergen's antidote to its more famous heavy-metal and rock scene. It has a loyal local following for its jazz and alternative concerts from September to May or June. At other times (including much of summer), it's a quiet bar.

Café Sanaa
LIVE MUSIC

(www.sanaa.no; Marken 31; ☉8pm-3am Fri & Sat) This lovely little cafe just back from the lake spills over onto the cobblestones and draws a fun, alternative crowd with live music and some of Bergen's most creative resident DJs. Music can be jazz, tango, blues or African, depending on where the mood takes them.

🛍 Shopping

The wooden alleyways of Bryggen have become a haven for artists and craftspeople, and there are stunning little shops and boutiques at every turn.

Per Vigeland
JEWELLERY

(www.pervigeland.no; Jacobsfjorden, Bryggen; ☉10am-6pm mid-May–Aug) A local jewellery designer working with silver and gold-plated silver.

(Continued on page 329)

Natural Wonders

Great Outdoors »
Winter Wonderland »
Summer Adventures »
Wildlife »

Beech forest in Skåne (p423), Sweden

ANDERS BLOMQVIST/GETTY IMAGES ©

Great Outdoors

The scenery in Scandinavia is one of its great attractions. Wild, rugged coasts and mountains, hundreds of kilometres of forest broken only by lakes and the odd cottage, and unspoilt Baltic archipelagos make up a varied menu of uplifting visual treats.

Forests

Mainland Scandinavia has some of the world's top tree cover, and the forests stretch much further than the eye can see. Mainly composed of spruce, pine and birch, these forests are responsible for the crisp, clean, aromatic northern air.

Iceland

Thrown up in the middle of the Atlantic by violent geothermal activity, Iceland offers bleak and epic scenery that is at once both harsh and gloriously uplifting. The juxtaposition of frozen glaciers and boiling geysers make it a wild scenic ride.

Norway

Fjords are famous for a reason; coastal views here take the breath away. There are spectacular views the length of this long country. Near the top, the Lofoten Islands present picturesque fishing villages against the awesome backdrop of glacier-scoured mountains.

Lakes

Once the ice melts, Scandinavia is a watery land. A Finnish or Swedish lake under a midnight sun, pines reflected in the calm, chilly water and a stillness broken only by the landing of waterbirds: these are enduring images.

Archipelagos

Thousands of islands lie offshore and the Baltic is the place to grab a boat and find an islet to call your own. Out in the Atlantic, the Faroes offer stern cliffs housing vast seabird colonies.

Clockwise from top left
1 Forest near Åre (458), Sweden 2 Strokkur (p239), Iceland 3 Preikestolen (p335), Norway

Winter Wonderland

Once the snows come, bears look for a place to sleep out the winter, but for the rest of us, there's no excuse. The ethereal beauty of the whitened land combines with numerous exciting activities to make this a great time to visit.

Skiing

There's not much you can teach Scandinavians about skiing; they invented it. There are numerous places to hit the powder, with excellent facilities for all levels. Cross-country is big, with lighted trails compensating for the long nights.

Winter Activities

Snowmobiles are a part of life up north, and it's lots of fun to whizz about on one. More sedate is ice fishing, but you'd better pack a warm drink. Ice climbing, nights in snow hotels, the aurora borealis (Northern Lights), snowshoe treks and kick sledding are other popular possibilities.

Sledding

The whoosh of the runners as a team of huskies or reindeer whisks you through the icy northern landscapes – it's tough to beat the feeling. Don't expect a pampered ride though – learn on the job or eat snow!

Landscapes

It's cold, but low winter light and the eerie blue colours the sky takes on make it spectacularly scenic. Trees glistening with ice crystals and snow carpeting the ground add to this magical landscape.

Saunas

If the cold has seeped into your bones, there's nothing like a log fire or, even better, a sauna, to warm the extremities again. Too hot? Get somebody to drill a hole in the lake and jump in. Good for the pores!

Clockwise from top left
1 Skiing in Norway 2 Northern Lights near Kiruna (p464), Sweden 3 Sledding in Levi (p197), Finland 4 Winter forest in Sweden

Summer Adventures

When the snows melt and the sun returns, it's like a blessing bestowed upon the land. Nature accelerates into top gear, and locals pack a year's worth of fun and festivals into the short but memorably vibrant summer season.

Nordic Peace

For many Scandinavians, summer is spent at a lakeside cottage or campsite where simple pleasures – swimming, fishing, chopping wood, picking berries – replace the stresses of urban life for a few blissful weeks.

Kayaking & Canoeing

It's a perfect time to get the paddles out and explore the rivers and lakes of the interior, or the coastal serrations and islands. Throughout the region, kayaking and canoeing are extremely popular and easy to organise.

Hiking

There's fabulous walking across the whole region, from the jaw-droppingly majestic Icelandic routes to the remote Finnish wilderness. Excellent facilities mean it's easy to plan short walks or multiday hiking adventures.

Midsummer

The summer solstice is celebrated throughout the region, whether with traditional midsummer poles and dancing, or beer, sausages and a lakeside barbecue and bonfire with friends.

Terraces

Once the first proper rays bathe the pavement, coat racks in bars and cafes disappear, and outdoor terraces sprout onto every square and street, packed with people determined to suck up every last drop of the precious summer sun.

Clockwise from top left
1 Coastal camping, Sweden 2 Kayaking in Sweden
3 Geirangerfjorden (p342) with Seven Sisters waterfall

Wildlife

Vast tracts of barely populated land away from the bustle of central Europe make Scandinavia an important refuge for numerous species, including several high-profile carnivores, myriad seabirds and lovable marine mammals.

Elk & Reindeer

If antlers are your thing, you won't be disappointed. The sizeable but ungainly elk (moose) is widespread in the mainland forests, often blundering onto roads or into towns. In Lapland, the domesticated reindeer is the herd animal of the indigenous Sámi.

Brown Bears

The ruler of the forest is deeply rooted in Finnish culture, and there's still a fairly healthy population of them in the east of the country, near the Russian border. Bear-watching trips offer a great opportunity to see these impressively large, shaggy beasts.

Polar Bears & Walrus

Svalbard is as close to the North Pole as most are going to get, and the wildlife is appropriately impressive. The mighty polar bear means you'll need a just-in-case weapon if you want to leave town, while the weighty walrus is also an impressive sight.

Whales & Seabirds

Iceland has important seabird colonies; they breed there in huge numbers. Off Iceland's and Norway's coastlines, several varieties of whale are in regular attendance, best seen on a dedicated boat trip.

Nordic Creatures

The region is stocked with a range of animals: lynx and wolves pace the forests, while golden eagles, ospreys, ptarmigans and capercaillie add feathered glory to the mix. Seals and dolphins are aplenty, and the lonely wolverine prowls the northern wastes in search of prey or carrion.

Right
1 Reindeer bull 2 Brown bear mother and cub

(Continued from page 320)

Juhls' Silver Gallery   JEWELLERY, HOMEWARES
(www.juhls.no; Bryggen 39; ⊙9am-8pm Mon-Fri, 9am-6pm Sat, noon-5pm Sun mid-Jun–Sep, shorter hr Oct–mid-Jun) This wonderful jewellery shop sells exquisite silver jewellery and other items crafted by Regine Juhls at her workshop high above the Arctic Circle.

Živa Jelnikar Design   JEWELLERY
(www.zj-d.com; Jacobsfjorden, Bryggen; ⊙10am-5pm Mon-Fri, 11am-4pm Sat & Sun Jun-Aug, shorter hr rest of yr, closed Sep-Oct) Located opposite the entrance to the Bryggen Visitors Centre, this shop features the highly original work of Slovenian designer Živa Jelnikar.

Kvams Flisespikkeri   ARTS & CRAFTS
(www.kvams-flisespikkeri.com; Bredsgården, Bryggen; ⊙9am-6pm mid-May–mid-Sep, noon-4pm Tue-Sat Oct-Apr) Sells lovely Bryggen-centric paintings, block prints and other artworks by Ketil Kvam.

Læverkstedet   CLOTHES, ACCESSORIES
(Jacobsfjorden, Bryggen; ⊙10am-8pm mid-May–mid-Aug) The purveyor of the softest moose leather, with jackets, bags and other knick-knacks.

Tabago   HANDICRAFTS
(☑41 02 08 80; www.tabago.no; Bryggen; ⊙noon-6pm Wed) Here you can buy a wooden pipe from Bård Hansen, one of only two wooden pipemakers left in Norway.

ⓘ Information

Bergen Turlag DNT Office (☑55 33 58 10; www.bergen-turlag.no; Tverrgaten 4; ⊙10am-4pm Mon-Wed & Fri, to 6pm Thu, to 3pm Sat) Maps and information on hiking and hut accommodation throughout western Norway.

Tourist office (☑55 55 20 00; www.visitbergen.com; Vågsallmenningen 1; ⊙8.30am-10pm Jun-Aug, 9am-8pm May & Sep, 9am-4pm Mon-Sat Oct-Apr) One of the best and busiest in the country.

ⓘ Getting There & Away

Air

The airport is in Flesland, 19km southwest of central Bergen. Direct flights connect Bergen with major cities in Norway, plus a handful of international destinations.

Boat

The *Hurtigruten* leaves from a newly built terminal east of Nøstegaten.

Flaggruten (☑53 40 91 20; www.tide.no; Strandkaiterminalen; one-way/return Nkr400/800) has express passenger catamarans to/from Stavanger (4½ hours, two daily).

Bus

Express buses run throughout the Western Fjords region, as well as to Ålesund (Nkr644, 10 hours, one to two daily), Trondheim (Nkr811, 12½ hours, two daily) and Stavanger (Nkr460, 5½ hours, five daily).

Train

The spectacular train journey between Bergen and Oslo (Nkr299 to Nkr804, 6½ to eight hours, five daily) runs through the heart of Norway. Other destinations include Voss (Nkr180, one hour, hourly) and Myrdal (Nkr271, 2¼ hours, up to nine daily) for connections for the Flåmsbana railway.

ⓘ Getting Around

To/From the Airport

Flybussen (www.flybussen.no; one-way/return adult Nkr100/160, child Nkr50/80) runs up to four times hourly (45 mintues) between the airport, the Radisson SAS Royal Hotel, the main bus terminal and opposite the tourist office.

Car & Motorcycle

Metered parking limited to 30 minutes or two hours applies all over central Bergen. The largest and cheapest indoor car park (Nkr120 per 24 hours) is the 24-hour Bygarasjen at the bus terminal; elsewhere you'll pay Nkr250.

Voss
POP 14,000

Voss has two personalities. At one level, it's a pretty lakeside town with fine views at every turn and the perfect place to break up a journey between Bergen and the fjords. At the same time, it has a world-renowned reputation as one of Norway's top adventure capitals, drawing both beginners and veterans of the thrill-seeking world for rafting, bungee jumping and just about anything you can do from a parasail; many of the activities take you out into the fjords.

⊙ Sights & Activities

Vangskyrkja   CHURCH
(Uttrågata; adult/child Nkr20/free; ⊙10am-4pm Mon-Sat, 1-4pm Sun Jun-Aug) Voss' stone church, the construction of which spans seven centuries, miraculously escaped destruction during the intense German bombing of Voss in 1940. Watch out for free concerts in summer and there are worship services every Sunday at 11am.

VOSS ACTIVITIES

If slow boats up the fjords seem like a pretty tame response to extraordinary Norwegian landscapes, Voss may be your antidote.

For booking any of the following, your best bet is to contact the operator directly. Another option is the tourist office, which can help with bookings for activities and accommodation. Most of the following activities only operate from May to September.

Paragliding, Parasailing & Bungee Jumping

Nordic Ventures (☎56 51 00 17; www.nordicventures.com; ☺Apr–mid-Oct) is one of the most professional operators of its kind in Norway, offering tandem paragliding flights (Nkr1500), parasailing (solo/dual flights Nkr575/950) and even 180m-high, 115km/h bungee jumps from a parasail (Nkr1800).

Kayak Fjord Expeditions

If you do one activity in Voss (or even anywhere in the fjords), make it this one. The perfect way to experience stunning Nærøyfjord, the guided kayak tours offered by Nordic Ventures also head to Hardangerfjord and come in a range of options.

One day (nine-hour) tours cost Nkr995 (including lunch and transport to/from the fjord), while the two-day version (Nkr2295) allows you to camp on the shores of the fjord. But our favourite is the three-day kayaking and hiking expedition (Nkr3095), which explores the fjords in kayaks and then takes you high above the fjords for unrivalled views.

Nordic Ventures also rents out kayaks (one/two/three days Nkr550/925/1295) if you'd rather branch out on your own.

Rafting

Voss Rafting Senter (☎56 51 05 25; www.vossrafting.no) specialises in rafting (Nkr1100 per person, grades III to IV) with some gentler, more family-friendly options (from Nkr600).

Other Activities

Voss Rafting Senter also organises canyoning (Nkr1100), waterfall abseiling (from Nkr850), riverboarding (Nkr1150), fishing (from Nkr420) and hiking (from Nkr500). Skiing is possible from early December until April. And then there's the latest addition to Voss' already impressive stable of activities – the **Wind Tunnel** (☎90 73 50 24; www. vossvind.no; ☺per person Nkr690) allows you to spend three minutes floating on air as if you were high above the earth with a parachute.

St Olav's Cross MONUMENT

In a field around 150m southeast of the tourist office stands the weathered stone erected in 1023 to commemorate the local conversion to Christianity.

Hangursbahnen CABLE CAR

(www.vossresort.no; adult/child Nkr100/60; ☺10am-5pm Jun-early Sep) Above Voss, the cable car whisks you to Mt Hangur (660m) for stunning panoramic views over the town. It's the nearest you'll get to paragliding without the adrenalin rush.

Prestegardsmoen Recreational & Nature Reserve HIKING

A series of hiking tracks through elm, birch and pine forests with 140 species of plant and 124 bird species. The reserve begins around 500m south of the town centre along the lake shore.

Festivals

Vossajazz MUSIC

(www.vossajazz.no) Held in March.

Extreme Sports Festival SPORT

(www.ekstremsportveko.com) A week-long festival in late June that combines all manner of extreme sports (skydiving, paragliding and base jumping) with local and international music acts.

🛏 Sleeping & Eating

TOP CHOICE Fleischer's Hotel HISTORIC HOTEL €€

(☎56 52 05 00; www.fleischers.no; Evangervegen; s/d from Nkr1290/1690; P🕸) For historic character, the beautiful Fleischer's Hotel, opened in its current form in 1889, oozes antique charm and is the best place in town. Some rooms have lake views and there's a swimming pool with a child's pool.

Park Hotel Vossevangen
HOTEL €€

(☑56 53 10 04; www.parkvoss.no; Uttrågata 1; s/d from Nkr1320/1720; ℗) While this place lacks the elegance of Fleischer's Hotel, the recently overhauled rooms are nonetheless extremely comfortable and many overlook Lake Vossevangen.

Voss Camping
CAMPGROUND €

(☑56 51 15 97; www.vosscamping.no; Prestegardsalléen 40; tent/caravan sites from Nkr150/220, cabins from Nkr600; ☺Easter-Sep; ℗@) Lakeside and centrally located, Voss Camping has basic facilities and can get a bit rowdy in summer.

TOP CHOICE Tre Brør Café
CAFE €

(www.vosscafe.no; Vangsgata 28; sandwiches & light meals Nkr65-155; ☺11am-7pm) This lovely little cafe in one of Voss' prettiest buildings is laid-back and stylish all at once and the food's also fantastic. There's a small selection of sandwiches, quiches and a changing menu of daily specials.

Ringheim Kafé
NORWEGIAN €€

(www.ringheimkafe.no; Vangsgata 32; mains Nkr120-165) One of numerous cafes lined up along the main Vangsgata thoroughfare, Ringheim has some real stars on the menu, including the elk burgers (Nkr155). If *hjortekoru*, the local smoked sausage with potato-and-cabbage stew (Nkr155), appears on the menu, you'd be mad to resist.

❶ Information

Tourist office (☑40 61 77 00; www.visitvoss. no; Vangsgata 20; ☺8am-7pm Mon-Fri, 9am-7pm Sat, noon-7pm Sun Jun-Aug, shorter hr rest of yr)

❶ Getting There & Away

BUS Frequent bus services connect Voss with Bergen (Nkr151, two hours), Flåm (Nkr133, 1¼ hours) and Sogndal (Nkr278, three hours).

TRAIN The **NSB** (☑56 52 80 00) rail services on the renowned Bergensbanen to/from Bergen (Nkr180, one hour, hourly) and Oslo (Nkr199 to Nkr718, 5½ to six hours, five daily) connect at nearby Myrdal (Nkr110, 50 minutes) with the scenic line down to Flåm.

Hardangerfjord

A notch less jagged and steep than Sognefjord, Hardangerfjord's slopes support farms and wildflowers, which picturesquely enhance the green hills as they plunge into the water. Norway's second-longest fjord network, it stretches inland from a cluster of rocky coastal islands to the frozen borders of the Folgefonn and Hardangerjøkulen icecaps. The area is known for its orchards (apples, cherries and plums) and bursts into bloom from mid-May to mid-June. Helpful regional information can be found at www. hardangerfjord.com.

At the innermost reaches of Hardangerfjorden you'll find the Eidfjord area, with sheer mountains, huge waterfalls, spiral road tunnels and the extraordinary Kjeåsen Farm, a deliciously inaccessible farm perched on a mountain ledge about 6km northeast of Eidfjord. Other Eidfjord highlights include Viking burial mounds and, on the road up to the Hardangervidda Plateau, the excellent Hardangervidda Natursenter (www.hardangerviddanatursenter.no; Øvre Eidfjord; adult/child/family Nkr120/60/280; ☺9am-8pm mid-Jun–mid-Aug, 10am-6pm Apr–mid-Jun & mid-Aug–Oct) with wonderful exhibits on the plateau, and the 182m-high Vøringfoss waterfall. For information, contact Eidfjord tourist office (☑53 67 34 00; www.visiteidfjord.no; ☺9am-7pm Mon-Fri, 10am-6pm Sat, 11am-6pm Sun mid-Jun–mid-Aug).

Tranquil Ulvik has extraordinary views from its fjordside walking paths, while at picturesque Utne you'll find an interesting collection of old buildings at the Hardanger Folk Museum (www.hardangerogvossmuseum. no; adult/child Nkr70/free; ☺10am-5pm May-Aug, to 3pm Mon-Fri Sep-Apr), and the pretty Utne Hotel.

For glacier hikes on the Buer arm of the Folgefonn ice sheet, contact the excellent Flat Earth (☑47 60 68 47; www.flatearth.no; adult incl crampons & ice axes Nkr700)in Odda. The hike up to Trolltunga, a narrow finger of rock that hangs out over the void high above the lake Ringedalsvatnet, and one of Norway's most precipitous vantage points, is another highlight close to Odda. For more information, contact Odda's tourist office (☑53 65 40 05; www.visitodda.com; ☺9am-7pm Mon-Fri, 10am-6pm Sat & Sun mid-Jun–mid-Aug).

NORWAY HARDANGERFJORD

🛏 Sleeping & Eating

TOP CHOICE **Eidfjord Gjestegiveri** GUESTHOUSE **€**

(📞53 66 53 46; www.ovre-eidfjord.com; Øvre Eidfjord; huts Nkr360, s/d without bathroom & incl breakfast Nkr590/745; P) This delightful guesthouse run by Dutch owners Eric and Inge has a homely feel, 6.5km from central Eidfjord. There are just five double rooms and one single; the six camping huts are only open from April to October. The other huge selling point of this place is its pancake cafe (Nkr75–Nkr119; open 11am-8pm), with around 20 varieties of fantastic and filling, sweet and salty Dutch pancakes.

🍽 Utne Hotel HISTORIC HOTEL **€€€**

(📞53 66 64 00; www.utnehotel.no; Utne; s/d annex Nkr1290/1690, main bldg Nkr1490/1890; P) The historic wooden Utne Hotel was built in 1722, making it Norway's oldest hotel. Restored in 2003, it overflows with period touches from the 18th and 19th centuries. It also has the best restaurant in town.

Vik Pensjonat GUESTHOUSE **€€**

(📞53 66 51 62; www.vikpensjonat.com; Eidfjord; d/f Nkr550/1580, s/d without bathroom Nkr440/500, cabins Nkr700-1150; P) This appealing place in the centre of Eidfjord, not far from the water's edge, is set in a lovely, renovated old home. It offers a friendly welcome and an excellent range of cosy accommodation. The attached cafe (light meals Nkr65 to Nkr90, mains Nkr145 to Nkr185) is one of the better places to eat in town, with everything from soups and sandwiches to main dishes such as mountain trout.

ℹ Getting There & Away

While thorough exploration of Hardangerfjord is best accomplished with a car, those with little time and no wheels would do well to book the 11-hour round-trip Hardanger in a Nutshell tour run by **Fjord Tours** (📞81 56 82 22; www.fjordtours.com; adult/child Nkr820/465). Combining bus, boat and train, it runs from Bergen to Norheimsund, Eidfjord, Ulvik and Voss, then back to Bergen again. Tickets can be purchased at Bergen's tourist office or online.

Infrequent Nor-Way Bussekspress buses connect Bergen with Hardangerfjord villages, with more frequent services in summer.

Stavanger

POP 123,487

Stavanger is one of our favourite cities in Norway. Said by some to be the largest wooden city in Europe, its old quarter climbs up the slopes around a pretty harbour. Here and elsewhere, the city is home to almost two-dozen museums. Stavanger is also one of Norway's liveliest urban centres – in summer the city's waterfront invariably courses with people. And as if all of that weren't enough, Stavanger is an excellent base from which to explore stunning Lysefjord.

⊙ Sights

TOP CHOICE **Gamle Stavanger** NEIGHBOURHOOD

Gamle (Old) Stavanger consists of cobblestone walkways passing between rows of 173 late-18th-century whitewashed wooden houses, all immaculately kept and adorned with cheerful, well-tended flower boxes. It well rewards an hour or two of ambling.

Norsk Oljemuseum MUSEUM

(Oil Museum; www.norskolje.museum.no; Kjeringholmen; adult/child/family Nkr100/50/250; ⊙10am-7pm Jun-Aug, to 4pm Mon-Sat, to 6pm Sun Sep-May) One of Norway's best museums, the Oil Museum is filled with hi-tech interactive displays, gigantic models and authentic reconstructions. Its many highlights include the world's largest drill bit; a 12-minute documentary by former Lonely Planet TV presenter Ian Wright and another on deep-sea diving; simulators; a petrodome re-creating millions of years of natural history; an escape chute that kids love and some amazing models of oil platforms.

Stavanger Domkirke CHURCH

(Håkon VII's gate; admission Nkr20, 4-7pm Mon-Fri free; ⊙8.30am-2pm & 4-7pm Mon-Fri, 9am-1pm Sat, 1-7pm Sun) This beautiful church is an impressive, but understated, medieval stone cathedral dating from approximately 1125. It was extensively renovated following a fire in 1272 and contains traces of Gothic, baroque, Romanesque and Anglo-Norman influences. Despite restoration through the centuries, the cathedral is, by some accounts, Norway's oldest medieval cathedral still in its original form. Watch out for organ recitals in summer.

Stavanger Museum MUSEUM

(📞51 84 27 00; www.museumstavanger.no; combined same-day admission adult/child Nkr60/40; ⊙11am-4pm mid-Jun–mid-Aug, shorter hr early Jun & late Aug, closed Mon rest of yr) The large eight-part museum, with its sites scattered around Stavanger, could easily fill a sightseeing day, but you'd have to keep up a brisk pace to fit them all in.

The main **Stavanger Bymuseum** (Muségata 16) reveals nearly 900 years of Stavanger's history, 'From Ancient Landscape to Oil Town'. Also in the same building is the **Norwegian Natural History Museum**.

More interesting is the **Maritime Museum** (Nedre Strandgate 17), in two restored warehouses, which gives a good glimpse of Stavanger's extensive nautical history. The fascinating **Canning Museum** (Øvre Strandgate 88a) occupies an old sardine cannery, where you'll see ancient machinery in action, learn about various soul-destroying jobs of the past and ogle a large collection of old sardine-can labels. There are also two 19th-century manor houses built by wealthy shipowners: the recently restored **Ledaal** (Eiganesveien 45), which serves as the residence for visiting members of the royal family, and the excellent **Breidablikk** (Eiganesveien 40a), a merchant's opulent villa built in 1881.

🛏 Sleeping

Book well in advance. This is an oil city and prices can soar on weekdays as businesspeople arrive, but return to more reasonable levels on weekends – try to plan your visit accordingly. The tourist office website (www.regionstavanger.com) has a list of small B&Bs in and around Stavanger.

📋TOP CHOICE Comfort Hotel Square   HOTEL €€

(☑51 56 80 00; www.nordicchoicehotels.no; Løkkeveien 41; s/d from Nkr670/870; ✳) In a wavy wooden building up behind Gamle Stavanger, this funky place has cool rooms with exposed concrete walls, Bang & Olufsen phones, creative lighting and wall-sized photos. The breakfast is better than average and the whole feel is contemporary without being overdone. If you're here on a weekend or can get a better rate through Fjord Pass (p379), it's outrageous value in this generally expensive city.

Stavanger B&B   B&B €€

(☑51 56 25 00; www.stavangerbedandbreakfast.no; Vikedalsgata 1a; s/d Nkr790/890, with shared bathroom Nkr690/790; Ⓟ) This quiet but popular place comes highly recommended by readers and it's not hard to see why. The simple rooms are tidy and come with satellite TV, shower and a smile from the friendly owners. There's free parking and waffles are served every night from 9pm.

Myhregaarden Hotel   BOUTIQUE HOTEL €€€

(☑51 86 80 00; www.myhregaardenhotel.no; Nygaten 24; s/d Nkr1995/2195; ✳) Stavanger's most stylish hotel has a more personal touch than most chain hotels. The refurbished early-20th-century building has some original features. All but five rooms have chandeliers and fireplaces; the remaining five have original wooden beams. The contemporary rooms have soothing colour schemes.

Skansen Hotel   HOTEL, GUESTHOUSE €€

(☑51 93 85 00; www.skansenhotel.no; Skansegata 7; r Mon-Thu Nkr995, Fri-Sun Nkr770) This centrally located place, opposite the old customs house, promises simple but comfortable, well-priced rooms that are slightly removed from the noise of the harbour yet still just a two-minute walk away.

Mosvangen Camping   CAMPGROUND €

(☑51 53 29 71; www.stavangercamping.no; Tjensvoll 1b; campsites without/with car Nkr150/200, with caravan or camper Nkr210, huts Nkr450-750; ☺Apr-Sep) During nesting season around Lake Mosvangen, campers are treated to almost incessant birdsong amid the green and agreeable surroundings. Take bus 78 or 79 (Nkr36) from opposite the cathedral to Ullandhaugveien, 3km to the south. Bus 4 also passes by.

🍴 Eating

Le Café Français   CAFE €

(Østervåg 30-32; sandwiches & light meals Nkr59-129; ☺9am-5pm Mon-Wed & Fri, to 7pm Thu, to 4pm Sat, 11am-5pm Sun) With the widest range of pastries and other sweet goodies in town and outdoor tables on the pedestrian street, this is a good place to wind down. It also serves sandwiches, miniquiches, French pancakes and good salads.

NB Sørensen's Damskibsexpedition   NORWEGIAN €€

(☑51 84 38 00; Skagen 26; mains Nkr125-329) One of the better places along the waterfront, this restaurant serves everything from fish to pork ribs, with a seasonal lunch menu that's excellent value. The atmospheric indoor dining area is ideal when the weather turns, and locals swear that the food and service is better upstairs. Try the grilled salmon.

Charlottenlund   NORWEGIAN, FRENCH €€€

(☑51 91 76 00; www.charlottenlund.no; Kongsgate 45; mains from Nkr298, 3-/4-/5-course set menus Nkr450/510/560; ☺5-11pm Mon-Sat) One of

Stavanger's classiest restaurants, Charlottenlund selecets the freshest Norwegian ingredients and uses French and Norwegian culinary traditions to prepare them. The results are as impeccable as the service and the set menus are excellent.

Kult Kafeen
CAFE €

(Sølvberggata 14; sandwiches & salads Nkr109-169; ⊙10am-8pm Wed-Fri, to 6pm Sat-Tue) Located in the Kulturhus in the centre of town, this cool place has won the affections of families and cool young professionals alike. Well-sized sandwiches, quiche, pasta and fresh salads are the high points, but many just come here for a quiet coffee.

Bølgen & Moi
NORWEGIAN €€

(Kjerringholmen, Norsk Oljemuseum; lunch specials Nkr149-189, 2-/3-course set menus Nkr295/395; ⊙cafe 11am-5pm daily, bar & brasserie 6pm-1am Tue-Sat) The imaginative menus in this stylish restaurant, which is attached to the Oil Museum, include dishes such as soy-and-honey-marinated salmon with potato salad, and well-priced lunch specials are huge. Try the mussel soup with apple and curry.

🍷 Drinking & Entertainment

Most of the livelier bars are right on the waterfront and cater to a younger crowd with a penchant for loud, energetic music. You'll hear them long before you see them and, as they're all similar, we've not listed them here – you should be able to find them easily on your own.

TOP CHOICE Bøker & Brøst
CAFE, BAR

(Øvre Holmegate 32; ⊙10am-2am) There are dozens of engaging little cafes in the lanes climbing the hillside west of the Oil Museum, but our favourite is Bøker & Brøst with its warm and eccentric decor, great coffee and laid-back feel whatever the time of day. Special mention must be made of the toilets, which have antique wallpaper and bookshelves filled to bursting – clearly they don't mind if you linger.

B.brormann B.bar
COCKTAIL BAR

(Skansegata 7; ⊙6pm-2am Mon-Thu, 4pm-2am Fri & Sat) One of Stavanger's coolest bars, where you can actually hear the conversation, and with contemporary artworks on the brick walls, this oddly named place draws a discerning over-30s crowd and serves half-litre beers and creative cocktails, some designed by Siv-Karin Helland, who won Norway's

2010 cocktail-mixing championship with her 'Monroe's Lemonade'.

Café Sting
CAFE, BAR, CLUB

(☑51 89 32 84; Valbergjet 3; ⊙noon-midnight Mon-Thu, to 3.30am Fri & Sat, 1pm-midnight Sun) Just up the hill but a world away from the harbour clamour, Café Sting is at once a mellow cafe and a funky cultural space with exhibitions, live jazz whenever the mood takes it, and a weekend nightclub where the DJs keep you on your toes, spinning house, hip hop and soul.

ℹ Information

Stavanger Turistforening DNT (off Muségata; ⊙10am-4pm Mon-Wed & Fri, to 6pm Thu, to 3pm Sat) Information on hiking and mountain huts.

Tourist office (☑51 85 92 00; www.regionstavanger.com; Domkirkeplassen 3; ⊙9am-8pm Jun-Aug, to 4pm Mon-Fri, to 2pm Sat Sep-May) Local information and advice on Lysefjord and Preikestolen.

ℹ Getting There & Away

To/From the Airport

Between early morning and mid- to late evening, **Flybussen** (☑51 52 26 00; www.flybussen.no/stavanger) runs every 15 minutes between the bus terminal and the airport at Sola (one way/return Nkr100/150).

Boat

Flaggruten (☑51 86 87 00; www.norled.no) runs express passenger catamarans to Bergen (one-way/return Nkr400/800, 4½ hours, two daily).

Norled (www.norled.no; ⊙Jun-Aug) has daily summer four-hour car ferries with tourist commentary along Lysefjord to Lysebotn (adult/child/car Nkr220/130/420) from Fiskepirterminalen. Departures are at 10am.

Bus

Nor-Way Bussekspress offers services to Oslo (Nkr477 to Nkr700, 9½ hours, up to five daily) and to Bergen (Nkr460, 5¾ hours, six daily).

Train

Trains run to Oslo (Nkr399 to Nkr904, eight hours, up to five daily) via Kristiansand (Nkr199 to Nkr450, 3½ hours).

Lysefjord

All along the 42km-long Lysefjord (Light Fjord), the granite rock glows with an ethereal, ambient light, even on dull days, all off-

VISITING LYSEFJORD

For general information on the region, check out www.lysefjordeninfo.no or www.visit-lysefjorden.no.

Pulpit Rock by Public Transport

From May to mid-September, five to seven ferries a day run from Stavanger's Fiskespiren Quay to Tau. Here the ferries are met by a bus, which runs between the Tau pier and the Preikestolhytta Vandrerhjem. From there, the two-hour trail leads up to Preikestolen. The first ferry leaves Stavanger at 8am and the last bus from Preikestolhytta to Tau leaves at 6.15pm. You can buy tickets at the Stavanger tourist office (p334) or Fiskespiren Quay. The return trip costs Nkr240/120 per adult/child.

Pulpit Rock by Car

If you have your own vehicle, take the car ferry from Stavanger's Fiskespiren Quay to Tau (adult/child/car Nkr44/22/133, 40 minutes, up to 24 departures daily). From the pier in Tau, a well-signed road (Rv13) leads 19km to Preikestolhytta Vandrerhjem (take the signed turn-off after 13km). It costs Nkr66/33 per car/motorcycle to park here.

An alternative route from Stavanger involves driving to Lauvik (via Sandnes along Rv13) from where a ferry crosses to Oanes (adult/child/car Nkr26/13/63, 10 minutes, departures almost every half hour).

Either way, the trip between Stavanger and the trailhead takes around 1½ hours.

Boat Tours to Lysefjord

In addition to the car ferries from Stavanger to Lysebotn, Norled (p334) offers two cruises: 'Lysefjord in a Nutshell' (adult/child Nkr600/460, 8½ hours) and 'Pulpit Rock Cruise' (adult/child Nkr360/250, three hours). Tickets can be purchased at the tourist office.

Also possible are the 'Pulpit Rock Cruise and Hike' tours offered by **Rødne Fjord Cruise** (☑51 89 52 70; www.rodne.no; ⊙departures 10am). They combine a cruise on Lysefjord plus time to hike up to Preikestolen and back for Nkr650/450 per adult/child. It also has three-hour cruises of Lysefjord that leave up to three times daily in summer and cost Nkr400/250 per adult/child.

Round Trips to Kjeragbolten

From mid-May to late August **Tide Reiser** (☑51 86 87 88; www.tidereiser.no; adult/child Nkr490/390; ⊙departures 8am late Jun–late Aug) runs 13½-hour bus-boat-hike return trips to Kjeragbolten, which can be otherwise difficult to reach. It includes a five-hour return hike and costs Nkr490/390 per adult/child.

set by almost-luminous mist. This is many visitors' favourite fjord and there's no doubt that it has a captivating beauty. Whether you cruise from Stavanger, hike up to Preikestolen, or drive the switchback road down to Lysebotn, it's one of Norway's must-sees.

The area's most popular outing is the two-hour hike to the top of the incredible **Preikestolen** (Pulpit Rock), 25km east of Stavanger. You can inch up to the edge of its flat top and peer 604m straight down a sheer cliff into the blue water of the Lysefjord for some intense vertigo. The other option is the **Kjeragbolten** boulder (chockstone), lodged between two rock faces about 2m apart but with 1000m of empty space underneath.

Sognefjorden

Sognefjorden, Norway's longest (204km) and deepest (1308m) fjord, cuts a deep slash across the map of western Norway. In places, sheer walls rise more than 1000m above the water, while elsewhere a gentler shoreline supports farms, orchards and villages. The broad, main waterway is impressive but by cruising into its narrower arms, such as the deep and lovely Nærøyfjord (on the Unesco World Heritage list) to Gudvangen, you'll see idyllic views of abrupt cliff faces and cascading waterfalls.

Find regional tourist information at www.sognefjord.no. **Fjord1** (☑57 75 70 00; www.fjord1.no) operates a daily (summer-only) express boat between Bergen and both Flåm (Nkr710, 5½ hours) and Sogndal (Nkr605, 4¾ hours), stopping along the way at 10 small towns including Vik (Nkr480, 3½ hours) and Balestrand (Nkr515, 3¾ hours). Outside the summer season, the boat only goes as far as Sogn with no onward ferry service to Flåm.

There are local ferries and buses linking the fjord towns. See www.ruteinfo.net and timetables available in tourist offices.

FLÅM
POP 575

Scenically set at the head of Aurlandsfjorden, Flåm is a tiny village of orchards and a handful of buildings. It's a jumping-off spot for travellers taking the Gudvangen ferry, the Sognefjorden express boat or the Myrdal train. It all gets a little overrun with people when a cruise ship's in port; it sees an amazing 500,000 visitors every summer. To rediscover solitude, walking a few minutes from the centre is all it takes – the tourist office has a list of 10 walks to help guide your step.

◉ Sights

Flåmsbana Railway   SCENIC RAILWAY
(www.flaamsbana.no; adult/child one way Nkr260/130, return Nkr360/260) Over the course of 20km, this engineering wonder hauls itself up 864m of altitude gain through 20 tunnels at a gradient of 1:18. The world's steepest railway that runs without cable or rack wheels, it takes a full 45 minutes to climb to Myrdal, on the bleak, treeless Hardangervidda Plateau, past thundering waterfalls (there's a photo stop at awesome Kjosfossen). It runs year-round with up to 10 departures daily in summer. For the best views, grab a seat on the right-hand side of the train. Late afternoon, when most of the cruise passengers have moved on, is the best time to make the trip.

FREE **Flåmsbana Museum**   MUSEUM
(www.flamsbana-museet.no; ⊙9am-7pm May-Sep shorter hr rest of yr) To prepare yourself for your rail journey, browse this little museum, right beside the train platform. It's not just about railways; there are fascinating photos of construction gangs and life in and around Flåm before the car era.

🏃 Activities

Riding the Rallarvegen   CYCLING
(www.rallarvegen.com) Cyclists can descend the Rallarvegen, the service road originally used by the navvies who constructed the railway, for 83km from Haugastøl (1000m) or an easier 56km from Finse. You can rent bicycles in Haugastøl (two days Nkr480/580 weekdays/weekend, including return transport from Flåm) and the company also offers packages that include accommodation.

Njord   KAYAKING
(⏱91 31 66 28; www.kajakk.com) Njord operates from Flåm's handkerchief of a beach. It offers a two-hour sea-kayaking induction (Nkr390), three-hour gentle fjord paddle (Nkr490) and four-hour paddle-and-hike trips (Nkr650), plus multiday kayaking, hiking and camping trips.

Fjord Safari   ADVENTURE TOUR
(www.fjordsafari.com; adult/child 1½hr trips Nkr480/290, 3hr Nkr690/420) Bounce along in a Zodiac/RIB inflatable to see more of the fjord in less time. The team supplies full-length waterproof kit – you'll need it for this exhilarating scoot across the waters.

SOGNEFJORDEN BY BOAT

Nærøyfjord, its 17km length a Unesco World Heritage Site, lies west of Flåm. Beside the deep blue fjord (only 250m across at its narrowest point) are towering 1200m-high cliffs, isolated farms, and waterfalls plummeting from the heights.

It may get overrun with tour groups in summer, but the classic boat trip from Flåm to Gudvangen (via Aurland and, upon request, Undredal) is one of the most beautiful boat trips on earth. Ferries between Gudvangen and Flåm (one way/return Nkr275/380) via Aurland (same price as Flåm) and Undredal (on request) leave Flåm at 3.10pm year-round and up to four times daily between May and September. In Gudvangen, buses to Voss and Oslo connect with the ferry arrival. Boat and bus tickets can be bought at the tourist offices in Flåm, Aurland and Gudvangen.

There's also at least one daily express boat to Bergen (Nkr706, 5½ hours) via Balestrand (Nkr237, 1½ hours).

🛏 Sleeping & Eating

Fretheim Hotel
HOTEL €€€

(☑57 63 63 00; www.fretheim-hotel.no; r from Nkr2150; ☺Feb–mid-Dec; **P@**) Haunt of the English aristocracy in the 19th century, the vast, 121-room, yet at the same time intimate and welcoming Fretheim is as much sports and social centre as hotel. In the original 1870s building, 17 rooms have been restored to their former condition – including replica claw-foot retro bathtubs – while equipped with 21st-century amenities. The restaurant (mains Nkr195 to Nkr365) serves the best cuisine in town with reindeer, local lamb or goat kid on the menu.

Flåm Camping & Youth Hostel
HOSTEL, CAMPGROUND €

(☑57 63 21 21; www.flaam-camping.no; car/caravan sites Nkr205/215, dm Nkr210-275, s/d/cabins from Nkr340/500/650; ☺Apr-Sep) This friendly spot is only a few minutes' walk from the station. In 2010 Hostelling International judged it to be Norway's best hostel and the ninth best in the world. You can see why; there's a brand-new block with en suite facilities, amenities are impeccable and the welcome couldn't be warmer.

Heimly Pensjonat
GUESTHOUSE €€

(☑57 63 23 00; www.heimly.no; s/d from Nkr895/1095) Overlooking the water on the fringe of the village and away from all the port hubbub, this place has straightforward rooms. There's a magnificent view along the fjord from the more expensive ones and from the small patch of lawn.

ⓘ Information

Tourist office (☑57 63 33 13; www.visitflam. com; ☺8.30am-4pm & 4.30-8pm Jun-Aug, 8.30am-4pm May & Sep) In summer the tourist office has the useful brochure *Sightseeing Tours from Flåm*, with timetables and prices.

ⓘ Getting There & Away

BOAT Sightseeing boat journeys from Flåm are possible, with a variety of ferries available (p336).

BUS Bus services run to Gudvangen, Aurland, Sogndal and Bergen.

AURLAND

Peaceful Aurland is Flåm's alter ego, so much less hectic than its neighbour a mere 10km south along the fjord. The views from here are more spectacular than than those from Flåm, and it's the starting point for some fine drives, hikes and boat trips.

SNØVEGEN

The 45km Snow Road, officially signed Aurlandsvegen, climbs from fjord level, twisting precipitously to the desolate, boulder-strewn high plateau that separates Aurland and Lærdalsøyri (Lærdal). This heart-stopping drive – strictly for summertime – has been designated as a National Tourist Route. Even if you don't opt for the whole route, drive the first 8km from Aurland to the magnificent, architect-designed observation point. Projecting out over the fjord way below, pine-clad, simple and striking like the best of Norwegian design, it's almost as impressive as the stunning panorama itself.

🛏 Sleeping & Eating

Aurland Fjordhotell
HOTEL

(☑57 63 35 05; www.aurland-fjordhotel.com; s/d from Nkr920/1240) At this friendly 30-room, family-owned hotel, most of the comfortable rooms have fabulous fjord views and there's a solarium, steam bath and sauna. To help you sleep, have a shot from the owner's huge collection of brandies and spirits in a couple of display cases beside reception.

Vangsgaarden
B&B €€

(☑57 63 35 80; www.vangsgaarden.no; d/f Nkr1050/1150, 4-bed cabins Nkr1250 plus bed linen & towels per person Nkr65) The complex embraces four 18th-century buildings and six cabins down at sea level with Aurland's best fjord views. Room decoration ranges from antique to Ikea; the dining room could be your Norwegian grandmother's parlour. Breakfast costs Nkr80. The cafe (mains Nkr110 to Nkr220) serves up local deer burgers, fish and chips and other reasonably priced dishes.

ⓘ Information

Aurland tourist office (☑57 63 33 13; www. alr.no; ☺9am-6pm Mon-Fri, 10am-5pm Sat & Sun Jun-Aug, shorter hr rest of yr)

ⓘ Getting There & Away

Buses run up to eight times daily between Aurland and Flåm (Nkr38, 15 minutes) and one to six times daily between Aurland and Lærdal (Nkr79, 30 minutes).

STALHEIM
POP 200

This gorgeous little spot high above the valley is an extraordinary place. Between

HIKES FROM STALHEIM

Norwegians delight in building their homes in the most inaccessible places, but **Husmannsplassen Nåli** (the Cotter's Farm of Nåli), along the ledge from Stalheim high above Nærøydalen, may just win the prize. Built in 1870 when the first cotter moved there with two cows, four sheep and 11 goats, it was occupied until 1930. Now overgrown, it's an evocative spot, although the route there (two hours return) is not for the faint-hearted – the path beneath the cliff wall is extremely narrow in parts and there's nothing between you and the valley floor far below; don't even think of walking here after rain. As long as you don't suffer from vertigo, it's one of Norway's most beautiful walks. Ask directions from the reception of the Stalheim Hotel.

The three-hour return hike to **Brekkedalen** leads up into the valley above Stalheim and locals in the know make a claim for this to be the region's prettiest walk. The views are, as you'd expect, magnificent, and it's a relatively easy way to leave behind the crowds at the hotel and have this stunning high country all to yourself. The tourist office (p331) in Voss has route descriptions, or ask at Stalheim Hotel for directions.

1647 and 1909, Stalheim was a stopping-off point for travellers on the Royal Mail route between Copenhagen, Christiania (Oslo) and Bergen. The mailmen and their weary steeds rested in Stalheim and changed to fresh horses after climbing up the valley and through the Stalheimskleiva gorge, flanked by the thundering Stalheim and Sivle waterfalls.

🛏 Sleeping

TOP CHOICE **Stalheim Hotel** HISTORIC HOTEL €€
(☏56 52 01 22; www.stalheim.com; s/d/superior from Nkr1160/1750/2150; ⌚mid-May–mid-Sep; P@) Arguably Norway's most spectacularly sited hotel, this stunning place has large rooms, around half of which have glorious views (all superior rooms have views). Not surprisingly, the hotel (room 324 in particular) once featured in Conde Nast's 'best rooms with a view'. The lunch/dinner buffets (Nkr280/395) are excellent, but lighter meals are available.

ℹ Getting There & Away

There's no public transport to Stalheim, but it's a favourite stop on the Norway in a Nutshell tours (p294) between Oslo and Bergen. Coming from Oslo, the bus arrives around 6pm, with a bus leaving the next morning for Bergen or Voss at 11.55am.

BALESTRAND

POP 1338

Balestrand sits comfortably beside the fjord; at its rear is an impressive mountain backdrop. Genteel and low-key, it has been a tranquil, small-scale holiday resort ever

since the 19th century and it's still one of our favourite bases for exploring Sognefjord.

◉ Sights & Activities

Balestrand is home to the charming wooden **Church of St Olav**, built in 1897 in the style of a traditional stave church, some **Viking-era burial mounds** and the excellent **Sognefjord Aquarium** (adult/child Nkr70/35; ⌚10am-7pm May-Sep).

The tourist office's free pamphlet *Outdoor Activities in Balestrand* has plenty of suggestions for marked walks, ranging from easy to demanding. It also rents out **bicycles** for Nkr50/150/250 per hour/half day/full day from May to September.

🛏 Sleeping & Eating

Kvikne's Hotel HOTEL €€
(☏57 69 42 00; www.kviknes.no; s/d from Nkr1150/1750; ⌚May-Sep; P@) The majestic pale-yellow, timber-built main building of Kvikne's Hotel, with exquisite antiques in its public areas, breathes late-19th-century luxury. Sadly, of its 190 rooms, 165 are in the newer building, erected in the 1960s. **Balholm Bar og Bistro** (mains Nkr249-519) is a reliable place for snacks and light meals. For a gastronomic delight, invest Nkr495 in the main restaurant's outstanding dinner buffet.

Balestrand Hotell HOTEL €€
(☏57 69 11 38; www.balestrand.com; s/d incl breakfast from Nkr670/990; ⌚mid-May–mid-Sep) This family-run, summertime-only hotel is a friendly place that eschews the tour groups that fill so many beds elsewhere in town. It's

well worth paying that little extra for inspirational views over the fjord.

Sjøtun Camping
CAMPGROUND €

(☑95 06 72 61; www.sjotun.com; per person/tent Nkr30/90, 4-/6-bed cabin with outdoor bathroom Nkr300/370; ☺Jun–mid-Sep) At this green camping ground, a 15-minute walk south along the fjord, you can pitch a tent on soft grass amid apple trees or rent a rustic cabin at a very reasonable price.

Ciderhuset
NORWEGIAN €€

(☑90 83 56 71; www.ciderhuset.no; Sjøtunsvegen 32; mains Nkr100-200; ☺4-10pm mid-Jun–mid-Aug) Within a fruit farm that produces organic juices, jams, bottled fruits, cider and cider brandy, this delightful restaurant fuses Nordic and Mediterranean culinary traditions. Bookings advisable.

ℹ Information
Tourist office (www.visitbalestrand.no; ☺10am-5.30pm Sun Jun-Aug, 10am-1pm & 3-5.30pm Mon-Sat May & Sep)

ℹ Getting There & Away
BOAT From June to August a car ferry (Nkr235/350 one way/return, 1½ hours, twice daily) follows the narrow Fjærlandsfjorden to Fjærland, gateway to the glacial wonderlands of Jostedalsbreen (in May and September there's a twice-daily passenger-ferry run).

BUS Express buses link Balestrand and Sogndal (Nkr112, one hour, three daily).

Jostedalsbreen

With an area of 487 sq km, the many-tongued Jostedalsbreen dominates the highlands between Nordfjord and Sognefjord and is mainland Europe's largest icecap; in some places it is 400m thick. Protected as a national park, the icecap provides extraordinary opportunities for otherworldly glacier hiking.

JOSTEDALEN & NIGARDSBREEN

The Jostedalen valley pokes due north from Gaupne, on the shores of Lustrafjord. This slim finger sits between two national parks and it's a spectacular drive as the road runs beside the milky turquoise river, tumbling beneath the eastern flank of the Nigardsbreen glacier. Of the Jostedalsbreen glacier tongues visible from below, Nigardsbreen is the most dramatic and easiest to approach.

◉ Sights
Breheimsenteret Visitors Centre
MUSEUM

(☑57 68 32 50; www.jostedal.com; display adult/child Nkr50/35; ☺9am-7pm mid-Jun–mid-Aug, 10am-5pm May–mid-Jun & mid-Aug–Sep) This state-of-the-art visitors centre burned to the ground in July 2011 and a new centre should have opened by the time you visit. The centre serves as the gateway to Nigardsbreen 34km up the valley from Lustrafjord. If all goes according to plan, it should have a display that tells how glaciers were formed and how they sculpt the landscape. It should also have a

---

SOGNEFJORDEN STAVE CHURCHES

Some 30km southeast of Lærdalsøyri along the E16, you'll find the 12th-century **Borgund stave church** (adult/child Nkr75/55; ☺8am-8pm mid-Jun–mid-Aug, 10am-5pm May–mid-Jun & mid-Aug–Sep). Dedicated to St Andrew, it's one of the best-known, most photographed – and certainly the best-preserved – of Norway's stave churches. Beside it is the only free-standing medieval wooden bell tower still standing in Norway.

There are two further examples in Vik. The **Hopperstad stave church** (adult/child Nkr60/45; ☺9am-6pm mid-Jun–mid-Aug, 10am-5pm mid-May–mid-Jun & mid-Aug–mid-Sep), originally built in 1140 and Norway's second oldest, escaped demolition by a whisker in the late 19th century and was painstakingly reconstructed. There's also the superb **Kaupanger Stave Church** (adult/child Nkr50/35; ☺10am-5pm Jun-Aug), dating from 1184.

Norway's oldest preserved place of worship, the **Urnes Stave Church** (adult/child Nkr60/45; ☺10.30am-5.30pm May-Sep) is a Unesco World Heritage site. Directly across the fjord from Solvorn, it gazes out over Lustrafjord. The original church was built around 1070, while the majority of today's structure was constructed a century later. Highlights are elaborate wooden carvings – animals locked in struggle, stylised intertwined bodies and abstract motifs – on the north wall, all recycled from the original church.

worthwhile free pamphlet, *Walking in Jostedal*, that describes a number of short (one- to 2½-hour) walks.

🏃 Activities

Most of the following activities are only available from June to September, although some only operate in July and August.

Ice Troll
GLACIER VISITS

(☑97 01 43 70; www.icetroll.com; 8-10hr excursions Nkr750-950) Andy and his team offer a couple of truly original glacier visits. After a kayak trip, enjoy an ice walk where those without paddles never get. The excursion is possible at three different sites and lasts eight to 10 hours. It also does longer overnight and two-day sorties.

Jostedalen Breførarlag
GLACIER VISITS

(☑57 68 31 11; www.bfl.no; family walk adult/child Nkr250/100, 2-/3-/5hr walks adult Nkr445/540/760) Leads several guided glacier walks on Nigardsbreen. Easiest is the family walk to the glacier snout and briefly along its tongue with around one hour on the ice. Fees for the two- to five-hour ice walks include the brief boat trip across Lake Nigardsvatnet.

Riverpig
RAFTING, RIVERBOARDING

(www.riverpig.no; rafting Nkr800, riverboarding Nkr1300) Run by the same outfit as Ice Troll, Riverpig does four-hour rafting trips on the Jostedalen River and, for the truly hardy, six-hour riverboarding expeditions.

Leirdalen Bre og Juv
ADVENTURE SPORTS

(Leirdal Glacier & Canyon; ☑47 02 78 78; www.breogjuv.no; canyoning Nkr500, hiking Nkr750) Offers canyon clambering and six- to eight-hour glacier hikes on Tunsbergsdalsbreen, Norway's longest glacier arm.

🛏 Sleeping

Jostedal Camping
CAMPGROUND €

(☑57 68 39 14; www.jostedalcamping.no; car/caravan sites Nkr110/125 plus per person Nkr30, cabins Nkr370-1150; ⊗May–mid-Oct) A trim, well-kept camping ground, right beside the Jostedal River. Facilities are impeccable and there's a lovely riverside terrace.

🌿 Jostedal Hotel
HOTEL €€

(☑57 68 31 19; www.jostedalhotel.no; s Nkr730-770, d Nkr930-1030, f Nkr1180-1280; @) Just 2.5km south of the visitors centre, this friendly place has been run by the same family for three generations. Meat, milk and vegetables for the restaurant come from their farm. There are also family rooms with self-catering facilities that can accommodate up to five guests.

ℹ Getting There & Around

BUS From mid-June to mid-September, **Jostedalsbrebussen** (No 160; The Glacier Bus; www.jostedal.com/brebussen) runs from Sogndal (with connections from Flåm, Balestrand and Lærdal) via Solvorn to the foot of the Nigardsbreen glacier, leaving at 8.45am and setting out on the return journey at 5pm.

CAR If you're driving, leave the Rv55 Sognefjellet Rd at Gaupne and head north up Jostedal along the Rv604.

FJÆRLAND
POP 300

The village of Fjærland (also called Mundal), at the head of scenic Fjærlandsfjorden, pulls in as many as 300,000 visitors each year. Most come to experience its pair of particularly accessible glacial tongues, Supphellebreen and Bøyabreen. Others come for the books. This tiny place, known as the **Book Town of Norway** (www.bokbyen.no), is a bibliophile's nirvana, with a dozen shops selling a wide range of used books, mostly in Norwegian but with lots in English and other European languages. Together the shops have almost 5km of bookshelves.

The village virtually hibernates from October onwards, then leaps to life in early May, when the ferry runs again.

⊙ Sights

Supphellebreen & Bøyabreen
GLACIER

You can drive to within 300m of the Supphellebreen glacier, then walk right up and touch the ice. Ice blocks from here were used as podiums at the 1994 Winter Olympics in Lillehammer.

At blue, creaking Bøyabreen, more spectacular than its brother over the hill Supphellebreen, you might happen upon glacial calving as a hunk tumbles into the meltwater lagoon beneath the glacier tongue.

Norwegian Glacier Museum
TOP CHOICE
MUSEUM

(Norsk Bremuseum; ☑57 69 32 88; www.bre.museum.no; adult/child Nkr120/60; ⊗9am-7pm Jun-Aug, 10am-4pm Apr-May & Sep-Oct) For the story on flowing ice and how it has sculpted the Norwegian landscape, visit this superbly executed museum, 3km inland from the ferry jetty. You can learn how fjords are formed, see an excellent 20-minute multiscreen

audiovisual presentation on Jostedalsbreen, touch 1000-year-old ice, wind your
way through a tunnel that penetrates the
mock-ice and even see the tusk of a Siberian
woolly mammoth, which met an icy demise
30,000 years ago.

🏃 Activities

At the small fjordside shack belonging to
Fjærland Kayak and Glacier (📞92 85 46
74; www.kayakglacier.no) you can hire a kayak,
canoe, motor or rowing boat or join one of
its daily guided kayaking trips (May to August), ranging from 2½ hours (Nkr420) to
a full day (Nkr950). It also offers more demanding guided glacier treks (Nkr700 to
Nkr750), leaving at 8.30am each morning.

The tourist office's free sheet, *Escape the
Asphalt,* lists 12 marked walking routes,
varying from 30 minutes to three hours. For
greater detail, supplement this with *Turkart
Fjærland* (Nkr70) at 1:50,000, which comes
complete with route descriptions and trails
indicated; pull on your boots and you're
away.

🛏 Sleeping & Eating

TOP CHOICE Hotel Mundal   HOTEL €€€
(📞57 69 31 01; www.hotelmundal.no; s/d from
Nkr1150/1750; �), May-Sep; [P] [@]) Retaining much
of its period furniture and run by the same
family since it was built in 1891, this place
features a welcoming lounge and a lovely
round tower. The restaurant serves truly
wonderful traditional four-course Norwegian dinners (Nkr375).

Fjærland Fjordstue Hotell   HOTEL €€
(📞57 69 32 00; www.fjaerland.no; r Nkr950-1580;
☉May–mid-Sep) The majority of this charming small family hotel's 17 rooms overlook
the fjord where, with a smattering of luck,
you might see porpoises playing. Its lounge
and restaurant both have stunning views
through their picture windows.

Bøyum Camping   CAMPGROUND €
(📞57 69 32 52; www.fjaerland.org/boyumcamping;
campsites Nkr120-170, dm Nkr175, d without bathroom Nkr280-360, 4-/8-bed cabins Nkr730/1030;
☉May-Sep) Beside the Glacier Museum and
3km from the ferry landing, Bøyum Camping has something for all pockets and sleeping preferences.

ℹ Getting There & Away

BOAT A car ferry (adult Nkr235/380 one way/
return, car/motorcycle Nkr360/420, 1½ hours)
runs twice daily between Balestrand and Fjærland from June to August (in May and September there's a twice-daily passenger-ferry run).

BUS Buses bypass the village and stop on the
Rv5 near the Glacier Museum. Three to six run
daily to/from Sogndal (Nkr81, 30 minutes) and
Stryn (Nkr225, two hours). There's also a twice-
daily, summer-only bus (adult/child Nkr165/85)
from the town centre and Glacier Museum up to
the glaciers and back.

BRIKSDALSBREEN

From the small town of **Olden** at the eastern
end of Nordfjord, a scenic road leads 23km
up Oldedalen past Brenndalsbreen, and
from there on to the twin glacial tongues of
Melkevollbreen and Briksdalsbreen. More
easily accessible, Briksdalsbreen attracts
hordes of tour buses. It's a temperamental glacier; in 1997 the tongue licked to its
furthest point for around 70 years, then
retreated by around 500m. In 2005 the
reaches where glacier walkers would clamber and stride cracked and splintered. So for
the moment, there are no guided hikes on
Briksdalsbreen, but it's a fickle creature and
this may change. For hiking on neighbouring Brenndalsbreen, contact **Briksdal Adventure** (📞i57 87 68 00; www.briksdal-adventure.
com).

Melkevoll Bretun (📞57 87 38 64; www.
melkevoll.no; per person/campsite Nkr30/100,
cabins Nkr500-750 plus per person Nkr70; cabins
without bathroom Nkr350 plus per person Nkr50;
☉May-Sep) is a gorgeous green camping
ground with accommodation for all pockets
and gorgeous views whichever way you turn.

Between June and August, buses leave
Stryn for Briksdal (Nkr82, one hour) once or
twice daily, calling by Loen and Olden.

Norangsdalen & Sunnmøresalpane

One of the most inspiring parts of the
Western Fjords is Norangsdalen, a hid-
den valley west of Hellesylt. The partially
unsealed Rv665 to the villages of **Øye** and
Urke, and the Leknes–Sæbø ferry on beauti-
ful **Hjørundfjorden** are served by bus from
Hellesylt once daily, Monday to Friday mid-
June to mid-August.

Hikers and climbers will enjoy the dramatic peaks of the adjacent **Sunnmør-
salpane**, including the incredibly steep
scrambling ascent of Slogen (1564m) from
Øye and the superb Råna (1586m), a long
and tough scramble from Urke.

Geirangerfjorden

Added to Unesco's World Heritage list in 2005, this king of Norwegian fjords boasts towering, twisting walls that curve inland for 20 narrow kilometres. Along the way abandoned farms cling to the cliffs and breathtakingly high waterfalls – with names such as the Seven Sisters, the Suitor and the Bridal Veil – drop straight into the sea from forests above.

The cruise by public ferry between Geiranger and Hellesylt is extraordinarily beautiful.

Around Geirangerfjorden

High mountains with cascading waterfalls and cliffside farms surround Geiranger, at the head of the crooked Geirangerfjorden. Although the village is tiny, it's one of Norway's most visited spots. Nevertheless, it's reasonably serene during the evening when all the cruise ships and tour buses have departed.

◉ Sights

Flydalsjuvet VIEWPOINT

Somewhere you've seen that classic photo, beloved of brochures, of the overhanging rock Flydalsjuvet, usually with a figure gazing down at a cruise ship in Geirangerfjord. The car park, signposted Flydalsjuvet, about 5km uphill from Geiranger on the Stryn road, offers a great view of the fjord and the green river valley, but doesn't provide the postcard view down to the last detail. For that, you'll have to drop about 150m down the hill, then descend a slippery and rather indistinct track to the edge. Your intrepid photo subject will have to scramble down gingerly and with the utmost care to the overhang about 50m further along.

Dalsnibba VIEWPOINT

(Nkr85 per car) For the highest and perhaps most stunning of the many stunning views of the Geiranger valley and fjord, take the 5km toll road (Nkr100 per vehicle) that climbs from the Rv63 to the Dalsnibba lookout (1500m). A **bus** (www.geirangerfjord.no; adult/child Nkr250/200 return) runs twice daily from Geiranger between mid-June and mid-August.

Norsk Fjordsenter MUSEUM

(www.verdsarvfjord.no; adult/child Nkr100/50; ☉10am-6pm May-Aug, to 3pm rest of yr) At the Geiranger Fjord Centre learn about the essentials that shaped culture in the middle of nowhere: mail packets, avalanches and building roads over impossible terrain.

🏃 Activities

Get away from the busy ferry terminal and life's altogether quieter. All around Geiranger there are great signed hiking routes to abandoned farmsteads, waterfalls and vista points. The tourist office's aerial-photographed *Hiking Routes* map (Nkr10) gives ideas for 18 signed walks of between 1.5km and 5km.

Coastal Odyssey KAYAKING, HIKING

(☑91 11 80 62; www.coastalodyssey.com; sea kayaks per hr/half day/day Nkr150/450/800, kayaking-hiking trips Nkr800-1250) Based at Geiranger Camping, this outfit is run by Jonathan Bendiksen, who rents sea kayaks and also does daily combined kayaking-hiking trips lasting from five to nine hours to the finest destinations around the fjord.

Geiranger Adventure CYCLING

(☑47 37 97 71; www.geiranger-adventure.com; per adult/child incl transport, bikes, helmet and other equipment Nkr450/225) This outfit will drive you up to Djupvasshytta (1038m), from where you can coast for 17 gentle, scenically splendid kilometres by bike down to the fjord; allow a couple of hours. It also rents bikes (Nkr75/250 per hour/day).

Geiranger Fjordservice BOAT

(☑70 26 30 07; www.geirangerfjord.no; boat tours adult/child Nkr190/100; ☉up to 4 sailings daily early May–mid-Sep) Does 1½-hour sightseeing boat tours, as well as a range of other bus, bike and boat possibilities around Geirangerfjord. Its kiosk is within the tourist office.

🛏 Sleeping & Eating

Hotel Utsikten HOTEL €€

(☑70 26 96 60; www.classicnorway.no/hotell-utsikten; s Nkr990, d Nkr1340-1600; ☉May-Sep; P@) High on the hill above Geiranger (take Rv63, direction Grotli), the venerable family-owned Utsikten, constructed in 1893, has stunning views over town and fjord, and atractive rooms.

Grande Fjord Hotel
HOTEL €€

(☎70 26 94 90; www.grandefjordhotel.com; d Nkr990-1250; P) This warmly recommended 48-room hotel does great buffet breakfasts and dinners. It's well worth paying the higher rate for a room with a balcony and magnificent view over the fjord.

Geiranger Camping
CAMPGROUND €

(☎70 26 31 20; www.geirangercamping.no; per person/campsite Nkr30/130; ☺mid-May–mid-Sep; P@) A short walk from the ferry terminal, Geiranger Camping is sliced through by a fast-flowing torrent. Though it's short on shade, it's pleasant and handy for an early-morning ferry getaway.

Laizas
CAFE €

(mains Nkr62-175; ☺10am-10pm mid-Apr–Sep) At the ferry terminal, just beside the tourist office, the young team at this airy, welcoming place puts on a handful of tasty hot dishes, good salads and snackier items such as focaccia, wraps and sandwiches.

ℹ Information

Tourist office (☎70 26 30 99; www.visitalesund-geiranger.com; ☺9am-6pm mid-May–mid-Sep)

ℹ Getting There & Away

Boat

The popular, hugely recommended run between Geiranger and Hellesylt (passenger/car with driver one way Nkr150/300, adult/child return Nkr200/100, one hour) is the most spectacular scheduled ferry route in Norway. It has four to eight sailings daily between May and mid-October (every 90 minutes until 6.30pm June to August).

Almost as scenic is the ferry that runs twice daily between Geiranger and Valldal (adult/child one way Nkr230/120, return Nkr350/180, 2¼ hours). It runs from mid-June to mid-August.

Bus

From mid-June to mid-August two buses daily make the spectacular run over Trollstigen to Åndalsnes (Nkr246, three hours) via Valldal (Nkr79, 1½ hours). For Molde, change buses in Åndalsnes; for Ålesund, change at Linge.

Åndalsnes

POP 2231

Two of the three approaches to Åndalsnes are dramatic by any standards: by road through the Trollstigen pass or along Roms-dalen as you ride (or follow the route of the spectacularly scenic Raumabanen). Badly bombed during WWII, the modern town, nestled beside Romsdalfjord, is nondescript, but the surrounding landscapes are magnificent.

◎ Sights

Trollveggen
CLIFF

Near Åndalsnes, dramatic Trollveggen (Troll Wall), first conquered in 1958 by a joint Norwegian and English team, rears skywards. The highest vertical mountain wall in Europe, its ragged and often cloud-shrouded summit, 1800m from the valley floor, is considered the ultimate challenge among mountaineers. The best views are via a walking trail accessible from the Trollstigen road – ask at the tourist office (p344) for details.

Raumabanen
SCENIC RAILWAY

(tourist train adult/child return Nkr440/220; 1 child per adult travels free) The rail route down from Dombås ploughs through a deeply cut glacial valley flanked by sheer walls and plummeting waterfalls; it's shadowed by the equally spectacular E136 highway. Trains run daily year-round along this spectacular route. There's also a tourist train with on-board commentary that runs twice daily from June to August from Åndalsnes' lakeside station up to Bjorli, at 600m. Book at the station or tourist office.

⚡ Activities

The best local climbs are the less-extreme sections of the 1500m-high rock route on Trollveggen and the 1550m-high Romsdalshorn, but there's a wealth of others. Serious climbers should buy *Klatring i Romsdal* (Nkr300), which includes rock and ice-climbing information in both Norwegian and English.

An excellent day hike, signed by red markers, begins in town and climbs to the summit of Nesaksla (715m), the prominent peak that rises above Åndalsnes. At the top, the payoff for a steep ascent is a magnificent panorama.

Another fabulous (and strenuous) day hike is the Romsdalseggen, an all-day hike (at least seven hours) along the ridge of the same name. In summer a bus (25 minutes) leaves from outside the Åndalsnes train station at 9.30am to the trailhead. The tourist office has detailed information on this hike.

🛏 Sleeping & Eating

Grand Hotel Bellevue HOTEL €€
(☏71 22 75 00; www.grandhotel.no; Åndalgata 5; s/d Nkr1195/1450, dinner mains Nkr135-289; ☺restaurant dinner only Mon-Sat; P@) This large whitewashed structure caps a hillock in the centre of town. Most of its 86 rooms have fine views, particularly those facing the rear. Its restaurant offers the town's most formal dining, but you can always nibble on a lighter dish for around Nkr100.

Åndalsnes Vandrerhjem Setnes HOSTEL €
(☏71 22 13 82; www.aandalsnesvandrerhjem.no; dm/s/d Nkr290/500/710; ☺Mar-Nov) This welcoming, HI-affiliated, sod-roofed hostel is 1.5km from the train station on the E136, in the direction of Ålesund. It's worth staying here for the pancakes-and-pickled-herring bumper breakfast alone.

Kaikanten CAFE, RESTAURANT €
(mains Nkr120-195; ☺10am-11pm Mon-Sat, noon-9pm Sun mid-May–Aug) Sit back, relax and enjoy a drink, a snack or something more substantial at this casual place by the water's edge. It serves wraps, sandwiches, pizzas and a range of lunch specials.

ℹ Information

Tourist Office (☏71 22 16 22; www.visit andalsnes.com; ☺9am-8.30pm Jun-Aug, to 3pm Mon-Fri rest of yr)

ℹ Getting There & Away

Bus
Buses along the spectacular National Tourist Route to Geiranger (Nkr246, three hours), via Trollstigen, the Linge–Eidsdal ferry and the steep Ørnevegen (Eagle Rd), run twice daily between mid-June and mid-August.

There are also services to Molde (Nkr139, 1½ hours, up to eight daily) and Ålesund (Nkr289, 2¼ hours, four times daily).

Train
Trains to/from Dombås (Nkr232, 1½ hours) run twice daily and are in synchronisation with Oslo-Trondheim trains. Unlike the tourist train, they don't stop for photos.

Åndalsnes to Geiranger

The **Trollstigen** (Troll's Ladder; www.trollstigen.net) winding south from Åndalsnes is a thriller of a road with 11 hairpin bends and a 1:12 gradient, and to add a daredevil element it's practically one lane all the way. On request, the bus makes photo stops at the thundering, 180m-high **Stigfossen waterfall** on its way up to the mountain pass. At the top, the bus usually stops long enough for you to walk to a lookout with a dizzying view back down the valley. The pass is usually cleared and open from late May to mid-October.

The pamphlet *Geiranger Trollstigen* (Nkr30) describes seven signed hiking trails in the Trollstigen area. You'll need to supplement this with the map *Romsdals-Fjella* at 1:80,000. The tourist office in Åndalsnes carries both.

There are waterfalls galore smoking down the mountains as you descend to **Valldal**. You could break your journey here – there are camping grounds, cabins and a hotel – though most travellers continue on, taking the short ferry ride from Linge across to **Eidsdal**. From there, a waiting bus continues along the **Ørnevegen** (Eagle's Hwy), with magnificent bird's-eye views of Geirangerfjorden during the descent into Geiranger village.

Ålesund
POP 40,419

The coastal town of Ålesund is, for many, just as beautiful as Bergen, if on a much smaller scale, and it is certainly far less touristy. Lucky for you, Ålesund burned to the ground in 1904. The amazing rebuilding created a town centre unlike anything else you'll see in Norway – a harmonious collection of pastel buildings almost entirely designed in the art nouveau tradition. All the loveliness is well staged on the end of a peninsula, surrounded by islands, water and hills.

◉ Sights & Activities

Sunnmøre Museum MUSEUM
(www.sunnmore.museum.no; Borgundgavlen; adult/child Nkr80/30; ☺11am-5pm Mon-Sat, noon-5pm Sun mid-Jun–mid-Aug, shorter hr rest of yr) Ålesund's celebrated open-air Sunnmøre Museum is 4km east of the city centre. Here, at the site of the old Borgundkaupangen trading centre, active from the 11th to 16th centuries, more than 50 traditional buildings have been relocated. Ship lovers will savour the collection of around 40 historic boats, including replicas of Viking-era ships and a commercial trading vessel from

around AD 1000. You can take bus 613, 618 or 624 to get here.

Jugendstil Art Nouveau Centre ARTS CENTRE
(Jugendstil Senteret; ☎70 10 49 70; www.jugend stilsenteret.no; Apotekergata 16; adult/child Nkr70/35; ☺10am-5pm Jun-Aug, 11am-4pm Tue-Sun Sep-May) Everyone from serious aesthetes to kids out for fun will get pleasure from this art centre. The introductory Time Machine capsule presents 'From Ashes to Art Nouveau', a 14-minute hi-tech, very visual story of the rebuilding of Ålesund after the great fire, while the displays offer carefully selected textiles, ceramics and furniture of the genre.

Atlanterhavsparken AQUARIUM
(Atlantic Ocean Park; www.atlanterhavsparken. no; Tueneset; adult/child Nkr140/65; ☺10am-7pm Sun-Fri, 10am-4pm Sat Jun-Aug, 11am-4pm Tue-Sun Sep-May) At the peninsula's western extreme, 3km from the town centre, the Atlantic Ocean Park can merit a whole day of your life. It introduces visitors to the North Atlantic's undersea world with glimpses of the astonishing richness of coastal and fjord submarine life. In summer a special bus (adult/child Nkr200/100 including admission) leaves from beside the town hall every half hour from around 10am to 4pm, Monday to Saturday.

Aalesunds Museum MUSEUM
(www.aalesunds.museum.no; Rasmus Rønnebergs gate 16; adult/child Nkr50/20; ☺9am-4pm Mon-Fri, 9am-3pm Sat, noon-4pm Sun mid-Jun–mid-Aug, shorter hr rest of yr) The town museum illustrates the history of sealing, fishing, shipping and industry in the Sunnmøre region, the fire of 1904, the Nazi WWII occupation and the town's distinctive art nouveau architecture.

Aksla VIEWPOINT
The 418 steps up Aksla hill lead to the splendid Kniven viewpoint over Ålesund and the surrounding mountains and islands. Follow Lihauggata from the pedestrian shopping street Kongensgata, pass the Rollon statue and begin the 15-minute puff to the top of the hill. There's also a road to the crest; take Røysegata east from the centre, then follow the Fjellstua signposts up the hill.

City Sightseeing Train TRAIN
(☎92 48 24 85; www.bytoget.no; adult/child Nkr150/70; ☺11am, 12.30pm, 2pm and 3.30pm) This toy sightseeing train does an hour-long circuit of the city, starting at St Olavs plass.

The commentary is reasonably informative and its major selling point is that it climbs the hill to the Aksla viewpoint with a 15-minute stop for photos.

🛏 Sleeping

TOP CHOICE Hotel Brosundet HOTEL €€
(☎70 11 45 00; www.brosundet.no; Apotekergata 5; s/d Nkr1390/1590, d with harbour view Nkr1890; P @) This boutique hotel, right on the waterfront, has oodles of charm. An ex-warehouse and protected building, it combines tradition with strictly contemporary comfort and style. Bedroom furnishings are of light pine, contrasting with the warm brown draperies and whitest of white sheets, while bathrooms, behind their smoked-glass walls, have the latest fittings. Original features (the wooden beams, for example) add character.

Clarion Collection Hotel Bryggen HOTEL €€
(☎70 10 33 00; www.choice.no; Apotekergata 1-3; s/d from Nkr880/1080; @) This wonderful waterfront option occupies a converted fish warehouse, artfully decorated with former tools and equipment. Rates include a light evening meal and free waffles throughout the day. There's a sauna, free to guests, too.

Rica Scandinavie Hotel HOTEL €€
(☎70 15 78 00; www.rica.no; Løvenvoldgata 8; d from Nkr875; P @) This fine place, Ålesund's oldest hotel, was the first to be constructed after the fire of 1904. With touches and flourishes of art nouveau (the furniture is original and in keeping with this theme, and even the lobby flat-screen TV seems to blend in) it exudes style and confidence.

Ålesund Vandrerhjem HOSTEL €
(☎70 11 58 30; www.hihostels.no; Parkgata 14; dm/s/d Nkr270/595/825; ☺year-round; @) This central, HI-affiliated hostel is in an attractive building (see the murals in the vast common room) that recently celebrated its first century. There are self-catering facilities and a heavy-duty washing machine.

🍴 Eating

TOP CHOICE Sjøbua SEAFOOD €€
(☎70 12 71 00; www.sjoebua.no; Brunholmgata 1a; mains Nkr298-356; ☺4pm-1am Mon-Fri) In a converted wharfside building with thick masonry walls skewered by stout beams and posts, atmospheric Sjøbua is one of northern Norway's finest fish restaurants. Choose

MOLDEJAZZ

Every year, Moldejazz pulls in up to 100,000 fans and a host of stars, mainly Scandinavian plus a sprinkling of international top liners. Molde, north-east of Ålesund, rocks all the way from Monday to Saturday in the middle of July. Of over 100 concerts, a good one-third are free, while big events are very reasonably priced at Nkr100 to Nkr350. For the low-down on this year's events, log onto www.moldejazz.no.

your crustacean, wriggling and fresh, from the lobster tank, or start with the sublime lobster-cream soup.

Maki   SEAFOOD €€€
(☑70 11 45 00; Apotekergata 5; mains Nkr275-329) The menu changes regularly at this ultracool restaurant in Hotel Brosundet. Sip a cocktail in its suave bar, then enjoy new takes on mussels, cod and other seafood dishes, presented to perfection.

Hummer & Kanari   BAR, RESTAURANT €
(www.hummerkanari.no; Kongensgata 19; dinner mains Nkr125-259; ⊙from 4pm Mon-Fri, from 2pm Sat & Sun) Behind the bar sit row upon row of liqueur and spirit bottles for mixers and shakers. Here at the downstairs bistro, you order at the counter. Upstairs, it's waiter service. But both call upon the same kitchen, which turns out ample portions of dishes such as *biffsnadder* (pan-fried slices of beef with vegetables and potatoes), fish burger and *kilippfisk* (cod with bacon).

Lyspunktet   CAFE, RESTAURANT €€
(www.lyspunktet.as; Kipervikgata 1; mains Nkr129-198; ⊙10am-10pm Tue-Fri, noon-5pm Sat & Sun) At this great-value, great-ambience, youthful place, loll back in its deep sofa. There are free refills for coffee and soft drinks, and dishes range from a fine fish soup through to pasta salad or teriyaki chicken. An excellent range of coffees rounds out a fine way to spend a couple of hours.

🔒 Shopping

Celsius   GLASS
(www.celsius-glass.com; Kaiser Wilhelmsgata 52; ⊙Tue-Sat) 'Luxury for everyday use' is the motto of this small glass studio, where each piece is designed to be stylish yet functional. The kiln is at the front, the shop at the rear.

They're hopefully back now from a sabbatical in Japan, so who knows what ideas they carried back with them.

Invit Interior   HOMEWARES
(☑70 15 66 44; Apotekergata 9; ⊙11am-4.25pm Tue-Sat) Appropriate for such a tasteful town, this shop-cum-gallery displays the very best of creative modern furniture and Scandinavian kitchenware and home appliances.

❶ Information

Tourist office (☑70 15 76 00; www.visitalesund-geiranger.com; Skaregata 1; ⊙8.30am-6pm Jun-Aug, 9am-4pm Mon-Fri Sep-May) Pick up the booklet *Along the Streets of Ålesund* (Nkr30), an excellent guide to the town's architectural highlights in a walking tour.

❶ Getting There & Away

Air
Ålesund has daily flights to Oslo, Bergen and Trondheim. Nettbuss airport buses (Nkr120, 20minutes) depart from Skateflukaia and the bus station approximately 90 minutes before the departure of domestic flights.

Boat
The *Hurtigruten* docks at Skansekaia Terminal.

Bus
There are buses to Bergen (Nkr639, 9¼ hours, one to three daily) and other destinations around the western fjord region.

Runde
POP 100

The squat island of Runde, 67km southwest of Ålesund, plays host to half a million seabirds of around 230 species, including 100,000 pairs of migrating puffins that arrive in April, breed and stay around until late July. There are also colonies of kittiwakes, gannets, fulmars, storm petrels, razor-billed auks, shags and guillemots, plus about 70 other species that nest here.

You'll see the best bird sites – as well as an offshore seal colony – on a **boat tour** (adult/child Nkr200/100). Three boats put out from Runde's small harbour, each two or three times daily.

Within the new **Runde Miljøsenter** (Runde Environmental Centre; ☑90 18 34 55; www.rundecentre.no; s/d Nkr1000/1500, 5-bed apt from Nkr2000; ℗), there's a seasonal **tourist office** (☑90 18 34 55; www.rundecentre.no; ⊙10am-6pm Jun-Aug, to 4pm May) and cafe.

Goksöyr Camping (☎70 08 59 05; www. goksoyr.no; per person/campsite Nkr20/120, 4-bed cabins Nkr540, 2-/4-bed cabin without bathroom Nkr280/450; ☺May-Sep) has a range of cabins and rooms around the camping ground itself, which is a fairly basic, waterside place.

NORTHERN NORWAY

With several vibrant cities and some wondrous natural terrain, you'll be mighty pleased with yourself for undertaking an exploration of this huge territory that spans the Arctic Circle. A vast plateau reaches across much of the interior, while small fishing villages cling to the incredibly steep and jagged Lofoten Islands, which erupt vertically out of the ocean. Medieval Trondheim, Norway's third-largest city, provides plenty of culture and charm, while Tromsø, the world's northernmost university town, parties year-round.

An alternative to land travel is the *Hurtigruten* coastal ferry, which pulls into every sizeable port, passing some of the best coastal scenery in Scandinavia. A good thing, too, since trains only run as far as Bodø.

Trondheim

POP 164,593

Trondheim, Norway's original capital, is Norway's third-largest city after Oslo and Bergen. With its wide streets and partly pedestrianised heart, it's an attractive city with a long history. Fuelled by a large student population, it buzzes with life. Cycles zip everywhere, it has some good cafes and restaurants, and it's rich in museums. You *can* absorb it in one busy day, but it merits more if you're to slip into its lifestyle.

Trondheim was founded at the estuary of the winding Nidelva in AD 997 by the Viking king Olav Tryggvason. After a fire razed most of the city in 1681, Trondheim was redesigned with wide streets and Renaissance flair by General Caspar de Cicignon. Today, the steeple of the medieval Nidaros Domkirke is still the highest point in the city centre.

◉ Sights

⬛ Nidaros Domkirke   CHURCH
(www.nidarosdomen.no; Kongsgårdsgata; adult/child/family Nkr60/30/150, tower Nkr30; ☺9am-

6pm Mon-Fri, to 2pm Sat, to 5pm Sun mid-Jun–mid-Aug, shorter hr rest of yr) Nidaros Cathedral is Scandinavia's largest medieval building. Outside, the ornately embellished west wall has top-to-bottom statues of biblical characters and Norwegian bishops and kings, sculpted in the early 20th century. Several are copies of medieval originals, housed nowadays in the museum.

The altar sits over the original grave of St Olav, the Viking king who replaced the Nordic pagan religion with Christianity. The original stone cathedral was built in 1153, when Norway became a separate archbishopric. The current transept and chapter house were constructed between 1130 and 1180 and reveal Anglo-Norman influences (many of the craftsmen were brought in from England), while the Gothic choir and ambulatory were completed in the early 14th century. The nave, repeatedly ravaged by fire across the centuries, is mostly a faithful 19th-century reconstruction.

Music lovers may want to time their visit to take in a recital on the church's magnificent organ.

From early June to early August, you can climb the cathedral's tower for a great view over the city. There are ascents every half-hour from its base in the south transept.

Archbishop's Palace   MUSEUM
(adult/child/family Nkr60/30/150, crown jewels Nkr85/40/200; ☺10am-5pm Mon-Fri, 10am-3pm Sat, noon-4pm Sun, shorter hr rest of yr) Beside the cathedral is the 12th-century archbishop's residence. It is Scandinavia's oldest secular building, commissioned around 1160. In its west wing, Norway's crown jewels shimmer and flash. Its museum is in the same compound. After visiting the well-displayed statues, gargoyles and carvings from the cathedral, drop to the lower level, where only a selection of the myriad artefacts revealed during the museum's construction in the

COMBINATION TICKET

If you're planning to visit all three sights within the Nidaros Domkirke complex, it's worth purchasing a combined ticket (adult/child/family Nkr120/60/300) that gives access to cathedral, palace museum and crown jewels.

Trondheim

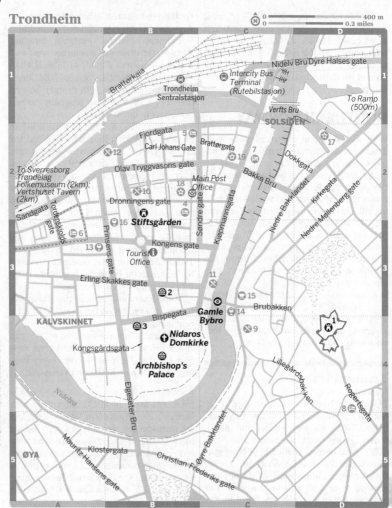

late 1990s are on show. Take in its enjoyable 15-minute audiovisual program.

Art Museums
GALLERY

The eclectic **Nordenfjeldske Kunstin-dustrimuseum** (Museum of Decorative Arts; Munkegata 5; adult/child Nkr60/30; ⊙10am-5pm Mon-Sat, noon-5pm Sun Jun–mid-Aug, shorter hr rest of yr) exhibits a fine collection of contemporary arts and crafts, including work by Hannah Ryggen, Norway's highly acclaimed tapestry artist. **Trondheim Kunstmuseum** (Bispegata 7b; adult/child Nkr50/30; ⊙9am-5pm mid-Jun–mid-Aug, 11am-4pm Tue-Sun rest of year)

has a corridor of Munch's lithographs and displays Norwegian and Danish art from 1850 onward.

Historic Buildings & Neighbourhoods
HISTORIC BUILDING

Scandinavia's largest wooden palace, the late-baroque **Stiftsgården** (Munkegata 23; adult/child Nkr60/30; ⊙10am-5pm Mon-Sat, noon-5pm Sun Jun-late Aug) was completed in 1778 and is now the official royal residence in Trondheim. Admission is by tour only, on the hour.

Trondheim

The picturesque old bridge **Gamle Bybro** originally dates from 1681, but the current wooden structure was built in 1861. From here, enjoy marvellous views over the **Bryggen**, an amazingly intact collection of tall red, yellow, green and orange 18th- and 19th-century warehouses reflected colourfully in the calm river.

On the east side of the bridge lies **Bakklandet**, a neighbourhood of cobblestone streets containing cafes and plenty of revived working-class residences from the 19th century.

Puff up the hill from this neighbourhood and there's a good view of the city from the top of the 17th-century **Kristiansten Fort** (Festningsgata; ⊙guided tours noon & 2pm daily Jun-Aug). Though its buildings open only during summer, the parklike grounds can be viewed year-round.

The **Sverresborg Trøndelag Folkemuseum** (www.sverresborg.no; Sverresborg Allé 13; adult/child incl guided tour Nkr100/45; ⊙11am-6pm Jun-Aug, 11am-3pm Mon-Fri, noon-4pm Sat & Sun rest of yr), set around the ruins of a medieval castle, is one of Norway's best open-air museums. Located on a hill with views over town, it displays more than 60 period buildings, including a small, 12th-century stave church (visit in winter to understand how cold, dark and miserable services must have been). Catch bus 8 or 9 from Dronningens gate.

Ringve Museum   MUSEUM
(www.ringve.no; Lade Allé 60; adult/child Nkr90/40; ⊙11am-4pm May-Aug) The Ringve Museum is a fascinating music-history museum set in an 18th-century manor. Music students give tours demonstrating the antique instruments on display on the hour. Take bus 3 or 4 from Munkegaten 3km northeast of the city centre.

A lavish **botanical garden** (Lade Allé 58; ⊙24hr) surrounds the estate, covering 14 hectares near Trondheimfjord.

🏃 Activities

West of town spreads the Bymarka, a gorgeous green woodland area laced with wilderness footpaths and ski trails. Take the Gråkallbanen tram, in itself a lovely scenic ride through the leafy suburbs, from the St Olavsgata stop to **Lian**. There you can enjoy excellent views over the city and a good swimming lake, **Lianvannet**. To the east of Trondheim, **Ladestien** (The Lade Trail) follows the shoreline of the Lade peninsula, beginning only 1km from the town centre.

The **Vassfjellet** mountains, south of town, offer both downhill and cross-country skiing. In season, a daily ski bus runs directly from Munkegata to the Vassfjellet Skisenter, only 8km beyond the city limits.

🎪 Festivals & Events

Kosmorama   FILM
(www.kosmorama.no) Trondheim's international film festival occupies an intensive week in late April.

Nidaros Blues Festival   MUSIC
(www.nidarosbluesfestival.com) In late April.

Olavsfestdagene   CITY
(www.olavsfestdagene.no) In honour of St Olav and held during the week around his saint's day, 29 July.

Trondelag Food Festival   FOOD

Coincides with or immediately follows Olavsfestdagene. Stalls selling local fare pack Kongens gate, east of Torvet.

UKA   CULTURE

(www.uka.no) Trondheim's 25,000 university students stage this three-week celebration, Norway's largest cultural festival. Every other year in October and November, it's a continuous party.

🛏 Sleeping

Pensjonat Jarlen   GUESTHOUSE €

(☑73 51 32 18; www.jarlen.no; Kongens gate 40; s/d Nkr540/690) Price, convenience and value for money are a winning combination here. After a recent overhaul, the rooms at this central spot are outstanding value, with a contemporary look (let down a little in some cases by the tired-looking bathrooms), some with polished floorboards, others carpet. Most have hotplates and a fridge thrown in.

Britannia Hotel   HOTEL €€

(☑73 80 08 00; www.britannia.no; Dronningens gate 5; r from Nkr1295; P❄@☀) This mastodon of a hotel with nearly 250 rooms was constructed in 1897. It exudes old-world grace from the mellow, wooden panelling of public areas to the magnificent oval Moorish-revival restaurant with its Corinthian pillars and central fountain.

Chesterfield Hotel   HOTEL €€

(☑73 50 37 50; www.bestwestern.no; Søndre gate 26; s/d from Nkr650/985; @) All 43 rooms at this venerable hotel are spacious. They were decorated and fundamentally renovated, with fresh beds and furniture, in 2006 following a major fire in the adjacent building. Those on the 7th (top) floor have huge skylights giving broad city views.

Radisson Blu Royal
Garden Hotel   HOTEL €€

(☑73 80 30 00; www.radissonblu.com; Kjøpmannsgata 73; s/d from Nkr795/995; P❄@☀) Opposite the Clarion, this first-class, contemporary riverside hotel (you can fish from your window in some rooms) is open and airy from the moment you step into the atrium, where the light streams in through its all-glass walls.

Singsaker Sommerhotel   HOTEL €

(☑73 89 31 00; http://sommerhotell.singsaker.no; Rogertsgata 1; dm NKR245, s/d Nkr598/798, s/d without bathroom Nkr475/649, ; ☺mid-Jun–mid-Aug; P) On a grassy knoll in a quiet residen-tial neighbourhood, this imposing building, usually a student hostel, was originally built as a club for occupying German officers. It represents great value. Bus 63 from the train station passes by.

Flakk Camping   CAMGROUND €

(☑72 84 39 00; www.flakk-camping.no; car/caravan site Nkr195/275, cabin without bathroom Nkr475-650; ☺May-Aug; P) Sitting right beside Trondheimfjord, this welcoming camping ground is about 10km from the city centre. Take Rv715 from Trondheim.

✗ Eating

🔝 Baklandet
Skydsstasjon   NORWEGIAN €€

(www.skydsstation.no; Øvre Bakklandet 33; mains Nkr130-255; ☺noon-1am) It began life as an 18th-century coaching inn and now contains several cosy rooms with poky angles and listing floors. It's a hyperfriendly place where you can tuck into tasty dishes, such as its renowned fish soup ('the best in all Norway,' a couple of diners assured us), shellfish salad, reindeer stew or oven-baked salmon.

Ravnkloa Fish Market   SEAFOOD €

(www.ravnkloa.no; Munkegata; snacks from Nkr45; ☺10am-5pm Mon-Fri, to 4pm Sat) You can munch on inexpensive fish cakes and other finny fare at this excellent, informal place, which also sells an impressive range of cheeses and other gourmet fare.

Havfruen   SEAFOOD €€€

(☑73 87 40 70; www.havfruen.no; Kjøpmannsgata 7; lunch mains from Nkr99, dinner mains Nkr279-299; ☺noon-midnight Mon-Sat) This charming riverside restaurant, all odd-angled pillars and rickety beams, specialises in the freshest of fish. The quality, reflected in the prices, is excellent, as are the accompanying wines, selected by the resident sommelier.

🖊 Ramp   BAR, RESTAURANT €

(Strandveien 25a; mains Nkr85-150; ☺noon-midnight) Well off the tourist route and patronised by in-the-know locals, friendly, alternative Ramp gets its raw materials, organic where possible, from local sources. It's renowned for its juicy house burgers filled with lamb, beef, fish or chickpeas.

Bari   CAFE, BAR €

(Munkegata 25; dishes around Nkr135) Eat in the stylish, modern, jazzy interior or choose the small streetside terrace. Bari has a reputation for, in particular, good Italian fare – pasta, superior burgers and bruschettas.

🍷 Drinking

As a student town, Trondheim offers lots of through-the-night life. The free paper *Natt & Dag* has listings, mostly in Norwegian. Solsiden (Sunnyside) is Trondheim's trendiest leisure zone. A whole wharfside of bars and restaurants nestle beneath smart new apartment blocks, converted warehouses and long-idle cranes.

TOP CHOICE **Den Gode Nabo**   PUB
(www.dengodenabo.com; Øvre Bakklandet 66; ⊙4pm-1.30am Sun-Fri, 1pm-1.30am Sat) The Good Neighbour, dark and cavernous within and nominated more than once as Norway's best pub, enjoys a prime riverside location. Indeed, part of it's on the water; reserve a table on the floating pontoon. There's a reproduction Wurlitzer jukebox, US visitors will find Sam Adams on draught while UK ale connoisseurs can savour Shepherd Neame's Bishop's Finger in the bottle.

Trondheim Microbryggeri   PUB
(Prinsens gate 39; ⊙5pm-midnight Mon, 3pm-2am Tue-Fri, noon-2am Sat) This splendid home-brew pub deserves a pilgrimage as reverential as anything accorded to St Olav from all committed øl (beer) quaffers. With up to eight of its own brews on tap and good light meals coming from the kitchen, it's a place to linger, nibble and tipple. It's down a short lane, just off Prinsens gate.

Bruk Bar   BAR
(Prinsens gate 19; ⊙11am-1.30am) Inside, a stuffed elk head gazes benignly down, candles flicker and designer lamps shed light onto the 30-somethings who patronise this welcoming joint. Outside there are leather sofas and a petrol bowser. The music is eclectic, varying at the whim of bar staff, but guaranteed loud.

Dromedar Kaffebar   CAFE
(Nedre Bakklandet 3; ⊙7am-6pm Mon-Fri, 10am-6pm Sat & Sun) The baristas of this cafe with outlets elsewhere in town have won the prize for Norway's best coffee in recent years. They do serve very good coffee indeed, in all sizes, squeezes and strengths. Inside is cramped so, if the weather permits, relax on the exterior terrace bordering the cobbled street. There's a second branch at Nødre

gate 2, similar in style, also with a streetside terrace.

☆ Entertainment

There's a cluster of nightclubs at the northern end of Nordre gate.

Dokkhuset   CONCERT VENUE
(www.dokkhuset.no; Dokkparken 4; ⊙11am-1am Mon-Thu, 11am-3am Fri & Sat, 1pm-1am Sun) In an artistically converted former pumping station (look through the glass beneath your feet at the old engines), the Dock House is at once auditorium (where if it's the right night you'll hear experimental jazz or chamber music), restaurant and cafe-bar. Sip a drink on the jetty or survey the Trondheim scene from its roof terrace.

Olavshallen   CONCERT VENUE
(☎73 99 40 50; www.olavshallen.no; Kjøpmannsgata 44) Trondheim's main concert hall is within the Olavskvartalet cultural centre. The home base of the Trondheim Symphony Orchestra, it also features international rock and jazz concerts, mostly between September and May.

Frakken   CLUB
(www.frakken.no; Dronningens gate 12; ⊙6pm-3am) This multistorey nightclub and piano bar features both Norwegian and foreign musicians and has live music nightly with karaoke thrown in Thursdays and Fridays.

ℹ️ Information

Tourist office (☎73 80 76 60; www.visittrondheim.no; Munkegata 19, Torvet; ⊙8.30am-7pm Jul, 9am-4pm Mon-Fri, 10am-2pm Sat rest of yr) The tourist office also runs two-hour guided walking/cycling tours (Nkr160/200) at 1pm from late June to mid-August.

ℹ️ Getting There & Away
Air
Værnes airport, 32km east of Trondheim, has both domestic and international flights.

NORWAY TRONDHEIM

MIDNIGHT SUN & POLAR NIGHT

Because earth is tilted on its axis, polar regions are constantly facing the sun at their respective summer solstices and are tilted away from it in the winter. The Arctic Circle, at N66° latitude, is the northern limit of constant daylight on its longest day of the year.

The northern half of mainland Norway, as well as Svalbard and Jan Mayen Island, lie north of the Arctic Circle but, even in southern Norway, the summer sun is never far below the horizon. Between late May and mid-August, nowhere in the country experiences true darkness. Conversely, winters here are dark, dreary and long, with only a few hours of twilight to break the long polar nights.

TOWN/AREA	LATITUDE	MIDNIGHT SUN	POLAR NIGHT
Bodø	67° 18'	4 Jun to 8 Jul	15 Dec to 28 Dec
Svolvær	68° 15'	28 May to 14 Jul	5 Dec to 7 Jan
Narvik	68° 26'	27 May to 15 Jul	4 Dec to 8 Jan
Tromsø	69° 42'	20 May to 22 Jul	25 Nov to 17 Jan
Alta	70° 00'	16 May to 26 Jul	24 Nov to 18 Jan
Hammerfest	70° 40'	16 May to 27 Jul	21 Nov to 21 Jan
Nordkapp	71° 11'	13 May to 29 Jul	18 Nov to 24 Jan
Longyearbyen	78° 12'	20 Apr to 21 Aug	26 Oct to 16 Feb

Boat

Trondheim is a major stop on the *Hurtigruten* coastal ferry route.

Bus

The intercity bus terminal (Rutebilstasjon) adjoins Trondheim Sentralstasjon (train station, also known as Trondheim S). Nor-Way Bussekspress services run at least daily to/from Ålesund (Nkr564, seven hours) via Molde (Nkr421, five hours) and Bergen (Nkr811, 14½ hours).

Train

There are two to four trains daily to/from Oslo (Nkr873, 6½ hours), while two head north to Bodø (Nkr1037, 9¾ hours).

ⓘ Getting Around

Flybussen (one-way/return Nkr120/190; 45 minutes) runs every 15 minutes from 4am to 9pm (less frequently at weekends), stopping at major landmarks such as the train station, Studentersamfundet and Britannia Hotel.

Trains run between Trondheim Sentralstasjon and the Værnes airport station (Nkr75, 35 minutes, hourly).

Bodø

TRANSPORT HUB / POP 37,834

Travellers generally use Bodø as a gateway to the Lofoten Islands. Most get off their boat or train, poke around for a few hours and then get on the first ferry. Those that linger tend to do so to behold Saltstraumen, one of the world's most impressive maelstroms.

The city's harbour is picturesque and chock-full of small fishing vessels, with steep granite islands rising behind. The town, hurriedly rebuilt after thorough destruction in WWII, is not. Even so, you'll find a passable cafe, a brewery and the closest thing to nightlife for hundreds of kilometres.

◉ Sights

Norsk Luftfartsmuseum   MUSEUM
(www.luftfart.museum.no; Olav V gata; adult/child Nkr110/55; ⊙10am-6pm mid-Jun–mid-Aug, 10am-4pm Mon-Fri, 11am-5pm Sat rest of yr) Norway's aviation museum is huge fun to ramble around if you have even a passing interest in flight and aviation history. Allow at least half a day to roam its 10,000 sq metres. Exhibits include a complete control tower, hands-on demonstrations and a simulator.

Nordlandmuseet   MUSEUM
(www.nordlandsmuseet.no; Prinsens gate 116; adult/child Nkr40/10; ⊙11am-6pm Mon-Fri, to 4pm Sat & Sun Jun-Aug, 9am-3pm Mon-Fri rest of yr) Recounting the short history of Bodø, this little gem of a museum has a cheerily entertaining and informative 25-minute film with English subtitles on the town's development.

🛏 Sleeping

Skagen Hotel   HOTEL €€
(☑75 51 91 00; www.skagen-hotel.no; Nyholmsgata 11; s/d from Nkr800/1000; @) Rooms here are attractively decorated in a vaguely antique style and are a continent away from chain-hotel clones. There's a bar and free afternoon waffles and coffee. Staff can also give advice on a whole raft of vigorous outdoor activities.

Clarion Collection Hotel Grand   HOTEL €€
(☑75 54 61 00; www.choice.no; Storgata 3; s/d from Nkr700/850; P@) With the Glasshuset shopping centre right beside it and the shortest of strolls from the quayside, the Grand is well positioned. All rooms were radically overhauled in 2009 and have parquet flooring, new bed linen and duvets, and freshly tiled bathrooms with large sinks.

Thon Hotel Nordlys   HOTEL €€
(☑75 53 19 00; www.thonhotels.no; Moloveien 14; s/d from Nkr795/995) Bodø's most stylish hotel, with touches of subtle Scandinavian design throughout, overlooks the marina and runs a reasonable restaurant.

🍴 Eating & Drinking

At the docks you can buy inexpensive fresh shrimp straight off the boat.

Bjørk   CAFE-BAR €€€
(www.restaurantbjork.no; Storgata 8, 1st fl, Glasshuset; lunch specials Nkr149-169, mains Nkr255-325) This pleasant place is a popular haunt, especially of Bodø's younger movers and shakers. It serves a variety of creative snacks, wood-fired pizzas, pasta, sushi and some local specialities such as grilled stockfish.

Løvolds   CAFE €
(www.lovold.no; Tollbugata 9; mains Nkr125-155; ⊙9am-6pm Mon-Fri, to 3pm Sat) This popular historic quayside cafeteria is Bodø's oldest eating choice. It offers sandwiches, grills and hearty Norwegian fare with quality quayside views at no extra charge.

ℹ Information

Tourist office (☑75 54 80 00; www.visitbodo.com; Tollbugata 13; ⊙9am-8pm Mon-Fri, 10am-6pm Sat, noon-8pm Sun mid-May–Aug, 9am-3.30pm Mon-Fri rest of yr)

ℹ Getting There & Around

AIR The airport is 2km away, with flights to Svolvær, Trondheim, Tromsø and more. Local buses (Nkr35) marked 'Sentrumsrunden' bring you to town.

BOAT Bodø is a stop on the *Hurtigruten* coastal-ferry route. Car ferries sail five to six times daily in summer (less frequently during the rest of the year) between Bodø and Moskenes in the Lofoten Islands (car ferries sail five to six times daily including driver/passenger Nkr558/156, 3½ hours). At least one calls in daily at the tiny southern Lofoten Islands of Røst and Værøy. Check www.thn.no for timetables and online bookings.

BUS Buses run to/from Narvik (Nkr575, 6½ hours) via Fauske (Nkr125, 1½ hours) twice daily.

TRAIN Bodø is the northern terminus of the Norwegian train network, with a service to Trondheim (Nkr399 to Nkr1037, 10 hours, twice daily).

Around Bodø

Sleepy **Kjerringøy** is 42km north of Bodø by the luminescent turquoise seas and soaring granite peaks. It's worth visiting for the timber-built 19th-century trading station, which is fantastically preserved as an **open-air museum** (☑75 50 35 05; www.nordlandsmuseet.no; adult/child Nkr90/45; ⊙11am-5pm late May-late Aug) set on a sleepy peninsula. Buses run from Bodø to Kjerringøy (Nkr95, 1½ hours, one daily). In summer it's possible to do a return trip on the same day.

The spectacular **Saltstraumen Maelstrom**, claimed to be the world's strongest, sufficiently boggles the mind (except on the rare off day when it appears about as powerful as a flushing toilet). At high tide 400 million cubic metres of water violently churns its whirlpool way through a 3km-long strait that empties one fjord into another. The spectacle occurs every six hours or so. Consult with the Bodø tourist office on when to arrive. Alternatively, if you read Norwegian, tide timetables are available at www.destinasjon-saltstraumen.com.

Narvik

POP 13,973

Narvik, whose waterfront is obliterated by a monstrous trans-shipment facility, is pincered by islands to the west and mountains in every other direction, while spectacular fjords stretch north and south.

◎ Sights

Ofoten Museum   MUSEUM
(Museum Nord; www.museumnord-narvik.no; Administrasjonsveien 3; adult/child Nkr50/free; ⊙10am-4.30pm Mon-Fri, noon-3pm Sat & Sun Jul-early Aug, 10am-3pm Mon-Fri rest of yr) This

engaging folk museum tells of Narvik's farming, fishing, railway-building and ore trans-shipment heritage.

Red Cross War Museum
MUSEUM

(Krigsminnemuseum; www.warmuseum.no; Kongens gate; adult/child Nkr75/25; ◷10am-9pm Mon-Sat, noon-6pm mid-Jun–mid-Aug, shorter hr rest of yr) This small but revealing museum illustrates the military campaigns fought hereabouts in the early years of WWII. The presentation may not be flash but it will still move you.

🏃 Activities

Narvikfjellet Cable Car
CABLE CAR

(www.narvikfjellet.no; Mårveien; adult one-way/return Nkr100/150, child free; ◷1-9pm or 1am Jun-Aug, shorter hr rest of yr) Climbing 656m above town, the cable car offers breathtaking views over the surrounding peaks and fjords – even as far as the Lofoten Islands on a clear day. Several marked walking trails radiate from its top station or you can bounce down a signed mountain-bike route. From February to April, it will whisk you up high for trail, off-piste and cross-country skiing with outstanding views.

Rallarveien
HIKING

This popular hike parallels the Ofotbanen railway, following the Rallarveien, an old navvy trail. Few walkers attempt the entire trail between Sweden's Abisko National Park and the sea, opting instead to begin at Riksgränsen, the small ski station just across the Swedish border, or Bjørnfell, the next station west. It's an undemanding descent as far as Katterat, from where you can take the evening train to Narvik.

🛌 Sleeping

TOP CHOICE Norumgården Bed & Breakfast
B&B €

(☎76 94 48 57; http://norumgaarden.narviknett.no; Framnesveien 127; s/d Nkr550/700, d with kitchen Nkr800; ◷late Jan-Nov) This little treasure of a place (it has only four rooms, so reservations are essential) offers excellent value. Used as a German officer's mess in WWII (the owner will proudly show you a 1940 bottle of Coca-Cola, made under licence in Hamburg), it nowadays brims with antiques and character.

Spor 1 Gjestegård
HOSTEL, GUESTHOUSE €

(☎76 94 60 20; www.spor1.no; dm Nkr300, s/d without bathroom Nkr500/600) This delightful place has the facilities of the best of hostels (especially the gleaming, well-equipped guest kitchen) and the comfort and taste of a guesthouse (bright, cheerful fabrics and decor, and soft duvets). Next door and run by the same family is a great pub open Tuesday to Saturday, and with an outdoor terrace.

Breidablikk Gjestehus
GUESTHOUSE €€

(☎76 94 14 18; www.breidablikk.no; Tore Hunds gate 41; dm Nkr350, s Nkr850-1150, d Nkr900-1350; P@) It's a steep but worthwhile walk from the centre to this pleasant hillside guesthouse with rooms for all budgets and sweeping views over town and fjord. There's a cosy communal lounge and it serves a delicious buffet breakfast.

🍴 Eating

Fiskehallen
CAFE €

(Kongens gate 42; mains Nkr99-199; ◷11am-4.30pm Mon-Fri) This tiny cafe, offshoot of the adjacent fish shop, offers tasty ready-to-eat dishes, such as fish cakes, bacalao-and-whale stew, to eat in or take away.

Kafferiet
NORWEGIAN €€

(Kongens Gate 44; lunch mains from Nkr99, dinner mains Nkr159-259; ◷10.30am-11pm) Just up the steps next to the long building that houses the Red Cross War Museum, this good choice makes a decent fish shop, including local dishes and the usual international staples. Most focus on fish and seafood, with grilled dried fish standing out amid the baguettes, salads and pasta dishes.

ℹ Information

Tourist office (☎76 96 56 00; www.destinationnarvik.com; ◷9am-7pm Mon-Fri, 10am-5.30pm Sat & Sun mid-Jun–mid-Aug, variable hr rest of yr)

ℹ Getting There & Away

AIR Nearly all flights leave from Harstad/Narvik Evenes airport, 1¼ hours away by road. Narvik's tiny Framneslia airport, about 3km west of the centre, serves only Bodø, Tromsø and Andenes.

BUS Express buses run northwards to Tromsø (Nkr345, 4¼ hours, three daily) and south to Bodø (Nkr308, 6½ hours, two daily). For the Lofoten Islands, two Lofotekspressen buses run daily between Narvik and Svolvær (Nkr250 to Nkr475, 4¼ hours) and continue to Å. Between late June and early September, bus 91 runs twice a day up the E10 to Riksgränsen (45 minutes) in Sweden and on to Abisko and Kiruna (three hours).

Around Narvik

The spectacular mountain-hugging **Ofotbanen railway** (☑76 92 31 21) trundles beside fjordside cliffs, birch forests and rocky plateaux as it climbs to the Swedish border. It was constructed by migrant labourers (navvies) at the end of the 19th century to connect Narvik with the iron-ore mines at Kiruna, in Sweden's far north. It was opened in 1903.

The train route from Narvik to Riksgränsen, the ski resort just inside Sweden (one way Nkr75 to Nkr125, one hour), features some 50 tunnels and snow sheds.

In Sweden, several long-distance trails radiate out from the railway, including the world-renowned Kungsleden, which heads south from Abisko into the heart of Sweden.

Lofoten Islands

You'll never forget your first approach to the Lofoten Islands by ferry. The islands spread their tall, craggy physique against the sky like some spiky sea dragon and you wonder how humans eked a living in such inhospitable surroundings.

The main islands, Austvågøy, Vestvågøy, Flakstadøy and Moskenesøy, are separated from the mainland by Vestfjorden. On each are sheltered bays, sheep pastures and picturesque villages. The vistas and the special quality of the Arctic light have long attracted artists, represented in galleries throughout the islands.

The four main islands are all linked by bridges or tunnels, with buses running the entire length of the Lofoten Islands road (E10) from Fiskebøl in the north to Å at road's end in the southwest.

Tourist information is available at www.lofoten.info.

SVOLVÆR
POP 4200

A compact town of old wooden buildings and modern concrete blocks, Lofoten Islands' principal town might be two notches less picturesque than its brothers, but it's still a pretty spot from which to base your explorations, with steep mountains rising sharply in the background and a busy harbour.

◉ Sights & Activities

Magic Ice   ICE BAR
(Fiskergata 36; adult/child Nkr100/70; ⊙noon-10.30pm mid-Jun–mid-Aug, 6-10pm rest of yr) Housed appropriately in what was once a fish-freezing plant, this is the ultimate place to chill out, perhaps with something to warm the spirit, served in an ice glass. The 500-sq-metre space is filled with huge ice sculptures, which illustrate life in the Lofoten Islands.

Hiking & Climbing   HIKING, CLIMBING
Daredevils like to scale **Svolværgeita** (the Svolvær Goat), a distinctive, two-pronged peak visible from the harbour, and then jump the 1.5m from one horn to the other – a graveyard at the bottom awaits those who miss. For phenomenal views, hikers can ascend the steep path to the base of the Goat and up the slopes behind it. There's also a rough route from the Goat over to the extraordinary **Devil's Gate**; ask the tourist office (p356) for details.

Trollfjord   CRUISE
(adult/child from Nkr500/200) From the port, several competing companies offer sailings into the constricted confines of nearby Trollfjord, spectacularly steep and narrowing to only 100m. Options range from speedboats to more leisurely cruises that may include the chance to dangle a line and bring home supper. Buy your ticket at the quayside.

Cycling   CYCLING
For 83km of breathtaking cycling, head to Holandshamn and make your way back to Svolvær along the **Kaiser Route**. Lonely shoreline, jagged mountains and abandoned farms will be your constant companion. Unlike the west side of The Lofoten Islands, this trip takes in parts of the islands that are largely undiscovered by tourists. A long stretch runs parallel to the Trollfjord.

⛏ Sleeping & Eating

⎣TOP⎤
⎣CHOICE⎦ **Svinøya Rorbuer**   CABIN €€
(☑76 06 99 30; www.svinoya.no; Gunnar Bergs vei 2; cabins & suites Nkr1550-3200) Across a bridge on the islet of Svinøya, site of Svolvær's first settlement, are several stunning cabins, some historic, most contemporary, and all cosy and comfortable. It also has other choices around the islands.

Svolvær Sjøhuscamp   SEA HOUSE €
(☑76 07 03 36; www.svolver-sjohuscamp.no; Parkgata 12; d/q from Nkr540/880, d with kitchen Nkr590, all without bathroom) This friendly sea house straddling the water is a convivial, excellent-value place to fetch up and meet fellow travellers. There's also a gem of an apartment with balcony and full facilities (Nkr1900) that sleeps up to six.

Lofoten Islands

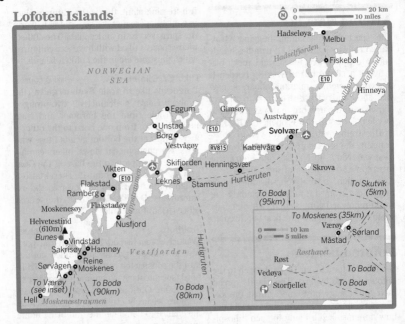

Rica Hotel Svolvær   HOTEL €€
(☑76 07 22 22; www.rica.no; Lamholmen; s/d from Nkr880/1010; ℗) The Rica is built on a tiny island, above the water and supported by piles. Some rooms have balconies, while room 121 has a hole in the floor so guests in the adjacent room can drop a fishing line directly into the briny. The restaurant has attractive lightweight wooden furnishings and does a gargantuan dinner buffet (Nkr350) in summer.

Lofoten Suite Hotel   HOTEL €€€
(☑47 67 01 00; www.lofoten-suitehotel.no; Havne-promenaden; ste from Nkr1500) Right on the main harbour in Svolvaer in a lovely wood-and-glass structure, this suites-only hotel has attractive modern rooms with wooden floorboards. Most rooms have fine harbour views and kitchenettes.

Norden & Du Verden   CAFE, RESTAURANT €€
(☑76 07 09 75; www.duverden.net; Havneprom-enaden; lunch buffet Nkr179, mains Nkr195-325, 2-/3-course set menu Nkr425/545; ⊙11am-11pm Mon-Sat) Sharing premises and kitchen, these two eateries complement each other. Norden, open daily, has an airy, modern interior and waterfront terrace. It's a very congenial cafe-restaurant serving lunches of salads and sandwiches, and dinner. To the rear, Du Verden offers fine gourmet dining in a more intimate ambience. Fish looms large on the menu and sushi is also possible.

Anker Brygge   NORWEGIAN €€€
(Kjøkkenet; ☑76 06 64 80; www.anker-brygge. no; Lamholmen; mains Nkr295-350) Originally a shack for salting fish and nowadays furnished like an old-time kitchen, this is a wonderfully cosy place to dine. The cuisine is just as traditional and the recommended menu choice is of course fish – try the kitchen's signature dish, *boknafisk* (semidried cod with salted fat and vegetables) or whole Arctic char.

ℹ Information

Tourist office (☑76 06 98 07; www.lofoten. info; Torget, Svolvær; ⊙9am-10pm Mon-Fri, to 8pm Sat, 10am-8pm Sun mid-June–mid-Aug, shorter hr rest of yr) Provides information on the entire archipelago.

ℹ Getting There & Away

AIR Svolvær has a small airport (4km from town) where you can catch flights to Bodø.

BOAT In addition to the *Hurtigruten* that connects Svolvaer and Bodø (sometimes in the wee small hours of the morning), there are the following services between the Lofoten Islands and the mainland:

» Bodø–Moskenes (adult/child/car/motorcycle Nkr166/84/604/274, 3½ to 4½ hours, one to

357

two daily) It's a two-hour drive from Moskenes to Svolvaer.

» Skutvik–Svolvaer (adult/child/car/motorcycle Nkr89/44/404/257, two hours, two to four daily)

BUS Buses to/from Vesterålen travel between Svolvær and Sortland (Nkr185, 2¼ hours, three to five daily). Buses to Leknes (Nkr147, 1½ hours, four to six daily) make connections to Å (Nkr265, 3½ hours, two to four daily), stopping at points west. Buses also run between Svolvær and Narvik (Nkr250 to Nkr475, 4¼ hours).

KABELVÅG

If you got off the boat and thought Svolvær's blend of traditional and modern wasn't cute enough, this pleasing village lies only 5km west and is connected by the E10 and a paved walking trail. Narrow channels lined with old warehouses lead to the circular cobbled *torget* (town square); its pattern of paving recalls the hulls of small fishing boats, themselves docked nearby.

⊙ Sights & Activities

Behind the old prison, a trail leads uphill to the **statue of King Øystein**, who in 1120 ordered the first *rorbu* (traditional seasonal house) to house fishermen who had been sleeping under their overturned rowing boats.

Some of these original *rorbuer* have been excavated as part of the **Lofotmuseet** (www. lofotmuseet.no; adult/child Nkr70/25; ⊙10am-6pm Jun-Aug, shorter hr rest of yr), a regional history museum on the site of the first town in the polar regions.

Nearby, the seafront **Lofoten Aquarium** (www.lofotakvariet.no; adult/child Nkr110/55; ⊙10am-6pm Jun-Aug, shorter hr rest of yr, closed Dec & Jan) shows you some of the personalities that have made the Lofoten Islands great, including the heroic cod and some harbour seals in an outdoor tank.

🛏 Sleeping & Eating

Kabelvåg Hotell   HOTEL €€
(☎76 07 88 00; www.kabelvaghotell.no; Kong Øysteinsgate 4; summer s/d Nkr795/1190; ⊙Jun–mid-Aug & late Feb-Apr) On a small rise close to the centre of Kabelvåg, this imposing seasonal hotel has been tastefully rebuilt in its original art deco style. Rooms overlook either the port or mountains. It also functions as a centre for skiing and a host of other winter activities.

Nyvågar Rorbuhotell   CABIN €€€
(☎76 06 97 00; www.nyvagar.no; Storvåganveien 22; 4-bed rorbu incl breakfast Nkr2100) At Storvågan,

below the museum complex, this snazzy, modern seaside place owes nothing to history, but its strictly contemporary *rorbuer* are attractive and fully equipped. Its acclaimed **Lorchstua restaurant** (mains Nkr175-375, 3-course menus Nkr425) serves primarily local specialities with a subtle twist, such as baked fillet of halibut in a cod brandade.

Ørsvågvær Camping   CAMPGROUND €
(☎76 07 81 80; www.orsvag.no; car/caravan sites Nkr160/200, 4-bed cabins Nkr900, 7-bed sea-house apt Nkr1250; ⊙May-Sep) Most *rorbuer* and the sea house here are right beside the fjord and offer splendid views.

Præstengbrygga   PUB, CAFE
(Torget; mains Nkr130-175) In central Kabelvåg, this friendly pub with all-wood interior and dockside terracing, front and rear, serves sandwiches, pizzas and tasty mains.

HENNINGSVÆR

A delightful 8km shoreside drive southwards from the E10 brings you to the still-active fishing village of Henningsvær, perched at the end of a thin promontory. Its nickname, 'the Venice of Lofoten', may be a tad overblown but it's certainly the lightest, brightest and trendiest place in the archipelago. It's also the region's largest and most active fishing port.

⊙ Sights & Activities

Ocean Sounds   WHALE CENTRE
(☎91 84 20 12; www.ocean-sounds.com; Hjellskjæret; adult/child Nkr200/free; ⊙2-6pm Jul–mid-Aug, by request mid-Apr–Jun & mid-Aug–Oct) Beside the Henningsvær Bryggehotel, this not-for-profit research centre has a series of multimedia presentations about cod, whales and other Arctic marine mammals. Or get out and about on a three- to four-hour marine safari in the Zodiac research boat (adult/child Nkr850/650, daily departures, weather permitting).

North Norwegian Climbing School   ROCK CLIMBING
(Nord Norsk Klatreskole; ☎90 57 42 08; www.nord norskklatreskole.no; Misværveien 10; ⊙Mar-Oct) This outfit offers a wide range of technical climbing and skiing courses all around northern Norway. Climbing the peaks with an experienced guide costs around Nkr2000, including equipment, for one to four people.

Lofoten Adventure   OUTDOORS
(☎90 58 14 75; www.lofoten-opplevelser.no; ⊙mid-Jun–mid-Aug) Based in Henningsvær, this

NORWAY LOFOTEN ISLANDS

outfit offers a cluster of maritime tours and activities including 1½-hour sea-eagle safaris (2.30pm, adult/child Nkr500/400), 2½-hour midnight safaris (10pm, Nkr750), three-hour whale safaris (on demand, November to mid-January, Nkr1350 to Nkr2100) and two-hour snorkelling activities including equipment (11am, Nkr750). Advance booking is essential.

Sleeping & Eating

Henningsvær Bryggehotel HOTEL €€€
(☑76 07 47 19; www.henningsvaer.no; Hjellskjæret; s/d from Nkr1070/1500) Overlooking the harbour, this attractive hotel is Henningsvær's finest choice. It's modern, with comfortable rooms furnished in contemporary design, yet constructed in a traditional style that blends harmoniously with its neighbours. Bluefish, its award-winning restaurant, is just as stylish; serving Arctic menu dishes and delicious desserts.

❶ Information
Tourist office (☑91 24 57 02; www.hennings-var.com; ☺10am-6pm Mon-Fri, 11am-4pm Sat & Sun mid-Jun–mid-Nov)

❶ Getting There & Away
In summer, bus 510 shuttles between Svolvær (40 minutes), Kabelvåg (35 minutes) and Henningsvær 10 times on weekdays (three services Saturday and Sunday).

LOFOTR VIKINGMUSEUM
This 83m-long chieftain's hall, Norway's largest Viking building, has been excavated at Borg, near the centre of Vestvågøy. The **museum** (www.lofotr.no; adult/child incl guided tour Nkr140/70; ☺10am-7pm Jun-Aug, shorter rest of yr) offers an insight into Viking life, complete with a scale-model reconstruction of the building, guides in Viking costume and a replica Viking ship, which you can sometimes help row.

The Svolvær–Leknes bus passes the museum's entrance.

STAMSUND
POP 1050
The traditional fishing village of Stamsund makes a fine destination largely because of its dockside hostel, a magnet for travellers who sometimes stay for weeks on end. Here, as elsewhere on the Lofoten Islands, highlights include hiking and fishing.

The wonderful old beach house **Justad Rorbuer og Vandrerhjem** (☑76 08 93 34; www.hihostels.no/stamsund; dm/s/d without bathroom Nkr150/350/470, 4-bed cabins Nkr550-900;

☺Mar–mid-Oct), 1.2km from the quay, attracts many repeat customers drawn by the waterside building, friendly manager (ask about hiking routes) and free loans of fishing gear and rowing boats. Bike rentals cost around Nkr100 per day.

The *Hurtigruten* coastal ferry stops en route between Bodø and Svolvær. In July and August buses from Leknes to Stamsund (25 minutes) run three to eight times daily.

REINE
Reine is a characterless place but gosh, it looks splendid from above, beside its placid lagoon and backed by the sheer rock face of Reinebringen. You get a great view from the head of the road that drops to the village from the E10.

From June to mid-August, **Aqua Lofoten** (www.aqualofoten.com; 3hr boat trip adult/child Nkr750/450) runs three-hour boat trips to the bird- and fish-rich Moskenesstraumen maelstrom.

In summer the **MS Fjordskyss** (www.reinefjorden.no) runs between Reine and Vindstad (adult/child return Nkr150/75, 25 minutes, three daily) through scenic Reinefjord. From Vindstad, it's a one-hour hike across the ridge to the abandoned beach-side settlement of **Bunes**, in the shadow of the brooding 610m **Helvetestind** rock slab.

Hamnøy Mat og Vinbu (☑76 09 21 45; Hamnøy; mains Nkr175-275; ☺May-early Sep) is a family-run place that serves stellar local specialities, including whale, bacalao and cod tongues. Grandmother takes care of the traditional dishes – just try her fish cakes – while her son is the main chef. Its fish is the freshest, bought daily from the harbour barely 100m away.

All buses from Leknes to Å stop in Reine.

SAKRISØY
Reine's rival for visual perfection, Sakrisøy is an incredibly charming and quiet village of ochre buildings set on some rocky outcroppings and surrounded by water, mountains and cod-drying racks. Here you can gawk at the scenery, grab a dockside fish cake, visit the **Museum of Dolls and Toys** (Dagmars Dukke og Leketøy Museum; www.lofoten.ws; adult/child Nkr60/30; ☺10am-6pm or 8pm mid-May-Aug, closed rest of yr), and sleep amid the postcard setting in a fine *robuer* at **Sakrisøy Rorbuer** (☑76 09 21 43; www.lofoten.ws; cabins Nkr800-1620).

Sakrisøy is 1km west of Reine towards Hamnøy.

Å

Å is a very special place at what feels like the end of the world on the western tip of the Lofoten Islands. A preserved fishing village perched on forbidding rocks connected by wooden footbridges, its shoreline is lined with red-painted *rorbuer,* many of which jut into the sea. Racks of drying cod and picture-postcard scenes occur at almost every turn. Visitors enliven the tiny place in summer, while in winter it's stark, haunting and empty.

Sights & Activities

Lofoten Tørrfiskmuseum　　MUSEUM
(adult/child Nkr50/40; ☺11am-4pm or 5pm Jun-Aug) The Lofoten Stockfish Museum is housed in a former fish warehouse. This personal collection, a passionate hobby of owner Steinar Larsen, illustrates the Lofoten Islands' traditional mainstay: the catching and drying of cod for export, particularly to Italy.

Norsk Fiskeværsmuseum　　MUSEUM
(adult/child Nkr60/30; ☺10am-6pm mid-Jun–mid-Aug, to 3.30pm Mon-Fri rest of yr) What is called collectively the Norwegian Fishing Village Museum is in fact a fair proportion of this hamlet: 14 of Å's 19th-century boathouses, storehouses, fishing cottages, farmhouses and commercial buildings.

Moskenesstraumen　　VIEWPOINT
Walk to the camping ground at the end of the village for a good hillside view of Værøy island, which lies on the other side of Moskenesstraumen, the swirling maelstrom that inspired the fictional tales of Jules Verne and Edgar Allen Poe.

Sleeping & Eating

Å-Hamna Rorbuer & Vandrerhjem　　HOSTEL €
(☎76 09 12 11; www.lofotenferie.com; hostel dm/s/d/tr Nkr200/230/420/600, 4–8-bed rorbuer Nkr900-1300) Sleep simple, sleep in more comfort; either way, this is an attractive choice. Newly affiliated to Hostelling International, it has dorms above the Stockfish Museum and in a quiet villa, set in its garden. For more space and privacy, choose one of the restored fishing huts.

Å Rorbuer　　HUT €€
(☎76 09 11 21; www.lofoten-rorbu.no; d Nkr750-1000, apt Nkr1600-1800) *Rorbuer* accommodation is dispersed throughout Å's historic buildings, the more expensive ones are fully equipped and furnished with antiques.

Brygga Restaurant　　SEAFOOD €€€
(☎76 09 11 21; lunch specials from Nkr129, mains Nkr175-325; ☺Jun-Sep) Hovering above the water, this is Å's one decent dining choice. The menu, as is right and proper in a village with such a strong fishing tradition, is mainly of things with fins.

❶ Getting There & Away

BOAT Car ferries sail five to six times daily in summer (less frequently during the rest of the year) between Moskenes (5km north of Å) and Bodø (adult/child/car/motorcycle Nkr166/84/604/274, 3½ to 4½ hours, one to two daily).

BUS Four to five buses connect Leknes and Å daily in summer, stopping in all major villages along the E10.

Vesterålen

Vesterålen is a group of islands to the north of the Lofoten Islands. Although the landscapes here aren't as dramatic, they tend to be much wilder and the forested mountainous regions of the island of Hinnøya are a unique corner of Norway's largely treeless northern coast.

Sights & Activities

Hurtigrutemuseet　　MUSEUM
(www.hurtigrutemuseet.no; Markedsgata 1; adult/child Nkr90/35; ☺10am-6pm mid-Jun–mid-Aug, shorter hr rest of yr) The *Hurtigruten* coastal ferry was founded in Stokmarknes in 1893 and the Hurtigruten Museum portrays the history of the line in text and image. Hitched to the quayside is the retired ship MS *Finnmarken,* claimed to be the world's largest museum piece, which plied the coastal route between 1956 and 1993.

Nyksund　　VILLAGE
(www.nyksund-info.com) Nyksund, on Langøya, is a former abandoned fishing village that's now re-emerging as an artists' colony. There's a great **walk** over the headland from Nyksund to Stø (three hours return), at the northernmost tip of Langøya.

FREE **Northern Lights Centre**　　EXHIBITION
(☺10am-6pm late Jun-late Aug) This impressive hi-tech aurora borealis exhibition in Andenes first featured at the 1994 Winter Olympics in Lillehammer.

Arctic Whale Tours　　WHALE WATCHING
(☎76 13 43 00; www.arcticwhaletours.com; adult/child Nkr870/550; ☺departures 9.30am & 4pm

mid-Jun–mid-Aug, 10.30pm Jul, 9.30am rest of season) From the small, distinctive fishing village of Stø on Langøya's northernmost tip, boats run from late May to mid-September for six-hour whale-watching cruises. On the way to the sperm whales' feeding grounds, boats pause to view seabird and seal colonies. If you don't see a whale or dolphin you get half your money back or a free second trip.

Whale Safari　　　　　　　　WHALE WATCHING
(☑76 11 56 00; www.whalesafari.no; Andenes; adult/child Nkr870/550) Far and away the island's biggest outfit, Whale Safari runs popular whale-watching cruises between late May and mid-September. It also operates the Whale Centre. Tours include a 1½- to four-hour boat trip and if you fail to sight at least one sperm whale, your money is refunded or you can take another trip for free. There's a good chance of spotting minke, pilot, humpback and killer whales (orcas).

Hvalsenteret　　　　　　　　MUSUEM
(Havnegate 1; adult/child Nkr60/30; ⊙8.30am-4pm or 8pm late May–mid-Sep) The Whale Centre in Andenes provides a perspective for whale watchers, with displays on whale research, hunting and the life cycle of these gentle monsters. Most people visit the centre in conjunction with a Whale Safari.

🛏 Sleeping & Eating

TOP
CHOICE **Hotell Marena**　　BOUTIQUE HOTEL €€
(☑91 58 35 17; www.hotellmarena.no; Storgata 15; s/d incl breakfast Nkr990/1250) Hotell Marena is an exciting and particularly tasteful recent addition to Andenes' accommodation choices. The 12 bedrooms have been individually designed with colours that match the tones of the blown-up photographs.

Sjøhus Senteret　　　GUESTHOUSE, CABIN €€
(☑76 12 37 40; www.lofoten-info.no/sjohussenteret; Ånstadsjøen; d/tr Nkr800/900, 3-/5-bed cabins Nkr1450/2200) Precisely 1.4km north of the bridge in Sortland, this appealing spot has both comfortable rooms and waterside cabins with views. Its **Sjøstua restaurant** (mains Nkr200-275; ⊙1-9.30pm Mon-Sat, to 8.30pm Sun) produces a delightful range of à la carte dishes.

Holmvik Brygge　　　GUESTHOUSE, CAFE €€
(☑76 13 47 96; www.nyksund.com; s/d Nkr500/850) This cosy, hugely welcoming guesthouse and cafe in itself justifies the detour. You can either cater for yourself or eat at its **Holmvik Stua** (lunch Nkr99-215, dinner Nkr175-375), where the food's locally sourced and the fish smoked on the premises.

ℹ Information

Andenes tourist office (☑76 14 12 03; www. andoyturist.no; Hamnegata 1; ⊙9am-6pm mid-Jun–Aug, 8am-3pm Mon-Fri rest of yr)

Sortland tourist office (☑76 11 14 80; www. visitvesteralen.com; Kjøpmannsgata 2; ⊙9am-5.30pm Mon-Fri, 10am-3.45pm Sat, noon-3.45pm Sun mid-Jun–mid-Aug, 9am-2.30pm Mon-Fri rest of yr) Covers the whole of the Vesterålen region.

ℹ Getting There & Away

Vesterålen is connected by ferry from Melbu on Hadseløya, to Fiskebøl on Austvågøy (Lofoten Islands). Sortland is the main transport hub in Vesterålen. Both Sortland and Stokmarknes are stops for the *Hurtigruten* coastal ferry.

Tromsø
POP 56,466

Simply put, Tromsø parties. By far the largest town in northern Norway and administrative centre of Troms county, it's lively with cultural bashes, buskers, an animated street scene, a midnight-sun marathon, a respected university, the hallowed Mack Brewery – and more pubs per capita than any other Norwegian town. Its corona of snow-topped peaks provides arresting scenery, excellent hiking in summer and great skiing and dog sledding in winter.

Although the city lies almost 400km north of the Arctic Circle, its climate is pleasantly moderated by the Gulf Stream. The long winter darkness is offset by round-the-clock activity during the perpetually bright days of summer.

◉ Sights

Tromsø's city centre and airport are on the island of Tromsøya, which is linked by bridges to overspill suburbs on both the mainland and the much larger outer island Kvaløya. Storgata is the principal drag.

Polaria　　　　　　　　　　EXHIBIT
(www.polaria.no; Hjalmar Johansens gate 12; adult/child Nkr120/60; ⊙10am-7pm mid-May–Aug, 11am-5pm Sep–mid-May) Daringly designed Polaria is an entertaining, informative, multimedia introduction to northern Norway and Svalbard. After a lush 14-minute film about

the latter or a nine-minute film on the aurora borealis (the two films alternate every 30 minutes), an Arctic walk leads to an aurora borealis display, aquariums of cold-water fish and – the big draw – a tank of energetic bearded seals.

Polar Museum   MUSEUM
(Polarmuseet; www.polarmuseum.no; Søndre Tollbodgata 11; adult/child Nkr50/25; ⊙10am-7pm mid-Jun–mid-Aug, 11am-4pm or 5pm rest of yr) The 1st floor of this harbourside museum, in a restored early-19th-century customs house, illustrates early polar research, especially the ventures of Nansen and Amundsen. Downstairs there's a well-mounted exhibition about the hunting and trapping of fuzzy Arctic creatures on Svalbard. Most labelling is in Norwegian only – the multilingual guides at the entrance fill in some of the gaps.

Ishavskatedralen   CHURCH
(Arctic Cathedral; www.ishavskatedralen.no; Hans Nilsensvei 41; adult/child Nkr35/free, organ recitals Nkr70-130; ⊙9am-7pm Mon-Sat, 1-7pm Sun) The 11 arching triangles of the Arctic Cathedral (1965), as the Tromsdalen Church is more usually called, suggest glacial crevasses and auroral curtains. The magnificent glowing stained-glass window that occupies almost the whole of the east end depicts Christ redescending to earth. Organ recitals take place at 11.30pm from June to mid-August as well as at 2pm in June and July. Take bus 20 or 24.

Tromsø University Museum   MUSEUM
(www.uit.no/tmu; Lars Thøringsvei 10; adult/child Nkr50/25; ⊙9am-6pm Jun-Aug, shorter hr rest of yr) Near the southern end of Tromsøya, this museum has well-presented displays on traditional and modern Sámi life, a relatively small section on the Vikings (who were of lesser importance in the history of northern Norway), geology and a number of thought-provoking themes (such as the role of fire, the consequences of global warming and loss of wilderness) with plenty of touch-screen involvement. Take bus 37.

Tromsø War Museum   MUSEUM
(www.tromsoforsvarsmuseum.no; Solstrandveien; adult/child Nkr50/25; ⊙noon-5pm Wed-Sun Jun-Aug, Sun only May & Sep) The cannons of a Nazi coastal artillery battery and a restored command bunker form the basis of the Tromsø Forsvarsmuseum. It also tells of the giant German battleship *Tirpitz*, sunk near the town on 12 November 1944, and the Nazi army's retreat from Leningrad, when many of its 120,000 troops were evacuated by ship from Tromsø. Take bus 12 or 28.

Mack Brewery   BREWERY
(Mack Ølbryggeri; ☑77 62 45 80; www.olhallen.no; Storgata 5) This venerable institution merits a pilgrimage. Established in 1877, it produces 18 kinds of beer, including the very quaffable Macks Pilsner, Isbjørn, Haakon and several dark beers. At 1pm year-round (plus 3pm June to August) tours (Nkr160, including a beer mug, pin and pint) leave from the brewery's own Ølhallen Pub, Monday to Thursday. It's wise to reserve in advance.

Fjellheisen   CABLE CAR
(www.fjellheisen.no; adult/child return Nkr130/50; ⊙10am-1am late May–July, to 10pm Aug, shorter hr rest of yr) For a fine view of the city and midnight sun, take the cable car to the top of Mt Storsteinen (421m). There's a restaurant at the top, from where a network of hiking routes radiates. Take bus 26.

Activities

In and around Tromsø (operators will normally collect you from your hotel) there's a whole range of robust activities in the winter twilight. You can experience the aurora borealis, go cross-country skiing and snowshoeing (including snowshoe safaris), reindeer- and dog sledding, and ice fishing.

To whet your winter appetite, check the tourist-office website and the following outfits:

Arctic Adventure Tours (www.arcticadventuretours.no)

Arctic Pathfinder (www.arcticpathfinder.no)

Natur i Nord (www.naturinord.no)

Tromsø Friluftsenter (www.tromso-friluftsenter.no)

Tromsø Villmarkssenter (www.villmarkssenter.no)

Festivals & Events

Northern Lights Festival   MUSIC
(www.nordlysfestivalen.no) Six days of music of all genres; late January.

Sámi Week   CULTURE
Includes the national reindeer-sledding championship, where skilled Sámi whoop and crack the whip along the main street; early February.

Midnight Sun Marathon
SPORT

(www.msm.no) The world's most northerly marathon, on a Saturday in June. In addition to the full-monty 42km, there's also a half-marathon and a children's race.

Insomnia Festival
MUSIC

(www.insomniafestival.no) A long, loud weekend of electronic music in October.

🛏 Sleeping

Tromsø's peak tourist time is June, when the university's still in full throe, summer tourism has begun and reservations are essential. Check out the homestay section of the tourist-office website for apartments and rooms in private homes.

⟨TOP CHOICE⟩ Rica Ishavshotel
HOTEL €€

(⟨☎⟩77 66 64 00; www.rica.no/ishavshotel; Fredrik Langes gate 2; s/d from Nkr995/1095; ⟨@⟩) Occupying a prime quayside position, this place is immediately recognisable by its tall spire resembling a ship's mast. It sometimes swallows as many as five tour groups per day, so summer reservations are advisable. Of its 180 attractive rooms, 74, including many singles, have superb views of the sound.

Ami Hotel
HOTEL €€

(⟨☎⟩77 62 10 00; www.amihotel.no; Skolegata 24; s/d Nkr700/870, without bathroom Nkr600/750; ⟨P⟩⟨@⟩) Beside a traffic-free road and park, this is a quiet, friendly, family-owned choice. There's a well-equipped kitchen for self-caterers and a couple of communal lounges, each with TV, internet access and free tea and coffee.

Clarion Hotel Bryggen
HOTEL €€

(⟨☎⟩77 78 11 00; www.nordicchoicehotels.no; Sjøgata 19/21; s/d from Nkr1070/1270; ⟨@⟩) This stylish 121-room waterside hotel, poking towards the sea like the prow of a ship, is architecturally stunning with its odd angles, aluminium trim, pictures on bedroom ceilings, sauna – and a top-floor spa where you can savour the picturesque harbour and mountain views as you bubble and boil in the hot tub. Its restaurant also has great fjord views.

Tromsø Camping
CAMPGROUND €

(⟨☎⟩77 63 80 37; www.tromsocamping.no; Tromsdalen; car/caravan site Nkr200/240, cabins Nkr450-1480; ⟨P⟩⟨@⟩) Tent campers enjoy leafy green campsites beside a slow-moving stream. However, bathroom and cooking facilities at this veritable village of cabins are stretched to the limit. Take bus 20 or 24.

Hotell Nord
HOTEL €

(⟨☎⟩77 68 31 59; www.hotellnord.no; Parkgata 4; s Nkr600-700, d Nkr650-850) This friendly place, up on the hillside just west of the centre, feels like an informal guesthouse. The cosy rooms are available with or without private bathroom, and rates include breakfast.

Radisson Blu Hotel Tromsø
HOTEL €€

(⟨☎⟩77 60 00 00; www.radissonblu.com; Sjøgata 7; s/d Nkr996/11156 mid-Jun–mid-Aug, prices vary rest of yr) Bedrooms have been comprehensively renovated and onto the solid, dull rectangular block of the original building has been grafted an attractive new wing. Of its 269 rooms (it's worth the Nkr100 extra for one in the new wing), around half have harbour views.

🍴 Eating

In Tromsø, the line is blurry between restaurants, cafes and pubs and many places function in all three modes, simultaneously or at different times of the day.

⟨TOP CHOICE⟩ Emma's Under
NORWEGIAN €€

(⟨☎⟩77 63 77 30; www.emmas.as; lunch mains Nkr139-245, dinner mains Nkr325-365; ⟨⊙⟩11am-midnight Mon-Fri, noon-midnight Sat) Intimate and sophisticated, Emma's Under is one of the most popular lunch spots in Tromsø, where mains often include northern Norwegian staples such as reindeer fillet, whale steak, lamb and stockfish. Upstairs is the more formal Emma's Drømekjøkken (⟨☎⟩77 63 77 30; mains Nkr325-365; ⟨⊙⟩6pm-midnight Mon-Sat), a highly regarded gourmet restaurant where advance booking is essential.

Aunegården
NORWEGIAN €€

(⟨☎⟩77 65 12 34; www.aunegarden.no; Sjøgata 29; lunch mains Nkr104-184, dinner mains Nkr248-295; ⟨⊙⟩11.30am-10pm Mon-Sat) You can almost lose yourself in this wonderful cafe-cum-restaurant that's all intimate crannies and cubbyholes. In a 19th-century building that functioned as a butcher's shop until 1996, it's rich in character and serves excellent salads, sandwiches and mains such as reindeer or wild boar.

Fiskekompaniet
SEAFOOD €€

(⟨☎⟩77 68 76 00; www.fiskekompani.no; Killengrens gate; lunch mains Nkr165-235, dinner mains Nkr296-495; ⟨⊙⟩noon-11pm) This classy and long-standing Tromsø fish-and-seafood favourite occupies a prime portside site. All dishes, subtly prepared and enhanced, are from the ocean and there are plenty of good wines to choose from.

Brasseriet
NORWEGIAN €€€

(☑77 66 64 00; mains Nkr210-375) Rica Ishavshotel's excellent restaurant serves creative dishes, such as fried fillet of reindeer with forest-mushroom sauce and lingonberries or saffron poached cod.

Driv
CAFE, RESTAURANT €

(www.driv.no; Tollbodgata 3; mains around Nkr129; ☺noon-6pm mid-Jun–mid-Aug, 2pm-2am rest of yr) This student-run converted warehouse serves meaty burgers, great salads, focaccias and pasta. It organises musical and cultural events. In winter you can steep yourself in good company within its open-air hot tub.

🍸 Drinking & Entertainment

Tromsø enjoys a thriving nightlife, with many arguing that it's the best scene in Norway. On Friday and Saturday, most nightspots stay open to 3.30am.

Ølhallen Pub
PUB

(☺9am-6pm Mon-Sat) At Mack Brewery's Ølhallen Pub you can sample its fine ales right where they're brewed. Perhaps the world's only, never mind most northerly, watering hole to be closed in the evening, it carries eight varieties on draught.

Verdensteatret
CAFE

(Storgata 93b; ☺11am-2am Mon-Thu, to 3.30am Fri & Sat, 1pm-2am Sun; 🛜) Norway's oldest film house will satisfy both cinephiles and drinkers after great cafes. The bar is a hip place with free wi-fi and weekend DJs. At other times, the bartender spins from a huge collection of vinyl records, so expect anything from classical to deepest underground. There are also bar snacks, Mack beers, great coffee and Spanish wines on the menu. Ask staff to let you peek into the magnificent cinema, its walls painted roof to ceiling with early-20th-century murals.

Blå Rock Café
BAR, LIVE MUSIC

(www.blarock.no; Strandgata 14/16; ☺11.30am-2am) The loudest, most raving place in town has theme evenings, almost 50 brands of beer, occasional live bands and weekend DJs. The music's rock, naturally. Every Monday hour is a happy hour.

Bastard
SPORTS BAR, LIVE MUSIC

(Strandgata 22; ☺8pm-2am Mon-Sat, 3-11pm Sun) Bastard (with the stress on the second syllable...) is a cool basement hang-out with low beams and white, furry walls. It engages art-house and underground DJs (Friday and Saturday) and bands (up to three times weekly). This sports bar carries UK and Norwegian football, so it also has a faithful following of armchair sporting regulars.

ℹ️ Information

Tourist office (☑77 61 00 00; www.visit-tromso.no; Kirkegata 2; ☺9am-7pm Mon-Fri, 10am-6pm Sat & Sun)

ℹ️ Getting There & Away

AIR Destinations with direct SAS flights to/from **Tromsø Airport** (☑77 64 84 00), the main airport for the far north, include Oslo, Narvik/Harstad, Bodø, Trondheim, Alta, Hammerfest, Kirkenes and Longyearbyen. **Norwegian** (www.norwegian.no) flies to and from London (Gatwick), Edinburgh, Dublin and Oslo.

BOAT Express boats connect Tromsø and Harstad (2½ hours), via Finnsnes (1¼ hours), two to four times daily. Tromsø is also a major stop on the *Hurtigruten* coastal ferry route.

BUS The main bus terminal (sometimes called Prostneset) is on Kaigata, beside the *Hurtigruten* quay. There are at least two daily express buses to/from Narvik (Nkr445, 4¼ hours) and one to/from Alta (Nkr535, 6½ hours).

ℹ️ Getting Around

AIR Tromsø's airport is about 5km from the centre, on the western side of Tromsøya island. Flybuss (adult/child Nkr60/30, 15 minutes) runs between the airport and Rica Ishavshotel, connecting with arriving and departing flights. Alternatively, take city bus 40 or 42 (Nkr28); when you arrive, wait for it on the road opposite the airport entrance.

BUS Local buses cost Nkr28 per ride; purchase your ticket on board.

TAXI Call ☑77 60 30 00.

FINNMARK

All along Norway's jagged northern coast, deeply cut by forbidding fjords, you'll find numerous isolated fishing villages, as well as some of the north's star attractions: Alta with its Stone Age rock carvings; Kirkenes, a frontierlike town sharing a border with Russia; and Nordkapp, reportedly but not quite mainland Europe's northernmost point.

Those who head inland will find the vast and empty Finnmarksvidda Plateau, a stark expanse with only two major settlements: Karasjok and Kautokeino. They and

SENJA

Senja, Norway's second-largest island, rivals the Lofoten Islands for natural beauty yet attracts a fraction of its visitors (we meandered the length of its northern coastline and saw only two non-Norwegian vehicles).

A broad agricultural plain laps at Innersida, the island's eastern coast facing the mainland. By contrast, birchwoods, moorland and sweet-water lakes extend beneath the bare craggy uplands of the interior. Along the northwestern coast, Yttersida, knife-ridged peaks rise directly from the Arctic Ocean. Here, the Rv86 and Rv862, declared a National Tourist Route, link isolated, still-active fishing villages such as Hamn and Mefjordvær, and traffic is minimal. The at-times-flat, then mildly bucking road, almost always within sight of the shore, is a cyclist's dream. On the way, pause at the **Tungeneset viewing point** and scramble over broad slabs of weathered rock to savour the spiky peaks to the west and, eastwards, more gently sculpted crests.

Finnmarksvidda are part of the heartland of the Sámi people, where reindeer herding has occurred for centuries. At either, enjoy a dog-sled journey across empty tundra half lit under the bruise blue winter sky.

One good source of information about the region is www.nordnorge.com.

Alta

POP 14,308

Although the fishing and slate-quarrying town of Alta lies at latitude N70°, it enjoys a relatively mild climate. The Alta Museum, with its ancient petroglyphs, is a must-see and the lush green Sautso-Alta Canyon, a quick hop away, is simply breathtaking.

◎ Sights

Alta Museum   MUSEUM
(www.alta.museum.no; Altaveien 19; adult/child Nkr90/20; ⊙8am-8pm mid-June–late Aug, shorter hr rest of yr) This superb award-winning museum in Hjemmeluft, at the western end of town, features exhibits and displays on Sámi culture, Finnmark military history, the Alta hydroelectric project and the aurora borealis. The rocks around it, a Unesco World Heritage Site, are incised with around 6000 late–Stone Age carvings, dating from 6000 to 2000 years ago. Themes include hunting scenes, fertility symbols, bear, moose, reindeer and crowded boats. It's a fascinating collection and the 3km loop around the carvings takes a maximum of 1½ hours. In winter the rock art is often buried under snow, but the museum remains open.

Northern Lights Cathedral   CHURCH
(Løkkeveien) Under construction when we visited, the daringly designed Northern Lights Cathedral, next to the Rica Hotel Alta, promises to be one of the architectural icons of the north, its swirling pyramid structure a rival to Tromsø's Ishavskatedralen (Arctic Cathedral; see p361).

☞ Tours

The Altaelva hydroelectric project has had very little effect on the most scenic stretch of river, which slides through 400m-deep **Sautso**, northern Europe's grandest canyon. The easiest way to see this impressive forested gorge is to take the 3½-hour tour (adult/child Nkr575/300) that the tourist office organises each Monday, Wednesday and Friday in July, leaving at 4pm, numbers permitting (minimum six people). Riverboat safaris are also possible; ask at the tourist office or Sorrisniva Igloo Hotel.

Alta is also renowned for its **salmon run**; several local companies organise fishing tours.

⊨ Sleeping & Eating

TOP
CHOICE⟩ **Rica Hotel Alta**   HOTEL €€€
(☑78 48 27 00; www.rica.no; Løkkeveien 61; s/d from Nkr910/1010) Alta's classiest hotel has attractive rooms – the massive photos of the aurora borealis are a lovely touch – and excellent service. Ask for a room overlooking the Northern Lights Cathedral. In the heart of town, it also has a bar and a fantastic restaurant (mains from Nkr265) serving up Arctic specialities such as reindeer or king crab,

with salmon and Arctic char also likely to feature.

Thon Hotel Vica
HOTEL €€

(☑78 48 22 22; www.thonhotels.no/Vica; Fogde-bakken 6; ⊙s/d from Nkr995/1095; 🅿@) In a timber-built former farmhouse, the Vica beckons you in. Until recently a family-run concern but now assimilated into the Thon chain, it has, at least for the moment, preserved its originality. There's a sauna (Nkr100) and a steaming outdoor hot tub (wonderful in winter when all around is snowcapped). It also has a terrific restaurant, Haldde (lunch Nkr100-200, dinner mains Nkr250-360), that relies almost entirely upon local ingredients in the preparation of choice dishes such as the Finnmark Platter of grouse, reindeer and elk, or its Flavour of Finnmark dessert of cloudberries and cowberry-blueberry sorbet within a nest of spun caramel.

Sorrisniva Igloo Hotel
HOTEL €€€

(☑78 43 33 78; www.sorrisniva.no; B&B s/d Nkr2450/4300; ⊙mid-Jan–mid-Apr; 🅿) Its 30 bedrooms – and beds too – are made entirely of ice, as are the chapel, bridal suite and stunning ice bar with its weird-and-wonderful sculptures lit by fibre optics. Then again, you might just want to drop by and visit (adult/child Nkr150/75).

Bårstua Gjestehus
GUESTHOUSE €€

(☑78 43 33 33; www.baarstua.no; Kongleveien 2a; s/d incl breakfast from Nkr630/830) This friendly B&B is set back from the E6. Its eight rooms, decorated with striking photographs, are spruce and well furnished. Each has self-catering facilities.

Alfa-Omega
CAFE, BAR €€

(Markedsgata 14-16; mains Nkr120-280; ⊙8am-10pm Mon-Sat) As its name suggests, this place has two parts: Omega, its contemporary cafe, open 11am to midnight, serves salads, sandwiches, pastas and cakes, not to mention a mean reindeer-steak sandwich. There's also a terrace, ideal for taking a little summer sunshine, overlooking Alta's bleak central square.

❶ Information

Tourist office (www.altatours.no; ⊙9am-8pm Jun-Aug, to 3.30pm Mon-Sat rest of yr) Alta's tourist office is looking for a home; ask at your hotel for its latest location.

❶ Getting There & Away

AIR The **airport** (☑78 44 95 55) is 4km east of the centre; follow the E6. Norwegian and SAS service Alta airport. Destinations include Oslo, Tromsø, Hammerfest, Lakselv and Vadsø.

BUS Buses run between Alta and Tromsø (Nkr535, 6½ hours, one daily), Kautokeino (Nkr250, 2¼ hours, daily except Saturday), Karasjok (Nkr430, 4¾ hours, two daily except Saturday), Honninsvåg (Nkr430, four hours, one daily) and Hammerfest (Nkr275, 2¼ hours, two daily).

Hammerfest
POP 7121

Most visitors to Hammerfest arrive by the *Hurtigruten* and have an hour or two to poke around. Unless you have unusual interests, that's about as much time as you'll need. The fishing town's oddest experience can be found at the Royal and Ancient Polar Bear Society.

Purporting to be Norway's northernmost town (other settlements lie further north, but they are too small to qualify as towns), Hammerfest has suffered as much as the walrus in the Polar Bear Society: a gale decimated it in 1856, a fire totalled it in 1890 and the Nazis burnt it again in 1944, after which it was rebuilt in the 'Finnmark Ugly' style. At night, an awe-inspiring fire from a nearby gas plant casts the place in an eerie red glow.

◉ Sights & Activities

Gjenreisningsmuseet
MUSEUM

(www.gjenreisningsmuseet.no; Kirkegata 21; adult/child Nkr50/free; ⊙10am-4pm mid-Jun–mid-Aug, 11am-2pm rest of yr) Hammerfest's Reconstruction Museum recounts the forced evacuation and decimation of the town during the Nazi retreat in 1944; the hardships that its citizens endured through the following winter; and Hammerfest's postwar reconstruction and regeneration.

Salen Hill
VIEWPOINT

For panoramic views over the town, coast and mountains, climb Salen Hill (86m), topped by the Turistua restaurant, a couple of Sámi turf huts and a lookout point. The 15-minute uphill walking trail begins at the small park behind the Rådhus.

FREE Royal & Ancient
Polar Bear Society MUSEUM
(www.isbjornklubben.no; ⊙6am-6pm Mon-Fri, to
4pm Sat & Sun Jun & Jul, 9am-4pm Mon-Fri, 10am-
2pm Sat & Sun Aug-May) Dedicated to preserving Hammerfest culture, the Royal and Ancient Polar Bear Society features exhibits on
Arctic hunting and local history, and shares
premises with the tourist office. The place
is, it must be said, a bit of a come-on. For
Nkr180, you can become a life member and
get a certificate, ID card, sticker and pin. For
a little more, you also receive a schnapps
glass and, as the demure young receptionist
will explain without blanching, get dubbed
with the bone from a walrus' penis. It's well
worth the extra for the conversation this
unique honour will generate down the pub,
once you're home.

⎍ Sleeping & Eating

Rica Hotel Hammerfest HOTEL €€
(☑78 42 57 00; www.rica.no; Sørøygata 15; s/d from
Nkr950/1200; P@) Constructed in agreeable
mellow brick, this hotel has an attractive bar
and lounge and well-furnished rooms, most
with harbour views. Its restaurant serves excellent local fare.

Camping Storvannet CAMPGROUND €
(☑78 41 10 10; storvannet@yahoo.no; Storvanns-
veien; car/caravan sites Nkr175/185, 2-/4-bed cabin
Nkr400/450; ⊙Jun-Sep) Beside a lake and
overlooked by a giant apartment complex,
this pleasant site, Hammerfest's only decent
camping option, is small, so do book your
cabin in advance.

Redrum CAFE, BAR €
(www.redrum.no; Storgata 23; snacks Nkr80-175;
⊙11am-5pm Mon-Thu, to 3am Fri-Sat) With its attractive contemporary decor and flickering
candles, Redrum saves its energy for weekend wildness, when there's regular live music. To the rear, there's a deep, more relaxed
wooden patio.

Qa Spiseri CAFE €
(Sjøgata 8; mains Nkr120-160; ⊙10am-5pm Mon-
Sat) Just off Sjøgata and run by a young
team, this popular place offers reliable cuisine with a great price-to-quality ratio with
a choice of Norwegian, Italian and Thai
dishes.

ⓘ Information

Tourist office (www.hammerfest-turist.no;
Hamnegata 3; ⊙6am-6pm Mon-Fri, to 4pm Sat
& Sun Jun-Jul, 9am-4pm Mon-Fri, 10am-2pm
Sat & Sun Aug-May)

ⓘ Getting There & Away

BOAT The *Hurtigruten* coastal ferry stops in
Hammerfest for 1½ hours in each direction. A
Hurtigruten hop to Tromsø (11 hours) or Honningsvåg (five hours) makes a comfortable alternative to a long bus journey.

BUS Buses run to/from Alta (Nkr275, 2¼ hours,
two daily), Honningsvåg (Nkr420, 3½ hours, one
to two daily) and Karasjok (Nkr395, 4¼ hours,
twice daily except Saturday), with one service
extending to Kirkenes (Nkr998, 10¼ hours)
via Tana Bru (Nkr715, eight hours) four times
weekly.

Nordkapp

POP 3000

Nordkapp is the one attraction in northern
Norway that everyone seems to visit even
if it is a tourist trap. Billing itself as the
northernmost point in continental Europe,
it sucks in visitors by the busload, some
200,000 every year. But it's the view that
thrills the most. In reasonable weather –
which is a lot of the time – you can gaze
down at the wild surf 307m below and
watch the mists roll in.

Nearer to the North Pole than to Oslo,
Nordkapp sits at latitude N71° 10' 21", where
the sun never drops below the horizon from
mid-May to the end of July. Long before
other Europeans took an interest, it was a
sacrificial site for the Sámi, who believed it
had special powers.

To reach the tip of the continent, by car,
by bike, on a bus or walking in, you have to
pay a toll (adult/child Nkr235/80).

Astoundingly, you can spend the night
in your own motor home or caravan at Nordkapp itself (fill up on water and electricity
though, because you won't find any there
for the taking).

The closest town of any size is **Honningsvåg**, 35km from Nordkapp.

⎍ Sleeping

All of the following hotels and hostels are in
Honningsvåg.

Northcape Guesthouse HOSTEL €
(☑47 25 50 63; www.northcapeguesthouse.com;
Elvebakken 5a, Honningsvåg; dm Nkr250, s/d/f
without bathroom Nkr550/700/1200; ⊙May-Aug;
P) A 1km walk from the *Hurtigruten* quay,
this bright, modern hostel is an excellent

budget choice. There's a cosy lounge, washing machine, a well-equipped kitchen for self-caterers and great views over the town below. It's often full so do reserve well in advance.

Rica Hotel Honningsvåg   HOTEL €€€
(☑78 47 72 20; www.rica.no; Nordkappgata 4; r from Nkr1195; [P]) An excellent hotel, the Rica maintains the high standards we've come to expect from this chain, with modern, comfortable rooms and good restaurants.

Nordkapp Vandrerhjem   HOSTEL €
(☑91 82 41 56; www.hihostels.no/nordkapp; Kobbhullveien 10, Honningsvåg; dm incl breakfast Nkr330, s/d Nkr450/760; [@]) A 156-bed HI hostel.

❶ Information

Tourist office (☑78 47 70 30; www.nordkapp. no; Fiskeriveien 4, Honningsvåg; ☉10am-10pm Mon-Fri, noon-8pm Sat & Sun mid-Jun–mid-Aug, 8.30am-4pm Mon-Fri rest of yr) In Honningsvåg.

❶ Getting There & Away

The *Hurtigruten* stops in Honningsvåg. Northbound ships stop for 3½ hours, long enough for the ship to offer its passengers a Nordkapp tour (around Nkr750 per person).

Buses for Honningsvåg run to/from Alta (Nkr430, four hours, one daily) and Hammerfest (Nkr420, 3¼ hours, one to two daily).

WORTH A TRIP

KNIVSKJELODDEN

Now here's a secret: Nordkapp isn't continental Europe's northernmost point. That award belongs to Knivskjelodden, an 18km round-trip hike away, less dramatic, inaccessible by vehicle – and to be treasured all the more for that. Lying about 3km west of Nordkapp, it sticks its finger a full 1457m further northwards. You can hike to the tip of this promontory from a marked car park 6km south of the Nordkapp toll booth. The 9km track, waymarked with giant cairns, isn't difficult despite some ups and downs, but it's best to wear hiking boots since it can be squelchy. When you get to the tall beehive-shaped obelisk at latitude N71° 11' 08", down at sea level, sign the guestbook. Allow five to six hours for the round trip.

❶ Getting Around

Between mid-May and late August, a local bus (adult/child Nkr100/50, 45 minutes) runs daily at 11am and 9.30pm between Honningsvåg and Nordkapp. It sets off back from the cape at 1.15pm and 12.45am (so that you can take in the midnight sun at precisely midnight). From 1 June to 15 August, there's a supplementary run at 5pm, though this returns at 6.15pm, giving you barely half an hour at Nordkapp unless you want to hang around for the service that returns at 12.45am. Check the departure times at Honningsvåg tourist office.

Kirkenes

POP 3440

This is it: you're as far east as Cairo, further east than most of Finland, a mere 15km from the border with Russia – and at the end of the line for the *Hurtigruten* coastal ferry. This tiny, nondescript place, anticlimactic for many, has a distinct frontier feel. You'll see street signs in Norwegian and Cyrillic script and hear Russian spoken by trans-border visitors and fishers.

The town reels with around 100,000 visitors every year, most stepping off the *Hurtigruten* to spend a couple of hours in the town before travelling onward. But you should linger a while here, not primarily for the town's sake but to take one of the many excursions and activities on offer.

🏃 Activities

For such a small place, Kirkenes offers a wealth of tours and activities in and around town. For an overview according to season, pick up one of the tourist office's comprehensive brochures, *Summer Activities* and *Winter Activities*.

There's also a summertime **reservation point** (☑48 18 97 97; www.incomingkirkenes.no; ☉10am-3pm Jun-Aug) in the lobby of the Rica Hotel. Otherwise, book through the tourist office, at most hotels or directly with tour operators.

King-crab safaris (adult/child Nkr1490/745) run year-round. Summer activities include half-day tours of the Pasvik Valley (adult/child Nkr790/495). You can also visit the Russian border and iron-ore mines (adult/child Nkr500/250) or take a boat trip along the Pasvik River, which demarcates the Norwegian–Russian border (adult/child Nkr1150/575).

For some winter fun, take a snowmobile safari (from Nkr1390) or a snowshoe walk

WORTH A TRIP

STABBURSNES

At Stabbursnes, en route between Honningsvåg and Karasjok, and beside one of the most attractive sectors of Porsangerfjord, there are a couple of important protected areas.

The **Stabbursnes Nature Reserve** extends over the wetlands and mudflats at the estuary of the Stabburselva River. Birdwatchers come to observe the many species of waterbird that rest in the area while migrating between the Arctic and more temperate zones. A signed nature trail (2.8km one way) leads along the estuary and beside the shore of Porsangerfjord. Ask at the visitors centre for its useful trail description in English.

No roads cross through the 747 sq km of **Stabbursdalen National Park**, which offers a spectacular glacial canyon and excellent hiking in the world's most northerly pine forest.

(Nkr850). Alternatively, try your hand at ice fishing (from Nkr800) or dog sledding (adult/child from Nkr1890/950).

Tours

Principal tour operators:

Arctic Adventure ADVENTURE
(www.arctic-adventure.no; Jarfjordbotn)

Barents Safari ADVENTURE
(www.barentssafari.no)

Pasvikturist ADVENTURE
(www.pasvikturist.no; Dr Wessels gate 9)

Radius ADVENTURE
(www.kirkenessnowhotel; Kongensgate 1-2) Can also help with visas for Russia.

Sleeping & Eating

TOP CHOICE **Sollia Gjestegård** HOTEL €€
(☑78 99 08 20; www.storskog.no; 2–6-bed cabins Nkr900-1350, s/d Nkr750/900, breakfast Nkr75) The air could scarcely be purer or the atmosphere more relaxed at this wonderful getaway haven, 13km southeast of Kirkenes and close to the Russian border. The whole family can sweat it out in the sauna and outdoor tub, while children will enjoy communing with the resident huskies. Just below, beside

the lake, its Gapahuken restaurant is just as enticing.

Thon Hotel Kirkenes HOTEL €€
(☑78 97 10 50; www.thonhotels.no/kirkenes; s/d from Nkr995/1195) This waterside hotel is boxy from the exterior. Within, though, it's open, vast and exciting, offering great views of the sound and a cluster of laid-up Russian trawlers to starboard.

Rica Arctic Hotel HOTEL €€
(☑78 99 11 59; www.rica.no/arctic; Kongensgate 1-3; d from Nkr1025; ℗@☀) The Rica Arctic, a pleasing modern block, boasts Norway's most easterly swimming pool, heated and open year-round. The other special attribute, its Arctic-menu restaurant (summer buffet Nkr325), is the best of the town's hotel dining options.

Kirkenes Snow Hotel HOTEL €€€
(☑78 97 05 40; www.kirkenessnowhotel.com; s/d incl transfer from Kirkenes, half board & sauna Nkr2900/2450; ⊗20 Dec–mid-Apr) Yes, the price is steep but you'll remember the occasion for life. And bear in mind that 25 tonnes of ice and 15,000 cu metres of snow are shifted each winter to build this ephemeral structure within Gabba Reindeer and Husky Park. For dinner, guests cook reindeer sausages over an open fire, then enjoy a warming main course of baked salmon.

TOP CHOICE **Gapahuken** NORWEGIAN €€€
(☑78 99 08 20; mains Nkr220-385; ⊗3-10pm Tue-Sat, to 7pm Sun mid-Jun–Aug, on demand rest of yr) From the broad picture windows of Gapahuken, restaurant of the Sollia Gjestegård hotel, there's a grand panorama of the lake at its feet and the Russian frontier post beyond. Discriminating diners drive out from Kirkenes to enjoy gourmet Norwegian cuisine based upon fresh local ingredients such as reindeer, king crab, Arctic salmon and halibut.

Information

Tourist office (☑78 97 11 77; www.kirkenes-info.no; Town Sq; ⊗10am-5pm Mon-Fri, to 2pm Sat & Sun)

Getting There & Around

AIR From **Kirkenes airport** (☑78 97 35 20), 13km southwest of town, there are direct flights to Oslo (SAS and Norwegian) and Tromsø (Widerøe). The airport is served by the Flybuss (Nkr85, 20 minutes), which connects the bus terminal and Rica Arctic Hotel with all arriving and departing flights.

BOAT Kirkenes is the terminus of the *Hurtigruten* coastal ferry, which heads southwards again at 12.45pm daily. A bus (Nkr95) meets the boat and runs into town and on to the airport.

BUS Buses run four times weekly to Karasjok (Nkr575, five hours), Hammerfest (Nkr998, 10¼ hours) and many points in between.

Karasjok

POP 1897

Kautokeino may have more Sámi residents, but Karasjok (Kárásjohka in Sámi) is Sámi Norway's indisputable capital. It's home to the Sámi Parliament and library, NRK Sámi Radio, a wonderful Sámi museum and an impressive Sámi theme park.

◉ Sights

Sápmi Park   AMUSEMENT PARK
(www.sapmi.no; Porsangerveien; adult/child Nkr120/65; ⊙9am-7pm mid-Jun–mid-Aug, shorter hr rest of yr) Sámi culture is big business here and it was only a matter of time before it was consolidated into a theme park. There's a wistful, hi-tech multimedia introduction to the Sámi in the 'Magic Theatre', plus Sámi winter and summer camps and other dwellings to explore in the grounds.

Sámi National Museum   MUSEUM
(Sámiid Vuorká Dávvirat; www.rdm.no; Museumsgata 17; adult/child Nkr75/free; ⊙9am-6pm Jun–mid-Aug, to 3pm Tue-Fri mid-Aug–May) The Sámi National Museum is also called the Sámi Collection. Devoted to Sámi history and culture, it has displays of colourful, traditional Sámi clothing, a bewildering array of tools and artefacts, and works by contemporary Sámi artists. Outdoors, you can roam among a cluster of traditional Sámi constructions and follow a short trail, signed in English, that leads past and explains ancient Sámi reindeer-trapping pits and hunting technique.

FREE **Sámi Parliament**   NOTABLE BUILDING
(Sámediggi; Kautokeinoveien 50) The Sámi Parliament was established in 1989 and meets four times annually. In 2000 it moved into a glorious new building, encased in mellow Siberian wood, with a birch, pine and oak interior. The main assembly hall is shaped like a Sámi tent, and the **Sámi library**, lit with tiny lights like stars, houses more than 35,000 volumes, plus other media. From late June to mid-August there are free 30-minute tours leaving hourly, on the half hour, between 8.30am and 2.30pm (except 11.30am). The rest of the year has tours at 1pm, Monday to Friday.

🏃 Activities

Sven Engholm, the 11-time winner of Finnmarksløpet, Europe's longest dog-sled race, oversees the outstanding **Engholm's Husky** (www.engholm.no), which offers winter dog-sled and cross-country skiing tours, as well as summer walking tours with a dog to carry most of your pack. All-inclusive expeditions range from one-/five-hour excursions (Nkr1100/1700) to five days of dog sledding (Nkr8900), with various variations on the theme. Consult the website for the full range of activities.

Also worth checking out is **Turgleder** (☑91 16 73 03; www.turgleder.com), run by Sven's daughter Liv. In summer they offer husky encounters and canoe rental with a full suite of winter activities as well.

🛏️ Sleeping & Eating

TOP CHOICE **Engholm Husky Design Lodge**   CABIN €€
(☑91 58 66 25; www.engholm.no; s/d full board from Nkr1300/2200) About 6km from Karasjok along the Rv92, Sven Engholm, the owner of Engholm's Husky, has built this wonderful haven in the forest with his own hands. Each rustic cabin is individually furnished with great flair, all have kitchen facilities and two have bathrooms. A fabulous place. Sven's place is also Karasjok's HI-affiliated youth hostel.

Rica Hotel Karasjok   HOTEL €€
(☑78 46 88 60; www.rica.no; Porsangerveien; s/d from Nkr1110/1360; P@) Adjacent to Sápmi Park, this is Karasjok's best business-style hotel. Its rooms sport subtle Sámi motifs throughout, plus, outside summertime, an impressive Arctic-menu restaurant.

Gammen   NORWEGIAN €€€
(☑78 46 88 60; mains Nkr225-385; ⊙11am-10pm mid-Jun–mid-Aug) It's very much reindeer or reindeer plus a couple of fish options (including juniper-smoked Arctic char) at this rustic complex of four large interconnected Sámi huts run by the Rica Hotel. You eat around a fire seated on reindeer-skin-clad chairs.

Shopping

Knivsmed Strømeng ARTS, CRAFTS
(☑78 46 71 05; Badjenjárga; ☺8.30am-4pm Mon-Fri) This craft shop calls on five generations of local experience to create unique and original handmade Sámi knives for everything from outdoor to kitchen use.

Information

Tourist office (www.sapmi.no; ☺9am-7pm Jun–mid-Aug, to 4pm Mon-Fri rest of yr)

Getting There & Away

Twice-daily buses (except Saturday) connect Karasjok with both Alta (Nkr430, 4¾ hours) and Hammerfest (Nkr395, 4¼ hours). There's a service to Kirkenes (Nkr575, five hours) four times weekly.

A daily Finnish Lapin Linjat bus runs to Rovaniemi (Nkr680, eight hours) via Ivalo (Nkr265, 3½ hours), in Finland.

Kautokeino

POP 1339

While Karasjok has made concessions to Norwegian culture, Kautokeino, the traditional winter base of the reindeer Sámi (as opposed to their coastal kin), remains more emphatically Sámi. Some 85% of the townspeople have Sámi as their first language and you may see a few non-tourist-industry locals in traditional dress.

Sights

TOP CHOICE Juhls' Sølvsmie GALLERY
(Juhls' Silver Gallery; www.juhls.no; Galaniitoluodda; ☺9am-8pm mid-Jun–mid-Aug, to 6pm rest of yr) This wonderful building, all slopes and soft angles, is on a hill above the town and clearly signed. It was designed and built by owners Regine and Frank Juhls, who first began working with the Sámi more than half a century ago. Their highly acclaimed gallery creates traditional-style and modern silver jewellery and handicrafts, and displays the best of Scandinavian design.

Kautokeino Museum MUSEUM
(Boaronjárga 23; adult/child Nkr40/free; ☺9am-6pm Mon-Sat, noon-6pm Sun mid-Jun–mid-Aug, 9am-3pm Mon-Fri rest of yr) Outside, this little museum has a fully fledged traditional Sámi settlement, complete with an early home, temporary dwellings and outbuildings such as the kitchen, sauna, and huts for storing fish, potatoes and lichen (also called 'reindeer moss' and prime reindeer fodder). Inside is a fascinating if cluttered display of Sámi handicrafts, farming and reindeer-herding implements, religious icons and winter transport gear.

Kautokeino Kirke CHURCH
(Suomalvodda; ☺9am-8pm Jun–mid-Aug) The timbered Kautokeino church, which dates from 1958, is one of Norway's most frequented, particularly at Easter. Its cheery interior, alive with bright Sámi colours, has some fixtures salvaged from the earlier 1701 church that was torched in WWII.

Sleeping & Eating

TOP CHOICE Thon Hotel Kautokeino HOTEL €€
(☑78 48 70 00; www.thonhotels.no/kautokeino; Biedjovaggeluodda 2; s/d Nkr1195/1395; P@) This brand-new hotel is a lovely structure with an exterior of mellow wood, built low to blend with its few neighbours. Within, rooms are cheerful and cosy and some have good views over the town. Duottar, its gourmet restaurant, serves fine cuisine (mains Nkr165 to Nkr329).

Arctic Motell & Camping CAMPGROUND €
(☑78 48 54 00; www.kauto.no; Suomaluodda 16; car/caravan sites Nkr175/220, cabins Nkr750-1800, without bathroom Nkr3450-400, motel r from Nkr850) This hyperfriendly place at the southern end of town has a communal kitchen for campers and cabin dwellers. Its *lavvo* (traditional Sami teepee-like house) is a warm and cosy spot to relax by a wood fire and sip steaming coffee, laid on nightly at 8pm. If you ask, the small cafe will also rustle up *bidos,* the traditional reindeer-meat stew served at Sámi weddings and other rites of passage.

Information

Tourist office (☑78 48 65 00; ☺10am-6pm Mon-Fri, to 5pm Sun mid-Jun–mid-Aug) Kautokeino's tourist office has had four different locations in our four recent visits. The Thon Hotel should know where they've migrated to.

Getting There & Away

Buses run between Kautokeino and Alta (Nkr250, 2¼ hours) daily except Saturday.

REISA NATIONAL PARK

Although technically in Troms county, Reisa National Park is most readily accessible by road from Kautokeino. For hikers, the 50km route through this remote Finnmarksvidda country is one of Norway's wildest and most physically demanding challenges. The northern trailhead at Sarelv is accessible on the Rv865, 47km south of Storslett, and the southern end is reached on the gravel route to Reisevannhytta, 4km west of Bieddju-vaggi on the Rv896, heading northwest from Kautokeino.

Most people walk from north to south. From Bilto or Sarelv, you can either walk the track up the western side of the cleft that channels the Reisaelva River or hire a riverboat for the three-hour, 27km trip upstream to Nedrefoss, where there's a Den Norske Turist-forening (DNT) hut. En route, notice the 269m Mollesfossen waterfall, east of the track on the tributary stream Molleselva. From Nedrefoss, the walking route continues for 35km south to the Reisavannhytta hut on Lake Reisajävri, near the southern trailhead.

SVALBARD

The world's most readily accessible piece of the polar north, and one of the most spectacular places imaginable, Svalbard is *the* destination for an unforgettable holiday. This wondrous archipelago is an assault on the senses: vast icebergs and floes choke the seas, and icefields and glaciers frost the lonely heights.

Svalbard also hosts a surprising variety of flora and fauna, including seals, walrus, Arctic foxes and polar bears.

Plan your trip well in advance. When you arrive, you'll almost certainly want to participate in some kind of organised trek or tour, and many need to be booked early. Travel outside Longyearbyen is both difficult and dangerous, but you miss out on a lot if you don't sign up for one.

History

Although the first mention of Svalbard occurs in an Icelandic saga from 1194, the official discovery of Svalbard (then uninhabited) is credited to Dutch voyager Willem Barents in 1596. He named the islands Spitsbergen (sharp mountains). The Norwegian name, Svalbard, comes from the Old Norse for 'cold coast'; ancient Norse sagas referred to 'a land in the far north at the end of the ocean'. During the 17th century, Dutch, English, French, Norwegian and Danish whalers slaughtered the whale population. They were followed in the 18th century by Russians hunting walrus and seals. The 19th century saw the arrival of Norwegians, who hunted polar bears and Arctic foxes. In 1906 commercial coal mining began and is continued today by the Russians (at Barentsburg) and the Norwegians (at Longyearbyen and Sveagruva). The 1920 Svalbard Treaty granted Norway sovereignty over the islands.

Tours

View dozens of exciting options on the tourist-office website (www.svalbard.net). Accommodation, transport and meals are usually included in longer tours, but day tours are also available.

Arctic Adventures ADVENTURE
(☎79 02 16 24; www.arctic-adventures.no) Small company offering the full range of activities.

Basecamp Spitsbergen ADVENTURE
(☎79 02 46 00; www.basecampspitsbergen.com) Mainly offers winter activities, including a stay aboard the *Noorderlicht,* a Dutch sailing vessel that's set into the fjord ice, and Isfjord Radio, the ultimate remote getaway on an upgraded, one-time radio station at the western tip of Spitsbergen Island.

Poli Arctici ADVENTURE
(☎79 02 17 05; www.poliartici.com) Poli Arctici is the trading name of Stefano Poli, originally from Milan and with 13 years as a Svalbard wilderness guide.

Spitsbergen Outdoor Activities ADVENTURE
(☎91 77 65 95; www.spitsbergenoutdooractivities.com) Kayaking, horse riding and hiking.

Spitsbergen Tours ADVENTURE
(☎79 02 10 68; www.terrapolaris.com) The owner, Andreas Umbreit, is one of the longest-standing operators on the archipelago.

Spitsbergen Travel ADVENTURE
(☎79 02 61 00; www.spitsbergentravel.no) One of the giants of the Svalbard travel scene, with a staggering array of options.

Svalbard Husky   DOG SLEDDING
(📞98 40 40 89; www.svalbardhusky.no) Year-round dog sledding.

Svalbard Snøscooterutleie   ADVENTURE
(📞79 02 46 61; www.scooterutleie.svalbard.no) Winter snowmobile safaris as well as a handful of summer activities.

Svalbard Villmarkssenter   DOG SLEDDING
(📞79 02 17 00; www.svalbardvillmarkssenter.no) Experts in dog mushing, whether by sledge over the snow or on wheels during summer.

Svalbard Wildlife Expeditions   ADVENTURE
(📞79 02 22 22; www.wildlife.no) Offering many of the usual and several unusual trips.

ℹ️ Information

Tourist Office (📞79 02 55 50; www.svalbard.net; ⏱10am-5pm May-Sep, noon-5pm Oct-Apr) Produces the comprehensive *Guide Longyearbyen* and a helpful weekly activities list.

ℹ️ Getting There & Away

SAS (www.flysas.com) flies to/from Oslo directly in summer (three flights weekly) or via Tromsø (once or twice daily) year-round. Norwegian (p383) also flies between Oslo and Longyearbyen three times weekly.

Longyearbyen

POP 2075

The frontier community of Longyearbyen, strewn with abandoned coal-mining detritus, enjoys a superb backdrop, including two glacier tongues, Longyearbreen and Lars Hjertabreen.

👁 Sights

In addition to the main sights, keep an eye out for wild reindeer and even the Arctic fox in and around the town.

Svalbard Museum   MUSEUM
(adult/child Nkr75/40, combined ticket with airship museum Nkr130/60; ⏱10am-5pm May-Sep) Museum is the wrong word for this impressive exhibition space. Themes include the life on the edge formerly led by whalers, trappers, seal- and walrus-hunters and, more recently, miners. It's an attractive mix of text, artefacts, and birds and mammals, stuffed and staring.

Spitsbergen Airship Museum   MUSEUM
(www.spitsbergenairshipmuseum.com; adult/child Nkr75/40, combined ticket with Svalbard Museum

Nkr130/60; ⏱10am-5pm mid-Jun–Aug) This museum is a fascinating complement to the main museum, with a stunning collection of artefacts, original newspapers and other documents relating to the history of polar exploration.

🏃 Activities

There's a dizzying array of short trips and day tours that vary with the season. The tourist office's weekly activities list provides details of many more. All outings can be booked through individual operators (directly or via their websites) or online at www.svalbard.net.

Birdwatching

More than 160 bird species have been reported in Svalbard, with the overwhelming number of these present during the summer months. Some tour operators run short boat trips to the 'bird cliffs' close to Longyearbyen, while birdwatchers should buy the booklet *Bird Life in Longyearbyen and surrounding area* (Nkr50), available from the tourist office.

Boat Trips

Polar Charter (📞97 52 32 50) sends out the *MS Polargirl* to Barentsburg and the Esmark Glacier (adult/child Nkr1390/1050, eight to 10 hours) four times a week, and to Pyramiden and Nordenskjöldbreen (adult/child Nkr1390/1050, eight to 10 hours). Prices include a lunch cooked on board.

Henningsen Transport and Guiding (📞79 02 13 11; www.htg.svalbard.no) runs a near-identical service, as well as six-hour Friday-evening trips to Tempelfjorden and the Van Post glacier (Nkr1090).

Spitsbergen Travel (📞79 02 61 00; www.spitsbergentravel.no; 3/6hr Nkr640/990) also arranges up to 13 weekly boat cruises around Isfjord, taking in birdwatching, fossil-hunting and glacier views.

Hiking & Fossil-Hunting

Summer hiking possibilities are endless and any Svalbard tour company worth its salt can organise half-, full- and multiday hikes.

The easiest options are three-hour fossil-hunting hikes, some of which take you up onto the moraine at the base of the Longyearbreen glacier.

Popular destinations for other hikes, many of which include glacier hikes, include Platåberget, up onto the Longyearbreen glacier itself, Sarkofagen (525m above sea level), Hiorthfjellet (900m above sea level), Nordenskjöldtoppen (1050m above sea level) and the Foxfonna ice field.

Kayaking

Svalbard Wildlife Expeditions runs seven-hour kayaking expeditions to Hiorthamn with an additional 10-hour hiking/kayaking challenge to Hiortfjellet.

Dog Sledding

Dedicated dog-sledding operators include Svalbard Husky (p372) and Svalbard Villmarkssenter (p372) and the standard four-hour expedition will give you a taste. For longer excursions (including some wonderful multiday trips), it's worth checking what Basecamp Spitsbergen (p371) has on offer.

Snowmobiling

Spitsbergen Travel has numerous single and multiday snowmobile expeditions. Among its single-day options are the East Coast Snowmobile Safari (eight to 10 hours), Barentsburg (seven to nine hours), Pyramiden (eight to 10 hours), Coles Bay (four hours), Elveneset (four hours) and the Polar Night Safari (three hours).

Svalbard Snøscooterutleie offers many of the same routes for similar prices as other tour companies, as well as offering snowmobile rental. To drive a snowmobile, you'll need your home driving licence.

⌖ Tours

Svalbard Maxi Taxi   MINIBUS
(✆79 02 13 05; per person Nkr250; ☼tours 10am & 4pm Jun-Aug) This local taxi company offers two-hour minibus tours that take you further than you might think possible around Longyearbyen.

✯ Festivals & Events

Polar Jazz   MUSIC
(www.polarjazz.no) A long winter (January or February) weekend of jazz.

Sunfest   CULTURE
Week-long celebrations in early March to dispel the polar night.

Blues Festival   MUSIC
(www.svalbardblues.com) Five-day jam session in late October to mark the onset of winter.

⌖ Sleeping

TOP CHOICE **Basecamp Spitsbergen**   LODGE €€€
(✆79 02 46 00; www.basecampexplorer.com; s Nkr1050-2090, d Nkr1500-2550) Imagine a re-created sealing hut, built in part from recycled driftwood and local slate. Add artefacts and decorations culled from the local refuse dump and mining cast-offs. Graft on 21st-century plumbing and design flair and you've got this place, also known as Trapper's Lodge.

Spitsbergen Guesthouse   GUESTHOUSE €
(✆79 02 63 00; www.spitsbergentravel.no; dm Nkr300-375, s Nkr510-710, d Nkr815-1015; ☼mid-Mar–mid-Sep) A subsidiary of Spitsbergen Travel, this guesthouse is spread over four buildings, one of which houses the large breakfast room (once the miners' mess hall), and can accommodate up to 136 people. The rooms are simple, but terrific value for money.

Mary-Ann's Polarrigg   HOTEL, GUESTHOUSE €€
(✆79 02 37 02; www.polarriggen.com; Skjæringa; s Nkr675-850, d Nkr895-2200) Run by the ebullient Mary-Ann and adorned with mining and hunting memorabilia, the Polarrigg brims with character, although most is in the public areas and rooms are quite simple. In the main wing, rooms have corridor bathrooms and doubles come with bunk beds. In the smart if somewhat overpriced annex, rooms have every comfort.

Longyearbyen Camping   CAMPGROUND €
(✆79 02 10 68; www.longyearbyen-camping.com; campsites per person Nkr100-150; ☼Apr & mid-Jun–mid-Sep) Near the airport on a flat stretch of turf, this particularly friendly camping ground overlooks Isfjorden and the glaciers beyond and has a kitchen and showers. You can hire a tent (per night Nkr100) and sleeping bag (first/subsequent nights Nkr50/30).

✕ Eating

TOP CHOICE **Huset**   NORWEGIAN, INTERNATIONAL €€
(✆79 02 25 00; cafe mains Nkr96-146, restaurant mains Nkr295-369, 3-/4-/5-course Arctic menu Nkr495/565/695; ☼cafe 4pm-midnight Sun-Fri, 2pm-midnight Sat, restaurant 7pm-midnight) It's something of a walk up here but it's worth it. Dining in the cafe-bar is casual, with

well-priced pasta, pizza and reindeer stew on the menu; the daily specials are wonderful. In the same building, the highly regarded restaurant serves up dishes such as terrine of Svalbard reindeer, fillet of reindeer and quail.

Kroa NORWEGIAN, INTERNATIONAL €€
(lunch mains Nkr75-150, dinner mains Nkr219-285; ⊙11.30am-2am) This pub and restaurant was reconstructed from the elements of a building brought in from Russian Barentsburg (the giant white bust of Lenin peeking from behind the bar gives a clue). Service is friendly and mains verge on the gargantuan. In high season it's worth booking a table if you don't want to wait.

ℹ Getting Around

Longyearbyen Taxi (☑79 02 13 75) charges up to Nkr150 between the town and the airport. The airport bus (Nkr50) connects with flights.

Around Svalbard

Independent travel around Svalbard is heavily regulated in order to protect both the virgin landscape and travellers. Travel to the very few settlements is usually done as part of a tour package. One of these settlements is **Barentsburg** (population 400), a Soviet-era relic. Simultaneously depressing and fascinating, this tiny Russian town still mines and exports coal, and a statue of Lenin still stares over the bleak built landscape and the impressive natural landscape that surrounds it. Almost-abandoned **Pyramiden** is a similar deal.

Tourist cruises might also bring you to **Ny Ålesund**, which, at latitude N 79°, is a wild place full of scientists and downright hostile Arctic terns. Remnants of past glories include a **stranded locomotive**, previously used for transporting coal, and an **airship pylon**, used by Amundsen and Nobile on their successful crossing of the North Pole in 1926.

The lovely blue-green bay of **Magdalenefjord**, flanked by towering peaks and intimidating tidewater glaciers, is the most popular anchorage along Spitsbergen's western coast and is one of Svalbard's prettiest corners.

UNDERSTAND NORWAY

History

Norway's first settlers arrived around 11,000 years ago with the end of the Ice Age. As the glaciers melted, the earliest hunter-gatherers moved in from Siberia, pursuing migrating reindeer herds. You can see the prehistoric rock drawings of these hunters in the far north on Alta. Shortly afterwards, nomadic European hunters arrived in the south of the country.

The Vikings

Norway greatly affected Western civilisation during the Viking Age, a period usually dated from the plundering of England's Lindisfarne monastery by Nordic pirates (AD 793). Through the next century, the Vikings conducted raids throughout Europe and established settlements in the Shetland, Orkney and Hebridean islands, the Dublin area (Ireland) and in Normandy (named after the 'North men'). The Viking leader Harald Hårfagre (Fairhair) unified Norway after the decisive naval battle at Hafrsfjord near Stavanger in 872. King Olav Haraldsson, adopting the religion of the lands he had conquered, converted the Norwegians to Christianity and founded the Church of Norway in 1024. You can see Viking artefacts firsthand in Oslo's Vikingskipshuset (p292) and the Lofotr Vikingmuseum (p358) in the Lofoten Islands.

The Viking Age declined after 1066, with the defeat of the Norwegian king, Harald Hardråda, at the Battle of Stamford Bridge in England. Norwegian naval power was finished off for good when Alexander III, King of Scots, defeated a Viking naval force at the Battle of Largs (Scotland) in 1263.

Under Occupation

In the early 14th century, Oslo emerged as a centre of power. A period of growth followed until 1349 when the bubonic plague swept the country, wiping out two-thirds of the population. In 1380 Norway was absorbed into a union with Denmark that lasted more than 400 years.

Denmark ceded Norway to Sweden in 1814. In 1884 a parliamentary government was introduced in Norway and a growing nationalist movement eventually led to a constitutional referendum in 1905. As expected, virtually no one in Norway favoured continued union with Sweden. The Swedish king, Oskar II, was forced to recognise Norwegian sovereignty, abdicate and reinstate a Norwegian constitutional monarchy, with Håkon VII on the throne. His descendants rule Norway to this day, with decisions on succession remaining under the authority of the *storting* (parliament). Oslo was declared the national capital of the Kingdom of Norway.

Independent Norway

Norway stayed neutral during WWI. Despite restating its neutrality at the start of WWII, it was attacked by the Nazis on 9 April 1940, falling to the Germans after a two-month struggle. King Håkon set up a government in exile in England, and placed most of Norway's merchant fleet under the command of the Allies. Although Norway remained occupied until the end of the war, it had an active Resistance movement, which you can ponder in Bergen's Theta Museum (p313) and Narvik's Red Cross War Museum (p354).

The royal family returned to Norway in June 1945. King Håkon died in 1957 and was succeeded by his son, Olav V, a popular king who reigned until his death in January 1991. The current monarch is Harald V, Olav's son, who was crowned in June 1991.

In the late 1960s oil was discovered in Norway's offshore waters, thereafter transforming Norway from one of Europe's poorest to arguably its richest. Although Norway joined the European Free Trade Association (EFTA) in 1960, it has been reluctant to forge closer bonds with other European nations, in part due to concerns about the effect on its fishing and small-scale farming industries. During 1994 a national referendum on joining the EU was held and rejected.

On 22 July 2011, a lone assailant killed 77 people in a bomb attack on government buildings in Oslo and a youth camp on the island of Utøya, close to Oslo. The killings, reportedly in protest at growing multiculturalism in the country, shocked and deeply traumatised the country. The perpetrator, a right-wing extremist, was later sentenced to 21 years for the attacks (the maximum possible sentence), with an option to renew the sentence thereafter.

People

Norway has 5.02 million people and one of Europe's lowest population densities. Most Norwegians are of Nordic origin (86.2% according to one recent study), and are thought to have descended from central and northern European tribes who migrated northwards around 8000 years ago. In addition, there are about 40,000 Sámi, the indigenous people of Norway's far north who now make up the country's second-largest ethnic minority (after the Polish community). Some Sámi still live a traditional nomadic life, herding reindeer in Finnmark.

Norway has become an increasingly multicultural society in recent years and was, at last count, home to 660,000 immigrants (around 13% of the population) from 216 countries (compared with just 1.5% of the population in 1970).

Around 80% of Norwegians belong to the Church of Norway, a Protestant Evangelical Lutheran denomination, but most Norwegians only attend church for Christmas and Easter. A growing Muslim population exists due to recent immigration.

Arts

In the late 19th century and into the early 20th century, three figures – playwright Henrik Ibsen, composer Edvard Grieg and painter Edvard Munch – towered over Norway's cultural life like no others. Their emergence came at a time when Norway was forging its path to independence and pushing the creative limits of a newly confident national identity.

Ibsen (1828–1906) became known as 'the father of modern drama', but to Norwegians he was the conscience of a nation. The enormously popular *Peer Gynt* (1867) was Ibsen's international breakthrough, while other well-known works include *The Doll's House* (1879), *Ghosts* (1881), *An Enemy of the People* (1882) and *Hedda Gabler* (1890).

Edvard Grieg (1843–1907) was greatly influenced by Norway's folk music and melodies and his first great, signature work, *Piano Concerto in A minor*, has come to represent Norway as no other work before or since. Thanks to his formidable repertoire (including *Ballad in G minor*, *The Mountain Thrall*, *Norwegian Dances for Piano* and the *Holberg Suite*), he became Norway's best-known composer. According to his biographer, it was impossible to listen to Grieg without sensing a light, fresh breeze from the blue waters, a glimpse of grand glaciers and a recollection of the mountains of western Norway's fjords.

Edvard Munch (1863–1944), Norway's most renowned painter, was a tortured soul: his first great work, *The Sick Child*, was a portrait of his sister Sophie shortly before her death. In 1890 he produced the haunting *Night*, depicting a lonely figure in a dark window. The following year he finished *Melancholy* and began sketches of what would become his best-known work, *The Scream*, which graphically represents Munch's own inner torment.

Literature

In the 20th century, three Norwegian writers – Bjørnstjerne Bjørnson (1832–1910), the hugely controversial Knut Hamsun (1859–1952) and Sigrid Undset (1882–1949) – won the Nobel Prize in Literature.

One of the best-known modern Norwegian writers is Jan Kjærstad (b 1953), whose *The Seducer* (2003) combines the necessary recipes for a best seller – a thriller with a love affair and a whiff of celebrity – with seriously good writing. Among other recent Norwegian winners of the prestigious Nordic Council Literature Prize is the prolific Per Petterson (b 1952), who won the prize in 2009 and whose works include *Out Stealing Horses, To Siberia* and *I Curse the River of Time*. If you're lucky enough to get hold of a copy, Angar Mykle's *Lasso Round the Moon* (1954) might be the best book you've never read.

Cinema

Though there aren't many, Norway has produced several good films, including *Elling* (2001), *Buddy* (2003) and *Beautiful Country* (2004). For a Norwegian classic, check out *Ni Liv* (1957), a story concerning the WWII Resistance. The Sámi film *Pathfinder* (1987) is a brutal adventure story set in Finnmark 1000 years ago. Information on festivals can be found at www.nfi.no.

Music

JAZZ

Norway has a thriving jazz scene, with world-class festivals throughout the year.

> **NORWAY'S BIGGEST SUPERGROUP: A-HA**
>
> Three decades after a-ha took the world by storm with 'Take on Me' (1985), this Norwegian supergroup remains the country's biggest-selling musical act. They released their ninth studio album *Foot of the Mountain* in 2009.

Jazz saxophonist Jan Garbarek is one of the most enduring Norwegian jazz personalities. His work draws on classical, folk and world-music influences and he has recorded 30 albums. His 1994 *Officium,* with its echoes of Gregorian chants, did well in the pop charts across Europe, while his 2005 *In Praise of Dreams* received a Grammy nomination. His daughter, Anja Garbarek, is seen as one of the most exciting and innovative performers on the Norwegian jazz scene, bringing pop and electronica into the mix.

Norway has some fine jazz festivals, including the following:

» Moldejazz (p346)
» Oslo International Jazz Festival (p294)
» Canal Street Jazz & Blues Festival (p301), Arendal
» Night Jazz Festival (p315), Bergen
» Vossajazz (p330), Voss
» Polar Jazz (p373), Longyearbyen

ELECTRONICA

Norway is at once one of Europe's most prolific producers and most devoted fans of electronica. Röyksopp (www.royksopp.com) took the international electronica scene by storm with its debut album *Melody A.M.* in 2001 and it's never really left the dance-floor charts since.

METAL

Metal is another genre that Norway has taken to heart. Although traditional heavy metal is popular, Norway is particularly known for its black-metal scene. For a time in the early 1990s, black metal became famous for its anti-Christian, Satanist philosophy with a handful of members of black-metal bands burning down churches. Among the better-known Norwegian black-metal bands are Darkthrone, Mayhem, Emperor, Enslaved, Gorgoroth, Satyricon and Arcturus.

Environment

The Land

Norway's geographical facts tell a story. The Norwegian mainland stretches 2518km from Lindesnes in the south to Nordkapp in the Arctic north, with a narrowest point of 6.3km wide. Norway also has the highest mountains in northern Europe and a land mass of 385,155 sq km (the fourth largest in Europe, behind France, Spain and Sweden).

Norway is also home to continental Europe's largest icecap (Jostedalsbreen), the world's second- and third-longest fjords (Sognefjorden and Hardangerfjord), Europe's largest and highest plateau (Hardangervidda) and several of the 10 highest waterfalls in the world. Norway's glaciers cover some 2600 sq km (close to 1% of mainland Norwegian territory and 60% of the Svalbard archipelago).

Wildlife

Norway has wild and semidomesticated reindeer herds, thriving elk populations and a scattering of Arctic foxes, lynxes, musk oxen, bears and wolverines. Lemmings occupy mountain areas through 30% of the country. Polar bears (population around 3000, or around one-eighth of the world's surviving population, and declining) and walrus are found in Svalbard. Several species of seal, dolphin and whale may be seen around most western and northern coasts.

Birdlife is prolific in coastal areas; puffins, fulmars and kittiwakes are common. Rarer species include ospreys, golden eagles and white-tailed sea eagles.

National Parks

At last count, Norway had 42 national parks (including seven in Svalbard, where approximately 65% of the land falls within park boundaries). Sixteen new national parks have been created since 2003, with a further four new parks and three extensions to existing parks planned. National parks cover 15% of the country. In many cases, the parks don't protect any specific features, nor do they necessarily coincide with the incidence of spectacular natural landscapes or ecosystem boundaries. Instead, they attempt to prevent development of remaining wilderness areas and many park boundaries simply follow contour lines around uninhabited areas.

Norwegian national parks are low profile and lack the traffic and overdeveloped facilities that have overwhelmed parks in other countries. Some parks, notably Jotunheimen and Rondane, are increasingly suffering from overuse, but in most places pollution and traffic are kept to a minimum.

Further national-park information is available at local tourist offices and from the **Directorate for Nature Management** (☎73 58 05 00; www.dirnat.no) in Trondheim.

Green Issues

Norway has led many contemporary environmental initiatives, such as the creation of the Svalbard Global Seed Vault (2008), where seeds are stored to protect biodiversity. In 2007 the government declared a goal of making Norway carbon-neutral by 2030, largely by purchasing offsets from developing countries.

Industrial waste is highly regulated and recycling is popular. There's little rubbish along the roadsides and general tidiness is a high priority in both urban and rural environments. Plastic bottles and cans may be exchanged for cash at supermarkets.

Loss of habitat has placed around 1000 species of plants and animals on the endangered or threatened species lists, and sport hunting and fishing are more popular here than in most of Europe. Hydroelectric schemes have devastated some mountain landscapes and waterfalls, and overfishing perpetually haunts the economy.

Whaling in Norway is regulated by the International Whaling Commission. Norway resumed commercial whaling of minke whales in 1993, defying an international ban. The government, which supports the protection of threatened species, contends that minke whales, with an estimated population of 100,000, can sustain a limited harvest.

Food & Drink

Norwegian food *can* be excellent. Abundant seafood and local specialities such as reindeer are undoubtedly the highlights, and most medium-sized towns have fine restaurants in which to eat. The only problem (and it's a significant one) is that prices are prohibitive, meaning that a full meal in a restaurant may become something of a luxury item for all but those on expense accounts.

What this does is push many visitors into eating fast-food meals in order to save money, at least at lunchtime, with pizzas, hot dogs and hamburgers a recurring theme.

Striking a balance between eating well and staying solvent requires a clever strategy. For a start, most Norwegian hotels and some hostels offer generous buffet breakfasts, ensuring that you'll rarely start the day on an empty stomach. Many restaurants, especially in larger towns, serve cheaper lunch specials (often from around Nkr79). These are often filling and well sized for those wanting more than a sandwich. Some hotels also lay on lavish dinner buffets in the evening – they're generally expensive, but excellent if it's your main meal of the day.

Staples & Specialities

Norwegian specialities include grilled or smoked *laks* (salmon), *gravat laks* (marinated salmon), *reker* (boiled shrimp), *torsk* (cod), *fiskesuppe* (fish soup), *hval* (whale) and other seafood. *Reinsdyrstek* (roast reindeer) is something every nonvegetarian visitor to Norway should try at least once; it's one of the tastier red meats.

Expect to see sweet brown goat's-milk cheese called *geitost*, and *sild* (pickled herring) with the breads and cereals in breakfast buffets. A fine Norwegian dessert is warm *moltebær syltetøy* (cloudberry jam) with ice cream. Also popular is *eplekake* (apple cake) served with fresh cream. *Lutefisk* (dried cod made almost gelatinous by soaking in lye) is popular at Christmas but it's an acquired taste.

If Norway has a national drink, it's strong black coffee. Most of the beer you'll drink is pilsner. At the other end of the taste spectrum is Norway's bitter aquavit, which does the job at 40% proof.

Where to Eat & Drink

Common throughout Norway is the *konditori,* a bakery with tables where you can sit and enjoy pastries and relatively inexpensive sandwiches. Other moderately cheap eats are found at *gatekjøkken* (food wagons and streetside kiosks), which generally have hot dogs for about Nkr40 and hamburgers for Nkr75. Marginally more expensive, but with more nutritionally balanced food, are *kafeterias,* with simple, traditional meals from about Nkr100. Restaurants vary widely in price, with mains going for Nkr120 to Nkr385.

Vegetarians & Vegans

Being vegetarian in Norway is a challenge and vegan almost impossible. In rural parts of the country, vegetarians will live out of a grocery store, though some cafes serve token dishes such as vegetables with pasta. Another easily found option is pizza, however Norwegian pizza is often bland and soggy. You'll find more options in bigger cities, although most menus are entirely based on fish and meat. About half of the kebab stands serve falafel. Norwegian restaurants aim to please and will often attempt to make you a special order if you ask (but don't expect exciting results).

Habits & Customs

Locals tend to eat breakfast at home, lunch between 11.30am and 2pm (often with their coworkers) and the evening meal between 6pm and 8pm (often later in larger cities).

SURVIVAL GUIDE

Directory A–Z

Accommodation

During summer, it's wise to book accommodation in advance.

The main tourist season runs from mid-June to mid-August. During the high season accommodation prices are at their lowest and many hotels offer their best deals. During the rest of the year, prices are much higher, except on weekends.

The following prices are for a high-season double room with private bathroom (usually including breakfast):

€€€	more than Nkr1400
€€	Nkr750 to Nkr1400
€	less than Nkr750

BED & BREAKFASTS

Some places operate as B&Bs, where prices (usually with shared bathrooms) start at Nkr350/500 for singles/doubles and can go up to Nkr650/1000. These options can be tracked down through **Bed and Breakfast Norway** (www.bbnorway.com).

CAMPING

Norway has more than 1000 camping grounds. Tent space ordinarily costs from Nkr100 at basic camping grounds, up to Nkr225 for those with better facilities. Quot ed prices usually include your car, motorcycle or caravan. A per-person charge is added in some places, electricity often costs a few kroner extra and most places charge Nkr10 for showers.

Most camping grounds also rent out cabins with cooking facilities, starting at around Nkr350 for a basic two- or four-bed bunkhouse. Bring a sleeping bag, as linen and blankets cost extra (from Nkr50 to Nkr100). There are also more-expensive deluxe cabins with shower and toilet facilities (Nkr750 to Nkr1500).

Norsk Camping (www.camping.no)

NAF Camp (www.nafcamp.no)

DNT & OTHER MOUNTAIN HUTS

Den Norske Turistforening (DNT; Norwegian Mountain Touring Club; ☑22 82 28 22; www.turistforeningen.no; Storgata 7, Oslo) is an important hiking resouce, which maintains a network of 460 mountain huts or cabins located a day's hike apart along the country's 20,000km of well-marked and maintained wilderness hiking routes. These include unstaffed huts with two beds, to large staffed lodges with more than 100 beds and renowned standards of service. DNT has lists of opening dates for each hut.

GUESTHOUSES & PENSIONS

Many towns have *pensjonat* (pensions) and *gjestehus* (guesthouses). Some, especially the latter, are family-run and offer a more intimate option than a hostel or hotel. Prices for a room with a shared bathroom usually start at Nkr500/750 for singles/doubles but can cost significantly more; linen and/or breakfast will only be included at the higher-priced places.

HOSTELS

In Norway, reasonably priced *vandrerhjem* (hostels) offer a dorm bed for the night, plus use of communal facilities that usually include a self-catering kitchen (you're advised to take your own cooking and eating utensils), internet access and bathrooms.

In most hostels, guests must bring their own sheet and pillowcase, although most hire sheets for a one-off fee (starting at Nkr50) regardless of the number of nights.

Most hostels have two- to six-bed rooms and beds cost from Nkr175 to Nkr400. Higher-priced hostels usually include a buffet breakfast, while other places may charge from Nkr70 to Nkr125 for breakfast.

The Norwegian hostelling association, **Norske Vandrerhjem** (☑23 12 45 10; www.hihostels.no), is HI-affiliated.

HOTELS

Norway's hotels are generally modern and excellent, although those with character are rare. The worthwhile **De Historiske** (☑55 31 67 60; www.dehistoriske.no) network links Norway's most historic old hotels and restaurants.

The main hotel chains or networks often have hotel passes, entitling you to a free night if you use the chain enough times; some passes only operate in summer. The major chains or networks include the following:

Best Western (www.bestwestern.no)

First Hotels (www.firsthotels.com)

Fjord Pass (www.fjordpass.no; 2 adults & any children under 15yr Nkr140) Available at around 150 hotels, guesthouses, cabins and apartments year-round. There are no free nights, but the discounts on nightly rates are considerable.

Nordic Choice Hotels (www.nordicchoicehotels.no) Covering Clarion, Quality and Comfort Hotels.

Rica Hotels (www.rica.no)

Thon Hotels (www.thonhotels.com)

Activities

SUMMER

Norway is a popular thrill-seeker destination thanks to professional operators and spectacular settings. Extreme sports include paragliding, parasailing, bungee jumping and skydiving. Voss (p330) is the centre of most of the action.

Norway has some of Europe's best hiking, including around 20,000km of marked trails that range from easy strolls through the green zones around cities, to long treks through national parks and wilderness areas. Many trails are maintained by DNT and marked with cairns or red Ts at 100m or 200m intervals.

The hiking season runs from late May to early October, with a much shorter season in the higher mountain areas and the far north. In the highlands, the snow often remains until June and returns in September, meaning many routes are only possible in July and August.

Norway's premier kayaking sites are clustered around the western fjords and there are numerous operators offering guided excursions.

The cascading, icy-black waters and white-hot rapids of central Norway are a rafting paradise from mid-June to mid-August. These range from Class II through to Class V.

WINTER

Downhill and cross-country skiing is possible throughout the country in winter.

Dog sledding is popular as it enables you to experience Arctic and sub-Arctic wilderness areas at a slow pace and free from engine noise. Expeditions can range from half-day to multiday trips with overnight stays in remote forest huts. Most operators will allow you to (depending on the number of travellers in your group) 'mush' your own sled (after a brief primer course) or sit atop the sled as someone else urges the dogs onwards.

Snowmobile operators usually allow you to ride as a passenger behind an experienced driver. For an additional charge you may be able to drive the snowmobile, but you will need a valid driving licence.

Business Hours

Standard opening hours are for high season (mid-June to mid-September) and tend to decrease outside that time.

Banks 8.15am to 3pm Monday to Wednesday and Friday, to 5pm Thursday

Drinking 6pm to 3am

Eating 8am to 11am, noon to 3pm and 6pm to 11pm

Entertainment 6pm to 3am

Offices 9am to 5pm Monday to Friday, 10am to 2pm Saturday

Post offices 9am to 5pm Monday to Friday, 10am to 2pm Saturday; large cities 8am to 8pm Monday to Friday, 9am to 6pm Saturday

Shops 10am to 5pm Monday to Wednesday and Friday, to 7pm Thursday, to 2pm Saturday

Children

Norway is a terrific destination in which to travel as a family. This is a country that is world-famous for creating family-friendly living conditions and most hotels, restaurants and many sights are accordingly child

friendly. It's worth remembering, however, that the old parental adage of not trying to be too ambitious in how far you travel is especially relevant in Norway – distances are vast and, due to the terrain, journey times can be significantly longer than for equivalent distances elsewhere.

Food

The price of an average main course:

€€€   more than Nkr200

€€   Nkr125 to Nkr200

€   less than Nkr125

Gay & Lesbian Travellers

Norwegians are generally tolerant of alternative lifestyles and on 1 January 2009 Norway became the sixth country in the world to legalise same-sex marriage. That said, public displays of affection are not common practice, except perhaps in some areas of Oslo. Oslo is generally Norway's most gay-friendly city and has the liveliest gay scene.

Internet Access

Good cybercafes that last the distance are increasingly hard to find; ask at the local tourist office. Prices per hour range from Nkr40 to Nkr80; students sometimes receive a discount. Free internet access is available in most municipal libraries (*biblioteket*). As it's a popular service, you may have to reserve a time slot earlier in the day; in busier places, you may be restricted to a half-hour slot.

Wireless is increasingly the norm in most hotels, guesthouses and even some camping grounds, as well as some cafes and bars.

Money

ATMs These machines accept most international cards and are available in most towns.

Currency The Norwegian kroner is most often written NOK in international money markets, Nkr in northern Europe and kr within Norway. We have used Nkr.

Changing money Not all banks will change money and in some places you may need to shop around to find one that does. Rates at post offices and tourist offices are generally poorer than at banks, but can be convenient for small amounts outside banking hours. Travellers cheques command a better exchange rate than cash (by about 2%), but attract commissions.

Public Holidays

Norway practically shuts down during the Christmas and Easter weeks.

New Year's Day (Nyttårsdag) 1 January

Maundy Thursday (Skjærtorsdag) March/April

Good Friday (Langfredag) March/April

Easter Monday (Annen Påskedag) March/April

Labour Day (Første Mai, Arbeidetsdag) 1 May

Constitution Day (Nasjonaldag) 17 May

Ascension Day (Kristi Himmelfartsdag) May/June, 40th day after Easter

Whit Monday (Annen Pinsedag) May/June, eighth Monday after Easter

Christmas Day (Første Juledag) 25 December

Boxing Day (Annen Juledag) 26 December

Telephone

MOBILE PHONES

More than 90% of the country has GSM mobile access; wilderness areas and national-park hiking trails are exceptions.

Norwegian SIM cards can be purchased from any 7-Eleven store and some Narvesen kiosks; prices start at Nkr200, including Nkr100 worth of calls. However, as the connection instructions are entirely in Norwegian, you're better off purchasing the card from any Telehuset outlet, where they'll help you connect on the spot.

The main service providers:

NetCom (www.netcom.no)

Network Norway (www.networknorway.no) Operates as Mobile Norway.

Telenor Mobil (www.telenor.com)

PHONE CODES

All Norwegian phone numbers have eight digits. Numbers starting with '800' usually indicate a toll-free number, while those beginning with '9' are mobile (cell-phone) numbers.

International access code ☑00

Norway country code ☑47

Directory assistance ☑180 (calls cost Nkr9 per minute)

PHONECARDS

Your best bet is to go for one of the phonecards issued by private companies. Usually costing Nkr100, they allow you to make more than six hours of calls using a scratch PIN number on the back and a local access number.

For international calls, internet-connected calls (eg www.skype.com) are the way to go, although unfortunately if you're not travelling with a laptop, few internet cafes are Skype-enabled and you cannot make phone calls from municipal-library computers.

Time

Time in Norway is one hour ahead of GMT/UTC, the same as Sweden, Denmark and most of Western Europe.

When telling time, in Norwegian the use of 'half' means 'half before' rather than 'half past'.

Norway observes daylight-saving time, with clocks set ahead one hour on the last Sunday in March and back an hour on the last Sunday in October. Timetables and business hours are posted according to the 24-hour clock.

Tourist Information

It's impossible to speak highly enough of tourist offices in Norway. Most serve as one-stop clearing houses for general information and bookings for accommodation and activities. Nearly every city and town has its own tourist office and most tourist offices in reasonably sized towns or major tourist areas publish comprehensive booklets giving the complete, up-to-date low-down on their town.

Offices in smaller towns may be open only during peak summer months, while in cities they're open year-round but with shorter hours in low season.

Visas

Norway is one of 26 member countries of the Schengen Agreement, under which EU countries (all but Bulgaria, Cyprus, Ireland, Romania and the UK) plus Iceland, Norway and Switzerland have abolished checks at common borders. Citizens of the USA, Canada, Australia and New Zealand need a valid passport to visit Norway, but do not need a visa for stays of less than three months. Citizens of EU countries and other Scandinavian countries do not require visas.

Getting There & Away

Crossing most borders into Norway is usually hassle-free; travellers from non-Western countries or those crossing by land into Norway from Russia should expect more rigorous searches.

All travellers – other than citizens of Denmark, Iceland, Sweden and Finland – require a valid passport to enter Norway.

Air

For a full list of Norwegian airports, visit www.avinor.no; the page for each airport has comprehensive information. The main

---

GETTING TO NORWAY BY LAND

Finland

Buses run between northern Norway and northern Finland with most cross-border services operated by the Finnish company **Eskelisen Lapin Linjat** (016-342 2160; www.eskelisen-lapinlinjat.com).

FROM	DESTINATION	PRICE (€)	DURATION (HR)
Rovaniemi	Alta	91	10
Rovaniemi	Karasjok	73	7
Rovaniemi	Tromsø	97.30	8-10
Rovaniemi	Vadsø	95.80	8

Russia

Buses run twice daily between Kirkenes and Murmansk (one way/return Nkr400/650, five hours). Once in Murmansk, trains connect to St Petersburg and the rest of the Russian rail network.

To cross the border, you'll need a Russian visa, which must usually be applied for and issued in your country of residence.

Sweden

BUS The largest, cheapest buses between Oslo and Sweden are with **Swebus Express** (0200 218 218; www.swebusexpress.se). **GoByBus** (www.gobybus.se) is also worth checking out.

FROM	PRICE (SKR)	DURATION (HR)	FREQUENCY
Stockholm	from 279	7½-15	around 4 daily
Gothenburg (Göteborg)	from 269	3¾	3 daily
Malmö	from 339	8	2-4 daily

Among the numerous cross-border services across the long land frontier between Sweden and Norway, there are services between Narvik and Kiruna, between Bodø and Skellefteå, and between Mo i Rana and Umeå.

TRAIN Rail services between Sweden and Norway are operated by **Swedish Railways** (in Sweden 0771-75 75 99; www.sj.se).

FROM	DESTINATION	PRICE (SKR)	DURATION (HR)	FREQUENCY
Gothenburg (Göteborg)	Oslo	from 256	4-7½	up to 5 daily
Stockholm	Oslo	from 480	6-12	up to 6 daily
Stockholm	Narvik	from 698	18-20	1-2 daily
Malmö	Oslo	from 591	7½-16½	6 daily

international Norwegian airports are: Gardermoen (Oslo), Flesland (Bergen), Sola (Stavanger), Tromsø, Værnes (Trondheim), Vigra (Ålesund), Karmøy (Haugesund), Kjevik (Kristiansand) and Torp (Sandefjord).

Dozens of international airlines fly to/from Norwegian airports. Airlines that use Norway as their primary base include the following:

Norwegian (www.norwegian.com) Low-cost airline.

SAS (www.sas.no)

Widerøe (www.wideroe.no) A subsidiary of SAS.

Sea

There are a number of international ferry routes to/from Norway (p491).

Getting Around

Norway has an extremely efficient public transport system and its trains, buses and ferries are often timed to link with each other. *NSB Togruter,* available free at most train stations, details rail timetables and includes information on connecting buses. Boat and bus *ruteplan* (timetables) are available from regional tourist offices.

Air

The major Norwegian domestic routes are competitive and you can travel for little more than the equivalent train fare if you're flexible about departure dates and book early.

Four airlines fly domestic routes:

DOT LT (www.flydot.no) Small planes with flights to Oslo from Røros.

Norwegian (www.norwegian.com) Low-cost airline with extensive network throughout Norway.

SAS (www.sas.no) The largest route network on mainland Norway and the only flights to Longyearbyen (Svalbard).

Widerøe (www.wideroe.no) Subsidiary of SAS with smaller planes and a handful of flights to small regional airports.

Bicycle

Given Norway's great distances, hilly terrain and narrow roads, extensive cycling can be arduous. Most of Norway's thousands of tunnels are closed to nonmotorised traffic; in many cases there are outdoor bike paths running parallel to the tunnels.

Rural buses, express ferries and non-express trains carry bikes for additional fees (around Nkr125), but express trains don't allow them. On international trains you'll need to pay excess baggage (around Nkr300). Nor-Way Bussekspress charges a child's fare to transport a bicycle.

Some tourist offices, hostels, camping grounds and *sykkelbutikken* (bicycle shops) rent out bicycles (around Nkr70 for an hour, up to Nkr300 per day).

Boat

An extensive network of ferries and express boats links Norway's offshore islands, coastal towns and fjord districts.

The Norwegian Tourist Board has schedules and prices; try *Rutebok for Norge* (www.rutebok.no). Tourist offices have timetables for local ferries.

The **Hurtigruten coastal ferry** (☑81 00 30 30; www.hurtigruten.com) links coastal towns and villages. One of 11 *Hurtigruten* ferries heads north from Bergen most nights, pulling into 35 ports on its six-day journey to Kirkenes. The return journey takes 11 days and covers 5200km. Meals are served in the dining room and you can buy snacks and light meals in the cafeteria.

You can book long-haul *Hurtigruten* trips online, but shorter legs should be booked once in Norway. All tickets can be purchased from most Norwegian travel agencies. The *Hurtigruten* website carries a list of international sales agents.

Summer fares (from mid-April to mid-September) are considerably more expensive than winter prices. Prices depend on the type of cabin, which range from those without view to supremely comfortable suites.

Cars can be carried for an extra fee. Children aged four to 16 years, students and seniors over the age of 67 all receive a 50% discount, as do accompanying spouses and children aged 16 to 25 years.

Bus

Nor-Way Bussekspress (☑81 54 44 44; www.nor-way.no), the main carrier, has routes connecting every main city. Cheaper buses are operated by **Lavprisekspressen** (www.lavprisekspressen.no), which sells tickets over the internet. Its buses travel the coast between Oslo and Stavanger (via Kristiansand and most towns in between) and along two north–south corridors linking Oslo with

Trondheim. Tickets bought online can cost as little as Nkr49 (Oslo to Trondheim).

Most local bus companies operate within a single county.

Bus timetables (and some prices) can be found in the free *Rutehefte*; available from most bus stations and some tourist offices.

Advance reservations are rarely required; Nor-Way Bussekspress has a 'Seat Guarantee – No Reservation' policy.

Car & Motorcycle

Some mountain passes close in winter and spring, until May or June. The **Road User Information Centre** (☎175) has the latest road conditions. Main highways, such as the E16 from Oslo to Bergen and the E6 from Oslo to Kirkenes, are open year-round.

Cars in snow-covered areas should have studded tyres or carry chains.

Norway's west coast is mountainous and deeply cut by fjords. Driving requires you to pass numerous ferry crossings, which can be time-consuming and costly. A full list of ferry schedules, fares and reservation phone number; are printed in *Rutebok for Norge,* the transport guide available in larger bookshops.

AUTOMOBILE ASSOCIATIONS
24-Hour Breakdown Assistance (☎08505)

Norges Automobil-Forbund (NAF; ☎92 60 85 05; www.naf.no)

DRIVERS LICENCE
Short-term visitors may hire a car with their home country's driving licence.

FUEL
Leaded and unleaded petrol and diesel are available at most petrol stations. At the time of writing prices ranged from Nkr11 to Nkr13 per litre. Diesel costs around Nkr1 per litre less. You can pay with major credit cards at most service stations.

In towns, petrol stations open until 10pm or midnight, but there are some 24-hour services (some are unmanned and you pay by credit card). In rural areas, many stations close early evening and don't open on weekends.

HIRE
Car hire is costly in Norway and geared to the business traveller. Walk-in rates for a compact car with 200km per day free are around Nkr1000 per day (including VAT insurance starts at Nkr60 per day extra). In summer ask about special offers.

Consider hiring your car in Sweden and returning it there afterwards, or negotiate a slightly more expensive one-way deal. Driving a Swedish rental car into Norway sometimes attracts an extra fee (around Skr1200), although usually only on summer rentals. The following online rental agencies act as clearing houses for cheap rates from major companies:

Auto Europe (www.auto-europe.com)

Autos Abroad (www.autosabroad.com)

Ideamerge (www.ideamerge.com)

INSURANCE
Third-party car insurance (unlimited cover for personal injury and Nkr1 million for property damage) is compulsory. If you're bringing a vehicle from abroad, an insurance

ROAD TOLLS

Driving around Norway, you'll soon become accustomed to the ominous 'Bomstasjon – Toll Plaza' signs. Apart from some smaller country roads, most of Norway's toll stations are automated. If you're driving a Norwegian rental car, they'll be fitted with an automatic sensor – after you return your car, the hire company adds up the accumulated tolls and charges your credit card.

If you're driving a foreign-registered car (including some rental cars from other countries), you're expected to register your credit card in advance online at www.autopass. no (and pay a deposit). The tolls are later deducted. The alternative is to stop at one of the pay stations (sometimes the first petrol station after the toll station) to pay there. If you don't pay, the authorities will, in theory, attempt to track you down once you return home (often six months later) and you may have to pay both the toll and a penalty fee of Nkr300.

company Green Card outlines the coverage granted by your home policy. Make sure your vehicle is insured for ferry crossings.

ROAD RULES

» Blood-alcohol limit 0.02%.

» Dipped headlights (including on motorcycles) are required at all times. Right-hand-drive vehicles must have beam deflectors to avoid blinding oncoming traffic.

» Legal age to drive a car: 18 years.

» Legal driving age to ride a motorcycle or scooter: 16 to 21 years (depending on the motorcycle's power); a licence is required.

» Motorcycles may not be parked on the pavement (sidewalk); they are subject to the same parking regulations as cars.

» Red warning triangles are compulsory in all vehicles.

» Drive on the right.

» Speed limits: open road (80km/h); if passing a house or business (60km/h to 70km/h); in villages (50km/h to 60km/h); in residential areas (30km/h). A few roads have segments allowing 90km/h or 100km/h. The speed limit for caravans (and cars pulling trailers) is usually 10km/h less than for cars.

Train

Norwegian State Railways (Norges Statsbaner; NSB; ☑81 50 08 88, press 9 for English; www.nsb.no) connects Oslo with Stavanger,

MINIPRIS – A TRAVELLER'S BEST FRIEND

On every long-distance train route, for every departure, Norwegian State Railways sets aside a limited number of tickets known as *minipris*. Those who book the earliest can get just about any route for just Nkr199. Once those are exhausted, the next batch of *minipris* tickets goes for Nkr299 and so on. These tickets cannot be purchased at ticket counters and must instead be bought over the internet (www.nsb. no) or in ticket-vending machines at train stations. *Minipris* tickets must be purchased at least one day in advance, reservations are nonrefundable and cannot be changed once purchased.

Bergen, Åndalsnes, Trondheim, Fauske and Bodø; lines also connect Sweden with Oslo, Trondheim and Narvik.

Most long-distance day trains have 1st- and 2nd-class seats and a buffet car or refreshment trolley service.

Reservations sometimes cost an additional Nkr50 and are mandatory on some long-distance routes.

There's a 50% discount for seniors (67 years and older), for travellers with disabilities, and for children (aged four to 15 years); children under four travel free. The student discount is 25% to 40%.

Sweden

Why Go?

As progressive and civilised as it may be, Sweden is a wild place. Its scenery ranges from barren moonscapes and impenetrable forests in the far north to sunny beaches and lush farmland further south. Its short summers and long winters mean that people cling to every last speck of sunshine on a late August evening – crayfish parties on seaside decks can stretch into the wee hours. In winter locals rely on candlelight and *glögg* to warm their spirits. But lovers of the outdoors will thrive here in any season: winter sees skiing and dog sledding while the warmer months invite long hikes, swimming and sunbathing, canoeing, cycling, you name it – if it's fun and can be done outdoors, you'll find it here. For less rugged types, there's always restaurant and nightclub hopping and museum perusing in cosmopolitan Stockholm, lively Göteborg and beyond.

Best Places to Eat

» Mat & Destillat (p427)
» Thörnströms Kök (p436)
» Frantzén/Lindeberg (p403)
» Salt och Brygga (p425)
» Camp Ripan Restaurang (p466)

Best Places to Stay

» Hotel Hellsten (p402)
» Icehotel (p465)
» Vandrarhem Högbonden (p456)
» Hotell Borgholm (p449)
» Avalon (p435)

When to Go
Stockholm

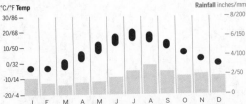

°C/°F Temp / Rainfall inches/mm

Jun-Aug Summers are short but intense, and the 'white nights' beyond the Arctic Circle magical.

Sep-Oct Nothing's open, but the countryside is stunning in autumn.

Dec-Mar Winter sports and the aurora borealis (Northern Lights) keep Norrland towns buzzing.

Connections

Trains and buses link Sweden with Norway, Finland and Denmark. Flights connect Göteborg and Stockholm to Iceland. Stockholm-Arlanda Airport connects Sweden with the rest of the world, and domestic flights connect the capital with the country's northern- and southernmost cities. Frequent ferries sail between Swedish ports and destinations in Denmark, Finland, Norway, Germany and parts of Eastern Europe.

ITINERARIES

One Week

Spend three days exploring Stockholm and Uppsala, and two days in and around Göteborg before continuing south to dynamic Malmö or flying to medieval Visby. In winter, get acclimatised in Stockholm before heading north to Kiruna and Abisko for dog sledding, aurora borealis–viewing and stays at the Icehotel.

Two Weeks

In summer, include a trip northwards to the Lake Siljan region, then head further up towards Sundsvall to explore the dramatic cliffs of Höga Kusten and to Abisko for great hiking. In winter, add skiing in Åre. Go in search of the lake monster in Östersund before detouring west to Åre for some extreme mountain biking and then head north to check out Sweden's most beautiful drive – the Wilderness Road.

Essential Food & Drink

» **Köttbullar och potatis** Meatballs and mashed potatoes, served with *lingonsylt* (lingonberry jam).

» **Gravlax** Cured salmon.

» **Sill & strömming** Herring, eaten smoked, fried or pickled and often accompanied by capers, mustard and onion.

» **Toast skagen** Toast with bleak roe, *crème fraiche* and chopped red onion.

» **Brännvin** Sweden's trademark spirit, also called aquavit and drunk as *snaps* (vodka).

AT A GLANCE

» **Capital** Stockholm

» **Area** 449,964 sq km

» **Population** 9.4 million

» **Country code** 46

» **Language** Swedish, plus the officially protected minority languages Romani, Finnish, Yiddish, Meänkieli (Finnish dialects) and Sámi (10 languages)

» **Currency** krona (Skr)

Exchange Rates

Australia	A$1	Skr6.70
Canada	C$1	Skr6.75
Euro Zone	€1	Skr8.64
Japan	¥100	Skr8.08
New Zealand	NZ$1	Skr5.59
UK	UK£1	Skr10.72
USA	US$1	Skr6.67

Set Your Budget

» **Budget hotel room** from Skr800

» **Two-course evening meal** Skr270

» **Museum entrance** Skr70–110

» **Beer** Skr52–60

» **Stockholm tunnelbana ticket (single trip)** Skr37

Resources

» **Visit Sápmi** (www.visitsapmi.com)

» **Visit Sweden** (www.visitsweden.com)

» **White Guide** (www.whiteguide.se) The best Swedish eating and drinking establishments.

Sweden Highlights

1 Tour the urban waterways, exploring top-notch museums and wandering the labyrinthine Old Town of **Stockholm** (p389)

2 Hike through wild landscapes, seeing herds of reindeer, absorbing Sámi culture and sleeping in the world-famous **Icehotel** (p465) in Jukkasjärvi

3 Dig into the art, fashion and originality that make Sweden's 'second city' of **Göteborg** (p430) first-rate

4 Celebrate Midsummer in the heartland villages surrounding lovely **Lake Siljan** (p420)

5 Join the feasting, archery and other medieval fun and frolics in historic **Visby** (p454)

6 Race a dog sled under the Northern Lights near **Kiruna** (p464)

7 Take a car for a spin on a frozen lake near **Arvidsjaur** (p462)

STOCKHOLM

📞 08 / POP 1.4 MILLION

Beautiful capital cities are no rarity in Europe, but Stockholm must surely be near the top of the list for sheer loveliness. The saffron-and-cinnamon buildings that cover its 14 islands rise starkly out of the surrounding ice-blue water, honeyed in sunlight and frostily elegant in cold weather. The city's charms are irresistible. From its movie-set Old Town (Gamla Stan) to its ever-modern fashion sense and impeccable taste in food and design, the city acts like an immersion school in aesthetics.

History

Legend has it that when the town of Sigtuna burned to the ground in 1187, the burghers put all their money into a hollow log and set it afloat, saying, 'Wherever this log washes up, that's where we'll settle next.' An equally reliable story holds that a rebellious fisherman in ancient times caught the biggest fish of his life and swore that it would grace the table of no bishop; so he swam off with the salmon, and where they landed became Stockholm.

Whichever origin story you believe, it's clear that the waterways had a hand in establishing Stockholm's location. Vikings moved their trade centre here from northern Mälaren lake for easier sea–lake trade. Around 1250, Stockholm's leaders wrote a town charter and signed a trade treaty with the Hanseatic port of Lübeck. Stockholm's official founder, Birger Jarl, commissioned the Tre Kronor castle in 1252.

A century later, Stockholm was hurting. The Black Death of 1350 wiped out a third of the population, and in 1391 the Danish Queen Margareta Valdemarsdotter besieged the city for four years. This led to the Union of Kalmar, which linked the crowns of Sweden, Norway and Denmark in 1397. But Sweden soon began to chafe under the union. Discontent peaked with the Stockholm Bloodbath of 1520, when Danish King Christian II tricked, trapped and beheaded 82 Swedish burghers, bishops and nobles on Stortorget in Gamla Stan. One of the 82 victims was the father of Gustav Eriksson Vasa; Gustav Vasa's quest to retaliate eventually led to widespread rebellion against Danish rule – and he became King of Sweden on 6 June 1523. These days, Swedes view Gustav Vasa as equal parts 'father of the country' and ruthless tyrant.

By the end of the 16th century, Stockholm's population was 9000 and had expanded beyond Gamla Stan to the neighbouring islands of Norrmalm and Södermalm. The city was officially proclaimed Sweden's capital in 1634, and by 1650 the city had a thriving artistic and intellectual culture and a grand new look, courtesy of father-and-son architects the Tessins. The next growth spurt came in 1871, when Sweden's northern and southern train lines met at Centralstationen (Central Station) and started an industrial boom. The city's population reached 245,000 in 1890.

Sweden's famed neutrality left it and its capital city in good shape through both World Wars, but modern times have seen some blemishes on Stockholm's rosy reputation – including the still-unsolved murder of Prime Minister Olof Palme in 1986 and the stabbing death of foreign minister Anna Lindh in 2003. These days, the capital is part of a major European biotechnology region, not to mention a rising star on the world stages of fashion and culinary arts.

⊙ Sights

Stockholm is a compact, walkable city, with sights distributed across all central neighbourhoods. The modern city spreads out from its historic core, Gamla Stan, home to the Royal Palace. Two smaller, satellite islands are linked to it by bridges: Riddarholmen, whose church is home to the royal crypt, to the west, and Helgeandsholmen, home of the Swedish parliament building, to the north. The tourist office is just across the street from Centralstationen, on the main island.

Many of Stockholm's best museums are on Djurgården, east of Gamla Stan, and the small island of Skeppsholmen. Södermalm, the city's funky, bohemian neighbourhood, lies south of Gamla Stan, just beyond the rather baffling traffic interchange called Slussen.

GAMLA STAN

Once you get over the armies of tourists wielding ice-cream cones and shopping bags, you'll discover that the oldest part of Stockholm is also its most beautiful. The city emerged here in the 13th century and grew with Sweden's power until the 17th century, when the castle of Tre Kronor, symbol of that power, burned to the ground. While ambling along Västerlånggatan, look out

Stockholm

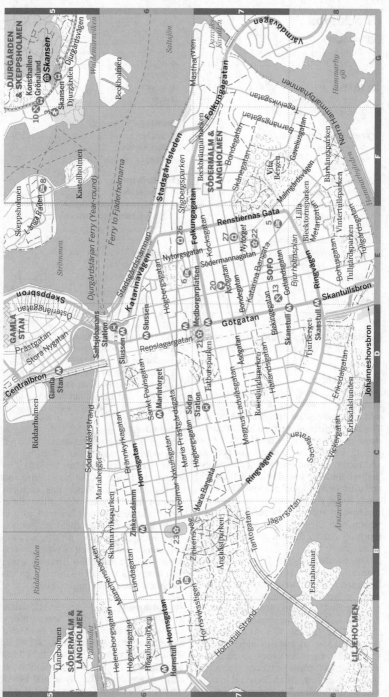

DJURGÅRDEN & SKEPPSHOLMEN

Konsthallen
Gröhalund
Skansen
10
3
Skansen
Djurgården Djurgårdsvägen

Skeppsholmen
Långa Raden
8
Kastellholmen
Beckholmen

GAMLA STAN
Skeppsbron
Östanänggatan
Prästgatan
Stora Nygatan
Gamla Stan
Centralbron
Riddarholmen

Waldemarsviken
Saltsjön
Djurgårdsfärjan Ferry (Year-round)
Ferry to Fjäderholmarna
Djurgårdshamnen
Stadsgårdshamnen
Stadsgårdsleden
Stadsgårdshamnen
Katarinavägen

SÖDERMALM & LÅNGHOLMEN
Beckbränmarbacken
Stigbergsparken
Stadsbergsparken

SÖDERMALM & LÅNGHOLMEN
Långholmen
Pålsundet
Riddarfjärden

Strömmen
Saltsjöbanans Station
Slussen
Slussen
Repslagargatan
Mariatorget
Mariatorget
Sankt Paulsgatan
Södra Station

Hornsgatan
Söder Mälarstrand
Brännkyrkagatan
Maria Prästgårdsgata
Högbergsgatan
Fatbursparken
Wollmar Yxkullsgatan
Maria Bangata

Folkungagatan
Nytorgsgatan
Högbergsgatan
Medborgarplatsen
Götgatan
Folkungagatan
26
6
20
21
Södermannagatan
Kocksgatan
Åsögatan
Bondegatan

Renstiernas Gata
27
Nytorget
22
5
SOFO
Katarina Bangata
Gotlandsgatan
13
Blekingegatan
Skanstull
Skanstull
Tjurberget
Skanstullsbron

Ringvägen
Björnholmsplan
Ringvägen
Skånegatan
Malmgårdsvägen
Vita Bergen
Lilla
Bleckthornsparken
Metargatan
Bondegatan
Vintertullsparken
Bohusgatan
Tullgårdsparken
Tullgårdsgatan

Barnängsparken
Norra Hammarbyhamnen
Tegelviksgatan
Tegelviksgatan
Barnängsgatan
Gaveliusgatan
Hammarbyleden
Hammarby sjö

Värmdövägen
Danviks Kanalen
Masthamnen
Masthamnen

Åsögatan
Magnus Ladulåsgatan
Rosenlundsparken
Hallandsgatan
Eriksdalsgatan
Eriksdalslunden
Eriksgatan
Johanneshovsbron

9
23
Zinkensdamm
Zinkensdamm
Zinkensvikparken
Zinkensväg
Hornstulls Strand
Hornsvikstigen
Hornstull
Hornstull
Hornsgatan
Ängslättsparken

Helenborgsgatan
Högalidsgatan
Högalidsparken
Lundagatan
Münchenbryggeriet
Skinnarviksparken
Mariaberget

Vintertullsparken
Sachsgatan
Vickergatan
Ringvägen
Tantogatan
Jägargatan

LILJEHOLMEN
Erstaholmar
Årstaviken

SÖDERMALM & LÅNGHOLMEN

Stockholm

for **Mårten Trotzigs Gränd** by No 81: this is Stockholm's narrowest lane, at less than 1m wide.

Kungliga Slottet   PALACE
(Royal Palace; Map p396; www.royalcourt.se; Slottsbacken; adult/student & child Skr150/75, valid for 7 days; ☺10am-5pm mid-May–mid-Sep) The 'new' Renaissance palace is built on the ruins of Tre Kronor, which burnt to the ground in the 17th century. Its baroque and rococo interior, comprising 608 rooms, makes it the largest royal palace in the world still used for its original purpose. The sumptuous **Royal Apartments** – two floors of royal pomp and princely portraits – overwhelm with their opulence and size – so much so that it's difficult to focus on individual detail.

The Swedish regalia – sceptres, royal swords, coronation gown and crowns are displayed at **Skattkammaren** (Royal Treasury), by the southern entrance to the palace near **Slottskyrkan** (Royal Chapel); the loveliest is the delicate crown of princess Sofia (1770). **Gustav III's Antikmuseum** (open mid-May to mid-Sep only) displays the Mediterranean treasures, in particular more than 200 classic sculptures, acquired by the eccentric monarch. Descend into the basement **Museum Tre Kronor** to see the foundations of 13th-century defensive walls and exhibits rescued from the medieval castle during the fire of 1697.

The **Changing of the Guard** takes place in the outer courtyard at 12.15pm Monday to Saturday and 1.15pm Sunday and public holidays from 23 April to the end of August.

Nobelmuseet   MUSEUM
(Map p396; http://nobelmuseet.se; Stortorget; adult/senior & student/child Skr80/60/free; ☺10am-6pm Jun-Aug, 11am-8pm Sep-May) Presenting the history of the Nobel Prize and its founder, Alfred Nobel, this excellent museum features great short films about the achievements of past laureates as well as changing exhibitions about art, science, creativity and inspiration. Befitting a museum dedicated to the spirit of creativity and invention, it's a beautifully designed space, with long sleek rows of information panels and subtly placed multimedia nooks.

Royal Armoury   MUSEUM
(Livrustkammaren; Map p396; www.livrustkammaren.se; Slottsbacken 3; adult/under 19yr Skr80/ free; ☺11am-5pm Fri-Wed, to 8pm Thu ; ☐2, 43, 55, 71, 76, 96 Slottsbacken, ⓂT13, 14, 17, 18,19 Gamla Stan) Highlights of this strategically-lit cellar armoury are the stuffed horse and bloodstained garments of Gustanv Adolf II who

died in the battle of Lützen in 1632, as well as a wealth of weaponry and suits of armour, an ermine-trimmed royal gown, and Cinderella-esque coaches that you can imagine turning into pumpkins at midnight.

Riddarholmskyrkan
CHURCH

(Riddarholmen Church; Map p396; www.kungahuset.se; Kungliga Slottet; adult/student & child Skr40/20; ⊙10am-5pm daily mid-May-mid-Sep; ☐2,43,55,71,76,96, Ⓜ Gamla Stan) The island of Riddarholmen has some of the oldest buildings in Stockholm, most prominently this church with its striking iron spire, where Sweden's past royals are seeing out eternity. Look out for the green marble sarcophagus of Gustav II Adolf. Guided tours (in English at 4pm) are highly recommended.

Storkyrkan
CHURCH

(Map p396; www.stockholmsdomkyrkoforsamling. se; Trångsund 1; adult/student Skr40/free; ⊙9am-4pm) Near the palace is the Great Church – the closest Stockholm comes to a cathedral, consecrated in 1306. Its most notable feature is the splendid life-sized *St George & the Dragon* sculpture, dating from the late 15th century. Free English tours at 11am Wednesday and 9.15am Thursday.

Medeltidsmuseet
MUSEUM

(Medieval Museum; Map p396; www.medeltids museet.stockholm.se; Strömparterren; adult/under 19 yr Skr70/free; ⊙noon-5pm Thu-Tue, to 7pm Wed Jul-Aug; 📷; ☐43, 62, 65, 71 Gustav Adolfs torg) This atmospheric, kid-friendly museum was built around the ancient walls found on this spot in the late 1970s, dating from the 1530s. There's a new medieval-themed exhibition every year, with engaging past exhibitions including 'Gambling Den' and 'Thine for Ever – Love and Alliances in the Middle Ages'.

DJURGÅRDEN

A former royal hunting reserve, Djurgården is an urban oasis of parkland with some of Stockholm's best museums. To get here, take bus or tram 47, or the Djurgården ferry from Nybroplan or Slussen. Walking or cycling is the best way to explore the island; you can rent bikes near the bridge in summer.

TOP CHOICE Vasamuseet
MUSEUM

(Map p390; www.vasamuseet.se; Galärvarvsvägen 14; adult/student/under 19yr Skr110/80/free; ⊙8.30am-6pm, to 8pm Wed; 📷; ☐7 Nordiska museet/Vasa) You'd think that people who came from Viking stock (sailing great distances in longboats etc) would be able to build a decent ship. But no, the massive warship *Vasa* didn't even make it out of the harbour. A whopping 69m long and 48.8m tall, the pride of the Swedish crown set off on its maiden voyage on 10 August 1628. Within minutes, the top-heavy vessel and its 100-member crew capsized tragicomically to the bottom of Saltsjön. The *Vasa* has since been raised from the bottom of the sea and stands proud and dramatically lit in the middle of the vast hall, with partially interactive, nautically themed exhibits occupying

---

STOCKHOLM IN...

Two Days

Beat the crowds to the labyrinthine streets of **Gamla Stan** for a coffee in an atmospheric, ancient cafe on **Stortorget**, the main square. Watch St George wrestle the dragon inside **Storkyrkan**, then join a tour of **Kungliga Slottet**, the royal palace, or simply watch the midday changing of the guard. Wander down to Slussen and catch a ferry across to **Skeppsholmen** for lunch and Lichtenstein at **Moderna Museet**, then walk back to Södermalm for dizzying views atop **Katarinahissen** and an evening of dinner and drinks in funky **Södermalm** (try the bar-lined street Skånegatan). Spend the next day visiting the dramatic **Vasamuseet** and its neighbours before dinner and drinks at **Mathias Dahlgren** – and if you have energy left, check out some of the clubs around **Stureplan**.

Four Days

Start with a little detour out of town on the third day – if the weather's nice, rent a bicycle and follow the bicycle path to **Drottningholm Slott**. You'll be hungry when you return, so how about a hearty dinner at **Båtfickan Djuret**? Next day, take a boat tour onto the archipelago, then dine at the Grand Hôtel's **Veranda** restaurant and finish in style with a drink at **Marie Laveau**.

MUSEUM ITINERARY: VASAMUSEET

As soon as you enter Vasamuseet, you can't help but marvel at the museum's centre-piece, subtly lit to great effect. The 17th century **Vasa galleon**, built to be Sweden's greatest warship, instead became the subject of great controversy, sinking within minutes of sailing. Divided into six levels that allow you to admire the salvaged and restored *Vasa* from keel to stern, the museum itself resembles the insides of a giant ship, blending skilfully presented exhibits with a wood-panelled interior.

Duck into the **screening room** by the entrance for an excellent video introduction to the ship's conception on King Gustav Vasa's orders, its watery demise, its rescue in 1961 and the challenge of preserving the world's largest wooden museum exhibit.

Head down to Level 2, where a combination of paintings and models takes you through the construction and sinking of **His Majesty's Ship**, including the fatal errors in the ship's construction that made her unseaworthy. The scale models at **Stockholm Shipyard** show how ships were built in 1620, and you can check out the *Vasa* during different stages of construction. Next, you come **Face to Face** with several of the ship's denizens through a mix of facial reconstruction and interactive displays. Fifteen skeletons from the ship have been dated by the radiocarbon method to determine age and health, their social status and possible occupation determined from their possessions and their location on the ship. Nearby, through a range of interactive displays, **Preserving the Vasa** explores various solutions to halting the ship's slow decomposition.

On main Level 4, **The Salvaging** walks you through the delicate process of the ship's recovery from the bottom of the harbour in 1961 via its discovery in 1956 by amateur archaeologist Anders Franzén.

If it hadn't been for the *Vasa's* ignominious sinking, the ship's destiny would have been victory or destruction on the high seas: **Battle!** on Level 5 puts you in the middle of a nautical skirmish. A rich collection of period objects gives you an insight into day-to-day **Life on Board** in between battles.

Finally, on Level 6, **The Sailing Ship** showcases the original preserved sails from the *Vasa*, while **Imagery of Power** explains the symbolism of the *Vasa's* 700 ornaments and sculptures that added to the ship's fatal weight.

---

several floors beside it. The most interesting of these are the reconstructions of some of the passengers on board based on the physical evidence at hand – down on the bottom level.

It's well worth taking a guided tour, as the guides explain the extraordinary and controversial 300-year story of the ship's death and resurrection, which saw the ship painstakingly raised in 1961 and reassembled like a giant 14,000-piece jigsaw. Almost all of what you see today is original. Guided tours are in English every 30 minutes in summer, and at least twice daily the rest of the year.

TOP CHOICE Skansen   MUSEUM
(Map p390; www.skansen.se; Djurgårdsvägen; adult/senior/child Skr150/130/60; ⊙10am-10pm late Jun-Aug; ⊕) The world's first open-air museum, Skansen was founded in 1891 by Artur Hazelius to give visitors an insight into how Swedes lived once upon a time. You and your kids could easily spend a day

here and still not see it all. It's 'Sweden in miniature', divided into regions, complete with traditional houses (check out the Sámi dwellings), nature, handicrafts, pastimes such as glass-blowing and even food stalls serving traditional foods. The **Nordic Zoo** enclosures, scattered throughout, showcase elk, reindeer, wolverine and other native wildlife, and are a particular highlight, especially in spring when baby critters scamper around. Check the website for individual workshop closing times.

Nordiska Museet   MUSEUM
(Map p390; www.nordiskamuseet.se; Djurgårds-vägen 6-16; adult/under 19yr Skr90/free; ⊙10am-5pm daily Jun-Aug, 10am-5pm Thu-Tue, to 8pm Wed Sep-May) The epic Nordiska really delves into Swedish culture with its enormous collection of all things Swedish, from 'Power of Fashion', spanning 300 years, to sacred Sámi objects and Strindberg paintings to folk art and embroidery, intricate dollhouses, festivals, weddings and rituals.

Gröna Lund Tivoli AMUSEMENT PARK
(Map p390; www.gronalund.com; Djurgårdsvägen; adult/senior & under 7yr Skr95/free; unlimited ride pass Skr299; ☺noon-10pm Mon-Sat, to 8pm Sun Jun, 11am-10pm Sun-Thu, to 11pm Fri & Sat Jul–early Aug, varies May & early Aug–mid-Sep; 🚇; ☐44 Stockholm Liljevalc Gröna Lund, 🚢977, ☐7 Stockholm Liljevalc Gröna Lund) This fun park has 30 rides and amusements – most are aimed at younger children, but thrill seekers can still lose their lunch on Fritt Fall, Free Fall Tilt, Insane and Catapult. Big-name concerts often held here in summer.

CENTRAL STOCKHOLM

The fashionable, high-heeled heart of modern-day Stockholm beats in bustling Norrmalm. Near T-Centralen station is **Sergels Torg**, a severely modern public square (actually round) bordered on one side by the imposing Kulturhuset. Norrmalm is also home to the beloved public park **Kungsträdgården** – home to an outdoor stage, winter ice-skating rink and restaurants, cafes and kiosks. Vasastan is the somewhat quieter, more residential area that extends to the north of Norrmalm.

Nationalmuseum MUSEUM
(National Art Museum; Map p396; www.national-museum.se; Södra Blasieholmshamnen; adult/senior & student/under 19yr Skr120/100/free; ☺11am-5pm Wed-Sun, to 8pm Tue Jun-Aug) Sweden's largest art museum is rather overpowering with its sheer collection of treasures from the Middle Ages to the present. Ground floor: temporary exhibitions of drawings and prints. First floor: applied arts – furniture that belonged to royals, and tapestries and more. Second floor: the unmissable, immense and once-controversial 'Midwinter Sacrifice,' one of several Carl Larsson paintings gracing the walls above the main stairway; works by Rembrandt, El Greco, various 16th to 18th century Swedish artists and Mediterranean and European sculpture. In summer 2013 the museum temporarily moved to the Academy of Art on Fredsgatan 12.

Historiska Museet MUSEUM
(Map p390; www.historiska.se; Narvavägen 13; adult/senior & student/under 19yr Skr80/60/free; ☺10am-5pm May-Sep) Sweden's main national historical collection covers prehistoric, Viking and medieval archaeology and culture. Don't miss the magnificent **Gold Room** with its 5th-century bling, including a seven-ringed gold collar. Another enthralling exhibit is a Stone Age home, as well as the Viking weaponry and boats.

Kulturhuset LEISURE COMPLEX
(Map p396; www.kulturhuset.stockholm.se; Sergels Torg; ☺11am-5pm; some sections closed Mon; 🚇; ☐52, 56, 59, 69, 91 Stockholm Sergels Torg, Ⓜ10, 11, 13, 14, 17, 18, 19 T-Centralen, ☐7 Stockholm Sergels Torg Spårv) This glass-fronted community centre in Sergels Torg houses temporary art and craft exhibitions (often with entry fee), a theatre, bookshop, design store, reading room, several cafes (including one upstairs with great views of central Stockholm), a comics library and bar.

SKEPPSHOLMEN

Moderna Museet MUSEUM
(Map p396; www.modernamuseet.se; Exercisplan 4; adult/senior & student/under 19yr Skr120/100/free; ☺10am-8pm Tue & Fri, to 6pm Wed, Thu, Sat & Sun) The sleek, impressive Moderna boasts a world-class collection of modern art, sculpture, photography and installations, temporary exhibitions and an outdoor sculpture garden. Besides standout works by Jackson Pollock, Salvador Dalí, Kandinsky, Yoko Ono and others, mesmerising temporary exhibits have included a crucifixion video involving plenty of pig's blood.

Östasiatiska Museet MUSEUM
(Museum of Far Eastern Antiquities; Map p396; www.ostasiatiska.se; Tyghusplan; adult/under 19yr Skr100/free; ☺11am-8pm Tue, 11am-5pm Wed-Sun; ☐65 Stockholm Östasiatiska museet) Famed for its world-class booty of ancient Eastern art, stoneware and porcelain, this museum showcases some incredible craftsmanship – from the miniature Japanese sculptures of demons and woodblock prints of the 'floating world' to Chinese ink-painting and elegant Korean pottery. Also noteworthy is the collection of wares from the Chinese dynasties of Song, Ming and Qing, as well as the museum's fresh temporary shows, which cover anything from manga to the art of Japanese tattoos.

KUNGSHOLMEN

Stadshuset NOTABLE BUILDING
(City Hall; Map p396; www.stockholm.se/stadshuset; Hantverkargatan 1; admission by tour only, adult/senior & student/child Skr100/80/40, tower admission Skr40; ☺10am, 11am, noon, 1pm, 2pm & 3pm; tower 9am-5pm Jun-Aug, 9am-4pm May & Sep; ☐3, 62 Stadshuset) Resembling a large church with two internal courtyards, the landmark Stadshuset, where visiting heads of state

Central Stockholm

SWEDEN STOCKHOLM

400 m
0.2 miles

NORRMALM & VASASTAN

ÖSTERMALM, GÄRDET & LADUGÅRDSGÄRDET

KUNGSHOLMEN

Streets & Places

Torsgatan
Kammakargatan
Wallingatan
Barnhusgatan
Olof Palmes Gata
Kungsgatan
Apelbergsgatan
Olofsgatan
Hötorget
Slöjdgatan
Drottninggatan
Sergelgatan
Sveavägen
Brunnsgatan
Malmskillnadsgatan
Regeringsgatan
Master Samuelsgatan
Lastmakargatan
Jakobsbergsgatan
Biblioteksgatan
Birger Jarlsgatan
Norrlandsgatan
Humlegårdsgatan
Grev Turegatan
Linnégatan
Artillerigatan
Storgatan
Skeppargatan
Grevgatan
Styrmansgatan
Strandvägen
Nybroplan
Nybrogatan
Sibyllegatan
Östermalmstorg
Riddargatan
Kaptensgatan

Östra Järnvägsgatan
Vasagatan
Klara Norra Kyrkogatan
Klara Östra Kyrkogatan
Klara Västra Kyrkogatan
Drottninggatan
Klarabergsgatan
Master Samuelsgatan
Bryggargatan
Gamla Brogatan
Målargatan
Kungsbron

Norra Bantorget
Hötorget
Norrmalmstorg
Stureplan
Norrlandsgatan
Smålandsgatan
Hamngatan
Kungsträdgården
Västra Trädgårdsgatan
Jakobs Torg
Gustav Adolfs Torg
Karl XII's Torg
Karl XIII's Torg
Kungsträdgårdsgatan
Brunkebergstorg
Malmtorgsgatan
Herkulesgatan
Vattugatan
Jakobsgatan
Fredsgatan
Strömgatan

T-Centralen
Sergels Torg
Stockholm Centralstationen
Cityterminalen
Swebus Express
Ybuss
Viking Line
Klarabergsviadukten
Centralplan
Tourist Office
Vasagatan
Tegelbacken
Rödbodgatan
Klarafaret
Tegelbacken
Stadshusbron
Centralbron
Norra Järnvägsbron
Vasabron
Bankkajen
Helgeandsholmen
Strömbron
Strömkajen
Skeppsbron
Slottsbacken

Nationalmuseum
Museiparken
Blasieholmsgatan
Södra Blasieholmshamnen
Blasieholmen
Nybrokajen
Strömma Kanalbolaget
Djurgården Boats
Djurgårdsfärjan Ferry (Summer Only)
Visit Skärgården
Ferry to Fjäderholmarna
Nybroviken
Nybrohamnen
Berzelii Park
Raoul Wallenbergs Torg
Waxholmsbolaget Office

Gustav III's Antikmuseum
Museum Tre Kronor
Tyghuset
Tyghusplan
Skeppsholmen

Kungsträdgården
Stallgatan

Kungsgatan
Olofsgatan
Hötorget
Kungsträdgårdsgatan

Norra Bantorget
Barnhusviken
Klara Sjö
Blekholmsfaret
Serafimerstranden
Klarabergsstranden
Klarastrandsleden
Kaplansbacken
Hantverkargatan
Ragnar Östbergs Plan
Norr Mälarstrand
Norr

Silja Line
Silja Stureplan

Vasagatan

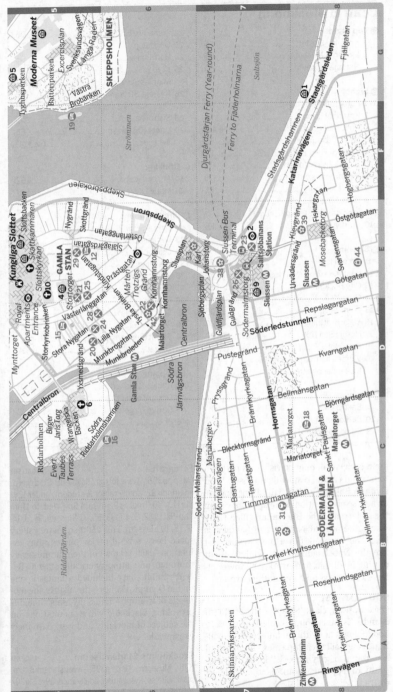

SWEDEN STOCKHOLM

Central Stockholm

are recevied, can only be visited as part of a tour. Inside is the resplendent mosaic-lined **Gyllene Salen** (Golden Hall), Prins Eugen's own fresco re-creation of the lake view from the gallery, and the **Blå Hallen** (Blue Hall), where the annual Nobel Prize banquet is held. You can walk down the staircase just like the Nobel laureates do, only without putting in all that hard work. The **tower** offers stellar views and a great thigh workout.

SÖDERMALM
Once-working-class 'Söder' – the southern island – is Stockholm's coolest neighbourhood, jammed with up-and-coming boutiques and galleries, hip cafes and bars and a museum of city history. 'SoFo' (the area south of Folkungagatan) is the trendiest district.

Fotografiska   GALLERY
(Map p396; www.fotografiska.eu; Stadsgårdshamnen 22; adult/senior & student/under 12yr Skr110/80/free; ⊙9am-9pm Sun-Wed, to 11pm Thu-Sat; 🚌2, 3, 43, 53, 55, 71 Slussen, Ⓜ13, 14, 17, 18, 19 Slussen) This 2500-sq-metre gallery space hosts several major photography exhibitions each year, all of them impressively thorough and atmospherically staged. Recent exhibits have included a fantastic one on the Olympic Games – the history, the moments of triumph – and Sally Mais' thought-provoking black-and-white meditations on the subject of mortality and loss. Extremely worthwhile.

Stockholms Stadsmuseum   MUSEUM
(City Museum; Map p396; www.stadsmuseum. stockholm.se; Ryssgården; adult/under 19yr Skr70/free; ⊙11am-5pm Tue-Sun, 11am-8pm Thu; 🛜👶;

13, 14, 17, 18, 19 Slussen) The city museum covers Stockholm's development from fortified port to modern metropolis via plague, fire and good old-fashioned scandal through a range of artefacts and interactive displays, and there's a special display on Raoul Wallenberg – the saviour of around 30,000 Hungarian Jews. Fans of Stieg Larsson's *Girl with the Dragon Tattoo* novel trilogy can take the museum's Millennium tour (in English at 11.30am and 2pm Saturday, tickets Skr120; self-guided tour map Skr40).

LADUGÅRDSGÄRDET

The vast parkland of Ladugårdsgärdet is part of the 27-sq-km **Ekoparken** (www.eko-parken.org), the world's first national park within a city. An impressive 14km long, its combo of forest and open fields stretches far into the capital's northern suburbs. This section of it, reached by bus 69 from Central-stationen or Sergels Torg, boasts three fine museums and one of Stockholm's loftiest views.

Etnografiska Museet   MUSEUM
(Museum of Ethnography; www.etnografiska.se; Djurgårdsbrunnsvägen 34; adult/under 18yr Skr60/free; ⊙11am-8pm Tue-Thu, 11am-5pm Fri-Sun; ♿; 🚍69 Museiparken) Highly original temporary exhibitions on non-European cultures (ranging from Amazon photography to the macabre etchings of Mexican artist José Guadalupe Posada) complement permanent collection highlights such as Mali crocodile masks, Mongolian temple tents and a Japanese teahouse.

Kaknästornet   VIEWPOINT
(www.kaknastornet.se; Mörka Kroken 28-30; adult/child Skr45/20; ⊙9am-10pm Jun-Aug; 🚍69 Stockholm Kaknästornet) This 155m-high TV tower has an observation deck with stunning 360-degree views, plus a restaurant.

🏃 Activities

Summer sees many head for the coast and the islands of the archipelago (with good swimming spots). Winter also sees some outdoor activity, including ice-skating on a rink set up in Kungsträdgården.

Sjöcafe   OUTDOOR ACTIVITIES
(Map p390; ☎08-660 57 57; canoes per hr/day Skr90/370; ⊙9am-9pm mid-Apr–mid-Sep; 🚍7 Djurgårdsbron) Next to the bridge leading to Djurgården, this place rents out bicycles, in-line skates, kayaks, canoes, rowing boats and pedal boats.

Stockholm City Bikes   CYCLING
(www.citybikes.se; 3-day/season card Skr165/300) Has around 90 self-service bicycle-hire stands across the city. To use, purchase a bike card from the tourist office.

👉 Tours

You're spoiled for choice when it comes to tours of the capital. You can take to the water with **Strömma Kanalbolaget** (☎08-12 00 40 00; www.stromma.se) for the excellent 'Under the Bridges of Stockholm' (Skr220, two hours) and 'Royal Canal Tour' (Skr160, 50 minutes) and trips to the archipelago, walk the streets in search of ghostly sightings and spooky tales with **Stockholm Ghost Walk** (www.stockholmghostwalk.com; adult/child Skr200/100), sate your artistic thirst with a tour of the Tunnelbana's diverse artwork with **Stockholm Metro Art Tours** (www.sl.se/art; ⊙Jun-Aug), and even follow in the footsteps of Blomqvist and Salander from *The Girl With the Dragon Tattoo* with **Millennium Tour** (www.stadsmuseum.stockholm.se; Skr120; ⊙11.30am & 2pm Sat).

✴️ Festivals & Events

Smaka På Stockholm   FOOD
(www.smakapastockholm.se) Taste samples from some of Stockholm's top kitchens and watch cooking duels at this week-long annual festival in Kungsträdgården, held in the first week of June.

Stockholm Pride   GAY & LESBIAN
(www.stockholmpride.org/en/) This annual parade and festival in late July to early August is dedicated to creating an atmosphere of freedom and support for gay, lesbian, bisexual and transgender people.

STOCKHOLM CARD

Available from tourist offices, camping grounds, hostels, hotels and Storstockholms Lokaltrafik (SL) public transport centres, the **Stockholm Card** (www.stockholmtown.com; adult 24/48/72/120hr Skr450/625/750/950, accompanying child Skr215/255/285/315) gives free entry to 80 attractions, free sightseeing by boat, free travel on public transport (including Katarinahissen, but excluding local ferries and airport buses), discounted boat trips to Drottingholm and more. For details, see the website.

GETTING HIGH IN STOCKHOLM

Now, we're not advocating anything illegal; rather, we're encouraging you to see the city from the following lofty viewpoints:

» **Katarinahissen** (Map p396; admission Skr10; ◷8am-10pm mid-May–Aug, 10am-6pm rest of yr) There's a great panoramic view over Stockholm from the top of this lift, dating from the 1930s. It takes you up 38m to the heights of Slussen. If you prefer, zigzagging wooden stairs also lead up the cliffs to the balcony. And if that weren't reason enough to ascend, at the top is one of the city's best restaurants, Gondolen (p404).

» **Gröna Lund Tivoli** (p395) Take a ride up Fritt Fall to cast your eye over the waterways...then scream as you plummet all the way down.

» **Stadshuset** (p395) – its tower offers stellar views and a great thigh workout.

Stockholm Jazz Festival　MUSIC
(www.stockholmjazz.com) Held in several different venues during the first week of October, this internationally known jazz festival brings artists from all over, such as Stacy Kent and the Bobo Stenson Trio; late night jam sessions at famed Stockholm jazz club Fasching are a highlight.

Stockholm International Film Festival　FILM
(www.stockholmfilmfestival.se) Screenings of new international and independent films, director talks and discussion panels draw cinephiles to this important annual festival in mid-November. Tickets go quickly, so book early if you're interested.

🛏 Sleeping

Whether you slumber in youth hostels, B&Bs, boutique digs or big-name chains, you can expect high-quality accommodation in Stockholm. It can be an expensive city to sleep in, but deals do exist! Major hotel chains are invariably cheaper if booked online and in advance, and most hotels offer discounted rates on weekends (Friday and Saturday) and Midsummer to mid-August, sometimes up to 50% off the listed price.

A number of agencies, including **Bed & Breakfast Agency** (✆08-643 80 28; www.bba.nu), can arrange single and double private rooms from Skr350 to Skr400 per person per night.

Stockholm has numerous Svenska Turistföreningen (STF) hostels affiliated with Hosteling International (HI), as well as Sveriges Vandrarhem i Förening (SVIF) and independent hostels (no membership cards required). Many have options for single, double or family rooms. Many hostels have breakfast available, usually for an additional Skr65 to Skr90. Sheets are almost always required; if you don't have your own, you'll need to rent them (around Skr55). Book in advance in summer.

Finding midrange rooms can be tricky outside peak season; in summer, many top-end hotels fall into the midrange category.

CENTRAL STOCKHOLM

City Backpackers TOP CHOICE　HOSTEL €
(Map p396; ✆08-20 69 20; www.citybackpackers.org; Upplandsgatan 2a; dm Skr190-290, s/d/tr Skr600/890/1190; ✳@) The closest hostel to Centralstationen is a great place to meet people without it being a party hostel; there are plenty of common spaces for mingling. Facilities include a sauna and guest kitchen, dorm beds have individual reading lights and excellent mattresses and the staff couldn't be more helpful. City tours are also offered, from a free weekly neighbourhood walk to themed, payable options such as 'Historic Horror'.

Berns Hotel　HOTEL €€€
(Map p396; ✆08-56 63 22 00; www.berns.se; Näckströmsgatan 8; r/ste from Skr1890/3500; ℗@☏; ⓜT-Kungsträdgården, ☏7 Kungsträdgården) Popular with rock stars, the rooms at forever-hip Berns come equipped with CD players and styles ranging from 19th-century classical to contemporary sleek. The balcony rooms are particularly impressive, while room 431 was once a dressing room used by Marlene Dietrich and Ella Fitzgerald. Complete with buzzing restaurants, bars and club, it's a sparkly choice for the party crew.

Grand Hôtel Stockholm　HOTEL €€€
(Map p396; ✆08-679 35 00; www.grandhotel.se; Södra Blasieholmshamnen 8; r/ste from Skr2040/6800; ℗@☏; ☏2,3,4,8,9,12Strömkajen,

Ⓜ T-Kungsträdgården) This is where the literati, glitterati and nobility call it a night. A waterfront landmark, with several exclusive restaurants, a piano bar and sumptuous spa, it remains Stockholm's most lux lodgings. Room styles span royal Gustavian to contemporary chic. Room 701 has a unique tower with a 360-degree view; room 702 is the astounding Nobel Room, where the literature-prize-winner slumbers overnight.

Castanea Old Town Hostel HOSTEL €
(Map p396; ☑08-22 35 51; www.castaneahostel .com; Kindstugatan 1; dm/s/d/q from Skr209/ 540/630/1100; ⏱reception 3-6pm; @🛜; Ⓜ T-13, T-14, T-17, T-18, T-19 Slussen, Gamla Stan) This hostel certainly has a lot going for it: a superb location in the middle of Gamla Stan, spic-and-span bathrooms, nice common areas and comfortable, if spartan, rooms. Perfect for those wanting a good night's sleep and a plethora of attractions right on their doorstep.

Lord Nelson Hotel HOTEL €€€
(Map p396; ☑08-50 64 01 20; www.lordnelsonhotel.se; Västerlånggatan 22; r from Skr1990; @🛜; 🚌3, 53 Riddarhustorget, Ⓜ Gamla Stan) Yo-ho-ho, me scurvy barnacles! At just 5m wide, Sweden's narrowest hotel – a glass-fronted 17th-century building – feels like a creaky old ship loaded with character. Its nautical theme extends to brass and mahogany furnishings, antique sea-captain trappings and a model ship in each of the small rooms, and the little rooftop sundeck is adorable.

Mälardrottningen HOTEL €€
(Map p396; ☑08-12 09 00 00; www.malardrott ningen.se; cabins from Skr1225; 🅿🛜; Ⓜ Gamla Stan) At one time the world's largest motor yacht, this stylish, cosy option features well-appointed cabins, each with en suite. Launched in 1924, it was once owned by American heiress Barbara Hutton (a modest gift from her father for her 18th birthday). Upper-deck, sea-side rooms offer the best views, and three rooms come with queen-sized beds for spacious slumber.

Nordic Sea Hotel HOTEL €€
(Map p396; ☑08-50 56 30 00; www.nordicseahotel. com; Vasaplan 4; s/d from Skr1280/1380; Ⓜ T-Centralen) This sister hotel to the smaller Nordic Light has modern rooms which won't wow you with the views, but which are super-convenient for sightseeing and departures from Centralstationen. Plus, Nordic Sea is

home to the famous Absolut Icebar, built entirely of ice, where you can throw on a parka and mittens and drink chilled vodka concoctions out of little ice glasses.

SKEPPSHOLMEN

Vandrarhem af Chapman & Skeppsholmen HOSTEL €
(Map p396; ☑08-463 22 66; www.stfchapman. com; dm/r Skr260/590; @🛜) The legendary *af Chapman* is a storied vessel, well anchored in a superb location off Skeppsholmen. It's moored off the west side of the island, off Västra Brobänken. To nab a bunk below decks, book seriously in advance; otherwise you'll end up rooming at the Skeppsholmen hostel on dry land, with the kitchen and TV lounge, but without the nautical atmosphere and the portholes. Friendly staff are knowledgeable about the city.

Hotel Skeppsholmen HOTEL €€€
(Map p390; ☑08-4072350; www.hotelskeppsholmen .com; Gröna gången 1; r/ste from Skr2195/3600; 🅿🛜; 🚌65 Arkitekt/Moderna mus, 🚢Slussen) A serene, forested location on Skeppsholmen, grand views, easy access to museums and ferries to Slussen almost on your doorstep – this elegant hotel has it all. The rooms are decked out in soothing creams and excellent breakfast is served in the light and airy dining room. Ask for a room with a sea view if possible.

SÖDERMALM

🔝 Rival Hotel HOTEL €€€
(Map p396; ☑08-54 57 89 00; www.rival.se; Mariatorget 3; r/ste from Skr1435/5215; @🛜; Ⓜ T-13, T-14 Mariatorget) Owned by ABBA's Benny Andersson and overlooking leafy Mariatorget, this ravishing design hotel is a chic retro gem, complete with vintage 1940s movie theatre and over-the-top art deco cocktail bar. The super-comfy rooms feature posters from great Swedish films, flat-screen TVs, and a

---

ⓘ **STOCKHOLM À LA CARTE**

Destination Stockholm (☑08-663 00 80; www.destination-stockholm.com; from Skr465) offers discount hotel-and-sightseeing packages that can be booked online. Its Stockholm à la Carte package is available weekends year-round and throughout the summer.

teddy bear to make you feel at home. There's a scrumptious designer bakery-cafe beside the foyer.

Columbus Hotell
HOTEL €€

(Map p390; ☑08-50 31 12 00; www.columbus. se; Tjärhovsgatan 11; s/d Skr1450/1750, budget s/d from Skr895/1035; @🛜) A Best Western member, this historic building is nestled in a quiet part of Södermalm and set around a cobblestone courtyard by a pretty park. In the Columbus Loft there are a few budget rooms with shared facilities and TV, comfy Jensen beds and bright furnishings; the other two floors boast larger, more luxurious rooms. No lift.

Bed & Breakfast 4 Trappor
B&B €€

(Map p390; ☑08-642 31 04; www.4trappor.se; Götlandsgatan 78; apt s/d Skr775/950, incl breakfast Skr850/1100; P🛜; ☐3, 53, 76, 96 Götlandsgatan) It's hard to beat this sassy, urbane home away from home, complete with cosy, floorboarded bedroom (maximum two guests), modern bathroom and well-equipped kitchen (espresso machine included!). Breakfast is served in the wonderful owners' next-door apartment, and the SoFo address means easy access to Stockholm's coolest shops and hang-outs. There's a two-night minimum stay. It's a huge hit, so book months ahead.

🌿 Zinkensdamm Hotell & Vandrarhem
HOTEL, HOSTEL €€

(Map p390; ☑08-616 81 00; www.zinkensdamm. com; Zinkens väg 20; dm Skr235-290, hostel d/tr Skr780/975, hotel r from Skr1545; P@🛜; MT-13, T-14 Zinkensdamm) In a quiet, leafy location in Södermalm, the Zinkensdamm STF is a large, attractive, well-equipped yellow house, complete with an ubersleek guest kitchen and personal lockers. Popular with families and backpackers, it has a decent restaurant pub and an upbeat vibe. Our one quibble is that some rooms are too small to swing even the tiniest of felines.

Långholmen Hotell & Vandrarhem
HOSTEL, HOTEL €

(☑08-720 85 00; www.langholmen.com; hostel dm adult/child Skr220/115, s Skr600, 2-/4-bed cells per person Skr275/220, hotel s/d Skr1595/1845; @🛜; ☐4, 40, 77, 94 Högalidsgatan, M13, 14 Hornstull T-Bana) We could make prison jokes here – that you'll wish they'd lock you up in this former prison and throw away the key – but we won't. You *will* sleep in a cell here, and

even if some of the bunks are a bit wobbly, you'll be far more comfortable than the former inmates. The restaurant serves meals all day, and Långholmen's popular summertime bathing spots are a towel flick away.

NORRMALM

🔲 Hotel Hellsten
HOTEL €€

(Map p390; ☑08-661 86 00; www.hellsten.se; Luntmakargatan 78; r from Skr1090; 🛜) Hip Hellsten is owned by anthropologist Per Hellsten and features objects from his travels and life, including Congan tribal masks and his grandmother's chandelier. Rooms are supremely comfortable and individually styled, with themes spanning rustic Swedish to Indian exotica; some feature four-poster beds and original tile stoves. The sleek bathrooms sport phones and hand-cut Greek slate. Extras include a sauna and small fitness room, as well as live jazz in the lounge on Thursday evenings.

OUTSIDE STOCKHOLM

STF Vandrarhem Gärdet
HOSTEL €

(☑08-463 22 99; www.svenskaturistforeningen. se; Sandhamnsgatan 59; s/d from Skr495/760; @🛜) Located in quiet Gärdet, a quick metro ride from Östermalm, Stockholm's first 'designer hostel' features smart, contemporary rooms that include red pin chairs. Each room comes equipped with a flat-screen TV, comfy beds and a hotel-grade private bathroom. Sheets and towels are included in the price. Take bus 1 from Centralstationen (or Gärdet tunnelbana stop) to Östhammarsgatan bus stop.

Jumbo Stay
HOSTEL €€

(☑08-59 36 04 00; www.jumbostay.com; Jumbovägen 4, Stockholm Arlanda Airport; dm Skr350-400, s/d Skr650/1150; P🛜) It's a hostel, Jim, but not as you know it. This converted jumbo jet at Arlanda Airport is hugely popular with flashpackers who've always dreamed of sleeping in style on a plane (no, we don't mean crammed into an economy class seat), thanks to the creative use of space and the 24-hour Jumbo bar for night owls. For the ultimate experience, treat yourself to a night in the cockpit suite. The free transfer bus 14 runs from the terminals to Jumbo Stay every 15 minutes between 5am and midnight.

✖ Eating

Stockholm, with eight Michelin-starred restaurants, has certainly earned its reputation as a foodie destination. For top-notch seafood with human scenery to match, head toward Östermalmstorg. Candlelit cafes dripping in history and charm line the crooked little streets of Gamla Stan. For solid everyman cuisine, head to Odenplan, and for inventive vegetarian fare try Södermalm's bohemian joints or Luntmakargatan and surrounding streets. Swedish food is not the only thing on offer; as in any cosmopolitan city, you can easily find good Japanese, Thai, Italian and even Ethiopian gastronomic delights to tempt your tastebuds.

CENTRAL STOCKHOLM

TOP CHOICE Frantzén/Lindeberg
INTERNATIONAL €€€

(Map p396; ☑08-20 85 50; www.frantzen-lindeberg.com; Lilla Nygatan 22; lunch/dinner Skr1650/2100; ⏰6.30pm-late Tue-Fri, from noon Sat; Ⓜ T-Gamla Stan) If anyone's culinary creations deserve the 'food as art' accolade, it must be Frantzén and Lindeberg, the two gastronomic geniuses who've more than earned their two Michelin stars. The menus – 14 courses for lunch, 20 for dinner – are dictated entirely by the seasons and by locally sourced produce such as fish from Mälaren, Northern Swedish cattle and organically grown vegetables, though exotic touches, such as wasabi and pineapple, do creep in.

Veranda
SWEDISH €€€

(Grand Hôtel Stockholm; Map p396; ☑08-679 35 86; www.grandhotel.se; Södra Blasieholmshamnen 8; breakfast buffet/smörgåsbord Skr242/425, 2-/3-course dinner Skr495/615; ⏰7.30am-3pm & 6-11pm Mon-Fri, 7am-4pm & 6-11pm Sat & Sun; Ⓜ T-Kungsträdgården) Located inside the venerable Grand Hôtel, the smörgåsbord here is Stockholm's best. Pace yourself like a marathon runner, and commence with the herring, helped down with snaps, before moving on to the gravlax (cured salmon) with a moreish mustard sauce, the charcuterie, the hot dishes (the meatballs! oh! the meatballs!), followed by dessert, coffee and punch. You needn't ever eat again.

Kryp In
SWEDISH €€€

(Map p396; ☑08-20 88 41; www.restaurangkrypin.nu; Prästgatan 17; mains Skr188-278; ⏰5-11pm Mon-Fri, 12.30-11pm Sat & Sun; Ⓜ T-Gamla Stan) Small but perfectly formed, this Gamla Stan spot wows diners with creative takes on traditional Swedish dishes. Expect the likes of chanterelle soup with cognac, with real depth of flavour, followed by beef cheeks in red wine or shellfish stew with saffron aioli. The

service is seamless and the atmosphere classy without being stuffy. Book ahead.

TOP CHOICE Hermitage
VEGETARIAN €€

(Map p396; Stora Nygatan 11; lunch/dinner Skr100/110; ⏰11am-8pm Mon-Sat, noon-4pm Sun; 🖋) We love this small vegetarian cafe. Its tables are too close together and it does get crowded when everyone from local students to vegie-hunting tourists pile in, but with good reason: the vegetarian dishes that make up the changing daily buffet are cooked with flair and a real understanding of flavours. Expect the likes of spicy vegetable fritters, brown rice, vegetable curry, macrobiotic salads and a fine choice of cold side dishes.

Mathias Dahlgren
INTERNATIONAL €€€

(Map p396; ☑08-679 35 84; www.mathiasdahlgren.com; Södra Blasieholmshamnen 6, Grand Hôtel Stockholm; Matbaren mains Skr255-405, Matsalen 5-/8-course menu Skr1375/1700; ⏰Matbaren noon-2pm Mon-Fri & 6pm-midnight Mon-Sat, Matsalen 7pm-midnight Tue-Sat; Ⓜ T-Kungsträndsgården) Chef Mathias Dahlgren's namesake restaurant, set in the Grand Hôtel, consists of the casual Matbaren (the Food Bar) and the more formal Matsalen (the Dining Room). The latter is where Dahlgren really delivers, experimenting with seasonal ingredients for his ever-changing menu: think foie gras terrine with mango, black sesame and black pepper, or fried apple with goat's milk ice cream, vanilla cream and rye bread. Book ahead for Matsalen.

Batfickan Djuret
ALTERNATIVE SWEDISH €€€

(Map p396; ☑08-50 64 00; www.djuret.se; Lilla Nygatan 5; 3-course lunch 395Skr; ⏰5.30pm-midnight Mon-Sat; Ⓜ T-Gamla Stan) 'Animal' is the carnivore's ultimate dream, the menu featuring nothing but beautifully-prepared cuts of meat, meat and more meat. Dig into wild duck with chestnuts, wild boar with apple sauce, and if you're truly hungry, order the Grande Deluxe – an endless mix of signature dishes until you are fully sated. **Svinet** (Pig), Djuret's summertime charcoal-grilled pork barbecue restaurant, is just the place to bring your sweetie – provided they are as carnivorously inclined as you are.

Siam Thai
THAI €€

(Map p396; ☑08-20 02 33; Stora Nygatan 25; lunch Skr90, mains Skr175-225; ⏰noon-3pm Mon-Sat, 6.30-10pm daily; 🖋; Ⓜ T-Gamla Stan) With its indoor rainforest effect, colourful Christmas lights and its real-deal Southeast Asian flavours, Siam Thai is always a reliable bet for large quantities of Thai dishes. Spice it up with anything from spicy papaya salad and prawns with eggplant in green curry to deep-fried chicken wrapped in pandanus leaves.

Bakfickan
SWEDISH €€€

(Map p396; www.operakallaren.se; Karl XII:S torg, Opera House; mains Skr160-290; ⊙11.30am-11pm Mon-Fri, noon-10pm Sat, to 7pm Sun; 🖉; MKungsträdgården) A relaxed corner of the Opera House's bar-and-dining complex, the 'back pocket' of Operakällaren is crammed with opera photographs and art deco–style lampshades. Old-school waiters serve traditional Swedish comfort food, from gravlax or pickled herring to *köttbullar och potatis* (meatballs and mash) and a daily vegie dish, and the counter seats make it a perfect spot for solo diners.

Under Kastanjen
CAFE €

(Map p396; www.underkastanjen.se; Kindstugatan 1; cakes from Skr40, salads from Skr70; ⊙8am-10pm Mon-Fri, 9am-10pm, to 7pm Sun; 🖉; MT-Gamla Stan) You are likely to be lured into this delightful cafe, with an enormous chestnut tree in front of it, by the smell of freshly-baked cinnamon buns, though its offerings are far more diverse than that. Opt for an imaginative salad of quinoa, cheese, fruit and more.

Chokladkoppen
CAFE €

(Map p396; www.chokladkoppen.se; Stortorget; cakes Skr40-80; ⊙9am-11pm summer, shorter hr rest of yr; 🖉; MT-Gamla Stan) One of Stockholm's best-loved cafes, Chokladkoppen sits slap bang on the Old Town's enchanting main square. It's a gay-friendly spot, with cute, gym-fit waiters, a look-at-me summer terrace and yummy grub such as broccoli-and-blue-cheese pie and white chocolate cheesecake to break your diet vows over.

SÖDERMALM

Pelikan
SWEDISH €€

(Map p390; www.pelikan.se; Blekingegatan 40; mains Skr80-180; ⊙4pm-midnight Mon-Thu, 1pm-1am Fri & Sat, to midnight Sun; MT-Skanstull) Lofty ceilings, wood panelling and waiters in waistcoats set the scene for classic *husmanskost* (traditional home cooking) at this century-old beer hall. The menu is unapologetically Swedish, so get your fill of herring assortments, meatballs, Arctic char and roast elk with chanterelles. Even if not eating, this is a wonderful place to just grab a beer.

Gondolen
SWEDISH €€€

(Map p396; 🕿08-641 70 90; www.eriks.se; Stadsgården 6; lunch Skr125, mains Skr285; ⊙11.30am-1am Mon-Fri, noon-1am Sat, 2pm-midnight Sun; MT-Slussen) Perched atop the iconic Katarinahissen (the vintage Slussen elevator), Gondolen combines killer city views with contemporary Nordic brilliance from chef Erik Lallerstedt. Play 'spot the landmark' while sampling the clean, beautiful flavours such as beef medallions with wild mushrooms and marsala wine gravy or cured salmon with lime and mustard.

Nystekt Strömming
SWEDISH €

(Map p396; Södermalmstorg; combo plates Skr45-75; ⊙generally 11am-8pm Mon-Fri, 11am-6pm Sat & Sun; MT-Slussen) There's so much more to Swedish cuisine than pickled herring, such as the beautiful, freshly fried *(stekt)* herring, for instance, served out of this humble cart outside the metro station at Slussen. The *strömming* burger makes a great snack on the go, but the full dinner combos are excellent if you want something more substantial.

ÖSTERMALM

Östermalms Saluhall
MARKET €€

(Map p396; www.ostermalmshallshallen.se; Östermalmstorg; mains Skr80-115; ⊙9.30am-6pm Mon-Thu, to 7pm Fri, to 4pm Sat; 🖉) Stockholm's historic blue-ribbon market spoils taste buds with fresh fish, seafood and meat, as well as fruits, vegetables and hard-to-find cheeses. In addition to the market, it's full of small eateries serving everything from sushi to falafel and lasagne. The building itself is a Stockholm landmark, designed as a Romanesque cathedral of food in 1885.

Cassi
FRENCH €€

(Map p390; 🕿08-661 74 61; www.cassi.se; Narvavägen 30; lunch Skr90, mains Skr69-275; ⊙noon-3pm & 6.30-10.30pm; 🛋; MT-Karlaplan) Cassi's been getting a little confused lately. A French bistro for more than 40 years, its menu now features distinctly un-French offerings, such as nasi goreng and lasagne. Still, its steak minute bearnaise is superb and so are the french fries. Separate menu for children, too.

KUNGSHOLMEN

Vurma
CAFE €

(Map p390; www.vurma.se; Polhemsgatan 15; salads Skr70-95; ⊙8am-6pm Mon-Fri, 9am-6pm Sat & Sun; 🖉) Squeeze in among the chattering punters, fluff up the cushions and eavesdrop over a vegan latte at this kitsch-hip cafe-bakery. The scrumptious sandwiches and salads are utterly inspired; try the chèvre cheese, marinated chicken, walnuts and honey. Four other branches include those in Vasastan (Map p390; www.vurma.se; Gästrikegatan 2; ⊙9am-7pm Mon-Sat, 10am-7pm Sun; ✐; Ⓜ T-S:t Eriksplan) and **Östermalm** (Map p390; www.vurma.se; Birger Jarlsgatan 36; ⊙11am-10pm Monday, to 11pm Tue & Wed, to midnight Fri & Sat; ✐; Ⓜ Östermalmstorg).

Roppongi   JAPANESE €€
(Map p390; www.roppongi.se; Hantverkargatan 76; lunch from Skr79, mains Skr139-239; ⊙11am-10pm Mon-Fri, to 9pm Sat, to 9pm Sun; ⊟3, 40, 62 Kronobergsgatan, Ⓜ T-Fridhemsplan) Finally, a sushi bar that does sushi rolls with ingredients other than salmon! Choose from the likes of tuna, spicy mayo and asparagus and tempura shrimp with chili mayo, or opt for some lamb gyoza (dumplings), steamed to perfection, along with a shot of sake to help it along. Takeaway available for those not feeling too sociable.

VASASTAN

Linguini   ITALIAN €€
(Map p390; ☑08-31 39 15; Frejgatan 48; mains Skr149-169; ⊙noon-10pm; ✐) True to the name, linguini does feature a lot on the menu of this friendly Italian joint in Norrmalm. Think: exposed brick walls, casual ambiance, and some of the best linguini with northern Italian sausage and porcini mushrooms you're likely to taste anywhere. Non-linguini offerings include ricotta and porcini torteloni and a superb panna cotta.

DJURGÅRDEN

Rosendals Trädgårdskafe   CAFE €€
(www.rosendalstrandgard.se; Rosendalsterrassen 12; mains Skr125-145; ⊙11am-5pm Mon-Fri, 11am-6pm Sat & Sun May-Sep; ✐; ⊟7 Bellmansro) Rosendals is an idyllic spot for heavenly carrot cake and an organic wine in summer or a warm cup of *glögg* (spicy mulled wine) and a *lussekatte* (saffron roll) in winter. Much of the produce is seasonal, biodynamic and grown on-site. To get here, walk up Sinshovsvägen from the Bellmansro tram stop and cut across the park.

Blå Porten Café   CAFE €€
(Map p390; ☑08-663 87 59; www.blaporten.com; Djurgårdsvägen 64; mains Skr85-155; ⊙11am-10pm Mon-Thu, 11am-7pm Fri-Sun; ✐; ⊟47 Liljevalc Gröna Lund, ⊟7 Liljevalc Gröna Lund) A good bet for lunch, Blå Porten is best on a sunny day when you can linger in the romantic garden courtyard over a plate of meatballs and other daily specials. Sunshine or not, the gluttonous table of fresh cakes and pastries is a constant, happy test of your self control (though some cakes are more looks than substance).

🍷 Drinking

From concrete-and-bare-bulb industrial spaces to raucous vintage beer halls and bricked-in underground vaults, there's a bar for every taste in this town. Good neighbourhood hang-outs *(kvarterskrog)* abound, but generally the shiny-miniskirt crowd hangs out in Östermalm, while the hipsters and arty types slink around Södermalm – any of the bars along Skånegatan are a good bet.

Absolut Icebar   BAR
(Map p396; ☑08-50 56 35 20; www.nordicseahotel .com; Vasaplan 4, Nordic Sea Hotel; prebooked online/drop in Skr180/195; ⊙11.15am-midnight Sun-Wed, to 1am Thu-Sat Jun-Aug) Okay, it's touristy. But you're intrigued, admit it: a bar built entirely out of ice, where you drink from glasses carved of ice at tables made of ice amidst ice sculptures. The admission price gets you warm booties, mittens, a parka and one drink (if you're looking for an inspiring cocktail avoid Wolfsbane – essentially neat vodka with a few frozen berries in it). Refill drinks costs Skr95.

Tudor Arms   PUB
(Map p390; www.tudorarms.com; Grevgatan 31; ⊟56, ⊟7 Styrmansgatan) With a name like that, how could it be anything other than a British pub. That said, it's the best of its kind, and with a loyal local clientele, going strong after 43 years. If you want to watch the game while nursing your pint of Fuller's London Pride, there's no place finer.

Marie Laveau   BAR
(Map p390; www.marielaveau.se; Hornsgatan 66; ⊙5pm-midnight Tue & Wed, to 3am Thu-Sat) Sip on inspired cocktails at this designer-grunge bar on one of the main drags through Södermalm – think chequered floor and subway-style tiled columns. DJs hit the deck in the raucous basement bar from Wednesday to Saturday, with theme nights including hip hop and breaks, funk and soul, and disco meets Ibiza house.

Vampire Lounge   BAR
(Map p390; www.vampirelounge.se; Östgötagatan 41; ⊙5pm-1am Mon-Fri, 7pm-1am Sat; Ⓜ T-Metborgarplatsen) This dark, cave-like watering hole

attracts creatures of the night with a taste for the macabre...and possibly some *Twilight* fans. Just in case a real bloodsucker turns up, follow the signs to cachets of holy water, garlic and crosses. The drink list, appropriately, features Bloody Marys and there are DJs hitting the decks on weekends.

Svartengrens
COCKTAIL BAR

(Map p390; www.svartengrens.se; Tulegatan 24; ⏰5pm-1am; ⓂT-Tekinska Högskolan) This cocktail bar inside a meat restaurant surprises with its stellar cocktails, each accompanied by a movie quote. The most unusual is the Finding Réno (vodka, beetroot syrup, lemon and bitters).

☆ Entertainment

Scan the local papers for up-to-date listings of entertainment events, particularly the Friday *På Stan* section of *Dagens Nyheter* newspaper. The monthly *What's On Stockholm* brochure, available free from the tourist office, is a more general guide.

Nightclubs

Café Opera
CLUB

(Map p396; ☎08-676 58 07; www.cafeopera.se; Karl XII:s Torg; admission from Skr160; ⏰10pm-3am Wed-Sun; ⓂT-Kungsträdgården) A night at the Café Opera has seen many a famous face pass through – David Bowie, Prince, Iron Maiden; after all, rock stars and wannabe playboys also need a suitably excessive place to schmooze, booze and groove – preferably one with bulbous chandeliers, ceiling frescos and a jet-set vibe. This bar/club combo fits the bill. The adjoining bar is a bartenders' hang-out, meaning a mediocre martini is strictly out of the question.

Sturecompagniet
CLUB

(Map p396; ☎08-54 50 76 00; www.sturecompagniet.se; Stureplan 4; admission Skr120; ⏰10pm-3am Thu-Sat; ⓂT-Östermalmstorg) Swedish soap stars, '80s-inspired glitz, and look-at-me attitude set the scene at this sprawling party playpen – the biggest in Stockholm. Choose your music style (there's something different happening on every floor), dress to the nines and get there early to charm the bouncers (it can be tough to get in after 1am).

Spy Bar
CLUB

(Map p396; www.thespybar.com; Birger Jarlsgatan 20; admission from Skr160; ⏰10pm-5am Wed-Sat; ⓂT-Östermalmstorg) Set in a turn-of-the-century flat (spot the tiled stoves), this party stalwart pulls in a 20- and 30-something media crowd, though it's not quite the heart and soul of the party. Expect three bars, electro, rock and hip-hop beats and no entry after 2am (unless you're well connected, darling). If you don't meet your James Bond here, try the chilled out Laroy bar on the ground floor.

Gay & Lesbian Venues

For club listings and events, pick up a free copy of street-press magazine *QX*, found at many clubs, stores and cafes around town. Its website (www.qx.se) is more frequently updated. *QX* also produces a free, handy *Gay Stockholm Map*.

Torget
BAR

(Map p396; www.torgetbaren.com; Mälartorget 13; ⓂT-Gamla Stan) Gamla Stan's premier gay bar has eye-candy staff, mock-baroque touches, a civilised salon vibe and DJs playing a mix of Scandinavian and international pop.

Roxy
BAR

(Map p390; www.roxysofo.se; Nytorget 6; ⏰5-11pm Mon, 5pm-midnight Tue-Thu, to 1am Fri & Sat, to 11pm Sun; ☐59 Närkesgatan) Chic resto-bar popular with publishing types and SoFo's creative set who come here to sample the great Mediterranean nibbles to a chilled-out soundtrack.

Paradise
CLUB

(Map p396; Gula Gången; admission Skr110-140; ⏰11pm-3am Fri) Stockholm's biggest gay club turns up the volume with mainstream hits on the main dance floor, serious house and tech-house in the basement and good, old-fashioned disco in the Panoramabar. The place gets packed and happily sweaty, and this may well be your idea of heaven.

Zipper
CLUB

(Map p390; www.zippersthlm.com; Sankt Eriksgatan 51; admission Skr140; ⏰10pm-3am Sat; ⓂT-Fridhemsplan) In a new location, Zipper is as wild as ever, with weekly events such as Candylicious (okay, let's have all your lollipop jokes now). Highly entertaining clubbing and cruising; prepare to get un-Zipped.

Live Music

Debaser
CLUB

(Map p396; ☎08-30 56 20; www.debaser.se; Karl Johanstorg 1, Slussen; ⏰7pm-1am Sun-Thu, 8pm-3am Fri & Sat) The king of rock clubs hides away under the Slussen interchange. Emerging or bigger-name acts play most nights, while the killer club nights span anything from rock steady to punk and electronica. One metre stop further south, **Debaser Medis** (Map p390; ☑08-694 7900; Medborgarplatsen 8; Ⓜ︎T-Medborgarplatsen) is its sprawling sister venue, with three floors rocking to live acts and DJ-spun tunes.

Södra Teatern   CLUB
(Map p396; ☑08-53 19 94 90; www.sodrateatern. se; Mosebacke torg 3; tickets free-Skr250; ⊗to 11pm Mon & Tue, to 1am Wed & Sun, to 2am Thu-Sat; Ⓜ︎T-Slussen) Eclectic theatre and club nights aside, this historic culture palace hosts a mixed line-up of live music. Tunes span anything from home-grown pop and acoustic sets to jazz and antipodean rock. The outdoor terrace combines dazzling city views with a thumping summertime bar.

Fasching   CONCERT HALL, CLUB
(Map p396; ☑08-53 48 29 60; www.fasching.se; Kungsgatan 63; ⊗6pm-1am Mon-Thu, to 4am Fri & Sat, 5pm-1am Sun; Ⓜ︎T-Centralen) Specialising primarily in jazz, this great all-rounder offers live music most nights. On weekends you can expect DJ nights featuring soul Afrobeat, Latin music and more.

Concerts, Theatre & Dance

Dramaten   THEATRE
(Map p396; ☑08-667 06 80; www.dramaten.se; Nybroplan; tickets Skr200-340; 🖈; Ⓜ︎T-Kungsträndsgården) The Royal Theatre stages a range of plays – from classical to international – in a sublime art nouveau environment. Dramaten's experimental stage Elverket at Linnégatan (same contact details) pushes all the boundaries with some edgier offerings that are performed within a converted power station.

Operan   OPERA
(Map p396; ☑08-791 44 00; www.operan.se; Gustav Adolfs Torg, Operahuset; tickets Skr60-800; Ⓜ︎T-Kungsträndsgården) The Royal Opera is the place to go for thunderous tenors, sparkling sopranos and classical ballet. It also has some bargain tickets in seats with poor views for as little as Skr60, and occasional lunchtime concerts for Skr200 (including a light lunch); the latter sell out pretty quickly.

Folkoperan   THEATRE
(Map p396; ☑08-616 07 50; www.folkoperan. se; Hornsgatan 72; tickets Skr285-475; Ⓜ︎T-Zinkensdamm) Folkoperan gives opera a thoroughly modern overhaul with its intimate, cutting-edge and sometimes controversial productions. Those aged under 26 years enjoy half-price tickets.

Sport

Bandy matches, a uniquely Scandinavian phenomenon, take place all winter at Stockholm's ice arenas. Catch a game at **Zinkensdamms Idrottsplats** (Map p390; Ringvägen 16; Ⓜ︎T-Zinkensdamm). The sport, a precursor to ice hockey but with more players (11 to a side) and less fighting, has grown massively popular since the late-1990s rise of the Hammarby team. The season lasts from November to March, so make sure you bring your own thermos of *kaffekask* – a warming mix of coffee and booze.

For the ultimate Scandi sport experience, head to an ice hockey game at **Globen** (☑077 131 0000; www.globen.se; Arenavägen; Ⓜ︎T-Globen); matches take place here up to three times a week from October to April.

🔒 Shopping

A design and fashion hub, Stockholm offers shoppers everything from top-name boutiques to the tiniest secondhand shops. Good local buys include edgy street wear, designer home decor and clever gadgets, and edible treats such as cloudberry jam, pickled herring and bottles of *glögg*. Södermalm's SoFo district (the streets south of Folkungagatan) is your best bet for home-grown fashion, while Östermalm is the place for high-end names like Marc Jacobs and Gucci.

Chokladfabriken   CHOCOLATE
(Map p390; www.chokladfabriken.com; Renstiernas Gata 12; ⊗10am-6.30pm Mon-Fri, 10am-5pm Sat; Ⓜ︎T-Metborgarplatsen) For an edible souvenir, head straight to this chocolate peddler, where seasonal Nordic ingredients are used to make some amazingly heavenly cocoa treats. There's a cafe for an on-the-spot fix, and smaller branches in **Norrmalm** (Map p396; Regeringsgatan 58) and **Östermalm** (Map p390; Grevgatan 37).

DesignTorget   HOMEWARES
(Map p396) If you love good design but don't own a Gold Amex, head to this chain, which sells the work of emerging designers – bright kitchenware, cool knick-knacks to have around the house – alongside established denizens. There are several branches around the city, including **Götgatan** (Map p396; ☑462 35 20; Götgatan 31, Götgatan; ⊗10am-7pm Mon-Fri, 10am-5pm Sat, noon-5pm Sun) and Sergels Torg.

WANT MORE?

For in-depth information, reviews and recommendations at your fingertips, head to the Apple App Store to purchase Lonely Planet's *Stockholm City Guide* iPhone app.

Alternatively, head to **Lonely Planet** (www.lonelyplanet.com/sweden/stockholm) for planning advice, author recommendations, traveller reviews and insider tips.

Tjallamalla CLOTHING
(Map p390; www.tjallamalla.com; Bondegatan 46; ⊙noon-6pm Mon-Fri, noon-5pm Sat, to 3pm Sun; ☐66, 96 Renstiernas gata) Raid the racks at this fashion icon for rookie designers such as Hot Sissy, Papagaio and organic Malmö street wear label Kärleksgatan. Graduates from Stockholm's prestigious Beckmans College of Design School sometimes sell their collections here on commission.

PUB DEPARTMENT STORE
(Map p396; Drottninggatan 72-6; ⊙10am-7pm Mon-Fri, 10am-6pm Sat, 11am-5pm Sun; Ⓜ T-Hötorget) Historic department store PUB famously once employed Greta Garbo and now stocks some of the hottest threads in town. Pick up Nordic fashion such as House of Dagmar and Stray Boys.

❶ Information

Emergency
Dial ☎112 for toll-free access to the fire service, police and ambulance.
24-hour Medical advice (☎08-32 01 00)
24-hour Police stations Kungsholmen (☎08-401 00 00; Kungsholmsgatan 37); Södermalm (☎08-401 03 00; Torkel Knutssonsgatan 20)

Internet Access
Most hostels and many hotels have a computer with internet access for guests, and nearly all also offer wi-fi access in rooms (sometimes for a fee). Wi-fi is also widely available in coffee shops and bars and in Centralstationen. Those without their own wi-fi enabled device have more-limited options, but the ubiquitous Sidewalk Express terminals are handy.
Sidewalk Express (www.sidewalkexpress.se; per hr Skr30) Rows of computer monitors and tall red ticket machines mark out these self-service internet stations, which dot the city. They're found at various locations, including City Bus Terminal, Centralstationen, Stockhom Arlanda Airport, and numerous 7-Eleven locations around town.

Media
Dagens Nyheter (www.dn.se) Daily paper with comprehensive culture section and weekend event listing (På Stan). Bar and restaurant news found on website.
Nöjesguiden (www.nojesguiden.se) Entertainment and events listings.

Medical Services
Apoteket CW Scheele (www.apoteket.se; Klarabergsgatan 64; Ⓜ T-Centralen) 24-hour pharmacy.
CityAkuten (☎020-150 150; www.cityakuten.se; Apelbergsgatan 48; ⊙8am-6pm Mon-Thu, to 5pm Fri, 10am-3pm Sat) Emergency health and dental care
Södersjukhuset (☎08-616 10 00; www.soderjukhuset.se; Ringvägen 52) The most central hospital.

Money
ATMs are plentiful, with a few at Centralstationen and airports; expect queues on Friday and Saturday nights.

The exchange company Forex has more than a dozen branches in the capital and charges Skr15 per travellers cheque. Two handy locations:
Stockholm-Arlanda Airport (www.forex.se; Terminal 2; ⊙5.30am-8pm Sun-Fri, to 5pm Sat)
Forex Bank (www.forex.se; Storgatan 17; ⊙9am-7pm Mon-Fri, 10am-3pm Sat; ☐62, 91)

Post
You can buy stamps and send letters at a number of city locations, including newsagencies and supermarkets – keep an eye out for the Swedish postal symbol (yellow on a blue background). There's a convenient outlet next to the Hemköp supermarket in the basement of central department store **Åhléns** (Klarabergsgatan 50; Ⓜ T-Centralen).

Telephones
Coin-operated phones are virtually nonexistent; payphones are operated with phonecards purchased from any Pressbyrån location (or with a credit card, although this is ludicrously expensive). Ask for a *telefonkort* for Skr50 or Skr120, which roughly equates to 50 minutes and 120 minutes of local talk time respectively. For calls abroad, buy a long-distance calling card, also available at Pressbyrån outlets. It's relatively inexpensive to use a mobile from another European country as rates are now standardised, but if you're staying in Sweden for a while, it's worth buying a cheap local mobile to reload with prepaid minutes.

Tourist Information

Tourist Office (☑08-50 82 85 08; www.
stockholmtown.se; Vasagatan 14; ☺9am-
6pm Mon-Fri, 10am-5pm Sat, 10am-4pm Sun
May–mid-Sep) Directly across the street from
Centralstationen. Busy but helpful, with plenty
of maps and brochures.

Websites

The Local (www.thelocal.se) News and features
about Sweden, written locally in English.

❶ Getting There & Away

Air

Stockholm Arlanda Airport (☑010-109 00 00;
www.swedavia.se) Stockholm's main airport,
45km north of the city centre, reached from
central Stockholm by bus and express train.

Bromma Stockholm Airport (☑010-109 00
00; www.swedavia.se) Located 8km west of
Stockholm, used for some domestic flights.

Stockholm Skavsta Airport (☑0155-28 04
00; www.skavsta-air.se) About 100km south of
Stockholm, near Nyköping, mostly used by
low-cost carriers such as Ryanair and Wizz Air.

Västerås Airport (☑021-80 56 10; www.
stockholmvasteras.se) About 100km northwest
of Stockholm on the E18 motorway, this tiny
airport is used by Ryanair.

Boat

Both **Silja Line** (☑08 22 21 40; www.tallinksilja.
com) and **Viking Line** (☑08-452 40 00; www.
vikingline.se) run ferries to Turku and Helsinki.

Tallink (☑08 22 21 40; www.tallinksilja.com)
Ferries head to Tallinn (Estonia) and Riga
(Latvia).Tallink–Silja Line ferries depart from
Frihamnen Terminal, reachable on foot from
Gärdet T-bana station or via Värtahamnen/
Frihamnen-bound buses 1, 72 or 76 from the
city centre. Viking Line ferries dock at Stads-
gårdskajen near Slussen in Central Stockholm,
reachable on foot from the Slussen T-bana stop.

St Peter Line ferries (www.stpeterline.com)
From St Petersburg via Helsinki, also depart
from Frihamnen. For more information, see p491
and p493.

Bus

Cityterminalen (www.cityterminalen.com;
☺7am-6pm) The main bus station, connected
to Centralstationen. The ticket counter sells
tickets for several bus companies, including Flygbussarna (airport coaches), Swebus
Express, Svenska Buss, Eurolines and Y-Buss.

Swebus Express (www.swebusexpress.com;
Cityterminalen) Runs daily to Malmö (9¼
hours), Göteborg (seven hours), Norrköping
(two hours), Kalmar (six hours), Mora (4¼
hours), Örebro (three hours) and Oslo (eight
hours). There are also direct runs to Gävle

(2½ hours), Uppsala (one hour) and Västerås
(1¾ hours).

Ybuss (www.ybuss.se; Cityterminalen) Runs
services to the northern towns of Sundsvall,
Östersund and Umeå.

Car & Motorcycle

The E4 motorway passes through the west of the
city, on its way from Helsingborg to Haparanda.
The E20 motorway from Stockholm to Göteborg
via Örebro follows the E4 as far as Södertälje.
The E18 from Kapellskär to Oslo runs from east
to west and passes north of central Stockholm.

Left Luggage

There are three sizes of left-luggage boxes (per
24 hours Skr40 to Skr120) at Centralstationen.
Similar facilities exist at the neighbouring bus
station and at major ferry terminals.

Train

Stockholm is the hub for national train services
run by **Sveriges Järnväg** (SJ; ☑0771-75 75 75;
www.sj.se) and Tågkompaniet (p481).

Centralstationen (Ⓜ T-Centralen) is the
central train station. In the main hall you'll find
the **SJ ticket office** (☺domestic tickets 7.30am-
7.45pm Mon-Fri, 8.30am-6pm Sat, 9.30am-7pm
Sun, international tickets 10am-6pm Mon-Fri,
general customer service 6am-11pm Mon-Fri,
6.30am-11pm Sat, 7am-11pm Sun). You'll also
find automated ticket machines (from 5am to
11.50pm).

Direct SJ trains to/from Copenhagen, Oslo
and Storlien (for Trondheim) arrive and depart
from Centralstationen, as do the overnight services from Göteborg (via Stockholm and Boden)
to Kiruna and Narvik; the Arlanda Express; and
the SL *pendeltåg* commuter services that run to/
from Nynäshamn, Södertälje and Märsta. Other
SL local rail lines (Roslagsbanan and Saltsjöba-
nan) run from Stockholm Östra (T-Tekniska
Högskolan) and Slussen, respectively.

In the basement at Centralstationen, you'll
find lockers costing Skr40, Skr60 or Skr120
(depending on size) for 24 hours, toilets for
Skr10 and showers (next to the toilets) for
Skr40. These facilities are open 5am to 12.30am
daily. There's also a left-luggage office, and a
lost property office (☑08-50 12 55 90; ☺9am-
7pm Mon-Fri); look for the 'Hittegods' sign.

❶ Getting Around

To/From the Airports

The **Arlanda Express** (www.arlandaexpress.
com) train from Centralstationen takes 20 minutes to reach Stockholm-Arlanda Airport; trains
run every 10 to 15 minutes from about 5am to
12.30am. Two adults travelling together can get
the discount Skr380 fare, but not every day.

Airport Cab (☑08-25 25 25; www.airportcab. se) charges Skr475 from Arlanda to Stockholm, Skr390 from Stockholm to Arlanda and Skr1100 between Stockholm and Skavsta airport.

The cheapest option is the **Flygbussarna** (www.flygbussarna.se) service between Stockholm-Arlanda, Bromma, Skavsta and Cityterminalen. Buses for Arlanda leave every 10 to 15 minutes (one way/return Skr99/198, 40 minutes); for Bromma every 20 to 30 minutes, less frequently on weekends (Skr79/150, 20 minutes) and for Skavsta every 30 minutes (Skr149/259, one hour 20 minutes).

Bicycle

Stockholm boasts a wide network of bicycle lanes, clearly marked with traffic signs.

Bicycles can be carried free on SL local trains, except during peak hour (6am to 9am and 3pm to 6pm Monday to Friday). They're not allowed in Centralstationen or on the T-bana.

There are around 90 self-service **Stockholm City Bikes** (www.citybikes.se; 3-day card Skr165, season card Skr300) stands across the city. Bicycles can be borrowed for three hours at a time and returned at any City Bikes stand. Purchase a bike card online or at the tourist office.

Boat

Djurgårdsfärjan city ferry (www.waxholmsbolaget.se) services connect Gröna Lund Tivoli on Djurgården with Nybroplan and Slussen as frequently as every 10 minutes in summer (less frequently in low season); a single trip costs Skr40 (free with the SL transport passes).

Car & Motorcycle

Driving in central Stockholm is hell on wheels. Skinny one-way streets and congested bridges are all part of the fun; Djurgårdsvägen is closed near Skansen at night, on summer weekends and some holidays. Don't attempt driving through the narrow streets of Gamla Stan.

Parking (www.stockholmparkering.se) is a major problem, but there are *P-hus* (parking stations) throughout the city; they charge up to Skr60 per hour, though the fixed evening rate is usually lower. If you do have a car, either park at one of the park-and-ride facilities outside the centre (per day Skr20) or stay on the outskirts of town and catch public transport into the centre.

Public Transport

Storstockholms Lokaltrafik (SL; www.sl.se) runs all tunnelbana (T or T-bana) metro trains, local trains and buses within the entire Stockholm county. There is an SL information office in the basement concourse at **Centralstationen** (☺6.30am-11.15pm Mon-Sat, from 7am Sun) and another near the Sergels Torg entrance (7am to 6.30pm Monday to Friday, 10am to 5pm Saturday and Sunday), which issues timetables and sells the SL Tourist Card and Stockholm Card. You can also call ☑600 10 00 for schedule and travel information.

The Stockholm Card (p399) covers travel on all SL trains and buses in greater Stockholm. International rail passes (eg Scanrail, Interrail) aren't valid on SL trains. SL offers several kinds of tickets and passes for buses and T-bana travel: individual ticket for one/two/three zones Skr25/37.50/50; prepaid strip of 16 tickets Skr200; 24-/72-hour unlimited travel Skr115/230.

Coupons, tickets and passes can be bought at T-bana stations, Pressbyrån kiosks, SL train stations and SL information offices. Tickets cannot be bought on buses, but it's possible to pay by text message if travelling with a mobile phone. Instructions are posted at bus stops; you text the number of zones you're crossing to ☑72150, receive a ticket by return message and show it to the driver.

Bus Bus timetables and route maps are complicated but worth studying as there are some useful connections to suburban attractions. Ask at the tourist office for the handy intercity route map (*Innerstadsbussar*, also available at www.sl.se).

Inner-city buses radiate from Sergels Torg, Odenplan, Fridhemsplan (on Kungsholmen) and Slussen. Bus 47 runs from Sergels Torg to Djurgården, and bus 69 runs from Centralstationen and Sergels Torg to the Ladugårdsgärdet museums and Kaknästornet. Useful buses for hostellers include bus 65, which goes from Centralstationen to Skeppsholmen, and bus 43 (Regeringsgatan to Södermalm).

Inner-city night buses run from 1am to 5pm on a few routes. Most leave from Centralstationen, Sergels Torg, Slussen, Odenplan and Fridhemsplan to the suburbs.

Train Local *pendeltåg* trains are useful for connections to Nynäshamn (for ferries to Gotland), to Märsta (for buses to Sigtuna and the short hop to Stockholm-Arlanda Airport) and Södertälje. SL coupons and SL travel passes are valid on these trains, and should be bought before boarding.

Tram The historic No 7 tram connects Norrmalmstorg and Skansen, passing most attractions on Djurgården. Both the Stockholm Card and SL Tourist Card as well as regular SL tickets are valid on board.

Metro (tunnelbana/T-Bana) The most useful mode of transport in Stockholm is the tunnelbana, run by SL. Its lines converge on T-Centralen, connected by an underground walkway to Centralstationen. There are three main tunnelbana lines with branches.

Taxi

Taxis are readily available but expensive, so check for a meter or arrange the fare first. The flag fall is Skr45, then about Skr11 to Skr13 per kilometre. Reputable firms include **Taxi Stockholm** (📞15 00 00; www.taxistockholm.se), **Taxi 020** (📞020-20 20 20; www.taxi020.se) and **Taxi Kurir** (📞0771-86 00 00; www.taxikurir.se).

AROUND STOCKHOLM

Most locals will tell you one thing not to miss about Stockholm is leaving it – whether for a journey into the lovely rock-strewn archipelago or an excursion into the surrounding countryside. Within easy reach of the capital are idyllic islands, Viking gravesites, cute fishing villages and sturdy palaces.

Suburbs

One of Stockholm's loveliest attractions is **Millesgården** (www.millesgarden.se; Carl Milles väg 2; adult/senior & student/child Skr100/80/free; ⊙11am-5pm May-Sep; ⓜT-Ropsten), a superb sculpture park and museum of works by Carl Milles and others. It's on Lidingö island with great views to the mainland; take the metro to T-Ropsten then bus 207.

The extensive **Naturhistoriska Riksmuseet** (www.nrm.se; Frescativägen 40; adult/child Skr80/free; ⊙10am-6pm Tue-Fri, 11am-6pm Sat & Sun; ♿; ⓜT-Universitetet) was founded by Carl von Linné in 1739. There are hands-on displays about nature and the human body, as well as whole forests worth of taxidermied wildlife, dinosaurs, marine life and the hardy fauna of the polar regions. The adjoining **Cosmonova** (www.nrm.se; Frescativägen 40; adult/child Skr90/50, no children under 5yr admitted; ♿; ⓜT-Universitetet) is a combined planetarium and Imax theatre.

One of Stockholm's more unusual attractions, **Skogskyrkogården** (Söckenvagen; admission free; ⊙24hr; ⓜT-Skogskyrkogården) is an arrestingly beautiful cemetery set in soothing pine woodland. Designed by the great Erik Gunnar Asplund and Sigurd Lewerentz, it's on the Unesco World Heritage list and famed for its functionalist buildings. Residents include Stockholm screen goddess Greta Garbo.

WORTH A TRIP

DROTTNINGHOLM

Still the royal family pad for part of the year, the Renaissance-inspired **Drottningholm Slott** (www.royalcourt.se; adult/student & child Skr100/50; combined ticket incl Chinese Pavillion Skr145/75; ⊙10am-4.30pm May-Aug), with its geometric baroque gardens, was designed by architectural great Nicodemius Tessin the Elder. Begun in 1662, about the same time as Versailles palace in France, it was completed by his son upon his death. You can walk around the wings open to the public on your own, but we recommend the one-hour guided tour (10am, noon, 2pm and 4pm daily from June to August, reduced schedule rest of the year).

The unique **Drottningholms Slottsteater** (www.dtm.se; admission by tour adult/student/child Skr90/70/free; ⊙hourly 11-4pm May-Aug, noon-3pm Sep) is the original 18th-century court theatre and the tours make use of ye olde backstage sound-effects, such as thunder machines and trapdoors; ask about opera, ballet and musical performances here in summer.

At the far end of the gardens is the 18th-century **Kina Slott** (Chinese Pavillion; adult/student & child Skr80/40; ⊙11am-4.30pm May-Aug, noon-3.30pm Sep), a lavishly decorated 'Chinese pavilion' – summer palace – that was built as a gift to Queen Lovisa Ulrika. Admission includes an entertaining guided tour.

If you're not short of time, you could cycle out here, otherwise take the metro to T-Brommaplan and change to bus 176, 177, 301 or 323. The most pleasant way to get to Drottningholm, however, is by **Strömma Kanalbolaget** (www.strommakanalbolaget.com; adult/child one way Skr135/65, return Skr180/90; combined ticket incl entry to Drottingholm & Kina Slott Skr320/160) boat. Frequent services depart from Stadshusbron (Stockholm) daily between May and mid-September, with less-frequent daily departures mid- to late September, and weekend-only services in October.

Around Stockholm

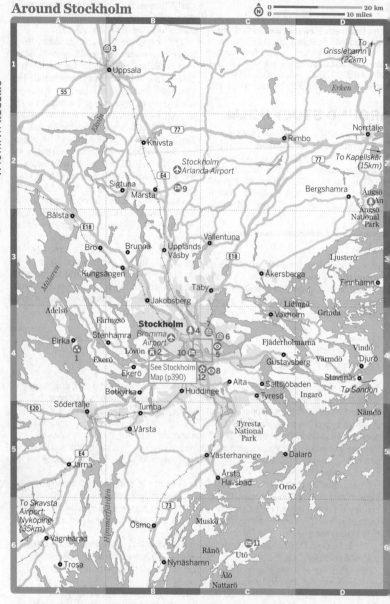

See Stockholm Map (p390)

Vaxholm

08 / POP 4857

Vaxholm, located about 35km northeast of Stockholm, is the gateway to the central and northern reaches of Stockholm's archi-pelago and it positively swarms with tour-ists in summer. It has a collection of quaint summer houses that were fashionable in the 19th century. The oldest buildings are in the Norrhamn area, a few minutes' walk north of the town hall, but there's also interesting

Around Stockholm

architecture along Hamngatan (the main street).

Bus 670 from Stockholm's T-Tekniska Högskolan metro station runs regularly to the town. **Waxholmsbolaget** (✆08-679 58 30; www.waxholmsbolaget.se) boats sail frequently between Vaxholm and Strömkajen in Stockholm (about 40 minutes). Strömma Kanalbolaget (p399) sails between Strandvägen and Vaxholm three times daily from mid-June to mid-August (return Skr230) and infrequently the rest of the year.

Stockholm Archipelago

✆08

South of the city, the land crumbles into myriad fragments. Depending on whom you ask, the archipelago has between 14,000 and 100,000 islands (the usual consensus is 24,000). Some are bare rocks sticking out of the water, others are covered in forest or dotted with the summer cottages of the well-do-to. The archipelago is the favourite time-off destination for Stockholm's locals, and everyone has their private spot to sunbathe and unwind.

Visit Skärgården (✆08-10 02 22; www.visitskargarden.se; Kajplats 18; ⊙9am-5pm Mon-Fri, 10am-4pm Sat, 11am-4pm Sun; Ⓜ T-Ropsten), a waterside information centre, can advise on (and book) accommodation and tours.

The biggest boat operator is **Waxholmsbolaget** (www.waxholmsbolaget.se). Time-

tables and information are available online. It divides the archipelago into three areas: Norra Skärgården is the northern section (north from Ljusterö to Arholma); Mellersta Skärgården is the middle section, taking in Vaxholm, Ingmarsö, Stora Kalholmen, Finnhamn, Möja and Sandhamn; and Södra Skärgården is the southern section, with boats south to Nämdö, Ornö and Utö. The 5-day Boat Hiker's Pass (Skr420) gives you unlimited rides.

If time is short, consider taking the Thousand Island Cruise, which is offered by **Stromma Kanabolaget** (✆08-12 00 40 00; www.strommakanalbolaget.com; Nybrokajen) and runs daily between late June and early August. The full-day tour departs from Stockholm's Nybrokajen at 9.30am and returns at 8.30pm; the cost of Skr1260 includes lunch, dinner, drinks and guided tours ashore and three island stops.

Sandhamn village on Sandön is popular with sailors and day trippers. One of the archipelago's best restaurants, **Seglarrestaurangen** (✆08-57 45 04 21; www.sandhamn.com; mains Skr225-295; ⊙year-round), inside the Seglarhotellet, serves high end Swedish food, from exceptional seared Lofoten cod to coffee-roasted venison.

The 900m-long **Finnhamn**, northeast of Stockholm, combines lush woods and meadows with sheltered coves, rocky cliffs and visiting eagle owls. While it's a popular summertime spot, there are enough quiet corners to indulge your inner hermit. **STF Vandrarhem Finnhamn** (✆08-54 24 62 12; www.svenskaturistforeningen.se; dm/s/d Skr270/415/540; ⊙year-round; @) is a hostel in a large wooden villa, with boat hire available. It's the largest hostel in the archipelago; advance booking is essential.

A cycling paradise in the southern archipelago, **Utö** has it all: sublime sandy beaches, lush fairy-tale forests, sleepy farms and abundant birdlife. Reception for the **STF hostel** (www.svenskaturistforeningen.se; dm Skr345, full board Skr1395; ⊙Sep-May) is at the nearby *värdshus* (former summer house), whose restaurant is ranked among the best in the archipelago.

Fjäderholmarna, one of the 'feather' islands at the entrance to the archipelago is the easiest to get to, with boats heading there every hour from Nybroplan (30 minutes). There are a couple of craft shops, restaurants, and a great fish smokehouse selling smoked prawns here, though the

BIRKA – PAST VIKING GLORY

On the island Björkö in Mälaren lake stand the remains of the Viking trading centre of Birka (www.stromma.se; ☉11am-6.30pm late Jun–mid-Aug, 11am-3pm May–late Jun & mid-Aug–early Sep), founded around AD 760 and now a Unesco World Heritage site. It is here that archaeologists have excavated the largest Viking cemetery in Sweden – more than 3000 graves, with most remains cremated, but some buried in coffins, which suggests the advent of Christianity. The harbour and fortress have also been excavated. Birka was abandoned in late 10th century – either because it was eclipsed by the up-and-coming commercial settlement of Sigtuna or else because the water level in the lake had dropped, cutting the island off from the Baltic Sea. However, you can still see objects from its heyday at the **museum**, where a scale model of the village puts things into perspective.

Daily cruises to Birka run from early May to early September; the round trip on Strömma Kanalbolaget's (p414) *Victoria* from Stadshusbron, Stockholm, is a full day's outing. The cruise price includes a visit to the museum and a guided tour in English of the settlement's burial mounds and fortifications. Boats leave between 9am and 10am (check website for schedule).

main activity is sunbathing on the rocks. The last boats leave the islands at around midnight, making them a perfect spot to soak up the long daylight hours.

Ekerö District

☑08 / POP 10,907

The pastoral Ekerö district, 20km west of Stockholm, is home to the romantic Drottningholm castle as well as several large islands in Mälaren lake, a dozen medieval churches and the Unesco World Heritage Site at Birka.

Sigtuna

☑08 / POP 8444

About 40km northwest of Stockholm is the picturesque lakeside village of Sigtuna, the oldest surviving town in Sweden. It was founded in about 980; the first Swedish coins were struck here in 995. There's a popular **Medieval Festival** in July and good holiday markets throughout December.

Ten rune stones still stand in various places around Sigtuna, and 150 more dot the surrounding landscape. Storagatan is probably Sweden's oldest main street, and there are ruins of 12th-century churches around town. The mid-13th-century church **Mariakyrkan**, Sigtuna's most arresting sight, contains restored medieval paintings. The friendly **Sigtuna Museum** (☑08-5912 6670; www.sigtunamuseum.se; Storagatan 55; adult/

student/child Skr20/10/free; ☉noon-4pm Jun-Aug) displays finds from excavations of the area, including ample amounts of coins and jewellery.

Sigtuna is easily doable as a day trip from Stockholm. Out of the numerous cafes to choose from, don't miss the delightful **Tant Brun Kaffestuga** (☑08-59 25 09 34; www.tantbrun-sigtuna.se; Laurentii gränd 3; cakes around Skr40; ☉10am-5pm Mon-Fri, to 6pm Sat & Sun), a 17th-century cafe with a worryingly saggy roof and pretty courtyard just off Storagatan.

To get here, take a local train (four hourly, 35 minutes) to Märsta, from where there are frequent buses to Sigtuna (570 or 575), or else travel in style by **Strömma Kanalbolaget** (☑08-12 00 40 00; www.stromma.se; adult/6-11 yr Skr340/170).

SVEALAND

This area, the birthplace of Sweden, offers evidence of the region's long history, including rune stones so plentiful you might stumble over them. Pre-Viking burial mounds in Gamla Uppsala light the imaginations of myth-builders and history buffs. There's also the trip into the bowels of the earth at the old mine in Falun, which accidentally provided the red paint for all those little cottages dotting the landscape. And, in Mora, the definitive Swedish king's path towards the crown is still retraced today by thousands of skiers each year in the Vasaloppet.

Uppsala

♪ 018 / POP 140,454

The historical and spiritual heart of the country, Uppsala has the upbeat party vibe of a university town to balance the weight of its castle, cathedral and university. Peaceful by day and lively by night, it makes an easy day trip from Stockholm, though it's worth lingering overnight to wander the deserted streets and soak in the atmosphere.

On the edge of the city is Gamla (Old) Uppsala, the original site of the town, which was once a flourishing 6th-century religious centre.

◉ Sights

Gamla Uppsala   ARCHAEOLOGICAL SITE
(www.arkeologigamlauppsala.se; 🖵115) If you wish to get to the root of Uppsala's beginnings, shrouded in legend and cloaked in mystery, head for Gamla Uppsala. The site's three **grave mounds**, named after the Norse god Odin, Thor and Frey, are said to be those of legendary pre-Viking kings who had descended from Frey, mentioned in *Beowulf* (although recent evidence suggests that at least one of the occupants is a woman) and lie in a field including about 300 smaller mounds and a great heathen temple (now with the Christian Gamla Uppsala kyrka planted on top of it). As fascinating as the grave mounds themselves are the myths surrounding them: a 17th-century professor, Olof Rudbeck, argued that Gamla Uppsala was actually the ancient sunken city of Atlantis, for example.

Nearby, the excellent **Gamla Uppsala Historical Centre** (adult/child Skr60/35, under 6yr free; ⊙11am-5pm May-Aug; ♿; 🖵115) shows off the finds from the burial mounds and the nearby archaeological sites, such as Viking weaponry and objects engraved with intricate, infinite patterns featuring the griffin. There's a timeline on the wall to help you make sense of the events and a kiddie area for budding archaeologists.

Christianity arrived in the 11th century, and with it the bishops and other church officials. From 1164 the archbishop had his seat in a cathedral on the site of the present **church**, which, by the 15th century, was enlarged and painted with frescos; inside there's the tomb of Celsius, responsible for thermometer measurements.

The site is located 4km north of the modern city; take bus 115 from Uppsala Centralstation (Srk30, every 30 minutes, 25 minutes).

Uppsala Slott   CASTLE
(www.uppsalaslott.se; admission by guided tour only, adult/child Skr80/15; ⊙tours in English 12.15pm, 1pm, 2pm & 3pm Tue-Sun Jul & Aug) Originally constructed by Gustav Vasa in the mid-16th century, Uppsala Slott features the state hall where kings were enthroned and a queen abdicated. Not much is left of the castle, since a large chunk of it was destroyed in a fire in 1702. Still, the view of Uppsala from its lofty hilltop position is worth a stroll.

WORTH A TRIP

SIGURDSRISTNINGEN

The vivid 3m-long Viking Age rock carving **Sigurdsristningen** (www.illustrata.com; admission free; ⊙24hr) illustrates the story of Sigurd the Dragon Slayer, a hero whose adventures are described in *Beowulf* and the Icelandic sagas. The story inspired Wagner's *Ring Cycle*, and *The Hobbit* and *Lord of the Rings* also borrow from it.

Carved into the bedrock around AD 1000, the carving shows Sigurd roasting the heart of the dragon Fafnir over a fire. Sigurd's stepfather, Regin, has persuaded him to kill Fafnir for the dragon's golden treasure. Sigurd touches the heart to see if it's cooked, then sucks his finger, and voila – he suddenly understands the language of birds. They warn him that Regin is plotting to kill him and keep the treasure, so Sigurd attacks first, chopping off his stepfather's head; the unfortunate fellow is shown in the left corner of the carving, among his scattered tools.

If you have a mobile phone with you, it can act as an audioguide for the price of a regular phone call; phone number given at the site.

The carving is situated near Sundbyholms Slott and Mälaren lake, 12km northeast of Eskilstuna. Get public transport details at the **Eskilstuna tourist office** (🕿016-710 70 00; www.eskilstuna.nu; Tullgatan 4, Rothoffsvillan; ⊙10am-5pm Mon-Fri, 10am-2pm Sat).

The castle is accessible through the frankly yawnsome **Uppsala Art Museum**; museum admission is included in the tour price. The **Botanical Gardens** (www.botan. uu.se; Villavägen 6-8; ☺7am-9pm daily May-Sep, to 7pm rest of yr), below the castle hill, show off more than 10,000 different species and are pleasant to wander through.

Museum Gustavianum MUSEUM
(www.gustavianum.uu.se; Akademigatan 3; adult/ senior & student/under 12yr Skr50/40/free; ☺10am-4pm Tue-Sun Jun-Aug) This pleasantly musty museum features such treasures as Egyptian sarcophagi, Greek vases, Roman oil lamps, the Augsburg Art Cabinet (a treasure chest of black oak belonging to Gustav II Adolf), and a room full of astrological measurement instruments. In the dome is a cleverly tucked away anatomical theatre dating back to 1663; if you're squeamish, don't look too closely at the creatures preserved in the formaldehyde.

Linnémuseet MUSEUM
(www.linnaeus.se; Svartbäcksgatan 27; adult/under 16yr Skr60/free; ☺11am-5pm Tue-Sun May-Sep) Memorabilia of groundbreaking botanist Carl von Linné's (aka Linnaeus) work in Uppsala. The gardens, with more than 1000 herbs, were designed according to an 18th-century plan and the former home of Linnaeus gives you a peek into the man's life.

Domkyrka CHURCH
(www.uppsaladomkyrka.se; Domkyrkoplan; ☺8am-6pm May-Sep) Scandinavia's largest cathedral, built to upstage the one in Trondheim, Norway, dominates the city, just as some of those buried here shaped their country, including Reformist Gustav Vasa, his son Johan III and botanist Carl von Linné. Relics of St Erik, Sweden's patron saint, are in a golden coffin in its own chapel.

Treasury MUSEUM
(Domkyrkan; adult/under 16 yr Skr40/free; ☺10am-5pm Mon-Sat, 12.30-5pm Sun May-Sep) The Domkyrka treasury, features a wealth of ecclesiastical wear, Gustav Vasa's funerary sword, Johan III's crown, and silver chalices aplenty.

Carolina Rediviva LIBRARY
(www.ub.uu.se; Dag Hammarskjölds väg 1; adult/ student & child Skr20/free, free Oct-May; ☺exhibition hall 9am-8pm Mon-Fri, 10am-5pm Sat) The display hall at the old university library contains some marvelous treasures, including one of the earliest maps of Mexico, cuneiform dating to the 7th century BC, the beautiful 6th-century *Codex Argentus* (aka Silver Bible), the first printed map of the Nordic countries and more, so much more.

🛌 Sleeping

Villa Anna HOTEL €€€
(☎018-580 20 00; www.villaanna.se; Odinslund 3; r from Skr1600; P🅿️🛜) A hotel that's not part of a chain? Right in the heart of town, with views of the historic centre? Hotel Anna is indeed all that – a rarity in these parts. Each spacious room is individually decorated in neutral shades, with the emphasis on comfort rather than gimmicks. There is an atmospheric cellar for wine tasting and the on-site restaurant is superb, serving elegant fusion dishes with an emphasis on local ingredients.

Hotell & Vandrarhem Kungsängstorg HOSTEL €
(☎018-444 20 10; www.vandrarhemuppsala.se; Kungsängstorg 6; hostel dm/s/d Skr200/425/500, hotel s/d/tr Skr790/990/1290; @) Quiet, intimate hostel in a beautifully restored house several blocks from the train station. The staff are lovely, the breakfast is ample, and the main difference between the 'hotel' and 'hostel' rooms is that the former has free bed linen and breakfast included. Hotel prices drop on weekends.

Fyrishov Camping CAMPGROUND €
(☎018-727 49 60; www.fyrishov.se; Idrottsgatan 2; sites Skr130, 4-bed cabins Skr895; ☺year-round; P🅿️🚣) This camping ground, situated 2km north of the city and popular with families, is attached to one of Sweden's largest water parks, with discounted swim-and-stay packages (cabins from Skr995). Take bus 1 from Dragarbrunnsgatan.

Best Western Hotel Svava HOTEL €€
(☎018-13 00 30; www.bestwestern.se; Bangårdsgatan 24; s/d from Skr675/1035; P🅿️🛜) Named after one of Odin's Valkyrie maidens and right opposite the train station, Svava is a very comfortable business-style hotel with a plethora of creature comforts. Weekend and summer discounts on offer that make it a smashing deal.

🍴 Eating

Casual dining options can be found inside **Saluhallen** (Sankt Eriks Torg; ☺10am-6pm Mon-Thu, to 7pm Fri, to 4pm Sat, restaurants 11am-4pm Sun), an indoor market between the cathedral and the river. Find groceries at the central **Hemköp supermarket** (Stora Torget; ☺8am-10pm).

TOP CHOICE Jay Fu   ASIAN, AMERICAN €€
(www.jayfu.se; Sankt Eriks torg 8; mains Skr185-285; ☺from 5pm Mon-Sat) The menu at this Asian–American joint, inspired by a kung fu stuntsman/Californian steakhouse owner, runs the gamut from such inspired creations as grilled scallops with green chilli mayo and grilled duck with apple kimchi to the No Shadow Burger and carrot cake with pistachio mousse. Be prepared for a leisurely dinner as the staff live on Zen time.

Hambergs Fisk   SEAFOOD €€
(www.hambergs.se; Fyristorg 8; mains Skr110-295; ☺11.30am-10pm Tue-Sat) No need to ask at the tourist office about where to eat: if you're there, you'll be close enough to smell the aromas of dill and seafood tempting you into this excellent fish restaurant, serving the likes of perch with hazelnut butter, shellfish platters to share and buillabaise. Fresh and fabulous.

Amazing Thai   THAI €€
(www.amazingthai.se; Bredgränd 14; mains Skr139-179; 🚗🚻) Authentic flavours (though ask them to turn up the heat if you like it Thai-style), fragrant stir-fries, noodle dishes and curries define this friendly restaurant, and while the food may fall short of 'amazing', it's pretty damn tasty and the portions are a good size. The all-you-can-gobble lunch buffet is a bargain at Skr85 and immensely popular with families.

Peppar Peppar   INTERNATIONAL €€€
(☏018-13 13 60; www.pepparpeppar.se; Suttings gränd 3; mains Skr228-296; 5-course tasting menu Skr496; ☺from 5pm Mon-Wed, from 4pm Thu-Sun) White linen, candles, a cosy atmosphere and dishes such as reindeer steak with chanterelles, pumpkin and truffle soup and pan fried sea bass make this a wonderful dinner option. The ingredients are locally sourced, but inspiration from abroad shows up in the likes of crème caramel with raspberries. Great service to boot.

Ofvandahls   CAFE €
(Sysslomansgatan 3-5; cakes & snacks around Skr45) An Uppsala institution, this classy *konditori* (bakery/confectionery/cafe) dates back to the 19th century and is a cut above your average coffee-and-bun shop.

UPPSALA KORTET

This handy little **discount card** (Skr195) gives 24 hours free or discounted admission to many of the town's museums and attractions, plus free local bus travel and parking and free travel to Arlanda Airport. There are also discounts at participating hotels, restaurants and shops. The card is valid from June to August, and can be bought from the tourist office. It covers one adult and up to two children.

ℹ Information

Tourist office (☏018-727 48 00; www.destinationuppsala.se; Fyristorg 8; ☺10am-6pm Mon-Fri, to 3pm Sat, also 11am-3pm Sun Jul-Aug) Pick up maps and the *What's On Uppsala* for event listings.

ℹ Getting There & Away

The Airbus (bus 801) departs at least twice an hour around the clock for nearby Stockholm Arlanda Airport (one way adult/child Skr120/70, 45 minutes); it leaves from outside Uppsala Central Station.

Swebus Express (☏0200-21 82 18; www.swebus.se) runs regular direct services to Stockholm (from Skr59, 1¼ hours, hourly), Västerås (Skr299, four hours, three daily), and Örebro (Skr229, five to 6½ hours, three daily).

There are frequent **SJ** (www.sj.se) trains to/from Stockholm (Skr82, 40 minutes, twice hourly), Falun (from Skr116, 2¼ to 3¼ hours, hourly), Gävle (from Skr96, 50 minutes to 1¼, at least hourly), Östersund (from Skr135, 4¼ to five hours, two daily) and Mora (from Skr152, 3¼ hours, two daily).

ℹ Getting Around

Upplands Lokaltrafik (☏0771-14 14 14; www.ul.se) runs traffic within the city and county. City buses leave from Stora Torget and the surrounding streets. Tickets for unlimited travel for 90 minutes cost from Skr30.

Örebro

☏019 / POP 107,038

A culturally rich city with a young vibe, Örebro buzzes around its central feature, the huge and romantic castle surrounded by a moat filled with water lilies. The city originally grew as a product of the textile industry, but it's now decidedly a university town –

students on bicycles fill the streets, and relaxed locals gather on restaurant patios and in parks.

◉ Sights

Slottet
CASTLE

(☎019-21 21 21; www.orebroslott.se; guided tours adult/child Skr70/30, history exhibition free; ☉daily Jun-Aug, 1pm Sat & Sun rest of yr, history exhibition 10am-5pm daily May-Aug) The magnificent **Slottet**, built in the 13th century to defend the town, now serves as the county governor's headquarters, so the exterior is more impressive than the interior, much of which is accessed by tour only. There's a historical one at 4.30pm (in Swedish or English, depending on numbers), or a 'Secrets of the Vasa Fortress' option at 2.30pm (in English) in summer which involves slightly cringeworthy costumed capering from the guides and some audience participation. Tickets purchased from the tourist office. The castle's northwest tower holds a small **history exhibition**.

Wadköping
MUSEUM

(admission Skr25; ☉11am-4pm or 5pm Tue-Sun, tours 1pm & 3pm Aug; ♿) A pleasant stroll east of the castle along the river will take you through Stadsparken, where the Stadsträdgården greenhouse precinct has a great cafe. Further east is the enjoyable Wadköping museum village, an open-air museum of enticing cobbled streets lined with craft workshops, a bakery, cafe and period buildings.

FREE Länsmuseum & Konsthall
MUSEUM

(www.orebrolansmuseum.se; Engelbrektsgatan 3; ☉9am-6pm Tue & Thu, 11am-9pm Wed, noon-4pm Fri-Sun) Outside the castle grounds, this combined regional and art museum mixes treasure – coins, jewellery – with other archaeological finds of Örebro County and some terrific temporary exhibitions, such as the trippy, colourful art of Karl Axel Pehrson.

St Nikolai Kyrka
CHURCH

(☉10am-5pm Mon-Fri, 11am-3pm Sat) The commercial centre and some grand buildings are around Stortorget, including the 13th-century St Nikolai Kyrka, where Jean Baptiste Bernadotte (Napoleon's marshal) was chosen in 1810 to take the Swedish throne in spite of not speaking a word of Swedish. The contemporary art exhibitions are well worth a gander, too.

⛵ Sleeping & Eating

Behrn Hotell
HOTEL €€€

(☎019-12 00 95; www.behrnhotell.se; Stortorget 12; s/d Skr1295/1595; ✳@🛜) Excellently situated on the main square, Behrn Hotell goes the extra mile, with homey rooms each individually decorated, ranging from strictly business to farmhouse to edgy modern Scandinavian. Do it right and get a room with a balcony, or a suite with old wooden beams, chandeliers and jacuzzi. There's also a spa and a restaurant that serves dinner from Tuesday to Friday.

STF Vandrarhem Livin
HOSTEL €

(☎019-31 02 40; www.livin.se; Järnvägsgatan 22; dm/s/d Skr250/500/640, hotel s/d Skr900/1100; 🛜) This large STF hostel is part of a modern budget-hotel building; spartan hostel rooms have the same basic features as the hotel rooms, including private bathroom and TV, but prices don't include sheets or breakfast. Rather impersonal, but well located and good, facilities-wise, with a large self-catering kitchen, laundry room and bicycle hire.

Karishma
INDIAN €€

(www.karishma.se; Kungsgatan 26; mains Skr149-189; ☉5-10.30pm Mon-Thu, to 11pm Fri, 4-11pm Sat, 3-9pm Sun; ☑) If you're hankering for authentic North Indian cuisine, look no further. Tandoori specials abound, as do stews and curries, and the sizzling prawn dish stands out. Wash it down with a superb salted lassi. Come hungry, as some of the mains are big enough for two.

Hälls Konditori Stallbacken
CAFE €

(www.hallsconditori.se; Engelbrektsgatan 12; pastries Skr20-45, lunch specials Skr79; ☉7.30am-6pm Mon-Fri, 10am-4pm Sat; ♿) One of two locations of this bakery-cafe (the other's in Järntorget), Hälls is a classic old-style *konditori*. Sensible light meals (salads, quiche, sandwiches) are available, plus there's teetering piles of creamy cakes and pastries.

ⓘ Information

Tourist office (☎019-21 21 21; www.orebrotown.se; ☉10am-6pm Mon-Fri, to 2pm Sat, noon-4pm Sun Jun-Aug) Inside the castle.

ⓘ Getting There & Away

Long-distance buses, which leave from opposite the train station, operate pretty much everywhere in southern Sweden. From here, **Swebus Express** (☎0771-218 218; www.swebus.se) has connections to Norrköping, Karlstad and Oslo (Norway), Mariestad and Göteborg, Västerås and Uppsala, and Eskilstuna and Stockholm.

Train connections are also good. Direct SJ trains run to/from Stockholm (Skr177, two hours, hourly), some via Västerås (Skr87, 50 minutes); and Göteborg (Skr221, 2¾ to 4¼ hours). Other trains run daily to Gävle (Skr227, three to four hours) and Borlänge (Skr194, two hours), where you can change for Falun and Mora.

Falun

📞 023 / POP 37,291

An unlikely combination of industrial and adorable, Falun is home to the region's most important mine and, as a consequence, the source of the deep-red paint that renders Swedish country houses so uniformly cute. It's the main city of the Dalarna region, putting it within easy striking distance of some of Sweden's best attractions, including the home of painter Carl Larsson, a work of art in itself.

⊙ Sights & Activities

TOP
CHOICE Kopparberget
Copper Mine MINE, MUSEUM
(📞023-78 20 30; www.falugruva.se; tours adult/child Skr210/80; ⊙tours 2pm Mon-Fri, noon & 2pm Sat & Sun; 🖪) The Kopparberget copper mine was the world's most important by the 17th century and only closed in 1992 (it's now on Unesco's World Heritage list). Here's your chance to descend into the bowels of the earth – perhaps with a brief prayer to the Lady of the Mine – (bring warm clothing; helmets provided) and find out what life was like for those who toiled here (including 17th-century miner Fet-Mats). Entertaining tours take one hour; unlike the miners of yore, you shan't have to descend by holding on to a giant bucket of ore and jumping off at designated points. Don't miss the royal graffiti.

If you're claustrophobic, it's worth taking the twee **mine train** (several departures daily) around the rim of the Stora Stöten ('Great Pit') to grasp its sheer size. The **mine museum** (adult/child Skr60/free; ⊙10am-6pm May-Sep) contains everything you could possibly want to know about the history, mythology, geology and copper production of the mine; the story of the mine hospital and Sweden's first pharmacy is most absorbing. Take bus 709.

Carl Larsson-gården HISTORIC HOME
(📞023-600 53; www.carllarsson.se; tour adult/child Skr145/50; ⊙10am-5pm May-Sep; 🖪) The beautiful early 20th-century home of the artist Carl Larsson and his wife Karin in the pretty village of Sundborn (13km from Falun; bus 64) is a bright, lively house with superb colour schemes, decoration and furniture, and the warmth of the family home is evident in Larsson's portraits of his family. Tapestries and embroidery woven by Karin Larsson reveal she was a skilled artist in her own right. Admission is by 45-minute guided tour only; call in advance for times of English tours.

There's more folk culture at **Dalarnas Museum** (www.dalarnasmuseum.se; Stigaregatan 2-4; ⊙noon-5pm Sun & Mon, 10am-5pm Tue-Sat; 🖪), plus Nobel Prize–winning author Selma Lagerlöf's preserved study and library and some cutting-edge temporary exhibits of Swedish artists.

Stora Kopparbergs Kyrka CHURCH
(Kyrkbacksvägen 8; ⊙10am-6pm Mon-Sat, 9am-6pm Sun) This late 14th-century church is Falun's oldest building, with brick vaulting and folk-art flowers running round the walls.

Hopptornen TOWER
(admission Skr25; ⊙10am-6pm Sun-Thu, 10am-11pm Fri & Sat mid-May–mid-Aug) This tower and ski jump in the hills behind the town has great views; you can either walk or take a lift to the top.

🛏 Sleeping & Eating

Främby Udde LODGE €€
(📞023-197 84; www.frambyudde.com; Främby Udde 20; 2-/4-person cottage from €116/151; 🅿🖪) It's difficult to get more Swedish than this: a lodge surrounded by cottages in a pine forest on a cape pretty much surrounded by the massive Runn lake. It embodies the whole *mens sana in corpore sano* (healthy mind in healthy body), and activities include canoeing and biking in summer and ice skating in winter. Around 4km southeast of Falun.

Falu Fängelse Vandrarhem HOSTEL €
(📞023-79 55 75; www.falufangelse.se; Villavägen 17; dm/s/f Skr260/360/670; ⊙reception 8am-6pm; @🛜) It's hard to beat this former prison cum SVIF hostel for atmosphere. Dorm beds are in cells, with heavy iron doors and thick walls, concrete floors and steel lockers for closets. The place is extremely friendly, and

A HORSEY HISTORY

The Dalecarlian or Dala horse originated as a simple wooden toy for children but grew into an art form, and its characteristic sturdy form, traditionally painted bright red but with a harness in green, yellow, white and blue, came to symbolise Dalarna village. Why a horse? Because horses were the most valuable of farm workers, and by the 19th century, these wooden creations were used as a form of barter.

A good place to see how today's Dala horses are made, and pick up some of your own, is **Nils Olsson Hemslöjd** (250-372 00; www.nohemslojd.se; 8am-6pm Mon-Fri, 9am-5pm Sat & Sun mid-Jun–mid-Aug) at Nusnäs, 10km southeast of Mora (bus 108, three daily Monday to Friday).

common areas are spacious and full of well-worn furniture. If you don't want to queue for the limited bathroom facilities, grab an en suite.

Banken Bar & Brasserie   INTERNATIONAL €€
(023-71 19 11; www.bankenfalun.se; Åsgatan 41; mains Skr145-235;) Based in a former bank, classy Banken has a splendid interior and matching service. The menu includes a *gott & enkelt* ('good and simple') category – featuring the likes of burgers and pasta – plus more upmarket 'world cuisine' dishes, such as reindeer steak. Inexpensive lunch menu (with vegie options) includes a salad buffet, main and drink (Skr130).

Kopparhattan Café & Restaurang   CAFE €€
(Stigaregatan 2-4; lunch buffet Skr85, mains Skr85-170) Funky, arty cafe-restaurant, attached to Dalarnas Museum and with a terrace overlooking the river, serving sandwiches, soup and vegetarian specials for lunch, and light vegie, fish and meat evening mains.

🛈 Information

Tourist Office (023-830 50; www.visit sodradalarna.se; Trotzgatan 10-12; 10am-6pm Mon-Fri, 10am-4pm Sat)

🛈 Getting There & Away

Falun isn't on the main train lines – change at Borlänge when coming from Stockholm or Mora – but there are direct trains to and from Gävle (Skr205, 1¼ hours, roughly every two hours), or regional buses (Skr120, two hours) equally often.

Swebus Express (0771-21 82 18; www.swebus.se) has buses on the Göteborg–Karlstad–Falun–Gävle route, and connections to buses on the Stockholm–Borlänge–Mora route.

Regional transport is run by **Dalatrafik** (0771-95 95 95; www.dalatrafik.se), which covers all corners of the county of Dalarna. Tickets cost Skr25 for trips within a zone and Skr15 extra for each new zone. A combination card for 10 journeys starts from Skr200. Regional bus 70 goes approximately hourly to Rättvik (Skr60, one hour) and Mora (Skr88, 1¾ hours).

Lake Siljan Region

Swedish friends tend to get all dewy-eyed at the mention of this picture-perfect, most intensely 'Swedish' region, complete with cute little red cottages with white window frames, rolling meadows and blue lakes. This gorgeous part of the country is an immensely popular summer destination (as testified by oodles of traffic around the lakes in peak season) and great for winter sports. **Dalarna** is well-known for its crafts, particularly those ubiquitous painted Dala horses you see everywhere, and its summer festivals; there's no better place to spend Midsummer, complete with the phallic pagan maypoles that Christianity couldn't get rid of.

Maps of **Siljansleden**, an excellent network of walking and cycling paths extending for more than 300km around Lake Siljan, are available from tourist offices for Skr25. Another way to enjoy the lake is by boat: in summer, **MS Gustaf Wasa** (070-542 10 25; www.wasanet.nu; cruises Skr80-275) runs a complex range of lunch, dinner and sightseeing cruises from the towns of Mora, Rättvik and Leksand. Ask at any tourist office or go online for a schedule.

LEKSAND
0247 / POP 15,292
Leksand's claim to fame is its Midsummer Festival, the most popular in Sweden, in which around 20,000 spectators fill the bowl-shaped green park on the first Friday evening after 21 June to sing songs and watch costumed dancers circle the maypole. **Leksands Kyrka** (Kyrkallén; 10am-6pm Jun–mid-Aug), with its distinctive onion dome, dates from the early 13th century. The **tourist office** (0248-79 72 00; leksand@siljan.se;

Kyrkallén 8; ⊙10am-5pm Mon-Fri, 10am-2pm Sat) is on the main drag.

Tiny **Tällberg**, midway between Rättvik and Leksand, is cuteness personified, with its smattering of adorable gingerbread houses scattered like a handful of rubies along a hillside, and it's nearly as expensive if you want to stay the night, as it's got eight upmarket hotels for a population of around 200. But it's a lovely place to have a wander and **Åkerblads** (⊘0247-508 00; www.akerblads. se; Sjögattu 2; s/d from Skr850/1430, discounted to Skr745/995) is one of the best lunch spots for miles around, with a fantastic buffet and weekend smörgåsbord.

Bus 58 between Rättvik and Leksand stops in the village regularly, and it's worth going just for the scenic landscape along the route. Tällberg is also on the train line that runs along Lika Siljan; the train station is around 2km below the village.

RÄTTVIK
⊘0248 / POP 4686

Laid-back Rättvik has sandy lakeside beaches for summer and ski slopes for winter. Don't miss the longest wooden pier in Sweden, the 625m **Långbryggan**. Views from surrounding hills are excellent.

By the lake northwest of the train station, the 13th-century **church**, rebuilt in 1793, has 87 well-preserved **church stables**, the oldest dating from 1470.

Inviting all sorts of bad puns about rocking out, **Dalhalla** (www.dalhalla.se) is an old limestone quarry 7km north of Rättvik used as an open-air theatre and concert venue in summer; the acoustics are incredible and the setting is stunning.

On the lake shore near the train station is shaded **Siljansbadets Camping** (⊘248-561 18; www.siljansbadet.com; campsite high season Skr160-265, 4-bed cabins from Skr605; ⊞), boasting its own Blue Flag beach.

By Enåbadets camping ground is the highly rated hostel **STF Vandrarhem Rättvik** (⊘0248-561 09; Centralgatan; s/d from Skr285/420; ⊙reception 8-10am & 5-6pm; P@ₐ), in a charming complex of old wooden buildings. Reception for the hostel is at the camping ground office.

Pizza joints abound, and Storgatan is home to a few supermarkets. **Frick's Konditori** (www.frickskonditori.se; Stora Torget; sandwiches from Skr40), in the square across from the train station, has great pastries, quiches and sandwiches, while the upmarket **Jöns-Andersgården** (⊘0248 130 15; www.jonsandersgarden.se; Bygatan 4; d with shared/private bathroom Skr750/1150, ste from Skr1300; ⊙mid-Apr–mid-Oct) hotel up the hill serves lovely Italian dishes, such as roast lamb with rosemary or monkfish risotto.

The **tourist office** (⊘0248-79 72 10; Riksvägen 40; ⊙10am-5pm Mon-Fri, 10am-2pm Sat) is at the train station.

Buses depart from outside the train station. Dalatrafik's bus 70 runs regularly between Falun, Rättvik and Mora. A couple of direct intercity trains per day from Stockholm (Skr332, 3½ hours) stop at Rättvik. Local trains run often between Rättvik and Mora (Skr70, 25 minutes).

MORA
0250 / POP 10,900

Legend has it that in 1520 Gustav Vasa arrived here in a last-ditch attempt to start a rebellion against the Danish regime. The people of Mora weren't interested, and Gustav was forced to put on his skis and flee for the border. After he left, the town reconsidered and two yeomen, Engelbrekt and Lars, volunteered to follow Gustav's tracks,

SWEDEN LAKE SILJAN REGION

WORTH A TRIP

SWEDEN'S PREDATOR PARK

Fat-bottomed roly-poly bear cubs are the star attraction at **Grönklitt Björnpark** (⊘0250-462 00; www.orsabjornpark.se; adult/child Skr190/130; ⊙10am-6pm mid-Jun–Aug, to 3pm rest of yr), the largest predator park in Europe, outside the town of Orsa (16km north of Mora). Even if there are no cubs around during your visit, there's plenty to see: polar bears, Kodiak bears, leopards, Amur tigers, lynx, wolves, red foxes and wolverines. The animals have a lot of space, woodland and water, which is ideal for them, but means there's plenty of room to hide, so you may not see the more skittish creatures. For the closest views, follow the posted feeding schedule. Buses 103 and 104 run from Mora to Grönklitt, via Orsa where you have to change to bus 118 to get to the Grönklitt Björnpark (twice daily Monday to Friday, once on Sunday).

finally overtaking him in Sälen and changing Swedish history.

Today the world's biggest cross-country ski race, **Vasaloppet**, which ends in Mora, commemorates this epic chase. Around 15,000 people take part on the first Sunday in March. In summer, you can walk the route on the 90km **Vasaloppsleden**.

◎ Sights

Zornmuseet
MUSEUM

(☎0250-59 23 10; www.zorn.se; Vasagatan 36; adult/senior & student/child Skr60/50/free; ☺9am-5pm Mon-Sat, 11am-5pm Sun mid-May–mid-Sep) Many of the best-loved portraits – such as the haunting *Midnatt* – and characteristic nudes of the Mora painter Anders Zorn (1860–1920), one of Sweden's most renowned artists, are on display here, along with some Julia Beck works and etchings by Rembrandt. Next door, the Zorn family house **Zorngården** (☎0250-59 23 10; Vasagatan 36; admission & tour adult/senior & student/child Skr90/75/40; ☺10am-4pm Mon-Sat, 11am-4pm Sun mid-May–mid-Sep) reflects Zorn's National Romantic aspirations (check out the Viking-influenced hall and entryway). Access is by guided tour (every 15 minutes in summer; phone ahead for English tours).

🛏 Sleeping & Eating

Mora Parken
CAMPGROUND, CABINS €

(☎0250-276 00; www.moraparken.se; site Skr195, 4-bed cabins from Skr645, hotel s/d Skr1095/1445; @) This fancy camping ground with rustic cabins and the sleek, modern hotel are combined in a great waterside spot, 400m northwest of the church. Perks include a swimming beach on your doorstep, kitchen for self-caterers and more.

Mora Hotell & Spa
HOTEL €€

(☎0250-59 26 50; www.morahotell.se; Strandgatan 12; r from Skr1445) There's been a hotel here since 1830, although the current version is as modern as it gets, with all the facilities you'd expect from a big chain – plus personality. Rooms combine clean lines, wooden floors and earthy tones with bright folk-art accents. Head to the spa for steam rooms, Jacuzzis, massage and body treatments.

Mora Kaffestuga
CAFE €

(Kyrkogatan 8; sandwiches from Skr55; ☺7am-7pm Mon-Sat) Along the main pedestrian shopping street are a few small cafes; this is the pick of them, for its stylish interior and heavenly baked goods and sandwiches.

China House
CHINESE €€

(www.morachina.se; Moragatan 1; lunch Skr82, mains Skr156-198; ☑) A surprisingly good Chinese restaurant, with friendly staff, an extensive menu and changing lunch specials on weekdays. Vegetarian options abound; as for the carnivorously-inclined, the best bet are the 'three small dishes' combos. There's a separate Thai menu also, but Chinese is what these guys do best.

ⓘ Information

Tourist Office (☎0248-79 72 00; www.siljan. se; Strandgatan 14a; ☺10am-5pm Mon-Fri, 10am-2pm Sat) Brochures, maps and helpful staff.

ⓘ Getting There & Away

All Dalatrafik buses use the bus station at Moragatan 23. Buses 70 and 270 runs to Rättvik and Falun, while buses 103, 104, and 105 and 45 serve Orsa.

Mora is an **SJ** (☎0771-75 75 75; www.sj.se) train terminus and the southern terminus of Inlandsbanan (Inland Railway), which runs north to Gällivare (mid-June to mid-August). The main train station is about 1km east of the town centre. The more central Mora Strand is a platform station in town, but not all trains stop there, so check the timetable. When travelling to Östersund, you can choose between Inlandsbanan (Skr482, 6¼ hours, one daily, June to August only) or bus 45 (Skr255, 5¼ hours, two daily).

WORTH A TRIP

KRONETORPS WINDMILL

Located 7km north of Malmö, on the way to Lund, the eye-catching **Kronetorps Mölla** (Dalbyvägen 63, ☎040-45 20 94) looms over the smattering of cottages that is Burlöv, as if challenging Don Quijotes. This Dutch-style, fully functional windmill was built in 1841 by a wealthy landowner, and it's possible to peek inside at the giant cogs responsible for turning the sails. Adjacent to the windmill is an indoor exhibition on life in bygone times. Guided tours are held on summer Sundays between 1 and 4pm; the rest of the time visits are by appointment only.

SKÅNE

Artists adore southern Sweden. Down here, the light is softer, the foliage brighter and the shoreline more dazzling and white. Sweden's southernmost county, Skåne (Scania) was Danish property until 1658 and still flaunts its differences. You can detect them in the strong dialect *(skånska)*, in the half-timbered houses and in Skåne's hybrid flag: a Swedish yellow cross on a red Danish background.

Malmö

☑ 040 / POP 280,400

Once dismissed as crime-prone and tatty, Sweden's third-largest city has rebranded itself as progressive and downright cool. Malmö's second wind blew in with the opening of the Öresund bridge and tunnel in 2000, connecting the city to bigger, cooler Copenhagen and creating a dynamic new urban conglomeration. Such a cosmopolitan outcome seems only natural for what is Sweden's most multicultural metropolis; 150 nationalities make up Malmö's headcount. Here, Nordic reserve meets exotic Middle Eastern street stalls, skater parks and head-turning contemporary architecture.

◉ Sights & Activities

The cobbled streets and interesting buildings around **Lilla Torg** are restored parts of the late-medieval town. Many are now occupied by galleries, boutiques and restaurants.

Malmö Museer   MUSEUM
(www.malmo.se/museer; Malmöhusvägen; adult/under 19yr Skr40/free; ⊙10am-4pm Jun-Aug) Various museums in and around the imposing **Malmöhus Slott** (castle) make up the maze-like Malmö Museer. You can walk through the royal apartments, learn about the castle's history, descend into the former prison with displays on crime and punishment, check out vehicles through the ages, and see works by important Swedish artists such as John Bauer and Sigrid Hjertén at the **Konstmuseum**.

Moderna Museet Malmö   MUSEUM
(www.modernamuseet.se; Gasverksgatan 22; adult/senior & student/under 18yr Skr50/40/free; ⊙11am-6pm Tue-Sun) This striking red-orange cube features ever-changing exhibitions – paintings, installations, photography and

sculpture – by contemporary artists, such as the recent 2013 Superrealism exhibition.

FREE **Form/Design Center**   ART GALLERY
(www.formdesigncenter.com; Lilla Torg 9; ⊙11am-5pm Tue-Sat, noon-4pm Sun) The Form/Design Center showcases cutting-edge design, architecture and art. The half-timbered houses in the surrounding cobbled streets now house **galleries** and **boutiques** selling arts and crafts.

Turning Torso   NOTABLE BUILDING
The northwest harbour redevelopment is home to the Turning Torso, a striking skyscraper and residential building that twists through 90 degrees from bottom to top. Designed by Spaniard Santiago Calatrava and inaugurated in 2005, it's now Sweden's tallest building (190m).

FREE **Malmö Konsthall**   ART GALLERY
(www.konsthall.malmo.se; St Johannesgatan 7; ⊙11am-5pm Thu-Tue, to 9pm Wed) One of Europe's largest contemporary art spaces, with exhibitions spanning both Swedish and foreign talent.

Stapelbädden Skatepark   SKATEBOARDING
(www.stpln.se; Stapelbäddsgatan 1) Intense urban jungle where skaters show off their skills. Even if you're not joining in, it makes for a heck of a spectacle.

City Boats Malmö   PEDAL BOATS
(☑0704-71 00 67; www.cityboats.se; Amiralsbron, Södra Promenaden; per 30/60min Skr90/150; ⊙11am-7pm May-Aug) To scoot around Malmö's canals in a pedal boat, head to this place just east of Gustav Adolfs Torg.

Malmö

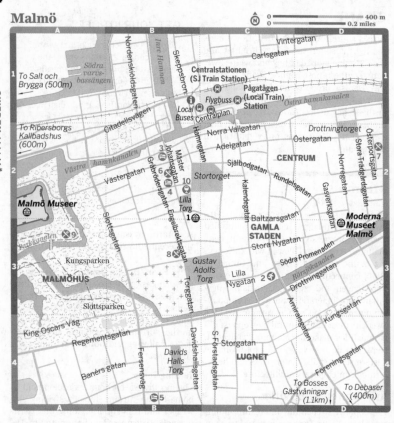

🛏 Sleeping

Centrally located private rooms and apartments are available through **City Room** (📞040-795 94; www.cityroom.se; s/d/apt from Skr400/500/600). The agency has no office address but can be reached by phone on weekdays from 9am to noon.

TOP CHOICE **Hotel Duxiana** HOTEL €€
(📞040-607 70 00; www.malmo.hotelduxiana .com; Mäster Johansgatan 1; s/d/ste from Skr795/ 1090/2140; P@🕾) Close to Centralstationen, ubersleek Hotel Duxiana is one for the style crew. In a palate of white, black and gunmetal grey, design features include Bruno Mattheson sofas and the same heavenly beds supplied to the world's first seven-star hotel in Dubai. Single rooms are small but comfy, while the decadent junior suites feature a clawed bathtub facing the bed.

Mäster Johan Hotel HOTEL €€
(📞040-664 64 00; www.masterjohan.se; Mäster Johansgatan 13; r/ste from Skr1290/1790; P@🕾) Just off Lilla Torg is one of Malmö's finest slumber spots, with spacious, elegantly understated rooms featuring beautiful oak floors and snow-white fabrics. Bathrooms flaunt Paloma Picasso–designed tiles, there's a sauna and gym, and the immaculate breakfast buffet is served in a glass-roofed courtyard.

STF Vandrarhem Malmö City HOSTEL €
(📞040-611 62 20; www.svenskaturistforeningen. se; Rönngatan 1; dm/s/d Skr190/455/510; @🖶) This central hostel has an excellent kitchen, outdoor patio, TV lounge and very helpful staff, and most sights are within easy walking distance. To reach the hostel, take buses 141 or 144 from the train station and get off at Malmö Teatern.

{"page": 425}

Malmö

Bosses Gästvåningar　　　　　HOSTEL €
(☑040-32 62 50; www.bosses.nu; Södra Förstadsgatan 110B; s/d/tr/q from Skr405/595/695/895; @; ☐1, 2, 3, 6, 7, 8, 34, 35, 131, 132) The quiet, clean rooms in this central SVIF hostel are like those of a budget hotel, with proper beds, TVs and shared bathrooms. Service is helpful and it's close to Möllevångstorget and opposite the town hospital (follow the signs for 'Sjukhuset' if arriving by car) or get off at Malmö Södervärn if travelling by bus.

✖ Eating

Malmö isn't short on dining experiences, whether it's vegan grub in a grungy left-wing hang-out or designer supping on contemporary Nordic flavours.

TOP
CHOICE Salt och Brygga　　　SWEDISH €€
(☑040-611 59 40; www.saltobrygga.se; Sundspromenaden 7; lunch mains Skr110-155, dinner mains Skr145-265; ⊙11am-2pm & 5-11pm Mon-Fri, 12.30-4pm & 5-11pm Sat; ☑) Overlooking the Öresund bridge, this stylish Slow Food restaurant serves contemporary organic Swedish cuisine. Flavours are clean and strictly seasonal – think smoked reindeer with chanterelles, seared walleye with kale and pumpkin, goat's cheese and spelt risotto, and fish so fresh it may have just jumped out of the sea in front of you. Book for dinner.

Mrs Saigon　　　　　VIETNAMESE €€
(www.mrs-saigon.se; Engelbrektsgatan 17; lunch buffet Skr88, mains Skr139-225; ⊙11.30am-3pm Mon-Sat, 5.30-11pm Tue-Sat; ☑) While the lunch buffet at this exposed-brick-and-red-velvet restaurant can only be described as 'miscellaneous Asian', in the evenings Mrs Saigon really wows you with authentic phô, grilled tiger prawns, steamed cod with black fungus and other Vietnamese delights. It's well worth going for the tasting plate of starters: the tiger prawn spring rolls and fish balls are superb.

Bastard　　　　　GASTROPUB €€€
(☑040-121 318; www.bastardrestaurant.se; Mäster Johansgatan 11; dishes from Skr180; ⊙5pm-midnight Tue-Thu, to 2am Fri & Sat) The place? Industrial-chic, with Bogart posters and rock on the stereo. The food? Gastropubbery at its finest. Perch on a stool by the U-shaped bar and watch the staff as they create imaginative tapas-style dishes such as salt cod with almonds, slow-cooked pig cheek and seared duck slices. The dishes are small, so they really add up.

Falafel No 1　　　MIDDLE EASTERN €
(www.falafel-n1.se; Österportsgatan 2; falafels Skr45; ☑) As the name suggests, this is Malmö's best falafel (trust us, we sampled plenty!), immortalised in songs by local band Timbuktu. Shwarma platters are also available, but to us, the falafel is the undisputed star of the show.

Slottsträdgården Kafé　　　CAFE €
(www.slotsstradgardenskafe.se; Grynbodgatan 9; sandwiches from Skr55; ⊙11am-5pm May-Sep; ☑) Organic coffee, filled sourdough baguettes, vegie dishes, chunky sandwiches and delectable cakes are all to be had at this little cafe, tucked away behind the castle.

♟ Drinking & Nightlife

Lilla Torg bars, such as **Victors** (www.victors.se; Lilla Torg), **Moosehead** (www.moosehead.se; Lilla Torg) and **Mello Yello** (www.melloyello.se;

MALMÖ CITY CARD

The Malmö City Kort discount card covers free bus transport, street parking, entry to several museums, and discounts at other attractions and on sightseeing tours. It costs Skr100 for one day and is now available as a smartphone app. Buy it at the tourist office.

Lilla Torg) have a great atmosphere and outdoor terraces.

Debaser   LIVE MUSIC
(www.debaser.se; Norra Parkgatan 2; ⏰7pm-3am Wed-Sun; 🚌5, 32 Malmö Folkets park) The Malmö branch of the Stockholm's music club heavyweight, with live gigs and club nights spanning anything from indie, pop and hip hop to soul, electronica and rock. There's a buzzing outdoor bar-lounge overlooking Folkets Park and decent grub till 10pm for a pre-party feed. To get here, follow Amiralsgatan about 600m south towards Möllevangstorget.

ℹ Information

Skånegården (☑040-34 12 00; www.malmotown.com; Skånegårdsvägen 5; ⏰9am-5pm Mon-Fri, 10am-2.30pm Sat & Sun) On the E20, 800m from the Öresund bridge tollgate.
Tourist office (☑040-34 12 00; www.malmotown.se; Skeppsbron 2; ⏰9am-7pm Mon-Fri, 10am-4pm Sat & Sun) Across the street from Centralstationen.

ℹ Getting There & Away

To/From the Airport

Flygbuss (www.flygbussarna.se; adult/senior & student Skr109/89) runs from Centralstationen to Sturup Airport (adult/student Skr109/89, 40 minutes); check the website for schedule. A taxi shouldn't cost more than Skr430.

Trains run directly from Malmö to Copenhagen's much larger main airport (Skr107, 20 minutes, every 20 minutes).

Air

Sturup Airport (☑010 10 945 00; www.swedavia.se) is situated 33km southeast of Malmö. SAS has numerous daily flights to Stockholm Arlanda Airport daily, as well as to Östersund. **Malmö Aviation** (www.malmoaviation.se) flies to Bromma Stockholm Airport and Visby, while **Direktflyg** (☑0243 44 47 00; www.direktflyg.com) serves Falun and Örebro. **Copenhagen**

Airport (☑45 3231 3231; www.copenhagenairport.org) is 24km west of Malmo.

Bus

There are two bus terminals with daily departures to Swedish and European destinations. Swebus Express (p420) runs two to four times daily to Stockholm (from Skr479, 8½ hours) and at least five daily to Göteborg (from Skr199, 3½ to four hours); at least two continue to Oslo (from Skr349, eight hours).

GoByBus (p478) has six buses per day on the Copenhagen–Malmö–Göteborg–Oslo route.

The second long-distance bus terminal, **Öresundsterminalen** (☑040-59 09 00; www.oresundsterminalen.se; Terminalgatan 10) is reached via bus 35 from Centralstationen towards Flansbjer (30 minutes). From here, **Svenska Buss** (☑0771-67 67 67; www.svenskabuss.se) runs to Stockholm (Skr350, 11 hours) via Karlskrona, four times weekly.

Train

Pågatågen (local trains), operated by **Skånetrafiken** (www.skanetrafiken.se), run to Helsingborg (Skr100, one hour, half-hourly), Lund (Skr47, 10 minutes, every 20 minutes) and Ystad (Skr82, 50 minutes, half-hourly). Bicycles are not allowed during peak times, except mid-June to mid-August.

The Malmö to Copenhagen Kastrup airport or Copenhagen central station trips take 20 and 35 minutes, respectively (Skr107, every 20 minutes).

Trains also serve Göteborg (from Skr199, 2½ hours, twice hourly) and Stockholm (from Skr299, 4½ to 5½ hours, hourly).

ℹ Getting Around

Skånetrafiken ((www.skanetrafiken.se) operates an extensive network of local buses, most leaving from in front of Centralstationen. Tickets cannot be purchased on buses; get them from the tourist office, ticket machines or the customer service desks in Centralstationen. Bus tickets start at Skr19, depending on the number of zones travelled. You can also pay for travel on local buses and train by SMS or else purchase the refillable Jojo card.

Lund

☑046 / POP 82,800

Centred around a striking cathedral (complete with a giant in the crypt and a magical clock), Lund is a soulful blend of leafy parks, medieval abodes and coffee-sipping bookworms. Like most university towns, however, it loses some of its buzz during the summer, when students head home for the holidays. Lund makes an easy day trip from Malmö.

The town's centrepiece is the splendid Romanesque **Domkyrkan** (Kyrkogatan; ⊗8am-6pm Mon-Fri, 9.30am-5pm Sat, to 6pm Sun), with some fantastic gargoyles over the side entrances, a giant turned to stone in the eerie crypt and an astronomical clock (noon and 3pm Monday to Saturday, 1pm and 3pm Sunday) that sends the wooden figures whirring into action.

Behind the cathedral, **Historiska Museet** (www.luhm.lu.se; Kraftstorg; adult/under 18yr Skr50/free; ⊗11am-4pm Tue-Fri, noon-4pm Sun) has a large collection of pre–Viking Age finds, including a 7000-year-old skeleton. It's joined with Domkyrkomuseet, which explores the history of the church in the area; the rooms filled with ominous-looking statues of the crucifiction put you in mind of a horror movie set.

The town's most engaging museum, **Kulturen** (www.kulturen.com; Tegnerplatsen; adult/student/under 19yr Skr90/45/free; ⊗10am-5pm May-Aug, noon-4pm Tue-Sat Sep-Apr; ⛴), is a huge open-air space where you can wander among birch-bark hovels, perfectly preserved cottages, churches, farms and grand 17th-century houses. The popular outdoor cafe flanks several rune stones.

🛏 Sleeping

Hotel Lundia BOUTIQUE €€
(☑046-280 65 00; info@lundia.se; Knut den Stores torg 2) The designers here have gone for a contemporary Scandinavian/Japanese look, leading to sleek but slightly Spartan-looking rooms. There's a stylish brasserie downstairs, serving international cuisine.

Lilla Hotellet i Lund HOTEL €€
(☑046-32 88 88; lillahotellet@telia.com; Bankgatan 7; s/d Skr1280/1480, discounted to Skr780/980; ⊗mid-Aug–mid-Jul) Partly housed in an old shoe factory, this homely spot peddles cosy rooms (think patchwork quilts and DVD players), as well as a sunny courtyard and guest lounge.

🍴 Eating

TOP CHOICE **Mat & Destillat** SWEDISH €€€
(☑046-12 80 00; www.matochdestillat.se; Kyrkogatan 17; lunch Skr95, mains Skr225-255; ⊗11.30am-11.30pm Mon-Thu, to 1am Fri, 1pm-1am Sat) This central restaurant and cocktail bar is akin to a culinary laboratory: you can always expect an unusual take on classic Swedish

dishes. There's a different dish of the day every lunchtime, while evening guests can expect the likes of beef with fois gras butter, poached cod with almonds and chocolate pudding to sell your children for.

Café Ariman CAFE €
(www.ariman.se; Kungsgatan 2B; mains from Skr70; ⊗11am-midnight Mon, to 1am Tue, Wed & Thu, to 3am Fri & Sat, 3-11pm Sun; ⛴) Head to this hip, grungy hang-out for cathedral views, strong coffee and cafe fare such as ciabatta, salads and vegetarian soup-of-the-week. It's popular with students: think nose-rings, dreadlocks and leisurely chess games. From September to May, DJs hit the decks on Friday and Saturday nights.

Gattostretto ITALIAN €€
(www.gattostretto.se; Kattesund 6A; lunch Skr75, mains Skr139-235; ⊗11am-11pm Mon-Sat) Located over medieval ruins and co-run by an affable Roman chef, this breezy cafe-restaurant serves a tasty slice of dolce vita. Guzzle down proper Italian espresso, have a slice of *torta rustica,* or long for Rome over expertly prepared seafood tagliatele or grilled lamb with rosemary potatoes.

🍷 Drinking & Entertainment

Glorias THEME BAR
(St Petri Kyrkogatan 9; ⊗11:30am-midnight Mon-Wed, to 1am Thu, to 3am Fri & Sat, 1-11pm Sun) The waft of booze that hits you in the doorway tells you that eating is secondary here. This often-rowdy American-style sports bar attracts a young crowd, and has somewhat pricey Cajun-style food and occasional live music. There's dancing until 3am on Fridays and Saturdays.

SF Bio Filmstaden CINEMA
(☑0856-26 00 00; Västra Mårtensgatan 12) Mainstream cinema.

ℹ Information

Tourist Office (☑046-35 50 40; www.lund.se; Botulfsgatan 1a; ⊗10am-6pm Mon-Fri, to 2pm Sat) Opposite the cathedral.

ℹ Getting There & Away

Long-distance buses leave from outside the train station. Most buses to/from Malmö run via Lund.

It's 10 to 15 minutes from Lund to Malmö by train, with frequent local Pågatågen departures (Skr47). Some trains continue to Copenhagen (Skr135, one hour). Other direct services run from Malmö to Kristianstad and Karlskrona via Lund. All long-distance trains from Stockholm or Göteborg to Malmö stop in Lund.

Trelleborg

📞 0410 / POP 28,300

Trelleborg is the main gateway between Sweden and Germany, with frequent ferry services (p491) but otherwise of little interest to the visitor; we suggest continuing on to Ystad or Malmö.

Simple and functional with shared bathrooms, **Night Stop** (📞 0410-410 70; www.hotelnightstop.com; Östergatan 59; s/d/tr/q Skr250/350/450/550; P) has the cheapest beds in town. Open 24 hours, it's about 500m from the ferry (turn right along Hamngatan after disembarking), diagonally opposite the museum.

Skånetrafiken (p426) bus 146 (Skr55, 45 minutes) runs roughly every half-hour between Malmö and Trelleborg's bus station, some 500m inland from the ferry terminals. Bus 165 has twice-hourly departures to Lund (Skr45, 1¼ hours).

Scandlines (📞 042-18 61 00; www.scandlines.se) ferries connect Trelleborg to Sassnitz (from Skr145, at least three daily) and Rostock (Skr210, two or three daily). **TT-Line** (📞 0450-280 181; www.ttline.com) ferries shuttle between Trelleborg and Travemünde (Skr420) three to five times daily, and between Trelleborg and Rostock (Skr420) up to three times daily. Buy tickets inside the building housing the **tourist office** (📞 0410-73 33 20; www.trelleborg.se/turism; Hamngatan 9; ⊙9am-7pm Mon-Fri, 10am-6pm Sat, 10am-5pm Sun Jun-Aug).

Ystad

📞 0411 / POP 18,400

Half-timbered houses, rambling cobbled streets and the haunting sound of a nightwatchman's horn give this medieval market town an intoxicating lure. Fans of writer Henning Mankell know it as the setting for his best-selling Inspector Wallander crime thrillers, while fans of drums and uniforms head in for the spectacular three-day Military Tattoo in August. Ystad is a terminal for ferries to Bornholm and Poland.

◎ Sights

Sankta Maria Kyrka CHURCH
(Stortorget; ⊙10am-6pm Jun-Aug, to 4pm Sep-May) Ever since 1250, a nightwatchman has blown his horn through the little window in the clock tower here (every 15 minutes from 9.15pm to 3am); the penalty for dozing off used to be beheading. Check out the hideous face beneath the baroque pulpit.

Klostret i Ystad MUSEUM
(www.klostret.ystad.se; St Petri Kyrkoplan; adult/under 16yr Skr40/free; ⊙noon-5pm Tue-Fri, noon-4pm Sat & Sun) The Middle Ages Franciscan monastery of Gråbrödraklostret, which doubled as a poorhouse, hospital and dump through the ages, includes the 13th-century deconsecrated **St Petri Kyrkan**, now used for art exhibitions, which has around 80 gravestones from the 14th to 18th centuries. Included in the same ticket, and with the same opening hours, is the **Ystads Konstmuseum** with its collection of Swedish and Danish art.

🛏 Sleeping & Eating

Station Bed & Breakfast Ystad B&B €
(📞 0708 577 995; www.vandrarhemsguiden.se; Spanienfararegatan 25; s/d/q Skr695/895/1395; P🖥) Not only has it featured in Inspector Wallander films, but this historic railway station building is home to a friendly B&B – in a super-convenient location. Rooms are spacious and well-heated and the breakfast buffet is free during high season (Skr60 at other times). It helps if you're not a terribly light sleeper.

Hos Morten Café CAFE €
(www.bookcafehosmorten.se; Gåsegränd; sandwiches Skr55-155; ⊙11am-4pm Tue-Sat, 12.30-8pm Sun; 🖋) For soup, Danish open sandwiches, filled baked potatoes, salads and pastries, seek out this adorable cafe, complete with book-crammed living room and a leafy courtyard outside.

Store Thor EUROPEAN €€
(📞 0411-185 10; www.storethor.se; Stortorget 1; lunch Skr100, mains Skr105-290) This atmospheric cellar restaurant inside the old town hall has rightly been lauded as one of Ystad's best by Inspector Wallander; the meats are cooked to perfection and you can expect such flights of the culinary imagination as cognac raw-spiced salmon. Lighter bites available in tapas form.

❶ Information

The **tourist office** (📞0411-57 76 81; www.ystad. se; St Knuts Torg; ⊙9am-7pm Mon-Fri, 10am-6pm Sat & Sun mid-Jun–mid-Aug) is inside the art museum. Pick up an *In the Footsteps of Wallander* brochure to follow along with everyone's favourite gloomy detective.

❶ Getting There & Away

Boat Unity Line (📞0411-55 69 00; www. unityline.se) and **Polferries** (📞040-12 17 00; www.polferries.se) operate daily crossings (p491) between Ystad and Świnoujście. Ystad's ferry terminal is within walking distance of the train station.

Bornholmstrafikken runs frequent ferries and catamarans between Ystad and Rønne, on the Danish island of Bornholm. Catamarans operate from a terminal directly behind the train station.

Bus Buses depart from outside Ystad train station. Skånetrafiken (p426) bus 190 runs from Ystad to Trelleborg (Skr65, one hour) hourly on weekdays, less frequently on weekends, while SkåneExpressen bus 6 runs to Lund (Skr93, 1¼ hours, at least four daily).

Train Pågatågen trains run every 30 minutes or so to/from Malmö (Skr82, 50 minutes).

Helsingborg

📞042 / POP 97,100

At its heart, Helsingborg is a sparkly showcase of rejuvenated waterfront, metro-glam restaurants, lively cobbled streets and lofty castle ruins. With Denmark looking on from a mere 4km across the Öresund, its flouncy, turreted buildings feel like a brazen statement.

◉ Sights & Activities

Dunkers Kulturhus   MUSEUM
(www.dunkerskulturhus.se; Kungsgatan 11; exhibitions adult/under 18yr Skr75/free; ⊙10am-6pm Mon-Fri, to 8pm Thu, to 5pm Sat & Sun) Just north of the transport terminals, the crisp, white Dunkers Kulturhus showcases the history of the town via the theme of water, as well as temporary art exhibitions (admission includes entry to both). The building's creator, Danish architect Kim Utzon, is the son of Sydney Opera House architect Jørn Utzon.

Fredriksdals Friluftsmuseum   MUSEUM
(www.fredriksdal.se; off Hävertgatan; adult/under 18yr Skr85/free May-Sep, admission free Oct-Mar; ⊙10am-6pm May-Aug, 11am-5pm Apr & Sep) Just 2km northeast of the centre, Fredriksdal is one of Sweden's best open-air museums, based around an 18th-century manor house, with a street of old houses, a children's farm, graphics museum and blissfully leafy grounds. The entrance is 250m south of the Zoégas bus stop.

Kärnan   RUINS
(⊙10am-6pm Jun-Aug, closed Mon rest of yr) Dramatic steps and archways lead up from Stortorget to this square tower, all that remains of the medieval castle. The view from the restored tower is regal indeed.

🛏 Sleeping

Hotel Maria   HOTEL €€
(📞042-24 99 40; www.hotelmaria.se; Mariagatan 8A; r from Skr950; 🅿@🛜) Tucked away behind Olsons Skafferi, Hotel Maria is utterly inspired, with each room flaunting a different historical style. Choose between Magnificent Baroque, Yuppie, Flower Power and others. Beds are divinely comfy, the staff are friendly, and there's a tapas bar downstairs.

Hotell Viking   HOTEL €€
(📞042-14 44 20; www.hotellviking.se; Fågelsångsgatan 1; r from Skr1474; 🅿🛜) The savvy, idiosyncratic rooms at this trendy, urbane hotel are constantly updated. Don't expect to be drinking out of enemy skulls; instead, styles range from sexy modern to classically romantic, and the plushest room features leather recliners and whirlpool massage bath.

Helsingborgs Vandrarhem   HOSTEL €
(📞042-14 58 50; www.cityvandrarhemmet.com; Järnvägsgatan 39; s/d/tr/f Skr445/595/795/950; 🅿🛜♿) Besides the central location (about 200m from Knutpunkten), this hostel is more akin to a budget hotel, with flat-screen

---

WORTH A TRIP

TO SAIL A STONE SHIP...

One of Skåne's most intriguing and remote attractions, Ales Stenar has all the mystery of England's Stonehenge but without the commercialism and the burnt-out druids. It's Sweden's largest stone ship setting, gorgeously located on a grassy knoll by the sea, 19km east of Ystad. According to legend, King Ale is buried here, but it may also have been a solar calendar. To get here, take bus 322 from Ystad (four times daily).

TVs and fridges in the rooms and nautically inspired decor.

 Eating

TOP CHOICE Gastro INTERNATIONAL €€€

(📞042-24 34 70; www.gastro.nu; Södra Storgatan 11-13; mains Skr109-250, multi-course taster menu Skr1190; ⊘6pm-midnight Wed-Sat) While we're not sold on the name, the dishes at this sharp, stylish award-winner will leave you smitten. On leather banquettes, diners swoon over the inventive multi-course taster menu. For the likes of pan-seared turbot with chanterelles, veal burgers with lingonberry, and dry aged beef with bearnaise sauce, stop by **Bistro G**, Gastro's little brother.

Sillen & Makrillen SEAFOOD €€€

(www.sillenmakrillen.se; Gröningen Norra; mains Skr255-289; ⊘5pm-1am Mon-Sat, 3pm-1am Sun; 🍴) As the name suggests, the Herring and Mackerel specialises in Poseidon's subjects, though there are always other options on the succinct menu. Prepare to be wowed by mussels with chorizo, hake loin with lobster and herring bouillabaise, with the main ingredients presumably fished out of the sea right by your table.

Olsons Skafferi CAFE €€

(📞042-14 07 80; www.olsonsskafferi.se; Mariagatan 6; lunch Skr75-95, dinner mains Skr149-259; ⊘lunch & dinner Mon-Sat; 🍴) Olsons is a super little spot, with alfresco seating on the pedestrian square right in front of Mariakyrkan. It doubles as an Italian deli and cafe, with spangly chandeliers and pasta that would make Bologna proud. The dinner menu is a wonderful melange of Swedish and Italian, such as wild boar with butternut squash and ravioli with truffle butter.

Ebbas Fik CAFE €€

(www.ebbasfik.se; Bruksgatan 20; burgers Skr115-135; ⊘9am-6pm Mon-Fri, 9am-4pm Sat; 🍴) It's still 1955 at this kitsch-tastic retro cafe, complete with jukebox, retro petrol pump and hamburgers (the bacon burger with mango chutney is inspired). The extensive cafe menu also includes (huge) sandwiches, baked potatoes and crazy layer cakes and buns.

🛈 Information

Tourist Office (📞042-10 43 50; www.helsingborg.se; Kungstgatan 11, Kulturhus; ⊘10am-6pm Mon-Fri, to 5pm Sat & Sun)

🛈 **Getting There & Away**

Boat Knutpunkten is the terminal for the frequent **Scandlines** (📞042-18 61 00; www.scandlines.se) car ferry to Helsingør (car with passengers Skr360).

Bus The bus terminal is at ground level in Knutpunkten. Regional **Skånetrafiken** (www.skanetrafiken.se) buses dominate but long-distance services are offered by Swebus Express (p420) and GoByBus (p478).

Both companies run north to Göteborg, continuing on to Oslo and south to Malmö. They also operate services northeast to Stockholm via Norrköping. Fares to Stockholm cost around Skr379 (7½ hours), to Göteborg Skr149 (2½ to three hours) and to Oslo Skr279 (seven hours).

Train Underground platforms in Knutpunkten serve trains, which depart daily for Göteborg (from Skr292, 2½ hours, up to 12 daily), Lund (Skr82, 30 to 40 minutes, every 30 minutes) and Malmö (Skr100, 40minutes to one hour, every hour), as well as Copenhagen and Oslo.

GÖTALAND

This region has a rich history and plenty to offer the visitor. For one, it's home to Sweden's second city, Göteborg (also known as Gothenburg), with an amusement park for the kids and a huge range of grown-up entertainment. Norrköping, an urban-restoration achievement, has turned its workmanlike heart into a lovely showpiece. Linköping's medieval cathedral is one of Sweden's largest, and in Vadstena there's the abbey established by the country's most important saint, Birgitta. There's also the overwhelming natural beauty of the Bohuslän coast.

Göteborg

📞031 / POP 549,900

Often caught in Stockholm's shadow, gregarious Göteborg (pronounced *yur*-te-borry, Gothenburg in English) socks a mighty good punch of its own. Some of the country's finest talent hails from its streets, including music icons José González and Soundtrack of Our Lives. Ornate architecture lines its tram-rattled streets and cafes hum with bonhomie. West of Kungsportsavenyn (dubbed the 'Champs Élysées' in brochures and a 'tourist trap' by locals), the Haga and Linné districts buzz with creativity. Fashionistas design fair-trade threads while artists collaborate over mean espressos. Stockholm may represent the 'big time', but many of

GÖTEBORG CITY CARD

The brilliant Göteborg City Card is well worth bagging, at least if you're planning to park in Göteborg (home to Sweden's priciest street parking and most dedicated traffic wardens). Perks include free or reduced admission to a bundle of attractions (including Liseberg and the museums), plus free city sightseeing tours, and travel by public transport within the region. The card costs Skr280/175 per adult/child for 24 hours and Skr395/275 for 48 hours. You'll need to efficiently cram in your museum time to get the most out of the pass; those planning to take the sightseeing tour will save the most. It's available at tourist offices, hotels, Pressbyrån newsagencies and online at www.goteborg.com; it is now also available as a smartphone app.

Göteborgspaketet (Göteborg Package) is an accommodation package offered at various hotels, with prices starting at Skr645 per person per night. It includes the Göteborg City Card for the number of nights you stay. Book online at www.goteborg.com or through the tourist office. More expensive packages include theatre or concert tickets, casino passes, spa visits etc.

the best and brightest ideas originate in this grassroots town.

◉ Sights

Liseberg   AMUSEMENT PARK
(www.liseberg.se; Södra Vägen; adult/under 90cm Skr95/free; ☺11am-11pm Jun–mid-Aug; ⛟) Scream yourself silly at this mighty theme park southeast of the city centre. Sweden's largest, it draws more than three million visitors every year. Blockbuster rides include the 90km/h wooden rollercoaster Balder, the stomach-churning Kanonen, where you're blasted from zero to 75km/h in less than two seconds, and Europe's tallest freefall tower, Atmosfear, where you plummet for more than 100m in three seconds. There are plenty of gentler rides for the little ones, and a pavillion where the seniors can go waltzing.

Each ride costs between one and four coupons (Skr20 each), so a pass might make more sense, depending on your ambitions and endurance. Enter from Örgrytevägen or Getebergsled.

Museums

TOP ⭐ CHOICE **Röda Sten**   GALLERY
(www.rodasten.com; Röda Sten 1; adult/under 21yr Skr40/free; ☺noon-5pm Tue-Sun, to 7pm Wed) Occupying a defunct, graffitied power station beside the giant Älvsborgsbron, Röda Sten is one of Sweden's coolest art centres. Its four gritty floors are home to any number of temporary exhibitions, featuring the likes of Nathalie Djurberg and ranging from edgy Swedish photography to New York sound installations. There's an indie-style cafe with summertime riverside seating, weekly live

music and club nights and offbeat one-offs like punk bike races, boxing matches and stand-up comedy. To get there, alight at Vagnhallen Majorna, walk towards Klippan, continue under Älvsborgsbron and look for the brown-brick building.

Universeum   MUSEUM
(www.universeum.se; Södra Vägen 50; adult/3-16yr Skr165/110; ☺10am-6pm; ⛟; ☐2, 4, 5, 6 , 8, 10 13 Korsvägen) There's no better place for kids than this incredible discovery centre. Think multistorey rainforest with marmosets jumping through the foilage, piranha pool and stingray lagoon demonstrating namesake denizens, hollow logs with snakes, and an engrossing science centre where you can have a go at mixing music, space rides and more.

Stadsmuseum   MUSEUM
(City Museum; www.stadsmuseum.goteborg.se; Norra Hamngatan 12, Östindiska huset; adult/under 25yr Skr40/free; ☺10am-5pm Tue-Sun, to 8pm Wed; ⛟) Treasures here include subtly lit Viking silver hoards, weaponry and Sweden's only original Viking ship. Other displays cover Göteborg's history, its guilds and a haul of East Indian pottery.

Konstmuseet   GALLERY
(www.konstmuseum.goteborg.se; Götaplatsen; adult/under 25yr Skr40/free; ☺11am-6pm Tue & Thu, to 9pm Wed, 11am-5pm Fri-Sun; ⛟) Works by the French Impressionists, Rubens, Van Gogh, Rembrandt, Picasso, as well as Scandinavian masters such as Bruno Liljefors, Edvard Munch, Anders Zorn and Carl Larsson, plus the Hasselblad photo collection. The temporary exhibitions, featuring the

Göteborg

Keillers
Park

Stalhandstegatan

HISINGEN

Lundby
Strand

Lindholm

Göta älv

Stena Line
Denmark
Terminal

Rosenlund

Älvsnabben

Skeppsbron

Södra

32

19

Otterhällegatan

Kungsgatan

Hvitfeldtsplatsen

Rosenlundsgatan

20

Stortorgsgatan

3

To Röda Sten
(2.0km)

Andreegatan

Masthamnsgatan

Förstalånggatan

34

Södra Allégatan

Järn-
torget

Haga Nygata

Stigbergsliden

15

Masthuggs-
torget

13

31

Andra Långgatan

Tredje Långgatan

24

LINNÉ

6

HAGA

Skansparken

Skans-
torget

Prinsgatan

Vegagatan

Nordhemsgatan

Linnégatan

Husargatan

August Kobbsgatan

14

Olivedalsgatan

Övre Husargatan

Västergatan

4

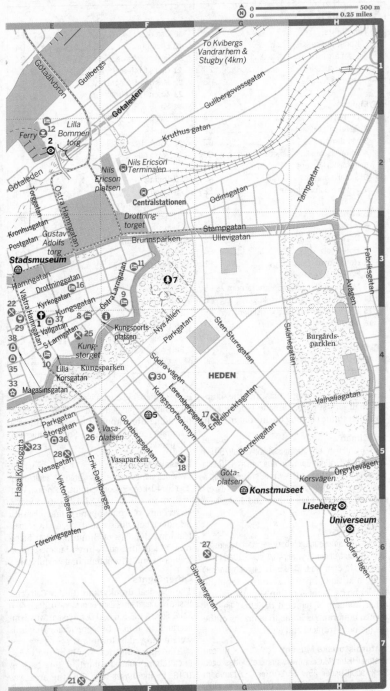

SWEDEN GÖTEBORG

0 ____ 500 m
0 ____ 0.25 miles

To Kvibergs
Vandrarhem &
Stugby (4km)

Gullbergsvassgatan

Götaleden

Kruthus gatan

Götaälvbron

Gullbergs

Lilla
Bommen
torg

12

Ferry

2

Nils Ericson
Terminalen

Nils
Ericson
platsen

Odinsgatan

Centralstationen

Tampgatan

Drottning-
torget

Stampgatan

Ullevigatan

Brunnsparken

Fabriksgatan

Götaleden

Torgatan

Östra Hamngatan

Kronhusgatan

Postgatan

Gustav
Adolfs
torg

Stadsmuseum

Hamngatan

Drottninggatan

16

11

Kyrkogatan

Östra Larmgatan

9

7

Kungsgatan

Avägen

22

Västra Hamngatan

29

1

37

8

Vallgatan

25

Kungsports-
platsen

Nya Allén

Parkgatan

Sten Sturegatan

Skånegatan

Burgårds-
parken

38

35

S Larmgatan

Kung-
storget

33

10

Lilla
Korsgatan

Kungsparken

Södra vägen

HEDEN

Valhallagatan

Magasinsgatan

30

Lorensbergsgatan

Kungsportsavenyn

Engelbrektsgatan

Berzeliigatan

Parkgatan

Storgatan

36

26

Vasa-
platsen

5

17

23

28

Vasagatan

Erik Dahlbergsg

Vasaparken

18

Göta-
platsen

Örgrytevägen

Korsvägen

Haga Kyrkogata

Viktoriagatan

Konstmuseet

Liseberg

Föreningsgatan

Universeum

Södra Vägen

27

Gibraltargatan

21

Göteborg

best of up-and-coming artists, and the sculpture hall, are superb. Outside is a hideous Poseidon statue choking the life out of a fish.

Maritiman
MUSEUM

(www.maritiman.se; Packhuskajen; adult/5-15yr Skr100/50; ⊙10am-6pm Jun-Aug; ⊞; ⊞5, 10 Lilla Bommen) Clamber all over a submarine, a destroyer, fishing boats and other vessels moored next to each other and linked by walkways.

Sjöfartsmuseet
MUSEUM

(www.sjofartsmuseum.goteborg.se; Karl Johansgatan 1-3; ⊙10am-5pm Tue-Sun, to 8pm Wed; ⊞3, 9, 11 Stigbergstorget) This maritime history features exquisite model boats, hands-on ship simulators and other manner of nautical delights. The attached aquarium is home to denizens of the deep – both tropical and local.

Naturhistoriska Museet
MUSEUM

(Natural History Museum; www.gnm.se; Slottsskogen Park; adult/under 25yr Skr90/free; ⊙11am-5pm Tue-Sun; ⊞; ⊞1, 2, 6, 101) Contains the world's

only stuffed blue whale, as well as fossils and pinned, pickled and stuffed examples of wildlife from around the world. Fantastic temporary exhibit on the South American highlands.

Röhsska Museet
MUSEUM

(www.designmuseum.se; Vasagatan 37; adult/under 25yr Skr40/free; ⊙noon-8pm Tue, noon-5pm Wed-Fri, 11am-5pm Sat & Sun; ⊞3, 4, 5, 7, 10 Valand) A clever mix of contemporary and classical Scandinavian design and decorative arts, featuring the likes of Bruno Mattson furniture, '80s politicised T-shirts, Japanese theatre masks and offbeat temporary exhibitions.

Other Sights

The classical **domkyrkan** (Gustavi Cathedral; Västra Hamngatan; ⊙8am-6pm Mon-Fri, 10am-4pm Sat & Sun; ⊞1, 2, 5, 6, 9, 11 Domkyrkan) was consecrated in 1815 – two previous cathedrals were destroyed by town fires.

The **Haga district**, south of the canal, is Göteborg's oldest suburb, dating back to 1648. In the 1980s and '90s, the area was thoroughly renovated and is now a cute, cobblestone maze of precious cafes and boutique shops.

There are some lovely green oases in the city, including **Trädgårdsföreningen** (www.trandardsforeningen.se; Nya Allén; ⏱7am-6pm; 🚊3, 4, 5, 7, 10 Kungsportsplatsen), laid out in 1842 and home to a couple of pretty cafes, a **rosarium** and a **palm house**. In Göteborg's southwest is **Slottsskogsparken**, the 'lungs' of the city; the **Botanic Gardens** – the largest in Sweden – are nearby.

🛏 Sleeping

TOP CHOICE Vanilla Hotel
BOUTIQUE HOTEL €€

(☎031-711 62 20; www.vaniljhotel.se; Kyrkogatan 38; s/d Skr1195/1345; 🅿@🛜) On a central street, this petite slumber spot is more akin to a homey B&B than a hotel. Light, bright rooms are individually decorated in sparing Scandinavian style, the bathrooms are spotless and breakfast is served in the buzzing cafe downstairs. Get there early for one of the five parking spaces.

TOP CHOICE Avalon
HOTEL €€€

(☎031-751 02 00; www.avalonhotel.se; Kungstorget 9; r from Skr1995; @🛜🏊; 🚊3, 4, 5, 7, 10 Kungsportsplatsen) The showy, design-conscious Avalon is in the most central location imaginable and perfect for sightseeing. Expect curvaceous furniture, bold colours, flat-screen TVs and heavenly pillows. Some rooms feature a mini-spa and mini-gym and the upmarket resto-bar is an after-work hot spot. The fabulous rooftop pool (open May to September) leans out over the edge for a dizzying dip.

Hotell Barken Viking
HOTEL €€

(☎031-63 58 00; www.liseberg.se; Gullbergskajen; r from Skr1395; @🛜; 🚊5, 10 Lilla Bommen) *Barken Viking* is an elegant four-masted sailing ship, converted into a stylish hotel and restaurant and moored near Lilla Bommen harbour. In your gently swaying, suitably nautical rooms, with their Hamptons-style linen and warm wood panelling, you can dream of Viking raids and pillaging. Discounted package deals include entry to Liseberg.

STF Vandrarhem Slottsskogen
HOSTEL €

(☎031-42 65 20; www.sov.nu; Vegagatan 21; hostel dm/s/d from Skr195/380/500, hotel s/d Skr590/890; @) Unlike many Swedish hostels, big, friendly Slottsskogen is a cracking place for meeting other travellers. For a

small extra payment there's access to a laundry, sauna and sunbed, and the buffet breakfast (Skr65) is brilliant, and if you choose the 'hotel' option, bed linen and breakfast are thrown in for free. Parking spaces can be booked for a fee.

Hotel Flora
BOUTIQUE HOTEL €€

(☎031-13 86 16; www.hotelflora.se; Grönsakstorget 2; r from Skr1295; @🛜; 🚊1, 2, 5, 6, 9, 10, 11 Grönsakstorget) Fabulous Flora boasts uberslick rooms flaunting black-and-white interiors, designer chairs, flat-screen TVs and sparkling bathrooms. The rooms are themed, and the ones on the top floor have air-conditioning; some offer river views and the chic split-level courtyard is perfect for sophisticated chilling.

Dorsia Hotel
BOUTIQUE HOTEL €€€

(☎031-790 10 00; www.dorsia.se; Trädgårdsgatan 6; r Skr1900-5800; ❄@🛜; 🚊3, 4, 5, 7, 10 Kungsportsplatsen) Opt for your own private kingdom in this luxurious establishment. Rooms are heavenly with their heavy velvet curtains, rich colour scheme, fine art on walls, luxurious beds and silk pillows. Yet this Old World-style decadence lives alongside the most modern of creature comforts – such as the Lava TV and internet combo.

Hotel Royal
HOTEL €€

(☎031-700 11 70; www.hotelroyal.nu; Drottninggatan 67; s/d Skr1395/1595; @🛜; 🚊1, 2, 5, 6, 9, 11 Domkyrkan) Göteborg's oldest hotel (1852) has aged enviably. The grand entrance has been retained, complete with painted glass ceiling and sweeping staircase, and the elegant, airy rooms make necessary 21st-century concessions like flat-screen TVs and renovated bathrooms. There's also homemade cake for guests and the breakfast is excellent.

Kvibergs Vandrarhem & Stugby
HOSTEL €

(☎43 50 55; www.vandrarhem.com; Kvibergsvägen 5; hostel d/tr/q Skr555/690/840, hotel d/tr/q Skr810/990/1060, 5-person cabin Skr1350; 🅿@🛜; 🚊6, 7, 11 Kviberg) If you'd like peace

---

ℹ FOUR FOR THE PRICE OF ONE

Museum hoppers take note: admission to one of four museums – the Röhsska Museet, Konstmuseet, Stadsmuseum or Sjöfartsmuseet – gets you into the other three for free.

DON'T MISS

GETTING HIGH IN GÖTEBORG

Not only does amusement park Liseberg (p431) make for an entertaining day out, but it also offers three great vantage points from which to survey the city.

» **Göteborgs Hjulet** – An enormous Ferris wheel of gondolas now installed in a new home.

» **Atmosfear** – Europe's tallest freefall ride; from 116m up, you'll enjoy unparalleled views of the city before plummeting that distance in 3 seconds and possibly losing your lunch.

» **Lisenberg Tower** – At 83m above the ground, it climaxes in a slow spinning dance with a breathtaking panorama.

and quiet and a full range of facilities, all within easy reach of the city, this sterling SVIF hostel, a few kilometres northeast of town, boasts super amenities, including flat-screen TVs, sauna, laundry, table tennis, two kitchens and two lounges. En suite hotel-style rooms and fully-equipped cabins for the whole family are on the menu also.

Masthuggsterrassens
Vandrarhem   HOSTEL €
(☎031-42 48 20; www.mastenvandrarhem.com; Masthuggsterrassen 10H; dm/d/tr/q Skr 210/500/690/840; @; ☐1, 3, 5, 6, 9, 10, 11, 101 Masthuggstorget) If you're after a good night's sleep, try this clean, quiet, well-run place, whose long hallways are plastered with vintage film posters. Facilities include three lounges, three kitchens and a little library (mostly Swedish books), and it's handy if you're catching an early ferry to Denmark. Follow the signs up the hill from the Masthuggstorget tram stop.

STF Vandrarhem
Stigbergsliden   HOSTEL €
(☎031-24 16 20; www.hostel-gothenburg.com; Stigbergsliden 10; dm/s/d/f from Skr180/470/675/975; ☺reception 4-6pm; @🖶) In a renovated seamen's institute, this homey hostel has history. Staff are helpful, and there's a big kitchen, laundry and TV room. Perks include an inexpensive cafeteria, sheltered garden and bike rental (per day Skr50).

✕ Eating

Cool cafes, cheap ethnic gems and foodie favourites abound around the Vasastan, Haga and Linné districts, often with lower prices than their Avenyn rivals. Göteborg also boasts plenty of great epicurean experiences in the form of Slow Food and Michelin-starred delights. For something quick, the Nordstan shopping complex has loads of fast-food outlets.

 Thörnströms Kök   SWEDISH €€€
(☎031-16 20 66; www.thornstromskok.com; 3 Teknologgatan; mains Skr235-275, 4-/6-/9-course menu Skr625/825/1125; ☺6pm-1am Mon-Sat; ☐7, 10 Kapellplatsen) Specialising in modern Scandinavian cuisine, chef Hakan shows you how he earned that Michelin star through creative use of local, seasonal ingredients and flawless presentation. Expect the likes of sweetbreads with hazelnut and Götland truffle, quail with port and apricot, and baked cod with blackened oysters. The white chocolate bavarois with cloudberry sorbet is truly inspired and if you're not feeling up to a multicourse menu, a number of dishes are available a la carte.

TOP CHOICE **Moon Thai Kitchen**   THAI €€
(☎031-774 2828; www.moonthai.se; Storgatan 1; mains Skr119-189; ☺11am-11pm Tue-Thu, to 1am Fri, noon-1am Sat, noon-11pm Sun; ☒; ☐1, 3, 5, 9, 11 Hagakyrkan or Vasa Viktoriagatan) The decor may be tacky, tropical 'anywhere in Asia', but the authentic Thai dishes will knock your socks off, particularly if you order 'full moon' (Thai-style spicy). The noodle dishes and the curries are well-represented, the som tam (spicy papaya salad) brings tears to our eyes and the only way to finish the meal is with the classic sticky rice with pandan leaf and mango.

Wasa Allé   SWEDISH €€€
(☎031-13 13 70; www.wasaalle.se; Vasagatan 24; business lunch Skr129, dishes Skr195-225; ☺11.30am-2pm Mon-Fri, 6pm-late Tue-Fri, 6pm-late Sat; ☒; ☐1, 2, 3 Vasa Viktoriagatan) At his flagship restaurant, chef Mats relies exclusively on sustainable and local produce, making your meal a guilt-free experience, and even the beer is sourced from small microbreweries. There are no starters or mains: choose from similar-sized dishes from the categories 'cold', 'warm' and 'sweet'. Standout offerings include elk tartar with black

chanterelle and lingonberries, hake with glazed beetroot, and caramelised rye bread with cream cheese and tarragon. Vegetarians are also well-catered for.

Smaka SWEDISH €€
(www.smaka.se; Vasaplatsen 3; mains Skr125-245; ☺5pm-1am Sun-Thu, to 2am Fri & Sat) You will smak-a your lips when you taste the old-school Swedish *husmanskost* such as the speciality meatballs with mashed potato and lingonberries and herring with crispbread. More unusual offerings include reindeer with vodka gravy, and the selection of Swedish farm cheeses is well worth a try.

Feskekörka MARKET €
(www.feskekörka.com; Rosenlundsgatan; ☺9am-5pm Tue-Thu, to 6pm Fri, 10am-3pm Sat; ☒3, 5, 9, 11 Hagakyrkan) Come and worship the creatures of the deep at the Fish Church – a market dedicated to all things fishy. Takeaway treats include fresh fish and chips, yummy shrimp and avocado salads and the ubiquitous smoked prawns.

Caleo MEDITERRANEAN €€
(☎031-708 9340; www.caleo.se; Engelbrektsgatan 39b; mains Skr159-259; ☺4pm-1am Mon-Thu, to 2am Fri, 2pm-2am Sat, 2pm-1am Sun; ☒3, 4, 5, 7, 10 Valand) Unlike many self-styled Mediterranean joints, this one truly does credit to the region. The likes of thyme-grilled lamb with feta-stuffed potatoes, chilli-seared tuna and duck with truffle risotto are both creative and beautifully presented without being too fussy. The service is spot on, too.

Magnus & Magnus EUROPEAN €€€
(☎031-13 30 00; www.magnusmagnus.se; Magasinsgatan 8; 2-/3-course menus Skr395/495; ☺from 6pm Mon-Sat; ☒1, 2, 5, 6, 9, 11 Domkyrkan) Ever-fashionable Magnus & Magnus serves inspired Euro-fusion dishes with unusual pairings of flavours, such as pork with langostine and hazelnuts, wild duck with pumpkin and coffee, and white chocolate with dill and cucumber, yet this mad alchemy works beautifully. The presentation is exceptional, the service anything but stuffy and the summer courtyard draws an uber-cool crowd in summer.

Bistro Merlot FRENCH €€
(☎031-20 10 21; Engelbrektsgatan 34; mains Skr125-259; ☺5pm-late Mon-Fri, 2pm-late Sat; ☒4, 5 Berzeliigatan) This compact bistro gets really packed with happy punters most evenings, drawn by the likes of *moules marinière* or

French onion soup with cognac and duck confit with apple compote. The prime-rib burger with goat's cheese is a winner in our book, but be prepared for a leisurely evening, as the staff find it hard to keep up.

Gao's Coffee & Sushi JAPANESE €
(www.gaosushi.se; Reutersgatan 2; sushi sets Skr65-168; ☒6, 7, 8, 10, 13 Wavrinskys Plats) It's well worth heading south of the centre to what is quite possibly Göteborg's best sushi joint. It's all about the sushi rolls here (the salmon, crab and avocado stand out) and there's usually a couple of hot dishes, such as chicken yakitori, to keep everyone happy.

Saluhallen MARKET €
(Kungstorget; ☺9am-6pm Mon-Fri, 9am-3pm Sat; ☒; ☒3, 4, 5, 7, 10 Kungsportsplatsen) Göteborg's main central market is jammed with tasty budget eateries and food stalls, and is the perfect place to stock up that picnic basket.

Saluhall Briggen MARKET €€
(www.saluhallbriggen.se; Nordhemsgatan 28; ☺9am-6pm Mon-Fri, to 3pm Sat; ☒) It might lack Saluhallen's size, but this covered market will have you drooling over its bounty of fresh bread, cheeses, quiches, seafood and takeaway Thai dishes and sushi. It's particularly handy for the hostel district.

⃝Ekostore SUPERMARKET €
(Ekelundsgatan 4; ☺10am-8pm Mon-Fri, 10am-2pm Sat; ☒1, 2, 5, 6, 9, 11 Domkyrkan) An eco-chic grocery store selling organic and fair-trade products.

⃝ Drinking

Kungsportsavenyn brims with beer-downing tourists; try the following places for a little more character. The Linné district is home to several student hang-outs serving extremely cheap beer.

⃝Lokal COCKTAIL BAR
(Kyrkogatan 11; ☺5pm-1am Mon-Sat) Arguably the best bar in Göteborg, this cool hang-out pulls everyone from artists and media types to the odd punk rocker. The drinks are inspired (think kiwi and ginger daiquiri), the fusion nibbles (including organic and vegie options) are excellent, and music spans soul, jazz and electro.

Sejdeln PUB
(Andra Långgatan 28; ☺4pm-1am Mon-Sat) Extremely popular with students and younger

clientele in general, this cosy, wood-panelled pub is the perfect spot for an inexpensive local beer or cider. Get here before the evening rush if you want to do anything other than prop up the bar.

Rose & Crown
PUB

(www.rosecrown.com; Kungsportsavenyn 6; 3, 4, 5, 7, 10 Valand) Yes, this 'English-style' pub is unashamedly touristy – mostly because it's in such a central location – but it's also popular with locals and undeniably a great spot for quaffing a pint while watching live sports.

☆ Entertainment

Clubs have varying minimum-age limits, ranging from 18 to 25 years, and many may charge admission depending on the night.

Bliss
CLUB

(www.blissresto.com; Magasinsgatan 3; 11.30am-2.30pm Mon-Fri, 6pm-1am or 2am Tue-Thu & Sat, 5pm-1am or 2am Fri; 1, 2, 5, 6, 9, 11 Domkyrkan) Bliss boasts one of the hippest interiors in Göteborg, with low designer seats and slick contemporary tones. It's a long-standing nocturnal favourite: you can sip on a cocktail to warm up and then groove to a DJ set on Fridays and Saturdays when the serious clubbers take over.

Nefertiti
LIVE MUSIC

(www.nefertiti.se; Hvitfeldtsplatsen 6; admission Skr50-250; 1, 5, 6, 9, 11 Grönsakstorget) A Göteborg institution, this effortlessly cool venue is famous for its smooth live jazz, blues and world music, usually followed by kicking club nights spanning techno, deep house and soul to hip hop and funk. Times vary, so check the website.

Pustervik
LIVE MUSIC, THEATRE

(www.pusterviksbaren.se; Järntorgsgatan 12; 1, 3, 5, 9, 11 Järntorget) Culture vultures and party people pack into this hybrid venue, with its heaving downstairs bar and upstairs club and stage. Gigs range from independent theatre and live music gigs (anything from emerging singer-songwriters to Neneh Cherry) to regular club nights spanning hip hop, soul and rock.

🔒 Shopping

Acne Jeans
CLOTHING

(www.acnestudios.com; Magasinsgatan 19; closed Sun; 1, 2, 5, 6, 9, 11 Domkyrkan) Sharing the same address with Prickig Katt and local label **Velour** (Magasinsgatan 19; closed Sun), this Stockholm giant stocks jeans as well as slick, stylish street wear for guys and girls.

DesignTorget
HOMEWARE

(www.designtorget.se; Vallgatan 14; 1, 2, 5, 6, 9, 11 Domkyrkan) Cool, affordable design objects from both established and up-and-coming Scandi talent – anything from brightly coloured kitchen utensils to suction cup bird feeders. Great for quirky gifts.

Prickig Katt
CLOTHING

(www.prickigkatt.se; Magasinsgatan 17; closed Sun; 1, 5, 6, 9, 11 Grönsakstorget) The flamboyant Spotted Cat sports retro-clad staff, idiosyncratic fashion from Dutch, Danish and home-grown labels, as well as kitschy wares and out-there handmade millinery and bling.

📋 DEM Collective
CLOTHING

(www.demcollective.com; Storgatan 11; Thu-Sat; 1, 2, 3 Vasa Viktoriagatan) Head to this bite-sized boutique for Scandi cool, fair-trade threads. Completely organic, designs are minimalist, street-smart and supremely comfortable.

ℹ Information

Solo women especially should take care around the Nordstand shopping complex late at night.

Internet Access
Sidewalk Express (www.sidewalkexpress.se; per hr Skr20) At Centralstationen and the 7-Eleven on Vasaplatsen.

Medical Services
Apotek Hjärtat (0771-45 04 50; Nordstan complex; 8am-10pm) Late-night pharmacy.
Östra Sjukhuset (031-343 40 00; www.sahlgrenska.se; 1) Major hospital about 5km northeast of central Göteborg, near the terminus at the end of tramline 1.

Money
Forex (www.forex.se) Centralstationen (7am-9pm Mon-Fri, 9am-7pm Sat & Sun); Kungsportsavenyn 22 (9am-7pm Mon-Fri, 10am-4pm Sat); Kungsportsplatsen (9am-7pm Mon-Fri, 10am-4pm Sat); Landvetter airport (5am-9pm Mon-Fri, to 8pm Sat & Sun); Nordstan shopping complex (9am-7pm Mon-Fri, 10am-6pm Sat, 11am-5pm Sun) Foreign-exchange office with numerous branches.

Tourist Office
Tourist office (031-368 4200; www.goteborg.com; Kungsportsplatsen 2; 9.30am-8pm daily mid-Jun–mid-Aug, 9.30am-6pm

Mon-Fri, 10am-2pm Sat & Sun May–mid-Jun & end Aug) Central and busy, it has a good selection of free brochures and maps.

ⓘ Getting There & Away

Air

About 25km east of the city, **Landvetter Airport** (☑010 109 0000; www.swedavia.se) has more than 20 direct daily flights to/from Stockholm's Arlanda and Bromma airports (with SAS and Malmö Aviation), as well as daily services to Umeå and several weekly services to Östersund, Borlänge, Visby and Sundsvall.

Direct European routes include Amsterdam (KLM), Brussels (Brussels Airlines), Copenhagen (SAS and Norwegian), Frankfurt (Lufthansa and SAS), Helsinki (Finnair and SAS), London (British Airways, SAS & Norwegian), Manchester (British Airways), Munich (Lufthansa), Oslo (Norwegian) and Paris (Air France).

Göteborg City Airport (www.goteborgairport. se), some 15km north of the city at Säve, is used for budget Ryanair, Wizz Air and Direktflyg flights to destinations including London Stansted, Visby, Edinburgh, and Frankfurt.

Boat

Göteborg is a major entry point for ferries, with several car and passenger services to Denmark, Germany and Norway. Take tram 3 or 9 to the **Stena Line** (www.stenaline.se) terminal.

Bus

Västtrafik (☑0771-41 43 00; www.vasttrafik. se) and **Hallandstrafiken** (www.hlt.se) provide regional transport links. The bus station, Nils Ericson Terminalen, is next to the train station. The Västtrafik information booth provides information and sells tickets for all city and regional

public transport within the Göteborg, Bohuslän and Västergötland area.

Swebus Express (p420) has an office located at the bus terminal and operates frequent buses to most of the major towns. Services to Stockholm (Skr379, seven hours) run at least four times daily. Other direct destinations include Copenhagen (Skr269, four to five hours, at least three daily), Halmstad (Skr129, 1¾ hours, six daily), Helsingborg (Skr129, three hours, five daily), Oslo (Skr219, 3¾ hours) and Malmö (Skr179, 3½ to four hours).

Car & Motorcycle

The E6 motorway runs north–south from Oslo to Malmö just east of the city centre and there's also a complex junction where the E20 motorway diverges east for Stockholm.

International car-hire companies Avis, Europcar and Hertz have desks at Landvetter and Göteborg City airports.

Train

From Centralstationen – Sweden's oldest train station – SJ and regional trains run to Stockholm (Skr540, three to 4½ hours, twice hourly), Copenhagen (Skr429, 3¾ hours, hourly), Malmö (Skr321, 3¼ hours, hourly), Linnköping and Norrköping as well as numerous other destinations in the southern half of Sweden.

ⓘ Getting Around

Västtrafik runs the city's public transport system of buses, trams and ferries.There are Västtrafik information booths selling tickets and giving out timetables inside **Nils Ericson Terminalen** (☑6am-10pm Mon-Fri, 9am-10pm Sat, 9am-7pm Sun), in front of the train station on **Drottningtorget** (☑6am-8pm Mon-Fri, 8am-8pm Sat & Sun) and at **Brunnsparken** (☑7am-7pm Mon-Fri, 9am-6pm Sat).

WORTH A TRIP

MARSTRAND

Pretty **Marstrand** (www.marstrand.nu), with its wooden buildings, island setting and relaxed air, conveys the essence of the Bohuslän fishing villages that dot the coast from Göteborg to the Norwegian border, and provides an idyllic area for sailing, cycling or driving. Car traffic is banned on the island itself, so those with their own wheels should take the frequent passenger ferry from Koön, 150m to the east.

The 17th-century **Carlstens Fästning** (www.carlsten.se; adult/7-15yr Skr75/25; ☑11am-6pm late Jun–late Jul, 11am-4pm rest of Jun & Aug) fortress reflects the town's martial and penal history. Entry price includes a guided tour; in the prison cells you are told the story of Lasse Maja, a local Robin Hood figure.

There are numerous eating options along the harbour, including fast-food stalls (one sells fresh fish and chips for about Skr60), cafes and upmarket restaurants.

From Göteborg you can take Västtrafik bus 312 or 302 to Arvidsvik (on Koön) then cross to Marstrand by frequent passenger-only ferry. The complete journey takes about an hour.

Holders of the Göteborg Pass travel free. Otherwise a city transport ticket costs from Skr24. A 24-hour Dagkort (day pass) for the whole city area costs Skr75, or Skr150 for 72 hours.

The easiest way to cover lengthy distances in Göteborg is by tram. Lines, numbered 1 to 13, converge near Brunnsparken (a block from the train station).

Västtrafik has regional passes for 24 hours (adult Skr265) that give unlimited travel on all *länstrafik* buses, trains and boats within Göteborg, Bohuslän and the Västergötland area. Other passes available, depending on where you wish to travel.

Cykelkungen (☑031-18 33 00; www.cykelkungen.se; Chalmersgatan 19; 24 hours/3 days/1 week Skr150/300/500) offers bike rental for Skr150/500 per day/week.

Strömstad

☑0526 / POP 6300

A resort, fishing harbour and spa town, Strömstad is laced with ornate wooden buildings echoing nearby Norway. Indeed, Norwegians head here en masse in summer to take advantage of Sweden's cheaper prices, lending a particularly lively air to the town's picturesque streets and bars. One of Sweden's largest, most magnificent **stone ship settings** (☺24hr) lies 6km northeast of Strömstad; ask for details at the tourist office.

No, **Crusellska Hemmet** (☑0526-101 93; www.crusellska.se; Norra Kyrkogatan 12; s/d Skr475/675; ☺Mar-Sep; [P][@][☂]) is not a Swedish cousin of the Disney villain; it's an exceptional hostel. Drifting white curtains, pale decor and wicker lounges lend the place a boutique vibe. The kitchen is seriously spacious, and there's a peaceful garden for alfresco contemplation, as well as a range of pampering spa treatments. Book ahead.

Try the fresh local *räkor* (shrimp) and delicious seafood in the many restaurants, or purchase from local fishmongers. One of the best places is **Rökeri is Strömstad** (www.rokerietistromstad.se; Torksholmen; mains Skr139-199; ☺noon-5pm Tue-Sat, 5pm-late Fri & Sat), a family-run smokehouse, fish shop and restaurant serving superb seafood baguettes, large bowls of hearty fish soup and seafood platters at lunchtime. Dinner is in a similar vein, only more refined.

The **tourist office** (☑0526-623 30; www.stromstad.se; Ångbåtskajen 2; ☺9am-8pm Mon-Sat, 10am-7pm Sun Jun-Aug) is located between the two harbours on the main square.

Buses and trains both use the train station near the southern harbour. Västtrafik runs bus 871 Göteborg to Strömstad (Skr165, four hours, five to six daily). There are also around six trains every day to/from Göteborg (Skr174, 2½ to three hours).

Norrköping

☑011 / POP 87,300

The envy of industrial has-beens across Europe, Norrköping has managed to cleverly regenerate its defunct mills and canals into a posse of cultural and gastronomic hang-outs fringing waterfalls and locks. Retro trams rattle down streets that are lined with eclectic architecture, while some 30km to the northeast, the animal park at Kolmården swaps urban regeneration for majestic Siberian tigers.

◉ Sights

Summer-only attractions include short guided tours on vintage trams; enquire at the tourist office.

FREE **Arbetets Museum**   MUSEUM
(www.arbetetsmuseum.se; Laxholmen; ☺11am-5pm, to 8pm Tue) Sweden's Museum of Work is in a 1917 building designed to mirror the island it sits on; named Strykjärnet (flatiron), it has seven sides, seven floors and a total of 7000 sq metres of floor space. Recent temporary exhibitions have covered the topics of hunting and the industrialisation of Sweden; don't miss the permanent exhibit about political cartoonists, primarily Ewert Karlsson, aka EWK, whose work appeared in the *New York Times* and *Le Monde*.

FREE **Konstmuseum**   MUSEUM
(www.norrkoping.se/konstmuseum; Kristinaplatsen; ☺noon-4pm Tue-Sun, to 8pm Wed Jun-Aug) Boasts important early 20th-century works with an emphasis on cubism and modernism, as well as Carl Larsson's dreamy *Frukost i det gröna* and a superb collection of graphic art.

Louis de Geer Konserthus   CONCERT VENUE
(☑011-15 50 30; www.louisdegeer.com; Dalsgatan 15) A modern addition to the riverside scenery is this extraordinary 1300-seat concert house in a former paper mill. Still containing the original balconies, it has great acoustics for orchestral, jazz and rock concerts.

Norrköping

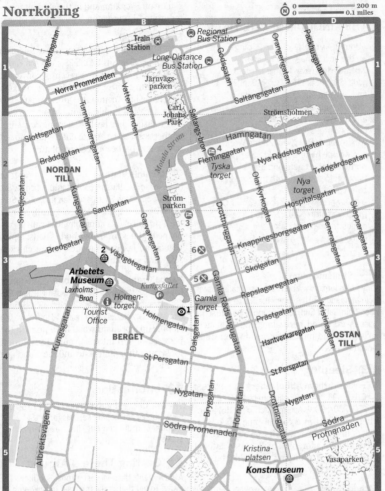

Norrköping

⦿ Top Sights
Arbetets Museum	B3
Konstmuseum	D5

⦿ Sights
1	Louis de Geer Konserthus	B4
2	Stadsmuseum	B3

🛏 Sleeping
3	Hotel Centric	B3
4	Strand Hotell	C2

⊗ Eating
	Fiskmagasinet	(see 5)
5	Mimmis Visthus	C3
6	Pappa Grappa Bar & Trattoria	C3

WORTH A TRIP

THE KINGDOM OF THE TIGER

About 35km north of Norrköping, on the north shore of Bråviken, **Kolmården** (www.kolmarden.com; adult/3-12yr Skr395/292; ⊙10am-7pm mid-Jun–mid-Aug) zoo is Scandinavia's largest, with around 750 residents from all climates and continents. It's divided into two areas: the main Djurparken, with a dolphin show in Marine World, and an ape hang-out; and Safariparken, home to lions, tigers and bears. The ticket gets you into both the zoo and safari park.

Kolmården is served by regular **Östgötatrafiken** (☑0771-21 10 10; www. ostgotatrafiken.se) bus 432 or 433 from Norrköping (Skr67, 40 minutes).

FREE **Stadsmuseum**　　　　　MUSEUM
(City Museum; www.norrkoping.se/stadsmuseet; Holmbrogränd; ⊙11am-5pm Tue-Fri, to 8pm Thu, noon-5pm Sat & Sun) Norrköping's industrial past is exhibited here alongside a particularly good and imaginative exhibit on traditional trades.

🛏 Sleeping

STF Vandrarhem Abborreberg　　HOSTEL €
(☑011-31 93 44; www.abborreberg.se; dm/s/d Skr250/300/500; ⊙Apr–mid-Oct; ⊕; ⊒116) Stunningly situated in a coastal pine wood 6km east of town, this sterling hostel offers accommodation in adorable small huts scattered through the surrounding park. Take bus 116 to Lindö (Skr22).

Strand Hotell　　　　BOUTIQUE HOTEL €€
(☑011-16 99 00; www.hotellstrand.se; Drottninggatan 2; s/d from Skr1171/1406; @⊗) Each of the 11 rooms inside this centrally located 1890 building has its own distinctive theme. Our favourite is the light, airy La Dolce Vita.

Hotel Centric　　　　　HOTEL €€
(☑011-12 90 30; www.centrichotel.se; Gamla Rådstugugatan 18; s Skr575, d Skr750-895; P@⊗) Spacious rooms, solid wooden furniture and friendly staff are the trademark at Norrköping's oldest hotel.

🍴 Eating

There are plenty of eateries in the shopping district along Drottninggatan, in the little square off Skogatan and in the student quarter around Kungsgatan.

Fiskmagasinet　　　　　SEAFOOD €€
(☑011-13 45 60; www.fiskmagasinet.se; Skolgatan 1; lunch Skr90, mains Skr135-285; ⊙lunch & dinner Mon-Sat) Housed in a recently converted 19th-century *snus* (snuff) factory, urbane Fiskmagasinet combines an intimate bar with a casually chic dining room serving savvy dishes like grilled herring with lingonberries, seared Arctic char with smoked bacon, and barbecue seafood platter.

🌿 **Mimmis Visthus**　　　　CAFE €€
(www.mimmisvisthus.se; Skolgatan1b; lunch Skr89 ⊙10am-6pm Mon-Fri, to 4pm Sat, noon-4pm Sun ⊘) With its emphasis on ecologically sound local produce, this adorable little cafe serves heaped plates of superfood salads, spicy vegetarian lasagne, quiches, cakes, chicken satay and smoothies.

Pappa Grappa Bar & Trattoria　　ITALIAN €€
(www.pappagrappa.se; Gamla Rådstugugatan 26-28; pizzas Skr83-109, mains Skr165-335; ⊙6pm-late Mon-Sat, pizzeria also open 4-11pm Sun; ⊘) Gobble up a brilliant wood-fired pizza in the pizzeria, or slip into the vaulted restaurant for scrumptious antipasto and meat and fish mains.

ⓘ Information

The well-stocked **tourist office** (☑011-15 50 00; www.upplev.norrkoping.se; Dalsgatan 16; ⊙10am-6pm Jul-mid-Aug) has free internet access.

ⓘ Getting There & Around

Air Sweden's third-largest airport is 60km away. To get there take the train to Nyköping, then catch a local bus. **Norrköping airport** (☑011-15 37 22; www.norrkopingflygplats.se) has direct flights from Copenhagen, Helsinki and Visby.

Bus The regional bus station is next to the train station, and long-distance buses leave from a terminal across the road. Swebus Express (p420) has frequent services to Stockholm (Skr149, 2¼ to 2½ hours, at least 11 daily), Göteborg (Skr289, 4¾ to five hours, at least five daily) and Kalmar (Skr279, 3¾ to four hours, four daily).

Train SJ trains depart for Stockholm (from Skr210, 1½ to two hours), Malmö (from Skr484, 3¼ to four hours), Nyköping (Skr82, 40 minutes, hourly) and Linköping (Skr76, 25 minutes, every 20 minutes).

Linköping

📍013 / POP 104,200

Most famous for its mighty medieval cathedral, Linköping is Norrköping's more upmarket cousin and also the site of the 'bloodbath of Linnköping'. In 1600, civil war flared between the Polish, Catholic King Sigismund (Sweden's legitimate but way-too-busy ruler) and his Protestant uncle, Duke Charles. Charles won, becoming King Charles IX and beheading five of Sigismund's supporters, cementing Protestant dominance in Sweden.

⊙ Sights & Activities

Domkyrka
CHURCH

(⊙9am-6pm) The enormous, copper-roofed cathedral with its 107m spire is the landmark of Linköping and one of Sweden's oldest and largest churches. Learn more about its history and architecture (and see the two mummified rats from the bishop's privy) at the museum inside the castle just across the way, the **Slotts & Domkyrkomuseum** (Castle & Cathedral Museum; www. lsdm.se; adult/student/7-18yr Skr50/40/20; ⊙noon-4pm Tue-Sun).

FREE Gamla Linköping
MUSEUM

(www.gamlalinkoping.info; ⊙10am-5pm Mon-Fri, 11am-4pm Sat & Sun; 🚻; 🚌12, 19) Some 2km west of the city is Gamla Linköping, one of the biggest open-air living-museum villages in Sweden. Among the 90 quaint houses are about a dozen theme museums, many handicraft shops, a small chocolate factory, a restaurant and a cafe. You can wander among the 19th-century buildings at will – the village and most museums are open daily. Just 300m through the forest behind the old village is the Valla Fritidsområde, a recreation area with domestic animals, gardens, a children's playground, minigolf, and a few small museums and old houses.

Östergötlands Länsmuseum
GALLERY

(www.ostergotlandsmuseum.se; Vasavägen; adult/under 26yr Skr70/free; ⊙10am-4pm Tue-Sun) Just north of the cathedral, this museum houses an extensive collection of art by a variety of European painters, including Cranach's view of Eden, *Original Sin*, with a cheeky-looking Eve.

Kinda Canal
BOAT TOUR

Upstaged by the Göta Canal, Linköping boasts its own canal system, the 90km Kinda Canal. Opened in 1871, it has 15 locks, including Sweden's deepest. Cruises include evening sailings, musical outings and winetasting trips. For a simple day excursion, from late June to early August **MS Kind** (📍0141-23 33 70; www.kindakanal.se; cruises from Skr140; ⊙May-Sep) leaves Tullbron dock at 10am on Tuesday, Thursday and Saturday, and travels to Rimforsa (Skr340, return by bus or train included).

🛏 Sleeping & Eating

Most places to eat and drink are on the main square or nearby streets, especially along buzzing Ågatan.

Park Hotel
HOTEL €€

(📍013-12 90 05; www.fawltytowers.se; Järnvägsgatan 6; s/d Skr1095/1295, budget r Skr795; 🅿@) Sweden's 'Fawlty Towers' (minus Manuel), this hotel across from the train station resembles that madhouse in appearance only (yes, there's an elk head at reception). A smart family-run establishment close to the train station, it's peppered with chandeliers, oil paintings and clean, modern, parquet-floored rooms. There's a restaurant on site and afternoon tea is served daily.

Linköping STF Vandrarhem & Hotell
HOSTEL €

(📍013-35 90 00; www.lvh.se; Klostergatan 52A; hostel dm/s/d Skr360/670/720, hotel s/d/f from Skr940/1090/1485; 🅿@🛜🚻; 🚌30, 52, 59, 72, 78) A swish central hostel with hotel-style accommodation, too, mostly with kitchenettes. All the spacious rooms have private bathroom and TV. Book ahead. To get here, head south of town along Drottninggatan. Limited parking.

Stångs Magasin
SWEDISH €€€

(www.stangsmagasin.se; Södra Stånggatan 1; lunch Skr115, mains Skr145-505; ⊙11.30am-2pm Mon-Fri, 6pm-midnight Tue-Fri, 5pm-midnight Sat Jul & Aug) In a 200-year-old warehouse down near the Kinda Canal docks, this elegant award winner fuses classic Swedish cuisine with Continental influences – think grlled trout with crayfish and yellow beets and venison with chanterelles and port wine reduction. The lunch specials are particularly good value.

Ammos Cafe Crepes
CREPERIE €

(Platensgatan 3; crepes from Skr45; 📍) Come to this little spot, decorated with spoof ad posters, for great atmosphere, absolutely enormous crepes with sweet and savoury fillings, sandwiches and cakes. Try the chicken, Västerbotten cheese and chanterelles crepe.

Ghingis ASIAN €€

(www.ghingis.se; Klostergatan; lunch/dinner buffet Skr95/209; ⊘11am-3pm & 5.30-11pm Mon-Fri, noon-3pm & 5-11pm Sat, noon-9pm Sun; ⚹) The choices at this hugely popular buffet restaurant run the gamut from Thai green curry and smoked sausage with pickled beets to chanterelle soup and grilled salmon with saffron sauce. Vegetarians are catered for. Dinner is Mongolian barbecue: pick a selection of meat, vegies and noodles, choose a sauce and watch them fry it up on the spot.

ⓘ Information

Tourist Office (☎013-190 0070; www.visitlinkoping.se; Storgatan 15; ⊘9am-6pm Mon-Fri, 11-3pm Sat & Sun)

ⓘ Getting There & Away

Air The **airport** (☎013-18 10 30; www.linkopingcityairport.se) is 2km east of town. **KLM** (www.klm.com) flies daily to Amsterdam, while **NextJet** (www.nextjet.se) serves Copenhagen. There's no airport bus, but taxi company **Taxibil** (☎013-14 60 00) charges around Skr160 for the ride.

Bus Regional and local buses, run by ÖstgötaTrafiken (p442), leave from the terminal next to the train station. Journeys cost from Skr22; a ticket valid for an hour costs Skr165/110 per adult/child. Tickets can be purchased at Pressbyrån outlets or at the train station. It's also possible to pay by SMS (text message).

Up to five express buses (65, 67, 68) per day go to Vadstena; otherwise change at Motala for bus 612 or 613.

Long-distance buses depart from a terminal 200m northwest of the train station. Swebus Express (p420) runs to Göteborg (Skr269, four hours, five to seven daily), and north to Norrköping (Skr49, 45 minutes, nine daily) and Stockholm (Skr199, three hours, eight daily).

Train Trains run to Stockholm (Skr272, 1¾ to two hours, hourly), Malmö (Skr235, three hours, hourly), Norrköping (Skr76, 25 minutes, every 20 minutes) and Kalmar (Skr220, three to 3¾ hours, hourly).

Vadstena

☎0143 / POP 5600

On Vättern lake, Vadstena is a legacy of both church and state power, and today St Birgitta's abbey and Gustav Vasa's castle compete for admiration. The atmosphere in the Old Town (between Storgatan and the abbey), with its wonderful cobbled lanes, evocative street names and wooden buildings, makes the place a satisfying pit stop.

◉ Sights & Activities

Vadstena Slott CASTLE

(www.vadstenadirect.se; Slottsvägen; tours adult/8-18yr Skr90/60; ⊘11am-4pm, to 6pm Jul-early Aug) Looming out of the moat surrounding it, this imposing Renaissance castle was originally built to thwart Danish attacks by the early Vasa kings. Guided tours (daily mid-May to mid-September) take in the upper apartments, stuffed with period furniture and featuring some very unflattering portraits of the Vasa family.

Klosterkyrkan CHURCH

(Abbey Church; ⊘9am-8pm Jul, 9am-7pm Jun & Aug) The superb 15th-century Klosterkyrkan, consecrated in 1430, was built in response to one of St Birgitta's visions and afterwards became the top pilgrimage site in Sweden. Check out the statue of St Birgitta 'in a state of ecstasy'; her mortal remains lie in a red velvet box in a glass case in the monks' choir stalls.

Near the church, the **Sankta Birgitta Klostermuseum** (www.sanctabirgitta.com; Lasarettsgatan; adult/8-17yr Sk60/30; ⊘10.30am-5pm Jul–mid-Aug, 11am-4pm Jun & rest of Aug) tells the story of St Birgitta's roller-coaster life (lady-in-waiting to King Magnus Eriksson, married at 13, was mother to eight unruly children...).

⌖ Sleeping & Eating

STF Vandrarhem Vadstena HOSTEL €

(☎0143-765 60; www.svenskaturistforeningen.se; Skänningegatan 20; dm/s/d Skr220/320/440; ⓟ@⟩) A short walk from the town centre sits this big hostel, with affable staff, sunny dorms and a large underground kitchen decorated with cheery Dala horses. Book ahead from late August to early June.

Vadstena Klosterhotel BOUTIQUE HOTEL €€€

(☎0143-315 30; www.klosterhotel.se; r from Skr1350; ⓟ@⟩) History and luxury merge at this wonderfully atmospheric hotel in St Birgitta's old convent. The bathrooms are a wee bit dated, but the medieval-style rooms are great, with chandeliers, high wooden beds, and heaven-sent coffeemakers. Most rooms boast lake views.

Vadstena Valven SWEDISH €€

(www.valven.se; Rådhustorget 9; lunch Skr78, mains Skr129-245; ⊘11.30am-2pm & 6-10pm Mon-Fri, 4-10pm Fri, noon-3pm & 6-10pm Sat, noon-3pm Sun) Vadstena's best restaurant in a vaulted cellar setting, serving a couple of daily lunch dishes and creative dinner mains, such as garlic-roasted lobster and elk fillet with truffled potato cake.

Rådhuskällaren
PUB **€€**

(www.radhuskallaren.com; Rådhustorget; mains Skr95-129; 🍴) Under the old courthouse, this affable 15th-century cellar restaurant dishes out simple but filling meat and fish meals. Its outdoor area is a favourite afternoon drinking spot in summer.

🛈 Information

Tourist Office (📞0143-315 70; www.vadstena. com; ⏰10am-6pm Jul, 10am-6pm Mon-Sat, to 4pm Sun Jun & early Aug) Located in Rödtornet (Sånggatan).

🛈 Getting There & Around

See p444 for regional transport information. Only buses run to Vadstena – you must take bus 610 to Motala (for trains to Örebro) or bus 661 to Mjölby (for trains to Linköping and Stockholm). Swebus Express (p420) runs on Friday and Sunday to/from Stockholm (Skr299, 4¼ hours).

SMÅLAND

The region of Småland is one of dense forests, glinting lakes and bare marshlands. Historically it served as a buffer zone between the Swedes and Danes; the eastern and southern coasts in particular witnessed territorial tussles. Today it's better known for the Glasriket (Kingdom of Crystal) in the central southeast.

Växjö

📞0470 / POP 60,900

A venerable old market town, Växjö (pronounced *vek*-choo, with the 'ch' sound as in the Scottish 'loch'), in Kronobergs *län* (Kronoberg county), is a good place to base yourself if you're interested in exploring the region's glassworks. It's also an important stop for Americans seeking their Swedish roots, since there had been mass emigration from Småland, one of Sweden's poorest regions, in the late 19th and early 20th century. In mid-August, **Karl Oscar Days** commemorates the 19th-century mass emigration, and the Swedish-American of the year is chosen.

🔘 Sights

Smålands Museum
MUSEUM

(www.kulturparkensmaland.se; Södra Järnvägsgatan 2; adult/under 19yr Skr50/free; ⏰10am-5pm Tue-Fri, 10am-4pm Sat & Sun; 🍴) This is really two museums in one: one features displays on Småland's manufacturing industries, archaeology and regional history, while the other, 'Five Hundred Years of Swedish Glass' is the star. The glassworks – from the 16th century onwards – include the record-holding collection of glass cheese-dish covers – hard to beat for obscure notoriety – and the strangely affecting examples of 'glass sickness'. The most incredible glass pieces, however, are contemporary, with their creators really letting their imagination take flight.

House of Emigrants
MUSEUM

(Utvandrarnas Hus; www.utvandrarnashus.se; Vilhelm Mobergs gata 4; adult/under 19yr Skr50/free; ⏰10am-5pm Tue-Fri, 10am-4pm Sat & Sun) Charting the poverty and hardships faced by impoverished Swedes (mostly from Småland) who emigrated to America between 1860 and 1930, this is an intensely moving museum, with the 'Dream of America' exhibition its main feature. You learn about the dreadful conditions aboard the immigrant ships, as well as about the experiences of recent immigrants to Sweden itself, coming from as far away as Somalia and Iran. The research centre has access to a vast database of information and is helpful when helping visitors with Swedish roots trace their origins.

🛏 Sleeping & Eating

Växjö Vandrarhem
HOSTEL **€**

(📞470-630 70; www.vaxjovandrarhem.nu; Brandts väg 11, Evedal; dm/s/d Skr200/380/500; ⏰reception 5-8pm Jun-Aug; 🅿@🛜) At Evedal, this pretty former spa hotel with a picturesque lakeside setting dates from the late 18th century. Most of the bright, but spartan, rooms have washbasins; there's a big kitchen, laundry, a wonderful lounge in the attic and bicycles for hire. It's well loved, so book early. Take bus 7 from town.

TOP CHOICE **PM & Vänner**
INTERNATIONAL **€€€**

(📞0470-70 04 44; www.pmrestauranger.se; Storgatan 22; restaurant tasting menu Skr995, bistro mains Skr209-365; ⏰6-10pm Wed-Sat) This stylish establishment serves up new-school Swedish flavours with global twists. This

WORTH A TRIP

ASTRID LINDGREN'S HOUSE

If you've grown up on stories of Pippi Longstocking, Karlsson-on-the-Roof, Kalle Blomkvist and other characters who'll stay with you all your life, you shouldn't miss the opportunity to visit the childhood home of Astrid Lindgren (1907–2002), Sweden's most prolific children's book author whose works have been translated into dozens of languages.

In Vimmerby, halfway between Linköping and Växjö, **Astrid Lindgrens Näs** (☑ tours 0492 76 94 00; www.astridlindgrensnas.se; Prästgården 24; adult/6-14yr Skr85/50, tours adult/under 15yr Skr95/50; ⊙10am-6pm Jun-Aug, shorter hr rest of yr) presents both her restored childhood home – an adorable cottage surrounded by rosebushes and visited by guided tour in summer – and a superb permanent exhibition titled 'The whole world's Astrid Lindgren' that takes you through this remarkable woman's life and achievements.

A girl with an idyllic childhood turned struggling single mother at 18, with energy to spare and a wild imagination, she took a stand against Hitler, was first published as an author in 1944, had a minor planet named after her and was found up a tree when she was well past the age of 70, saying that there's no rule that old women shouldn't climb trees. That's just the tip of the iceberg. To discover more, stop by.

is the place to splurge on a six-course tasting menu, accompanied by expertly chosen vintages. Local produce sparkles in dishes such as barbot (fish) with pear and truffle and wood pigeon 'with flavours from the deep forest of Småland'. The upscale bistro next door also offers wonderfully inventive dishes featuring bleak roe, elk, herring, 'Jannson's Temptation' and other Swedish delights. Don't miss Jon's dessert featuring sea buckthorn.

ℹ Information

Tourist office (☑ 470-73 32 80; www.turism.vaxjo.se; Stortorget, Residencet; ⊙9.30am-6pm Mon-Fri, 10am-2pm Sat Jun-Aug) On the main square.

ℹ Getting There & Away

Småland airport (☑ 0470-75 85 00; www.smalandairport.se) is 9km northwest of Växjö. SAS (p479) and **NextJet** (☑ 08-639 85 38; www.nextjet.se) have direct flights to Stockholm Arlanda Airport, **Fly Smaland** (☑ 0900 20 71 720; www.flysmaland.com) to Stockholm's Bromma, and **Ryanair** (www.ryanair.com) to Düsseldorf Weeze. Bus 50 connects with Ryanair flights from Växjö's Centralstation; otherwise take a **taxi** (☑ 0470-135 00) for Skr310.

Länstrafiken Kronoberg (☑ 0470-72 75 50; www.lanstrafikenkron.se) runs the regional bus network, with daily buses to Halmstad, Jönköping and Kosta. Long-distance buses depart beside the train station. Svenska Buss (p426) runs daily services daily to Eksjö (Skr220, 1½ hours), Linköping (Skr290, 3¼ hours) and Stockholm (Skr380, six hours).

Växjö is served by SJ trains running to Kalmar (Skr136, 1¼ hours, hourly), Malmö (Skr181, two hours, hourly) and Göteborg (Skr275, 2¾ hours, four daily).

Glasriket

What comes in a myriad of colours and shapes, is both beautiful and useful, and alternately brittle and pliable? If you've guessed glass, then you're absolutely right, and there's no better place to see traditional glass-blowing than here, in its birthplace, the so-called 'Kingdom of Crystal'. **Glasriket** (www.glasriket.se) is the most visited area of Sweden outside Stockholm and Göteborg, featuring a dozen or so glass factories (look for *glasbruk* signs), most with long histories: Kosta, for example, was founded in 1742.

The glassworks have similar opening hours, usually 10am to 6pm Monday to Friday, 10am to 4pm Saturday and noon to 4pm Sunday. Expert glass designers produce some extraordinary avant-garde pieces, often with a good dollop of Swedish wit. Factory outlets have substantial discounts on seconds (around 30% to 40% off), and larger places can arrange shipping to your home country.

If you're serious about purchasing glass, it's worth picking up a **Glasriket Pass** (www.glasriket.se; Skr95) that gets you a 10% to 15% discount off purchases and more.

KOSTA

Kosta is where it all began in 1742. Today, the **Kosta Boda** (www.kostaboda.se) complex pulls in coachloads of visitors, who raid the vast discount outlets The exhibition gallery contains some inspired creations, there are plenty of glass-blowing demos in the old factory quarters and **Kosta Boda Art Hotel** (☑0487-348 30; www.kostabodaarthotel.se; Stora vägen 75; s/d Skr995/1350; P🐾🖕) combines seriously inspired design with seriously good *smörgasbord* lunches (Skr255) at the attached Linnéa Art Restaurant.

ORREFORS

Established in 1888, **Orrefors** (www.orrefors .se) features arguably the most famous of Sweden's glassworks. Demonstrations abound and you're likely to spend hours admiring the unconventional creations in the sleek museum-gallery. The attached cafe-bar does very good sandwiches.

The friendly, well-equipped **Vandrarhem Orrefors** (☑0481-300 20; www.orrefors vandrarhem.se; Silversparregatan 14; s/d/f from Skr350/420/660; ☺May-Sep) is located conveniently near the factory. Quaint red houses surround a grassy garden, and the peaceful rooms have proper beds. Breakfast is available on request.

NYBRO

Quiet Nybro has two excellent glassworks worth visiting and was once an important centre for hand-blown light bulbs(!). Of the two glassworks, 130-year-old (don't laugh!) **Pukeberg** (www.pukeberg.se; Pukebergarnas väg), just southeast of the centre, is perhaps more interesting for its quaint setting. **Nybro** (www.nybro-glasbruk.se; Herkulesgatan) is smaller and laced with quirky items (think Elvis Presley glass platters).

The local STF hostel, **Nybro Lågprishotell & Vandrarhem** (☑0481-109 32; www.nybrovandrarhem.se; Vasagatan 22; dm/s/d Skr250/350/450, hotel s/d Skr490/790; P🖕), near Pukeberg, is clean and comfortable, with a kitchen on each floor as well as a sauna. More expensive hotel rooms have cable TV, nonbunk beds and private showers and toilets, with breakfast included.

Nybro's **tourist office** (☑0481-450 85; www.nybro.se; Stadshusplan; ☺6.45am-5pm Mon-Fri, noon-4pm Sun) is inside the town hall.

❶ Getting There & Around

Apart from the main routes, bus services around the area are practically nonexistent. The easiest way to explore is with your own transport (beware of elk). Bicycle tours on the unsurfaced country roads are excellent; there are plenty of hostels, and you can camp almost anywhere except near the military area on the Kosta–Orrefors road.

Kalmar Länstrafik (☑010 21 21 000; www.klt. se) bus 139 runs from mid-June to mid-August only and calls at a few of the glass factories. The service operates four times daily on weekdays and once on Saturday, and runs from Nybro to Orrefors and Målerås. Kosta is served by regular bus 218 from Växjö (two or three daily).

SJ trains between Alvesta and Kalmar stop in Nybro every hour or two; Nybro is also connected by regional bus 131 to Kalmar.

Oskarshamn

TRANSPORT HUB

Oskarshamn is useful mostly for its regular boat connections with Gotland.

The well-run **STF Vandrarhem Oskar & Hotel Rum Oscar** (☑0491-158 00; www. forumoscarhamn.se; Södra Långgatan 15-17; hostel dm/s/d Skr180/305/410, hotel s/d Skr780/1050; P@) is a brilliant budget option, with sleek modern rooms and private bathrooms, a snazzy TV lounge and dining room, and a tidy kitchen for self-caterers.

Oskarshamn airport (www.oskarhamnairport.se) is 12km north of town, with several daily flights to Stockholm Arlanda Airport.

Boats to Visby depart from the Gotland Ferry Terminal, daily in winter and twice daily in summer. The **MS Solund** (www.olandsfarjan.se) ferry to Öland departs from the ferry terminal off Skeppsbron.

Long-distance bus services stop at the very central bus station. Regional bus services run up to six times daily from Oskarshamn to Kalmar (Skr85, 1½ hours).

Swebus Express (p420) has two to three daily buses between Stockholm and Kalmar calling in at Oskarshamn.

Kalmar

☑0480 / POP 36,400

Dashing Kalmar claims one of Sweden's most spectacular castles, where the crowns of Sweden, Denmark and Norway agreed to the short-lived Union of Kalmar in 1397. Other local assets include Sweden's largest gold hoard, from the 17th-century ship *Kronan*, and the storybook cobbled streets of Gamla Stan (Old Town) to the west of Slottshotellet.

⊙ Sights

Kalmar Slott
CASTLE

(www.kalmarslott.kalmar.se; adult/student/under 17yr Skr100/60/25; ⊙10am-6pm daily Jul–mid-Aug, shorter hr rest of yr; ⊞) Looming across the moat, the once powerful Renaissance Kalmar Slott has everything a good castle should: an imposing presence, turrets, a dungeon and secret passages – not that the latter did much good to King Erik, Gustav Vasa's son, when his brother Johan slipped arsenic into his pea soup. The highlight is the interior – the panelled **King Erik chamber**, the eerie Burnt Hall hung with painted glass, the ceiling frescos, the tapestries. In summer there are jesters and jousters entertaining the kids in the yard. **Guided tours** are included in the price.

Kalmar Konstmuseum
MUSEUM

(www.kalmarkonstmuseum.se; Stadsparken; adult/senior & student/under 20yr Skr50/40/free; ⊙noon-5pm Tue-Sun, to 7pm Wed) Striking on the outside, this modern-art museum hosts excellent contemporary exhibitions, such as 'Don't You Wish Your Girlfriend Was a Freak Like Me?'

Kalmar Länsmuseum
MUSEUM

(County Museum; www.kalmarlansmuseum.se; Skeppsbrogatan; adult/under 19 yr Skr80/free; ⊙10am-4pm Mon-Fri, to 8pm Wed, 11am-4pm Sat & Sun; ⊞) Mounds of gold, exceptionally well-preserved period costumes, cannons and more – an epic nautical disaster is your gain! In 1676 the flagship *Kronan* sank controversially off Öland, taking with it almost 800 souls. But that means that you can view the booty – over 20,000 objects – right here, as well as the video of its salvaging.

Domkyrkan
CHURCH

(Cathedral; www.kalmardomkyrka.se; Stortorget; ⊙8am-3.30pm Mon-Fri, to 6.30pm Wed, 9am-4pm Sat & Sun) Home to a spectacular pulpit, this baroque beauty was designed by Tessin, King Karl X Gustav's favourite architect.

🛏 Sleeping

Slottshotellet
HOTEL €€€

(☑480-882 60; www.slottshotellet.se; Slottsvägen 7; r/ste from Skr1395/1795; P@🛜) Kalmar's top pick is this wonderfully romantic, cosy hotel based in four buildings in a gorgeous green setting near the castle. Most rooms have antique furnishings, some feature vintage Swedish tile stoves, and the atmospheric junior suite is *the* place to woo your sweetie. Staff are wonderful and there's an onsite summer restaurant.

Calmar Stadshotel
HOTEL €€

(☑480-49 69 00; www.profilhotels.se; Stortorget 14; s/d from Skr1195/1405; P@🛜) Quiet, comfortable rooms equipped with mod cons in a you-can't-get-more-central-than-this location on the main square in an attractive Art Nouveau style building. The epic buffet breakfast will ensure that you needn't eat all day.

Hotell Svanen
HOSTEL, HOTEL €

(☑480-255 60; www.hotellsvanen.se; Rappegatan 1; hostel dm/s/d from Skr195/385/490, hotel s/d Skr595/830; P🛜) On the quiet island of Ängö, about 1km north of town, these are the best budget digs in town. Hotel Svanen and the SVIF hostel share the same building. The sparsely furnished, compact hostel rooms downstairs mostly share facilities; the hotel rooms have bathroom and are light, bright and nicely furnished. Take bus 402 in the 'Skogsrået' direction and alight at 'Ängöleden'.

🍴 Eating

Gröna Stugan
EUROPEAN €€€

(www.gronastuganikalmar.se; Larmgatan 1; mains Skr210-285; ⊙5-11pm Mon-Sat, to 9pm Sun) Somewhat nautically themed Green House thrills your tastebuds with the likes of cod cheek with apple puree and wasabi, and duck breast with cherry sauce. In summer, wallet-friendly lunches are served on the town green.

Da Ernesto
ITALIAN €€

(www.ernestokalmar.se; Larmtorget 4; mains Skr130-280; ⊙5-11pm Mon-Fri, noon-midnight Sat, 1-10pm Sun; 🚼) Run by a real-deal Neapolitan, this Italian cafe, restaurant and bar attracts scores of people with its baristas, extensive menu (including Neapolitan-style pizzas), homemade pasta (try the linguine with saffron) and well-mixed drinks.

ℹ Information

Tourist office (☑480-41 77 00; www.kalmar.se/turism; Ölandskajen 9; ⊙9am-9pm Mon-Fri, 10am-5pm Sat & Sun late Jun–mid-Aug, sorter hr other times) About 100m south of the train station.

ℹ️ Getting There & Away

Air

The **airport** (📞480-45 90 00; www.kalma-rairport.se) is 6km west of town. SAS (p479) flies several times daily to Stockholm Arlanda Airport, while **Kalmarflyg** (www.kalmarflyg.se) flies to Stockholm's Bromma airport. Bus 402 (Skr45, 20 minutes) provides connections to central Kalmar.

Bus

All regional and long-distance buses depart from the train station; local town buses have their own station on Östra Sjögatan. Regional buses are run by **Kalmar Länstrafik** (📞010 21 21 000; www.klt.se), including buses to Öland.

Swebus (p420) services run north to Norr-köping (Skr289, four hours, two daily), Stock-holm (Skr359, 6½ hours, two daily); and south to Karlskrona (Skr61, 1¼ hours, one or two daily) and Malmö (Skr189, 4½ hours, two or three daily). Svenska Buss (p426) has four services per week on the same route; journey times and prices are similar. **Silverlinjen** (📞0485-261 11; www.silverlinjen.se) runs one to three daily direct buses to Stockholm (Skr300, 5¾ hours); reservations are essential.

Train

SJ trains run every hour or two between Kalmar and Alvesta (from Skr157, 1¼ hours), where you can connect with the main Stockholm–Malmö line and with trains to Göteborg. Trains run to Linköping up to six times daily (Skr220, 3¼ hours), also with connections to Stockholm.

Öland

📞0485 / POP 24,600

Like a deranged vision of Don Quixote's, the skinny island of Öland is covered in old wooden windmills. Symbols of power and wealth in the mid-18th century, there are still 400 or so left.

Öland is doable as a long day trip from Kalmar, but is best explored at leisure. Hav-ing a car will allow you to reach such iso-lated spots as Trollskogen on the island's northernmost tip, a dense pine forest full of delightful walking trails, and the remains of the Iron Age fortresses in the southern half of the island. A slower, equally scenic way of exploring is by bicycle; check **Cykla På Öland** (www.cyklapaoland.se) for cycling routes and other handy info.

FÄRJESTADEN & AROUND

South of Färjestaden the entire island is a Unesco World Heritage Site, lauded for its unique agricultural landscape, in continu-ous use from the Stone Age to today, and peppered with rune stones and ancient burial cairns.

The bridge from Kalmar lands you on the island just north of Färjestaden, where there's a well-stocked **tourist office** (📞485-89 000; www.olandsturist.se; ⊘9am-7pm Mon-Fri, to 6pm Sat, to 5pm Sun Jul–mid-Aug) at the Träff-punkt Öland centre. Staff can book island accommodation (for a fee). There are few hotels, but more than 25 camping grounds and at least a dozen hostels (book ahead). Camping between midsummer and mid-August can cost up to Skr320 per campsite.

Silverlinjen (www.silverlinjen.se) runs twice-daily direct buses from Öland to Stockholm (Skr300, six hours), calling at Kalmar – res-ervations essential.

BORGHOLM & AROUND

Öland's 'capital' and busiest town, Borgholm exudes a vaguely tacky air with its discount shops and summer crowds. Just outside town, **Borgholms Slott** (www.borgholmsslott. se; adult/12-17yr Skr70/40; ⊘10am-6pm Jun-Aug; 🅿️), Northern Europe's largest ruined castle, is a most dramatic sight. These four grey walls and four grey towers were burnt and abandoned early in the 18th century, but now there's a terrific museum inside fo-cussing on the castle's history, and summer concerts in the courtyard. Three kilometres south of Borgholm, and boasting exception-al gardens, is the more compact **Solliden Palace** (www.sollidensslot.se; adult/student/child Skr75/55/44; ⊘11am-6pm mid-May–mid-Sep), still used by the Swedish royal family.

🛏️ Sleeping & Eating

The tourist offices in Borgholm and Färjes-taden can help you find inexpensive private rooms in the area.

| TOP |
| CHOICE |

Hotell Borgholm HOTEL €€

(📞0485-770 60; www.hotellborgholm.com; Träd-gårdsgatan 15-19; s/d Skr1335/1535; ❄️@🛜) The beautifully renovated rooms at this fine hotel feature smart, comfortable beds, pine wooden floors and bold touches of colour on the feature walls. The restaurant here is the best on the island, with chef/owner Karin Fransson whipping up such delights as duck leg with red cabbage marmalade and for-est mushrooms for the seven-course taster menu (Skr995). Book ahead.

Ebbas Vandrarhem & Trädgårdscafé
HOSTEL €

(☎0485-103 73; www.ebbas.se; Storgatan 12; dm/s/d Skr270/350/540; ☺May-Sep; 🛜) Right in the thick of things, Ebbas cafe has a small STF hostel above it. Five of the compact lemon-yellow rooms overlook the gorgeous rose-laced garden, and four of the rooms face the bustling pedestrianised main street. There's a kitchen for self-catere, or just pop downstairs for decent hot and cold grub (lunch Skr105), served until 9pm in the summer (earlier at other times).

Öländsk Mat
SWEDISH €€

(☎070-577 5704; Trädgårdsgatan 18; mains Skr85; ☺11am-4pm daily; 🍴) What this friendly little cafe does best are two typical Öland specialities: *kroppkakor* (large potato dumplings filled with bacon and onions and served with lingonberry jam) and *isterband* sausage (coarsely ground, with grain), though there's always a vegie dish as well. Enjoy.

Robinson Crusoe
EUROPEAN €€

(www.robinsoncrusoe.se; Hamnvägen; lunch buffet Skr110, mains Skr158-495) At this harbourfront restaurant, the menu flits between the likes of Öland flounder and Devil Steak, its spicy sauce a secret recipe. The scrumptious lunchtime buffet is all about meat and fish, though there's a large salad bar attached.

Karlskrona

☎0455 / POP 35,200

If you like your Swedes in uniform, you'll appreciate Karlskrona. Marine cadets pepper the streets of what has always been an A-league naval base. In 1998 the entire town was added to the Unesco World Heritage list for its impressive collection of 17th- and 18th-century naval architecture. Karlskrona's archipelago of almost 1000 islands makes for a great boat excursion in summer.

⊙ Sights & Activities

TOP CHOICE Marinmuseum
MUSEUM

(www.marinmuseum.se; Stumholmen; adult/under 19yr Skr100/free; ☺10am-6pm Jun-Aug, to 4pm rest of yr; 🚹) This striking naval museum is Karlskrona's tour de force. The engaging displays, some interactive, cover scale models of famous ships, the history of the Swedish navy, naval battles (shoot your own cannon), navigation at sea and life on board the ships. There's a hall of splendid figureheads and a recent display on the Cold War. The attached restaurant does an excellent lunch buffet (Skr90).

Kungsholms Fort
FORT

(guided tours adult/under 17yr Skr210/50; ☺10am-2pm Jun-Aug) The extraordinary offshore Kungsholms Fort, with its curious circular harbour, was established in 1680 to defend the town. Four-hour boat tours of the archipelago, including a visit to the fortress, depart from Fisktorget; book at the tourist office or Marinmuseum (bring ID).

FREE Drottningskärs kastell
CASTLE

(☺Skärgårdstrafiken boat Jun-Aug) Bristling with cannons, this tower on the island of Aspö was described by Admiral Nelson of the British Royal Navy as 'impregnable'. You can visit it on an **Äspoleden**, a free car ferry that runs up to twice hourly in July and August from Handelshamnen, north of the Marinmuseum.

Amiralitetskyrkan
CHURCH

(Vallgatan 11) Sweden's oldest wooden church is the stocky **Amiralitetskyrkan**, whose gorgeous pastel interior is worth a peek. Inside is the original wooden statue of **Old Rosenbom** who saved Nils Holgersson in the Selma Lagerlöf classic, *The Wonderful Adventures of Nils.*

🛏 Sleeping & Eating

First Hotel Ja
HOTEL €€

(☎0455-555 60; www.firsthotels.se; Borgmästaregatan 13; r from Skr1056; 🅿@) Karlskrona's top slumber spot boasts slick, hip, recently renovated rooms in white and charcoal hues, with blissful beds and flat-screen TVs. Hotel perks include a sauna, bar-restaurant and a great breakfast buffet.

STF Vandrarhem Trossö Karlskrona
HOSTEL €

(☎0455-100 20; www.karlskronavandrarhem.se; Drottninggatan 39; dm/s/d from Skr160/280/370; 🛜🚹) Modern, clean and friendly, this hostel has a laundry, TV room and backyard for kids to play in; parking on the opposite side of the street is free.

Glassiärens Glassbar
ICE CREAM

(Stortorget 4; ☺May-Sep) The queues at this legendary ice-cream seller are matched by the mammoth serves. Piled high in a heavenly waffle cone, the two-flavour option (Skr37) is a virtual meal.

Nivå INTERNATIONAL €€
(☑0455-103 71; www.niva.nu; Norra Kungsgatan
3; burgers & salads Skr115-149, mains Skr189-355;
⊙5-11pm Mon-Thu, 4pm-1am Fri, noon-1am Sat)
Just off Stortorget, this slinky steakhouse
has an excellent menu of light, well-priced
dishes (nachos, burgers, salads), plus beautifully grilled steaks. It's also a popular
evening bar.

❶ Information

Tourist office (☑455-30 34 90; www.karl-
skrona.se/tourism; Stortorget 2; ⊙9am-7pm
Jul–mid-Aug; shorter hr rest of yr) Has internet
access and info on archipelago cruises.

❶ Getting There & Away

Air Ronneby Airport (☑010 109 54 00; www.
swedavia.com) is 33km west of Karlskrona;
the Flygbuss leaves from Stortorget (adult/
child Skr90/45). There are several SAS and
Blekingeflyg flights to Stockholm Arlanda and
Bromma, respectively.

Boat Stena Line ferries to Gdynia (Poland)
depart from Verkö, 10km east of Karlskrona
(take bus 6).

Bus The bus and train stations are just north
of central Karlskrona. **BlekingeTrafiken**
(☑0455-569 00; www.blekingetrafiken.se)
operates regional buses. Svenska Buss (p426)
runs between Stockholm and Malmö every day
except Saturday, calling at Karlskrona, while
Kustbussen bus 500 serves Kalmar (Skr170, 1½
hours, two to six daily).

Train Destinations include Lund (Skr205, 2½
hours, hourly) and Malmö (Skr205, 2¾ hours,
hourly).

GOTLAND

Gorgeous Gotland has much to brag about:
a Unesco-lauded medieval capital, truffle-
sprinkled woods, A-list dining hot spots, tal-
ented artisans, and more hours of sunshine
than anywhere else in Sweden. It's also one
of the country's richest historical regions,
with around 100 medieval churches and
countless prehistoric sites.

The island is situated nearly halfway
between Sweden and Latvia, in the middle
of the Baltic Sea. Just off its northeast tip
you'll find the island of Fårö, most famous
as the home of Sweden's great director, the
late Ingmar Bergman. The island national
park of Gotska Sandön is located 38km further north, while the petite islets of Stora
Karlsö and Lilla Karlsö sit just off the western coast.

Check out www.gotland.net and www.
guteinfo.com (in Swedish) – both are good
websites for local info. Gotland is primarily
a summer holiday destination, and much of
the island shuts down between September
and May, so plan ahead if you're thinking of
a low-season visit.

❶ Getting There & Away

Air

Visby is served by a number of airlines, including SAS (p479), Malmö Aviation (p479) and
the cheaper local airline, Gotlandsflyg (p479),
with regular flights between Visby and Bromma
airport (one to 10 times daily). Prices start at
around Skr450 one way; book early for discounts.
Popular summer-only routes include Göteborg,
Oslo and Helsinki.

The island's airport is 5km northeast of Visby.
There are several Flygbussarna buses daily
running between the bus station and the airport,
but the schedule is irregular. Your best bet is to
catch a taxi into/from town (around Skr150).

Boat

Year-round car ferries between Visby and both
Nynäshamn and Oskarshamn are operated by
Destination Gotland (☑0771-22 33 00; www.
destinationgotland.se). There are departures to
and from Nynäshamn (one to six daily, 3¼ hours)
and Oskarshamn (one to three daily, three to
four hours). Ferry passengers are allowed two
pieces of luggage, one to check; there are also
lockers in the ferry terminals (small/large per 24
hour Skr50/60).

Prices vary by season, route and departure
time, but adult/student &senior/3-12yr tickets
start from Skr258-391/206-313/52-78. Some
overnight, evening and early-morning sailings in
the middle of the week tend to be cheaper.

Transporting a bicycle costs Skr50; a car
usually costs from Skr350, although again in
the peak summer season a tiered price system
operates. Booking a nonrefundable ticket three
weeks in advance will save you money. If you're
thinking of taking a car on the ferry between
mid-June and mid-August, make sure you reserve a place well in advance.

❶ Getting Around

There are several bike-rental places in Visby,
including Visby Hyrcykel.

Kollektiv Trafiken (☑0498-21 41 12; www.
gotland.se) runs buses via most villages to all
corners of the island. The most useful routes,
which have connections up to seven times daily,
operate between Visby and Burgsvik in the far
south, Visby and Fårösund in the north (also with
bus connections on Fårö), and Visby and Klinte-
hamn. A one-way ticket will not cost you more
than Skr75 (although if you take a bike on board
it will cost an additional Skr45).

Visby

☎ 0498 / POP 22,600

The port town of Visby is medieval eye candy and enough to warrant a trip to Gotland all by itself. Inside its thick city walls await twisting cobbled streets, fairy-tale wooden cottages, evocative ruins and steep hills with impromptu Baltic views. The city wall, with its 40-plus towers and the spectacular church ruins within, at-test to the town's former Hanseatic trading glories.

Visby

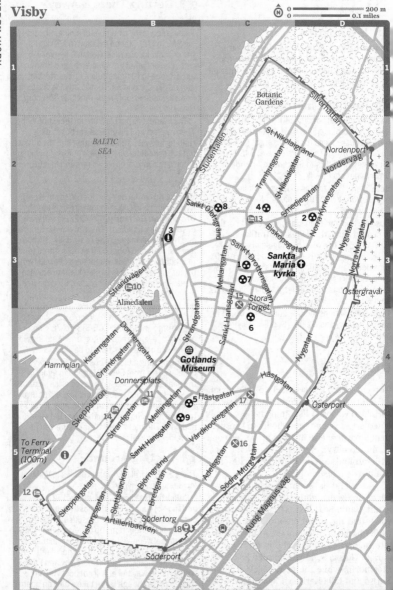

◉ Sights

Gotlands Museum
MUSEUM

(www.gotlandsmuseum.se; Strandgatan 14; adult/child Skr100/80; ⊙10am-6pm; 🖼) Highlights at this superb, beautifully-presented regional museum include a hall of strategically lit, intricately carved 5th to 11th century picture stones and the the legendary Spillings Hoard: at 85kg, it's the world's largest booty of preserved silver treasure, found as recently as 1999. Don't miss the Hall of Prehistoric Graves, either, with its chambered tombs and funeral objects, or the medieval wooden sculptures. The rest of the exhibits take you through the history of Visby, from Viking roots to bustling medieval trade centre to the 1900s. In the museum there's a sandpit with buried treasure for budding archaeologists, while upstairs is the superb Phenomena Science Center Auditorium with plenty of hands-on activities for kids.

Medieval Ruins
RUINS

Visby's 13th-century wall of 40 towers makes for an impressive sight, best explored on a leisurely walk around the perimeter (3.5km). Ask at the tourist office about guided walking tours, conducted in English twice a week in summer (Skr120), or buy a copy of *Visby on Your Own* (Skr35) for a self-guided tour.

Within the town walls are the ruins of 10 **medieval churches**, as well as the stoic **Sankta Maria kyrka** (Cathedral of St Maria; www.visbydf.se; Norra Kyrkogatan 2; ⊙9am-9pm Jul & Aug, to 5pm rest of yr), built in the late 12th and early 13th centuries, with a cosy, candle-lit interior and beautiful stained glass windows, decorated in symmetrical patterns. As the sign says, leave your sword at the door.

🛏 Sleeping

Book accommodation well in advance if possible. Gotland's hotel prices increase on summer weekends and in the peak tourist months.

TOP CHOICE Clarion Hotel Wisby
HOTEL €€€

(☎498-25 75 00; www.clarionwisby.com; Strandgatan 6; s/d from Skr1870/2170; 🅿@🛜🏊) Top of the heap in Visby is the luxurious and landmark Wisby. Medieval vaulted ceilings and look-at-me candelabra contrast with funky contemporary furnishings. The gorgeous pool – complete with medieval pillar – occupies a converted merchant warehouse.

Hotel Stenugnen
HOTEL €€

(☎0498-21 02 11; www.stenungen.nu; Korsgatan 6; r Skr545-899; 🅿🛜🖼) At this adorable little hotel, bright whitewashed rooms are designed to make you feel as if you're sleeping in a yacht and the location is practically on top of the medieval wall. Plenty of rainy day distractions provided for kids and the homemade bread is just delicious.

Hotel St Clemens
HOTEL €€

(☎0498-21 90 00; www.clemenshotell.se; Smedjegatan 3; r from Skr1195-1795, ste from Skr2195; 🅿🛜) In a peaceful location a stone's throw from the Botanical Gardens, this hotel is run by a friendly hunband-and-wife team and comes with its very own church ruins. The rooms – some spartan doubles and their plusher, newer sisters – are scattered throughout several buildings. The iPad in the dining room with links to international newspapers is a nice touch.

SWEDEN VISBY

Visby

Fängelse Vandrarhem · HOSTEL €

(☑0498-20 60 50; www.visbyfangelse.se; Skepps-bron 1; dm/s/d from Skr290/400/500; ☎) As hard to get into as it once was to get out of, this former prison offers compact converted cells to bed down in year-round. There's a cute terrace bar in summer to counterbalance the inconvenience of queuing for the bathroom. Reserve well in advance and don't forget to write down the door code that's emailed to you.

Almedalens Hotell · HOTEL €€€

(☑0498-27 18 66; www.almedalen.com; Strand-vägen 8; s/d from Skr1295/1695; P☎🛜🛗) If you wish to stay practically on the sea, with views of either the medieval wall or the restless waves, then this small hotel, with crisp linens and airy, bright rooms, is the place. The kitchenettes in most rooms are a boon for self-caterers and the proprietor goes out of her way to make you feel welcome.

✖ Eating

There are more restaurants per capita in Visby than in any other Swedish city. Most are clustered around the Old Town squares, on Adelsgatan or at the harbour. Wherever you choose, do not pass up a chance to try the island's speciality – a saffron pancake *(saffranspankaka)* with berries and cream.

Skafferiet · SWEDISH €

(www.skafferietvisby.se; Adelsgatan 38; sandwiches from Skr85; ⏲11am-6pm Mon-Fri, to 4pm Sat, noon-4pm Sun; 🚲) This old-school Swedish cafe, with its low ceilings, stubby candles, rough-hewn wood tables and copper saucepans on the walls, is equally good for lingering over coffee or a quick, convenient lunch of chunky sandwiches and salads. Don't miss

out on the saffron pancakes or the home-made ice cream.

Visby Crêperie & Logi · CREPERIE €

(www.creperielogi.se; Wallérs Plats; crepes Skr45-135; ⏲11am-11pm May-Aug, 11am-2pm & 4-11pm Tue-Sun Sep-Apr; 🚲) The small dining room and balcony at this wonderful spot gets absolutely packed with diners hankering after crepes – crepes with goat's cheese, honey and rocket, with whitefish roe and crème fraiche, with salmon and crayfish, with saffron ice cream... The portions are massive and there's a selection of French ciders to complement your choice. There's a single suite upstairs (Skr2250) if you can't bear to leave.

Bakfickan · SEAFOOD €€

(www.bakfickan-visby.nu; Stora Torget; lunch specials Skr95, mains Skr139-235) White tiled walls, merrily strung lights and boisterous crowds define this foodie-loved hole in the wall, where the menu is succinct but everything perfectly executed. Standout mains include the rich, hearty seafood stew flavoured with saffron and aioli, and grilled cod with chanterelles. Light bites include smoked shrimp, while the chocolate truffle is not to be missed.

☗ Drinking

Tretton Tinnar · PUB

(www.trettontinnar.se; Adelsgatan 2) This pub is used as a venue for live music and events as well as a regular, grungy watering hole. It's built into the town wall and is a good place to check out the vaguely rockish party crowd (as opposed to the shiny-shirts-only party crowd found in most Visby bars). There's an outdoor courtyard in summer.

❶ Information

Tourist office (☑0498-20 17 00; www.gotland.info; Skeppsbron 4-6; ⏲8am-7pm in summer, to 4pm Mon-Fri, 10am-4pm Sat & Sun rest of yr) Friendly, helpful tourist office with plenty of brochures and maps. Arranges tours, including classic tour of Visby (11.30am Wednesday and Saturday July and August; adult/child Skr120/65).

DON'T MISS

MEDIEVAL WEEK

Undoubtedly the most exciting time to be in Visby is during **Medieval Week** (www.medeltidsveckan.se) in early August, when everyone walks around dressed in medieval garb and you see such anachronisms as knights taking money out of an ATM. All week festivities abound, with archery and axe-throwing competitions, live music, a craft market and feasting like in the days of yore. Book way, way ahead.

Around the Island

Renting a bicycle and following the well-marked **Gotlandsleden cycle path** is one of the best ways to spend time on Gotland. It loops all around the island, sometimes joining the roadways but more often winding through quiet fields and forests. You can hire cycles at several locations in Visby. There's an excellent hostel network along the cycle route, with particularly good facilities in Bunge, Lummelunda, Lärbro and the small northern islet of Fårö.

NORRLAND

Norrland, the northern half of Sweden, is remote enough for travellers not to see much of the tour-bus crowd – or, for that matter, much of anyone else. The population is sparse – reindeer outnumber cars on the roads, and much of the landscape consists of deep-green forest. It's a paradise for nature lovers who enjoy hiking, skiing and other outdoor activities; in winter in particular, the landscape is transformed by snowmobiles, dog sleds and eerie natural phenomena – the aurora borealis. The north is home to the Sámi people, and it's possible to take part in traditional Sámi pastimes, such as reindeer herding.

Norrland also boasts a rarely glimpsed monster lurking in a lake and a disappearing hotel made of ice. Inlandsbanan, the historic railway line from Mora to Gällivare via Östersund, Arvidsjaur and Jokkmokk, is a fun if not particularly fast way to see the north in summertime.

Sundsvall

🖉 060 / POP 50,700

When Sundsvall burned to the ground in 1888, a decision was made to adopt the dragon as the town's symbol in a bid to fight fire with fire. Just in case, though, the old wooden houses were rebuilt in stone, separated by wide avenues, making the other towns along the Bothnian coast look like country bumpkins by comparison. You'll find brightly painted dragons all over the city centre, each annually decorated by a local artist.

Housed inside the **Kulturmagasinet**, a beautifully-restored old warehouse, the **Sundsvall Museum** (www.sundsvall.se/museum; Sjögatan, Kulturmagasinet; ☺10am-7pm Mon-Thu, to 6pm Fri, 11am-4pm Sat & Sun) has engaging exhibits of the history of Sundsvall, natural history and geology. There's a permanent art display upstairs featuring 20th century Swedish artists, while superb temporary exhibitions have recently included Edward C Curtis's early 20th century photography of Native Americans.

A great budget spot nearby is the **Sundsvall City Hostel** (🖉060-12 60 90; www.sundsvallcityhostel.se; Sjögatan 11; hostel dm/s/d Skr220/400/500, hotel s/d Skr500/595; 🛜), with bright, en-suite rooms and dorms, sauna and large guest kitchen. But if you're looking for opulence and old-world charm, then **Elite Hotel Knaust** (🖉060-608 0000; www.elite.se; Storgatan 13; r/ste from Skr1050/2250; 🅿🛜), with its high ceilings, classical decor and superb breakfast buffet may be more your style.

Head to the adorable organic cafe **Tant Anci & Fröcken Sara** (Bankgatan 15; mains Skr89-110; ☺10am-10pm Mon-Fri, 11am-10pm Sat, noon-6pm Sun; 🍴) for hearty sandwiches, giant bowls of pasta, soup and pastries, or else to **Casiopeija** (🖉060-14 11 50; www.casino-cosmopol.se; Parkhusplatsen 7, inside Casino Cosmopol; mains Skr185-315, 5-course tasting menu Skr795; ☺6-11.30pm Mon-Sat), inside the Casino Cosmopol, for high-end Swedish cuisine, such as reindeer steak with chanterelles and walleye with crayfish.

The helpful **tourist office** (🖉060-658 5800; www.visitsundsvall.se; Stora Torget; ☺10am-7pm Mon-Fri, 10am-4pm Sat, noon-4pm Jun-Aug) has information on attractions in the area.

❶ Getting There & Away

Air From **Midlanda airport** (🖉010 109 6000; www.swedavia.se), 22km north of Sundsvall, SAS flies to Stockholm, while Malmö Aviation serves Stockholm and Visby and Direktflyg serves Göteborg and Luleå. **Airport bus** (🖉060 207 63; www.torpshammarsbuss.se) runs at least four times daily.

Bus Buses depart from the Sundsvall bus station, near Kulturmagasinet. **Ybuss** (🖉060-17 19 60; www.ybuss.se) runs to Östersund (Sk215, 2½ hours, twice daily) and Stockholm (Skr300, six hours, four to five daily). Länstrafiken Västerbotten bus 100 runs twice daily to Umeå (Skr310, 5¾ hours), where you can find connections to Luleå and beyond.

Train SJ trains run west to Östersund (Skr301, 2¾ hours, daily) and south to Stockholm (from Skr373, 3¼ hours to 4¾ hours, up to 11 daily). The station is just east of the town centre on Köpmangatan.

Höga Kusten

🖉0613

Cross the 1867m Höga Kustenbron – Norrland's answer to the Golden Gate Bridge – and you find yourself amidst some of the most dramatic scenery on the Swedish

THE HIGH COAST TRAIL

Starting at the northern end of the Höga Kustenbron and finishing at the summit of the hill overlooking Örnsköldsvik, the 129km-long Höga Kustenleden (High Coast Trail) spans the entire length of the Höga Kusten. The trail is divided into 13 sections, each between 15km and 24km in length, with accommodation at the end of each section consisting mostly of rustic cabins.

Parts of the trail involve an easy ramble, whereas other sections will challenge you with steep, uneven ground. Take food and plenty of drinking water with you.

The trail takes in some of the most beautiful coastal scenery in Sweden – from cliffs and sandy coves to lush countryside, dense evergreen forest, and the Slåtterdalskrevan, a 200m-deep canyon. The forest is home to lynx, roe deer and mink, as well as all four of Sweden's game birds: the black grouse, willow grouse, capercallie and hazel hen.

Recommended detours include Mount Skuleberget, north of Docksta and towards Norrgällsta (1.4km) – you can either hike up Mt Skuleberget or take a cable car (open 10am to 5pm June to August; Skr90) to the top; Dalsjöfallet (1.5km), a waterfall that lies halfway between Skuleberget and Gyltberget mountains, and crystal-clear Lake Balestjärn in the middle of the small peninsula to the north of Köpmanholmen.

The trail is well-signposted but it is best to pick up a detailed booklet and map beforehand.

Buses running along the E4 stop at either end of the trail, as well as at several villages along that way that are close to different sections of the trail.

coastline. The secret to the rugged beauty of the Höga Kusten (High Coast) is elevation; nowhere else on the coast do you find such a mountainous landscape, with sheer rocky cliffs plunging straight down to the sea, as well as lakes, fjords, and dozens of tranquil islands covered in dense pine forest. The region, recognised as geographically unique, was recently listed as a Unesco World Heritage area.

It's a real delight to drive the scenic, winding roads between the minute fishing villages and even more rewarding to stay on the tiny islands of Högbonden, Ulvön and Trysunda, or to walking the 129km Höga Kustenleden (High Coast Trail), a hiking trail that spans the coast.

THE ISLANDS

Högbonden is a tiny island in the southern part of Höga Kusten, only fifteen minutes by boat from Bönhamn or Barsta villages. It's famous for its 100-year-old lighthouse atop the forested island's rocky plateau. It's an easy day trip, but it's best to stay overnight at the simple **Vandrarhem Högbonden** (☎0613-230 05; www.hogbonden.se; dm Skr300-350; ☺May-Oct). The main attractions here are sunset watching or diving off the jetty and relaxing in the wood-burning sauna by the sea. Book well in advance.

Ulvön is the largest island in the Höga Kusten archipelago, famous for its regatta

(14 to 18 July) and for the production of *surströmming* – utterly noxious (or delightful, depending on your perspective) fermented herring, traditionally eaten in August. It's possible to do a day trip to Ulvöhamn, the island's one-street village with a tiny 17th-century chapel decorated with colourful murals inside. The restaurant at the **Ulvö Hotell** (☎0660-22 40 09; www.ulvohotell.se; mains Skr195-345; ☜) by the quay offers a superb seasonal menu featuring local ingredients.

Trysunda is a small island with cute fishermen's houses clustered around a little U-shaped bay. There are also some great secluded spots for bathing, reachable by the walking paths through the woods. You can walk around the whole of Trysunda in an hour or two.

ℹ Information

Naturum (☎0613-700 200; www.naturumhogakusten.se; ☺9am-7pm late Jun-mid-Aug), by the E4 north of the village of Docksta, has exhibitions and lots of information on hiking routes along the coast and around Skuleberget (285m), the looming mountain.

The regional **tourist office** (☎0613-504 80; www.hogakusten.com; ☺10am-6pm Jun-Aug) located inside Hotell Höga Kusten, just north of the suspension bridge, is open year-round and has a detailed map of the scenic byways, boat timetables and more.

❶ Getting There & Around

This area is virtually impossible to explore without your own set of wheels, though you can reach most boat departure points by public transport.

Bus

Frequent Länstrafiken Västerbotten buses 10 and 100 run along the E4, stopping at Docksta, while bus 421 runs to Köpmanholmen (up to 11 daily) from Örnsköldsvik. Bönhamn and Barsta are not reachable by public transport.

Boat

M/S Ronja (www.hkship.se) ferries to Högbonden run from Barsta only mid-May to mid-June and mid-August to October (noon Friday to Sunday), and from both Barsta and Bönhamn in peak summer (mid-June to mid-August) four times daily.

M/S Kusttrafik ferry (☑0613-105 50; www.hkship.se) to Ulvön leaves from Docksta daily at 9.30am, returning at 3pm between June and August.

MF Ulvön (☑070 651 92 65; www.ornskolvik-shamn.se; a; ☉mid-Jun–mid-Aug) ferry leaves Köpmanholmen for Ulvön four times daily, and twice daily for Trysunda.

Östersund

☑063 / POP 44,300

This pleasant town by Lake Storsjön, in whose chilly waters is said to lurk Sweden's answer to the Loch Ness monster, is an excellent gateway town for further explorations of Norrland.

⊙ Sights & Activities

Östersund is a major winter sports centre. You can also ask at the tourist office about monster-spotting **lake cruises** (adult/child Skr100/45; ☉Jun-Sep). Bring your binoculars.

Jamtli   MUSEUM

(www.jamtli.com; adult/under 18yr mid-Jun–Aug Skr240/free, rest of yr Skr60/free; ☉11am-5pm Tue-Sun mid-Aug–late Jun, 11am-5pm daily late Jun–mid-Aug; ⊞) Ultra-popular Jamtli combines an open-air museum park with a first-rate regional culture museum. In the outdoor section, guides in period costume encourage visitor participation in milking, baking, grass cutting and more amidst painstakingly reconstructed wooden buildings – bakery, smithy, woodman's cottage and 18th-century farm. Indoors, the regional museum exhibits the **Överhogdal tapestry**, a Viking relic from around 1100 – one of the

oldest of its kind in Europe. Monster spotters can check out the display devoted to the creature; those with a taste for the macabre will appreciate the pickled monster embryo.

Frösön   ISLAND

(viewing tower adult/child Skr10/5; ☉viewing tower 9am-9pm mid-Jun–mid-Aug) Just across the footbridge on Frösön island is Sweden's northernmost rune stone, which commemorates the arrival of 'East Man', the first Christian missionary, in 1050. A good place to keep the kids entertained is the 17-hectare, family-owned **Frösön Zoo** (www.frosozoo.se; adult/child Skr200/100; ☉10am-4pm mid-Jun–mid-Aug, to 6pm Jul), which specialises in exotic animals. Also on the island is the late-12th-century **Frösöns Kyrka** (☉8am-8pm summer, Mon-Fri rest of year; ⊞3), with its distinctive bell tower, built on a sacrificial site to the ancient gods (*æsir*). Catch buses 5 and 3, respectively.

🛏 Sleeping & Eating

Hotel Jämteborg   HOTEL €

(☑063-51 01 01; www.jamteborg.se; Storgatan 54; hostel d/tr Skr590/840, B&B s/d/tr Skr490/690/890, hotel s/d from Skr995/1190; ▣☎) Accommodation in just about every possible form – hostel beds, B&B or hotel – in several centrally located buildings. The hotel section has cheerful rooms in bright colours; all hotel rooms include private bathrooms and breakfast. Rooms across the street in Pensionat Svea have shared shower and bath but include breakfast; the summer-only hostel rooms don't include breakfast.

Hotel Emma   HOTEL €€

(☑063-51 78 40; www.hotelemma.com; Prästgatan 31; s/d Skr940/1095; ▣@☎) Emma is on the main pedestrian shopping street, right above a whisky bar, with all the comforts of

---

STORSJÖODJURET – THE LAKE MONSTER

Just imagine...you're sitting by Lake Storsjön at dusk when you notice a dark shadow rise out of the water. Could it be the head of **Storsjöodjuret** (ww.storsjoodjuret.com) – the lake monster that dwells somewhere in the 91m depths? There are new sightings every summer, and the lake monster has had such a grip on the public imagination that in 1894, an (unsuccessful) hunt for it was organised by King Oscar II.

a fancy chain but with personality: its rooms are nestled into crooked passages on two floors, with homey touches such as squishy armchairs and imposing ceramic stoves; some rooms have French doors facing the courtyard and buttery wood floors. Parking costs Skr60.

TOP CHOICE Innefickan
FUSION €€€

(☎063-12 90 99; www.innefickan.se; Postgränd 11; mains Skr198-289) Funky cellar setting brightened up by modern art pieces and a succinct, inspired menu. You can't go wrong with the 'Thai-style' veal carpaccio or mains such as slow-cooked lamb with polenta and grilled Arctic char. Add a divine truffle to finish.

Brunkullans Krog
SWEDISH €€

(www.brunkullanskrog.se; Postgränd 5; mains Skr139-259; ⊘from 5pm Wed-Sat) A local favourite for its outdoor patio, Brunkullans also has a wonderfully atmospheric, candle-lit 19th-century interior space. The menu features Swedish classics (meatballs, steak) and upmarket versions of basic bar food, such as a decadent bacon-cheeseburger.

ⓘ Information

Tourist Office (☎063-14 40 01; www.visitostersund.se; Rådhusgatan 44; ⊘9am-5pm Mon-Fri) Opposite the town hall; has free internet access.

ⓘ Getting There & Away

The **airport** (☎063-19 30 00; www.swedavia. com) is on Frösön, 11km west of the town centre; the **airport bus** (www.stadsbussarna.se) leaves regularly from the bus terminal (adult/child Skr75/38). SAS serves Stockholm, Göteborg and Malmö, while Direktflyg (p426) flies to Luleå and Umeå.

Länstrafiken (www.ltnbd.se) bus 45 runs south to Mora (5½ hours, two to four daily) and north to Gällivare (Skr507, 11 hours, daily), stopping in all major towns on the way, while bus 155 runs west to Åre (1½ hours, daily).

Three SJ trains (including an overnighter) run from Stockholm (from Skr483, five to 7¾ hours) via Uppsala, and one continues to Åre, (Skr211, 1½ hours) from where you can carry on to Trondheim, Norway. In summer the Inlandsbanan (p481) train runs once daily, north to Gällivare (Skr1116, 14½ hours) via Arvidsjaur and Jokkmokk, and south to Mora (Skr482, five hours).

Åre

☑0647 / POP 10,200

Beautifully situated in a mountain valley by the shores of Åresjön, Åre is Sweden's most popular skiing resort (www.skistar.com/are) and a party town during the November to mid-May season. In winter, you can also engage in heli-skiing, kite-boarding, snowferring (snow and ice sailing) and other variations on regular skiing and snowboarding.

In July Åre hosts the **Åre Bike Festival** and the hardcore **Åre Extreme Challenge**, with zorbing, mountain boarding, hillcarting, hiking, rafting and paragliding also on the menu, with spa treatments available to those worn out by all the sporty stuff. With all the outdoor adventures, it's a wonder the place hasn't yet become backpacker central.

◉ Sights & Activities

Åre Bike Park
MOUNTAIN BIKING

(www.arebikepark.com) In summer, the slopes of Mt Åreskutan become an enormous bike playground, with more than 30 trails spanning over 40km of track, ranging from beginner to extreme. The Kabinbanan cable car, the Bergbanan funicular, and the VM6:an and Hummelliften chairlifts are fitted with bike racks to help you up the mountain. You can rent bikes and safety equipment at **Åre Bikes** (☎0647-500 96; www.aremtb.se; Årevägen 138).

Kabinbana
CABLE CAR, VIEWPOINT

(adult/child Skr130/100; ⊘10am-4pm daily late Jun–late Sep) Taking you almost to the top of Mt Åreskutan, the only cable car in Sweden gives you awesome views of the surrounding area. It departs from behind Åre's main square and goes up to a viewing platform (1274m) – the starting point for hiking and biking tracks.

🛏 Sleeping & Eating

Accommodation fills up quickly in winter and not all hotels stay open in summer.

STF Vandrarhem Åre
HOSTEL €

(☎0647-301 38; www.brattlandsgarden.se; dm Skr200, s/d from Skr300/400; P) A lovely spot on an old farmstead, run by a warm, helpful family. Rooms are tucked into red wooden buildings and there's a huge combined living room and dining area and a large, well-equipped kitchen. The hostel is 6km east of Åre, in Brattland; a daily bus connects it to town, although service is spotty.

Tott Hotel   HOTEL €€€
(📞0647-150 00; www.tottare.com; Tott vägen 111; d/ste from Skr1759/4440; P🐕🛜🏊) High enough up the slope to give you a grand view of the town below, but not so high that you need a chairlift to get there, Tott is all modern efficiency, with spacious rooms in neutral shades, and a pool and luxurious spa.

TOP
CHOICE **Åre Bageri**   BAKERY €€
(www.arebageri.se; Årevägen 55; breakfast buffet Skr115; ⊙7am-4pm; 🖋) A sprawling organic cafe and stone-oven bakery with a comfy atmosphere, this place lends itself to lingering. In addition to great coffee, pastries and huge sandwiches, it does a fairly epic all-you-can-eat breakfast spread. More substantial Mediterranean-style buffet lunch, too.

Broken   AMERICAN €€
(www.broken-are.com; Torggränd 4; mains Skr115-194) Just off the main square, this American-style diner dishes up what every hungry hiker/biker/boarder secretly craves: philly cheese steak, mega fajitas, ribs and jumbo hamburgers, followed by banana splits and washed down with frozen margaritas.

ⓘ Information

The **tourist office** (📞0647-163 21; www.visitare. se; ⊙10am-6pm Mon-Fri, 10am-3pm Sat & Sun), at the library inside the train station complex, has free internet access. The same building contains luggage lockers (small/large per day Skr40/80), a sporting-goods store and an ICA supermarket.

ⓘ Getting There & Away

Bus 155 runs east to Östersund (Skr142, 1½ hours, one or two daily).

Åre has east-bound trains for Östersund (from Skr86, 1½ hours, up to six daily) and Stockholm (from Skr399, 7½ to 9½ hours, two or three daily), and west-bound services to Trondheim, Norway (from Skr89, 2½ hours, two daily).

Umeå

🔵090 / POP 79,600

With the vibrant feel of a college town (it has around 30,000 students), Umeå is an agreeable place to hang out, wind down or stock up for an outdoor adventure.

The town's main attraction is **Gammlia** (www.vsb.se; 10am-5pm mid-Jun–mid-Aug; ♿), an entertaining cluster of museums, the centrepiece of which is the excellent **Västerbottens Museum**, which traces the history of the province from prehistoric times to Umeå today, its exhibitions including photographs of the Sámi and an absolutely enormous historica collection of skis (including the world's oldest ski – 5200 years old!). **Bildmuséet**, the modern art space, features striking photography, installations and more. These are surrounded by the **Friluftsmuséet**, an open-air historic village where staff in period garb demonstrate traditional homestead life. It takes around 20 minutes to walk to Gammlia; or else you can take buses 2 or 7.

Stay at the friendly, centrally located **STF Vandrarhem Umeå** (📞090-77 16 50; www. umeavandrarhem.com; Västra Esplanaden 10; dm/s/d from Skr170/300/360; @), and try to nab a space in one of the newer rooms with beds rather than bunks, or else opt for the more upmarket **Hotel Pilen** (📞090-16 16 16; www. hotellpilen.se; Pilgatan 5; s/d/tr Skr775/975/1125; P🐕🛜🏊) by the river, with the added perks of pool and sauna.

Several boat restaurants moored on the river by the main square serve fresh herring and the like in summer. Otherwise, **Rex Bar och Grill** (📞090-70 60 50; www.rexbar.com; Rådhustorget; mains Skr180-320) is the place for a happy marriage of Northern Swedish and French brasserie dishes, as well as American-style weekend brunch, while the **Allstar** (www.allstarbar.se; Kungsgatan 50A; mains Skr100-185; ⊙3-11pm Mon-Thu, noon-2am Fri & Sat, 2-10pm Sun) sports bar is your one-stop shop for quesadillas, nachos and all that jazz.

The **tourist office** (📞090-16 16 16; www.visit umea.se; Renmarkstorget 15; ⊙9am-7pm Mon-Fri, 10am-4pm Sat, noon-4pm Sun Jun–mid-Aug) has plenty of info on attractions in and around town.

ⓘ Getting There & Away

Air The **airport** (📞010 109 5000; www.swedavia.com) is 4km south of the city centre. SAS flies to Stockholm and Kiruna, Malmö Aviation to Göteborg and Stockholm and Direktflyg to Luleå and Östersund.

Boat RG Line (www.rgline.com) operates ferries between Umeå and Vaasa (Finland) once or twice daily (Sunday to Friday).

Bus Ybuss (p455) runs twice-daily services south to Stockholm (Skr430, 9½ to 10 hours), via Sundsvall (Skr257, 3¾ hours), while **Länstrafiken i Västerbotten** (📞077-10 01 10; www.tabussen.nu) destinations include Luleå (Skr310, four to five hours, up to nine daily).

Train Two SJ trains leave daily for Stockholm (from Skr450, 6½ to nine hours), while the

DON'T MISS

LULEÅ ARCHIPELAGO

This extensive archipelago consists of some 1700 islands, most of them uninhabited and therefore perfect for skinny dipping, berry picking, camping wild…we can go on! The larger islands are accessible by boat from Luleå in summer (ask the tourist office in Luleå for updated boat schedules); for the rest you'll need your own. In winter, the archipelago becomes a different kind of playground, with snowmobiling, skating, ice sailing, kiting and ice fishing all on the menu.

Here's a brief guide to the bigger islands:

Sandön The largest island, with an attractive beach in Klubbviken bay.

Junkön Famous for its 16th century windmill.

Rödkallen Numerous seabird species and an 1872 lighthouse.

Kluntarna All-rounder, with holiday cottages, pine forest, seabird colonies and fishing villages.

Småskär Rocky, semi-wild bird sanctuary with a few secluded cottages.

Brändöskär Bleakly beautiful, wind-lashed dot in the outermost archipelago.

north-bound trains run to Luleå (Skr286, 4½ hours, daily) from where there are connections to Kiruna and Narvik, Norway.

Luleå

☎0920 / POP 46,600

Pretty Luleå is a pedestrian-friendly university town with several parks and a sparkling bay with a marina. The capital of Norrboten, Luleå moved to its present location from Gammelstad in 1649 because of the falling sea level (8mm per year), due to postglacial uplift of the land.

However, **Gammelstad** (☎0920-45 70 10; www.lulea.se/gammelstad; admission free; ⏰24hr) remains its biggest attraction: this Unesco World Heritage–listed smattering of little red Swedish cottages with the white trim and lace curtains was the medieval centre of northern Sweden. The stone church (from 1492), 424 wooden houses (where the pioneers stayed overnight on their weekend pilgrimages) and six church stables remain. Many of the buildings are still in use, but some are open to the public and the site is lovely to walk around. Contact the Gammelstad visitor centre about guided tours (Skr35) that leave hourly from mid-June to mid-August.

Norrbottens Museum (www.norrbottensmuseum.nu; Storgatan 2; admission free; ⏰10am-4pm Mon-Fri, noon-4pm Sat & Sun Jun-Aug; 👪) is worth a visit just for the collection of photos, tools, dioramas depicting traditional reindeer-herding Sámi life, and the 19th-century playrooms for kiddies. For something more hands-on, head out to the **Teknikens Hus** (www.teknikenshus.se; adult/under 4 yr Skr70/free; ⏰10am-4pm daily mid-Jun–Aug, Tue-Sun rest of year; 👪; 🚌4, 5) where interactive displays let you fly a rocket, sit in a helicopter, attend a simulated mine explosion and learn about the aurora borealis (Northern Lights). It's on the university campus, 4km north of Centrum.

Sleeping & Eating

SVIF Vandrarhem Kronan/Luleå HOSTEL €
(☎0920-43 40 50; www.vandrarhemmetkronan.se; Kronan H7; dm/s/d/tr Skr175/270/390/560; P@Wi-Fi) About 3km from the centre, this year-round hostel is the best budget option in the area, with good facilities set in a forested location. To get here, take any bus heading towards Kronanområdet.

Hotell Aveny HOTEL €€
(☎0920-22 18 20; www.hotellaveny.com; Hermelinsgatan 10; s/d Skr790/970; P Wi-Fi) This homey hotel has individually designed rooms, decorated in soft pastel shades and, true to its name, corridors decorated to look like avenues and shopping streets. There's a sauna to chill out in and an extensive breakfast buffet.

Cook's Krog SWEDISH €€€
(☎0920-20 10 25; www.cookskrog.se; Storgatan 17; mains Skr192-315, 5-course taster menu Srk695) This is Luleå's top spot for reindeer and other Northern Swedish specialities. Treat yourself to the exquisite five-course menu

which includes whitefish, grilled reindeer steak and cloudberries with ice cream.

Baan Thai THAI €€
(Kungsgatan 22; mains Skr130-240; 🍴) Authentic Thai dishes. The curries and *chu chi pla* (deep fried fish) are particularly good here but ask the staff to spice it up if you want the true Thai fire.

ℹ️ Information

Tourist office (☎0920-45 70 00; www. visitlulea.se; Skeppsbrogatan 17; ⏰10am-7pm Mon-Fri, 10am-4pm Sat & Sun) Inside Kulturens Hus.

ℹ️ Getting There & Around

Air From the **airport** (☎010 109 4800; www. swedavia.se), 9km southwest of town, SAS flies regularly to Stockholm, while Direktflyg serves Kiruna, Sundsvall and Umeå. Bus 230 runs to the airport from the bus station.

Bus Buses 20 and 100 run north to Haparanda (Skr163, 2¼ to 2¾ hours, up to six daily) and south to Umeå (Skr310, four to 4½ hours, up to nine daily). Buses 44 and 10 connect Luleå with Lapland destinations such as Jokkmokk (Skr217, three hours, four daily) and Gällivare (Skr285, 3½ to 4½ hours, four daily).

Train There are two overnight trains to Stockholm (from Skr307, 13 to 14 hours) via Uppsala (from Skr307, 12 to 13 hours), as well as trains bound for Narvik, Norway (Skr482, eight hours, two daily) via Kiruna (Skr354, 4½ hours) and Abisko (Skr463, 6¼ hours).

Haparanda

☎092 / POP 10,100

Haparanda was founded in 1821 to compensate the loss of Finland's Tornio to Russia in 1809. Haparanda and Tornio are now a single Eurocity, separated by a river and with the two halves within easy walking distance of each other. But while Tornio has the art galleries and the vibrant nightlife, what does Haparanda have? The world's largest IKEA. Unless you're on the hunt for flat-packed furniture, you're only likely to be passing through en route to or from Finland.

If you have to stay overnight, try **Svefi Hotel & Vandrarhem** (☎0922-688 00; www. swefi.net; Torget 3; hostel s/d Skr400/550, hotel from Skr500/700; ⏰reception 8am-5pm Mon-Fri, 1-5pm Sat & Sun; 🅿️🛜), with its super-central location on the main square, modern rooms with bright, bold furnishings, and a simple canteen-style restaurant. You'll find a few eateries scattered around Torget, the main square, and there's a good canteen inside IKEA.

WORTH A TRIP

VILDMARKSVÄGEN – THE WILDERNESS ROAD

Branching off Route 45 at Strömsund (located between Ostersund and Arvidsjaur) is one of the most spectacular drives in Sweden. Route 342, known as the **Wilderness Road** (www.wildernessroad.eu), stretches for around 500km, first running northwest towards the mountains before skirting the Norwegian border and then joining the E45 3km north of Vilhelmina. The first section runs through dense evergreen forest, punctuated by numerous lakes – perfect for skinny dipping, since you're unlikely to encounter anyone else. The surrounding forest is also home to elk, lynx, wolverine, fox and Sweden's highest population of bears, so if you're lucky (or unlucky!) you may well spot one.

Just left of Bågede, a rocky track leads towards the impressive 43m-high Hällsingsåfallet, a waterfall that tumbles into an 800m-long canyon.

Beyond Stora Blåsjon lake, Route 345 climbs up onto the enormous, desolate Stekkenjokk plateau dotted with stone cairns before descending to the tiny village of Klimpfjäll (this stretch of road is closed October to early June); 13km east, a turnoff leads to the late-18th-century Sámi church village at **Fatmomakke** (www.fatmomakke. se) where you find traditional Sámi *kota* and log cabins.

About 20km further east, you reach the fishing paradise of Saxnäs. **Saxnäsgården** (☎940-37 700; www.saxnas.se; hostel s/d Skr400/550, hotel s/d Skr850/1100, 5-person cabin Skr950; 🅿️🛜🏊) hotel is a great base for all sorts of outdoor adventures – from heli-skiing, snow-mobile safaris and dog sledding in winter to guided hikes, tours of Fatmo-makke, boating and fishing in summer; there's a good restaurant to boot.

Allow a full day for driving the Vildmarksvägen and fill up on petrol, as the only petrol station is in Gäddede, halfway along.

WORTH A TRIP

THE SILVER AND THE SÁMI

Tiny Arjeplog, 85km northwest of Arvidsjaur, is well worth a detour for two big reasons: silver and Sámi culture. The tour de force of the wonderful **Silver Museum** (Silvermuseet; www.silvermuseet.se; Torget, Arjeplog; adult/under 16 yr Skr60/free; ☉9am-6pm mid-Jun–mid-Aug) is the vast collection of Sámi silver objects – the most extensive of its kind – including belt buckles, ornate spoons and goblets and collars that would traditionally have been passed down from mother to daughter. Linger in the basement cinema to catch the engaging slideshow and voiceover describing life in Arjeplog.

If you want to learn more about reindeer herding and Sámi livelihood, watch reindeer being lassoed, stay in a Sámi *kota* (traditional Forest Sámi dwelling) and have your dinner cooked over a campfire, take the road running immediately south of Arjeplog or else the E45 west of Arvidsjaur for 50km and turn north at the village of Slagnäs; the **Båtsuoj Sámi Camp** (☎0960 651 026; www.batsuoj.se; short tour/long tour/overnight stay Skr220/600/1100) is signposted near the village of Gasa.

The main **tourist office** (☎in Finland 050-590 0562, in Sweden 0922-120 10; www.haparandatornio.com; Pakkahuoneenkatu 1; ☉9am-7pm Mon-Fri, 10am-6pm Sat & Sun Jun-early Aug) in Haparanda is shared with the office in Tornio (in Finland) on the 'green line'.

Tapanis Buss (☎0922-129 5508; www.tapanis.se) runs express coaches from Stockholm to Haparanda two to three times a week (Skr600, 15 hours) as well as daily buses over the border to Tornio (Skr20, 10 minutes). Buses 20 and 100 run between Haparanda and Luleå (Skr163, 2½ to three hours, up to 11 daily) with connections to coastal towns further south and Lapland.

Arvidsjaur
☎0960 / POP 4640

If you've dreamed of taking a Porsche for a spin on ice, or flying through the snowy wilderness on a snowmobile or dog sled, here's your chance. The small settlement of Arvidsjaur was established as a Sámi marketplace, but it's most famous now as a centre for winter activities – most notably, for professional drivers putting fast cars through their paces on nearby frozen lakes.

The first church was built in Arvidsjaur in 1607, in hopes of introducing the Sámi to Christianity. Church attendance laws imposed a certain amount of pew time upon the nomadic Sámi, so to give them a place to rest their weary heads after travelling from afar, they built small cottages, or *gåhties*. Some 80 of these are preserved now in **Lappstaden** (Storgatan; tours Skr50; ☉10am-7pm, tours 6pm Jun-Aug) – the biggest Sámi church town in Sweden – and are still in use.

In winter, **Nymånen** (☎070 625 40 32; www.nymanen.com) organise dog sledding trips in the area, while **Super Safari** (☎0960-104 57; www.supersafari.info; 2-/4-hour tours from Skr700/950) takes visitors out on guided snowmobile tours; you can choose to share or drive your own. Consult the helpful **tourist office** (☎0960-175 00; www.polcirkeln.nu; Östra Skolgatan 18C; ☉9.30am-6pm Mon-Fri, noon-4.30 Sat & Sun Jun-Aug) if you wish to learn to drive on ice.

Friendly accommodation and good pub grub can be found at **Hotell Laponia** (☎0960-555 00; www.hotell-laponia.se; Storgatan 45; P ☎), where you're likely to rub shoulders with professional test drivers in winter, or at the **Silver Cross 45** (☎070 644 2862; www.silvercross45.se; Villavägen 56; s/d/f Skr250/400/700; P ☎ ☎) hostel, with compact wood-panelled rooms and shared facilities (including kitchenette). Storgatan is lined with eateries.

Arvidsjaur airport (☎0960-173 80; www.ajr.nu), 11km from town, has daily links to Stockholm Arlanda with NextJet (p446). From the bus station on Storgatan Länstrafiken (p458) bus 45 runs north to Gällivare (Skr285, four to six hours, one or two daily) and south to Östersund (Skr440, 7¼ hours, one or two daily). In summer the Inlandsbanan (p481) train can take you north to Gällivare (Skr408, six hours) via Jokkmokk (Skr259, three hours), or south to Östersund (Skr708, 8¾ hours).

Jokkmokk
☎0971 / POP 2790

The capital of Sámi culture, and the biggest handicraft centre in Lappland, Jokkmokk has not only the definitive Sámi museum but it's the only town in Sweden which has a further education college that teaches reindeer husbandry, craft-making and ecology using the Sámi language. Jokkmokk is the jumping-off point for visiting the four nearby national parks which are part of the **Laponia World Heritage site** (www.laponia. nu) and it makes a great base for all manner of outdoor adventures year-round.

The illuminating **Ájtte Museum** (www. ajtte.com; Kyrkogatan 3; adult/child Skr70/35; ☺9am-6pm mid-Jun–mid-Aug, 10am-4pm Tue-Fri & 10am-2pm Sat & Sun rest of yr) is Sweden's most thorough introduction to different aspects of Sámi culture – from colourful traditional costume, crafts, silverware and 400-year-old magical painted shamans' drums to Sámi creation myths, traditional everyday life, replicas of sacrificial sites and a diagram explaining the uses and significance of various reindeer entrails. One section details the widespread practice of harnessing the rivers in Lappland for hydroelectric power and the consequences this has had for the Sámi people and their territory. The beautifully showcased collection of traditional silver jewellery features collars which are now making a comeback among the Sámi after a long absence.

If you're then inspired to obtain some beautiful Sámi handiwork for yourself, **Sami Duodji** (www.sameslodjstiftelsen.se; Porjusvägen 4; ☺10am-5pm Mon-Fri) offers an excellent selection of silver jewellery, woodwork, leatherwork, knives and more.

🛏 Sleeping & Eating

Book your accommodation months in advance for the **Jokkmokk Winter Festival**.

STF Vandrarhem Åsgård HOSTEL €
(☎0971-55 977; www.jokkmokkhostel.com; Åsgatan 20; dm/s/d from Skr130/320/380; ☺reception 8-10am & 5-8.30pm summer, 5-7pm rest of yr; @☞✈) This family-run STF hostel, popular with Inlandsbanan travellers, has a lovely setting among green lawns and trees, right near the tourist office. It's a quiet, comfortable place with simple rooms, a kitchen, a TV lounge and basement sauna (per person Skr20).

Hotel Jokkmokk HOTEL €€
(www.hoteljokkmokk.se; Solgatan 45; s/d Skr890/1095; P☞) Overlooking picturesque Lake Talvatis, Jokkmokk's nicest hotel features cosy rooms, a sauna in the basement

and another by the lake (for that refreshing hole-in-the-ice dip in winter). The large restaurant, shaped like a Sámi *kota,* appropriately serves the likes of elk fillet and smoked reindeer with juniper berry sauce. There's a great sculpture trail along the lake.

TOP CHOICE **Ájtte Museum Restaurant** SÁMI €€
(mains Skr90-130; ☺noon-4pm) This fine Sámi restaurant inside the museum makes it possible to enhance what you've learned about the local wildlife by sampling some of them – from *suovas* (smoked and salted reindeer meat) to grouse with local berries. The weekday lunchtime buffet serves home-style Swedish dishes.

Restaurang Thai Maung Isaan THAI €
(Porjusvägen 4 ; mains from Skr65; ✈) In a handy location just off the main street, this cheerful cheapie serves large portions of authentic Thai dishes – from noodles, stir fries and curries. If you want the authentic spice levels, request it when ordering.

❶ Information

Tourist office (☎0971-222 50; www.turism. jokkmokk.se; Stortorget 4; ☺9am-7pm Mon-Fri, 10am-6pm Sat & Sun mid-Jun–Aug) Plenty of info on the area, including winter activities, such as dog sledding.

DON'T MISS

JOKKMOKK WINTER MARKET

One of the biggest highlights of travelling in Lappland in winter is Jokkmokk's annual **Winter Market** (www.jokkmokksmarknad.com), attracting some 30,000 people annually. It's the biggest sales opportunity of the year for Sámi traders who come to see old friends, while the visitors can splurge on the widest array of Sámi *duodji* (handicraft) in the country. The Winter Market itself is held on the first Thursday through Saturday in February and is preceded by several days of folk music, plays, parades, local cinematography, photography exhibitions, food tasting sessions and talks on different aspects of Sámi life. Highlights include the merry chaos of the reindeer races on the frozen Lake Talvatissjön behind Hotell Jokkmokk, and the splendid traditional Sámi costumes.

❶ Getting There & Away

From the bus station on Klockarvägen buses 44 and 45 run to Gällivare (Skr130, 1½ hours, four daily), while bus 45 serves Arvidsjaur daily (Skr197, 2½ hours). Bus 47 runs to Kvikkjokk (Skr163, 2¾ hours) daily.

In summer, **Inlandsbanan** trains stop in Jokkmokk.

Gällivare

❷ 0970 / POP 8450

Gällivare – the last stop on the Inlandsbanan – and its northern twin, Malmberget, are surrounded by forest and dwarfed by the bald Dundret hill. After Kiruna, Malmberget (Ore Mountain) is the second-largest iron-ore mine in Sweden, and – you've guessed it! – Gällivare's main attraction is a trip into the bowels of the earth. Contact the Gällivare tourist office for details of the mine tours – one to the **LKAB iron-ore mine** (Skr340; ⊗9.30am mid-Jun–early-Aug, by appointment in winter), and the other to the **Aitik open-pit copper mine** (Skr340; ⊗tours 2pm Mon, Wed, Fri & Sat mid-Jun–early Aug).

Vast holes in the earth aside, you can go up **Dundret** (821m), a nature reserve and excellent vantage point for watching the midnight sun (2 June to 12 July). In winter there are four Nordic courses and 10 ski runs of varying difficulty, and the mountaintop resort rents out gear and organises numerous activities. If you have your own car, it's a rather hair-raising drive to the top. You can also book a tour by **taxi** (❷0970-10 000; www.gellivaretaxi.se) or via the tourist office.

🛏 Sleeping & Eating

Grand Hotel Lapland　　　　　　HOTEL €€
(❷0970-77 22 90; www.grandhotellapland.com; Lasarettsgatan 1; s/d from Skr1295/1675; P⊛🐾) Modern hotel opposite the train station with comfortable, airy rooms. The ground level **Vassara Pub** serves sumptuous local specialities such as reindeer, Arctic char and cloudberry tiramisu, as well as the less expensive burgers and fries.

Nittaya Thai Catering　　　　　　THAI €
(www.nittayathaicatering.se; Storgatan 21B; lunch buffet Skr85; ⊗10am-2pm Mon-Fri) Authentic Thai cuisine in attractive surroundings. The changing weekday lunch buffet is a bargain and the red curries stand out.

❶ Information

Tourist office (❷0970-166 60; www.gellivare-lapland.se; Storgatan 16; ⊗9am-6pm Mon-Fri, to 3pm Sat & Sun mid-Jun–mid-Aug) Organises tours of the mine and midnight sun tours.

Visit Sápmi (❷070 688 1577; www.visit-sapmi.com; Östra Kyrkallén 2, 2nd fl) Started in 2010, Visit Sápmi aims to become the first port of call for any visitor to Sweden with an interest in any aspect of Sámi life. With an emphasis on sustainable ecotourism, Visit Sápmi aims to have contact with every Sámi entrepreneur in Sweden, awarding the Sápmi Experience quality label to operators who meet their criteria regarding sustainable practices, and putting visitors in touch with relevant outfits.

❶ Getting There & Away

Regional buses depart from the train station. Bus 45 runs daily to Östersund (Skr507, 11 hours) via Jokkmokk and Arvidsjaur; buses 10 and 52 go to Kiruna (Skr163, 1½ to two hours); and bus 44 runs to Luleå (Skr285, 3½ hours).

Tågkompaniet (www.tagkompaniet.se) trains come from Luleå and Stockholm (sometimes changing at Boden), and from Narvik in Norway. More exotic is the summer-only **Inlandsbanan** (www.inlandsbanan.se), which terminates at Gällivare.

Kiruna

❷ 0980 / POP 18.100

Thousands of visitors flock to Kiruna every year and at first glance, it's difficult to say why: it's a sprawl of a mining town on the verge of collapsing into the enormous pit mine, the landscape around it scarred by iron ore extraction. However, Kiruna is also the gateway to the Icehotel in nearby Jukkasjärvi – northern Sweden's biggest attraction – and the Kungsleden in Abisko, as well as a fantastic base for all manner of outdoor adventures – dog sledding, snowmobiling and Northern Lights tours in winter and biking, hiking and canoeing in summer. Kiruna is also an important centre for Sámi culture.

Whether you consider it a marvel of modern engineering or a monumental eyesore, a descent into the depths of the **LKAB iron-ore mine** (off Gruvvägen; tours Skr195) – the world's largest underground mine – 540m underground, is an eye-opener. Some of the stats you'll hear on a tour are mind-blowing and you'll find yourself dwarfed by the immense machinery. Tours leave daily from the

DON'T MISS

ICEHOTEL

From a humble start in 1989 as a small igloo, the winter wonderland that is the **Icehotel** (☎980 66 800; www.icehotel.com; Jukkasjärvi; cold r from Skr3200, warm r from Skr2500; P📶👪) in Jukkasjärvi, 18km east of Kiruna, has since grown into an international phenomenon.

The enormous hotel is built using 30,000 tonnes of snow and 4000 tonnes of ice with international artists and designers coming to contribute innovative ice sculptures every year.

In the ice rooms, the beds are made of compact snow and covered with reindeer skins and sleeping bags used by the Swedish army for Arctic survival training – guaranteed to keep you warm despite the -5°C temperature inside the rooms. Come morning, guests are revived with a hot drink and a spell in the sauna. There are 30 satellite bungalows scattered around the frozen monolith for those not wanting to brave the cold.

The attached **Ice Church** is popular for weddings (giving new meaning to the expression 'cold feet'!), while the Absolut Icebar (drinks served in ice glasses) is the first of its kind. In June 2011, a smaller version of the Icehotel opened inside the Icebar warehouse.

Winter adventures include snowmobile safaris, skiing, ice-fishing, dog sledding, Sámi culture tours, and Northern Lights safaris, while summer activities comprise hiking, rafting, canoeing, fishing and Ranger all-terrain buggy tours.

Nonguests can visit the Icehotel in summer and winter and take part in guided tours or eat at the exquisite restaurant.

From 2014 Sir Richard Branson's **Virgin Galactic** (www.virgingalactic.com) venture is due to offer suborbital space flights to the general public (for out-of-this-world prices of $200,000 per ticket!), combined with stays at the Icehotel.

tourist office mid-June to mid-August; less frequently the rest of the year; book English tours via the tourist office.

Activities

Nutti Sámi Siida REINDEER SLEDDING
(☎980-213 29; www.nutti.se; Marknadsvägen 84, Jukkasjärvi) Certified Nature's Best, this specialist in sustainable Sámi ecotourism arranges short reindeer sledding excursions (Skr2490) and its tour de force – an eight-day reindeer sleigh trip through the tundra to the Norwegian border, staying in Sámi tents and wilderness huts (Skr33,000).

Active Lapland DOG SLEDDING
(☎076-104 55 08; www.activelapland.com; Solbacksvägen 22) Longstanding dog sledding operator offering anything from two-hour dog sled rides (Skr1050) and rides under the Northern Lights (Skr1100) to airport pick-up by dog sleigh (Skr5200 per sled of one to four people).

Kiruna Guidetur SNOW MOBILING
(☎980-811 10; www.kirunaguidetur.com; Vänortssgatan 8) Great all-rounder, offering snowmobiling (from Skr850), dog sledding, snowshoeing, overnighting in igloos and elk safaris in winter, and mountain biking, rafting and midnight sun tours in summer.

Sleeping

TOP CHOICE **Hotel Arctic Eden** BOUTIQUE HOTEL €€
(☎0980-611 86; www.hotelarcticeden.se; Förargatan 18; s/d Skr990/1600; P📶🏊) What do Sámi art, Thai food and swimming pools have in common? Nothing, except that they all come together at Kiruna's most luxurious lodgings. The hotel's rooms are an effortless blend of Sámi decor and modern creature comforts (including incredible power showers) and the two restaurants on the premises serve fine Northern Swedish and Thai cuisines, respectively. The plush spa (featuring Swedish massage, of course) is a nice extra.

STF Vandrarhem/Hotell City HOSTEL, HOTEL €
(☎hostel 0980-171 95, hotel 0980-666 55; www.hotellcity.se; Bergmästaregatan 7; dm/s/d from Skr200/440/500, hotel s/d from Skr850/990; P@📶) A catch-all hotel-and-hostel combo, with a gleaming red-and-white colour scheme in the modern hotel rooms, and cosy dorms. Sauna and breakfast costs extra for hostel guests.

Camp Ripan   CAMPGROUND, HOTEL €€
(☑0980-630 00; www.ripan.se; Campingvägen 5;
campsites from Skr135, s/d from Skr1450/1610,
cabins from Skr995; P@🛜🏊🐾) This large
and well-equipped camping ground with
swimming pool has hotel-standard chalets
and stylish rooms with Sámi-inspired art
in addition to its caravan and tent sites; in
winter, you can now sleep in an igloo. Numerous guided excursions on offer, ample
play facilities for children, and the on-site
restaurant is one of the best in town.

 ## Eating

TOP
CHOICE **Camp Ripan Restaurang**   SWEDISH €€
(www.ripan.se; Campingvägen; lunch buffet Skr89,
mains Skr145-275; ⊘lunch 11am-2pm; 🍴) Located
at the camping ground (of all places!), the
unusually expansive lunch buffet that's heavy
on the vegies is very good value, but the real
draw is the Sámi-inspired a la carte menu
featuring local seasonal produce. Go for the
a la carte menu to sample smoked reindeer
with cowberries, mouse ragout, ptarmigan,
and sponge cake with cloudberries.

Café Safari   CAFE €
(www.cafesafari.se; Geologsgatan 4; cakes from
Skr35, sandwiches from Skr65; ⊘8am-6pm Mon-
Fri, 10am-4pm Sat) This is the nicest cafe in
town – a long, skinny room with good coffee, outstanding cakes (try the pecan pie!)
plus light meals such as sandwiches, quiche
and baked potatoes. The sunny terrace is a
people-watching magnet in warm weather.

Thai Kitchen   THAI €
(Vänortsgatan 8; mains Skr75-120; 🍴) Don't let
the plastic tablecloths fool you – this greasy
spoon cooks up excellent Thai dishes, though
if you like it hot, ask the girls to kick it up
a notch. The sour and spicy glass noodles
are superb.

❶ Information

Tourist office (☑0980-188 80; www.lap-
pland.se; Lars Janssonsgatan 17, Folkets Hus;
⊘8.30am-9pm Mon-Fri, to 6pm Sat & Sun
May-Sep, to 5pm Mon-Fri, to 3pm Sat Oct-Apr)
The tourist office, on the main square, has
internet access and can book mine tours and
accommodation as well as various activities,
including rafting, dog-sledding and snow-
scooter trips.

❶ Getting There & Away

Air Kiruna airport (☑010-109 4600; www.
swedavia.com), 7km east of the town, has

direct flights to Stockholm, Umeå and Copenhagen with SAS (p479), and to Luleå and
Gällivare with Direktflyg (p426). The **airport
bus** (☑980-156 90; www.kirunatrafik.se) runs
two or three times daily during peak summer
season (adult/child Skr50/20)

Bus Regional buses to and from the **bus station** (Hjalmar Lundbohmsvägen) include bus
10 twice daily to Gällivare (Skr163, 1½ hours)
and Luleå (Skr356, 5¼ hours), bus 92 goes
twice daily in summer to Nikkaluokta (Skr120)
for the Kebnekaise trailhead, while bus 91 runs
to Narvik, Norway (Skr275, 2½ hours) daily via
Abisko.

Train There is a daily overnight train to Stock-
holm (from Skr403, 17 hours) via Uppsala (from
Skr403, 15¾ hours). Other destinations include
Luleå (Skr354, 3¾ to four hours, two daily),
Gällivare (Skr130, 1¼ hours, two daily) and
Narvik, Norway (Srk230, 3¼ hours, two daily)
via Abisko (Skr122, 1½ hours).

Abisko
☑0980

The one-elk town of Abisko is the main gateway to the Kungsleden – a 500km-long hiking trail that starts in the 75-sq-km **Abisko
National Park**, by the southern shore of
Torneträsk lake. This is the driest part of
Sweden, giving the area a completely distinct landscape – it's wide open and arid,
and consequently has a relatively long (for
northern Sweden) hiking season.

Abisko's location far beyond the Arctic
Circle and its relative remoteness make it
an ideal location for observing the Northern Lights and the midnight sun. From December through March, and also between
mid-June and mid-July a chairlift takes
you up the local mountain Nuolja to the
Aurora Sky Station (www.auroraskystation.
se; Northern Lights Skr595, chairlift one way/return
Skr135/170; overnight stay Skr3075 ; ⊘8pm-mid-
night Dec-Mar, 9.30am-4pm & 10pm-1am Tue, Thu
& Sat mid-Jun–mid-Jul). In winter, overnight
stays are possible.

Abisko has two train stops: Östra station puts you in the centre of the tiny village, while Abisko Turiststation is across the
highway from the STF lodge – where most
visitors are heading.

The STF Abisko Turiststation/Mountain
Lodge (p467) provides information on local
hikes and runs a variety of tours – from hiking excursions to Sámi camp tours. There's
a small supply shop selling snacks and renting camping equipment (8am to 8pm June,

8am to 9pm July and August), though its far cheaper to bring your own.

Naturum (📞0980-401 77; www.naturumabisko.se; ⏱9am-6pm Tue-Sat early Jul–Sep, Feb-Apr) has an office and exhibition space next to STF Turiststation, with detailed maps, booklets and extensive information on the Kungsleden, and the helpful staff are happy to answer questions and make suggestions based on the amount of time you have. There's a good display on local fauna and flora.

🏃 Activities

Hiking is the big activity here – trails are varied in both distance and terrain, and they're easy to reach. You can opt for anything from a 10km to 20km hike in the vicinity of Abisko to a trek along the entire Kungsleden. In winter, dog sledding and snow mobiling take over; parts of the Kungsleden are marked with snowmobile tracks.

🛏 Sleeping & Eating

Abisko Fjällturer   HOSTEL €
(📞980-40103; www.abisko.net; dm/d Skr225/600) This backpackers' delight has comfortable doubles and dorms with wide bunks, sharing two guest kitchens and a wonderful wooden sauna. Brothers Tomas and Andreas keep a large team of sled dogs; day packages in winter (Skr1000/1500) include accommodation, two or four hours' driving your own dog sled, sauna, snowshoes and skis. To find the place, cross the railway tracks 150m east of Abisko Östra station.

STF Abisko Turiststation   HOSTEL €€
(📞980-402 00; www.abisko.nu; dm/d from Skr290/840; P🅿🛜) Bustling hiker central, 2km from Abisko village, with 300 beds in dorms, cabins and private rooms. Guest kitchens, a basement sauna, excellent facilities and knowledgeable, friendly staff ensure the hostel's popularity, so book in advance. There's a terrific restaurant where you can treat yourself to pre- or post-hike organic breakfast (Skr130) and sumptuous three-course dinners (Skr360).

❶ Getting There & Away

Bus Bus 91 runs east to Kiruna (Skr170, 1¾ hours, two daily) and west to Narvik (Skr175, 1¼ hours, daily).

Train Trains run to Kiruna (Skr122, 1½ hours, three daily) and to Narvik (Skr119, 1¾ hours, three daily).

HIKING MAPS

There are two series of detailed maps (1:100,000) that cover every section of the Kungsleden: Fjällkartan and **Calazo** (www.calazo.se). Fjällkartan maps cover a slightly wider area around the Kungsleden and and are one-sided, whereas Calazo are double-sided and water-resistant.

Maps for specific trail sections:

Abisko–Nikkaluokta Fjällkartan BD6 Calazo Kungsleden

Nikkaluokta–Saltoluokta Fjällkartan BD8/Calazo Kebnekaisefjällen

Saltoluokta–Kvikkjokk Fjällkartan BD10/Calazo Sarek & Padjelanta

Kvikkjokk–Ammarnäs Fjällkartan BD14 (north), BD16 (south)/ Calazo Kvikkjokk-Ammarnäs

Ammarnäs–Hemavan Fjällkartan AC2/Calazo Ammarnäs-Hemavan

Kungsleden

Kungsleden (The King's Trail) is Sweden's most important hiking and skiing route, running for 450km from Abisko to Hemavan. The route is split into five mostly easy or moderate sections, with **STF mountain huts** (dm Skr370, campsites Skr85; ⏱mid-Feb–early May & late Jun–mid-Sep), each manned by a custodian, spaced out along the route 10km to 20km from one another (first come, first served basis). Eleven of the 16 huts sell provisions and full kitchen facilities are provided. You'll need your own sleeping bag and there's no electricity. The section between Kvikkjokk and Ammarnäs is not covered by STF, so you can stay in private accommodation in villages or camp wild. The most popular section is from Abisko to Nikkaluokta; Sweden's highest mountain, Kebnekaise (2111m), is a glorious extra. During summer, you are likely to meet the local Sámi herding their reindeer all along the Kungsleden.

ABISKO TO KEBNEKAISE (5-7 DAYS, 105KM)

From Abisko it's 86km to Kebnekaise Fjällstation and 105km to Nikkaluokta if you're leaving the trail at Kebnekaise. This section of Kungsleden runs through the dense vegetation of Abisko National Park, mostly following the valley, with wooden boardwalks over the boggy sections and bridges over streams. The highest point along the trail is the Tjäkta Pass (1150m), with great views over the Tjäktavagge Valley. There are five STF huts along the trail: Abiskojaure, Alesjaure, Tjäktja, Sälka (a good base for a day's hiking in the surrounding area) and Singi. The STF has mountain lodges at Abisko and Kebnekaise.

KEBNEKAISE TO SALTOLUOKTA (THREE TO FOUR DAYS, 52KM)

This section is 52km from Kebnekaise Fjällstation and 38km from Singi to Saltoluokta. In summer, you can shorten the extra 19km hike from Nikkaluokta to Kebnekaise Fjällstation by 5km by catching a boat across Ladjojaure lake. South of Singi, 14km from Kebnekaise, this quieter section of the trail runs through scenery more understated and less dramatic than around Kebnekaise. You may have to row yourself 1km across lake Teusajaure (there's an STF boat service in peak season) and then cross the bare plateau before descending to Vakkotavare through beech forest. There's excellent fishing at the Kaitumjaure and Teusajaure lakes and the views of Sarek National Park on the approach to Vakkotavare are fabulous. Everyone takes the bus along the road from Vakkotavare to the quay at Kebnats (Skr85), where there's an STF ferry across the Langas lake to Saltoluokta Fjällstation. STF has mountain lodges at Kebnekaise and Saltoluokta, and four huts en route: Singi, Kaitumjaure, Teusajaure and Vakkotavare.

SALTOLUOKTA TO KVIKKJOKK (FOUR DAYS, 73KM)

From Saltoluokta, it's a long and relatively steep climb to Sitojaure (6 hours), where you cross a lake using the boat service run by the hut's caretaker, followed by a boggy stretch with wooden walkways over the worst sections. At Aktse, on the shores of Laitaure Lake, you are rewarded with views of the bare mountainous terrain and you then cross the lake using the rowboats provided.

Aktse makes an excellent base for side trips into Sarek National Park. To reach Kvikkjokk, you pass through pine forest.

STF has lodges at Saltoluokta and Kvikkjokk and huts at Sitojaure, Aktse and Pårte.

KVIKKJOKK TO AMMARNÄS (EIGHT TO 10 DAYS, 157KM)

This is the wildest and most difficult section of the trail; for experienced hikers only. You have to take a tent, as accommodation is very spread out. First, you take the boat across Saggat lake from Kvikkjokk before walking to Tsiellejåkk, from where it's 55km to the next hut at Vuonatjviken. You then cross Riebnesjaure lake and another one from Hornavan to the village of Jäkkvikk, from where the trail runs through Pieljekaise National Park. From Jäkkvikk, it's only 8km until the next hut, followed by another stop at the village of Adolfström; then you cross the lake before making for the cabins at Sjnjultje. There the trail forks: you can either take the direct 34km route to Ammarnäs or a 24km detour to Rävfallet and then an additional 20km to Ammarnäs.

You can find private accommodation at Tsielejåkk, Vuonatjviken, Jäkkvikk, Pieljekaise, Adolfström, Sjnjultje, Rävfallet and Ammarnäs.

AMMARNÄS TO HEMAVAN (FOUR DAYS, 78KM)

The trail is the easiest of the five sections, mostly consisting of a gentle ramble through beech forest and wetlands, and over low hills. There's a long steep climb (8km) through beech forest between Ammarnäs and Aigert; at the top you are rewarded with an impressive waterfall. From Aigert, you can do a detour up Stor Aigert (1100m) for great surrounding views. It's possible to bypass Aigert altogether by taking a boat across the marsh towards Serve, the next hut. To reach Syter, you cross the wetlands (Tärnasjö Archipelago) using the network of bridges, stopping at the hut by Tärnasjö Lake for a spell in the sauna; it's also possible to catch a boat across the lake to shorten your hike. The hike up to Syter peak (1768m) from Syter hut is greatly recommended and the view on the way down from Viterskalet to Hemavan, taking in Norway's Okstindarnas glaciers, is particularly spectacular.

The STF has hostels at Ammarnäs and Hemavan and five huts en route at Aigert, Serve, Tärnasjö, Syter and Viterskalet, which all sell provisions.

ℹ Getting There & Away

Frequent trains stop at Abisko en route from Kiruna to Narvik, Norway, and Inlandsbanan (p481) stops at Jokkmokk in summer.

Following are handy bus routes to other starting points along the Kungsleden:

Kiruna to Nikkaluokta Bus 92 (Skr122, one hour, two daily)

Gällivare to Ritsem (via Kebnats and Vakkotavare) Bus 93 (Skr300, 3½ hours, one daily)

Jokkmokk to Kvikkjokk Buses 47, 94 (Skr162, 2½ hours, two to three daily)

Arjeplog to Jäkkvik Buses 104, 200 (Skr99, one hour, one or two daily except Saturday)

Sorsele to Ammarnäs Bus 341 (Skr124, 1¼ to 1¾ hours, one to three daily)

Umeå to Hemavan Bus 31, 319 from Tärnaby (Skr269, six hours, one or two daily)

UNDERSTAND SWEDEN

History

Sweden's history can be seen as a play in three acts.

Act I Fur-clad hunter-gatherers – the predecessors of the Sámi – step onto the stage, followed by the Vikings' raiding and plundering, only to be subdued by Christians.

Act II The action is split between the court and the battlefield. Royal dynasties follow one another in rapid succession; there's fratricide by poisoned pea soup; an androgynous girl-king ascends the throne only to flee dressed as a man; a king is assassinated at a masked ball and another during battle. Sweden's territory expands and then rapidly constricts.

Act III Sweden is largely untouched by the turmoil of the World Wars and focuses on improving the lives of her own citizens before turning her sights to the rest of the world. Sweden welcomes scores of refugees and the homogenous-looking cast quickly becomes a diverse one.

From first settlement to Christianity

Around 9000 BC, hunter-gatherers followed the retreating ice into Sweden.

By AD 600, the Svea people of the Mälaren valley (just west of Stockholm) had gained supremacy, and their kingdom, Svea Rike, gave the country of Sweden its name: Sverige.

The Viking Age was under way by the 9th century, and initial hit-and-run raids along the European coast were followed by major military expeditions, settlement and trade.

Stubbornly pagan for many centuries, Sweden turned to Christianity in the 10th century, and by 1160 King Erik Jedvarsson (Sweden's patron saint, St Erik) had virtually wiped out paganism.

NOBEL ACHIEVEMENTS

In his will, Alfred Nobel (1833–96), the inventor of dynamite, used his vast fortune to establish the Nobel Institute and the international prizes in 1901. This idea was reportedly sparked by an erroneous report in a French newspaper, a premature obituary in which the writer condemned Nobel for his explosive invention ('the merchant of death is dead,' it declared). Prizes are awarded annually for physics, chemistry, medicine and literature, as well as the Peace Prize. An awards ceremony is held in Stockholm on 10 December, while the Peace Prize is awarded in Oslo in the presence of the King of Norway.

Intrigue & Empire-building

In 1319 Sweden and Norway were united as one kingdom, but after the Black Death in 1350 created a shortage of candidates for the throne, Denmark intervened and, together with Norway, joined Sweden in the Union of Kalmar in 1397, resulting in Danish monarchs on the Swedish throne.

A century of Swedish nationalist grumblings erupted in rebellion under the young nobleman Gustav Vasa. Crowned Gustav I in 1523, he introduced the Reformation and a powerful, centralised nation state. The resulting period of expansion gave Sweden control over much of Finland and the Baltic countries. Gustav Vasa's sons did not get on – to the point of Johan allegedly poisoning King Erik's pea soup.

The last of the Vasa dynasty – Kristina – was a tomboy and a willful, controversial character who eventually abdicated the throne in 1654 and fled to Rome, dressed as a man.

King Karl XII's adventures in the early 18th century cost Sweden its Baltic territories. The next 50 years saw greater parliamentary power, but Gustav III led a coup that brought most of the power back to the crown. An aristocratic revolt in 1809 fixed that (and lost Finland to Russia). The constitution produced in that year divided legislative powers between king and *riksdag* (parliament).

During a gap in royal succession, Swedish agents chose Napoleon's marshal Jean-Baptiste Bernadotte (renamed Karl Johan) as regent. He became king of Norway and

Sweden in 1818, and the Bernadotte dynasty still holds the Swedish monarchy.

World Wars & Beyond

In spite of rapid industrialisation, around a million Swedes fled poverty for a brighter future in America in the late 19th and early 20th centuries.

Sweden declared herself neutral in 1912, and remained so throughout the bloodshed of WWI. Swedish neutrality during WWII was ambiguous: letting German troops march through to occupy Norway and selling iron ore to both warring sides tarnished Sweden's image, leading to a crisis of conscience at home and international criticism.

On the other hand, Sweden was a haven for refugees from Finland, Norway, Denmark and the Baltic states; downed allied aircrew who escaped the Gestapo; and many thousands of Jews who escaped persecution and death.

Throughout the 1950s and '60s the Social Democrats continued with the creation of *folkhemmet* (the welfare state), with the introduction of unemployment benefit, childcare and paid holidays. The standard of living for ordinary Swedes rose rapidly.

Recent Years

The world recession of the early 1990s forced a massive devaluation of the Swedish krona, and with both their economy and national confidence shaken, Swedes voted narrowly in favour of joining the European Union (EU) in 1995.

MURDER MOST MYSTERIOUS

In 1986 Social Democrat Prime Minister Olof Palme (1927–86) was shot dead by a mystery man as he walked home from the cinema with his wife on a frigid February night. What followed resembles an absurd play, complete with a cast of incompetent police, hysterical wife, a number of improbable suspects including members of the Kurdish separatist movement (PKK), a violent alcoholic and a right-wing ladies' man, and various assorted lunatics. Decades later, conspiracy theories abound, key questions remain unanswered and the murderer has still not been brought to justice.

Since then, Sweden's economy has improved considerably, with falling unemployment and inflation. A 2003 referendum on whether Sweden should adopt the euro resulted in a 'no' vote.

In October 2006, the long-entrenched Social Democrats lost their leadership position in parliament. The centre-right Alliance Party won the election, with new Prime Minister Fredrik Reinfeldt campaigning on a 'work first' platform.

The global economic crisis again affected Sweden towards the end of 2008. As ever, economic tensions fed social anxieties. An annual survey about ethnic diversity, conducted by Uppsala University researchers, indicated twice as many Swedes had an 'extremely negative' attitude towards racial diversity in 2008 than in 2005. (Researchers added, however, that Sweden is still well ahead of the rest of Europe in terms of encouraging diversity.)

People

With 9.5 million people spread over the third-largest area in Western Europe, Sweden has one of the lowest population densities on the continent. Most Swedes live in the large cities of Stockholm, Göteborg, Malmö and Uppsala. Conversely, the interior of Norrland is sparsely populated.

The majority of Sweden's population is considered to be of Nordic stock, and about 30,000 Finnish speakers form a substantial minority in the northeast, near Torneälven (the Torne river). More than 160,000 citizens of other Nordic countries live in Sweden.

Around 17% of Sweden's population are either foreign born or have at least one non-Swedish parent. The 10 largest immigrant groups are from Finland, former Yugoslavia, Iraq, Poland, Iran, Germany, Denmark, Norway, Turkey and Somalia, and there are around 45,000 Roma.

Swedish music stars José González and Salem Al Fakir and film director Josef Fares are testament to Sweden's increasingly multicultural make-up. Some 200 languages are now spoken in Sweden.

Sweden first opened its borders to mass immigration during WWII. At the time it was a closed society, and new arrivals were initially expected to assimilate and 'become Swedish'. In 1975 parliament adopted a new set of policies that emphasised the freedom to preserve and celebrate traditional native cultures.

Not everyone in Sweden is keen on this idea, with random hate crimes – including the burning down of a Malmö mosque in 2004 – blemishing the country's reputation for tolerance. As hip hop artist Timbuktu (himself the Swedish-born son of a mixed-race American couple) told the *Washington Post*, 'Sweden still has a very clear picture of what a Swede is. That no longer exists – the blond, blue-eyed physical traits. That's changing. But it still exists in the minds of some people.'

The Sámi in Sweden

Europe's only indigenous people, the ancestors of the Sámi migrated to the north of present-day Scandinavia, following the path of the retreating ice, and lived by hunting reindeer in the area spanning from Norway's Atlantic coast to the Kola Peninsula in Russia, collectively known as Sápmi. By the 17th century, the depletion of reindeer herds had transformed the hunting economy into a nomadic herding economy. Until the 1700s, the Sámi lived in *siida* – village units or communities, migrating for their livelihoods, but only within their own defined areas. Those areas were recognised and respected by the Swedish government until colonisation of Lappland began in earnest and the Sámi found their traditional rights and livelihoods threatened both by the settlers and by the establishment of borders between Sweden, Norway, Finland and Russia.

Though Sweden's Sámi population numbers around 15,000 to 20,000, according to the Sámediggi (Sámi parliament) statutes, a Sámi is a person who feels oneself to be Sámi, who either knows the Sámi language or who has had at least one parent or grandparent who spoke Sámi as their mother tongue.

Particularly precise when it comes to describing natural phenomena, the landscape and reindeer, there are 10 Sámi languages spoken across Sápmi, which belong to the Finno-Ugrian language group and are not related to any Scandinavian language. Sámi education is now available in government-run Sámi schools or regular municipal schools. Of the 6000 or so Sámi who still speak their mother tongue, 5000 speak the North Sámi dialect.

Sámi beliefs and mythology have traditionally revolved around nature, with the *noaidi* (shamans) bridging the gap between the physical and the spiritual worlds. In 1685, it was decided that the Sámi must be converted to Christianity. Idolatry trails were held, shaman drums burned and sacred sites desecrated. From the 1800s onwards, Sweden's policies regarding the Sámi were tinted with social Darwinism, deeming them to be an inferior race fit only for reindeer herding. The use of the Sámi language was discouraged and it wasn't until after until after WWII that the Sámi began to actively participate in the struggle for their rights, forming numerous associations and pressure groups.

The Sámi in Sweden are represented by the Sámediggi (Sámi parliament), which oversees matters such as reindeer herding interests and promotes Sámi culture. However, while it acts in an advisory capacity to the Swedish government, the Sámediggi does not have the power to make decisions regarding land use. The Swedish Sámi take part in the Sámiráđđi, the unifying body for the Sámi organisations across Sápmi and an active participant in the WCIP (World Council of Indigenous Peoples).

Sámi claim the right to traditional livelihoods, land and water, citing usufruct (age-old usage) and the traditional property rights of the Sámi *siida*, which are not formally acknowledged by Sweden. The Swedish State is yet to ratify the International Labour Organisation's Convention 169, which would recognise the Sámi as an aboriginal people with property rights, as opposed to just an ethnic minority.

One of the cornerstones of Sámi identity is the *yoik* – a rhythmic poem or song composed for a specific person, event or object to describe and remember their innate nature.

From the 1970s onwards, there has been a revival of traditional Sámi handicraft, such as leatherwork, textiles, knife-making, woodwork and silverwork. Since then, genuine Sámi handwork that uses traditional designs and materials has borne the Sámi Duodji (Sámi Handicraft) trademark and can be found all over Lappland.

The booklet *The Saami – People of the Sun & Wind*, published by Ájtte Museum (p463) in Jokkmokk, describes Sámi traditions in all four countries of the Sápmi region and is available at tourist shops around the area. Visitors interesting in learning more about the Sámi and in experiencing

Sámi culture should consult Visit Sápmi (p464), an excellent resource for all thing Sámi. Also, look for the 'Naturens Bäst' logo, which indicates that an excursion or organisation has been approved by **Svenska Ekoturismföreningen** (www.ekoturism.org), the country's first ecotourism regulating body.

Arts

Painting & Sculpture

Sweden's 19th-century artistic highlights include the warm art nouveau oil paintings of Carl Larsson (1853–1919), the nudes and portraits of Anders Zorn (1860–1920), August Strindberg's violently moody seascapes, and the nature paintings of Bruno Liljefors (1860–1939). Carl Milles (1875–1955) is Sweden's greatest sculptor, once employed as Rodin's assistant.

Literature

Well-known Swedish writers include the poet Carl Michael Bellman (1740–95), playwright August Strindberg (1849–1912), Nobel Prize winner Selma Lagerlöf (1858–1940) and prolific children's writer Astrid Lindgren (1907–2002) – the 18th most translated author in the world. Vilhelm Moberg (1898–1973) won international acclaim with *Utvandrarna* (The Emigrants; 1949) and *Nybyggarna* (The Settlers; 1956). More recently, Stieg Larsson's Millennium trilogy (*The Girl with the Dragon Tattoo* et al) has been a worldwide phenomenon and has inspired at least two feature-film adaptations.

Design

Sweden is a living gallery of inspired design, from Jonas Bohlin 'Tutu lamps' to Tom Hedquist milk cartons. While simplicity still defines the Nordic aesthetic, new designers are challenging Scandi functionalism with bold, witty work. A claw-legged 'Bird Table' by Broberg Ridderstråle and a table made entirely of ping-pong balls by Don't Feed the Swedes are two examples of playful creations from design collectives such as Folkform, DessertDesign and Defyra.

Aesthetic prowess also fuels Sweden's thriving fashion scene. Since the late 1990s and continuing today, local designers have aroused global admiration: Madonna dons Patrik Söderstam trousers, and Acne Jeans sell like hot cakes at LA's hip Fred Segal. In fact, these days Sweden is exporting more fashion than pop.

Frozen art – the ice sculptures at the Icehotel (p465) – has become a focus for collaboration between Swedish artists and designers and those from around the world.

And if you haven't come across IKEA furniture, then you have probably been living on a desert island for the last few decades.

Cinema

Swedish cinema is inextricably linked with the name of Ingmar Bergman. His deeply contemplative films (*The Seventh Seal; Through a Glass Darkly; Persona*) explore alienation, the absence of god, the meaning of life, the certainty of death and other lighthearted themes. Recently, Trollhättan and Ystad have become film-making centres, thanks to younger directors like Lukas Moodysson, whose *Lilja 4-Ever, Show Me Love* and *Tillsammans* have all been hits. Director Tomas Alfredson's atmospheric teen-vampire film *Let the Right One In* also became a cult hit and inspired an American remake and Stieg Larsson's trilogy, starting with *The Girl With a Dragon Tattoo*, has also been immortalised on the big screen.

Pop Music

Any survey of Swedish music must at least mention ABBA, the iconic, dubiously outfitted winners of the 1974 Eurovision Song Contest (with 'Waterloo'). More current Swedish successes are pop icon Robyn, indie melody-makers Peter Björn & John, and the exquisitely mellow José González, whose cover of the Knife's track 'Heartbeats' catapulted the Göteborg native to international stardom. Other Swedish exports include Roxette, The Hives, Mando Diao, The Cardigans, Kent, Lisa Ekdahl, The Hellacopters and Ace of Base.

Environment

Sweden occupies the eastern side of the Scandinavian peninsula, sharing borders with Norway, Finland and Denmark (the latter a mere 4km to the southwest of Sweden and joined to it by a spectacular bridge and tunnel).

Sweden's surface area (450,000 sq km) is stretched long and thin. Around one-sixth of the country lies within the Arctic Circle, yet Sweden is surprisingly warm thanks to the Gulf Stream: minimum northern temperatures are around –20°C (compared with –45°C in Alaska).

The country has a 7000km-long coastline, with myriad islands – the Stockholm archipelago alone has up to 24,000. The largest and most notable islands are Gotland and Öland on the southeast coast, and the best sandy beaches are down the west coast, south of Göteborg.

Forests take up nearly 60% of Sweden's landscape and the land is dotted with around 100,000 lakes. Vänern is the largest lake in Western Europe, at 5585 sq km. Kebnekaise (2111m), part of the glaciated Kjölen Mountains along the Norwegian border, is the highest mountain in Sweden. The southern part of the country is mostly farmland.

Wildlife

Thanks to Sweden's geographical diversity, it has a great variety of European animals, birds and plants. The big carnivores – bear, wolf, wolverine, lynx and golden eagle – are all protected species. The elk (moose in the USA), a gentle, knobby-kneed creature that grows up to 2m tall, is the symbol of Sweden. Elk are a serious traffic hazard, particularly at night: they can dart out in front of your car at up to 50km/h. Around 260,000 domesticated reindeer, also no fun to run into on a highway, roam the northern areas under the watchful eyes of Sámi herders. The musk ox is another large herbivore you may encounter. Forests, lakes and rivers support beaver, otter, mink, badger and pine marten, and hundreds of bird species (including numerous sea birds) populate the country.

National Parks

Sweden had the distinction of being the first country in Europe to establish a national park (1909). There are now 29, along with around 2600 smaller nature reserves; together they cover about 9% of the country. The organisation **Naturvårdsverket** (www.swedishepa.se) oversees and produces pamphlets about the parks in Swedish and English, along with the excellent book *Nationalparkerna i Sverige* (National Parks in Sweden).

Four of Sweden's large rivers (Kalixälven, Piteälven, Vindelälven and Torneälven) have been declared National Heritage Rivers in order to protect them from hydroelectric development.

Environmental Issues

Ecological consciousness in Sweden is very high and reflected in concern for native animals, clean water and renewable resources. Swedes are fervent believers in sorting and recycling household waste – you'll be expected to do the same in hotels, hostels and camping grounds. Most plastic bottles and cans can be recycled in supermarkets with around Skr1 returned per item.

Two organisations that set standards for labelling products as ecologically sound are the food-focused **KRAV** (www.krav.se), a member of the International Federation of Organic Agriculture Movements, and **Swan** (www.svanen.se), which has a wider scope and certifies entire hotels and hostels.

Linked to the environmental concerns is the challenge of protecting the cultural heritage of the Sámi people. The harnessing of rivers can have massive (negative) impact on what has historically been Sámi territory, whether by flooding reindeer feeding grounds or by diverting water and drying up river valleys. In general, the mining, forestry and space industries have wreaked havoc on Sámi homelands.

ARCTIC PHENOMENA

The north of Sweden offers two unparalleled shows of nature. The mesmerising **aurora borealis** (Northern Lights) consists of ghostly whisps, streaks and haloes of faint green, yellow and even crimson light, caused by the interaction of charged particles in the atmosphere, and best seen between October and March.

Beyond the Arctic Circle, the **midnight sun** can be seen between mid-June and early July and the endless hours of daylight give lakes and rivers a wonderful pearly sheen.

Food & Drink

Epicureans around the world are smitten with Sweden's new-generation chefs and their inventive creations. Current luminaries include Bocuse d'Or recipient Mathias Dahlgren, TV chef Niklas Ekstedt and New York–based Marcus Samuelsson.

Staples & Specialities

While new-school Swedish nosh thrives on experimentation, it retains firm roots in Sweden's culinary heritage. Even the most avant-garde chefs admire simple, old-school *husmanskost* (everyman cuisine) like *toast skagen* (toast with bleak roe, crème fraiche and chopped red onion) and *köttbullar och potatis* (meatballs and potatoes, usually served with lingonberry jam, or *lingonsylt*). Seafood staples include caviar, gravlax (cured salmon) and the ubiquitous *sill* (herring), eaten smoked, fried or pickled and often accompanied by capers, mustard and onion. The most contentious traditional food is the pungent *surströmming* (fermented Baltic herring), guaranteed to knock out your sense of smell and traditionally eaten in August and September in a slice of *tunnbröd* (thin, unleavened bread) with boiled potato and onions and ample amounts of *snaps* (vodka). In the north of Sweden, you will come across reindeer and elk steak, Arctic char (fish) and cloudberry-based desserts.

Where to Eat & Drink

Most hotels and some hostels provide breakfast buffets laden with cereals and yogurt plus bread, fruit, cold cuts, cheese and the like. Sweden is the inventor of the *smörgåsbord* – a vast buffet of Swedish specialities and served as brunch in many establishments. Many cafes and restaurants offer a daily lunch special called *dagens rätt* or *dagens lunch* (main course, salad, bread, cold drink and coffee) at a fixed price between 11.30am and 2pm, which makes it considerably cheaper to eat out in the middle of day than in the evenings.

To counter the mid-afternoon slump, Swedes enjoy *fika,* an almost mandatory coffee break. *Konditori* are old-fashioned bakery-cafes where you can get a pastry or a *smörgås* (sandwich), but there are also many stylish, modern cafes where you can enjoy people watching over pricier Italian coffees, gourmet salads, bagels and muffins.

Pure vegetarian restaurants (especially buffets) are increasingly common, and there will usually be at least one vegetarian main-course option on the menu at ordinary restaurants.

Drinking

Lättöl (light beer, less than 2.25% alcohol) and *folköl* (folk beer, 2.25% to 3.5% alcohol) account for about two-thirds of all beer sold in Sweden and can be bought in supermarkets everywhere. *Mellanöl* (medium-strength beer, 3.6% to 4.5% alcohol), *starköl* (strong beer, over 4.5% alcohol) and wines and spirits can be bought only at outlets of the state-owned alcohol store – Systembolaget – which is open until about 6pm on weekdays and slightly shorter hours on Saturday.

Sweden's trademark spirit, *brännvin,* also called aquavit and drunk as *snaps,* is a fiery and strongly flavoured drink that's usually distilled from potatoes and spiced with herbs.

The legal drinking age in Sweden is 18 years, although you have to be 20 years old to buy alcohol at a Systembolaget.

SURVIVAL GUIDE

Directory A–Z
Accommodation

In much of Sweden prices go *down* in high season (July and August) by up to 50%. Most hotels in Sweden also offer steep discounts (up to 50%) on Friday and Saturday nights and from mid-May through August. Many hotels also have discounts for rooms booked online ahead of time. The following price categories are for a standard double room with private bathroom in high season (June to August):

€€€   more than Skr1600
€€   Skr800 to Skr1600
€   less than Skr800

CABINS & CHALETS

Daily rates for *stugor* (cabins and chalets, often found at camping grounds or in the countryside) offer good value for small groups and families, and range in both quality and price (Skr400 to Skr1000). Some are simple, with bunk beds and little else (you share the bathroom and kitchen facilities with campers); others are fully equipped with their own kitchen, bathroom and living room. Local and regional tourist offices have listings of cabins and cottages that may be rented by the week; these are often in idyllic forest, lakeside or coastal locations. See the Stuga (www.stuga.nu) website for more.

CAMPING

Sweden has hundreds of camping grounds; a free English-language guide with maps is available from tourist offices. Some are open year-round, but the best time for camping is from May to August. Prices vary with facilities, from Skr160 for a basic site to around Skr260 for the highest standards. Most camping grounds have kitchens and laundry facilities, and many have the works – swimming pool, bike and canoe rental, restaurant, store etc.

You must have a Camping Key Europe (150Skr per year) to stay at most Swedish camping grounds; it also gives you discounts in participating cafes, museums and more. Apply for one in advance filling out an online form at the **Sveriges Camping & Stugföretagares Riksorganisation** (www.camping.se) website; otherwise pick up a temporary card at any Swedish camping ground.

Visit www.camping.se for lots of useful information.

HOSTELS

Sweden has well over 450 hostels *(vandrarhem)* with excellent facilities. Outside major cities, hostels are used as holiday accommodation by Swedish families, couples or retired people. Dorms are often absent, meaning you often have to rent a room rather than a bed. Some hostels also have en suite singles and doubles that are almost of hotel quality. About half of hostels open year-round; many others open from May to September, while some open only from mid-June to mid-August.

Swedish hostels keep very short reception hours (except in Stockholm and Göteborg): 5pm to 7pm, occasionally also 8am to 10am. Pre-book by telephone or online – reservations are highly recommended. Some hostels email you a door code to get in after hours.

Almost 400 hostels, mountain huts and lodges are affiliated with **Svenska Turistföreningen** (STF; ☑08-463 21 00; www.svenskaturistforeningen.se), part of Hostelling International (HI). Holders of HI membership cards pay the same rates as STF members. Nonmembers can pay Skr50 extra (Skr100 at some mountain lodges), or join up at hostels (adult/under 26yr/under 15yr Skr295/150/30 per calendar year). We quote member prices for any STF hostels. Children aged under 16 years pay about half the adult price.

Around 200 hostels belong to **Sveriges Vandrarhem i Förening** (SVIF; ☑031-828 800; www.svif.se). No membership is required. Rates are similar to those of STF hostels.

Most SVIF hostels have kitchens. Pick up the free guide at tourist offices or SVIF hostels.

HOTELS

Most hotels in Sweden tend to belong to big hotel chains. Hotel prices include a breakfast buffet unless stated otherwise. Ask at tourist offices for the free booklet *Hotels in Sweden* or visit the website www.hotelsinsweden.net; budget travellers should check out **Ibis** (www.ibishotel.com); the Ibis Budget range offers simple and cheap rooms with private facilities.

Activities

Sweden is a canoeing and kayaking paradise (canoes are more common). The national canoeing body is **Kanotförbundet** (Kayak & Canoe Federation; www.kanot.com). It provides general advice and lists approved canoe centres that hire out canoes.

There are thousands of kilometres of hiking trails in Sweden, particularly in the north. The best hiking time is between late June and mid-September, when trails are mostly snow-free.

Large ski resorts cater to downhill skiing and snowboarding. **SkiStar** (www.skistar.com) manages the largest resorts and has good information on its website.

Winter activities in the north include dog sledding, snowmobiling, and cross-country skiing.

Business Hours

Opening hours can vary significantly between high and low seasons. Any hours provided here are for the high season, from June to August.

Banks 9.30am to 3pm Monday to Friday; some city branches open from 9am to 5pm or 6pm

Bars & pubs 11am or noon to 1am or 2am

Department stores 10am to 7pm Monday to Saturday (sometimes later), noon to 4pm Sunday

Government offices 9am to 5pm Monday to Friday

Post offices 9am to 5pm Monday to Friday

Restaurants Lunch from 11.30am to 2pm, dinner 6pm to 10pm; often closed on Sunday and/or Monday

Shops 9am to 6pm Monday to Friday, 9am to 1pm Saturday

Supermarkets 8am or 9am to 7pm or 9pm

Systembolaget 10am to 6pm Monday to Friday, 10am to 2pm (often to 5pm) Saturday, sometimes with extended hours on Thursday and Friday evenings

Children

Sweden is a very easy, friendly place to travel with children. Museums almost always have dedicated playrooms with hands-on learning tools. Restaurants offer high chairs and kids' menus. There are safety features for children in hire cars. Hostels generally have family rooms and camping grounds are often equipped with swimming pools and playgrounds.

Discount Cards

Göteborg, Malmö, Stockholm and Uppsala offer tourist cards that offer discounts on major attractions, transport and more (see individual city sections for details).

The **International Student Identity Card** (ISIC; www.isic.org; $25) offers discounts on admission to museums, sights, public transport and more.

Seniors get discounts on entry to museums, sights, cinema and theatre tickets, air tickets and other transport. No special card required. Show your passport as proof of age (the minimum qualifying age is 60 or 65).

Food

The following price ranges refer to a standard main course:

€€€ more than Skr185
€€   Skr75 to Skr185
€   less than Skr75

Gay & Lesbian Travellers

Sweden recognises civil unions or 'registered partnerships' that grant general marriage rights to gay and lesbian couples.

Riksförbundet för Sexuellt Likaberättigande (RFSL; ☎08-501 62 900; www.rfsl.se; Sveavägen 59, 2nd fl, Stockholm) National organisation for gay and lesbian rights.

QX (www.qx.se) Free monthly magazine in Stockholm, Göteborg, Malmö and Copenhagen.

Internet Access

Sweden is a wired country. Most hotels have wireless LAN connections. Hostels and tourist offices frequently have at least one internet-enabled computer available for use, often free of charge.

Nearly all public libraries offer free internet access, but often the time slots are booked for days in advance by locals.

Internet cafes are rarely found outside big cities and typically charge around Skr1 per online minute, or Skr60 per hour. Wireless internet is almost universal at coffee shops, train stations, bars, cafes and hotels, although often there's a fee for access.

Bring a universal AC adaptor and plug adaptor for your laptop.

Money

Sweden uses the krona (plural: kronor), denoted Skr (or SEK in Sweden) and divided into 100 öre. Coins are one, five and 10 kronor, and notes are 20, 50, 100, 500 and 1000 kronor. Swedes round to the nearest krona when paying cash, as there are no öre coins any more.

ATMS

ATMs are easy to find in all major towns and cities. They accept major credit cards as well as Plus and Cirrus.

CREDIT CARDS

Visa and MasterCard are widely accepted; American Express, Discover and Diners Club less so.

MONEYCHANGERS

Forex (☎0771-22 22 21; www.forex.se) is the biggest foreign money exchange company in Sweden; it has branches in major airports, ferry terminals and city centres.

TIPPING

Hotels Optional; Skr10 per day for house-keeping appreciated

Restaurants 5% is considered very generous, no need to tip unless rewarding exceptional service

Taxis Optional; round up the bill to the nearest 10Skr

Public Holidays

Many businesses close early the day before and all day after official public holidays, including the following:

Nyårsdag (New Year's Day) 1 January

Trettondedag Jul (Epiphany) 6 January

Långfredag, Påsk, Annandag Påsk (Good Friday, Easter Sunday & Monday) March/April

Första Maj (Labour Day) 1 May

Kristi Himmelsfärds dag (Ascension Day) May/June

Pingst, Annandag Pingst (Whit Sunday & Monday) Late May or early June

Midsommardag (Midsummer's Day) First Saturday after 21 June

Alla Helgons dag (All Saints' Day) Saturday, late October or early November

Juldag (Christmas Day) 25 December

Annandag Jul (Boxing Day) 26 December

Photography

Photographing military establishments is forbidden. Ask permission before taking photos of the Sámi.

Telephone

Directory Assistance (☏118 118) Within Sweden.

Directory assistance (☏118 119) International.

Emergency Services (☏112) Toll-free.

Mobile phones Using a mobile phone from another EU country is relatively inexpensive due to standardised rates. For longer stays in Sweden, consider buying a Swedish SIM card (around Skr100) from one of the three main providers: Telia, Tele2 or Telenor.

Phone codes Swedish phone numbers have area codes followed by varying numbers of digits. To call Sweden from abroad, dial the country code (☏46) followed by the area code and telephone number (omitting the first zero in the area code). For international calls dial ☏00 followed by the country code and the local area code. Toll-free codes include ☏020 and ☏0200 (but not from public phones or abroad). Mobile phone numbers usually begin with ☏010, ☏070, ☏073, ☏076, and ☏0730.

Phonecards All public pay phones take coins and prepaid phonecards available at Pressbyrå newsagents.

Time

Sweden is one hour ahead of GMT/UTC and observes daylight-saving time (with changes in March and October). Timetables and business hours generally use the 24-hour clock.

Toilets

Public toilets in parks, shopping malls, libraries and bus or train stations are rarely free in Sweden. Except at the larger train stations (where an attendant is on duty), pay toilets are coin operated, and usually cost Skr5 to Skr10 (so keep coins handy). In some places it's also possible to pay by SMS (text message).

Tourist Information

Most Swedish towns have a centrally located tourist office (turistbyrå), with plenty of brochures on attractions, accommodation and transport. Most are open long hours in summer and short hours (until 4pm on weekdays or not at all) during winter.

Visit Sweden (www.visitsweden.com) Sweden's official travel and tourism information site in many languages.

Travellers with Disabilities

Sweden is one of the easiest countries to travel around in a wheelchair. People with disabilities will find transport services with adapted facilities, ranging from trains to taxis, but contact the operator in advance for the best service. Public toilets and some hotel rooms have facilities for people with disabilities; **Hotels in Sweden** (www.hotels insweden.net) indicates whether hotels have adapted rooms.

De Handikappades Riksförbund (☏08-685 80 00; www.dhr.se) National association for people with disabilities.

Visas

Non-EU passport holders from the USA, Canada, Australia and New Zealand do not need a visa for stays of less than three months. Citizens of EU countries and other Scandinavian countries with a valid passport or national identification card do not require visas. Other nationalities should check with **Migrationsverket** (☑0771 235 235; www.migrationsverket.se) to see whether they require a visa before arriving in Sweden.

Getting There & Away

Air

The main airport is Stockholm Arlanda, linking Sweden with major European and North American cities. Göteborg Landvetter is Sweden's second-biggest international airport. Stockholm Skavsta (100km south of Stockholm, near Nyköping) and Göteborg City act as airports for budget airline Ryanair. Stockholm's Västerås airport also serves Ryanair.

Göteborg City Airport (www.goteborg airport.se)

Göteborg Landvetter Airport (www.swedavia.se)

Stockholm Arlanda Airport (☑010-109 00 00; www.swedavia.se)

Stockholm Skavsta Airport (☑0155-28 04 00; www.skavsta-air.se)

Scandinavian Airlines System (SAS) is the regional carrier and has a good safety record. Most of the usual airlines fly into Sweden, including the following:

Air France (www.airfrance.com)

British Airways (www.britishairways.com)

Norwegian Air (www.norwegian.com)

Lufthansa (www.lufthansa.com)

Ryanair (www.ryanair.com)

SAS (www.flysas.com)

Wizz Air (www.wizzair.com)

Land

Direct access to Sweden by land is possible from Norway, Finland and Denmark (via the Öresund toll bridge). Border-crossing formalities are nonexistent.

Train and bus journeys between Sweden and the continent go directly to ferries. Include ferry fares (or Öresund tolls) in your budget if you're driving from Europe.

Eurolines Scandinavia (www.eurolines.se) Has an office in Malmö. Full schedules and fares are listed on the company's website.

GoByBus (www.gobybus.se) Long-distance buses within Sweden and to Oslo and Copenhagen.

Sveriges Järnväg (www.sj.se) National network covering most main lines, especially in the south. Train services to Copenhagen also.

Swebus (www.swebusexpress.se)

CONTINENTAL EUROPE

Eurolines services run between Göteborg and London via Copenhagen and Brussels (Skr1349, 27 hours, daily) and Göteborg and Berlin (Sk688, 15 hours, three or four weekly) via Copenhagen.

DENMARK

Bus Eurolines (www.eurolines.se) runs buses between Stockholm and Copenhagen (Skr447, 9¾ hours, at least three per week), and between Göteborg and Copenhagen (Skr319, 4½ hours, daily). **Swebus Express** (www.swebusexpress.se) and **Go-ByBus** (www.gobybus.se) both run regular buses on the same routes. All companies offer student, youth (under 26) and senior discounts.

Train Öresund trains operated by **Skånetrafiken** (www.skanetrafiken.se) run every 20 minutes from 6am to midnight (and once an hour thereafter) between Copenhagen and Malmö (one way Skr105, 35 minutes) via the bridge. The trains usually stop at Copenhagen airport.

From Copenhagen, change in Malmö for Stockholm trains. Frequent services operate directly between Copenhagen and Göteborg (Skr416, four hours) and between Copenhagen, Kristianstad and Karlskrona.

Car & Motorcycle You can drive from Copenhagen to Malmö across the Öresund bridge on the E20 motorway. Tolls are paid at Lernacken, on the Swedish side, in either Danish or Swedish currency (single crossing per car Skr375), or by credit or debit card.

FINLAND

Bus Frequent bus services run from Haparanda to Tornio (Skr20, 10 minutes). **Tapanis Buss** (www.tapanis.se) runs express coaches from Stockholm to Tornio via Haparanda twice weekly (Skr600, 15 hours). **Länstrafiken i Norrbotten** (www. ltnbd.se) operates buses as far as Karesuando, from where it's only a few minutes' walk across the bridge to Kaaresuvanto (Finland).

There are also regular services from Haparanda to Övertorneå (some continue to Pello, Pajala and Kiruna) – you can walk across the border at Övertorneå or Pello and pick up a Finnish bus to Muonio, with onward connections from there to Kaaresuvanto and Tromsø (Norway).

Car & Motorcycle The main routes between Sweden and Finland are the E4 from Umeå to Kemi and Rd45 from Gällivare to Kaaresuvanto.

NORWAY

Bus Swebus Express (☎0771-21 82 18; www. swebus.se) runs from Stockholm to Oslo (Sk447, six hours, at least two daily), and from Göteborg to Oslo (Skr259, 3¾ hours, at least three daily).

In the north, buses run once daily from Umeå to Mo i Rana (eight hours) and from Skellefteå to Bodø (nine hours, daily except Saturday); for details, contact **Länstrafiken i Västerbotten** (☎077-10 01 10; www.tabussen. nu) and **Länstrafiken i Norrbotten** (www. ltnbd.se).

Train Trains run daily from Stockholm to Oslo (Skr1024, 8½ to 11 hours, two daily) and at night to Narvik (Skr874, 22 hours, daily) via Luleå and Kiruna. There are also trains from Göteborg to Oslo (Skr347, four hours, three daily).

Car & Motorcycle The main roads between Sweden and Norway are the E6 from Göteborg to Oslo, the E18 from Stockholm to Oslo, the E14 from Sundsvall to Trondheim, the E12 from Umeå to Moi i Rana and the E10 from Kiruna to Bjerkvik.

Sea

Ferry connections between Sweden and its neighbours are frequent and straightforward. See p493 for full details.

Getting Around

Air

Domestic airlines in Sweden tend to use **Stockholm Arlanda Airport** (www.arlanda.se)

as a hub, but there are 30-odd regional airports. Flying domestic is expensive on fullprice tickets, but substantial discounts are available on internet bookings, student and youth fares, off-peak travel, return tickets booked at least seven days in advance and low-price tickets for accompanying family members and seniors.

Sweden's internal flight operators and their destinations include the following:

Gotlandsflyg (☎077 44 44 141; www.gotlands flyg.se) Ängelholm, Stockholm Bromma/ Arlanda, Göteborg, Kalmar, Malmö, Mora, Stockholm Bromma/Arlanda/ Skavsta, Sundsvall, Umeå, Visby, Växjö.

Malmö Aviation (☎040-660 28 20; www.mal moaviation.se) Göteborg, Stockholm, Malmö, Umeå, Visby, Kalmar and more.

SAS (☎0770-72 77 27; www.flysas.com) Göteborg, Kalmar, Kiruna, Luleå, Malmö, Karlskrona, Skellefteå, Stockholm, Sundsvall/ Härnösand, Umeå, Visby, Åre/Östersund, Ängelholm/Helsingborg.

Boat

CANAL BOAT

The canals provide cross-country routes linking the main lakes. The longest cruises, on the Göta Canal from Söderköping (south of Stockholm) to Göteborg, run from mid-May to mid-September, take at least four days and include the lakes in between.

Rederiaktiebolaget Göta Kanal (☎031-80 63 15; www.gotacanal.se) operates three ships over the whole distance at fares from Skr9475 to Skr15,975 per person for a fourday cruise, including full board and guided excursions.

FERRY

An extensive boat network and the five-day Båtluffarkortet boat pass (Skr420) open up the attractive Stockholm archipelago. Gotland is served by regular ferries from Nynäshamn and Oskarshamn, and the quaint fishing villages off the west coast can normally be reached by boat with a regional transport pass – enquire at the Göteborg tourist offices.

Bus

Swebus Express (☎0771-21 82 18; www.swe bus.se) has the largest network of express buses, but they serve only the southern half of the country (as far north as Mora in Dalarna).

Svenska Buss (☑0771-67 67 67; www.svenska buss.se) and GoByBus (www.gobybus.se) also connect many southern towns and cities with Stockholm; prices are often slightly cheaper than Swebus Express, but services are less frequent.

North of Gävle, regular connections with Stockholm are provided by several smaller operators, including Ybuss (☑060-17 19 60; www.ybuss.se), which has services to Sundsvall, Östersund and Umeå.

Länstrafiken i Norrbotten (www.ltnbd. se) serves many destinations in the north of the country, as does its sister company, Länstrafiken i Västerbotten (☑077-10 01 10; www.tabussen.nu).

You don't have to reserve a seat on Swebus Express services. Generally, tickets for travel between Monday and Thursday are cheaper, or if they're purchased over the internet, or more than 24 hours before departure. If you're a student or senior, it's worth asking about fare discounts.

BUS PASSES
Good-value daily or weekly passes are usually available from local and regional transport offices, and many regions have 30-day passes for longer stays, or a special card for peak-season summer travel.

REGIONAL NETWORKS
The *länstrafik* bus networks are well integrated with the regional train system, with one ticket valid on any local or regional bus or train. Rules vary but transfers are usually free if used within one to four hours. Fares on local buses and trains are often identical, though they can vary wildly, depending on when you travel and how far in advance you purchase your tickets.

Car & Motorcycle
Sweden has good-standard roads, and the excellent E-class motorways rarely have traffic jams.

LOCAL TRANSPORT
In Sweden, public transport is heavily subsidised and well organised. It's divided into 24 regional networks (*länstrafik*), with local transport always linked to regional transport, but with an overarching Resplus (www.samtrafiken. se) system, where one ticket is valid on trains and buses.

AUTOMOBILE ASSOCIATIONS
The Swedish national motoring association is Motormännens Riksförbund (☑08 690 38 00; www.motormannen.se).

BRING YOUR OWN VEHICLE
If bringing your own car, you'll need your vehicle registration documents, unlimited third-party liability insurance and a valid driving licence. A right-hand drive vehicle brought from the UK or Ireland should have deflectors fitted to the headlights to avoid dazzling oncoming traffic. You must carry a reflective warning breakdown triangle.

DRIVING LICENCE
An international driving permit isn't necessary; your domestic licence will do.

HIRE
To hire a car you have to be at least 20 (sometimes 25) years of age, with a recognised licence and a credit card.

International rental chains Avis, Hertz and Europcar have desks at Stockholm Arlanda and Göteborg Landvetter airports and offices in most major cities. The best car-hire rates (though subject to length of rental) are generally from larger petrol stations (such as Statoil and OK-Q8) – look out for signs saying *biluthyrning* or *hyrbilar*.

Avis (☑0770-82 00 82; www.avis.se)

Europcar (☑0770-77 00 50; www.europcar.se)

Hertz (☑0771-21 12 12; www.hertz.se)

Mabi Hyrbilar (☑020-110 1000; www.mabi-rent.se) National company with competitive rates.

OK-Q8 (☑020-65 65 65; www.okq8.se) Click on *Hyrbilar* in the website menu to see car-hire pages. If renting for less than a certain number of days, you won't get unlimited mileage.

Statoil (☑08-429 63 00; www.statoil.se) Click on *Uthyrningsstationer* to see branches with car hire, and on *Priser* for prices.

ROAD HAZARDS
In the northern part of Sweden, reindeer and elk are serious road hazards, particularly around dawn and dusk. Look out for black plastic bags tied to roadside trees or poles – this is a sign from local Sámi that they have reindeer herds grazing in the area. Report all incidents to police – failure to do so is an offence. Sandboxes on many roads may be helpful in mud or snow. Also, if driving in Göteborg and Norrköping, be aware

ROAD RULES

» You drive on and give way to the right.

» Dipped headlights must be on at all times when driving.

» Seatbelt use is obligatory and children under the age of seven should be in the appropriate harness or car seat.

» The maximum blood-alcohol limit is a stringent 0.02%.

» The speed limit on motorways (signposted in green and called E1, E4, etc) is 110km/h; highways 90km/h; narrow rural roads 70km/h and built-up areas 50km/h. Police using hand-held radar speed detectors impose on-the-spot fines.

COSTS

Ticket prices vary tremendously, depending on the type of train, class, time of day and how far in advance you buy the ticket. Super-fast X2000 trains are pricier than other trains. Full-price 2nd-class tickets for longer journeys cost about twice as much as equivalent bus trips, but there are various discounts available, especially for booking a week or so in advance (*förköpsbiljet*), online, or at the last minute. Students, pensioners and people aged under 26 get a steep discount on the standard adult fare.

All SJ ticket prices drop from late June to mid-August. Most SJ trains don't allow bicycles to be taken onto trains (they have to be sent as freight), but those in southern Sweden do; check when you book your ticket.

TRAIN PASSES

The Sweden Rail Pass and international passes, such as Inter-Rail and Eurail, are accepted on SJ services and most regional trains.

The **Eurail Scandinavia Pass** (www.eurail.com) entitles you to unlimited rail travel in Denmark, Finland, Norway and Sweden; it is valid in 2nd class only and is available for three, four, five, six or eight days of travel within a one-month period (prices start at adult/youth US$261/196). All rail-pass holders are required to pay a small supplement (including the obligatory seat reservation) for X2000 trains. The pass also provides free travel on Scandlines' Helsingør–Helsingborg route, and 20% to 50% discounts on various ship routes, including the following:

ROUTE	OPERATOR
Frederikshavn–Göteborg	Stena Line
Grenå–Varberg	Stena Line
Helsinki–Åland–Stockholm	Silja Line
Turku–Mariehamn–Stockholm	Silja Line
Turku/Helsinki–Stockholm	Viking Line
Stockholm–Tallinn	Silja Line
Stockholm–Riga	Silja Line

of trams, which have priority; overtake on the right.

Train

Sweden has an extensive and reliable railway network, and trains are certainly faster than buses. Many destinations in the northern half of the country, however, cannot be reached by train alone, and Inlandsbanan, the historic train line through Norrland, runs only during summer. The following are the main train operators in the country:

Inlandsbanan (☎0771-53 53 53; www.inlandsbanan.se) Slow and scenic 1300km route from Kristinehamn to Gällivare. Some sections must be travelled by bus, but the all-train section starts at Mora. Trains run June to August. Two weeks' unlimited travel costs Skr1795.

Sveriges Järnväg (SJ; ☎0771-75 75 75; www.sj.se) National network covering most main lines, especially in the south. Train services to Copenhagen also.

Tågkompaniet (☎0771-44 41 11; www.tagkompaniet.se) Operates excellent overnight trains from Göteborg and Stockholm north to Boden, Kiruna, Luleå and Narvik, and the lines north of Härnösand.

Survival Guide

Directory A–Z

Accommodation

Accommodation listings have been divided into budget, midrange and top-end categories.

Cheap hotels are virtually unknown in far-northern Europe, but hostels, guest-houses, pensions, private rooms, farm accommodation and B&Bs can be good value. Self-catering cottages and flats are an excellent option if travelling in a family or group. The following options are useful for bookings.

Train stations Often have a hotel-booking desk.

Tourist offices Have extensive accommodation lists. Usually for a small fee, the more helpful offices will go out of their way to find you somewhere to stay.

Internet A powerful resource both for scope and discounted rooms.

Agencies For private rooms, agencies can be good value; you may lack privacy, but staying with a local family brings you closer to the spirit of the country.

B&Bs, Guesthouses & Hotels

» B&Bs, where you get a room and breakfast in a private home, can often be real bargains. Pensions and guesthouses are similar but usually slightly more upmarket.

» Most Scandinavian hotels are geared to business travellers and have prices to match. But excellent hotel discounts are often available at certain times (eg at weekends and in summer in Finland, Norway and Sweden) and for longer stays. Breakfast in hotels is usually included in the price of the room.

» If you think a hotel is too expensive, ask if it has a cheaper room. In nonchain places it can be easy to negotiate a discount in quiet periods if you're with a group or are planning to stay for any length of time.

Camping

» Camping is cheap (usually a charge per tent or camp-site, per vehicle and per person) and immensely popular throughout the region. There are camping cards that offer good benefits and discounts.

» National tourist offices have booklets or brochures listing camping grounds all over their country.

» In most larger towns and cities, camping grounds are some distance from the centre. If you've got no transport, the money you save by camping can quickly be outweighed by the money spent commuting in and out of town.

» Nearly all mainland Scandinavian camping grounds rent simple cabins – a good budget option if you're not carrying a tent. Many also have more upmarket cottages with bedrooms, bathrooms and proper kitchens, great for families who want to self-cater.

» Camping other than in designated camping grounds is not always straightforward but in many countries there's a right of common access that applies. Tourist offices usually stock official publications in English explaining your rights and responsibilities.

Hostels

Hostels generally offer the cheapest roof over your head, and in Scandinavia you don't have to be young to use them: hostels are geared for budget travellers of all ages, including families with kids, and most have dorms and private rooms.

BOOK YOUR STAY ONLINE

For more accommodation reviews by Lonely Planet authors, check out http://hotels.lonelyplanet.com. You'll find independent reviews, as well as recommendations on the best places to stay. Best of all, you can book online.

Most hostels are part of national Youth Hostel Associations (YHAs), known collectively throughout the world as **Hostelling International** (HI; www.hihostels.com).

You'll have to be a YHA or HI member to use some affiliated hostels (indicated by a blue triangle symbol) but in practice most are open to anyone. Without an HI card you may have to pay a bit extra, but this can be offset against future membership. Prices listed in this guide are HI member prices. To join HI, ask at any hostel, contact your local or national hostelling office, or register over the internet. If you'll be spending more than four or five nights in hostels in Scandinavia, it's worth doing. There's a particularly huge network of HI hostels in Denmark and Sweden.

Comfort levels and facilities vary markedly. Some hostels charge extra if you don't want to sweep your room out when you leave.

Many hostel guides are available, including HI's annually updated *Official International Youth Hostels Guide*.

Breakfast Many hostels (exceptions include most hostels in Iceland) serve breakfast, and almost all have communal kitchens where you can prepare meals.

Bookings Some hostels accept reservations by phone; they'll often book the next hostel you're headed to for a small fee. The HI website has a booking form you can use to reserve a bed in advance – but not all hostels are on the network. Popular hostels in capital cities can be heavily booked in summer and limits may be placed on how many nights you can stay.

Linen You must use a sleeping sheet and pillowcase or linen in hostels in most Scandinavian countries; sleeping bags are not

permitted. It's worth carrying your own sleeping sheet or linen, as hiring these at hostels is comparatively expensive.

Travellers with Disabilities
Specially adapted rooms for visitors with disabilities are becoming more common, but check with the hostel first.

Self-Catering

» There's a huge network (especially in Norway, Sweden, Denmark and Finland) of rental cottages that make excellent, peaceful places to stay and offer a chance to experience a traditional aspect of Scandinavian life.

» Many Scandinavians traditionally spend their summers in such places. Renting a cottage for a few days is highly recommended as part of a visit to the region.

University Accommodation

» Some universities and colleges rent out students' rooms (sometimes called 'summer hotels') to tourists from June to mid-August.

» Usually single or twin rooms with a kitchenette (but often no utensils). Enquire directly at the college or university, student information services or local tourist offices.

Children

Most of Scandinavia is very child friendly, with domestic tourism largely dictated by children's needs. Iceland is something of an exception: children are liked and have lots of freedom, but they're treated as mini adults, and there aren't many attractions tailored particularly for children.

Accommodation The bigger camping grounds and spa hotels are particularly kid-conscious, with heaps of facilities and activities

designed with children in mind. Cots (cribs) are standard in many hotels but numbers may be limited.

Activities In Denmark, Finland, Norway and Sweden you'll find excellent theme parks, water parks and holiday activities. Many museums have a dedicated children's section with toys, games and dressing-up clothes.

Food Choice of baby food, infant formulas, soy and cow's milk, disposable nappies (diapers) etc is wide in Scandinavian supermarkets.

Restaurants High chairs are standard in many restaurants but numbers may be limited. Restaurants will often have children's menu options, and there are lots of chain eateries aimed specifically at families.

Transport Car-rental firms hire out children's safety seats at a nominal cost, but advance bookings are essential.

Want more? Pick up a copy of Lonely Planet's *Travel with Children*.

Customs Regulations

From non-EU to EU countries For EU countries (ie Denmark, Sweden, Finland and Estonia), travellers arriving from outside the EU can bring duty-free goods up to the value of €300 (or €430 if you arrive by air or sea) without declaration. You can also bring in up to 16L of beer, 2L of wine and 1L of spirits, plus 200 cigarettes or 250g of tobacco. These allowances change occasionally, so before departure check out www.ec.europa.eu/taxation_customs; click on the 'Travellers' link on the left hand side of the web page for current details.

Within the EU If you're coming from another EU country, there is no restriction on the value of purchases for your own use.

Åland islands Arriving on or from the Åland islands (although technically part of the EU), carries the same import restrictions as arriving from a non-EU country.

Other Nordic countries Norway, Iceland, the Faroe Islands and St Petersburg have lower limits.

Discount Cards

» **Camping Key Europe** (www.campingkeyeurope.com) Discounts at many camping grounds and attractions in Scandinavia and Northern Europe, with built-in third-party insurance. In Denmark and some Swedish camping grounds, it's obligatory to have this or a similar card. If you're just getting a camping card to use in Scandinavia, we recommend this one, as it's accepted in more places than others. One card covers you whether you're an individual, a couple or a family with children under 18. Order through regional camping websites, or buy from camping grounds throughout the region (this is sometimes cheaper). It costs around €16 depending slightly on what country and whereabouts you get it.

» **Camping Card International** (www.campingcardinternational.com) Similar to Camping Key Europe, also widely accepted in the region.

» **European Youth Card** (Euro<26; www.eyca.org) This card offers discounts to those aged under 30. Available through student unions, hostelling organisations or youth-oriented travel agencies.

» **Hostelling International** (www.hihostels.com) Not mandatory in Scandinavia but gives a sizeable discount every time you check in to an affiliated hostel. Best to buy from your national hostelling association before you set off, although some Scandinavian hostels will issue one on the spot or after six stays (generally more expensive than getting one at home).

» **International Student Identity Card** (ISIC; www.isic.org) This card offers discounts on many forms of transport, either reduced or free admission to museums and sights, and cheap meals in student cafeterias – a worthwhile way of cutting costs. Check the website for a list of discounts by country. Because of the proliferation of fake ISIC cards, carry your home student ID as back up. Some places won't give student discounts without it.

» **International Teacher Identity Card** (ITIC; www.isic.org) Just for teachers and academics. The discounts for flashing these cards have reduced over the years due to widespread fraud, but you will still be able to make a few savings here and there.

» **International Youth Travel Card** (IYTC; www.isic.org) Discounts for under-26ers. Buy as per European Youth Card.

» **Seniors Cards** Discounts for retirees, pensioners and those over 60 (sometimes slightly younger for women; over 65 in Sweden) at museums and other sights, public swimming pools, spas and transport companies. Make sure you carry proof of age around with you.

» **Student cards** If you are studying in Scandinavia, a local student card will get you megadiscounts on transport and more.

Electricity

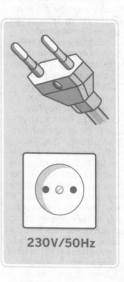

230V/50Hz

Embassies & Consulates

Travellers can visit the website of their home country's national department or ministry of foreign affairs to locate embassies and consulates in Scandinavia.

Australian Department of Foreign Affairs & Trade www.dfat.gov.au/missions

Canadian Foreign Affairs & International Trade www.international.gc.ca/ciw-cdm/embassies-ambassades.aspx

French Ministry of Foreign Affairs www.mfe.org/index.php/Annuaires/Ambassades-et-consulats-francais-a-l-etranger

German Federal Foreign Office www.auswaertiges-amt.de/DE/Laender informationen/03-WebseitenAV/Uebersicht_node.html

Irish Department of Foreign Affairs www.dfa.ie/home/index.aspx?id=285

Netherlands Ministry of Foreign Affairs www.mfa.nl

New Zealand Ministry of Foreign Affairs & Trade www.nzembassy.com

UK Foreign & Commonwealth Office www.fco. gov.uk/en/travel-and-living-abroad/find-an-embassy

US Department of State www.usembassy.gov

Gay & Lesbian Travellers

» Denmark, Finland, Iceland, Norway and Sweden are very tolerant nations, although public displays of affection are less common in rural areas, particularly Lapland.

» See this book's individual country chapters for more information.

Health

Travel in Scandinavia presents very few health problems. The standard of health care is extremely high and English is widely spoken by doctors and medical-clinic staff. Tap water is safe to drink, the level of hygiene is high and there are no endemic diseases.

Extreme climate risks Be aware of hypothermia, frostbite or viral infections (influenza). Biting insects, such as mosquitoes, are more of an annoyance than a real health risk.

Health insurance (EEA) Citizens of the European Economic Area (EEA) are covered for emergency medical treatment in other EEA countries (including Denmark, Finland, Iceland, Norway and Sweden) on presentation of a European Health Insurance Card (EHIC), which replaced the old E111 form. Enquire about EHICs at your health centre, travel agency or (in some countries) post office well in advance of travel.

Health insurance (non-EEA) Citizens from countries outside the EEA should find out if there is a reciprocal arrangement for free medical care between their country and the country visited. If not, travel health insurance is recommended.

Vaccinations Not specifically required for visitors to Scandinavia but you should be up to date with all normal childhood vaccinations.

Insurance

A travel-insurance policy to cover theft, personal liability, loss and medical problems is recommended. There are a variety of policies available and travel agencies will have recommendations. Travel insurance also usually covers cancellation or delays in travel arrangements, for example, if you fall seriously ill two days before departure. If you're driving, don't forget to consider car insurance (p495).

Worldwide travel insurance is available at www. lonelyplanet.com/travel-insurance. You can buy, extend and claim online anytime – even if you're already on the road.

» Buy insurance as early as possible. If you buy it the week before you are due to fly, you may find that you're not covered for delays to your flight caused by strikes or other industrial actions

that may have been in force before you took out the insurance.

» Get a policy that covers you for the worst-possible health scenario if you aren't already covered by a reciprocal health-care agreement. Make sure your policy also covers you for any activities you plan to do, like skiing – check the small print. Find out in advance if your insurance plan will make payments directly to providers or reimburse you later for overseas health expenditure.

» If you plan to travel more than once in a 12-month period, you may find it cheaper to take out an annual policy rather than two single-trip policies.

» Paying for your airline ticket with a credit card often provides limited travel accident insurance, and you may be able to reclaim the payment if the operator doesn't deliver. Certain bank accounts also offer their holders automatic travel insurance.

Internet Access

» There are internet cafes throughout Scandinavia. Libraries provide free/very cheap internet service – but there may be a waiting list and locals may have priority.

» Public internet access in some post offices, tourist

SCANDINAVIAN CURRENCIES

COUNTRY	CURRENCY
Denmark	Danish krone (Dkr)
Finland	euro (€)
Iceland	Icelandic króna (Ikr)
Norway	Norwegian krone (Nkr)
Sweden	Swedish krona (Skr)
Tallinn, Estonia	euro (€)

offices, hostels, hotels and universities.

» Wireless (wi-fi) hot spots are rife. An astonishing number of cafes, bars, hostels and hotels offer the service for free. A growing number of towns and cities in the region have free public wi-fi across the centre.

» It can also be reasonably priced to buy a USB modem and pay-as-you-go SIM card, though in some countries you'll need to register an address.

Money

ATMs Widespread, even in small places. This is the best way to access cash in Scandinavia. Find out what your home bank will charge you per withdrawal before you go as you may be better off taking out larger sums.

Cash cards A good alternative to travellers cheques. These are much like debit or credit cards but are loaded with a set amount of money. They also have the advantage of lower withdrawal fees than your bank might otherwise charge you.

Changing money All Scandinavian currencies are fully convertible.

Charge cards Includes cards like American Express and Diners Club. Less widely accepted than credit cards because they charge merchants high commissions.

Debit and credit cards Scandinavians love using plastic, even for small transactions, and you'll find that debit and credit cards are the way to go here.

Foreign currencies Easily exchanged, with rates usually slightly better at exchange offices rather than banks. Avoid exchanging in airports if possible; you'll get better rates downtown. Always ask about the rate and commission before handing over your cash.

Tax A value-added tax (VAT) applies to most goods and services throughout Scandinavia. International visitors from outside the EEA can claim back the VAT above a set minimum amount on purchases that are being taken out of the country. The procedure for making the claim is usually pretty straightforward.

Tipping Isn't required in Scandinavia. But if you round up the bill or leave a little something in recognition of good service, it won't be refused.

Travellers cheques Rapidly disappearing but still accepted in big hotels and exchange offices.

TELEPHONE CODES

COUNTRY	☑CC	☑IAC
Denmark	45	00
Finland	358	00
Iceland	354	00
Norway	47	00
Sweden	46	00
Tallinn	372	00

Use the country code (CC) to call into that country. Use the international access code (IAC) to call abroad from that country.

Telephone

To call abroad dial the international access code (IAC) for the country you are calling from, the country code (CC) for the country you are calling, the local area code (usually dropping the leading zero if there is one) and then the number. If, for example, you are in Norway (which has an international access code of ☑00) and want to make a call to Sweden (country code ☑46) in the Stockholm area (area code ☑08, number ☑123 4567), dial ☑00-46-8-123 4567.

Emergencies The emergency number is the same throughout Scandinavia: ☑112.

Internet Calling via the internet is a practical and cheap solution for making international calls.

Mobile phones Bring a mobile that's not tied to a specific network (unlocked) and buy a local SIM card in each country you visit. If coming from outside Europe, check that the phone will work in Europe's GSM 900/1800 network; most modern phones will.

Phone boxes Almost nonexistent in most of Scandinavia.

Phonecards Easily bought for cheaper international calls.

Reverse-charge (collect) calls Usually possible, and communicating with the local operator in English should not be much of a problem.

Time

Scandinavia sprawls across several time zones. The 24-hour clock is widely used. Note that Europe and the US move clocks forward and back at slightly different times. The following table is a seasonal guide only.

TIME

CITY	TIME IN WINTER	TIME IN SUMMER
New York	11am (UTC -5)	noon (UTC -4)
Reykjavík	4pm (UTC)	4pm (UTC; no summer time)
London	4pm (UTC)	5pm (UTC +1)
Oslo, Copenhagen, Stockholm	5pm (UTC +1)	6pm (UTC +2)
Helsinki, Tallinn	6pm (UTC +2)	7pm (UTC +3)

Tourist Information

Facilities Generally excellent, with piles of regional and national brochures, helpful free maps and friendly employees. Staff are often multilingual, speaking Scandinavian languages, English, German and French.

Locations Offices at train stations or centrally (often in the town hall or central square) in most towns.

Opening hours Longer office hours over summer, reduced hours over winter; smaller offices may open only during peak summer months.

Services Will book hotel and transport reservations and tours; a small charge may apply.

Travellers with Disabilities

» Scandinavia leads the world as the best-equipped region for the traveller with disabilities. By law, most institutions must provide ramps, lifts and special toilets for people with disabilities; all new hotels and restaurants must install disabled facilities. Most trains and city buses are also accessible by wheelchair.

» Some national parks offer accessible nature trails, and cities have ongoing projects in place designed to maximise disabled access in all aspects of urban life.

» Iceland is a little further behind the rest of the region; check access issues before you travel. Scandinavian tourist-office websites generally contain good information on disabled access.

» Before leaving home, get in touch with your national support organisation – preferably the 'travel officer' if there is one. They often have complete libraries devoted to travel and can put you in touch with agencies that specialise in tours for the disabled. One such in the UK is **Can Be Done** (☎+44 (0)20-8907 2400; www.canbedone.co.uk).

Visas

» Denmark, Estonia, Finland, Iceland, Norway and Sweden are all part of the Schengen area. A valid passport or EU identity card is required to enter the region.

» Citizens of the EU, USA, Canada, Australia and New Zealand don't need a tourist visa for stays of less than three months; others may need a Schengen visa. New Zealanders are allowed consecutive 90-day stays in several Schengen states.

» A Schengen visa can be obtained by applying to an embassy or consulate of any country in the Schengen area.

Women Travellers

» Scandinavia is one of the safest places to travel in all of Europe and women travellers should experience little trouble.

» In smaller towns, and especially north of Sweden and Finland, bars can be fairly unreconstructed places, and women may get a bit of nonthreatening but unpleasant hassle from drunk locals.

Transport

GETTING THERE & AWAY

Scandinavia is easily accessed from the rest of Europe and beyond. There are direct flights from numerous destinations into Sweden, Norway, Denmark and Finland, and less choice to Iceland. Denmark, Sweden and Norway can be accessed by train from Western Europe, while Baltic and Atlantic ferries are another good option for accessing these Nordic countries.

Flights, cars and tours can be booked online at lonelyplanet.com.

Air

As well as the many national carriers that fly directly into Scandinavia's airports, there is a host of budget options. These change frequently, and are best investigated on websites such as www.whichbudget.com. Budget airlines have the extra advantage of well-priced one-way tickets, making it easy to fly into one of the region's cities and out from another.

The following are major hubs in Scandinavia.

Arlanda Airport (www.swedavia.se/arlanda) Stockholm, Sweden

Gardermoen International Airport (www.osl.no) Oslo, Norway

Helsinki-Vantaa Airport (www.helsinki-vantaa.fi) Helsinki, Finland

Kastrup International Airport (www.cph.dk) Copenhagen, Denmark

Keflavík Airport (www.kefairport.is) Reykjavík, Iceland

Land

Bus

Without a rail pass, the cheapest overland transport from Europe to Scandinavia is the bus, though a cheap flight deal will often beat it on price. **Eurolines** (www.eurolines.com), a conglomeration of coach companies, is the biggest and best-established express-bus network, and connects Scandinavia with the rest of Europe. Advance ticket purchases are usually necessary.

Car & Motorcycle

Driving to Scandinavia means driving into Denmark from Germany (and then on across to Sweden via the bridge and tunnels), going through Russia or taking a car ferry.

Hitching & Car-Ride Services

Summer hitching is possible but expect some looong waits. Hitching is never entirely safe, and we therefore don't recommend it. Travellers who hitch should understand that they are taking a small but potentially serious risk.

After hitching, the cheapest way to head further north in Europe is as a paying passenger in a private car. Various car-sharing websites across Europe are good places to start. Try www.mitfahrzentrale.de, www.covoiturage.fr or www.roadsharing.com. Local tourist-information offices can help you locate agencies.

Train

FROM GERMANY

» Apart from trains into Finland from Russia, the rail route into Scandinavia goes from Germany into Denmark, then on to Sweden and then Norway via the Copenhagen–Malmö bridge and tunnel connection. Hamburg and Cologne are the main gateways in Germany for this route.

» There are several direct Hamburg–Copenhagen trains daily (2nd class from €81, cheaper if booked in advance, five to seven hours); some go via the ferry between Puttgarten and Rødby (included; the train actually boards the ferry).

» Overnight trains head from Cologne to Copenhagen (11 hours) via Odense.

FROM LONDON

Various options, see the exceptional **Man in Seat 61** (www.seat61.com) for details. Contact **Deutsche Bahn UK** (www.bahn.com) for details of frequent special offers and for reservations and tickets.

For more information on international rail travel (including Eurostar services), contact the **Rail Europe Travel Centre** (www.raileurope.co.uk; 178 Piccadilly, London). You can also book via its website.

Sea

Services are year-round between major cities: book ahead in summer, at weekends and if travelling with a vehicle. Many boats are amazingly cheap if you travel deck class (without a cabin). Many ferry lines offer 50% discounts for holders of Eurail, Scanrail and InterRail passes. Some offer discounts for seniors, and for ISIC and youth-card holders; inquire when purchasing your ticket. There are usually discounts for families and small groups travelling together. Ferry companies have detailed timetables and fares on their websites. Fares vary according to season.

Baltic Countries

There are numerous sailings between Tallinn, Estonia and Helsinki, Finland, operated by Eckerö Line, Linda Line (fast boats), Tallink/Silja Line and Viking Line. Tallink/Silja also sails from Tallinn to Stockholm via Mariehamn and DFDS Seaways runs from Paldiski (Estonia) to Kappelskär (Sweden). Navirail crosses from Paldiski to Hanko (Finland).

Stena Line runs from Nynäshamn, Sweden to Ventspils, Latvia several times weekly. Tallink/Silja does a Stockholm to Riga run.

DFDS operates between Karlshamn (Sweden) and Klaipėda (Lithuania).

Germany

Denmark Bornholmer Færgen runs between the island of Bornholm and Sassnitz, in eastern Germany. Scandlines runs from Rødby, on

FERRY COMPANIES

The following is a list of the main ferry companies operating to and around Scandinavia, with their websites and major routes. See websites for contact telephone numbers, times, durations and sample fares.

BornholmerFærgen (www.faergen.com) Denmark–Sweden, Denmark–Germany

Color Line (www.colorline.com) Norway–Denmark, Norway–Germany, Norway–Sweden

DFDS Seaways (www.dfdsseaways.com) Norway–Sweden–Denmark, Denmark–UK, Lithuania–Sweden, Estonia–Sweden

Eckerö Line (www.eckeroline.fi) Finland–Tallinn, Finland–Sweden

Finnlines (www.finnlines.com) Finland–Sweden, Finland–Germany, Finland–Poland, Sweden–Germany

Fjord Line (www.fjordline.com) Norway–Denmark

HH Ferries (www.hhferries.se) Sweden–Denmark

Linda Line (www.lindaline.fi) Finland–Estonia

Navirail (www.navirail.com) Finland–Estonia

Polferries (www.polferries.pl) Sweden–Poland, Denmark–Poland

Regina Line (www.reginaline.dk) Denmark–UK

RG Line (www.rgline.com) Finland–Sweden

St Peter Line (www.stpeterline.com) Finland–St Petersburg plus a St Petersburg–Helsinki–Stockholm–Tallinn–St Petersburg circuit

Scandlines (www.scandlines.com) Sweden–Denmark, Denmark–Germany

Smyril Line (www.smyrilline.com) Denmark–Faroe Islands–Iceland

Stena Line (www.stenaline.com) Denmark–Norway, Denmark–Sweden, Sweden–Germany, Sweden–Poland, Sweden–Latvia

Syltfaehre (www.syltfaehre.de) Denmark–Germany (Sylt)

Tallink/Silja Line (www.tallinksilja.com) Finland–Sweden, Finland–Tallinn, Sweden–Tallinn, Sweden–Latvia

TT-Line (www.ttline.com) Sweden–Germany

Unity Line (www.unityline.pl) Sweden–Poland

Viking Line (www.vikingline.fi) Finland–Sweden, Finland–Tallinn

Train & Ferry Routes

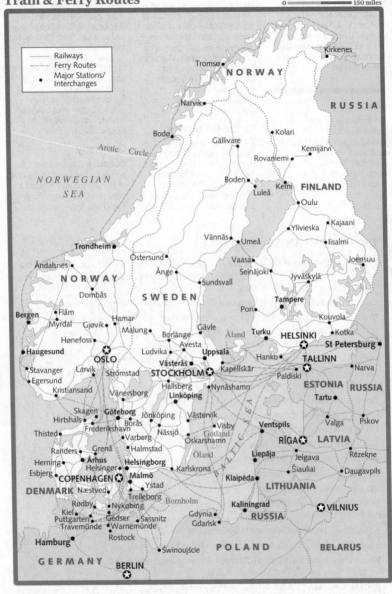

- Railways
- Ferry Routes
- Major Stations/Interchanges

the island of Lolland, to Puttgarten, and between Gedser, on the island of Falster, and Rostock. There's also a service from Havneby, at the southern tip of the Danish island of Rømø, to List on the German island of Sylt; this is run by Syltfaehre.

Finland Finnlines runs from Helsinki to Travemünde and Helsinki to Rostock.

Norway Color Line runs daily from Oslo to Kiel.

Sweden Stena Line runs Trelleborg to Rostock, Trelleborg to Sassnitz and Göteborg to Kiel. TT-Line runs Trelleborg to Travemünde and Trelleborg to Rostock. Finnlines runs Malmö to Travemünde.

Poland

Denmark Polferries operates to Świnoujście from Copenhagen.

Finland Finnlines runs from Helsinki to Gdynia.

Sweden Polferries runs Ystad to Świnoujście, as does Unity Line, which also runs Trelleborg to Świnoujście. Polferries also links Nynäshamn with Gdańsk. Stena Lines runs between Karlskrona and Gdynia.

UK DFDS Seaways has ferries from Harwich to Esbjerg in Denmark, as does Regina Line.

GETTING AROUND

Getting around the populated areas of Scandinavia is generally a breeze, with efficient public-transport systems and snappy connections. Remote regions usually have trustworthy but infrequent services.

Air

» Flights are safe and reliable. Can be expensive, but often cheaper than land-based alternatives for longer journeys, and can save days of travelling time.

» There are reduced rates for internet bookings on internal airline routes, with several budget operators offering domestic and intra-Scandinavian flights.

» Good bus and train networks between airports and city centres.

» Visitors flying **SAS** (www. flysas.com) or code-shared flights on a return ticket to Scandinavia from Asia or the USA can buy Visit Scandinavia/Europe Airpass coupons. The passes allow one-way travel on direct flights between any two Scandinavian cities serviced by SAS and some other operators, with stopovers limited to one in each city.

Children fly for around 70% of the adult price. Tickets can be purchased after arriving in Scandinavia if you have a return SAS international ticket.

Bicycle

Scandinavia is exceptionally bike friendly, with loads of cycle paths, courteous motorists, easy public-transport options and flattish, picturesque terrain.

Bike clubs The wonderful **Cyclists' Touring Club** (www.ctc.org.uk) offers cycling conditions, routes, itineraries, maps and specialised insurance.

Bike shops Widespread in towns and cities, but worth taking sufficient tools and spare parts if visiting more remote areas.

Hire From train station bike-rental counters; in some cases it's possible to return hire bikes to another outlet so you don't have to double back.

No-nos Cycling across the Øresund bridge between Denmark and Sweden is prohibited.

On public transport Bikes can be transported as luggage, either free or for a small fee, on slower trains and local buses in Scandinavia.

Theft Not uncommon in places like Helsinki and Copenhagen; take a decent lock and use it when you leave your bike unattended.

Boat

Ferry

You can't really get around Scandinavia without using ferries extensively. The shortest routes from Denmark (Jutland) to Norway and from southern Sweden to Finland are ferry routes. Denmark is now well connected to mainland Europe and Sweden by bridges.

Ferry tickets are cheap on competitive routes, although transporting cars can be costly. Bicycles are usually carried free. On some routes, train-pass holders are entitled to free or discounted travel.

Weekend ferries, especially on Friday night, are significantly more expensive. Teenagers are banned from travelling on some Friday-night ferries due to problems with drunkenness.

For Tallinn and Estonia connections see p218.

Denmark–Norway There are several connections. From Hirtshals, Fjord Line sails to Bergen, Kristiansand, Langesund and Stavanger. Color Line goes to Kristiansand and Larvik. From Frederikshavn, Stena Line goes to Oslo. From Copenhagen, DFDS Seaways also goes to Oslo.

Denmark–Sweden Stena Line runs the connections Grenaa to Varberg and Frederikshavn to Göteborg. The short Helsingør to Helsingborg crossing is covered by Scandlines and HH Ferries, while BornholmerFærgen goes from Rønne on Bornholm to Ystad.

Norway–Sweden Color Line and Fjord Line connect Strömstad, Sweden, with Sandefjord, Norway.

Sweden–Finland Connections from Stockholm to Helsinki or Turku via Mariehamn are operated by Tallink/Silja and Viking Line. Viking also runs to Åland from Kapellskär. Eckerö Line runs from Grisslehamn to Eckerö on Åland, Finnlines runs Kapellskär to Naantali, while further north, RG Line connects Umeå with Vaasa.

Steamer

» Scandinavia's main lakes and rivers are served by diesel-powered boats and steamers during summer. Treat these as relaxing, scenic miniholidays; if you view them merely as a way to get from A to B, they can seem quite expensive.

THE ICELAND FERRY

The popular *Nörrona* ferry travels from Denmark to the Faroe Islands and on to Iceland. LP author Mark Elliott has some handy hints:

It can be confusing to piece together the reality from the **Smyril Line** (☑in Denmark 96 55 03 60, in Faroe Islands 345 900; www.smyril-line.com) website. The cheapest fares will get you a bed in a claustrophobic 'couchette' (windowless six-bed dorm) in the bowels of the ship, but neither linen nor pillow is provided. Upgrading to a two-person cabin (linen, pillow, TV etc included) offers a vast improvement in comfort and means you have somewhere to leave your luggage during the day without paying Dkr20/40 for small/large lockers every time you need something. If driving, note that the car deck is inaccessible during the voyage. Buffet meals (breakfast/dinner €14/27) are ample but bring plenty of drinking water if you don't want to pay per bottle once aboard. Wi-fi is available by credit/debit card and there are power points in the corridors and cafeteria. Live music and evening magic shows are free as is use of the deck 1 swimming pool (bring your own towel).

A massively important thing is to realise that when it suggests that passengers should arrive two to three hours ahead of time for check-in it is dead serious – I arrived just over two hours before departure and was only just in time to board.

» Sweden has the largest fleets in Scandinavia. Most leave from Stockholm and sail east to the Stockholm archipelago and west to historic Lake Mälaren. You can also cruise the Göta Canal, the longest water route in Sweden.

» Legendary *Hurtigruten* ferry provides a link between Norway's coastal fishing villages.

» In Finland, steamships ply the eastern lakes, connecting the towns on their shores.

Bus

Buses provide a viable alternative to the rail network in Scandinavian countries, and are the only option in Iceland and parts of northern Sweden, Finland and Norway.

Cost Compared to trains, they're usually cheaper (Finland is the exception) and slightly slower. Connections with train services (where they exist) are good.

Advance reservation Rarely necessary. But you do need to prepurchase your ticket before you board many city buses, and then validate your ticket on board.

International routes There are regular bus services between Denmark and Sweden, and Sweden and Norway. Services between Finland and Norway run in Lapland, and there's a bus between Finland and Sweden at the border towns of Tornio/Haparanda.

Car & Motorcycle

Travelling with a vehicle is the best way to get to remote places and gives you independence and flexibility. Drawbacks include cost, being isolated in your own little car bubble and stressful city-centre driving.

Scandinavia is excellent for motorcycle touring, with good-quality winding roads, stunning scenery and an active motorcycling scene – just make sure your wet-weather gear is up to scratch. The best time for touring is May to September. On ferries, motorcyclists rarely have to book ahead as they can generally be squeezed in.

Bringing Your Own Vehicle

Documentation Proof of ownership of a private

vehicle should always be carried (this is the Vehicle Registration Document for British-registered cars) when touring Europe. You'll also need an insurance document valid in the countries you are planning to visit. Contact your local automobile association for further information.

Border crossings Vehicles crossing an international border should display a sticker showing their country of registration. (The exception is cars with Euro-plates being taken into another EU country.)

Safety It's compulsory to carry a warning triangle in most places, to be used in the event of breakdown, and several countries require a reflective jacket. You must also use headlamp beam reflectors/converters on right-hand-drive cars.

Driving Licence

An EU driving licence is acceptable for driving throughout Scandinavia, as are North American and Australian licences, for example. If you have any other type of licence, you should check to see if you need to obtain an International Driving Permit (IDP) from your motoring organisation before you leave home.

If you're thinking of going snowmobiling, you'll need to bring your driving licence with you.

Fuel & Spare Parts

Fuel is heavily taxed and very expensive in Scandinavia. Most types of petrol, including unleaded 95 and 98 octane, are widely available; leaded petrol is no longer sold. Diesel is significantly cheaper than petrol in most countries. Always check the type of fuel being supplied – usually pumps with green markings deliver unleaded fuel, and black pumps supply diesel.

Hire

Cost Renting a car is more expensive in Scandinavia than in other European countries. Be sure you understand what's included in the price (unlimited or paid kilometres, injury insurance, tax, collision damage waiver etc) and what your liabilities are. Norway is the most expensive so it may pay to rent a car in neighbouring Sweden and take it across.

Insurance It's usually worth taking the collision damage waiver, although you may be covered for this and injury insurance if you have a travel-insurance policy: check.

Companies The big international firms – Hertz, Avis, Budget and Europcar – are all present, but using local firms can mean a better deal. Big firms give you the option of returning the car to a different outlet when you've finished with it, but this is heavily charged.

Booking Try to prebook your vehicle, which always works out cheaper. Online brokers often offer substantially cheaper rates than the company websites themselves.

Fly/drive combination SAS and Icelandair often offer cheaper car rentals to their international passengers. Check their websites for deals.

Border crossings Ask in advance if you can drive a rented car across borders. In Scandinavia it's usually no problem.

Age The minimum rental age is usually 21, sometimes even 23, and you'll need a credit card (or a mountain of cash) for the deposit.

Motorcycle and moped rental Not particularly common in Scandinavian countries, but possible in major cities.

Insurance

Third-party motor insurance A minimum requirement in most of Europe. Most UK car-insurance policies automatically provide third-party cover for EU and some other countries. Ask your insurer for a Green Card – an internationally recognised proof of insurance (there may be a charge) – and check that it lists all the countries you intend to visit.

Breakdown assistance Check whether your insurance policy offers breakdown assistance overseas. If it doesn't, a European breakdown-assistance policy, such as those provided by the AA or the RAC, is a good investment. Your motoring organisation may also offer reciprocal coverage with affiliated motoring organisations.

Road Conditions & Hazards

Conditions and types of roads vary widely across Scandinavia, but it's possible to make some generalisations.

Iceland Specific challenges include unsealed gravel roads, long, claustrophobic single-lane tunnels, frequent mist and the wild, lonely, 4WD-only F-roads. See the video at www.drive.is for more info.

Main roads Primary routes, with the exception of some roads in Iceland, are universally in good condition. There are comparatively few motorways.

Minor roads Road surfaces on minor routes are not so reliable, although normally adequate.

Norway Has some particularly hair-raising roads; serpentine examples climb from sea level to 1000m in what seems no distance at all on a map. These roller coasters will use plenty of petrol and strain the car's engine and brakes, not to mention your nerves! Driving a campervan on this kind of route is not recommended.

Tolls In Norway, there are tolls for some tunnels, bridges, roads and entry into larger towns, and for practically all ferries crossing fjords. Roads, tunnels, bridges and car ferries in Finland and Sweden are usually free, although there's a hefty toll of €43 per car on the Øresund bridge (www.oresundsbron.com) between Denmark and Sweden.

Winter Snow tyres are compulsory in winter except in Denmark. Chains are allowed in most countries but almost never used.

Livestock on roads Suicidal stock, including sheep, elk, horses and reindeer, is a potential hazard. If you are involved in an animal incident, by law you must report it to the police.

Road Rules

» Drive on the right-hand side of the road in all Scandinavian countries.

» Seatbelts are compulsory for driver and all passengers.

» Headlights must be switched on at all times.

» In the absence of give way or stop signs, priority is given to traffic approaching from the right.

» It's compulsory for motorcyclists and their passengers to wear helmets.

» Take care with speed limits, which vary from country to country.

» Many driving infringements are subject to on-the-spot fines in Scandinavian countries. In Norway they are stratospheric. Drink-driving regulations are strict.

Hitching

» Hitching is never entirely safe in any country in the world. Travellers, particularly women, who decide to hitch are taking a small but potentially serious risk – even in 'safe' Scandinavia.

» It's neither popular nor particularly rewarding to hitch in most of the region. In fact, it's some of the slowest in the world. Your plans need to be flexible.

» It's sometimes possible to arrange a lift privately: scan student notice boards in colleges or contact car-sharing agencies.

Train

Trains in Scandinavia are comfortable, frequent and punctual. As with most things in the region, prices are relatively expensive, although train passes can make travel affordable. There are no trains in Iceland nor in far-north Finland and Norway.

Costs Full-price tickets can be expensive; book ahead for discounts. Rail passes are worth buying if you plan to do a reasonable amount

of travelling within a short space of time. Seniors and travellers under 26 years of age are eligible for discounted tickets in some countries, which can cut fares by between 15% and 40%.

Reservations It's a good idea (sometimes obligatory) to make reservations at peak times and on certain train lines, especially long-distance trains. In some countries it can be a lot cheaper to book in advance and online.

Express Trains There are various names for fast trains throughout Scandinavia. Supplements usually apply on fast trains and it's wise (sometimes obligatory) to make reservations at peak times and on certain lines.

Overnight Trains

These trains usually offer couchettes or sleepers. Reservations are advisable, particularly as sleeping options are generally allocated on a first-come, first-served basis.

Couchettes Basic bunk beds numbering four (1st class) or six (2nd class) per compartment that are comfortable enough, if lacking a little privacy. In Scandinavia, a bunk costs around €25 to €50 for most trains, irrespective of the length of the journey.

Sleepers The most comfortable option, offering beds for one or two passengers

in 1st class and two or three passengers in 2nd class.

Food Most long-distance trains have a dining car or snack trolley – bring your own nibbles to keep costs down.

Car Some long-distance trains have car-carrying facilities.

Train Passes

There are a variety of passes available for rail travel within Scandinavia, or in various European countries including Scandinavia. There are cheaper passes for students, people under 26 and seniors. Supplements (eg for high-speed services) and reservation costs are not covered by passes, and terms and conditions change – check carefully before buying. Pass-holders must always carry their passport on the train for identification purposes.

EURAIL PASSES

Eurail (www.eurail.com) offers a good selection of different passes available to residents of non-European countries, which should be purchased before arriving in Europe.

Eurail Scandinavia Pass Gives a number of days in a two-month period, and is valid for travel in Denmark, Sweden, Norway and Finland. It costs €250 for four days, and up to €388 for 10 days. A similar but cheaper pass includes Sweden and one of the following: Norway, Denmark or Finland. There are also single-country passes.

CLIMATE CHANGE & TRAVEL

Every form of transport that relies on carbon-based fuel generates CO_2, the main cause of human-induced climate change. Modern travel is dependent on aeroplanes, which might use less fuel per kilometre per person than most cars but travel much greater distances. The altitude at which aircraft emit gases (including CO_2) and particles also contributes to their climate change impact. Many websites offer 'carbon calculators' that allow people to estimate the carbon emissions generated by their journey and, for those who wish to do so, to offset the impact of the greenhouse gases emitted with contributions to portfolios of climate-friendly initiatives throughout the world. Lonely Planet offsets the carbon footprint of all staff and author travel.

Eurail Global Pass Offers travel in 23 European countries – either 10 or 15 days in a two-month period or unlimited travel from 15 days up to three months. It's much better value for under 26s, as those older have to buy a 1st-class pass.

Discounts Most passes offer discounts of around 25% for those under 26, or 15% for two people travelling together. On most Eurail passes, children between four and 11 get a 50% discount on the full adult fare. Eurail passes give a 30%

to 50% discount on several ferry lines in the region; check the website for details.

INTERRAIL PASSES

If you've lived in Europe for more than six months, you're eligible for an **InterRail** (www.interrailnet.com) pass. InterRail scrapped its complex zonal system and now offers two passes valid for train travel in Scandinavia.

InterRail One Country Pass Offers travel in one country of your choice for three/four/six/eight days in a one-month period, costing

€119/150/201/243 in 2nd class for Denmark or Finland, and €181/205/267/311 for Sweden or Norway.

Global Pass Offers travel in 30 European countries and costs from €267 for five days' travel in any 10, to €638 for a month's unlimited train travel.

Discounts On both the above passes, there's a 33% discount for under 26s. InterRail passes give a 30% to 50% discount on several ferry lines in the region; check the website for details.

Language

WANT MORE?

For in-depth language information and handy phrases, check out Lonely Planet's *Western Europe Phrasebook*. You'll find it at **shop.lonelyplanet.com**, or you can buy Lonely Planet's iPhone phrasebooks at the Apple App Store.

This chapter offers basic vocabulary to help you get around Scandinavia. If you read our coloured pronunciation guides as if they were English, you'll be understood. Note that the stressed syllables are indicated with italics.

Some phrases in this chapter have both polite and informal forms (indicated by the abbreviations 'pol' and 'inf' respectively). The abbreviations 'm' and 'f' indicate masculine and feminine gender respectively.

DANISH

Danish has official status in Denmark and the Faroe Islands.

All vowels in Danish can be long or short. Note that aw is pronounced as in 'saw', eu as the 'u' in 'nurse', ew as 'ee' with rounded lips, oh as the 'o' in 'note', ow as in 'how', and dh as the 'th' in 'that'.

Basics

Hello.	Goddag.	go·da
Goodbye.	Farvel.	faar·vel
Excuse me.	Undskyld mig.	awn·skewl mai
Sorry.	Undskyld.	awn·skewl
Please.	Vær så venlig.	ver saw ven·lee
Thank you.	Tak.	taak
You're welcome.	Selv tak.	sel taak
Yes.	Ja.	ya
No.	Nej.	nai

How are you?
Hvordan går det? — vor·dan gawr dey

Good, thanks.
Godt, tak. — got taak

What's your name?
Hvad hedder De/du? (pol/inf) — va hey·dha dee/doo

My name is ...
Mit navn er ... — mit nown ir ...

Do you speak English?
Taler De/du engelsk? (pol/inf) — ta·la dee/doo eng·elsk

I don't understand.
Jeg forstår ikke. — yai for·stawr i·ke

Accommodation

campsite	campingplads	kaam·ping·plas
guesthouse	gæstehus	ges·te·hoos
hotel	hotel	hoh·tel
youth hostel	ungdoms-herberg	awng·doms·heyr·beyrg

Signs – Danish	
Indgang	Entrance
Udgang	Exit
Åben	Open
Lukket	Closed
Forbudt	Prohibited
Toilet	Toilets

Numbers – Danish		
1	*en*	in
2	*to*	toh
3	*tre*	trey
4	*fire*	feer
5	*fem*	fem
6	*seks*	seks
7	*syv*	sew
8	*otte*	aw·te
9	*ni*	nee
10	*ti*	tee

Do you have a ... room?	*Har I et ... værelse?*	haar ee it ... verl·se
single	*enkelt*	eng·kelt
double	*dobbelt*	do·belt

How much is it per ...?	*Hvor meget koster det per ...?*	vor maa·yet kos·ta dey peyr ...
night	*nat*	nat
person	*person*	per·sohn

Eating & Drinking

Can you recommend a ...?	*Kan De/du anbefale en ...?* (pol/inf)	kan dee/doo an·bey·fa·le in ...
bar	*bar*	baar
cafe	*café*	ka·fey
restaurant	*restaurant*	res·toh·rang

What would you recommend?
Hvad kan De/du anbefale? (pol/inf) — va kan dee/doo an·bey·fa·le

Do you have vegetarian food?
Har I vegetarmad? — haar ee vey·ge·taar·madh

I'll have ...
..., tak. — ... taak

Cheers!
Skål! — skawl

I'd like the ..., please.	*Jeg vil gerne have ..., tak.*	yai vil gir·ne ha ... taak
bill	*regningen*	rai·ning·en
menu	*menuen*	me·new·en
breakfast	*morgenmad*	morn·madh
lunch	*frokost*	froh·kost
dinner	*middag*	mi·da

beer	*øl*	eul
coffee	*kaffe*	ka·fe
tea	*te*	tey
water	*vand*	van
wine	*vin*	veen

Emergencies

Help!	*Hjælp!*	yelp
Go away!	*Gå væk!*	gaw vek

Call ...!	*Ring efter ...!*	ring ef·ta ...
a doctor	*en læge*	in le·ye
the police	*politiet*	poh·lee·tee·et

I'm lost.
Jeg er faret vild. — yai ir faa·ret veel

I'm ill.
Jeg er syg. — yai ir sew

I have to use the telephone.
Jeg skal bruge en telefon. — yai skal broo·e en tey·ley·fohn

Where's the toilet?
Hvor er toilettet? — vor ir toy·le·tet

Shopping & Services

I'm looking for ...
Jeg leder efter ... — yai li·dha ef·ta ...

How much is it?
Hvor meget koster det? — vor maa·yet kos·ta dey

That's too expensive.
Det er for dyrt. — dey ir for dewrt

Where's ...?	*Hvor er der ...?*	vor ir deyr ...
an ATM	*en hæveautomat*	in he·ve·ow·toh·mat
a foreign exchange	*et vekselkontor*	it veks·le·kon·tohr
market	*marked*	maar·kedh
post office	*postkontor*	post·kon·tohr
tourist office	*turistkontoret*	too·reest·kon·toh·ret

Transport & Directions

Where's ...?
Hvor er ...? — vor ir ...

What's the address?
Hvad er adressen? — va ir a·draa·sen

Can you show me (on the map)?
Kan De/du vise mig   kan dee/doo vee·se mai
det (på kortet)? (pol/inf)   dey (paw kor·tet)

Where can I buy a ticket?
Hvor kan jeg købe   vor ka yai *keu*·be
en billet?   in bi·*let*

What time's the ... bus?	*Hvad tid er den ... bus?*	va teedh ir den ... boos
first	*første*	*feurs*·te
last	*sidste*	*sees*·te
One ... ticket (to Odense), please.	*En ... billet (til Odense), tak.*	in ... bee·*let* (til oh·dhen·se) taak
one-way	*enkelt*	*eng*·kelt
return	*retur*	rey·*toor*
boat	*båden*	*w*·dhen
bus	*bussen*	*boo*·sen
plane	*flyet*	*flew*·et
train	*toget*	*taw*·et

ESTONIAN

Double vowels in written Estonian indicate they are pronounced as long sounds.

Note that air is pronounced as in 'hair', aw as in 'law', ea as in 'ear', eu as in 'nurse', ew as ee with rounded lips, oh as the 'o' in 'note', ow as in 'how', uh as the 'a' in 'ago', kh as in the Scottish *loch*, and zh as the 's' in 'pleasure'.

Basics

Hello.	*Tere.*	*te*·re
Goodbye.	*Nägemist.*	*nair*·ge·mist
Excuse me.	*Vabandage.* (pol)	va·ban·da·ge
	Vabanda. (inf)	va·ban·da
Sorry.	*Vabandust.*	va·ban·dust
Please.	*Palun.*	*pa*·lun
Thank you.	*Tänan.*	*tair*·nan
You're welcome.	*Palun.*	*pa*·lun
Yes.	*Jaa.*	yaa
No.	*Ei.*	ay

Signs – Estonian

Sissepääs	Entrance
Väljapääs	Exit
Avatud/Lahti	Open
Suletud/Kinni	Closed
WC	Toilets

Numbers – Estonian

1	*üks*	ewks
2	*kaks*	kaks
3	*kolm*	kolm
4	*neli*	*ne*·li
5	*viis*	vees
6	*kuus*	koos
7	*seitse*	*say*·tse
8	*kaheksa*	ka·hek·sa
9	*üheksa*	ew·hek·sa
10	*kümme*	*kewm*·me

How are you?
Kuidas läheb?   ku·i·das *lair*·hep

Fine. And you?
Hästi. Ja teil?   *hairs*·ti ya tayl

What's your name?
Mis on teie nimi?   mis on *tay*·e *ni*·mi

My name is ...
Minu nimi on ...   *mi*·nu *ni*·mi on ...

Do you speak English?
Kas te räägite   kas te *rair*·git·te
inglise keelt?   *ing*·kli·se keylt

I don't understand.
Ma ei saa aru.   ma ay saa *a*·ru

Eating & Drinking

What would you recommend?
Mida te soovitate?   *mi*·da te *saw*·vit·tat·te

Do you have vegetarian food?
Kas teil on taimetoitu?   kas tayl on *tai*·met·toyt·tu

I'll have a ...
Ma tahaksin ...   ma *ta*·hak·sin ...

Cheers!
Terviseks!   *tair*·vi·seks

I'd like the ..., please.	*Ma sooviksin ..., palun.*	ma *saw*·vik·sin ... *pa*·lun
bill	*arvet*	*ar*·vet
menu	*menüüd*	*me*·newt
breakfast	*hommikusöök*	*hom*·mi·ku·seuk
dinner	*õhtusöök*	*uhkh*·tu·seuk
lunch	*lõuna*	*luh*·u·na
beer	*õlu*	*uh*·lu
coffee	*kohv*	kokv
tea	*tee*	tey
water	*vesi*	*ve*·si
wine	*vein*	vayn

Emergencies

| Help! | Appi! | ap·pi |
| Go away! | Minge ära! | ming·ke air·ra |

Call ...!	Kutsuge ...!	ku·tsu·ge ...
a doctor	arst	arst
the police	politsei	po·li·tsay

I'm lost.
Ma olen ära eksinud.　ma o·len air·ra ek·si·nud

Where are the toilets?
Kus on WC?　kus on ve·se

Shopping & Services

I'm looking for ...
Ma otsin ...　ma o·tsin

How much is it?
Kui palju see maksab?　ku·i pal·yu sey mak·sab

That's too expensive.
See on liiga kallis.　sey on lee·ga kal·lis

bank	pank	pank
market	turg	turg
post office	postkontor	post·kont·tor

Transport & Directions

Where's the ...?
Kus on ...?　kus on ...

Can you show me (on the map)?
Kas te näitaksite　kas te nair·i·tak·sit·te
mulle (kaardil)?　mul·le (kaar·dil)

Where can I buy a ticket?
Kust saab osta pileti?　kust saab os·ta pi·let·ti

What time's the ... bus?	Mis kell väljub ... buss?	mis kel vairl·yub ... bus
first	esimene	e·si·me·ne
last	viimane	vee·ma·ne

One ... ticket (to Pärnu), please.	Üks ... pilet (Pärnusse), palun.	ewks ... pi·let (pair·nus·se) pa·lun
one-way	ühe otsa	ew·he o·tsa
return	edasi-tagasi	e·da·si·ta·ga·si

boat	laev	laiv
bus	buss	bus
plane	lennuk	len·nuk
train	rong	rongk

FINNISH

Double consonants are held longer than their single equivalents. Note that eu is pronounced as the 'u' in 'nurse', ew as 'ee' with rounded lips, oh as the 'o' in 'note', ow as in 'how', and uh as the 'u' in 'run'.

Basics

Hello.	Hei.	hay
Goodbye.	Näkemiin.	na·ke·meen
Excuse me.	Anteeksi.	uhn·tayk·si
Sorry.	Anteeksi.	uhn·tayk·si
Please.	Ole hyvä.	o·le hew·va
Thank you.	Kiitos.	kee·tos
You're welcome.	Ole hyvä.	o·le hew·va
Yes.	Kyllä.	kewl·la
No.	Ei.	ay

How are you?
Mitä kuuluu?　mi·ta koo·loo

Fine. And you?
Hyvää. Entä itsellesi?　hew·va en·ta it·sel·le·si

What's your name?
Mikä sinun nimesi on?　mi·ka si·nun ni·me·si on

My name is ...
Minun nimeni on ...　mi·nun ni·me·ni on ...

Do you speak English?
Puhutko englantia?　pu·hut·ko en·gluhn·ti·uh

I don't understand.
En ymmärrä.　en ewm·mar·ra

Eating & Drinking

What would you recommend?
Mitä voit suositella?　mi·ta voyt su·o·si·tel·luh

Do you have vegetarian food?
Onko teillä　on·ko teyl·la
kasvisruokia?　kuhs·vis·ru·o·ki·uh

I'll have a ...
Tilaan ...　ti·laan ...

Cheers!
Kippis!　kip·pis

Signs – Finnish

Sisään	Entrance
Ulos	Exit
Avoinna	Open
Suljettu	Closed
Kielletty	Prohibited
Opastus	Information

Numbers – Finnish

1	yksi	ewk·si
2	kaksi	kuhk·si
3	kolme	kol·me
4	neljä	nel·ya
5	viisi	vee·si
6	kuusi	koo·si
7	seitsemän	sayt·se·man
8	kahdeksan	kuhk·dek·suhn
9	yhdeksän	ewh·dek·san
10	kymmenen	kewm·me·nen

I'd like the ..., please.

	Saisinko ...	sai·sin·ko ...
bill	laskun	luhs·kun
menu	ruoka-listan	ru·o·kuh·lis·tuhn
breakfast	aamiaisen	aa·mi·ai·sen
lunch	lounaan	loh·naan
dinner	illallisen	il·luhl·li·sen
bottle of (beer)	pullon (olutta)	pul·lon (o·lut·tuh)
(cup of) coffee/tea	(kupin) kahvia/teetä	(ku·pin) kuh·vi·uh/tay·ta
glass of (wine)	lasillisen (viiniä)	luh·sil·li·sen (vee·ni·a)
water	vettä	vet·ta

Emergencies

Help!	Apua!	uh·pu·uh
Go away!	Mene pois!	me·ne poys
Call ...!	Soittakaa paikalle ...!	soyt·tuh·kaa pai·kuhl·le ...
a doctor	lääkäri	la·ka·ri
the police	poliisi	po·lee·si

I'm lost.
Olen eksynyt.   o·len ek·sew·newt

Where are the toilets?
Missä on vessa?   mis·sa on ves·suh

Shopping & Services

I'm looking for ...
Etsin ...   et·sin ...

How much is it?
Mitä se maksaa?   mi·ta se muhk·saa

That's too expensive.
Se on liian kallis.   se on lee·uhn kuhl·lis

Where's the ...?	Missä on ...?	mis·sa on ...
bank	pankki	puhnk·ki
market	kauppatori	kowp·pa·to·ri
post office	posti-toimisto	pos·ti·toy·mis·to

Transport & Directions

Where's ...?
Missä on ...?   mis·sa on ...

Can you show me (on the map)?
Voitko näyttää sen   voyt·ko na·ewt·ta sen
minulle (kartalta)?   mi·nul·le (kar·tuhl·tuh)

Where can I buy a ticket?
Mistä voin ostaa lipun?   mis·ta voyn os·taa li·pun

What time's the ... bus?	Mihin aikaan lähtee ... bussi?	mi·hin ai·kaan lah·tay ... bus·si
first	ensimmäinen	en·sim·mai·nen
last	viimeinen	vee·may·nen

One ... ticket, please.	Saisinko yhden ... lipun.	sai·sin·ko ewh·den ... li·pun
one-way	yksisuun-taisen	ewk·si·soon·tai·sen
return	meno-paluu	me·no·pa·loo

Where does this ... go?	Minne tämä ... menee?	min·ne ta·ma ... me·nay
boat	laiva	lai·vuh
bus	bussi	bus·si
plane	lentokone	len·to·ko·ne
train	juna	yu·nuh

ICELANDIC

Double consonants are given a long pronunciation. Note that eu is pronounced as the 'u' in 'nurse', oh as the 'o' in 'note', ow as in 'how', öy as the '-er y-' in 'her year' (without the 'r'), dh as the 'th' in 'that', and kh as the throaty 'ch' in the Scottish loch.

Basics

Hello.	Halló.	ha·loh
Goodbye.	Bless.	bles
Please.	Takk.	tak
Thank you.	Takk fyrir.	tak fi·rir
You're welcome.	Það var ekkert.	thadh var e·kert

Signs – Icelandic

Inngangur	Entrance
Útgangur	Exit
Opið	Open
Lokað	Closed
Bannað	Prohibited
Snyrting	Toilets

Excuse me.	Afsakið.	af·sa·kidh
Sorry.	Fyrirgefðu.	fi·rir·gev·dhu
Yes.	Já.	yow
No.	Nei.	nay

How are you?
Hvað segir þú gott?   kvadh se·yir thoo got

Fine. And you?
Allt fínt. En þú?   alt feent en thoo

What's your name?
Hvað heitir þú?   kvadh hay·tir thoo

My name is ...
Ég heiti ...   yekh hay·ti ...

Do you speak English?
Talar þú ensku?   ta·lar thoo ens·ku

I don't understand.
Ég skil ekki.   yekh skil e·ki

Eating & Drinking

What would you recommend?
Hverju mælir þú með?   kver·yu mai·lir thoo medh

Do you have vegetarian food?
Hafið þið   ha·vidh thidh
grænmetisrétti?   grain·me·tis·rye·ti

I'll have a ...
Ég ætla að fá ...   yekh ait·la adh fow ...

Cheers!
Skál!   skowl

I'd like the ..., please.	Get ég fengið ... takk.	get yekh fen·gidh ... tak
bill	reikninginn	rayk·nin·gin
menu	matseðillinn	mat·se·dhit·lin
breakfast	morgunmat	mor·gun·mat
lunch	hádegismat	how·de·yis·mat
dinner	kvöldmat	kveuld·mat
bottle of (beer)	(bjór)flösku	(byohr)·fleus·ku
(cup of) coffee/tea	kaffi/te (bolla)	ka·fi/te (bot·la)
glass of (wine)	(vín)glas	(veen)·glas
water	vatn	vat

Emergencies

Help!	Hjálp!	hyowlp
Go away!	Farðu!	far·dhu

Call ...!	Hringdu á ...!	hring·du ow ...
a doctor	lækni	laik·ni
the police	lögregluna	leu·rekh·lu·na

I'm lost.
Ég er villtur/villt. (m/f)   yekh er vil·tur/vilt

Where are the toilets?
Hvar er snyrtingin?   kvar er snir·tin·gin

Shopping & Services

I'm looking for ...
Ég leita að ...   yekh lay·ta adh ...

How much is it?
Hvað kostar þetta?   kvadh kos·tar the·ta

That's too expensive.
Þetta er of dýrt.   the·ta er of deert

Where's the ...?	Hvar er ...?	kvar er ...
bank	bankinn	bown·kin
market	markaðurinn	mar·ka·dhu·rin
post office	pósthúsið	pohst·hoo·sidh

Transport & Directions

Where's ...?
Hvar er ...?   kvar er ...

Can you show me (on the map)?
Geturðu sýnt mér   ge·tur·dhu seent myer
(á kortinu)?   (ow kor·ti·nu)

Where can I buy a ticket?
Hvar kaupi ég miða?   kvar köy·pi yekh mi·dha

Numbers – Icelandic

1	einn	aydn
2	tveir	tvayr
3	þrír	threer
4	fjórir	fyoh·rir
5	fimm	fim
6	sex	seks
7	sjö	syeu
8	átta	ow·ta
9	níu	nee·u
10	tíu	tee·u

What time's the ... bus?	Hvenær fer ... strætisvagninn?	kve·nair fer ... strai·tis·vag·nin
first	fyrsti	firs·ti
last	síðasti	see·dhas·ti

One ... ticket (to Reykjavík), please.	Einn miða ... (til, Reykjavíkur) takk.	aitn mi·dha ... (til Reykja·vee·kur) tak
one-way	aðra leiðina	adh·ra lay·dhi·na
return	fram og til baka	fram okh til ba·ka

Is this the ... to (Akureyri)?	Er þetta ... til (Akureyrar)?	er the·ta ... til (a·ku·ray·rar)
boat	ferjan	fer·yan
bus	rútan	roo·tan
plane	flugvélin	flukh·vye·lin

NORWEGIAN

There are two official written forms of Norwegian, *Bokmål* and *Nynorsk*. They are actually quite similar and understood by all speakers. It's estimated that around 85% of Norwegian speakers use *Bokmål* and about 15% use *Nynorsk*. In this section we've used *Bokmål* only.

Each vowel can be either long or short. Generally, they're long when followed by one consonant and short when followed by two or more consonants. Note that aw is pronounced as in 'law', eu as the 'u' in 'nurse', ew as 'ee' with pursed lips, and ow as in 'how'.

Basics

Hello.	God dag.	go·daag
Goodbye.	Ha det.	haa·de
Please.	Vær så snill.	veyr saw snil
Thank you.	Takk.	tak
You're welcome.	Ingen årsak.	ing·en awr·saak
Excuse me.	Unnskyld.	ewn·shewl
Sorry.	Beklager.	bey·klaa·geyr
Yes.	Ja.	yaa
No.	Nei.	ney

How are you?
Hvordan har du det?   vor·dan haar doo de

Fine, thanks. And you?
Bra, takk. Og du?   braa tak aw doo

What's your name?
Hva heter du?   vaa hey·ter doo

Signs – Norwegian

Inngang	Entrance
Utgang	Exit
Åpen	Open
Stengt	Closed
Forbudt	Prohibited
Toaletter	Toilets

My name is ...
Jeg heter ...   yai hay·ter ...

Do you speak English?
Snakker du engelsk?   sna·ker doo eyng·elsk

I don't understand.
Jeg forstår ikke.   yai fawr·stawr i·key

Accommodation

campsite	campingplass	keym·ping·plas
guesthouse	gjestgiveri	yest·gi·ve·ree
hotel	hotell	hoo·tel
youth hostel	ungdoms-herberge	ong·dawms-heyr·beyrg

Do you have a single/double room?
Finnes det et enkeltrom/dobbeltrom?   fi·nes de et eyn·kelt·rom/daw·belt·rom

How much is it per night/person?
Hvor mye koster det pr dag/person?   vor mew·e kaws·ter de peyr daag/peyr·son

Eating & Drinking

Can you recommend a ...?	Kan du anbefale en ...?	kan doo an·be·fa·le en ...
bar	bar	baar
cafe	kafé	ka·fe
restaurant	restaurant	res·tu·rang

I'd like the menu.
Kan jeg få menyen, takk.   kan yai faw me·new·en tak

What would you recommend?
Hva vil du anbefale?   va vil doo an·be·fa·le

Do you have vegetarian food?
Har du vegetariansk mat her?   har doo ve·ge·ta·ree·ansk maat heyr

I'll have ...
Jeg vil ha ...   yai vil haa ...

Cheers!
Skål!   skawl

I'd like the bill.
Kan jeg få regningen, takk.   kan yai faw rai·ning·en tak

Numbers – Norwegian		
1	*en*	en
2	*to*	taw
3	*tre*	trey
4	*fire*	*fee*·re
5	*fem*	fem
6	*seks*	seks
7	*sju*	shoo
8	*åtte*	*aw*·te
9	*ni*	nee
10	*ti*	tee

breakfast	*frokost*	fro·kost
lunch	*lunsj*	loonsh
dinner	*middag*	mi·da
beer	*øl*	eul
coffee	*kaffe*	*kaa*·fe
tea	*te*	te
water	*vann*	van
wine	*vin*	veen

Emergencies

Help!	*Hjelp!*	yelp
Go away!	*Forsvinn!*	fawr·*svin*

Call a doctor/the police!
Ring en lege/politiet!   ring en *le*·ge/po·lee·*tee*·ay

I'm lost.
Jeg har gått meg vill.   yai har gawt mai vil

I'm ill.
Jeg er syk.   yai er sewk

I have to use the telephone.
Jeg må låne   yai maw *law*·ne
telefonen.   te·le·*fo*·nen

Where are the toilets?
Hvor er toalettene?   vor eyr to·aa·*le*·te·ne

Shopping & Services

I'm looking for ...
Jeg leter etter ...   yai *ley*·ter e·*ter* ...

How much is it?
Hvor mye koster det?   vor *mew*·e *kaws*·ter de

That's too expensive.
Det er for dyrt.   de eyr fawr dewrt

Where's ...?	*Er det ...?*	eyr de ...
an ATM	*en minibank*	en *mi*·nee·bank
a foreign exchange	*valuta veksling*	va·*lu*·ta· *vek*·sling

market	*marked*	*mar*·ked
post office	*postkontor*	pawst·*kawn*·tawr
tourist office	*turist- informasjon*	tu·*reest*· in·fawr·ma·*shawn*

Transport & Directions

Where is ...?
Hvor er ...?   vor ayr ...

What is the address?
Hva er adressen?   va ayr aa·*dre*·seyn

Can you show me (on the map)?
Kan du vise meg   kan du vee·se ma
(på kartet)?   (paw *kar*·te)

Where can I buy a ticket?
Hvor kan jeg kjøpe   vor kan yai *sheu*·pe
billett?   bee·*let*

One one-way/return ticket (to Bergen), please.
Jeg vil gjerne ha   yai vil *yer*·ne haa
enveisbillett/   en·veys·bee·*let*/
returbillett   re·*toor*·bi·let
(til Bergen), takk.   (til *ber*·gen) tak

What time's the ... bus?	*Når går ... buss?*	nawr gawr ... bus
first	*første*	*feur*·ste
last	*siste*	*si*·ste

boat	*båt*	bawt
bus	*buss*	bus
plane	*fly*	flew
train	*tåg*	tawg

SWEDISH

Swedish is the national language of Sweden and it also has official status in neighbouring Finland.

Vowel sounds can be short or long – generally the stressed vowels are long, except when followed by double consonants. Note that aw is pronounced as in 'saw', air as in 'hair', eu as the 'u' in 'nurse', ew as 'ee' with rounded lips, oh as the 'o' in 'note', and fh is a breathy sound pronounced with rounded lips, like saying 'f' and 'w' at the same time.

Signs – Swedish	
Ingång	Entrance
Utgång	Exit
Öppet	Open
Stängt	Closed
Förbjudet	Prohibited
Toaletter	Toilets

Basics

Hello.	*Hej.*	hey
Goodbye.	*Hej då.*	hey daw
Please.	*Tack.*	tak
Thank you.	*Tack.*	tak
You're welcome.	*Varsågod.*	var·sha·*gohd*
Excuse me.	*Ursäkta mig.*	oor·*shek*·ta mey
Sorry.	*Förlåt.*	feur·*lawt*
Yes.	*Ja.*	yaa
No.	*Nej.*	ney

How are you?
Hur står det till?   hoor stawr de til

Fine, thanks. And you?
Bra, tack. Och dig?   braa tak o dey

What's your name?
Vad heter du?   vaad *hey*·ter doo

My name is ...
Jag heter ...   yaa *hey*·ter ...

Do you speak English?
Talar du engelska?   *taa*·lar doo *eng*·el·ska

I don't understand.
Jag förstår inte.   yaa feur·*shtawr in*·te

Accommodation

campsite	*campingplats*	*kam*·ping·*plats*
guesthouse	*gästhus*	*yest*·hoos
hotel	*hotell*	hoh·*tel*
youth hostel	*vandrarhem*	*van*·drar·hem

Do you have a single/double room?
Har ni ett enkelrum/   har nee et *en*·kel·rum/
dubbelrum?   *du*·bel·rum

How much is it per night/person?
Hur mycket kostar det   hoor *mew*·ket *kos*·tar de
per natt/person?   peyr nat/*peyr*·shohn

Eating & Drinking

Can you recommend a ...?	*Kan du rekommendera en ...?*	kan doo re·ko·men·*dey*·ra eyn ...
bar	*bar*	bar
cafe	*kafé*	ka·*fey*
restaurant	*restaurang*	res·taw·*rang*

I'd like the menu.
Jag skulle vilja ha   yaa *sku*·le *vil*·ya *haa*
menyn.   me·*newn*

What would you recommend?
Vad skulle ni anbefalla?   vaad *sku*·le nee *an*·be·fa·la

Numbers – Swedish

1	*ett*	et
2	*två*	tvaw
3	*tre*	trey
4	*fyra*	*few*·ra
5	*fem*	fem
6	*sex*	seks
7	*sju*	fhoo
8	*åtta*	*o*·ta
9	*nio*	*nee*·oh
10	*tio*	*tee*·oh

Do you have vegetarian food?
Har ni vegetarisk mat?   har nee ve·ge·*taa*·risk maat

I'll have ...
Jag vill ha ...   yaa vil haa ...

Cheers!
Skål!   skawl

I'd like the bill.
Jag skulle vilja ha   yaa *sku*·le *vil*·ya *haa*
räkningen.   *reyk*·ning·en

breakfast	*frukost*	*froo*·kost
lunch	*lunch*	lunsh
dinner	*middag*	*mi*·daa

beer	*öl*	eul
coffee	*kaffe*	*ka*·fe
tea	*te*	tey
water	*vatten*	*va*·ten
wine	*vin*	veen

Emergencies

Help!	*Hjälp!*	yelp
Go away!	*Försvinn!*	feur·*shvin*

Call a doctor!
Ring efter en doktor!   ring *ef*·ter en *dok*·tor

Call the police!
Ring efter polisen!   ring *ef*·ter poh·*lee*·sen

I'm lost.
Jag har gått vilse.   yaa har got *vil*·se

I'm ill.
Jag är sjuk.   yaa air fhook

I have to use the telephone.
Jag måste använda   yaa *maws*·te an·*ven*·da
telefonen.   te·le·*foh*·nen

Where are the toilets?
Var är toaletten?   var air toh·aa·*le*·ten

Shopping & Services

I'm looking for ...
Jag letar efter ...   yaa *ley*·tar ef·ter ...

How much is it?
Hur mycket kostar det?   hoor *mew*·ke *kos*·tar de

That's too expensive.
Det är för dyrt.   de air feur *dewrt*

Where's ...?	*Var finns det en ...?*	var fins de eyn ...
an ATM	*bankomat*	ban·koh·*maat*
a foreign exchange	*växlings- kontor*	*veyk*·slings· kon·tohr
market	*torghandel*	*tory*·han·del
post office	*posten*	*pos*·ten
tourist office	*turistbyrå*	too·*rist*·bew·raw

Transport & Directions

Where's ...?
Var finns det ...?   var finns de ...

What's the address?
Vilken adress är det?   *vil*·ken a·*dres* air de

Can you show me (on the map)?
Kan du visa mig (på kartan)?   kan doo *vee*·sa mey (paw *kar*·tan)

Where can I buy a ticket?
Var kan jag köpa en biljett?   var kan yaa *sheu*·pa eyn bil·*yet*

A one-way/return ticket (to Stockholm), please.
Jag skulle vilja ha en enkelbiljett/returbiljett (till Stockholm).   yaa *sku*·le *vil*·ya haa eyn en·kel·bil·*yet*/re·toor·bil·*yet* (til *stok*·holm)

What time's the ... bus?	*När går ... bussen?*	nair gawr ... *bu*·sen
first	*första*	*feursh*·ta
last	*sista*	*sis*·ta

boat	*båt*	bawt
bus	*buss*	bus
plane	*flygplan*	*flewg*·plaan
train	*tåg*	tawg

behind the scenes

SEND US YOUR FEEDBACK

We love to hear from travellers – your comments keep us on our toes and help make our books better. Our well-travelled team reads every word on what you loved or loathed about this book. Although we cannot reply individually to postal submissions, we always guarantee that your feedback goes straight to the appropriate authors, in time for the next edition. Each person who sends us information is thanked in the next edition – the most useful submissions are rewarded with a selection of digital PDF chapters.

Visit **lonelyplanet.com/contact** to submit your updates and suggestions or to ask for help. Our award-winning website also features inspirational travel stories, news and discussions.

Note: We may edit, reproduce and incorporate your comments in Lonely Planet products such as guidebooks, websites and digital products, so let us know if you don't want your comments reproduced or your name acknowledged. For a copy of our privacy policy visit lonelyplanet.com/privacy.

OUR READERS

Many thanks to the travellers who used the last edition and wrote to us with helpful hints, useful advice and interesting anecdotes: Richard Hulin, Wanda Serkowska, Allen Sooredoo, Stephan Stevnsborg, Lena Torsvik, Colin Wojtowycz

AUTHOR THANKS

Andy Symington

Andy owes many thanks once again to Gustav, Marja, Mirjam and Meri Schulman for their warm Finnish welcome whenever I visit. Thanks also go to helpful Finns in tourist offices and elsewhere, Cristina Sandoval, Alexis Kouros, Satu Natunen and her team, and to the brilliant group of authors and editors that made coordinating this book a very light task. Lastly, love and gratitude to my parents for their support and to Elena Vázquez Rodríguez, excellent travel companion and so much more, *kiitos paljon mí amor*.

Carolyn Bain

Much love and thanks go to Graham Harris and Kate Johns for pre-Estonia fun and games, and to Brandon Presser for Nordic-Baltic inspiration (and for seeing the same Tallinn cafe from many different angles). In Tallinn, warmest thanks to Priit and Beatrice for excellent chats and food, Geli for her usual fine apartment assistance, Elina and Triin at Chado for their tips, and especially to Estonia's finest tea-meister, Steve Kokker.

Cristian Bonetto

A huge *tak* to the countless locals who offered their expert insights on everything from Danish art and architecture, to foraged native herbs. Special thanks to Morten Heide, Martin Kalhøj and Therese Haddad Vester. Thanks also to Rasmus Kofoed, Magnus Høegh Kofoed, Ane Katrine Vig and Henrik Lorentsen. At Lonely Planet, special thanks to Katie O'Connell and Andy Symington.

Anthony Ham

Thanks to so many people who have made Norway one of my favourite places on earth. Special thanks to Sonja (Bergen), Jonas (Svolvaer) and Andreas (Svalbard). At Lonely Planet, thanks especially to Andy Symington, Miles Roddis and Stuart Butler. Special thanks to Jan and Ron, and to Marina and Alberto for sharing the journey. To my three girls, Marina, Carlota and Valentina: *Os quiero, os quiero, os quiero*.

Anna Kaminski

Many people to thank, not least Katie – for entrusting me with this chapter – Andy and the rest of the *Scandinavia* 11 team, to Ellen and Genie Khmelnitski for sharing part of my journey, and to everyone who helped me along the way, including Ali (Luleå), Katja, Pia and Vitaly and wife (Göteborg), Lennart (Visit Sápmi), Akshey and Britta in Malmö, as well as Peter, Emma, Krister, Amelie and Erik in Stockholm.

ACKNOWLEDGMENTS

Cover photograph: Kronetorps windmill, Burlöv, Sweden; Anders Blomqvist/Getty Images©.

This Book

This 11th edition of Lonely Planet's *Scandinavia* guidebook is part of Lonely Planet's Europe series. Other titles in this series include *Western Europe, Mediterranean Europe, Central Europe, South-eastern Europe, Eastern Europe* and *Europe on a Shoestring*. Lonely Planet also publishes phrasebooks for these regions. This guidebook was commissioned in Lonely Planet's London office, and produced by the following:

Commissioning Editors Lucy Monie Hall, Katie O'Connell, Helena Smith, Anna Tyler

Coordinating Editor Karyn Noble

Coordinating Cartographer Valentina Kremenchutskaya

Coordinating Layout Designer Clara Monitto

Managing Editors Barbara Delissen, Brigitte Ellemor, Angela Tinson

Managing Cartographer Adrian Persoglia

Managing Layout Designer Jane Hart

Assisting Editors Penny Cordner, Kate Daly, Justin Flynn, Kellie Langdon, Charlotte Orr, Monique Perrin

Assisting Cartographers Alex Leung, James Leversha

Cover Research Kylie McLaughlin

Internal Image Research Aude Vauconsant

Language Content Branislava Vladisavljevic

Thanks to Nigel Chin, Ryan Evans, Larissa Frost, Chris Girdler, Genesys India, Jouve India, Anne Mason, Trent Paton, Kerrianne Southway, Gerard Walker

index

000 Map pages
000 Photo pages

how to use this book

These symbols will help you find the listings you want:

- ⦿ Sights
- 🏖 Beaches
- 🏃 Activities
- 🎓 Courses
- 👉 Tours
- 🎊 Festivals & Events
- 🛌 Sleeping
- ✖ Eating
- 🍷 Drinking
- ☆ Entertainment
- 🛍 Shopping
- ℹ Information/Transport

These symbols give you the vital information for each listing:

- ☎ Telephone Numbers
- ☺ Opening Hours
- P Parking
- ⊖ Nonsmoking
- ❄ Air-Conditioning
- @ Internet Access
- 🛜 Wi-Fi Access
- 🏊 Swimming Pool
- 🥗 Vegetarian Selection
- 📖 English-Language Menu
- 👪 Family-Friendly
- 🐾 Pet-Friendly
- 🚌 Bus
- ⛴ Ferry
- Ⓜ Metro
- Ⓢ Subway
- 🚊 Tram
- 🚆 Train

Reviews are organised by author preference.

Look out for these icons:

TOP CHOICE   Our author's recommendation

FREE   No payment required

🌿   A green or sustainable option

Our authors have nominated these places as demonstrating a strong commitment to sustainability – for example by supporting local communities and producers, operating in an environmentally friendly way, or supporting conservation projects.

Map Legend

Sights
- 🏖 Beach
- 🛕 Buddhist
- 🏰 Castle
- ✝ Christian
- 🕉 Hindu
- ☪ Islamic
- ✡ Jewish
- 🗿 Monument
- 🏛 Museum/Gallery
- 🏚 Ruin
- 🍇 Winery/Vineyard
- 🦁 Zoo
- ⦿ Other Sight

Activities, Courses & Tours
- 🤿 Diving/Snorkelling
- 🛶 Canoeing/Kayaking
- ⛷ Skiing
- 🏄 Surfing
- 🏊 Swimming/Pool
- 🚶 Walking
- 🏄 Windsurfing
- 🎯 Other Activity/Course/Tour

Sleeping
- 🛏 Sleeping
- ⛺ Camping

Eating
- ✖ Eating

Drinking
- ☕ Drinking
- 🍵 Cafe

Entertainment
- 🎭 Entertainment

Shopping
- 🛍 Shopping

Information
- ✉ Post Office
- ℹ Tourist Information

Transport
- ✈ Airport
- ⊗ Border Crossing
- 🚌 Bus
- 🚡 Cable Car/Funicular
- 🚲 Cycling
- ⛴ Ferry
- 🚝 Monorail
- P Parking
- Ⓢ S-Bahn
- 🚕 Taxi
- 🚆 Train/Railway
- 🚊 Tram
- ⊖ Tube Station
- Ⓤ U-Bahn
- Ⓜ Underground Train Station
- ● Other Transport

Routes
- Tollway
- Freeway
- Primary
- Secondary
- Tertiary
- Lane
- Unsealed Road
- Plaza/Mall
- Steps
- ⊨ ⊨ Tunnel
- Pedestrian Overpass
- Walking Tour
- Walking Tour Detour
- Path

Boundaries
- International
- State/Province
- Disputed
- Regional/Suburb
- Marine Park
- Cliff
- Wall

Population
- ✪ Capital (National)
- ⊙ Capital (State/Province)
- ● City/Large Town
- ○ Town/Village

Geographic
- 🏠 Hut/Shelter
- 🚩 Lighthouse
- 👁 Lookout
- ▲ Mountain/Volcano
- 🌴 Oasis
- 🌳 Park
-)(Pass
- 🏕 Picnic Area
- 💧 Waterfall

Hydrography
- River/Creek
- Intermittent River
- Swamp/Mangrove
- Reef
- Canal
- Water
- Dry/Salt/Intermittent Lake
- Glacier

Areas
- Beach/Desert
- + + + Cemetery (Christian)
- × × × Cemetery (Other)
- Park/Forest
- Sportsground
- Sight (Building)
- Top Sight (Building)

Anthony Ham
Norway Anthony fell in love with Norway the first time he laid eyes on her. His true passion is the Arctic north, especially spending time with the Sámi or scouring the horizon for polar bears in the wilds of Svalbard. When he's not travelling for Lonely Planet, Anthony writes and photographs for magazines and newspapers around the world.

Read more about Anthony at:
lonelyplanet.com/members/anthonyham

Anna Kaminski
Sweden Anna has been dreaming of Scandinavia ever since reading Norse myths and legends as an impressionable five-year-old. Already a huge fan of Swedish Lapland and Stockholm, this time around Anna was lucky enough to travel the whole country, trying her luck in a medieval archery competition in Visby and at glass-blowing in Glasriket, and visiting the childhood home of her favourite childhood author – Astrid Lindgren.

OUR STORY

A beat-up old car, a few dollars in the pocket and a sense of adventure. In 1972 that's all Tony and Maureen Wheeler needed for the trip of a lifetime – across Europe and Asia overland to Australia. It took several months, and at the end – broke but inspired – they sat at their kitchen table writing and stapling together their first travel guide, *Across Asia on the Cheap*. Within a week they'd sold 1500 copies. Lonely Planet was born.

Today, Lonely Planet has offices in Melbourne, London, Oakland and Delhi, with more than 600 staff and writers. We share Tony's belief that 'a great guidebook should do three things: inform, educate and amuse'.

OUR WRITERS

Andy Symington

Coordinating Author; Finland, Iceland Andy hails from Australia, lives in Spain, learned to ski as a child in Norway, was entranced by wintertime Finland as a backpacking teenager and has been a regular visitor to the Nordic lands ever since. He has travelled extremely widely throughout the region, and is a regular contributor on Finland and Scandinavia to Lonely Planet guides and other publications. His highlights have included close encounters with bears, rowing-boat odysseys on enormous lakes and a near-terminal swim in a seriously cold Arctic Ocean. In a never-ending bid for honorary citizenship of the north, he has a huge stockpile of Nordic CDs, ranging from contemporary Sámi *yoiks* to epic '80s Viking metal.

Read more about Andy at:
lonelyplanet.com/members/andy_symington

Carolyn Bain

Tallinn Melbourne-based Carolyn has investigated great pockets of northern Europe in the name of work, including Sweden, Denmark, Iceland and the Baltic countries. For this book she returned to the northeast, where Estonia combines the best of Eastern Europe and Scandinavia and delivers something heartwarmingly unique.

Cristian Bonetto

Denmark Despite his love of long, hot summers, Cristian Bonetto has an intense passion for all things Danish. What started with a weakness for Lego blocks has since blossomed into an obsession with Danish design, art, cuisine and all things *hyggelig* (cosy). The country's effortless cool is a constant source of inspiration for the former playwright and soap scribe, whose musings on travel and pop culture have appeared in various international publications. To date, Cristian contributed to over a dozen Lonely Planet guides.

OVER MORE
PAGE WRITERS

Published by Lonely Planet Publications Pty Ltd
ABN 36 005 607 983
11th edition – Oct 2013
ISBN 978 1 74220 420 8
© Lonely Planet 2013   Photographs © as indicated 2013
10 9 8 7 6 5 4 3 2 1
Printed in China

Although the authors and Lonely Planet have taken all reasonable care in preparing this book, we make no warranty about the accuracy or completeness of its content and, to the maximum extent permitted, disclaim all liability arising from its use.